Fundamentals of Managerial Economics

Sixth Edition

MARK HIRSCHEY

University of Kansas

JAMES L. PAPPAS

University of South Florida

THE DRYDEN PRESS

Chicago   New York   San Francisco   Philadelphia
Montreal   Toronto   London   Sydney   Tokyo

Acquisitions Editor	GARY NELSON
Developmental Editor	STACEY SIMS
Project Editor	REBECCA DODSON
Art Director	BILL BRAMMER
Production Manager	LOIS WEST
Permissions Editor	ANNETTE COOLIDGE
Product Manager	KATHLEEN SHARP
Marketing Coordinator	CRISTIN WESTHOFF
Compositor	THE CLARINDA CO.
Text Type	10/12 TIMES ROMAN
Cover Image	MARK HUMPHRIES

ADDRESS FOR ORDERS
THE DRYDEN PRESS
6277 SEA HARBOR DRIVE
ORLANDO, FL 32887-6777
1-800-782-4479 OR 1-800-433-001 (IN FLORIDA)

ADDRESS FOR EDITORIAL CORRESPONDENCE
THE DRYDEN PRESS
301 COMMERCE STREET, SUITE 3700
FORT WORTH, TX 76102

ISBN: 0-03-024583-4

LIBRARY OF CONGRESS CATALOG CARD NUMBER: 97-065946
PRINTED IN THE UNITED STATES OF AMERICA
7 8 9 0 1 2 3 4 5 6   039   9 8 7 6 5 4 3 2 1

THE DRYDEN PRESS
HARCOURT BRACE COLLEGE PUBLISHERS

The Dryden Press Series in Economics

Baldani, Bradfield, and Turner
MATHEMATICAL ECONOMICS

Baumol and Blinder
ECONOMICS: PRINCIPLES AND POLICY
Seventh Edition (Also available in micro and macro paperbacks)

Baumol, Panzar, and Willig
CONTESTABLE MARKETS AND THE
THEORY OF INDUSTRY STRUCTURE
Revised Edition

Breit and Elzinga
THE ANTITRUST CASEBOOK: MILESTONES IN
ECONOMIC REGULATION
Third Edition

Brue
THE EVOLUTION OF ECONOMIC THOUGHT
Fifth Edition

Edgmand, Moomaw, and Olson
ECONOMICS AND CONTEMPORARY ISSUES
Fourth Edition

Gardner
COMPARATIVE ECONOMIC SYSTEMS
Second Edition

Gwartney and Stroup
ECONOMICS: PRIVATE AND PUBLIC CHOICE
Eighth Edition (Also available in micro and macro paperbacks)

Gwartney and Stroup
INTRODUCTION TO ECONOMICS:
THE WEALTH AND POVERTY OF NATIONS

Heilbroner and Singer
THE ECONOMIC TRANSFORMATION
OF AMERICA: 1600 TO THE PRESENT
Third Edition

Hess and Ross
ECONOMIC DEVELOPMENT: THEORIES,
EVIDENCE, AND POLICIES

Hirschey and Pappas
MANAGERIAL ECONOMICS
Eighth Edition

Hyman
PUBLIC FINANCE: A CONTEMPORARY
APPLICATION OF THEORY TO POLICY
Fifth Edition

Kahn
THE ECONOMIC APPROACH TO
ENVIRONMENTAL AND NATURAL RESOURCES
Second Edition

Kaserman and Mayo
GOVERNMENT AND BUSINESS:
THE ECONOMICS OF ANTITRUST
AND REGULATION

Kaufman
THE ECONOMICS OF LABOR MARKETS
Fourth Edition

Kennett and Lieberman
THE ROAD TO CAPITALISM: THE
ECONOMIC TRANSFORMATION OF EASTERN
EUROPE AND THE FORMER SOVIET UNION

Kreinin
INTERNATIONAL ECONOMICS:
A POLICY APPROACH
Eighth Edition

Lott and Ray
APPLIED ECONOMETRICS WITH DATA SETS

Mankiw
PRINCIPLES OF ECONOMICS
*(Also available in micro and macro
paperbacks)*

Marlow
PUBLIC FINANCE: THEORY AND PRACTICE

Nicholson
INTERMEDIATE MICROECONOMICS
AND ITS APPLICATION
Seventh Edition

Nicholson
MICROECONOMIC THEORY:
BASIC PRINCIPLES AND EXTENSIONS
Seventh Edition

Puth
AMERICAN ECONOMIC HISTORY
Third Edition

Ragan and Thomas
PRINCIPLES OF ECONOMICS
*Second Edition (Also available in micro
and macro paperbacks)*

Ranamathan
INTRODUCTORY ECONOMETRICS
WITH APPLICATIONS
Fourth Edition

Rukstad
CORPORATE DECISION MAKING IN THE
WORLD ECONOMY: COMPANY CASE
STUDIES

Rukstad
MACROECONOMIC DECISION MAKING IN
THE WORLD ECONOMY: TEXT AND CASES
Third Edition

Samuelson and Marks
MANAGERIAL ECONOMICS
Second Edition

Scarth
MACROECONOMICS: AN INTRODUCTION TO
ADVANCED METHODS
Third Edition

v

Stockman
INTRODUCTION TO ECONOMICS
(Also available in micro and macro paperbacks)

Walton and Rockoff
HISTORY OF THE AMERICAN ECONOMY
Eighth Edition

Welch and Welch
ECONOMICS: THEORY AND PRACTICE
Sixth Edition

Yarbrough and Yarbrough
THE WORLD ECONOMY: TRADE AND FINANCE
Fourth Edition

Preface

The first edition of *Fundamentals of Managerial Economics* was written and published to help students both understand and improve the managerial decision-making process. Today, the role of managers in corporations, not-for-profit institutions, and government agencies has become even more important, and the need to improve resource use in all types of organizations has become much more visible. The information age of the 1990s has put so much more data at the disposal of managers that "information overload" and the "paralysis of analysis" have become common complaints. Widespread volatility in input prices and availability, the rapid pace of technical change, plus ongoing globalization of the marketplace all combine to make difficult the efficient use of economic resources and information. Dynamic change in the economic environment also makes it difficult to accurately assess demand and supply conditions, as it increases the need for timely and effective managerial decision making. Sound economic analysis has never been more important—regardless of whether the decision-making unit is an individual, household, firm, nonprofit organization, or government agency.

Fundamentals of Managerial Economics, Sixth Edition, is designed to provide a solid foundation of economic understanding for use in managerial decision making. This text offers an intuitive *noncalculus-based* treatment of economic theory and analysis. A wide variety of examples and simple numerical problems are used to illustrate the application of managerial economics to a wide variety of practical situations. The nature of the decision process and the role that economic analysis plays in that process are emphasized throughout.

A key feature of this text is its attempt to depict the firm as a cohesive, unified organization. The basic valuation model is constructed and used as the underlying economic model of the firm. Each topic in the text is then related to an element of the value maximization model. In this manner, effective management is seen to involve an integration of the accounting, finance, marketing, personnel, and production functions. This integrative approach demonstrates that important managerial decisions are *interdisciplinary* in the truest sense of the word. Over the years, we have come to appreciate that students find the presentation of the business firm as a unified whole, rather than a series of discrete, unrelated parts, as one of the most valuable lessons of managerial economics.

While both microeconomic and macroeconomic relations have implications for managerial decision making, this text concentrates on microeconomic topics of particular importance. Following the development of the economic model of the firm, the vital role of profits is examined. Because the decision-making process often requires a elementary understanding of economic and statistical relations, a number of basic economic relations, statistical concepts, and optimization techniques are described early in the text. Since the demand for a firm's products plays a major role in determining its profitability and ongoing success, demand analysis and estimation is an essential area of study. An important part of this investigation is a study of the basic forces of demand and supply. This naturally leads to a discussion of economic forecasting and methods for assessing forecast reliability. Production theory, cost analysis, and linear programming techniques are then explored as means for understanding the economics of resource allocation and employment.

Another important topic is market structure analysis, which provides a foundation for studying the external economic environment and for examining the pricing practices needed for successful management. The role of government in the market economy, including the constraints it imposes on business, requires a careful examination of regulation and antitrust law. Given the government's increasing role in the demand and supply for basic services, such as education and health care, a careful consideration of the use of economic principles in public management is also provided. Finally, risk analysis and capital budgeting are shown as methods for introducing marginal analysis into the long-range strategic planning and control process. The risk analysis and capital budgeting process is not only important within firms, hospitals, and other economic organizations; it is also vital to society as a whole because it pertains to the allocation of scarce capital resources.

Fundamentals of Managerial Economics, Sixth Edition, takes a practical problem-solving approach to the study of managerial economics. The text focuses on the economics—not the mathematics—of the managerial decision process. When appropriate, quantitative methods and tools are introduced to give greater insight into the technique of economic analysis and to facilitate the practical use of economics in decision situations. However, the emphasis throughout the text is clearly on economic intuition as a practical tool for problem solving.

Changes in the Sixth Edition

The environment in which managerial decisions are made is constantly changing. To maintain its value as an educational resource, a textbook must be modified and updated. This revision of *Fundamentals of Managerial Economics* contains a number of important additions and refinements. Indeed, every chapter has been updated in response to valuable suggestions provided by students and instructors and to reflect recent developments in the field. The following section highlights some of most important changes in the fifth edition.

CONTENT

■ Chapter 3, *Statistical Analysis of Economic Relations,* has been further simplified to show how basic statistical tools can be used to provide valuable information concerning demand, production, cost, and market structure relations.

■ Chapter 5, *Demand Analysis and Estimation,* now focuses on the intuitive appeal of elasticity analysis and better illustrates the use of real-world data in the regression-based approach to demand estimation.

- Chapter 6, *Forecasting,* has been simplified to emphasize on the comparative strengths and weaknesses of alternative forecasting techniques. Important strengths and limitations of macroeconomic and microeconomic forecasting techniques are stressed.
- Chapter 10, *Perfect Competition and Monopoly,* and Chapter 11, *Monopolistic Competition and Oligopoly,* have been extensively revised to better illustrate the use of economic methodology to devise and execute an effective competitive strategy in light of market structure considerations.
- Chapter 12, *Pricing Practices,* has been rewritten to improve our explanation of essential elements of markup pricing policies and transfer pricing principles.
- Chapter 13, *Government Regulation of the Market Economy,* has undergone comprehensive revision to offer perspective on recent moves to deregulate and reregulate various types of private-market activity. Added perspective on the size-efficiency issue is provided by considering the link between firm size and profitability for both U.S. and global competitors. New types of incentive-based regulation are also examined more fully as means for achieving socially desirable objectives through public and private sector cooperation.
- Chapter 14, *Risk Analysis,* offers a clearer presentation of the wide variety of business risks and the special risks borne by firms with multinational operations. The use of game theory to aid in decision making under uncertainty is also more fully examined.
- Chapter 16, *Public Management,* has been revised and simplified to show how how economic principles can be used to understand and improve the allocation of public-sector resources.

LEARNING AIDS

- Each chapter incorporates a wide variety of simple numerical examples and detailed practical illustrations of chapter concepts. These features portray the valuable use and real-world implications of covered material.
- Each chapter now includes *three* Managerial Applications boxes to show current examples of how the concepts introduced in managerial economics are actually used in real-world situations. New Managerial Applications based on articles from *Barron's, Business Week, Forbes, Fortune,* and *The Wall Street Journal* are provided. This feature stimulates student interest in the material and offers a popular basis for classroom discussion.
- The text also incorporates several new regression-based illustrations of chapter concepts using actual company data, or data adapted from real-world situations. These illustrations build on the introduction to the statistical analysis of economic relations given in Chapter 3. Like all aspects of the text, this material is self-contained and intuitive.
- Effective managers in the 1990s must be sensitive to the special challenges posed by an increasingly global marketplace. To increase student awareness of such issues, the text also features a number of examples, Managerial Applications, and

case studies that relate to global business topics. A special global icon in the margin indicates the location of these effective learning aids.

- Each chapter is now accompanied by a case study that provides in-depth treatment of chapter concepts. To meet the needs of all instructors and students, many of these case studies are written to allow, but do not require, a computer-based approach. These case studies, identified by a computer disk symbol in the margin, are fully self-contained. Both 3.5″ and 5.25″ floppy diskettes for IBM PC® and IBM® compatible computers that contain case-study data and detailed solutions are provided to adopters with the *Instructor's Manual*. These case studies are especially helpful to instructors who wish to more fully incorporate the use of basic spreadsheet and statistical software in their courses.

- Over 300 new end-of-chapter questions and problems are also provided, after having been subject to necessary revision and class testing. Questions are designed to give students the opportunity to grasp basic concepts on an intuitive level and express their understanding in a nonquantitative fashion. Problems cover a wide variety of decision situations and illustrate the role of economic analysis from within a simple numerical framework.

- Each chapter also now includes *two* self-test problems to show students how economic tools and techniques can be used to solve practical business problems. These self-test problems are a proven study aid that greatly enhances the learning value of end-of-chapter questions and problems.

ANCILLARY PACKAGE

Fundamentals of Managerial Economics, Sixth Edition, is supported by the most comprehensive ancillary package available in managerial economics to make teaching and learning the material both easy and enjoyable.

INSTRUCTOR'S MANUAL

The *Instructor's Manual* offers learning suggestions, plus detailed answers and solutions for all chapter questions and problems. As mentioned previously, diskettes for IBM PC® and IBM® compatible computers that contain case-study data and detailed solutions are provided to adopters with the *Instructor's Manual*.

STUDY GUIDE

The *Study Guide* furnishes a detailed line summary of major concepts for each chapter, a brief discussion of important economic relations as they are covered in the text, and an expanded set of more than 150 solved problems. This completely new edition has undergone extensive class testing and analysis. Based on the comments of students and instructors alike, this new study guide is highly recommended as a valuable learning resource.

TEST BANK

A comprehensive *Test Bank* is also provided that offers a variety of multiple-choice questions, one-step, and multistep problems for every chapter. Full solutions are included, of course. With a selection of over 500 questions and problems, the *Test Bank* is a valuable tool for exam preparation.

ACKNOWLEDGMENTS

A number of people have aided in the preparation of *Fundamentals of Managerial Economics,* Sixth Edition. Helpful suggestions and constructive comments have been received from a great number of instructors and students who have used previous editions. Numerous reviewers have also provided insights and assistance in clarifying difficult material. Among those who have been especially helpful in the development of this edition are: Trent Boggess, Plymouth State College; John Deming, Seattle Pacific University; Peter Frederiksen, Naval Postgraduate School; Stanley Ghosh, Hawaii Pacific University; Constantine Glezakos, California State University–Long Beach; Charles Hegji, Auburn University; James Henderson, Baylor University; Agha Khan, Virginia State University; Douglas J. Lamdin, University of Maryland, Balitmore County; Rajan Sampath, Colorado State University; Charles Sullivan, Husson College.

The University of Kansas, the University of South Florida, students, and colleagues have together provided a stimulating environment and general intellectual support. We are grateful for their efforts. We want to thank Greg Freix and Romano Delcore, M.D., for their problem-checking and proofreading assistance on this revision.

We are also indebted to The Dryden Press staff and would like to thank the following people for their special efforts: Gary Nelson, Acquisitions Editor; Stacey Sims, Developmental Editor; Rebecca Dodson, Project Editor; Bill Brammer, Art Director; Lois West, Production Manager; Annette Coolidge, Permissions Editor; Kathleen Sharp, Product Manager, and Cristin Westhoff, Marketing Coordinator.

Finally, we want to thank our wives, Chris and Bonnie, for their encouragement, support, and assistance.

Every effort has been made to minimize errors in the text. However, errors do occasionally slip through despite diligent efforts to provide an error-free package of text and ancillary materials. Readers are invited to correspond with us directly concerning any corrections or other suggestions.

Finally, more than ever before, it is obvious that economic efficiency is an essential ingredient in the successful management of both private-sector and public-sector organizations. Like any dynamic area of study, the field of managerial economics continues to undergo profound change in response to the challenges imposed by a rapidly evolving environment. It is stimulating and exciting to participate in these developments. We sincerely hope that the sixth edition of *Fundamentals of Managerial Economics* contributes to a better understanding of the usefulness of economic theory and methodology to managerial practice.

Mark Hirschey
James L. Pappas
August 1997

MARK HIRSCHEY, PH.D. (University of Wisconsin-Madison), is a Professor in the School of Business at the University of Kansas, where he teaches undergraduate and graduate courses in managerial economics and finance. Professor Hirschey is president of the Association of Financial Economists as well as a member of several professional organizations. He has published articles in the *American Economic Review, Journal of Accounting Research, Journal of Business, Journal of Business and Economic Statistics, Journal of Finance, Journal of Financial Economics, Journal of Industrial Economics, Review of Economics and Statistics,* and other leading academic journals. He is editor of *Advances in Financial Economics,* past editor of *Managerial and Decision Economics,* and co-author of *Managerial Economics,* Eighth Edition, with James Pappas.

JAMES L. PAPPAS, PH.D. (UCLA), is Lykes Professor of Banking and Finance in the College of Business Administration at the University of South Florida. He is a member of several professional organizations and has served as an officer of the Financial Management Association. Articles by Professor Pappas have appeared in *Decision Sciences, Engineering Economist, Financial Analysts' Journal, Journal of Business, Journal of Finance, Journal of Industrial Economics, Journal of Marketing Research, Southern Economic Journal,* and other leading academic journals. He has served on the editorial boards of *Financial Management* and *Managerial and Decision Economics,* and is co-author of *Managerial Economics,* Eighth Edition, with Mark Hirschey. Active in executive education, Professor Pappas also serves as Academic Dean of the Graduate School of Banking, which is offered by the Central States Conference of Bankers Associations and the University of Wisconsin–Madison.

Contents

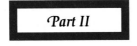

Part II

DEMAND ANALYSIS   127

Part III

PRODUCTION AND COST ANALYSIS   261

Part IV

MARKET STRUCTURE ANALYSIS AND ESTIMATION   419

Part V

Overview of Managerial Economics

1

The Nature and Scope of Managerial Economics

Warren E. Buffett, the renowned chairman and chief executive officer of Omaha, Nebraska-based Berkshire Hathaway, Inc., started an investment partnership with $100 in 1956 and has gone on to accumulate a personal net worth in excess of $16 billion. What is intriguing about Buffett is that he credits his success to a basic understanding of managerial economics.

Berkshire is a collection of extraordinarily profitable operating businesses, including the GEICO Insurance Company, Buffalo News newspaper, See's Candies, and the Nebraska Furniture Mart, among others. Despite the fact that many of these wholly owned subsidiaries operate in fairly mundane industries, they commonly earn in excess of 30% to 50% per year on invested capital. This is astonishingly good performance in light of the the fact that a return of 10% to 12% per year is more typical of industry in general and that Berkshire subsidiaries operate without the benefits of leverage. A second and equally important contributor to Berkshire's outstanding performance is a handful of substantial holdings in publicly traded common stocks, such as The American Express Company, The Coca-Cola Company, and Wells Fargo & Company, among others.

As a manager, Buffett thinks like an investor. As both manager and investor, Buffett looks for "wonderful businesses" with outstanding economic characteristics: high rates of return on invested capital, substantial profit margins on sales, and consistent earnings growth. Complicated businesses that face fierce competition or require large capital investment and ongoing innovation are shunned. Buffett prefers simple-to-understand businesses that require little capital investment and feature enduring competitive advantages.[1]

Buffett's success is powerful testimony to the practical usefulness of managerial economics. Managerial economics is worth studying because it answers fundamental questions: How do managers make good operating and planning decisions? When are the characteristics of a market so attractive that entry becomes appealing? When are these attributes so unattractive that exit is preferable to continued operation? Why do some professions pay well, while others offer only minimal financial rewards? Answers to these questions illustrate the vital importance of managerial economics. Successful managers make good decisions, and one of the most useful tools employed by successful managers is the methodology of managerial economics.

---

[1] See Warren E. Buffett, "Buffett's Bully Pulpit," Fortune, April 14, 1997, 197–198.

The Managerial Decision-Making Process

Managerial Economics
Applies economic tools and techniques to business and administrative decision making.

Managerial economics applies economic theory and methods to business and administrative decision making. Managerial economics prescribes rules for improving managerial decisions. It tells managers how things should be done to achieve organizational objectives efficiently. Managerial economics also helps managers recognize how economic forces affect organizations and describes the economic consequences of managerial behavior. It links traditional economics with the decision sciences to develop vital tools for managerial decision making. This process is illustrated in Figure 1.1.

Managerial economics identifies ways to efficiently achieve goals of the organization. For example, suppose a small business seeks rapid growth to reach a size that permits efficient use of national media advertising. Managerial economics can be used to identify pricing and production strategies to help meet this short-run objective quickly and effectively. Similarly, managerial economics provides production and marketing rules that permit the company to maximize net profits once it has achieved its growth objectives.

Managerial economics has applications in both profit and not-for-profit sectors. For example, an administrator of a nonprofit hospital strives to provide the best medical care possible given limited medical staff, equipment, and related resources. Using the tools and concepts of managerial economics, the administrator can determine the optimal allocation of these limited resources. In short, managerial economics helps managers arrive at a set of operating rules that aid in the efficient use of scarce human and capital resources. By following these rules, businesses, nonprofit organizations, and government agencies are able to meet their objectives efficiently.

To establish appropriate decision rules, managers must understand the economic environment in which they operate. Managerial economics also describes how economic forces affect managerial decisions. For example, a grocery retailer may offer consumers a highly price-sensitive product, such as milk, at an extremely low markup over cost—say, 1% to 2%—while offering less price-sensitive products, such as nonprescription drugs, at markups of as high as 40% over cost. Managerial economics describes the logic of this pricing practice with respect to the goal of profit maximization. Similarly, managerial economics reveals that imposing auto import quotas reduces the availability of substitutes for domestically produced cars, raises auto prices, and creates the possibility of monopoly profits for domestic manufacturers. It does not tell us whether imposing quotas is good public policy; that is a decision involving broader political considerations. Managerial economics only describes the predictable economic consequences of such actions.

Managerial economics offers a comprehensive application of economic theory and methodology to managerial decision making. It is just as relevant to the management of nonbusiness, nonprofit organizations, such as government agencies, cooperatives, schools, hospitals, museums, and similar institutions, as it is to the management of profit-oriented businesses. Although this text focuses primarily on business applications, it also includes examples and problems from the government and nonprofit sectors to illustrate the broad relevance of managerial economics concepts and tools.

Figure 1.1

THE ROLE OF MANAGERIAL ECONOMICS
IN MANAGERIAL DECISION MAKING

Managerial economics uses economic concepts and decision science techniques to solve managerial problems.

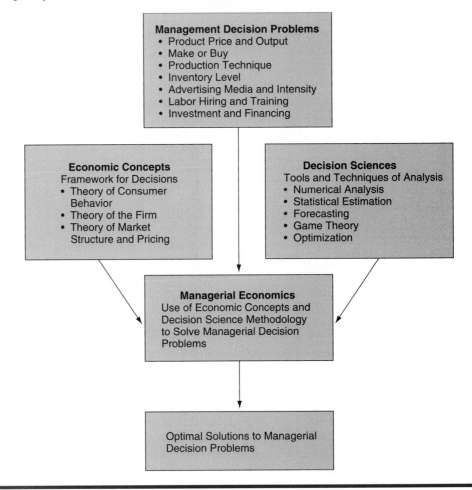

Theory of the Firm

A business enterprise is a combination of people, physical and financial assets, and information (financial, technical, marketing, etc.). People directly involved include customers, stockholders, management, labor, and suppliers. Society in general is affected by business because the business community uses scarce resources, pays taxes, provides employment, and produces much of society's material and services output. Firms exist because they are useful for producing and distributing goods and services.

Managerial Ethics

Pick up *The Wall Street Journal,* or a leading business magazine, like *Forbes,* and it's not hard to find evidence of unscrupulous behavior. Indeed, it can be discouraging to note the amount of press coverage and other attention showered upon companies or top management cited for fraud or simple waste of shareholder assets. Intense media coverage sometimes gives the mistaken impression that base, immoral, or unscrupulous behavior is common in business. Sometimes it's far too easy to gain the mistaken impression that "dirty" business is standard operating procedure in corporate America.

Often overlooked is the fact that unethical conduct is neither consistent with the long-run interests of stockholders, nor with the enlightened self-interest of management and other employees. While famous examples of unscrupulous behavior are unfortunate, it is important to recognize that such scandals occur only infrequently. Every business day on Wall Street, and on Main Street, thousands of business transactions, some involving billions of dollars in cash and securities, are made on the basis of simple phone conversations. Fraud and other scandals are the stark exception to standard operating procedure in business.

If honesty and trust didn't pervade corporate America, the ability to conduct business would be more than hampered—it would founder. Management guru Peter Drucker has written that the purpose of business is to create a customer—someone who will want to do business with you and your company on a regular basis. The only way this can be done is to make sure that you continually take the customer's perspective. How can customer needs be met better, cheaper, or faster? Don't wait for customers to complain or seek alternate suppliers; seek out ways of helping before they become obvious. When customers benefit, so do you and your company. In dealing with employees, it's best to be honest and forthright. If you make a mistake, admit it and go on. By accepting responsibility for your failures, employees will come to trust you and help find solutions for the inevitable problems that are encountered. Similarly, it's best to see every business transaction from the standpoint of those with whom you are dealing. In a job interview, for example, strive to see how you can create value for a potential employer. It's natural to see things from one's own viewpoint; it is typically much more beneficial to see things from the perspective of the person sitting on the other side of the table.

To become successful in business, everyone must adopt a set of principles. For better or worse, we are known by the standards we adopt. For some ethical rules to keep in mind when conducting business, you may want to consider the following:

■ Above all else, keep your word. Say what you mean, and mean what you say.

■ Do the right thing. A handshake with an honorable person is worth more than a ton of legal documents from an unscrupulous individual.

■ Accept responsibility for your mistakes and fix them. Be quick to share credit for success.

■ Leave something on the table. Make sure you profit *with* the customer, not *off* the customer.

■ Stick by your principles. Principles are not for sale at any price.

To gain some perspective on the conduct of notorious "corporate losers," consider the experience of one of America's most famous "winners"—Omaha multibillionaire Warren E. Buffett, chairman of Berkshire Hathaway, Inc. Buffett and Charlie Munger, the number two man at Berkshire, are famous for doing multimillion dollar deals on the basis of a simple handshake. At Berkshire, management relies upon the character of the people with whom they are dealing rather than expensive accounting audits, detailed legal opinions, or liability insurance coverage. Buffett says that after some early mistakes he learned to go into business only with people whom he likes, trusts, and admires. While a company won't necessarily prosper because its managers display admirable qualities, Buffett says he has never made a good deal with a bad person.

Doing the right thing not only makes sense from an ethical perspective, it makes good business sense as well. In business, nice guys, like Warren Buffett, often finish first.

See: John Rutledge, "The Portrait on My Office Wall," *Forbes,* December 30, 1996, 78.

They are economic entities and are best analyzed in the context of an economic model.

Theory of the Firm

The basic model of the business enterprise.

The model of business is called the **theory of the firm.** In its simplest version, the basic firm is thought to have profit maximization as its primary goal. The firm's owner-manager is assumed to be working to maximize the firm's short-run profits. Today, the emphasis on profits has been broadened to encompass uncertainty and the time value of money. In this more complete model, the primary goal of the firm is long-term **expected value maximization.**

Expected Value Maximization

Optimization of profits in light of uncertainty and the time value of money.

DEFINING VALUE

Value of the Firm

The present value of the firm's expected future net cash flows.

Many concepts of value are found in economics and business-book value, market value, liquidating value, going-concern value, and so on. The **value of the firm** is the present value of the firm's expected future net cash flows. If cash flows are equated to profits for simplicity, the value of the firm today, or its **present value,** is the value of expected profits or cash flows, discounted back to the present at an appropriate interest rate.[2]

Present Value

Worth in current dollars.

This model is employed throughout this book and can be expressed as follows:

Value of the Firm = Present Value of Expected Future Profits

$$= \frac{\pi_1}{(1+i)^1} + \frac{\pi_2}{(1+i)^2} + \cdots + \frac{\pi_N}{(1+i)^N}$$

$$= \sum_{t=1}^{N} \frac{\pi_t}{(1+i)^t}$$

(1.1)

Here, $\pi_1, \pi_2, \ldots \pi_N$ represent expected profits in each year, t, and i is the appropriate interest, or discount, rate. The final form for Equation 1.1 is simply a shorthand expression in which sigma (Σ) stands for "sum up" or "add together." The term

$$\sum_{t=1}^{N}$$

means, "Add together as t goes from 1 to N the values of the term on the right." For Equation 1.1, the process is as follows: Let $t = 1$ and find the value of the term $\pi_1/(1+i)^1$, the present value of year 1 profit; then let $t = 2$ and calculate $\pi_2/(1+i)^2$, the present value of year 2 profit; continue until $t = N$, the last year included in the analysis; then add up these present-value equivalents of yearly profits to find the current or present value of the firm.

---

[2]Discounting is required because profits obtained in the future are less valuable than profits earned presently. To understand this concept, one needs to recognize that $1 in hand today is worth more than $1 to be received a year from now, because $1 today can be invested and, with interest, grow to a larger amount by the end of the year. If we had $1 and invested it at 10 percent interest, it would grow to $1.10 in one year. Thus, $1 is defined as the present value of $1.10 due in one year when the appropriate interest rate is 10 percent. A primer on present value and the time value of money is provided in Appendix A.

Because profits (π) are equal to total revenues (*TR*) minus total costs (*TC*), Equation 1.1 can be rewritten as

$$\text{Value} = \sum_{t=1}^{N} \frac{TR_t - TC_t}{(1 + i)^t}. \tag{1.2}$$

This expanded equation can be used to examine how the expected value maximization model relates to a firm's various functional departments and activities. The marketing department of a firm often has primary responsibility for sales (*TR*); the production department has primary responsibility for costs (*TC*); and the finance department has primary responsibility for acquiring capital and, hence, for the discount factor (*i*) in the denominator. Many important overlaps exist among these functional areas. The marketing department can help reduce costs associated with a given level of output by influencing customer order size and timing. The production department can stimulate sales by improving quality and reducing delivery lags. Other departments, for example, accounting, personnel, transportation, and engineering, provide information and services vital to sales growth and cost control. The determination of *TR* and *TC* is a complex task that requires recognizing important interrelations among the various areas of firm activity. All of these activities affect the firm's risks and the discount rate used to determine present values. An important concept in managerial economics is that managerial decisions should be analyzed in terms of their effects value, as expressed in Equations 1.1 and 1.2.

CONSTRAINTS AND THE THEORY OF THE FIRM

Managerial decisions are often made in light of constraints imposed by technology, resource scarcity, contractual obligations, and government laws and regulations. To make decisions that will maximize value, managers must consider both short-run and long-run implications as well as how external constraints affect their ability to achieve organization objectives.

Firms and other organizations frequently face limited availability of essential inputs, such as skilled labor, raw materials, energy, specialized machinery, and warehouse space. Managers often face limitations on the amount of investment funds available for a particular project or activity. Decisions can also be constrained by contractual requirements. For example, labor contracts limit flexibility in worker scheduling and job assignments. Contracts sometimes require that a minimum level of output be produced to meet delivery requirements. In most instances, output must also meet quality requirements. Some common examples of output quality constraints are nutritional requirements for feed mixtures, audience exposure requirements for marketing promotions, reliability requirements for electronic products, and customer service requirements for minimum satisfaction levels.

Legal restrictions, which affect both production and marketing activities, can also play an important role in managerial decisions. Laws that define minimum wages, health and safety standards, pollution emission standards, fuel efficiency requirements, and fair pricing and marketing practices all limit managerial flexibility.

The role that constraints play in managerial decisions makes the topic of constrained optimization a basic element of managerial economics. Later chapters consider important economic implications of both self-imposed and social constraints. This analysis is important because value maximization and allocative efficiency in society depend on the efficient use of scarce economic resources.

LIMITATIONS OF THE THEORY OF THE FIRM

Optimize
Seek the best solution.

Satisfice
Seek satisfactory rather than optimal results.

Some critics question why the value maximization criterion is used as a foundation for studying firm behavior. Are not managers interested, at least to some extent, in power, prestige, leisure, employee welfare, community well-being, and society in general? Further, do managers really try to **optimize** (seek the best result) or merely **satisfice** (seek satisfactory rather than optimal results)? Does the manager of a firm really seek the sharpest needle in a haystack (optimize), or does he or she stop after finding one sharp enough for sewing (satisfice)? How can one tell whether company support of United Way, for example, leads to long-run value maximization? Are high salaries and substantial stock options necessary to attract and retain managers who can keep the firm ahead of the competition? When a risky venture is turned down, can one say that this reflects inefficient risk avoidance on the part of management? Or does it, in fact, reflect an appropriate decision from the standpoint of value maximization?

It is impossible to give definitive answers to questions like these, and this dilemma has led to the development of alternative theories of firm behavior. Some of the more prominent alternatives are models in which size or growth maximization is the assumed primary objective of management, models that argue that managers are most concerned with their own personal utility or welfare maximization, and models that treat the firm as a collection of individuals with widely divergent goals rather than as a single, identifiable unit. Each of these alternative theories, or models, of managerial behavior has added to our knowledge and understanding of the firm. Still, none can supplant the basic value maximization model of the firm as a foundation for analyzing managerial decisions. Examining why provides additional insight into the value of studying managerial economics.

The theory of the firm states that managers maximize the value of the firm subject to constraints imposed by resource limitations, technology, and society. The theory does not explicitly recognize other goals, including the possibility that managers take actions that benefit parties other than stockholders—perhaps the managers themselves or society in general—and *reduce* stockholder wealth. The model seems to ignore the possibilities of satisficing, managerial self-dealing, and voluntary social responsibility on the part of business. Given that firms assert the existence of multiple goals, engage in "social responsibility" programs, and sometimes exhibit what appears to be satisficing behavior, is the economic model of the firm an adequate basis for the study of managerial decision making? Based on the evidence, the answer is yes.

Research shows that vigorous competition in markets for most goods and services typically forces managers to seek value maximization in their operating decisions. Competition in the capital markets forces managers to seek value maximization in their financing decisions as well. Stockholders are, of course, interested in value maximization because it affects their rates of return on common stock investments. Managers who pursue their own interests instead of stockholders' interests run the risk of losing their job. Buyout pressure from unfriendly firms ("raiders") has been considerable during recent years. Unfriendly takeovers are especially hostile to inefficient management, which is usually replaced. Further, because recent studies show a strong correlation between firm profits and managerial compensation, managers have strong economic incentives to pursue value maximization through their decisions.

It is also sometimes overlooked that managers must fully consider costs and benefits before they can make reasoned decisions. Would it be wise or profitable to seek the best technical solution to a problem if the costs of finding this solution greatly exceed resulting benefits? Of course not. What often appears to be satisficing on the part of management can be interpreted as value-maximizing behavior once the costs of information gathering and analysis are considered. Similarly, short-run growth maximization strategies are often consistent with long-run value maximization when the production, distribution, or promotional advantages of large firm size are better understood.

Finally, the value maximization model also offers insight into a firm's voluntary "socially responsible" behavior. The criticism that the neoclassical theory of the firm emphasizes profits and value maximization while ignoring the issue of social responsibility is important and will be discussed later in the chapter. For now, it will prove useful to examine the concept of profits, which is central to the theory of the firm.

Profits

Profits are such a key element in the free enterprise system that the system would fail without profits and the profit motive. Even in planned economies, where state ownership rather than private enterprise is typical, the profit motive is increasingly used to spur efficient resource use. In the former Eastern Bloc countries, the former Soviet Union, China, and other nations, new profit incentives for managers and workers have led to higher product quality and cost efficiency. Thus, profits and the profit motive play an important and growing role in the efficient allocation of economic resources worldwide.

BUSINESS VERSUS ECONOMIC PROFIT

The general public and the business community typically define profit using an accounting concept. This gives rise to a general understanding of profit as the residual of sales revenue minus the explicit costs of doing business. It is the amount available to fund equity capital after payment for all other resources used by the firm. This definition of profit is often referred to as accounting profit, or **business profit.**

Business Profit
Residual of sales revenue minus the explicit accounting costs of doing business.

The economist also defines profit as the excess of revenues over the costs of doing business. However, inputs provided by the owners, including entrepreneurial effort and capital, are resources that must be paid for as well if they are to be employed. The economist includes a normal rate of return on equity capital plus an opportunity cost for the effort of the owner-entrepreneur as costs of doing business, just as the interest paid on debt and the wages paid to labor are considered costs in calculating business profit. The risk-adjusted **normal rate of return** on capital is the minimum return necessary to

Normal Rate of Return
Minimum profit necessary to attract and retain investment.

attract and retain investment. Similarly, the opportunity cost of owner effort is determined by the value that could be received in an alternative activity. In economic terms, profit is business profit minus the implicit costs of capital and other owner-provided inputs used by the firm. This profit concept is frequently referred to as **economic profit** to distinguish it from business profit.

The concepts of business profit and economic profit can be used to explain why profits exist and their role in a free enterprise economy. There is a normal rate of return, or profit, that is necessary to induce individuals to invest funds in one activity rather than elsewhere or spending them for current consumption. This normal profit is simply a cost for capital; it is no different from the cost of other resources, such as labor, materials, and energy. A similar price exists for the entrepreneurial effort of a firm's owner-manager and for other resources that owners bring to the firm. These opportunity costs for owner-provided inputs offer a primary explanation for the existence of business profits.

Economic Profit
Business profit minus the implicit costs of capital and any other owner-provided inputs.

THE VARIABILITY OF BUSINESS PROFITS

What explains the difference between the economist's concept of normal profits as a cost of equity capital and other owner-provided inputs and the actual business profits earned by firms? In equilibrium, economic profits would be zero if all firms operated in perfectly competitive markets. All firms would report business profits reflecting only a normal rate of return on equity investment and payment for other owner-supplied inputs.

In actual practice, reported profits fluctuate widely. In Table 1.1, business profits are shown for a well-known sample of 30 industrial giants, those companies that comprise the Dow Jones Industrial Average. Income is measured by accounting net profits in dollar terms, and as a percentage of sales revenue and the book value of stockholders' equity. As shown in Table 1.1, business profits during the mid-1990s have been unusually low for leading firms such as Alcoa in the aluminum industry, IBM in computer equipment, and International Paper. Business profits have been unusually high for Coca-Cola in soft drinks, Merck in pharmaceuticals, and Philip Morris in branded food and tobacco products. Industrial giants such as Caterpillar, General Motors, and Union Carbide have lost enormous amounts of money during recent years.

Profit Margin
Net profit divided by sales.

Return on Stockholders' Equity
Accounting net income divided by the book value of total assets minus total liabilities.

While business profits can be measured in dollar terms or as a percentage of sales revenue, called **profit margin,** as in Table 1.1, the economist's concept of a normal rate of profit is typically assessed in terms of the realized rate of **return on stockholders' equity** (ROE). Return on stockholders' equity is defined as accounting net income (profit) divided by the book value of the firm. As seen in Table 1.1, the average ROE for industrial giants found in the Dow Jones Industrial Average is within a broad range around 15 to 20% per year. However, while an average annual ROE of roughly 10% can be regarded as a typical or normal rate of return in the United States and Canada, this standard is routinely exceeded by companies such as Coca-Cola, which has consistently earned a ROE in excess of 45% per year. It is a standard seldom met by International Paper, a company that has suffered massive losses in an attempt to cut costs and increase product quality in the face of tough environmental regulations and foreign competition.

Table 1.1

THE PROFITABILITY OF INDUSTRIAL GIANTS INCLUDED
IN THE DOW JONES INDUSTRIAL AVERAGE

COMPANY NAME	INDUSTRY NAME	SALES	NET WORTH	NET PROFIT	RETURN ON SALES PROFIT (MARGIN)	RETURN ON EQUITY (ROE)
Alcoa	Aluminum	$12,984.0	$4,301.2	$527.6	4.1%	12.3%
Allied Signal	Diversified Co.	14,271.0	4,027.0	983.0	6.9%	24.4%
American Express	Financial Services	16,031.0	8,243.0	1,676.0	10.5%	20.3%
AT&T Corp.	Telecom Services	80,763.0	21,053.0	1,609.0	2.0%	7.6%
Boeing	Aerospace & Defense	20,708.0	9,873.0	1,059.0	5.1%	10.7%
Caterpillar, Inc.	Construction & Mining Machinery	16,267.0	3,979.0	1,280.0	7.9%	32.2%
Chevron Corp.	Integrated Petroleum	41,539.0	15,496.0	1,725.0	4.2%	11.1%
Coca-Cola	Soft Drinks	18,436.0	6,235.0	3,378.0	18.3%	54.2%
Disney (Walt)	Recreation	16,561.1	16,234.0	1,142.0	6.9%	7.0%
DuPont (E.I.)	Basic Chemical	44,185.0	9,756.0	3,405.0	7.7%	34.9%
Eastman Kodak	Precision Instruments	16,018.0	4,839.0	1,399.0	8.7%	28.9%
Exxon Corp.	Integrated Petroleum	128,242.0	41,469.0	6,695.0	5.2%	16.1%
General Electric	Electrical Equipment	75,937.0	29,999.0	7,078.0	9.3%	23.6%
General Motors	Auto & Truck	173,028.5	21,799.1	5,144.3	3.0%	23.6%
Goodyear Tire	Tire & Rubber	13,109.4	3,711.3	656.3	5.0%	17.7%
Hewlett-Packard	Computer & Peripherals	31,519.0	11,839.0	2,433.0	7.7%	20.6%
IBM	Computer & Peripherals	74,724.0	21,115.0	5,097.0	6.8%	24.1%
International Paper	Paper & Forest Products	20,075.0	9,414.0	571.0	2.8%	6.1%
Johnson & Johnson	Medical Supplies	18,842.0	9,045.0	2,403.0	12.8%	26.6%
McDonald's Corp.	Restaurant	10,450.4	7,961.1	1,503.7	14.4%	18.9%
Merck & Co.	Drug	18,979.5	11,396.5	3,695.6	19.5%	32.4%
Minnesota Mining & Mfg.	Diversified Chemical	13,918.0	6,295.0	1,044.0	7.5%	16.6%
Morgan (J.P.)	Bank	15,259.0	10,384.0	1,521.0	10.0%	14.6%
Philip Morris	Tobacco	68,150.0	14,375.0	6,104.0	9.0%	42.5%
Procter & Gamble	Household Products	35,160.0	10,133.0	3,026.0	8.6%	29.9%
Sears	Retail Store	36,990.0	4,462.0	1,120.5	3.0%	25.1%
Travelers Group	Financial Services	NA	11,710.0	1,628.0	NA	13.9%
Union Carbide	Basic Chemical	5,997.0	2,084.0	672.0	11.2%	32.2%
United Technologies	Diversified Co.	23,341.0	4,260.0	835.0	3.6%	19.6%
Wal-Mart Stores	Retail Store	93,627.0	14,756.0	2,740.0	2.9%	18.6%
Averages		$38,503.7	$11,674.8	$2,405.0	7.5%	22.2%

Notes: All dollar figures are in millions; NA means "not applicable."

Data Source: Value/Screen II Database, January 1, 1997.

Some of the variation in ROE depicted in Table 1.1 represents the influence of risk premiums necessary to compensate investors if one business is inherently riskier than another. In the pharmaceuticals industry, for example, hoped-for discoveries of effective therapies for important diseases are often a long shot at best. Thus, the 32.4% rate of return reported by Merck overstates the relative profitability of the drug industry; it could be cut by one-half or more with proper risk adjustment. Similarly, reported profit rates can overstate differences in economic profits if accounting error or bias causes investments of a long-term benefit to be omitted from the balance sheet. For example, current accounting practice often fails to consider advertising or research and development expenditures as intangible investments with long-term benefits. Since advertising and research and development expenditures are immediately expensed rather than capitalized and written off over their useful lives, intangible assets can be grossly understated for certain companies. The balance sheet of Coca-Cola fails to reflect the hundreds of millions of dollars spent to establish and maintain the good reputation of its soft drink products, just as Merck's balance sheet fails to reflect the research dollars spent to develop such important product names as *Mevacor, Prinivil,* and *Vasotec.* As a result, business profit rates for both Coca-Cola and Merck overstate each company's true economic performance.

However, even after risk adjustment, and modification to account for the effects of accounting error and bias, ROE numbers reflect significant variation in economic profits. The observed variation in business profits makes it clear that many firms earn significant economic profits or experience meaningful economic losses at any given point. To better understand these real-world differences in firm profit rates, it is necessary to examine a number of theories used to explain profit variations and why economic profits exist.

FRICTIONAL THEORY OF ECONOMIC PROFITS

Frictional Profit Theory
Abnormal profits observed following unanticipated changes in demand or cost conditions.

One explanation of economic profits or losses is **frictional profit theory.** It states that markets are sometimes in disequilibrium because of unanticipated changes in demand or cost conditions. Shocks occur in the economy and produce disequilibrium conditions that lead to positive or negative economic profits for some firms.

For example, the use of automatic teller machines (ATMs) makes it possible for the customers of financial institutions to easily obtain cash, enter deposits, and make loan payments. At the same time, ATMs render obsolete many of the functions that used to be carried out at branch offices and foster ongoing consolidation in the industry. Similarly, a new generation of user-friendly computer software leads to a marked increase in the demand for high-powered personal computers (PCs) and a rapid growth in returns for efficient PC manufacturers. Alternatively, a rise in the use of plastics or aluminum in automobiles might drive down the profits of steel manufacturers. Over time, barring impassable barriers to entry and exit, resources would flow into or out of financial institutions, computer manufacturers, and steel manufacturers, thus driving rates of return back to normal levels. During interim periods, profits might be above or below normal because of frictional factors that prevent instantaneous adjustment to new market conditions.

MONOPOLY THEORY OF ECONOMIC PROFITS

Monopoly Profit Theory
Above-normal profits
caused by barriers to entry
that limit competition.

A further explanation of above-normal profits, **monopoly profit theory,** is an extension of frictional profit theory. This theory asserts that some firms are sheltered from competition by high barriers to entry. Economies of scale, high capital requirements, patents, or import protection enable some firms to build monopoly positions that allow above-normal profits for extended periods. Monopoly profits can even arise because of luck or happenstance (being in the right industry at the right time) or from anticompetitive behavior. Unlike other potential sources of above-normal profits, monopoly profits are often seen as unwarranted. Thus, monopoly profits are usually taxed or otherwise regulated. Monopoly, a most interesting topic, is discussed at length in Chapters 10, 11, and 13, which consider the causes and consequences of monopoly and how society attempts to mitigate its potential costs.

INNOVATION THEORY OF ECONOMIC PROFITS

Innovation Profit Theory
Above-normal profits that
follow successful invention
or modernization.

An additional theory of economic profits, **innovation profit theory,** describes the above-normal profits that arise following successful invention or modernization. For example, innovation profit theory suggests that Microsoft Corporation has historically earned a superior rate of return because it successfully developed, introduced, and marketed the Graphical User Interface, a superior image-based rather than command-based approach to computer software instructions. Microsoft has continued to receive these supernormal returns as other firms have scrambled to offer a wide variety of "user-friendly" software for personal and business applications. Only after competitors have introduced and successfully saturated the market for such user-friendly software will Microsoft profits be driven down to normal levels. Similarly, McDonald's Corporation earned above-normal rates of return as an early innovator in the fast-food business. With increased competition from Burger King, Wendy's, and a host of national and regional competitors, McDonald's, like Apple, IBM, Xerox, and other early innovators, has seen its above-normal returns decline. As in the case of frictional or disequilibrium profits, profits that are due to innovation are susceptible to the onslaught of competition from new and established competitors.

COMPENSATORY THEORY OF ECONOMIC PROFITS

Compensatory Profit Theory
Above-normal rates of
return that reward
efficiency.

Compensatory profit theory describes above-normal rates of return that reward firms for being extraordinarily successful in meeting customer needs, maintaining efficient operations, and so forth. If firms that operate at the industry's average level of efficiency receive normal rates of return, it is reasonable to expect firms operating at above-average levels of efficiency to earn above-normal rates of return. Inefficient firms can be expected to earn unsatisfactory, below-normal rates of return.

Compensatory profit theory also recognizes economic profit as an important reward to the entrepreneurial function of owners and managers. Every firm and product starts as an idea for better serving some established or perceived need of existing or potential customers. This need remains unmet until an individual takes the initiative to design, plan, and implement a solution. The opportunity for economic profits is an important motivation for such entrepreneurial activity.

THE ROLE OF PROFITS IN THE ECONOMY

Each of the preceding four theories describes economic profits obtained for different reasons. In some cases, several reasons might apply. For example, a very efficient manufacturer may earn an above-normal rate of return in accordance with compensatory theory, but, during a strike by a competitor's employees, the above-average profits may be augmented by frictional profits. Similarly, Microsoft's profit position might be partly explained by all four theories: The company has earned high frictional profits while Adobe Systems, Computer Associates, Computervision, Lotus, Netscape, Oracle, and a host of other software companies tool up in response to the rapid growth in demand for user-friendly software; it has earned monopoly profits because it has some patent

---

MANAGERIAL APPLICATION
1.2

The "Marlboro" Question

Philip Morris Companies, Inc., is a holding company whose subsidiaries manufacture and sell a wide variety of branded consumer products. Kraft General Foods, Inc., Miller Brewing Company, and other top subsidiaries help make Philip Morris one of the largest and most successful consumer packaged goods companies in the world. Nevertheless, while *Coca-Cola* and *See's Candies* are the wonderful products of wonderful companies, Philip Morris is famous for *Marlboro* cigarettes, a product that is known for killing its customers. Is it possible for such a product to be the basis for a wonderful business?

The "tobacco" issue is charged with emotion these days, and it is important to recognize two different issues tied to the decision to enter or exit the tobacco business. From the standpoint of a business manager or individual investor, there is the economic question of whether it is *possible* to earn above-normal returns by investing in Philip Morris, RJR Nabisco, or other parts of the tobacco business. From a philosophical standpoint, there is the ethical question of whether it is *desirable* to earn such abnormal returns, if available.

Among the well-known *gloomy* particulars are:

- During the last several years, the link between smoking and cancer seems to have moved from a "pre-

ponderance of the evidence" to "beyond a reasonable doubt."

- Recent medical studies suggest that breaking the tobacco habit may be as difficult as curing heroin addiction. This fuels the fire of those who seek to restrict smoking opportunities.

- Given general recognition of the link between smoking and cancer, and even fewer smokers among potential jurors, the potential for adverse jury decisions, particularly regarding passive smoke, would seem to be increasing.

- Prospects for additional "sin" and "health care" taxes on smoking appear high.

- *Nicoderm* and other products have the potential to break the habit for a high-income, and therefore less-price-sensitive, smoker.

- Smoking is now most common among the less educated and less affluent, and hence price-sensitive, sector of society.

Some underappreciated *positive* counterpoints to consider are:

- Given that adverse jury decisions have not emerged to date, it is simply not possible to make an appropri-

protection; it has certainly benefited from successful innovation; and it is well managed and thus has earned compensatory profits.

Economic profits play an important role in a market-based economy. Above-normal profits serve as a valuable signal that firm or industry output should be increased. Expansion by established firms or entry by new competitors often occurs quickly during high-profit periods. Just as above-normal profits provide a signal for expansion and entry, below-normal profits provide a signal for contraction and exit. Economic profits are one of the most important factors affecting the allocation of scarce economic resources. Above-normal profits can also constitute an important reward for innovation and efficiency, just as below-normal profits can serve as a penalty for stagnation and inefficiency. Thus, profits play a critical role both in providing an incentive for innovation and productive efficiency and in allocating scarce resources.

An understanding of how profits affect business behavior provides important insight into the relationship between the firm and society.

Continued

- ate judgment regarding the probability of successful product liability suits in tobacco.
- Business managers and investors tend to overweigh the cost of disaster scenarios, such as the potential risk to tobacco from "long tail" passive smoke litigation.
- Additional "sin" and "health care" taxes on smoking increase the government's interest in legal smoking.
- Higher excise taxes will kill price competition in the tobacco industry. Huge percentage increases in manufacturer prices will barely budge retail prices; huge manufacturer price cuts would barely dent retail prices.
- Continued tobacco use is more voluntary than ever since antidotes such as *Nicoderm* are now available.
- Even though smoking is now most common in the more price-sensitive sector of society, it remains a very high-margin, relatively low-cost product.

Taken as a whole, these considerations suggest it might be quite *possible* to make above-average returns by investing in the tobacco business. However, there may be something of a "greater fool" theory at work in this analysis because, knowing full well the faults of tobacco products, tobacco companies and their investors can only benefit by finding "greater fools" to pay high prices for products that they themselves would not buy. Moreover, while it is dangerous to argue against the right of consumers to make their own consumption decisions, such decisions can be troubling when they involve chemical dependency.

None of the above addresses the question of whether it is *desirable* to profit from the sale of clearly injurious tobacco products. Legendary investor John Templeton has compiled an enviable investment record despite a policy of not investing in tobacco, alcohol, or gaming stocks. At the same time, mutual fund giant Peter Lynch has compiled an even more enviable investment record with the Magellan Fund's Philip Morris investments. While there is no easy answer to the "tobacco" question, all managers and investors routinely face such issues. From both economic and ethical perspectives, what do *you* think?

See: Mike France, "Is Big Tobacco Ready to Deal?," *Business Week*, December 23, 1996, 32-34.

Role of Business in Society

Evidence that business contributes significantly to social welfare is clear and convincing. The economy in the United States and several other countries has sustained a notable rate of growth over many decades. Benefits of that growth have also been widely distributed. Suppliers of capital, labor, and other resources all receive substantial returns for their contributions. Consumers benefit from an increasing quantity and quality of goods and services available for consumption. Taxes on the business profits of firms, as well as on the payments made to suppliers of labor, materials, capital, and other inputs, provide revenues needed to increase government services. All of these contributions to social welfare stem directly from the efficiency of business in serving the economic needs of customers.

WHY FIRMS EXIST

Firms exist by public consent to serve the needs of society. If social welfare could be measured, business firms might be expected to operate in a manner that would maximize some index of social well-being. Maximization of social welfare requires answering the following important questions: What combination of goods and services (including negative by-products, such as pollution) should be produced? How should goods and services be provided? And how should goods and services be distributed? These are some of the most vital questions faced in a free enterprise system, and they are important issues in managerial economics.

In a free market economy, the economic system produces and allocates goods and services according to the forces of demand and supply. Firms must determine what products customers want, bid for necessary resources, and then offer their products for sale. In this process, each firm actively competes for a share of the customer's dollar. Suppliers of capital, labor, and raw materials must then be compensated out of sales proceeds. The share of revenues paid to each supplier depends on relative productivity, resource scarcity, and the degree of competition in each input market.

THE ROLE OF SOCIAL CONSTRAINTS

Although the process of market-determined production and allocation of goods and services is highly efficient, there are potential difficulties in an unconstrained market economy that can prevent the maximization of social welfare. Society has developed a variety of methods for alleviating these problems through the political system. One possible difficulty with an unconstrained market economy is that certain groups could gain excessive economic power, permitting them to obtain too large a share of the value created by firms. To illustrate, the economics of producing and distributing electric power are such that only one firm can efficiently serve a given community. Furthermore, there are no good substitutes for electric lighting. As a result, electric companies are in a position to exploit consumers; they could charge high prices and earn excessive profits. Society's solution to this potential exploitation is direct regulation. Prices charged by electric companies and other utilities are controlled and held to a level that is thought to be just sufficient to provide stockholders with a fair rate of return on their investment. In theory, the regulatory process is simple; in practice, it is costly, difficult to implement, and in many ways arbitrary. It is a poor but sometimes necessary substitute for competition.

An additional problem can occur in a market economy when, because of economies of scale or other barriers to entry, a limited number of firms serve a given market. If firms compete fairly with each other, no difficulty arises. However, if they conspire with one another in setting prices, they may be able to restrict output, obtain excessive profits, and reduce social welfare. Antitrust laws are designed to prevent such collusion as well as the merging of competing firms when the effect of the merger would be to lessen competition substantially. Like direct regulation, antitrust laws contain arbitrary elements and are costly to administer, but they too are necessary if economic justice, as defined by society, is to be served.

A further problem relates to workers being exploited under certain conditions. Because of the potential for exploitation, laws have been developed to equalize the bargaining power of employers and workers. These labor laws require firms to allow collective bargaining and to refrain from unfair practices. The question of whether labor's bargaining position is too strong in some instances also has been raised. For example, can powerful national unions such as the Teamsters use the threat of a strike to obtain excessive increases in wages, which may in turn be passed on to consumers in the form of higher prices? Those who believe this to be the case have suggested that the antitrust laws should be applied to labor unions, especially those that bargain with numerous small employers.

A market economy also faces difficulty when firms can impose external costs on society through their production activities. For example, firms can impose costs on others when they dump wastes into the air or water or when they deface the earth, as in strip mining. If a factory pollutes the air, causing nearby residents to suffer lung ailments or other health impairments, a meaningful cost is imposed on these people and society in general. Failure to shift these costs back onto the firm and, ultimately, to the consumers of its products, means that the firm and its customers benefit unfairly by not having to pay the full costs of its activities. The presence of pollution and other externalities may result in an inefficient and inequitable allocation of resources. In both government and business, considerable attention is being directed to the problem of internalizing social costs. Some of the practices used to internalize social costs include setting health and safety standards for products and work conditions, establishing emissions limits on manufacturing processes and on products that pollute, and imposing fines or closing firms that do not meet established standards.

THE SOCIAL RESPONSIBILITY OF BUSINESS

All of these measures—utility regulation, antitrust laws, labor laws, and the direct regulation of products and operations—are examples of actions taken by society to modify the behavior of business firms and to make this behavior more consistent with broad social goals. These constraints have an important bearing on the firm's operations and, hence, on managerial decision making.

The World Is Turning to Capitalism and Democracy

MANAGERIAL APPLICATION
1.3

Capitalism is based on voluntary exchange between self-interested parties. Given that the exchange is voluntary, both parties must perceive benefits, or profit, for market transactions to take place. If only one party were to benefit from a given transaction, there would be no incentive for the other party to cooperate and no voluntary exchange would take place. A self-interested capitalist must also have in mind the interest of others. In contrast, a truly selfish individual is only concerned with himself or herself, without regard for the well-being of others. As such, selfish behavior is inconsistent with the capitalistic system. Self-interested behavior leads to profits and success under capitalism; selfish behavior does not.

Like any economic system, capitalism has far-reaching political and social consequences. Similarly, democracy has far-reaching economic consequences. What is sometimes not understood is that capitalism and democracy are mutually reinforcing. Some philosophers have gone so far as to say that capitalism and democracy are intertwined. Without capitalism, democracy is impossible. Without democracy, capitalistic systems fail. To better understand the relation between capitalism and democracy, it becomes necessary to consider the fundamentally attractive characteristics of a decentralized exchange economy.

Capitalism is socially desirable because of its decentralized and customer-oriented nature. The menu of products to be produced is derived from market price and output signals originating in free and competitive markets, not from the output schedules of a centralized planning agency. As such, production is freely directed by self-interested producers seeking to meet the demands of individual customers. Resources and products are impartially allocated through market forces. They are not allocated on the basis of favoritism due to social status or political persuasion. Through their purchase decisions, customers are able to influence the quantity and quality of products brought to market. Any producer who is able to meet these demands is allowed to compete.

A freely competitive market gives customers a broad choice of goods and services and gives all producers the opportunity to succeed. As such, capitalism reinforces the individual freedoms protected in a democratic society. In democracy, government does not grant individual freedom. Instead, the political power of government emanates from the people. Similarly, the flow of economic resources originates with the individual customer in a capitalistic system. It is not centrally directed by government.

Competition among producers is also a fundamentally attractive feature of the capitalistic system because it tends to keep costs and prices as low as possible. By operating efficiently, firms are able to produce the maximum quantity and quality of goods and services possible, given scarce productive resources. Even though efficiency in resource allocation is an often recognized virtue of capitalism, the egalitarian nature of capitalistic production methods is sometimes overlooked. Mass production is, by definition, production for the masses. By its nature, capitalism seeks to satisfy a broad rather than narrow constituency. Competition by entrant and nonleading firms typically limits the concentration of economic and political power. When economic forces tend to reduce rather than increase the number of viable competitors, antitrust or regulation policy is sometimes used to avoid potentially harmful consequences. On balance, and especially when compared to centrally planned economies, competitive processes in a capitalistic system tend to further the principles of individual freedom and self-determination. From this perspective, capitalism and democracy are mutually reinforcing. Strong market forces tend to undermine the economic favoritism that occurs under totalitarian systems of government. Similarly, the democratic form of government is inconsistent with concentrated economic influence and decision making.

Today, communism and totalitarian forms of government are in retreat around the globe. China has experienced violent upheaval as the country embarks on much-needed economic and political reforms. In the Soviet Union, Eastern Europe, India, and Latin America, years of economic failure have forced governments to dismantle entrenched bureaucracy and install economic incentives. Rising living standards and political freedom have made life in the West the envy of the world. Against this backdrop, the future is bright indeed for capitalism *and* democracy!

See: Tad Szulc, "First Money, Then the Flag," *Forbes*, April 7, 1997, 52-55.

What does all this mean with respect to the value maximization theory of the firm? Is the model adequate for examining issues of social responsibility and for developing rules for business decisions that reflect the role of business in society? Business firms are primarily economic entities and, as such, can be expected to analyze social responsibility from within the context of the economic model of the firm. This is an important consideration when examining the set of inducements used to channel the efforts of business in directions that society desires. Similar considerations should also be taken into account before applying political pressure or regulations to constrain firm operations. For example, from the consumer's standpoint it is desirable to pay low rates for gas, electric, and telephone services. If public pressures drive rates down too low, however, utility profits could fall below the level necessary to provide an adequate return to investors. In that event, capital would not flow into the regulated industries, innovation would cease, and service would deteriorate. When such issues are considered, the economic model of the firm provides useful insight. This model emphasizes the close relation between the firm and society, and it indicates the importance of active business participation in the development and achievement of social objectives.

Structure of This Text

OBJECTIVES

This text should help you accomplish the following objectives:

- Develop a clear understanding of economic theory and methods as they relate to managerial decision making;
- Acquire a framework for understanding the nature of the firm as an integrated whole as opposed to a loosely connected set of functional departments; and
- Recognize the relation between the firm and society and the key role of business as a tool for social betterment.

Throughout the text, the emphasis is on the *practical* application of economic analysis to managerial decision problems.

DEVELOPMENT OF TOPICS

The value maximization framework offers useful perspective for characterizing actual managerial decisions and a means for developing rules that can be used to improve those decisions. The basic test of the value maximization model—indeed, of any model—is its ability to explain behavior in the real world of managerial decision making. As basic elements of managerial economics are introduced, it is important to recognize how they relate to real-world practice. This text highlights the complementary relation between theory and practice. Theory is used to improve managerial decision making, and practical experience leads to the development of better theory.

Chapter 2, Basic Economic Relations, begins by examining the important role that marginal analysis plays in the optimization process. The balancing of marginal revenues and marginal costs to determine the profit-maximizing output level is explored, as are other fundamental economic relations that help organizations efficiently employ scarce resources. All of these economic relations are considered based on the simplifying assumption that cost and revenue relations are known with certainty. Later in the book, this assumption is relaxed, and the more realistic circumstance of decision making under conditions of uncertainty is examined. This material shows how optimization concepts can be effectively employed in situations when managers have extensive information about the chance or probability of certain outcomes, but the end result of managerial decisions cannot be forecast precisely. Given the challenges posed by a rapidly changing global environment, a careful statistical analysis of economic relations is often conducted to provide the information necessary for effective decision making. Tools used by managers in the statistical analysis of economic relations are the subject of Chapter 3, Statistical Analysis of Economic Relations.

The concepts of demand and supply are basic to understanding the effective use of economic resources. The general overview of demand and supply in Chapter 4 provides a framework for the more detailed inquiry that follows. In Chapter 5, Demand Analysis and Estimation, attention is turned to a careful consideration of demand analysis and estimation. The successful management of any organization requires understanding of the demand for its products. The demand function relates the sales of a product to such important factors as the price of the product itself, prices of other goods, income, advertising, and even weather. The role of demand elasticities, which measure the strength of the relations expressed in the demand function, is also emphasized. Issues addressed in the prediction of demand and cost conditions are explored more fully in Chapter 6, Forecasting. The material in this chapter provides a useful framework for the ongoing estimation of important demand and cost relations.

Chapters 7, 8, and 9 examine production and cost concepts. The economics of resource employment in the manufacture and distribution of goods and services is the focus of this material. These chapters present economic analysis as a context for understanding the underlying logic of managerial decisions and as a means for developing improved operating and planning practices. Chapter 7, Production Analysis and Estimation, develops and illustrates rules for optimal resource combination and employment levels. This material demonstrates how resources can be combined in a profit-maximizing manner. Chapter 8, Cost Analysis and Estimation, focuses on the identification of cost-output relations so that appropriate decisions regarding product pricing, plant size and location, and so on can be made. Chapter 9, Linear Programming, introduces a tool from the decision sciences which can be applied to many important optimization problems. This technique offers managers highly useful input for short-run operating decisions, as well as information helpful in the long-run planning process.

The remainder of the book builds on the foundation provided in Chapters 1 through 9 to examine a variety of topics in the theory and practice of managerial economics. Chapters 10 and 11 explore market structures and their implications for the development and implementation of effective competitive strategy. The analyses of demand and supply relations are integrated to examine the dynamics of economic markets. Chapter 10, Perfect Competition and Monopoly, offers perspective on how product differentiation, barriers to entry, and the availability of information interact to determine the vigor of competition. Chapter 11, Monopolistic Competition and Oligopoly, considers "competition among the few" for industries in which interactions among competitors are normal. Chapter 12, Pricing Practices, shows how the forces of supply and demand interact under a variety of market settings to signal appropriate pricing policies. Importantly, this chapter analyzes pricing practices commonly observed in business and shows how they reflect the predictions of economic theory.

Chapter 13, Government Regulation of the Market Economy, focuses on the role of government by considering how the external economic environment affects the managerial decision-making process. This chapter investigates how interactions among business, government, and the public result in antitrust and regulatory policies with direct implications for the efficiency and fairness of the economic system. Chapter 14, Risk Analysis, illustrates how the predictions of economic theory can be applied in the real-world setting of uncertainty. Chapter 15, Capital Budgeting, examines the key elements necessary for an effective planning framework for managerial decision making. It investigates the capital budgeting process and how firms combine demand, production, cost, and risk analyses to effectively make strategic long-run investment decisions. Finally, Chapter 16, Public Management, studies how the tools and techniques of managerial economics can be used to analyze decisions in the public and not-for-profit sectors and how that decision-making process can be improved.

Summary

Managerial economics links traditional economics with the decision sciences to develop important tools for managerial decision making. This approach is successful because it focuses on the application of the tools and techniques of economic analysis to practical business problem solving.

- **Managerial economics** applies economic theory and methods to business and administrative decision making.
- The basic model of the business enterprise is called the **theory of the firm.** The primary goal is seen as long-term **expected value maximization.** The **value of the firm** is the present value of the firm's expected future net cash flows, where **present value** is the value of expected cash flows discounted back to the present at an appropriate interest rate.
- Valid questions are sometimes raised about whether managers really **optimize** (seek the best solution) or merely **satisfice** (seek satisfactory rather than optimal results). Most often, especially when information costs are considered, managers can be seen as optimizing.
- **Business profit,** or accounting profit, is the residual of sales revenue minus the explicit accounting costs of doing business. Business profit often incorporates a **normal rate of return** on capital, or the minimum return necessary to attract and retain investment for a particular use. **Economic profit** is business profit minus the implicit costs of equity and other owner-provided inputs used by the firm. **Return on**

stockholders' equity, or accounting net income divided by the book value of total assets minus total liabilities, is a useful, practical indicator of firm performance.

■ One explanation of economic profits or losses is **frictional profit theory,** in which abnormal profits are observed following unanticipated changes in product demand or cost conditions. **Monopoly profit theory** asserts that above-normal profits are sometimes caused by barriers to entry that limit competition. **Innovation profit theory** describes above-normal profits that arise as a result of successful invention or modernization. **Compensatory profit theory** holds that above-normal rates of return can sometimes be seen as a reward to firms that are extraordinarily successful in meeting customer needs, maintaining efficient operations, and so forth.

The use of economic theory and methods to analyze and improve the managerial decision-making process combines the study of theory and practice to gain a useful and practical perspective. Although the logic and consistency of managerial economics are intuitively appealing, the primary virtue of managerial economics lies in its usefulness. It works!

QUESTIONS

Q1.1   Why is it appropriate to view firms primarily as economic entities?

Q1.2   Explain how the valuation model given in Equation 1.2 could be used to describe the integrated nature of managerial decision making across the functional areas of business.

Q1.3   Describe the effects of each of the following managerial decisions or economic influences on the value of the firm:
A.   The firm is required to install new equipment to reduce air pollution.
B.   Through heavy expenditures on advertising, the firm's marketing department increases sales substantially.
C.   The production department purchases new equipment that lowers manufacturing costs.
D.   The firm raises prices. Quantity demanded in the short run is unaffected, but in the longer run, unit sales are expected to decline.
E.   The Federal Reserve System takes actions that lower interest rates dramatically.
F.   An expected increase in inflation causes generally higher interest rates, and, hence, the discount rate increases.

Q1.4   It is sometimes argued that managers of large, publicly owned firms make decisions to maximize their own welfare as opposed to that of stockholders. Would such behavior create problems in using value maximization as a basis for examining managerial decision making?

Q1.5   How is the popular notion of business profit different from the economic profit concept described in the chapter? What role does the idea of normal profits play in this difference?

Q1.6   Which concept—the business profit concept or the economic profit concept—provides the more appropriate basis for evaluating the operations of a business? Why?

Q1.7   What factors should be considered in examining the adequacy of profits for a firm or industry?

Q1.8   Why is the concept of self-interest important in economics?

Q1.9   "In the long run, a profit-maximizing firm would never knowingly market unsafe products. However, in the short run, unsafe products can do a lot of damage." Discuss this statement.

Q1.10   Is it reasonable to expect firms to take actions that are in the public interest but are detrimental to stockholders? Is regulation always necessary and appropriate to induce firms to act in the public interest?

Case Study for Chapter 1

DO BOARDS OF DIRECTORS MAKE GOOD CORPORATE WATCHDOGS?

Is the large publicly-traded corporation in eclipse? Some say yes. Harvard financial economist Michael Jensen, for example, argues that the experience of the past two decades indicates that corporate internal control systems have failed to deal effectively with economic changes, especially slow growth and the requirement for exit from declining industries. In some parts of the economy, new and smaller organizations are emerging to take the place of giant corporations. While corporate in form, these agile organizations eschew public shareholders. Their major source of capital is public and private debt rather than publicly-traded equity.

In analyzing the late-1980s trend toward leveraged buyouts (LBOs), Jensen observed that LBOs differ from publicly-held conglomerates in at least four important respects: management incentives are closely tied to performance, decentralization is common, a heavy reliance on leverage is typical, and obligations to creditors and residual claimants are clearly specified. In suggesting ways for public corporations to "heal" themselves, Jensen advised that public companies should become more like LBOs by decentralizing, borrowing to repurchase stock or pay large dividends, or increasing equity ownership among corporate directors, managers, and other employees.

Of course, given recent experience it is quite valid to express concern with respect to the adaptive capability of some large corporations. Still, pronouncements concerning the "death" of the modern corporation may be premature. The corporate form has endured and flourished because it is a useful and effective means for gathering and deploying economic resources. Questions about corporate effectiveness are ultimately questions about what is referred to as *corporate governance*. Corporate governance is the system of controls that helps the corporation effectively manage, administer, and direct economic resources.

Problems in corporate governance exist to the extent that unresolved material conflicts endure between the self-seeking goals of (agent) managers and the value maximization goal of (principal) stockholders. "Agency costs" incurred by stockholders are reflected in expenses for managerial monitoring, the over-consumption of perquisites by managers, and lost opportunities due to excessive risk avoidance. While this agency cost characterization of the corporate governance issue is fairly recent, modern concern with the topic began more than sixty years ago when Berle and Means predicted that managers with little direct ownership interest, and thus having their "own" rather than stockholder interests in mind, would come to run the bulk of U.S. business enterprise. Interestingly, economists' concern with this "other people's money" problem dates from 1776 and the work of Adam Smith. One of the most important corporate governance mechanisms is a board of directors that is focused and motivated to further shareholder interests. Within this context, a relevant question is: Do company boards of directors make good corporate watchdogs?

To gain insight on this important issue, it is interesting to consider some recent experience. For example, financier Kirk Kerkorian and former Chrysler Chairman Lee Iacocca dropped a bombshell in 1995 when they announced a hostile bid to take over Chrysler. Prior to the bid, Kerkorian and Iacocca held roughly 10% of Chrysler shares. Far from dissatisfied with the performance of Chrysler management or Chairman Robert Eaton, Iacocca's hand-picked successor, Kerkorian and Iacocca were merely disappointed that Chrysler's stock price had failed to reflect the dramatic turnaround in Chrysler's fortunes. Since taking the helm in 1992, Eaton had guided Chrysler through tricky new product introductions for its flagship Jeep and minivan brands, pared debt, and boosted return on equity to a sparkling 30%+. Under Eaton's leadership, Chrysler had also accumulated a cash hoard of nearly $7.5 billion, to guide Chrysler through the next downturn in the auto industry. Therein lies the rub—Kerkorian and Iacocca argued that Chrysler's cash hoard was far in excess of required cash reserves. Chrysler management and the company's board of directors quickly responded to the Kerkorian and Iacocca bid. Within months, Chrysler announced a dividend increase and share buyback program that returned billions of dollars to Chrysler shareholders, while retaining sufficient reserves to fund an innovative new vehicle program. By the start of 1997, Chrysler stock had rebounded to a level more than 50% above the Kerkorian and Iacocca bid.

The resurgence at Chrysler mirrors the rebound at GM following a board revolt caused by its long downward spiral in market share and profitability during the 1980s. Not only was Chairman and CEO Roger Smith fired, but his successor Robert C. Stempel was also sacked when Stempel failed to stem the tide of dismal profit performance and bungled corporate strategy. John F. Smith, Jr., the former chief of GM's profitable foreign operations, was promoted to

THE BEST AND WORST BOARDS OF DIRECTORS

Table 1.2

THE BEST BOARDS OF DIRECTORS		THE WORST BOARDS OF DIRECTORS	
NAME	DETAILS	NAME	DETAILS
Campbell Soup	Wins admiration for governance practices and candid self-review policy.	Archer Daniels Midland	Investors scorn board for nepotism and general lack of independence.
General Electric	CEO wins plaudits for focusing on GE and shunning other boards; each outside director owns roughly $500,000 in GE stock.	Champion International	Directors own little stock; under-performing CEO sits on two boards of companies run by fellow directors
IBM	Board's hiring of outside CEO and spectacular turnaround have won investor favor.	H.J. Heinz	Geriatric board is loaded with insiders who fail to represent shareholder interests.
Compaq Computer	Outside chairman reviews both company and director performance.	Rollins Environmental	Board comprised solely of management insiders; perhaps the least independent board of any public company.
Colgate Palmolive	Colgate sports an independent board with an excellent reputation.	NationsBank	A top performing bank despite featuring a board that flunks tests of independence and accountability.
Chrysler	Directors communicate openly with top institutional investors; dividend boost and share buybacks placate shareholders.	AT&T	AT&T features professional directors who sit on too many boards, own little stock, and lack high-tech expertise.

THE BEST BOARDS OF DIRECTORS		THE WORST BOARDS OF DIRECTORS	
NAME	DETAILS	NAME	DETAILS
Johnson & Johnson	Board known for managerial expertise and for being sensitive to shareholder interests.	Kmart	Board acted slowly in replacing under-performing CEO; too little stock ownership among too many directors.
Merck & Co.	Outside-dominated committee evaluates company and board performance.	UNISYS	Outside directors own little stock; investors remain disenchanted with abysmal stock performance.
Hercules	High-quality board known for independence; administers tough self-evaluation for effectiveness.	Ethyl Corp.	Investors remain unhappy with subpar returns and the company's once-clubby board.
Exxon	Exxon's annual election of board members, significant stock ownership requirement, and no board pensions win shareholder approval.	Fleming Cos.	Lackluster stock returns frustrate investors, who view board as too cozy with management.

See: John A. Byrne, "The Best and Worst Boards," *Business Week,* November 25, 1996, 82-106.

the post of GM president and given the unenviable task of turning the company around. John Smith's reign at the head of GM has been marked by stunning success. Nonessential businesses, like EDS, have been shed and refocused attention on the company's core operations has produced the most innovative and high-quality line of cars, trucks, and sport utility vehicles in GM history.

Also bowing to unrelenting pressure from shareholders during the mid-1990s, retail giant Sears shed its Dean Witter brokerage, Discover charge card, and Allstate insurance operations—and refocused attention on its key retailing operations. In another case, poor performance at travel and financial services giant American Express forced the board of directors to sack its chairman and CEO in 1993. Harvey Golub, former head of American Express' mutual fund divi-

sion, assumed the top job and promptly moved to divest the First Data Corp. transaction processing subsidiary, Shearson brokerage, and Lehman Brothers investment banking business. Like Chrysler, GM, and Sears, American Express and its shareholders enjoyed a strong rebound in operating performance during the mid-1990s.

In many other instances, shareholder-led boardroom revolts have led to dramatically improved performance for trimmed down and refocused corporate giants. After such stunning success in improving management strategy and operating performance, stockholders and stockholder groups have finally gotten the attention they deserve from refocused and energized corporate boards of directors. The "best" corporate boards have clearly gotten the message; some of the "worst" corporate boards have much to learn.

A. Do documented cases of incompetence by top management and corporate boards of directors invalidate the value-maximization theory of the firm?

B. Many shareholder groups prefer to split the chairman and CEO posts, and install an outsider as chairman of the board of directors. From the shareholder viewpoint, discuss some of the advantages and disadvantages of an "outside" chairman.

C. Shareholders often want change when corporate performance is poor, top executive pay is excessive, or management is unresponsive. However, removing corporate directors by shareholder vote remains almost impossible. In annual proxy contests, shareholders are generally offered only one slate of candidates, and they can express their dissatisfaction only by withholding votes from would-be board members. Does this mean that the current shareholder voting process is an ineffectual means of corporate control? How might this process be improved?

D. In addition to casting their vote in annual proxy contests, shareholders "vote with their feet" when they sell the stocks of poorly performing companies. How is this likely to influence inferior performance by top management and the board of directors?

Basic Economic Relations

Managers have always had to make tough choices that involve benefits and costs. Until recently, however, it was simply impractical to compare the relative pluses and minuses of a large number of managerial decisions under a wide variety of operating conditions. Now with the low-cost and highly powerful desktop computers of the late-1990s, it is possible to analyze a broad assortment of managerial decisions and operating scenarios. Powerful and inexpensive desktop computers empower managers in both large and small organizations to make useful projections and insightful operating decisions.

Effective managers in the late-1990s must be able to collect, organize, and process a vast assortment of relevant operating information. However, efficient information processing requires more than electronic computing capability; it requires a fundamental understanding of basic economic relations. Without such knowledge, the computing capability of powerful desktop computers is wasted. With such a framework, powerful desktop computers become an awesome aid to managerial decision making.[1]

This chapter introduces a number of basic economic concepts and fundamental principles of economic analysis. These ideas form the basis for describing all demand, cost, and profit relations. Once the basics of economic relations are understood, the tools and techniques of optimization can be applied to find the best course of action for any given managerial decision problem.

Economic Optimization

Effective managerial decision making is the process of efficiently arriving at the best possible solution to a given problem. If only one solution is possible, then no decision problem exists. When alternative courses of action are available, the best decision is the one that produces the result most consistent with managerial objectives. The process of arriving at the best managerial decision is the process of economic optimization.

OPTIMAL DECISIONS

Should input quality be enhanced to better meet low-cost import competition? Is a reduction in labor costs efficiently achieved through an across-the-board decrease in staffing, or is it better to make targeted cutbacks? Following an increase in product demand, is it preferable to increase managerial staff, line personnel, or both? These are the

---

[1] See I. Jeanne Dugan, "The Best Performers," *Business Week,* March 24, 1997, 80-90.

types of questions that require a careful consideration of basic economic relations. Answers to these questions clearly depend on the objectives and preferences of management. Just as there is no single "best" purchase decision for all customers at all times, there is no single "best" investment decision for all managers at all times. When alternative courses of action are available, the decision that produces the result most consistent with managerial objectives is the **optimal decision.**

A major challenge that must be met in the decision-making process is characterizing the relative desirability of decision alternatives in terms of the objectives of the organization. Decision makers must recognize all available choices and portray them in terms of appropriate decision variables, costs, and benefits. The description of decision alternatives is greatly enhanced through application of the principles of managerial economics. Managerial economics also provides tools for analyzing and evaluating decision alternatives. Economic concepts and methodology are used to select the optimal course of action in light of available options and objectives.

Fundamental principles of economic analysis form the basis for describing demand, cost, and profit relations. Once basic economic relations are understood, the tools and techniques of optimization can be used to find the best course of action. Most important, the theory and process of optimization gives practical insight concerning the value maximization theory of the firm. Understanding optimization techniques is helpful because these methods offer a realistic means for dealing with the complexities of goal-oriented managerial activities.

MAXIMIZING THE VALUE OF THE FIRM

In managerial economics, the primary objective of management is assumed to be maximization of the value of the firm. This *value maximization* objective was introduced in Chapter 1 and is again expressed in Equation 2.1:

$$\text{Value} = \sum_{t=1}^{N} \frac{\text{Profit}_t}{(1+i)^t} = \sum_{t=1}^{N} \frac{\text{Total Revenue}_t - \text{Total Cost}_t}{(1+i)^t}. \qquad \textbf{(2.1)}$$

Maximizing Equation 2.1 is a complex task that involves detailed consideration of future revenues, costs, and discount rates. Total revenues are determined by the quantity sold and the prices received. Factors that affect prices and the quantity sold include marketing strategies, pricing and distribution policies, the nature of competition, and the general state of the economy. Complex cost relations are also encountered in the production process. Cost analysis requires a detailed examination of the prices and availability of various input factors, alternative production methods, and so on. Finally, the relation between an appropriate discount rate and the company's mix of products and both operating and financial leverage must be determined. All of these factors affect the value of the firm as described in Equation 2.1 and must be considered.

To determine the optimal course of action, marketing, production, and financial decisions must all be integrated within the decision analysis framework. Decisions related to personnel retention and development, organization structure, and long-term business strategy must be combined in a framework that shows how any managerial initiative

Does Good Theory Always Work in Practice?

Have you ever been a spectator at a golf, tennis, or racquetball tournament when a particular athlete's play became the center of attention? As people admired the performance, some questions inevitably arose. Have you ever heard people ask, "Where did that athlete study physics?" or "Wow, who taught that guy physiology?" Chances are you haven't. Instead, the discussion probably centered on the player's skill, finesse, or tenacity. Natural talent developed through long hours of dedicated training and intense competition is commonly regarded as the chief prerequisite for becoming an accomplished amateur or professional athlete. But if you think about it, an accomplished racquetball player must also know a great deal about angles, speed, and acceleration. Likewise, a successful tennis competitor must fully understand his or her physical limits as well as the competition's.

While success in these sports requires that one understand the basic principles of physics and physiology, most athletes develop their "feel" for these subjects on the tennis court, golf course, baseball diamond, or gridiron. In fact, some successful athletes have had little or no formal textbook instruction in these subjects. Their understanding more often is based, for example, on the "applied physics" courses offered daily on the tennis court. What is critical is that these "students" have mastered their subject; how they came about this expertise is often much less important.

Similarly, some very successful businesses are run by people with little or no formal training in accounting, finance, management, or marketing. This is especially true of older executives who came up through the ranks before the post-World War II college education boom. These executives' successes testify to their ability to develop a feel for business in much the same way that the successful athlete develops a feel for his or her sport. Although the term *optimization* may be foreign to such individuals, the methodology of optimization is familiar to each of them in terms of their everyday business practices. Adjusting prices to avoid stockout situations, increasing product quality to "meet the competition," and raising salaries to retain valued employees all involve a basic, practical understanding of optimization concepts.

The behavior of both the successful athlete and the successful executive can be described, or modeled, as being consistent with a process of optimization. In the case of, say, the tennis player, the pursuit of on-the-court success can be described as being consistent with performance maximization, given his or her skill and other capabilities. In the case of the successful business executive, the day-to-day activities incorporated into ongoing business practice typically are quite consistent with long-term value maximization. The fact that some successful sport and business practitioners learn their "lessons" through hands-on experience rather than in the classroom doesn't diminish the value of the formal educational experience. In the classroom, one can discuss and analyze the basic lessons and themes that emerge in the business practices of successful managers and firms. When described in model form, such as in the value maximization model, the generality of these lessons and themes becomes apparent, thereby enhancing the classroom experience.

The usefulness of economic models and optimization analysis lies in the logical framework they provide for characterizing and *predicting* practical managerial experience. The old saw, "That may be OK in theory, but it doesn't work in practice," is plainly incorrect. Useful theory describes and predicts actual business decisions. If a given theory doesn't describe and predict actual practice, it should be rejected in favor of theory and models that actually describe and predict real-world behavior. The reason why economic theory and methodology form the basis for the study of managerial decision making is quite simple—it works. Managerial economics works not just in the classroom, but more importantly, it works in the everyday "lab" of business practice. There is no conflict between theory and practice. The study of theory is helpful because the task of successful business management is made easier through the careful combination of theory and practical business experience.

See: Nina Munk and Suzanne Oliver, "They Know Something That Their Competitors Don't," *Forbes,* November 4, 1996, 158-159.

affects all parts of the firm. The value maximization model provides an attractive basis for such analysis. Using the principles of economic analysis, it is also possible to compare the higher costs or lower benefits of alternative, suboptimal courses of action.

The complexity of completely integrated decision analysis—or global optimization—often confines its use to major planning decisions. For many day-to-day operating decisions, managers typically employ less complicated, partial optimization techniques. Partial optimization concentrates on limited objectives within the firm's various operating departments. For example, the marketing department is usually required to determine the price and advertising strategy that achieves some sales goal given the firm's current product line and marketing budget. Alternatively, a production department might minimize the cost of a target output level at a given level of quality. In both instances, the fundamentals of economic analysis provide the basis for optimal managerial decisions.

The decision process, regardless of whether it is applied to fully integrated or partial optimization problems, involves two steps. First, economic relations must be expressed in a form suitable for analysis; the managerial decision problem must be expressed in analytical terms. Second, optimization techniques must be applied to determine the best, or optimal, solution in light of managerial objectives. The following material introduces a number of concepts that are useful for expressing decision problems in an economic framework. Several economic relations used to determine the firm's optimal price and output combination are investigated.

Basic Economic Relations

Tables
A list of economic data.

Spreadsheet
A table of electronically stored data.

Graph
Visual representation of data.

Equation
Analytical expressions of functional relationships.

Tables are the simplest form for presenting economic data. When these data are displayed electronically in the format of an accounting income statement or balance sheet, the tables are referred to as **spreadsheets.** When the underlying relation between economic data is very simple, tables and spreadsheets may be sufficient for analytical purposes. In such instances, a simple **graph** or visual representation of the data provides valuable insight. Complex economic relations require more sophisticated methods of expression. An **equation** is an analytical expression of functional relationships that characterizes the connection among economic variables. When the underlying relation among economic variables is uncomplicated, equations offer a useful, compact means for data description. When underlying relations are complex, equations are helpful because they permit the powerful tools of mathematical and statistical analysis to be employed.

FUNCTIONAL RELATIONS: EQUATIONS

The easiest way to examine basic economic concepts is to consider the functional relations incorporated in the basic valuation model. Consider first the relation between output, Q, and total revenue, TR. Using functional notation, a total revenue is:

$$TR = f(Q). \tag{2.2}$$

Table 2.1

RELATION BETWEEN TOTAL REVENUE AND OUTPUT:
TOTAL REVENUE = $1.50 × OUTPUT

TOTAL REVENUE	OUTPUT
$1.50	1
3.00	2
4.50	3
6.00	4
7.50	5
9.00	6

Equation 2.2 is read, "Total revenue is a function of output." The value of the dependent variable (total revenue) is determined by the independent variable (output). In an equation such as this, the variable to the left of the equal sign is called the **dependent variable.** Its value depends on the size of the variable or variables to the right of the equal sign. Variables on the right-hand side of the equal sign are called **independent variables.** Their values are determined independently of the functional relation expressed by the equation.

Dependent Variable
Y-variable determined by *X* values.

Independent Variable
X-variable determined separately from the *Y*-variable.

Equation 2.2 does not indicate the specific relation between output and total revenue; it merely states that some relation exists. Equation 2.3 provides a precise expression of this functional relation:

$$TR = P \times Q, \tag{2.3}$$

where *P* represents the price at which each unit of *Q* is sold. Total revenue is equal to price times the quantity of output sold. If price is constant at $1.50 regardless of the quantity sold, the relation between quantity sold and total revenue is

$$TR = \$1.50 \times Q. \tag{2.4}$$

The data in Table 2.1 are specified by Equation 2.4 and graphically illustrated in Figure 2.1.

TOTAL, AVERAGE, AND MARGINAL RELATIONS

Total, average, and marginal relations are very useful in optimization analysis. Whereas the definitions of totals and averages are well known, the meaning of marginals needs further explanation. A **marginal** relation is the change in the dependent variable caused by a one-unit change in an independent variable.[2] For example, **marginal**

Marginal
Change in the dependent variable caused by a one-unit change in an independent variable.

Marginal Revenue
Change in total revenue associated with a one-unit change in output.

[2]Appendix 2A provides a comprehensive review of mathematical techniques from simple algebra through differential calculus. Most students will find a review of algebra helpful. A basic understanding of calculus helps students to fully appreciate the material covered in the text, and many instructors make modest use of calculus in their courses.

Figure 2.1

GRAPH OF THE RELATION BETWEEN TOTAL REVENUE AND OUTPUT

When P = $1.50, a one-unit increase in the quantity sold will increase total revenue by $1.50.

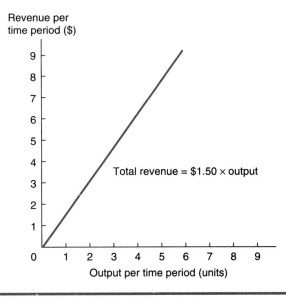

Revenue per
time period ($)

Total revenue = $1.50 × output

Output per time period (units)

Marginal Cost
Change in total cost
following a one-unit change
in output.

Marginal Profit
Change in total profit due to
a one-unit change in output.

revenue is the change in total revenue associated with a one-unit change in output; **marginal cost** is the change in total cost following a one-unit change in output; and **marginal profit** is the change in total profit due to a one-unit change in output.

Table 2.2 shows the relation among totals, marginals, and averages for a simple profit function. Columns 1 and 2 display the relation between output and total profits. Column 3 shows the marginal profit earned for a one-unit change in output, while Column 4 gives the average profit per unit at each level of output. The marginal profit earned on the first unit of output is $19. This is the change from $0 profits earned when zero units of output are sold to the $19 profit earned when one unit is produced and sold. The $33 marginal profit associated with the second unit of output is the increase in total profits (= $52 − $19) that results when output is increased from one to two units. When the marginal is positive, the total is increasing; when the marginal is negative, the total is decreasing. The data in Table 2.2 illustrate this point. The marginal profit associated with each of the first seven units of output is positive, and total profits increase with output over this range. Since the marginal profit of the eighth unit is negative, profits are reduced if output is raised to that level. Maximization of the profit function—or any function, for that matter—occurs at the point where the marginal switches from positive to negative.

When the marginal is greater than the average, the average must be increasing. For example, if a firm operates five retail stores with average annual sales of $350,000 per

	TOTAL, MARGINAL, AND AVERAGE RELATIONS
Table 2.2	**FOR A HYPOTHETICAL FUNCTION**

UNITS OF OUTPUT Q (1)	TOTAL PROFITS π^a (2)	MARGINAL PROFITS $\Delta\pi^b$ (3)	AVERAGE PROFITS $\overline{\pi}^c$ (4)
0	$0	—	—
1	19	$19	$19
2	52	33	26
3	93	41	31
4	136	43	34
5	175	39	35
6	210	35	35
7	217	7	31
8	208	−9	26

store and it opens a sixth store (the marginal store) that generates sales of $400,000, average sales per store will increase. If sales at the new (marginal) store are less than $350,000, average sales per store will decrease. Table 2.2 also illustrates the relation between marginal and average values. In going from four units of output to five, the marginal profit of $39 is greater than the $34 average profit at four units; therefore, average profit increases to $35. The $35 marginal profit of the sixth unit is the same as the average profit for the first five units, so average profit remains identical between five and six units. Finally, the marginal profit of the seventh unit is below the average profit at six units, causing average profit to fall.

GRAPHING TOTAL, MARGINAL, AND AVERAGE RELATIONS

Knowledge of the geometric relations among totals, marginals, and averages can prove useful in managerial decision making. Figure 2.2a presents a graph of the profit-to-output relation given in Table 2.2. Each point on the curve represents a combination of output and total profit, as do Columns 1 and 2 of Table 2.2. Marginal and average profit figures from Table 2.2 have been plotted in Figure 2.2b.

Just as there is an arithmetic relation among the totals, marginals, and averages in the table, so too there is a corresponding geometric relation. To see this relation, consider first the average profit per unit of output at any point along the total profit curve. The average profit figure is equal to total profit divided by the corresponding number of units of output. Geometrically, this relation is represented by the slope of a line from the origin to the point of interest on the total profit curve. For example, consider the slope of the line from the origin to point *B* in Figure 2.2a. **Slope** is a measure of the steepness of a line, and is defined as the increase (or decrease) in height per unit of movement

Slope
A measure of the steepness of a line.

Figure 2.2

GEOMETRIC REPRESENTATION OF TOTAL, MARGINAL, AND AVERAGE
RELATIONS: (A) TOTAL PROFITS; (B) MARGINAL AND AVERAGE PROFITS

(a) Marginal profit is the slope of the total profit curve; it is maximized at point C. More importantly, total profit is maximized at point E, where marginal profit equals zero. (b) Average profit rises (falls) when marginal profit is greater (less) than average profit.

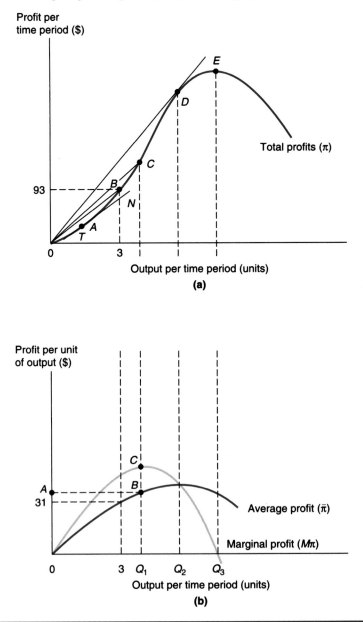

along the horizontal axis. The slope of a straight line passing through the origin is determined by dividing the Y coordinate at any point on the line by the corresponding X coordinate. Using Δ (read *delta*) to designate change, slope $= \Delta Y / \Delta X = (Y_2 - Y_1) / (X_2 - X_1)$. Since X_1 and Y_1 are zero for any line going through the origin, slope $= Y_2 / X_2$ or, more generally, slope $= Y/X$. Thus, the slope of the line $0B$ can be calculated by dividing \$93, the Y coordinate at point B, by 3, the X coordinate at point B. This process involves dividing total profit by the corresponding units of output. Thus, *at any point along a total curve, the corresponding average figure is given by the slope of a straight line from the origin to that point.* These average figures can also be graphed directly, as in Figure 2.2b, where each point on the average profit curve is the corresponding total profit divided by quantity.

The marginal relation has a similar geometric association with the total curve. In Table 2.2, each marginal figure is shown to be the change in total profit associated with the last unit increase in output. This rise (or fall) in the total profit associated with a one-unit increase in output is the *slope* of the total profit curve at that point.

Tangent
A line that touches but does not intersect a given curve.

Slopes of nonlinear curves are typically found geometrically by drawing a line tangent to the curve at the point of interest and determining the slope of the tangent. A **tangent** is a line that touches but does not intersect a given curve. In Figure 2.2a, for example, the marginal profit at point A is equal to the slope of the total profit curve at that point and equals the slope of the tangent labeled *TAN*. Therefore, *at any point along a total curve, the corresponding marginal figure is given by the slope of a line drawn tangent to the total curve at that point.* Slope or marginal figures can also be graphed directly as shown by the marginal profit curve in Figure 2.2b.

Inflection Point
A point of maximum slope.

Several important relations among totals, marginals, and averages become apparent when considering Figure 2.2a. First, note that the slope of the total profit curve is increasing from the origin to point C. Lines drawn tangent to the total profit curve become steeper as the point of tangency approaches point C, so marginal profit is increasing up to this point. This is also illustrated in Figure 2.2b, where the marginal profit curve increases up to output Q_1, corresponding to point C on the total profit curve. At point C, called an **inflection point,** the slope of the total profit curve is maximized; marginal, but not average or total profits, are maximized at that output. Between points C and E, total profit continues to increase because marginal profit is still positive even though it is declining. At point E, the total profit curve has a slope of zero and thus is neither rising nor falling. Marginal profit at this point is zero, and total profit is maximized. Beyond E (output Q_3 in Figure 2.2b), the total profit curve has a negative slope and marginal profit is negative.

In addition to the total-average and total-marginal relations, Figure 2.2b shows the relation between marginals and averages. At low output levels, where the marginal profit curve lies above the average, the average is rising. Although marginal profit reaches a maximum at output Q_1 and declines thereafter, the average curve continues to rise so long as the marginal lies above it. At output Q_2, marginal and average profits are equal, and the average profit curve reaches its maximum value. Beyond Q_2, the marginal curve lies below the average and the average is falling.

The application of marginal analysis in managerial decision making can be illustrated using the example of Payless Furniture, Inc., a San Francisco-based retailer. The company is faced with the important decision of how it should allocate its cable TV advertising budget of $5,000 per week between its Bay Area and Sacramento markets. In the allocation of the advertising budget between each market, the company seeks to maximize the total profit generated. For simplicity, assume that a prime-time advertisement on local cable TV in each market costs an identical $1,000. Moreover, assume that each advertisement addresses a different segment of Payless' customer base, so there is no synergy obtained from running a mix of advertisements. Since profits average a flat 8% of sales revenue, the profit-maximizing advertising allocation also results in maximum sales revenue. According to Payless' best estimate, the relation between weekly gross revenues before advertising costs and the number of advertisements per week is shown in Table 2.3.

Clearly, the first best use of advertising dollars is for promotion in the Bay Area market. A first advertisement in the Bay Area generates $50,000 in marginal revenues; a second advertisement generates $30,000; a third advertisement generates $25,000; a fourth advertisement generates $20,000. Rather than run a fifth advertisement in the Bay Area, it would be wise to run a first advertisement in the Sacramento market. This advertisement would generate $20,000 in marginal revenue, the same amount produced by a fourth advertisement in the Bay Area market. Because a fourth advertisement in the Bay Area market generates the same amount as a first advertisement in the Sacramento market, at the margin Payless is indifferent between these two advertising alternatives. With only $5,000 to spend, Payless should spend $4,000 for promotion in the Bay Area, and $1,000 for advertising in the Sacramento market. With this advertising allocation, $200,000 in Bay Area revenue plus $25,000 in Sacramento market revenue—a total of $225,000 per week would be generated. Since gross profits before advertising expenses average a flat 8% of sales, a total of $18,000 (= 0.08 × $225,000) per week in gross profits and $13,000 (= $18,000 − $5,000) per week in net profits after advertising costs would be generated. No other allocation of a $5,000 advertising budget would be as profitable. Subject to a $5,000 advertising budget constraint, this is the profit-maximizing allocation of advertising between Payless' two markets.

Table 2.3

WEEKLY GROSS REVENUES BEFORE ADVERTISING COSTS AND THE NUMBER OF ADS PER WEEK

BAY AREA MARKET			SACRAMENTO MARKET		
NUMBER OF ADS	REVENUE	MARGINAL REVENUE	NUMBER OF ADS	REVENUE	MARGINAL REVENUE
0	$ 75,000	—	0	$ 5,000	—
1	125,000	$50,000	1	25,000	$20,000
2	155,000	30,000	2	40,000	15,000
3	180,000	25,000	3	52,500	12,500
4	200,000	20,000	4	60,000	7,500
5	210,000	10,000	5	65,000	5,000

Before concluding that this advertising budget allocation represents the best that Payless can do in terms of producing profits, it is necessary to ask if profits would be increased or decreased following an expansion in the advertising budget. When gross profit before advertising expenditures average a flat 8%, expansion is called for so long as an additional advertisement generates *more than* $12,500 in revenues. This stems from the fact that the marginal cost of a single advertisement is $1,000, and *more than* $1,000 (= 0.08 × $12,500) in marginal gross profit before advertising expenses will be generated with more than $12,500 in additional revenues. Notice that a second advertisement in the Sacramento market results in an additional $15,000 per week in revenues. Given an 8% of revenues gross profit before advertising expenditures, such an advertisement would produce an additional $1,200 (= 0.08 × $15,000) in gross profits and $200 (= $1,200 − $1,000) in net profits per week. Expansion in Payless' advertising budget from $5,000 to $6,000 per week is clearly appropriate. With a $6,000 advertising budget, $4,000 should be spent in the Bay Area market and $2,000 should be spent in the Sacramento market. A total of $240,000 in revenues, $19,200 (= 0.08 × $240,000) in gross profits before advertising expenses, and $13,200 (= $19,200 − $6,000) in net profits per week would thus be generated. Since a third advertisement in the Sacramento market would produce only breakeven additional revenues of $12,500, running such an advertisement would neither increase nor decrease Payless profits. As a result, Payless would be indifferent as to running or not running a third advertisement in the Sacramento market.

Marginal Analysis in Decision Making

Geometric relations between totals and marginals offer a fruitful basis for examining the role of marginal analysis in economic decision making. Managerial decisions frequently require finding the maximum value of a function. For a function to be at a maximum, its marginal value (slope) must be zero. Evaluating the slope, or marginal value, of a function, therefore, enables one to determine the point at which the function is maximized. To illustrate, consider the following profit function:

$$\pi = - \$10,000 + \$400Q - \$2Q^2.$$

Here π = total profit and Q is output in units. As shown in Figure 2.3, if output is zero, the firm incurs a $10,000 loss since fixed costs equal $10,000. As output rises, profits increase. A breakeven point is reached at 28 units of output; total revenues equal total costs and profit is zero at that activity level. Profit is maximized at 100 units and declines thereafter. The marginal profit function graphed in Figure 2.3 begins at a level of $400 and declines continuously. For output quantities from 0 to 100 units, marginal profit is positive and total profit increases with each additional unit of output. At $Q =$ 100, marginal profit is zero and total profit is at its maximum. Beyond $Q = 100$, marginal profit is negative and total profit is decreasing.

Another example of the importance of the marginal concept in economic decision analysis is provided by the important fact that marginal revenue equals marginal cost at

How Entrepreneurs Shape the Economy

Sometimes it is easy to overlook the fact that firms are made up of people. Firms often are started by a single individual with no more than an idea for a better product or service—the entrepreneur. Taken from the Old French word *entreprendre,* meaning "to undertake," the term *entrepreneur* refers to one who organizes, operates, and assumes the risk of a business venture. Until recently, there appeared to be little academic or public policy interest in this key function or in the entrepreneur's role in the economy's overall performance. The entrepreneur's skill was simply considered part of the labor input in production. Now, both academicians and practitioners are beginning to better understand the critical role of the entrepreneur, partly because entrepreneurship has become a formal field of study at many leading business schools.

As a catalyst, the entrepreneur brings economic resources together in the risky attempt to meet consumers' needs and desires. This process often leads to failure—in fact, the odds against success are long. Seldom do more than one in ten start-up businesses enjoy even minimal economic success. Even those select few that see their product or service reach a national market find stable long-term success elusive. Once established, they in turn become targets for future entrepreneurs. As entrepreneurs create new opportunities, they destroy the old way of doing things. Thus, entrepreneurship plays an important role in what economist Joseph Schumpeter once called the "creative destruction of capitalism." This is the process of replacing the old with the new, the inefficient with the efficient, and low quality with a superior product.

Given the long odds against success, you might wonder why so many willingly embark on ventures (adventures?) that appear doomed to fail. One reason is that one-in-a-million chance of developing "the" truly revolutionary product or service that will fundamentally change how people live, work, play, or shop. Sam Walton, the founder of retailer Wal-Mart, Inc., made *billions* of dollars bringing brand-name merchandise at bargain prices to rural America—and created thousands of well-paid job opportunities for Wal-Mart "associates." Even though the opportunity for wealth is surely an important motivation, the impact and recognition that come with creating a truly unique good or service often are equally important to entrepreneurs. Many simply want to "make a difference."

What is the entrepreneur's role from the standpoint of society in general? Clearly, everyone benefits from the innovative products, services, and delivery systems that result from entrepreneurs' efforts. Consider the benefits resulting from the efforts of such entrepreneurs as Thomas Edison, Chester Carlson, and Bill Gates. Their fame and fortune only partly reflect the benefits enjoyed from phonography, electric lighting, photography, xerography, the "graphic desktop," and other "user friendly" computer software. Like all entrepreneurs, they have played an important role in determining the types of products that become available in the marketplace. Just as importantly, entrepreneurs help determine *when* they become available. In the modern information age, entrepreneurs succeed by meeting the demands of the consumer for products that are better, cheaper, and faster.

Evidence of private and social benefits from entrepreneurship is widespread. Note the outstanding growth for small-firm sales, profits, and employment in emerging industries such as biotechnology, computer software and services, industrial services, recreation, and telecommunications. High rates of return on tangible and intangible assets also imply a wise use of resources in smaller entrepreneurial firms. Larger companies also have sought to reinvent themselves in a process called *intrapreneurship,* in which the entrepreneur works within the overall framework of an existing large organization. Titans, such as Merck & Co. and the DuPont Co., have come to recognize and benefit from the importance of the intrapreneur. Thus, entrepreneurship plays a key role in both the initial development and ongoing revitalization of firms. The opportunity to earn a normal business profit plus an attractive salary or wage is the realistic objective of every entrepreneur. The hope of above-normal economic profits is the dream that spurs our market-based "bottoms up" method of economic development.

See: Stephanie N. Mehta, "As Ideas Beget Entrepreneurs, So Does a Plan," *The Wall Street Journal,* February 19, 1997, B1, B2.

PROFIT AS A FUNCTION OF OUTPUT

Figure 2.3

Total profit is maximized at 100 units, where marginal profit equals zero. Beyond that point, marginal profit is negative and total profit decreases.

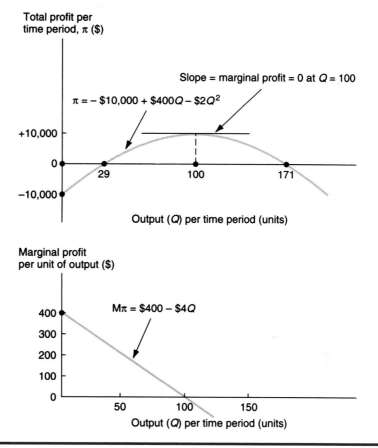

Total profit per
time period, π ($)

Slope = marginal profit = 0 at $Q = 100$

$\pi = -\$10,000 + \$400Q - \$2Q^2$

+10,000

0

29   100   171

−10,000

Output (Q) per time period (units)

Marginal profit
per unit of output ($)

400    $M\pi = \$400 - \$4Q$

300

200

100

0

50   100   150

Output (Q) per time period (units)

Profit Maximization
Activity level that generates
highest profit, $MR = MC$
and $M\pi = 0$.

the point of **profit maximization.** Figure 2.4 illustrates this relation using hypothetical revenue and cost functions. Total profit is equal to total revenue minus total cost and is, therefore, equal to the vertical distance between the total revenue and total cost curves at any output level. This distance is maximized at output Q_B. At that point, marginal revenue, MR, and marginal cost, MC, are equal; $MR = MC$ at the profit-maximizing output level.

The reason why Q_B is the profit-maximizing output can be intuitively explained by considering the shapes of the revenue and cost curves to the right of point Q_A. At Q_A and Q_C, total revenue equals total cost and two breakeven points are illustrated. As seen in Figure 2.4, a **breakeven point** identifies output quantities where total profits are zero. At output quantities just beyond Q_A, marginal revenue is greater than marginal cost, meaning that total revenue is rising faster than total cost. Thus, the total revenue and

Breakeven Point
Output level where total
profit is zero.

Figure 2.4

TOTAL REVENUE, TOTAL COST, AND PROFIT MAXIMIZATION

The difference between the total revenue and total cost curves is greatest when their slopes are equal. At that point, marginal revenue equals marginal cost, marginal profit equals zero, and profit is maximized.

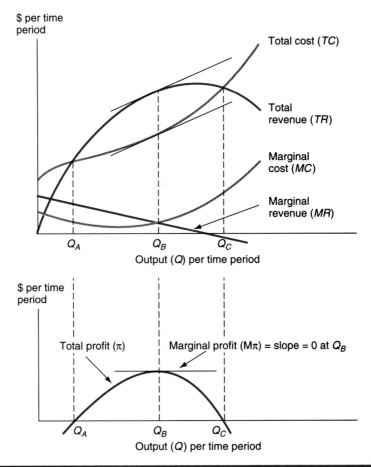

total cost curves are spreading farther apart and profits are increasing. The divergence between total revenue and total cost curves continues so long as total revenue is rising faster than total cost—in other words, so long as $MR > MC$. Notice that marginal revenue is continuously declining while marginal cost first declines but then begins to increase. Once the slope of the total revenue curve is exactly equal to the slope of the total cost curve and marginal revenue equals marginal cost, the two curves will be parallel and stop diverging. This occurs at output Q_B. Beyond Q_B, the slope of the total cost curve is greater than that of the total revenue curve. Marginal cost is then greater than marginal revenue so the distance between the total revenue and total cost curves is decreasing and total profits are declining.

The relations among marginal revenue, marginal cost, and profit maximization can also be demonstrated by considering the general profit expression, $\pi = TR - TC$. Because total profit is total revenue minus total cost, marginal profit ($M\pi$) is marginal revenue (MR) minus marginal cost (MC):

$$M\pi = MR - MC.$$

Since maximization of any function requires that the marginal of the function be set equal to zero, profit maximization occurs when:

$$M\pi = MR - MC = 0$$

or where:

$$MR = MC.$$

Therefore, in determining the optimal activity level for a firm, the marginal relation tells us that so long as the increase in revenues associated with expanding output exceeds the increase in costs, continued expansion will be profitable. The optimal output level is determined when marginal revenue is equal to marginal cost, marginal profit is zero, and total profit is maximized.

To further illustrate the use of marginal analysis in managerial decision making, consider the case of the Storrs Manufacturing Company, located in West Hartford, Connecticut. The company has developed and test-marketed the "Golden Bear Golf Cart," a new and highly energy-efficient golf cart. The product is unique, and preliminary indications are that Storrs can obtain a substantial share of the national market if it acts quickly to expand production from its current level of 400 units per month. Data from independent marketing consultants retained by Storrs indicate the following monthly demand, total revenue, and marginal revenue relations:

$$P = \$7{,}500 - \$3.75Q \qquad \text{(Demand)}$$

$$TR = \$7{,}500Q - \$3.75Q^2 \qquad \text{(Total revenue)}$$

$$MR = \$7{,}500 - \$7.5Q. \qquad \text{(Marginal revenue)}$$

where P is price and Q is output.

In addition, Storrs' accounting department has estimated monthly total cost and marginal cost relations of:

$$TC = \$1{,}012{,}500 + \$1{,}500Q + \$1.25Q^2 \qquad \text{(Total cost)}$$

$$MC = \$1{,}500 + \$2.5Q. \qquad \text{(Marginal cost)}$$

These relations can be used to determine the optimal activity level for the firm. Profit will be maximized where $MR = MC$. This suggests an activity level of 600 units, since:

$$MR = MC$$

$$\$7{,}500 - \$7.5Q = \$1{,}500 + \$2.5Q$$

$$\$10Q = \$6{,}000$$

$$Q = 600 \text{ units.}$$

At this optimal activity level, price, total revenue, and the maximum total profit can be calculated as:

$$P = \$7,500 - \$3.75Q$$
$$= \$7,500 - \$3.75(600)$$
$$= \$5,250 \text{ per unit}$$
$$TR = \$7,500Q - \$3.75Q^2$$
$$= \$7,500(600) - \$3.75(600^2)$$
$$= \$3,150,000$$
$$\pi = TR - TC$$
$$= \$7,500Q - \$3.75Q^2 - \$1,012,500 - \$1,500Q - \$1.25Q^2$$
$$= -\$5Q^2 + \$6,000Q - \$1,012,500$$
$$= -\$5(600^2) + \$6,000(600) - \$1,012,500$$
$$= \$787,500$$

To maximize short-run profits, Storrs should expand from its current level of 400 units to 600 units per month. Any deviation from an output of 600 units and price of $5,250 per unit would lower Storrs' short-run profits.

In some instances, however, a company such as Storrs might wish to deviate from this short-run profit-maximizing activity level in order to achieve certain long-run objectives. For example, suppose Storrs fears that short-run profits as high as $787,500 per month (or 25% of sales) would provide a powerful enticement for new competitors. To limit an increase in present and future competition, Storrs may decide to lower prices to rapidly penetrate the market and preclude entry by new rivals. For example, Storrs might wish to adopt a short-run operating philosophy of **revenue maximization** as part of a long-run value maximization strategy. In this instance, Storrs' short-run operating philosophy would be to set $MR = 0$, which would result in the following activity level:

Revenue Maximization Activity level that generates highest revenue, $MR = 0$.

$$MR = 0$$
$$\$7,500 - \$7.5Q = 0$$
$$\$7.5Q = \$7,500$$
$$Q = 1,000 \text{ units}$$
$$P = \$7,500 - \$3.75(1,000)$$
$$= \$3,750$$
$$TR = \$7,500(1,000) - \$3.75(1,000^2)$$
$$= \$3,750,000$$

$$\pi = -\$5(1{,}000^2) + \$6{,}000(1{,}000) - \$1{,}012{,}500$$

$$= -\$12{,}500 \text{ (A loss)}$$

Notice that revenue maximization involves a consideration of revenue or "demand-side" influences only. In this instance, the revenue-maximizing activity occurs when a loss of $12,500 per month is incurred. In other instances, profits may be high or low at the point of revenue maximization. Unlike profit maximization, cost relations are not considered at all. Relative to profit maximization, revenue maximization increases both unit sales and total revenue, but substantially decreases short-run profitability. These effects are typical and a direct result of the lower prices that accompany a revenue maximization strategy. Since revenue maximization involves setting $MR = 0$, whereas profit maximization involves setting $MR = MC$, the two strategies will only lead to identical activity levels in the unlikely event that $MC = 0$. While marginal cost sometimes equals zero when services are provided, such as allowing a few more fans to watch a scarcely attended baseball game, such instances are rare. Most goods and services involve at least some variable production and distribution costs, and hence marginal costs typically will be positive. Thus, revenue maximization typically involves moving down along the demand and marginal revenue curves to lower prices and greater unit sales levels than would be indicated for profit maximization. Of course, for this strategy to be optimal, the long-run benefits derived from greater market penetration and scale advantages must be sufficient to overcome the short-run disadvantage of lost profits.

Finally, consider the implications of still another possible short-run strategy for Storrs. Suppose that instead of short-run profit or revenue maximization, the company decides on an intermediate strategy of expanding sales beyond the short-run profit-maximizing activity level but to a lesser extent than that suggested by revenue maximization. This might be appropriate if, for example, Storrs is unable to finance the very high rate of growth necessary for short-run revenue maximization. Given the specific nature of Storrs' total cost and profit relations, the company might decide on a short-run

Average Cost Minimization
Activity level that generates lowest average cost, $MC = AC$.

operating strategy of **average cost minimization.** To find this activity level, remember that average cost is falling when $MC < AC$, rising when $MC > AC$, and at a minimum when $MC = AC$. Therefore, the average cost minimizing activity level for Storrs is:

$$MC = AC = \frac{TC}{Q}$$

$$\$1{,}500 + \$2.5Q = \frac{\$1{,}012{,}500 + \$1{,}500Q + \$1.25Q^2}{Q}$$

$$\$1{,}500 + \$2.5Q = \frac{\$1{,}012{,}500}{Q} + \$1{,}500 + \$1.25Q$$

$$\$1.25Q = \frac{\$1{,}012{,}500}{Q}$$

$$Q^2 = 810{,}000 \qquad\qquad\qquad \textbf{(2.2)}$$

$$Q = 900 \text{ units}$$

$$P = \$7,500 - \$3.75(900)$$
$$= \$4,125$$
$$TR = \$7,500(900) - \$3.75(900^2)$$
$$= \$3,712,500$$
$$\pi = -\$5(900^2) + \$6,000(900) - \$1,012,500$$
$$= \$337,500$$

For Storrs, average cost minimization involves operation at an activity level that lies between those indicated by profit maximization and revenue maximization strategies. Since average cost minimization reflects a consideration of cost relations or "supply-side" influences only, however, either greater or lesser activity levels than those indicated by profit maximization and revenue maximization strategies might result. In Storrs' case, average cost minimization leads to some of the market penetration advantages of revenue maximization, but achieves some of the greater profits associated with lower activity levels. As such, it might be an attractive short-run strategy for the company.

Do Companies Really Maximize Value?

MANAGERIAL APPLICATION
2.3

Prominent illustrations of flawed corporate strategy and asset mismanagement at top companies can be cited on a regular basis. While such cases sometimes offer evidence that is inconsistent with the value maximization theory of the firm, value maximization theory can still be described as the *typical* motivation of management. This stems from the fact that inefficiency and waste often lead to a change in management and dramatic corporate restructuring.

A classic case of how boards of directors have come to respond aggressively to flawed corporate strategy is provided by the early-1990s shakeup at General Motors, Inc. A deep slump in auto sales drove worldwide losses for GM to a whopping $4.5 billion during 1991. North American auto operations did even worse—they lost a stunning $7.1 billion. Despite an avalanche of new cars and trucks, GM's U.S. market share plummeted from more than 40% in the mid-1980s to roughly 35%, and a dangerous hemorrhaging of red ink had erupted with no quick relief in sight.

During April 1992, after having stood idly by while GM deteriorated badly throughout the 1980s, GM's board of directors had finally seen enough. In unprecedented ac-

tion, the GM board removed GM chairman Robert C. Stempel from his post as head of the board's influential executive committee. The executive committee is the policy and strategy setting arm of GM's board, and the base from which all key operating and planning decisions emanate. At the same time, the board demoted Stempel's hand-picked president of GM, Lloyd E. Reuss. To replace Reuss, the board promoted John F. Smith, Jr., the former chief of GM's international operations.

While the board announced it would not involve itself in the day-to-day details of running GM, it was clear that the board had lost confidence in Stempel and the top management of the company. Clearly, the board wanted immediate action. In fact, more than just shaking up the generals, these GM board actions directly led to Stempel's resignation from the company.

By 1995, it had become crystal clear that GM's boardroom rebellion was contagious. After ignoring investor concerns for years, Kmart CEO Joseph Antonini lost his title of chairman of the board in February 1995. Despite some evidence of long-awaited improvement, boards of directors at ITT and Baxter International also

In general, revenue and cost relations as well as entry conditions must be considered before settling on an appropriate short-run operating strategy. Once such a strategy is identified, a study of the specific revenue and cost relations and other influences facing the firm will suggest an appropriate activity level.

The Incremental Concept in Economic Analysis

The marginal concept is a key element of the economic decision-making process. It is important to recognize, however, that marginal relations only measure the impact associated with *unitary changes* in output or some other important independent variable. Many managerial decisions involve changes that are much broader in scope. For example, a manager might be interested in analyzing the potential effects on revenues, costs, and profits of a 25% increase in production. Alternatively, a manager might want to analyze the profit impact of introducing a new product line, or assess the cost impact of changing an entire production system.

Continued

moved to split the jobs of chairman and CEO. Top management at Caesars World, USAir, and United States Shoe were also put on notice that outside directors would not sit idly by while corporate performance continues to deteriorate. Captive boards have also been informed in no uncertain terms that stockholders won't tolerate mediocre performance indefinitely.

Ongoing mergers and acquisitions also send a clear signal to outside directors to be on their guard. Shareholders are watching closely to see how they discharge their fiduciary duties, and move swiftly to discipline inefficient management. Critics of underperforming companies have proposed a variety of mechanisms that shareholders can use to hold management accountable:

- There should be a majority of outside directors.
- Independent members of the board should select a lead director.
- Independent directors should meet alone in executive session on a regularly scheduled basis.
- Independent directors should take responsibility for all board procedures.
- The board should have basic responsibility for selection of its own members.

- The board should conduct regularly scheduled performance reviews of the CEO and key executives.
- The board must understand and fully endorse the company's long-term strategies.
- The board must give an adequate amount of attention to its most important responsibility: the selection of the CEO.

Such suggestions for improving board member performance have intriguing potential for improving the accountability of top management and company performance. Similarly, operating performance and stockholder returns typically improve when top executives and other employees hold a substantial equity interest. Innovations on both fronts are sure to continue to increase the shareholder accountability of both boards of directors and top management. As a result, value maximization theory continues to provide the fundamental motivation for everyday managerial decision making.

See: Anthony Bianco and John A. Byrne, "The Rush to Quality on Corporate Boards," *Business Week,* March 3, 1997, 34-35.

In all managerial decisions, the study of *differences* or *changes* is vital to selecting an optimal course of action. While correct for analyzing unitary changes, the marginal concept is too narrow to provide a general methodology for evaluating all such alternative courses of action. The incremental concept is the economist's generalization of the marginal concept. Incremental analysis involves examining the impact of alternative managerial *decisions* on revenues, costs, and profit. The **incremental change** is the comprehensive impact from a given managerial decision. For example, the incremental revenue associated with adding a new item to a firm's product line is the difference in total revenue that stems from the new product introduction.

Incremental Change
Comprehensive impact resulting from a decision.

INCREMENTAL PROFITS

Incremental Profit
Gain or loss associated with a given managerial decision.

The fundamental relations of incremental analysis are essentially the same as those of marginal analysis. **Incremental profit** is the profit gain or loss associated with a given managerial decision. Total profit increases when incremental profit is positive. When incremental profit is negative, total profit declines. Similarly, incremental profit is positive (and total profit increases) if the incremental revenue associated with a decision exceeds incremental cost. The incremental concept is so intuitively obvious that it is easy to overlook its significance in managerial decision making and its potential complexity.

For example, a firm may refuse to sublet excess warehouse space for $5,000 per month because it figures its cost is $7,500 per month—the price that it paid for a long-term lease on the facility. However, if the warehouse space represents true excess capacity with no current value to the company, its historical cost of $7,500 per month is irrelevant and should be disregarded. The firm would forego $5,000 in profits by turning down the offer to sublet the excess warehouse space. Similarly, any firm that adds a standard allocated charge for fixed costs and overhead to the true incremental cost of production runs the risk of turning down profitable sales.

On the other hand, care must be exercised to ensure against incorrectly assigning overly low incremental costs to a decision. Incremental decisions involve a time dimension that cannot be ignored. Not only must all current revenues and costs be considered, future revenues and costs must also be incorporated in the analysis. For example, assume that the excess warehouse space described earlier came about following a downturn in the overall economy. Furthermore, assume that the excess warehouse space was in fact sublet for one year at a price of $5,000 per month, or a total of $60,000. An incremental loss might be experienced if the firm must later go out and lease additional space to accommodate an increase in production following a subsequent upturn in economic activity. If $75,000 had to be spent to replace the sublet warehouse facility, the decision to sublet would involve an incremental loss of $15,000. To be sure, making accurate projections concerning the future pattern of revenues and costs is risky and subject to error. Nevertheless, they cannot be ignored in incremental analysis.

Another interesting example of the incremental concept involves the measurement of the incremental revenue resulting from the introduction of a new product. Incremental revenue in this case would include new product revenues plus any change in the revenues generated by the rest of the firm's product line. Thus, incremental revenues would include any revenue gain from increased sales of related products, where that increase was the result of adding the new product to the firm's line. Similarly, if the new item took sales away from another of the firm's products, this loss in revenue would have to be accounted for in measuring the incremental revenue of the new product.

AN ILLUSTRATION OF THE INCREMENTAL CONCEPT

A more detailed illustration of the incremental concept is found in the financing decision that is typically associated with real estate and equipment financing. Consider a small business whose $100,000 purchase offer has been accepted by the seller of a small retail facility. The firm must obtain financing to complete the transaction. The best rates it has found are at a local financial institution that offers a renewable five-year mortgage at 8% interest with a down payment of 20%, or 8.5% interest on a loan with only 10% down. In the first case, the borrower is able to finance up to 80% of the purchase price; in the second case, the borrower is able to finance up to 90%. For simplicity, assume that both loans only require interest payments during these five years. After five years, either note is renewable at then-current interest rates and would be restructured with monthly payments designed to amortize the loan over 20 years. An important question facing the firm is: What is the incremental financing cost of the additional funds borrowed when 90% versus 80% of the purchase price is financed?

Since no principal payments are required, the annual financing cost under each loan alternative can be easily calculated. For the 80% loan, the annual financing cost in dollar terms is:

$$\text{Financing Cost} = \text{Interest Rate} \times \text{Loan Percentage} \times \text{Purchase Price}$$

$$= (0.08)(0.8)(\$100,000) \tag{2.3}$$

$$= \$6,400.$$

For a 90% loan, the corresponding annual financing cost is:

$$\text{Financing Cost} = (0.085)(0.9)(\$100,000)$$

$$= \$7,650. \tag{2.4}$$

To calculate the incremental cost of the added funds borrowed under the 90% financing alternative, the firm must compare the additional financing costs incurred to the additional funds borrowed. In dollar terms, the incremental annual financing cost is:

$$\begin{array}{c} \text{Incremental} \\ \text{Cost} \end{array} = \begin{array}{c} 90\% \text{ Loan Financing} \\ \text{Cost} \end{array} - \begin{array}{c} 80\% \text{ Loan Financing} \\ \text{Cost} \end{array}$$

$$= \$7,650 - \$6,400 \tag{2.5}$$

$$= \$1,250.$$

In percentage terms, the incremental cost of the additional funds borrowed under the 90% financing alternative is:

$$\frac{\text{Incremental Cost}}{\text{in Percentage Terms}} = \frac{\text{Incremental Financing Costs}}{\text{Incremental Funds Borrowed}}$$

$$= \frac{\$7,650 - \$6,400}{\$90,000 - \$80,000}$$

$$= \frac{\$1,250}{\$10,000}$$

$$= 0.125, \text{ or } 12.5\%.$$

The true incremental cost of funds for the last $10,000 borrowed under the 90% financing alternative is 12.5%, not the 8.5% interest rate quoted for the loan. While this high incremental cost of funds is perhaps surprising, it is not unusual. It results from the fact that with a 90% loan the higher 8.5% interest rate is charged on the entire loan balance, not just on the incremental $10,000 in funds borrowed.

The incremental concept is important for managerial decision making, because it focuses attention on the changes or differences between the available alternatives. It also indicates that revenues and costs unaffected by the decision are irrelevant and should not be included in the analysis. This incremental concept is examined in somewhat greater detail in Chapters 8 and 12.

Summary

Effective managerial decision making is the process of finding the best possible solution to a given problem. Both the methodology and tools of managerial economics play an important role in this process.

- The decision alternative that produces a result most consistent with managerial objectives is the **optimal decision.**
- **Tables** are the simplest and most direct way used to list economic data. When these data are displayed electronically in the format of an accounting income statement or balance sheet, tables are referred to as **spreadsheets.** In many instances, a simple **graph** or visual representation of the data can provide valuable insight. In other instances, complex economic relations are typified using an **equation,** or analytical expressions of functional relationships.
- The value of a **dependent variable** in an equation depends on the size of the variable or variables to the right of the equals sign. Variables on the right-hand side of the equals sign are called **independent variables,** because their values are determined outside or independently of the functional relation expressed by the equation.
- A **marginal** relation is the change in the dependent variable caused by a one-unit change in an independent variable. **Marginal revenue** is the change in total

revenue associated with a one-unit change in output. **Marginal cost** is the change in total cost following a one-unit change in output; **marginal profit** is the change in total profit due to a one-unit change in output.

- In graphic analysis, **slope** is a measure of the steepness of a line and is defined as the increase (or decrease) in height per unit of movement along the horizontal axis. A **tangent** is a line that touches but does not intersect a given curve. An **inflection point** reveals a point of maximum slope.

- Marginal revenue equals marginal cost at the point of **profit maximization,** so long as total profit is falling as output expands from that point. The **breakeven point** identifies an output quantity where total profit is zero. Marginal revenue equals zero at the point of **revenue maximization,** so long as total revenue is falling beyond that point. **Average cost minimization** occurs when marginal and average costs are equal and average cost is increasing as output expands.

- The incremental concept is often employed as the practical equivalent of marginal analysis. **Incremental change** is the comprehensive impact resulting from a decision. **Incremental profit** is the profit gain or loss associated with a given managerial decision.

Each of these concepts is fruitfully applied in the practical analysis of managerial decision problems. As seen in later chapters, basic economic relations provide the underlying framework necessary for the analysis of all profit, revenue, and cost relations.

QUESTIONS

Q2.1 What key ingredients are crucial to the optimization process?

Q2.2 What is the difference between global and partial optimization techniques?

Q2.3 Why do you think electronic spreadsheets are rapidly growing in popularity as a means for expressing economic relations?

Q2.4 Describe the relation between totals and marginals, and explain why the total is maximized when the marginal is set equal to zero.

Q2.5 Why must a marginal curve always intersect the related average curve at either a maximum or a minimum point?

Q2.6 Would you expect total revenue to be maximized at an output level that is typically greater or less than the profit-maximizing output level? Why?

Q2.7 Does the point of minimum long-run average costs always represent the optimal activity level?

Q2.8 Economists have long argued that if you want to tax away excess profits without affecting allocative efficiency, you should use a lump-sum tax instead of an excise or sales tax. Use the concepts developed in the chapter to support this position.

Q2.9 "It is often impossible to obtain precise information about the pattern of future revenues, costs, and interest rates. Therefore, the process of economic optimization is futile." Discuss this statement.

Q2.10 Distinguish the incremental concept from the marginal concept.

SELF-TEST PROBLEMS AND SOLUTIONS

ST2.1 **Profit vs. Revenue Maximization.** Presto Products, Inc., manufactures small electrical appliances and housewares, including pressure cookers, heaters, canners, fry pans, griddles, roaster/ dutch ovens, deep fryers, and so on. Due to extremely competitive conditions in its markets, Presto is finding it very difficult to show price or volume gains in many of its traditional product lines. Luckily, the company has recently introduced an innovative new dessert maker for frozen yogurt and tofu that has the clear potential to offset the weak pricing and sluggish volume growth experienced during recent periods.

Monthly demand and cost relations for Presto's frozen dessert maker are as follows:

$$P = \$60 - \$0.005Q.$$

$$MR = \$60 - \$0.01Q.$$

$$TC = \$100,000 + \$5Q + \$0.0005Q^2.$$

$$MC = \$5 + \$0.001Q.$$

A. Set up a table or spreadsheet for Presto output (Q), price (P), total revenue (TR), marginal revenue (MR), total cost (TC), marginal cost (MC), total profit (π), and marginal profit ($M\pi$). Establish a range for Q from 0 to 10,000 in increments of 1,000 (i.e., 0, 1,000, 2,000, . . . , 10,000).

B. Using the Presto table or spreadsheet, create a graph with TR, TC, and π as dependent variables, and units of output (Q) as the independent variable. At what price/output combination is total profit maximized? Why? At what price/output combination is total revenue maximized? Why?

C. Determine these profit-maximizing and revenue-maximizing price/output combinations analytically. In other words, use Presto's profit and revenue equations to confirm your answers to Part B.

D. Compare the profit-maximizing and revenue-maximizing price/output combinations, and discuss any differences. When will short-run revenue maximization lead to long-run profit maximization?

ST2.1 **SOLUTION**

A. A table or spreadsheet for Presto output (Q), price (P), total revenue (TR), marginal revenue (MR), total cost (TC), marginal cost (MC), total profit (π), and marginal profit ($M\pi$) appears at the bottom of this page.

B. Using the Presto table or spreadsheet, a graph with TR, TC, and π as dependent variables and units of output (Q) as the independent variable appears on page 51.

The price/output combination at which total profit is maximized is $P = \$35$ and $Q = 5,000$ units. At that point, $MR = MC$ and total profit is maximized at \$37,500.

The price/output combination at which total revenue is maximized is $P = \$30$ and $Q = 6,000$ units. At that point, $MR = 0$ and total revenue is maximized at \$180,000.

C. To find the profit-maximizing output level analytically, set $MR = MC$, or set $M\pi = 0$, and solve for Q. Since,

$$MR = MC$$

$$\$60 - \$0.01Q = \$5 + \$0.001Q$$

$$0.011Q = 55$$

$$Q = 5,000$$

UNITS	PRICE	TOTAL REVENUE	MARGINAL REVENUE	TOTAL COST	MARGINAL COST	TOTAL PROFIT	MARGINAL PROFIT
0	$60	$0	$60	$100,000	$5	($100,000)	$55
1,000	55	55,000	50	105,500	6	(50,500)	44
2,000	50	100,000	40	112,000	7	(12,000)	33
3,000	45	135,000	30	119,500	8	15,500	22
4,000	40	160,000	20	128,000	9	32,000	11
5,000	35	175,000	10	137,500	10	37,500	0
6,000	30	180,000	0	148,000	11	32,000	(11)
7,000	25	175,000	(10)	159,500	12	15,500	(22)
8,000	20	160,000	(20)	172,000	13	(12,000)	(33)
9,000	15	135,000	(30)	185,500	14	(50,500)	(44)
10,000	10	100,000	(40)	200,000	15	(100,000)	(55)

PRESTO PRODUCTS, INC.
Profit vs. Revenue Maximization

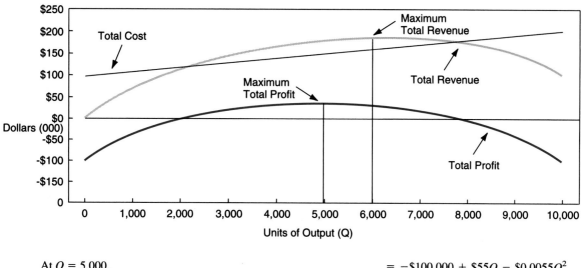

At $Q = 5,000$,

$$P = \$60 - \$0.005(5,000)$$

$$= \$35$$

$$\pi = -\$100,000 + \$55(5,000)$$
$$- \$0.0055(5,000^2)$$

$$= \$37,500$$

(Note: This is a maximum since total profit is falling for $Q > 5,000$.)

To find the revenue-maximizing output level, set $MR = 0$, and solve for Q. Thus,

$$MR = \$60 - \$0.01Q = 0$$

$$0.01Q = 60$$

$$Q = 6,000$$

At $Q = 6,000$,

$$P = \$60 - \$0.005(6,000)$$

$$= \$30$$

$$\pi = TR - TC$$

$$= (\$60 - \$0.005Q)Q - \$100,000$$
$$- \$5Q - \$0.0005Q^2$$

$$= -\$100,000 + \$55Q - \$0.0055Q^2$$

$$= -\$100,000 + \$55(6,000)$$
$$- \$0.0055(6,000^2)$$

$$= \$32,000$$

(Note: This is a revenue maximum since total revenue is decreasing for output beyond $Q > 6,000$.)

D.   Given downward sloping demand and marginal revenue curves, and positive marginal costs, the profit-maximizing price/output combination is *always* at a higher price and lower production level than the revenue-maximizing price-output combination. This stems from the fact that profit is maximized when $MR = MC$, whereas revenue is maximized when $MR = 0$. It follows that profits and revenue are only maximized at the same price/output combination in the unlikely event that $MC = 0$.

In pursuing a short-run revenue rather than profit-maximizing strategy, Presto can expect to gain a number of important advantages, including enhanced product awareness among consumers, increased customer loyalty, potential economies of scale in marketing and promotion, and possible limitations in competitor entry and growth. To be consistent with long-run profit maximization, these advantages of short-run revenue maximization must be at least worth Presto's short-run sacrifice of $5,500 (= $37,500 − $32,000) in monthly profits.

ST2.2 **Average Cost-Minimization.** Pharmaceutical Laboratories, Inc., is an international manufacturer and marketer of products for the over-the-counter health care market, and bulk antibiotics for the animal feed market. Dr. Indiana Jones, head of marketing and research, seeks your advice on an appropriate pricing strategy for Pharmed Caplets, a bulk antibiotic for sale to the veterinarian and feedlot-operator market. This product has been successfully launched during the past few months in a number of test markets, and reliable data is now available for the first time.

The marketing and accounting departments have provided you with the following monthly total revenue and total cost information:

$$TR = \$900Q - \$0.1Q^2.$$

$$MR = \$900 - \$0.2Q.$$

$$TC = \$36,000 + \$200Q + \$0.4Q^2.$$

$$MC = \$200 + \$0.8Q.$$

A. Set up a table or spreadsheet for Pharmed Caplets output (Q), price (P), total revenue (TR), marginal revenue (MR), total cost (TC), marginal cost (MC), average cost (AC), total profit (π), and marginal profit ($M\pi$). Establish a range for Q from 0 to 1,000 in increments of 100 (i.e., 0, 100, 200, . . . , 1,000).

B. Using the Pharmed Caplets table or spreadsheet, create a graph with AC and MC as dependent variables and units of output (Q) as the independent variable. At what price/output combination is total profit maximized? Why? At what price/output combination is average cost minimized? Why?

C. Determine these profit-maximizing and average-cost minimizing price/output combinations analytically. In other words, use Pharmed Caplets' revenue and cost equations to confirm your answers to Part B.

D. Compare the profit-maximizing and average-cost minimizing price/output combinations, and discuss any differences. When will average-cost minimization lead to long-run profit maximization?

ST2.2 **SOLUTION**

A. A table or spreadsheet for Pharmed Caplets output (Q), price (P), total revenue (TR), marginal revenue (MR), total cost (TC), marginal cost (MC), average cost (AC), total profit (π), and marginal profit ($M\pi$) appears at the bottom of this page.

B. Using the Pharmed Caplets table or spreadsheet, a graph with AC and MC as dependent variables and units of output (Q) as the independent variable appears on page 53.

The price/output combination at which total profit is maximized is $P = \$830$ and $Q = 700$ units. At that point, $MR = MC$ and total profit is maximized at $209,000.

The price/output combination at which average cost is minimized is $P = \$870$ and $Q = 300$ units. At that point, $MC = AC = \$440$.

Units	Price	Total Revenue	Marginal Revenue	Total Cost	Marginal Cost	Average Cost	Total Profit	Marginal Profit
0	$900	$0	$900	$36,000	$200	—	($36,000)	$700
100	$890	89,000	$880	$60,000	$280	600.00	29,000	600
200	$880	176,000	$860	$92,000	$360	460.00	84,000	500
300	$870	261,000	$840	$132,000	$440	440.00	129,000	400
400	$860	344,000	$820	$180,000	$520	450.00	164,000	300
500	$850	425,000	$800	$236,000	$600	472.00	189,000	200
600	$840	504,000	$780	$300,000	$680	500.00	204,000	100
700	$830	581,000	$760	$372,000	$760	531.43	209,000	0
800	$820	656,000	$740	$452,000	$840	565.00	204,000	(100)
900	$810	729,000	$720	$540,000	$920	600.00	189,000	(200)
1,000	$800	800,000	$700	$636,000	$1,000	636.00	164,000	(300)

PHARMACEUTICAL LABORATORIES, INC.
Average Cost Minimization

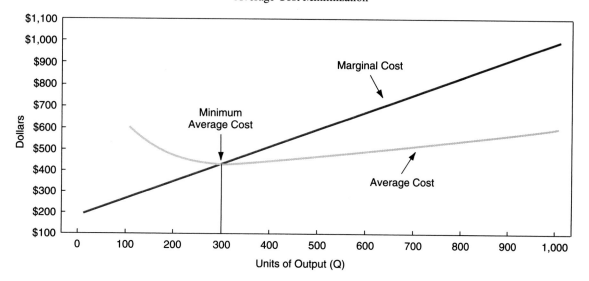

C. To find the profit-maximizing output level analytically, set $MR = MC$, or set $M\pi = 0$, and solve for Q. Since,

$$MR = MC$$

$$\$900 - \$0.2Q = \$200 + \$0.8Q$$

$$Q = 700$$

At $Q = 700$,

$$P = TR/Q$$

$$= (\$900Q - \$0.1Q^2)/Q$$

$$= \$900 - \$0.1(700)$$

$$= \$830$$

$$\pi = TR - TC$$

$$= \$900Q - \$0.1Q^2 - \$36,000 - \$200Q - \$0.4Q^2$$

$$= -\$36,000 + \$700(700) - \$0.5(700^2)$$

$$= \$209,000$$

(Note: This is a profit maximum since profits are falling for $Q > 700$.)

To find the average-cost minimizing output level, set $MC = AC$, and solve for Q. Since,

$$AC = TC/Q$$

$$= (\$36,000 + \$200Q + \$0.4Q^2)/Q$$

$$= \$36,000Q^{-1} + \$200 + \$0.4Q,$$

it follows that:

$$MC = AC$$

$$\$200 + \$0.8Q = \$36,000Q^{-1} + \$200 + \$0.4Q$$

$$0.4Q = 36,000Q^{-1}$$

$$0.4Q^2 = 36,000$$

$$Q^2 = 36,000/0.4$$

$$Q^2 = 90,000$$

$$Q = 300$$

At $Q = 300$,

$$P = \$900 - \$0.1(300)$$

$$= \$870$$

$$\pi = -\$36,000 + \$700(300) - \$0.5(300^2)$$

$$= \$129,000$$

(Note: This is an average-cost minimum since average cost is rising for $Q > 300$.)

D. Given downward sloping demand and marginal revenue curves, and a U-shaped or quadratic AC function, the profit-maximizing price/output combination will *often* be at a different price and production level than the average-cost minimizing price-output combination. This stems from the fact that profit is maximized when $MR = MC$, whereas average cost is minimized when $MC = AC$. Profits are maximized at the same price/output combination as where average costs are minimized in the unlikely event that $MR = MC$ and $MC = AC$ and, therefore, $MR = MC = AC$.

It is often true that the profit-maximizing output level differs from the average-cost minimizing activity level. In this instance, expansion beyond $Q = 300$, the average-cost minimizing activity level, can be justified because the added gain in revenue more than compensates for the added costs. Note that total costs rise by $240,000, from $132,000 to $372,000 as output expands from $Q = 300$ to $Q = 700$, as average cost rises from $440 to $531.43. Nevertheless, profits rise by $80,000, from $129,000 to $209,000, because total revenue rises by $320,000, from $261,000 to $581,000. The profit-maximizing activity level can be less than, greater than, or equal to the average-cost minimizing activity level depending on the shape of relevant demand and cost relations.

PROBLEMS

P2.1 **Graph Analysis**
A. Given the output (Q) and price (P) data in the following table, calculate the related total revenue (TR), marginal revenue (MR), and average revenue (AR) figures:

Q	P	TR	MR	AR
0	$10			
1	9			
2	8			
3	7			
4	6			
5	5			
6	4			
7	3			
8	2			
9	1			
10	0			

B. Graph these data using "dollars" on the vertical axis and "quantity" on the horizontal axis. At what output level is revenue maximized?
C. Why is marginal revenue less than average revenue at each price level?

P2.2 A. Fill in the missing data for price (P), total revenue (TR), marginal revenue (MR), total cost (TC), marginal cost (MC), profit (π), and marginal profit ($M\pi$) in the following table:

Q	P	TR	MR	TC	MC	π	$M\pi$
0	$160	$0	$—	$0	$—	$0	$—
1	150	150	150	25	25	125	125
2	140			55	30		100
3		390			35	300	75
4			90	130		350	
5	110	550		175			
6		600	50		55	370	
7		630		290	60		-30
8	80	640		355		285	
9					75		-85
10		600		525			

B. At what output level is profit maximized?
C. At what output level is revenue maximized?
D. Discuss any differences in your answers to Parts B and C.

P2.3 **Marginal Analysis.** Characterize each of the following statements as true or false, and explain your answer.
A. If marginal revenue is less than average revenue, the demand curve will be downward sloping.
B. Profits will be maximized when total revenue equals total cost.
C. Given a downward-sloping demand curve and positive marginal costs, profit-maximizing firms will always sell less output at higher prices than will revenue-maximizing firms.

D. Marginal cost must be falling for average cost to decline as output expands.

E. Marginal profit is the difference between marginal revenue and marginal cost and will always equal zero at the profit-maximizing activity level.

P2.4   Marginal Analysis: Tables. Sarah Berra is a regional sales representative for Dental Laboratories, Inc. Berra sells alloy products created from gold, silver, platinum, and other precious metals to several dental laboratories in Maine, New Hampshire, and Vermont. Berra's goal is to maximize her total monthly commission income, which is figured at 7.5% of gross sales. In reviewing her monthly experience over the past year, Berra found the following relations between days spent in each state and monthly sales generated:

MAINE		NEW HAMPSHIRE		VERMONT	
DAYS	GROSS SALES	DAYS	GROSS SALES	DAYS	GROSS SALES
0	$ 4,000	0	$ 0	0	$ 2,500
1	10,000	1	3,500	1	5,000
2	15,000	2	6,500	2	7,000
3	19,000	3	9,000	3	8,500
4	22,000	4	10,500	4	9,500
5	24,000	5	11,500	5	10,000
6	25,000	6	12,000	6	10,000
7	25,000	7	12,500	7	10,000

A. Construct a table showing Berra's marginal sales per day in each state.

B. If administrative duties limit Berra to only ten selling days per month, how should she spend them?

C. Calculate Berra's maximum monthly commission income.

P2.5   Marginal Analysis: Tables. Climate Control Devices, Inc., estimates that sales of defective thermostats cost the firm an average of $25 each for replacement or repair. An independent engineering consultant has recommended hiring quality control inspectors so that defective thermostats can be identified and corrected before shipping. The following schedule shows the expected relation between the number of quality control inspectors and the thermostat failure rate, defined in terms of the percentage of total shipments that prove to be defective.

NUMBER OF QUALITY CONTROL INSPECTORS	THERMOSTAT FAILURE RATE (PERCENT)
0	5.0
1	4.0
2	3.2
3	2.6
4	2.2
5	2.0

The firm expects to ship 250,000 thermostats during the coming year, and quality control inspectors each command a salary of $30,000 per year.

A. Construct a table showing the marginal failure reduction (in units) and the dollar value of these reductions for each inspector hired.

B. How many inspectors should the firm hire?

C. How many inspectors would be hired if additional indirect costs (lost customer goodwill and so on) were to average 30% of direct replacement or repair costs?

P2.6   Profit Maximization: Equations. Rochester Instruments, Inc., operates in the highly competitive electronics industry. Prices for its RII-X control switches are stable at $50 each. This means that $P = MR = \$50$ in this market. Engineering estimates indicate that relevant total and marginal cost relations for the RII-X model are:

$$TC = \$78,000 + \$18Q + \$0.002Q^2$$

$$MC = \$18 + \$0.004Q.$$

A. Calculate the output level that will maximize the RII-X profit.

B. Calculate this maximum profit.

P2.7   Profit Maximization: Equations. 21st Century Insurance offers mail-order automobile insurance to preferred-risk drivers in the Los Angeles area. The company is the low-cost provider of insurance in this market but doesn't believe its $750 annual premium can be raised for competitive reasons. Its rates are expected to remain stable during coming periods; hence, $P = MR = \$750$. Total and marginal cost relations for the company are as follows:

$$TC = \$2,500,000 + \$500Q + \$0.005Q^2$$

$$MC = \$500 + \$0.01Q.$$

A. Calculate the profit-maximizing activity level.

B. Calculate the company's optimal profit and return-on-sales levels.

P2.8 **Not-for-Profit Analysis.** The Denver Athlete's Club (DAC) is a private, not-for-profit athletic club located in Denver, Colorado. DAC currently has 3,500 members but is planning on a membership drive to increase this number significantly. An important issue facing Jessica Nicholson, DAC's administrative director, is the determination of an appropriate membership level. In order to efficiently employ scarce DAC resources, the board of directors has instructed Nicholson to maximize DAC's operating surplus, defined as revenues minus operating costs. They have also asked Nicholson to determine the effects of a proposed agreement between DAC and a neighboring club with outdoor recreation and swimming pool facilities. Plan A involves paying the neighboring club $100 per DAC member. Plan B involves payment of a fixed fee of $400,000 per year. Finally, the board has determined that the membership fee for the coming year will remain constant at $2,500 per member irrespective of the number of new members added and whether Plan A or Plan B is adopted.

In the calculations for determining an optimal membership level, Nicholson regards price as fixed; therefore, $P = MR = \$2,500$. Before considering the effects of any agreement with the neighboring club, Nicholson projects total and marginal cost relations during the coming year to be as follows:

$$TC = \$3,500,000 + \$500Q + \$0.25Q^2$$

$$MC = \$500 + \$0.5Q,$$

where Q is the number of DAC members.

A. Before considering the effects of the proposed agreement with the neighboring club, calculate DAC's optimal membership and operating surplus levels.

B. Calculate these levels under Plan A.

C. Calculate these levels under Plan B.

P2.9 **Revenue Maximization.** Desktop Publishing Software, Inc., develops and markets software packages for business computers. Although sales have grown rapidly during recent years, the company's management fears that a recent onslaught of new competitors may severely retard future growth opportunities. Therefore, it believes that the time has come to "get big or get out."

The marketing and accounting departments have provided management with the following monthly demand and cost information:

$$P = \$1,000 - \$1Q.$$

$$MR = \$1,000 - \$2Q.$$

$$TC = \$50,000 + \$100Q.$$

$$MC = \$100.$$

A. Calculate monthly quantity, price, and profit at the short-run revenue-maximizing output level.

B. Calculate these same values for the short-run profit-maximizing level of output.

C. When would short-run revenue maximization lead to long-run profit maximization?

P2.10 **Average-Cost Minimization.** Giant Screen TV, Inc., is a San Diego-based manufacturer and distributor of customized, 60-inch, high-resolution television monitors for individual and commercial customers. Revenue and cost relations are as follows:

$$TR = \$5,100Q - \$0.25Q^2.$$

$$MR = \$5,100 - \$0.5Q.$$

$$TC = \$7,200,000 + \$600Q + \$0.2Q^2.$$

$$MC = \$600 + \$0.4Q.$$

A. Calculate output, marginal cost, average cost, price, and profit at the average cost-minimizing activity level.

B. Calculate these values at the profit-maximizing activity level.

C. Compare and discuss your answers to Parts A and B.

> ## *Case Study for Chapter 2*

A SPREADSHEET APPROACH TO FINDING THE
ECONOMIC ORDER QUANTITY

A spreadsheet is a table of data that is organized in a logical framework similar to an accounting income statement or balance sheet. At first, this marriage of computers and accounting information might seem like a minor innovation. However, it is not. For example, with computerized spreadsheets it becomes possible to easily reflect the effects on revenue, cost, and profit of a slight change in demand conditions. Similarly, the effects on the profit-maximizing or breakeven activity levels can be easily determined. Various "what if?" scenarios can also be tested to determine the optimal or profit-maximizing activity level under a wide variety of operating conditions. Thus, it becomes easy to quantify in dollar terms the pluses and minuses (revenues and costs) of alternate decisions. Each operating and planning decision can be easily evaluated in light of available alternatives. Through the use of spreadsheet formulas and so-called "macros," managers are able to locate maximum or minimum values for any objective function based on the relevant marginal relations. Therefore, spreadsheets are a very useful tool that can be employed to analyze a variety of typical optimization problems.

To illustrate the use of spreadsheets in economic analysis, consider the case of The Neighborhood Pharmacy, Inc. (NPI), a small but rapidly growing operator of a number of large-scale discount pharmacies in the greater Boston, Massachusetts, metropolitan area. A key contributor to the overall success of the company is a system of tight controls over inventory acquisition and carrying costs. The company's total annual costs for acquisition and inventory of pharmaceutical items are composed of the purchase cost of individual products supplied by wholesalers (purchase costs); the clerical, transportation, and other costs associated with placing each individual order (order costs); and the interest, insurance, and other expenses involved with carrying inventory (carrying costs). The company's total inventory-related costs are given by the expression:

$$TC = P \cdot X + \Theta \cdot X/Q + C \cdot Q/2,$$

where TC is inventory-related total costs during the planning period, P is the purchase price of the inventory item, X is the total quantity of the inventory item that is to be ordered (used) during the planning period (use requirement), Θ is the cost of placing an individual order for the inventory item (order cost), C is inventory carrying costs expressed on a per unit of inventory basis (carrying cost), and Q is the quantity of inventory ordered at any one point in time (order quantity). Here Q is NPI's decision variable, whereas each other variable contained in the total cost function is beyond control of the firm (exogenous). In analyzing this total cost relation, NPI is concerned with picking the order quantity that will minimize total inventory-related costs. The optimal or total cost minimizing order quantity is typically referred to as the "economic order quantity."

During the relevant planning period, the per unit purchase cost for an important prescribed (ethical) drug is $P = \$4$, the total estimated use for the planning period is $X = 5,000$, the cost of placing an order is $\Theta = \$50$, and the per unit carrying cost is $C = \$0.50$, calculated as the current interest rate of 12.5% multiplied by the per unit purchase cost of the item.

A. Set up a table or spreadsheet for NPI's order quantity (Q), inventory-related total cost (TC), purchase price (P), use requirement (X), order cost (Θ), and carrying cost (C). Establish a range for Q from 0 to 2,000 in increments of 100 (i.e., 0, 100, 200, . . . , 2,000).

B. Based on the NPI table or spreadsheet, determine the order quantity that will minimize the company's inventory-related total costs during the planning period.

C. Placing inventory-related total costs, TC, on the vertical or *y*-axis and the order quantity, Q, on the horizontal or *x*-axis, plot the relation between inventory-related total costs and the order quantity.

D. Based on the same data as previously, set up a table or spreadsheet for NPI's order quantity (Q), inventory-related total cost (TC), and each component part of total costs, including inventory purchase (acquisition) costs, $P \cdot X$; total order costs, $\Theta \cdot X/Q$; and total carrying costs, $C \cdot Q/2$. Placing inventory-related total costs, TC, and each component cost category as dependent variables on the vertical or y-axis and the order quantity, Q, as the independent variable on the horizontal or x-axis, plot the relation between inventory-related cost categories and the order quantity.

Math Analysis for Managers

This appendix provides a brief and selective discussion of mathematical terms and methods commonly employed in managerial economics. The first section covers basic properties of real numbers that help us understand how to solve equations. It is followed by an explanation of the use of exponents and radicals. The next section describes the fundamentals of equations, their different forms, and the operations used to manipulate them. The following section explains the use of logarithms. The final section covers some basic rules of calculus.

Properties of Real Numbers

In this section, we will review some important properties of real numbers. These properties are basic to our understanding of how to manipulate numerical values.

TRANSITIVE PROPERTY

If X, Y, and Z are real numbers, then:

$$\text{if } X = Y \text{ and } Y = Z, X = Z.$$

This means that if two numbers are both equal to a third number, they are equal to each other. For example, if $X = Y$ and $Y = 5$, then $X = 5$.

COMMUTATIVE PROPERTIES

If X and Y are real numbers, then:

$$X + Y = Y + X \text{ and } XY = YX.$$

This means that you can add or multiply numbers in any order. For example, $2 + 3 = 3 + 2 = 5$ and $2(3) = 3(2) = 6$.

ASSOCIATIVE PROPERTIES

If X, Y, and Z are real numbers, then:

$$X + (Y + Z) = (X + Y) + Z \text{ and } X(YZ) = (XY)Z.$$

This means that for purposes of addition or multiplication, numbers can be grouped in any convenient manner. For example, $3 + (4 + 5) = (3 + 4) + 5 = 12$ and $3(4 \times 5) = (3 \times 4)5 = 60$.

DISTRIBUTIVE PROPERTIES

If X, Y, and Z are real numbers, then:

$$X(Y + Z) = XY + XZ \text{ and } (X + Y)Z = XZ + YZ.$$

This means that within the context of an equation, the order of addition or multiplication is immaterial; that is, it is possible to first multiply and then add, or vice versa. For example, $3(4 + 5) = 3(4) + 3(5) = 27$ and $3(4 + 5) = 3(9) = 27$.

INVERSE PROPERTIES

For each real number X, there is a number $-X$, called the *additive inverse* or *negative* of X, where:

$$X + (-X) = 0.$$

For example, since $5 + (-5) = 0$, the additive inverse of 5 is -5. Similarly, the additive inverse of -5 is 5. For each real number X, there also is a unique number, X^{-1}, called the *multiplicative inverse* or *reciprocal* of X, where:

$$X \cdot \frac{1}{X} = \frac{X}{X} = 1.$$

The expression $1/X$ can be written X^{-1}, so $X(1/X) = X \cdot X^{-1} = X/X = 1$. For example, $4(1/4) = 4 \cdot 4^{-1} = 4/4 = 1$. This property holds for all real numbers except 0, for which the reciprocal is undefined.

EXPONENTS AND RADICALS

Exponents and radicals can be thought of as abbreviations in the language of mathematics. For example, the product:

$$X \cdot X \cdot X = X^3.$$

In general, for a positive integer n, X^n is an abbreviation for the product of n X's. In X^n, the letter X is called the *base* and the letter n the *exponent* (or *power*). If $Y = X^n$, X is called the nth root of Y. For example, $2 \cdot 2 \cdot 2 = 2^3 = 8$ and 2 is the third root of 8. Any number raised to the first power equals itself, $X^1 = X$ (for example, $7^1 = 7$), and any number raised to the zero power equals one—that is, $X^0 = 1$ for $X \neq 0$ (0^0 is not defined). Some numbers do not have an nth root that is a real number. For example, since the second power, or square, of any real number is nonnegative, there is no real number that is the second, or square, root of -9.

It is also common to write:

$$\frac{1}{X \cdot X \cdot X \dots \cdot X} = \frac{1}{X^n} = X^{-n}.$$

n factors

This implies that $1/X^{-n} = X^n$. In general, whenever we move a number raised to a power from the numerator (top) to the denominator (bottom) of an expression, the sign of the exponent, or power, is multiplied by -1, as vice-versa. For example, $1/(2 \cdot 2 \cdot 2) = 1/2^3 = 2^{-3} = 0.125$.

The symbol $\sqrt[n]{X}$ is called a *radical*. Here n is the *index*, $\sqrt{}$ is the *radical sign*, and X is the *radicand*. For convenience, the index is usually omitted in the case of principal square roots; $\sqrt{X}$ is written instead of $\sqrt[2]{X}$. Therefore, $\sqrt{16} = \sqrt[2]{16} = 4$. If X is positive and m and n are integers where n is also positive, then:

$$\sqrt[n]{X^m} = X^{m/n}.$$

For example, $\sqrt{2^4} = 2^{4/2} = 2^2 = 4$. Similarly, $\sqrt{9} = 9^{1/2} = 3$.

The basic rule for multiplication is $X^m \cdot X^n = X^{m+n}$ and for division is $X^m/X^n = X^{m-n}$. For example, $3^3 \cdot 3^2 = 3^{3+2} = 3^5 = 243$, and $3^3/3^2 = 3^{3-2} = 3^1 = 3$.

Equations

A statement that two algebraic expressions are related is called an *equation*. The two expressions that make up an equation are called its *members* or *sides*. They are often separated by the symbol $=$, which is called an *equality* or *equals sign*. In solving an equation or finding its roots, we often manipulate the original equation in order to generate another equation that will be somewhat easier to solve.

EQUIVALENT OPERATIONS

There are three operations that can be performed on equations without changing their solution values; hence, the original and subsequent equations are called *equivalent*. These operations are:

Addition (Subtraction) Operation. Equivalence is maintained when adding (subtracting) the same variable to (from) both sides of an equation, where the variable is the same as that occurring in the original equation. For example, if $6X = 20 + 2X$, subtracting $2X$ from both sides gives the equivalent equation $4X = 20$.

Multiplication (Division) Operation. Equivalence is maintained when multiplying (dividing) both sides of an equation by the same nonzero constant. For example, if $4X = 20$, dividing both sides by 4 gives the equivalent equation $X = 5$.

Replacement Operation. Equivalence is maintained when replacing either side of an equation by an equivalent expression. For example, if $X(X - 4) = 3$, replacing the left side by the equivalent expression $X^2 - 4X$ gives an equivalent equation $X^2 - 4X = 3$.

It is worth emphasizing that each of these operations can be applied to any equation with the effect that the resulting equation will be mathematically identical to the original.

Equations may take a wide variety of functional forms. Three of the more frequently encountered are described next.

LINEAR EQUATIONS

An equation *linear* in the variable X can be written:

$$aX + b = 0,$$

where a and b are constants and a is called the slope *coefficient* and b the *intercept*.

A linear equation is sometimes referred to as a *first-degree equation* or *equation of degree one*. To solve the linear equation $2X + 6 = 14$, we apply the subtraction and division operations to find $2X = 8$ and $X = 4$.

QUADRATIC EQUATIONS

An equation *quadratic* in the variable X can be written:

$$aX^2 + bX + c = 0.$$

where a, b, and c are constants and $a \neq 0$. Here a and b are slope coefficients and c is the intercept.

A quadratic equation is sometimes referred to as a *second-degree equation* or *equation of degree two*. Whereas linear equations have only one root, quadratic equations sometimes have two different roots. The solutions to quadratic equations are easily found through application of the *quadratic* formula. If $aX^2 + bX + c = 0$ and a, b, and c are constants where $a \neq 0$, then:

$$X = \frac{-b \pm \sqrt{b^2 - 4ac}}{2a}.$$

The solutions for the values of X are called the *roots* of the quadratic equation. For example, if $2X^2 - 15X + 18 = 0$, then $X = +15 \pm \sqrt{225 \ 4(2)(18)/2(2)} = (15 \pm 9)/4 = 6$ and 1.5. In many instances, one or both of the solved values for a quadratic equation will be negative. If the quadratic equation is a profit function and X is output, for example, any root $X < 0$, implying negative output, will be mathematically correct but meaningless from an economic standpoint. Therefore, when applying the quadratic formula to problems in managerial economics, one must use judgment to identify those solution values that are both mathematically correct and economically relevant.

MULTIPLICATIVE EQUATIONS

An equation *multiplicative* in the variables X and Z can be written:

$$Y = aX^{b_1}Z^{b_2},$$

where a is the constant and b_1 and b_2 are exponents.

For example, $Y = 5X^2Z^3$ where $X = 3$ and $Z = 4$ has the solution $Y = 5(3^2)(4^3) = 5(9)(64) = 2,880$. Multiplicative equations are often employed in managerial economics, particularly in demand, production, and cost analyses.

EXPONENTIAL FUNCTIONS

Certain multiplicative functions are referred to as *exponential functions.* The function $Y = b^x$, where $b > 0$, $b \neq 1$, and X is any real number, is referred to as an *exponential function to the base b.* Exponential functions often are constructed using e, the Naperian Constant ($=2.71828\cdots$) as a base. Thus, for example, the equation $Y = e^2$ means $Y = (2.71828\cdots)^2$. While e may seem a curious number to adopt as the base in an exponential function, it is usefully employed in economic studies of compound growth or decline.

LOGARITHMIC FUNCTIONS

For the purposes of economic analysis, multiplicative or exponential relations often are transformed into a linear *logarithmic form,* where:

$$Y = \log_b X \text{ if and only if } X = b^Y.$$

Here Y is a *logarithmic function to the base b.* $Y = \log_b X$ is the logarithmic form of the exponential $X = b^Y$. For example, $\log_{10} 1{,}000 = 3$ is the logarithmic equivalent of the exponential $10^3 = 1{,}000$. For much of the work in managerial economics, logarithms are written using either the base 10, called *common logarithms,* or the base e ($=$ Naperian Constant $= 2.71828\cdots$), called *natural logarithms.* Natural logarithms typically are denoted by the notation "ln" rather than "log e."

Some important basic properties of logarithms are:

Product Property. The logarithm of a product is the sum of logarithms:

$$\ln XY = \ln X + \ln Y.$$

For example, $\ln 6 = \ln (3 \cdot 2) = \ln 3 + \ln 2 = 1.099 + 0.693 = 1.792$. It is important to note that the logarithm of a sum is *not* the sum of logarithms.

Quotient Property. The logarithm of a quotient is the difference of logarithms:

$$\ln \frac{X}{Y} = \ln X - \ln Y.$$

For example, $\ln 1.5 = \ln 3/2 = \ln 3 - \ln 2 = 1.099 - 0.693 = 0.406$. Here note that the logarithm of a quotient is *not* the quotient of logarithms.

Power Property. The logarithm of a number X raised to the exponent n, X^n, is the exponent times the logarithm of X:

$$\ln X^n = n \ln X.$$

For example, $\ln 9 = \ln 3^2 = 2 \ln 3 = 2(1.099) = 2.198$.

Using the properties of logarithms, we see that there is a simple logarithmic transformation for any multiplicative or exponential function. For example, the logarithmic transformation of the multiplicative equation $Y = 5X^2Z^3$ can be written $\ln Y = \ln 5 + 2 \ln X + 3 \ln Z$. Here we have used the natural logarithm of X, although the transformation would be the same using common logs or logs to any other base.

It is important to recognize the symmetry between the logarithmic and exponential functions. It is an important property of each that:

$$\ln e^X = X \text{ and } e^{\ln X} = X.$$

In words, the logarithm to the base e of the number e raised to the power X equals X. Similarly, the number e raised to the power $\ln X$ equals X. For example, $\ln e^1 = 1$ and $e^{\ln 1} = 1$. This means that any number or equation transformed into logarithmic form through use of logarithms can be converted back into original form through exponential transformation. For example, recall from earlier discussion that the multiplicative equation $Y = 5X^2Z^3$ has the logarithmic equivalent $\ln Y = \ln 5 + 2 \ln X + 3 \ln Z$. It follows that if $X = 3$ and $Z = 4$, then $Y = 5(3^2)(4^3) = 5(9)(64) = 2{,}880$ and $\ln Y = \ln 5 + 2 \ln 3 + 3 \ln 4 = 1.609 + 2.197 + 4.159 = 7.965$. Equivalence requires that $\ln 2{,}880 = 7.965$ and $e^{7.965} = 2{,}880$, which is indeed the case.

The practical relevance of this symmetry between logarithms and exponential functions is that, for example, a multiplicative demand relation can be analyzed in linear logarithmic form using widely available computer-software regression packages and converted back into original form through exponential transformation for purposes of numerical evaluation.

Concept of a Marginal

In Chapter 2, a *marginal* is defined as the change in the value of the dependent variable associated with a one-unit change in an independent variable. This relationship can be more precisely specified by examining the nature of a change in a function. Consider the unspecified function $Y = f(X)$, which is read "Y is a function of X." Using Δ (delta) to denote change, the change in the value of the independent variable, X, is given by the notation ΔX and the change in the dependent variable, Y, is given by ΔY.

The ratio $\Delta Y/\Delta X$ provides a very general specification of the marginal concept:

$$\text{Marginal } Y = \frac{\Delta Y}{\Delta X}. \qquad (2A.1)$$

The change in Y, ΔY, divided by the change in X, ΔX, indicates the change in the dependent variable associated with a one-unit change in the value of X.

Figure 2A.1, which graphs a function relating Y to X, illustrates this relation. For values of X close to the origin, a relatively small change in X creates a large change in Y. Thus, the value of $\Delta Y/\Delta X$—for example, $(Y_2 - Y_1)/(X_2 - X_1)$—is relatively large, showing that a small increase in X induces a large increase in Y. The situation is reversed the farther out one moves along the X axis. A large increase in X—say, from X_3 to X_4—produces only a small increase in Y, from Y_3 to Y_4; thus $\Delta Y/\Delta X$ is small.

In Figure 2A.1, the marginal relation between X and Y changes at different points along the curve. When the curve is relatively steep, the dependent variable, Y, is highly responsive to changes in the independent variable, X; but when the curve is relatively flat, Y responds less significantly to changes in X. Notice, however, that the general

ILLUSTRATION OF CHANGING $\Delta Y/\Delta X$ OVER THE RANGE OF A CURVE

Figure 2A.1

The ratio $\Delta Y/\Delta X$ changes continuously along a curved line.

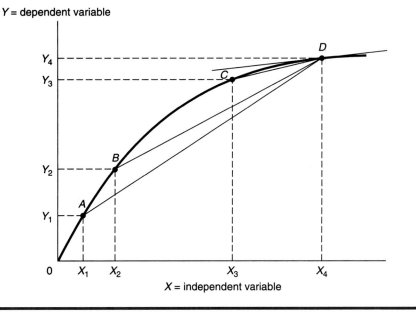

expression of the marginal relation in Equation 2A.1 does not necessarily capture this changing marginal relation. For example, using that equation one could estimate the marginal relation as:

$$\frac{\Delta Y}{\Delta X} = \frac{Y_4 - Y_1}{X_4 - X_1}.$$

This measure of the marginal is shown in Figure 2A.1 as the slope of the line connecting points A and D. We can see that this measure of the marginal is considerably smaller than the estimate one would obtain looking at the change $(Y_2 - Y_1)/(X_2 - X_1)$, the slope of a straight line connecting points A and B, and larger than the marginal found for the change $(Y_4 - Y_3)/(X_4 - X_3)$, the slope of a straight line connecting points C and D.

The problem is that $(Y_4 - Y_1)/(X_4 - X_1)$ measures the average change in Y for a one-unit change in X between points A and D. Since this "average" marginal value may differ significantly from the actual marginal at a point such as D, it has limited value for decision making and could, in fact, lead to incorrect decisions.

If a decision maker wanted to know how Y varies for changes in X around point D, the relevant marginal would be found as $\Delta Y/\Delta X$ for a very small change in X around X_4. The mathematical concept for measuring the nature of such very small changes is called a *derivative*. A derivative, then, is simply a precise specification of the marginal value at a particular point on a function. The mathematical notation for a derivative is:

$$\frac{dY}{dX} = \frac{\text{limit}}{\Delta X \to 0} \frac{\Delta Y}{\Delta X},$$

which is read, "The derivative of Y with respect to X equals the limit of the ratio $\Delta Y/\Delta X$, as ΔX approaches zero."[2]

This concept of the derivative as the limit of a ratio is precisely equivalent to the slope of a curve at a point. Figure 2A.1 also presents this idea. Notice that the *average* slope of the curve between points A and D is measured as:

$$\frac{\Delta Y}{\Delta X} = \frac{Y_4 - Y_1}{X_4 - X_1}$$

and is shown as the slope of the line connecting the two points. Similarly, the average slope of the curve can be measured over smaller and smaller intervals of X and shown by other chords, such as those connecting points B and C with D. At the limit, as ΔX approaches zero around point D, the ratio $\Delta Y/\Delta X$ is equal to the slope of a line drawn tangent to the curve at point D. *The slope of this tangent is defined as the derivative, dY/dX, of the function at point D; it measures the marginal change in Y associated with a very small change in X at that point.*

To illustrate the relation between the mathematical concept of a derivative and the economic concept of a marginal, the dependent variable, Y, might be total revenue and the independent variable, X, might be output. The derivative dY/dX then shows precisely how revenue and output are related at a specific output level. Since the change in revenue associated with a change in output is defined as the marginal revenue, the derivative of the total revenue provides a precise measure of marginal revenue at any specific output level. A similar situation exists for total cost: The derivative of the total cost function at any output level indicates the marginal cost at that output.

Derivatives provide much useful information in managerial economics. Therefore, it is important to examine the rules for finding the derivatives of certain frequently encountered functions.

---

[2] If the value of a function $Y = f(X)$ approaches a constant Y^* as the value of the independent variable, X, approaches X^*, Y^* is called the *limit* of the function $f(x)$ as X approaches X^*. This would be written:

$$\frac{\text{limit}}{x \to X^*} f(X) = Y^*.$$

For example, if $Y = X - 4$, the limit of this function as X approaches 5 is 1; that is:

$$\frac{\text{limit}}{X \to 5} (X - 4) = 1.$$

This says that the value of X approaches but does not quite reach 5; the value of the function $Y = X - 4$ comes closer and closer to 1. This concept of a limit is examined in detail in any introductory calculus textbook.

Rules for Differentiating a Function

Determining the derivative of a function is not a particularly difficult task; it simply involves applying a basic formula to the function. This section presents the basic formulas or rules for differentiation. Proofs are omitted here, but can be found in any introductory calculus textbook.

CONSTANTS

The derivative of a constant is always zero; that is, if Y is a constant:

$$\frac{dY}{dX} = 0.$$

This situation is graphed in Figure 2A.2 for the example $Y = 2$. Since Y is defined as a constant, its value does not vary as X changes and, hence, dY/dX must be zero.

POWERS

The derivative of a power function such as $Y = aX^b$, where a and b are constants, is equal to the exponent b multiplied by the coefficient a times the variable X raised to the $b - 1$ power:

$$Y = aX^b$$

$$\frac{dY}{dX} = b \cdot a \cdot X^{(b-1)}.$$

Figure 2A.2

GRAPH OF A CONSTANT FUNCTION: Y = CONSTANT; $dY/dX = 0$

If the value of Y does not vary with changes in X, then $dY/dX = 0$.

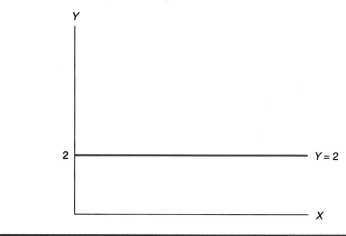

For example, given the function:

$$Y = 2X^3,$$

then

$$\frac{dY}{dX} = 3 \cdot 2 \cdot X^{(3-1)}$$

$$= 6X^2.$$

Two further examples of power functions should clarify this rule. The derivative of the function $Y = X^3$ is given as:

$$\frac{dY}{dX} = 3 \cdot X^2.$$

The exponent, 3, is multiplied by the implicit coefficient, 1, and in turn by the variable, X, raised to the second power.

Finally, the derivative of the function $Y = 0.5X$ is:

$$\frac{dY}{dX} = 1 \cdot 0.5 \cdot X^0 = 0.5.$$

The implicit exponent, 1, is multiplied by the coefficient, 0.5, times the variable, X, raised to the zero power. Since any number raised to the zero power equals 1, the result is 0.5.

Again a graph may help clarify the power function concept. In Figure 2A.3, the last two power functions given above, $Y = X^3$ and $Y = 0.5X$, are graphed. Consider first

Figure 2A.3

GRAPHS OF POWER FUNCTIONS

The derivative of the linear function $Y = 0.5X$ is constant. The derivative of the nonlinear function $Y = X^3$ rises as X increases.

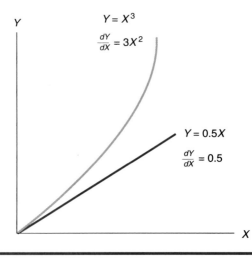

$Y = 0.5X$. The derivative of this function, $dY/dX = 0.5$, is a constant, indicating that the slope of the function is a constant. This can be readily seen from the graph. The derivative measures the *rate of change*. If the rate of change is constant, as it must be if the basic function is linear, the derivative of the function must be constant. The second function, $Y = X^3$, rises at an increasing rate as X increases. The derivative of the function, $dY/dX = 3X^2$, also increases as X becomes larger, indicating that the slope of the function is increasing or that the rate of change is increasing.

SUMS AND DIFFERENCES

The following notation is used throughout the remainder of this section to express a number of other important rules of differentiation:

$$U = g(X): U \text{ is an unspecified function, } g, \text{ of } X$$

$$V = h(X): V \text{ is an unspecified function, } h, \text{ of } X$$

The derivative of a sum (difference) is equal to the sum (difference) of the derivatives of the individual terms. Thus, if $Y = U + V$, then:

$$\frac{dY}{dX} = \frac{dU}{dX} + \frac{dV}{dX}.$$

For example, if $U = g(X) = 2X^2$, $V = h(X) = -X^3$, and $Y = U + V = 2X^2 - X^3$, then:

$$\frac{dY}{dX} = 4X - 3X^2.$$

Here the derivative of the first term, $2X^2$, is found to be $4X$ by the power rule; the derivative of the second term, $-X^3$, is found to be $-3X^2$ also by that rule; and the derivative of the total function is the sum of the derivatives of the parts.

Consider a second example of this rule. If $Y = 300 + 5X + 2X^2$, then:

$$\frac{dY}{dX} = 0 + 5 + 4X.$$

The derivative of 300 is 0 by the constant rule; the derivative of $5X$ is 5 by the power rule; and the derivative of $2X^2$ is $4X$ by the power rule.

PRODUCTS

The derivative of the product of two expressions is equal to the sum of the first term multiplied by the derivative of the second *plus* the second term times the derivative of the first. Thus, if $Y = U \cdot V$, then:

$$\frac{dY}{dX} = U \cdot \frac{dV}{dX} + V \cdot \frac{dU}{dX}.$$

For example, if $Y = 3X^2(3 - X)$, then, letting $U = 3X^2$ and $V = (3 - X)$, we get:

$$\frac{dY}{dX} = 3X^2 \left(\frac{dV}{dX} \right) + (3 - X) \left(\frac{dU}{dX} \right)$$

$$= 3X^2(-1) + (3 - X)(6X)$$

$$= -3X^2 + 18X - 6X^2$$

$$= 18X - 9X^2.$$

The first factor, $3X^2$, is multiplied by the derivative of the second, -1, and added to the second factor, $3 - X$, times the derivative of the first, $6X$. Simplifying the expression results in the preceding final expression.

QUOTIENTS

The derivative of the quotient of two expressions is equal to the denominator multiplied by the derivative of the numerator *minus* the numerator times the derivative of the denominator, all divided by the square of the denominator. Thus, if $Y = U/V$, then:

$$\frac{dY}{dX} = \frac{V \cdot \dfrac{dU}{dX} - U \cdot \dfrac{dV}{dx}}{V^2}.$$

For example, if $U = 2X - 3$ and $V = 6X^2$, then:

$$Y = \frac{2X - 3}{6X^2}$$

and

$$\frac{dY}{dX} = \frac{6X^2 \cdot 2 - (2X - 3)12X}{36X^4}$$

$$= \frac{12X^2 - 24X^2 + 36X}{36X^4}$$

$$= \frac{36X - 12X^2}{36X^4}$$

$$= \frac{3 - X}{3X^3}.$$

The denominator, $6X^2$, is multiplied by the derivative of the numerator, 2. Subtracted from this is the numerator, $2X - 3$, times the derivative of the denominator, $12X$. The result is then divided by the square of the denominator, $36X^4$. Algebraic reduction results in the final expression of the derivative.

LOGARITHMIC FUNCTIONS

The derivative of a logarithmic function $Y = \ln X$ is given by the expression:

$$\frac{dY}{dX} = \frac{d \ln X}{dX} = \frac{1}{X}$$

This also implies that if $Y = \ln X$, then $dY = (1/X)dX = dX/X$. Since dX is the change in X by definition, dX/X is the percentage change in X. Derivatives of logarithmic functions have great practical relevance in managerial economics given the prevalence of multiplicative (and hence linear in the logarithms) equations used to describe demand, production, and cost relations. For example, the expression $Y = aX^b$ has an equivalent logarithmic function $\ln Y = \ln a + b \ln X$, where $d \ln Y/d \ln X = (dY/Y)/(dX/X) = b$. Here b is called the *elasticity* of Y with respect to X, since it reflects the percentage effect on Y of a 1% change in X. The concept of elasticity is introduced and extensively examined in Chapter 5 and discussed throughout the remaining chapters.

FUNCTION OF A FUNCTION (CHAIN RULE)

The derivative of a function of a function is found as follows: If $Y = f(U)$, where $U = g(X)$, then:

$$\frac{dY}{dX} = \frac{dY}{dU} \cdot \frac{dU}{dX}.$$

For example, if $Y = 2U - U^2$ and $U = 2X^3$, then dY/dX is found as follows:
Step 1:

$$\frac{dY}{dU} = 2 - 2U.$$

Substituting for U, creates the expression:

$$\frac{dY}{dU} = 2 - 2(2X^3)$$

$$= 2 - 4X^3$$

Step 2:

$$\frac{dU}{dX} = 6X^2.$$

Step 3:

$$\frac{dY}{dX} = \frac{dY}{dU} \cdot \frac{dU}{dX}$$

$$= (2 - 4X^3) \cdot 6X^2$$

$$= 12X^2 - 24X^5.$$

Further examples of this rule should indicate its usefulness in obtaining derivatives of many functions.

Example 1: $Y = \sqrt{X^2 - 1}$

Let $U = X^2 - 1$. Then $Y = \sqrt{U} = U^{1/2}$.

$$\frac{dY}{dU} = \frac{1}{2}U^{-1/2}$$

$$= \frac{1}{2U^{1/2}}.$$

Substituting $X^2 - 1$ for U in the derivative results in:

$$\frac{dY}{dU} = \frac{1}{2(X^2 - 1)^{1/2}}.$$

Since $U = X^2 - 1$,

$$\frac{dU}{dX} = 2X.$$

Using the function of a function rule, $dY/dX = dY/dU \cdot dU/dX$, so:

$$\frac{dY}{dX} = \frac{1}{2(X^2 - 1)^{1/2}} \cdot 2X$$

$$= \frac{X}{\sqrt{X^2 - 1}}.$$

Example 2:

$$Y = \frac{1}{X^2 - 2}$$

Let $U = X^2 - 2$. Then $Y = 1/U$, and the quotient rule yields:

$$\frac{dY}{dU} = \frac{U \cdot 0 - 1 \cdot 1}{U^2}$$

$$= -\frac{1}{U^2}.$$

Substituting $(X^2 - 2)$ for U obtains:

$$\frac{dY}{dU} = -\frac{1}{(X^2 - 2)^2}.$$

Since $U = X^2 - 2$,

$$\frac{dU}{dX} = 2X.$$

Therefore:

$$\frac{dY}{dX} = \frac{dY}{dU} \cdot \frac{dU}{dX} = -\frac{1}{(X^2 - 2)^2} \cdot 2X$$

$$= -\frac{2X}{(X^2 - 2)^2}$$

Example 3: $Y = (2X + 3)^2$
Let $U = 2X + 3$. Then $Y = U^2$ and

$$\frac{dY}{dU} = 2U.$$

Since $U = 2X + 3$,

$$\frac{dY}{dU} = 2(2X + 3)$$

$$= 4X + 6$$

and

$$\frac{dU}{dX} = 2.$$

Thus,

$$\frac{dY}{dX} = \frac{dY}{dU} \cdot \frac{dU}{dX} = (4X + 6)2$$

$$= 8X + 12.$$

It is common knowledge that average scores achieved by U.S. students on the Scholastic Aptitude Test have been declining for years. It is less known that average SAT test scores among whites and blacks, Asians, Mexicans, and Puerto Ricans have generally risen over the past two decades. Average test scores have been declining while the "average" student is doing better. How can the overall average go down if sub-averages for all of the constituent sub-groups are going up? What has changed is not student performance, but demographics. Minority students, whose scores are rising the fastest, but from a lower base, are a rapidly growing part of the test pool. By focusing on the overall average, rather than the averages of constituent subgroups, a picture of declining performance has been painted when performance has instead been improving. In business, the client of a major auditing firm encountered a similar problem. The company feared a loss in market share, as it noted a disturbing erosion in overall profit margins. Upon closer examination the auditing firm found that profit margins were holding steady or rising in each product line, but that the product mix was changing in favor of lower margin products. As in the case of declining SAT scores, the "lie of averages" had emerged. Statistics such as overall averages do not lie, but they can be easily manipulated.[1]

Effective managers are adept at information processing made difficult by an environment that is complex and constantly changing. In this chapter, methods for characterizing the central tendency and dispersion of economic data are presented. This provides the background necessary for a more detailed examination of the statistical analysis of economic relations.

Data Summary and Description

The population of potential buyers includes those persons who may be favorably disposed to purchase a given product. Just as a complete census of city, county, and state residents is a time-consuming and expensive means for determining characteristics of the local population, a complete census of potential buyers is a costly means for determining the likely customer response to a change in product design, quality, or price. Rather than conduct a cursory analysis of each and every potential buyer, it is often desirable to conduct a detailed analysis of a sample or subset of buyers. Similarly, it is often too expensive or otherwise impractical to test the reliability or cost of each and

---

[1] See Fred R. Bleakley, "Some Economists Motives Questioned," *The Wall Street Journal,* March 25, 1997, A2, A4.

every unit produced, so the reliability or cost of a sample of products is analyzed instead. In the absence of a complete and detailed census of the entire population, summary and descriptive measures of the overall population, called **population parameters,** are not known and must be estimated. The most effective means for doing so is to rely on **sample statistics,** or summary and descriptive measures that describe a representative subset of the overall population.

Population Parameters
Summary and descriptive measures for the population.

Sample Statistics
Summary and descriptive measures for a sample.

A complete and detailed study of all those factors and individuals that influence the firm's economic environment is seldom practical or even possible. Therefore, the statistical analysis of economic relations usually focuses on the estimation and interpretation of sample statistics rather than population parameters. In the design and application of statistical methods, managers wish to draw important inferences about overall population parameters based on a detailed analysis of sample statistics. The first important class of sample summary and descriptive statistics that managers must consider involves measures of central tendency.

Measures of Central Tendency

A number that tells the "typical" value of sales, costs, profits, or any amount is called a measure of central tendency. Measures of central tendency are often the most important summary and descriptive statistics available because they indicate a standard level that can be expected under normal operating conditions. Such measures offer less information than is provided by a more complete description of the data, but have advantages in terms of brevity. Measures of central tendency present important features of the data in a concise fashion that offers managers a reasonable basis for operating and planning decisions. While statisticians have constructed several useful measures of central tendency, managers often focus on the mean, median, and mode. Which among these is most appropriate for a given task depends on the nature of the underlying data, and the need being addressed by the manager.

MEAN

Mean
Average.

The arithmetic **mean** or average is the sum of numbers included in a given sample divided by the number of observations. If n is the number of sample observations, X_1 is the first observation, X_2 is the second observation, X_3 is the third observation, and so on, then the sample mean is calculated as:

$$\overline{X} = \frac{X_1 + X_2 + X_3 \cdots + X_n}{n}. \tag{3.1}$$

Alternatively, the arithmetic mean or average is sometimes expressed as:

$$\overline{X} = \frac{\sum_{i=1}^{n} X_i}{n}, \tag{3.2}$$

| Table 3.1 | | | | |

ANNUAL NET PROFIT, PROFIT MARGIN, AND SALES REVENUE IN 25
REGIONAL TELECOMMUNICATIONS SERVICES MARKETS

REGIONAL MARKET	NET PROFIT ($ IN MILLIONS)	NET PROFIT MARGIN (PERCENT)	SALES REVENUE ($ IN MILLIONS)
A	4.2	16.0	26.2
B	6.1	15.0	40.7
C	4.9	14.9	32.8
D	3.5	14.2	24.6
E	4.7	16.4	28.7
F	3.5	14.4	24.3
G	7.6	15.7	48.4
H	3.9	14.4	27.0
I	6.2	12.7	48.9
J	4.7	13.0	36.2
K	5.2	14.4	36.1
L	3.5	16.1	21.7
M	3.3	15.6	21.1
N	4.4	12.2	36.1
O	7.6	16.0	47.6
P	6.5	14.8	43.8
Q	7.1	14.3	49.7
R	5.8	14.3	40.6
S	2.9	14.3	20.3
T	4.7	15.3	30.8
U	7.4	15.1	49.0
V	3.2	15.4	20.8
W	4.4	14.9	29.5
X	5.6	15.3	36.6
Y	3.3	16.2	20.4
MEAN	5.0	14.8	33.7
SAMPLE VARIANCE	2.2	1.2	104.4
SAMPLE STANDARD DEVIATION	1.5	1.1	10.2

where the greek letter sigma, Σ, is referred to as the mathematical summation sign. Σ signals to sum over the sample observations from $i = 1$, the first sample observation, to $i = n$, the last sample observation.

To illustrate, consider the net profit, profit margin, and sales revenue data contained in Table 3.1 for a hypothetical sample of small regional markets for a leading provider of telecommunications services. Profit margin, defined as net profit divided by sales revenue, is the rate of profitability expressed as a percentage of sales. Although the data are hypothetical, they are representative of actual figures. Both net profit and profit margin, expressed in percentage terms, are common measures of firm performance. Sales revenue is a commonly used measure of firm size. Each row of information shows relevant data for each market in the sample, when sample markets are numbered in sequential order. Average net profit per market is $5 million, the average profit margin is 14.8%, and average sales revenue is $33.7 million. In each instance, the sample average reflects a simple sum of each respective value over the entire sample of $n = 25$ markets, all divided by 25, the total number of sample observations. In this particular sample, no individual observation has exactly the sample average level of net profit or sales revenue. With a net profit of $4.9 million, Regional Market C comes closest to the sample average net profit. With $32.8 million in sales, Regional Market C is also closest to the sample average revenue. Regional Market P has exactly the sample average net profit margin of 14.8%.

Any individual observations may coincide with averages for the overall sample, but this is mere happenstance. When profit, profit margin, and sales revenue data are measured in very small increments, it is quite rare to find individual observations that exactly match sample averages. Based on the sample mean criterion, each sample observation that is near sample averages can be described as typical of sample values. It is important to note, however, that there is substantial variation around these sample averages and the chance of atypical sample values is correspondingly high.

The mean represents an attractive measure of central tendency when upward and downward divergences from the mean are fairly balanced. If the number of sample observations above the sample mean is roughly the same as the number of observations below the sample mean, then the mean provides a useful indicator of a typical observation. However, when the number of sample observations above or below the mean is unusually large, as sometimes occurs when there is a significant divergence between extremely large or extremely small observations, the sample mean has the potential to provide a biased view of typical sample values.

MEDIAN

Median
"Middle" observation.

The sample **median,** or "middle" observation, sometimes has the potential to provide a measure of central tendency that is more useful than the sample mean. When the number of sample observations either above or below the mean is unusually large, then the sample mean can be far different from the value for a typical observation. Such divergences exist whenever a sample includes values that are either very small or very large in relation to the typical observation. For example, annual sales revenue can range from a few million dollars per year for small- to medium-size regional competitors into the tens of billions of dollars per year for large multinational corporations such as IBM, GE, or AT&T. Despite the fact that the overwhelming majority of firms in most industries are relatively small, the average level of sales per firm can be relatively high—given the influence of revenues generated by industrial giants. Not only sales revenue, but also profit numbers, wealth, and many other types of important economic data tend to be skewed. It is typical to find most observations at relatively modest levels of revenue, profit, or wealth, while a small and declining number can be found along a diminishing "tail" that reaches upward to the end of the sample distribution. In such instances, the sample median can provide a very useful indicator of central tendency.

| Table 3.2 | SAMPLE RANK ORDER OF ANNUAL NET PROFIT, PROFIT MARGIN, AND SALES REVENUE IN 25 REGIONAL TELECOMMUNICATIONS SERVICES MARKETS |

		NET PROFIT		NET PROFIT MARGIN		SALES REVENUE	
	ROW NUMBER	($ IN MILLIONS)	MARKET	(PERCENT)	MARKET	($ IN MILLIONS)	MARKET
	1	7.6	G	16.4	E	49.7	Q
	2	7.6	O	16.2	Y	49.0	U
	3	7.4	U	16.1	L	48.9	I
	4	7.1	Q	16.0	A	48.4	G
	5	6.5	P	16.0	O	47.6	O
	6	6.2	I	15.7	G	43.8	P
	7	6.1	B	15.6	M	40.7	B
	8	5.8	R	15.4	V	40.6	R
	9	5.6	X	15.3	X	36.6	X
	10	5.2	K	15.3	T	36.2	J
	11	4.9	C	15.1	U	36.1	N
	12	4.7	E	15.0	B	36.1	K
MEDIAN OBSERVATION	**13**	**4.7**	**J**	**14.9**	**C**	**32.8**	**C**
	14	4.7	T	14.9	W	30.8	T
	15	4.4	W	14.8	P	29.5	W
	16	4.4	N	14.4	H	28.7	E
	17	4.2	A	14.4	K	27.0	H
	18	3.9	H	14.4	F	26.2	A
	19	3.5	D	14.3	R	24.6	D
	20	3.5	L	14.3	S	24.3	F
	21	3.5	F	14.3	Q	21.7	L
	22	3.3	M	14.2	D	21.1	M
	23	3.3	Y	13.0	J	20.8	V
	24	3.2	V	12.7	I	20.4	Y
	25	2.9	S	12.2	N	20.3	S
MEAN		5.0		14.8		33.7	
SAMPLE VARIANCE		2.2		1.2		104.4	
SAMPLE STANDARD DEVIATION		1.5		1.1		10.2	

To illustrate, Table 3.2 presents the net profit, profit margin, and sales revenue data contained in Table 3.1 in a new rank order from largest to smallest values. Sample observations are now simply numbered from 1 to 25, since the values in any given row no longer refer to any single market. The sample average (and standard deviation discussed later) is not affected by this new sample ordering. In Table 3.2, sample medians for net profit, profit margin, and sales revenue can be determined by simply counting from the largest to the smallest values to find the middle observation. With an overall sample size of $n = 25$, the middle observation occurs at the 13th sample observation, given exactly 12 larger and 12 smaller observations. For this sample of regional telecommunications services markets, median net profit is $4.7 million, median profit margin is 14.9%, and median sales revenue is $32.8 million. Based on the sample median criterion, each of these observations is typical of sample values.

Sample averages for both net profit and sales revenue are slightly biased or skewed upward because sample mean values are somewhat above median levels. This reflects the fact that a few very large regional markets can cause sample average values to be greater than the typically observed level. As discussed earlier, differences between sample means and medians are to be expected for much economic data given the long upward "tail" provided by the giants of industry. However, there is no necessary reason to suspect any relation between profit margins and firm size. Profit margins are net profit as a percentage of sales revenue. Since sales revenue is a commonly used measure of firm size, profit margin data are an example of "normalized" or size-adjusted data. The sample average profit margin of 14.8% is very close to the sample median of 14.9%. This indicates that the distribution of profit margin data is fairly centered around the sample mean observation, as is often the case when "normalized" or size-adjusted data are considered. There is however, substantial variation around the sample averages for net profit, profit margin, and sales revenues, and the chance of atypical sample values is correspondingly high.

MODE

Mode
Most common value.

Another commonly employed measure of central tendency is the **mode,** or the most frequently encountered value in the sample. The mode is not often relied on in cases where continuous data are employed. Continuous data are numbers, such as net profit, profit margin, or sales revenue data, that can vary by small amounts—or continuously. For example, it is quite rare to find instances where several firms in an industry have exactly the same levels of net profits in *dollars,* whereas many firms might report the same profit level in millions of dollars. In the regional telecommunications services markets example, three regional markets generate exactly the same $4.7 million profit level. This modal profit level is slightly below the mean profit level, but exactly equals the median profit level. Thus, these net profit data are reasonably well centered in the sense that the mean, median, and mode measures of central tendency converge on a narrow range of values. By way of comparison, three markets each have a net profit margin of 14.4% while three others have a net profit margin of 14.3%. Given the very small difference between these modal profit margin levels, the sample median of 14.9%, and the sample average of 14.8%, it appears reasonable to conclude that profit margins are also centered in a very narrow range. However, no two markets have exactly the same level of revenue when sales is measured in millions of dollars—so there is no modal level for this series of sales data.

The mode is most attractive as a measure of central tendency in instances when only a modest amount of variation in continuous data is observed or when grouped data are being analyzed. For example, if only a limited variety of colors and sizes are offered to customers, identification of the modal or most popular color and size class is important for both marketing and production purposes. If customer classes are analyzed in terms of age groupings, identifying important characteristics of the modal age group becomes similarly important.

If a sample of observations has more than one mode, it is called multimodal; a bimodal distribution, for example, has two modes. Samples with more than one mode often include groups of data that are quite different on some important dimension. The distribution of customer weight and height is likely to be bimodal since both weight or height tend to vary by sex. The mode weight and height of women is far less than that for men, so any analysis of customer weight and height that does not control for sex is likely to be bimodal. In instances where measurements of sample groups have a multimodal distribution, it is often appropriate to construct separate frequency distributions for each sample subgroup, rather than to ignore the important underlying causes of modal differences.

COMPARING MEASURES OF CENTRAL TENDENCY

The mean, median, and mode are all useful measures of central tendency, but their value can be limited by unique characteristics of the underlying data. A comparison across alternate measures is useful for determining the extent to which a consistent pattern of central tendency emerges. If the mean, median, and mode all coincide at a single sample observation, the sample data are said to be **symmetrical.** If the data are perfectly symmetrical, then the distribution of data above the mean is a perfect mirror image of the data distribution below the mean. A perfectly symmetrical distribution is illustrated in Figure 3.1b. Whereas a symmetrical distribution implies balance in sample dispersion, **skewness** implies a lack of balance. If the greater bulk of sample observations are found to the left of the sample mean, then the sample is said to be skewed downward or to the left as in Figure 3.1a. If the greater bulk of sample observations are found to the right of the mean, then the sample is said to be skewed upward or to the right as in Figure 3.1c.

When alternate measures of central tendency converge on a single value or narrow range of values, managers can be confident that an important characteristic of a fairly homogeneous sample of observations has been discovered. When alternate measures of central tendency fail to converge on a single value or range of values, then it is likely that underlying data comprise a heterogeneous sample of observations with important subsample differences. A comparison of alternate measures of central tendency is usually an important first step to determining whether a more detailed analysis of subsample differences is necessary.

Symmetrical
A balanced distribution.

Skewness
A lack of balance.

Measures of Dispersion

In addition to knowing the "typical" value for a given sample of data, it is important to know the degree to which individual observations vary around this level. Are the data tightly clustered around the typical value, or are the data widely dispersed? If the data

THE MEAN, MEDIAN, AND MODE

Differences between the mean, median, and mode reflect skewness.

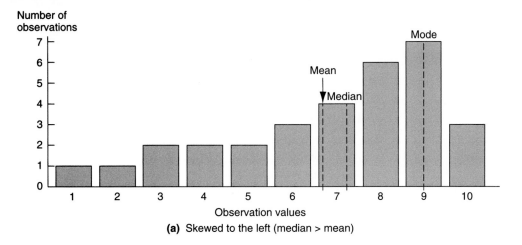

(a) Skewed to the left (median > mean)

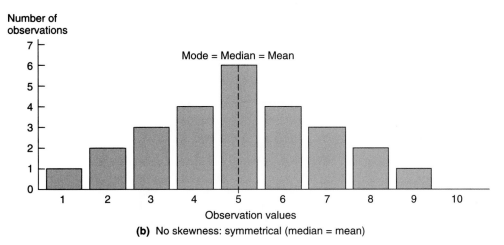

(b) No skewness: symmetrical (median = mean)

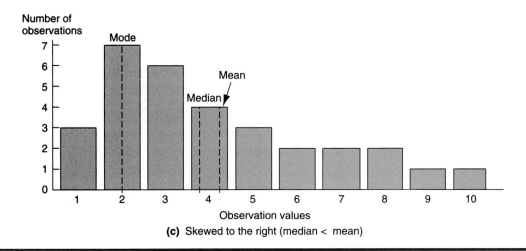

(c) Skewed to the right (median < mean)

Statistical Literacy Is an Awesome Tool

Until recently, it was common to teach statistics the old-fashioned way, with blackboard, chalk, and a seemingly endless repetition of problem-solving exercises. During the 1990s, many talented students and innovative educators have come to reject this traditional approach as antiquated. Rather than denying the importance of state-of-the-art technology in the teaching and learning of modern statistics, many have decided that traditional approaches must be updated to become more relevant to the needs of students.

When handheld calculators first appeared, some parents and educators became concerned that students would no longer see the need to learn basic arithmetic. They feared that students would lose the fundamental understanding of numbers that is essential for everyday living in a quantified, high-tech, market economy. Instead, experience emphatically demonstrates that the use of handheld calculators doesn't diminish numerical literacy; indeed, it has proved an extraordinarily useful means for instruction, and facilitates the student's appreciation of the usefulness of statistics.

In a similar fashion, powerful desktop computers are now fundamentally changing the methods of advanced forms of mathematical instruction and analysis. Until recently, when an engineer or business manager needed to calculate the flow of heat through the metal wall of an engine cylinder, relevant equations were solved with paper and pencil and the tedious application of high-level calculus. Today, engineers and mathematicians who face such problems employ computer-based numerical solution methods. Millions of simple calculations performed in a split second by powerful desktop computers substitute for pages of painstaking calculation. When it comes to real-world problems, important equations in engineering and physics are no longer solved using tools developed by 19th-century French and German mathematicians. In the 1990s, these problems are solved with millions of simple calculations performed by powerful desktop computers.

The ongoing revolution in the teaching and learning of statistics illustrates a fundamental lesson from history: when the basic tools of a discipline suddenly become a billion-fold more powerful, the discipline changes completely. The invention of supersonic jets doesn't make it essential to become a faster walker; the entire nature of

travel is transformed. Computers are causing the same fundamental transformation of the statistical analysis of basic economic relations. College students from campuses all over the United States and Canada now produce computer-based numerical solutions to problems that would have baffled yesterday's numerical prodigies. While the results appear as pictures or numbers, and not symbols or equations, they are what you need to build things that work. Similarly, inexpensive and easy-to-use business software packages now allow almost anyone to crunch numbers, draw graphs, and conduct sophisticated statistical analyses. Other bargain-priced and user-friendly software programs allow almost anyone to solve otherwise daunting statistical problems.

Doomsayers are always quick to point out when students from the United States fall behind foreign counterparts on measured exams. German and Japanese students are obviously good at math; they whip U.S. students on every standardized math test available. However, standardized test scores and international math olympiads may not be the most useful bases for comparison. While many foreign students learn partial differential equations, ours write innovative software programs, worm their way into computer data banks, and wreak havoc with business and government records. Interestingly, after not finding much that was useful in the traditional approach to mathematics, Bill Gates, now chairman of software titan Microsoft, Inc., dropped out of Harvard. While many talented students might indeed compare favorably with Gates on a standardized high school math test, Gates is obviously capable of providing a practical computer-based solution to a variety of vexing problems in mathematics and statistics.

In short, statistical literacy is an awesome component in the toolbox of business managers and public sector decision makers. By taking advantage of the amazing accomplishments of Bill Gates and other titans of the computer revolution, managers today find it easier than ever before to offer products and services that are better, cheaper, and faster.

See: Diane Ravitch, "Dumb Students? Or Dumb Textbooks?," *Forbes*, December 16, 1996, 118.

are tightly clustered about the typical level, then measures of central tendency provide a close approximation to individual values drawn from the sample. If the data are widely dispersed around typical values, then measures of central tendency offer only a poor approximation to individual values that might be drawn from the sample. As in the case of measures of central tendency, statisticians have constructed several useful measures of such dispersion. In general, measures of dispersion describe variation in the data in terms of the distance between selected observations or in terms of the average deviation among sample observations. Managers often focus on the range, variance and standard deviation, and coefficient of variation. Which among these is most appropriate for a given task depends on the nature of the underlying data and the need being addressed by the manager.

RANGE

Range
Scope from largest to smallest observations.

The simplest and most commonly employed measure of dispersion is the sample **range,** or the difference between the largest and smallest sample observations. In the telecommunications services example, the sample range in net profit is defined by the $7.6 million earned in the most profitable sample market, to the $2.9 million earned in the least profitable sample observation. Note the very high degree of dispersion in net profits over the sample. The highest level of firm profits earned is more than two and one-half times, or 150%, greater than the lowest profit level. The range in net profit margin, though substantial, is much lower because these data are implicitly size-adjusted. The 16.4% earned in the market with the highest net profit margin is only 34% greater than the 12.2% margin earned in the market with the lowest profit margin. Profit variation is much less when one explicitly controls for firm size differences. As might be expected, the range in market size as measured by sales revenue is substantial. The $49.7 million in sales revenue earned in the largest market is roughly 150% greater than the $20.3 million size of the smallest market in the sample.

Range has intuitive appeal as a measure of dispersion because it identifies the distance between the largest and smallest sample observations. Range can be used to identify likely values that might be associated with "best case" and "worst case" scenarios. While range is a popular measure of variability that is easy to compute, it has the unfortunate characteristic of ignoring all but the two most extreme observations. As such, the range measure of dispersion can be unduly influenced by highly unusual outlying observations. The effects of outliers are sometimes minimized by relying on interquartile or percentile range measures. For example, the interquartile range identifies the spread that bounds the middle 50th percent of sample observations by measuring the distance between the first and third quartiles. Similarly, by measuring the distance between the 90th and 10th percentile of sample observations, the bounds on the middle 80% of sample observations can be determined. Both interquartile and percentile range measures are attractive because they retain the ease of calculation and intuitive appeal of the range measure of dispersion. However, like any range measure, they do not provide detailed information on the degree of variation among all sample observations. For this reason, range measures are often considered in conjunction with measures of dispersion that reflect the average deviation among all sample observations.

VARIANCE AND STANDARD DEVIATION

Population Variance
Average squared deviation
from the overall mean.

Despite their ease of calculation and intuitive interpretation, the usefulness of range measures of dispersion is limited by the fact that only two data points, the high and low observations, are reflected. For this reason, range measures of dispersion are often supplemented by measures that reflect dispersion through the sample or entire population. A measure of dispersion throughout the population is given by the **population variance,** or the arithmetic mean of the squared deviation of each observation from the overall mean. The squared deviation of each observation from the overall mean is considered in order to give equal weight to upside as well as downside variation within the population. Without this squaring process, positive and negative deviations would tend to cancel and result in an understatement of the degree of overall variability. Population variance is calculated using the following expression:

$$\sigma^2 = \frac{(X_1 - \mu)^2 + (X_2 - \mu)^2 + \cdots + (X_N - \mu)^2}{N}, \tag{3.3}$$

$$= \frac{\sum_{i=1}^{N} (X_i - \mu)^2}{N},$$

**Population Standard
Deviation**
Square root of the
population variance.

where the greek letter mu, μ, is used to represent the mean of the population, and N is the number of observations in the overall population. The population variance is expressed in units of squared deviations, or squared values of individual observations, rather than in the same units as the individual observations. In the case of net profit and sales revenue, variance is expressed in terms of dollars squared. In the case of net profit margin, variance is expressed in terms of squared percentages. The **population standard deviation,** or square root of the population variance, is a measure that describes dispersion throughout the entire population in the same units as is characteristic of the underlying data (e.g., dollars or percentages). The standard deviation for a measure that describes the overall population is given by:

$$\sigma = \sqrt{\frac{\sum_{i=1}^{N} (X_i - \mu)^2}{N}}. \tag{3.4}$$

Like the population variance, the population standard deviation reflects both upside and downside variation throughout the entire population. Because the population standard deviation is expressed in the same units as individual observations, it is also a measure of dispersion that has a very simple and intuitive interpretation. For both reasons, it is possibly the most commonly employed measure of dispersion that managers rely on.

Of course, it is often too expensive and impractical to measure the variance or standard deviation of the entire population. When a subset or sample of the overall population is analyzed, a slightly different formula must be employed to properly

Sample Variance
Average squared deviation
from the sample mean.

calculate variance and standard deviation. The **sample variance** is given by the expression:

$$s^2 = \frac{(X_1 - \overline{X})^2 + (X_2 - \overline{X})^2 + \cdots + (X_n - \overline{X})^2}{n - 1}, \tag{3.5}$$

$$= \frac{\sum_{i=1}^{n} (X_i - \overline{X})^2}{n - 1},$$

**Sample Standard
Deviation**
Square root of the
population variance.

where $\overline{X}$ denotes mean for a sample of n observations. The **sample standard deviation** is given by the expression:

$$s = \sqrt{\frac{\sum_{i=1}^{n} (X_i - \overline{X})^2}{n - 1}}. \tag{3.6}$$

Three differences between these formulas and those for the population variance and standard deviation are obvious: the sample mean $\overline{X}$ is substituted for the population mean μ, squared deviations are measured over the sample observations rather than over the entire population, and the denominator is $n - 1$ rather than n. The answer as to why $n - 1$ is used rather than n is quite complex, but reflects the fact that dispersion in the overall population would be underestimated if n were used in the denominator of the sample variance and standard deviation calculations. It is therefore necessary to rely on the population variance and standard deviation formulas when calculating measures of dispersion for an entire population. If the list of markets in the telecommunications services example comprises a complete list of the markets served by a given firm, then it would be appropriate to calculate the dispersion in net profits, profit margins, and sales revenue using formulas for the population variance and standard deviation. If this list comprised only a sample or subset of all markets served by the firm, then it would be appropriate to calculate the dispersion in net profits, profit margins, and sales revenue using formulas for the sample variance and standard deviation.

From a practical standpoint, when a relatively large number of sample observations is involved, only a modest difference results from using $n - 1$ versus n in the calculation of variance and standard deviation. Table 3.1 shows variance and standard deviation calculations based on the assumptions that the list of telecommunications services markets comprise only a subset or sample of relevant markets versus the overall population. When as few as 25 observations are considered, only modest differences would be noted between the population parameter calculations for variance and standard deviation and the relevant sample statistics.

COEFFICIENT OF VARIATION

The variance and standard deviation are absolute measures of dispersion that are directly influenced by size and the unit of measurement. The variance and standard deviation for sales revenue will almost always exceed those for net profit because net profit (defined as revenue minus cost) is almost always less than total revenues. In a true economic sense, however, profits tend to be more unpredictable than sales revenue because profit variation reflects the underlying variability in both sales (demand) and cost (supply) conditions. As a result, managers often rely on a measure of dispersion that does not depend on size or the unit of measurement. The **coefficient of variation** compares the standard deviation to the mean in an attractive relative measure of dispersion within a population or sample. For a population, the coefficient of variation equals:

Coefficient of Variation
Standard deviation divided by the mean.

$$V = \frac{\sigma}{\mu}. \tag{3.7}$$

For a sample, the coefficient of variation equals:

$$V = \frac{s}{\overline{X}}. \tag{3.8}$$

Because it is unaffected by size or the unit of measure, the coefficient of variation can be used to compare relative dispersion across a wide variety of data. In capital budgeting, for example, managers use the coefficient of variation to compare "risk/reward" ratios for projects of widely different investment requirements or profitability. Since managers are sometimes only able to withstand a fixed dollar amount of loss or foregone profit, the coefficient of variation is often used in conjunction with absolute risk measures such as the variance and standard deviation. Taken together, absolute and relative measures give managers an especially useful means for assessing the magnitude of dispersion within a population or sample of data.

Hypothesis Testing

Experiments involving measures of central tendency and measures of dispersion are often used to provide the information necessary for informed managerial decisions. A **hypothesis test** is a statistical experiment used to measure the reasonableness of a given theory or premise. In hypothesis testing, two different types of experimental error are encountered. **Type I error** is the incorrect rejection of a true hypothesis; **Type II error** is the failure to reject a false hypothesis. Because both can lead to bad managerial decisions, the probability of both types of error must be quantified and entered into the decision analysis. While a wide variety of different hypothesis tests are often employed by managers, the basics of the technique can be illustrated using a simple means test example.

Hypothesis Test
Statistical experiment.

Type I Error
Incorrect rejection of a true hypothesis.

Type II Error
Failure to reject a false hypothesis.

MEANS TESTS FOR LARGE SAMPLES

The first step in hypothesis testing is to formally state the basic premise or null hypothesis, along with the converse premise or alternative hypothesis. The significance level of the test and the test statistic must then be determined, and the decision rule must be stated. Finally, data must be collected and the test must be performed so that an in-formed managerial decision can be made.

The sample mean can be compared to the population mean to learn if any given sample is typical or atypical of the population. A typical sample has a mean that is "close" to the population mean; an atypical sample has a mean that is "not close." To decide the cutoff point, a standardized variable or test statistic must be constructed. Commonly referred to as the **z-statistic,** this test statistic is normally distributed with a mean of zero and a standard deviation of one. For the means test, the test statistic is based on the difference between the mean of a sample and the mean of the overall population, divided by the standard deviation of the sample. Therefore, a z-statistic $= 2$ implies that the sample mean is two standard deviations larger than the population mean, a z-statistic $= 3$ implies that the sample mean is three standard deviations larger than the population mean, and so on.

z-**Statistic**
Normally distributed test
statistic with zero mean and
standard deviation of one.

For large samples where $n > 30$ and the standard deviation of the overall popula-tion is known, the test statistic is:

$$z = \frac{\overline{X} - \mu}{\sigma/\sqrt{n}},$$

(3.9)

where $\overline{X}$ is the sample mean, μ is the known mean of the population, σ is the population standard deviation, and n is sample size. This test statistic is the difference between the sample and overall mean, $\overline{X} - \mu$, divided by the standard deviation of the sample mean, $\sigma/\sqrt{n}$. It describes the difference between the sample and population means in "stan-dardized units." A confidence interval for the true mean μ is from $\overline{X} - z(\sigma/\sqrt{n})$ to $\overline{X} + z(\sigma/\sqrt{n})$, where z is the value from the normal table in Appendix C corresponding to the relevant confidence level.

As seen in Figure 3.2, 95% of the area under the z-statistic's normal or bell-shaped curve falls within ± 1.96 standard deviations of the mean, and 99% of this area falls within ± 2.576 standard deviations. In other words, there can be 95% confidence that the sample is typical of the overall population if the sample average falls within roughly *two* sample standard deviations of the average for the overall population. There can be 99% confidence that the sample is typical of the overall population if the sam-ple average falls within roughly *three* sample standard deviations of the population average.

To illustrate, consider the case of a retailer that receives a large shipment of light bulbs from a new supplier and wishes to learn if these new bulbs are of standard qual-ity. Light bulbs received from the retailer's current supplier have an average life of 2,000 hours, with a standard deviation of 200 hours. The retailer's null hypothesis is that the new bulbs are of equal quality, or H_0: $\mu = 2,000$ hours. The alternate hypothe-sis is that the new bulbs are not of equal quality, or H_a: $\mu \neq 2,000$. Obviously, all new bulbs cannot be tested. To test the null hypothesis, the retailer might decide to test the life of a random sample of 100 bulbs. The retailer would be inclined to reject the new bulbs if this sample had a dramatically shorter mean life than bulbs from its current supplier. To minimize the Type I error of incorrectly deciding to reject new bulbs of

Figure 3.2

THE z DISTRIBUTION

The z-statistic is normally distributed with a mean of zero and a standard deviation of one.

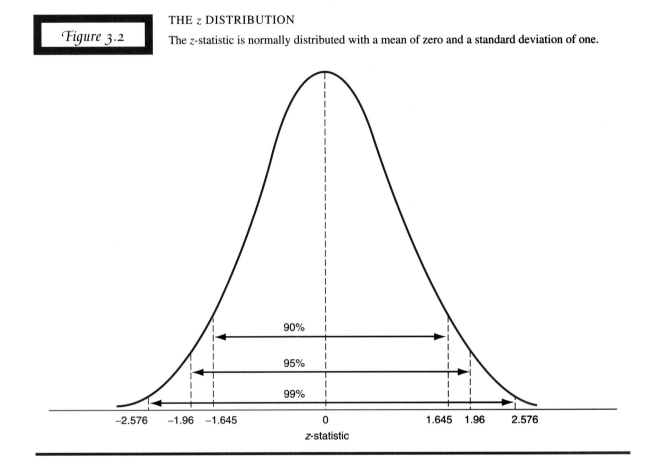

equal quality, the significance level of the hypothesis test might be set at $\alpha = 0.05$ or $\alpha = 0.01$. The retailer will purchase the new bulbs provided the chance of incorrectly rejecting equal quality bulbs is only 5% or 1%, respectively.

In the light bulb example, the relevant test statistic $z = (\overline{X} - 2{,}000) \div 20$, since $\mu = 2{,}000$ hours, $\sigma = 200$ hours, and $n = 100$ sample observations. So long as the computed value for this test statistic is within roughly ± 2, the retailer could safely infer with 95% confidence that the new bulbs are of the same quality as those obtained from current suppliers. The chance of incorrectly rejecting equal quality bulbs is 5% when the test statistic falls in the range between ± 2. Such a value for the test statistic requires a sample average bulb life within the range from 1,960 hours to 2,040. The 99% confidence interval requires the test statistic to fall within the range ± 3, and a sample average bulb life of 1,940 hours to 2,060 hours. By accepting bulbs with a sample average life that falls within this broader range, the chance of wrongly rejecting equal quality bulbs (Type I error) can be cut to 1%.

If the population standard deviation σ is unknown and the sample size is large, $n >$ 30, the sample standard deviation s can be substituted for σ in the test statistic calculation:

$$z = \frac{\overline{X} - \mu}{s/\sqrt{n}}, \tag{3.10}$$

where $\overline{X}$ is the sample mean, μ is the known mean of the population, s is the sample standard deviation, and n is sample size. Again, a confidence interval for the true mean μ is from $\overline{X} - z(s/\sqrt{n})$ to $\overline{X} + z(s/\sqrt{n})$, where z is from the normal table in Appendix C for the relevant confidence level. This test statistic formula, like that given in Equation 3.9, is based on the assumption that the sample is "small" relative to the size of the overall population. If sample size exceeds 5% of the overall population, then the denominator of each equation must be multiplied by what is known as the finite population correction factor, or $\sqrt{(N - n)/(N - 1)}$ where N is the size of the overall population and n is sample size.

MEANS TESTS FOR SMALL SAMPLES

For meaningful statistical analysis, sample size must be sufficiently large to accurately reflect important characteristics of the overall population. While it is typically desirable to have 30 or more sample observations, this is not always possible. Sometimes, managers must rely on very small samples of data, say $n < 30$. In such instances, the test statistic formula must be altered slightly.

If the population is normally distributed, the distribution around the small sample mean will be *approximately* normal. In this situation, the test statistic formula is written:

$$t = \frac{\overline{X} - \mu}{s/\sqrt{n}}, \tag{3.11}$$

where $\overline{X}$ is the sample mean, μ is the known mean of the population, s is the sample standard deviation, and n is sample size. A confidence interval for the true mean μ can be calculated as $\overline{X} - t(s/\sqrt{n})$ to $\overline{X} + t(s/\sqrt{n})$ where t is from the t-table in Appendix C for $(n - 1)$ degrees of freedom and the relevant confidence level.

t-Statistic
Approximately normal test statistic.

This so-called **t-statistic** is a test statistic that has an *approximately* normal distribution with a mean of zero and a standard deviation of one. The t-statistic (or t-value) is normally distributed for large samples, but is less so in the case of small samples. Like the z-statistic, it describes the difference between the sample and population means in "standardized units," or by the number of sample standard deviations. Since the t-statistic is only approximately normal, the rules of thumb of two standard deviations for the 95% confidence interval and three standard deviations for the 99% confidence interval hold only for large samples where $n > 30$. The "hurdle" or critical t-value is adjusted upward when sample size is reduced. The amount of upward adjustment depends on the test statistic's **degrees of freedom,** or the number of observations beyond the absolute minimum required to calculate the statistic. Since at least two observations are

Degrees of Freedom
Number of observations beyond the minimum required to calculate a statistic.

necessary before a mean can be calculated, degrees of freedom for a means test are calculated as $df = n - 1$. The precise critical t-value to use in a means test for very small sample sizes are obtained from a t-table, such as that found in Appendix C. For example, when sample size is $n = 10$ observations, the critical t-value for a means test with $df = 10 - 1 = 9$ is 2.262 at the $\alpha = 0.05$ significance level, and 3.25 at the $\alpha = 0.01$ significance level. The population mean is expected to be found within $\pm$ 2.262 standard deviations of the sample mean with 95% confidence, and within $\pm$ 3.25 standard deviations of the sample mean with 99% confidence.

To this point, measures of central tendency and measures of dispersion have been considered useful for describing populations and samples of data. These measures are very useful to managers who seek a detailed statistical profile of customer characteristics, cost experience, industry profits, and a host of other important economic variables. However, managers are often interested in the central tendency and dispersion of these data and in the extent to which these patterns can be described. For this reason, successful real-world managers devote significant effort to describing the causes and consequences of important economic relations.

Regression Analysis

Regression Analysis
Statistical method for describing XY relations.

The most compelling challenge faced by management is the accurate estimation of demand, cost, and profit relations. Not only must the range of important factors that affect demand, costs, and profits be determined but the relative magnitude of each influence must also be assessed. **Regression analysis** is a powerful and extremely useful statistical technique that describes the way in which one important economic variable is related to one or more other economic variables. While there are clear limitations to the technique, regression analysis is often used to provide successful managers with valuable insight concerning a variety of significant economic relations. Given the widespread success of regression analysis in real-world applications, it is well worth gaining a careful understanding of the technique.

WHAT IS A STATISTICAL RELATION?

To understand when the use of regression analysis is appropriate, one must appreciate a basic difference between two broad classes of economic relations.

Deterministic Relation
A relation known with certainty.

A **deterministic relation** is one that is known with certainty. For example, total profit equals total revenue minus total cost, or $\pi = TR - TC$. Once the levels of total revenue and total cost are known with certainty, total profits can be exactly determined. The profit relation is an example of a deterministic relation. If total cost = $5 \times$ quantity, then total cost can be exactly determined once the level of quantity is known, just as quantity can be determined once the total cost level is known. If all economic relations were deterministic, then managers would never be surprised by higher or lower than expected profits; total revenues and total costs could be exactly determined at the start of every planning period. As it turns out, few economic relations are deterministic in nature. It is far more common that economic variables are related to each other in

Lies, Damn Lies, and Government Statistics

Once a reliable source of timely and accurate statistics on the U.S. economy, the federal government's system for gathering and interpreting economic data has fallen on hard times. To illustrate, consider the problems faced by the Bureau of Labor and Statistics (BLS). The BLS attempts to measure unemployment by monthly surveys of some 60,000 representative households are bedeviled by demographic and structural shifts. Among the important questions that the survey cannot answer are: How many of the "unemployed" work in the underground economy? What proportion of the roughly 85 million Americans putting in 35 or more hours a week and counted as full-time workers actually hold two or more part-time jobs? What about laid-off managers who adopt the label "consultant" to mask the reality of joblessness? Until these questions are answered, the true unemployment rate could be higher, or lower, than the official numbers.

The problem isn't just measurement error. In a large and complex modern economy, *nobody* has or can have precisely accurate macroeconomic measures of employment, inflation, productivity. The problem is that admittedly imperfect government-provided estimates increasingly involve errors and bias of large and unpredictable magnitudes. Penny-pinching is partly to blame; real government spending on data gathering and analysis has barely grown since the late 1970s, though the economy today is nearly 30% larger and infinitely more complex. Efforts to reduce the burden of paperwork on business have also made it more difficult to gather detailed data in a timely fashion. More important, government statisticians often find themselves analyzing yesterday's news. Federal agencies that crank out most of the economic data we rely upon haven't kept pace with enormous technological and structural changes that have transformed the economy.

For example, government statisticians are slow to recognize the effects of new technology and better products. With help from leading manufacturers, the BLS revised its methods for calculating computer price indexes by taking into account increases in computing speed. As a result, computer prices adjusted for quality changes are plunging at a double-digit rate per year. In most other areas, the task of adjusting price indexes for changes in

product quality is woefully inadequate. The producer price index, which contains thousands of values for products such as bolts and valves, still has no accurate measure for semiconductors or for communications equipment, a $58-billion-a-year industry and the biggest category of producer durables.

In recent studies, management consulting firms report that productivity in major service industries is far higher in the U.S. than it is in Europe and Japan. In banking, it's nearly 50% higher than in Europe, largely because U.S. banks were quicker during the 1980s to apply computer technology to their back-office clearing operations, install automated teller machines, and adopt new, more efficient organizational structures. Economists also point to mismeasurement problems as the main explanation for the perceived stagnation in productivity growth. During recent years, the rapidly expanding service sector has created almost all of the economy's new jobs, and productivity measurement in services is treacherously difficult. In the securities industry, for example, the number of shares traded per day on the New York Stock Exchange has jumped from 8 to 10 million during the 1960s to an average in excess of 400 million shares in the mid-1990s. Moreover, this surge in industry output has occurred despite a modest increase in industry employment. By and large, the BLS fails to accurately account for such brisk productivity growth throughout the rapidly growing financial sector. Serious productivity measurement problems also are present in the supposedly unproductive banking, real estate, and insurance industries.

What should be done about the current situation? To better measure consumer prices, BLS could tap into the electronic scanning data now widely used by retailers and their suppliers. Price and production indexes must also reflect quality adjustments for new products and technologies, and surveys of changes in employment must be refined. Americans and their government need to know what's *really* happening in the economy.

See: Gene Epstein, "Not Adding Up," *Barron's,* March 10, 1997, 18-21.

ways that cannot be predicted with absolute accuracy. Almost all economic relations must be estimated.

Statistical Relation
An inexact relation.

A **statistical relation** exists between two economic variables if the average of one is related to another, but it is impossible to predict with certainty the value of one based on the value of another. In the earlier example, if $TC = \$5Q$ *on average,* then a one-unit increase in quantity would tend to result in an average $5 increase in total cost. Sometimes the actual increase in total cost would be more than $5; sometimes it would be less. In such circumstances, a statistical relation exists between total costs and output.

When a statistical relation exists, the exact or "true" relation between two economic variables is not known with certainty and must be estimated. Perhaps the most common means for doing so is to gather and analyze historical data on the economic

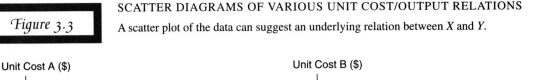

Figure 3.3

SCATTER DIAGRAMS OF VARIOUS UNIT COST/OUTPUT RELATIONS

A scatter plot of the data can suggest an underlying relation between X and Y.

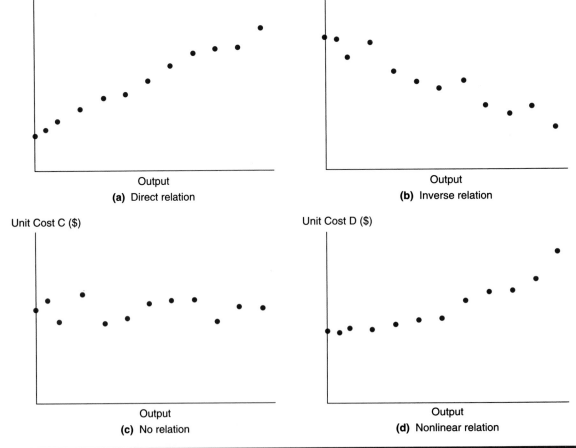

Unit Cost A ($)

Output
(a) Direct relation

Unit Cost B ($)

Output
(b) Inverse relation

Unit Cost C ($)

Output
(c) No relation

Unit Cost D ($)

Output
(d) Nonlinear relation

Time Series
A daily, weekly, monthly, or annual sequence of data.

Cross-Section
Data from a common point in time.

variables of interest. A **time series** of data is a daily, weekly, monthly, or annual sequence of data on an economic variable such as price, income, cost, or revenue. To judge the trend in profitability over time, a firm would analyze the time series of profit numbers. A **cross-section** of data is a group of observations on an important economic variable at any point in time. If a firm were interested in learning the relative importance of market share versus advertising as determinants of profitability, it might analyze a cross-section of profit, advertising, and market share data for a variety of regional or local markets. To assess the effectiveness of a quality management program, the firm might consider both time series and cross-section data.

Scatter Diagram
A plot of *XY* data.

The simplest and most common means for analyzing a sample of historical data is to plot and visually study the data. A **scatter diagram** is a plot of data where the *dependent* variable is plotted on the vertical or *Y*-axis, and the *independent* variable is plotted on the horizontal or *X*-axis. Figure 3.3 shows scatter diagrams that plot the relation between four different unit cost categories and output. The data underlying these plots are given in Table 3.3. In these examples, each unit cost category represents a different dependent or *Y*-variable because these unit costs depend on, or are determined by, the level of output. The level of output is the independent or *X*-variable. In Figure 3.3a, a direct relation between unit cost category A and output is shown. This means that an increase in output will cause an increase in the level of these costs. Conversely Figure 3.3b depicts an inverse relation between unit cost category B and output. An increase in output will cause a decrease in unit cost category B. No relation is evident between output and unit cost category C. In panel 3.3d, a nonlinear relation between unit costs and output is illustrated.

Scatter diagrams are analyzed to gain an instinctive "feel" for the data. The method is entirely inductive and intuitive. While the examination of scatter diagrams has undeniable value as a starting point in the analysis of simple statistical relations, its inherent lack of structure can also limit its value. For example, the choice of which variable to call "dependent" or "independent" is often haphazard. The fact that an increase in

Table 3.3

DATA INPUT FOR SCATTER DIAGRAMS OF OUTPUT AND UNIT COSTS

UNITS OF OUTPUT	UNIT COST A	UNIT COST B	UNIT COST C	UNIT COST D
0	$2.14	$7.91	$5.59	$4.41
25	2.47	7.81	6.10	4.29
50	2.99	6.72	4.84	4.56
100	3.67	7.57	6.44	4.50
150	4.36	5.81	4.78	4.79
200	4.58	5.21	5.04	5.07
250	5.38	4.80	5.87	5.18
300	6.28	5.25	6.07	6.21
350	7.03	3.78	6.17	6.73
400	7.32	3.23	4.83	6.79
450	7.41	3.70	5.73	7.49
500	8.53	2.48	5.56	9.14

output causes a change in unit costs may seem obvious. However, in some circumstances, the directional nature of the link between economic variables is not apparent. Scatter diagrams can be helpful by illustrating the linkage or simple correlation between variables, but by themselves they do not establish causality. To warrant the inference of cause and effect, the correlation between two series of data must be interpreted in light of previous experience or economic theory. In the study of regression analysis techniques, it is important to keep in mind that economic theory provides the underlying rationale for model specification.

SPECIFYING THE REGRESSION MODEL

The first step in regression analysis is to specify the variables to be included in the regression equation or model. Product demand, measured in physical units, is the dependent variable when specifying a demand function. The list of independent variables, or those that influence demand, always includes the price of the product and generally includes such factors as the prices of complementary and competitive products, advertising expenditures, consumer incomes, and population of the consuming group. Demand functions for expensive durable goods, such as automobiles and houses, include interest rates and other credit terms; those for ski equipment, beverages, or air conditioners include weather conditions. Determinants of demand for capital goods, such as industrial machinery, include corporate profitability, capacity utilization ratios, interest rates, trends in wages, and so on. Total or unit cost is the dependent variable when specifying a cost function. The independent variables always include the level of output and typically include wage rates, interest rates, raw material prices, and so on.

The second step in regression analysis is to obtain reliable data. Data must be gathered on total output or demand, measures of price, credit terms, capacity utilization ratios, wage rates, and the like. Obtaining accurate data is not always easy, especially if the study involves time series data over a number of years. Moreover, some key variables may have to be estimated. Consumer attitudes toward product quality and expectations about future business conditions, both quite important in demand functions for many consumer goods, often have to be estimated. Unfortunately, survey questionnaire and interview techniques sometimes introduce an element of subjectivity into the data and the possibility of error or bias.

Once variables have been specified and the data have been gathered, the functional form of the regression equation must be determined. This form reflects the way in which independent variables are assumed to affect the dependent or Y-variable. The most common specification is a **linear model,** such as the following demand function:

Linear Model
A straight-line relation.

$$Q = a + bP + cA + dI. \tag{3.12}$$

Here Q represents the unit demand for a particular product, P is the price charged, A represents advertising expenditures, and I is per capita disposable income. Unit demand is assumed to change in a linear fashion with changes in each independent variable. For example, if $b = -1.5$, the quantity demanded will decline by one and one-half units with each one-unit increase in price. This implies a linear, or straight line, demand curve. Each coefficient measures the change in Y following a one-unit change in each respective X-variable. Note that the size of this influence does not depend on the size of the X-variable. In a linear regression model, the marginal effect of each X-variable on Y is constant. The broad appeal of linear functions stems from the fact that many demand and cost relations are in fact approximately linear. Furthermore, the most popular regression technique, the method of least squares, can be used to estimate the coefficients a, b, c, and d for linear equations.

Multiplicative Model
A log-linear relation.

Another common regression model form is the **multiplicative model:**

$$Q = aP^{b}A^{c}I^{d}. \tag{3.13}$$

A multiplicative model is used when the marginal effect of each independent variable is thought to depend on the value of all independent variables in the regression equation. For example, the effect on quantity demanded of a price increase often depends not just on the price level, but also on the amount of advertising, competitor prices and advertising, and so on. Similarly, the effect on costs of a wage hike can depend on the output level, raw material prices, R&D expenditures, and so on. Allowing for such changes in the marginal relation is sometimes more realistic than the implicit assumption of a constant marginal, as in the linear model.

Happily, the benefits of added realism for the multiplicative model have no offsetting costs in terms of added complexity or difficulty in estimation. As described in Appendix 2A, Equation 3.13 can be transformed into a linear relation using logarithms, and then estimated by the least squares technique. Thus, Equation 3.13 is equivalent to:

$$\log Q = \log a + b \cdot \log P + c \cdot \log A + d \cdot \log I. \tag{3.14}$$

When written in the form of Equation 3.12, the coefficients of Equation 3.14 ($\log a$, b, c, and d) can be easily estimated. Given the multiplicative or log-linear form of the regression model, these coefficient estimates can also be interpreted as estimates of the constant *elasticity* of Y with respect to X, or the percentage change in Y due to a one percent change in X (see Appendix 2A). Much more will be said about elasticity later in the book, but for now it is worth noting that multiplicative or log-linear models imply constant elasticity.

To summarize, multiplicative models imply a changing absolute effect on the Y-variable due to changes in the various independent variables. This is sometimes attractive in demand analysis because the marginal effect of a dollar spent on advertising, for example, can vary according to overall levels of advertising, prices, income, and so on. Similarly, this is sometimes appealing in cost analysis since the effect on costs of a one-unit change in output can depend on the level of output, wages, raw material prices, and so on. The changing marginal effect implicit in the multiplicative or log-linear model contrasts with the constant marginal effect of independent variables in linear models. Multiplicative demand and cost functions are also based on the assumption of constant elasticities, whereas elasticity varies along linear demand functions. Of course, the specific form of any regression model—linear, multiplicative, or otherwise—should always be chosen to reflect the true relation among the economic variables being studied. Care must be taken to ensure that the model chosen is consistent with underlying economic theory.

THE LEAST SQUARES METHOD

Regression equations are typically estimated or "fitted" by the method of least squares. The method can be illustrated by considering a simple total cost function example.

Assume the manager of the Tucson branch of the First National Bank has asked you to estimate the relation between the total number of new checking accounts opened per month and the costs of processing new account applications. Table 3.4 shows the relevant total cost and number of new account applications data for the past year (12 monthly observations). When a linear regression model is used to describe the relation between the total cost of processing new account applications and the number of applications, the general form of the First National Bank regression equation is:

$$Total\ Cost = Y = a + bX, \qquad (3.15)$$

where total cost is the dependent or Y-variable, and output is the dependent or X-variable. Such a regression equation is called a **simple regression model,** because it involves only one dependent Y-variable and one independent X-variable. A **multiple regression model** also entails one Y-variable, but includes two or more X-variables.

Simple Regression Model
A relation with one dependent Y-variable and one independent X-variable.

Multiple Regression Model
A relation with one dependent Y-variable and more than one independent X-variable.

The method of least squares estimates or fits the regression line that minimizes the sum of the squared deviations between the best fitting line and the set of original data points. The technique is based on the minimization of squared deviations to avoid the problem of having positive and negative deviations cancel each other out. By employing the least squares technique, it is possible to estimate the intercept a and slope coefficient b that correspond to the best fitting regression line. The exact form of the First National Bank regression equation to be estimated using the monthly data contained in Table 3.4 is:

$$Total\ Cost_t = Y_t = a + bX_t + u_t, \qquad (3.16)$$

Table 3.4

NEW ACCOUNT APPLICATION PROCESING COSTS AND THE NUMBER OF NEW ACCOUNTS AT THE FIRST NATIONAL BANK

MONTH	TOTAL COSTS (Y_t)	"FITTED" TOTAL COST ESTIMATE (Y_t)	NUMBER OF NEW ACCOUNTS (X_t)
January	$4,950	$4,755.91	205
February	4,275	5,061.00	220
March	6,050	5,467.78	240
April	5,350	5,569.48	245
May	5,125	5,671.17	250
June	6,650	6,179.65	275
July	7,450	6,993.22	315
August	6,850	7,094.92	320
September	8,250	7,603.40	345
October	8,700	9,332.23	430
November	9,175	9,433.92	435
December	9,975	9,637.32	445
Average	$6,900	$6,900.00	310

where total cost in month t is the dependent or Y-variable, and the number of new account applications in month t is the independent output or X-variable. u_t is a residual or disturbance term that reflects the influences of stochastic or random elements, and of any other determinants of total costs that have been omitted from the regression equation. When time series data are being examined, as they are in this example, the term t is used to signify subscript. If cross-section data were being examined—for example, processing costs at a number of branch offices during any given month—the various branch offices would be designated using the subscript i.

The a intercept marks the intersection of the regression line with the sales axis. The b slope coefficient is the slope of the regression line, and the u_t error term measures the vertical deviation of each tth data point from the fitted regression line. The least squares technique minimizes the total sum of squared u_t values by the choice of the a and b coefficients. When the a and b coefficients are combined with actual data on the independent X-variable (the number of applications) as shown in Equation 3.15, the estimated or fitted total cost values shown in Table 3.4 can be calculated. These fitted values are connected by the fitted regression line drawn in Figure 3.4. Fitted values for the dependent Y-variable, called $\hat{Y}$ or "Y hat," are extremely valuable because they indicate the expected total cost level associated with a given number of new account applications, or X-variable. However, regression analysis also provides management with a number of additional insights concerning the total cost-output relation. In the next section, important insights offered by commonly reported regression statistics are investigated.

Regression Statistics

Just a few years ago, the process of estimating economic relations was painstaking and costly. Only the largest and most advanced organizations could afford the necessary investment in sophisticated computers and highly trained staff. Today, powerful desktop personal computers (PCs) with sophisticated but user-friendly statistical software make the estimation of even complex economic relations both quick and easy. As a result, the accurate estimation of statistical relations has become a standard tool of the successful manager in organizations of all sizes. The two leading software programs used for this purpose are *Minitab* statistical software, published by Minitab, Inc., and *SPSS Advanced Statistics,* published by SPSS, Inc. Both are inexpensive, easy to learn, and offer a wealth of powerful techniques for data analysis and regression model estimation. Less comprehensive statistical software that run along with *Lotus 1-2-3* and other spreadsheet programs can also be useful, especially when detailed statistical analysis is unnecessary. This section focuses on the interpretation of regression output.

Standard Error of the Estimate
Standard deviation of the dependent Y-variable after controlling for all X-variables.

STANDARD ERROR OF THE ESTIMATE

A useful measure for examining the accuracy of any regression model is the **standard error of the estimate,** S.E.E., or the standard deviation of the dependent Y-variable after controlling for the influence of all X-variables. The standard error of the estimate

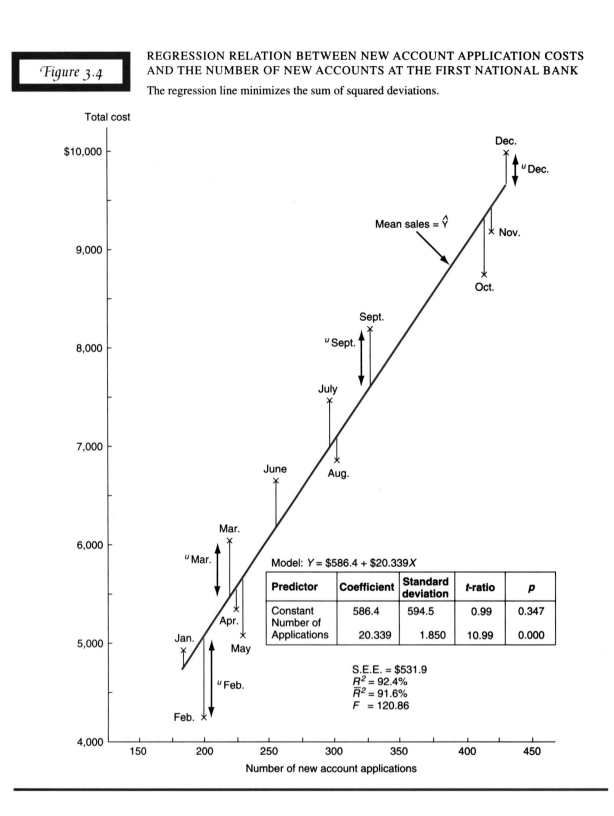

Figure 3.4

REGRESSION RELATION BETWEEN NEW ACCOUNT APPLICATION COSTS
AND THE NUMBER OF NEW ACCOUNTS AT THE FIRST NATIONAL BANK

The regression line minimizes the sum of squared deviations.

Total cost

$10,000

Dec.

^{u}Dec.

Mean sales = $\hat{Y}$

9,000

Nov.

Oct.

Sept.

^{u}Sept.

8,000

July

Aug.

June

7,000

Mar.

6,000

^{u}Mar.

Model: $Y = \$586.4 + \$20.339X$

Predictor	Coefficient	Standard deviation	t-ratio	p
Constant	586.4	594.5	0.99	0.347
Number of Applications	20.339	1.850	10.99	0.000

Apr.

Jan.

May

5,000

S.E.E. = $531.9
$R^2 = 92.4\%$
$\bar{R}^2 = 91.6\%$
$F = 120.86$

^{u}Feb.

Feb.

4,000

150   200   250   300   350   400   450

Number of new account applications

increases with the amount of scatter about the sample regression line. If each data point were to lie exactly on the regression line, then the standard error of the estimate would equal zero since each $\hat{Y}_t$ would exactly equal Y_t. No scatter about the regression line exists when the standard error of the estimate equals zero. If there is a great deal of scatter about the regression line, then $\hat{Y}_t$ often differs greatly from each Y_t, and the standard error of the estimate will be large.

The standard error of the estimate provides a very useful means for estimating confidence intervals around any particular $\hat{Y}_t$ estimate, *given* values for the independent X-variables. In other words, the standard error of the estimate can be used to determine a range within which the dependent Y-variable can be predicted with varying degrees of statistical confidence based on the regression coefficients and values for the X-variables. Since the best estimate of the tth value for the dependent variable is $\hat{Y}_t$, as predicted by the regression equation, the standard error of the estimate can be used to determine just how accurate a prediction $\hat{Y}_t$ is likely to be. If the u_t error terms are normally distributed about the regression equation, as would be true when large samples of more than 30 or so observations are analyzed, there is a 95% probability that observations of the dependent variable will lie within the range $\hat{Y}_t \pm (1.96 \times$ S.E.E.$)$, or within roughly *two* standard errors of the estimate. The probability is 99% that any given $\hat{Y}_t$ will lie within the range $\hat{Y}_t \pm (2.576 \times$ S.E.E.$)$, or within roughly *three* standard errors of its predicted value. When very small samples of data are analyzed, "critical" values slightly larger than two or three are multiplied by the S.E.E. to obtain the 95% and 99% confidence intervals. Precise values can be obtained from a t-table such as that found in Appendix C, as described in the following discussion of t-statistics. For both small and large samples of data, greater predictive accuracy for the regression model is obviously associated with smaller standard errors of the estimate.

The standard error of the estimate concept is portrayed graphically in Figure 3.5. The least squares regression line is illustrated as a bold straight line; the upper and lower 95% confidence interval limits are shown as broken curved lines. On average, 95% of all actual data observations will lie within roughly two standard errors of the estimate. Given a value X_t, the interval between the upper and lower confidence bounds can be used to predict the corresponding Y_t value with a 95% probability that the actual outcome will lie within that confidence interval. Notice that this confidence interval widens for sample observations that are much higher or much lower than the sample mean. This is because the standard error of the estimate calculation is based on observations drawn from the sample rather than the overall population and provides only an approximation to the true distribution of errors. Confidence bounds are closest to the regression line in the vicinity of mean values for X_t and Y_t, or at the center of the scatter diagram. Confidence bounds diverge from the regression line toward the extreme values of the sample observations. An obvious implication worth remembering is that *relatively little confidence can be placed in the predictive value of a regression equation extended beyond the range of sample observations.*

In the First National Bank cost estimation example, the standard error of the estimate is 531.9. This means that the standard deviation of actual Y_t values about the regression line is \$531.90, since the standard error of the estimate is always in the same

Figure 3.5

ILLUSTRATION OF THE USE OF THE STANDARD ERROR OF THE ESTIMATE TO DEFINE CONFIDENCE INTERVALS

The standard error of the estimate (S.E.E.) is used to construct a confidence interval.

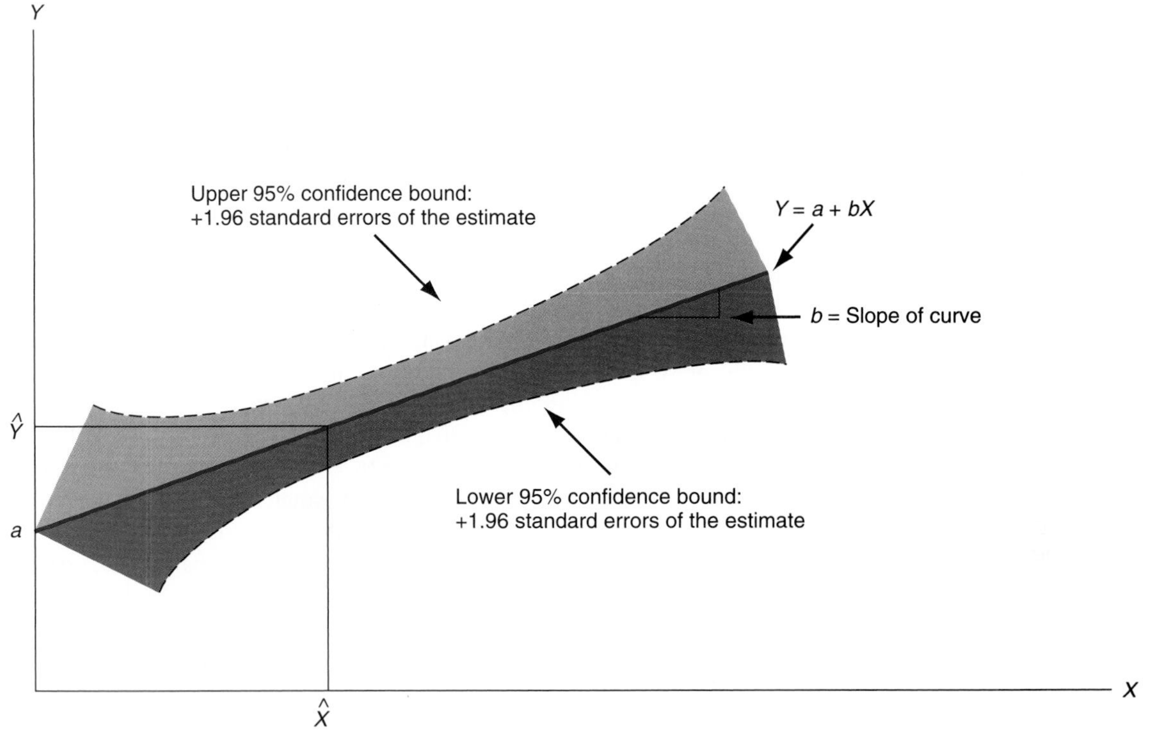

units as the dependent Y-variable. There is a 95% probability that any given observation Y_t will lie within roughly two standard errors of the relevant $\hat{Y}_t$ estimate.[2] For example, the number of new account applications during the month of July is 315 per month, and the expected or fitted total cost level is $6,993.19 (= $586.4 + $20.339(315)). The corresponding confidence bounds for the 95% confidence interval are $6,993.19 ± (2 × $531.9). This means that there is roughly a 95% chance that actual total costs per month

---

[2]The precise "critical" number used in the multiplication of S.E.E. is found in a t-table such as that in Appendix C. This value is adjusted downward when sample size n is small relative to the number of coefficients k estimated in the regression model. To find the precise critical value, calculate the number of degrees of freedom, defined as $df = n - k$, and read the appropriate t-value from the table. In this example, $df = n - k = 12 - 2 = 10$ and there is a 95% probability that any given observation Y_t will lie within precisely 2.228 standard errors of the relevant $\hat{Y}_t$ estimate. There is a 99% probability that actual total costs will fall within precisely 3.169 standard errors of the predicted value. Therefore, even for the very small sample size analyzed in this example, the rough rules of thumb of two standard deviations for the 95% confidence bounds and three standard deviations for the 99% confidence bounds work quite well.

for the 315 unit activity level will fall in a range from $5,929.39 to $8,056.99. Similarly, there is a 99% probability that actual total costs will fall within roughly three standard errors of the predicted value, or in the range from $5,397.49 to $8,588.89. The wider the confidence interval, the higher is the confidence level that actual values will be found within the predicted range. Greater predictive accuracy is obviously also associated with smaller standard errors of the estimate.

GOODNESS OF FIT, r AND R^2

Correlation Coefficient
Goodness of fit measure for a simple regression model.

In a simple regression model with only one independent variable the **correlation coefficient, r,** measures goodness of fit. The correlation coefficient falls in the range between 1 and -1. If $r = 1$, there is a perfect direct linear relation between the dependent Y-variable and the independent X-variable. If $r = -1$, there is a perfect inverse linear relation between Y and X. In both instances, actual values for Y_t all fall exactly on the regression line. The regression equation explains all of the underlying variation in the dependent Y-variable in terms of variation in the independent X-variable. If $r = 0$, zero correlation exists between the dependent and independent variables; they are autonomous. When $r = 0$, there is no relation at all between actual Y_t observations and fitted $\hat{Y}_t$ values.

Coefficient of Determination
Percentage of Y-variation explained by the regression model.

In multiple regression models where more than one independent X-variable is considered, the squared value of the coefficient of multiple correlation is used in a similar manner. The square of the coefficient of multiple correlation, called the **coefficient of determination** or R^2, shows how well a multiple regression model explains changes in the value of the dependent Y-variable. R^2 is defined as the proportion of the total variation in the dependent variable that is explained by the full set of independent variables. In equation form, R^2 is written:

$$R^2 = \frac{\text{Variation Explained by Regression}}{\text{Total Variation of } Y}. \tag{3.17}$$

Accordingly, R^2 can take on values ranging from 0, indicating that the model provides no explanation of the variation in the dependent variable, to 1.0, indicating that all the variation has been explained by the independent variables. The coefficient of determination for the regression model illustrated in Figure 3.4 is 92.4, indicating that 92.4% of the total variation in First National Bank new account application costs can be explained by the underlying variation in the number of new account applications. If R^2 is relatively high, deviations about the regression line will be relatively small, as shown in Figure 3.6. In such instances, actual Y_t values will be close to the regression line and values for u_t will be small. As the size of the deviations about the regression line increases, the coefficient of determination falls. At the extreme, the sum of the squared error terms equals the total variation in the dependent variable, and $R^2 = 0$. In this case, the regression model is unable to explain *any* variation in the dependent Y-variable.

A relatively low value for R^2 indicates that a given model is inadequate in terms of its overall explanatory power. The most general cause for this problem is the omission of important explanatory variables. In practice, the coefficient of determination will seldom equal either 0 or 100%. In the First National Bank example, $R^2 = 92.4\%$ and a relatively high level of explanatory power is realized by the regression model. Fully

Figure 3.6

EXPLAINED AND UNEXPLAINED VARIATIONS OF THE DEPENDENT
VARIABLE IN A REGRESSION MODEL

R^2 is high when unexplained variation is low.

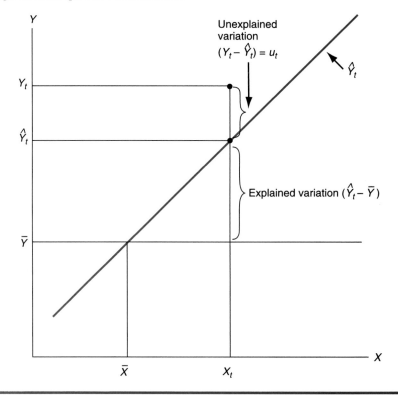

92.4% of cost variation is explained by the variation in new account applications—a level of explanation that is often very useful for planning purposes. In empirical demand estimation, values for R^2 of 80%, indicating that 80% of demand variation has been explained, are often quite acceptable. For goods with highly stable and predictable demand patterns, demand function R^2s as high as 90% to 95% are sometimes achieved. Very high levels of R^2 can also be attained in cost function analysis of output produced under controlled conditions. Generally speaking, demand and cost analysis for a given firm or industry over time (time series analysis) will lead to higher levels for R^2 than would a similar analysis across firms or industries at a given point in time (cross-sectional analysis). This is because most economic phenomena are closely related to the overall pace of economic activity and thus have an important time or trend element. Such exogenous forces are held constant in cross-section analyses and cannot contribute to the overall explanatory power of the regression model. In judging whether or not a given R^2 is sufficiently high to be satisfactory, the type of analysis conducted and the anticipated use of statistical results must be considered.

THE CORRECTED COEFFICIENT OF DETERMINATION, $\overline{R}^2$

As stated previously, an R^2 of 100% results when each data point lies exactly on the regression line. Although one might think that any regression model with an $R^2 = 100\%$ would prove highly reliable as a predictive device, this is not always true. The coefficient of determination for any regression equation is artificially high when too small a sample is used to estimate the model's coefficients. At the extreme, R^2 always equals 100% when the number of estimated coefficients equals or exceeds the number of observations because each data point can then be placed exactly on the regression line.

To conduct meaningful regression analysis, the sample used to estimate the regression equation must be sufficiently large to accurately reflect the important characteristics of the overall population. This typically means that 30 or more data observations are needed to adequately fit a regression model. More precisely, what is typically needed is 30 or more degrees of freedom (*df*). Degrees of freedom are the number of observations beyond the absolute minimum required to calculate a given regression statistic. For example, to calculate an intercept term, at least one observation is needed; to calculate an intercept term plus one slope coefficient, at least two observations are needed; and so on. Since R^2 approaches 100% as degrees of freedom approach zero for any regression model, statisticians developed a method for correcting or adjusting R^2 to account for the number of degrees of freedom. The corrected coefficient of determination, denoted by the symbol $\overline{R}^2$, can be calculated using the expression:

$$\overline{R}^2 = R^2 - \left(\frac{k-1}{n-k}\right)(1 - R^2), \tag{3.18}$$

where n is the number of sample observations (data points) and k is the number of estimated coefficients (intercept plus the number of slope coefficients). Note that the $\overline{R}^2$ calculation always involves a downward adjustment to R^2. The downward adjustment to R^2 is large when n, the sample size, is small relative to k, the number of coefficients being estimated. This downward adjustment to R^2 is small when n is large relative to k. In the First National Bank example, $\overline{R}^2 = 91.6\%$—a relatively modest downward adjustment to the $R^2 = 92.4\%$, and suggests that the high level of explanatory power achieved by the regression model cannot be attributed to an overly small sample size.

Like R^2, statistical software programs typically perform the $\overline{R}^2$ adjustment, so there is often no need to actually make such calculations in practice. Still, knowing what is involved makes the reasons for the practice obvious. Clearly, confidence in the reliability of a given regression model will be higher when both R^2 and the number of degrees of freedom are substantial.

THE *F*-STATISTIC

F-Statistic
Offers evidence if
explained variation in *Y* is
significant.

Both the coefficient of determination, R^2, and corrected coefficient of determination, $\overline{R}^2$, provide evidence on whether or not the proportion of explained variation is relatively "high" or "low." However, neither tells if the independent variables as a group explain a *statistically significant* share of variation in the dependent *Y*-variable. The **F-statistic** provides evidence on whether or not a statistically significant proportion of total variation in the dependent variable has been explained. Like $\overline{R}^2$, the F-statistic is adjusted for degrees of freedom and is defined as:

$$F_{k-1,n-k} = \frac{\textit{Explained Variation}/(k-1)}{\textit{Unexplained Variation}/(n-k)}. \tag{3.19}$$

Once again, n is the number of observations (data points) and k is the number of estimated coefficients (intercept plus the number of slope coefficients). Also like $\overline{R}^2$, the F-statistic can be calculated in terms of the coefficient of determination, where:

$$F_{k-1,n-k} = \frac{R^2/(k-1)}{(1-R^2)/(n-k)}. \tag{3.20}$$

The F-statistic is used to indicate whether or not a significant share of the variation in the dependent variable is explained by the regression model. The hypothesis actually tested is that the dependent Y-variable is *unrelated* to all of the independent X-variables included in the model. If this hypothesis cannot be rejected, the total explained variation in the regression will be quite small. At the extreme, if $R^2 = 0$, then $F = 0$ and the regression equation provides absolutely no explanation of the variation in the dependent Y-variable. As the F-statistic increases from zero, the hypothesis that the dependent Y-variable is not statistically related to one or more of the regression's independent X-variables becomes easier to reject. At some point, the F-statistic becomes sufficiently large to reject the independence hypothesis and warrants the conclusion that at least some of the model's X-variables are significant factors in explaining variation in the dependent Y-variable.

The F-test is used to determine whether a given F-statistic is statistically significant. Performing F-tests involves comparing F-statistics with critical values from a table of the F-distribution. If a given F-statistic *exceeds* the critical value from the F-distribution table, the hypothesis of no relation between the dependent Y-variable and the set of independent X-variables can be rejected. Taken as a whole, the regression equation can then be seen as explaining significant variation in the dependent Y-variable. Critical values for the F-distribution are provided at the 10%, 5%, and 1% significance levels in Appendix C. If the F-statistic for a given regression equation exceeds the F-value in the table, there can be 90%, 95%, or 99% confidence, respectively, that the regression model explains a significant share of variation in the dependent Y-variable. The 90%, 95%, and 99% confidence levels are popular for hypothesis rejection, because they imply that a true hypothesis will be rejected only 1 out of 10, 1 out of 20, or 1 out of 100 items, respectively. Such error rates are quite small and typically quite acceptable.

Critical F-values depend on degrees of freedom related to both the numerator and denominator of Equation 3.17. In the numerator, the degrees of freedom equal one less than the number of coefficients estimated in the regression equation ($k-1$). The degrees of freedom for the denominator of the F-statistic equal the number of data observations minus the number of estimated coefficients ($n-k$). The critical value for F can be denoted as $F_{f1,f2}$, where $f1$, the degrees of freedom for the numerator, equals

$k - 1$, and $f2$, the degrees of freedom for the denominator, equals $n - k$. For example, the F-statistic for the First National Bank example involves $f1 = k - 1 = 2 - 1 = 1$, and $f2 = n - k = 12 - 2 = 10$ degrees of freedom. Also note that the calculated $F_{1,10} = 120.86 > 10.04$, the critical F-value for the $\alpha = 0.01$ or 99% confidence level. This means there is less than a 1% chance of observing such a high F-statistic when there is in fact no variation in the dependent Y-variable explained by the regression model. Alternatively, the hypothesis of no link between the dependent Y-variable and the entire group of X-variables can be rejected with 99% confidence. Given the ability to reject the hypothesis of no relation at the 99% confidence level, it will always be possible to reject this hypothesis at the lower 95% and 90% confidence levels. Since the significance with which the no-relation hypothesis can be rejected is an important indicator of overall model fit, rejection should always take place at the highest possible confidence level.

As a rough rule of thumb, and assuming a typical regression model including four or five independent X-variables plus an intercept term, a calculated F-statistic greater than *three* permits rejection of the hypothesis that there is no relation between the dependent Y-variable and the X-variables at the $\alpha = 0.05$ significance level (with 95% confidence). As seen in Figure 3.7, a calculated F-statistic greater than *five* typically permits rejection of the hypothesis that there is no relation between the dependent Y-variable and the X-variables at the $\alpha = 0.01$ significance level (with 99% confidence). However, as seen in the earlier discussion, critical F-values are adjusted upward when sample size is small in relation to the number of coefficients included in the regression model. In such instances, precise critical F-values must be obtained from an F-table, such as that found in Appendix C.

JUDGING VARIABLE SIGNIFICANCE

The standard error of the estimate indicates the precision with which the regression model can be expected to predict the dependent Y-variable. The standard deviation (or standard error) of each individual coefficient provides a similar measure of precision for the relation between the dependent Y-variable and a given X-variable. When the standard deviation of a given estimated coefficient is small, a strong relation is suggested between X and Y. When the standard deviation of a coefficient estimate is relatively large, the underlying relation between X and Y is typically weak.

A number of interesting statistical tests can be conducted based on the size of a given estimated coefficient and its standard deviation. These tests are based on alternate versions of the previously described t-statistic. Generally speaking, a t-test is performed to test whether the estimated coefficient $\hat{b}$ is significantly different from some hypothesized value. By far, the most commonly tested hypothesis is that $b = 0$. This stems from the fact that if X and Y are indeed unrelated, then the b slope coefficient for a given X-variable will equal zero. If the $b = 0$ hypothesis can be rejected, then it is possible to infer that $b \neq 0$ and that a relation between Y and a given X-variable does in fact exist.

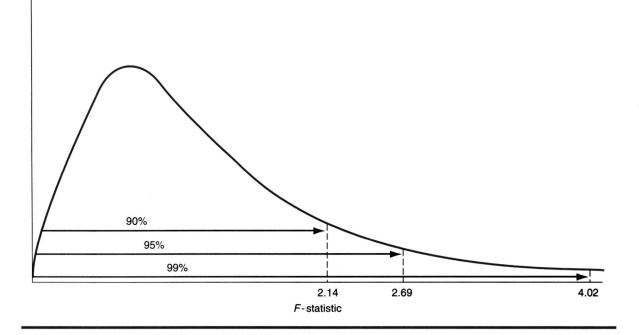

| Figure 3.7 |

THE *F* DISTRIBUTION WITH 4 AND 30 DEGREES OF FREEDOM (FOR A REGRESSION MODEL WITH AN INTERCEPT PLUS FOUR *X* VARIABLES TESTED OVER 35 OBSERVATIONS)

The *F* distribution is skewed to the right but tends toward normality as both numbers of degrees of freedom become very large.

The *t*-statistic with $n - k$ degrees of freedom used to test the $b = 0$ hypothesis is given by the expression:

$$t_{n-k} = \frac{\hat{b}}{\text{Standard Deviation of } \hat{b}}, \qquad (3.21)$$

where, once again, n is the number of observations (data points) and k is the number of estimated coefficients (intercept plus the number of slope coefficients). Notice that this *t*-statistic measures the size of an individual coefficient estimate relative to the size of its underlying standard deviation.

This popular *t*-statistic measures the size of the b coefficient relative to its standard deviation because both the size of b and its underlying stability are important in determining if, on average, $b \neq 0$. The *t*-statistic measures the number of standard deviations between the estimated regression coefficient, $\hat{b}$, and zero. If the calculated *t*-statistic is greater than the relevant critical *t*-value, taken from a table of values such as that found in Appendix C, the hypothesis that $b = 0$ can be rejected. Conversely, if the calculated

t-statistic is not greater than the critical t-value, it is not possible to reject the $b = 0$ hypothesis. In that case, there is no evidence of a relation between Y and a given X-variable.

Returning to the First National Bank example, the estimated coefficient for the number of new account applications X-variable is 20.339. Given a standard deviation of only 1.85, the calculated t-statistic $= 10.99 > 3.169$, the critical t-value for $n - k = 10$ degrees of freedom at the $\alpha = 0.01$ significance level. With 99% confidence, the hypothesis of no effect can be rejected. Alternatively, the probability of encountering such a large t-statistic is less than 1% [hence the probability (p) value of 0.000 in Figure 3.4] when there is in fact no relation between the total costs Y-variable and the number of new account applications X-variable.

As a rough rule of thumb, assuming a large $n > 30$ sample size and a typical regression model of four or five independent X-variables plus an intercept term, a calculated t-statistic greater than *two* permits rejection of the hypothesis that there is no relation between the dependent Y-variable and a given X-variable at the $\alpha = 0.05$ significance level (with 95% confidence). A calculated t-statistic greater than *three* typically permits rejection of the hypothesis that there is no relation between the dependent Y-variable and a given X-variable at the $\alpha = 0.01$ significance level (with 99% confidence). However, as described earlier, critical t-values are adjusted upward when sample size is small in relation to the number of coefficients included in the regression model. In such instances, precise critical t-values can be obtained from a t-table, such as that found in Appendix C.

A Demand Estimation Example

An example of demand estimation can be used to illustrate how regression models are estimated—or fitted—by the method of least squares. Assume that monthly data have been assembled by Electronic Data Processing (EDP), Inc., a small but rapidly growing firm that provides electronic data processing services to companies, hospitals, and other organizations. EDP's main business is to maintain and monitor payroll records on a contractual basis and issue payroll checks, W-2 forms, and so on, to the employees of client customers. The company has aggressively expanded its personal selling efforts and experienced a rapid expansion in annual revenues during the past year. In a tough economic environment, year-end sales revenue grew to an annual rate of $79.2 million per year. Table 3.5 shows EDP data on contract sales (Q), personal selling expenses (PSE), advertising expenditures (AD), and average contract price (P) over the past year (12 observations). Because of a stagnant national economy, industry-wide growth was halted during the year, and the usually positive effect of income growth on demand was missing. Thus, the trend in national income was not relevant during this period. For simplicity, assume that the data contained in Table 3.5 include all relevant factors influencing EDP's monthly sales.

If a linear relation among unit sales, contract price, personal selling expenditures, and advertising is hypothesized, the EDP regression equation takes the following form:

$$Sales = Y_t = a + bP_t + cPSE_t + dAD_t + u_t, \tag{3.22}$$

Spreadsheet and Statistical Software for the PC

The personal computer revolution in business began with the publication of *Lotus 1-2-3*® spreadsheet software. A spreadsheet is a tabular collection of business data in the style of an accounting worksheet that can be easily manipulated and analyzed by computer. An instant hit that still leads the market for basic spreadsheet software, *Lotus 1-2-3 for Windows*® makes income statement and balance sheet analysis quick and easy. Recent versions incorporate a broad range of tools for analysis, including: net present value, internal rate of return, linear programming, and regression. Using *Lotus 1-2-3 for Windows,* managers are also able to analyze and display operating data using a wide variety of charting and graphing techniques. Sometimes, a simple bar chart or line plot is all that's needed to convey a basic message or suggest an obvious solution. In other instances, more detailed statistical analysis is required. *Lotus 1-2-3 for Windows,* and other leading spreadsheet software programs like *Microsoft Excel,* offer sophisticated but easy to use statistical capabilities like regression and correlation analysis.

For more detailed study, users of *Lotus 1-2-3 for Windows* are able to take advantage of numerous "add in macros," or customized routines, to solve specialized business problems. For example, *@Risk* is a *Lotus 1-2-3* add-in software application that allows managers to employ proven risk analysis techniques in the evaluation of any uncertain business situation. To prepare for the possibility of lower than forecast sales, it is often not enough to test worst case, most likely, and best case scenarios. *@Risk* can be used to run thousands of simulations to show the likelihood of each possible scenario, and calculate the economic consequences. *Solver,* a fully integrated feature in *Lotus 1-2-3,* provides linear, nonlinear, and mixed integer optimization with full sensitivity analysis—for up to 120 variables and 120 constraints. Other more sophisticated linear programming add-in programs are available, of course. *ForeCalc* makes it possible to use a wide variety of broadly accepted exponential smoothing models to generate sales and cost forecasts without leaving the spreadsheet. *Ready-To-Run Accounting* incorporates powerful tools for financial analysis in a best-selling general ledger add-in software. In addition to regular

business editions, each of these four *Lotus 1-2-3* add-ins is published in user-friendly student editions with excellent written documentation.

Faster processors, tons of memory, and the graphical user interface of Windows has led to a new generation of powerful user-friendly statistical software for detailed analysis of product demand and cost data. In business and in many leading business schools around the country, *Minitab Statistical Software*, published by Minitab, Inc., is an acknowledged leader. *Minitab* was traditionally command-driven software, meaning that users had to type a command sequence to perform a given statistical analysis. To run a regression of the data in column one on one predictor (*x*-variable) contained in column two, the command is simply: REGRESS C1 1 C2. The command for correlation is CORRELATE, for the arithmetic mean it is MEAN, and so on. While the language of *Minitab* is intuitive and easy to learn, many users now prefer the newer *Windows* version that employs an easy-to-learn menu-driven approach. For nonspecialized users who want to get up and running in a hurry on a statistical package that can handle all but the most knotty problems, *Minitab* is a top choice.

Advanced statistical software packages allow users to conduct a broad range of highly sophisticated statistical analyses on large data sets. Multivariate analysis, time-series analysis, factor analysis, and nonlinear regression are typical capabilities that distinguish advanced statistical packages from more basic offerings. *SPSS for Windows,* the best advanced statistical software program written for the PC, features comprehensive statistical capability, excellent documentation, and a user-friendly interface. Using *SPSS for Windows,* it is possible to easily conduct a detailed analysis of problems facing the smallest firm or Fortune 500 company. *SPSS for Windows* is a comprehensive package of statistical and graphics software that offers users a complete solution to data modeling, analysis, and report preparation needs.

See: Michael J. Himowitz, "Microsoft Delivers a Real Bargain—Honest," *Forbes,* April 14, 1997, 172.

| Table 3.5 | DEMAND FUNCTION REGRESSION ANALYSIS FOR ELECTRONIC DATA PROCESSING, INC. |

Unit Sales	Unit Price	Selling Expenses	Advertising Expenditures	Fitted Values	Residuals
100	$3,800	$14,250	$13,500	99.69	0.31
110	3,700	15,000	15,000	111.53	−1.53
130	3,500	17,000	17,250	136.26	−6.26
170	3,200	18,750	22,500	170.76	−0.76
140	3,900	21,750	18,000	144.84	−4.84
210	2,500	23,250	16,500	213.91	−3.91
230	2,300	22,500	24,000	235.35	−5.35
250	2,100	24,000	15,000	233.03	16.97
200	3,400	21,000	24,750	178.45	21.55
220	2,500	24,750	19,500	228.41	−8.41
240	2,400	25,500	24,750	248.38	−8.38
200	3,300	29,250	12,000	199.40	0.60
Mean 183.33	$3,050.00	$21,416.67	$18,562.50	183.33	−0.00

where Y_t is the number of contracts sold, P_t is the average contract price per month, PSE_t is personal selling expenses, and AD_t is advertising expenditures, and u_t is a random disturbance term—all measured on a monthly basis over the past year.

When this linear regression model is estimated over the EDP data, the following regression equation is estimated:

$$Sales_t = 169.0 - 0.046\ P_t + 0.005\ PSE_t + 0.002\ AD_t$$

$$(3.97) \quad (-6.77) \quad\quad (5.69) \quad\quad\quad (2.72)$$

where P_t is price, PSE_t is selling expense, AD_t is advertising, and t-statistics are indicated within parentheses. The standard error of the estimate, or S.E.E., is 11.2 units; the coefficient of determination or $R^2 = 96.6\%$; the adjusted coefficient of determination is $\overline{R}^2 = 95.3\%$; and the relevant F-statistic $= 76.17$.

How might the values of these coefficient estimates be interpreted? To begin with, the intercept term $a = 169.0$ has no economic meaning. Caution must always be exercised when interpreting points outside the range of observed data and this intercept, like most, lies far from typical values. This intercept cannot be interpreted as the expected level of sales at a zero price, and assuming both personal selling expenses and advertising are completely eliminated. Similarly, it would be hazardous to use this regression model to predict sales at prices, selling expenses, or advertising levels well in excess of sample norms.

Slope coefficients provide estimates of the change in sales that might be expected following a one-unit increase in price, selling expenses, or advertising expenditures. In this example, sales are measured in units, and each independent variable is measured in dollars. Therefore, a $1 increase in price can be expected to lead to a 0.046-unit reduction in sales volume per month. Similarly, a one-dollar increase in selling expenses can be expected to lead to a 0.005-unit increase in sales; a one-dollar increase in advertising can be expected to lead to a 0.002-unit increase in sales. In each instance, the effect of independent X-variables appears quite consistent over the entire sample. The t-statistics for both price and selling expenses exceed a value of three.[3] The chance of observing such high t-statistics when in fact no relation exists between sales and these X-variables is less than 1%. Though less strong, the link between sales and advertising expenditures is also noteworthy. The t-statistic for advertising exceeds the value of two, meaning that there can be 95% confidence that advertising has an effect on sales. The chance of observing such a high t-statistic for advertising expenditures when in fact advertising has no effect on sales is less than 5%. Again, caution must be used when interpreting these individual regression coefficients. It is important not to extend the analysis beyond the range of data used to estimate the regression coefficients.

The standard error of the estimate or S.E.E. of 11.2 units can be used to construct a confidence interval within which actual values are likely to be found based on the size of individual regression coefficients and various values for the X-variables. For example, given this regression model and values of $P_t = \$3,200$, $PSE_t = \$18,750$, and $AD_t = \$22,500$ for the independent X-variables, the fitted value $\hat{Y}_t = 170.76$ can be calculated (see Table 3.5). Given these values for the independent X-variables, 95% of the time actual observations will lie within roughly two standard errors of the estimate; 99% of the time actual observations will lie within roughly three standard errors of the estimate. Thus, the bounds for the 95% confidence interval are given by the expression $170.76 \pm (2 \times 11.2)$, or from 148.36 to 193.16 units. Bounds for the 99% confidence interval are given by the expression $170.76 \pm (3 \times 11.2)$, or from 137.16 to 204.36. units.

Finally, the coefficient of determination $R^2 = 96.6\%$ and indicates the share of variation in EDP demand explained by the regression model. Only 3.4% is left unexplained. Moreover, the adjusted coefficient of determination is $\bar{R}^2 = 95.3\%$ and reflects only a modest downward adjustment to R^2 based on the size of the sample analyzed relative to the number of estimated coefficients. This suggests that the regression model explains a significant share of demand variation—a suggestion that is supported by the F-statistic. $F_{3,8} = 76.17$ and is far greater than five, meaning that the hypothesis of no relation between sales and this group of independent X-variables can be rejected with 99% confidence. There is less than a 1% chance of encountering such a large F-statistic when in fact there is no relation between sales and these X-variables as a group.

---

[3]The t-statistics for both price and selling expenses exceed 3.355, the precise critical t-value for the $\alpha = 0.01$ level and $n - k = 12 - 4 = 8$ degrees of freedom. The t-statistic for advertising exceeds 2.306, the critical t-value for the $\alpha = 0.05$ level and 8 degrees of freedom, meaning that there can be 95 percent confidence that advertising has an effect on sales. Note also that $F_{3,8} = 76.17 > 7.58$, the precise critical F-value for the $\alpha = 0.01$ significance level.

Summary

This chapter introduces various methods for characterizing central tendency and dispersion throughout samples and populations of data. An understanding of these statistics is a necessary prelude to the detailed examination of the highly useful regression analysis technique for the study of statistical relations.

- Summary and descriptive measures of the overall population, called **population parameters,** are seldom known and must typically be estimated. The most effective means for doing so is to rely on **sample statistics,** or summary and descriptive measures that describe a representative sample.
- Useful measures of central tendency include the arithmetic **mean** or average, **median** or "middle" observation, and **mode** or most frequently encountered value in the sample. If the data are perfectly balanced or **symmetrical,** then measures of central tendency will converge on a single typical value. Otherwise, **skewness** and a lack of symmetry in sample dispersion is implied.
- Commonly employed measures of dispersion include the **range,** or the difference between the largest and smallest sample observations, **variance,** or average squared deviation from the mean, and **standard deviation,** or square root of the variance. The standard deviation measures dispersion in the same units as the underlying data. The **coefficient of variation** compares the standard deviation to the mean in an attractive relative measure of dispersion. The **coefficient of determination** shows the share of variation in Y that is explained by the regression model.
- A **hypothesis test** is a statistical experiment used to measure the reasonableness of a given theory or premise. **Type I error** is the incorrect rejection of a true hypothesis; **Type II error** is the failure to reject a false hypothesis. The z-**statistic** is a test statistic that is normally distributed with a mean of zero and a standard deviation of one. A t-**statistic** has the same distribution for large samples, but is *approximately* normal over small samples. Critical t-values are adjusted upward as sample size is reduced, depending on **degrees of freedom,** or the number of observations beyond the absolute minimum required to calculate the statistic.
- A **deterministic relation** is one that is known with certainty. A **statistical relation** exists if the average of one variable is related to another, but it is impossible to predict with certainty the value of one based on the value of another.
- A **time series** of data is a daily, weekly, monthly, or annual sequence of economic data. A **cross-section** of data is a group of observations on an important economic variable at any given point in time.
- A **scatter diagram** is a plot of data where the *dependent* variable is plotted on the vertical or Y-axis, and the *independent* variable is plotted on the horizontal or X-axis.
- The most common specification for economic relations is a **linear model,** or straight-line relation, where the marginal effect of each X-variable on Y is constant. Another common regression model form is the **multiplicative model,** or log-liner relation, used when the marginal effect of each independent variable is thought to depend on the value of all independent variables in the regression equation.

- A **simple regression model** involves only one dependent Y-variable and one independent X-variable. A **multiple regression model** also entails one Y-variable, but includes two or more X-variables.
- The **standard error of the estimate,** or S.E.E., measures the standard deviation of the dependent Y-variable after controlling for the influence of all X-variables.
- In a simple regression model with only one independent variable, the **correlation coefficient,** r, measures goodness of fit. The **coefficient of determination,** or R^2, shows how well a multiple regression model explains changes in the value of the dependent Y-variable.
- The **F-statistic** provides evidence on whether or not a statistically significant share of variation in the dependent Y-variable has been explained by all the X-variables. t-statistics are used to measure the significance of the relation between a dependent Y-variable and a given X-variable.

Methods examined in this chapter are commonly employed by both large and small corporations and other organizations in their ongoing statistical analysis of economic relations. Given the continuing rise in both the diversity and complexity of the economic environment, the use of such tools is certain to grow in the years ahead.

QUESTIONS

Q3.1 Is the mean or the median more likely to provide a better measure of the typical profit level for corporations?

Q3.2 What important advantage do the variance and standard deviation have over the range measure of dispersion?

Q3.3 When dispersion in dollars of total cost is being analyzed, in what units are the variance and standard deviation measured?

Q3.4 If a regression model estimate of total monthly profits is $50,000 with a standard error of the estimate of $25,000, what is the chance of an actual loss?

Q3.5 A simple regression $TC = a + bQ$ is unable to explain 19% of the variation in total costs. What is the coefficient of correlation between TC and Q?

Q3.6 In a regression-based estimate of a demand function, the b-coefficient for advertising equals 3.75 with a standard deviation of 1.25 units. What is the range within which there can be 99% confi-

dence that the actual parameter for advertising can be found?

Q3.7 Describe the benefits and risks entailed with an experimental approach to regression analysis.

Q3.8 Describe a circumstance in which a situation of very high correlation between two independent variables, called multicollinearity, is likely to be a problem, and discuss a possible remedy.

Q3.9 When residual or error terms are related over time, serial correlation is said to exist. Is serial correlation apt to be a problem in a time series analysis of quarterly sales data over a ten-year period? Identify a possible remedy, if necessary.

Q3.10 Managers often study the profit margin-sales relation over the life cycle of individual products, rather than the more direct profit-sales relation. In addition to the economic reasons for doing so, are there statistical advantages as well? (Note: profit margin equals profit divided by sales.)

SELF-TEST PROBLEMS AND SOLUTIONS

ST3.1 **Data Description and Analysis.** Max Miller, a staff research assistant with Market Research Associates, Ltd., has conducted a survey of households in the affluent Denver suburb of Genesee,

Colorado. The focus of Miller's survey is to gain information on the buying habits of potential customers for a local new car dealership. Among the data collected by Miller is the following information on number of cars per household and household disposable income for a sample of $n = 15$ households:

NUMBER OF CARS	HOUSEHOLD INCOME (IN $000)
1	100
3	100
0	30
2	50
0	30
2	30
2	100
0	30
2	100
2	50
3	100
2	50
1	50
1	30
2	50

A.   Calculate the mean, median, and mode measures of central tendency for the number of cars per household and household disposable income. Which measure does the best job of describing central tendency for each variable?
B.   Based on this $n = 15$ sample, calculate the range, variance, and standard deviation for each data series, and the 95% confidence interval within which you would expect to find each variable's true population mean.
C.   Consulting a broader study, Miller found a $60,000 mean level of disposable income per household for a larger sample of $n = 196$ Genesee households. Assume Miller knows that disposable income per household in the Denver area has a population mean of $42,500 and $\sigma = $3,000$. At the 95% confidence level, can you reject the hypothesis that the Genesee area has a typical average income?

ST3.1   **SOLUTION**
A.   The mean, or average number of 1.533 cars per household, and mean household disposable income of $60,000 are calculated as follows:

$$\text{CARS: } \overline{X} = (1 + 3 + 0 + 2 + 0 + 2 + 2$$
$$+ 0 + 2 + 2 + 3 + 2 + 1$$
$$+ 1 + 2)/15 = 23/15$$
$$= 1.533$$

$$\text{INCOME: } \overline{X} = (100 + 100 + 30 + 50 + 30$$
$$+ 30 + 100 + 30 + 100 + 50$$
$$+ 100 + 50 + 50 + 30$$
$$+ 50)/15$$
$$= \$60,000$$

By inspection of a rank-order from highest to lowest values, the "middle" or median values are two cars per household and $50,000 in disposable income per household. The mode for the number of cars per household is two cars, owned by seven households. The distribution of disposable income per household is *trimodal* with five households each having income of $30,000, $50,000, and $100,000.

In this instance, the median appears to provide the best measure of central tendency.
B.   The range is from zero to three cars per household, and from $30,000 to $100,000 in disposable income. For the number of cars per household, the sample variance is 0.98 (cars squared), and the sample standard deviation is 0.9809 cars. For disposable income per household, the sample variance is 928.42 (dollars squared), and the standard deviation is $30.47. These values are calculated as follows:

$$\text{Cars: } s^2 = [(1 - 1.533)^2 + (3 - 1.533)^2$$
$$+ (0 - 1.533)^2 + (2 - 1.533)^2$$
$$+ (0 - 1.533)^2 + (2 - 1.533)^2$$
$$+ (2 - 1.533)^2 + (0 - 1.533)^2$$
$$+ (2 - 1.533)^2 + (2 - 1.533)^2$$
$$+ (3 - 1.533)^2 + (2 - 1.533)^2$$
$$+ (1 - 1.533)^2 + (1 - 1.533)^2$$
$$+ (2 - 1.533)^2]/14$$

$$= 13.733/14$$

$$= 0.9809$$

$$s = \sqrt{s^2} = 0.990$$

$$\text{Income: } s^2 = [(100 - 60)^2 + (100 - 60)^2$$
$$+ (30 - 60)^2 + (50 - 60)^2$$
$$+ (30 - 60)^2 + (30 - 60)^2$$
$$+ (100 - 60)^2 + (30 - 60)^2$$
$$+ (100 - 60)^2 + (50 - 60)^2$$
$$+ (100 - 60)^2 + (50 - 60)^2$$
$$+ (50 - 60)^2 + (30 - 60)^2$$
$$+ (50 - 60)^2]/14$$

$$= 13{,}000/14$$

$$= 928.42$$

$$s = \sqrt{s^2} = \$30.470(000)$$

Given the very small sample size involved, the t-test with $df = n - 1 = 15 - 1 = 14$ is used to determine the 95% confidence intervals within which you would expect to find each variable's true population mean. The exact confidence intervals are from 0.985 cars to 2.082 cars per household, and from \$43,120 to \$76,880 in disposable income per household, calculated as follows:

Cars: $\overline{X} - t(s/\sqrt{n})$
$$= 1.533 - 2.145(0.99/3.873)$$
$$= 0.985 \text{ (lower bound)}$$

$\overline{X} + t(s/\sqrt{n})$
$$= 1.533 + 2.145(0.99/3.873)$$
$$= 2.082 \text{ (upper bound)}$$

Income: $\overline{X} - t(s/\sqrt{n})$
$$= 60 - 2.145(30.47/3.873)$$
$$= 43.12 \text{ (lower bound)}$$

$\overline{X} + t(s/\sqrt{n})$
$$= 60 + 2.145(30.47/3.873)$$
$$= 76.88 \text{ (upper bound)}$$

Of course, if the rule-of-thumb of $t = 2$ were used rather than the exact critical value of $t = 2.145$ ($df = 14$), then a somewhat narrower confidence interval would be calculated.

C. Yes. The z-statistic can be used to test the hypothesis that the mean level of income in Genesee is the same as that for the Denver area given this larger sample size, since disposable income per household has a known population mean and standard deviation. Given this sample size of $n = 196$, the 95% confidence interval for the mean level of income in Genesee is from \$58,480 to \$61,520—both well above the population mean of \$42,500:

$\overline{X} - z(\sigma/\sqrt{n})$
$$= \$60{,}000 - 1.96(\$3{,}000/\sqrt{196})$$
$$= \$59{,}580 \text{ (lower bound)}$$

$\overline{X} + z(\sigma/\sqrt{n})$
$$= \$60{,}000 + 1.96(\$3{,}000/\sqrt{196})$$
$$= \$60{,}420 \text{ (upper bound)}$$

Had the rule of thumb $z = 2$ been used rather than the exact $z = 1.96$, a somewhat wider confidence interval would have been calculated.

The hypothesis to be tested is that the mean income for the Genesee area equals that for the overall population, H_0: $\mu = \$42{,}500$, when $\sigma = \$3{,}000$. The test-statistic for this hypothesis is $z = 81.67$, meaning that the null hypothesis can be rejected:

$$z = \frac{\overline{X} - \mu}{\sigma/\sqrt{n}} = \frac{\$60{,}000 - \$42{,}500}{\$3{,}000/\sqrt{196}} = 81.67$$

The probability of finding such a high sample average income when Genesee is in fact typical of the overall population average income of \$42,500 is less than 5%. Genesee area income appears to be higher than that for the Denver area in general.

ST3.2 **Simple Regression.** The global aerospace industry is dominated by Boeing and McDonnell Douglas from the United States, and Airbus Industrie, the European consortium. During the early-1990s, the end of the Cold War with the former Soviet Union led to a dramatic downshifting in orders for military-related purchases at the same time a global recession cut sharply into the commercial demand for aircraft. Against this backdrop, a number of analysts began to question the wisdom and profitability of the industry's massive long-term investments in research and development (R&D).

The following table shows sales revenue, profit, and R&D data for a $n = 19$ sample of firms taken from the U.S. aerospace industry. Data are for 1993 and are limited to those companies reporting sales of \$58 million or more and R&D expenditures of at least \$1 million. R&D expenses are the dollar amount of company-sponsored R&D during the most recent fiscal year, as reported to the Securities and Exchange Commission on Form 10-K. Excluded from such numbers is R&D under contract to others, such as U.S. government agencies. All figures are in \$ millions.

COMPANY NAME	SALES	PROFITS	R&D EXPENSE
Abex	$728.4	($194.0)	$11.6
Boeing	30,184.0	2,256.0	1,846.0
Curtiss-Wright	179.7	32.7	1.6
GenCorp	1,937.0	37.0	36.0
General Dynamics	3,472.0	227.0	66.0
K&F Industries	295.5	(14.7)	14.1
Kaman	782.9	29.0	17.8
Lockeed	10,100.0	549.0	420.0
Martin Marietta	5,954.3	512.4	200.0
McDonnell Douglas	17,373.0	1,086.0	509.0
Northrop	5,550.0	180.0	93.0
OEA	88.1	23.1	2.6
Orbital Sciences	174.6	5.4	6.0
Pacific Scientific	172.6	8.1	8.2
Sequa	1,868.3	43.8	17.6
Sunstrand	1,672.7	130.1	115.4
Thiokol	1,311.7	101.8	14.2
United Technologies	21,641.0	200.0	1,219.0
Woodward Governor	374.2	33.0	16.0
Averages	$5,466.3	$276.1	$242.8

Data Source: "R&D Scoreboard," *Business Week,* June 28, 1993, 105.

A.   A simple regression model with sales revenue as the dependent *Y*-variable and R&D expenditures independent *X*-variable yields the following results:

SALES AS A FUNCTION OF R&D
REGRESSION OUTPUT:

Constant	$1,364.797
Std Err of *Y* Est	$2,259.882
R^2	93.4%
No. of Observations	19
Degrees of Freedom	17

	R&D
X Coefficient	$16.889
Std Err of Coef.	1.093
t-statistic	15.46

How would you interpret these findings?
B.   A simple regression model with net income (profits) as the dependent *Y*-variable and R&D ex-

penditures independent *X*-variable yields the following results:

PROFITS AS A FUNCTION OF
R&D REGRESSION OUTPUT:

Constant	$45.073
Std Err of *Y* Est	$317.105
R^2	69.4%
No. of Observations	19
Degrees of Freedom	17

	R&D
X Coefficient(s)	$0.951
Std Err of Coef.	0.153
t-statistic	6.20

How would you interpret these findings?
C.   Discuss any differences between your answers to Parts A and B.

ST3.2   **SOLUTION**

A.   First of all, the constant in such a regression typically has no meaning. Clearly, the intercept should not be used to suggest the value of sales revenue that might occur for a firm that had zero R&D expenditures. As discussed in the problem, this sample of firms is restricted to those companies having at least $1 million in R&D spending. The R&D coefficient is statistically significant at the $\alpha = 0.01$ level with a calculated *t*-statistic value of 15.46, meaning that it is possible to be more than 99% confident that R&D expenditures affect firm sales. The probability of observing such a large *t*-statistic when there is in fact no relation between sales revenue and R&D expenditures is less than 1%. The R&D coefficient estimate of $16.889 implies that a $1 rise in R&D expenditures leads to an average $16.889 increase in sales revenue.

The $R^2 = 93.4\%$ indicates the share of sales variation that can be explained by the variation in R&D expenditures. This suggests that R&D expenditures are a key determinant of sales in the aerospace industry. The standard error of the *Y*-estimate, or S.E.E. = $2,259.882, is the average amount of error encountered in estimating the level of sales for any given level of R&D spending. If the u_i error terms are normally distributed about the regression equation, as would be true when large samples of more than 30 or so observations are analyzed, there is a 95% probability that observations of the dependent variable will lie within the range $\hat{Y}_i \pm (1.96 \times \text{S.E.E.})$, or within roughly *two* standard errors of the estimate. The probability is 99% that any given $\hat{Y}_i$ will lie within the range $\hat{Y}_i \pm (2.576 \times \text{S.E.E.})$, or within roughly *three* standard errors of its predicted value. When very small samples of data are analyzed, as is the case here, "critical" values slightly larger than two or three are multiplied by the S.E.E. to obtain the 95% and 99% confidence intervals.

Precise critical *t*-values obtained from a *t*-table, such as that found in Appendix C, are $t^*_{17,\alpha=0.05} = 2.110$ (at the 95% confidence level) and $t^*_{17,\alpha=0.01} = 2.898$ (at the 99% confidence level) for $df = 19 - 2 = 17$. This means that actual sales revenue Y_i can be expected to fall in the range $\hat{Y}_i \pm (2.110 \times \$2,259.882)$, or $\hat{Y}_i \pm \$4,768.351$, with 95% confidence; and within the range $\hat{Y}_i \pm (2.898 \times \$2,259.882)$, or $\hat{Y}_i \pm \$6,549.138$, with 99% confidence.

B. As in Part A, the constant in such a regression typically has no meaning. Clearly, the intercept should not be used to suggest the level of profits which might occur for a firm that had zero R&D expenditures. Again, the R&D coefficient is statistically significant at the $\alpha = 0.01$ level with a calculated *t*-statistic value of 6.20, meaning that it is possible to be more than 99% confident that R&D expenditures affect firm sales. The probability of observing such a large *t*-statistic when there is in fact no relation between profits and R&D expenditures is less than 1%. The R&D coefficient estimate of $0.951 suggests that a $1 rise in R&D expenditures leads to an average 95.1¢ increase in current-year profits.

The $R^2 = 69.4\%$ indicates the share of profit variation that can be explained by the variation in R&D expenditures. This suggests that R&D expenditures are a key determinant of profits in the aerospace industry. The standard error of the Y-estimate of S.E.E. = $317.105 is the average amount of error encountered in estimating the level of profit for any given level of R&D spending. Actual profits Y_i can be expected to fall in the range $\hat{Y}_i \pm (2.110 \times \$317.105)$, or $\hat{Y}_i \pm \$669.092$, with 95% confidence; and within the range $\hat{Y}_i \pm (2.898 \times \$317.105)$, or $\hat{Y}_i \pm \$918.970$, with 99% confidence.

C. Clearly, a strong link between both sales revenue and profits and R&D expenditures is suggested by a regression analysis of the aerospace industry. Still, there appears to be less variation in the sales-R&D relation than in the profits-R&D relation. As indicated by R^2, the linkage between sales and R&D seems somewhat stronger than the relation between profits and R&D. This stems from the fact that the selection technique limited the overall sample to firms with positive and substantial levels of both sales revenue and R&D expenditures, whereas no such screen for profitability was included.

PROBLEMS

P3.1 **Data Description.** Universal Package Service, Ltd., delivers small parcels to business addresses in the Greater Boston area. To learn more about the demand for its service, UPS has collected the following data on the number of deliveries per week for a sample of ten customers:

3 3 4 2 4 2 3 3 23 3

A. Calculate the mean, median, and mode measures of central tendency for the number of deliveries per week. Which measure does the best job of describing central tendency for this variable?
B. Calculate the range, variance, and standard deviation for this data series. Which measure does the best job of describing the dispersion in this variable?

P3.2 **Data Description.** Scanning America, Inc., is a small but rapidly growing firm in the digitized document translation business. The company reads architectural and engineering drawings into a scanning device that translates graphic information into a digitalized format that can be manipulated on a personal computer or work station. During recent weeks, the company has added a total of ten new clerical and secretarial personnel to help answer customer questions and process orders. Data on the number of years of work experience for these ten new workers are as follows:

5 3 3 5 4 5 4 3 4 3

A. Calculate the mean, median, and mode measures of central tendency for the number of years of work experience. Which measure does the best job of describing central tendency for this variable?

B. Calculate the range, variance, and standard deviation for this data series, and the 95% confidence interval within which you would expect to find the population's true mean.

P3.3 Hypothesis Testing: z-tests. Olae Oil Beauty Lotion is a skin moisturizing product that contains rich oils, blended especially for overly dry or neglected skin. The product is sold by a wide range of retail outlets in 5-ounce bottles. In an ongoing review of product quality and consistency, the manufacturer of Olae Oil Beauty Lotion found a sample average product volume of 5.2 ounces per unit with a sample standard deviation of 0.12 ounces, when a sample of $n = 144$ observations was studied.

A. Calculate the range within which the population average volume can be found with 99% confidence.

B. Assuming that $s = 0.12$ cannot be reduced, and a sample size of $n = 144$, what is the minimum range within which the sample average volume must be found to justify with 99% confidence the advertised volume of 5 ounces?

P3.4 Hypothesis Testing: t-tests. Syndicated Publications, Inc., publishes a number of specialty magazines directed at dairy producers located throughout the midwest. As part of its sales trainee program, the company closely monitors the performance of new advertising space sales

SERVICE CALLS PER DAY

STAFF MEMBER A	STAFF MEMBER B
8	6
7	6
5	5
5	6
6	7
6	6
4	6
7	6
5	6
7	6

personnel. During a recent two-week period, the number of customer contacts were monitored and recorded for two new sales representatives; see the table at the bottom of the first column.

A. Calculate the 95% confidence interval for the population mean number of customer contacts for each sales representative.

B. At this confidence level, is it possible to reject the hypothesis that these two representatives call on an equal number of potential clients?

P3.5 Hypothesis Testing: t-tests. Onyx Corporation designs and manufactures a broad range of fluid handling and industrial products. While fluid handling products have been a rapidly growing market for Onyx during recent years, operating margins dipped recently as customers have complained about lower reliability for one of the company's principal products. Indeed, one of its leading customers provided Onyx with two years of data on the customer's downtime experience:

ONYX CORP. HOURS OF DOWNTIME PER MONTH

MONTH	LAST YEAR	THIS YEAR
January	4	8
February	6	7
March	5	8
April	3	9
May	6	9
June	6	8
July	6	9
August	5	8
September	5	9
October	4	7
November	5	6
December	5	8

A. Calculate the 95% confidence interval for the population mean downtime for each of the two years.

B. At this confidence level, is it possible to reject the hypothesis that downtime experience is the same during each of these two years?

P3.6 Simple Regression and Correlation. Market Research, Inc., has conducted a survey to learn the car buying intentions of a $n = 15$ sample of service department customers. The survey asked each service department customer the age of the oldest automobile in their household and whether or not they intend to buy a new car during the next six months. Survey results were as follows:

MARKET RESEARCH, INC. SURVEY RESULTS

BUY IN 6 MO. (1 = YES, 0 = NO)	AGE OF OLDEST AUTOMOBILE IN HOUSEHOLD (IN YEARS)
0	1
1	5
0	3
0	1
0	2
1	3
1	2
1	6
1	4
0	2
0	3
1	5
0	1
0	3
1	5

A. Interpret the coefficient of correlation between the "Buy" and "Age" variables of 0.727.

B. Interpret the following results for a simple regression over this sample where "Buy" is the dependent Y-variable and "Age" is the independent X-variable.

The regression equation is:

$$BUY = -0.242 + 0.231\ AGE$$

Predictor	Coef	Stdev	t-ratio	p
Constant	−0.2419	0.2087	−1.16	0.267
AGE	0.23105	0.06057	3.81	0.002

S.E.E. = 0.3681 $R^2 = 52.8\%$
$\bar{R}^2 = 49.2\%$
F-statistic = 14.55
($p = 0.002$)

P3.7 **Simple Regression and Correlation.** The toiletries and cosmetics industry has long been one of the most profitable industries in the United States. The stocks of such firms have also been favored by investors who prefer the "safe harbor" provided by companies able to achieve a mod-

icum of earnings growth in both good and poor economic environments. This began to change in the mid-1990s as sluggish economic activity in the United States and overseas added to investor concerns about the inroads achieved by private-label goods. All of this has led investors to prize those companies with predictable rates of growth in earnings per share (EPS).

The table below shows the Value Line EPS growth estimates and five-year EPS growth for a sample of $n = 7$ firms taken from the U.S. toiletries and cosmetics industry. Value Line estimates are for the three- to five-year time horizon ending in 1999–2001; historical rates of EPS growth are taken from the 1991–1995 period. All figures are in percentage terms.

COMPANY NAME	PRJ EPS GROWTH	5-YR EPS GROWTH
Alberto Culver	11.5	8.0
Avon Products	13.0	12.0
Carter-Wallace	7.5	−10.5
Gillette	16.5	18.0
Helen of Troy	15.0	6.0
Tambrands, Inc.	9.5	5.5
Windmere-Durable Holdings	12.5	−7.5
Averages	12.2	4.5

Data Source: Value/Screen II Data Base, July 1, 1996.

A. A simple regression model with the Value Line EPS growth estimate as the dependent Y-variable and the five-year historical rate of growth in EPS as the independent X-variable yields the following results:

PROJECTED EPS GROWTH AS A FUNCTION OF HISTORICAL EPS GROWTH:

Constant	11.275
Std Err of Y Est	2.441
R^2	47.7%
No. of Observations	7
Degrees of Freedom	5
X Coefficient(s)	0.209
Std Err of Coef.	0.098
t-statistic	2.13

How would you interpret these findings?

B. Use the information provided to calculate and interpret the coefficient of correlation between the Value Line EPS growth estimate (dependent Y-variable) and the five-year rate of growth in EPS (independent X-variable).

P3.8 **Simple Regression.** The Environmental Controls Corporation (ECC) is a multinational manufacturer of materials handling, accessory, and control equipment. During the past year, ECC has had the following cost experience after introducing a new fluid control device:

THE ENVIRONMENTAL CONTROLS CORPORATION

OUTPUT	COST 1	COST 2	COST 3
0	$17,000	$11,000	$0
100	10,000	7,000	1,000
200	8,000	13,000	2,000
500	20,000	10,000	6,000
900	14,000	12,000	10,000
1,000	8,000	19,000	11,000
1,200	15,000	16,000	13,000
1,300	14,000	15,000	15,000
1,400	6,000	16,000	18,000
1,500	18,000	23,000	19,000
1,700	8,000	21,000	22,000
1,900	16,000	25,000	24,000

A. Calculate the mean, median, range, and standard deviation for output and each cost category variable.

B. Describe each cost category as fixed or variable based upon the following simple regression results where COST is the dependent Y-variable and OUTPUT is the independent X-variable. The first simple regression equation is:

$$\text{COST1} = \$13,123 - \$0.30 \text{ OUTPUT}$$

Predictor	Coef	Stdev	t-ratio	p
Constant	13123	2635	4.98	0.000
OUTPUT	−0.297	2.285	−0.13	0.899

$$\text{S.E.E.} = \$4,871 \ R^2 = 0.2\%$$
$$\overline{R}^2 = 0.0\% \ F\text{-statistic} = 0.02$$
$$(p = 0.899)$$

The second simple regression equation is:

$$\text{COST2} = \$8,455 + \$7.40 \text{ OUTPUT}$$

Predictor	Coef	Stdev	t-ratio	p
Constant	8455	1550	5.45	0.000
OUTPUT	7.397	1.345	5.50	0.000

$$\text{S.E.E.} = \$2,866 \ R^2 = 75.2\%$$
$$\overline{R}^2 = 72.7\% \ F\text{-statistic} = 30.26$$
$$(p = 0.000)$$

The third simple regression equation is:

$$\text{COST3} = -\$662 + \$12.7 \text{ OUTPUT}$$

Predictor	Coef	Stdev	t-ratio	p
Constant	−661.5	488.4	−1.35	0.205
OUTPUT	12.7298	0.4236	30.05	0.000

$$\text{S.E.E.} = \$902.8 \ R^2 = 98.9\%$$
$$\overline{R}^2 = 98.8\% \ F\text{-statistic} = 903.1$$
$$(p = 0.000)$$

P3.9 **Multiple Regression.** The current performance and long-term prospects of soft drink and alcoholic beverage companies are a study in contrasts. The current profitability and long-term growth prospects for soft drink companies are excellent and a number have worthwhile long-term investment potential. While demand for soft drinks in the United States and Canada continues to be strong, some of the more exciting areas for growth include Eastern Europe, China, and India, where Coca-Cola and Pepsi have limited market penetration or have been prohibited for years. "New Age" drinks such as teas, fruit juices, and flavored water add to the industry's growth potential in both developed and developing countries. By way of contrast, the near-term and long-term outlook for the alcoholic beverage companies is uninspiring. Recessions in major markets, price wars, the threat of higher excise taxes, and growing restrictions on alcohol consumption have all diminished the industry's current performance and long-term growth potential.

To learn how investors assess the long-term growth potential of beverage firms, the table below shows price/earnings ratios, profitability as measured by the return on stockholders' equity

(ROE), the 12-month growth in earnings per share, and the current dividend yield for a $n = 8$ sample of beverage companies. Generally speaking, investors accord higher P/E ratios to companies with relatively attractive growth potential; low P/E ratios are common for stagnant or declining companies. Data are for the most recent fiscal year. P/E data are in ratio form, whereas ROE, EPS growth, and the current dividend yield are in percentage terms.

COMPANY NAME	CUR-RENT P-E	% RETURN NET WORTH	12-MONTH EPS % CHG	CUR-RENT YIELD
Anheuser-Busch	18.4	22.2	−2.3	2.6
Brown-Forman 'B'	17.0	27.2	7.0	2.8
Cadbury Schwepp	15.8	13.3	−16.1	4.1
Canandaigua 'A'	15.6	12.0	12.6	0.0
Coca-Cola	36.4	55.4	17.3	1.1
Coors (Adolph)	17.5	4.9	−27.7	2.9
Molson Cos 'A'	12.5	5.1	−57.3	3.3
Pepsico, Inc.	24.1	27.2	13.2	1.3
Averages	19.7	20.9	−6.7	2.3

Data Source: Value/Screen II, Data Base Information, July 1, 1996.

A. A multiple regression model with the company's P/E ratio as the dependent Y-variable, and ROE, EPS growth, and current yield as independent X-variables yields the following results:

DETERMINANTS OF P/E RATIOS:

Constant	12.419
Std Err of Y Est	3.519
R^2	87.5%
No. of Observations	8
Degrees of Freedom	4

	%ROE	%EPS CHG.	%YIELD
X Coefficient(s)	0.458	−0.075	−1.252
Std Err of Coef.	0.113	0.091	1.363
t-statistic	4.04	−0.82	−0.92

How would you interpret these findings?

B. What suggestions might you make for a more detailed study of the determinants of P/E ratios for beverage firms?

P3.10 **Multiple Regression.** Retailing is one of the largest industries in terms of sales, profits, and employment. Everyday low prices, made popular by Wal-Mart and other discount retailers, have swept the industry and become standard operating procedure. In this environment, the way to survive and prosper is to reduce operating expenses, increase product quality, and improve customer service. Perhaps more than any other single industry, retailers have taken advantage of advances in computer-based methods of data collection and analysis to improve their relation with suppliers, keep inventories lean, and boost sales by better serving customer demands.

To learn how investors assess the investment potential of retail companies, the table below shows the market value of common equity, the accounting book value of total assets, accounting net income, and the five-year rate of growth in earnings per share for a $n = 18$ sample of retailers. The market value effects of accounting book values indicate how investors capitalize the current value of assets in place; valuation effects of net profits and earnings growth reflect investor views of the firms' longer-term growth potential. See the top table on page 121.

A. A multiple regression model with each retailer's market value of common stock as the dependent Y-variable, and total assets, net profit, and the five-year rate of growth in earnings per share gives the results in the bottom table on page 121. How would you interpret these findings?

B. What suggestions might you make for a more detailed study of the determinants of the market value of common stock for retailers versus other types of companies?

COMPANY NAME	MARKET VALUE	TOTAL ASSETS	NET PROFIT	5-YR EPS GROWTH (%)	TOTAL DEBT
Consol. Stores	$1,636.3	$639.8	$64.4	49.5	$50.0
Dayton Hudson	7,322.4	12,570.0	311.0	0.0	9,918.0
Dillard Dept St.	4,00.51	4,778.5	245.7	8.5	2,356.0
Dollar General	2,580.5	680.0	87.8	38.0	6.0
Family Dollar	950.5	636.2	58.1	18.5	0.0
Fred Meyer	777.8	1,671.6	30.3	10.0	1,339.2
Hudson's Bay Co.	1,202.9	4,208.3	34.6	0.5	2,725.4
Jacobson Stores	65.0	262.5	−4.2	−40.0	239.4
Kmart Corp.	5,777.3	15,397.0	−490.0	−44.5	11,128.0
Mac Frugal's	458.3	419.1	36.3	5.5	192.8
May Dept. Stores	10,888.1	10,122.0	700.0	8.5	6,666.0
Mercantile Sts.	2,204.0	2,074.7	123.2	−4.5	509.8
Nordstrom, Inc.	3,493.0	2,732.6	165.1	7.5	731.4
Penney (J.C.)	11,396.0	17,102.0	838.0	6.5	8,160.0
Price/CostCo.	3,964.4	4,437.4	217.2	25.5	2,189.2
Sears, Roebuck	18,988.1	33,130.0	1,025.0	1.0	20,088.0
Service Mdse.	548.3	1,940.6	50.3	−2.5	1,246.6
Wal-Mart Stores	58,758.1	37,541.0	2,740.0	19.0	21,200.0
Averages	$7,500.6	$8,352.4	$346.3	5.9	$4,930.4

Data Source: Value/Screen II, Data Base Information, July 1, 1996.

DETERMINANTS OF THE MARKET VALUE OF THE FIRM:

Constant	$125.340
Std Err of Y Est	$3,739.962
R^2	94.3%
No. of Observations	18
Degrees of Freedom	13

	TOTAL ASSETS	NET PROFIT	EPS GROWTH	TOTAL DEBT
X Coefficient(s)	−0.472	17.284	−31.581	1.119
Std Err of Coef.	0.779	3.131	48.984	1.145
t-statistic	−0.61	5.52	−0.64	0.98

Case Study for Chapter 3

SIZE AND PROFITABILITY IN THE GLOBAL TELECOMMUNICATIONS SERVICES INDUSTRY

Net profit, profit margin, and sales revenue data are provided in Table 3.6 for a $n = 43$ sample of large firms in the global telecommunications services industry. Each row of information shows relevant data for one firm, with sample observations ranked in alphabetical order. In the fourth column of data, the number one is used to indicate if a firm is domiciled in the United States, the number zero is used to indicate if a firm is non–U.S. based. Average net profit for all firms is $735.6 million, the average profit margin is 10.5%, and average sales revenue is $8,847.6 million. In each instance, the sample average reflects a simple sum of each respective value over the entire sample of $n = 43$ firms, all divided by 43, the total number of sample observations. In this particular sample, no individual observation has exactly the sample average level of net profit, profit margin, or sales revenue. With a net profit of $819.1 million, Sweden's Ericsson Telephone comes closest to the sample average net profit. Similarly, NYNEX Corp. with a profit margin of 10.4% and Cable & Wireless, PLC, from the UK, with sales revenue of $8,467.5 million are relatively close to the sample average net profit margin and sales revenue levels, respectively. Based on the sample mean criterion, each of these observations can be described as typical of sample values. It is important to note, however, that there is substantial variation around the sample averages and the chance of atypical sample values appears to be correspondingly high.

Within this sample, non–U.S.-based firms appear somewhat larger but much less profitable than U.S.-based telecommunications companies. For the subsample of $n = 28$ U.S.-based companies, average net profit is $684.3 million, the average profit margin is 8.5%, and average sales revenue is $8,536.4 million. For the subsample of $n = 15$ non–U.S.-based companies, average net profit is $831.5 million, the average profit margin is 14.1%, and average sales revenue is $9,428.4 million. This reflects the fact that the United States is the most hotly competitive telecommunications market in the world. In fact, many of the

non–U.S.-based telecommunications firms listed in Table 3.6 have monopoly or near-monopoly positions in their domestic markets.

Since profit, profit margin, and sales revenue data are not rank-ordered from highest to lowest in the table on page 123, such a ranking is necessary before median levels can be easily calculated. When the sample is rank-ordered from highest to lowest according to net profit, profit margin, or sales revenue, the 22nd sample observation falls exactly in the middle of the distribution of the $n = 43$ the global telecommunications services industry sample. This middle observation is, by definition, the sample median. Exactly 21 sample observations have values above this median value; exactly 21 sample observations have values below this median value. Thus, the median net profit level of $401.8 million is earned by Telecom New Zealand. The sample median profit margin, or return on sales, of 9.2% is earned by the Southern New England Telephone Company from the U.S. The sample median size or sales revenue of $3,45.0 million is generated by Hong Kong Telecom. Based on the sample median criterion, each of these observations is typical of sample values.

Sample averages for both net profit and sales revenue appear to be skewed upward in that sample median values are far below average levels. This reflects the fact that a few very large firms in the industry cause sample average values to be far greater than typically observed levels. As discussed previously, differences between sample means and medians are to be expected for much economic data given the long upward "tail" provided by the giants of industry. However, there is no necessary reason to suspect any relation between profit margins and firm size. This is because profit margins are defined here, and typically, as net profit as a percentage of sales revenue, and sales revenue is a commonly used measure of firm size. Profit margin data are an example of "normalized" or size-adjusted data. The sample average profit margin of 10.5% is close to the sample median of 10.4%. This indicates that the distribution of profit

Table 3.6

NET PROFITS, PROFIT MARGINS, AND SALES REVENUE IN THE GLOBAL
COMMUNICATIONS MARKET

COMPANY NAME	NET PROFIT	PROFIT MARGIN	SALES	U.S. (1) NON-US. (0)
Airtouch Communications	$131.9	8.1%	$1,618.6	1
Alcatel Alsthom	871.2	2.8%	31,366.3	0
ALLTEL Corp.	335.6	10.8%	3,109.7	1
Ameritech Corp.	1,887.6	14.1%	13,427.8	1
AT&T Corp.	1,866.5	2.3%	79,609.0	1
BC Telecom	185.5	7.8%	2,390.6	0
BCE, Inc.	492.8	2.7%	17,975.5	0
Bell Atlantic	1,699.6	12.7%	13,429.5	1
Bellsouth Corp.	2,227.0	12.5%	17,886.0	1
British Telecom	2,763.2	12.5%	22,102.4	0
Cable & Wireless	838.0	9.9%	8,467.5	0
Century Telephone	110.5	17.1%	644.8	1
Cincinnati Bell	114.2	8.5%	1,336.1	1
Citizens Util B	159.5	14.9%	1,069.0	1
Comsat Corp.	50.0	5.9%	852.1	1
Ericsson Telephone	819.1	5.5%	14,876.5	0
Frontier Corp.	141.9	6.6%	2,143.7	1
GTE Corp.	2,527.0	12.7%	19,957.0	1
Hong Kong Telecom	1,098.6	31.8%	3,450.0	0
LCI International	50.8	7.5%	672.9	1
Lincoln Telecom	29.0	12.9%	225.1	1
MCI Communications	866.0	5.7%	15,265.0	1
Northern Telecom	395.0	3.7%	10,672.0	0
NYNEX Corp.	1,396.3	10.4%	13,406.9	1
Pacific Telesis	1,048.0	11.6%	9,042.0	1
Paging Network	−44.2	−6.8%	646.0	1
Reuters ADR	567.3	13.5%	4,189.7	0
SBC Communications	1,889.3	14.9%	12,669.7	1
Southern New England Telephone	168.8	9.2%	1,838.5	1
Sprint Corp.	946.1	7.4%	12,765.1	1
Telecom de Chile	225.2	22.3%	1,009.0	0
Telecom N. Zealand	401.8	21.6%	1,860.2	0
Telefon de Espana	949.0	7.9%	11,961.0	0
Telefonos de Mexico	1,893.2	32.4%	5,843.0	0
Telephone Danmark	643.4	18.9%	3,395.7	0
Telephone & Data Systems	63.4	6.6%	954.4	1
US West Communications	1,107.0	11.7%	9,484.0	1
US West Media	71.0	3.0%	2,374.0	1
U.S. Cellular	43.9	8.9%	492.4	1
U.S. Long Distance	12.0	5.3%	225.0	1
Vanguard Cellular	−7.0	−3.0%	236.1	1
Vodafone Group	329.3	17.6%	1,867.2	0
Worldcom, Inc.	267.7	7.4%	3,639.9	1
Averages	$735.6	10.5%	$8,847.6	0.7
Standard Deviation	$767.9	7.6%	$13,307.7	0.5

Data Source: Value/Screen II, July 1, 1996.

margin data is fairly centered around the sample mean observation, as is often the case when "normalized" or size-adjusted data are considered. It is important to note, however, that there is substantial variation around the sample averages for net profit, profit margin, and sales revenues, and the chance of atypical sample values appears correspondingly high.

The wide variation in profits and profit margins in global communications reflects the fact that individual firms in the industry have important underlying differences in their businesses. Cellular companies tend to be highly leveraged and risky given the relatively new nature of the industry and potential competition from new technology, like wireless systems and personal communications networks. Long-distance carriers benefit greatly from the growth of global communications traffic and from the growing use of phone lines for data transmission. Both cellular companies and long-distance carriers have fundamental differences from the independent phone companies and regional operators, such as Ameritec, Bell Atlantic, and Pacific Telesis. Perhaps nowhere is the stark difference among leaders in the industry's subcategories so apparent as when firms are ranked according to profitability and profit margins. The global leader in current profits is U.K.-giant British Telecom with $2,763.2 million in profits; the global leader in profit margin is Mexico's Telefonos de Mexico at a whopping 32.4%. In both instances, the bottom performer according to these performance measures is U.S.-based Paging Network with losses of $442.2 million and a profit margin of −6.8%. However, rather than reflecting abysmal operating performance, the losses encountered by Paging Network reflect the embryonic stage of development of the radio-transmitted paging services industry. Plano, Texas-based Paging Network is engaged in the acquisition, construction, and operation of radio-transmitted paging services under the PageNet trade name throughout the United States. The future for this segment of the industry is very bright.

A regression model estimate of the relation between net profits and sales revenue for the overall sample of $n = 43$ global telecommunications services companies provides insight concerning the size-profitability relation for telecommunications companies. To contrast the nature of this relation for U.S.-based versus non–U.S.-based companies, each firm was assigned a dummy or binary variable called where U.S. = 1 for companies domiciled in the

United States, and U.S. = 0 if the company is based outside the United States. By considering the effect of dummy or binary variables in a regression model, it becomes possible to learn whether or not country of origin has an influence on profit levels or profit rates. These OLS regression results are as follows (standard errors in parentheses):

REGRESSION OUTPUT: PROFIT AS A FUNCTION OF SALES

Constant	$513.129
Std Err of Y Est	$634.114
R^2	35.1%
No. of Observations	43
Degrees of Freedom	40

	SALES	U.S.
X Coefficient(s)	$0.034	−$117.122
Std Err of Coef.	0.007	203.004
t-statistic	4.59	−0.58

A. How would you interpret these results?
B. A regression model estimate of the relation between net profit margin and sales revenue for the overall sample of $n = 43$ firms is (standard errors in parentheses):

REGRESSION OUTPUT: PROFIT MARGIN AS A FUNCTION OF SALES

Constant	0.152
Std Err of Y Est	0.071
R^2	16.7%
No. of Observations	43
Degrees of Freedom	40

	SALES	U.S.
X Coefficient(s)	−1.167E-06	−0.056
Std Err of Coef.	8.210E-07	0.023
t-statistic	1.42	−2.49

Why is the R^2 from this regression model so much lower than that found for the net profit-sales relation?
C. Regression model estimates of the relation between net profits and sales, and between profit margin and sales revenue for the subsamples of

$n = 28$ U.S.-based firms and $n = 15$ non–U.S.-based firms, are shown in the following tables (standard errors in parentheses):

What is the fundamental difference between these estimation results and those reported previously?

PROFIT AS A FUNCTION OF SALES
(U.S. COMPANIES):

Constant	$394.366
Std Err of Y Est	$640.884
R^2	40.6%
No. of Observations	28
Degrees of Freedom	26

X Coefficient(s)	$0.034	
Std Err of Coef.	0.008	
t-statistic	4.22	

PROFIT MARGIN AS A FUNCTION OF SALES
(U.S. COMPANIES):

Constant	0.087
Std Err of Y Est	0.054
R^2	0.3%
No. of Observations	28
Degrees of Freedom	26

X Coefficient(s)	−1.953E-07	
Std Err of Coef.	6.771E-07	
t-statistic	−0.29	

PROFIT AS A FUNCTION OF SALES
(NON–U.S. COMPANIES):

Constant	$523.554
Std Err of Y Est	$644.707
R^2	17.9%
No. of Observations	15
Degrees of Freedom	13

X Coefficient(s)	$0.033	
Std Err of Coef.	0.019	
t-statistic	1.68	

PROFIT MARGIN AS A FUNCTION OF SALES
(NON–U.S. COMPANIES):

Constant	0.204
Std Err of Y Est	0.081
R^2	37.2%
No. of Observations	15
Degrees of Freedom	13

X Coefficient(s)	−6.751E-06	
Std Err of Coef.	2.431E-06	
t-statistic	−2.78	

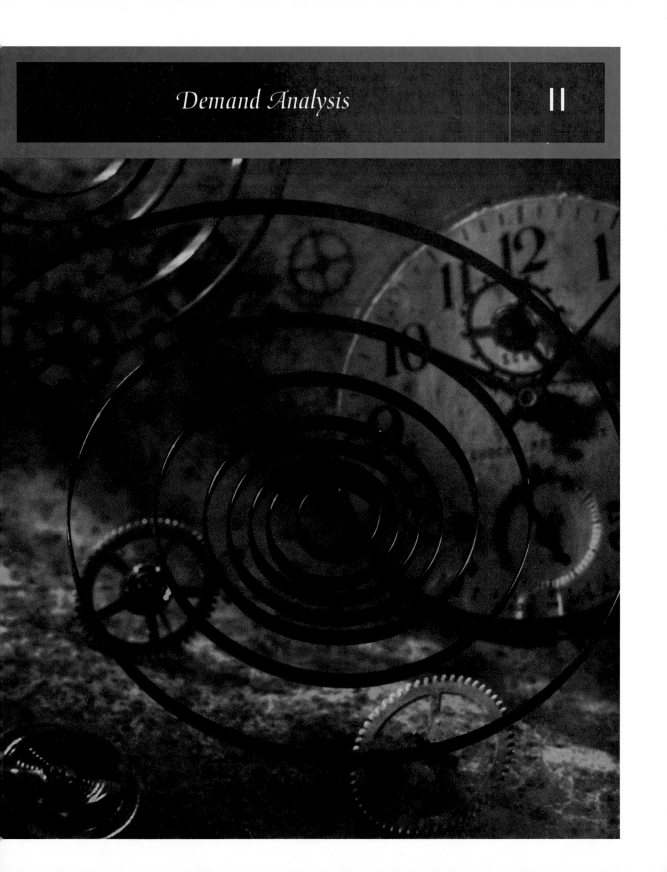

Demand Analysis

II

Demand and Supply

4

In September 1992, financier George Soros made more than $1.5 billion in only a few days by betting that the laws of demand and supply are more powerful than the combined will of the British and German governments. To understand how Soros made such a killing one has only to look at the flawed logic behind Europe's Exchange Rate Mechanism. Since 1987, major European currencies have been narrowly fixed in price relative to each other, with Germany's mark the "anchor" or reference point currency. However, government-set prices seldom balance currency supply and demand. When the demand for British exports rises, foreign demand for British pounds also rises. If the supply of pounds is constant, rising foreign demand gives birth to higher "prices" for pounds, when the price of a pound is expressed in foreign currencies. On the other hand, when the British government boosts the supply of pounds to revive a sluggish economy, it can lower the value of the pound vis-á-vis foreign currencies. In 1992, wily speculators like Soros knew that based upon the laws of demand and supply the pound was overpriced relative to the German mark. When government bankers allowed the financial currency markets to set the pound price, the pound fell in value and Soros made a killing.[1] The upshot is that the laws of demand and supply are so powerful that they even dictate the value of currencies.

The concepts of demand, supply, and market equilibrium contribute the basis necessary to analyze the markets for all goods and services. The overview presented in this chapter offers a useful framework for more detailed study in Chapters 5 through 12. The importance of demand and supply as determinants of both business practice and public policy is investigated in Chapters 10 through 16.

The Basis for Demand

Demand
The total quantity customers are willing and able to purchase.

Demand is the quantity of a good or service that customers are willing and able to purchase during a specified period under a given set of economic conditions. The time frame might be an hour, a day, a month, or a year. The conditions to be considered include the price of the good in question, prices and availability of related goods, expectations of price changes, consumer incomes, consumer tastes and preferences, advertising expenditures, and so on. The amount of the product that consumers are prepared to purchase, its demand, depends on all these factors.

---

[1]See Rita Koselka and Matthew Schifrin, "Brother Can You Spare an EMU?" *Forbes,* December 30, 1996, 120.

For managerial decision making, the primary focus is on market demand. Market demand is the aggregate of individual, or personal, demand. Insight into market demand relations is gained by first understanding the nature of individual demand. Individual demand is determined by the value associated with acquiring and using any good or service and the ability to acquire it. Both are necessary for effective individual demand. Desire without purchasing power may lead to want, but not to demand.

DIRECT DEMAND

Direct Demand
Demand for consumption products.

Utility
Value.

There are two basic models of individual demand. One, known as the theory of consumer behavior, relates to the **direct demand** for personal consumption products. This model is appropriate for analyzing individual demand for goods and services that directly satisfy consumer desires. The value or worth of a good or service, its **utility**, is the prime determinant of direct demand. Individuals are viewed as attempting to maximize the total utility or satisfaction provided by the goods and services they acquire and consume. This optimization process requires that consumers consider the marginal utility (gain in satisfaction) of acquiring additional units of a given product or acquiring one product rather than another. Product characteristics, individual preferences (tastes), and the ability to pay are all important determinants of direct demand.

DERIVED DEMAND

Derived Demand
Demand for inputs used in production.

Goods and services are also acquired not for their direct consumption value but because they are important inputs in the manufacture and distribution of other products. The outputs of engineers, production workers, sales staff, managers, lawyers, consultants, office business machines, production facilities and equipment, natural resources, and commercial airplanes are all examples of goods and services demanded not for direct final personal consumption but rather for their use in providing other goods and services. Their demand is derived from the demand for the products they are used to providing. The demand for all inputs used by a firm is **derived demand.**

The demand for mortgage money is an example. The quantity of mortgage credit demanded is not determined directly; it is derived from the more fundamental demand for housing. The demand for air transportation to major resort areas is not a direct demand but is derived from the demand for recreation. Similarly, the demand for all producers' goods and services used in manufacturing products for final consumption is derived. The aggregate demand for consumption goods and services determines demand for the capital equipment, materials, labor, and energy used to manufacture them. For example, the demands for steel, aluminum, and plastics are all derived demands, as are the demands for machine tools and labor. None of these producers' goods are demanded because of their direct value to consumers but because of the role they play in the production of goods and services.

The demand for producers' goods and services is closely related to the demand for the final products they make. Therefore, an examination of final product demand is an important part of the demand analysis for intermediate, or producers', goods. For products whose demand is derived rather than direct, the theory of the firm provides the basis for analyzing individual demand. Demand for these goods stems from their value in the manufacture and sale of other products. They have value because their employment has the potential to generate profits. Key components in the determination of derived demand are the marginal benefits and marginal costs associated with employing a given input or factor of production. The amount of any good or service employed rises when its marginal benefit, measured in terms of the value of resulting output, is greater than the marginal costs of employing the input, measured in terms of wages, interest, raw material costs, or related expenses. Conversely, the amount of any input employed in production falls when the resulting marginal benefits are less than the marginal cost of employment. In short, derived demand is related to the profitability of employing a good or service.

Regardless of whether a good or service is demanded by individuals for final consumption (direct demand) or as an input used in providing other goods and services (derived demand), the fundamentals of economic analysis offer a basis for investigating the characteristics of demand. For final consumption products, utility maximization as described by the theory of consumer behavior explains the basis for direct demand. For inputs used in the production of other products, profit maximization provides the underlying rationale for derived demand. Since both demand models are based on the optimization concept, while various characteristics that affect demand may differ, the fundamental relations are essentially the same. The principles of managerial economics, and particularly the principles of optimal resource use, provide a basis for understanding demand by both firms and consumers.

The Market Demand Function

Demand Function
The relation between demand and factors influencing its level.

The market **demand function** for a product is a statement of the relation between the aggregate quantity demanded and all factors that affect this quantity. In functional form, a demand function may be expressed as:

$$\text{Quantity of Product } X \text{ Demanded} = Q_x = f(\text{Price of } X, \text{Prices of Related Goods, Expectations of Price Changes, Consumer Incomes, Tastes and Preferences, Advertising Expenditures, and so on}). \quad (4.1)$$

The generalized demand function expressed in Equation 4.1 lists variables that commonly influence demand. For use in managerial decision making, the demand function must be made explicit. The relation between quantity and each of the demand-determining variables must be specified. To illustrate what is involved, assume that the demand function for the automobile industry has been specified as follows:

$$Q = a_1P + a_2PI + a_3I + a_4Pop + a_5i + a_6A. \quad (4.2)$$

This equation states that the number of new domestic automobiles demanded during a given year (in millions), Q, is a linear function of the average price of new domestic cars (in $), P; the average price for new import cars (in $), PI; disposable income per household (in $), I; population, (in millions), Pop; average interest rate on car loans (in percent), i; and advertising expenditures (in $ millions), A. The terms a_1, a_2, . . ., a_6 are called the parameters of the demand function. Assume that the parameters of this demand function are known with certainty as shown in the following equation:

$$Q = -0.002P + 0.001PI + 0.0008I + 0.22Pop - 800i + 0.002A \qquad \textbf{(4.3)}$$

Equation 4.3 states that automobile demand falls by 0.002 units for each $1 increase in the average price charged by domestic manufacturers; it rises by 0.001 units with every $1 increase in the average price of imports, a prime substitute; it increases by 0.0008 units for each $1 increase in disposable income per household; it increases by 0.22 units for each additional million persons in the population; it decreases by 800 units for every 1% rise in interest rates; and it increases by 0.002 units for each $1 million spent on advertising. Remember here and throughout, Q is measured in units of one million cars. This means that each of the unit changes referred to in Equation 4.3 must be multiplied by one million to derive the magnitude of change measured in the number of cars: -0.002 units implies a decline of 2,000 cars, 0.001 units implies an increase of 1,000 cars, and so on.

To derive an estimate of industry demand in any given year, each parameter in Equation 4.3 is multiplied by the value of the related variable and then summed. Table 4.1 illustrates this process, showing that the estimated annual demand for new domestic automobiles is 16 million cars, assuming the stated values of each independent variable.

Table 4.1

ESTIMATING INDUSTRY DEMAND FOR THE DOMESTIC AUTOMOBILE INDUSTRY

INDEPENDENT VARIABLE (1)	PARAMETER (2)	ESTIMATED VALUE FOR INDEPENDENT VARIABLE DURING THE COMING YEAR (3)	ESTIMATED DEMAND (4) = (2) × (3)
Average price for new domestic cars (P) ($)	−0.002	$20,000	−40
Average price for new import cars (PI) ($)	0.001	$22,000	22
Disposable income, per household (I) ($)	0.0008	$40,000	32
Population (Pop) (millions)	0.22	250	55
Average interest rate (i) (percent)	−800	8%	−64
Industry advertising expenditures (A) ($million)	0.002	$5,500	11
Total demand (millions of cars)			16

INDUSTRY DEMAND VERSUS FIRM DEMAND

Market demand functions can be specified for an entire industry or for an individual firm, though somewhat different variables would typically be used in each case. Most important, variables representing competitors' actions would be stressed in firm demand functions. For example, a firm's demand function would typically include competitors' prices and advertising expenditures. Demand for the firm's product line is negatively related to its own prices but positively related to the prices charged by competing firms. Demand for the firm's products would typically increase with its own advertising expenditures, but it could increase or decrease with additional advertising by other firms.

The parameters for specific variables ordinarily differ in industry versus firm demand functions. Consider the positive influence of population on the demand for Ford automobiles as opposed to automobiles in general. While the effect is positive in each instance, the parameter value in the Ford demand function would be much smaller than that in the industry demand function. Only if Ford had 100% of the market—that is, if Ford were the industry—would the parameters for firm and industry demand be identical.

Since firm and industry demand functions differ, different models or equations must be estimated for analyzing these two levels of demand. However, it is important to recognize that the demand concepts developed in this chapter apply to both firm and industry demand functions.

The Demand Curve

Demand Curve
The relation between price and the quantity demanded, holding all else constant.

The demand function specifies the relation between the quantity demanded and all variables that determine demand. The **demand curve** is the part of the demand function that expresses the relation between the price charged for a product and the quantity demanded, holding constant the effects of all other variables. Frequently, a demand curve is shown in the form of a graph, and all variables in the demand function except the price and quantity of the product itself are held fixed at specified levels. In the automobile demand function given in Equation 4.3, for example, one must hold income, population, interest rates, and advertising expenditures constant to identify the demand curve with which to examine the relation between automobile new domestic prices and the quantity demanded.

DEMAND CURVE DETERMINATION

To illustrate the demand curve determination process, consider the relation depicted in Equation 4.3 and Table 4.1. Assuming that import car prices, income, population, interest rates, and advertising expenditures are all held constant at their Table 4.1 values, the relation between the quantity demanded of new domestic cars and price is expressed as:

$$Q = -0.002P + 0.001(\$22,000) + 0.0008(\$40,000) + 0.22(250)$$

$$-800(0.08) + 0.002(\$5,500) \qquad \textbf{(4.4)}$$

$$= 56 - 0.002P$$

Alternatively, when price is expressed as a function of output, the industry demand curve (Equation 4.4) can be written:

$$P = \$28{,}000 - \$500Q \qquad \textbf{(4.5)}$$

Equations 4.4 and 4.5 both represent the demand curve for automobiles given specified values for all of the other variables in the demand function. Equation 4.5 is shown graphically in Figure 4.1 since it is common to show price as a function of quantity in demand analysis. As is typical, a reduction in price increases the quantity demanded and, conversely, an increase in price decreases the quantity demanded. The -0.002 slope coefficient for the price variable in Equation 4.4 means that a \$1 increase in the

Figure 4.1

A HYPOTHETICAL AUTOMOBILE INDUSTRY DEMAND CURVE FOR NEW DOMESTIC AUTOMOBILES

The parameter estimate (slope coefficient) for the automobile demand curve reveals that a \$1 increase in the price of new automobiles will decrease the quantity demanded by 0.002 units, when units are expressed in millions. Thus, a decline in quantity demanded of 2,000 autos follows a \$1 increase in price.

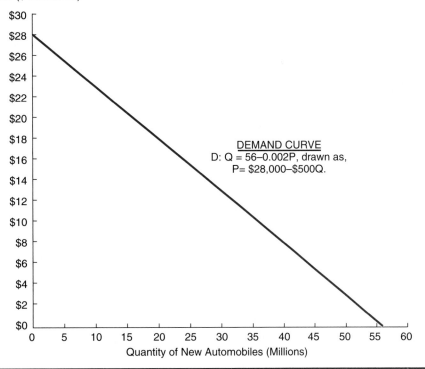

Average Price Per Auto (\$ thousands)

DEMAND CURVE
D: Q = 56–0.002P, drawn as,
P= \$28,000–\$500Q.

Quantity of New Automobiles (Millions)

average price of new domestic automobiles would reduce the quantity demanded by 0.002 units, or 2,000 cars ($= -0.02 \times 1,000,000$) since units are in millions of new domestic cars. Similarly, a $1 decrease in the average price of new domestic automobiles would increase quantity demanded by 0.002 units, or 2,000 cars. When price is expressed as a function of quantity, as in Equation 4.5, a one-unit (or one-million car) increase in Q would lead to a $500 reduction in the average price of new domestic cars. A one-unit (or one-million car) decrease in Q would lead to a $500 increase in average prices.

RELATION BETWEEN THE DEMAND CURVE AND DEMAND FUNCTION

The relation between the demand curve and the demand function is important and worth considering in somewhat greater detail. Figure 4.2 shows three demand curves for automobiles. Each curve is constructed in the same manner as that depicted in Equations 4.4 and 4.5 and then portrayed in Figure 4.1. In fact, D is the same automobile demand curve characterized by Equation 4.5 and Figure 4.1. If D is the appropriate demand curve, then 16 million new domestic automobiles can be sold at an average price of $20,000, whereas 24 million automobiles could be sold at an average price of $16,000, but only 10 million automobiles can be sold at an average price of $23,000.

Change in the Quantity Demanded
Movement along a given demand curve reflecting a change in price and quantity.

This variation is described as a **change in the quantity demanded,** defined as a movement along a single given demand curve. As average price drops from $23,000 to $20,000 to $16,000 along D, the quantity demanded rises from 10 million to 16 million to 24 million automobiles. A change in the quantity demanded refers to the effect on sales of a change in price, holding constant the effects of all other demand-determining factors.

Shift in Demand
Switch from one demand curve to another following a change in a nonprice determinant of demand.

A **shift in demand,** or switch from one demand curve to another, reflects a change in one or more of the nonprice variables in the product demand function. In the automobile demand-function example, a decrease in interest rates causes an increase in automobile demand, because the interest rate parameter of -800 indicates that demand and interest rates are inversely related—that is, they change in opposite directions. When demand is inversely related to a factor such as interest rates, a reduction in the factor leads to rising demand and an increase in the factor leads to falling demand.

D_A is another automobile demand curve. The sole difference between D and D_A is that D assumes an interest rate of 8% rather than the 6.5% interest rate used to construct D_A. Since the interest rate parameter is negative, a decrease in interest rates causes an increase in automobile demand. Holding all else equal, a 1.5% reduction in interest rates leads to a 12-unit [$= -800 \times (-0.015)$] increase in automobile demand. A 1.5% decrease in average interest rates leads to an upward or rightward shift in the original demand curve D to the new demand curve D_A. This also means that a 1.5% interest rate reduction will increase automobile demand by 12 units at each price level, where units are expressed in millions of cars. Thus, a 12-unit increase represents an increase of 12 million cars. At an average price of $20,000, for example, a 1.5% reduction in interest rates increases automobile demand from 16 million to 28 million units per year, as shown on D_A. Also as shown on D_A, after a 1.5% decrease in interest rates, the original

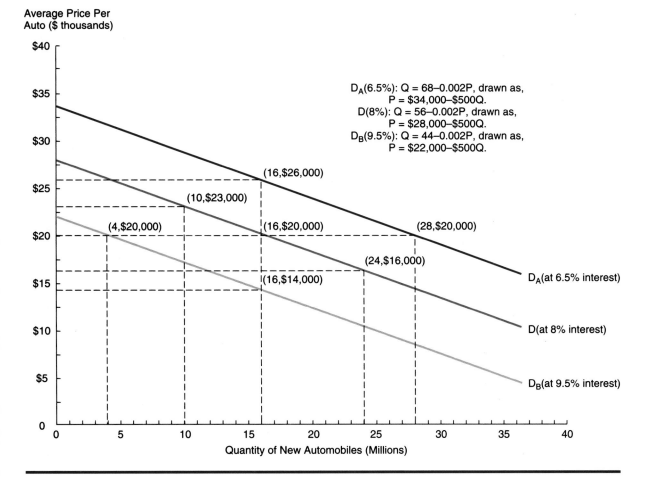

Figure 4.2

HYPOTHETICAL INDUSTRY DEMAND CURVES FOR NEW DOMESTIC AUTOMOBILES AT INTEREST RATES OF 9.5%, 8%, AND 6.5%

A shift in the original demand curve from D to D_A follows a 1.5% fall in interest rates from 8% to 6.5%; a shift from D to D_B reflects a 1.5% rise in interest rates from 8% to 9.5%.

Average Price Per Auto ($ thousands)

$D_A(6.5\%): Q = 68 - 0.002P$, drawn as, $P = \$34,000 - \$500Q$.
$D(8\%): Q = 56 - 0.002P$, drawn as, $P = \$28,000 - \$500Q$.
$D_B(9.5\%): Q = 44 - 0.002P$, drawn as, $P = \$22,000 - \$500Q$.

(16,\$26,000)
(10,\$23,000)
(4,\$20,000)   (16,\$20,000)   (28,\$20,000)
(24,\$16,000)
(16,\$14,000)

D_A(at 6.5% interest)

D(at 8% interest)

D_B(at 9.5% interest)

Quantity of New Automobiles (Millions)

quantity of 16 million automobiles could be sold at a higher average price of $26,000. Notice that demand curve D indicates that only 16 million units could be sold at an average industry price of $20,000, when interest rates average 8% per year.

On the other hand, a 1.5% increase in interest rates, from 8% to 9.5%, causes an inward or leftward shift in the original demand curve D to the new demand curve D_B. A 1.5% increase in interest rates reduces automobile demand by 12 million cars at each price level. At a price of $20,000, a 1.5% increase in interest rates reduces demand for new domestic cars from 16 million cars, the D level, to only 4 million units, the D_A level. With interest rates at 9.5%, demand for 16 million cars would only arise at the lower average price of $14,000, the D_B level, again holding all other demand-determining factors constant.

From the advertising parameter of 0.002, it is possible to infer that demand and advertising are positively related. Rising demand follows increases in advertising, and falling demand follows reductions in advertising. The shift from D to D_A in Figure 4.2, for example, could also have resulted from a $6 billion increase in industry advertising rather than a 1.5% reduction in interest rates, or it could be the result of a $3 billion increase in industry advertising coupled with a 0.75% reduction in interest rates. In each case, the resulting demand curve is given by the equation $Q = 68 − 0.002P$, or $P = \$34,000 − \$500Q$. On the other hand, the downward shift from D to D_B in Figure 4.2 could have resulted from a $6 billion decrease in industry advertising rather than a 1.5% increase in interest rates, or it could be the result of a $3 billion decrease in industry advertising coupled with a 0.75% increase in interest rates. In each case, the resulting demand curve is given by the equation $Q = 44 − 0.002P$, or $P = \$22,000 − \$500Q$.

The distinction between changes in the quantity demanded, which reflect movements along a given demand curve, and changes in demand, which reflect shifts from one demand curve to another, is extremely important. Failure to understand the causes of changes in demand for a company's products can lead to costly, even disastrous, mistakes in managerial decision making. The task of demand analysis is made especially difficult by the fact that under normal circumstances, not only prices but also prices of other goods, income, population, interest rates, advertising, and most other demand-related factors vary from period to period. Sorting out the impact of each factor makes demand analysis one of the most challenging aspects of managerial economics. This important topic is investigated in Chapter 5.

The Basis for Supply

Supply
The total quantity offered for sale.

The term **supply** refers to the quantity of a good or service that producers are willing and able to sell during a certain period under a given set of conditions. Factors that must be specified include the price of the good in question, prices of related goods, the current state of technology, levels of input prices, weather, and so on. The amount of product that producers bring to the market—the supply of the product—depends on all these factors.

FACTORS THAT INFLUENCE SUPPLY

The supply of a product in the market is merely the aggregate of the amounts supplied by individual firms. The theory of the firm provides the basis for analyzing factors related to both individual firm and market supply. The supply of products arises from their ability to enhance the firm's value-maximization objective. Key components in this supply determination are the marginal benefits and marginal costs associated with expanding output. The amount of any good or service supplied will rise when the marginal benefit to producers, measured in terms of the value of output, is greater than the

The Import Supply Battle in the U.S. Auto Industry

The U.S. auto industry provides an interesting case study of the dynamics of changing demand and supply conditions. In contrast to just a few years ago, when the Big Three auto makers dominated the industry, today six major companies have a substantial share of the U.S. market, and a handful of other companies are able to profitably exploit important market niches.

On an overall basis, the "Big Three" U.S. manufacturers account for 60% to 65% of the U.S. market, Japanese nameplates account for roughly 25%, and European makes are responsible for the remainder. Despite a continuing erosion in market share during the 1970s and 1980s, General Motors remains by far the largest company in the U.S. auto market. GM's current market share is in the 30% to 35% range, followed by the Ford Motor Company with roughly 25%, Chrysler and Toyota with 10% to 15% each, Honda roughly 8%, and Nissan roughly 5%; other companies, such as Mazda, Mitsubishi, Subaru, and Volkswagen, account for the rest.

There is widespread concern in the industry that the sluggish economic growth of the mid-1990s will cause a lingering drop in the demand for automobiles and trucks. A continuing flood of new products is consequently emerging as the companies fight for market share. Many of these new products are aimed at market segments that didn't even exist during the mid-1970s, when the industry suffered its last major downturn. Chrysler, for example, was able to return from the edge of bankruptcy to record profits largely on the basis of its astonishing success with minivans. By the late 1990s, however, there will be at least a dozen new vehicles aimed at this market, some with highly popular four-wheel drive. To counter this attack on its most profitable market segment, Chrysler introduced a new generation of minivans—some with value pricing packages that cut prices to levels not seen since the mid-1980s. At the same time, Ford took aim at Chrysler's lucrative Jeep franchise with the Ford Explorer and outran both Jeep and Chevrolet to take first place in the sport-utility truck market.

To gain entry into a large number of important market niches, some companies are entering into joint ventures. Mazda Motor Corporation and Ford, for example, work closely together in both automobile and truck segments of the industry. Ford has long been recognized as an innovative industry leader in trucks and has agreed to share its expertise with Mazda. Meanwhile, Mazda designs and builds cars for Ford. Ford also began to market minivans made with Nissan during the mid-1990s. Mitsubishi makes cars with Chrysler, and three Japanese companies and one Korean company make cars marketed by GM. Interestingly, each of the three largest U.S. manufacturers has taken important equity interests in a number of foreign producers, thus blurring the distinction between foreign and domestic vehicles.

One important difference that remains between domestically produced and imported autos and trucks stems from the tariff and quota protection that domestic manufacturers have been able to obtain from Congress. Not satisfied with voluntary quotas on Japanese auto imports, domestic manufacturers successfully fought during the late 1980s to extend a 25% import tariff on imported vans and sport-utility vehicles. Although vans and sport-utility vehicles account for 20% of all vehicles sold in the United States, imports enjoy only a modest share of this market segment and such vehicles are among the most profitable in the industry.

Unfortunately, import tariffs and quotas during the 1970s and 1980s allowed the domestic auto industry to raise both prices and profits while product quality lagged behind the imports. In the more competitive market of the 1990s, price increases have been restrained while the quality of domestically produced cars and light trucks has surged. From a consumer's standpoint, import competition has been a highly beneficial spur to innovation and quality improvement, as it keeps the lid on auto industry prices and profits. The active interplay of demand and supply is the best guarantee of efficiently functioning markets.

See: Brian Bremner, "Toyota's Crusade," *Business Week*, April 7, 1997, 104-114.

marginal cost of production. The amount of any good or service supplied will fall when the marginal benefit to producers is less than the marginal costs of production. Thus, individual firms will expand or reduce supply based on the expected profits of each action.

Among the factors influencing the supply of a product, the price of the product itself is perhaps the most important. Higher prices increase the quantity of output producers want to bring to market. When marginal revenue exceeds marginal cost, firms increase supply to earn the greater profits associated with expanded levels of output. Higher prices allow firms to pay the higher production costs that are sometimes associated with expansions in output. Conversely, lower prices typically cause producers to supply a lower quantity of output. At the margin, lower prices can have the effect of making previous levels of production unprofitable.

The prices of related goods and services can also play an important role in determining supply of a product. If a firm employs limited resources that can be used to produce several different products, it can be expected to switch production from one product to another depending on market conditions. For example, the supply of gasoline typically declines in autumn when the price of heating oil rises. Gasoline supply typically increases during the spring and summer months with the seasonal decline in heating oil prices. Whereas the substitution of one output for another can cause an inverse relation between the supply of one product and the price of a second, complementary production relationships result in a positive relation between supply and the price of a related product. For example, ore deposits containing lead often also contain silver. An increase in the price of lead can therefore lead to an expansion in both lead and silver production.

Technology is a key determinant of product supply. The current state of technology refers to the manner in which inputs are transformed into output. An improvement in the state of technology, including any product invention or process innovation that reduces production costs, increases the quantity and/or quality of products offered for sale at a given price.

Changes in input prices also affect supply in that an increase in input prices will raise costs and reduce the quantity that can be supplied profitably at a given market price. Alternatively, a decrease in input prices increases profitability and the quantity supplied at a given price.

For some products, especially agricultural products, weather can play an important role in determining supply. Temperature, rainfall, and wind all influence the quantity that can be supplied. Heavy rainfall in early spring, for example, can delay or prevent the planting of crops, significantly limiting supply. Abundant rain during the growing season, on the other hand, can greatly increase the available supply at harvest time. An early freeze that prevents full maturation or heavy rain or snow that limits harvesting activity both reduce the supply of agricultural products.

Managerial decision making requires understanding both individual firm supply and market supply conditions. Market supply is the aggregate of individual firm supply, so it is ultimately determined by factors affecting firm supply. Firm supply is examined in greater detail in Chapters 7 and 8. For now, meaningful insight can be gained by understanding the nature of market supply.

The Market Supply Function

Supply Function
The relation between supply and all factors influencing its level.

The market **supply function** for a product is a statement of the relation between the quantity supplied and all factors affecting that quantity. In functional form, a supply function can be expressed as:

$$\text{Quantity of Product } X \text{ Supplied} = Q = f(\text{Price of } X, \text{ Prices of Related Goods, Current State of Technology, Input Prices, Weather, and so on}). \qquad (4.6)$$

The generalized supply function expressed in Equation 4.6 lists variables that influence supply. As is true with the demand function, the supply function must be made explicit to be useful for managerial decision making.

DETERMINANTS OF SUPPLY

To illustrate, consider the automobile industry example discussed previously and assume that the supply function has been specified as follows:

$$Q = b_1 P + b_2 PT + b_3 W + b_4 S + b_5 E + b_6 i. \qquad (4.7)$$

This equation states that the number of new domestic automobiles supplied during a given period (in millions), Q, is a linear function of the average price of new domestic cars (in $), P; average price of new domestic trucks (in $), PT; average hourly price of labor (wages in $ per hour), W; average cost of steel ($ per ton), S; average cost of energy ($ per mcf natural gas), E; and average interest rate (price of capital in %), i. The terms $b_1, b_2, \ldots, b_6$ are the parameters of the supply function. Note that no explicit term describes technology, or the method by which inputs are combined to produce output. The current state of technology is an underlying or implicit factor in the industry supply function.

Substituting a set of assumed parameter values into Equation 4.7 gives the following supply function for the automobile industry:

$$Q = 0.004P - 0.001PT - 0.12W - 0.04S - 0.8E - 400i. \qquad (4.8)$$

Equation 4.8 indicates that automobile supply increases by 0.004 units for each $1 increase in the average price charged; it decreases by 0.001 units for each $1 increase in the average price of new domestic trucks; it decreases by 0.12 units for each $1 increase in wage rates, including fringes; it decreases by 0.04 units with each $1 increase in the average cost of steel; it decreases by 0.8 units with each $1 increase in the average cost of energy; and it decreases by 400 units if interest rates rise 1%. Each parameter indicates the effect of the related factor on supply from domestic manufacturers where, once again, units are measured in terms of millions of cars. Thus, 0.004 units translate into 4,000 ($= 0.004 \times 1,000,000$) cars, 0.001 units translate into 1,000 cars, and so on.

In order to estimate the supply of automobiles during the coming period, each parameter in Equation 4.8 is multiplied by the value of its respective variable and these products are then summed. Table 4.2 illustrates this process, showing that the supply of autos, assuming the stated values of the independent variables, is 16 million units.

| Table 4.2 | ESTIMATING INDUSTRY SUPPLY FOR THE DOMESTIC AUTOMOBILE INDUSTRY |

INDEPENDENT VARIABLE (1)	PARAMETER (2)	ESTIMATED VALUE FOR INDEPENDENT VARIABLE DURING THE COMING YEAR (3)	ESTIMATED SUPPLY (4) = (2) × (3)
Average price for new domestic cars (P) ($)	0.004	$20,000	80
Average price for new domestic trucks (PT) ($)	−0.001	$16,000	−16
Average hourly wage rate, including fringe benefit (W) ($)	−0.12	$50	−6
Average cost of steel, per ton (S) ($)	−0.04	$200	−8
Average cost of energy input, per mcf natural gas (E) ($)	−0.8	$2.50	−2
Average interest rate (i) (in percent)	−400	8%	−32
Total Demand (millions of cars)			16

INDUSTRY SUPPLY VERSUS FIRM SUPPLY

Just as in the case of demand, supply functions can be specified for either an entire industry or an individual firm. Even though factors affecting supply are highly similar in industry versus firm supply functions, the relative importance of such influences can differ dramatically. At one extreme, if all firms used identical production methods and identical equipment, had salaried and hourly employees who were equally capable and identically paid, and had equally skilled management, then individual firm and industry supply functions would have an obvious and close relation. One would expect each firm to be similarly affected by changes in the factors underlying supply. Each parameter in the individual firm supply functions would be smaller than in the industry supply function, however, and would reflect each firm's relative share of the market.

More typically, firms within a given industry adopt somewhat different production methods, use equipment of different vintage, and employ labor of varying skill and compensation level. In such cases, individual firms' supply levels can be affected quite differently by various factors. Japanese and Korean automakers, for example, may be able to offer subcompacts profitably at average industry prices as low as, say, $14,500 per automobile. On the other hand, U.S. auto manufacturers, who have historically operated with a labor cost disadvantage, may only be able to offer a supply of subcompacts at average industry prices in excess of, say, $16,000. This means that at relatively high average prices for the industry above $16,000 per unit, both foreign and domestic auto manufacturers would be actively engaged in car production. At relatively low average prices below $16,000, only foreign producers would offer cars. This would be reflected by different parameters describing the relation between price and quantity supplied in the individual firm supply functions for Japanese, Korean, and U.S. automobile manufacturers.

Individual firms supply output only when doing so is profitable. When industry prices are high enough to cover the marginal costs of increased production, individual firms expand output, thereby increasing total profits and the value of the firm. To the extent that the economic capabilities of industry participants vary, so too does the scale of output supplied by individual firms at various industry prices.

Similarly, supply is affected by the production technology of various firms. Firms operating with highly automated facilities incur large fixed costs and relatively small variable costs. The supply of product from such firms is likely to be relatively insensitive to price changes when compared to less automated firms, for which variable production costs are higher and thus more closely affected by production levels. Relatively low-cost producers can and do supply output at relatively low market prices. Of course, both relatively low-cost and high-cost producers are able to supply output profitably when market prices are high.

The Supply Curve

Supply Curve
The relation between price and the quantity supplied, holding all else constant.

The supply function specifies the relation between the quantity supplied and all variables that determine supply. The **supply curve** is the part of the supply function that expresses the relation between the price charged for a product and the quantity supplied, holding constant the effects of all other variables. As is true with demand curves, supply curves are often shown graphically, and all independent variables in the supply function except the price of the product itself are assumed to be fixed at specified levels. In the automobile supply function given in Equation 4.8, for example, it is important to hold constant the price of trucks and the prices of labor, steel, energy, and other inputs in order to examine the relation between automobile price and the quantity supplied.

SUPPLY CURVE DETERMINATION

To illustrate the supply determination process, consider the relation depicted in Equation 4.8. Assuming that the price of trucks, the prices of labor, steel, energy, and interest rates are all held constant at their Table 4.2 values, the relation between the quantity supplied and price is:

$$Q = 0.004P - 0.001(\$16,000) - 0.12(\$50) - 0.04(\$200)$$
$$- 0.8(\$2.50) - 400(0.08) \qquad \textbf{(4.9)}$$
$$= -64 + 0.004P.$$

Alternatively, when price is expressed as a function of output, the industry supply curve (Equation 4.9) can be written:

$$P = \$16,000 + \$250Q. \qquad \textbf{(4.10)}$$

Equations 4.9 and 4.10, which represent the supply curve for automobiles given the specified values of all other variables in the supply function, are shown graphically in Figure 4.3. When the supply function is pictured with price as a function of quantity, or as $P = \$16,000 + \$250Q$, industry supply will rise by one unit, or one million new domestic cars, if average price rises by \$250, or 1/0.004. Industry supply increases by 0.004 units, or 4,000 cars ($= 0.004 \times 1,000,000$), with each \$1 increase in average price above the \$16,000 level. The \$16,000 intercept in this supply equation implies that the domestic car industry would not supply any new cars at all if the industry average price fell below \$16,000. At average prices below that level, low-cost imports would supply the entire industry demand.

RELATION BETWEEN SUPPLY CURVE AND SUPPLY FUNCTION

Like the relation between the demand curve and the demand function, the relation between the supply curve and the supply function is very important in managerial decision making. Figure 4.4 shows three supply curves for automobiles: S_A, S, and S_B. S is the

Figure 4.3

A HYPOTHETICAL INDUSTRY SUPPLY CURVE FOR NEW DOMESTIC AUTOMOBILES

For industry prices above \$16,000, the supply-curve parameter estimate (slope coefficient) shows that a \$1 increase in the average price of new automobiles will increase the quantity supplied by 0.004 unit, when units are expressed in millions. Thus, a 4,000-auto rise in quantity demanded follows a \$1 increase in price.

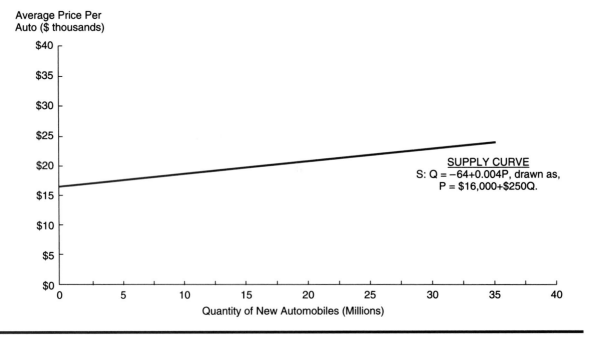

SUPPLY CURVE
S: Q = −64+0.004P, drawn as,
P = \$16,000+\$250Q.

Average Price Per Auto (\$ thousands)

Quantity of New Automobiles (Millions)

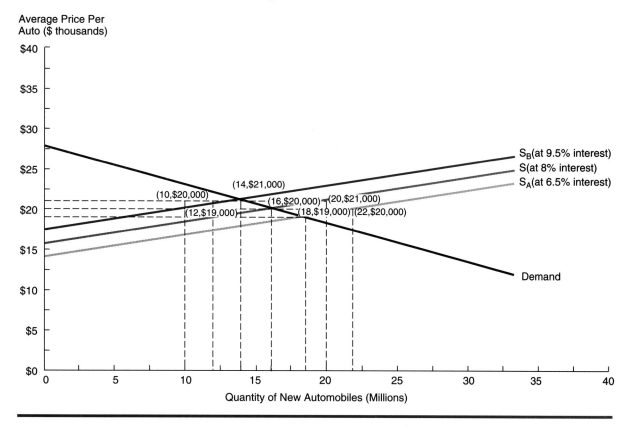

Figure 4.4

HYPOTHETICAL INDUSTRY SUPPLY CURVES FOR NEW DOMESTIC AUTOMOBILES AT INTEREST RATES OF 9.5%, 8%, AND 6.5%

A shift in the original supply curve from S to S_B follows a 1.5% rise in interest rates from 8% to 9.5%; a shift from S to S_A reflects a 1.5% fall in interest rates from 8% to 6.5%.

Average Price Per Auto ($ thousands)

same automobile supply curve determined by Equations 4.9 and 4.10 and shown in Figure 4.3. If S is the appropriate supply curve, then 16 million automobiles would be offered for sale at an industry average price of $20,000. Only 12 million automobiles would be offered for sale at an average price of $19,000; but industry supply would total 20 million automobiles at an average price of $21,000. Such movements along a given supply curve reflect a **change in the quantity supplied.** As average price rises from $19,000 to $20,000 to $21,000 along S, the quantity supplied increases from 12 million to 16 million to 20 million automobiles.

Change in the Quantity Supplied
Movement along a given supply curve reflecting a change in price and quantity.

Supply curves S_A and S_B are similar to S. The differences are that S_A is based on a 6.5% interest rate, whereas S_B assumes a 9.5% interest rate. Recall that S is based on an interest rate assumption of 8%. Since the supply function interest rate parameter is -400, a 1.5% fall in interest rates leads to a 6-unit [$= -400 \times (-0.015)$] increase in automobile supply at each automobile price level. This increase is described as a downward or rightward shift in the original supply curve S to the new supply curve S_A. Conversely, a 1.5% rise in interest rates leads to a 6-unit ($= -400 \times 0.015$) decrease in automobile supply at each automobile price level. This reduction is described as an upward or leftward shift in the original supply curve S to the new supply curve S_B.

To avoid confusion, remember that S_B lies *above* S in Figure 4.4, whereas D_B lies *below* D in Figure 4.2. Similarly, it is important to keep in mind that S_A lies *below* S in Figure 4.4, but D_A lies *above* D in Figure 4.2. These differences stem from the fact that a rise in demand involves an *upward* shift in the demand curve, whereas a fall in demand involves a *downward* shift in the demand curve. Conversely, a rise in supply involves a *downward* shift in the supply curve; a fall in supply involves an *upward* shift in the supply curve.

At a price of $20,000, for example, a 1.5% rise in interest rates reduces automobile supply from 16 million units, the S level, to 10 million units, the S_B level. This reduction in supply reflects the fact that previously profitable production no longer generates a profit because of the increase in capital costs. At a price of $20,000, a 1.5% reduction in interest rates increases automobile supply from 16 million units, the S level, to 22 million units, the S_A level. Supply rises following this decline in interest rates because, given a decline in capital costs, producers find that they can profitably expand output at the $20,000 price level from 16 million to 22 million units.

A **shift in supply,** or a switch from one supply curve to another, indicates a change in one or more of the nonprice variables in the product supply function. In the automobile supply-function example, an increase in truck prices leads to a decrease in automobile supply, since the truck price parameter of -0.001 indicates that automobile supply and truck prices are inversely related. This reflects the fact that as truck prices rise, holding all else constant, auto manufacturers have an incentive to shift from automobile to truck production. When automobile supply is inversely related to a factor such as truck prices, rising truck prices lead to falling automobile supply, and falling truck prices lead to rising automobile supply. From the negative parameters for the price of labor, steel, energy, and interest rates, it is also possible to infer that automobile supply is inversely related to each of these factors as well.

A change in interest rates is not the only factor that might be responsible for a change in the supply curve from S to S_A or S_B. From the steel cost parameter of -0.04, it is possible to infer that supply and steel costs are inversely related. Falling supply follows an increase in steel costs, and rising supply follows a decrease in steel costs. The shift from S to S_B in Figure 4.4, which reflects a decrease in supply, could have resulted from a $150 per ton increase in industry average steel costs rather than a 1.5% increase in interest rates from 8% to 9.5%. Alternatively, this change could result from a $75 per ton increase in industry-average steel costs plus a 0.75% increase in interest rates. In each case, the resulting supply curve is given by the equation $Q = -70 + 0.004P$, or $P = \$17,500 + \$250Q$. Similarly, the shift from S to S_A in Figure 4.4, which reflects an increase in supply, could have resulted from a $150 per ton decrease in industry average steel costs rather than a 1.5% decrease in interest rates from 8% to 6.5%. This change could also result from a $75 per ton decrease in industry average steel costs plus a 1.5% decrease in interest rates. In each case, the resulting supply curve is given by the equation $Q = -58 + \$0.004P$, or $P = \$14,500 + \$250Q$.

For some products, a positive relation between supply and other factors such as weather is often evident. This is especially true for agricultural products. If supply were positively related to weather, perhaps measured in terms of average temperature, then rising supply would follow rising average temperature and falling supply would accompany falling average temperature. Weather is not included in the automobile supply function described here, meaning that there is no close relation between automobile supply and weather.

The distinction between changes in the quantity supplied, which reflect movements along a given supply curve, and a shift in supply, which reflects movement from one supply curve to another, is important, as was the distinction between changes in the quantity demanded and a shift in demand. Since the prices of related products, input prices, taxes, weather, and other factors affecting supply can be expected to vary from one period to the next, assessing the individual importance of each factor becomes a challenging aspect of managerial economics. This topic is explored more fully in Chapters 7 and 8.

Market Equilibrium

Equilibrium
Perfect balance in demand and supply.

Integrating the concepts of demand and supply establishes a framework for understanding how they interact to determine market prices and quantities for all goods and services. When the quantity demanded and the quantity supplied of a product are in perfect balance at a given price, the market for the product is said to be in **equilibrium.** An equilibrium is stable when the factors underlying demand and supply conditions remain unchanged in both the present and the foreseeable future. During those instances when the factors underlying demand and supply are dynamic rather than constant, a change in current market prices and quantities is likely. A temporary market equilibrium of this type is often referred to as an unstable equilibrium. To understand the forces that drive market prices and quantities either up or down to achieve equilibrium, the concepts of surplus and shortage must be introduced.

SURPLUS AND SHORTAGE

Surplus
Excess supply.

Shortage
Excess demand.

A **surplus** is created when producers supply more of a product at a given price than buyers demand. Surplus describes a condition of excess supply. Conversely, a **shortage** is created when buyers demand more of a product at a given price than producers are willing to supply. Shortage describes a condition of excess demand. Neither surplus nor shortage will occur when a market is in equilibrium, since equilibrium is defined as a condition in which the quantities demanded and supplied are exactly in balance at the current market price. Surplus and shortage describe situations of market disequilibrium because either will result in powerful market forces being exerted to change the prices and quantities offered in the market.

To illustrate the concepts of surplus and shortage and, in the process, the concept of market equilibrium, consider the demand and supply curves for the automobile industry

Demand and Supply Conditions for Economists

The forces of demand and supply exert a powerful influence on the market for goods and services, and in the markets for labor and other inputs. An interesting case in point is the economics industry itself.

The demand for economists originates in the private sector, where they are employed in business—usually in staff rather than line positions—as consultants and commentators; in government, where economic analysis often guides public policy; and in academia, where economists are employed in teaching capacities, primarily at the college and university levels.

During recent years, financial economists have made quite a splash on Wall Street, offering their services in the pricing and marketing of complex financial instruments. Although perhaps no more than 500 to 1,000 economists are actually employed in this capacity, the rapid growth of the industry, and bonus-based compensation plans that run into several hundred thousand dollars per year for a handful of stars, have made this business highly visible. Many more economists, perhaps a few thousand, are employed in industry for their forecasting input concerning trends in macroeconomic conditions, as well as for their microeconomic advice concerning pricing, output, and other decisions. The National Association of Business Economists, for example, counts roughly 3,000 members in a wide variety of industries. However, employment in this sector of the industry can be quite cyclical. During the recession of 1991, for example, several brokerages, banks, and other financial institutions trimmed their economics staff considerably. Consulting and speech making, representing a fairly small segment, are the glamour end of the business. Stars such as Lester Thurow, Dean of the Sloan School of Management at the Massachusetts Institute of Technology, have the capacity to earn hundreds of thousands of dollars per year in fees for consulting, speaking engagements, and publishing. The earnings of celebrity economists such as Milton Friedman, John Kenneth Galbraith, Robert Heilbroner, Michael Porter, Paul Samuelson, and Lester Thurow are high in large part because they are so rare. The supply of such "superstars" is severely limited.

In terms of sheer numbers of jobs, the best employment opportunities for economists are in academia, especially for those who hold the doctoral degree. According to *Job Openings for Economists,* a publication of the American Economic Association, roughly 80% to 90% of the total number of job opportunities in economics are in four-year colleges and universities. An overwhelming majority of the roughly 20,000 members of the AEA hold academic jobs.

Since the mid-1970s, the number of new Ph.D.'s in economics has held steady at approximately 750 to 800 per year. This means that the supply of new academic economists is quite high when compared to the number of new Ph.D.'s in related disciplines like accounting, finance, management, and marketing. Each year the number of new Ph.D.'s in economics is basically equivalent to the number of Ph.D.'s granted in all of the functional areas of business administration combined. Academic job market candidates from leading programs in economics count themselves lucky to receive two or three attractive job offers after graduation, whereas similar candidates from leading business programs often enjoy many job opportunities and substantially greater starting salaries.

New Ph.D.'s in accounting, for example, total no more than 75 to 100 per year. At that pace, it will take 20 years to fill current vacancies in accounting. Therefore, it is perhaps not surprising that salaries for new academic Ph.D.'s in economics are in the $40,000 per year range, but they are in excess of $75,000 to $100,000 for Ph.D.'s in business disciplines like financial economics and accounting. What is surprising is how slowly the supply of Ph.D.'s from high-quality doctoral programs in business has grown during recent years. Employment opportunities in the private sector are so attractive that talented accounting undergraduates, for example, do not find the Ph.D. sufficiently rewarding to encourage them to pursue advanced degrees. This might explain the failure of accounting students to pursue advanced degrees, but why don't economics Ph.D. students switch to accounting?

See: John A. Byrne, "Gold Rush in the Ivory Tower," *Business Week,* October 21, 1996, 124-130.

SURPLUS, SHORTAGE, AND MARKET EQUILIBRIUM

Figure 4.5

At an industry average price of $22,000, excess supply creates a surplus of 12 million units exerting downward pressure on both price and output levels. Similarly, excess demand at a price of $18,000 creates a shortage of 12 million units and upward pressure on both prices and output. Market equilibrium is achieved when demand equals supply at a price of $20,000 and quantity of 16 million units.

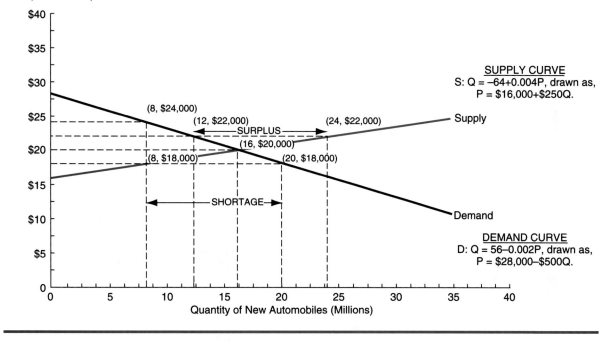

example depicted in Figure 4.5. Note that the demand curve is the same hypothetical demand curve shown in Figure 4.1, and it is also *D* in Figure 4.2. The supply curve shown is the same one illustrated in Figure 4.3, and shown as *S* in Figure 4.4. To clarify the concepts of surplus, shortage, and market equilibrium, it becomes useful to focus on the relation of the quantity supplied and the quantity demanded at each of three different hypothetical market prices.

At a market price of $22,000, the quantity demanded is 12 million units. This is easily derived from Equation 4.4, the market demand curve; $Q_D = 56 - 0.002$ ($22,000) = 12 units, where units are measured in millions of cars. The quantity supplied at an industry average price of $22,000 is derived from the market supply curve, Equation 4.9, which indicates that $Q_S = -64 + 0.004($22,000) = 24$ units, or 24 million cars. At an average automobile price of $22,000, the quantity supplied greatly exceeds the quantity demanded. This difference of 12 million cars per year (= 24 − 12) constitutes a surplus.

An automobile surplus results in a near-term buildup in inventories and pressure for a decline in market prices and production. This is typical for a market with a surplus of product. Prices tend to decline as firms recognize that consumers are unwilling to purchase the quantity of product available at prevailing prices. Similarly, producers cut back on production as inventories build up and prices soften, reducing the quantity of product supplied in future periods. The automobile industry has used rebate programs and dealer-subsidized low-interest-rate financing on new cars to effectively combat the problem of periodic surplus automobile production in the United States and Canada during recent years.

A different type of market imbalance is also illustrated in Figure 4.5. At an average price for new domestic cars of $18,000, the quantity demanded rises to 20 million cars, $Q_D = 56 - 0.002(\$18,000) = 20$. At the same time, the quantity supplied falls to 8 million units, $Q_S = -64 + 0.004(\$18,000) = 8$. This difference of 12 million cars per year $(= 20 - 8)$ constitutes a shortage. Shortage, or excess demand, reflects the fact that, given the current productive capability of the industry (including technology, input prices, and so on), producers cannot profitably supply more than 8 million units of output per year at an average price of $18,000, despite buyer demand for more output.

Shortages exert a powerful upward force on both market prices and output levels. In this example, the demand curve indicates that with only 8 million automobiles supplied, buyers would be willing to pay an industry average price of $24,000 (= $28,000 − $500(8)). Consumers would bid against one another for the limited supply of automobiles and cause prices to rise. The resulting increase in price motivates manufacturers to increase production while reducing the number of buyers willing and able to purchase cars. The resulting increase in the quantity supplied and reduction in quantity demanded work together to eventually eliminate the shortage.

The market situation at a price of $20,000 and a quantity of 16 million automobiles per year is displayed graphically as a balance between the quantity demanded and the quantity supplied. This is a condition of market equilibrium. There is no tendency for change in either price or quantity at a price of $20,000 and a quantity of 16 million units. The graph shows that any price above $20,000 results in surplus production. Prices in this range create excess supply, a buildup in inventories, and pressure for an eventual decline in prices to the $20,000 equilibrium level. At prices below $20,000, shortage occurs, which creates pressure for price increases. With prices moving up, producers are willing to supply more product and the quantity demanded declines, thus reducing the shortage.

Market Equilibrium Price
Market clearing price.

Only a market price of $20,000 brings the quantity demanded and the quantity supplied into perfect balance. This price is referred to as the **market equilibrium price,** or the market clearing price, since it just clears the market of all supplied product. Table 4.3 shows the surplus of quantity supplied at prices above the market equilibrium price and the shortage that results at prices below the market equilibrium price.

In short, surplus describes an excess in the quantity supplied over the quantity demanded at a given market price. A surplus results in downward pressure on both market prices and industry output. Shortage describes an excess in the quantity demanded over the quantity supplied at a given market price. A shortage results in upward pressure on

	SURPLUS, SHORTAGE, AND MARKET EQUILIBRIUM IN THE DOMESTIC AUTOMOBILE INDUSTRY WITH 8% INTEREST RATES

Table 4.3

AVERAGE PRICE FOR DOMESTIC AUTOMOBILES ($) (1)	QUANTITY SUPPLIED (Q_S) (MILLIONS OF CARS) (2)	QUANTITY DEMANDED (Q_D) (MILLIONS OF CARS) (3)	SURPLUS (+) OR SHORTAGE (−) (MILLIONS OF CARS) (4) = (2) − (3)
$30,000	56	0	56
29,000	52	0	52
28,000	48	0	48
27,000	44	2	42
26,000	40	4	36
25,000	36	6	30
24,000	32	8	24
23,000	28	10	18
22,000	24	12	12
21,000	20	14	6
20,000	16	16	0
19,000	12	18	−6
18,000	8	20	−12
17,000	4	22	−18
16,000	0	24	−24
15,000	0	26	−26
14,000	0	28	−28
13,000	0	30	−30
12,000	0	32	−32
11,000	0	34	−34
10,000	0	36	−36

both market prices and industry output. Market equilibrium describes a condition of perfect balance in the quantity demanded and the quantity supplied at a given price. In equilibrium, there is no tendency for change in either price or quantity.

COMPARATIVE STATICS: CHANGING DEMAND

Managers typically control a number of the factors that affect product demand or supply. To make appropriate decisions concerning those variables, it is often useful to know how altering them changes market conditions. Similarly, the direction and magnitude of changes in demand and supply that are due to uncontrollable external factors, such as income or interest rate changes, need to be understood so that managers can develop strategies and make decisions that are consistent with the market conditions they face.

One relatively simple but useful analytical technique is to examine the effects on market equilibrium of changes in economic factors underlying product demand and

$\mathcal{A}O\mathcal{L}$ "Netheads" Learn About Demand and Supply

In December 1996, America Online, Inc. succumbed to competitive pressure from AT&T Corp., MCI, Sprint, and a host of other internet service providers and cut its price for unlimited access to the internet to the industry standard of $19.95 per month. Within a month, usage skyrocketed and subscribers found it tough to log on and access the AOL system. Since flat-rate pricing doesn't penalize unlimited usage, many subscribers simply decided to log on to the AOL service on their desktop PC and leave their connection running all day and night. Because of surging popularity among novice users, longtime subscribers found themselves locked out of the AOL system. Dedicated users became especially irate when AOL kept running TV commercials and offering promotional rates to new subscribers when it was clearly unable to handle the traffic such promotions generated. Subscriber frustration turned to litigation as AOL was hit with several lawsuits charging the company with negligence and consumer fraud because members couldn't access the system for which they had paid.

Overloaded and facing lawsuits and massive defections from dissatisfied customers, AOL made a radical decision. In January 1997, AOL decided to slash marketing efforts aimed at recruiting new subscribers until its system could be upgraded to handle the 8 million customers it already had. That meant pulling a barrage of TV ads and cutting AOL's "carpet bombing" practice of mailing free trial diskettes to millions of PC users. AOL also announced a plan to step up investment in network capacity, from $250 million to $350 million per year.

After touting its achievement of attracting 8 million subscribers, an important selling point to potential advertisers on the AOL system, AOL's marketing retrenchment was a stunning blow to the company's long-term plans. Given the high costs of attracting and retaining subscribers in a viciously price competitive environment, and the enormous computing expenses involved with building the AOL network, the company had been banking on a rapid increase in advertising revenues to stem a growing tide of red ink. In 1996, AOL had been severely criticized for accounting policies that capitalized direct-marketing expenses and amortized such expenditures over a two-

year period. When the company switched to a more realistic approach of writing such sign-up expenses off during the year incurred during the fall of 1996, one-time charges eclipsed all earnings reported since the company became a public entity. Worse still, skyrocketing marketing and infrastructure expenses placed the company in a dangerous position of hemorrhaging cash flow during early 1997. Without a quick infusion of cash from new subscribers and advertisers, AOL's very survival remains in doubt.

To be sure, other internet providers also have problems. AT&T Corp. and NetCom, among others, have suffered embarrassing and costly service interruptions. Like AOL, these other internet service providers suffer from a business plan featuring fixed-rate pricing that encourages unlimited demand, and time-dependent supply costs that are variable with usage. Even with massive new additions to industry capacity, internet technology may simply not work well when scaled up into the millions of subscribers who have no incentive to curtail usage. Unlike local phone service, where fixed costs predominate and marginal usage costs are near zero, a working model for internet service providers may more closely resemble that for long-distance telephone service providers. When costs are closely tied to time of usage, as they are in long-distance service, service provider pricing must be on a per unit basis.

As the internet service provider industry matures, pricing will evolve to reflect the amount and time of usage. With time-based pricing, demand will be curtailed during peak hours and the practice of novice users logging on for days at a time will end. Added revenues will also make possible necessary additions to industry infrastructure (supply). In the meantime, AOL netheads and the frustrated customers of other internet service providers will suffer from demand/supply imbalances created by the industry's fixed-rate pricing plans.

See: Thomas E. Webber, "AOL Plans to Trim Ad Campaign, Boost Network Spending to Tackle Traffic," *The Wall Street Journal,* January 17, 1997, B2.

Comparative Statics Analysis
The study of changing demand and supply conditions.

supply. This is called **comparative statics analysis.** In comparative statics analysis, the role of factors influencing demand is often analyzed while holding supply conditions constant. Similarly, the role of factors influencing supply can be analyzed by studying changes in supply while holding demand conditions constant. Comparing market equilibrium price and output levels before and after various hypothetical changes in demand and supply conditions has the potential to yield useful predictions of expected changes.

Figures 4.6 and 4.7 illustrate the comparative statics of changing demand and supply conditions. Figure 4.6a combines the three automobile demand curves shown in Figure 4.2 with the automobile supply curve *S* of Figure 4.4. The demand-related effects of changes in interest rates on the market price and quantity of automobiles are

Figure 4.6a

THE COMPARATIVE STATICS OF (A) CHANGING DEMAND
OR (B) CHANGING SUPPLY

(a) Holding supply conditions constant, demand will vary with changing interest rates. Demand increases with a fall in interest rates; demand falls as interest rates rise.

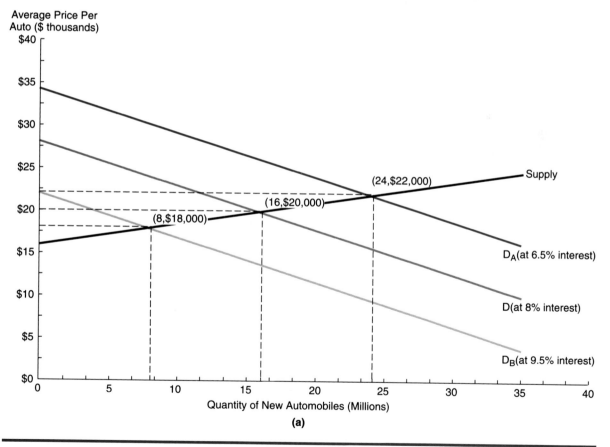

(a)

FIGURE 4.6 CONTINUED

(b) Holding demand conditions constant, supply will vary with changing interest rates. Supply falls with a rise in interest rates; supply rises as interest rates decline.

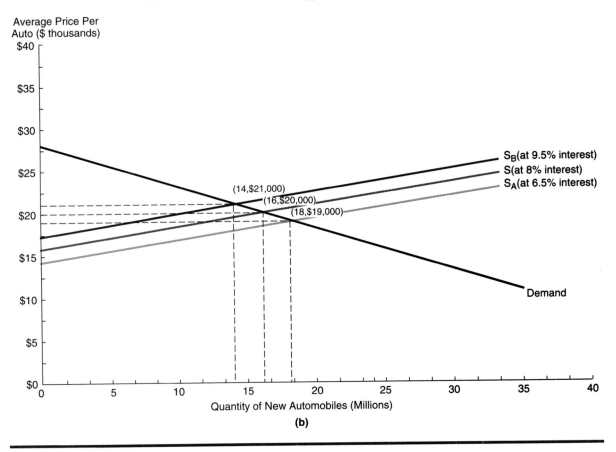

(b)

illustrated. Given the supply curve S, *and assuming for the moment that supply does not change in response to changes in interest rates,* the intersections of the three demand curves with the supply curve indicate the market price and quantity combinations expected at different interest rates.

At the intersection of D_A, which corresponds to a 6.5% interest rate, and the supply curve S, supply and demand are equal at a price of $22,000 and quantity of 24 million units. This result is obtained by simultaneously solving the equations for D_A and S to find the single price and quantity that satisfies both:

$$D_A: Q_D = 68 - 0.002P.$$

$$S: Q_S = -64 + 0.004P.$$

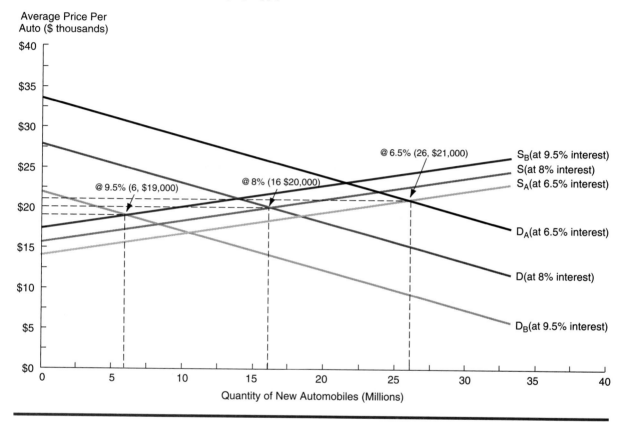

Figure 4.7

THE COMPARATIVE STATICS OF CHANGING DEMAND
AND CHANGING SUPPLY CONDITIONS

The market equilibrium price/output combination reflects the combined effects of changing demand *and* changing supply conditions.

Demand and supply are equal at a price of $22,000 because:

$$Q_D = Q_S$$

$$68 - 0.002P = -64 + 0.004P$$

$$0.006P = 132$$

$$P = \$22,000.$$

The related quantity is found by substituting this $22,000 price into either the demand curve D_A or the supply curve S:

$$D_A: Q_D = 68 - 0.002(\$22,000)$$

$$= 24 \text{ units}$$

$$S: Q_S = -64 + 0.004(\$22,000)$$
$$= 24 \text{ units}$$

Using the same procedure to find the market clearing price-quantity combination for the intersection of D (the demand curve for an 8% interest rate), with S, an equilibrium price of $20,000 and quantity of 16 million units is found. With interest rates at 9.5% (curve D_B), the market clearing price and quantity is $18,000 and 8 million units. Clearly, the level of interest rates plays an important role in the buyer's purchase decision. With higher interest rates, car buyers purchase fewer automobiles and only at progressively lower prices. In part, this reflects the fact that most car purchases are financed, and at higher interest rates the total cost of buying an automobile is greater.

COMPARATIVE STATICS: CHANGING SUPPLY

Figure 4.6b combines the three automobile supply curves shown in Figure 4.4 with the automobile demand curve D of Figure 4.2. The market equilibrium price and quantity effects of changing interest rates are illustrated, holding demand conditions constant *and, in particular, assuming that demand does not change in response to changes in interest rates.* Given the market demand curve D, a 1.5% fall in interest rates from 9.5% to 8% causes the equilibrium quantity supplied to rise from 14 million units on S_B to 16 million units on S; a further 1.5% drop in interest rates from 8% to 6.5% causes the equilibrium quantity supplied to rise from 16 million units on S to 18 million units on S_A. Similarly, in light of the market demand curve D, a 1.5% fall in interest rates from 9.5% to 8% causes the equilibrium price to fall from $21,000 to $20,000; a further 1.5% drop in interest rates from 8% to 6.5% causes the equilibrium price to fall from $20,000 to $19,000. As interest rates fall, producers find that they can profitably supply more output, even as average price falls, given the capital cost savings that would accompany lower interest rates. The effects of lower interest rates on supply are dramatic and reflect the highly capital-intensive nature of the automobile industry.

COMPARATIVE STATICS: CHANGING DEMAND *AND* SUPPLY

From this analysis of hypothetical automobile demand and supply relations, it is clear that interest rates are an important factor influencing demand *and* supply. This is a typical circumstance: Factors related to overall economic activity often have important influences on both demand and supply. Figure 4.7 illustrates the comparative statics of changing demand *and* changing supply conditions by showing the net effects of changing interest rates. Here S_A and D_A, both of which assume a 6.5% interest rate, yield an equilibrium price-output combination of $21,000 and 26 million cars; S and D, which assume an 8% interest rate, yield an equilibrium price-output combination of $20,000 and 16 million units; S_B and D_B, which assume a 9.5% interest rate, result in a price-output equilibrium of $19,000 and 6 million units. These price-output combinations reflect the combined effects of changing interest rates on demand and supply. The comparative statics of changes in any of the other factors that influence demand and supply can be analyzed in a similar fashion.

Summary

This chapter illustrates how the forces of supply and demand combine to establish the prices and quantities observed in the markets for all goods and services.

- **Demand** is the quantity of a good or service that customers are willing and able to purchase during a specified period under a given set of economic conditions. **Direct demand** is the demand for personal consumption products that directly satisfy consumer desires. The value or worth of a good or service, its **utility,** is the prime determinant of direct demand. The demand for all inputs used by a firm is **derived demand** and is determined by the profitability of using various inputs to produce output.

- The market **demand function** for a product is a statement of the relation between the aggregate quantity demanded and all factors that affect this quantity. The **demand curve** is the part of the demand function that expresses the relation between the price charged for a product and the quantity demanded, holding constant the effects of all other variables.

- A **change in the quantity demanded** is a movement along a single given demand curve. A **shift in demand,** or shift from one demand curve to another, reflects a change in one or more of the nonprice variables in the product demand function.

- The term **supply** refers to the quantity of a good or service that producers are willing and able to sell during a certain period and under a given set of conditions. The market **supply function** for a product is a statement of the relation between the quantity supplied and all factors affecting that quantity. A **supply curve** expresses the relation between the price charged for a product and the quantity supplied, holding constant the effects of all other variables.

- Movements along a given supply curve reflect a **change in the quantity supplied.** A **shift in supply,** or a switch from one supply curve to another, indicates a change in one or more of the nonprice variables in the product supply function.

- A market is in **equilibrium** when the quantity demanded and the quantity supplied of a product are in perfect balance at a given price. **Surplus** describes a condition of excess supply. A **shortage** is created when buyers demand more of a product at a given price than producers are willing to supply. The **market equilibrium price,** or market clearing price, just clears the market of all supplied product.

- In **comparative statics analysis,** the role of factors influencing demand or supply is analyzed while holding all else equal.

A fundamental understanding of demand and supply concepts is essential to the successful operation of any economic organization. The concepts introduced in this chapter provide the structure for the more detailed analysis of demand and supply in subsequent chapters and thereby make an important contribution to managerial economics.

QUESTIONS

Q4.1   What key ingredients are necessary for the creation of economic demand?

Q4.2   Describe the difference between direct demand and derived demand.

Q4.3 Explain the rationale for each of the demand variables in Equation 4.1.

Q4.4 Distinguish between a demand function and a demand curve. What is the difference between a change in the quantity demanded and a shift in the demand curve?

Q4.5 What key ingredients are necessary for the creation of economic supply?

Q4.6 Explain the rationale for each of the supply variables in Equation 4.5.

Q4.7 Distinguish between a supply function and a supply curve. What is the difference between a change in the quantity supplied and a shift in the supply curve?

Q4.8 "Dynamic rather than static demand and supply conditions are typically observed in real-world markets. Therefore, comparative statics analysis has only limited value." Discuss this statement.

Q4.9 Contrast the supply and demand conditions for new Ph.D.'s in economics and accounting. Why do such large differences in starting salaries seem to persist over time?

Q4.10 "A famous economist once argued, 'Supply creates its own demand.' It would have been more accurate to argue 'Demand creates its own supply.'" Discuss this statement.

SELF-TEST PROBLEMS AND SOLUTIONS

ST4.1 **Demand and Supply Curves.** The following relations describe demand and supply conditions in the lumber/forest products industry:

$$Q_D = 80,000 - 20,000P, \quad \text{(Demand)}$$

$$Q_S = -20,000 + 20,000P, \quad \text{(Supply)}$$

where Q is quantity measured in thousands of board feet (one square foot of lumber, one inch thick) and P is price in dollars.

A. Set up a table or spreadsheet to illustrate the effect of price (P), on the quantity supplied (Q_S), quantity demanded (Q_D), and the resulting surplus (+) or shortage (−) as represented by the difference between the quantity demanded and the quantity supplied at various price levels. Calculate the value for each respective variable based on a range for P from $1.00 to $3.50 in increments of 10¢ (i.e., $1.00, $1.10, $1.20, . . . $3.50).

B. Using price (P) on the vertical or y-axis and quantity (Q) on the horizontal or x-axis, plot the demand and supply curves for the lumber/forest products industry over the range of prices indicated previously.

ST4.1 **SOLUTION**

A. A table or spreadsheet that illustrates the effect of price (P), on the quantity supplied (Q_S), quantity demanded (Q_D), and the resulting surplus (+) or shortage (−) as represented by the difference between the quantity demanded and the quantity supplied at various price levels is shown in the next column:

LUMBER AND FOREST INDUSTRY SUPPLY
AND DEMAND RELATIONSHIPS

PRICE	QUANTITY DEMANDED	QUANTITY SUPPLIED	SURPLUS (+) OR SHORTAGE (−)
$1.00	60,000	0	−60,000
1.10	58,000	2,000	−56,000
1.20	56,000	4,000	−52,000
1.30	54,000	6,000	−48,000
1.40	52,000	8,000	−44,000
1.50	50,000	10,000	−40,000
1.60	48,000	12,000	−36,000
1.70	46,000	14,000	−32,000
1.80	44,000	16,000	−28,000
1.90	42,000	18,000	−24,000
2.00	40,000	20,000	−20,000
2.10	38,000	22,000	−16,000
2.20	36,000	24,000	−12,000
2.30	34,000	26,000	−8,000
2.40	32,000	28,000	−4,000
2.50	30,000	30,000	0
2.60	28,000	32,000	4,000
2.70	26,000	34,000	8,000
2.80	24,000	36,000	12,000
2.90	22,000	38,000	16,000
3.00	20,000	40,000	20,000
3.10	18,000	42,000	24,000
3.20	16,000	44,000	28,000
3.30	14,000	46,000	32,000
3.40	12,000	48,000	36,000
3.50	10,000	50,000	40,000

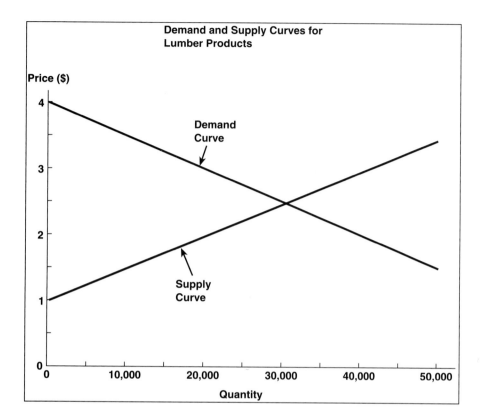

B. Using price (P) on the vertical or y-axis and quantity (Q) on the horizontal or x-axis, a plot of the demand and supply curves for the lumber/forest products industry is shown above.

ST4.2 **Supply Curve Determination.** Information Technology, Inc., is a supplier of math coprocessors (computer chips) used to speed the processing of data for analysis on personal computers. Based on an analysis of monthly cost and output data, the company has estimated the following relation between the marginal cost of production and monthly output:

$$MC = \$100 + \$0.004Q.$$

A. Calculate the marginal cost of production at 2,500, 5,000, and 7,500 units of output.

B. Express output as a function of marginal cost. Calculate the level of output when $MC = \$100$, $\$125$, and $\$150$.

C. Calculate the profit-maximizing level of output if wholesale prices are stable in the industry at $\$150$ per chip and, therefore, $P = MR = \$150$.

D. Derive the company's supply curve for chips assuming $P = MR$. Express price as a function of quantity and quantity as a function of price.

ST4.2 **SOLUTION**

A. Marginal production costs at each level of output are:

$$Q = 2{,}500:\ MC = \$100 + \$0.004(2{,}500)$$
$$= \$110$$

$$Q = 5{,}000:\ MC = \$100 + \$0.004(5{,}000)$$
$$= \$120$$

$$Q = 7{,}500:\ MC = \$100 + \$0.004(7{,}500)$$
$$= \$130$$

B. When output is expressed as a function of marginal cost:

$$MC = \$100 + \$0.004Q$$

$$0.004Q = -100 + MC$$

$$Q = -25{,}000 + 250MC$$

The level of output at each respective level of marginal cost is:

$$MC = \$100: Q = -25{,}000 + 250(\$100) = 0$$

$$MC = \$125: Q = -25{,}000 + 250(\$125)$$
$$= 6{,}250$$

$$MC = \$150: Q = -25{,}000 + 250(\$150)$$
$$= 12{,}500$$

C. Note from Part B that $MC = \$150$ when $Q = 12{,}500$. Therefore, when $MR = \$150$, $Q = 12{,}500$ will be the profit-maximizing level of output. More formally:

$$MR = MC$$

$$\$150 = \$100 + \$0.004Q$$

$$0.004Q = 50$$

$$Q = 12{,}500$$

D. Since prices are stable in the industry, $P = MR$, this means that the company will supply chips at the level of output where:

$$MR = MC$$

and, therefore, that:

$$P = \$100 + \$0.004Q$$

This is the supply curve for math chips, where price is expressed as a function of quantity. When quantity is expressed as a function of price:

$$P = \$100 + \$0.004Q$$

$$0.004Q = -100 + P$$

$$Q = -25{,}000 + 250P$$

PROBLEMS

P4.1 **Demand and Supply Curves.** The following relations describe monthly demand and supply conditions in the metropolitan area for recyclable aluminum:

$$Q_D = 317{,}500 - 10{,}000P, \text{ (Demand)}$$

$$Q_S = 2{,}500 + 7{,}500P, \quad \text{(Supply)}$$

where Q is quantity measured in pounds of scrap aluminum and P is price in cents.
Complete the following table:

PRICE (1)	QUANTITY SUPPLIED (2)	QUANTITY DEMANDED (3)	SURPLUS (+) OR SHORTAGE (−) (4) = (2) − (3)
15¢			
16			
17			
18			
19			
20			

P4.2 **Demand and Supply Curves.** The following relations describe monthly demand and supply rela-

tions for dry cleaning services in the metropolitan area:

$$Q_D = 500{,}000 - 50{,}000P, \quad \text{(Demand)}$$

$$Q_S = -100{,}000 + 100{,}000P, \quad \text{(Supply)}$$

where Q is quantity measured by the number of items dry cleaned per month and P is average price in dollars.
A. At what average price level would demand equal zero?
B. At what average price level would supply equal zero?
C. Calculate the equilibrium price/output combination.

P4.3 **Demand Analysis.** The demand for housing is often described as being highly cyclical and very sensitive to housing prices and interest rates. Given these characteristics, describe the effect of each of the following in terms of whether it would increase or decrease the quantity demanded or the demand for housing. Moreover, when price is expressed as a function of quantity, indicate whether the effect of each of the following is an upward or downward

movement along a given demand curve or involves an outward or inward shift in the relevant demand curve for housing. Explain your answers.
A. An increase in housing prices
B. A fall in interest rates
C. A rise in interest rates
D. A severe economic recession
E. A robust economic expansion

P4.4 **Demand and Supply Curves.** Demand and supply conditions in the market for unskilled labor are important concerns to business and government decision makers. Consider the case of a federally mandated minimum wage set above the equilibrium, or market clearing, wage level. Some of the following factors have the potential to influence the demand or quantity demanded of unskilled labor. Influences on the supply or quantity supplied may also result. Holding all else equal, describe these influences as increasing or decreasing, and indicate the direction of the resulting movement along or shift in the relevant curve(s).
A. An increase in the quality of secondary education.
B. A rise in welfare benefits.
C. An increase in the popularity of self-service gas stations, car washes, and so on.
D. A fall in interest rates.
E. An increase in the minimum wage.

P4.5 **Demand Function.** The Creative Publishing Company (CPC) is a coupon book publisher with markets in several southeastern states. CPC coupon books are either sold directly to the public, sold through religious and other charitable organizations, or given away as promotional items. Operating experience during the past year suggests the following demand function for CPC's coupon books:

$$Q = 5,000 - 4,000P + 0.02Pop + 0.5I$$
$$+ 1.5A,$$

where Q is quantity, P is price ($), Pop is population, I is disposable income per household ($), and A is advertising expenditures ($).
A. Determine the demand faced by CPC in a typical market in which $P = \$10$, $Pop = 1,000,000$ persons, $I = \$30,000$, and $A = \$10,000$.

B. Calculate the level of demand if CPC increases annual advertising expenditures from $10,000 to $15,000.
C. Calculate the demand curves faced by CPC in Parts A and B.

P4.6 **Demand Curves.** The Eastern Shuttle, Inc., is a regional airline providing shuttle service between New York and Washington, D.C. An analysis of the monthly demand for service has revealed the following demand relation:

$$Q = 26,000 - 500P - 250P_{OG} + 200I_B$$
$$- 5,000S,$$

where Q is quantity measured by the number of passengers per month, P is price ($), P_{OG} is a regional price index for other consumer goods (1967 = 1.00), I_B is an index of business activity, and S, a binary or dummy variable, equals 1 in summer months and 0 otherwise.
A. Determine the demand curve facing the airline during the winter month of January if $P_{OG} = 4$ and $I_B = 250$.
B. Determine the demand curve facing the airline, quantity demanded, and total revenues during the summer month of July if $P = \$100$ and all other price-related and business activity variables are as specified previously.

P4.7 **Supply Function.** A review of industrywide data for the jelly and jam manufacturing industry suggests the following industry supply function:

$$Q = -59,000,000 + 500,000P - 250,000P_L$$
$$- 500,000P_K + 2,000,000W,$$

where Q is cases supplied per year, P is the wholesale price per case ($), P_L is the average price paid for unskilled labor ($), P_K is the average price of capital (in percent), and W is weather measured by the average seasonal rainfall in growing areas (in inches).
A. Determine the industry supply curve for a recent year when $P_L = \$4$, $P_K = 10$ percent, and $W = 20$ inches of rainfall. Show the industry supply curve with quantity expressed as a function of price and price expressed as a function of quantity.
B. Calculate the quantity supplied by the industry at prices of $50, $60, and $70 per case.
C. Calculate the prices necessary to generate a supply of 4 million, 6 million, and 8 million cases.

P4.8 **Supply Curve Determination.** Olympia Natural Resources, Inc., and Yakima Lumber, Ltd., supply cut logs (raw lumber) to lumber and paper mills located in the Cascade Mountain region in the state of Washington. Each company has a different marginal cost of production depending on its own cost of landowner access, labor and other cutting costs, the distance cut logs must be shipped, and so on. The marginal cost of producing one unit of output, measured as one thousand board feet of lumber (where one board foot is one square foot of lumber, one inch thick), is:

$$MC_O = \$350 + \$0.00005Q_O. \text{ (Olympia)}$$

$$MC_Y = \$150 + \$0.0002Q_Y. \quad \text{(Yakima)}$$

The wholesale market for cut logs is vigorously price competitive, and neither firm is able to charge a premium for its products. Thus, $P = MR$ in this market.

A. Determine the supply curve for each firm. Express price as a function of quantity and quantity as a function of price. (Hint: Set $P = MR = MC$ to find each firm's supply curve.)

B. Calculate the quantity supplied by each firm at prices of $325, $350, and $375. What is the minimum price necessary for each individual firm to supply output?

C. Assuming these two firms make up the entire industry in the local area, determine the industry supply curve when $P < \$350$.

D. Determine the industry supply curve when $P > \$350$. To check your answer, calculate quantity at an industry price of $375 and compare your result with Part B.

P4.9 **Supply Curve Determination.** Cornell Pharmaceutical, Inc., and Penn Medical, Ltd., supply generic drugs to treat a wide variety of illnesses. A major product for each company is a generic equivalent of an antibiotic used to treat postoperative infections. Proprietary cost and output information for each company reveal the following relations between marginal cost and output:

$$MC_C = \$10 + \$0.004Q_C. \quad \text{(Cornell)}$$

$$MC_P = \$8 + \$0.008Q_P. \quad \text{(Penn)}$$

The wholesale market for generic drugs is vigorously price competitive, and neither firm is able to charge a premium for its products. Thus, $P = MR$ in this market.

A. Determine the supply curve for each firm. Express price as a function of quantity and quantity as a function of price. (Hint: Set $P = MR = MC$ to find each firm's supply curve.)

B. Calculate the quantity supplied by each firm at prices of $8, $10, and $12. What is the minimum price necessary for each individual firm to supply output?

C. Assuming these two firms make up the entire industry, determine the industry supply curve when $P < \$10$.

D. Determine the industry supply curve when $P > \$10$. To check your answer, calculate quantity at an industry price of $12 and compare your answer with Part B.

P4.10 **Market Equilibrium.** Eye-de-ho Potatoes is a product of the Coeur d'Alene Growers' Association. Producers in the area are able to switch back and forth between potato and wheat production depending on market conditions. Similarly, consumers tend to regard potatoes and wheat (bread and bakery products) as substitutes. As a result, the demand and supply of Eye-de-ho Potatoes are highly sensitive to changes in both potato and wheat prices.

Demand and supply functions for Eye-de-ho Potatoes are as follows:

$$Q_D = -1,450 - 25P + 12.5P_W + 0.2Y,$$
$$\text{(Demand)}$$

$$Q_S = -100 + 75P - 25P_W - 12.5P_L + 10R,$$
$$\text{(Supply)}$$

where P is the average wholesale price of Eye-de-ho Potatoes ($ per bushel), P_W is the average wholesale price of wheat ($ per bushel), Y is income (GNP in $ billions), P_L is the average price of unskilled labor ($ per hour), and R is the average annual rainfall (in inches). Both Q_D and Q_S are in millions of bushels of potatoes.

A. When quantity is expressed as a function of price, what are the Eye-de-ho Potatoes demand and supply curves if $P = \$2$, $P_W = \$4$, $Y = \$7,500$ billion, $P_L = \$8$, and $R = 20$ inches?

B. Calculate the surplus or shortage of Eye-de-ho Potatoes when $P = \$1.50, \$2$, and $2.50.

C. Calculate the market equilibrium price/output combination.

Case Study for Chapter 4

A SPREADSHEET ANALYSIS OF PRODUCT DEMAND
AND SUPPLY CONDITIONS

Spreadsheet analysis is an appropriate means for studying the demand and supply effects of possible changes in various exogenous and endogenous variables. Endogenous variables include all important demand and supply-related factors that are within the control of the firm. Examples include product pricing, advertising, product design, and so on. Exogenous variables consist of all significant demand and supply-related influences that are beyond the control of the firm. Examples include competitor pricing, competitor advertising, weather, general economic conditions, and related factors.

In comparative statics analysis, the marginal influence on demand and supply of a change in any one factor can be isolated and studied in depth. The advantage of this approach is that causal relationships can be identified and responded to, if appropriate. The disadvantage of this marginal approach is that it becomes rather tedious to investigate the marginal effects of a wide range of demand and supply influences. It is here that spreadsheet analysis of demand and supply conditions becomes useful. Using spreadsheet analysis, it is possible to learn the demand and supply implications of an almost limitless range of operating scenarios. Rather than calculating the effects of only a few possibilities, it is feasible to consider even rather unlikely outcomes. A complete picture can be drawn of the firm's operating environment, and strategies for responding to a host of operating conditions can be drawn up.

To illustrate this process, consider the case of Sunbest Orange Juice, a product of California's Orange County Growers' Association. Both demand and supply of the product are highly sensitive to changes in the weather. During hot summer months, demand for Sunbest and other beverages grows rapidly. On the other hand, hot, dry weather has an adverse effect on supply by reducing the size of the orange crop.

Demand and supply functions for Sunbest are as follows:

$$Q_D = 12,275,000 - 2,500,000P + 200,000P_S \\ + 75Y + 5,000T \qquad \text{(Demand)}$$

$$Q_S = -27,450 + 6,000,000P - 240,000P_L \\ - 220,000P_K - 200,000T \qquad \text{(Supply)},$$

where P is the average wholesale price of Sunbest (\$ per case), P_S is the average wholesale price of canned soda (\$ per case), Y is disposable income per household (\$), T is the average daily high temperature (degrees), P_L is the average price of unskilled labor (\$ per hour), and P_K is the risk-adjusted cost of capital (in percent).

During the coming planning period, a wide variety of operating conditions is possible. To gauge the sensitivity of demand and supply to changes in these operating conditions, a number of scenarios that employ a range from optimistic to relatively pessimistic assumptions are shown on page 162.

OPERATING ENVIRONMENT FOR DEMAND	PRICE OF SUNBEST (P)	PRICE OF SODA (P_S)	DISPOSABLE INCOME (I)	TEMPERATURE (T)
Optimistic Scenario 1	$5.00	$4.00	$39,500	78.75
2	4.80	4.10	39,400	79.00
3	4.60	4.20	39,300	79.25
4	4.40	4.30	39,200	79.50
5	4.20	4.40	39,100	79.75
6	4.00	4.50	39,000	80.00
7	3.80	4.60	38,900	80.25
8	3.60	4.70	38,800	80.50
9	3.40	4.80	38,700	80.75
Pessimistic Scenario 10	3.20	4.90	38,600	81.00

OPERATING ENVIRONMENT FOR SUPPLY	PRICE OF SUNBEST (P)	PRICE OF LABOR (P_L)	COST OF CAPITAL (P_K)	TEMPERTURE (T)
Optimistic Scenario 1	$5.00	$8.00	9.00%	78.00
2	4.80	8.15	9.25%	77.75
3	4.60	8.30	9.50%	77.50
4	4.40	8.45	9.75%	77.25
5	4.20	8.60	10.00%	77.00
6	4.00	8.75	10.25%	76.75
7	3.80	8.90	10.50%	76.50
8	3.60	9.05	10.75%	76.25
9	3.40	9.20	11.00%	76.00
Pessimistic Scenario 10	3.20	9.35	11.25%	75.75

Demand and supply functions for Sunbest orange juice can be combined with data on the operating environment to construct estimates of demand, supply, and the amount of surplus or shortage under each operating scenario.

A. Set up a table or spreadsheet to illustrate the effects of changing economic assumptions on the demand for Sunbest orange juice. Use the demand function to calculate demand based on three different underlying assumptions concerning changes in the operating environment. First, assume that all demand factors change in unison from levels indicated in the Optimistic Scenario #1 to the levels indicated in Pessimistic Scenario #10. Second, fix all demand factors except the price of Sunbest at Scenario #6 levels, and then calculate the quantity demanded at each scenario

price level. Finally, fix all demand factors except temperature at Scenario #6 levels, and then calculate demand at each scenario temperature level.

B. Set up a table or spreadsheet to illustrate the effects of changing economic assumptions on the supply of Sunbest orange juice. Use the supply function to calculate supply based on three different underlying assumptions concerning changes in the operating environment. First, assume that all supply factors change in unison from levels indicated in the Optimistic Scenario #1 to the levels indicated in Pessimistic Scenario #10. Second, fix all supply factors except the price of Sunbest at Scenario #6 levels, and then calculate the quantity supplied at each scenario price level. Finally, fix all supply factors except temperature at Scenario

#6 levels, and then calculate supply at each scenario temperature level.

C.   Set up a table or spreadsheet to illustrate the effect of changing economic assumptions on the surplus or shortage of Sunbest orange juice that results from each scenario detailed in Part A and

Part B. Which operating scenario results in market equilibrium?

D.   Are demand and supply more sensitive to changes in the price of Sunbest or to changes in temperature?

Wired Ventures, Inc., American Cybercast, and Slate, *Microsoft's Web-based political magazine, all thought the internet was a pot of gold at the end of the information highway. They were wrong. In late-1996, Wired canceled an initial public offering of its common stock amid investor skepticism that the company will ever make money. Similarly, California-based American Cybercast, known for its Generation X drama called "The Spot," announced that it would fold in January 1997 unless it found a buyer. In a tongue-in-cheek announcement, editor Michael Kinsley said that* Slate *would forego a planned charge of $19.95 per year because, "Right now there are too many people that are too dammed cheap . . . er, we mean . . . too engaged by the novelty of the medium to pay extra for content."[1] Even in a communications revolution, there is no getting around business fundamentals. Successful companies must meet customer preferences at price points that offer real value.*

Identifying profitable price points is especially difficult in a medium so new as Web publishing. For example, Dow Jones, Inc. was delighted with the initial response to publication of the Wall Street Journal Interactive edition; about 600,000 signed on as registered users when the service was offered for free before September 1996. However, demand fell to only 50,000 users when a modest fee was imposed—just $29 per year for subscribers to the Journal's print edition, $49 per year for nonsubscribers. Apparently, quantity demanded is especially sensitive, or elastic, with respect to price in cyberspace.

Nothing is more important in business than the need to identify and effectively meet customer demand. This chapter examines the elasticity concept as a useful means for quantifying the magnitude and sensitivity of demand to changes in underlying conditions.

Demand Sensitivity Analysis: Elasticity

For constructive managerial decision making, the firm must know the sensitivity or responsiveness of demand to changes in factors that make up the underlying demand function.

---

[1]See Don Clark, "Facing Early Losses, Some Web Publishers Begin to Pull the Plug," *The Wall Street Journal*, January 17, 1997, A1.

THE ELASTICITY CONCEPT

Elasticity
The percentage change in a dependent variable resulting from a 1% change in an independent variable.

One measure of responsiveness employed not only in demand analysis but throughout managerial decision making is **elasticity,** defined as the percentage change in a dependent variable, Y, resulting from a 1% change in the value of an independent variable, X. The equation for calculating elasticity is

$$Elasticity = \frac{Percentage\ Change\ in\ Y}{Percentage\ Change\ in\ X}. \tag{5.1}$$

The concept of elasticity simply involves the percentage change in one variable associated with a given percentage change in another variable. In addition to being used in demand analysis, the concept is used in finance, where the impact of changes in sales on earnings under different production levels (operating leverage) and different financial structures (financial leverage) are measured by an elasticity factor. Elasticities are also used in production and cost analysis to evaluate the effects of changes in input on output as well as the effects of output changes on costs.

Endegenous Variables
Factors controlled by the firm.

Exogenous Variables
Factors outside the control of the firm.

Factors such as price and advertising that are within the control of the firm are called **endogenous variables.** It is important that management know the effects of altering these variables when making decisions. Other important factors outside the control of the firm, such as consumer incomes, competitor prices, and the weather, are called **exogenous variables.** The effects of changes in both types of influences must be understood if the firm is to respond effectively to changes in the economic environment. For example, a firm must understand the effects on demand of changes in both prices and consumer incomes to determine the price cut necessary to offset a decline in sales caused by a business recession (fall in income). Similarly, the sensitivity of demand to changes in advertising must be quantified if the firm is to respond appropriately with price or advertising changes to an increase in competitor advertising. Determining the effects of changes in both controllable and uncontrollable influences on demand is the focus of demand analysis.

POINT ELASTICITY AND ARC ELASTICITY

Point Elasticity
Elasticity at a given point on a function.

Arc Elasticity
Average elasticity over a given range of a function.

Elasticity can be measured in two different ways, point elasticity and arc elasticity. **Point elasticity** measures elasticity at a given point on a function. The point elasticity concept is used to measure the effect on a dependent variable Y of a very small or marginal change in an independent variable X. Although the point elasticity concept can often give accurate estimates of the effect on Y of very small (less than 5%) changes in X, it is not used to measure the effect on Y of large-scale changes, because elasticity typically varies at different points along a function. To assess the effects of large-scale changes in X, the arc elasticity concept is employed. **Arc elasticity** measures the average elasticity over a given range of a function.

Using the lowercase epsilon as the symbol for point elasticity, the point elasticity formula is written

$$Point\ Elasticity = \epsilon_X = \frac{Percentage\ Change\ in\ Y}{Percentage\ Change\ in\ X},$$

$$= \frac{\Delta Y/Y}{\Delta X/X}, \tag{5.2}$$

$$= \frac{\Delta Y}{\Delta X} \times \frac{X}{Y}.$$

The $\Delta Y/\Delta X$ term in the point elasticity formula is the marginal relation between Y and X, and it shows the effect on Y of a one-unit change in X. Point elasticity is determined by multiplying this marginal relation by the relative size of X to Y, or the X/Y ratio at the point being analyzed.

Point elasticity measures the percentage effect on Y of a percentage change in X at a given point on a function. If $\epsilon_X = 5$, a 1% increase in X will lead to a 5% increase in Y, and a 1% decrease in X will lead to a 5% decrease in Y. Thus, when $\epsilon_X > 0$, Y changes in the same positive or negative direction as X. Conversely, when $\epsilon_X < 0$, Y changes in the opposite direction of changes in X. For example, if $\epsilon_X = -3$, a 1% increase in X will lead to a 3% decrease in Y, and a 1% decrease in X will lead to a 3% increase in Y.

An example can be used to illustrate the calculation and use of a point elasticity estimate. Assume that management is interested in analyzing the responsiveness of movie ticket demand to changes in advertising for the Empire State Cinema, a regional chain of movie theaters. Also assume that analysis of monthly data for six outlets covering the past year suggests the following demand function:

$$Q = 6,600 - 5,000P + 3,500P_V + 35I + 1,000A, \tag{5.3}$$

where Q is the quantity of movie tickets, P is average ticket price (in dollars), P_V is the three-day movie rental price at video outlets in the area (in dollars), I is average disposable income per household (in thousands of dollars), and A is monthly advertising expenditures (in thousands of dollars). (Note that I and A are expressed in thousands of dollars in this demand function.) For a typical theater, $P = \$6$, $P_V = \$2$, and income and advertising are \$40,000 and \$20,000, respectively. The demand for movie tickets at a typical theater can be estimated as

$$Q = 11,600 - 5,000(6) + 3,500(2) + 35(40) + 1,000(20)$$

$$= 10,000.$$

The numbers that appear before each variable in Equation 5.3 are called coefficients or parameter estimates. They indicate the expected change in movie ticket sales associated with a one-unit change in each relevant variable. For example, the number 5,000 indicates that the quantity of movie tickets demanded falls by 5,000 units with every \$1 increase in the price of movie tickets, or $\Delta Q/\Delta P = -5,000$. Similarly, a \$1 increase in the price of videocassette rentals causes a 3,500-unit increase in movie ticket demand, or $\Delta Q/\Delta P_V = 3,500$; a \$1,000 (one-unit) increase in disposable income per household leads to a 35-unit increase in demand. In terms of advertising, the expected change in demand following a one-unit (\$1,000) change in advertising, or $\Delta Q/\Delta A$, is

1,000. With advertising expenditures of $20,000, the point advertising elasticity at the 10,000-unit demand level is

$$\epsilon_A = Point\ Advertising\ Elasticity$$

$$= \frac{Percentage\ Change\ in\ Quantity\ (Q)}{Percentage\ Change\ in\ Advertising\ (A)}$$

$$= \frac{\Delta Q/Q}{\Delta A/A}$$

$$= \frac{\Delta Q}{\Delta A} \times \frac{A}{Q}$$

(5.4)

$$= 1,000 \times \frac{\$20}{10,000}$$

$$= 2.$$

Thus, a 1% change in advertising expenditures results in a 2% change in movie ticket demand. This elasticity is positive, indicating a direct relation between advertising outlays and movie ticket demand. An increase in advertising expenditures leads to higher demand; a decrease in advertising leads to lower demand.

For many business decisions, managers are concerned with the impact of substantial changes in a demand-determining factor, such as advertising, rather than with the impact of very small (marginal) changes. In these instances the point elasticity concept suffers a conceptual shortcoming.

To see the nature of the problem, consider the calculation of the advertising elasticity of demand for movie tickets as advertising increases from $20,000 to $50,000. Assume that all other demand-influencing variables retain their previous values. With advertising at $20,000, demand is 10,000 units. Changing advertising to $50,000 ($\Delta A = 30$) results in a 30,000-unit increase in movie ticket demand, so total demand at that level is 40,000 tickets. Using Equation 5.2 to calculate the advertising point elasticity for the change in advertising from $20,000 to $50,000 indicates that

$$Advertising\ Elasticity = \frac{\Delta Q}{\Delta A} \times \frac{A}{Q} = \frac{30,000}{\$30} \times \frac{\$20}{10,000} = 2.$$

The advertising point elasticity is $\epsilon_A = 2$, just as that found previously. Consider, however, the indicated elasticity if one moves in the opposite direction—that is, if advertising is decreased from $50,000 to $20,000. The indicated elasticity point is

$$Advertising\ Elasticity = \frac{\Delta Q}{\Delta A} \times \frac{A}{Q} = \frac{-30,000}{-\$30} \times \frac{\$50}{40,000} = 1.25.$$

The indicated elasticity $\epsilon_A = 1.25$ is now quite different. This problem occurs because elasticities are not typically constant but vary at different points along a given demand function. The advertising elasticity of 1.25 is the advertising point elasticity when advertising expenditures are $50,000 and the quantity demanded is 40,000 tickets.

To overcome the problem of changing elasticities along a demand function, the arc elasticity formula was developed to calculate an average elasticity for incremental as opposed to marginal changes. The arc elasticity formula is

$$E = \text{Arc Elasticity} = \frac{\dfrac{\text{Change in } Q}{\text{Average } Q}}{\dfrac{\text{Change in } X}{\text{Average } X}} = \frac{\dfrac{Q_2 - Q_1}{(Q_2 + Q_1)/2}}{\dfrac{X_2 - X_1}{(X_2 + X_1)/2}}$$

$$= \frac{\dfrac{\Delta Q}{(Q_2 + Q_1)}}{\dfrac{\Delta X}{(X_2 + X_1)}} = \frac{\Delta Q}{\Delta X} \times \frac{X_2 + X_1}{Q_2 + Q_1}$$

(5.5)

The percentage change in quantity demanded is divided by the percentage change in a demand-determining variable, but the bases used to calculate percentage changes are averages of the two data endpoints rather than the initially observed value. The arc elasticity equation eliminates the problem of the elasticity measure depending on which end of the range is viewed as the initial point. This yields a more accurate measure of the relative relation between the two variables over the *range* indicated by the data. The advertising arc elasticity over the $20,000–$50,000 range of advertising expenditures can be calculated as

$$\text{Advertising Arc Elasticity} = \frac{\text{Percentage Change in Quantity } (Q)}{\text{Percentage Change in Advertising } (A)}$$

$$= \frac{(Q_2 - Q_1)/(Q_2 + Q_1)}{(A_2 - A_1)/(A_2 + A_1)}$$

$$= \frac{\Delta Q}{\Delta A} \times \frac{A_2 + A_1}{Q_2 + Q_1}$$

$$= \frac{30,000}{\$30} \times \frac{\$50 + \$20}{40,000 + 10,000}$$

$$= 1.4.$$

Thus, a 1% change in the level of advertising expenditures in the range of $20,000 to $50,000 results, on average, in a 1.4% change in movie ticket demand.

To summarize, it is important to remember that point elasticity is a marginal concept. It measures the elasticity at a specific point on a function. Proper use of point elasticity is limited to analysis of very small changes, say 0% to 5%, in the relevant independent variable. Arc elasticity is a better concept for measuring the average elasticity over an extended range when the change in a relevant independent variable is 5% or more. It is the appropriate tool for incremental analysis.

	MANAGERIAL APPLICATION
What's in a Name?	**5.1**

When words become unforgettably associated with innovative new products, the result can spell trouble. Aspirin, brassiere, cellophane, escalator, linoleum, yo-yo, and zipper are all products that lost distinctiveness because their trademarks fell into common usage. All of these products and trademarks suffered from *too much* success. Either their product was as new and innovative as its name, or the trademark seemed to be especially well suited to the underlying product.

Owners of such modern-day trademarks as *Astroturf, Coke, Frisbee, Kleenex, Kitty Litter, Styrofoam, Walkman,* and *Xerox* employ a veritable army of lawyers in an endless struggle against the dreaded lower case "generic" treatment. Actually, the threat of such "genericide" is quite remote, at least in the U.S. and Canada. The courts and Congress bend over backwards to preserve trademarks for companies that advertise or otherwise expend significant effort and expense to establish and maintain distinctive product recognition. Brand-name marketers recognize that the payoff from such advertising can be huge. Companies that offer well-established brand-name products to immense consumer markets have enjoyed a stream of enormous profits over the years. Owning strong brands has allowed them to price their products at a premium, and to reap literally billions of dollars in above-normal profits. Top-selling brands like *Coca-Cola, Gillette,* and *Ivory* have retained a remarkable level of brand-name recognition over time; others like *IBM* and *Twinkies* appear to be in trouble. Companies that do not spend enough on advertising to support valuable brand-name assets, and the products that carry them, are losing their premium status.

Cost-conscious retailers have recently been forcing manufacturers to divert dollars from brand-name advertising into costly trade promotions, such as payments for space on store shelves. That dims the prominence of brand names. Advertising effectiveness has also faded because of a decline in mass media that has made it harder to hammer home a single, coherent message. TV viewers no longer flock to the networks as they once did, and advertisers now find it necessary to address narrower and more specialized audiences on cable and through printed media. The net effect of all of this is that some important brands are being devalued. While they aren't disappearing, consumers seem more willing than ever before to switch to cheaper, generic products. Recent studies show the seriousness of this trend. Market surveys show that less than two-thirds of all consumers currently restrict their buying to well-known brand names, compared with roughly three-quarters of all consumers during the mid-1970s. Most consumers abandoning name-brand products are trading down to private label or generic products.

Even as the powerful pull of some brand names is diminishing, the cost and risk of launching new brand names are rising. Roughly 90% of all new brands fail, according to marketing specialists, and mistakes can cost dearly. Most successful new brands are simply brand-name extensions, like *Ultra Tide* detergent, *Lipton* flavored teas, and so on. However, even normally safe product line extensions involve risks. Clorox Co. spent hundreds of millions of dollars to develop a new line of laundry detergents, then dropped the product in 1991 when shoppers refused to buy detergent from a company famous for bleach.

Not all marketing managers agree that the trend away from brands names is serious. Brands are more important than ever at Campbell Soup Co.'s North American operations, which is spending millions of dollars on ads to revive the Campbell Kids. Brand-name advertising is also important at Philip Morris, Frito-Lay, Inc., and Coca-Cola, which continue to advertise heavily. The fortunes of these and other companies with heavily entrenched brands wax and wane slowly. It took years for once-powerful monikers such as *Pepsodent* toothpaste and *Oxydol* laundry detergent to become marketing also-rans. Still, recent evidence suggests that it's not too soon for some firms to start worrying about their good names.

See: Holman W. Jenkins, Jr., "Business World: Brand Managers Get Old-Time Religion," *The Wall Street Journal,* April 23, 1996, A23.

Price Elasticity of Demand

The most widely used elasticity measure is the **price elasticity of demand,** which measures the responsiveness of the quantity demanded to changes in the price of the product, holding constant the values of all other variables in the demand function.

Using the formula for point elasticity, price elasticity of demand is found as

$$\epsilon_P = Point\ Price\ Elasticity = \frac{Percentage\ Change\ in\ Quantity\ (Q)}{Percentage\ Change\ in\ Price\ (P)}$$

$$= \frac{\Delta Q/Q}{\Delta P/P}, \tag{5.6}$$

$$= \frac{\Delta Q}{\Delta P} \times \frac{P}{Q},$$

where $\Delta Q/\Delta P$ is the marginal change in quantity following a one-unit change in price, and P and Q are price and quantity, respectively, at a given point on the demand curve.

The concept of point price elasticity can be illustrated by referring to Equation 5.3:

$$Q = 11,600 - 5,000P + 3,500P_V + 35I + 1,000A.$$

The coefficient for the price variable indicates the effect on quantity demanded of a one-unit change in price:

$$\frac{\Delta Q}{\Delta P} = -5,000, \text{ a constant.}$$

At the typical values of $P_V = \$2$, $I = \$40,000$, and $A = \$20,000$, the demand curve is calculated as

$$Q = 11,600 - 5,000P + 3,500(2) + 35(40) + 1,000(20)$$

$$= 40,000 - 5,000P.$$

This demand curve relation can be used to calculate ϵ_P at two points: (1) where $P_1 = \$6$ and $Q_1 = 10,000$ and (2) where $P_2 = \$7$ and $Q_2 = 5,000$. This implies $\epsilon_{P_1} = -3$ and $\epsilon_{P_2} = -7$ because:

$$(1)\ \epsilon_{P_1} = -5,000 \times \left(\frac{\$6}{10,000}\right) = -3.$$

$$(2)\ \epsilon_{P_2} = -5,000 \times \left(\frac{\$7}{5,000}\right) = -7.$$

Therefore, a 1% increase in price from the $6 movie ticket price level results in a 3% reduction in the quantity demanded. At the $7 price level, a 1% increase results in a 7% reduction in the quantity demanded. This indicates that movie ticket buyers, like most consumers, become increasingly price sensitive as average price increases. This example illustrates how price elasticity tends to vary along a linear demand curve, with ϵ_P

increasing in absolute value at higher prices and lower quantities. Although price elasticity always varies along a linear demand curve, under certain conditions it can be constant along a curvilinear demand curve. This point will be illustrated in a later section.

When evaluating price elasticity estimates, recognize that price elasticities are uniformly negative. This is because the quantity demanded for all goods and services is inversely related to price. In the previous example, at a $6 price, a 1% *increase* in price leads to a 3% *decrease* in the quantity of movie tickets demanded. Conversely, a 1% *decrease* in price leads to a 3% *increase* in the quantity demanded. For expository convenience, the equation for price elasticity is sometimes multiplied by -1 to change price elasticities to positive numbers. Therefore, when price elasticities are reported as positive numbers, or in absolute value terms, it is important to remember the underlying inverse relation between price and quantity.

Using the arc elasticity concept, the equation for price elasticity is

$$E_P = Arc\ Price\ Elasticity = \frac{Percentage\ Change\ in\ Quality\ (Q)}{Percentage\ Change\ in\ Price\ (P)}$$

$$= \frac{(Q_2 - Q_1)/[(Q_2 + Q_1)/2]}{(P_2 - P_1)/[(P_2 + P_1)/2]} \tag{5.7}$$

$$= \frac{\Delta Q}{\Delta P} \times \frac{P_2 + P_1}{Q_2 + Q_1}$$

This form is especially useful for analyzing the average sensitivity of demand to price changes over an extended range of prices. For example, the average price elasticity over the price range from $6 to $7 is

$$E_P = \frac{\Delta Q}{\Delta P} \times \frac{P_2 + P_1}{Q_2 + Q_1}$$

$$= \frac{-5,000}{1} \times \frac{\$7 + \$6}{5,000 + 10,000}$$

$$= -4.33.$$

This means that, on average, a 1% change in price leads to a 4.33% change in quantity demanded when price is between $6 and $7 per ticket.

PRICE ELASTICITY AND TOTAL REVENUE

One of the most important features of price elasticity is that it provides a useful summary measure of the effect of a price change on revenues. Depending on the degree of price elasticity, a reduction in price can increase, decrease, or leave total revenue unchanged. A good estimate of price elasticity makes it possible to accurately estimate the effect of price changes on total revenue.

For decision-making purposes, three specific ranges of price elasticity have been identified. Using $|\epsilon_P|$ to denote the absolute value of the price elasticity, three ranges for price elasticity are

1. $|\epsilon_P| > 1.0$, defined as elastic demand.
    Example: $\epsilon_P = -3.2$ and $|\epsilon_P| = 3.2$.

2. $|\epsilon_P| = 1.0$, defined as unitary elasticity.
    Example: $\epsilon_P = -1.0$ and $|\epsilon_P| = 1.0$.

3. $|\epsilon_P| < 1.0$, defined as inelastic demand.
    Example: $\epsilon_P = -0.5$ and $|\epsilon_P| = 0.5$.

Elastic Demand
A situation in which a price change leads to a more than proportionate change in quantity demanded.

Unitary Elasticity
A situation in which price and quantity changes exactly offset each other.

Inelastic Demand
A situation in which a price change leads to a less than proportionate change in quantity demanded.

With **elastic demand**, $|\epsilon_P| > 1$ and the relative change in quantity is larger than the relative change in price. A given percentage increase in price causes quantity to decrease by a larger percentage. If demand is elastic, a price increase lowers total revenue and a decrease in price raises total revenue. **Unitary elasticity** is a situation in which the percentage change in quantity divided by the percentage change in price equals -1. Since price and quantity are inversely related, a price elasticity of -1 means that the effect of a price change is *exactly* offset by the effect of a change in quantity demanded. The result is that total revenue, the product of price times quantity, remains constant. With **inelastic demand** a price increase produces less than a proportionate decline in the quantity demanded, so total revenues rise. Conversely, when demand is inelastic, a price decrease generates a less than proportionate increase in quantity demanded, so total revenues fall. These relations are summarized in Table 5.1.

Price elasticity can range from completely inelastic, where $\epsilon_P = 0$, to perfectly elastic, where $\epsilon_P = -\infty$. To illustrate, consider first an extreme case in which the quantity demanded is independent of price so that some fixed amount, Q^*, is demanded regardless of price. When the quantity demanded of a product is completely insensitive to price, $\Delta Q / \Delta P = 0$, and price elasticity will equal zero, irrespective of the value of P/Q. The demand curve for such a good or service is perfectly vertical, as shown in Figure 5.1.

The other limiting case, that of infinite price elasticity, describes a product that is completely sensitive to price. The demand curve for such a good or service is perfectly horizontal, as shown in Figure 5.2. Here the ratio $\Delta Q / \Delta P = -\infty$ and $\epsilon_P = -\infty$, regardless of the value of P/Q.

The economic as well as mathematical properties of these limiting cases should be understood. A firm faced with a vertical or perfectly inelastic demand curve could charge any price and still sell Q^* units. Theoretically, such a firm could appropriate all of its customers' income or wealth. Conversely, a firm facing a horizontal or perfectly elastic demand curve could sell an unlimited quantity of output at the price P^*, but it would lose all sales if it raised prices by even a small amount. Such extreme cases are

---

Table 5.1

THE RELATIONSHIP BETWEEN PRICE ELASTICITY AND TOTAL REVENUE

ELASTICITY	IMPLIES	FOLLOWING A PRICE INCREASE:	FOLLOWING A PRICE DECREASE:
Elastic demand, $|\epsilon_P| > 1$.	$\%\Delta Q > \%\Delta P$	Revenue decreases.	Revenue increases.
Unitary elasticity, $|\epsilon_P| = 1$.	$\%\Delta Q = \%\Delta P$	Revenue unchanged.	Revenue unchanged.
Inelastic demand, $|\epsilon_P| < 1$.	$\%\Delta Q < \%\Delta P$	Revenue increases.	Revenue decreases.

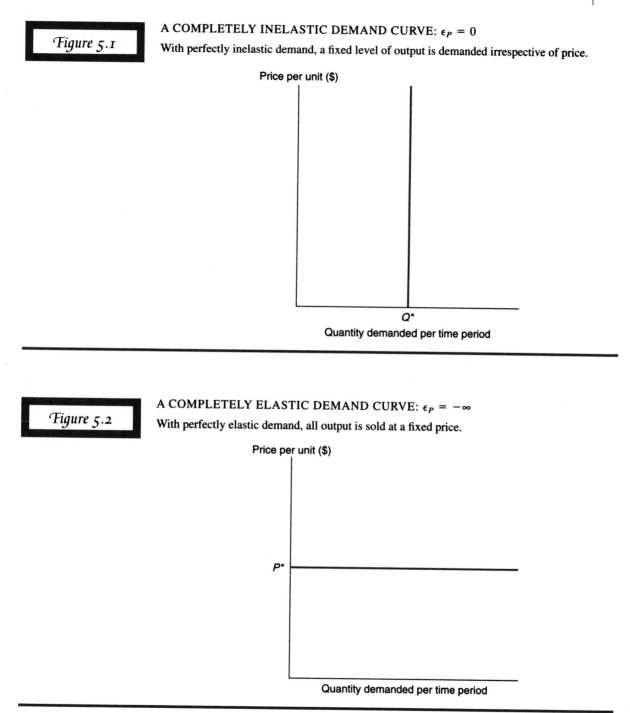

Figure 5.1

A COMPLETELY INELASTIC DEMAND CURVE: $\epsilon_P = 0$

With perfectly inelastic demand, a fixed level of output is demanded irrespective of price.

Price per unit ($)

Q^*

Quantity demanded per time period

Figure 5.2

A COMPLETELY ELASTIC DEMAND CURVE: $\epsilon_P = -\infty$

With perfectly elastic demand, all output is sold at a fixed price.

Price per unit ($)

P^*

Quantity demanded per time period

rare in the real world, but monopolies that sell necessities such as pharmaceuticals enjoy relatively inelastic demand, whereas firms in highly competitive industries such as grocery retailing face highly elastic demand curves.

THE PRICE ELASTICITY OF DEMAND FOR AIRLINE PASSENGER SERVICE

Southwest Airlines likes to call itself the Texas state bird. It must be some bird, because the U.S. Transportation Department regards Southwest as Texas' dominant carrier. Fares are cut in half and traffic doubles, triples, or even quadruples whenever Southwest enters a new market. Airport authorities rake in millions of extra dollars in landing fees, parking and concession fees soar, and added business is attracted to the local area—all because Southwest has arrived! Could it be that Southwest has discovered what many airline passengers already know? Customers absolutely crave cut-rate prices for friendly service with arrival and departure times that are convenient and reliable. The once-little upstart airline from Texas is growing by leaps and bounds because nobody knows how to meet the demand for regional airline service like Southwest Airlines.

Table 5.2 shows information that can be used to infer the industry arc price elasticity of demand in selected regional markets served by Southwest. In 1991, for example, Southwest saw an opportunity because airfares out of San Francisco were high and the nearby Oakland airport was underused. By offering cut-rate fares out of Oakland to Burbank, a similarly underused airport in Southern California, Southwest was able to spur dramatic traffic gains and revenue growth. During the first 12 months of operation, Southwest induced a growth in airport traffic on the Oakland–Burbank route from 246,555 to 1,053,139 passengers, an increase of 806,584 passengers, following an average one-way fare cut from $86.50 to $44.69. Using the arc price elasticity formula, an arc price elasticity of demand of $E_P = -1.95$ for the Oakland–Burbank market is suggested. Given elastic demand in the Oakland–Burbank market, city-pair annual revenue grew from $21.3 million to $47.1 million over this period.

A very different picture of the price elasticity of demand for regional airline passenger service is portrayed by Southwest's experience on the Kansas City–St. Louis route. In 1992, Southwest began offering cut-rate fares between Kansas City and St. Louis and was, once again, able to spur dramatic traffic growth. However, in the Kansas City–St. Louis market, traffic growth was not sufficient to generate added revenue. During the first 12 months of Southwest's operation in this market, traffic growth in the Kansas City–St. Louis route was from 428,711 to 722,425 passengers, an increase of 293,714 passengers, following an average one-way fare cut from $154.42 to $45.82. Again using the arc price elasticity formula, a market arc price elasticity of demand of only $E_P = -0.47$ is suggested. With inelastic demand, Kansas City–St. Louis market revenue fell from $66.2 million to $33.1 million over this period.

In considering these arc price elasticity estimates, remember that they correspond to each market rather than to Southwest Airlines itself. If Southwest were the single carrier or monopolist in the Kansas City–St. Louis market, it could gain revenues and cut variable costs by raising fares and reducing the number of daily departures. As a monopolist, such a fare increase would lead to higher revenues and profits. However, given

Table 5.2	**HOW PRICES PLUNGE AND TRAFFIC SOARS WHEN SOUTHWEST AIRLINES ENTERS A MARKET**	

BURBANK–OAKLAND

Passengers in 12 months before Southwest	246,555
Passengers in 12 months after Southwest	1,053,139
Increase in passengers	806,584
Average one-way fare before Southwest	$86.50
Average one-way fare after Southwest	$44.69
Decrease in one-way fares	−$41.81
Market revenue in 12 months before Southwest	$21,327,008
Market revenue in 12 months after Southwest	$47,064,782
Increase in market revenue	$25,737,774
Implied arc price elasticity of demand (E_P)	−1.95

KANSAS CITY–ST. LOUIS

Passengers in 12 months before Southwest	428,711
Passengers in 12 months after Southwest	722,425
Increase in passengers	293,714
Average one-way fare before Southwest	$154.42
Average one-way fare after Southwest	$45.82
Decrease in one-way fares	−$108.60
Market revenue in 12 months before Southwest	$66,201,553
Market revenue in 12 months after Southwest	$33,101,514
Decrease in market revenue	−$33,100,039
Implied arc price elasticity of demand (E_P)	−0.47

the fact that other airlines operate in each market, Southwest's own demand is likely to be much more price elastic than the market demand elasticity estimates shown in Table 5.2. To judge the profitability of any fare, it is necessary to consider Southwest's revenue *and* cost structure in each market. For example, service in the Kansas City–St. Louis market might allow Southwest to more efficiently utilize aircraft and personnel used to serve the Dallas–Chicago market and thus be highly profitable even when bargain-basement fares are charged.

As this pricing example from the airline passenger industry illustrates, the arc price elasticity of demand can vary widely from one region to another. Successful product design, development, and pricing in any market requires a clear understanding of the breadth and depth of product demand. Effective execution of the firm's marketing function is necessary to ensure the firm's economic viability. In the case of Southwest

Airlines, the company and the Oakland airport authority even handed out bilingual promotional brochures to appeal to San Francisco's large Chinese immigrant population. Southwest's message is clear: It is impossible to operate profitably unless product demand exists or can be created.

VARYING ELASTICITY AT DIFFERENT POINTS ON A DEMAND CURVE

All linear demand curves, except perfectly elastic or perfectly inelastic ones, are subject to varying elasticities at different points on the curve. In other words, any linear demand curve is price elastic at some output levels but inelastic at others. To see this, recall again the definition of point price elasticity expressed in Equation 5.6:

$$\epsilon_P = \frac{\Delta Q}{\Delta P} \times \frac{P}{Q}.$$

The slope of a linear demand curve, $\Delta P/\Delta Q$, is constant; thus, its reciprocal, $1/(\Delta P/\Delta Q) = \Delta Q/\Delta P$, is also constant. However, the ratio P/Q varies from 0 at the point where the demand curve intersects the horizontal axis and price = 0, to $+\infty$ at the vertical price axis intercept where quantity = 0. Since the price elasticity formula for a linear curve involves multiplying a negative constant by a ratio that varies between 0 and $+\infty$, the price elasticity of a linear curve must range from 0 to $-\infty$.

Figure 5.3 illustrates this relation. As the demand curve approaches the vertical axis, the ratio P/Q approaches infinity and ϵ_P approaches minus infinity. As the demand curve approaches the horizontal axis, the ratio P/Q approaches 0, causing ϵ_P also to approach 0. At the midpoint of the demand curve $(\Delta Q/\Delta P) \times (P/Q) = -1$; this is the point of unitary elasticity.

PRICE ELASTICITY AND REVENUE RELATIONS

The relation between price elasticity and total revenue can be further clarified by examining Figure 5.4 and Table 5.3. Figure 5.4(a) reproduces the demand curve shown in Figure 5.3 along with the associated marginal revenue curve. The demand curve shown in Figure 5.4(a) is of the general linear form

$$P = a - bQ, \tag{5.8}$$

where a is the intercept and b is the slope coefficient. It follows that total revenue *(TR)* can be expressed as

$$TR = P \times Q$$
$$= (a - bQ) \times Q$$
$$= aQ - bQ^2.$$

By definition, marginal revenue *(MR)* is the change in revenue following a one-unit expansion in output, $\Delta TR/\Delta Q$, and can be written

$$MR = \Delta TR/\Delta Q = a - 2bQ. \tag{5.9}$$

| **Figure 5.3** | **THE PRICE ELASTICITY OF DEMAND VARIES ALONG A LINEAR DEMAND CURVE** |

The price elasticity of demand will vary from 0 to $-\infty$ along a linear demand curve.

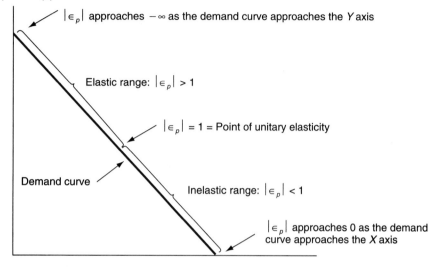

| **Table 5.3** | **PRICE ELASTICITY AND REVENUE RELATIONS: A NUMERICAL EXAMPLE** |

PRICE, P	QUANTITY, Q	TOTAL REVENUE, $TR = P \times Q$	MARGINAL REVENUE, $MR = \Delta TR$	ARC ELASTICITY[a], E_P
$100	1	$100	—	—
90	2	180	$80	−6.33
80	3	240	60	−3.40
70	4	280	40	−2.14
60	5	300	20	−1.44
50	6	300	0	−1.00
40	7	280	−20	−0.69
30	8	240	−40	−0.47
20	9	180	−60	−0.29
10	10	100	−80	−0.16

Figure 5.4

RELATIONS AMONG PRICE ELASTICITY AND MARGINAL, AVERGE, AND TOTAL REVENUE: (A) DEMAND (AVERAGE REVENUE) AND MARGINAL REVENUE CURVES; (B) TOTAL REVENUE

In the range in which demand is elastic with respect to price, marginal revenue is positive and total revenue increases with a reduction in price. In the inelastic range, marginal revenue is negative and total revenue decreases with price reductions.

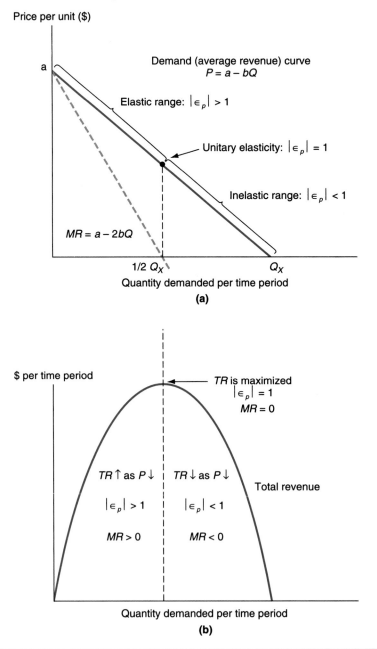

Price per unit ($)

a

Demand (average revenue) curve
$P = a - bQ$

Elastic range: $|\epsilon_p| > 1$

Unitary elasticity: $|\epsilon_p| = 1$

Inelastic range: $|\epsilon_p| < 1$

$MR = a - 2bQ$

1/2 Q_X

Q_X

Quantity demanded per time period

(a)

$ per time period

TR is maximized
$|\epsilon_p| = 1$
$MR = 0$

$TR \uparrow$ as $P\downarrow$ $TR \downarrow$ as $P\downarrow$

Total revenue

$|\epsilon_p| > 1$ $|\epsilon_p| < 1$

$MR > 0$ $MR < 0$

Quantity demanded per time period

(b)

The relation between the demand (average revenue) and marginal revenue curves becomes clear when one compares Equations 5.8 and 5.9. Each equation has the same intercept a. This means that both curves begin at the same point along the vertical price axis. However, the marginal revenue curve has twice the negative slope of the demand curve. This means that the marginal revenue curve intersects the horizontal axis at 1/2 Q_X, given that the demand curve intersects at Q_X. Figure 5.4(a) shows that marginal revenue is positive in the range where demand is price elastic, zero where $\epsilon_P = -1$, and negative in the inelastic range. Thus, there is an obvious relation between price elasticity and both average and marginal revenue.

As shown in Figure 5.4(b), price elasticity is also closely related to total revenue. Total revenue increases with price reductions in the elastic range (where $MR > 0$) because the increase in quantity demanded at the new lower price more than offsets the lower revenue per unit received at that reduced price. Total revenue peaks at the point of unitary elasticity (where $MR = 0$), since the increase in quantity associated with the price reduction exactly offsets the lower revenue received per unit. Finally, total revenue declines when price is reduced in the inelastic range (where $MR < 0$). Here the quantity demanded continues to increase with reductions in price, but the relative increase in quantity is less than the percentage decrease in price, and thus is not large enough to offset the reduction in revenue per unit sold.

The numerical example in Table 5.3 illustrates these relations. It shows that from 1 to 5 units of output, demand is elastic, $|\epsilon_P| > 1$, and a reduction in price increases total revenue. For example, decreasing price from \$80 to \$70 increases the quantity demanded from 3 to 4 units. Marginal revenue is positive over this range, and total revenue increases from \$240 to \$280. For output above 6 units and prices below \$50, demand is inelastic, $|\epsilon_P| < 1$. Here price reductions result in lower total revenue, because the increase in quantity demanded is not large enough to offset the lower price per unit. With total revenue decreasing as output expands, marginal revenue must be negative. For example, reducing price from \$30 to \$20 results in revenue declining from \$240 to \$180 even though output increases from 8 to 9 units; marginal revenue in this case is $-\$60$.

PRICE ELASTICITY AND OPTIMAL PRICING POLICY

Firms use price discounts, specials, coupons, and rebate programs to test the price sensitivity of demand for their products. As a practical matter, firms often maintain current and detailed information concerning the price elasticity of demand for their products, even when they may be unable to completely derive underlying demand functions. Price elasticity estimates along with relevant cost data represent sufficient information for setting a pricing policy that is consistent with value maximization. This is because a relatively simple mathematical relation exists between marginal revenue, price, and the point price elasticity of demand. Given any point price elasticity estimate, relevant marginal revenues can be determined easily. When this marginal revenue information is combined with pertinent marginal cost data, the basis for an optimal pricing policy is created. The relation between marginal revenue, price, and the point price elasticity of demand follows directly from the mathematical definition of a marginal relation.[2] In equation form, the link between marginal revenue, price, and the point price elasticity of demand is:

$$MR = P\left(1 + \frac{1}{\epsilon_P}\right).$$ (5.10)

AN OPTIMAL PRICING POLICY EXAMPLE

This simple relation between marginal revenue, price, and the point price elasticity is very useful in the setting of pricing policy. To see the usefulness of Equation 5.10 in practical pricing policy, consider the pricing problem faced by a profit-maximizing firm. Recall from Chapter 2 that profit maximization requires operating at the activity level where marginal cost equals marginal revenue. Most firms have extensive cost information and can estimate marginal cost reasonably well. By equating marginal costs with marginal revenue as identified by Equation 5.10, the profit-maximizing price level

---

[2]Marginal revenue is the derivative of the total revenue function. That is, $MR = dTR/dQ$. Since total revenue equals price times quantity $(TR = P \times Q)$, marginal revenue is found by taking the derivative of the function $P \times Q$ with respect to Q:

$$MR = \frac{d(P \times Q)}{dQ}.$$

Because price and quantity are interdependent in the typical demand situation, the rule for differentiating a product must be employed in taking the preceding derivative:

$$MR = \frac{dTR}{dQ} = \frac{d(P \times Q)}{dQ} = P \times \frac{dQ}{dQ} + Q \times \frac{dP}{dQ}$$

$$= P \times 1 + Q \times \frac{dP}{dQ}$$

$$= P + Q \times \frac{dP}{dQ}.$$

This relation is a completely general specification of marginal revenue, which, if P is factored out from the right-hand side, can be rewritten as

$$MR = P\left(1 + \frac{Q}{P} \times \frac{dP}{dQ}\right).$$

Note that the term $Q/P \times dP/dQ$ in the preceding expression is the reciprocal of the definition for point price elasticity, $\epsilon_P = dQ/dP \times (P/Q)$:

$$\frac{Q}{P} \times \frac{dP}{dQ} = \frac{1}{\frac{dQ}{dP} \times \frac{P}{Q}} = \frac{1}{\epsilon_P}.$$

Thus, marginal revenue can be rewritten as

$$MR = P\left(1 + \frac{1}{\epsilon_P}\right).$$

can be easily determined. Using Equation 5.10, set marginal cost equal to marginal revenue, where

$$MC = MR$$

and, therefore,

$$MC = P\left(1 + \frac{1}{\epsilon_P}\right),$$

which implies that the optimal or profit-maximizing price, P^*, equals

$$P^* = \frac{MC}{\left(1 + \dfrac{1}{\epsilon_P}\right)} \qquad \textbf{(5.11)}$$

This simple relation between price, marginal cost, and the point price elasticity of demand is the most useful pricing tool offered by managerial economics.

To illustrate the usefulness of Equation 5.11, suppose that manager George Stevens notes a 2% increase in weekly sales following a 1% price discount on *The Kingfish* fishing reels. The point price elasticity of demand for *The Kingfish* fishing reels is:

$$\epsilon_P = \frac{\textit{Percentage Change in Q}}{\textit{Percentage Change in P}}$$

$$= \frac{2\%}{-1\%}$$

$$= -2.$$

What is the optimal retail price for *The Kingfish* fishing reels if the company's wholesale cost per reel plus display and marketing expenses—or relevant marginal costs—total $25 per unit? With marginal costs of $25 and $\epsilon_P = -2$, the profit-maximizing price is:

$$P = \frac{\$25}{\left(1 + \dfrac{1}{-2}\right)}$$

$$= \$50.$$

Therefore, the profit-maximizing price on *The Kingfish* fishing reels is $50.

To see how Equation 5.11 can be used for planning purposes, suppose Stevens can order reels through a different distributor at a wholesale price that reduces marginal costs by $1 to $24 per unit. Under these circumstances, the new optimal retail price is

$$P = \frac{\$24}{\left(1 + \dfrac{1}{-2}\right)}$$

$$= \$48.$$

Thus, the optimal retail price would fall by $2 following a $1 reduction in *The King-fish's* relevant marginal costs.

Equation 5.11 can serve as the basis for calculating profit-maximizing prices under current cost and market-demand conditions, as well as under a variety of circumstances. Table 5.4 shows how profit-maximizing prices vary for a product with a $25 marginal cost as the point price elasticity of demand varies. Note that the less elastic the demand, the greater the difference between the optimal price and marginal cost. Conversely, as the absolute value of the price elasticity of demand increases (that is, as demand becomes more price elastic), the profit-maximizing price gets closer and closer to marginal cost. This important demand relation will be examined further in Chapter 12, where pricing practices are analyzed.

DETERMINANTS OF PRICE ELASTICITY

Why is the price elasticity of demand high for some products and low for others? In general, there are three major causes of differential price elasticities: (1) the extent to which a good is considered to be a necessity; (2) the availability of substitute goods to satisfy a given need; and (3) the proportion of income spent on the product. A relatively constant quantity of a service such as electricity for residential lighting will be purchased almost irrespective of price, at least in the short run and within price ranges customarily encountered. There is no close substitute for electric service. However, goods such as designer jeans, while desirable, face considerably more competition, and their demand depends more on price.

Similarly, the demand for "big ticket" items such as automobiles, homes, and vacation travel accounts for a large share of consumer income and will be relatively sensitive to price. Demand for less expensive products, such as soft drinks, movies, and candy, can be relatively insensitive to price. Given the low percentage of income spent on "small ticket" items, consumers often find that searching for the best deal available is not worth the time and effort. Accordingly, the elasticity of demand is typically higher for major purchases than for small ones. The price elasticity of demand for compact disc players, for example, is higher than that for compact discs.

Price elasticity for an individual firm is seldom the same as that for the entire industry. The reason for this is discussed in detail in Chapters 10 and 11, which deal with market structure, but an intuitive explanation can be given here. In pure monopoly, the firm demand curve is also the industry demand curve, so obviously the elasticity of

---

Table 5.4

PRICE ELASTICITY AND OPTIMAL PRICING POLICY

POINT PRICE ELASTICITY	MARGINAL COST	PROFIT-MAXIMIZING PRICE
−1.25	$25	$125.00
−1.50	25	75.00
−2.50	25	41.67
−5.00	25	31.25
−10.00	25	27.78
−25.00	25	26.04

Sports Merchandising Is Cooling Down

Have you ever been to Anaheim to watch the Mighty Ducks play NHL hockey? Do you marvel firsthand at the terrific home-court advantage enjoyed by the Chicago Bulls? How about Coors Stadium—do you like the intimacy of the Colorado Rockies' new baseball park? What about those new NFL Carolina Panthers—do you have your season tickets yet?

If you haven't been to California to see the Mighty Ducks or to Chicago to see (and hear!) the Bulls, to Colorado to enjoy the Rockies, or to North Carolina to observe the Panthers, don't worry—there is still ample opportunity for you to express your affinity for them and other sports favorites. Just head on down to the sporting goods retailer at your local mall and you will find that manufacturers have slapped sports logos onto everything from T-shirts to authentic jerseys, warm ups, and cologne. (What does a Mighty Duck smell like?)

During the early 1990s sports-product sales skyrocketed. Marketing of NFL-licensed products, such as New York Giants' wastebaskets, more than doubled from $1.5 billion to more than $3.25 billion per year over the 1990–1995 period. Close behind, products with NBA logos generated roughly $3 billion in 1995 revenues, up from less than $1 billion in 1990. Retail sales of products licensed by Major League Baseball also rose from roughly $1.5 billion in 1990 to $3 billion in 1993, before plummeting to roughly $2 billion per year following the 1994–1995 baseball strike. Also hit by labor strife woes, marketing of products with NHL logos flattened out at roughly $1 billion in 1995, after exploding from near-zero levels in 1990.

Merchandisers have found labor-market woes to be a large and growing threat to the industry. Sports merchandising began a rapid cool down when the major league baseball season was scrapped for good on September 14, 1994. Retailers were stuck with large inventories of unsold goods bought to take advantage of the traditional surge in late-season interest associated with the baseball playoffs and the World Series. Then, in 1994, a bad situation became much worse when the National Hockey League canceled the start of its season because of a long-simmering labor dispute. Anything that interrupts fan interest in sports is bad for all sports merchandising. Fans

like winners, and without any games there are no winners. Some continuing fallout from fan disenchantment is inevitable in an industry with such immense new-found wealth, and the concomitant bickering between owners and players. Major League Baseball Properties, for example, used to be the biggest beneficiary of sports merchandising, with $2.8 billion in 1993 revenues. By 1995, MLB properties saw merchandise sales slip to $2.1 billion, third among major sports. The baseball and hockey strikes hurt not just baseball-related and hockey-related paraphernalia; also hit were sports merchandise sales for basketball and football.

A cooling in the torrid early 1990s pace of sports merchandising was inevitable. The National Basketball Association, which saw licensing sales quadruple during the 1990–1994 period, just couldn't expect that pace to continue. While the loss of "sizzle" following the retirement of Michael Jordan is partly to blame, sizable gains from a base of $3 billion in sales are difficult. Similarly, the demand for authentic football and hockey jerseys can become fairly limited when costs begin to exceed $100 per unit.

To protect themselves from future player strikes, leading retailers have established new marketing arrangements that tie professional-league royalties to the number of games played. Other retailers have begun to emphasize college sports at the expense of the professional leagues. Despite some rumblings of concern about low graduation rates and the abuse of student athletes, labor strife at the college level seems years away. Still other retailers downplay tie-ins with specific teams or sports, and instead emphasize generic sports attitudes such as "Just Do It" or "Life Is a Contact Sport." After suffering through the misery of recent player strikes, retailers of sports merchandising must feel like sports merchandising itself is a contact sport!

See: John Heylar, "Licensed Sports Gear Takes a Hit From Alienated Fans," *The Wall Street Journal,* February 23, 1995, B1, B11; and A. Craig Copetas, "Sports: Europe Is U.S. Sports' New Classroom," *The Wall Street Journal,* November 29, 1996, B7.

demand faced by the firm at any output level is the same as that faced by the industry. Consider the other extreme—pure competition, as approximated by wheat farming. The industry demand curve for wheat is downward sloping: the lower its price, the greater the quantity of wheat that will be demanded. However, the demand curve facing any individual wheat farmer is essentially horizontal. A farmer can sell any amount of wheat at the going price, but if the farmer raises the price by the smallest fraction of a cent, sales collapse to zero. The wheat farmer's demand curve—or that of any firm operating under pure competition—is perfectly elastic. Figure 5.2 illustrates such a demand curve.

As explained in Chapter 4, the demand for producer goods and services is indirect, or derived from their value in use. Because the demand for all inputs is derived from their usefulness in producing other products, their demand is derived from the demand for final products. In contrast to the terms *final product* or *consumer demand,* the term *derived demand* describes the demand for all producer goods and services. Although the demand for producer goods and services is related to the demand for the final products that they are used to make, this relation is not always as close as one might suspect.

In some instances, the demand for intermediate goods is less price sensitive than demand for the resulting final product. This is because intermediate goods sometimes represent only a small portion of the cost of producing the final product. For example, suppose the total cost to build a small manufacturing plant is $1 million, and $25,000 of this cost represents the cost of electrical fixtures and wiring. Even a doubling in electrical costs from $25,000 to $50,000 would have only a modest effect on the overall costs of the plant—which would increase by only 2.5% from $1 million to $1,025,000. Rather than being highly price sensitive, the firm might select its electrical contractor based on the timeliness and quality of service provided. In such an instance, the firm's price elasticity of demand for electrical fixtures and wiring is quite low, even if its price elasticity of demand for the overall project is quite high.

In other situations, the reverse might hold. Continuing with our previous example, suppose that steel costs represent $250,000 of the total $1 million cost of building the plant. Because of its relative importance, a substantial increase in steel costs has a significant influence on the total costs of the overall project. As a result, the price sensitivity of the demand for steel will be close to that for the overall plant. If the firm's demand for plant construction is highly price elastic, the demand for steel is also likely to be highly price elastic.

Although the derived demand for producer goods and services is obviously related to the demand for resulting final products, this relation is not always close. When intermediate goods or services represent only a small share of overall costs, the price elasticity of demand for such inputs can be much different than that for the resulting final product. The price elasticity of demand for a given input and the resulting final product must be similar in magnitude only when the costs of that input represent a significant share of overall costs.

USES OF PRICE ELASTICITY INFORMATION

Price elasticity information is useful for a number of purposes. Obviously, firms are required to be aware of the price elasticity of demand when they price their products. For example, a profit-maximizing firm would never choose to lower its prices in the inelastic range of the demand curve. Such a price decrease would decrease total revenue and at the same time increase costs, since the quantity demanded would rise. A dramatic decrease in profits would result. Even over the range in which demand is elastic, a firm will not necessarily find it profitable to cut price. The profitability of a price cut in the elastic range of the demand curve depends on whether the marginal revenues generated exceed the marginal cost of added production. Price elasticity information can be used to answer questions such as

- What is the expected impact on sales of a 5% price increase?
- How great a price reduction is necessary to increase sales by 10%?
- Given marginal cost and price elasticity data, what is the profit-maximizing price?

The worldwide energy crisis that developed following the OPEC oil embargo illustrates the importance of price elasticity information. Electric utilities were forced to raise prices dramatically because of a rapid increase in fuel costs. The question immediately arose: How much of a cutback in quantity demanded and, hence, how much of a reduction in future capacity needs would these price increases cause? In other words, what was the price elasticity of electricity? In view of the long lead times required to build electricity-generating capacity and the major economic dislocations that arise from power outages, this was a critical question for both consumers and producers of electricity.

Price elasticity information has also played a major role in the debate over national energy policy. Some industry and government economists argue that the price elasticity of demand for energy is sufficiently large that an equilibrium of demand and supply will occur following only modest price changes. Others argue that energy price elasticities are so low that unconscionable price increases are necessary to reduce the quantity demanded to meet pending supply shortfalls. Meanwhile, the collapse of oil prices during the late 1980s and early 1990s raises fears among some that low oil prices might increase demand so much that they may increase the Western world's already heavy reliance on imported oil. These same issues have also become a focal point in controversies surrounding nuclear energy, natural gas price deregulation, and alternative renewable energy sources. In this debate on energy policy, the relation between price and quantity supplied—the price elasticity of supply—is also an important component. As with most economic issues, both demand and supply sides of the marketplace must be analyzed to arrive at a rational decision. Strongly interrelated energy issues continue to have important implications for all sectors of the economy, and price elasticity analysis is playing an increasingly important role in the search for solutions.

Another example of the importance of price elasticity information relates to the widespread discounts or reduced rates offered different customer groups. *The Wall Street Journal* offers students bargain rates; airlines, restaurants, and most hotel chains offer discounts to vacation travelers and senior citizens; large corporate customers get discounts or rebates on desktop computers, auto leases, and many other items. Many such discounts are substantial, sometimes in the range of 30% to 40% off standard list prices. The question of whether reduced prices attract sufficient additional customers to offset lower revenues per unit is directly related to the price elasticity of demand. All group-based customer discounts must be supported by detailed estimates of differences in the relevant price elasticity of demand.

Additional uses of price elasticity information are examined in later chapters. At this point, it becomes useful to consider some other important demand elasticities.

Cross-Price Elasticity of Demand

The demand for most products is influenced by prices of other products. For example, the demand for beef is related to the price of chicken. As the price of chicken increases, so does the demand for beef; consumers substitute beef for the now relatively more expensive chicken. On the other hand, a price decrease for chicken leads to a decrease in the demand for beef as consumers substitute chicken for the now relatively more expensive beef. In general, a direct relation between the price of one product and the demand for a second product holds for all **substitutes.** A price increase for a given product will increase demand for substitutes; a price decrease for a given product will decrease demand for substitutes.

Substitutes
Related products for which a price increase for one leads to an increase in demand for the other.

Some goods and services—for example, cameras and film—exhibit a completely different relation. Here price increases in one product typically lead to a reduction in demand for the other. Goods that are inversely related in this manner are known as **complements;** they are used together rather than in place of each other.

Complements
Related products for which a price increase for one leads to a reduction in demand for the other.

The concept of **cross-price elasticity** is used to examine the responsiveness of demand for one product to changes in the price of another. Point cross-price elasticity is given by the following equation:

Cross-Price Elasticity
Responsiveness of demand for one product to changes in the price of another.

$$\epsilon_{PX} = \frac{Percentage\ Change\ in\ Quantity\ of\ Y}{Percentage\ Change\ in\ Price\ of\ X}$$

$$= \frac{\Delta Q_Y/Q_Y}{\Delta P_X/P_X} \tag{5.12}$$

$$= \frac{\Delta Q_Y}{\Delta P_X} \times \frac{P_X}{Q_Y},$$

where Y and X are two different products. The arc cross-price elasticity relationship is constructed in the same manner as was previously described for price elasticity:

$$E_{PX} = \frac{Percentage\ Change\ in\ Quantity\ of\ Y}{Percentage\ Change\ in\ Price\ of\ X}$$

$$= \frac{(Q_{Y2} - Q_{Y1})/[(Q_{Y2} + Q_{Y1})/2]}{(P_{X2} - P_{X1})/[(P_{X2} + P_{X1})/2]} \tag{5.13}$$

$$= \frac{\Delta Q_Y}{\Delta P_X} \times \frac{P_{X2} + P_{X1}}{Q_{Y2} + Q_{Y1}},$$

The cross-price elasticity for substitutes is always positive; the price of one good and the demand for the other always move in the same direction. Cross-price elasticity is negative for complements; price and quantity move in opposite directions for complementary goods and services. Finally, cross-price elasticity is zero, or nearly zero, for unrelated goods where variations in the price of one good have no effect on demand for the second.

The concept of cross-price elasticity can be illustrated by considering the demand function for monitored in-home healthcare services provided by Home Medical Support (HMS), Inc.:

$$Q_Y = f(P_Y, P_D, P_H, P_T, i, I).$$

Here, Q_Y is the number of patient days of service per year; P_Y is the average price of HMS service; P_D is an industry price index for prescription drugs; P_H is an index of the average price of hospital service, a primary competitor; P_T is a price index for the travel industry; i is the interest rate; and I is disposable income per capita. Assume that the parameters of the HMS demand function have been estimated as follows:

$$Q_Y = 25,000 - 5P_Y - 3P_D + 10P_H + 0.0001P_T - 0.02i + 2.5I.$$

The effects on Q_Y caused by a one-unit change in the prices of other goods are

$$\frac{\Delta Q_Y}{\Delta P_D} = -3.$$

$$\frac{\Delta Q_Y}{\Delta P_H} = +10.$$

$$\frac{\Delta Q_Y}{\Delta P_T} = 0.0001 \approx 0.$$

Since both prices and quantities are always positive, the ratios P_D/Q_Y, P_H/Q_Y, and P_T/Q_Y are also positive. Therefore, the signs of the three cross-price elasticities in this example are determined by the sign of each relevant parameter estimate in the HMS demand function:

$$\epsilon_{PD} = (-3)(P_D/Q_Y) < 0.$$

HMS service and prescription drugs are complements.

$$\epsilon_{PH} = (+10)(P_H/Q_Y) > 0.$$

HMS service and hospital service are substitutes.

$$\epsilon_{PT} = (+0.0001)(P_T/Q_Y) \approx 0, \text{ so long as the ratio } P_T/Q_Y \text{ is not extremely large.}$$

Demand for travel and HMS service are independent.

The concept of cross-price elasticity serves two main purposes. First, it is important for the firm to be aware of how demand for its products is likely to respond to changes in the prices of other goods. Such information is necessary for formulating the firm's own pricing strategy and for analyzing the risks associated with various products. This is particularly important for firms with a wide variety of products, where meaningful substitute or complementary relations exist within the firm's own product line. Second, cross-price elasticity information allows managers to measure the degree of competition in the marketplace. For example, a firm might appear to dominate a particular market or market segment, especially if it is the only supplier of a particular product. However, if the cross-price elasticity between a firm's output and products produced in related industries is large and positive, the firm is not a monopolist in the true sense and is not immune to the threat of competitor encroachment. In the banking industry, for example, individual banks clearly compete with money market mutual funds, savings and loan associations, credit unions, and commercial finance companies. The extent of competition can be measured only in terms of the cross-price elasticities of demand for various services offered by banks and all relevant potential competitors.

The importance of the concept of cross-price elasticity of demand is explored further in Chapters 12 and 13, where market structure is examined, and in Chapter 14, where its role in multiple product pricing is analyzed.

Income Elasticity of Demand

For many goods, income is another important determinant of demand. Income is frequently as important as price, advertising expenditures, credit terms, or any other variable in the demand function. This is particularly true of luxury items such as big-screen televisions, country club memberships, elegant homes, and so on. In contrast, the demand for such basic commodities as salt, bread, and milk is not very responsive to income changes. These goods are bought in fairly constant amounts regardless of changes in income. Of course, income can be measured in many ways—for example, on a per capita, per household, or aggregate basis. Gross national product, national income, personal income, and disposable personal income have all served as income measures in demand studies.

NORMAL VERSUS INFERIOR GOODS

Income Elasticity
Responsiveness of demand to changes in income, holding constant the effect of all other variables.

The **income elasticity** of demand measures the responsiveness of demand to changes in income, holding constant the effect of all other variables that influence demand. Letting I represent income, income point elasticity is defined as

$$\epsilon_I = \frac{\text{Percentage Change in Quantity } (Q)}{\text{Percentage Change in Income } (I)}$$

$$= \frac{\Delta Q/Q}{\Delta I/I} \qquad \qquad \textbf{(5.14)}$$

$$= \frac{\Delta Q}{\Delta I} \times \frac{I}{Q}.$$

Inferior Goods
Products for which consumer demand declines as income rises.

Income and the quantity purchased typically move in the same direction; that is, income and sales are directly rather than inversely related. Therefore, $\Delta Q/\Delta I$ and hence ϵ_I are positive. This does not hold for a limited number of products termed **inferior goods.** Individual consumer demand for such products as beans and potatoes, for example, is sometimes thought to decline as income increases, because consumers replace them with more desirable alternatives. More typical products, whose individual and aggregate demand is positively related to income, are defined as **normal goods** or **superior goods.**

Normal or Superior Goods
Products for which demand is positively related to income.

To examine income elasticity over a range of incomes rather than at a single level, the arc elasticity relation is employed:

$$E_I = \frac{Percentage\ Change\ in\ Quantity\ (Q)}{Percentage\ Change\ in\ Income\ (I)}$$

$$= \frac{(Q_2 - Q_1)/[(Q_2 + Q_1)/2]}{(I_2 - I_1)/[(I_2 + I_1)/2]} \qquad (5.15)$$

$$= \frac{\Delta Q}{\Delta I} \times \frac{I_2 + I_1}{Q_2 + Q_1}.$$

Arc income elasticity provides a measure of the average responsiveness of demand for a given product to a relative change in income over the range from I_1 to I_2.

In the case of inferior goods, individual demand actually rises during an economic downturn. As workers get laid off from their jobs, for example, they might tend to substitute potatoes for meat, hamburgers for steak, bus rides for automobile trips, and so on. As a result, demand for potatoes, hamburgers, bus rides, and other inferior goods can actually rise during recessions. Their demand is **countercyclical.**

Countercyclical
Inferior goods whose demand falls with rising income, and rises with falling income.

TYPES OF NORMAL GOODS

For most products, income elasticity is positive, indicating that demand rises as the economy expands and national income increases. The actual size of the income elasticity coefficient is very important. Suppose, for example, that ϵ_I for a particular product is 0.3. This means that a 1% increase in income causes demand for the product to increase by only .3%. Given growing national income over time, such a product would not maintain its relative importance in the economy. Another product might have an income elasticity of 2.5; its demand increases 2.5 times as fast as income. If $\epsilon_I < 1.0$ for a particular good, its producers will not share proportionately in increases in national income. On the other hand, if $\epsilon_I > 1.0$, the industry will gain more than a proportionate share of increases in income.

Noncyclical Normal Goods
Products for which demand is relatively unaffected by changing income.

Goods for which $0 < \epsilon_I < 1$ are often referred to as **noncyclical normal goods,** since demand is relatively unaffected by changing income. Sales of most convenience goods, such as toothpaste, candy, soda, movie tickets, and so on, account for only a small share of the consumer's overall budget, and spending on such items tends to be relatively unaffected by changing economic conditions. For goods having $\epsilon_I > 1$, referred to as **cyclical normal goods,** demand is strongly affected by changing economic conditions. Purchase of "big ticket" items such as homes, automobiles, boats, and recreational vehicles can be postponed and tend to be put off by consumers during economic downturns. As a result, housing demand, for example, can collapse during recessions

Cyclical Normal Goods
Products for which demand is strongly affected by changing income.

and skyrocket during economic expansions. These relations between income and product demand are summarized in Table 5.5.

These relations have important policy implications for both firms and government agencies. Firms whose demand functions have high income elasticities enjoy good growth opportunities in expanding economies, so forecasts of aggregate economic activity figure importantly in their plans. Companies faced with low income elasticities, in contrast, are relatively unaffected by the level of overall business activity. This is relatively desirable from the standpoint that such a business is harmed relatively little by economic downturns. Nevertheless, since such a company cannot expect to share fully in a growing economy, it might seek to enter industries that provide better growth opportunities.

Income elasticity can also play an important role in the marketing activities of a firm. If per capita or household income is found to be an important determinant of demand, this can affect the location and type of sales outlets. It can also have an impact on advertising and other promotional activities. For example, firms that provide goods or services with high income elasticities often target promotional efforts at young professionals, given their potential for increased future business over time.

At the national level, the question of income elasticity has figured importantly in several key areas. Agriculture, for example, has had problems for many years, partly because of the low income elasticity for most food products. This has made it difficult for farmers' incomes to keep up with those of urban workers, a problem that, in turn, has caused concern in Washington and in national capitals throughout the world.

A somewhat similar problem arises in housing. Congress and every U.S. president since the end of World War II have stated that improving the housing stock is a primary national goal. If, on the one hand, the income elasticity for housing is high and $\epsilon_I > 1$, an improvement in the housing stock will be a natural by-product of a prosperous economy. On the other hand, if the housing income elasticity $\epsilon_I < 1$, a relatively small percentage of additional income will be spent on houses. As a result, housing stock would not improve much over time despite a growing economy and increasing incomes. In the event that $\epsilon_I < 1$, direct government investment in public housing or rent and interest subsidies might be necessary to bring about a dramatic increase in the housing stock over time. Not only has the income elasticity of housing been an important issue in debates on national housing policy, but these very debates have created a stimulus for economic research into the theory and measurement of income elasticities.

THE RELATIONSHIP BETWEEN INCOME AND PRODUCT DEMAND

Table 5.5

GOODS CATEGORY	INCOME ELASTICITY	EXAMPLES
Inferior goods (countercyclical)	$\epsilon_I < 0$	Basic foodstuffs, generic products, bus rides
Noncyclical normal goods	$0 < \epsilon_I < 1$	Toiletries, movies, liquor, cigarettes
Cyclical normal goods	$\epsilon_I > 1$	Automobiles, housing, vacation travel, capital equipment

Additional Demand Elasticity Concepts

The elasticity concept is a simple way to measure the effect of change in an independent variable on a dependent variable in any functional relation. The dependent variable in this chapter is the demand for a product, and the demand elasticity for any variable in the firm's demand function can be calculated. The three most common demand elasticities—price elasticity, cross-price elasticity, and income elasticity—are emphasized in this chapter. Examples of other demand elasticities can be used to reinforce the generality of the concept.

OTHER DEMAND ELASTICITIES

Advertising elasticity plays an important role in marketing activities for a broad range of goods and services. A low advertising elasticity means that a firm must spend substantial sums to shift demand for its products through advertising. In such cases, alternative marketing approaches are often more productive.

In the housing market, mortgage interest rates are an important determinant of demand. Accordingly, interest rate elasticities have been used to analyze and forecast the demand for housing construction. To be sure, this elasticity coefficient varies over time as other conditions in the economy change. Other things are held constant when measuring elasticity, but in the real world other things do not typically remain constant. Studies indicate that the interest rate elasticity of residential housing demand averages about -0.15. This means that a 10% rise in interest rates decreases the demand for housing by 1.5%, provided that all other variables remain unchanged. If Federal Reserve policy is expected to cause interest rates to rise from 8% to 9.6% (a 20% increase), a 3% decrease ($-0.15 \times 20 = -3$) in housing demand can be projected, on average.

Not surprisingly, public utilities calculate the weather elasticity of demand for their services. They measure weather using degree days as an indicator of average temperatures. This elasticity factor is used, in conjunction with weather forecasts, to anticipate service demand and peak-load conditions.

THE TIME FACTOR IN ELASTICITY ANALYSIS

Time itself is also an important factor in demand elasticity analysis, given the lack of instantaneous responses in the marketplace. Consumers often react slowly to changes in prices and other demand conditions. To illustrate this delayed or lagged effect, consider the demand for electric power. Suppose that an electric utility raises its rates by 30%. How will this affect the quantity of electric power demanded? In the very short run, any effects will be slight. Customers may be more careful to turn off unneeded lights, but total demand, which is highly dependent on the appliances owned by the residential customers and the equipment operated by their industrial and commercial customers, will probably not be greatly affected. Prices will go up and quantity demanded will not fall much, so total revenue will increase substantially. In other words, the short-run demand for electric power is relatively inelastic.

Retailers Go Global

One of the most striking economic differences between the U.S. and Canada and the rest of the world is the extreme lack of competition in many local retail markets around the globe. U.S. and Canadian consumers have a plethora of department stores, specialty outlets, and discount retailers to choose among, while Japanese consumers, for example, typically face severely limited shopping alternatives. Whereas U.S. and Canadian shoppers have access to a wide variety of domestic and imported goods and services, Japanese consumers typically have only Japanese-made products at their disposal. In fact, the typical Japanese consumer is completely unaware of how the lack of competition in Japanese retail trade restricts purchase options and raises prices. As a result, Japanese consumers have never lobbied government trade officials for greater retail competition, and for access to large retail stores that offer bargain prices.

Thanks to relentless pressure by foreign trade representatives, government officials in Japan and other countries have moved to free up anticompetitive retail trade laws. Before recent changes, mom-and-pop retail stores in Japan were able to delay the opening of any large chain or retail store for as long as 10 years. Since trade reforms instituted in the early 1990s, stores like U.S. retail giant Toys "R" Us are opening at a quicker pace. This growing number of large domestic and foreign retailers is creating chaos in a Japanese distribution system that has traditionally been more interested in keeping wholesalers and retailers happy than in lowering prices for consumers.

As global trade barriers have fallen, retailers have responded with a massive deployment of new stores that undercut local retailers on price, while greatly expanding the variety and quality of goods and services. In Malaysia, for example, Asian shoppers now buy American products in a Dutch-owned store called Makro, Southeast Asia's largest store group. Makro enjoys booming success as it brings shoppers lower prices, and previously unheard-of choice and convenience. In Shanghai, China, Japanese retailer Yaohan is building the Nextage Tower, a flagship store designed to handle *one million* shoppers on a typical weekend. Yaohan envisions opening an additional 1,000 modern supermarkets in South China alone during the next few years. In Madrid, Spain, children play at the Discovery Zone, as local retailers discover the big purchasing power that can be tapped in serving little tykes. Mexican shoppers buy fresh tortillas daily at the local Kmart, while mega-merchants like Wal-Mart and Carrefour build monster stores worldwide at a breakneck pace.

While bargain hunting is a long-ingrained habit among many U.S. and Canadian shoppers, it is a startling change in behavior for some consumers. During the robust economic environment of the 1980s, for example, many Japanese consumers were willing to pay top-dollar prices for high-value products. Discount stores were regularly shunned by the Japanese consumer as sellers of low-quality products or miscellaneous goods obtained from dubious manufacturers. Discounters were limited to offering only a limited range of products, like electronic goods. As global retailers find it easier to penetrate intricate local distribution networks, consumers who identify a simple link between high prices and high quality will shift strategy. Global merchants are also finding that it pays to look for customers away from traditional shopping districts. A few years ago, the British Airport Authority decided to dramatically cut sky-high airport prices, and garnered big-time sales as customer traffic boomed. With such successes, continuing innovation in global retailing is inevitable. How about global catalogs for *Eddie Bauer, L.L. Bean,* and *Lands' End?*

Global retailers have clearly "let the cat out of the bag." Bargain hunting has become the rage among global consumers. Like shoppers taught U.S. and Canadian retailers long ago, local retailers around the world are coming to find that you've got to have quality products at reasonable prices.

See: Carla Rapoport and Justin Martin, "Retailers Go Global," *Fortune,* February 20, 1995, 102–108.

In the long run, however, an increase in power rates can have a substantial effect on electricity demand. Residential users will reduce their purchases of air conditioners, electric heating units, and other appliances; and appliances that are purchased will be more energy efficient. This will reduce the long-run demand for power. Industrial users will also tend to switch to other energy sources, employ less energy-intensive production methods, or relocate to areas where electric costs are lower. Thus, the ultimate effect of a price increase on electricity demand may be substantial, but it might take a number of years before its full impact is felt.

In general, opportunities to respond to price changes tend to increase with time as consumers obtain more information or better perceive the price effects and as more substitutes are made available. There is a similar phenomenon with respect to income changes. It takes time for consumers' purchasing habits to respond to changed income levels. For these reasons, long-run elasticities tend to be greater than short-run elasticities for most demand variables.

Summary

Product demand is a critical determinant of profitability, and demand estimates are key considerations in virtually all managerial decisions. This chapter considers methods for quantifying and interpreting demand relations.

- **Elasticity** is the percentage change in a dependent variable, Y, resulting from a one-percent change in the value of an independent variable, X. **Point elasticity** measures elasticity at a point on a function. **Arc elasticity** measures the average elasticity over a given range of a function.

- Factors such as price and advertising that are within the control of the firm are called **endogenous variables;** factors outside the control of the firm such as consumer incomes, competitor prices, and the weather are called **exogenous variables.**

- The **price elasticity of demand** measures the responsiveness of the quantity demanded to changes in the price of the product, holding constant the values of all other variables in the demand function. With **elastic demand,** a price increase will lower total revenue and a decrease in price will raise total revenue. **Unitary elasticity** describes a situation in which the effect of a price change is *exactly* offset by the effect of a change in quantity demanded. Total revenue, the product of price times quantity, remains constant. With **inelastic demand,** a price increase produces a less than proportionate decline in quantity demanded, so total revenue rises. Conversely, a price decrease produces less than a proportionate increase in quantity demanded, so total revenue falls.

- A direct relation between the price of one product and the demand for another holds for all **substitutes.** A price increase for a given product will increase demand for substitutes; a price decrease for a given product will decrease demand for substitutes. Goods that are inversely related in terms of price and quantity are known as **complements;** they are used together rather than in place of each other. The concept of **cross-price elasticity** is used to examine the responsiveness of demand for one product to changes in the price of another.

■ The **income elasticity** of demand measures the responsiveness of demand to changes in income, holding constant the effect of all other variables that influence demand. For a limited number of **inferior goods,** individual consumer demand is thought to decline as income increases because consumers replace them with more desirable alternatives. Demand for such products is **countercyclical,** actually rising during recessions and falling during economic booms. More typical products, whose individual and aggregate demand is positively related to income, are defined as **normal** or **superior goods.** Goods for which $0 < \epsilon_I < 1$ are often referred to as **noncyclical normal goods,** since demand is relatively unaffected by changing income. For goods having $\epsilon_I > 1$, referred to as **cyclical normal goods,** demand is strongly affected by changing economic conditions.

Demand analysis and estimation is one of the most interesting and challenging topics in managerial economics. This chapter provides a valuable, albeit brief, introduction to several key concepts that are useful in the practical analysis and estimation of demand functions. As such, this material offers constructive input that is useful for understanding the underlying economic causes of demand.

QUESTIONS

Q5.1   Is the economic demand for a product determined solely by its usefulness?

Q5.2   Assume that the price of *Coca-Cola* in soda machines is increased from 50¢ to $1 per can, while the price of *Pepsi* and all other soft drinks remains the same. Is likely to discover a negative value for the price elasticity of demand for *Coca-Cola* following such a price increase? Is it possible to find a positive value?

Q5.3   Name products for which you believe the price elasticity of demand might in fact be positive. What errors in demand analysis and estimation might lead to the erroneous conclusion that the price elasticity of demand is positive when in fact it is negative?

Q5.4   Describe how cents-off coupons can be used as an effective device for estimating the price elasticity of demand for grocery items. Why do retailers and manufacturers offer such coupons in lieu of across-the-board price cuts?

Q5.5   Describe the income, substitution, and total effects on consumption following a price increase.

Q5.6   Define each of the following terms, giving each a verbal explanation and an equation:
   A.   Point elasticity
   B.   Arc elasticity
   C.   Price elasticity
   D.   Cross-price elasticity
   E.   Income elasticity

Q5.7   When is use of the arc elasticity concept valid as compared with the use of the point elasticity concept?

Q5.8   Why is the price elasticity of demand typically greater for an industry than for a single firm in the industry?

Q5.9   Is the cross-price elasticity concept useful for identifying the boundaries of an industry or market?

Q5.10   Individual consumer demand declines for inferior goods as personal income increases because consumers replace them with more desirable alternatives. Is an inverse relation between demand and national income likely for such products?

SELF-TEST PROBLEMS AND SOLUTIONS

ST5.1   **Elasticity Estimation.** Distinctive Designs, Inc., imports and distributes dress and sports watches. At the end of the company's fiscal year, brand manager Karla Wallace has asked you to evaluate sales of the sports watch line using the following data:

Month	Number of Sports Watches Sold	Sports Watch Advertising Expenditures	Sports Watch Price, P	Dress Watch Price, P_D
July	4,500	$10,000	26	50
August	5,500	10,000	24	50
September	4,500	9,200	24	50
October	3,500	9,200	24	46
November	5,000	9,750	25	50
December	15,000	9,750	20	50
January	5,000	8,350	25	50
February	4,000	7,850	25	50
March	5,500	9,500	25	55
April	6,000	8,500	24	51
May	4,000	8,500	26	51
June	5,000	8,500	26	57

In particular, Wallace has asked you to estimate relevant demand elasticities. Remember that to estimate the required elasticities, you should consider months only when the other important factors considered in the preceding table have not changed. Also note that by restricting your analysis to consecutive months, changes in any additional factors not explicitly included in the analysis are less likely to affect estimated elasticities. Finally, the average arc elasticity of demand for each factor is simply the average of monthly elasticities calculated during the past year.

A. Indicate whether there was or was not a change in each respective independent variable for each month pair during the past year.

Month-Pair	Sports Watch Advertising Expenditures, A	Sports Watch Price, P	Dress Watch Price, P_D
July–August	_____	_____	_____
August–September	_____	_____	_____
September–October	_____	_____	_____
October–November	_____	_____	_____
November–December	_____	_____	_____
December–January	_____	_____	_____
January–February	_____	_____	_____
February–March	_____	_____	_____
March–April	_____	_____	_____
April–May	_____	_____	_____
May–June	_____	_____	_____

B. Calculate and interpret the average advertising arc elasticity of demand for sports watches.

C. Calculate and interpret the average arc price elasticity of demand for sports watches.

D. Calculate and interpret the average arc cross-price elasticity of demand between sports and dress watches. See the table on page 195.

ST5.1 **SOLUTION**

A.

MONTH-PAIR	SPORTS WATCH ADVERTISING EXPENDITURES, A	SPORTS WATCH Price, P	DRESS WATCH Price, P_D
July–August	No change	Change	No change
August–September	Change	No change	No change
September–October	No change	No change	Change
October–November	Change	Change	Change
November–December	No change	Change	No change
December–January	Change	Change	No change
January–February	Change	No change	No change
February–March	Change	No change	Change
March–April	Change	Change	Change
April–May	No change	Change	No change
May–June	No change	No change	Change

B. In calculating the arc advertising elasticity of demand, only consider consecutive months when there was a change in advertising but no change in the prices of sports and dress watches:

August–September

$$E_A = \frac{\Delta Q}{\Delta A} \times \frac{A_2 + A_1}{Q_2 + Q_1}$$

$$= \frac{4{,}500 - 5{,}500}{\$9{,}200 - \$10{,}000} \times \frac{\$9{,}200 + \$10{,}000}{4{,}500 + 5{,}500}$$

$$= 2.4$$

January–February

$$E_A = \frac{\Delta Q}{\Delta A} \times \frac{A_2 + A_1}{Q_2 + Q_1}$$

$$= \frac{4{,}000 - 5{,}000}{\$7{,}850 - \$8{,}350} \times \frac{\$7{,}850 + \$8{,}350}{4{,}000 + 5{,}000}$$

$$= 3.6$$

On average, $E_A = (2.4 + 3.6)/2 = 3$ and demand will rise 3%, with a 1% increase in advertis-

ing. Thus, demand appears quite sensitive to advertising.

C. In calculating the arc price elasticity of demand, only consider consecutive months when there was a change in the price of sports watches, but no change in advertising nor the price of dress watches:

July–August

$$E_P = \frac{\Delta Q}{\Delta P} \times \frac{P_2 + P_1}{Q_2 + Q_1}$$

$$= \frac{5{,}500 - 4{,}500}{\$24 - \$26} \times \frac{\$24 + \$26}{5{,}500 + 4{,}500}$$

$$= -2.5.$$

November–December

$$E_P = \frac{\Delta Q}{\Delta P} \times \frac{P_2 \; P_1}{Q_2 + Q_1}$$

$$= \frac{15{,}000 - 5{,}000}{\$20 - \$25} \times \frac{\$20 + \$25}{15{,}000 + 5{,}000}$$

$$= -4.5$$

April–May

$$E_P = \frac{\Delta Q}{\Delta P} \times \frac{P_2 + P_1}{Q_2 + Q_1}$$

$$= \frac{4,000 - 6,000}{\$26 - \$24} \times \frac{\$26 + \$24}{4,000 + 6,000}$$

$$= -5$$

On average, $E_P = [(-2.5) + (-4.5) + (-5)]/3 = -4$. A 1% increase (decrease) in price will lead to a 4% decrease (increase) in the quantity demanded. The demand for sports watches is, therefore, elastic with respect to price.

D.   In calculating the arc cross-price elasticity of demand, only consider consecutive months when there was a change in the price of dress watches, but no change in advertising or the price of sports watches:

September–October

$$E_{PX} = \frac{\Delta Q}{\Delta P_X} \times \frac{P_{X2} + P_{X1}}{Q_2 + Q_1}$$

$$= \frac{3,500 - 4,500}{\$46 - \$50} \times \frac{\$46 + \$50}{3,500 + 4,500}$$

$$= 3$$

May–June

$$E_{PX} = \frac{\Delta Q}{\Delta P_X} \times \frac{P_{X2} + P_{X1}}{Q_2 + Q_1}$$

$$= \frac{5,000 - 4,000}{\$57 - \$51} \times \frac{\$57 + \$51}{5,000 + 4,000}$$

$$= 2$$

On average, $E_{PX} = (3 + 2)/2 = 2.5$. Since $E_{PX} > 0$, sports and dress watches are substitutes.

ST5.2   **Cross-Price Elasticity.** Surgical Systems, Inc., makes a proprietary line of disposable surgical stapling instruments. The company grew rapidly during the early 1990s as surgical stapling procedures continued to gain wider hospital acceptance as an alternative to manual suturing. However, price competition in the medical supplies industry is growing rapidly in the increasingly price-conscious mid-1990s. During the past year, Surgical Systems sold 6 million units at a price of

$14.50, for total revenues of $87 million. During the current term, Surgical Systems' unit sales have fallen from 6 million units to 3.6 million units following a competitor price cut from $13.95 to $10.85 per unit.

A.   Calculate the arc cross-price elasticity of demand for Surgical Systems' products.

B.   Surgical Systems' director of marketing projects that unit sales will recover from 3.6 million units to 4.8 million units if Surgical Systems reduces its own price from $14.50 to $13.50 per unit. Calculate Surgical Systems' implied arc price elasticity of demand.

C.   Assuming the same implied arc price elasticity of demand calculated in Part B, determine the further price reduction necessary for Surgical Systems to fully recover lost sales (i.e., regain a volume of 6 million units).

ST5.2   **SOLUTION**

A. $$E_{PX} = \frac{Q_{Y2} - Q_{Y1}}{P_{X2} - P_{X1}} \times \frac{P_{X2} + P_{X1}}{Q_{Y2} + Q_{Y1}}$$

$$= \frac{3,600,000 - 6,000,000}{\$10.85 - \$13.95}$$

$$\times \frac{\$10.85 + \$13.95}{3,600,000 + 6,000,000}$$

$$= 2 \text{ (Substitutes)}$$

B. $$E_P = \frac{Q_2 - Q_1}{P_2 - P_1} \times \frac{P_2 + P_1}{Q_2 + Q_1}$$

$$= \frac{4,800,000 - 3,600,000}{\$13.50 - \$14.50}$$

$$\times \frac{\$13.50 + \$14.50}{4,800,000 + 3,600,000}$$

$$= -4 \text{ (Elastic)}$$

C. $$E_P = \frac{Q_2 - Q_1}{P_2 - P_1} \times \frac{P_2 + P_1}{Q_2 + Q_1}$$

$$-4 = \frac{6,000,000 - 4,800,000}{P_2 - \$13.50}$$

$$\times \frac{P_2 + \$13.50}{6,000,000 + 4,800,000}$$

$$-4 = \frac{P_2 + \$13.50}{9(P_2 - \$13.50)}$$

$$-36P_2 + \$486 = P_2 + \$13.50$$

$$37P_2 = \$472.50$$

$$P_2 = \$12.77$$

This implies a further price reduction of 73¢:

$$\Delta P = \$12.77 - \$13.50 = -\$0.73.$$

PROBLEMS

P5.1 **Price Elasticity.** Characterize each of the following goods and services in terms of its price elasticity of demand. In so doing, indicate whether a steeply sloped (vertical) and relatively inelastic demand curve, or a flat (horizontal) and relatively elastic demand curve, is typical under normal market conditions. Why?
A. Unleaded gasoline.
B. Wheat.
C. Individual income tax preparation services.
D. A cure for AIDS.
E. Lottery tickets.

5.2 **Cross-Price Elasticity.** Characterize each of the following pairs of goods and/or services in terms of their cross-price elasticity of demand. In so doing, indicate whether the cross-price elasticity of demand is apt to be positive, negative, or zero. Similarly, describe each of these pairs of products as substitutes, complements, or independent goods. Why?
A. Computer memory chips and user-friendly software.
B. Self-service and unskilled labor.
C. Video games and "surfing the web."
D. Movies and popcorn.
E. Spreadsheet software and bookkeeper labor.

P5.3 **Income Elasticity.** During recent years, the U.S. president and the Congress have complained about skyrocketing public and private expenditures for Medicare and Medicaid services. At the same time, the demand for privately financed medical care has also increased significantly.
A. Use the concept of the income elasticity of demand to explain why the demand for medical services has grown over time.
B. Is it surprising that the share of national income devoted to medical services in the U.S. is greater than the share of national income devoted

to medical care in less prosperous countries around the world?

P5.4 **Elasticity.** The demand for personal computers can be characterized by the following point elasticities: price elasticity $= -5$, cross-price elasticity with software $= -4$, and income elasticity $= 2.5$. Indicate whether each of the following statements is true or false, and explain your answer.
A. A price reduction for personal computers will increase both the number of units demanded and the total revenue of sellers.
B. The cross-price elasticity indicates that a 5% reduction in the price of personal computers will cause a 20% increase in software demand.
C. Demand for personal computers is price elastic and computers are cyclical normal goods.
D. Falling software prices will increase revenues received by sellers of both computers and software.
E. A 2% price reduction would be necessary to overcome the effects of a 1% decline in income.

P5.5 **Demand Curves.** KRMY-TV is contemplating a T-shirt advertising promotion. Monthly sales data from T-shirt shops marketing the "Eye Watch KRMY-TV" design indicate that

$$Q = 1,500 - 200P,$$

where Q is T-shirt sales and P is price.
A. How many T-shirts could KRMY-TV sell at $4.50 each?
B. What price would KRMY-TV have to charge to sell 900 T-shirts?
C. At what price would T-shirt sales equal zero?
D. How many T-shirts could be given away?
E. Calculate the point price elasticity of demand at a price of $5.

P5.6 **Optimal Pricing.** In an effort to reduce excess end-of-the-model-year inventory, Harrison Ford offered a 2.5% discount off the average list price of Contours sold during the month of August. Customer response was enthusiastic, with unit sales rising by 10% over the previous month's level.

A. Calculate the point price elasticity of demand for Harrison Ford Contours.

B. Calculate the profit-maximizing price per unit if Harrison Ford has an average wholesale cost of $10,000 and incurs marginal selling costs of $875 per unit.

P5.7 **Cross-Price Elasticity.** Kitty Russell's Longbranch Cafe in Sausalito recently reduced Nachos Supreme appetizer prices from $5 to $3 for afternoon "early bird" customers and enjoyed a resulting increase in sales from 60 to 180 orders per day. Beverage sales also increased from 30 to 150 units per day.

A. Calculate the arc price elasticity of demand for Nachos Supreme appetizers.

B. Calculate the arc cross-price elasticity of demand between beverage sales and appetizer prices.

C. Holding all else equal, would you expect an additional appetizer price decrease to $2.50 to cause both appetizer and beverage revenues to rise? Explain.

P5.8 **Income Elasticity.** Ironside Industries, Inc., is a leading manufacturer of tufted carpeting under the Ironside brand. Demand for Ironside's products is closely tied to the overall pace of building and remodeling activity and, therefore, is highly sensitive to changes in national income. The carpet manufacturing industry is highly competitive, so Ironside's demand is also very price-sensitive.

During the past year, Ironside sold 15 million square yards (units) of carpeting at an average wholesale price of $7.75 per unit. This year, income per capita is expected to surge from $17,250 to $18,750 as the nation recovers from a steep recession. Without any price change, Ironside's marketing director expects current-year sales to rise to 25 million units.

A. Calculate the implied income arc elasticity of demand.

B. Given the projected rise in income, the marketing director believes that the current volume of 15 million units could be maintained despite an increase in price of 50¢ per unit. On this basis, calculate the implied arc price elasticity of demand.

C. Holding all else equal, would a further increase in price result in higher or lower total revenue?

P5.9 **Cross-Price Elasticity.** B. B. Lean is a catalog retailer of a wide variety of sporting goods and recreational products. Although the market response to the company's spring catalog was generally good, sales of B. B. Lean's $140 deluxe garment bag declined from 10,000 to 4,800 units. During this period, a competitor offered a whopping $52 off its regular $137 price on deluxe garment bags.

A. Calculate the arc cross-price elasticity of demand for B. B. Lean's deluxe garment bag.

B. B. B. Lean's deluxe garment bag sales recovered from 4,800 units to 6,000 units following a price reduction to $130 per unit. Calculate B. B. Lean's arc price elasticity of demand for this product.

C. Assuming the same arc price elasticity of demand calculated in Part B, determine the further price reduction necessary for B. B. Lean to fully recover lost sales (i.e., regain a volume of 10,000 units).

P5.10 **Advertising Elasticity.** Enchantment Cosmetics, Inc., offers a line of cosmetic and perfume products marketed through leading department stores. Product Manager Erica Kane recently raised the suggested retail price on a popular line of mascara products from $9 to $12 following increases in the costs of labor and materials. Unfortunately, sales dropped sharply from 16,200 to 9,000 units per month. In an effort to regain lost sales, Enchantment ran a coupon promotion featuring $5 off the new regular price. Coupon printing and distribution costs totaled $500 per month and represented a substantial increase over the typical advertising budget of $3,250 per month. Despite these added costs, the promotion was judged to be a success, as it proved to be highly popular with consumers. In the period prior to expiration, coupons were used on 40% of all purchases and monthly sales rose to 15,000 units.

A. Calculate the arc price elasticity implied by the initial response to the Enchantment price increase.

B. Calculate the effective price reduction resulting from the coupon promotion.

C. In light of the price reduction associated with the coupon promotion and assuming no change in the price elasticity of demand, calculate Enchantment's arc advertising elasticity.

D. Why might the true arc advertising elasticity differ from that calculated in Part C?

Case Study for Chapter 5

DEMAND ESTIMATION FOR BRANDED CONSUMER PRODUCTS

Demand estimation for brand-name consumer products is made difficult by the fact that managers must rely on proprietary data. There simply is not any publicly available data that can be used to estimate demand elasticities for brand-name orange juice, frozen entrees, pies, and the like—and with good reason. Competitors would be delighted to know profit margins across a broad array of competing products so that advertising, pricing policy, and product development strategy could all be targeted for maximum benefit. Product demand information is valuable and jealously guarded.

To see the process that might be undertaken to develop a better understanding of product demand conditions, consider the example of Mrs. Smyth's Inc., a Chicago-based food company. In early 1997, Mrs. Smyth's initiated an empirical estimation of demand for its deluxe frozen fruit pies. The firm is formulating pricing and promotional plans for the coming year, and management is interested in learning how pricing and promotional decisions might affect sales. Mrs. Smyth's has been marketing frozen fruit pies for several years, and its market research department has collected quarterly data over two years for six important marketing areas, including sales quantity, the retail price charged for the pies, local advertising and promotional expenditures, and the price charged by a major competing brand of frozen pies. Statistical data published by Sales Management magazine on population and disposable income in each of the six market areas were also available for analysis. It was therefore possible to include a wide range of hypothesized demand determinants in an empirical estimation of fruit pie demand. These data appear in Table 5.6.

Table 5.6

MRS. SMYTH'S FROZEN FRUIT PIE REGIONAL MARKET DEMAND DATA, 1995–1 TO 1996–4

	YEAR-QUARTER	UNIT SALES (Q)	PRICE (cents)	ADVERTISING EXPENDITURE ($000)	COMPETITORS' PRICE (cents)	INCOME ($000)	POPULATION (000)	TIME VARIABLE (T)
ATLANTA, GA	1996–4	27,500	550	$10.0	375	$41.5	2,650	8
	1996–3	25,000	600	7.5	375	40.5	2,500	7
	1996–2	25,000	575	10.0	375	40.0	2,450	6
	1996–1	25,000	575	5.0	400	39.5	2,350	5
	1995–4	27,500	525	10.0	400	39.5	2,300	4
	1995–3	22,500	500	7.5	325	39.0	2,250	3
	1995–2	25,000	525	7.5	375	39.5	2,150	2
	1995–1	22,500	600	5.0	425	39.5	2,150	1

continued

Table 5.6

YEAR-QUARTER	UNIT SALES (Q)	PRICE (cents)	ADVERTISING EXPENDITURE ($000)	COMPETITORS' PRICE (cents)	INCOME ($000)	POPULATION (000)	TIME VARIABLE (T)
BALTIMORE, MD							
1996–4	27,500	600	5.0	425	40.0	2,300	8
1996–3	25,000	600	5.0	400	39.5	2,300	7
1996–2	27,500	525	10.0	425	39.5	2,250	6
1996–1	25,000	550	5.0	400	39.0	2,200	5
1995–4	22,500	600	5.0	400	39.0	2,250	4
1995–3	22,500	550	5.0	375	39.0	2,200	3
1995–2	22,500	625	5.0	400	39.0	2,200	2
1995–1	22,500	600	7.5	400	38.5	2,150	1
CHICAGO, IL							
1996–4	32,500	600	5.0	400	46.0	6,200	8
1996–3	32,500	550	15.0	375	45.5	6,150	7
1996–2	27,500	600	5.0	375	45.0	6,100	6
1996–1	22,500	600	10.0	350	44.5	6,150	5
1995–4	30,000	550	5.0	375	45.0	6,200	4
1995–3	30,000	575	15.0	350	44.5	6,250	3
1995–2	25,000	600	5.0	450	44.5	6,100	2
1995–1	27,500	575	5.0	375	44.0	6,050	1
DENVER, CO							
1996–4	35,000	500	15.0	400	47.5	1,600	8
1996–3	32,500	575	10.0	400	47.0	1,650	7
1996–2	32,500	550	7.5	425	47.0	1,600	6
1996–1	30,000	600	12.5	400	46.5	1,550	5
1995–4	27,500	550	5.0	350	46.0	1,550	4
1995–3	25,000	600	5.0	325	46.5	1,500	3
1995–2	27,500	575	10.0	350	47.0	1,450	2
1995–1	30,000	550	10.0	425	46.5	1,450	1
ERIE, PA							
1996–4	17,500	600	2.5	375	35.5	300	8
1996–3	17,500	625	2.5	375	35.0	290	7
1996–2	15,000	600	5.0	375	34.5	285	6
1996–1	17,500	575	2.5	350	34.5	270	5
1995–4	15,000	625	2.5	325	34.0	265	4
1995–3	17,500	575	2.5	375	34.0	270	3
1995–2	15,000	575	5.0	350	34.0	275	2
1995–1	17,500	575	2.5	400	34.0	280	1
FORT LAUDERDALE, FL							
1996–4	27,500	625	5.0	400	46.0	1,500	8
1996–3	27,500	625	12.5	350	46.0	1,450	7
1996–2	27,500	625	5.0	450	45.0	1,300	6
1996–1	25,000	625	5.0	375	44.5	1,450	5
1995–4	30,000	550	7.5	425	44.5	1,350	4
1995–3	30,000	575	12.5	425	44.0	1,100	3
1995–2	27,500	600	12.5	400	43.5	1,050	2
1995–1	25,000	575	10.0	400	43.5	1,025	1

The following regression equation was fit to these data:

$$Q_{it} = b_0 + b_1P_{it} + b_2A_{it} + b_3PX_{it} + b_4Y_{it} \\ + b_5Pop_{it} + b_6T_{it} + u_{it}.$$

Q is the quantity of pies sold during the tth quarter; P is the retail price in cents of Mrs. Smyth's frozen pies; A represents the dollars (in thousands) spent for advertising and promotional activities; PX is the price, measured in cents, charged for competing pies; Y is thousands of dollars of disposable income per household; Pop is the population of the market area (in thousands of persons); T is the trend factor (1995–1 = 1, . . ., 1996–4 = 8); and u_{it} is a residual (or disturbance) term. The subscript i indicates the regional market from which the observation was taken, whereas the subscript t represents the quarter during which the observation occurred. Least squares estimation of the regression equation on the basis of the 48 data observations (eight quarters of data for each of six areas) resulted in the estimated regression coefficients and other statistics given in Table 5.7.

The individual coefficients for the Mrs. Smyth's pie demand regression equation can be interpreted as follows. The intercept term, −4,516.291, has no economic meaning in this instance; it lies far outside the range of observed data and obviously cannot be interpreted as the demand for Mrs. Smyth's frozen fruit pies when all the independent variables take on zero values. The coefficient for each independent variable indicates the marginal relation between that variable and sales of pies, holding constant the effect of all the other variables in the demand function. For example, the −35.985 coefficient for P, the price charged for Mrs. Smyth's pies, indicates that when the effects of all other demand variables are held constant, each 1¢ increase in price causes quarterly sales to decline by roughly 36 pies. Similarly, the 203.713 coefficient for A, the advertising and promotion variable, indicates that for each $1,000 (one-unit) increase in advertising during the quarter, roughly 204 additional pies are sold. The 37.960 coefficient for the competitor-price variable indicates that demand for Mrs. Smyth's pies rises by roughly 38 pies with every 1¢ increase in competitor prices. The 777.051 coefficient for the Y variable indicates that, on average, a $1,000 (one-unit) increase in the average disposable income per household for a given market leads to roughly a 777-unit increase in quarterly pie demand. Similarly, a 1,000 person (one-unit) increase in the population of a given market area leads to a small 0.256-unit increase in quarterly pie demand. Finally, the 356.047 coefficient for the trend variable indicates that pie demand is growing in a typical market by roughly 356 units per quarter. This means that Mrs. Smyth's is enjoying secular growth in pie demand, perhaps as a result of the growing popularity of Mrs. Smyth's products or of frozen foods in general.

Individual coefficients provide useful estimates of the expected marginal influence on demand following a one-unit change in each respective variable.

Table 5.7

ESTIMATED DEMAND FUNCTION FOR MRS. SMYTH'S FROZEN FRUIT PIES

VARIABLE (1)	COEFFICIENT (2)	STANDARD ERROR OF COEFFICIENT (3)	t-STATISTIC (4) = (2) ÷ (3)
Intercept	−4,516.291	4,988.242	−0.91
Price (P)	−35.985	7.019	5.13
Advertising (A)	203.713	77.292	2.64
Competitor price (PX)	37.960	7.065	5.37
Income (Y)	777.051	66.423	11.70
Population (Pop)	0.256	0.125	2.04
Time (T)	356.047	92.288	3.86

Coefficient of determination = R^2 = 92.7%
Standard error of estimate = S.E.E. = 1,442

However, they are only estimates. For example, it would be very unusual for a 1¢ increase in price to cause exactly a −35.985-unit change in the quantity demanded. The actual effect could be more or less. For decision-making purposes, it would be helpful to know if the marginal influences suggested by the regression model are stable or instead tend to vary widely over the sample analyzed.

In general, if it is known with certainty that $Y = a + bX$, then a one-unit change in X will always lead to a b-unit change in Y. If $b > 0$, X and Y will be directly related; if $b < 0$, X and Y will be inversely related. If no relation at all holds between X and Y, then $b = 0$. Although the true parameter b is unobservable, its value is estimated by the regression coefficient $\hat{b}$. If $\hat{b} = 10$, a 1-unit change in X will increase Y by 10 units. This effect may appear to be large, but it will be statistically significant only if it is stable over the entire sample. To be statistically reliable, $\hat{b}$ must be large relative to its degree of variation over the sample.

In a regression equation, there is a 68% probability that b lies in the interval $\hat{b} \pm$ one standard error (or standard deviation) of the coefficient $\hat{b}$. There is a 95% probability that b lies in the interval $\hat{b} \pm$ two standard errors of the coefficient. There is a 99% probability that b is in the interval $\hat{b} \pm$ three standard errors of the coefficient. When a coefficient is at least twice as large as its standard error, one can reject at the 95% confidence level the hypothesis that the true parameter b equals zero. This leaves only a 5% chance of concluding incorrectly that $b \neq 0$ when in fact $b = 0$. When a coefficient is at least three times as large as its standard error (standard deviation), the confidence level rises to 99% and chance of error falls to 1%.

A significant relation between X and Y is typically indicated whenever a coefficient is at least twice as large as its standard error; significance is even more likely when a coefficient is at least three times as large as its standard error. The independent effect of each independent variable on sales is measured using a two-tail t-statistic where:

$$t\text{-statistic} = \frac{\hat{b}}{\text{Standard error of } \hat{b}}.$$

This t-statistic is a measure of the number of standard errors between $\hat{b}$ and a hypothesized value of zero. If the sample used to estimate the regression parameters is large (for example, $n > 30$), the t-statistic follows a normal distribution and properties

of a normal distribution, can be used to make confidence statements concerning the statistical significance of $\hat{b}$. Hence $t = 1$ implies 68% confidence, $t = 2$ implies 95% confidence, $t = 3$ implies 99% confidence, and so on. For small sample sizes (for example, $d.f. = n - k < 30$), the t-distribution deviates from a normal distribution, and a t-table should be used for testing the significance of estimated regression parameters.

Another regression statistic, the standard error of the estimate (S.E.E.), is used to predict values for the dependent variable given values for the various independent variables. Thus, it is helpful in determining a range within which one can predict values for the dependent variable with varying degrees of statistical confidence. Although the best estimate of the value for the dependent variable is $\hat{Y}$, the value predicted by the regression equation, the standard error of the estimate can be used to determine just how accurate this prediction $\hat{Y}$ is likely to be. Assuming that the standard errors are normally distributed about the regression equation, there is a 68% probability that actual observations of the dependent variable Y will lie within the range $\hat{Y} \pm$ one standard error of the estimate. The probability that an actual observation of Y will lie within two standard errors of its predicted value increases to 95%. There is a 99% chance that an actual observed value for Y will lie in the range $\hat{Y} \pm$ three standard errors. Obviously, greater predictive accuracy is associated with smaller standard errors of the estimate.

Mrs. Smyth's could forecast the total demand for its pies by forecasting sales in each of the six market areas, then summing these area forecasts to obtain an estimate of total pie demand. Using the results from the demand estimation model and data from each individual market, it would also be possible to construct a confidence interval for total pie demand based on the standard error of the estimate.

A. Describe the statistical significance of each individual independent variable included in the Mrs. Smyth's frozen fruit pie demand equation.

B. Interpret the coefficient of determination (R^2) for the Mrs. Smyth's frozen fruit pie demand equation.

C. What is the expected value of next quarter's unit sales in the Baltimore, Maryland, market?

D. To illustrate use of the standard error of the estimate statistic, derive the 95% confidence interval for next quarter's actual unit sales in the Baltimore, Maryland, market.

Forecasting

Harvard economist John Kenneth Galbraith is credited with the quip, "We have two classes of forecasters: Those who don't know—and those who don't know they don't know." There is more than a bit of truth to this witticism.

Experienced economists know that economic forecasting is fraught with uncertainty. To see why, consider the interrelated nature of economic forecasts. One might ask an economist, will the pace of real economic growth in the U.S. average an anemic 2%, a healthy 3%, or a robust 3.5%? What will be the rate of inflation? How will investors respond to a proposed cut in the capital gains tax, if and when such a tax cut is passed by both Houses of Congress and signed into law by the president? Most importantly, how is the rate of growth in the overall economy related to inflation, and how are both apt to be affected by an important change in tax law that, at this point, is only at the proposal stage? When chemists and physicists run experiments, they have carefully controlled laboratory environments. Economists enjoy no such luxury; they must make assumptions based on volatile conditions subject to random and violent shocks. No wonder that economic forecasters lament the difficulty of making accurate economic projections.[1]

Predicting trends in the overall economy and its impact on the cost or demand for company goods and services is one of the most difficult responsibilities facing management. However, it is a necessary task because, for better or worse, all decisions are made on the basis of future expectations. This chapter illustrates a number of forecasting techniques that have proven successful in forming accurate expectations in a wide variety of real-world applications.

What Is Economic Forecasting?

Everybody forecasts, whether they realize it or not. When undergraduate students decide on a major in college, or graduate students decide to pursue the Masters in Business Administration, it is based on personal skills and interests and individual forecasts of personal satisfaction, job market opportunities, and so on. When companies hire new

---

[1]See Andrew J. Kessler, "The Database Economy," *Forbes,* April 21, 1997, 168.

workers or managers, they must forecast the relative productivity of a wide variety of individuals with disparate skills, work histories, and personalities. Businesses must forecast future events before preparing even the simplest business plan or making the most mundane decisions. How much inventory should be carried? What price should be charged during the coming holiday season? Which market is the most natural path for regional expansion? All of these decisions require that managers make informed forecasts of future economic events.

WHY IS FORECASTING USEFUL?

Much business forecasting is intuitive and judgmental. Sometimes this is appropriate; sometimes it is not. Managers sometimes must integrate quantitative and nonquantitative information in a way not easily modeled or characterized by numbers. In such instances, there is no substitute for the extraordinary pattern recognition capabilities of the human mind. Experienced managers sometimes "know" the correct level of inventory to order, or price to set, despite the fact that they are unable to easily explain all of the factors that weigh in their decisions. While there is no good substitute for the accurate intuition of an experienced manager, some firms err in their overreliance on judgmental forecasting methods. In particular, the concept of forecasting is sometimes confused with goal setting. If a company asks its staff to forecast sales for the Mid-Atlantic region, for example, these "forecasts" are sometimes used as yardsticks to judge sales performance. If forecast sales are exceeded, sales performance is "good"; if forecast sales are not achieved, sales performance is "poor." This sometimes leads sales staffs to underestimate future sales in a effort to boost perceived performance. Just as a successful college football coach predicts a tough year to enhance the popular perception of a winning record, sales personnel have incentives to be overly conservative in their sales projections for new or improved products. Coaches of teams with 8-3 records sometimes lose their jobs if fans had expected a perfect 11-0 season; brand managers of even highly successful new product introductions sometimes get fired if rosy predictions are not met.

A primary advantage of the wide variety of statistical techniques commonly employed in economic forecasting is that they separate the process of forecasting from the firm's goal-setting activity. When sales are forecast in an objective, systematic, and unbiased manner, the potential for accurate forecasts increases, as does the capacity for appropriate operating and planning decisions. When these forecasts involve outcomes and precipitating factors that can be quantified, it also becomes possible to access the direct ramifications of changes in controllable and uncontrollable conditions. Optimistic through pessimistic scenarios can be tested and analyzed for their performance implications and for their significance in terms of the decision-making process. Forecasting that is objective and quantitative has the potential to help almost any business; accurate business forecasting is a value-added undertaking.

COMMON TYPES OF FORECASTING PROBLEMS

Macroeconomic Forecasting
Prediction of aggregate economic activity.

A great deal of the attention devoted to business forecasting relates to the prediction of aggregate economic activity. **Macroeconomic forecasting** involves predicting aggregate measures of economic activity at the international, national, regional, or state level. Predictions of Gross Domestic Product (GDP), unemployment, and interest rates by "blue chip" business economists capture the attention of national media, business, government, and the general public on a daily basis.[2] Other macroeconomic forecasts commonly reported in the press include predictions of consumer spending, business investment, homebuilding, exports, imports, federal purchases, state and local government spending, and so on. These macroeconomic predictions are important because they are, to a greater or lesser extent, used by businesses and individuals to make day-to-day and long-term investment decisions. If interest rates are projected to rise, homeowners may rush to refinance fixed-rate mortgages, while businesses float new bond and stock offerings to refinance existing debt or take advantage of investment opportunities. When such predictions are accurate, significant cost savings or revenue gains become possible. When such predictions are inaccurate, higher costs and lost marketing opportunities occur. The tremendous profit potential from accurate macroeconomic forecasts makes the subject a topic of keen interest to all types of businesses in a wide variety of industries.

Despite the obvious potential for significant benefits from accurate macroeconomic forecasts, the many challenges facing macroeconomic forecasting can limit its usefulness. The accuracy of any forecast is subject to the influence of controllable and uncontrollable factors. In the case of macroeconomic forecasting, uncontrollable factors loom large in both number and influence. Take interest rate forecasting, for example. The future course of short-term interest rates depends on both the demand for and supply of funds. The demand for credit and short-term interest rates rises if businesses seek to build inventories or expand plant and equipment, or if consumers wish to increase installment credit. The supply of credit rises and short-term interest rates fall if the Federal Reserve System acts to increase the money supply, or if consumers cut back on spending to increase savings rates. Interest rate forecasting is made difficult by the fact that business decisions to build inventories, for example, are largely based on the expected pace of overall economic activity—which itself depends on interest-rate expectations. The macroeconomic environment is interrelated in ways that are unstable and cannot be easily predicted. Even policy decisions are hard to predict. For example, Federal Reserve System policy meeting minutes are confidential until months after the fact.

---

[2] GDP measures aggregate business activity as described by the value at final point of sale of all goods and services produced in the domestic economy during a given period by both domestic and foreign-owned enterprises. Gross national product (GNP) is the value at final point of sale of all goods and services produced by *domestic* firms. As such, GNP does not reflect domestic production by foreign-owned firms (e.g., Toyota Camrys produced in Kentucky).

Is it any wonder that "Fed watching" is a favorite pastime of business economists and that accurate macroeconomic forecasting is difficult?

In contrast with macroeconomic forecasting, **microeconomic forecasting** involves the prediction of desegregate or partial economic data at the industry, firm, plant, or product level. Unlike predictions of GDP growth, which are widely followed in the press, the general public often ignores microeconomic forecasts of scrap prices for aluminum, the demand for new cars, or production costs for *Crest* toothpaste. For example, it is exceedingly unlikely that the *CBS Evening News* will ever be interrupted to discuss an upward trend in used car prices, even though these data are an excellent predictor of the future path of new car demand. When used car prices surge, new car demand often grows rapidly; when used car prices sag, new car demand typically drops. The fact that used car prices and new car demand are closely related is not surprising given the strong substitute-good relation that exists between used cars and new cars.

Trained and experienced analysts often find it easier to accurately forecast microeconomic trends, like the demand for new cars, than macroeconomic trends in the overall economy, such as GDP growth. This is because microeconomic forecasts abstract from the profusion of important variables and variable interrelationships that together determine the macroeconomy. With specialized knowledge about changes in new car prices, car import tariffs, car loan rates, and used car prices, among other factors, it is possible to isolate and focus on the fairly narrow range of important factors that influence new car demand. In contrast, a similarly precise model of aggregate economic demand in the macroeconomy might involve literally thousands of economic variables and hundreds of functional relationships. This is not to say that microeconomic forecasting is easy and that forecast results are always precise. In late 1993, for example, the head of Ford forecast 1994 new car and truck demand of 14.5 million units, the head of General Motors forecast 14 million units, while the head of Chrysler forecast 16 million units. According to industry surveys, the actual number of new vehicles sold in 1994 was 15.4 million units. This was up from 14.2 million units in 1993, and roughly the same as industry sales of 15.5 million units in 1995 and 15 million units in 1996. Clearly, accurate auto and truck demand forecasting is tough even for industry experts.

In sum, both macroeconomic and microeconomic forecasting face important challenges that can limit their effectiveness. A careful analyst considers and models the influences of both controllable and uncontrollable factors. Where the influence of uncontrollable factors looms especially large, as in macroeconomic forecasting, it is only prudent to allow for the potential of significant forecast error.

THE PROBLEM OF CHANGING EXPECTATIONS

A subtle problem bedevils both macroeconomic and microeconomic forecasting: the problem of changing expectations. If business purchasing agents are optimistic about future trends in the economy and boost inventories in anticipation of surging customer demand, the resulting inventory buildup can itself contribute to economic growth. Conversely, if purchasing agents fear an economic recession and cut back on orders and inventory growth, they themselves can be a main contributor to any resulting economic downturn. The expectations of purchasing agents and other managers can become a self-fulfilling prophecy because the macroeconomic environment represents the sum of the investment and spending decisions of business, government, and the public. Indeed, the link between expectations and realizations has the potential to create an optimistic bias in government-reported statistics.

Government economists are sometimes criticized for being overly optimistic about the rate of growth in the overall economy, the future path of interest rates, or the magnitude of the federal deficit. As consumers of the economic statistics, managers must realize that it can pay for government or politically motivated economists to be optimistic. If business leaders can be led to make appropriate decisions for a growing economy or falling interest rates, their decisions can in fact help lead to a growing economy and/or lower interest rates. Unlike many business economists from the private sector, government-employed and/or politically motivated economists often actively seek to manage the economic expectations of business leaders and the general public.

It is vital for managers to appreciate the link between economic expectations and realizations and to be wary of the potential for forecast bias.

THE DATA QUALITY PROBLEM

It is impossible to derive accurate forecasts from data that are carelessly collected. Accurate forecasts require an appropriately detailed collection of pertinent data that are current, complete, and free from error. At one time or another, everyone has heard the familiar warning about the relation between data quality and forecast accuracy: "garbage in, garbage out." However, this statement is true in ways that are not immediately obvious. For example, if a manager wants to forecast demand for consumer or producer goods, it is often better to input incoming orders rather than shipments because shipments are sometimes subject to production delays. Similarly, the timing of order fulfillment is sometimes subject to delays in transit that are beyond the control of the shipping firm.

In addition to carefully considering the quality of data input to be used to generate forecasts, the quantity of available data is also an important consideration. A general rule is: The more data that can be subject to analysis, the better. Some advanced forecasting software that works on desktop personal computers can function with as few as five data points. However, the forecasts that result from such paltry bodies of data are often simplistic, if not trivial. Although the collection of large samples of data on market transactions can be expensive and tedious, the payoff in forecast accuracy can justify the effort.

If monthly data are seasonal in nature, it is important to have an extended time series of information to facilitate forecast accuracy. Most forecasting software programs used to monitor monthly activity require a minimum of two years of data (24 observations) to build a seasonally adjusted forecast model. This is because such models build an index for each monthly forecast period, and this requires at least two data points for each month. Practically speaking, two years of monthly data are often not enough; three years or five years of monthly data (36 to 60 observations) are typically necessary before a high level of monthly forecast accuracy can be achieved. Of course, most forecast software works with data of any periodicity, be it hourly, daily, weekly, monthly, or annual in nature. The ultimate consideration that must be addressed is whether the quantity and quality of data analyzed are sufficient to shed meaningful light on the forecast problem being addressed. The ultimate answer to this question is empirical. The acid test is: Can useful forecasts be generated?

One of the most vexing data quality problems encountered in forecasting is the obstacle presented by government-supplied data that are often tardy and inaccurate. For example, the Commerce Department's Bureau of Economic Analysis "advanced" estimate of GDP for the fourth quarter of the year is typically published in late January of the following year. A "preliminary" revision to this estimate is then released by the Bureau of Economic Analysis on March 1; an official final revision is not made available until March 31, or until 90 days after the fact. Such delays cause problems by inducing uncertainty for those seeking to make projections about future trends in economic activity. Worse still, preliminary and final revisions to official GDP estimates are often large and in unpredictable directions. An advanced estimate of a robust 5% rate of growth in real GDP may be revised to a more typical 3% rate of expansion in the official preliminary estimate, only to be downgraded to a sluggish 2% rate of growth in the final estimate. Extreme variation in the official estimates of key economic statistics is a primary cause of forecast error among business economists.

Finally, before discussing alternative forecast techniques, it is worth remembering that forecasts are, by definition, never perfect. All forecasting methods rely heavily on historical data and historical relationships. Future events are seldom, if ever, explicitly accounted for in popular forecasting techniques. Computer-based forecasting software rarely takes into account future events such as a large upcoming sale event, new product introduction, increased consumer confidence, and so on. Managers are always well advised to combine the output of traditional forecast methods with personal insight and knowledge of future events to create the best and most useful forecasts.

COMMON FORECAST TECHNIQUES

Several techniques are available for forecasting economic variables. They range from simple forecasting methods that are somewhat naive and relatively inexpensive to approaches that are complex and costly. Some forecasting techniques are basically quantitative; others are largely qualitative. In general, the most commonly applied forecasting techniques can be divided into the following broad categories:

Economic Forecasting: The Art and the Science

Accurate forecasts of future economic activity are valuable to firms making hiring, inventory, and other investment decisions. Consumers making purchase and career decisions also find accurate forecasts of short- and long-term economic trends exceptionally useful. Because firms and consumers base important decisions on expectations about the pace of future economic activity, a substantial demand for economic forecasts results. So extensive is this demand that the supply of economic forecasting services has exploded during recent years. Economic forecasts by academic, business, and government economists are prominently featured on television and radio and in the print media. The high level of business and consumer interest, and resulting media coverage, gives rise to a high level of visibility for economists who provide forecasting services.

This high level of visibility has focused attention on both the strengths and limitations of economic forecasting. In terms of limitations, the accuracy of economic forecasts is often criticized. For example, it is very difficult to decipher if real economic growth will be 2.0% or 2.5%. The difference, although small, can be crucial for sectors such as capital equipment, where business conditions are closely tied to aggregate economic activity. The demand for capital equipment might rebound vigorously with a 2.5% growth in GDP, but remain sluggish with a 2.0% rise. Thus, a difference of only 0.5% in GDP growth might make a difference of millions of dollars in revenues and profits. If a weather forecast calls for sunny skies and a high of 75°, the forecaster is applauded if sunny skies and a high of 80° results. Not so with the economic forecaster. You and I may not notice any difference between 2.0% or 2.5% rates of economic growth, but companies blame (or fire) their economists when projections for robust economic growth fail to materialize and spending plans go awry. Patience with forecast error in business tends to be low.

Many of us also do not understand why disagreement among forecasting economists is common and why this disagreement can produce divergent economic forecasts. These concerns sometimes reflect too little appreciation of difficulty of economic forecasting. In the real world, "all else held equal" doesn't hold very often, if ever. To forecast the future course of GDP, for example, one must be able to accurately predict the future pattern of government spending, tax and monetary policy, consumer and business spending, dollar strength against foreign currencies, weather, and so on. Although typical patterns can be inferred on the basis of past trends, atypical departures often have economic consequences that complicate matters. An unexpected drought, winter storm, or labor strike can disrupt economic activity, and upset the accuracy of economic forecasts in the process.

In light of the uncertainties involved, it seems reasonable that different forecasting economists would accord differing importance to a wide variety of economic influences. Just as individual forecasters assess different probabilities to an increase in government spending, they might also interpret consequences differently. Forecasters' judgment is reflected not only in the interpretation they give to the data generated by complex computer models but also in the models themselves. Computers may generate economic forecasts, but they do so on the basis of programs written by economists. Computer-generated economic forecasts are only as sophisticated as the data employed, model analyzed, and the subsequent analysis.

Given the criticism often aimed at forecasters, it is ironic to note that the success of economic forecasting is responsible, at least in part, for some of its failures. Users have come to expect a nearly unattainable level of forecast accuracy. At the same time, users forget that forecasts can, by themselves, have important economic consequences. When consumers and businesses cut back on spending in reaction to the forecast of an impending mild recession, for example, they change the basis for the forecasters' initial prediction. By their behavior, they may also cause a steeper recession. This is the forecaster's dilemma: The future as we know it doesn't exist. In fact, it can't.

See: James C. Cooper and Kathleen Madigan, "A Toast for the New Year: Happy Rebound," *Business Week,* January 13, 1997, 31-32.

- Qualitative analyses
- Trend analysis and projection
- Exponential smoothing
- Econometric methods

It is impossible to argue that any one of these forecasting approaches is inherently superior to the others. Each method has its strengths and weaknesses. The best forecast methodology for a particular task depends on the nature of a specific forecasting problem. When making a choice among forecast methodologies, a number of important factors must be considered. It is always worth considering the distance into the future that one must forecast, the lead time available for making decisions, the level of accuracy required, the quality of data available for analysis, the stochastic or deterministic nature of forecast relations, and the cost and benefits associated with the forecasting problem.

Techniques such as trend analysis, market experiments, consumer surveys, and the leading indicator approach to forecasting are well suited for short-term projections. Forecasting with complex econometric models and systems of simultaneous equations have proven somewhat more useful for long-run forecasting. The level of sophistication also varies within each class of forecasting technique. Typically, the greater the level of sophistication, the higher the cost. If the required level of accuracy is low, less sophisticated methods can provide adequate results at a minimal cost.

Qualitative Analysis

Qualitative Analysis
An intuitive judgmental approach to forecasting based on opinion.

Qualitative analysis, an intuitive judgmental approach to forecasting, can be a highly useful technique if it allows for the systematic collection and organization of data derived from unbiased, informed opinion. However, qualitative methods can produce biased results when specific individuals dominate the forecasting process through reputation, force of personality, or strategic position within the organization.

EXPERT OPINION

Personal Insight
Forecast method based on personal or organizational experience.

The most basic form of qualitative analysis used in forecasting is **personal insight,** in which an informed individual uses personal or company experience as a basis for developing future expectations. Although this approach is highly subjective, the reasoned judgment of informed individuals often provides valuable insight. When the informed opinion of several individuals is relied on, the approach is called forecasting through

Panel Consensus
Forecast method based on the informed opinion of several individuals.

panel consensus. The panel consensus method assumes that several experts can arrive at forecasts that are superior to those that individuals generate. Direct interaction among experts is used in the panel consensus method with the hope that resulting forecasts embody all available objective and subjective information.

Although the panel consensus method often results in forecasts that embody the

Delphi Method
Method that uses forecasts derived from an independent analysis of expert opinion.

collective wisdom of consulted experts, it can sometimes be unfavorably affected by the forceful personality of one or a few key individuals. A related approach, the **delphi method,** has been developed to counter this disadvantage. In the delphi method, members of a panel of experts individually receive a series of questions relating to the underlying forecasting problem. Responses are analyzed by an independent party, who then tries to elicit a consensus opinion by providing feedback to panel members in a manner that prevents direct identification of individual positions. This method helps limit the steamroller or bandwagon problems of the basic panel consensus approach.

SURVEY TECHNIQUES

Survey Techniques
An interview or mailed questionnaire approach to forecasting.

Survey techniques that skillfully employ interviews or mailed questionnaires constitute another important forecasting tool, especially for short-term projection. Designing surveys that provide unbiased and reliable information is a challenging task. When properly carried out, however, survey research can provide managers with valuable information that would otherwise be unobtainable.

Surveys generally use interviews or mailed questionnaires asking business firms, government agencies, and individuals about their future plans. Business firms plan and budget virtually all their expenditures in advance of actual purchase or production decisions. Surveys asking about capital budgets, sales budgets, and operating budgets can thus provide much useful information for forecasting. Government departments also prepare formal budgets and surveys of budget material, congressional appropriations hearings, and the like can provide a wealth of information to the forecaster. Finally, even individual consumers routinely plan expenditures for such major items as automobiles, furnitures, housing, vacations, and education ahead of the purchase date, so surveys of consumer intentions often accurately predict future spending on consumer goods.

Survey information may be all that is obtainable in certain forecasting situations, as, for example, when a firm is attempting to project the demand for a new product. Although surveys sometimes serve as an alternative to quantitative forecasting techniques, they frequently supplement rather than replace quantitative analysis. Their value stems from two influences. First, a nonquantifiable psychological element is inherent in most economic behavior; surveys and other qualitative methods are especially well suited to picking up this phenomenon. Second, quantitative models generally assume stable consumer tastes. If these tastes are actually changing, survey data can suggest the nature and direction of such changes.

COMMON SOURCES OF SURVEY INFORMATION

Surveys useful for forecasting business activity in various sectors of the U.S. economy are published periodically by both private and government sources. Some of the most

Table 6.1

BARRON'S WEEKLY MARKET LABORATORY: PULSE OF THE ECONOMY

ECONOMIC GROWTH AND INVESTMENT	LATEST DATE	LATEST DATA	PRECEDING PERIOD	YEAR AGO
Durable goods produced a	Dec.	p144.7	r142.8	134.8
Capacity utilization %	Dec.	p83.8	r83.4	82.9
Gross domestic product	3rd qtr	+2.1	r+4.7	+2.2
Industrial output a	Dec.	p129.1	r128.1	122.8
Manufacturing a	Dec.	p131.8	r130.4	124.8
Nondurable goods produced a	Dec.	p117.6	r116.7	113.8
Personal income, (Bil. $)	Nov.	6,574	r6,542	6,229
All fixed investment	3rd qtr	1,057.5	1,031.1	981.0
Nonresidential investment	3rd qtr	781.4	750.5	719.7
Residential investment	3rd qtr	277.8	281.5	262.3

PRODUCTION				
Electric Power, (Mil. kw hrs)	Jan. 11	65,741	57,896	67,271
Lumber, (Mil. bd ft)	Oct.	3,158	r2,858	2,902
Mining a	Dec.	p104.0	r102.7	98.1
Newsprint, U.S. & Can., (Thous. metric tons)	Oct.	1,357	r1,259	1,337
Petroleum, daily runs, (Thous. bbls)	Jan. 10	13,774	14,083	13,597
Petroleum, rated capacity, %	Jan. 10	90.7	92.3	89.8
Rotary rigs running U.S. & Can. (Hughes)	Jan. 10	1,235	1,203	1,056
Steel, (Thous. tons)	Jan. 11	1,994	1,999	2,031
Steel, rated capacity, % (AISI)	Jan. 11	86.5	87.9	91.9
Utilities a	Dec.	p124.1	r128.4	125.1

CONSUMPTION AND DISTRIBUTION				
Autos, domestic units sold	Dec.	500,112	488,293	544,849
Autos, import units sold	Dec.	104,430	102,874	109,273
Business sales, (Bil. $)	Nov.	729.83	r725.79	690.26
Consumer spending, (Bil. $)	Nov.	5,406	5,377	XXXX
Durable goods, (Bil. $)	Nov.	170.10	r168.70	161.36
Factory Shipments, (Bil. $)	Nov.	318.28	315.42	301.28
Light trucks, domestic units	Dec.	483,289	494,166	485,984
Light trucks, import units	Dec.	36,514	39,942	32,027
Lumber shipments, (Mil. board ft)	Oct.	3,184	r2,813	2,900
New home sales, (Thous. units)	Oct.	714	782	673
Personal consumption	3rd qtr	4,693.5	4,687.6	3,701.1
Retail store sales, (Bil. $)	Nov.	206.06	r206.84	197.91
Wholesale sales, (Bil. $)	Nov.	204.58	r202.79	191.57

[a]-1987 equals 100. [b]-1982–1984 equals 100. [c]-1987 equals 100. [e]-Estimate. [p]-Preliminary. [r]-Revised.

Source: *Barron's,* January 27, 1997, MW102.

widely used are those employed to forecast plant and equipment expenditures. Surveys of business intentions to expand plant and equipment are conducted by the U.S. Department of Commerce, the Securities and Exchange Commission, the National Industrial Conference Board, and McGraw-Hill, Inc., among others. Several trade associations also publish expenditure surveys for specific industries. For example, the Edison Electric Institute and the American Gas Association publish information that is widely employed in forecasting capacity utilization and investment expenditure plans for the energy sector. Changes in inventories and sales revenue expectations are published by the U.S. Department of Commerce and private organizations such as McGraw-Hill, Dun and Bradstreet, and the National Association of Purchasing Agents. These surveys, although not nearly as accurate as those for long-term investment, provide a useful check on other forecasting methods. Consumer intentions surveys of the Census Bureau, the University of Michigan Research Center, and the Sindlinger-National Industrial Conference Board all provide information on planned purchases of specific products, such as automobiles, housing, and appliances. In addition, these surveys often indicate consumer confidence in the economy and, therefore, spending expectations in general.

Some of the most readily available survey information is that published regularly in leading business newspapers and magazines. For example, *Barron's* is a national business and financial weekly that offers a wide range of useful survey information. As shown in Table 6.1, *Barron's* weekly market survey of economic indicators depicts the rate of change in the overall level of economic activity as indicated by gross national product (GNP), durable and nondurable manufacturing, factory utilization, and other statistics. Also provided are more specific data on the level of production in a wide range of basic industries such as autos, electric power, paper, petroleum, and steel, among others. Data published weekly in *Barron's* include not only the level of production (what is made), but also distribution (what is sold), inventories (what is on hand), new orders received, unfilled orders, purchasing power, employment, and construction activity. *Forbes* magazine publishes its own biweekly index of economic activity using government data on consumer prices, manufacturer's new orders and inventories, industrial production, new housing starts, personal income, new unemployment claims, retail sales, and consumer installment credit. To measure these eight elements of the *Forbes Index,* ten series of U.S. government data are monitored over a 14-month period.

Fortune and *Business Week* magazines also offer interesting regular coverage and analysis of data on current and projected levels of economic activity. For instance, the quarterly *Fortune Forecast* of economic activity is based on a proprietary econometric model developed by the company's own staff economists. At a minimum, the forecast data and analysis published in these leading business newspapers and magazines provide managers with a useful starting point in the development of their own future expectations. Managers of large and small organizations will find both the data and the analysis provided helpful in developing the background of information necessary for successful forecasting.

Trend Analysis and Projection

Trend Analysis
Forecasting the future path of economic variables based on historical patterns.

Trend analysis is based on the assumption that economic performance follows an established pattern and, therefore, historical data can be used to predict future business activity. Trend analysis techniques involve characterizing the historical pattern of an economic variable and then projecting or forecasting its future path based on past experience.

The many variations of forecasting by trend projection are all predicated on a continuation of the past relation between the variable being projected and the passage of time, so all of them employ time series data. As described in Chapter 3, an economic time series is a sequential array of data on the value of an economic variable. Weekly, monthly, or annual series of data on sales and costs, personal income, population, labor force participation rates, and GNP are all examples of economic time series.

TRENDS IN ECONOMIC DATA

Trend
Long-run pattern of increase or decrease.

Cyclical Fluctuation
Rhythmic fluctuation in an economic series due to expansion or contraction in the overall economy.

Seasonality
Rhythmic annual patterns in sales or profits.

Irregular or Random Influences
Unpredictable shocks to the economic system.

All time series, regardless of the nature of the economic variable involved, can be described in terms of a few important underlying characteristics. A **trend** is the long-run pattern of increase or decrease in a series of economic data. **Cyclical fluctuation** describes the rhythmic variation in economic series that is due to a pattern of expansion or contraction in the overall economy. Seasonal variation, or **seasonality,** is a rhythmic annual pattern in sales or profits caused by weather, habit, or social custom. **Irregular or random influences** are unpredictable shocks to the economic system and the pace of economic activity caused by wars, strikes, natural catastrophes, and so on.

These four patterns are illustrated in Figure 6.1. Figure 6.1(a) shows secular and cyclical trends in sales of women's clothing. Figure 6.1(b) shows a seasonal pattern superimposed over the long-run trend (which, in this case, is a composite of the secular and cyclical trends), and random fluctuations around the seasonal curve.

Time series analysis can be as simple as projecting or extrapolating the unadjusted trend. When one applies either simple graphic analysis or least squares regression techniques, historical data can be used to determine the average increase or decrease in the series during each period and then projected into the future. Time series analysis can also be considerably more complex and sophisticated, allowing examination of seasonal and cyclical patterns in addition to the basic trend.

Since extrapolation techniques assume that a variable will follow an established path, the problem is to determine the appropriate trend curve. In theory, one could fit any mathematical function to the historical data and extrapolate to estimate future values. In practice, linear, simple power, or exponential curves are typically used for economic forecasting.

Selection of the appropriate curve is guided by both empirical and theoretical considerations. Empirically, it is a question of finding the curve that best fits historical movements in the data. Theoretical considerations intervene when logic dictates that a particular pattern of future events should prevail. For example, output in a particular industry may have been expanding at a constant rate historically, but because of known

Figure 6.1

TIME SERIES CHARACTERISTICS: (A) SECULAR TREND AND CYCLICAL
VARIATION IN WOMEN'S CLOTHING SALES; (B) SEASONAL PATTERN
AND RANDOM FLUCTUATIONS

(a) The cyclical pattern in sales varies significantly from the normal secular trend. (b) Seasonal
patterns, random fluctuations, and other influences cause deviations around the cyclical patterns
of sales.

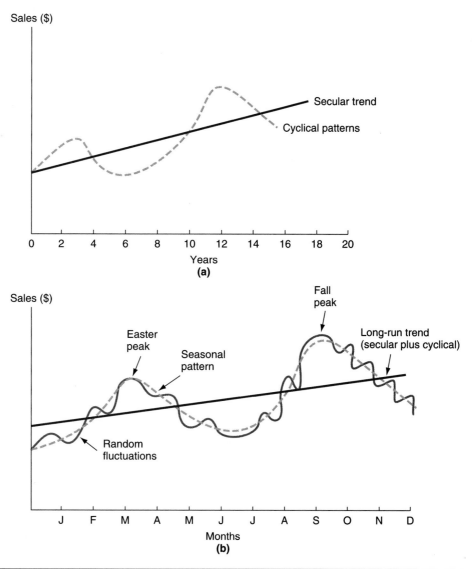

resource limitations, one might use a declining growth-rate model to reflect the expected slowdown in growth.

LINEAR TREND ANALYSIS

Linear Trend Analysis
Assumes Constant *unit* change over time.

Linear trend analysis assumes a constant period-by-period *unit* change in an important economic variable over time. Such a trend is illustrated in Figure 6.2, which displays the 15 years of actual sales data for The American Express Company given in Table 6.2, along with a curve representing a linear relation between sales and time over the 1977–1991 period.

A linear relation between firm sales and time, such as that illustrated in Figure 6.2, can be written as

$$S_t = a + b \times t. \tag{6.1}$$

The coefficients of this equation can be estimated using American Express sales data for the 1977 to 1991 period and the least squares regression method as follows (*t*-statistics in parentheses):

$$S_t = -\$982 + \$1,773.4t \qquad R^{-2} = 94.5\%$$
$$(-0.94) \ (15.48) \tag{6.2}$$

Although a linear trend projection for firm sales is relatively naive, an important trend element is obvious in American Express sales data. Using the linear trend equation estimated over the 1977 to 1991 period, it is possible to forecast firm sales for future periods. To do so, it is important to realize that in this model, $t = 1$ for 1977, $t = 2$ for 1978, and so on. This means that $t = 0$ in the 1976 base period. To forecast sales in any future period, simply subtract 1976 from the year in question to determine a relevant value for t.

For example, a sales forecast for 1998 using Equation 6.2 is

$$t = 1998 - 1976 = 22$$

$$S_{1998} = -\$982 + \$1,773.4(22)$$

$$= \$38,032.8 \text{ million.}$$

Similarly, a sales forecast for American Express in the year 2003 is

$$t = 2003 - 1976 = 27$$

$$S_{2003} = -\$982 + \$1,773.4(27)$$

$$= \$46,899.8 \text{ million.}$$

Note that these sales projections are based on a linear trend line, which implies that sales increase by a constant dollar amount each year. In this example, American Express sales are projected to grow by $1,773.4 million per year. However, there are important reasons for believing that the true trend for American Express sales is nonlinear and that the forecasts generated by this constant change model will be relatively poor estimates of actual values. To see why a linear trend relation may be inaccurate, consider the rela-

THE AMERICAN EXPRESS COMPANY SALES REVENUE, 1977–1991

Sales data points lie in a pattern around the fitted regression line, indicating that the slope of the sales/time line may not be constant.

Figure 6.2

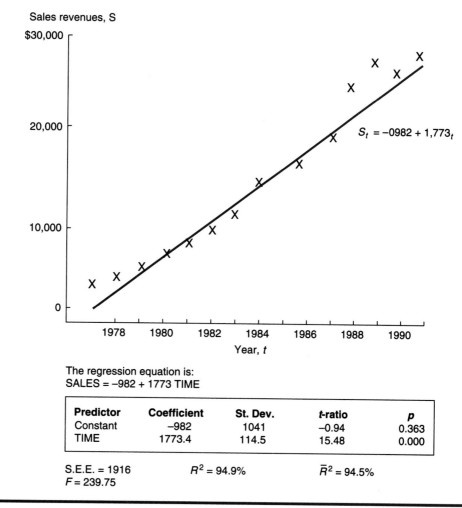

Sales revenues, S

$S_t = -0982 + 1{,}773_t$

Year, t

The regression equation is:
SALES = −982 + 1773 TIME

Predictor	Coefficient	St. Dev.	t-ratio	p
Constant	−982	1041	−0.94	0.363
TIME	1773.4	114.5	15.48	0.000

S.E.E. = 1916 $R^2 = 94.9\%$ $\bar{R}^2 = 94.5\%$
F = 239.75

tion between actual sales data and the linear trend shown in Figure 6.2. Remember that the least squares regression line minimizes the sum of squared residuals between actual and fitted values over the sample data. As is typical, actual data points lie above and below the fitted regression line. Note, however, that the pattern of differences between actual and fitted values varies dramatically over the sample period. Differences between actual and fitted values are generally positive in both early (1977 to 1979) and later (1988 to 1990) periods, whereas they are generally negative in the intervening 1980 to

Table 6.2	SALES REVENUE FOR THE AMERICAN EXPRESS COMPANY, 1977–91			
YEAR	SALES REVENUE ($ MILLIONS)	NATURAL LOGARITHM OF SALES REVENUE (BASE E)	COMMON LOGARITHM OF SALES REVENUE (BASE 10)	TIME PERIOD
1991	$25,763	10.1567	4.4110	15
1990	24,332	10.0995	4.3862	14
1989	25,047	10.1285	4.3988	13
1988	23,132	10.0490	4.3642	12
1987	17,626	9.7771	4.2462	11
1986	14,652	9.5923	4.1659	10
1985	11,850	9.3801	4.0737	9
1984	12,895	9.4646	4.1104	8
1983	9,770	9.1871	3.9899	7
1982	8,093	8.9988	3.9081	6
1981	7,210	8.8832	3.8579	5
1980	5,505	8.6134	3.7408	4
1979	4,666	8.4481	3.6689	3
1978	4,086	8.3153	3.6113	2
1977	3,447	8.1453	3.5374	1

Data Source: R. Daniel Oshinskie, "American Express," *The Value Line Investment Survey,* September 6, 1996, 2142.

Note: Source only has column 1 data.

1988 period. These differences suggest that the slope of the sales/time relation may not be constant but rather may be generally increasing over the 1977 to 1991 period. Under these circumstances, it may be more appropriate to assume that sales are changing at a constant annual *rate* rather than a constant annual *amount.*

GROWTH TREND ANALYSIS

Growth Trend Analysis Assumes constant *percentage* change over time.

Growth trend analysis assumes a constant period-by-period *percentage* change in an important economic variable over time. Such a forecast model has the potential to better capture the increasing annual sales pattern described by the 1977 to 1991 American Express sales data. This model is appropriate for forecasting when sales appear to change over time by a constant proportional amount rather than by the constant absolute amount assumption implicit in a simple linear model. The constant annual rate of growth model, assuming *annual* compounding, is described as follows:

$$\text{Sales in } t \text{ Years} = \text{Current Sales} \times (1 + \text{Growth Rate})^t$$

$$S_t = S_0(1 + g)^t.$$

(6.3)

In words, Equation 6.3 means that sales in *t* years in the future are equal to current-period sales, S_0, compounded at a constant annual growth rate, *g,* for a period of *t* years.

Use of the constant annual rate of growth model involves determining the average historical rate of growth in a variable such as sales and then using that rate of growth in a forecast equation such as Equation 6.3 to project future values. This approach is identical to the compounding value model used in finance.

Just as it is possible to estimate the constant rate of unit change in an economic time series by fitting historical data to a linear regression model of the form $Y = a + bt$, a constant annual rate of growth can be estimated using that same technique. In this case, the relevant growth rate is estimated using a linear regression model that is fit to a logarithmic transformation of the historical data. Taking common logarithms (to the base 10) of both sides of Equation 6.3 results in the expression

$$log\ S_t = log\ S_0 + log\ (1 + g) \times t. \tag{6.4}$$

Notice that Equation 6.4 is an expression of the form

$$Y_t = a + bt,$$

where $Y_t = log\ S_t$, $a = log\ S_0$, $b = log\ (1 + g)$, and t is an independent, or X variable. The coefficients $log\ S_0$ and $log\ (1 + g)$ can be estimated using the least squares regression technique.

Applying this technique to the American Express sales data for the 1977 to 1991 period results in the linear constant annual rate of growth regression model (t-statistics in parentheses):

$$log\ S_t = 3.498 + 0.067t \qquad \bar{R}^2 = 97.8\% \tag{6.5}$$
$$(143.33)\ (24.84)$$

Sales revenue forecasts (in millions of dollars) can be determined by transforming this estimated equation back to its original form:

$$S_t = (Antilog\ 3.498) \times (Antilog\ 0.067)^t,$$

or $\tag{6.6}$

$$S_t = \$3,147.75(1.17^t).$$

In this model, \$3,147.75 million is the adjusted level of sales for $t = 0$, or 1976, because the first year of data used in the regression estimation, $t = 1$, was 1977. The number 1.17 equals 1 plus the average rate of growth using annual compounding, meaning that American Express sales increased at a 17% annual rate from 1977 to 1991.

To forecast sales in any future year using this model, subtract 1976 from the year being forecast to determine t. Thus, a constant annual rate of growth model forecast for sales in 1998 is:

$$t = 1998 - 1976 = 22$$

$$S_{1998} = \$3,147.75(1.17^{22})$$

$$= \$99,561\ million.$$

Similarly, a constant growth model forecast of American Express sales in the year 2000 is:

$$t = 2003 - 1976 = 27$$

$$S_{2003} = \$3,147.75(1.17^{27})$$

$$= \$218,282 \text{ million.}$$

Another frequently used form of the constant growth model is based on an underlying assumption of *continuous,* as opposed to annual, compounding. The continuous growth model is expressed by the exponential equation:

$$Y_t = Y_0 e^{gt}. \tag{6.7}$$

Taking the natural logarithm (to the base *e*) of Equation 6.7 gives:

$$\ln Y_t = \ln Y_0 + gt.$$

Under an exponential rate of growth assumption, the regression model estimate of the slope coefficient, *g,* is a direct estimate of the continuous rate of growth. For example, a continuous growth model estimate for American Express sales is (*t* statistics in parentheses):

$$\ln S_t = 8.054 + 0.154t \qquad \bar{R}^2 = 97.8\%.$$
$$(143.33)\ (24.84) \tag{6.8}$$

In this equation, the coefficient 0.154 (= 15.4%) is a direct estimate of the continuous compounding growth rate for American Express sales. Notice that *t* statistics for the intercept and slope coefficients are identical to those derived for the constant annual rate of growth regression model (Equation 6.5).

Again, sales revenue forecasts (in millions of dollars) can be derived by transforming this estimated equation back to its original form:

$$S_t = (Exponentiate\ 8.054) \times (Exponentiate\ 0.154)^t,$$

or $$\tag{6.9}$$

$$S_t = \$3,146.35(1.17^t).$$

The very small difference between the intercept estimates for Equations 6.6 and 6.9 can be attributed to rounding error; otherwise they are identical. Subject to rounding error, identical 1998 and 2003 sales forecasts result using either the constant annual rate of growth or the continuous compounding assumption. Either method can be relied on with an equal degree of confidence as a useful basis for a constant growth model approach to forecasting.

LINEAR AND GROWTH TREND COMPARISON

The importance of selecting the correct structural form for a trending model can be demonstrated by comparing the sales projections that result from the two basic approaches that have been considered. Recall that with the constant change model, sales

The Security Analyst Forecasting Follies

Buyers of growth stocks bet that superior future growth in earnings per share will bring above-normal rates of return. Because investors often rely upon security analysts for guidance in the formation of future earnings expectations, they are implicitly depending upon security analysts for accurate earnings forecasts. In practice, the earnings forecasts of security analysts are seldom on the mark. Small high-tech stocks with high revenue and earnings growth rate expectations embedded in their stock prices often plummet 25% to 50% when quarterly earnings per share came in only a few pennies below analyst expectations. When such companies announce that security analyst earnings estimates were overly optimistic, the natural temptation is to conclude that such forecasting errors can be attributed to the always-hard-to-predict nature of small high-tech companies. However, security analysts are not able to boast of a markedly better record in forecasting earnings and revenue growth for large companies in relatively stable industries.

To document the typical forecast error of security analyst forecasts of company earnings per share, money managers and financial economists have conducted exhaustive studies of earnings per share estimates. Typically, researchers find that average forecast error falls in a range from 25%–50% of actual reported earnings per share. Worse yet, this abysmal average performance is not typically due to the influence of a few bad forecasts for a handful of statistical outliers. Less than 25% of the consensus earnings per share estimates by security analysts tend to come within a broad band of plus or minus 5% of reported earnings; less than 50% come within a broader band of plus or minus 10%. Big negative and positive earnings surprises are also common. It is not unusual for large, well-known companies to surprise analysts with earnings per share that are 50% or 150% of expected levels. In short, security analysts consistently fail to accurately forecast earnings per share for companies that they know intimately, in industries that they study continually, and for periods of less than *three months* in duration. Given the magnitude of these earnings per share forecast errors, it becomes questionable whether security analyst forecasts are useful to stock market investors. If security analysts cannot fine-tune their profit forecasts within 5% or 10% boundaries, it is impossible for them to consistently differentiate between growth stocks expanding at, say, 15% per year and stagnant companies growing at 5% or less.

Why is the earnings per share forecasting problem so daunting as to frustrate the efforts of such a talented and high-paid group of forecasters? Based on the evidence, it is obviously difficult to forecast changes in aggregate or macroeconomic conditions that include interest rates, inflation, unemployment, taxes, government spending, trade imbalances, and so on. More difficult still is the problem of forecasting how such changes will affect industry competition, imports, and firm-specific factors such as costs, revenues, and accounting policy choice decisions. All of this begs a very important question. Of what investment value are earnings estimates that are seriously wrong two-thirds or three-quarters of the time? In most instances, not much. To complicate matters further, the price of stocks today is not based on today's earnings, but on expected earnings during the still distant future. Clearly, for individual investors to put money on these estimates is to make a bet with the odds stacked high against them. Case after case can be used to illustrate how stock market investors who rely upon notoriously unreliable security analyst estimates get battered in the stock market.

If security analyst forecasts of earnings per share are not to be relied upon, how should investors make their investment decisions? Many in the field of finance argue that a well-diversified portfolio of stocks held for long-term appreciation is the best investment strategy. Professionals like Peter Lynch argue that you can beat the averages by investing in companies with well-documented growth prospects that sell at low prices relative to earnings. In any event, the empirical evidence clearly suggests that reliance on the accuracy of security analyst forecasts is not likely to be a successful investment strategy.

See: John H. Christy, "The *Forbes* 500s On Wall Street," *Forbes,* April 21, 1997, 286-318.

were projected to be $38.0 billion in 1998 and $46.9 billion in 2003. Compare these sales forecasts with the projections of $99.6 billion in 1998 and $218.3 billion in 2003 for the constant growth rate model. Notice that the difference in the near-term forecasts (1998) is smaller than the difference between longer-term (2003) projections. This shows that if an economic time series is growing at a constant rate rather than increasing by a constant dollar amount, forecasts based on a linear trend model will tend to be less accurate the further one forecasts into the future.

Of course, the pattern of future sales for any company, and therefore the reasonableness of a linear trend projection using either a constant change model or a constant growth model, remains a matter for conjecture. Whether a firm is able to maintain a rapid pace of growth depends on a host of factors both within and beyond its own control. Successfully managing rapid growth over extended periods is extraordinarily difficult and is rarely observed in practice. In fact, the sales pattern shown in Figure 6.2 might describe a company experiencing phases of rapid growth (1970s), maturation (1980s), and then decline (1990s). Individual products often display such a sales pattern, as do some firms and industries. When applying trend projection methods, it is important to establish the degree of similarity in growth opportunities between the historical and forecast periods. Prudence also suggests that the forecast horizon be limited to a relatively short time frame (five or ten years, maximum).

Although trend projection methods provide adequate results for some forecasting purposes, a number of serious shortcomings limit their usefulness. One problem is that simple trend projection techniques lack the ability to predict cyclical turning points or other short-term fluctuations. Another is that trend projections implicitly assume that historical patterns will continue unabated into the future. This is not always the case. There are many examples of the disastrous effects of using this forecasting method just prior to economic recessions in 1975, 1982, and 1991. Finally, trend analysis does not reflect any underlying causal relations and hence offers no help in describing *why* a particular series moves as it does. As a result, the method is incapable of predicting the effects of policy decisions or exogenous shocks.

Cyclical and Seasonal Variation

Many important economic time series are regularly influenced by cyclical and seasonal variations. Figure 6.1 illustrated how such variations can influence demand patterns for a typical consumer product. It is worth considering these influences further, since the treatment of cyclical and seasonal variations plays an important role in time series analysis and projection.

THE BUSINESS CYCLE

Business Cycle
Rhythmic pattern of contraction and expansion in the overall economy.

One of the most fascinating topics in managerial economics is the **business cycle,** or rhythmic pattern of contraction and expansion observed in the overall economy. On any given business day, a wide variety of news reports, press releases, and analyst comments can be found concerning the current state and future direction of the overall economy. The reason for such intense interest is obvious. The profit and sales performance of all companies depends to a greater or lesser extent on the vigor of the overall economy. On average, business activity in the United States expands at a rate of 2.5% to 3% per year when measured in terms of inflation-adjusted, or real-dollar, GDP. During robust expansions, the pace of growth in real GDP can increase to an annual rate of 5% or more for brief periods. During especially severe recessions, real GDP can actually decline for an extended period. In the case of firms that employ significant financial and operating leverage, a difference of a few percentage points in the pace of overall economic activity can make the difference between vigorous expansion and gut-wrenching contraction.

Table 6.3 shows the pattern of business cycle expansion and contraction that has been experienced in the United States from the mid-1800s to the mid-1990s. Between December 1854 and March 1991, there have been 31 complete business cycles. The average duration of each cyclical contraction is 18 months, when duration is measured from the previous cyclical peak to the low point or trough of the subsequent business contraction. The average duration of each cyclical expansion is 35 months, as measured by the amount of time from the previous cyclical trough to the peak of the following business expansion. In the post–World War II period, there have been nine complete business cycles, with the typical contraction lasting only 11 months, less than a year, and the typical expansion lasting 50 months, or slightly more than four years. Clearly, periods of economic expansion predominate, which indicates a healthy and growing economy.

Whether the current economy is in a state of boom, moderate expansion, moderate contraction, or outright recession, there is sure to be widespread disagreement among analysts concerning current or future business prospects. This reflects the fact that, despite intense interest and widespread news coverage, the causes of economic contractions and expansions remain something of a mystery. *Why* the economy shifts from boom to bust and how such shifts might be predicted and controlled are still largely beyond our knowledge. Hopefully, the ever-increasing quality of economic data from both private sources and the government, and the amazing power of new computer hardware and software, will allow analysts to unlock further mysteries of the business cycle during the 1990s. In the meantime, changes in the pattern and pace of economic activity remain a matter for intense debate and conjecture.

ECONOMIC INDICATORS

Whereas cyclical patterns in most economic time series are erratic and make simple projection a hazardous short-term forecasting technique, a relatively consistent relation often exists among various economic variables over time. Even though many series of economic data do not exhibit a consistent pattern over time, it is often possible to find a high degree of correlation *across* these series. Should the forecaster have the good fortune to discover an economic series that leads the one being forecast, the leading series can be used as a barometer for forecasting short-term change, just as a meteorologist uses changes in a mercury barometer to forecast changes in the weather.

Table 6.3

BUSINESS CYCLE EXPANSIONS AND CONTRACTIONS

				CYCLE	
		CONTRACTION (TROUGH FROM PREVIOUS PEAK)	EXPANSION (TROUGH TO PEAK)	TROUGH FROM PREVIOUS TROUGH	PEAK FROM PREVIOUS PEAK
TROUGH	**PEAK**				
December 1854	June 1857	—	30	—	—
December 1858	October 1860	18	22	48	40
June 1861	April 1865	8	*46*	30	*54*
December 1867	June 1869	*32*	18	*78*	50
December 1870	October 1873	18	34	36	52
March 1879	March 1882	65	36	99	101
May 1885	March 1887	38	22	74	60
April 1888	July 1890	13	27	35	40
May 1891	January 1893	10	20	37	30
June 1894	December 1895	17	18	37	35
June 1897	June 1899	18	24	36	42
December 1900	September 1902	18	21	42	39
August1904	May 1907	23	33	44	56
June 1908	January 1910	13	19	46	32
January 1912	January 1913	24	12	43	36
December 1914	August 1918	23	*44*	35	*67*
March 1919	January 1920	*7*	10	*51*	17
July 1921	May 1923	18	22	28	40
July 1924	October 1926	14	27	36	41
November 1927	August 1929	13	21	40	34
March 1933	May 1937	43	50	64	93
June 1938	February 1945	13	*80*	63	*93*
October 1945	November 1948	*8*	37	*88*	45
October 1949	July 1953	11	*45*	48	*56*
May 1954	August 1957	*10*	39	*55*	49
April 1958	April 1960	8	24	47	32
February 1961	December 1969	10	*106*	34	*116*
November 1970	November 1973	*11*	36	*117*	47
March 1975	January 1980	16	58	52	74
July 1980	July 1981	6	12	64	18
November 1982	July 1990	16	92	28	108
March 1991		8	—	100	—
Average all cycles:					
1854–1991 (31 cycles)		18	35	53	53[1]
1854–1919 (16 cycles)		22	27	48	49[2]
1919–1945 (6 cycles)		18	35	53	53
1945–1991 (9 cycles)		11	50	61	61

Table 6.3

continued

TROUGH	PEAK	CONTRACTION (TROUGH FROM PREVIOUS PEAK)	EXPANSION (TROUGH TO PEAK)	TROUGH FROM PREVIOUS TROUGH	PEAK FROM PREVIOUS PEAK
Average, peacetime cycles:					
1854–1991 (26 cycles)		19	29	48	48^3
1854–1919 (14 cycles)		22	24	46	47^4
1919–1945 (5 cycles)		20	26	46	45
1945–1991 (7 cycles)		11	43	53	53

Source: *Survey of Current Business,* October 1994, C51.

1.   30 cycles.

2.   15 cycles.

3.   25 cycles.

4.   13 cycles.

Note—Figures printed in bold italic are the wartime expansions (Civil War, World Wars I and II, Korean war, and Vietnam war), the postwar contractions, and the full cycles that include the wartime expansions.

The Survey of Current Business, a monthly publication of the Bureau of Economic Analysis of the Department of Commerce, provides extensive data on a wide variety of

Economic Indicators
Data that describe projected, current, or past economic activity.

economic indicators, or data series that successfully describe the pattern of projected, current, or past economic activity. Table 6.4 lists 11 leading, 4 roughly coincident, and 7 lagging economic indicators of business cycle peaks that are described in that publication and broadly relied upon in business cycle forecasting. Figure 6.3 shows the pattern displayed by composite indexes of these leading, coincident, and lagging indicators

Composite Index
A weighted average of leading, coincident, or lagging economic indicators.

from the mid-1950s through the mid-1990s. A **composite index** is a weighted average of leading, coincident, or lagging economic indicators. Combining individual series into a composite index results in a forecasting series with less random fluctuation, or noise. These composite series are smoother than the underlying individual data series and have less tendency to produce false signals of change in economic conditions. Notice how the composite index of leading indicators consistently turns down just prior to the start of each recessionary period. Similarly, notice how this data series bottoms out and then starts to rise just prior to the start of each subsequent economic expansion. Just as leading indicators seem to earn that description based on their performance, coincident and lagging indicators perform as expected over this period.

BAROMETRIC FORECASTING

Barometric Forecasting
Predictive method based on the observed relation among economic time series.

Barometric forecasting is a predictive method based on the observed relation among economic time series. Changes in some series appear to be consistently related to changes in one or more other series. The theoretical basis for some of these leads and lags is obvious. For example, building permits precede housing starts, and orders for plant and equipment lead production in durable goods industries. Each of these indicators directly

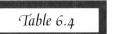

LEADING, COINCIDENT, AND LAGGING ECONOMIC INDICATORS OF BUSINESS CYCLE PEAKS

11 Leading Indicators	Average workweek for manufacturing workers
	Average weekly initial claims for state unemployment insurance
	New orders for consumer goods and materials
	Vendor performance measured by companies receiving slower deliveries
	Contracts and orders for plant and equipment
	Index of new building permits for private housing units
	Change in unfilled factory orders for durable goods
	Change in sensitive materials prices
	Index of stock prices for 500 common stocks
	Money supply
	Index of consumer expectations
4 Roughly Coincident Indicators	Employees on nonagricultural payrolls
	Personal income minus transfer payments
	Index of total industrial production
	Manufacturing and trade sales
7 Lagging Indicators	Average duration of unemployment
	Ratio of constant-dollar inventories to sales for manufacturing and trade
	Change in labor cost per unit of manufacturing output
	Average prime rate charged by banks
	Commercial and industrial loans outstanding
	Ratio of consumer installment credit to personal income
	Change in prices for consumer services

Source: *Survey of Current Business,* February 1995, C1.

reflects plans or commitments for the activity that follows. Other barometers are not so directly related to the economic variables they forecast. An index of common stock prices is a good leading indicator of general business activity. Although the causal linkage may not be readily apparent, stock prices reflect aggregate profit expectations by business managers and investors and thus describe future business conditions.

Barometric methods of forecasting require the identification of an economic time series that consistently leads the series being forecast. Once this relation is established, forecasting directional changes in the lagged series involves keeping track of movement in the leading indicator. In practice, several problems prevent such an easy solution to the forecasting problem. Few series always correctly indicate changes in another economic variable. Even the best leading indicators forecast directional changes in business conditions with no more than 80% to 90% accuracy. Also, even indicators that have good records of forecasting directional changes generally fail to lead by a consistent period. If a series is to be an adequate barometer, it must not only indicate directional changes but must also provide a relatively constant lead time. Few series meet the test of lead-time consistency. Finally, barometric forecasting suffers in that, even when leading indicators prove to consistently indicate directional changes with stable lead times, they provide very little information about the magnitude of change in the forecast variable.

Figure 6.3

COMPOSITE INDEXES OF 11 LEADING, 4 COINCIDENT, AND 7 LAGGING
INDICATORS (INDEX: 1987 = 100)

P indicates a "peak" in an economic expansion; T indicates a "trough" in an economic recession.
Therefore, PT shows the time frame of an economic recession.

Source: *Survey of Current Business,* February 1995, C7.

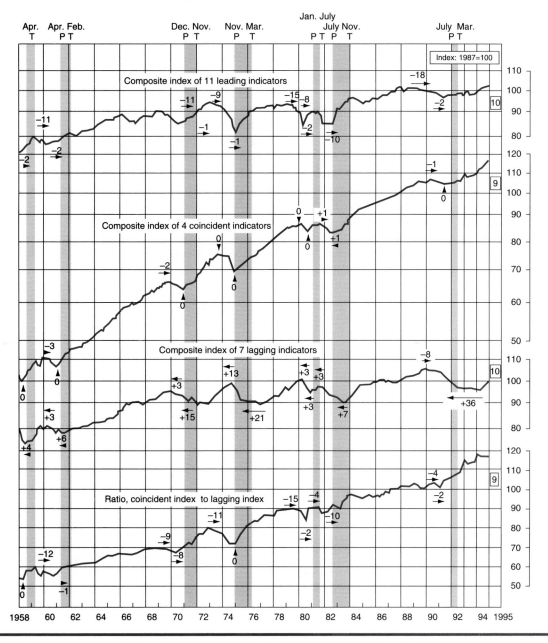

Note: The numbers and arrows indicate length of leads (−) and lags (+) in months from business cycle
turning dates.

To partially overcome the difficulties of barometric forecasting, economists use both composite and diffusion indexes. Unlike a composite index, which combines a number of leading indicators into a single standardized index, a **diffusion index** indicates the percentage of leading, coincident, or lagging indicators that are rising at any point in time. Figure 6.4 shows the pattern displayed by diffusion indexes for the 11 leading indicator components, 4 coincident indicator components, and 7 lagging indicator components from the mid-1950s through the mid-1990s. If all 11 leading indicators are relatively reliable advance indicators of heavy equipment sales, a diffusion, or pressure, index shows the percentage of those indicators that is increasing at the present time. If 7 are rising, the diffusion index of leading indicators is 7/11, or 64%. With only 3 rising, the diffusion index registers 27%. Forecasting with diffusion indexes typically involves projecting an increase in a given economic variable if the relevant diffusion index is above 50% and a decline when it is below 50%.

There is evidence that the leading indicator, or barometric, approach to business forecasting is nearly as old as business itself. More than 2,000 years ago, merchants used the arrival of trading ships as indicators of business activity. More than 100 years ago, Andrew Carnegie is reported to have used the number of smoking industrial chimneys to forecast business activity and hence the demand for steel. Today, the barometric approach to forecasting has been refined considerably, primarily through the work of the National Bureau of Economic Research and the U.S. Department of Commerce. However, even with the use of composite and diffusion indexes, the barometric forecasting technique is a relatively poor tool for estimating the magnitude of change in an economic variable. Although barometric methods represent a considerable improvement over simple extrapolation techniques, the barometric forecasting methodology is not a fool-proof solution to the problem of calling turning points in economic conditions.

SEASONAL VARIATION

Many important series of economic data are influenced not only by cyclical variation but also by seasonal patterns of business activity. For example, new housing starts constitute an important economic time series that is regularly influenced by both seasonal and cyclical variations. Understandably, housing starts tend to be high in the months of May, June, and July and relatively low in November, December, and January. The obvious reason for such variation is the weather. In many northern states, it is difficult, if not impossible, to maintain a high level of housing starts during colder winter months. After adjusting for the seasonal element in housing starts, a regular pattern of cyclical variation is typically observed. Seasonally adjusted annual data show that housing starts declined precipitously just prior to and during the economic downturns of 1975, 1982, and 1991 and illustrate why housing starts are considered a leading economic indicator.

Although housing starts are an obvious and classic example of economic data subject to seasonal and cyclical variation, they are by no means a unique case. For example, economic activity in the retailing, recreation, travel, automobile, and related industries are all affected by seasonal variation. Even in grocery retailing, an important seasonal element is reflected in the demand for meats. For example, turkey demand skyrockets at Thanksgiving and Christmas, whereas hamburger and hot dog demand surges on the

Figure 6.4

RATES OF CHANGE AND DIFFUSION INDEXES FOR CYCLICAL
INDICATOR COMPOSITE INDEXES

P indicates a "peak" in an economic expansion; T indicates a "trough" in an economic recession.
Therefore, PT shows the time frame of an economic recession.

Source: *Survey of Current Business,* November/December 1995, C8.

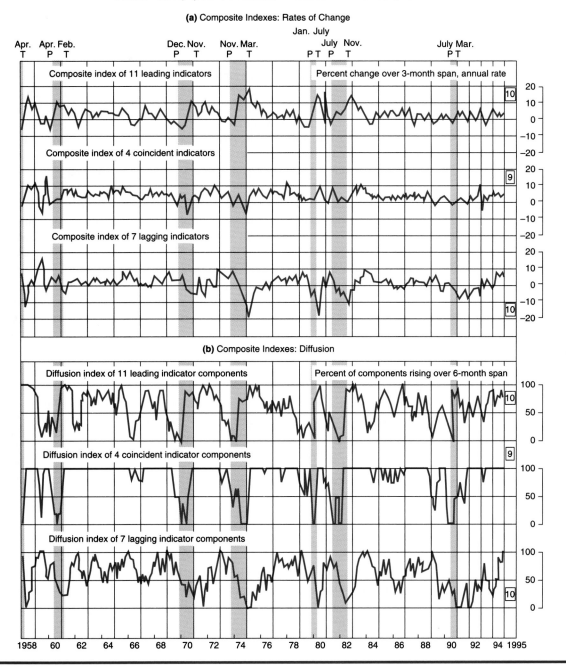

Fourth of July. Similarly, summertime demand is especially strong for grocery products such as soda, charcoal, shampoo, deodorant soap, and so on. As a result, controlling for seasonal and cyclical variations is an important aspect of time series analysis and projection. For many economic projections, an analysis of seasonal and cyclical fluctuations can vastly improve forecasting results, especially for short-run forecasting.

There are several techniques for estimating seasonal variations. A simple one examines the ratio of actual monthly data to the trend projection. For example, if monthly sales for a product indicate that, on average, December volume is 20% above trend, a seasonal adjustment factor of 1.20 can be applied to the trend projection to forecast December sales. If February sales are typically 15% below trend, an adjustment factor of 0.85 can be used to project February sales. To illustrate, annual sales might be forecast at $1.2 million, or $100,000 a month. When the seasonal factor is introduced, however, December sales would be projected at $120,000 ($100,000 × 1.20) and February sales at $85,000 ($100,000 × 0.85). Production, inventory, and financing requirements could be scheduled accordingly.

The Box-Jenkins technique is one of many advanced methods for time series analysis that provide sophisticated means for analyzing the various components—trend, seasonal, cyclical, and random—that make up an economic time series. Such techniques enable one to analyze the wide variety of complex patterns that might exist in actual profit and sales data. For many forecasting applications, they provide a substantial improvement over simple extrapolation procedures.

Exponential Smoothing Techniques

There is a wide variety of statistical forecasting techniques used to predict unit sales growth, revenue, costs, and profit performance. These techniques range from simple to sophisticated. In practice, many companies concentrate on different methods of exponential smoothing, or estimating the moving average of a time series of data. This section briefly introduces the exponential smoothing concept and discusses three common ways in which the exponential smoothing concept is used in real-world forecasting applications.

THE EXPONENTIAL SMOOTHING CONCEPT

Exponential Smoothing
Averaging method for forecasting time series of data.

Exponential smoothing is a method for forecasting time series of data. Examples of data series that have been successfully forecast using the method include trends in unit sales, unit costs, wage expenses, and so on. This technique identifies historical patterns of trend or seasonality in the data series one wishes to forecast and then extrapolates these patterns forward into the forecast period. Its accuracy depends on the degree to which established patterns of change are apparent and their degree of constancy over time. The more regular the pattern of change in any given data series, the easier it is to forecast.

Exponential smoothing (or "averaging") techniques are among the most widely used forecasting methods in business today. While extensive historical records are required for accurate future projections, data requirements seldom limit the application of the technique. Many firms collect a wealth of pertinent sales and revenue information using bar-code information, point-of-sale data, or statistics collected by sales representatives. Still, it is worth remembering that several years of information are required for accurate forecasting of annual data, particularly when strong seasonal or cyclical influences are present.

All leading methods of exponential smoothing involve the same essential process of data averaging. In these approaches, the data series to be forecast is assumed to be modeled by one, two, or three essential components. These key components represent the level, trend, or seasonality of the data being forecast. The level of the time series to be forecast is the local mean or average about which it fluctuates. This level may be constant or slowly changing. As discussed previously, trend is any systematic change in the level of the time series of data. If a given forecast model includes a trend, then that trend is either projected as a straight line into the future or it is projected as a gradually diminishing exponential that eventually dies out to a constant level. This type of dampened exponential is essentially just a change in level, where change is achieved gradually over time. As mentioned already, the seasonality of a time series is a periodic pattern of change in the data, usually tied to weather, custom, or tradition. Retail sales typically exhibit a strong seasonal trend over the course of the year. Many stores book 30% or more of annual sales during the busy Christmas selling season. Seasonal components can be additive, meaning that seasonal patterns remain constant over time, or multiplicative, meaning that seasonal patterns grow with the average level of the series over time.

Figure 6.5 shows nine common profiles of data that can be forecast using popular exponential smoothing techniques. They range in complexity from the very simple nonseasonal constant level of data shown in Figure 6.5(a), to the more complex dampened trend with a multiplicative seasonal influence shown in Figure 6.5(i). To ensure that the correct exponential smoothing technique is chosen, a method with sufficient flexibility to conform to the underlying data must be employed. Thus, a good first step in the exponential smoothing process is to graph the data series to be forecast and then choose the exponential smoothing method with sufficient flexibility to best resemble the data.

As a case in point, Figure 6.6 shows a typical pattern of sales for the life cycle of a product. Product life cycles often progress from the introduction point to rapid growth and market penetration, to a mature phase of sales stability, to periods of declining market share and abandonment. Over this life cycle, different methods of sales forecasting may be appropriate. In the initial phase, and before the generation of significant market data, qualitative analyses and market experiments are highly appropriate. Once the product has been launched and is rapidly gaining market acceptance, in Phase II, three-parameter exponential smoothing methods that involve level, trend, and seasonal components become relevant. In the mature phase of sales stability, Phase III, or two-parameter exponential smoothing models (econometric models) that incorporate level and seasonal components are suitable. In the fourth and final phase of declining market share and abandonment, three-parameter exponential smoothing methods that involve level, trend, and seasonal components again become relevant. The important point is that the choice of an appropriate forecasting method depends on the pattern of time series data that is to be forecast.

Figure 6.5

NINE COMMON TRENDS IN ECONOMIC TIME SERIES CAN BE FORECAST USING EXPONENTIAL SMOOTHING METHODS

Forecasting economic time series often involves a consideration of changes in the level, trend, and/or seasonality of the data.

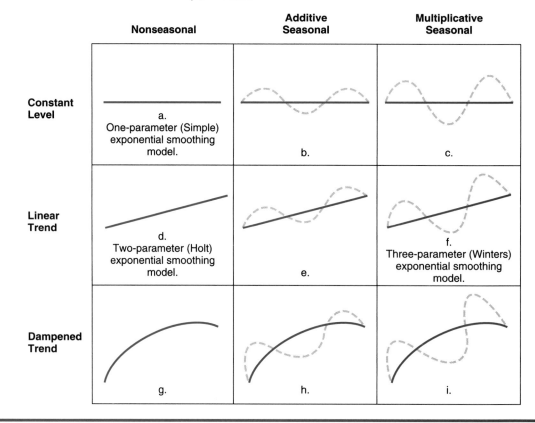

	Nonseasonal	Additive Seasonal	Multiplicative Seasonal
Constant Level	a. One-parameter (Simple) exponential smoothing model.	b.	c.
Linear Trend	d. Two-parameter (Holt) exponential smoothing model.	e.	f. Three-parameter (Winters) exponential smoothing model.
Dampened Trend	g.	h.	i.

ONE-PARAMETER (SIMPLE) EXPONENTIAL SMOOTHING

One-Parameter (Simple) Exponential Smoothing Method for forecasting slowly changing levels.

In **one-parameter (simple) exponential smoothing,** the sole regular component is the level of the forecast data series. It is implicitly assumed that the data consist of irregular fluctuations around a constant or very slowly changing level. Simple exponential smoothing is appropriate for forecasting sales in mature markets with stable activity; it is inappropriate for forecasting in markets that are growing rapidly or are seasonal.

In the simple exponential smoothing model, each smoothed estimate of a given level is computed as a weighted average of the current observation and past data. Each weight decreases in an exponential pattern. The rate of decrease in the influence of past levels depends on the size of the smoothing parameter that controls the model's relative sensitivity to newer versus older data. The larger the value of the smoothing parameter, the more emphasis is placed on recent versus distant observations. On the other hand, if

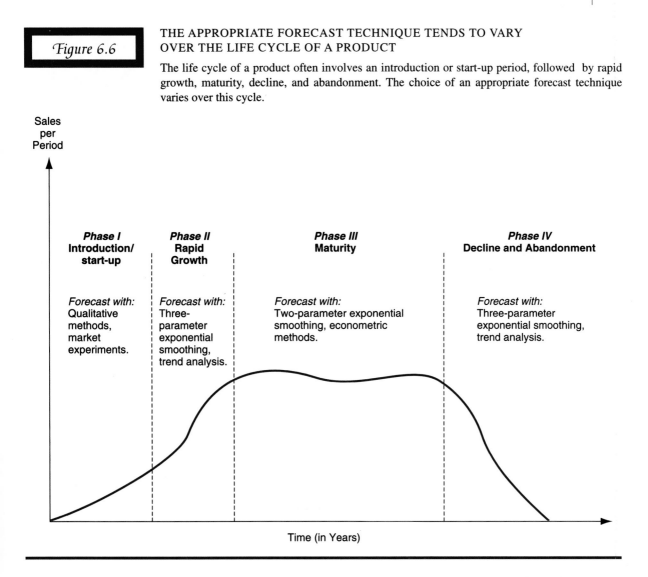

Figure 6.6

THE APPROPRIATE FORECAST TECHNIQUE TENDS TO VARY OVER THE LIFE CYCLE OF A PRODUCT

The life cycle of a product often involves an introduction or start-up period, followed by rapid growth, maturity, decline, and abandonment. The choice of an appropriate forecast technique varies over this cycle.

Sales per Period

Phase I
Introduction/ start-up

Forecast with:
Qualitative methods, market experiments.

Phase II
Rapid Growth

Forecast with:
Three-parameter exponential smoothing, trend analysis.

Phase III
Maturity

Forecast with:
Two-parameter exponential smoothing, econometric methods.

Phase IV
Decline and Abandonment

Forecast with:
Three-parameter exponential smoothing, trend analysis.

Time (in Years)

the smoothing parameter is very small, then a large number of data points receive nearly equal weights. In this case, the forecast model displays a long "memory" of past values.

TWO-PARAMETER (HOLT) EXPONENTIAL SMOOTHING

Two-Parameter (Holt) Exponential Smoothing
Method for forecasting stable growth.

Simple exponential smoothing is not appropriate for forecasting data that exhibit extended trends. In **two-parameter (Holt) exponential smoothing,** the data are assumed to consist of fluctuations about a level that is changing with some constant or slowly drifting linear trend. Two-parameter exponential smoothing is often called the Holt

How Good Is Your Forecasting Ability?

MANAGERIAL APPLICATION
6.3

When making predictions of economic and social change, it is vitally important to be aware of broad trends in the overall economy. One valuable source of information on the U.S. economy is the *Statistical Abstract of the United States*. This annual publication of the U.S. Bureau of the Census offers a wealth of economic and demographic data that private and public sector analysts rely upon.

The following table offers insight concerning a number of important economic and social trends during the 1980s, and year 2000 estimates based upon a simple trend extrapolation. Which forecasts do you believe will prove accurate? Which forecasts are apt to be wide of the mark?

CATEGORY	1980	1990	PERCENT CHANGE	2000 (EST.)
College enrollment	7,475,000	7,989,000	6.9%	8,538,344
College tuition, public avg.	$583	$1,356	132.6%	$3,154
College tuition, private avg.	$3,130	$8,174	161.2%	$21,346
Commercial banks	14,435	12,345	−14.5%	10,558
Credit cards (mil.)	526	1,027	95.2%	2,005
Credit card debt (bil.)	$80.2	$257.9	221.6%	$829.3
Daily NYSE volume (mil.)	49.5	213.4	331.1%	920.0
Dentists	141,000	186,000	31.9%	245,362
Divorces, U.S.	1,189,000	1,175,000	−1.2%	1,161,165
Doctors of medicine	467,700	615,400	31.6%	809,744
Fishing licenses	35,200,000	37,000,000	5.1%	38,892,045
Gold price per ounce	$612.60	$384.90	−37.2%	$241.83
Government revenue, total (bil.)	$932.0	$2,047.0	119.6%	$4,495.9
Government expenditures, total (bil.)	$959.0	$2,219.0	131.4%	$5,134.5
Government debt, total (bil.)	$1,250.0	$4,127.0	230.2%	$13,625.7
Gross domestic product, current dollars (bil.)	$2,708.0	$5,522.2	103.9%	$11,261.0
Gross domestic product, 1987 dollars (bil.)	$3,776.3	$4,877.5	29.2%	$6,299.8
High school dropouts	5,212,000	3,854,000	−26.1%	2,849,830
Hunting licenses	27,000,000	30,000,000	11.1%	33,333,333
Income of household $75,000 and over, 1991 dollars	7.2%	10.8%	50.0%	16.2%
Immigration, U.S.	530,639	1,536,483	189.6%	4,448,938
Life expectancy at birth (female)	77.4	78.8	1.8%	80.2
Life expectancy at birth (male)	70.0	71.8	2.6%	73.6

Method, after its originator C. C. Holt.[3] Two-parameter exponential smoothing is quite appropriate for forecasting sales in established markets with stable growth; it is inappropriate in either stable or rapidly growing markets.

---

[3]C.C. Holt, *Forecasting Seasonals and Trends by Exponentially Weighted Moving Averages* (Pittsburgh, PA: Carnegie Institute of Technology, 1957).

Managerial Application continued

Category	1980	1990	Percent Change	2000 (est.)
Marriages, U.S.	2,390,000	2,448,000	2.4%	2,507,408
Mergers and acquisitions, $1 million or more	1,558	4,168	167.5%	11,150
Money income of households, 1991 dollars	$29,309	$31,203	6.5%	$33,219
Mortgage interest rate	12.3%	9.7%	−21.1%	7.6%
National health expenditures (bil.)	$250.1	$675.0	169.9%	$1,821.8
National health expenditures (per capita)	$1,064	$2,601	144.5%	$6,358
Oil price per barrel, avg.	$38.23	$22.97	−39.9%	$13.80
Patents issued	66,200	99,200	49.8%	148,650
Air travel	$13.5	$26.5	96.3%	$52.0
Education and research	$33.6	$86.4	157.1%	$222.2
Tobacco products	$20.9	$43.4	107.7%	$90.1
Persons attending church or synagogue	40.0%	40.0%	0.0%	40.0%
Persons below poverty level (mil.)	29.3	33.6	14.7%	38.5
Population, City of Chicago	3,005,000	2,784,000	−7.4%	2,579,253
Population, New York City	7,072,000	7,323,000	3.5%	7,582,909
Population, U.S.	227,726,000	249,900,000	9.7%	274,233,113
Population, U.S. 65 years and over	25,549,000	31,079,000	21.6%	37,805,951
Postage stamp, first class	$0.15	$0.25	66.7%	$0.42
Poverty level, households, 1991 dollars	$8,414	$13,359	58.8%	$21,210
Purchasing power of $1	$1.00	$0.63	−37.0%	$0.40
R&D expenditures, current dollars (bil.)	$62.6	$146.2	133.5%	$341.4
Return on stockholders equity, manufacturing	13.9%	10.7%	−23.0%	8.2%
Scholastic Aptitude Test (SAT) verbal score, avg.	424	424	0.0%	424
Scholastic Aptitude Test (SAT) math score, avg.	466	476	2.1%	486
Spending on legal services (bil.)	$13.6	$49.7	265.4%	$181.6
Television households	97.9%	98.2%	0.3%	98.5%
Television households with cable	19.9%	58.9%	196.0%	174.3%
Unmarried couples, U.S.	1,589,000	2,856,000	79.7%	5,133,251
Unmarried couples, U.S. with children under age 15	431,000	891,000	106.7%	1,841,951
U.S. 3-month Treasury bill rate	11.4%	7.5%	−34.2%	4.9%
U.S. long-term Treasury bond rate	10.8%	8.7%	−19.1%	7.1%

Data Source: U.S. Bureau of the Census, *Statistical Abstract of the United States: 1993*, (113th edition), Washington, D.C., 1993.

Holt's exponential smoothing model uses a smoothed estimate of the trend component as well as the level component to produce forecasts. In the two-parameter exponential smoothing forecast equation, the current smoothed level is added to a linear trend to forecast future values. The updated value of the smoothed level is computed as the weighted average of new data and the best estimate of the new level based on old data. The Holt method combines old and new estimates of the one period change of the smoothed level, thus defining the current linear or local trend.

THREE-PARAMETER (WINTERS) EXPONENTIAL SMOOTHING

Three-Parameter (Winters) Exponential Smoothing
Method for forecasting seasonally adjusted growth.

The **three-parameter (Winters) exponential smoothing** method extends the two-parameter technique by including a smoothed multiplicative index to account for the seasonal behavior of the forecast series. The three-parameter exponential smoothing technique is often called the Winters Method, after its originator P. R. Winters.[4] Because much economic data involve both growth trend and seasonal considerations, three-parameter exponential smoothing is one of the most commonly used forecasting methods employed in business today. Three-parameter exponential smoothing is best suited for forecasting problems that involve rapid and/or changing rates of growth combined with seasonal influences. Three-parameter exponential smoothing is suitable for forecasting sales in both rapidly growing markets and in rapidly decaying markets with seasonal influences.

Winters' three-parameter exponential smoothing model assumes that each observation is the product of a deseasonalized value and a seasonal index for that particular month or quarter. The deseasonalized values are assumed to be described by the Holt model. The Winters model involves three smoothing parameters to be used in level, trend, and seasonal index smoothing equations. The Winters model forecast is computed similarly to the Holt model forecast and then multiplied by the seasonal index for the current period. Smoothing in the Winters model is similar to the Holt model, except that in the Winters model the measurement of level is deseasonalized through dividing by the seasonal index calculated one year before. The trend smoothing equations of the two models are identical. The seasonal index is estimated as the ratio of the current observation to the current smoothed level, averaged with the previous value for that particular period.

In sum, each of the three common exponential forecast techniques uses recursive (or backward-linked) equations to obtain smoothed values for model components. The simple exponential smoothing method uses one equation to estimate the appropriate level, the Holt method uses two equations to estimate the appropriate level and trend, and the Winters method uses three equations to estimate level, trend, and seasonal components of the forecast time series. Experience has shown that each method can be used to generate business forecasts that lead to better managerial decisions.

Econometric Methods

Econometric Methods
Use of economic theory and mathematical and statistical tools to forecast economic relations.

Econometric methods of forecasting combine economic theory with mathematical and statistical tools to analyze economic relations. Econometric forecasting techniques have several distinct advantages over alternative methods. For one, they force the forecaster to make explicit assumptions about the linkages among the variables in the economic

---

[4]P. R. Winters, "Forecasting Sales by Exponentially Weighted Moving Averages," *Management Science* 6 (April 1960), 324–342.

system being examined. In other words, the forecaster must deal with causal relations. This process reduces the probability of logical inconsistencies in the forecast model and increases the reliability and acceptability of the results.

A second advantage of econometric methods is the consistency of the techniques from period to period. The forecaster can compare forecasts with actual results and use the insights gained to improve the forecast model. By feeding past forecasting errors back into the model, new parameter estimates can be generated that should improve future forecasting results.

The type of output provided by econometric forecasts is another major advantage of this technique. Since econometric models offer estimates of actual values for forecasted variables, these models indicate not only the direction of change but also the magnitude of change. This is a notable improvement over the barometric approach, which provides little information about the magnitude of expected changes.

Perhaps the most important advantage of econometric models relates to their basic characteristic of *explaining* economic phenomena. In the vast majority of business forecasting problems, management has a degree of control over some of the variables in the relationship being examined. For example, when forecasting sales of a product, the firm must take into account the price it will charge, the amount it has spent and will spend on advertising, and many other variables over which it may or may not have any influence. Only by thoroughly understanding the interrelations involved can management hope to forecast accurately and to make optimal decisions as it selects values for controllable variables.

SINGLE-EQUATION MODELS

Many managerial forecasting problems can be adequately addressed with single-equation econometric models. The first step in developing an econometric model is to express relevant economic relations in the form of equations. When constructing a model for forecasting the regional demand for portable personal computers, one might hypothesize that computer demand (C) is determined by price (P), disposable income (I), population (Pop), interest rates (i), and advertising expenditures (A). A linear model expressing this relation is:

$$C = a_0 + a_1P + a_2I + a_3Pop + a_4i + a_5A. \qquad \textbf{(6.10)}$$

The next step in econometric modeling is to estimate the parameters of the system, or values of the coefficients, as in Equation 6.10. The most frequently used technique for parameter estimation is the application of least squares regression analysis with either time series or cross section data.

Once the coefficients of the model have been estimated, forecasting with a single-equation model consists of evaluating the equation with specific values for the independent variables. This means that an econometric model used for forecasting purposes must contain independent or explanatory variables whose values for the forecast period can be readily obtained.

MULTIPLE-EQUATION SYSTEMS

Although forecasting problems can often be analyzed with a single-equation model, in some cases complex relations among economic variables require use of multiple-equation systems. Variables whose values are determined within such a model are referred to as *endogenous,* meaning originating from within, and those determined outside, or external to, the system are referred to as *exogenous.* The values of endogenous variables are determined by the model; the values of exogenous variables are given externally. Endogenous variables are equivalent to the dependent variable in a single-equation system; exogenous and predetermined variables are equivalent to the independent variables.

Multiple-equation econometric models are composed of two basic kinds of expressions—identities and behavioral equations. **Identities** express relations that are true by definition. The statement that profits (π) equal total revenue (TR) minus total cost (TC) is an example of an identity:

Identities
Economic relations that are true by definition.

$$\pi = TR - TC. \tag{6.11}$$

Profits are *defined* by the relation expressed in Equation 6.11.

Behavioral Equations
Economic relations that are hypothesized to be true.

The second group of equations encountered in econometric models, **behavioral equations,** reflects hypotheses about how the variables in a system interact with each other. Behavioral equations may indicate how individuals and institutions are expected to react to various stimuli, or they may be technical, as, for example, a function that indicates production system relations.

Perhaps the easiest way to illustrate the use of multiple-equation systems is to examine a simple three-equation model of equipment and related software sales for a personal computer retailer. As you recall, Equation 6.10 expressed a single-equation model that might be used to forecast regional demand for portable personal computers. However, total revenues for a typical retailer usually include not only sales of personal computers but also sales of software programs (including computer games) and sales of peripheral equipment (e.g., video display terminals, printers, and so on). Although actual econometric models used to forecast total sales revenue from these items might include several equations and many important economic variables, the simple system described in this section should suffice to provide insight into the multiple-equation approach without being overly complex. The three equations are:

$$S_t = b_0 + b_1 TR_t + u_1 \tag{6.12}$$

$$P_t = c_0 + c_1 C_{t-1} + u_2 \tag{6.13}$$

$$TR_t = S_t + P_t + C_t, \tag{6.14}$$

where S is software sales, TR is total revenue, P is peripheral sales, C is personal computer sales, t is the current time period, $t - 1$ is the previous time period, and u_1 and u_2 are error, or residual, terms.

Equations 6.10 and 6.13 are behavioral hypotheses. Equation 6.12 hypothesizes that current-period software sales are a function of the current level of total revenues; Equation 6.13 hypothesizes that peripheral sales depend on previous-period personal computer sales. The last equation in the system, Equation 6.14, is an identity. It defines total revenue as being equal to the sum of software, peripheral equipment, and personal computer sales.

The stochastic disturbance terms in the behavioral equations, u_1 and u_2, are included because the hypothesized relations are not exact. In other words, other factors that can affect software and peripheral sales are not accounted for in the system. So long as these stochastic elements are random and their expected values are zero, they do not present a barrier to empirical estimation of system parameters. However, if the error terms are not randomly distributed, parameter estimates will be biased and the reliability of model forecasts will be questionable. Large error terms, even if they are distributed randomly, reduce forecast accuracy.

Empirical estimation of the parameters for multiple equation systems (the bs and cs in Equations 6.12 and 6.13) often requires using statistical techniques beyond the scope of this text. However, the use of such a system for forecasting purposes can be illustrated.

To forecast next year's software and peripheral sales and total revenue for the firm represented by this illustrative model, it is necessary to express S, P, and TR in terms of variables whose values are known or can be estimated at the moment the forecast is generated. In other words, each endogenous variable (S_t, P_t, and TR_t) must be expressed in terms of the exogenous and predetermined variables (C_{t-1} and C_t). Such relations are called reduced-form equations because they reduce complex simultaneous relations to their most basic and simple form. Consider the manipulations of equations in the system necessary to solve for TR via its reduced-form equation.

Substituting Equation 6.12 into 6.14—that is, replacing S_t with Equation 6.12—results in[5]

$$TR_t = b_0 + b_1 \ TR_t + P_t + C_t. \tag{6.15}$$

A similar substitution of Equation 6.13 for P_t produces

$$TR_t = b_0 + b_1 \ TR_t + c_0 + c_1 C_{t-1} + C_t. \tag{6.16}$$

Collecting terms and isolating TR in Equation 6.16 gives

$$(1 - b_1)TR_t = b_0 + c_0 + c_1 C_{t-1} + C_t$$

or, alternately,

$$
\begin{aligned}
TR_t &= \frac{b_0 + c_0 + c_1 C_{t-1} + C_t}{(1 - b_1)} \\
&= \frac{b_0 + c_0}{(1 - b_1)} + \frac{c_1}{(1 - b_1)} C_{t-1} + \frac{1}{(1 - b_1)} C_t.
\end{aligned} \tag{6.17}
$$

---

[5]The stochastic disturbance terms (us) have been dropped from the illustration because their expected values are zero. The final equation for TR, however, is stochastic in nature.

Equation 6.17 now relates current total revenues to previous-period and current-period personal computer sales. Assuming that data on previous-period personal computer sales can be obtained and that current-period personal computer sales can be estimated using Equation 6.10, Equation 6.17 provides a forecasting model that accounts for the simultaneous relations expressed in this simplified multiple-equation system. Of course, in real-world situations, it is possible, perhaps even likely, that personal computer sales depend on the price, quantity, and quality of available software and peripheral equipment. Then S, P, and C, along with other important factors, may all be endogenous, involving a large number of relations in a highly complex multiple-equation system. Disentangling the important but often subtle relations involved in such a system makes forecasting with multiple-equation systems both intriguing and challenging.

Judging Forecast Reliability

One of the most challenging aspects of forecasting is judging the reliability of forecasts obtained from various models. How well do various methodologies deal with specific forecasting problems? In comparing forecast and actual values, how close is close enough? Is **forecast reliability,** or predictive consistency, over one sample or time period necessarily transferable to other samples and time periods? Each of these questions is fundamentally important and must be adequately addressed prior to the implementation of any successful forecasting program.

Forecast Reliability
Predictive consistency.

TESTS OF PREDICTIVE CAPABILITY

Ideally, to test predictive capability, a model generated from data of one sample or period is used to forecast data for some alternative sample or period. Thus, the reliability of a model for predicting firm sales, such as that shown in Equation 6.2, can be tested by examining the relation between forecast and actual data for years beyond 1991, given that the model was generated using data from the 1977 to 1991 period. However, it is often desirable to test a model without waiting for new data to become available. In such instances, one can divide available data into two subsamples, called a **test group** and a **forecast group.** The forecaster then estimates a forecasting model using data from the test group and uses the resulting model to forecast the data of interest in the forecast group. A comparison of forecast and actual values can then be conducted to test the stability of the underlying cost or demand relation.

Test Group
Subsample of data used to generate a forecast model.

Forecast Group
Subsample of data used to test a forecast model.

CORRELATION ANALYSIS

In analyzing a model's forecast capability, the correlation between forecast and actual values is of substantial interest. The formula for the simple correlation coefficient, r, for forecast and actual values, f and x, respectively, is:

$$r = \frac{\sigma_{fx}}{\sigma_f \sigma_x},$$

(6.18)

where σ_{fx} is the covariance between the forecast and actual series, and σ_f and σ_x are the sample standard deviations of the forecast and actual series, respectively. Most basic statistical software programs and many hand-held calculators readily provide these data, making the calculation of r a relatively simple task. Generally speaking, correlations between forecast and actual values in excess of 0.99 (99%) are highly desirable and indicate that the forecast model being considered constitutes an effective tool for analysis. However, in cross-section analysis, in which the important trend element in most economic data is held constant, a correlation of 99% between forecast and actual values is rare. When unusually difficult forecasting problems are being addressed, correlations between forecast and actual data of 90% or 95% may prove satisfactory. In contrast, in critical decision situations, forecast values may have to be estimated at very precise levels. In such instances, forecast and actual data may have to exhibit an extremely high level of correlation, 99.5% or 99.75%, to generate a high level of confidence in forecast reliability. The correlation between forecast and actual values necessary to reach a threshold reliability acceptance level depends in large part on the difficulty of the forecasting problem being analyzed and the cost of forecast error.

SAMPLE MEAN FORECAST ERROR ANALYSIS

Sample Mean Forecast Error
Estimate of average forecast error.

Further evaluation of a model's predictive capability can be made through consideration of a measure called the **sample mean forecast error,** which provides a useful estimate of the average forecast error of the model. It is sometimes called the root mean squared forecast error and is denoted by the symbol U. The sample mean forecast error is calculated as:

$$U = \sqrt{\frac{1}{n} \sum_{i=1}^{n} (f_i - x_i)^2}, \tag{6.19}$$

where n is the number of sample observations, f_i is a forecast value, and x_i is the corresponding actual value. The deviations between forecast and actual values are squared in the calculation of the mean forecast error to prevent positive and negative deviations between forecast and actual values from canceling each other out. The smaller the sample mean forecast error, the greater the accuracy associated with the forecasting model.

Choosing the Best Forecast Technique

To select an appropriate forecast method, managers must understand the nature of the forecasting problem and data under investigation. The range of potentially useful forecast techniques, including information regarding their capabilities and limitations, must also be understood, and finally, managers must be aware of the set of criteria on which the forecast method selection decision is to be made.

Typically, managers review forecast problems with others to assess past successes and failures in using alternative forecast methods. Staff or company colleagues may be available for consultation; otherwise, industry associations, nonprofit business research organizations, such as the Conference Board, and government agencies, such as the Commerce Department, may be consulted. If the scope of the forecast problem is large and requires extensive and ongoing consultation, outside consulting firms might be contacted for assistance. After conducting this initial research, managers are in a good position to select the most appropriate approach to solving the forecast problem at hand. Among the factors to be considered are data characteristics and requirements, the relevant time horizon, computer and related costs, and the role of judgment (see Table 6.5).

DATA REQUIREMENTS

A major factor influencing the selection of forecast techniques relates to the variable for which the forecast is being developed: namely, the identification and understanding of historical patterns of data. If trend, cyclical, seasonal, or irregular patterns can be recognized, then forecast techniques that are capable of handling those patterns can be readily selected. For example, if the data are relatively stable, a simple exponential smoothing approach may be quite adequate. Other exponential smoothing models are appropriate for trending and seasonal data; the same model will not be applicable in all cases. Notice, for example, that the simple exponential smoothing model can only handle nontrending, nonseasonal data.

As the forecast horizon increases, the cyclical pattern of economic data may also become a significant feature of the overall trend. In these cases, the need to relate the forecast variable to economic, market, and competitive factors increases, since simple trend projections may no longer be appropriate.

The selection of a given forecast technique is based on the assumption that stable patterns are evident in historical time series of economic data. To select an appropriate forecast method, managers must make judgments as to what historical data are representative of patterns that are likely to occur throughout the forecast period. The choice of an appropriate forecast technique will often hinge on the amount of relevant historical data that is readily available and any obvious patterns of that data. For many important forecast problems, ten years of monthly data (120 observations) are available and appropriate for forecasting future activity. In such cases, the full range of advanced forecast techniques can be considered. If only more restricted samples of data are available for analysis, then simpler forecast methods must be employed.

TIME HORIZON CONSIDERATIONS

Experience has shown that technically sophisticated time-series models can provide accurate short-term forecasts. For a long-range forecast, say, for a five-year plan, the forecaster will also want to use regression or econometric models. In the short term, the momentum of existing consumer behavior often resists dramatic change. Over a five-year period, however, customers can find new suppliers, and their needs may change. Therefore, in the long term, it is essential to relate the item being forecast to its "drivers," as explanatory factors are sometimes called.

The accuracy of econometric models during volatile forecast periods depends on the accuracy with which explanatory factors can be predicted. While these models can

Table 6.5 A SUBJECTIVE COMPARISON OF ALTERNATIVE FORECAST TECHNIQUES

| | QUALITATIVE FORECASTING METHODS | | | | QUANTITATIVE FORECASTING METHODS | | | | | | |
| | Personal Insight | Delphi Method | Panel Consensus | Market Research | STATISTICAL | | | | DETERMINISTIC | | |
					Summary Statistics	Trend Projections	Exponential Smoothing	Econometric Models	Market Survey	Leading Indicator	Econometric Models
Pattern of data that can be recognized and handled easily.											
Trend	✓	✓	✓	✓	✓	✓	✓	✓	✓	✓	✓
Seasonal	✓	✓	✓	✓	✓	✓	✓	✓	✓	✓	✓
Cyclical	✓	✓	✓	✓	✓	✓	✓	✓	✓	✓	✓
Minimum data requirements.	Low	Low	Low	Low	Low	Medium	Medium	High	Low	Medium	High
Time horizon for which method is appropriate.											
Short term (0–3 mos.)	✓	✓	✓	✓	✓	✓	✓	✓	✓	✓	✓
Medium term (12–24 mos.)	✓	✓	✓	✓	✓	✓	✓	✓	✓	✓	✓
Long term (2 yrs. or more)	✓	✓	✓	✓	✓	✓	NA	✓	NA	NA	✓
Accuracy											
Predicting patterns.	Medium	Medium	Medium	Medium	Low	Medium	Low	High	Low	Low	Low
Predicting turning points.	Low	Medium	Medium	Medium	Low	Low	Low	High	Low	Low	Low
Applicability											
Time required to obtain forecast.	Medium	Medium	Medium	High	Low	Low	Low	Medium	High	Medium	Medium
Ease of understanding and interpreting the results.	High	High	High	High	High	High	Medium	Medium	Medium	Medium	High
Computer costs											
Development.	Low	Low	Low	Low	Low	Low	High	High	High	High	Medium
Storage requirements.	Low	Low	Low	Low	Medium	Medium	High	Medium	Low	Medium	High
Running.	Low	High	Low	Low	Low	Medium	Low	Medium	Low	Low	High

also be used in the short term, they are costlier and more complex than simpler exponential smoothing models. When economic or market conditions are stable, econometric models are seldom more accurate than more simple trend projections and exponential smoothing methods.

For three-year to five-year forecasts, simple trend, econometric models, and exponential smoothing methods are typically employed. Over this intermediate term, trend projection techniques are relatively inexpensive to apply, but may produce forecasts that are often not as accurate as those resulting from econometric methods. When sufficient data exist and the need for accuracy is great, the use of exponential smoothing or econometric models is often recommended. Then, the generally superior short-term forecasting abilities of smoothing models emerge. Also evident over the intermediate term are the advantages of econometric models, which are superior in relating the item to be forecast to economic conditions, price changes, competitive activities, and other explanatory variables.

When both smoothing and econometric models yield similar forecasts, managers can be reasonably certain that the forecast is consistent with underlying assumptions and has a good chance of being accurate. When the forecasts produced by two or more methods are significantly different, this is a warning to exercise extreme care. The risks associated with such forecasts are also greater than when different methods produce inconsistent forecasts.

In sum, the time horizon for a forecast has a direct bearing on the selection of an appropriate forecast technique. In general, the longer the time horizon, the greater the reliance on qualitative methods. For short- and medium-term forecasts, a variety of quantitative methods can be applied. As the horizon increases, however, a number of quantitative techniques become less appropriate. For example, exponential smoothing time-series models are poor predictors of turning points. For predicting business activity more than two years into the future, their use is not recommended. Econometric models may be more useful for the short, medium, *and* long term. Trend projection techniques are appropriate for short and medium time horizons, as are econometric techniques.

COMPUTER AND RELATED COSTS

Computer costs are rapidly becoming an insignificant part of forecast technique selection. The recent proliferation of forecast software has also lessened the need for sophisticated support staff. Still, while computer costs are decreasing, other costs associated with forecast development and implementation cannot be ignored. Some of the major forecast cost considerations include: processing costs, connect-time and data storage costs, supplementary charges for use of software packages and data base retrievals, maintenance and support charges, and special hardware needs. Start-up costs for developing forecasts for new products and services, analysis, and modeling work tend to escalate over time, especially when the experience level of the forecasting staff is low. The maintenance of a complex forecasting system, on the other hand, can be relatively inexpensive provided adequate programming documentation and standards are kept current.

ROLE OF JUDGMENT

The choice of an appropriate forecasting methodology depends on both the underlying characteristics of the forecasting problem and the level of accuracy required. In all instances, the most sophisticated forecast methodology to employ is that which provides sufficiently accurate results at minimum cost. No one flies a jet to the grocery store—similarly, no manager would find costly and difficult methods appropriate for solving trivial forecasting problems.

To determine a suitable level of forecast accuracy, one must compare the costs and benefits of increased accuracy. When forecast accuracy is low, the probability of significant forecasting error is high, as is the chance of making suboptimal managerial decisions. Conversely, when forecast accuracy is high, the probability of substantial forecasting error is reduced and the chance of making erroneous managerial decisions is low. It is reasonable to require a relatively high level of forecast accuracy when the costs of forecast error are high. When only minor costs result from forecast error, only inexpensive and typically less precise methods can be justified.

The material in this chapter highlights advantages and limitations of various forecast techniques. By understanding the strengths and weaknesses of such methodologies, managers can select the appropriate method to generate required forecast values. In many instances, especially when difficult forecasting problems are being addressed, managers find it helpful to employ multiple forecasting approaches. When a variety of forecast techniques yield highly comparable results, managers can be confident of a high degree of forecast accuracy. If different methods yield widely divergent forecast results, managers must be cautious in their interpretation and use of forecast information.

Finally, it is worth emphasizing that the objective of economic forecasting is to improve on the subjective judgments made by managers. All managers must forecast; the goal is to make better forecasts. Nowhere in the forecasting process is the subjective judgment of managers relied on so heavily as it is in the selection of an appropriate forecast method. Each forecast technique must be evaluated in terms of its general reliability and applicability to the problem at hand and in terms of its relative cost effectiveness. To select the best technique to address a given forecast problem, managers must be knowledgeable about the strengths and weaknesses of various forecast methods, the amount and quality of available data, and the human and other costs associated with generating reliable forecasts. When it comes to the selection of the best forecast technique, as in every step of the forecasting process, there is no substitute for seasoned business judgment.

Summary

Managerial decision making is often based on forecasts of future events. This chapter examines several techniques for economic forecasting, including qualitative analysis, trend analysis and projection, econometric models, and input-output methods.

- **Qualitative analysis** is an intuitive judgmental approach to forecasting that is useful when it provides for the systematic analysis of data derived from unbiased, informed opinion. The **personal insight** method is one in which an informed individual uses personal or organizational experience as a basis for developing future expectations. The **panel consensus** method relies on the informed opinion of several individuals. In the **delphi method,** responses from a panel of experts are analyzed by an independent party to elicit a consensus opinion.

- **Survey techniques** that skillfully employ interviews or mailed questionnaires constitute another important forecasting tool, especially for short-term projections.

- **Trend analysis** involves characterizing the historical pattern of an economic variable and then projecting or forecasting its future path based on past experience. A **secular trend** is the long-run pattern of increase or decrease in a series of economic data. **Cyclical fluctuation** describes the rhythmic variation in economic series that is due to a pattern of expansion or contraction in the overall economy. Seasonal variation, or **seasonality,** is a rhythmic annual pattern in sales or profits caused by weather, habit, or social custom. **Irregular or random influences** are unpredictable shocks to the economic system and the pace of economic activity caused by wars, strikes, natural catastrophes, and so on.

- A simple **linear trend analysis** assumes a constant period-by-period *unit* change in an important economic variable over time. **Growth trend analysis** assumes a constant period-by-period *percentage* change in an important economic variable over time.

- **Macroeconomic forecasting** involves predicting the pace of economic activity, employment, or interest rates at the international, national, or regional level. **Microeconomic forecasting** involves predicting economic performance, say, profitability, at the industry, firm, or plant level.

- The **business cycle** is the rhythmic pattern of contraction and expansion observed in the overall economy. **Economic indicators** are series of data that successfully describe the pattern of projected, current, or past economic activity. A **composite index** is a weighted average of leading, coincident, or lagging economic indicators. **Barometric forecasting** is a predictive method based on the observed relation among economic time series. A **diffusion index** indicates the percentage of leading, coincident, or lagging indicators that are rising at any point in time.

- **Exponential smoothing** (or "averaging") techniques are among the most widely used forecasting methods in business today. In **two-parameter (Holt) exponential smoothing,** the data are assumed to consist of fluctuations about a level that is changing with some constant or slowly drifting linear trend. The **three-parameter (Winters) exponential smoothing** method extends the two-parameter technique by including a smoothed multiplicative seasonal index to account for the seasonal behavior of the forecast series.

- **Econometric methods** use economic theory and mathematical and statistical tools to forecast economic relations. **Identities** are economic relations that are true by definition. **Behavioral equations** are hypothesized economic relations that are estimated using econometric methods.

- **Forecast reliability,** or predictive consistency, must be accurately judged in order to assess the degree of confidence that should be placed in economic forecasts. A given forecast model is often estimated using a **test group** of data and evaluated using **forecast group** data. No forecasting assignment is complete until reliability has been quantified and evaluated. The **sample mean forecast error** is one useful measure of predictive capability.

All forecasting methods have particular strengths and shortcomings. The appropriate technique to apply in a given forecasting situation depends on such factors as the distance into the future being forecast, the lead time available, the accuracy required, the quality of data available for analysis, and the nature of the economic relations involved in the forecasting problem. In many instances, comparing results from multiple forecasting techniques provides a useful basis for judging forecast reliability.

QUESTIONS

Q6.1   What is the delphi method? Describe its main advantages and limitations.

Q6.2   Describe the main advantages and limitations of survey data.

Q6.3M   What is trend projection, and why is this method often employed in economic forecasting?

Q6.4   What is the basic shortcoming of trend projection that barometric approaches improve on?

Q6.5   What advantage do diffusion and composite indexes provide in the barometric approach to forecasting?

Q6.6   Explain how the econometric model approach to forecasting could be used to examine various "what if" questions about the future.

Q6.7   Describe the data requirements that must be met if regression analysis is to provide a useful basis for forecasting.

Q6.8   Would a linear regression model of the advertising/sales relation be appropriate for forecasting the advertising levels at which threshold or saturation effects become prevalent?

Q6.9   Cite some examples of forecasting problems that might be addressed using regression analysis of complex multiple-equation systems of economic relations.

Q6.10   What are the main characteristics of accurate forecasts?

SELF-TEST PROBLEMS AND SOLUTIONS

ST6.1   Gross Domestic Product (GDP) is a measure of overall activity in the economy. It is defined as the value at the final point of sale of all goods and services produced during a given period by both domestic and foreign-owned enterprises. GDP data for the 1966–95 period offer the basis to test the abilities of simple constant change and constant growth models to describe the trend in GDP over time. However, regression results generated over the entire 1966–95 period cannot be used to forecast GDP over any subpart of that period. To do so would be to overstate the forecast capability of the regression model since, by definition, the regression line minimizes the sum of squared deviations over the estimation period. To test forecast reliability, it is necessary to test the predictive capability of a given regression model over data that was not used to generate that very model. In the absence of GDP data for future periods, say, 1996–2000, the reliability of alternative forecast techniques can be illustrated by arbitrarily dividing historical GDP data into two subsamples: a 1966–90 25-year test group and a 1991–95 5-year forecast group. Regression models estimated over the 1966–90 test group can be used to "forecast" actual GDP over the 1991–95 period. In other words, estimation results over the 1966–90 subperiod provide a forecast model that can be used to evaluate the predictive reliability of constant change and constant growth models over the 1991–95 forecast period.

The accompanying table shows GDP figures for the U.S. economy for the 30-year period from 1966–95.

GROSS DOMESTIC PRODUCT, 1966–95 (IN BILLIONS OF DOLLARS)

YEAR	GDP	LN GDP	TIME PERIOD
1995	$7,245.8	8.8882	30
1994	6,931.4	8.8438	29
1993	6,550.2	8.7873	28
1992	6,020.2	8.7029	27
1991	5,724.8	8.6526	26
1990	5,546.1	8.6209	25
1989	5,250.8	8.5661	24
1988	4,900.4	8.4971	23
1987	4,539.9	8.4207	22
1986	4,268.6	8.3590	21
1985	4,038.7	8.3037	20
1984	3,777.2	8.2367	19
1983	3,405.0	8.1330	18
1982	3,149.6	8.0550	17
1981	3,030.6	8.0165	16
1980	2,708.0	7.9040	15
1979	2,488.6	7.8195	14
1978	2,232.7	7.7110	13
1977	1,974.1	7.5879	12
1976	1,768.4	7.4778	11
1975	1,585.9	7.3689	10
1974	1,458.6	7.2852	9
1973	1,349.6	7.2076	8
1972	1,207.0	7.0959	7
1971	1,097.2	7.0005	6
1970	1,010.7	6.9184	5
1969	959.5	6.8664	4
1968	889.3	6.7904	3
1967	814.3	6.7023	2
1966	769.8	6.6461	1

Sources: *Economic Report of the President,* (Washington, DC: U.S. Government Printing Office, 1995), 274, and *Federal Reserve Bulletin,* July 1996, A48.

A.   Use the simple regression model approach to estimate the linear relation between GDP and time (*T*) over the entire 1966–95 period, and the 1966–90 subperiod, where

$$GDP_t = b_0 + b_1 T_t + u_t,$$

and GDP_t is GDP in year *t*, and *T* is a time trend variable (where $T_{1966} = 1$, $T_{1967} = 2$, $T_{1968} = 3$, . . ., and $T_{1995} = 30$); and *u* is a residual term

that includes the effects of all factors that have been omitted from the regression model and the influences of random or stochastic elements. This is called a constant change model because it is based on the assumption of a constant dollar growth in economic activity per year. How well does the constant change model fit actual GDP data over each period?

B.   Use the simple regression model approach to estimate the linear relation between the natural logarithm of GDP and time (*T*) over the entire 1966–1995 period, and the 1966–90 subperiod, where

$$ln\ GDP_t = b_0 + b_1 T_t + u_t,$$

and $ln\ GDP_t$ is the natural logarithm of GDP in year *t*, and *T* is a time trend variable (where $T_{1966} = 1$, $T_{1967} = 2$, $T_{1968} = 3$, . . ., and $T_{1995} = 30$); and *u* is a residual term. This is called a constant growth model because it is based on the assumption of a constant percentage growth in economic activity per year. How well does the constant growth model fit actual GDP data over each period?

C.   Create a spreadsheet that shows actual GDP and constant change model GDP forecasts over the 1991–95 period. Subtract forecast values from actual figures to obtain annual estimates of forecast error, and squared forecast error, for each year over the 1991–95 period.

Finally, compute the correlation coefficient between actual and forecast values for each GDP_t value over the 1991–95 period. Also compute the sample average (or root mean squared) forecast error. Based upon these findings, how well does the constant change model generated over the 1966–90 period forecast actual GDP data over the 1991–95 period?

D.   Create another spreadsheet that shows constant growth model GDP forecasts over the 1991–95 period alongside actual figures. Then, subtract forecast values from actual figures to obtain annual estimates of forecast error, and squared forecast error, for each year over the 1991–95 period.

Finally, compute the correlation coefficient between actual and forecast values for each GDP_t variable over the 1991–95 period. Also compute the sample average (or root mean squared) forecast error. Based upon these findings, how well does the constant growth model generated over the 1966–90 period forecast actual GDP data over the 1991–95 period?

ST6.1 **SOLUTION**

A. The constant change model estimated using the simple regression model technique illustrates the linear relation between GDP and time.

A descriptive constant change regression model covering the 1966–90 period (*t*-statistic in parentheses) is:

$$GDP_t = -\$318.983 + \$228.552T_t,$$
$$(26.88)$$
$$R^2 = 95.27\%$$

An $R^2 = 96.27\%$ and a highly significant *t*-statistic for the time trend variable indicate that the constant change model closely describes the change in GDP over the entire 1966–95 period.

A constant change regression model estimated over the 1966–90 25-year period (*t*-statistic in parentheses), used to forecast GDP over the 1991–95 5-year period, is:

$$GDP_t = -\$74.130 + \$203.304T_t,$$
$$(22.70)$$
$$R^2 = 95.73\%$$

As before, $R^2 = 95.73\%$ and a highly significant *t*-statistic for the time trend variable indicate that the constant change model closely describes the change in GDP over the 1966–90 subperiod. Nevertheless, some differences are noted over this subperiod and the overall period from 1966–95. Notice the large differences in the intercept term and slope coefficients estimated over the 1966–95 and 1966–90 periods. This may portend significant differences in growth conditions and difficulty in accurately forecasting GDP between these two periods.

B. The constant growth model estimated using the simple regression model technique illustrates the linear relation between the natural logarithm of GDP and time.

A descriptive constant growth regression model covering the 1966–90 period (*t*-statistic in parentheses) is:

$$ln\ GDP_t = 6.583 + 0.082T_t,\ R^2 = 99.01\%.$$
$$(52.97)$$

An $R^2 = 99.01\%$ and a highly significant *t*-statistic for the time trend variable indicate that the constant growth model closely describes the change in GDP over the entire 1966–95 period.

A constant growth regression model estimated over the 1966–90 25-year period (*t*-statistic in parentheses), used to forecast GDP over the 1991–96 5-year period, is:

$$ln\ GDP_t = 6.529 + 0.087T_t,\ R^2 = 99.50\%.$$
$$(67.49)$$

As before, $R^2 = 99.50\%$ and a highly significant *t*-statistic for the time trend variable indicate that the constant growth model closely describes the change in GDP over the 1966–90 subperiod. Nevertheless, some differences are again noted over this subperiod and the overall period from 1966 to 95. Even modest differences in the intercept term and slope coefficient estimated over the 1966–95 and 1966–90 periods can lead to large forecast errors.

C. Each constant change GDP forecast is derived using the constant change model coefficients estimated in Part A, along with values for each respective time trend variable over the 1991–95 period. Remember that $T_{1991} = 26$, $T_{1992} = 27$, $T_{1993} = 28$, . . ., and $T_{1995} = 30$. The following spreadsheet shows actual and constant change model GDP forecasts for the 1991–95 forecast period. (See table at top of page 252.)

The correlation coefficient between actual and constant change model forecast GDP is $r_{GDP,}$ $_{FGDP} = 99.58\%$. The sample root mean squared forecast error is $918.6 billion (= $\sqrt{\$843,891.4}$), or 14.1% of average actual GDP over the 1991–95 period. Despite the fact that the correlation between actual and constant change forecast model values is relatively high, forecast error appears substantial. Economic growth was unusually tepid during the early part of the 1990s, and this led to large forecast errors for constant change forecasts of GDP based upon more rapidly growing prior periods.

D. Each constant growth GDP forecast is derived using the constant growth model coefficients estimated in Part B, along with values for each respective time trend variable over the 1991–95 period. Again, remember that $T_{1991} = 26$, $T_{1992} =$

YEAR	GDP	GDP FORECAST	FORECAST ERROR (GDP-FORECAST)	SQUARED FORECAST ERROR (GDP-FORECAST)^2	TIME PERIOD
1995	$7,245.8	$6,025.0	$1,220.8	$1,490,365.8	30
1994	6,931.4	5,821.7	1,109.7	1,231,455.3	29
1993	6,550.2	5,618.4	931.8	868,276.8	28
1992	6,020.2	5,415.1	605.1	366,167.6	27
1991	5,724.8	5,211.8	513.0	263,191.6	26
Average	$6,494.5	$5,618.4	$876.1	$843,891.4	

27, $T_{1993} = 28$, . . ., and $T_{1995} = 30$ and that the constant growth model provides predicted, or forecast, values for ln GDP$_t$. To obtain forecast values for GDP$_t$, simply take the antilog (ex-ponent) of each predicted ln GDP$_t$ variable.

The following spreadsheet shows actual and constant growth model GDP forecasts for the 1991–95 forecast period:

YEAR	GDP	LN GDP	LN GDP FORECAST	GDP FORECAST	FORECAST ERROR (GDP-FORECAST)	SQUARED FORECAST ERROR (GDP-FORECAST)^2	TIME PERIOD
1995	$7,245.8	8.8882	9.1476	$9,391.6	−$2,145.8	$4,604,661.9	30
1994	6,931.4	8.8438	9.0603	8,606.6	−1,675.2	2,806,301.0	29
1993	6,550.2	8.7873	8.9730	7,887.2	−1,337.0	1,787,509.6	28
1992	6,020.2	8.7029	8.8857	7,227.9	−1,207.7	1,458,515.8	27
1991	5,724.8	8.6526	8.7984	6,623.7	−898.9	808,043.6	26
Average	$6,494.5	8.7749	8.9730	$7,947.4	−$1,452.9	$2,293,006.4	

The correlation coefficient between actual and constant growth model forecast GDP is $r_{GDP, FGDP} = 99.32\%$. The sample root mean squared forecast error is $1,514.3 billion (= $\sqrt{\$2,293,006.4}$), or 23.3% of average actual GDP over the 1991–95 period. Again, and despite the fact that the the correlation between actual and constant change forecast model values is relatively high, forecast error appears very high. As before, unusually modest economic growth during the early 1990s has led to large forecast errors when the forecast model for GDP is based upon more rapidly growing prior periods.

ST6.2 **Multiple Regression.** Branded Products, Inc., based in Oakland, California, is a leading producer and marketer of household laundry detergent and bleach products. About a year ago, Branded Products rolled out its new Super Detergent in four western states, following success in more limited test markets. This isn't just a "me too" product in a commodity market. Branded Products' detergent contains Branded 2 bleach, a successful laundry product in its own right. At the time of the introduction, management wondered whether the company could successfully crack this market, dominated as it is by Procter & Gamble and other big players.

The following spreadsheet (or table) shows weekly demand data and regression model forecast results for Super Detergent over the past seven months (30 weeks). See the table on page 253.

A. Interpret the coefficient estimate for each respective independent variable.

B. Characterize the overall explanatory power of this multiple regression model in light of R^2 and the following plot of forecast and actual demand per week.

BRANDED PRODUCTS DEMAND ESTIMATION PROBLEM

WEEKLY SALES PERIOD	DEMAND IN CASES, Q	PRICE PER CASE, P	COMPETITOR PRICE, P_X	ADVERT., Ad	INCOME, Y	MONTH, T	FORECAST DEMAND, Q
1	1,290	$137	$94	$814	$42,498	1	1,287
2	1,177	147	81	896	41,399	2	1,187
3	1,155	149	89	852	39,905	3	1,188
4	1,299	117	92	854	34,871	4	1,311
5	1,166	135	86	810	34,239	5	1,175
6	1,186	143	79	768	44,452	6	1,200
7	1,293	113	91	978	30,367	7	1,317
8	1,322	111	82	821	37,757	8	1,321
9	1,338	109	81	843	40,130	9	1,359
10	1,160	129	82	849	31,264	10	1,172
11	1,293	124	91	797	34,610	11	1,262
12	1,413	117	76	988	41,033	12	1,349
13	1,299	106	90	914	30,674	13	1,341
14	1,238	135	88	913	31,578	14	1,196
15	1,467	117	99	867	41,201	15	1,430
16	1,089	147	76	785	30,247	16	1,032
17	1,203	124	83	817	33,177	17	1,222
18	1,474	103	98	846	37,330	18	1,453
19	1,235	140	78	768	44,671	19	1,230
20	1,367	115	83	856	37,950	20	1,333
21	1,310	119	76	771	43,478	21	1,316
22	1,331	138	100	947	36,053	22	1,306
23	1,293	122	90	831	35,333	23	1,300
24	1,437	105	86	905	44,304	24	1,484
25	1,165	145	96	996	30,925	25	1,214
26	1,328	138	97	929	36,867	26	1,300
27	1,515	116	97	1,000	41,799	27	1,485
28	1,223	148	84	951	40,684	28	1,238
29	1,293	134	88	848	43,637	29	1,331
30	1,215	127	87	891	30,468	30	1,235
Averages	1,285.8	127.0	87.3	870.2	37,430.0	15.5	1,285.8

REGRESSION OUTPUT:

Constant	850.042
Std Err of Y Est	33.640
R^2	91.47%
No. of Observations	30
Degrees of Freedom	24

	P	P_X	Ad	Y	T
X Coefficient(s)	−5.033	4.744	0.277	0.011	1.309
Std Err of Coef.	0.439	0.970	0.105	0.001	0.753
t-statistic	−11.45	4.89	2.65	11.00	1.74

ST6.2   **SOLUTION**

A.   Each respective independent X-variable has a statistically significant effect on QUANTITY at the 99% confidence level, except for the TIME trend variable. This implies that there is no obvious growth trend in demand for super detergent. PRICE has the predictably negative influence on QUANTITY, whereas the effects of COMPETITOR PRICE ADVERTISING and INCOME are positive as expected. The chance of finding such large t-statistics is less than 1% if, in fact, there

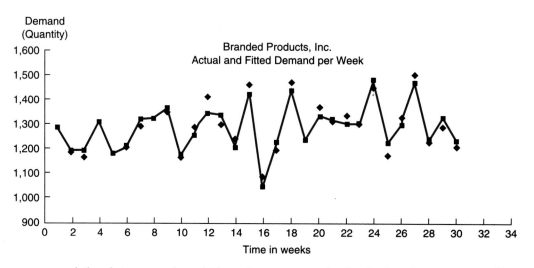

were no relation between each variable and QUANTITY.

B. The R^2 = 91.47% obtained by the model means that roughly 91% of demand variation is explained by the underlying variation in all five independent variables. This is a relatively high level of explained variation and implies an attrac-

tive level of explanatory power. Moreover, as shown in the graph of actual and forecast demand, the multiple regression model closely tracks week-by-week changes in demand with no worrisome divergences between actual and forecast demand over time.

PROBLEMS

P6.1   **Sales Trend Analysis.** Rent-A-Car, Inc., provides daily auto rental service to individuals while their own cars are being repaired. Annual sales revenue has grown rapidly from $2.5 million to $10 million during the past five-year period.

A. Calculate the five-year growth rate in sales using the constant growth model with annual compounding.

B. Calculate the five-year growth rate in sales using the constant growth model with continuous compounding.

C. Compare your answers to Parts A and B, and discuss any differences.

P6.2   **Growth Rate Estimation.** Mr. Ed's BBQ is a small restaurant featuring Texas-style barbecue. Wilbur Post, owner of Mr. Ed's, is concerned about the restaurant's erratic revenue pattern during recent years.

A. Complete the following table showing annual sales data for Mr. Ed's during the 1991–96 period.

YEAR (1)	SALES (2)	CURRENT SALES ÷ PREVIOUS PERIOD SALES (3)	GROWTH RATE (4) = [(3) − 1] × 100
1991	$250,000	—	—
1992	200,000		
1993	400,000		
1994	500,000		
1995	500,000		
1996	250,000		

B. Calculate the geometric average annual rate of growth for the 1991–96 period. (Hint: Calculate this growth rate using sales from 1991 and 1996.)

C. Calculate the arithmetic average annual rate of growth for the 1991–96 period. (Hint: This is the average of Column 4 figures.)

D. Discuss any differences in your answers to Parts B and C.

P6.3 **Sales Trend Analysis.** Environmental Designs, Inc., produces and installs energy-efficient window systems in commercial buildings. During the past ten years, sales revenue has increased from $25 million to $65 million.

A. Calculate the company's growth rate in sales using the constant growth model with annual compounding.

B. Derive a five-year and a ten-year sales forecast.

P6.4 **Cost Forecasting.** Bullwinkle J. Moose, a quality-control supervisor for Rocket Devices, Inc., is concerned about unit labor cost increases for the assembly of electrical snap-action switches. Costs have increased from $80 to $100 per unit over the previous three years. Moose thinks that importing switches from foreign suppliers at a cost of $115.90 per unit may soon be desirable.

A. Calculate the company's unit labor cost growth rate using the constant rate of change model with continuous compounding.

B. Forecast when unit labor costs will equal the current cost of importing.

P6.5 **Unit Sales Forecast Modeling.** Joyce Davenport has discovered that the change in Product A demand in any given week is inversely proportional to the change in sales of Product B in the previous week. That is, if sales of B rose by $X\%$ last week, sales of A can be expected to fall by $X\%$ this week.

A. Write the equation for next week's sales of A, using the variables A = sales of Product A, B = sales of Product B, and t = time. Assume that there will be no shortages of either product.

B. Last week, 100 units of A and 90 units of B were sold. Two weeks ago, 75 units of B were sold. What would you predict the sales of A to be this week?

P6.6 **Sales Forecast Modeling.** H. M. Murdock must convince the loan officer at a local bank of the viability of Mr. T's, a retail outlet for T-shirts, posters, and novelty items. In doing so, Murdock must generate a sales forecast. Murdock assumes that next-period sales are a function of current income, advertising, and advertising by a competing retailer.

A. Write an equation for predicting sales if Murdock assumes that the percentage change in sales is twice as large as the percentage change in income and advertising but that it is only one-half as large as, and of the opposite sign of, the percentage change in competitor advertising. Use the variables S = sales, Y = income, A = advertising, and CA = competitor advertising.

B. During the current period, sales total $500,000, median family income is $35,700, advertising is $20,000, and competitor advertising is $66,000. Previous period levels were $35,000 (income), $25,000 (advertising), and $60,000 (competitor advertising). Forecast next-period sales.

P6.7 **Cost Forecast Modeling.** Tonya Harding is product safety manager at Lillehammer Products, Inc., a Norwegian-based manufacturer of petite hand tools. Harding is evaluating the cost effectiveness of a preventive maintenance program. Harding believes that monthly downtime on the packaging line caused by equipment breakdown is related to the hours spent each month on preventive maintenance.

A. Write an equation to predict next month's downtime using the variables D = downtime, M = preventive maintenance, t = time, a_0 = constant term, a_1 = regression slope coefficient, and u = random disturbance. Assume that downtime in the forecast (next) month decreases by the same percentage as preventive maintenance increased during the month preceding the current one.

B. If 40 hours were spent last month on preventive maintenance and this month's downtime was 500 hours, what should downtime be next month if preventive maintenance this month is 50 hours? Use the equation developed in Part A.

P6.8 **Sales Forecast Modeling.** Toys Unlimited Ltd., must forecast sales for a popular adult computer game to avoid stockouts or excessive inventory charges during the upcoming Christmas season. In percentage terms, the company estimates that game sales fall at double the rate of price increases and that they grow at triple the rate of customer traffic increases. Furthermore, these effects seem to be independent.

A. Write an equation for estimating the Christmas season sales, using the variables S = sales, P = price, T = traffic, t = time, and u = a random disturbance term.

B. Forecast this season's sales if Toys Unlimited sold 10,000 games last season at $15 each, this season's price is anticipated to be $16.50, and customer traffic is expected to rise by 15% over previous levels.

P6.9 **Simultaneous Equations.** Mid-Atlantic Cinema, Inc., runs a chain of movie theaters in the east-central states and has enjoyed great success with a Tuesday Night at the Movies promotion. By offering half off its regular $6 admission price, average nightly attendance has risen from 500 to 1,500 persons. Popcorn and other concession revenues tied to attendance have also risen dramatically. Historically, Mid-Atlantic has found that 50% of all moviegoers buy a $2 cup of buttered popcorn. Eighty percent of these popcorn buyers, plus 40% of the moviegoers who do not buy popcorn, each spend an average of $1.25 on soda and other concessions.

A. Write an expression describing total revenue from tickets plus popcorn plus other concessions.

B. Forecast total revenues for both regular and special Tuesday night pricing.

C. Forecast the total profit contribution earned for the regular and special Tuesday night pricing strategies if the profit contribution is 25% on movie ticket revenues and 80% on popcorn and other concession revenues.

P6.10 **Simultaneous Equations.** Supersonic Industries, based in Seattle, Washington, manufactures a wide range of parts for aircraft manufacturers. The company is currently evaluating the merits of building a new plant to fulfill a new contract with the federal government. The alternatives to expansion are to use additional overtime, to reduce other production, or both. The company will add new capacity only if the economy appears to be expanding. Therefore, forecasting the general pace of economic activity for the United States is an important input to the decision-making process. The firm has collected data and estimated the following relations for the U.S. economy:

Last year's total profits (all corporations) $P_{t-1} =$ $500 billion

This year's government expenditures $G =$ $1,500 billion

Annual consumption expenditures $C =$ $300 billion $+ 0.75Y + u$

Annual investment expenditures $I =$ $550 billion $+ 0.9P_{t-1} + u$

Annual tax receipts $T = 0.2GDP$

National income $Y = GDP - T$

Gross domestic product $(GDP) = C + I + G.$

Forecast each of the preceding variables through the simultaneous relations expressed in the multiple equation system. Assume that all random disturbances average out to zero.

Case Study for Chapter 6

FORECASTING GLOBAL PERFORMANCE FOR A MICKEY MOUSE ORGANIZATION

The Walt Disney Company is one of the best known and best managed entertainment companies in the world. As the cornerstone of a carefully integrated entertainment marketing strategy, the company owns and operates the world's most acclaimed amusement parks and entertainment facilities. Some of the best known and most successful among these are Disneyland, California, and Walt Disney World, Florida—an immense entertainment center that includes the Magic Kingdom, Epcot Center, and Disney-MGM Studios. During recent years, the company has extended its amusement park business to foreign soil with Tokyo Disneyland and Euro Disneyland, located just outside of Paris, France. Disney's foreign operations provide an interesting example of the company's shrewd combination of marketing and financial skills. To conserve scarce capital resources, Disney was able to entice foreign investors to put up

100% of the financing required for both the Tokyo and Paris facilities. In turn, Disney is responsible for the design and operation of both operations, retains an important equity interest, and enjoys significant royalties on all gross revenues. Disney's innovative means for financing foreign operations has enabled the company to greatly expand its revenue and profit base without any commensurate increase in capital expenditures. As a result, the success of its foreign operations has allowed the company to increase its already enviable rate of return on stockholders' equity to more than 20% per year.

Disney is also a major force in the movie picture production business with Buena Vista, Touchstone, and Hollywood Pictures, in addition to the renowned Walt Disney Studios. The company is famous for recent hit movies such as *Beauty and the Beast, The Lion King,* and *Pocahontas,* in addition to a film library including hundreds of movie classics like *Fantasia, Snow White,* and *Mary Poppins,* among others. Disney employs an aggressive and highly successful video marketing strategy for new films and re-releases from the company's extensive film library. The Disney Store, a chain of retail specialty shops, profits from the sale of movie tie-in merchandise, books, and recorded music. Also making a significant contribution to the bottom line are earnings from the cable TV Disney Channel. In February 1996, the Disney empire grew further with the acquisition of Capital Cities/ABC, a print and television media behemoth, for stock and cash. The company's family entertainment marketing strategy is so broad in its reach that Disney characters such as Mickey Mouse, Donald Duck, and Goofy have become an integral part of the American culture. Given its ability to turn whimsy into outstanding operating performance, the Walt Disney Company is one firm that doesn't mind being called a "Mickey Mouse Organization."

Table 6.6 shows a variety of accounting operating statistics, including revenues, cash flow, capital spending, dividends, earnings, book value, and year-end share prices for the Walt Disney Corporation during the 1980–95 period. All data are expressed in dollars per share to illustrate how individual shareholders have benefited from the company's consistently superior rates of growth. During this time frame, for example, revenue per share grew at an annual rate of 18.6% per year, and earnings per share grew by 16.4% per year. These performance measures

exceed industry and economy-wide norms by a substantial margin. Disney employees, CEO Michael D. Eisner, and all stockholders have profited greatly from the company's outstanding performance. Over the 1980–95 period, Disney common stock exploded in price from roughly $3 per share to $58 7/8, after adjusting for stock splits. This represents more than a 21% annual rate of return, and makes Disney one of the truly outstanding stockmarket performers during recent years.

Of course, present-day investors want to know how the company will fare during coming years. Will the company be able to continue sizzling growth, or, like many companies, will Disney find it impossible to maintain such stellar performance? On the one hand, Tokyo Disneyland and Euro Disneyland promise significant future revenues and profits from previously untapped global markets. Anyone with young children who has visited Disneyland or Disney World has seen their delight and fascination with Disney characters. It is also impossible not to notice how much foreign travelers to the United States seem to enjoy the Disney experience. Donald Duck and Mickey Mouse will do a lot of business abroad. Future expansion possibilities in Malaysia, China, or the former Soviet Union also hold the potential for rapid growth into the next century. On the other hand, growth of 20% per year is exceedingly hard to maintain for any length of time. At that pace, the 81,000 workers employed by Disney in 1996 would grow to 168,000 by the year 2000, and to over 1 million by the year 2010. Maintaining control with such a rapidly growing workforce would be challenging, to say the least; maintaining Disney's high level of creative energy might not be possible.

Given the many uncertainties faced by Disney and most major corporations, long-term forecasts of operating performance by industry analysts are usually restricted to a fairly short time perspective. *The Value Line Investment Survey,* one of the most widely respected forecast services, focuses on a three- to five-year time horizon. To forecast performance for any individual company, *Value Line* starts with an underlying forecast of the economic environment three to five years hence. During late-1996, for example, *Value Line* forecast a 1999–2001 economic environment in which unemployment will average 5.8% of the workforce, compared to 5.6% in 1995. Industrial production will be expanding about 3.5% per year;

Table 6.6

OPERATING STATISTICS FOR THE WALT DISNEY COMPANY
(ALL DATA IN DOLLARS PER SHARE)

YEAR	REVENUES	CASH FLOW	CAPITAL SPENDING	DIVIDENDS	EARNINGS	BOOK VALUE	YEAR-END SHARE PRICE
1980	$1.77	$0.34	$0.31	$0.05	$0.26	$2.08	$3.20
1981	1.94	0.31	0.64	0.06	0.23	2.25	3.27
1982	1.93	0.27	0.64	0.06	0.23	2.25	3.95
1983	2.37	0.33	0.60	0.08	0.17	2.54	3.29
1984	3.07	0.40	0.36	0.08	0.19	2.14	3.74
1985	3.89	0.55	0.36	0.08	0.32	2.29	7.06
1986	4.73	0.71	0.34	0.08	0.46	2.71	10.78
1987	5.46	1.02	0.53	0.08	0.71	3.50	14.81
1988	6.45	1.26	1.12	0.10	0.95	4.43	16.44
1989	8.49	1.65	1.39	0.12	1.28	5.62	28.00
1990	11.09	1.95	1.36	0.14	1.50	6.62	25.38
1991	11.87	1.73	1.78	0.17	1.20	7.43	28.63
1992	14.31	2.16	1.04	0.20	1.52	8.97	43.00
1993	15.93	2.34	1.48	0.24	1.63	9.39	42.63
1994	19.19	2.90	1.96	0.29	2.04	10.51	46.00
1995	23.10	3.46	1.71	0.35	2.53	12.68	58.88
1999–2001*	53.65	4.85	3.50	0.80	4.85	37.45	

*indicates *Value Line* estimates.

Data Source: *The Value Line Investment Survey,* August 30, 1996, 1779; *Compustat PC+,* January 1996.

inflation measured by the Consumer Price Index will continue at a modest 3% per year. Long-term interest rates are projected to be about 7.5%, and gross domestic product will average $9,050 billion in the years 1999 through 2001, or about 25% above the 1995 total of $7,254 billion. As *Value Line* states, things may turn out differently, but these plausible assumptions offer a fruitful basis for measuring the relative growth potential of various firms like Disney.[6]

The most interesting economic statistic for Disney stockholders is, of course, its stock price during some future period, say 1999 through 2001. In economic terms, stock prices represent the net present value of future cash flows, discounted at an appropriate risk-adjusted rate of return. To forecast Disney's

stock price during the 1999–2001 period, one might use any or all of the data in Table 6.6. Historical numbers for a recent period, like 1980 to 1995, often represent a useful context for projecting future stock prices. For example, Fidelity's legendary mutual fund investor Peter Lynch argues that stock prices are largely determined by the future pattern of earnings per share. In fact, stock prices typically rise following an increase in earnings per share and plunge when earnings per share plummet. Another legendary investor, Sir John Templeton, the father of global stock market investing, focuses on book value per share. Templeton contends that future earnings are closely related to the book value of the firm, or accounting net worth. According to Templeton, "bargains" can be found when stock can be purchased in companies that sell in the marketplace at a significant discount to book value, or when book value per share is expected to rise dramatically. Both Lynch and Templeton have built a large following among investors who have

[6]See: "Economic Series," *The Value Line Investment Survey,* October 25, 1996, 1000.

profited mightily using their stockmarket selection techniques.

As an experiment, it will prove interesting to employ the data provided in Table 6.6 to estimate regression models that can be used to forecast the average common stock price for The Walt Disney Company over the 1999–2001 period.

A. Estimate a simple regression model over the 1980–95 period where the y-variable is the Disney year-end stock price and the x-variable is Disney's earnings per share. Then, use this model to forecast Disney's average stock price for the 1999–2001 period using the Value Line estimate of Disney's average earnings per share for 1999 through 2001. Discuss this share-price forecast.

B. Estimate another simple regression model over the 1980–95 period where the y-variable is the Disney year-end stock price and the x-variable is Disney's book value (net worth) per share. Then, use this model to forecast Disney's average stock price for the 1999–2001 period using the Value Line estimate of Disney's average book value per share for 1999 through 2001. Discuss this share-price forecast.

C. Estimate a multiple regression model over the 1980–95 period where the y-variable is the Disney year-end stock price and the x-variables are Disney's earnings per share and book value (net worth) per share. Then, use this model to forecast Disney's average stock price for the 1999–2001 period using the Value Line estimate of Disney's average earnings per share and book value per share for 1999-2001. Discuss this share-price forecast.

D. Estimate another multiple regression model over the 1980–95 period where the y-variable is the Disney year-end stock price and the x-variables include each of the operating statistics (accounting performance numbers) shown in Table 6.6. Then, use this model and Value Line estimates to forecast Disney's average stock price for the 1999–2001 period. Discuss this share-price forecast.

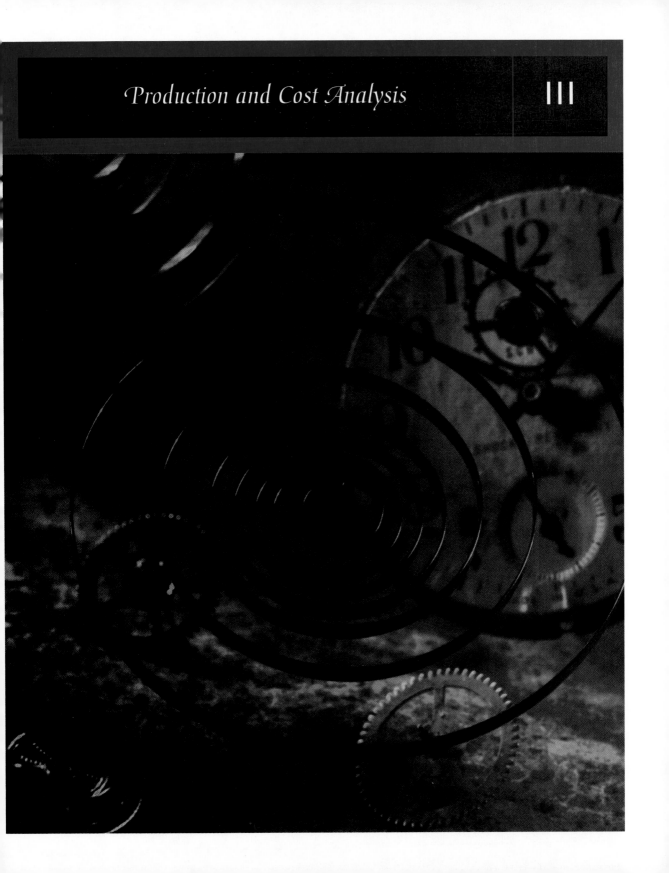

Production and Cost Analysis

III

Production Analysis and Estimation

McAfee Associates earns the highest margins in the software business by delivering virus protection, use monitoring, and backup storage programs over the internet. McAfee's dazzling 16% profit margin is earned by offering superior products and services at prices 50% of those charged by competitors. While rivals sell major upgrades every 18 months or so, McAfee sends licensees free mini-upgrades every quarter as a means of building customer loyalty. Continuous improvement is also evident at disposable latex glove maker Safeskin, Inc.—a 25% market share leader in the $500 million market for acute care exam gloves. By talking to doctors, Safeskin has discovered and exploited a market niche for state-of-the-art rubber gloves that are sterile, comfortable to wear, and easy to work with. Safeskin's secret: talking directly to customers and continuously striving to meet their changing needs. Talking to customers is also a fine art at Southern Energy Homes, a maker of energy-efficient mobile homes that cater to the affluent but cost-conscious customer. If you want to move the bathroom, add a fireplace or skylight, or build a television set into the wall, just fax your plan to Southern for a same-day price quote. Southern's "customized" profits are among the highest in the industry.[1]

Like other industry leaders, these companies have learned that product quality is more than defect prevention and production time reduction. It is about producing exciting products that customers want at prices that beat the competition. This chapter considers all aspects of this production process. Hiring workers, personnel training, and the organizational structure adopted to maximize efficiency are all part of the process of making things better, faster, or cheaper. As such, production analysis is a key element in the value maximization process.

Production Functions

The production process is the creative endeavor at the heart of every successful organization. To be successful, the production process must reflect an efficient use of human and capital resources in the creation of needed products. Not only must resources be used effectively, but products must meet customer specifications in terms of price, quality, and timely delivery. To successfully master the production process, organizations must focus on how to effectively meet customer needs. The corporate landscape is littered with examples of firms that once introduced innovative product and process improvements only

---

[1] See Scott Wooley, "The New Distribution," *Forbes,* November 4, 1996, 164–165; Lusia Kroll, "We Aim to Please," *Forbes,* November 4, 1996, 169–170; and Matthew Schifrin, "I Happen to Be Very Lucky," *Forbes,* November 4, 1996, 177–178.

to see their early lead and dominant position in the marketplace eroded by later and more efficient rivals. Similarly, a number of firms have fallen prey to the mistake of striving and succeeding at being the low-cost producer in a vanishing market. Productive efficiency is not simply about *what* or *how* to produce; it is about *both*.

The Production Process

Production Function
The maximum output that can be produced for a given amount of input.

A **production function** is a descriptive statement that relates inputs to outputs. It specifies the maximum output that can be produced for a given amount of input or, alternatively, the minimum quantity of input necessary to produce a given level of output. Production functions are determined by the technology available for employing plant, equipment, labor, materials, and so on. Any improvement in technology, such as better equipment or a training program that enhances worker productivity, results in a new production function.

Basic properties of production functions can be illustrated by examining a simple two-input, one-output system. Consider a production process in which various quantities of two inputs, X and Y, can be used to produce a product, Q. Inputs X and Y might represent resources such as labor and capital or energy and raw materials. The product Q could be physical goods such as television sets, baseball gloves, or breakfast cereal; Q could also represent services such as medical care, education, or banking.

The production function for such a system can be written

$$Q = f(X, Y). \tag{7.1}$$

Table 7.1 is tabular representation of a two-input, single-output production system. Each element in the table shows the maximum quantity of Q that can be produced with a specific combination of X and Y. Table 7.1 shows, for example, that 2 units of X and 3

Table 7.1

A REPRESENTATIVE PRODUCTION TABLE

UNITS OF Y
EMPLOYED

Units of Y				OUTPUT QUANTITY					
10	52	71	87	101	113	122	127	129	130	131
9	56	74	89	102	111	120	125	127	128	129
8	59	75	91	99	108	117	122	124	125	126
7	61	77	87	96	104	112	117	120	121	122
6	62	72	82	91	99	107	111	114	116	117
5	55	66	75	84	92	99	104	107	109	110
4	47	58	68	77	85	91	97	100	102	103
3	35	49	59	68	76	83	89	91	90	89
2	15	31	48	59	68	72	73	72	70	67
1	5	12	35	48	56	55	53	50	46	40
	1	2	3	4	5	6	7	8	9	10

UNITS OF X EMPLOYED

units of *Y* can be combined to produce 49 units of output; 5 units of *X* coupled with 5 units of *Y* results in 92 units of output; 4 units of *X* and 10 units of *Y* produce 101 units of *Q*, and so on. The units of input could represent *hours* of labor, *dollars* of capital, *cubic feet* of natural gas, *tons* of raw materials, and so on. Units of *Q* could be *numbers* of television sets or baseball gloves, *cases* of cereal, *patient days* of hospital care, customer *transactions* at an ATM banking facility, and so on.

Figure 7.1

REPRESENTATIVE PRODUCTION SURFACE

This discrete production function illustrates the output level resulting from each combination of inputs *X* and *Y*.

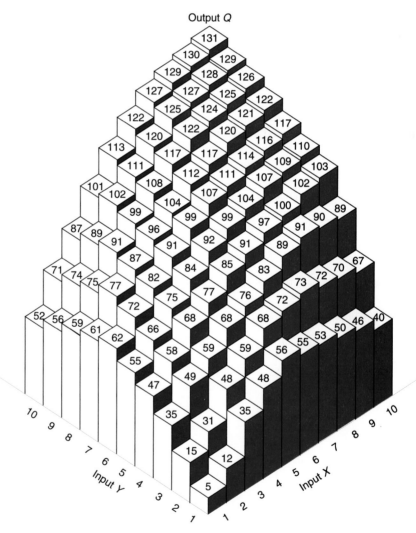

Discrete Production Function
A production function with distinct input patterns.

The **discrete production function** described in Table 7.1 involves distinct, or "lumpy," patterns for input combination that can be illustrated graphically, as in Figure 7.1. The height of the bars associated with each input combination indicates the output produced. The tops of the output bars map the production surface for the system.

Continuous Production Function
A production function where inputs can be varied in an unbroken marginal fashion.

The discrete production data shown in Table 7.1 and Figure 7.1 can be generalized by assuming that the underlying production function is continuous. A **continuous production function** is one in which inputs can be varied in an unbroken marginal fashion rather than incrementally, as in the preceding example.

RETURNS TO SCALE AND RETURNS TO A FACTOR

In studying production functions, two important relations between inputs and outputs are of interest. One is the relation between output and the variation in *all inputs* taken together. This is known as the **returns to scale** characteristic of a production system. Returns to scale play an important role in managerial decisions. They affect the optimal scale, or size, of a firm and its production facilities. They also affect the nature of competition in an industry and thus are important in determining the profitability of investment in a particular economic sector.

Returns to Scale
The output effect of a proportional increase in all inputs.

Returns to a Factor
The relation between output and variation in only one input.

A second important relation in any production system is that between output and variation in only *one of the inputs* employed. **Returns to a factor** denotes the relation between the quantity of an individual input (or factor of production) employed and the level of output produced. Factor productivity is the key to determining the optimal combination of inputs that should be used to manufacture a given product. Factor productivity analysis provides the basis for efficient resource employment in all production systems. Because an understanding of factor productivity aids in the study of returns to scale, it is worth considering factor productivity concepts first.

Total, Marginal, and Average Product

The economic concept of factor productivity or returns to a factor is important in the process of determining optimal input combinations for any production system. Because the process of optimization entails an analysis of the relation between the total and marginal values of a function, it is useful to introduce the concepts of total, average, and marginal products for the resources employed in a production system.

TOTAL PRODUCT

Total Product
The whole output from a production system.

Total product is the output from a production system. It is synonymous with Q in Equation 7.1. Total product is a measure of the total output or product that results from employing a specific quantity of resources in a given production system.

The total product concept is used to investigate the relation between output and variation in only one input in a production function. For example, suppose that Table 7.1 represents a production system in which Y is a capital resource and X represents a labor input. If a firm is operating with a given level of capital (say, $Y = 2$), then the relevant production function for the firm in the short run is represented by the row in Table 7.1 corresponding to that level of fixed capital.[2] Operating with two units of capital, output or total product depends on the quantity of labor (X) employed. This total product of X can be read from the $Y = 2$ row in Table 7.1. It is also shown in Column 2 of Table 7.2 and is illustrated graphically in Figure 7.3.

More generally, the total product for a factor of production, such as labor, can be expressed as a function relating output to the quantity of the resource employed. Continuing the example, the total product of X is given by the production function

$$Q = f(X/Y = 2).$$

This equation relates the output quantity Q (the total product of X) to the quantity of Input X employed, fixing the quantity of Y at two units. One would, of course, obtain other total product functions for X if the factor Y were fixed at levels other than two units.

Figure 7.3(a) illustrates the more general concept of the total product of an input as the schedule of output obtained as that input increases, *holding constant the amounts of other inputs employed.* This figure depicts a continuous production function where inputs can be varied in a marginal unbroken fashion rather than discretely. Suppose the firm wishes to fix, or hold constant, the amount of Input Y at the level Y_1. The total product curve of Input X, holding Input Y constant at Y_1, originates at Y_1 and rises along the production surface as the use of Input X is increased.

Table 7.2	TOTAL PRODUCT, MARGINAL PRODUCT, AND AVERAGE PRODUCT OF FACTOR X, HOLDING $Y = 2$

INPUT QUANTITY (X)	TOTAL PRODUCT OF THE INPUT (Q)	MARGINAL PRODUCT OF INPUT X ($MP_X = \Delta Q/\Delta X$)	AVERAGE PRODUCT OF INPUT X ($AP_X = Q/X$)
1	15	+15	15.0
2	31	+16	15.5
3	48	+17	16.0
4	59	+11	14.8
5	68	+ 9	13.6
6	72	+ 4	12.0
7	73	+ 1	10.4
8	72	− 1	9.0
9	70	− 2	7.8
10	67	− 3	6.7

[2]In economic terminology the *short run* is a period of time during which at least one resource in a production system is fixed; that is, the quantity of that resource is constant regardless of the quantity of output produced. This concept is further developed in Chapter 8.

Figure 7.2

TOTAL, AVERAGE, AND MARGINAL PRODUCT FOR INPUT X, GIVEN $Y = 2$

(a) Holding Y at two units, total production first rises but then falls as the amount of X employed grows. (b) Total product rises as long as marginal product is positive.

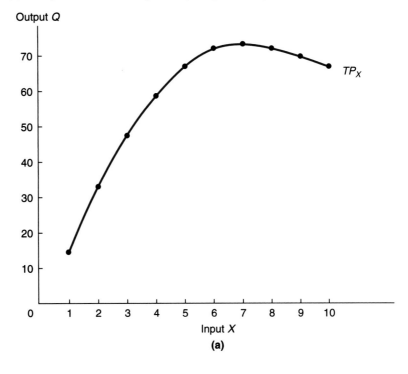

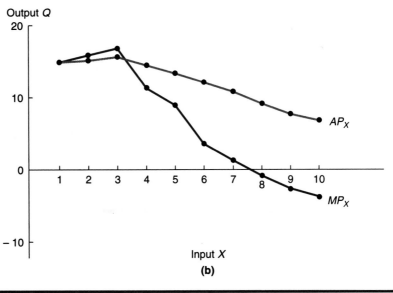

MARGINAL PRODUCT

Given the total product function for an input, both marginal and average products can be easily derived. The **marginal product** of a factor, MP_X, is the change in output associated with a one-unit change in the factor input, holding all other inputs constant. For a total product function such as that shown in Table 7.2 and Figure 7.2(a), the marginal product is expressed as:

$$MP_X = \frac{\Delta Q}{\Delta X},$$

where ΔQ is the change in output resulting from a one-unit change, ΔX, in the variable factor. This expression assumes that the quantity of the other input, Y, remains unchanged.

AVERAGE PRODUCT

Average product is total product divided by the number of units of input employed:

$$AP_X = \frac{Q}{X}. \tag{7.2}$$

The average product for X given $Y = 2$ units is shown in Column 4 of Table 7.2 and in Figure 7.2(b).

For a continuous total product function, as illustrated in Figure 7.3(a), marginal product equals the slope of the total product curve, whereas the average product equals the slope of a line drawn from the origin to a point on the total product curve. The average and marginal products for Input X can be determined in this manner, and these points are plotted to form the average and marginal product curves shown in Figure 7.3(b).

Three points of interest, A, B, and C, can be identified on the total product curve in Figure 7.3(a). Each has a corresponding location on the average or marginal curves. Point A is the inflection point of the total product curve. The marginal product of X (the slope of the total product curve) increases until this point is reached, after which it begins to decrease. This phenomenon can be seen in Figure 7.3(b), as MP_X is at a maximum at A'.

The second point on the total product curve, B, indicates the output at which the average product and marginal product are equal. The slope of a line from the origin to any point on the total product curve measures the average product of X at that point, whereas the slope of the total product curve equals the marginal product. At Point B, where X_2 units of Input X are employed, a line from the origin is tangent to the total product curve, so $MP_X = AP_X$. Note also that the slopes of successive lines drawn from the origin to the total product curve increase until Point B, after which their slopes decline. The average product curve rises until it reaches B, then declines; this feature is also shown in Figure 7.3(b) as Point B'. Here again $MP_X = AP_X$ and AP_X is at a maximum.

The third point, C, indicates where the slope of the total product curve is zero and the curve is at a maximum. Beyond C the marginal product of X is negative, indicating that increased use of Input X results in a *reduction* of total product. The corresponding

Figure 7.3

TOTAL, MARGINAL, AND AVERAGE PRODUCT CURVES:
(A) TOTAL PRODUCT CURVE FOR X, HOLDING $Y = Y_1$;
(B) MARGINAL PRODUCT CURVE FOR X, HOLDING $Y = Y_1$

MP_X reaches a maximum at point A', where the slope of the TP_X curve is the greatest. AP_X is at a maximum where $MP_X = AP_X$. At point C, TP_X is at a maximum and $MP_X = 0$.

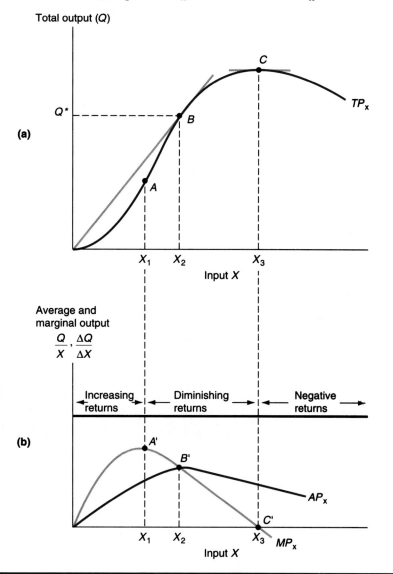

One of the hottest management concepts from the 1980s—the Total Quality Management, or TQM approach—has failed to deliver promised results in many companies. As a result, the concept has lost favor in some circles. Cynics suggest that the devastation of TQM programs has produced a new type of consultant who specializes in turning around faltering quality programs, or what skeptics call "Totaled Quality Management" programs.

While this new backlash of cynicism suggests that the TQM movement may be a dying fad, important reasons suggest that the approach will continue to remain a cornerstone of enlightened management. First and foremost, quality management programs are a vital component of prosperity because customers demand continuous improvement in the goods and services that they buy. In today's global economic environment, both large and small companies have come to recognize that improved quality is an essential ingredient for success. Still, quality management programs are not painless. Many firms that jumped on the TQM bandwagon were simply not ready or were unwilling to invest the time or resources that a successful TQM program requires.

TQM requires a major commitment that many organizations have not been willing to undertake for a number of reasons. In simplest terms, TQM involves a keen attention to the production process, a high level of commitment to the customer, and the involvement of employees in identifying and continuously improving upon the best production practices. The fact that many firms have not yet benefitted from TQM programs widely adopted during the 1980s may say more about how some managers search for a quick fix or cure-all for complex and deep-seated problems. TQM is not a quick fix; TQM is a basic reengineering of the firm's entire operation. TQM starts with a basic question—Should we be doing this at all? If affirmative, TQM then asks, "How can we do this cheaper, faster, or better?" While the term *total quality* has sometimes been naively limited to firms in the manufacturing sector, creative companies have used TQM techniques in services sectors to improve firm performance measured on the basis of product cost, service quality, rate of speed, and pace of innovation.

Analysts agree that adherence to basic concepts determines the success of any single total quality effort.

Among those factors thought to be most important are:

■ The CEO must be actively and visibly behind it.
■ Tunnel vision must be avoided. Ask what change does for the customer.
■ Limit yourself to a few critical goals.
■ Link change to a clear financial payback.
■ Customize the TQM concept to meet the specific needs of customers.

Like any sound theory, these principles are not only good in terms of setting an enlightened operating philosophy, they work well in practice too. Top executives at Analog Devices, General Electric, Pepsi-Cola, a subsidiary of PepsiCo, Inc., and United Parcel Service of America have all learned that effective TQM programs require the close involvement of top management. Continuous monitoring is also required to ensure that the TQM process itself retains an effective customer focus.

TQM must be outward rather than inward looking. Customer focus is vital to the success of TQM programs. At industrial giant GE, everything from the installation of new technology to methods of improving billing accuracy is judged against an assortment of financial yardsticks, such as potential sales gains and the return on capital. Instead of simply attracting new customers, GE's quality-control program emphasizes customer retention and development, both of which can be promoted through extensive surveys to determine what customers really want.

In assessing GE's quality-control program, GE Chairman Jack Welch exemplifies the importance of involvement at the very top of the organization. According to Welch, when it comes to quality, you can't behave in a "calm, rational manner," you have to be out there on the "lunatic fringe." Everyone must be convinced that quality improvement is absolutely critical to survival. GE's quality-control program, and TQM programs in general, are successful to the extent that they become an emphatic way of putting the customer first.

See: William M. Carley, "To Keep GE's Profits Rising, Welch Pushes Quality-Control Plan," *The Wall Street Journal*, January 13, 1997, A1, A8.

point in Figure 7.3(b) is C′, the point where the marginal product curve intersects the *x* axis.

THE LAW OF DIMINISHING RETURNS TO A FACTOR

Law of Diminishing Returns
As the quantity of a variable input increases, the resulting rate of output increase eventually diminishes.

The total and the marginal product curves in Figure 7.3 demonstrate the property known as the **law of diminishing returns.** This law states that as the quantity of a variable input increases, with the quantities of all other factors being held constant, the resulting rate of increase in output eventually diminishes. Alternatively, the law of diminishing returns states that the marginal product of a variable factor must eventually decline as increasingly more of the variable factor is combined with other fixed resources. The law of diminishing returns is sometimes called the law of diminishing marginal returns to emphasize the fact that it deals specifically with the diminishing marginal product of a variable input factor. The law of diminishing returns cannot be derived deductively. It is a generalization of an empirical regularity associated with every known production system. The basis for this relation is easily demonstrated for the labor input in a production process in which a fixed amount of capital is employed.

Consider a factory with an assembly line for the production of refrigerators. If only one employee is put to work, that individual must perform each of the activities necessary to assemble refrigerators. Output from such a combination of labor and capital is likely to be quite small. In fact, it may be less than could be achieved with a smaller amount of capital, given the inefficiency of having one employee accompany a refrigerator down an assembly line rather than building it at a single station. As additional units of labor are added to this production system—holding capital input constant—output is likely to expand rapidly. The intensity with which the capital resource is used increases with additional labor, and increasingly efficient input combinations result. The improved use of capital resulting from the increase in labor could cause the marginal product or rise in output associated with each successive employee to actually increase over some range of additional labor. This increasing marginal productivity might result from each unit of labor using a more manageable quantity of capital than is possible with less total labor input. Worker specialization that often accompanies increased employment is another factor that might lead to increasing returns to labor as successive workers are employed.

An illustration of a production situation in which the marginal product of an input increases over some range is presented in Table 7.2. The first unit of labor (Input *X*) results in 15 units of production. With 2 units of labor, 31 units can be produced. The marginal product of the second unit of labor $MP_{X=2} = 16$ exceeds that of the $MP_{X=1} = 15$. Similarly, the addition of another unit of labor results in output increasing to 48 units, indicating a marginal product of $MP_{X=3} = 17$ for the third unit of labor.

Eventually, sufficient labor is combined with the fixed capital input so that the benefits of further labor additions will not be as large as the benefits achieved earlier. When this occurs, the rate of increase in output per additional unit of labor, the marginal product of labor, will drop. Although the marginal product of labor is positive and total output increases as more units of labor are employed, the rate of increase in output eventually declines. In other words, the marginal product of labor remains positive but ultimately decreases. This diminishing marginal productivity of labor is exhibited by the fourth, fifth, sixth, and seventh units of Input X in Table 7.2.

Finally, a point might be reached where the quantity of the variable input factor is so large that total output actually begins to decline with additional employment of that factor. In the refrigerator assembly example, this might occur when the labor force became so large that additional employees actually got in each other's way and hindered the manufacturing process. This happens in Table 7.2 when more than 7 units of Input X are combined with 2 units of Input Y. The eighth unit of X results in a 1-unit reduction in total output, $MP_{X=8} = -1$; units 9 and 10 cause output to fall by 2 and 3 units, respectively. In Figure 7.3b, regions where the variable input factor X exhibits increasing, diminishing, and negative returns have been labeled. The concepts of total and marginal product and the law of diminishing returns to a factor are important in identifying efficient as opposed to inefficient input combinations. This can be illustrated with yet another example.

Suppose Tax Advisors, Inc., has an office for processing tax returns in Scranton, Pennsylvania. Table 7.3 provides information on the production function for processing tax returns in that office. If the office employs one certified public accountant (CPA), it can process 0.2 tax returns per hour. Adding a second CPA increases production to 1 return per hour, and with a third, output jumps to 2.4 returns processed per hour. In this production system, the marginal product for the second CPA is 0.8 returns per hour as compared with 0.2 for the first CPA employed. The marginal product for the third CPA is 1.4 returns per hour.

It is instructive to examine the source of this relative burst in productivity for the second and third CPAs. After all, $MP_{CPA=2} = 0.8$ seems to indicate that the second CPA is four times as productive as the first, and $MP_{CPA=3} = 1.4$ says that the third CPA is more productive still. In production analysis, however, it is assumed that each unit of an input factor is like all other units of that same factor, meaning that each CPA is equally competent and efficient. If individual differences in the CPA inputs do not account for this increasing productivity, what does?

Typically, increased specialization and better utilization of other factors in the production process allow factor productivity to grow. As the number of CPAs increases,

Table 7.3

PRODUCTION FUNCTION FOR TAX-RETURN PROCESSING

UNITS OF LABOR INPUT EMPLOYED (CPAs)	TOTAL PRODUCT OF CPAs—TAX RETURNS PROCESSED/HOUR ($TP_{CPA} = Q$)	MARGINAL PRODUCT OF CPAs ($MP_{CPA} = \Delta Q$)	AVERAGE PRODUCT OF CPAs ($AP_{CPA} = Q/X$)
1	0.2	0.2	0.20
2	1.0	0.8	0.50
3	2.4	1.4	0.80
4	2.8	0.4	0.70
5	3.0	0.2	0.60
6	2.7	-0.3	0.45

each can specialize, for example, in processing personal returns, partnership returns, or corporate returns. Also, additional CPAs may be better able to fully utilize computer, clerical, and other resources employed by the firm. Advantages from specialization and increased coordination among all resources cause output to rise at an increasing rate, from 0.2 to 1 return processed per hour as the second CPA is employed, and from 1 to 2.4 returns per hour as the third CPA is added.

In practice it is very rare to see input combinations that exhibit increasing returns for any factor. With increasing returns to a factor, an industry would come to be dominated by one very large producer—and this is seldom the case. Input combinations in the range of diminishing returns are commonly observed. If, for example, four CPAs could process 2.8 returns per hour, then the marginal product of the fourth CPA $MP_{CPA=4} = 0.4$ would be less than the marginal product of the third CPA ($MP_{CPA=3} = 1.4$) and diminishing returns to the CPA labor input would be encountered.

The irrationality of employing inputs in the negative returns range, beyond X_3 in Figure 7.3, can be illustrated by noting that adding a sixth CPA would cause total output to fall from 3.0 to 2.7 returns per hour. The marginal product of the sixth CPA is -0.3 ($MP_{CPA=6} = -0.3$), perhaps because of problems with coordinating work among greater numbers of employees or limitations in other important inputs. Would the firm pay an additional employee's salary when employing that person reduces the level of salable output? Obviously not, which demonstrates the irrationality of employing inputs in the range of negative returns.

Input Combination Choice

The concept of factor productivity can be more fully explored using isoquant analysis, which explicitly recognizes the potential variability of both factors in a two-input, one-output production system. This technique is introduced in the following section to examine the role of input substitutability in determining efficient input combinations.

PRODUCTION ISOQUANTS

Although one can examine the properties of production functions graphically using three-dimensional production surfaces, a two-dimensional representation using isoquants is simpler to use and equally instructive. The term **isoquant**—derived from *iso,* meaning equal, and *quant,* from quantity—denotes a curve that represents the different combinations of inputs that can be efficiently used to produce a specified quantity of output. Efficiency in this case refers to **technical efficiency,** meaning the least-cost production of a target level of output. If 2 units of X and 3 units of Y can be combined to produce 49 units of output, but they can also be combined less efficiently to produce only 45 units of output, the $X = 2$, $Y = 3$ input combination will lie only on the $Q = 49$ isoquant. The $X = 2$, $Y = 3$ combination resulting in $Q = 45$ is not technologically efficient, because this same input combination can produce a larger output quantity. This combination would not appear in the production function nor on the $Q = 45$ isoquant. Production theory assumes that only the most efficient techniques are used to convert

Isoquant
Different input combinations used to efficiently produce a specified output.

Technical Efficiency
Least-cost production of a target level of output.

resource inputs into products. For example, from Table 7.1 it is clear that 91 units of output can be produced efficiently using the input combinations $X = 3$, $Y = 8$; $X = 4$, $Y = 6$; $X = 6$, $Y = 4$; or $X = 8$, $Y = 3$. These four input combinations all lie on the $Q = 91$ isoquant. Similarly, the combinations $X = 6$, $Y = 10$; $X = 7$, $Y = 8$; $X = 10$, $Y = 7$ all result in 122 units of production and, hence, lie on the $Q = 122$ isoquant.

These two isoquants are illustrated in Figure 7.4. Each point on the $Q = 91$ isoquant indicates a different combination of X and Y that can produce 91 units of output. For example, 91 units can be produced with 3 units of X and 8 units of Y, with 4 units of X and 6 units of Y, or with any other combination of X and Y on the isoquant $Q = 91$. A similar interpretation can be given the isoquant for $Q = 122$ units of output.

Isoquants for a continuous production function also represent different levels of output. Every point on the Q_1 isoquant, for example in Figure 7.5(c)—that is, all points along curve Q_1—represent input combinations that can be used to produce an equal quantity, or isoquant, of Q_1 units of output. The isoquant curve Q_2 maps out the locus of all input combinations that result in Q_2 units of production, and so on.

INPUT FACTOR SUBSTITUTION

The shapes of isoquants reveal a great deal about the substitutability of input factors—that is, the ability to replace one input for another in the production process. This point is illustrated in Figure 7.5(a), (b), and (c).

Figure 7.4

REPRESENTATIVE ISOQUANTS FROM TABLE 7.1

Each point on an isoquant represents a different combination of Inputs X and Y that can be used to produce the same level of output.

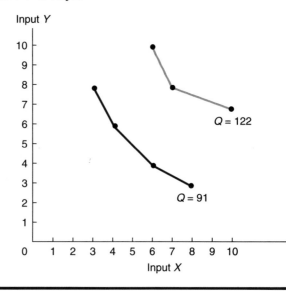

| Figure 7.5 | ISOQUANTS FOR INPUTS WITH VARYING DEGREES OF SUBSTITUTABILITY: (A) ELECTRIC POWER GENERATION; (B) BICYCLE PRODUCTION; (C) DRESS PRODUCTION |

(a) Straight-line isoquants indicate perfect substitution. (b) A right-angle shape for isoquants reflects inputs that are perfect complements. (c) C-shaped isoquants indicate imperfect substitutability among inputs.

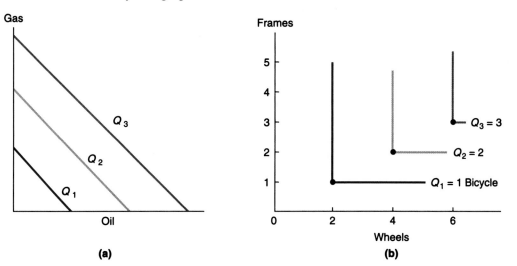

(a)

(b)

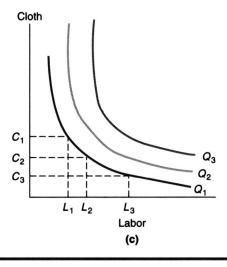

(c)

Input Substitution
The systematic replacement of productive factors.

In some production systems, **input substitution** or replacement is readily accomplished. In the production of electricity, for example, fuels used to power generators often represent readily substitutable inputs. Figure 7.5(a) shows isoquants for such an electric power generation system. The technology, a power plant with boilers equipped to burn either oil or gas, is given. Various amounts of electric power can be produced by burning gas only, oil only, or varying amounts of each. In this instance, gas and oil are perfect substitutes, and the electricity isoquants are straight lines. Other examples of readily substitutable inputs include fish meal and soybeans to provide protein in a feed mix, energy and time in a drying process, and United Parcel Service and the U.S. Postal Service for package delivery. In each case, production isoquants are linear.

At the other extreme of input substitutability lie production systems in which inputs are perfect complements for each other. In these situations, exact amounts of each input are required to produce a given quantity of output. Figure 7.5(b) illustrates isoquants for bicycles and completely fixed input combinations. Exactly two wheels and one frame are required to produce a bicycle, and in no way can wheels be substituted for frames, or vice versa. Pants and coats for suits, engines and bodies for trucks, barbers and shears for haircuts, and chemicals in compounds for prescription drugs are further examples of complementary inputs. Production isoquants for complementary inputs take the shape of right angles, as indicated in Figure 7.5(b).

Figure 7.5(c) shows a production process in which inputs can be substituted for each other within limits. A dress can be made with a relatively small amount of labor (L_1) and a large amount of cloth (C_1). The same dress can also be made with less cloth (C_2) if more labor (L_2) is used because the dressmaker can cut the material more carefully and reduce waste. Finally, the dress can be made with still less cloth (C_3), but workers must be so extremely painstaking that the labor input requirement increases to L_3. Although a relatively small addition of labor, from L_1 to L_2, reduces the input of cloth from C_1 to C_2, a very large increase in labor, from L_2 to L_3, is required to obtain a similar reduction in cloth from C_2 to C_3. The substitutability of labor for cloth diminishes from L_1 to L_2 to L_3. The substitutability of cloth for labor in the manufacture of dresses also diminishes, as can be seen by considering the quantity of cloth that must be added to replace each unit of reduced labor in moving from L_3 to L_1.

Most labor-capital substitutions in production systems exhibit this diminishing substitutability. Energy and insulation used to provide home heating exhibit diminishing substitutability, as do doctors and medical technicians in providing health care services.

MARGINAL RATE OF TECHNICAL SUBSTITUTION

Marginal Rate of Technical Substitution
The amount of one input that must be substituted for another to maintain constant output.

Isoquant slope provides the key input substitutability. In Figure 7.5(c), the slope of the isoquant is simply the change in Input Y (cloth) divided by the change in Input X (labor). The **marginal rate of technical substitution**[3] **(MRTS)** is the amount of one input

---

[3]The term **marginal rate of technical substitution** is often shortened to *marginal rate of substitution*.

factor that must be substituted for one unit of another input factor to maintain a constant level of output. Algebraically,

$$MRTS = \frac{\Delta Y}{\Delta X} = Slope\ of\ an\ Isoquant. \tag{7.3}$$

The marginal rate of technical substitution usually diminishes as the amount of substitution increases. In Figure 7.5(c), for example, as more and more labor is substituted for cloth, the increment of labor necessary to replace cloth increases. At the extremes, isoquants may even become positively sloped, indicating that the range over which input factors can be substituted for each other is limited. A classic example is the use of land and labor to produce a given output of wheat. At some point, as labor is substituted for land, the farmers will trample the wheat. As more labor is added, more land eventually must be added if wheat output is to be maintained. The farmers must have some place to stand.

The input substitution relation indicated by the slope of a production isoquant is directly related to the concept of diminishing marginal productivity introduced earlier. This is because the marginal rate of technical substitution is equal to -1 times the ratio of the marginal products of the input factors $[MRTS = -1(MP_X/MP_Y)]$. To see this, note that the loss in output resulting from a small reduction in Y equals the marginal product of Y, MP_Y, multiplied by the change in Y, ΔY. That is,

$$\Delta Q = MP_Y \times \Delta Y. \tag{7.4}$$

Similarly, the change in Q associated with the increased use of Input X is given by the expression

$$\Delta Q = MP_X \times \Delta X. \tag{7.5}$$

With substitution of X for Y along an isoquant, the absolute value of ΔQ in Equations 7.4 and 7.5 must be the same. That is, the change in output associated with the reduction in Input Y must be exactly offset by the change in output resulting from the increase in Input X for output to remain constant—as it must along an isoquant. Thus, the ΔQs in Equations 7.4 and 7.5 must be of equal size and opposite sign. Therefore, along an isoquant,

$$-(MP_X \times \Delta X) = (MP_Y \times \Delta Y). \tag{7.6}$$

Transposing the variables in Equation 7.6 produces

$$-\frac{MP_X}{MP_Y} = \frac{\Delta Y}{\Delta X}. \tag{7.7}$$

In other words, this means that the marginal rate of technical substitution is equal to the slope of a production isoquant:

$$MRTS_{XY} = Slope\ of\ an\ Isoquant.^4$$

The slope of a production isoquant such as in Equation 7.3 is equal to $\Delta Y/\Delta X$ and is determined by the ratio of the marginal products of both inputs. In Figure 7.5(c) the isoquant Q_1 has a very steep negative slope at the point (L_1, C_1). When cloth is relatively abundant, the marginal product of labor is relatively high as compared with the marginal product of cloth. When labor is relatively abundant at, say, point (L_3, C_3), the marginal product of labor is low relative to the marginal product of cloth.

Equation 7.7 provides a basis for examining the concept of irrational input combinations. It is irrational for a firm to combine resources in such a way that the marginal product of any input is negative, since this implies that output could be increased by using less of that resource.[5] Note from Equation 7.6 that if the inputs X and Y are combined in proportions such that the marginal product of either factor is negative, then the slope of the production isoquant will be positive. For a production isoquant to be positively sloped, one of the input factors must have a negative marginal product. From this it follows that input combinations lying along a positively sloped portion of a production isoquant are irrational and would be avoided by the firm.

In Figure 7.6, the rational limits of input substitution are where the isoquants become positively sloped. Limits to the range of substitutability of X for Y are indicated by the points of tangency between the isoquants and a set of lines drawn perpendicular to the Y axis. Limits of economic substitutability of Y for X are shown by the tangents of lines perpendicular to the X axis. Maximum and minimum proportions of Y and X that would be combined to produce each level of output are determined by points of tangency between these lines and the production isoquants.

Ridge Lines
Graphic bounds for positive marginal products.

It is irrational to use any input combination outside these tangents, or **ridge lines,** as they are called. Such combinations are irrational because the marginal product of the

---

[4]This result can also be demonstrated using calculus by noting that along any isoquant the total differential of the production function must be zero (output is fixed along an isoquant). Thus, for the production function given by Equation 7.1, setting the total differential equal to zero gives

$$\frac{\partial Q}{\partial X}dX + \frac{\partial Q}{\partial Y}dY = 0,$$

and, rearranging terms,

$$(-)\frac{\partial Q/\partial X}{\partial Q/\partial Y} = \frac{dY}{dX}.$$

Or, since $\partial Q/\partial X = MP_X$ and $\partial Q/\partial Y = MP_Y$,

$$(-)\frac{MP_X}{MP_Y} = \frac{dY}{dX} = Slope\ of\ the\ Isoquant.$$

[5]This is technically correct only if the resource has a positive cost. Thus, for example, a firm might employ additional workers even though the marginal product of labor was negative if it received a government subsidy for that employment that more than offset the cost of the output reduction.

Figure 7.6

MAXIMUM VARIABLE PROPORTIONS FOR INPUTS X AND Y

The rational limits of substitution between Y and X occur where the isoquants become positive.

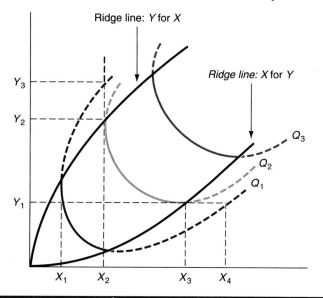

relatively more abundant input is negative outside the ridge lines. The addition of the last unit of the excessive input factor actually reduces output. Obviously, it would be irrational for a firm to buy and employ additional units that cause production to decrease. To illustrate, suppose a firm is currently operating with a fixed quantity of Input Y equal to Y_1 units, as shown in Figure 7.6. In such a situation the firm would never employ more than X_3 units of Input X, because employment of additional units of X results in production of successively lower output quantities. For example, if the firm combines Y_1 and X_4, output is equal to Q_1 units. By reducing usage of X from X_4 to X_3, output can be increased from Q_1 to Q_2.

A similar relation is shown for Input Y. In the area above the upper ridge line, the relative amount of Y is excessive. In this area it is possible to increase production and move to a higher isoquant by reducing the amount of Y employed. For example, the input combination (X_2, Y_3) results in Q_1 units of output. By reducing the amount of Y employed to Y_2 while holding X constant at X_2, the firm produces a higher level of output, Q_2. This means that the marginal product of Y is negative, since reducing its usage increases production. In the area above the upper ridge line, Input Y is excessive relative to Input X, and Y's marginal product is negative. Below the lower ridge line, Input X is excessive relative to Y, and X's marginal product is negative. Only for input combinations lying between the ridge lines will *both* inputs have positive marginal products. It is here and along the negatively sloped portion of the isoquant that optimal input combinations are found.

How Work Is Changing

The average size of companies in the United States and Canada, measured by the number of workers employed, will have decreased by the time Saturday, January 1, 2000 rolls around. More people will have started their own businesses, industrial dinosaurs will have perished, new industrial giants will have sprung up. The post-World War II trend toward an increase in the relative importance of services will also have increased. Today, roughly 2/3 of Gross Domestic Product and 3/4 of total employment is devoted to the production of services, only 1/3 of GDP and 1/4 of total employment is devoted to the production of services. As incomes grow, people will continue to spend a greater part of the increment on services rather than goods. It's hard to imagine anyone who would buy two or three new refrigerators every year, but it is easy to imagine taking two or three exotic vacations per year, if only one could afford it. In the year 2000, consumer preferences for high quality services will surpass 1990s levels.

Workers on the job in the year 2000 will feel increased pressure to specialize in a new age of computational infrastructure. Economies of the post-World War II period have revolved around electrical power, the electric motor, the internal combustion engine, and the telephone. The development of these technologies made possible the shift from an agricultural to a manufacturing economy. In the process, they accelerated urbanization, the growth of corporations, and the rise of professional management. Another shift is now taking place because of growing knowledge on how to convert electronic and mechanical impulses into digitally encoded information. As such information is transmitted across vast distances, industry is gradually enabled to replace its traditional electromechanical infrastructure with a computational infrastructure. Computers are now able to take over more of the work that has been routinized. More important, computers are able to routinize more economic activity, from guiding robots that make things to transmitting information within and among organizations. Flexible manufacturing, program trading, and point-of-sale terminals wired into the supplier's factory are all examples of how computers have transformed work, and will continue to do so. Experts on this transformation argue that people in business are rethinking, rein-

venting, and reengineering the structure of work—all with the aid of computer technology.

In many instances, companies evolving their way toward 2000 have found that to get more efficient they need to get smaller. Computer industry giants IBM and Digital Equipment shed *hundreds* of thousands of employees during the early 1990s. It is perhaps shocking to see these two old-line computer companies stumble badly in competition against much smaller competitors like Dell, Cisco, and Microsoft. While noteworthy, the decline of computer goliaths is not unique. Smaller, more nimble, competitors have crippled former leaders in the auto, banking, entertainment, insurance, and telecommunications industries, among others. In fact, during recent years *all* net job growth has been created by new companies with 25 or fewer employees, with most coming from new firms with fewer than 10.

Why is more and more economic activity being generated in smaller and smaller companies? The answer lies in the significant enabling effects of computer technology. Computers replace routine workers while augmenting knowledge workers. Routine work is best organized in large hierarchical companies; innovation and cognitive analysis thrive in small firms. In economic terms, economies of scale remain in auto assembly, but there are none when it comes to generating new product and process innovations.

As computerized coordination substitutes for human effort, back office clerks or managers that pass information up and down the chain of command will continue to be eliminated. The increasing use of information technology expands the importance of market mechanisms as opposed to a company's internal control systems. As the benefits of vertical integration melt away, flatter, more horizontal organizations will evolve. In such organizations, it is vital that employees justify the compensation they receive in terms of tangible benefits provided to their employers. With authority comes responsibility, and the worker's primary responsibility is to create value for the employer.

See: Eric S. Hardy, "The Forbes 500s—Jobs and Productivity," *Forbes*, April 21, 1997, 220-248.

The Roles of Revenue and Cost in Production

To determine the optimal input combination, technical relations must be supplemented with information about revenues and costs. In an advanced market economy, productive activity results in goods and services that are sold rather than consumed by producers. Returns earned by the providers of labor, materials, capital, and other inputs are important. To gain an understanding of how the factors of production should be combined for maximum efficiency, it is necessary to shift from the analysis of the *physical* productivity of inputs to an examination of their *economic* productivity, or net revenue-generating capability.

MARGINAL REVENUE PRODUCT

Marginal Revenue Product
The amount of revenue generated by employing the last input unit.

The economic productivity of an input is its **marginal revenue product,** or the additional net revenue generated by the last unit employed. In equation form, the marginal revenue product of input X, MRP_X, equals the input marginal product multiplied by the marginal revenue of output:

$$MRP_X = \frac{\Delta TR}{\Delta X}$$

$$= \frac{\Delta Q}{\Delta X} \times \frac{\Delta TR}{\Delta Q} \qquad (7.8)$$

$$= MP_X \times MR_Q.$$

Marginal revenue product is the economic value of a marginal unit of an input factor. For example, if the addition of one more worker generates two incremental units of a product that can be sold for $5 each, the marginal product of labor is 2, and its marginal revenue product is $10 (= 2 × $5). Table 7.4 illustrates marginal revenue product for a simple one-factor production system. The marginal revenue product values shown in Column 4 assume that each unit of output can be sold for $5. The marginal revenue product of the first unit of X employed equals the 3 units of output produced times the $5 revenue received per unit, or $MRP_{X=1} = \$15$. The second unit of X adds 4 units of production so $MRP_{X=2} = 4$. For the second unit of input, $MRP_{X=2} = \$20$. Marginal revenue products for each additional unit of X are all determined in this manner.

OPTIMAL LEVEL OF A SINGLE INPUT

To illustrate how the economic productivity of an input, as defined by its marginal revenue product, is related to factor use, consider the following question: If the price of input X in the production system depicted in Table 7.4 is $12, how many units of X will a firm use? Clearly, the firm will employ 3 units of X because the value of adding each of these units as measured by their marginal revenue products exceeds their marginal cost. When 3 units of X are employed, the third and marginal unit causes total revenues to rise by $15 while costing only $12. At the margin, employing the third unit of X

Table 7.4

MARGINAL REVENUE PRODUCT FOR A SINGLE INPUT

Units of Input (X)	Total Product of X (Q)	Marginal Product of X ($MP_X = \Delta Q$)	Marginal Revenue Product of X ($MP_X \times \$5$)
1	3	3	$15
2	7	4	20
3	10	3	15
4	12	2	10
5	13	1	5

increases total profit by $3 (= \$15 - \$12)$. A fourth unit of X would not be employed because the value of its marginal product ($10) is less than the cost of employment ($12); profit would decline by $2.

The relation between resource productivity, as measured by marginal revenue product, and optimal employment or factor use can be generalized by referring to the basic marginal principles of profit maximization developed in Chapter 2. Recall that so long as marginal revenue exceeds marginal cost, profits must increase. In the context of production decisions, this means that profit will increase so long as the marginal revenue generated by an input, or its marginal revenue product, exceeds the marginal cost of employment. Conversely, when marginal revenue product is less than the cost of employing the factor, marginal profit is negative, and the firm would reduce employment.

The concept of optimal resource use can be clarified by examining a simple production system in which a single variable labor input, L, is used to produce a single product, Q. Profit maximization requires production at a level such that marginal revenue equals marginal cost. Because the only variable factor in the system is Input L, the marginal cost of production is

$$MC_Q = \frac{\Delta Total\ Cost}{\Delta Output}$$

$$= \frac{P_L}{MP_L}. \tag{7.9}$$

Dividing P_L, the price of a marginal unit of L, by MP_L, the number of units of output gained by the employment of an added unit of L, provides a measure of the marginal cost of producing each additional unit of output.

Marginal revenue must equal marginal cost at the profit-maximizing output level. Therefore, MR_Q can be substituted for MC_Q in Equation 7.9, resulting in the expression

$$MR_Q = \frac{P_L}{MP_L}. \tag{7.10}$$

Equation 7.10 must hold for profit maximization because its right-hand side is just another expression for marginal cost. Solving Equation 7.10 for P_L results in

$$P_L = MR_Q \times MP_L,$$

or, since $MR_Q \times MP_L$ is defined as the marginal revenue product of L,

$$P_L = MRP_L. \tag{7.11}$$

Equation 7.11 states the rule that *a profit-maximizing firm will always set marginal revenue product equal to marginal cost (price) for every input.* If marginal revenue product exceeds the cost of an input, profits could be increased by employing additional units of that input factor. Conversely, when the marginal cost of an input factor is greater than its marginal revenue product, profit would increase by reducing employment. Only when $MRP = P$ is profit maximized for individual firms. Optimal employment and **economic efficiency** is achieved in the overall economy when all firms employ resources so as to equate each input's marginal revenue product and marginal cost.

Economic Efficiency
Achieved when all firms equate input marginal revenue product and marginal cost (maximize profits).

Determination of the optimal input level can be clarified by reconsidering the Tax Advisors, Inc., example, illustrated in Table 7.3. If three CPAs can process 2.4 returns per hour and employing a fourth CPA increases total output per hour to 2.8, then employing a fourth CPA reduces marginal product from $MP_{CPA=3} = 1.4$ to $MP_{CPA=4} = 0.4$. This describes a situation in which employment is in a range of diminishing returns to the labor factor. For optimal resource employment, the question must be answered: Should a fourth CPA be hired? The answer depends on whether expanding employment will increase or decrease total profits. A fourth CPA should be hired if doing so will increase profits; otherwise, a fourth CPA should not be hired.

For simplicity, assume that CPA time is the only input required to process additional tax returns and that CPAs earn $35 per hour, or roughly $70,000 per year including fringe benefits. If Tax Advisors, Inc., receives $100 in revenue for each tax return prepared by the fourth CPA, a comparison of the price of labor and marginal revenue product for the fourth CPA reveals

$$P_{CPA} < MRP_{CPA=4} = MR_Q \times MP_{CPA=4}$$

because

$$\$35 < \$40 = \$100 \times 0.4.$$

This implies that if a fourth CPA is hired, total profits will rise by $5 per hour (= $40 − $35). The additional CPA should be employed.

Since the marginal product for the fifth CPA equals 0.2, $MP_{CPA=5} = 0.2$, and the marginal revenue product falls to only $20 per hour, or less than the $35-per-hour cost of hiring that person. The firm would incur a $10-per-hour loss by expanding hiring to that level and would, therefore, stop at an employment level of four CPAs.

For simplicity, this example assumes that CPA time is the only variable input involved in tax-return preparation. In reality, for this product, like most, other inputs are likely to be necessary to increase output. Additional computer time, office supplies, and clerical support may also be required to increase output. If such were the case, determining the independent contribution or value of CPA input would be more complex. If *variable* overhead for CPA support staff and supplies equals 50% of sales revenue, then the **net marginal revenue,** or marginal revenue after all variable costs, for CPA time

Net Marginal Revenue
Marginal revenue after all variable costs.

would be only $50 per unit ($= 0.5 \times MR_Q$). In this instance, Tax Advisors, Inc., would find that the $20 ($= 0.4 \times (0.5)(\$100)$) net marginal revenue product generated by the fourth CPA would not offset the necessary $35-per-hour cost (wage rate). It would, therefore, employ no more than three CPAs, a level at which $MRP = 1.4 \times (0.5)(\$100) = \$70 > \$35 = P_{CPA}$. The firm will employ additional CPAs only so long as their net marginal revenue product equals or exceeds their marginal cost (price of labor).

This explains why, for example, a law firm might hire new associates at annual salaries of $80,000 when it expects them to generate $150,000 per year in gross billings, or 1,500 billable hours at a rate of $100 per hour. If variable costs are $70,000 per associate, only $80,000 is available to cover associate salary expenses. When customers pay $100 per hour for legal services, they are in fact paying for attorney time and expertise plus the support of legal secretaries, law clerks, office staff, supplies, facilities, and so on. By itself, new associate time is worth much less than $100 per hour, or $150,000 per year. The net marginal revenue of new associate attorney time, or CPA time in the preceding Tax Advisors, Inc., example, is the *marginal* value created after allowing for the variable costs of all other inputs that must be increased to provide service.

The simple concept that inputs will be employed so long as their value in production as measured by their net marginal revenue product exceeds their cost is the foundation of production analysis. The section that follows shows that it is the basis for determining optimal input combinations and the profit-maximizing level of output. As is illustrated in Figure 7.7, it also underlies the demand for input factors.

THE INPUT DEMAND FUNCTION

Data on the marginal revenue product of labor and wage rates present firms with clear incentives regarding the level of employment. If $MRP_L > P_L$, it will pay to expand labor usage; when $MRP_L < P_L$, it will pay to cut back. When $MRP_L = P_L$, the level of employment is optimal. When an unlimited supply of labor can be employed at a given wage rate, determining the optimal level of employment involves a simple comparison of MRP_L and P_L. However, when higher wages are necessary to expand the level of employment, this fact must be taken into account in the determination of an optimal level of employment.

To illustrate, consider the case of Micromachines, Inc., in Chapel Hill, North Carolina. Micromachines is a high-tech company that assembles and markets Lilliputian-size machines: tiny gears and cranks the size of large specks of dust. The firm plans to introduce a new microscopic motor with the following demand conditions:

$$Q = 187,500 - 2,500P$$

or

$$P = \$75 - \$0.0004Q.$$

Motor parts are purchased from a number of independent subcontractors and then put together at Micromachines' assembly plant. Each unit of output is expected to require two hours of labor. Total costs for parts acquisition *before* assembly labor costs are as follows:

$$TC = \$250,000 + \$15Q.$$

Business is booming for Micromachines' established products, and the company has no excess assembly staff. To assemble this additional product, the firm will need to hire and train a new staff of technical assistants. Given tight labor market conditions, Micromachines expects that an increase in employment will be possible only at higher wage rates. Based on data compiled by its director of human resource management, the firm projects the following labor supply curve in the highly competitive local labor market:

$$L_S = 10,000P_L.$$

Based on the above information, it is possible to derive Micromachines' demand curve for labor. To do so, simply note that because two hours of labor are required for each unit of output, the company's profit function can be written as

$$\pi = TR - TC_{PARTS} - TC_{ASSEMBLY}$$
$$= (\$75 - \$0.0004Q)Q - \$250,000 - \$15Q - 2P_LQ$$
$$= -\$0.0004Q^2 + \$60Q - 2P_LQ - \$250,000.$$

To find Micromachines' labor demand curve, it is necessary to determine the firm's optimal level of output. The profit-maximizing level of output is found by setting marginal profit equal to zero ($M\pi = \Delta\pi/\Delta Q = 0$), where

$$M\pi = -\$0.0008Q + \$60 - 2P_L = 0.$$

This implies a direct relation between the price of labor, P_L, and the firm's optimal level of output:

$$2P_L = \$60 - \$0.0008Q.$$
$$P_L = \$30 - \$0.0004Q.$$

This expression can be used to indicate a profit-maximizing level of output and the optimal employment level. In setting $M\pi = MR - MC = 0$, the firm has also implicitly set $MR = MC$. In terms of employment, this means that $MRP_L = P_L$ for each and every input at the profit-maximizing activity level. Therefore, Micromachines' marginal revenue product of labor is given by the expression $MRP_L = \$30 - \$0.0004Q$.

To identify Micromachines' optimal level of employment at any given price of labor, simply determine the amount of labor required to produce the relevant profit-maximizing level of output. Because each unit of output requires *two* units of labor, $L = 2Q$ and $Q = 0.5L$. By substitution, the firm's demand curve for labor is

$$P_L = MRP_L$$
$$= \$30 - \$0.0004(0.5L)$$
$$= \$30 - \$0.0002L$$

or

$$L_D = 150,000 - 5,000P_L.$$

At any given wage rate, this expression indicates Micromachines' optimal level of employment. At any given employment level, this expression also indicates Micromachines' optimal wage rate. As can be expected, a higher wage results in a lower level of labor demand, and the amount of labor demanded rises as the wage rate falls.

The equilibrium wage rate and employment level in the local labor market can be determined by setting the demand for labor equal to the supply of labor:

$$\text{Labor Demand} = \text{Labor Supply}$$

$$150,000 - 5,000P_L = 10,000P_L$$

$$15,000P_L = 150,000$$

$$P_L = \$10 \text{ (wage rate).}$$

To determine the equilibrium employment level, set labor demand equal to labor supply at a wage rage of $10:

$$\text{Labor Demand} = \text{Labor Supply}$$

$$150,000 - 5,000(\$10) = 10,000(\$10)$$

$$100,000 = 100,000 \text{ (worker hours).}$$

This implies that Micromachines has a profit-maximizing activity level of 50,000 micromotors (units of output) because $Q = 0.5L = 0.5(100,000) = 50,000$ units.

Using the firm's demand curve for micromotors and total profit function, it is now possible to calculate the optimal output price and profit levels:

$$P = \$75 - \$0.0004(50,000)$$

$$= \$55.$$

$$\pi = -\$0.0004(50,000^2) + \$60(50,000) - 2(\$10)(50,000) - \$250,000$$

$$= \$750,000.$$

From this example, it becomes clear that the input demand function and the optimal level of employment can be derived by calculating the profit-maximizing level of output and then determining the amount of labor necessary to produce that output level. In the earlier Tax Advisors, Inc., example, the point where $MRP_L = P_L$ indicates the optimal employment level. This is similar to setting $MR = MC$ for each input. In the Micromachines, Inc., example, labor costs are directly incorporated into the profit function and the point where $M\pi = 0$ is found. Both approaches yield the same profit-maximizing result because if $M\pi = MR - MC = 0$, then $MR = MC$ and $P_L = MRP_L$. Either method can be used to determine an optimal employment level.

Figure 7.7 shows the marginal revenue product for an input, L, along with its market price, P_L^*. Over the range OL^*, expanding L usage increases total profits, since the marginal revenue product gained from employing each unit of L exceeds its price.

THE *MRP* CURVE IS AN INPUT DEMAND CURVE

Figure 7.7

Profits are maximized at L^*, where $P_L^* = MRP_L$

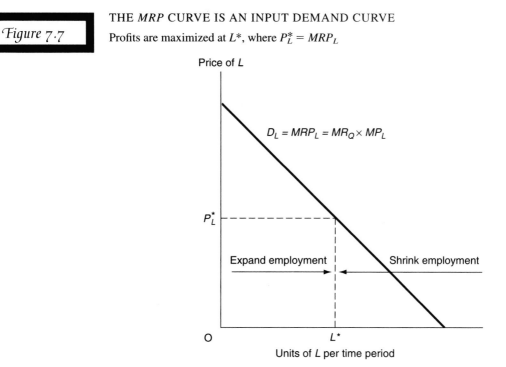

Beyond L^*, increased usage of L reduces profits, because the benefits gained (MRP_L) are less than the costs incurred (P_L). Only at L^*, where $P_L^* = MRP_L$, is total profit maximized. Of course, if P_L^* were higher, the quantity of L demanded would be reduced. Similarly, if P_L^* were lower, the quantity of L purchased would be greater.

OPTIMAL COMBINATION OF MULTIPLE INPUTS

Isocost Curve
Line of constant costs.

The results of preceding sections can be extended to determine the optimal input proportions in production systems employing several input factors. Among the several possible approaches to this task, one of the simplest involves combining technical and market relations through the use of isoquant and isocost curves. Optimal input proportions can be found graphically for a two-input, single-output system by adding an **isocost curve,** a line of constant costs, to the diagram of production isoquants. Each point on the isocost curve represents a combination of inputs, say, X and Y, whose cost equals a constant expenditure. The budget lines illustrated in Figure 7.8 are constructed in the following manner: Let $P_X = \$500$ and $P_Y = \$250$, the prices of X and Y. For a given budget, say $B_1 = \$1,000$, the firm can purchase 4 units of Y ($= \$1,000/\$250$) and no units of X, or 2 units of X ($= \$1,000/\$500$) and none of Y. These two quantities represent the X and Y intercepts of a budget line, and a straight line connecting them identifies all combinations of X and Y that $\$1,000$ can purchase.

The equation for a budget line is merely a statement of the various combinations of inputs that can be purchased for a given dollar amount. For example, the various combinations of X and Y that can be purchased for a fixed budget, B, are given by the expression

$$B = P_X \times X + P_Y \times Y.$$

Solving this expression for Y so that it can be graphed, as in Figure 7.8, results in

$$Y = \frac{B}{P_Y} - \frac{P_X}{P_Y}X. \tag{7.12}$$

Note that the first term in Equation 7.12 is the Y-axis intercept of the isocost curve. It indicates the quantity of Input Y that can be purchased with a given budget or expenditure limit, *assuming zero units of Input X are bought*. The slope of a budget line $\Delta Y / \Delta X$ equals $-P_X/P_Y$ and measures relative input prices. A change in the budget level, B, leads to a parallel shift in the budget line; changes in input prices alter the slope of the budget line.

These relations can be clarified by considering further the example illustrated in Figure 7.8. With a $1,000 budget, the Y-axis intercept of the budget line has already been shown to be 4 units. Relative prices determine the slope of the budget line. Thus, in Figure 7.8 the slope of the isocost curves is given by the expression:

ISOCOST CURVES

Figure 7.8

Each point on an isocost line represents a different combination of inputs that can be purchased at a given expenditure level.

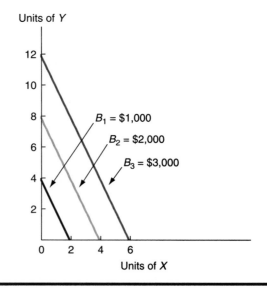

$$Slope = \frac{-P_X}{P_Y} = \frac{-\$500}{\$250} = -2.$$

Suppose that a firm has only \$1,000 to spend on inputs for the production of Q. Combining a set of production isoquants with the budget lines of Figure 7.8 to form Figure 7.9 indicates that the optimal input combination occurs at Point A, the point of tangency between the budget line and a production isoquant. At that point, X and Y are combined in proportions that maximize the output attainable for an expenditure B_1. No other combination of X and Y that can be purchased for \$1,000 will produce as much output. All other (X, Y) combinations along the budget line through (X_1, Y_1) must intersect isoquants representing lower output quantities. Alternatively, the combination (X_1, Y_1) is the least-cost input combination that can produce output Q_1. All other (X, Y) combinations on the Q_1 isoquant lie on higher budget lines. Similarly, X_2, Y_2 is the least-cost input combination for producing Q_2, and so on. All other possible combinations for producing Q_1, Q_2, and Q_3 are intersected by higher budget lines. By connecting points of tangency between isoquants and budget lines (Points A, B, and C), an

Figure 7.9

OPTIMAL INPUT COMBINATIONS

The points of tangency between the isoquant and isocost curves depict optimal input combinations at different activity levels.

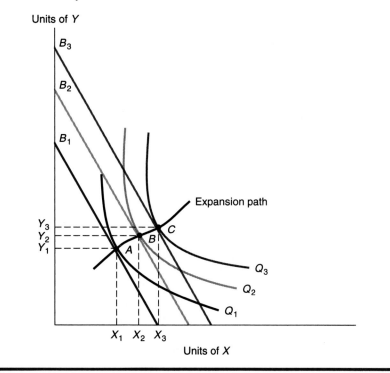

Expansion Path
Optimal input combinations
as the scale of production
expands.
expansion path is identified that depicts optimal input combinations as the scale of production expands.

The fact that optimal input combinations occur at points of tangency between a production isoquant and an isocost curve leads to a very important economic principle. The slope of an isocost curve equals $-P_X/P_Y$. The slope of an isoquant curve equals the marginal rate of technical substitution of one input factor for another when the quantity of production is held constant. The marginal rate of technical substitution was shown in Equation 7.6 to equal -1 times the ratio of input marginal products, $-MP_X/MP_Y$.

At the point of optimal input combination, isocost and the isoquant curves are tangent and have equal slope. Therefore, for optimal input combinations, the ratio of input prices must equal the ratio of input marginal products, as is shown in Equation 7.13:

$$\frac{P_X}{P_Y} = \frac{MP_X}{MP_Y}. \tag{7.13}$$

Alternatively, the ratios of marginal product to price must be equal for each input:

$$\frac{MP_X}{P_X} = \frac{MP_Y}{P_Y}. \tag{7.14}$$

The economic rule for a least-cost combination of inputs, as given in Equation 7.14, means that *optimal input proportions are employed when an additional dollar spent on any input yields the same increase in output.* Any input combination violating this rule is suboptimal because a change in input proportions could result in the same quantity of output at lower cost.

The Tax Advisors, Inc., example can further illustrate these relations. Assume that in addition to three CPAs, four bookkeepers are employed at a wage (including fringes) of $15 per hour and that $MP_{B=4} = 0.3$. This compares with a CPA wage of $35 per hour and $MP_{CPA=3} = 1.4$. Based on these assumptions, the marginal product per dollar spent on each input is

$$\frac{MP_{B=4}}{P_B} = \frac{0.3}{\$15} = 0.02 \text{ Units per Dollar (for bookkeepers)}$$

and

$$\frac{MP_{CPA=3}}{P_{CPA}} = \frac{1.4}{\$35} = 0.04 \text{ Units per Dollar (for CPAs).}$$

Such an input combination violates the optimal proportions rule since the ratios of marginal products to input prices are not equal. The last dollar spent on bookkeeper labor input produces ("buys") 0.02 units of output (tax-return preparations), whereas the last dollar spent on CPA time produces twice as much, 0.04 units. By transferring $1 of cost from bookkeeper time to CPA time, the firm could increase total output by 0.02 tax-return preparations per hour without increasing total cost. Expenditures on the CPA input represent a better use of firm resources, and the company should reallocate resources to employ relatively more CPAs and relatively fewer bookkeepers.

In Equation 7.9, it was shown that the marginal product to price ratio indicates the marginal cost of output from a marginal unit of input X or Y. In terms of this example, this implies that

$$MC_Q = \frac{P_B}{MP_{B=4}} = \frac{\$15}{0.3} = \$50 \text{ per unit (using bookkeepers)}$$

and

$$MC_Q = \frac{P_{CPA}}{MP_{CPA=3}} = \frac{\$35}{1.4} = \$25 \text{ per unit (using CPAs).}$$

Again, the superior economic productivity of CPAs is indicated; they are able to produce output at one-half the marginal cost of output produced by bookkeepers.

It is important to recognize that the preceding analysis for determining optimal proportions of multiple inputs considers input price and input marginal product (productivity) relations only. Since the economic value of output is not considered, these data are insufficient to allow calculation of optimal employment *levels*. Notice in the Tax Advisors, Inc., example that the marginal cost of output using either input is much less than the $100 marginal revenue per tax return. It is quite possible that more CPAs *and* more bookkeepers should be hired. The next section introduces output value to determine the optimal level of resource employment in production systems with multiple inputs.

OPTIMAL LEVELS OF MULTIPLE INPUTS

Combining inputs in proportions that satisfy Equations 7.13 and 7.14 ensures that any output quantity is produced at minimum cost. Cost minimization requires only that the ratios of marginal product to price be equal for all inputs. Alternatively, cost minimization dictates that inputs be combined in optimal proportions for a given or target level of output. Profit maximization, however, requires that a firm employ optimal input proportions *and* produce an optimal quantity of output. Therefore, *cost minimization and optimal input proportions are necessary but not sufficient conditions for profit maximization.*

Profit maximization requires that the firm employ inputs up to the point where $MC_Q = MR_Q$. As a result, profit maximization requires for each and every input that

$$\frac{P_X}{MP_X} = MR_Q \tag{7.15}$$

and

$$\frac{P_Y}{MP_Y} = MR_Q. \tag{7.16}$$

Rearranging produces

$$P_X = MP_X \times MR_Q = MRP_X \tag{7.17}$$

MANAGERIAL APPLICATION
7.3

Is Raising the Minimum Wage a Good Idea?

In 1996, the federal minimum wage was increased by 50 cents per hour to $4.75, and to $5.15 in 1997. Offered as a well-deserved raise for hardworking Americans, President Clinton argued that a boost was the right thing to do since the minimum wage had been relatively stagnant during recent years. The federal minimum wage was raised from $3.35 to $3.80 during 1990, and bumped further to $4.25 during 1991. Clinton and Labor Secretary Robert Reich justified a boost in the minimum wage on the grounds that it would help the working poor. While most middle- and high-income people seem to be enjoying peace and prosperity during the 1990s, the Administration argued that too many low-income people are working harder for less in real or after-inflation dollars. Moreover, they argued that a modest increase does not cost jobs and may even lure people back into the labor market.

However, critics note that by raising the minimum wage, labor-market competition from low-wage workers is made illegal. It is not only against the law for employers to pay less than the federal mandate, it is illegal for workers to seek employment at wage rates below the federal minimum wage. Therefore, a rise in the federal minimum wage is sought by labor unions who seek to eliminate competition from low-wage workers. From a political standpoint, cynics suggest that an increase in the minimum wage is an astute means of helping organized labor by favoring a measure that appears, at least on the surface, to help the working poor.

From a balanced point of view, it is worth examining the economic costs and benefits associated with an increase in the minimum wage. It is also important to recognize the equity implications of a minimum-wage boost. From an equity standpoint, it is important to recognize that part-time workers dominate the minimum-wage work force. When workers retain their jobs after the minimum wage has been boosted, it's mainly teenagers in part-time service occupations, like fast-food restaurants, who benefit. The overwhelming majority of minimum-wage workers tend to be young, part-time workers from households that lie above, not below, the poverty line.

The potential benefits of an increase in the minimum wage, namely higher incomes for the working poor, are obvious. What is less obvious is the potential cost in terms of lost employment opportunities. Whenever the decision of adding or subtracting workers is faced, an employer compares the marginal revenue product of the last worker hired to the marginal cost of employment. At the margin, each worker's job must be justified by bringing to the employer at least as much in added revenue as is necessary to pay the marginal cost of employment. When the minimum wage is increased from $4.25 to $5.15 per hour, low-skill workers unable to produce more than $4.25 per hour in employer benefits get laid off.

Because almost all minimum-wage workers are employed in the services sector, self-service is the most common alternative to the employment of minimum-wage labor. Thirty years ago, teenagers had a variety of low-wage income opportunities, including jobs as a car washer, dish washer, gas pump "jockey," golf caddie, grocery store carryout, movie theater usher, waitress, and so on. However, with rising minimum wage rates, consumers balked at paying the higher prices necessary to provide such services. Now, most of those jobs are gone. Self-service car washes and gas stations, do-it-yourself grocery retailers, and self-serve restaurants have all become popular as minimum wage hikes have outstripped consumers' willingness to pay. History tells us that teenage unemployment jumps following minimum-wage increases; unemployment skyrockets among black teenagers. Perhaps the most damaging effect of increases in the minimum wage is that it denies entry-level job opportunities to the poorest and least educated portion of the workforce.

The bottom line is simple: worker productivity must be enhanced if you want to increase incomes among the working poor. Raising the minimum wage while holding job skills constant will *reduce* not enhance income opportunities for minimum-wage workers.

See: Rob Norton, "The Minimum Wage Is Unfair," *Fortune,* May 27, 1996, 53.

and

$$P_Y = MP_Y \times MR_Q = MRP_Y \qquad (7.18)$$

Profits are maximized when inputs are employed so that price equals marginal revenue product for each input. The difference between cost minimization and profit maximization is quite simple. Cost minimization and the employment of optimal input proportions requires considering only the supply-related factors of input prices and marginal productivity. Profit maximization requires consideration of these supply-related factors *and* the demand-related marginal revenue of output. When a firm employs each input in a production system so that input *MRP* = Price, the firm ensures that inputs are being combined in optimal proportions *and* that the total level of resource employment is optimal.

A final look at the Tax Advisors, Inc., example illustrates these relations. Recall that for a production system with three CPAs and four bookkeepers the ratio of marginal products to price for each input indicates a need to employ more CPAs relative to the number of bookkeepers. Assume that hiring one more bookkeeper leaves unchanged their marginal product of 0.3 tax returns processed per hour ($MP_{B=5} = 0.3$). In addition, assume that with this increased employment of bookkeepers the marginal product of the fourth CPA increases from 0.4 to 0.7 tax returns processed per hour. This assumption reflects the fact that the marginal productivity of an input factor (CPAs) is typically enhanced when used in conjunction with more of a complementary input, bookkeepers in this case. Now $MP_{B=5} = 0.3$ and $MP_{CPA=4} = 0.7$. With the costs of each input remaining constant at $P_B = \$15$ and $P_{CPA} = \$35$, the marginal product-to-price ratios are now equal:

$$\frac{MP_{B=5}}{P_B} = \frac{0.3}{\$15} = 0.02 \text{ Units per Dollar (for bookkeepers)}$$

and

$$\frac{MP_{CPA=4}}{P_{CPA}} = \frac{0.7}{\$35} = 0.02 \text{ Units per Dollar (for CPAs).}$$

The combination of four CPAs and five bookkeepers is now optimal from a cost-minimizing standpoint, and input *proportions* are optimal. However, it is still unclear whether an optimal *level* of input has been employed. In other words, does the resulting output level maximize profit? To answer this question, it becomes necessary to determine if marginal revenue product equals the marginal cost of each input. If net marginal revenue (*NMR*) per return remains at $50 = (\$100 \times 0.5)$, then

$$MRP_B = MP_B \times NMR_Q$$
$$= 0.3 \times \$50 = \$15$$
$$MRP_B = \$15 = P_B$$

and

$$MRP_{CPA} = MP_{CPA} \times NMR_Q$$
$$= 0.7 \times \$50 = \$35$$
$$MRP_{CPA} = \$35 = P_{CPA}.$$

Marginal revenue product equals cost for each input. The combination of four CPAs and five bookkeepers is an optimal *level* of employment because the resulting output quantity maximizes profit.

Returns to Scale

Constant Returns to Scale
When a given percentage increase in all inputs leads to an identical percentage increase in output.

Increasing Returns to Scale
When the proportional increase in output is larger than an underlying proportional increase in input.

Decreasing Returns to Scale
When output increases at a rate less than the proportionate increase in inputs.

Closely related to the productivity of individual inputs is the question of how a proportionate increase in all inputs will affect total production. This is the question of returns to scale, and there are three possible situations. First, **constant returns to scale** exist when a given percentage increase in all inputs leads to that same percentage increase in output. For example, if a simultaneous doubling of all inputs leads to a doubling of output, then returns to scale are constant. **Increasing returns to scale** are prevalent if the proportional increase in output is larger than the underlying proportional increase in inputs. If output increases at a rate less than the proportionate increase in inputs, **decreasing returns to scale** are present.

EVALUATING RETURNS TO SCALE

The returns-to-scale concept can be clarified by reexamining the production data in Table 7.1. Assume that the production system represented by those data is currently operating with 1 unit of Input X and 3 units of Input Y. Production from such an input combination would be 35 units. Doubling X and Y results in an input combination of $X = 2$ and $Y = 6$. Output from this input combination would be 72 units. A 100% increase in both X and Y increases output by 37 units ($= 72 - 35$), a 106% increase ($= 37/35 = 1.06$). Over this range, output increases more than proportionately to the increase in the productive factors. The production system exhibits increasing returns to scale over this range of input use.

The returns to scale of a production system can vary over different levels of input usage. Consider, for example, the effect of a 50% increase in X and Y from the input combination $X = 2$, $Y = 6$. Increasing X by 50% results in employment of 3 units of that factor ($= 2 \times 1.5$), whereas a 50% increase in Y leads to 9 units ($= 6 \times 1.5$) of that input being used. The new input combination results in 89 units of production. Therefore, a 50% increase in input employment generates only a 24% [$= (89 - 72)/72$] increase in output. Since the increase in output is less than proportionate to the underlying increase in input, the production system exhibits decreasing returns to scale over this range.

Isoquant analysis can be used to examine returns to scale for a two-input, single-output production system. Consider the production of Q_1 units of output using the input combination of (X_1, Y_1). If doubling both inputs shifts production to Q_2, and if Q_2 is precisely twice as large as Q_1, the system is said to exhibit constant returns to scale over the range (X_1,Y_1) to $(2X_1,2Y_1)$. If Q_2 is greater than twice Q_1, returns to scale are increasing; if Q_2 is less than double Q_1, the system exhibits decreasing returns to scale.

The returns to scale implicit in a given production function can also be examined graphically, as in Figure 7.10. In this graph, the slope of a curve drawn from the origin up the production surface indicates whether returns to scale are constant, increasing, or decreasing.[5] In the production system illustrated in Figure 7.10, a curve drawn from the origin with a constant slope indicates that returns to scale are constant. In Figure 7.10, if a curve from the origin exhibits a constantly increasing slope, increasing returns to scale are indicated. If a production function increases at a decreasing rate, decreasing returns to scale are indicated.

A more general condition is a production function with first increasing, then decreasing, returns to scale. The region of increasing returns is attributable to specialization. As output increases, specialized labor can be used and efficient, large-scale machinery can be employed in the production process. Beyond some scale of operation,

Figure 7.10

RETURNS TO SCALE MAY BE CONSTANT, DECREASING, OR INCREASING

A straight-line production function indicates constant returns to scale, and a given percentage change in all inputs will cause the same percentage change in output. When the slope of such a line from the origin is falling, decreasing returns to scale are indicated. If the slope of such a line from the origin is rising, increasing returns to scale are revealed. If decreasing returns to scale are present, total output grows slower than input use; when returns to scale are present, total output grows faster than input use.

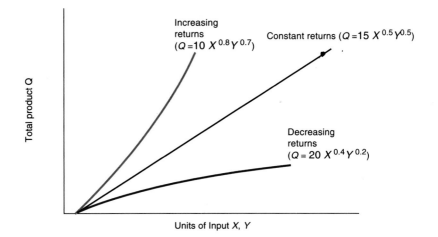

Increasing returns $(Q = 10\,X^{0.8}Y^{0.7})$

Constant returns $(Q = 15\,X^{0.5}Y^{0.5})$

Decreasing returns $(Q = 20\,X^{0.4}Y^{0.2})$

Total product Q

Units of Input X, Y

---

[5]Both inputs X and Y can be plotted on the horizontal axis of Figure 7.10 because they bear constant proportions to one another. What is actually being plotted on the horizontal axis is the number of units of some fixed input combination.

however, not only are further gains from specialization limited, but problems of coordination may also begin to increase costs substantially. When coordination expenses more than offset additional benefits of specialization, decreasing returns to scale set in.

OUTPUT ELASTICITY AND RETURNS TO SCALE

Output Elasticity
The percentage change in output associated with a 1% change in all inputs.

Even though graphic representations of returns to scale like Figure 7.10 is intuitively appealing, returns to scale can be more accurately determined for production functions through analysis of output elasticities. **Output elasticity,** ϵ_Q, is the percentage change in output associated with a 1% change in all inputs, and a practical means for returns to scale estimation. Letting $\underline{X}$ represent the entire set of input factors,

$$\epsilon_Q = \frac{\text{Percentage Change in Output } (Q)}{\text{Percentage Change in All Inputs } (\underline{X})} \tag{7.19}$$

$$= \frac{\Delta Q/Q}{\Delta \underline{X}/\underline{X}} = \frac{\Delta Q}{\Delta \underline{X}} \times \frac{\underline{X}}{Q},$$

where $\underline{X}$ refers to a complete set of input factors (i.e., $\underline{X}$ = capital, labor, energy, etc.), then the following relations hold:

IF	THEN	RETURNS TO SCALE ARE:
Percentage change in $\underline{Q}$ > Percentage change in $\underline{X}$,	$\epsilon_Q > 1$.	Increasing.
Percentage change in $\underline{Q}$ = Percentage change in $\underline{X}$,	$\epsilon_Q = 1$.	Constant.
Percentage change in $\underline{Q}$ < Percentage change in $\underline{X}$,	$\epsilon_Q < 1$.	Diminishing.

Thus, returns to scale can be analyzed by examining the relationship between the rate of increase in inputs and the quantity of output produced. For example, assume that all inputs in the unspecified production function $Q = f(X, Y, Z)$ are increased using the constant factor k, where $k = 1.01$ for a 1% increase, $k = 1.02$ for a 2% increase, and so on. Then the production function can be rewritten as

$$hQ = f(kX, kY, kZ), \tag{7.20}$$

where h is the proportional increase in Q resulting from a k-fold increase in each input factor. From Equation 7.20, it is evident that the following relationships hold:

- If $h > k$, then the percentage change in Q is greater than the percentage change in the inputs, $\epsilon_Q > 1$, and the production function exhibits increasing returns to scale.
- If $h = k$, then the percentage change in Q equals the percentage change in the inputs, $\epsilon_Q = 1$, and the production function exhibits constant returns to scale.
- If $h < k$, then the percentage change in Q is less than the percentage change in the inputs, $\epsilon_Q < 1$, and the production function exhibits decreasing returns to scale.

For certain production functions, called homogeneous production functions, when each input factor is multiplied by a constant k, the constant can be completely factored out of the production function expression. Following a k-fold increase in all inputs, the production function takes the form $hQ = k^n f(X,Y,Z)$. The exponent n provides the key to returns-to-scale estimation. If $n = 1$, then $h = k$ and the function exhibits constant returns to scale. If $n > 1$, then $h > k$, indicating increasing returns to scale, whereas $n < 1$ indicates $h < k$ and decreasing returns to scale. In all other instances, the easiest means for determining the nature of returns to scale can be easily determined through numerical example.

To illustrate, consider the production function $Q = 2X + 3Y + 1.5Z$. Returns to scale can be determined by learning how an arbitrary, say 2%, increase in all inputs affects output. If, initially, $X = 100$, $Y = 200$, and $Z = 200$, output is found to be

$$Q_1 = 2(100) + 3(200) + 1.5(200)$$

$$= 200 + 600 + 300 = 1,100 \text{ units.}$$

Increasing all inputs by 2% (letting $k = 1.02$) leads to the input quantities $X = 102$, $Y = 204$, and $Z = 204$, and

$$Q_2 = 2(102) + 3(204) + 1.5(204)$$

$$= 204 + 612 + 306 = 1,122 \text{ units.}$$

Because a 2% increase in all inputs has led to a 2% increase in output ($1.02 = 1,122/1,100$), this production system exhibits constant returns to scale.

Production Function Estimation

From a theoretical standpoint, the most appealing functional form for production function estimation might be cubic, such as the equation

$$Q = a + bXY + cX^2Y + dXY^2 - eX^3Y - fXY^3. \tag{7.21}$$

This form is general in that it exhibits stages of first increasing and then decreasing returns to scale. The marginal products of the input factors exhibit a pattern of first increasing and then decreasing returns, as was illustrated in Figure 7.3.

Given enough input/output observations, either over time for a single firm or at a single point in time for a number of firms in an industry, regression techniques can be used to estimate the parameters of the production function. Frequently, however, the data observations do not exhibit enough dispersion to indicate the full range of increasing and then decreasing returns. In these cases, simpler functional specifications can be used to estimate the production function within the range of available data. In other words, the full generality of a cubic function may be unnecessary, and an alternative linear or log-linear model specification can be usefully applied in empirical estimation. The multiplicative production function described in the next section is one such approximation that has proven extremely useful in empirical studies of production relationships.

POWER PRODUCTION FUNCTIONS

Power Production Function
A multiplicative relation between input and output.

One function commonly employed in production studies is the **power production function,** a multiplicative relation between output and input that takes the form

$$Q = b_0 X^{b_1} Y^{b_2}. \tag{7.22}$$

Power functions have properties that are useful in empirical research. Most important, power functions allow the marginal productivity of a given input to depend on the levels of *all* inputs employed, a condition that often holds in actual production systems. Power functions are also easy to estimate in log-linear form using least squares regression analysis (see Chapter 3). That is, Equation 7.22 is equivalent to

$$\log Q = \log b_0 + b_1 \log X + b_2 \log Y. \tag{7.23}$$

The least squares technique can be used to easily estimate the coefficients of Equation 7.23 and thus the parameters of Equation 7.22. Returns to scale are also easily calculated by summing the exponents of the power function or, alternatively, by summing the log-linear model coefficient estimates. As seen in Figure 7.10, if the sum of power function exponents is less than 1, diminishing returns are indicated. A sum greater than 1 indicates increasing returns. If the sum of exponents is exactly 1, returns to scale are constant, and the powerful tool of linear programming, described in Chapter 11, can be used to determine optimal input-output relations for the firm.

Power functions have been successfully employed in a large number of empirical production studies since Charles W. Cobb and Paul H. Douglas's pioneering work in the late 1920s. The impact of their work is so great that power production functions are now frequently referred to as Cobb–Douglas production functions.

FUNCTIONAL FORM SELECTION FOR EMPIRICAL STUDIES

Many functional forms are available for empirical production study. As with empirical demand estimation, the primary determinant of the functional form used to estimate any model of production depends on the relation hypothesized by the researcher. A simple linear approach will be adequate in many instances. In others a power function or log-linear approach can be justified. When specification uncertainty is high, a number of plausible alternative model specifications can be fitted to the data to determine which form seems most representative of actual conditions.

Summary

This chapter introduces and analyzes the creative process of production. Several important properties of production systems are examined in some detail.

- A **production function** specifies the maximum output that can be produced for a given amount of inputs. A **discrete production function** involves distinct, or "lumpy," patterns for input combinations. In a **continuous production function,** inputs can be varied in an unbroken marginal fashion.

- The **returns to scale** characteristic of a production system describes the output effect of a proportional increase in all inputs. The relation between output and variation in only one of the inputs employed is described as the **returns to a factor.**

- The **total product** indicates the total output from a production system. The **marginal product** of a factor, MP_X, is the change in output associated with a one-unit change in the factor input, holding all other inputs constant. A factor's **average product** is the total product divided by the number of units of that input employed.

- The **law of diminishing returns** states that as the quantity of a variable input increases, with the quantities of all other factors being held constant, and the resulting rate of increase in output eventually diminishes.

- An **isoquant** represents the different combinations of inputs that can be used efficiently to produce a specified quantity of output. Efficiency in this case refers to **technical efficiency,** meaning the least-cost production of a target level of output.

- **Input substitution,** or the systematic replacement of productive factors, is an important consideration when judging the efficiency of any production system. The **marginal rate of technical substitution** measures the amount of one input that must be substituted for another to maintain a constant level of output. It is irrational for a firm to use any input combination outside the **ridge lines** that indicate the bounds of positive marginal products.

- The **marginal revenue product** of an input is found by multiplying the marginal product of the input by the marginal revenue resulting from the sale of goods or services produced. This is the amount of revenue generated by employing the last input unit. Profit maximization requires that marginal revenue product and marginal cost be set equal for each input. **Economic efficiency** is achieved in the overall economy when all firms employ resources in order to equate each input's marginal revenue product and marginal cost. In all instances, it is important to consider the **net marginal revenue** of each input, or marginal revenue after all variable costs. Similarly important is the firm's **isocost curve,** or line of constant costs. An **expansion path** depicts optimal input combinations as the scale of production expands.

- **Constant returns to scale** exist when a given percentage increase in all inputs leads to that same percentage increase in output. **Increasing returns to scale** are prevalent if the proportional increase in output is larger than the underlying proportional increase in inputs. If output increases at a rate less than the proportionate increase in inputs, **decreasing returns to scale** are present.

- **Output elasticity,** ϵ_Q, is the percentage change in output associated with a 1% change in all inputs, and it is a practical means for returns-to-scale estimation. **Power production function** indicates a multiplicative relation between input and output and is often used in production function estimation.

The successful analysis and estimation of production relations is fundamental to the ongoing success of any organization. Concepts developed in this chapter can be used to understand, refine, and improve the policies of successful companies.

QUESTIONS

Q7.1   Use the total product curve illustrated on the following diagram to answer the following questions.

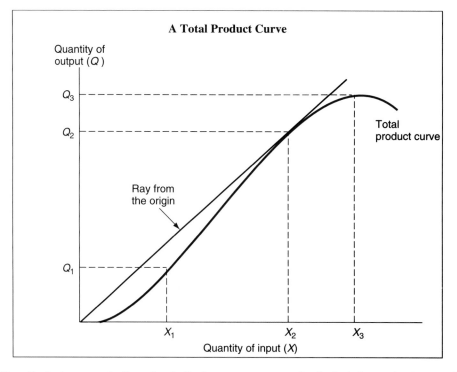

A Total Product Curve

A.   Describe both geometrically and verbally the marginal product and the average product associated with Output Q_1.

B.   At what points along the curve will the marginal and the average products be maximized?

C.   How could you use the related marginal product curve to identify the maximum rational quantity of input for Factor X, holding constant the amounts of all other inputs?

Q7.2   Review the following isoquant diagram (in which L^* and K^* indicate the optimal combination for producing Output Q^* as determined by the point of tangency between an isocost curve and an isoquant curve). See the figure at the top of page 301.

A.   What would be the effect in this production system on the isocost and isoquant curves and on the optimal input combination of an increase in the relative productivity of labor, L?

B.   What would be the effect on the curves and on the input combination referred to in Part A of a technological change that increased the productivity of capital, K?

C.   What would be the effect of a change that proportionally increased the effectiveness of both labor and capital simultaneously?

Q7.3   Using a diagram of isoquant and isocost curves like the ones that follow, demonstrate that both relative input prices and factor productivity play roles in determining optimal input combinations. See the figure at the bottom of page 301 and the top of page 302.

Q7.4   Is the use of least-cost input combinations a necessary condition for profit maximization? Is it a sufficient condition? Explain.

Q7.5   "Output per worker is expected to increase by 10% during the next year. Therefore, wages can also increase by 10% with no harmful effects on employment, output prices, or employer profits." Discuss this statement.

Q7.6   Commission-based and piece-rate-based compensation plans are commonly employed by

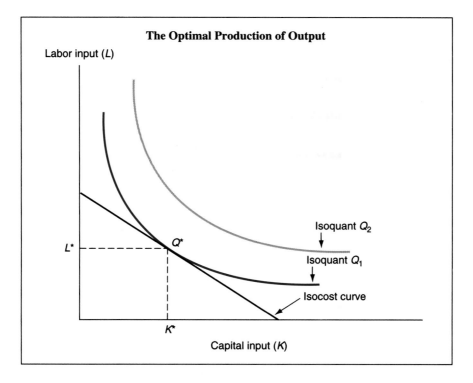

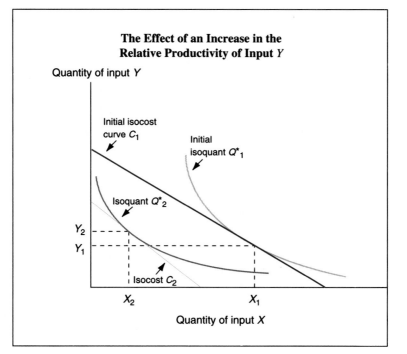

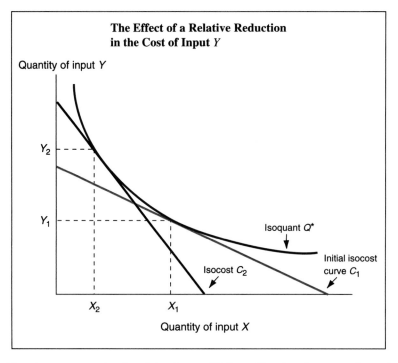

The Effect of a Relative Reduction in the Cost of Input Y

Quantity of input Y

Y_2

Y_1

Isoquant Q^*

Initial isocost curve C_1

Isocost C_2

X_2 X_1

Quantity of input X

businesses. Use the concepts developed in the chapter to explain these phenomena.

Q7.7   "Hourly wage rates are an anachronism. Efficiency requires incentive-based pay tied to performance." Discuss this statement.

Q7.8   Explain why the *MP/P* relation is deficient as the sole mechanism for determining the optimal level of resource employment.

Q7.9   Develop the appropriate relations for determining the optimal quantities of all inputs to employ in a production system, and explain the underlying rationale.

Q7.10   Suppose that labor, capital, and energy inputs must be combined in fixed proportions. Does this mean that returns to scale will be constant?

SELF-TEST PROBLEMS AND SOLUTIONS

ST7.1   **Optimal Input Usage.** Medical Testing Labs, Inc., provides routine testing services for blood banks in the Los Angeles area. Tests are supervised by skilled technicians using equipment produced by two leading competitors in the medical equipment industry. Records for the current year show an average of 27 tests per hour being performed on the Testlogic-1 and 48 tests per hour on a new machine, the Accutest-3. The Testlogic-1 is leased for $18,000 per month, and the Accutest-3 is leased at $32,000 per month. On average, each machine is operated 25 eight-hour days per month.

A.   Describe the logic of the rule used to determine an optimal mix of input usage.

B.   Does Medical Testing Lab usage reflect an optimal mix of testing equipment?

C.   Describe the logic of the rule used to determine an optimal level of input usage.

D.   If tests are conducted at a price of $6 each while labor and all other costs are fixed, should the company lease more machines?

ST7.1   **SOLUTION**

A.   The rule for an optimal combination of Testlogic-1 (*T*) and Accutest-3 (*A*) equipment is

$$\frac{MP_T}{P_T} = \frac{MP_A}{P_A}.$$

This rule means that an identical amount of additional output would be produced with an additional dollar expenditure on each input. Alternatively, an equal marginal cost of output is incurred irrespective of which input is used to expand output. Of course, marginal products and equipment prices must both reflect the same relevant time frame, either hours or months.

B. On a per hour basis, the relevant question is

$$\frac{27}{\$18,000/(25 \times 8)} \overset{?}{=} \frac{48}{\$32,000/(25 \times 8)}$$

$$0.3 \overset{\checkmark}{=} 0.3$$

On a per month basis, the relevant question is

$$\frac{27 \times (25 \times 8)}{\$18,000} \overset{?}{=} \frac{48 \times (25 \times 8)}{\$32,000}$$

$$0.3 \overset{\checkmark}{=} 0.3$$

In both instances, the last dollar spent on each machine increased output by the same 0.3 units, indicating an *optimal mix* of testing machines.

C. The rule for optimal input employment is

$$MRP = MP \times MR_Q = \text{Input Price.}$$

This means that the level of input employment is optimal when the marginal sales revenue derived from added input usage is just equal to input price, or the marginal cost of employment.

D. For each machine hour, the relevant question is

Testlogic-1

$$MRP_T = MP_T \times MR_Q \overset{?}{=} P_T$$

$$27 \times \$6 \overset{?}{=} \$18,000/(25 \times 8)$$

$$\$162 > \$90.$$

Accutest-3

$$MRP_A = MP_A \times MR_Q \overset{?}{=} P_A$$

$$48 \times \$6 \overset{?}{=} \$32,000/(25 \times 8)$$

$$\$288 > \$160.$$

Or, in per month terms:

Testlogic-1

$$MRP_T = MP_T \times MR_Q \overset{?}{=} P_T$$

$$27 \times (25 \times 8) \times \$6 \overset{?}{=} \$18,000$$

$$\$32,400 > \$18,000.$$

Accutest-3

$$MRP_A = MP_A \times MR_Q \overset{?}{=} P_A$$

$$48 \times (25 \times 8) \times \$6 \overset{?}{=} \$32,000$$

$$\$57,600 > \$32,000.$$

In both cases, each machine returns more than its marginal cost (price) of employment, and expansion would be profitable.

ST7.2 **Production Function Estimation.** Washington-Pacific, Inc., manufactures and sells lumber, plywood, veneer, particle board, medium-density fiberboard, and laminated beams. The company has estimated the following multiplicative production function for basic lumber products in the Pacific Northwest market using monthly production data over the past two and one-half years (30 observations):

$$Q = b_0 L^{b_1} K^{b_2} E^{b_3},$$

where

Q = output,

L = labor input in worker hours,

K = capital input in machine hours, and

E = energy input in BTUs.

Each of the parameters of this model was estimated by regression analysis using monthly data over a recent three-year period. Coefficient estimation results were as follows:

$$\hat{b}_0 = 0.9; \ \hat{b}_1 = 0.4; \ \hat{b}_2 = 0.4; \text{ and } \hat{b}_3 = 0.2.$$

The standard error estimates for each coefficient are:

$$\sigma_{\hat{b}_0} = 0.6; = 0.1; \ \sigma_{\hat{b}_2} = 0.2; \ \sigma_{\hat{b}_3} = 0.1$$

A. Estimate the effect on output of a 1% decline in worker hours (holding K and E constant).

B. Estimate the effect on output of a 5% reduction in machine hours availability accompanied by a 5% decline in energy input (holding L constant).

C. Estimate the returns to scale for this production system.

ST7.2 SOLUTION

A. For Cobb–Douglas production functions, calculations of the elasticity of output with respect to individual inputs can be made by simply referring to the exponents of the production relation. Here a 1% decline in L, holding all else equal, will lead to a 0.4% decline in output. Notice that:

$$\frac{\Delta Q/Q}{\Delta L/L} = \frac{\Delta Q}{\Delta L} \times \frac{L}{Q}$$

$$= \frac{(b_0 b_1 L^{b_1-1} K^{b_2} E^{b_3}) \times L}{Q}$$

$$= \frac{b_0 b_1 L^{b_1-1+1} K^{b_2} E^{b_3}}{b_0 L^{b_1} K^{b_2} E^{b_3}}$$

$$= b_1$$

And since $(\Delta Q/Q)/(\Delta L/L)$ is the percent change in Q due to a 1% change in L,

$$\frac{\Delta Q/Q}{\Delta L/L} = b_1$$

$$\Delta Q/Q = b_1 \times \Delta L/L$$

$$= 0.4(-0.01)$$

$$= -0.004 \text{ or } -0.4\%$$

B. From Part A it is obvious that:

$$\Delta Q/Q = b_2(\Delta K/K) + b_3(\Delta E/E)$$

$$= 0.4(-0.05) + 0.2(-0.05)$$

$$= -0.03 \text{ or } -3\%$$

C. In the case of Cobb–Douglas production functions, returns to scale are determined by simply summing exponents since:

$$Q = b_0 L^{b_1} K^{b_2} E^{b_3}$$

$$hQ = b_0(kL)^{b_1}(kK)^{b_2}(kE)^{b_3}$$

$$= k^{b_1 + b_2 + b_3} b_0 L^{b_1} K^{b_2} E^{b_3}$$

$$= k^{b_1 + b_2 + b_3} Q$$

Here $b_1 + b_2 + b_3 = 0.4 + 0.4 + 0.2 = 1$ indicating constant returns to scale. This means that a 1% increase in all inputs will lead to a 1% increase in output, and average costs will remain constant as output increases.

PROBLEMS

P7.1 Marginal Rate of Technical Substitution. The following production table provides estimates of the maximum amounts of output possible with different combinations of two input factors, X and Y. (Assume that these are just illustrative points on a spectrum of continuous input combinations.)

UNITS OF Y USED	ESTIMATED OUTPUT PER DAY				
5	210	305	360	421	470
4	188	272	324	376	421
3	162	234	282	324	360
2	130	188	234	272	305
1	94	130	162	188	210
	1	2	3	4	5
	Units of X Used				

A. Do the two inputs exhibit the characteristics of constant, increasing, or decreasing marginal rates of technical substitution? How do you know?

B. Assuming that output sells for $3 per unit, complete the following tables at the top of page 305.

C. Assume that the quantity of X is fixed at 2 units. If output sells for $3 and the cost of Y is $120 per day, how many units of Y will be employed?

D. Assume that the company is currently producing 162 units of output per day using 1 unit of X and 3 units of Y. The daily cost per unit of X is $120 and that of Y is also $120. Would you recommend a change in the present input combination? Why or why not?

X FIXED AT 2 UNITS

UNITS OF Y USED	TOTAL PRODUCT OF Y	MARGINAL PRODUCT OF Y	AVERAGE PRODUCT OF Y	MARGINAL REVENUE PRODUCT OF Y
1				
2				
3				
4				
5				

Y FIXED AT 3 UNITS

UNITS OF X USED	TOTAL PRODUCT OF X	MARGINAL PRODUCT OF X	AVERAGE PRODUCT OF X	MARGINAL REVENUE PRODUCT OF X
1				
2				
3				
4				
5				

E. What is the nature of the returns to scale for this production system if the optimal input combination requires that $X = Y$?

P7.2 **Production Function Concepts.** Indicate whether each of the following statements is true or false. Explain your answers.

A. Decreasing returns to scale and increasing average costs are indicated when $\epsilon_Q < 1$.

B. If the marginal product of capital falls as capital usage grows, the returns to capital are decreasing.

C. L-shaped isoquants describe production systems in which inputs are perfect substitutes.

D. Marginal revenue product measures the profit earned through expanding input usage.

E. The marginal rate of technical substitution will be affected by a given percentage increase in the marginal productivity of all inputs.

P7.3 **Factor Productivity.** During recent years, computer-aided design (CAD) and computer-aided manufacturing (CAM) have become prevalent in many U.S. industries. Holding all else equal, indicate whether each of the following factors would be responsible for increasing or decreasing this prevalence. Explain your answers.

A. Rising worker pension costs

B. Technical advances in computer mainframe design

C. An increase in the import share of the market

D. Falling prices for industry output

E. Computer software that is increasingly user-friendly

P7.4 **Returns to Scale.** Determine whether the following production functions exhibit constant, increasing, or decreasing returns to scale.

$$A.\ Q = 0.5X + 2Y + 40Z$$

$$B.\ Q = 3L + 10K + 500$$

$$C.\ Q = 4A + 6B + 8AB$$

$$D.\ Q = 7L^2 + 5LK + 2K^2$$

$$E.\ Q = 10L^{0.5}K^{0.3}$$

P7.5 **Optimal Input Mix.** World Wide Sports, Inc., based in St. Paul, Minnesota, distributes a complete line of sporting equipment. President Frank Furillo is reviewing the company's sales force compensation plan. Currently, the company pays its three experienced sales staff members a salary based on years of service, past contributions to the company, and so on. New sales trainee Phil Esterhaus is paid a more modest salary. Monthly sales and salary data for each employee are as follows:

SALES STAFF	AVERAGE MONTHLY SALES	MONTHLY SALARY
Lucy Bates	$160,000	$6,000
Mick Belker	100,000	4,500
Joe Coffey	90,000	3,600
Phil Esterhaus	75,000	2,500

Esterhaus has shown great promise during the past year, and Furillo believes that a substantial raise is clearly justified. At the same time, some adjustment to the compensation paid to other sales personnel also seems appropriate. Furillo is considering changing from the current compensation plan to one based on a 5% commission. He sees such a plan as being fairer to the parties involved and believes it would also provide strong incentives for needed market expansion.

A. Calculate World Wide's salary expense for each employee expressed as a percentage of the monthly sales generated by that individual.

B. Calculate monthly income for each employee under a 5% of monthly sales commission-based system.

C. Will a commission-based plan result in efficient relative salaries, efficient salary levels, or both?

P7.6 **Optimal Input Mix.** The First National Bank received 3,000 inquiries following the latest advertisement describing its 30-month IRA accounts in the *Boston World,* a local newspaper. The most recent ad in a similar advertising campaign in *Massachusetts Business,* a regional business magazine, generated 1,000 inquiries. Each newspaper ad costs $500, whereas each magazine ad costs $125.

A. Assuming that additional ads would generate similar response rates, is the bank running an optimal mix of newspaper and magazine ads? Why or why not?

B. Holding all else equal, how many inquiries must a newspaper ad attract for the current advertising mix to be optimal?

P7.7 **Optimal Input Level.** The I-70 Truck Stop, Inc., sells gasoline to both self-service and full-service customers. Those who pump their own gas benefit from the lower self-service price of $1.25 per gallon. Full-service customers enjoy the service of an attendant, but they pay a higher price of $1.30 per gallon. The company has observed the following relation between the number of attendants employed per day and full-service output:

I-70 TRUCK STOP, INC.

NUMBER OF ATTENDANTS PER DAY	FULL-SERVICE OUTPUT (GALLONS)
0	0
1	2,000
2	3,800
3	5,400
4	6,800
5	8,000

A. Construct a table showing the net marginal revenue product derived from attendant employment.

B. How many attendants would I-70 employ at a daily wage rate of $64?

C. What is the highest daily wage rate I-70 would pay to hire three attendants per day?

P7.8 **Optimal Input Level.** Ticket Services, Inc., offers ticket promotion and handling services for concerts and sporting events. The Chicago branch office makes heavy use of spot radio advertising on WNDY-AM, with each 30-second ad costing $100. During the past year, the following relation between advertising and ticket sales per event has been observed:

$$\text{Sales (units)} = 5,000 + 100A - 0.5A^2.$$

$$\Delta\text{Sales (units)}/\Delta\text{Advertising} = 100 - A.$$

Here, A represents a 30-second radio spot ad, and sales are measured in numbers of tickets.

Harry Stone, manager for the Chicago office, has been asked to recommend an appropriate level of advertising. In thinking about this problem, Stone noted its resemblance to the optimal resource employment problem he had studied in a managerial economics course that was part of his M.B.A. program. The advertising/sales relation could be thought of as a production function, with advertising as an input and sales as the output. The problem is to determine the profit-maximizing level of employment for the input, advertising, in this "production" system. Stone recognized that to solve the problem, he needed a measure of output value. After reflection, he determined that the value of output is $2 per ticket, the net marginal revenue earned by Ticket Services (price minus all marginal costs except advertising).

A. Continuing with Stone's production analogy, what is the marginal product of advertising?

B. What is the rule for determining the optimal amount of a resource to employ in a production system? Explain the logic underlying this rule.

C. Using the rule for optimal resource employment, determine the profit-maximizing number of radio ads.

P7.9 **Net Marginal Revenue.** Robert Hartley & Associates is a large human resource management consulting firm with offices located throughout the United States. Output at the firm is measured in billable hours, which vary between partners and associates.

Partner time is billed to clients at a rate of $100 per hour, whereas associate time is billed at a rate of $50 per hour. On average, each partner generates 25 billable hours per 40-hour workweek, with 15 hours spent on promotion, administrative, and supervisory responsibilities. Associates generate an average of 35 billable hours per 40-hour workweek and spend 5 hours per week in administrative and training meetings. Variable overhead costs average 50% of revenues generated by partners and, given supervisory requirements, 60% of revenues generated by associates.

A. Calculate the annual (50 workweeks) net marginal revenue product of partners and associates.

B. Assuming that partners earn $65,000 and associates earn $30,000 per year, does the company have an optimal combination of partners and associates? If not, why not? Make your answer explicit and support any recommendations for change.

P7.10 **Production Function Estimation.** Consider the following Cobb–Douglas production function for bus service in a typical metropolitan area:

$$Q = b_0 L^{b_1} k^{b_2} F^{b_3},$$

where

Q = output in millions of passenger miles,

L = labor input in worker hours,

K = capital input in bus transit hours, and

F = fuel input in gallons.

Each of the parameters of this model was estimated by regression analysis using monthly data over a recent three-year period. Results obtained were as follows (standard errors in parentheses):

$$\hat{b}_0 = 1.2; \ \hat{b}_1 = 0.28; \ \hat{b}_2 = 0.63; \ \text{and} \ \hat{b}_3 = 0.12.$$

The standard error estimates for each coefficient are:

$$\sigma_{b_0} = 0.4; \ \sigma_{b_1} = 0.15; \ \sigma_{b_2} = 0.12; \ \sigma_{b_3} = 0.07$$

A. Estimate the effect on output of a 4% decline in worker hours (holding K and F constant).

B. Estimate the effect on output of a 3% reduction in fuel availability accompanied by a 4% decline in bus transit hours (holding L constant).

C. Estimate the returns to scale for this production system.

Case Study for Chapter 7

PRODUCTIVITY MEASUREMENT AND ENHANCEMENT IN THE SERVICES SECTOR

The measurement and enhancement of worker productivity is an important challenge facing all managers. Productivity enhancement is vital given the role of labor as a key input in the production of goods and services and in light of the generally increasing vigor of domestic and import competition. Of course, before incentives to enhance worker productivity can be introduced, the multiple dimensions of worker productivity must be made explicit and accurately measured. Management must be able to clearly articulate the many important dimensions of worker output and communicate this information effectively to workers.

The business and popular press is replete with examples of firms and industries that have foundered because of problems tied to the inaccurate measurement of "blue-collar" worker productivity. When worker incentives are carelessly tied to piece-rate production, mass quantities of low-quality output sometimes result. Similarly, worker incentive pay plans that emphasize high-quality output can fail to provide necessary incentives for timely delivery. What is often overlooked in the discussion of workers' efficiency and labor productivity is that the definition and measurement of productivity is perhaps even more difficult in the case of managers and other "white-collar" workers. Problems encountered in the definition and measurement of white-collar-worker productivity can be illustrated by considering the productivity of college and university professors.

For most two-year and four-year college and university professors, teaching is a primary component of their work assignment. Faculty members have a standard teaching load, defined by the number of class hours per term, number of students taught, or a multiple of the two, called "student contact hours." However, not all student contact hours are alike. For example, it is possible to generate large numbers of student contact hours per faculty member simply by offering courses in a mass lecture setting with hundreds of students per class. In other cases, a faculty member might work with a very small number of students in an advanced seminar or laboratory course, generating relatively few student credit hours. The teaching "product" in each of these course settings is fundamentally similar, and few would argue that the number of students taught is an irrelevant basis for comparing the productivity of professors teaching these different types of classes.

On the other hand, few would suggest defining teaching productivity solely in terms of the sheer quantity of students taught. Student course evaluations are typically required to provide evidence from student "customers" concerning the quality of instruction. Many schools rely on such data as an exclusive measure of teaching quality. At other schools, student course-evaluation data are supplemented by peer review of teaching methods and materials, interviews of former students, and so on. Measures of both the quantity and quality of instruction must be employed in the measurement of teaching productivity.

In addition to their important teaching role, faculty members are expected to play an active role in the ongoing administration of their academic institution. At a minimum, they participate in the peer review of faculty, in student and faculty recruiting, and in curriculum and program development. Faculty often play an active role on committees that conduct the everyday management of the institution. This faculty governance system is an important organizational difference between most academic and nonacademic institutions. Faculty members are both workers and management. Measuring "output" as related to these activities, and hence productivity, is very difficult.

At many schools, faculty members also play an important liaison role with external constituents. Alumni provide important financial resources to colleges and universities and appreciate programs designed for their benefit. Nondegree "short courses" are often offered on topical subjects at nominal charge for the benefit of alumni and the community at large. Similarly, faculty are asked to give lectures to local groups, interviews for local media, and informal consulting services to local firms and organizations. Often these services are provided for free or at nominal charge as part of the faculty member's "service" function. Similarly, faculty are sometimes called on to provide service to external academic and professional organizations. Participation at national and regional academic conventions, editing academic journals, and helping design and write professional exams are typical examples of expected but unpaid services.

The preceding duties are supplemented by faculty research requirements at most four-year colleges and universities and at all graduate institutions. This requirement is fundamental to the growth and development of colleges and universities but is often misunderstood by those outside of academia. To be granted the doctoral degree, doctoral candidates must complete a rigorous series of courses and exams and meet a dissertation requirement. A doctoral dissertation is a book-length independent study that makes an important contribution to knowledge in a scholarly discipline. In fulfilling this requirement, doctoral students demonstrate their capacity to participate in the discovery of new knowledge. A key difference between the role of university professors and that of other teachers is that professors must be intimately involved with the creation and dissemination of new knowledge. Thus, the research component is a key ingredient of professorial output.

Research output is extremely varied. In the physical sciences, new compounds or other physical products may result. Similarly, such research may lead to new process techniques. In most academic fields, the primary research product is new knowledge communicated in the form of research reports or other scholarly publications. As with teaching, measuring the quantity and quality of research output proves to be most challenging. Judging the value of a research product is often quite subjective, and its worth may not be recognized for years.

Given the difficulties involved with evaluating highly specialized and detailed research, many institutions consider the dollar amount of research funds awarded to an individual to be a useful indicator of the quantity and quality of research output. It is anomalous that a school's best researchers and highest-paid faculty members may be the least expensive in terms of their net costs to the institution. When established researchers are able to consistently obtain external funding in excess of incremental costs, their net employment costs can be nil. In such instances, the disadvantages to an institution of losing a star researcher are obvious.

Of course, just as in the case of measuring teaching quality, difficulties are encountered in measuring the quality of published research output. In most instances, the quality of published articles and books is judged in terms of the reputation of the publisher or editor, the level of readership enjoyed, and so on. Over time, the number of new research outlets has grown to keep pace with the growing level of specialization in the various disciplines. In economics, for example, there are as many as 200 possible research outlets. However, only a relative handful are widely read in any given subdiscipline. Competition for scarce journal space in such outlets is fierce. Acceptance rates at leading journals often average no more than 5% to 10% of those articles submitted. When one considers that a productive scholar is typically able to complete no more than one or two substantial research projects per year, the odds are very much against achieving publication of one or two first-rate

journal articles per year. Thus, research productivity is usually measured in terms of both the quantity and quality of published research.

In sum, defining the role of professors at colleges and universities provides an interesting example of the difficulties involved in measuring worker productivity. Each individual academic institution must define on an ongoing basis the relative importance of the teaching, research, and service components of faculty output. Once this has been determined, the difficult task of defining and measuring faculty-member productivity on each dimension must begin.

Based on the preceding information and in light of the focus of your academic institution, answer the following questions:

A.   How would you define faculty-member productivity?

B.   Do you agree with the view that many elements of professorial output do not easily lend themselves to quantitative evaluation? How might you measure such productivity?

C.   Would productivity clauses for professors' contracts make sense economically? What problems do you see in implementing such clauses in actual practice?

D.   Reconsider your answers to Parts A through C for other service-industry occupations (for example, doctors, lawyers, and legislators). Are the issues discussed unique to academia?

Cost Analysis and Estimation

Proctor & Gamble Co. (P&G) is a consumer-products behemoth that really helps consumers clean up. Households around the world rely on "new and improved" Tide to clean their clothes, Ivory and Ariel detergents to wash dishes, and Pantene Pro-V to shampoo and condition hair. Other P&G products dominate a wide range of lucrative, but slow-growing, product lines, including: disposable diapers (Pampers), feminine hygiene (Always), and facial moisturizers (Oil of Olay). P&G's ongoing challenge is to figure out ways of continuing to grow aggressively outside the United States, while it cultivates the profitability of dominant consumer franchises here at home. P&G's challenge is made difficult by the fact that the company already enjoys a dominant market position in many of its slow-growing domestic markets. Worse yet, most of its brand names are aging, albeit gracefully. Tide, for example, has been "new and improved" almost continuously over its more than 60-year history. Ivory virtually introduced the concept of bar soap nearly 100 years ago; Jif peanut butter and Pampers disposable diapers are roughly 40 years old.

P&G is clearly winning the battle to grow profits. With savage cost cutting that has trimmed expenses by over $3 billion since 1992, record revenues have translated into smashing earnings and a soaring stock price. Through careful attention to cost analysis and estimation, P&G has demonstrated that successful corporate restructuring is a continual process of making things faster, better, and cheaper. This chapter illustrates that corporate rejuvenation requires a fundamental appreciation of the cost implications of all pertinent decision alternatives.[1]

What Makes Cost Analysis Difficult?

Cost analysis is made difficult by the effects of unforeseen inflation, unpredictable changes in technology, and the dynamic nature of input and output markets. Wide divergences between economic costs and accounting valuations are common. This makes it extremely important to consider whether or not unadjusted accounting data offer an appropriate basis for managerial decisions.

---

[1]See Raju Narisetti, "P&G, Seeing Shoppers Were Being Confused, Overhauls Marketing," *The Wall Street Journal,* January 15, 1997, A1, A8.

THE LINK BETWEEN ACCOUNTING AND ECONOMIC VALUATIONS

Corporate restructuring during the 1990s often involves eliminating nonstrategic operations to redeploy assets and strengthen core lines of business. When nonessential assets are disposed of in a depressed market, there is often no relation between low "fire sale" proceeds and book value, historical cost, or replacement cost. Conversely, when assets are sold to others who can more effectively use such resources, sale proceeds can approximate replacement valuations and greatly exceed historical costs and book values. Even under normal circumstances, the link between economic and accounting values can be tenuous. Economic worth as determined by profit-generating capability, rather than accounting value, is always the most relevant consideration when determining the cost and use of specific assets.

Accurate cost analysis involves careful consideration of all relevant decision alternatives. In many instances, the total costs of making a given decision are clear only when viewed in light of what is actually done *and* what is not done. For example, suppose that a company is contemplating closing satellite distribution facilities in Houston and St. Louis and opening a major regional distribution center in Dallas. Careful decision analysis includes comparing the relative costs and benefits of each decision alternative. Neither option can be viewed in isolation; each choice plays an important role in shaping the relevant costs and benefits of *both* decision alternatives. The process of cost analysis is one of measuring and weighing the relative costs of decision alternatives.

Cost analysis plays an essential role in managerial economics because virtually every managerial decision requires a careful comparison between costs and benefits. Evaluation of a proposal to expand output necessitates that the increased revenues gained from added sales be compared with the higher production costs incurred. In weighing a recommendation to expand capital resources, managers must compare the revenues derived from investment and the cost of needed funds. The expected benefits of advertising promotion must be measured in relation to the costs of personal selling, media promotion, and direct marketing. Even a decision to pave the employees' parking lot or to refurbish the company lunchroom involves a comparison between projected costs and the expected benefits derived from improved morale and worker productivity. In every case, the decision-making process involves a comparison between the costs and the benefits resulting from various decision alternatives.

HISTORICAL VERSUS CURRENT COSTS

The term *cost* can be defined in a number of ways, and the correct definition varies from situation to situation. In popular terminology, cost generally refers to the price that must be paid for an item. If a firm buys an input for cash and uses it immediately, few problems arise in defining and measuring its cost. However, if an input is purchased, stored for a time, and then used, complications can arise. The problem is even more acute if the item is a long-lived asset like a machine tool or a building that will be used at varying rates for an indeterminate period.

Historical Cost
Actual cash outlay.

When costs are calculated for a firm's income tax returns, the law requires use of the actual dollar amount spent to purchase the labor, raw materials, and capital equipment used in production. For tax purposes, **historical cost,** or actual cash outlay, is the relevant cost. This is also generally true for annual 10-K reports to the Securities and Exchange Commission and for reports to stockholders.

Current Cost
Amount paid under prevailing market conditions.

Historical costs are not appropriate for many managerial decisions. Current costs or projected future costs are typically much more relevant. **Current cost** is the amount that must be paid for an item under prevailing market conditions. Current cost is influenced by market conditions measured by the number of buyers and sellers, the current state of technology, inflation, and so on. For assets purchased recently, historical cost and current cost are typically the same. For assets purchased several years ago, historical cost and current cost are often quite different. Since World War II, inflation has been an obvious source of large differences between current and historical costs throughout most of the world. With an inflation rate of roughly 5% per year, prices double in less than 15 years and triple in roughly 22 years. Land purchased for $50,000 in 1970 often has a current cost in excess of $150,000. In California, Florida, Texas, and other rapidly growing areas, current costs can and do run much higher. Just as no homeowner would sell his or her home for a lower price based on lower historical costs, no manager can afford to sell assets or products for less than current costs.

A firm also cannot assume that the accounting historical cost is the same as the relevant economic cost of using a given piece of equipment. For example, it is not always appropriate to assume that use costs equal zero just because a machine has been fully depreciated using Accelerated Cost Recovery System (ACRS) accounting methods. If a machine could be sold for $10,000 now, but its market value is expected to be only $2,000 one year from now, the relevant cost of using the machine for one additional year is $8,000.[2] Again, there is little relation between the $8,000 relevant cost of using the machine and the zero cost that would be reported on the firm's income statement.

Historical costs provide a measure of the market value of an asset at the time of purchase. Current costs are a measure of the market value of an asset at the present time. Traditional accounting methods and the IRS rely heavily on the historical cost concept because it can be applied consistently across firms and is easily verifiable. However, when historical and current costs differ markedly, reliance on historical costs can sometimes lead to operating decisions with disastrous consequences. The recent savings and loan (S&L) industry debacle is a clear case in point. On a historical cost basis, almost all thrifts appeared to have solid loan assets to back up deposit liabilities. On a current cost basis, however, many S&Ls proved insolvent because loan assets had a current market value below the current market value of liabilities. The present move by federal and state bank regulators toward market-value-based accounting methods is motivated by a desire to avoid S&L-type disasters in the future.

---

[2]This statement involves a slight oversimplification. The economic cost of using a machine for one year is its current market value minus the discounted present value of its worth one year from now. This adjustment is necessary to account for the fact that future dollars have a lower *present* value than dollars received today.

REPLACEMENT COST

Replacement Cost
The cost of duplicating productive capability using current technology.

Although it is typical for current costs to exceed historical costs, this is not always the case. Computers and many types of electronic equipment cost much less today than they did just a few years ago. In these high-tech industries, the rapid pace of advancement in technology has overcome the general rate of inflation. As a result, current costs are falling. Current costs for used computers and electronic equipment are determined by what is referred to as **replacement cost,** or the cost of duplicating productive capability using current technology. Business computers and workstations purchased in 1990 are much cheaper today. In many instances, costs have fallen by 25 to 40% or more. In valuing such assets, the appropriate measure is the much lower replacement cost—not the historical cost. Similarly, if a company holds electronic components in inventory, the relevant cost consideration for pricing purposes is replacement costs.

In a more typical example, consider a construction company that has an inventory of 1,000,000 board feet of lumber, purchased at a historical cost of $200,000, or $200 per 1,000 board feet (a board foot of lumber is one square foot of lumber, one inch thick). Assume that lumber prices rise by 50%, and the company is asked to bid on a construction project that would require lumber. What cost should the construction company assign to the lumber, the $200,000 historical cost or the $300,000 replacement cost? The answer is the current or replacement cost of $300,000. The company will have to pay $300,000 to replace the lumber it uses on the new construction project. In fact, should it choose to do so, the construction company could sell its current inventory of lumber to others for the prevailing market price of $300,000. Under current market conditions, the lumber has a value, worth, and cost of $300,000. The amount of $300,000 is the relevant economic cost for purposes of bidding on the new construction project. For income tax purposes, however, the appropriate cost basis for the lumber inventory is still the $200,000 historical cost.

Opportunity Costs

The preceding replacement cost discussion is based on an alternative-use concept. Economic resources like lumber have value because they can be used to produce products that consumers desire. When a firm uses such a resource for producing a particular product, it bids against alternative users. Thus, the firm must offer a price at least as great as the resource's value in alternative use. The role played by choice alternatives in cost analysis is formalized by the opportunity cost concept.

THE OPPORTUNITY COST CONCEPT

Opportunity Cost
Foregone value associated with current rather than next-best use of an asset.

Opportunity cost is the foregone value associated with the current rather than next-best use of a given asset. In other words, the cost of a given asset is determined by the highest-valued *opportunity* that must be foregone to allow current use. The cost of aluminum used in the manufacture of soft drink containers, for example, is determined by its value in alternative uses. Soft drink bottlers must pay an aluminum price equal to this value or the aluminum will be used in the production of alternative goods, such as airplanes, building materials, cookware, and so on. Similarly, if a firm owns capital equipment that can be used to produce either Product A or Product B, the relevant cost of Product A includes the profit of the alternative Product B that cannot be produced because the equipment is tied up in manufacturing Product A.

The opportunity cost concept explains asset use in a wide variety of circumstances. Gold and silver are pliable yet strong precious metals. As such, they make excellent material for dental fillings. However, when precious metals speculation drove prices skyrocketing during the 1970s, plastic and ceramic materials became a common substitute for dental gold and silver. More recently, lower market prices have again allowed widespread dental use of both metals. Still, dental customers must be willing to pay a price for dental gold and silver that is competitive with the price paid by jewelry customers and industrial users.

EXPLICIT AND IMPLICIT COSTS

Explicit Cost
Out-of-pocket
expenditures.

Implicit Cost
Noncash costs.

Typically, the costs of using resources in production involve both out-of-pocket costs, or **explicit costs,** and other noncash costs, called **implicit costs.** Wages paid, utility expenses, payment for raw materials, interest paid to the holders of the firm's bonds, and rent on a building are all examples of explicit expenses. The implicit costs associated with any decision are much more difficult to compute. These costs do not involve cash expenditures and are therefore often overlooked in decision analysis. Since cash payments are not made for implicit costs, the opportunity cost concept must be used to measure them. The rent that a shop owner could receive on buildings and equipment if they were not used in the business is an implicit cost of the owner's own retailing activity, as is the salary that an individual could receive by working for someone else instead of operating his or her own retail establishment.

An example should clarify these cost distinctions. Consider the costs associated with the purchase and operation of a law practice. Assume that an established practice and office space can be bought for $225,000, with an additional $25,000 needed for initial working capital. Grace Van Owen has personal savings of $250,000 to invest in such an enterprise; Michael Kuzak, another possible buyer, must borrow the entire $250,000 at a cost of 15%, or $37,500 per year. Assume that operating costs are the same no matter who owns the practice and that Van Owen and Kuzak are equally capable of completing the purchase. Does the $37,500 in annual interest expenses make Kuzak's potential operating cost greater than that of Van Owen? For managerial decision purposes, the answer is no. Even though Kuzak has higher explicit interest costs, true financing costs may well be the same for both individuals. Van Owen has an implicit interest cost equal to the amount that could be earned on an alternative $250,000 investment. If a 15% return can be earned by investing in other assets of equal risk, then Van Owen's implicit investment opportunity cost is also $37,500 per year. In this case, Van Owen and Kuzak each have a financing cost of $37,500 per year. Van Owen's cost is implicit and Kuzak's is explicit.

Will total operating costs be identical for both individuals? Not necessarily. Just as the implicit cost of Van Owen's capital must be included in the analysis, so too must implicit labor costs be included for each individual. If Van Owen is a senior partner in a major Los Angeles law firm earning $150,000 a year and Kuzak is a junior partner earning $100,000 annually, implicit labor costs will be different. The implicit labor expense for each potential buyer is the amount of income foregone by quitting his or her present job. Thus, implicit labor costs are $150,000 for Van Owen and $100,000 for Kuzak. On an annual basis, Van Owen's total capital plus labor costs are $187,500, all of which are implicit. Kuzak's total annual costs are $137,500, including explicit capital costs of $37,500 plus implicit labor costs of $100,000.

Incremental and Sunk Costs in Decision Analysis

Value maximization requires that every managerial decision be justified on the basis of its contributing more in added benefits than in added costs. Relevant costs and benefits for any decision are limited to those that are affected by it. Factors that are relevant to a managerial decision can be obscured by introducing extraneous cost information. To limit the confounding influence of irrelevant cost information, it is helpful to focus on the causal relation between costs and a given managerial decision, as well as on the reversible or nonreversible nature of some cost categories.

INCREMENTAL COST

Incremental Cost
Change in cost caused by a given managerial decision.

Incremental cost is the change in cost caused by a given managerial decision. Like marginal cost, the incremental cost concept plays an important role in the optimization process. The difference between the two concepts is that marginal cost is defined as the change in cost following a one-unit change in output, whereas incremental costs typically involve multiple units of output. For example, incremental costs are the relevant consideration when an air carrier considers the cost of adding an additional departure from New York's La Guardia Airport to upstate New York. When all current departures are full, it is impractical for the carrier to consider adding a single additional passenger-mile unit of output. Similarly, the incremental cost concept comes into play when judging the costs of adding a new product line, advertising campaign, production shift, or organization structure.

Inappropriate managerial decisions can result when the incremental concept is ignored or applied incorrectly. Consider, for example, a commercial real estate firm that refuses to rent excess office space for $750 per month because it figures cost as $1,000 per month—or incremental operating costs of $150 plus interest and overhead charges of $850. If the relevant incremental cost is indeed only $150 per month, turning away

Profit Contribution
Profit before fixed charges.

the prospective renter causes a $600 (= $750 − $150) per month loss in **profit contribution**, or profit before fixed charges. Interest and overhead charges will be incurred irrespective of whether the excess space is rented. By adding the prospective renter, the landlord has the same interest and overhead expenses as before, *plus* $600 in added revenues after incremental operating expenses. The net effect of rejecting such a renter would be to reduce profit contribution and net profits by $600.

Care must be also exercised to ensure against incorrectly assigning a lower than appropriate incremental cost. If excess capacity results from a temporary reduction in demand, this must be taken into account. Accepting the $750 per month renter in the

The ABCs of Cost Analysis

During the 1980s, companies found that antiquated accounting systems were leading them to charge too much or too little for their products. As managers raced to modernize their bookkeeping, they discovered an innovative system that helped them estimate manufacturing costs more accurately and manage their companies more effectively. This innovation in managerial and cost accounting is called activity-based costing, or ABC. Companies that have "gotten the ABC religion" are reaping rewards in terms of better product design and factory layouts. They are also using the new method to trim waste, improve service, evaluate quality initiatives, and push for continuous improvement.

Traditional accounting systems look at companies as huge machines made of components, or "departments" such as human resources, purchasing, or maintenance that operate together to make products or provide a service. By contrast, ABC sees businesses as an assembly of individuals that perform a wide variety of activities to satisfy customer demands. An important advantage of ABC is that it allows companies to more accurately decipher the variable component of overhead costs, and to allocate those variable costs to the appropriate activity tied to the production of a given product or service. This is an important consideration in modern manufacturing systems because hard-to-allocate variable overhead costs can run as much as 50%–75% of total charges in some industries.

At the heart of ABC is a detailed management information system that tracks the time spent by workers on specific activities. For example, in the material-control department, which buys factory components and fills customer orders, a customer service rep might spend 30% of the day taking orders and 50% processing them. Based upon that information, traditional expenses for fixed costs, supplies, salaries, and fringe benefit expenses were totaled and spread over each order. With ABC, workers in all areas of the plant define their basic activities. Then, the costs of each activity are assessed and prices are set to cover both direct and indirect variable costs. Both traditional and ABC accounting methods reach the same bottom line, but ABC permits accountants to charge costs to products much more accurately because it breaks down

variable overhead far more precisely than old-fashioned systems do.

For example, traditional accounting focuses on valuing a company's inventory for financial reporting purposes. To satisfy the Internal Revenue Service and shareholders, accountants take the cost of materials and add in direct labor. Then they compute allocated overhead from rent to R&D expenses, based on the number of direct labor hours it takes to make a product. To get "fully allocated" costs, accountants add direct costs to overhead costs per unit, computed according to the number of items made during the period under consideration. This system works fine when direct labor accounts for most of total costs and a company produces just a few products requiring the same processes. Most companies fit that description in the 1920s, when traditional cost accounting methods were first devised. Today, most companies run complex operations and offer a wide assortment of products. When a company makes a variety of products, it must finance and maintain large inventories. When production lines stop and restart to turn out different styles, costs for downtime and reprogramming production control machinery can skyrocket. Many companies are discovering that when customers demand specialized production, or a customized mix of goods and services, ABC is the only effective means for measuring and tracking cost.

The ability to make better product-mix and pricing decisions is only the most obvious benefit of employing ABC. If managers focus too narrowly on the cost estimation aspect of ABC, they run the risk of losing far greater potential benefits. The immense amount of information collected when creating an ABC database reveals a lot about how business processes operate. Smart managers can use this knowledge to make their processes faster, higher quality, and more efficient. Thus, ABC can become the cornerstone of a management information system vital to the competitive success of the company.

See: Srikumar S. Rao, "Overhead Can Kill You," *Forbes*, February 10, 1997, 97.

previous example might well be a mistake if doing so causes full-price and more profitable renters to be turned away. When excess capacity is caused by an unpredictable temporary drop in demand, only short-term or month-to-month leases should be offered at the bargain price of $750 per month. In this way, pricing flexibility can be maintained while the net cost of temporary excess capacity is minimized. In any event, all incremental costs, including those that might be incurred in the future, must be considered.

SUNK COSTS

Inherent in the incremental cost concept is the principle that any cost not affected by a decision is irrelevant to that decision. A cost that does not vary across decision alternatives is called a **sunk cost;** such costs do not play a role in determining the optimal course of action.

For example, suppose a firm has spent $5,000 on an option to purchase land for a new factory at a price of $100,000. Also assume that it is later offered an equally attractive site for $90,000. What should the firm do? The first thing to recognize is that the $5,000 spent on the purchase option is a sunk cost that must be ignored. To understand this, consider the firm's current decision alternatives. If the firm proceeds to purchase the first property, it must pay a price of $100,000. The newly offered property requires an expenditure of $90,000 and results in a $10,000 savings. In retrospect, purchase of the $5,000 option was a mistake. It would be a compounding of this initial error to follow through with purchase of the first property and lose an additional $10,000.

In managerial decision making, care must be taken to ensure that only those costs actually affected by a decision are considered. These incremental costs can include both implicit and explicit costs. If long-term commitments are involved, both current and future incremental costs must also be accounted for. Any costs not affected by available decision alternatives are sunk and irrelevant.

Sunk Cost
Cost that does not vary across decision alternatives.

Short-Run and Long-Run Costs

Cost Function
The cost-output relation.

Short-Run Cost Functions
Basis for day-to-day operating decisions.

Long-Run Cost Functions
Basis for long-range planning.

Short Run
Operating period during which at least one input is fixed.

Long Run
Planning period with complete input flexibility.

Proper use of relevant cost concepts requires an understanding of the relation between cost and output, or the **cost function.** Cost functions depend on the underlying production function and input prices. Production functions specify the technical relation between inputs and output and, when combined with input prices, determine cost functions. Two basic cost functions are used in managerial decision making: **short-run cost functions,** used for day-to-day operating decisions, and **long-run cost functions,** used for long-range planning.

HOW IS THE OPERATING PERIOD DEFINED?

The **short run** is the operating period during which the availability of at least one input is fixed. In the **long run,** the firm has complete flexibility with respect to input use. In the short run, operating decisions are typically constrained by prior capital expenditures. In the long run, no such restrictions exist. For example, a management consulting firm operating out of rented office space might have a short-run period as brief as several weeks, the time remaining on the office lease. In contrast, a firm in the hazardous waste disposal business with 25- to 30-year leases on disposal sites has significant long-lived assets and faces a lengthy period of operating constraints.

The economic life of an asset and the degree of specialization affect the time length of operating period constraints. Consider, for example, a health maintenance organization's (HMO) automobile purchase for making prescription deliveries. If the car is a standard model without modification, it represents an unspecialized input factor with a resale market based on the used car market in general. However, if the car has been modified by adding refrigeration equipment for transporting perishable medicines, it becomes a more specialized input with full value only for those who need a vehicle with refrigeration equipment. In this case, the market price of the car might not equal its value in use to the HMO; hence, the short run is extended. To the extent that specialized input factors are employed, the short run is lengthened. When only unspecialized factors are used, the short run becomes a very condensed period.

The amount of time required to order, receive, and install new assets also influences the duration of the short run. Many manufacturers face delays of several months when ordering new plant and equipment. Air carriers must place their equipment orders five or more *years* in advance with Boeing, McDonnell Douglas, and other airplane manufactures. Electric utilities frequently require eight or more *years* to bring new generating plants on line. For all such firms, the short-run operating period involves an extended amount of time.

In summary, the long run is a period of sufficient length to permit a complete change in productive facilities. The short run is a period during which at least some productive inputs cannot be altered. Long-run cost curves are called *planning curves;* short-run cost curves are called *operating curves.* In the long run, plant and equipment are variable, so management can plan the most efficient physical plant, given an estimate of the firm's demand function. Once the optimal plant has been determined and the resulting investment in equipment has been made, operating decisions will be constrained by these prior decisions.

FIXED AND VARIABLE COSTS

Fixed Cost
Expense that does not vary with output.

Fixed costs do not vary with output. These costs include interest expenses, rent on leased plant and equipment, depreciation charges associated with the passage of time, property taxes, and salaries for employees not laid off during periods of reduced activity. Since all costs are variable in the long run, long-run fixed costs always equal zero. The concept of fixed costs is applicable only in the short run. **Variable costs** fluctuate with output. Expenses for raw materials, depreciation associated with the use of equipment, the variable portion of utility charges, some labor costs, and sales commissions are all examples of variable expenses. In the short run, both variable and fixed costs are often incurred. In the long run, all costs are variable.

Variable Cost
Expense that fluctuates with output.

A sharp distinction between fixed and variable costs is not always possible nor realistic. For example, CEO and staff salaries may be largely fixed, but during severe business downturns, even CEOs take a pay cut. Similarly, salaries for line managers and supervisors are fixed only within certain output ranges. Below a lower limit, supervisors and managers would be laid off. Above an upper limit, additional supervisors and managers would be hired. The longer the duration of abnormal demand, the greater the likelihood that some fixed costs will actually vary. In recognition of this, such costs are sometimes referred to as *semivariable*.

Short-Run Cost Curves

Short-Run Cost Curve
Cost-output relation for a specific plant and operating environment.

A **short-run cost curve** shows the minimum cost impact of output changes for a specific plant size and in a given operating environment. Such curves reflect the optimal or least-cost input combination for producing output under fixed circumstances. Wage rates, interest rates, plant configuration, and all other operating conditions are held constant.

Any change in the operating environment leads to a *shift* in short-run cost curves. For example, a general rise in wage rates leads to an upward shift; a fall in wage rates leads to a downward shift. Such changes must not be confused with *movements along* a given short-run cost curve caused by a change in production levels. For an existing plant, the short-run cost curve illustrates the minimum cost of production at various output levels under current operating conditions. Short-run cost curves are a useful guide to operating decisions.

SHORT-RUN COST CATEGORIES

Both fixed and variable costs affect short-run costs. Total cost at each output level is the sum of total fixed costs (a constant) and total variable costs. Using TC to represent total cost, TFC for total fixed cost, TVC for total variable cost, and Q for the quantity of output produced, various unit costs are calculated as follows:

$$Total\ Cost = TC = TFC + TVC. \tag{8.1}$$

$$Average\ Fixed\ Cost = AFC = \frac{TFC}{Q}. \tag{8.2}$$

$$Average\ Variable\ Cost = AVC = \frac{TVC}{Q}. \tag{8.3}$$

$$Average\ Total\ Cost = ATC = \frac{TC}{Q} = AFC + AVC. \tag{8.4}$$

$$Marginal\ Cost = MC = \frac{\Delta TC}{\Delta Q}. \tag{8.5}$$

These cost categories are portrayed in Table 8.1. Using these data, it is possible to identify the various cost relations as well as to examine cost behavior. Table 8.1 shows that *AFC* declines continuously with increases in output. *ATC* and *AVC* also decline as long as they exceed *MC,* but they increase when they are less than *MC*. Alternatively, as long

Table 8.1

SHORT-RUN COST RELATIONS

Q	TC	TFC	TVC	ATC	AFC	AVC
1	$120	$100	$20	$120.0	$100.0	$20.0
2	138	100	38	69.0	50.0	19.0
3	151	100	51	50.3	33.3	17.0
4	162	100	62	40.5	25.0	15.5
5	175	100	75	35.0	20.0	15.0
6	190	100	90	31.7	16.7	15.0
7	210	100	110	30.0	14.3	15.7
8	234	100	134	29.3	12.5	16.8
9	263	100	163	29.2	11.1	18.1
10	300	100	200	30.0	10.0	20.0

as *MC* is less than *ATC* and *AVC,* both average cost categories will decline. When *MC* is greater than *ATC* and *AVC,* both average cost categories will rise. Also note that *TFC* is invariant with increases in output and that *TVC* at each level of output equals the sum of *MC* up to that output.

Marginal cost is the change in cost associated with a one-unit change in output. Because fixed costs do not vary with output, fixed costs do not affect marginal costs. Only variable costs affect marginal costs. Therefore, marginal costs equal the change in total costs *or* the change in total variable costs following a one-unit change in output:

$$MC = \frac{\Delta TC}{\Delta Q} = \frac{\Delta TVC}{\Delta Q}.$$

SHORT-RUN COST RELATIONS

The relations among short-run cost categories are shown in Figure 8.1. Figure 8.1(a) illustrates total cost and total variable cost curves. The shape of the total cost curve is determined entirely by the total variable cost curve. The slope of the total cost curve at each output level is identical to the slope of the total variable cost curve. Fixed costs merely shift the total cost curve to a higher level. This means that marginal costs are totally independent of fixed cost.

The shape of the total variable cost curve, and hence the shape of the total cost curve, is determined by the productivity of the variable input factors employed. The variable cost curve in Figure 8.1 increases at a decreasing rate up to output level Q_1, then at an increasing rate. Assuming constant input prices, this implies that the marginal productivity of variable inputs first increases, then decreases. Variable input factors exhibit increasing returns in the range from 0 to Q_1 units and show diminishing returns thereafter. This is a typical finding. Fixed plant and equipment are usually designed to operate at a target production level. Operating below the target output level results in some excess capacity. In the below-target output range, production can be increased

SHORT-RUN COST CURVES

Figure 8.1

(a) The productivity of variable input factors determines the slope of both the total and variable cost curves. An increase (decrease) in fixed costs shifts the total cost curve upward (downward), but it has no effect on variable cost curves. (b) Marginal cost declines to Q_1. Both average total cost and average variable costs fall (rise) when marginal cost is lower (higher).

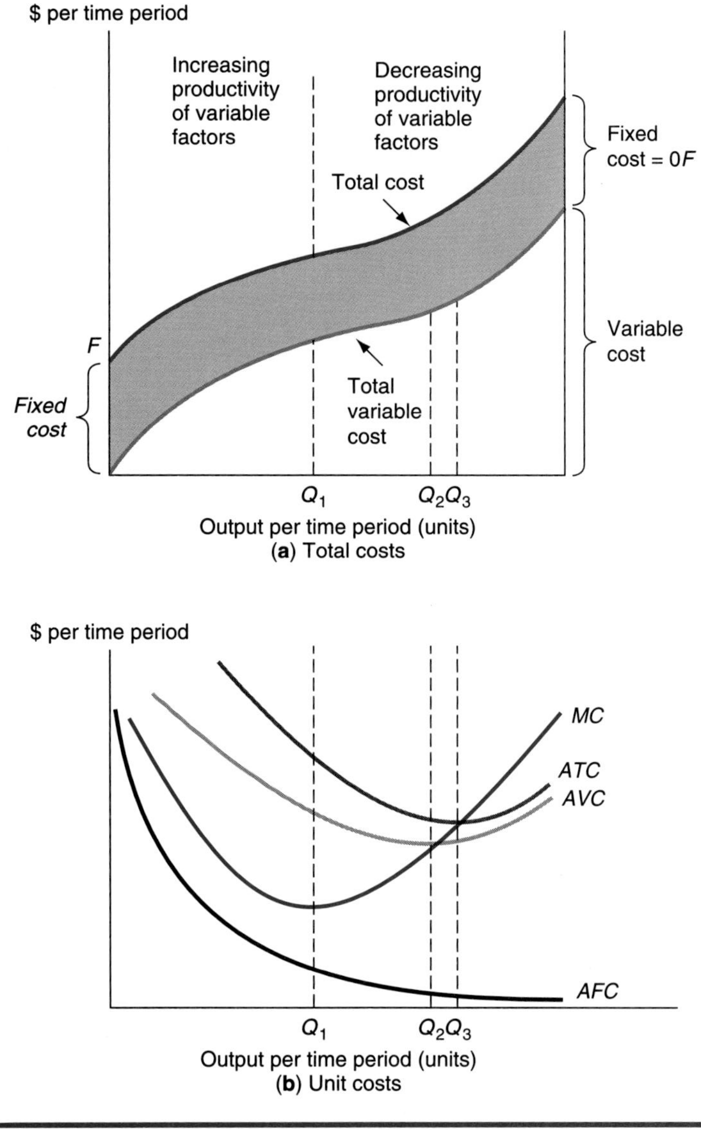

$ per time period

Increasing
productivity
of variable
factors

Decreasing
productivity
of variable
factors

Fixed
cost = 0F

Total cost

Variable
cost

F

Fixed
cost

Total
variable
cost

Q_1 Q_2Q_3

Output per time period (units)
(a) Total costs

$ per time period

MC

ATC
AVC

AFC

Q_1 Q_2Q_3

Output per time period (units)
(b) Unit costs

more than proportionately to increases in variable inputs. At above-target output levels, fixed factors are intensively used, and the law of diminishing returns takes over. There, a given percentage increase in variable inputs results in a smaller relative increase in output.

The relation between short-run costs and the productivity of variable input factors is also reflected by short-run unit cost curves, as shown in Figure 8.1(b). Marginal cost declines over the range of increasing productivity and rises thereafter. This imparts the familiar *U*-shape to average variable cost and average total cost curves. At first, marginal cost curves also typically decline rapidly in relation to the average variable cost curve and the average total cost curve. Near the target output level, the marginal cost curve turns up and intersects each of the *AVC* and *ATC* short-run curves at their respective minimum points.[3]

Long-Run Cost Curves

Long-Run Cost Curve
Cost-output relation for the optimal plant in the present operating environment.

In the long run, the firm has complete input flexibility. Therefore, all long-run costs are variable. A **long-run cost curve** shows the minimum cost impact of output changes for the optimal plant size in the present operating environment. Such curves reflect the optimal or least-cost input combination for producing output assuming an *ideal* input selection. As in the case of short-run cost curves, wage rates, interest rates, plant configuration, and all other operating conditions are held constant. Any change in the operating environment leads to a shift in long-run cost curves. For example, product inventions and process improvements that occur over time cause a downward *shift* in long-run cost curves. Such changes must not be confused with *movements along* a given long-run cost curve caused by changes in the output level. Long-run cost curves reveal the nature of returns to scale and optimal plant sizes. They are a helpful guide to planning decisions.

LONG-RUN TOTAL COSTS

If input prices are not affected by the amount purchased, a *direct* relation exists between cost and production functions. A production function that exhibits constant returns to scale is linear, and doubling inputs leads to doubled output. With constant input prices, doubling inputs doubles total cost and results in a linear total cost function. If increasing returns to scale are present, output doubles with less than a doubling of inputs and total cost. If production is subject to decreasing returns to scale, inputs and total cost must more than double to cause a twofold increase in output. A production function exhibiting first increasing and then decreasing returns to scale is illustrated, along with its implied cubic cost function, in Figure 8.2. Here, costs increase less than proportionately with output over the range in which returns to scale are increasing but at more than a proportionate rate after decreasing returns set in.

---

[3]Relations among total, average, and marginal curves are discussed in greater detail in Chapter 2.

Figure 8.2

TOTAL COST FUNCTION FOR A PRODUCTION SYSTEM EXHIBITING INCREASING, THEN DECREASING, RETURNS TO SCALE

With increasing returns to scale, total cost rises slower than total output. With decreasing returns to scale, total cost rises faster than total output. Total cost functions often display an S-shape, reflecting varying returns to scale at various activity levels.

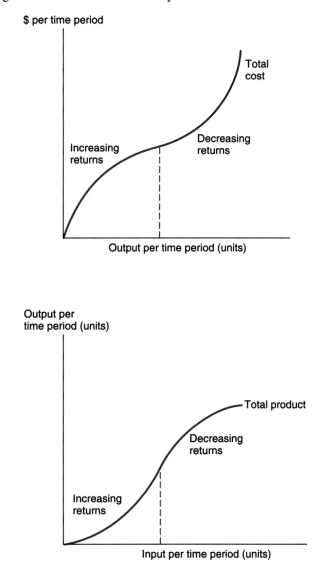

The direct relations between production and cost functions illustrated to this point are based on constant input prices. If input prices are a function of output, cost functions will reflect this relationship. Large-volume discounts can lower unit costs as output rises, just as costs rise with the need to pay higher wages to attract additional workers at high output levels. The cost function for a firm facing constant returns to scale but rising input prices as output expands takes the shape shown in Figure 8.3. Costs rise more than proportionately as output increases. Quantity discounts, however, produce a cost function that increases at a decreasing rate, as in the increasing returns section of Figure 8.2.

Although cost and production are clearly related, the nature of input prices must be examined before any cost function can be related to the underlying production function. Input prices and productivity jointly determine cost functions.

RETURNS TO SCALE

Economies of Scale
Decreasing long-run
average costs.

Many factors combine to produce the frequently encountered pattern of first increasing, then constant, then decreasing returns to scale. Increasing returns, or **economies of scale,** which originate from production and market-related sources, cause long-run average costs to decline. Labor specialization often gives rise to economies of scale. In small firms, workers generally do several jobs, and proficiency sometimes suffers from a lack of specialization. Labor productivity can be higher in large firms, where individuals are hired to perform specific tasks. This can reduce unit costs for large-scale operations.

Technical factors can also lead to economies of scale. Large-scale operation permits the use of highly specialized equipment, as opposed to the more versatile but less efficient machines used in smaller firms. Also, the productivity of equipment frequently increases with size much faster than its cost. A 500,000-kilowatt electricity generator costs considerably less than two 250,000-kilowatt generators, and it also requires less fuel and labor when operated at capacity. Quantity discounts give rise to money-related pecuniary economies through large-scale purchasing of raw materials, supplies, and other inputs. These economies extend to the cost of capital when large firms have greater access to capital markets and can acquire funds at lower rates.

At some output level, economies of scale are typically exhausted, and average costs level out or begin to rise. Increasing average costs at high output levels are often attributed to limitations in the ability of management to coordinate large-scale organizations. Staff overhead also tends to grow more than proportionately with output, again raising unit costs. The trend toward small to medium-sized businesses during the 1980s and 1990s indicates that diseconomies do indeed limit firm sizes in many industries.

COST ELASTICITIES AND RETURNS TO SCALE

Cost Elasticity
Percentage change in total
cost associated with a 1%
change in output.

Figure 8.2 is useful for illustrating the total returns to scale concept. Still, it is often easier to calculate scale economies for a given production system by considering cost elasticities. **Cost elasticity,** ϵ_C measures the percentage change in total cost associated with a 1% change in output.

Algebraically, the elasticity of cost with respect to output is

$$\epsilon_C = \frac{Percentage\ Change\ in\ Total\ Cost\ (TC)}{Percentage\ Change\ in\ Output\ (Q)}$$

$$= \frac{\Delta TC/TC}{\Delta Q/Q}$$

$$= \frac{\Delta TC}{\Delta Q} \times \frac{Q}{TC}.$$

Cost elasticity is related to economies of scale as follows:

IF	THEN	RETURNS TO SCALE ARE
Percentage change in TC < Percentage change in Q,	$\epsilon_C < 1.$	Increasing.
Percentage change in TC = Percentage change in Q,	$\epsilon_C = 1.$	Constant.
Percentage change in TC > Percentage change in Q,	$\epsilon_C > 1.$	Decreasing.

With a cost elasticity of less than one ($\epsilon_C < 1$), costs increase at a slower rate than output. Given constant input prices, this implies higher output-to-input ratios and increasing returns to scale. If $\epsilon_C = 1$, output and costs increase proportionately, implying constant returns to scale. Finally, if $\epsilon_C > 1$, for any increase in output, costs increase by a greater relative amount, implying decreasing returns to scale. To prevent confusion concerning cost elasticity and returns to scale, remember that an inverse relation holds between costs and scale economies and a direct relation holds between resource usage and scale economies. Thus, although $\epsilon_C < 1$ implies increasing returns to scale, because costs are increasing more slowly than output, recall from Chapter 7 that an output elasticity greater than 1 ($\epsilon_Q > 1$) implies increasing returns to scale, because output is increasing faster than input usage. Similarly, decreasing returns to scale are implied by $\epsilon_C > 1$ and by $\epsilon_Q < 1$.

LONG-RUN AVERAGE COSTS

Additional insight into scale economies and the relation between long-run and short-run costs is obtained by examining long-run average cost ($LRAC$) curves. Short-run cost curves relate costs and output for a specific scale of plant, whereas long-run cost curves identify optimal scales of plant for each production level. $LRAC$ curves can be thought of as an envelope of short-run average cost ($SRAC$) curves. This concept is illustrated in Figure 8.3, which shows four short-run average cost curves representing four different scales of plant. Each of the four plants has a range of output over which it is most efficient. Plant A, for example, provides the least-cost production system for output in the range 0 to Q_1 units; Plant B provides the least-cost system for output in the range Q_1 to Q_2; Plant C is most efficient for output quantities Q_2 to Q_3; and Plant D provides the least-cost production process for output above Q_3.

The solid portion of each curve in Figure 8.3 indicates the minimum long-run average cost for producing each level of output, assuming only four possible scales of plant. This can be generalized by assuming that plants of many sizes are possible, each only slightly larger than the preceding one. As shown in Figure 8.4, the long-run average cost curve is then constructed tangent to each short-run average cost curve. At each point of tangency, the related scale of plant is optimal; no other plant can produce that particular level of output at so low a total cost. Cost systems illustrated in Figures 8.3 and 8.4 display first increasing, then decreasing returns to scale. Over the range of output produced by Plants *A, B,* and *C* in Figure 8.3, average costs are declining; these declining costs mean that total costs are increasing less than proportionately with output. Since Plant *D*'s minimum cost is greater than that for Plant *C*, the system exhibits decreasing returns to scale at this higher output level.

Production systems that reflect first increasing, then constant, then diminishing returns to scale result in U-shaped long-run average cost curves such as the one illustrated in Figure 8.4. With a U-shaped long-run average cost curve, the most efficient plant for each output level is typically not operating at the point where short-run average costs are minimized, as can be seen in Figure 8.3. Plant *A*'s short-run average cost curve is minimized at Point *M*, but at that output level, Plant *B* is more efficient; *B*'s short-run average costs are lower. In general, when returns to scale are increasing, the least-cost

---

Figure 8.3

SHORT-RUN COST CURVES FOR FOUR SCALES OF PLANT

Short-run cost curves represent the most efficient range of output for a given plant size. The solid portion of each *SRAC* curve indicates the minimum long-run average cost for each level of output.

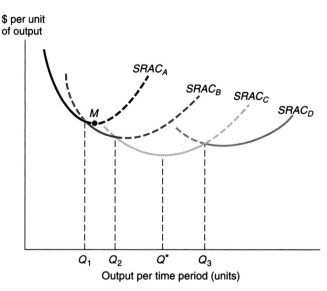

Figure 8.4

LONG-RUN AVERAGE COST CURVE AS THE ENVELOPE OF SHORT-RUN AVERAGE COST CURVES

The long-run average cost curve is the envelope of short-run average cost curves. The optimal scale for a plant is found at the point of minimum long-run average costs.

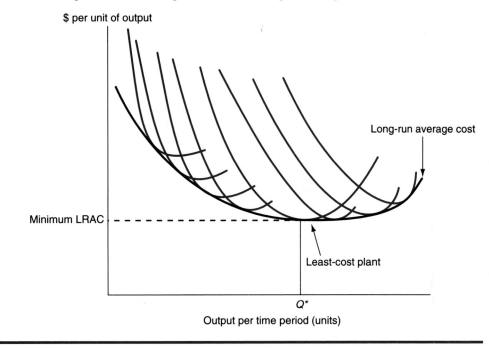

Capacity
Output level at which short-run average costs are minimized.

plant will operate at less than full capacity. Here, **capacity** refers not to a physical limitation on output but rather to the point at which short-run average costs are minimized. Only for that single output level at which long-run average cost is minimized (output Q^* in Figures 8.3 and 8.4) is the optimal plant operating at the minimum point on its short-run average cost curve. At any output level greater than Q^*, decreasing returns to scale prevail, and the most efficient plant is operating at an output level slightly greater than capacity.

Minimum Efficient Scale

The shape of long-run average cost curves is important not only because of implications for plant scale decisions but also because of effects on the potential level of competition. Even though U-shaped cost relations are quite common, they are not universal. In some industries, firms encounter first increasing, then constant returns to scale. In such

What'n Heck Is a FASB?

The Financial Accounting Standards Board (FASB) is a nongovernmental body empowered by the Securities and Exchange Commission with responsibility for determining the nature and scope of accounting information. Started in 1973 as the logical successor to the accounting profession's Accounting Principles Board, the FASB develops new accounting standards in an elaborate process that reflects the views of accountants, business executives, security analysts, and the public. As a result, the FASB plays a key role in defining the specific information that must be incorporated in published corporate financial statements. FASB provides essential input concerning the framework for accounting balance sheets that define the current financial status of a company ("where it is"), and for accounting income statements that show changes in a company's financial performance ("where it is going"). By standardizing the content and format of such reports, FASB helps investors better monitor their investments.

The FASB is also instrumental in the resolution of a broad range of important and controversial accounting issues. For example, the FASB plays a key role in the debate over accounting policy issues, including the controversy on whether to require firms to use current market values rather than historical-cost book values for accounts receivables, bonds, and intangible assets like brand names and patents. This is a highly controversial issue, because the market-value approach would lead to a much different picture of corporate assets and liabilities for many companies.

Corporate executives typically resist the FASB's efforts to install new accounting rules, citing the higher operating expenses sometimes required to meet new guidelines. Most new standards require the capture of new data or the reworking of existing accounting information. At times, however, more subtle unspoken interests may be responsible for corporate opposition to new FASB standards. During inflationary periods, as has been the case in the United States since World War II, the use of historical book values tends to overstate net income numbers, and to understate the value of tangible plant and equipment. As a result, reported profit rates, such as the key return-on-stockholders'-equity measure, can be inflated when book-value data are used. Because of the effects of inflation, a market-value standard provides a more economically meaningful picture of "true" corporate profitability, but it typically results in lower profit rates. The fact that a market-value standard lowers reported profits is an important concern to many executives, especially those with compensation plans tied to reported profits.

One of the most important accounting innovations promoted by the FASB during recent years involves the cash-flow statements that all companies are now required to provide. By minimizing distortions that are sometimes introduced by imperfect accrual accounting methods, cash-flow data are intended to provide a clearer picture of current corporate performance. Needless to say, many corporations oppose cash-flow reporting requirements, especially when meeting them causes perceived (reported) performance to falter.

On Wall Street, some observers view ongoing disputes between the FASB and the corporate community on the accounting treatment of executive stock options, for example, as being based on a rather myopic view of the information-processing capability of both professional and institutional investors. Clearly, the takeover and corporate restructuring boom of the late 1980s was based on a sophisticated awareness of corporate cash flows, an awareness that preceded FASB cash-flow reporting requirements. Still, cash-flow statements help individual investors by providing them with another low-cost basis for evaluating corporate performance, while new reporting requirements allow investors to determine the economic impact of executive stock-option grants.

Given the wide range of important accounting issues being addressed, the role played by the FASB has grown steadily. At times, the public perception of the FASB has failed to match this pace. This is changing as the FASB's public visibility increases. FASB-inspired guidelines allow companies to report assets and incomes that are closer to real economic values. For investors, more detailed disclosure of income, assets, and liabilities are an important benefit of standardized accounting rules.

See: Phillip L. Zweig, "Corporate America Is Fed Up With FASB," *Business Week,* April 21, 1997, 108–110.

instances, an L-shaped long-run average cost curve emerges, and very large plants are at no relative cost disadvantage compared with smaller plants. The number of competitors and ease of entry is typically greater in industries with U-shaped long-run average cost curves than in those with L-shaped or continuously downward-sloping long-run average cost curves. Insight on the competitive implications of cost/output relations can be gained by considering the minimum efficient scale concept.

COMPETITIVE IMPLICATIONS OF MINIMUM EFFICIENT SCALE

Minimum Efficient Scale
Output level at which long-run average costs are minimized.

Minimum efficient scale (MES) is the output level at which long-run average costs are minimized. Thus, MES is at the minimum point on a U-shaped long-run average cost curve (output Q^* in Figures 8.3 and 8.4) and at the corner of an L-shaped long-run average cost curve.

Generally speaking, the number of competitors is large and competition is vigorous when MES is low relative to total industry demand. This fact follows from the correspondingly low barriers to entry from capital investment and skilled labor requirements. Competition can be less vigorous when MES is large relative to total industry output, because barriers to entry tend to be correspondingly high and can limit the number of potential competitors. When considering the competitive impact of MES, industry size must always be considered. Some industries are large enough to accommodate substantial numbers of very large competitors. In such instances, even though MES is large in an absolute sense, it can be quite small in a relative sense and can allow vigorous competition.

When the cost disadvantage of operating plants that are of less than MES size is relatively small, there will seldom be serious anticompetitive consequences. The somewhat higher production costs of small producers can be overcome by superior customer service and regional location to cut transport costs and delivery lags. In such instances, statistically significant advantages to large-scale operation have little economic relevance. Therefore, the barrier-to-entry effects of MES depend on the size of MES relative to total industry demand *and* the slope of the long-run average cost curve at points of less-than-MES-size operations. Both must be considered.

TRANSPORTATION COSTS AND MES

Transportation costs play an important role in determining the efficient scale of operation. Transportation costs include terminal, line-haul, and inventory charges associated with moving output from production facilities to customers. Terminal charges consist of handling expenses necessary for loading and unloading shipped materials. Since terminal charges do not vary with the distance of shipment, they are as high for short hauls as for long hauls.

Line-haul expenses include equipment, labor, and fuel costs associated with moving a given commodity a specified distance. They vary directly with the distance shipped. Although line-haul expenses are relatively constant on a per mile basis, they vary widely from one commodity to another. It costs more to ship a ton of fresh fruit 500 miles than to ship a ton of coal a similar distance. Fresh fruit comes in odd shapes and sizes and requires more container space than a product like coal, which can be compactly loaded. Any product that is perishable, fragile, or particularly susceptible to theft (e.g., consumer electronics, cigarettes, liquor) has high line-haul expenses because of greater equipment, insurance, and labor costs.

Finally, there is an inventory cost component to transportation costs related to the time element involved in shipping goods. The time required for transit is extremely important because slower modes such as railroads and barges delay the receipt of sale proceeds from customers. Even though out-of-pocket expenses are greater, air cargo or motor carrier shipment can reduce the total economic costs of transportation because of their greater speed in delivery.

Transportation costs play an important role in determining optimal plant sizes. As more output is produced at a given plant, it becomes necessary to reach out to more distant customers. This can lead to increased transportation costs per unit sold. Figure 8.5 illustrates an L-shaped long-run average cost curve reflecting average production costs that first decline and then become nearly constant. Assuming relatively modest terminal and inventory costs, greater line-haul expenses cause transportation costs per unit to increase at a relatively constant rate. Before transportation costs, Q_A^* represents the MES plant size. Including transportation expenses, the MES plant size falls to Q_B^*. In general, as transportation costs become increasingly important, MES will fall. In the extreme,

Figure 8.5

EFFECT OF TRANSPORTATION COSTS ON OPTIMAL PLANT SIZE

High transportation costs reduce the *MES* plant size from Q_A^* to Q_B^*. As transportation costs rise relative to production costs, *MES* plant size will fall.

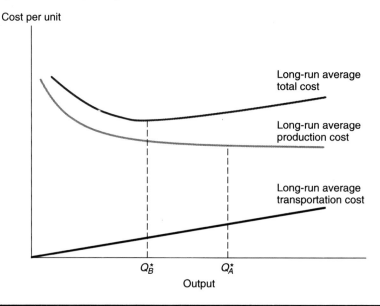

when transportation costs are large in relation to production costs, as is the case with milk, bottled soft drinks, gravel, cement, and many other products with high weight-to-value (or bulk-to-value) ratios, even small, relatively inefficient production facilities can be profitable when located near important markets. In contrast, when transportation costs are relatively insignificant—as is the case for relatively low-weight, compact, high-value products such as writing pens, electronic components, and medical instruments—markets are national or international in scope, and increasing returns to scale cause output to be produced at only a few large plants.

Firm Size and Plant Size

Production and cost functions exist at the level of the individual plant and, for multiplant firms, at the level of the entire firm. The cost function for a multiplant firm can be the sum of the cost functions for individual plants. It can also be greater or less than this figure. For this reason, it becomes important to examine the relative importance of economies of scale that arise within production facilities, intraplant economies, and those that arise between and among plants, or multiplant economies of scale.

MULTIPLANT ECONOMIES AND DISECONOMIES OF SCALE

Multiplant Economies of Scale
Cost advantages from operating multiple facilities in the same line of business or industry.

Multiplant Diseconomies of Scale
Cost disadvantages from managing multiple facilities in the same line of business or industry.

Multiplant economies of scale are cost advantages that arise from operating multiple facilities in the same line of business or industry. Conversely, **multiplant diseconomies of scale** are cost disadvantages that arise from managing multiple facilities in the same line of business or industry.

To illustrate, assume a U-shaped long-run average cost curve for a given plant, as shown in Figure 8.4. If demand is sufficiently large, the firm will employ N plants, each of optimal size and producing Q^* units of output. In this case, what is the shape of the firm's long-run average cost curve? Figure 8.6 shows three possibilities. Each possible long-run average cost curve has important implications for the minimum efficient firm size, Q_F^*. First, the long-run average cost curve can be L-shaped, as in Figure 8.6(a), if no economies or diseconomies result from combining plants. Second, costs could decline throughout the entire range of output, as in (b), if multiplant firms are more efficient than single-plant firms. When they exist, such cases are caused by economies of multiplant operation. For example, all plants may use a central billing service, a common purchasing or distribution network, centralized management, and so on. The third possibility, shown in (c), is that costs first decline beyond Q^*, the output of the most efficient plant, and then begin to rise. In this case, multiplant economies of scale dominate initially, but they are later overwhelmed by the higher costs of coordinating many operating units.

All three shapes of cost curves shown in Figure 8.6 are found in the U.S. economy. Since optimal plant and firm sizes are identical only when multiplant economies are negligible, the magnitude of both influences must be carefully considered in evaluating

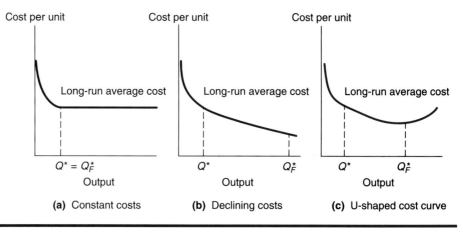

THREE POSSIBLE LONG-RUN AVERAGE COST CURVES FOR A MULTIPLANT FIRM

(a) Constant costs characterize a multiplant facility that has neither economies nor diseconomies of scale. **(b)** Average costs decline if a multiplant firm is more efficient than a single-plant firm. **(c)** The average costs of operating several plants can eventually rise when coordinating costs overcome multiplant economies.

the effect of scale economies. Both intraplant and multiplant economies can have an important impact on minimum efficient firm size.

THE ECONOMICS OF MULTIPLANT OPERATION: AN EXAMPLE

An example can help clarify the relation between firm size and plant size as well as the important minimum efficient scale concept. Consider Plainfield Electronics, a New Jersey-based company that manufactures a line of large industrial control panels for a national market. Currently, the firm's production is consolidated at a single Eastern-seaboard facility. Because of growth in demand for the firm's products, a multiplant alternative to centralized production is being considered. Estimated demand, marginal revenue, and *single-plant* production plus transportation cost curves for the firm are as follows:

$$P = \$940 - \$0.02Q.$$

$$MR = \frac{\Delta TR}{\Delta Q} = \$940 - \$0.04Q.$$

$$TC = \$250{,}000 + \$40Q + \$0.01Q^2.$$

$$MC = \frac{\Delta TC}{\Delta Q} = \$40 + \$0.02Q.$$

Plainfield's total profit function is

$$\pi = TR - TC$$

$$= P \times Q - TC$$

$$= (\$940 - \$0.02Q)Q - \$250{,}000 - \$40Q - \$0.01Q^2$$

$$= -\$0.03Q^2 + \$900Q - \$250{,}000.$$

The profit-maximizing activity level with centralized production is identified by locating the output level at which $M\pi = MR - MC = 0$ and, therefore, $MR = MC$.

Setting marginal revenue equal to marginal cost and solving for the related output quantity gives

$$MR = MC$$

$$\$940 - \$0.04Q = \$40Q + \$0.02Q$$

$$\$0.06Q = \$900$$

$$Q = 15{,}000.$$

At $Q = 15{,}000$,

$$P = \$940 - \$0.02Q$$

$$= \$940 - \$0.02(15{,}000)$$

$$= \$640,$$

and

$$\pi = -\$0.03(15{,}000)^2 + \$900(15{,}000) - \$250{,}000$$

$$= \$6{,}500{,}000.$$

Therefore, profits are maximized at the $Q = 15{,}000$ output level under the assumption of centralized production. At that activity level, $MC = MR = \$640$, and $M\pi = 0$.

To gain insight regarding the possible advantages of operating multiple smaller plants as opposed to one large centralized production facility, the average cost function for a single plant must be examined. To simplify matters, assume that multiplant production is possible under the same cost conditions described previously. That is, over the range of reasonable plant-size options, the firm's individual plant cost functions are the same with either single or multiplant operations. Also assume that there are no other multiplant economies or diseconomies of scale with which to contend.

The activity level at which average cost is minimized is found by setting marginal cost equal to average cost and solving for Q:

$$AC = TC/Q$$

$$= (\$250{,}000 + \$40Q + \$0.01Q^2)/Q$$

$$= \$250{,}000Q^{-1} + \$40 + \$0.01Q$$

and

$$MC = AC$$

$$\$40 + \$0.02Q = \$250{,}000Q^{-1} + \$40 + \$0.01Q$$

$$250{,}000Q^{-1} = 0.01Q$$

$$Q^2 = \frac{250{,}000}{0.01}$$

$$Q = \sqrt{25{,}000{,}000}$$

$$= 5{,}000.$$

Average cost is minimized at an output level of 5,000. This output level is the minimum efficient plant scale. Since the average cost-minimizing output level of 5,000 is far less than the single-plant profit-maximizing activity level of 15,000 units, the profit-maximizing level of total output occurs at a point of rising average costs. Assuming centralized production, Plainfield would maximize profits at an activity level of $Q = 15{,}000$ rather than $Q = 5{,}000$ because market-demand conditions are such that, despite the higher costs experienced at $Q = 15{,}000$, the firm can profitably supply output up to that level. Profit maximization requires consideration of both revenue and cost conditions.

Since centralized production maximized profits at an activity level well beyond that at which average cost is minimized, Plainfield has an opportunity to reduce costs and increase profits by adopting the multiplant alternative. Although the single-plant $Q = 15{,}000$ profit-maximizing activity level and the $Q = 5{,}000$ average cost-minimizing activity level might suggest that multiplant production at three facilities is optimal, this is incorrect. Profits were maximized at $Q = 15{,}000$ under the assumption of centralized production because at that activity level both marginal revenue and marginal cost equal \$340. However, with multiplant production and each plant operating at the $Q = 5{,}000$ activity level, marginal cost will be lowered and multiplant production will entail a new, higher profit-maximizing activity level. At $Q = 5{,}000$,

$$MC = \$40 + \$0.02Q$$

$$= \$40 + \$0.02(5{,}000)$$

$$= \$140.$$

With multiple plants all operating at 5,000 units per year, $MC = \$140$. Therefore, it is profitable to expand production as long as the marginal revenue obtained exceeds this minimum $MC = \$140$. This assumes, of course, that each production facility is operating at the optimal activity level of $Q = 5{,}000$ per plant.

The optimal multiplant activity level for the firm, assuming optimal production levels of $Q = 5{,}000$ at multiple plants, can be calculated by equating MR to the multiplant $MC = \$140$:

$$MR = \$140 = MC$$

$$\$940 - \$0.04Q = \$140$$

$$\$0.04Q = \$800$$

$$Q = 20{,}000.$$

Given optimal multiplant production of 20,000 units and average cost-minimizing activity levels of 5,000 units for each plant, multiplant production at four facilities is suggested:

$$\text{Optimal Number of Plants} = \frac{\text{Optimal Multiplant Activity Level}}{\text{Optimal Production per Plant}}$$

$$= \frac{20{,}000}{5{,}000}$$

$$= 4.$$

At $Q = 20{,}000$,

$$P = \$940 - \$0.02(20{,}000)$$

$$= \$540,$$

and

$$\pi = TR - TC$$

$$= P \times Q - 4 \times TC \text{ per plant}$$

$$= \$540(20{,}000) - 4[\$250{,}000 + \$40(5{,}000) + \$0.01(5{,}000^2)]$$

$$= \$8{,}000{,}000.$$

Given these cost relations, multiplant production is much more preferable to the centralized production alternative because it results in maximum profits that are $1.5 million larger. As shown in Figure 8.7, this follows from the firm's ability to concentrate production at the minimum point on the single-plant U-shaped average cost curve.

The multiplant cost advantages indicated in this example could stem from a variety of factors. One possibility, given that Plainfield's product is a large, heavy industrial control panel, is transportation cost savings from regional rather than centralized production. The role of distribution costs can be significant for industries in which final-product transport costs are large relative to production costs.

Finally, it is important to recognize that the optimal multiplant activity level of 20,000 units described in this example is based on the assumption that each production facility produces exactly 5,000 units of output and, therefore, $MC = \$140$. Marginal

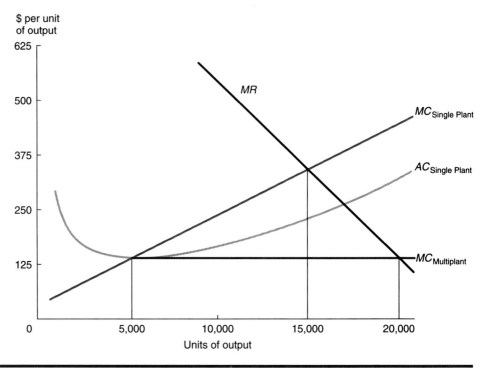

Figure 8.7

PLAINFIELD ELECTRONICS: SINGLE VERSUS MULTIPLANT OPERATION

In this example, profit is maximized at a production level well beyond that at which average cost is minimized for a single plant. Profits are greater with four plants because output can then be produced at minimum cost.

cost will equal only $140 when $Q = 5,000$ or some round multiple thereof (e.g., $Q = 10,000$ from two plants, $Q = 15,000$ from three plants, and so on). The optimal multiplant activity-level calculation is somewhat more complicated when this assumption is not met. Plainfield could not produce $Q = 21,000$ at $MC = \$140$. For an output level in the 20,000 to 25,000 range, it is necessary to equate marginal revenue with the marginal cost of each plant at its optimal activity level. This reemphasizes the point that determination of the optimal multiplant activity level always depends on the comparison of relevant marginal revenues and marginal costs.

PLANT SIZE AND FLEXIBILITY

Is the plant that can produce a given output at the lowest possible cost the optimal plant for producing that expected level of output? Not necessarily. Consider the following situation. Although actual demand for a product is uncertain, it is expected to be 5,000 units per year. Two possible probability distributions for this demand are given in Figure 8.8. Distribution *L* exhibits a low degree of variability in demand, and Distribution *H* indicates substantially higher variation in possible demand levels.

Now suppose that two plants can be employed to produce the required output. Plant *A* is quite specialized and is geared to produce a specified output at a low cost per unit. If, however, more or less than the specified output is produced (in this case 5,000 units), unit production costs rise rapidly. Plant *B*, on the other hand, is more flexible. Output can be expanded or contracted without excessive cost penalties, but unit costs are not as low as those of Plant *A* at the optimal output level. These two cases are shown in Figure 8.9.

Plant *A* is more efficient than Plant *B* between 4,500 and 5,500 units of output; outside this range, *B* has lower costs. Which plant should be selected? The answer depends on relative cost differentials at different output levels and the probability distribution for demand. The firm should make its plant-size decision on the basis of the level and variability of expected average total costs. If the demand probability distribution with low variation, Distribution *L*, is correct, the more specialized facility is optimal. If probability Distribution *H* more correctly describes the demand situation, the lower minimum cost of more specialized facilities is more than offset by the possibility of very high costs of producing outside the 4,500- to 5,500-unit range. Plant *B* could then have lower expected costs or a more attractive combination of expected costs and potential variation.

PROBABILITY DISTRIBUTIONS OF DEMAND

Distribution *L* has a low degree of variability from the expected demand level. Distribution *H* varies substantially from the expected demand level.

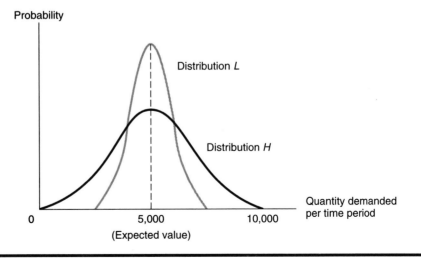

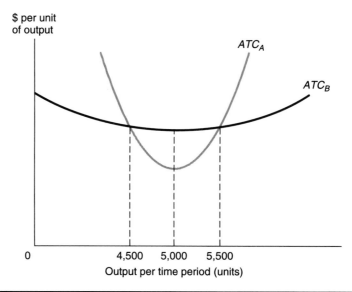

Figure 8.9

ALTERNATIVE PLANTS FOR PRODUCTION OF EXPECTED 5,000 UNITS OF OUTPUT

Unit costs are lower for Plant *A* than for Plant *B* between 4,500 and 5,500 units of output. Outside this range, Plant *B* has lower unit costs.

Learning Curves

For many manufacturing processes, average costs decline substantially as *cumulative total output* increases. This results as both management and labor become more knowledgeable about production techniques and their experience levels increase. Improvements in the use of production equipment and procedures are important in this process, as are reduced waste from defects and reduced labor requirements as workers become more proficient in their jobs.

THE LEARNING CURVE CONCEPT

Learning Curve
Average cost reduction over time due to production experience.

When knowledge gained from manufacturing experience is used to improve production methods so that output is produced with increasing efficiency, the resulting decline in average costs is said to reflect the effects of the firm's **learning curve.** The learning curve or experience curve phenomenon affects average costs in a way similar to that for any technical advance that improves productive efficiency. Both involve a downward shift in the long-run average cost curve at all levels of output. Learning through production experience permits the firm to produce output more efficiently at each and every output level.

To illustrate, consider Figure 8.10, which shows hypothetical long-run average cost curves for periods t and $t + 1$. With increased knowledge about production methods gained through the experience of producing Q_t units in period t, long-run average costs have declined for every output level in period $t + 1$, which means that Q_t units could be produced during period $t + 1$ at an average cost of B rather than the earlier cost of C. The learning curve cost savings is BC. If output were expanded from Q_t to Q_{t+1} between these periods, average costs would fall from C to A. This decline in average costs reflects both the learning curve effect, BC, and the effect of economies of scale, AB.

To isolate the effect of learning or experience on average cost, it is necessary to identify carefully that portion of average-cost changes over time that is due to other factors. One of the most important of these changes is the effect of economies of scale. As seen before, the change in average costs experienced between periods t and $t + 1$ can reflect the effects of both learning and economies of scale. This is a typical situation. Similarly, the effects of important technical breakthroughs, causing a downward shift in *LRAC* curves, and input-cost inflation, causing an upward shift in *LRAC* curves, must be constrained to examine learning curve characteristics. Only when output scale, technology, and input prices are all held constant can the learning curve relation be accurately represented.

LONG-RUN AVERAGE COST CURVE EFFECTS OF LEARNING

Learning will cause a downward shift from $LRAC_t$ to $LRAC_{t+1}$. An average cost decline from C to A reflects the effects of both learning and economies of scale.

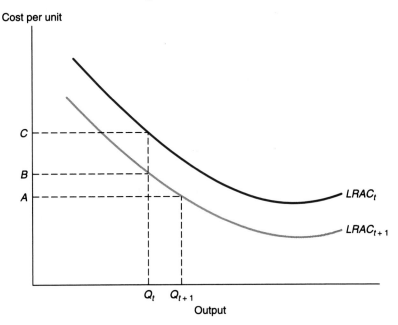

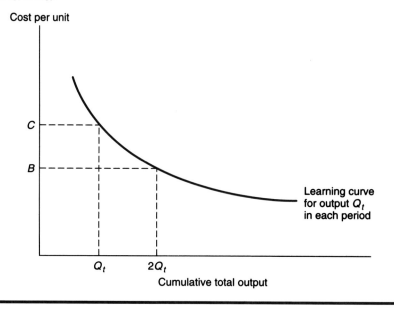

| Figure 8.11 |

LEARNING CURVE OF AN ARITHMETIC SCALE

The learning curve reflects the percentage decline in average cost as total cumulative output doubles from Q_t to $2Q_t$.

Figure 8.11 depicts the learning curve relation suggested by Figure 8.10. Note that learning results in dramatic average cost reductions at low total production levels, but it generates increasingly modest savings at higher cumulative production levels. This reflects the fact that many improvements in production methods become quickly obvious and are readily adopted. Later gains often come more slowly and are less substantial.

A LEARNING CURVE EXAMPLE

Given this typical shape of the learning curve relation, the learning curve, or experience curve, phenomenon is often characterized as a constant percentage decline in average costs as cumulative output increases. This percentage represents the proportion by which unit costs decline as the cumulative quantity of total output doubles. Suppose, for example, that average costs per unit for a new product were $100 during 1995 but fell to $90 during 1996. Furthermore, assume that average costs are in constant dollars, reflecting an accurate adjustment for input-price inflation and an identical basic technology being used in production. Given equal output in each period to ensure that the effects of economies of scale are not incorporated in the data, the learning or experience rate, defined as the percentage by which average cost falls as output doubles, is the following:

$$\text{Learning Rate} = \left(1 - \frac{AC_2}{AC_1}\right) \times 100$$

$$= \left(1 - \frac{\$90}{\$100}\right) \times 100$$

$$= 10\%$$

Thus, as *cumulative* total output doubles, average cost is expected to fall by 10%. If annual production is projected to remain constant, it will take two additional years for cumulative output to double again. One would project that average unit costs will decline to $81 (90% of $90) in 1998. Since cumulative total output at that time will equal four years' production, at a constant annual rate, output will again double by 2002. At that time, the learning curve will have reduced average costs to $72.90 (90% of $81).

Because of the frequency with which one finds the learning curve concept described as a cause of economies of scale, it is worth repeating that although related, the two are distinct concepts. Scale economies relate to cost differences associated with different output levels during a single production period. They are specified in terms of the cost output relation measured *along* a single *LRAC* curve. Learning curves relate cost differences to total cumulative output for a product. They are measured in terms of *shifts* in *LRAC* curves over time. These shifts result from improved production efficiencies stemming from knowledge gained through production experience. Care must be exercised to separate learning and scale effects in cost analysis.

Research in a number of industries, ranging from aircraft manufacturing to semiconductor memory-chip production, has shown that a constant percentage of savings in average costs as a result of learning or experience can be very important in some production systems. Learning or experience rates of 20% to 30% are sometimes reported. These high learning rates imply rapidly declining manufacturing costs as cumulative total output increases. It should be noted, however, that many learning curve studies fail to account adequately for the expansion of annual production levels. Therefore, reported learning or experience rates include the effects of both learning and economies of scale. Nevertheless, actual learning rates can sometimes be quite significant. Indeed, managers in a wide variety of industries have found that the learning curve concept has considerable strategic implications.

STRATEGIC IMPLICATIONS OF THE LEARNING CURVE CONCEPT

The learning curve can play a central role in determining long-run success or failure and, thereby, assumes an important role in competitive strategy. What makes the learning curve phenomenon important for competitive strategy is its possible contribution to achieving and maintaining a dominant position in a given market. By virtue of their large relative volume, dominant firms have greater opportunity for learning than do smaller, nonleading firms. In some instances, the market share leader is able to drive down its average cost curve faster than its competitors, underprice them, and permanently maintain a leadership position. Nonleading firms face an important and perhaps insurmountable barrier to relative improvement in performance. Where the learning

Is Bigger Always Better?

When economies of scale are substantial, larger firms are able to achieve lower costs of production or distribution than their smaller rivals. These cost advantages translate into higher and more stable profits, and a permanent competitive advantage for larger firms in some industries. Diseconomies of large-scale organizations work in the opposite direction. When diseconomies of scale are operative, larger firms suffer a cost disadvantage when compared to their smaller rivals. Smaller firms are then able to translate the benefits of small size into a distinct competitive advantage. Rather than losing profits and sales opportunities to their larger rivals, these smaller firms can enjoy higher profit rates and a gain in market share over time.

In general, industries dominated by large firms tend to be those in which there are significant economies of scale, important advantages to vertical integration, and a prevalence of mass marketing. As a result, large organizations with sprawling plants emphasize large quantities of output at low production costs. Use of national media, especially TV advertising, is common. In contrast, industries in which "small is beautiful" tend to be those characterized by diseconomies of scale, considerable advantages to subcontracting for "just in time" assembly and manufacturing, and niche marketing that emphasizes the use of highly skilled individuals adept at personal selling. Small factories with flexible production schedules are common. Rather than mass quantity, many smaller companies emphasize quality. Instead of the sometimes slow-to-respond hierarchical organizations of large companies, smaller companies feature "flat" organizations with decentralized decision making and authority.

Even though the concept of diseconomies of large size is well known, it is sometimes not appreciated how common the phenomenon is in actual practice. In many sectors, smaller companies have emerged as a dominant competitive force. In many industries offering business and consumer services, smaller firms are typically better able to quickly meet the specialized needs of their customers and have successfully met competition from large companies. Many sectors of industrial manufacturing have found that the highly flexible and customer-sensitive nature of many smaller companies can lead to distinct competitive advantages. For example, although early advances in large mainframe computers were historically the domain of larger companies such as IBM, the vast majority of innovations in the computer industry during the 1980s and 1990s—the personal computer, minicomputer, supercomputer, and user-friendly software—have been started or commercialized by venture-backed entrepreneurial companies.

The villain sometimes encountered by large-scale firms is not any diseconomy of scale in the production process itself, but rather the burden that size places on effective management. Big often means complex, and complexity results in inefficiencies and bureaucratic snarls that can strangle effective communication. In the former Soviet Union, a huge, highly centralized, run-from-the-top system came crashing down from its own gigantic weight. Hoping to avoid a similar fate, many large organizations are now splitting assets into smaller independent operating units that can react quickly to customer needs without the long delays typical of large organizations. IBM, for example, has split into independent operating units that compete directly with one another in providing customers with the latest in computer equipment and software. GM, seeking to become more like lean and agile Japanese competitors, established Saturn as an independent operating unit. This suggests that the Corporate America is going through a metamorphism that will favor large organizations that are especially adept at reallocating capital among nimble, entrepreneurial operating units.

In the past, when foreign visitors wanted to experience firsthand the latest innovations in U.S. business and administrative practice, they found it mandatory to stop and visit major corporations in Chicago, Detroit, New York, and Pittsburgh. Today, it is more likely that they would make stops at Boston's Route 128, California's Silicon Valley, or North Carolina's Research Triangle. From electronics instruments to specialized steel, smaller companies have replaced larger companies in positions of industry leadership. Many larger companies are finding that meeting the needs of the customer sometimes requires a dramatic downsizing of the large-scale organization.

See: Greg Ip, "Investors Seek Out Blue Chip Companies More for Their Bottom Line Than Size," *The Wall Street Journal*, January 20, 1997, C1, C2.

curve advantages of leading firms are important, it may be prudent to relinquish non-leading positions and redeploy assets to markets in which a dominant position can be achieved or maintained.

A classic example illustrating the successful use of the learning curve concept is Texas Instruments (TI). TI is a large and highly profitable growth company headquartered in Dallas, Texas. Despite some well-publicized problems in its consumer products division (personal computers, calculators, and video games), TI has long enjoyed a dominant position as a supplier in the electronics industry. TI's main business is producing semiconductor chips, which are key components used to store information in computers and a wide array of electronic products. With growing applications for computers and "intelligent" electronics during recent years, the demand for semiconductors is growing rapidly. Some years ago, TI was one of a number of leading semiconductor manufacturers. At this early stage in the development of the industry, TI made the decision to price its semiconductors well below then-current production costs, given expected learning curve advantages in the 20% range. TI's learning curve strategy proved spectacularly successful. With low prices, volume increased dramatically. Since TI was making so many chips, average costs were even lower than anticipated, it could price below the competition, and dozens of competitors were knocked out of the world market. Given a relative cost advantage and strict quality controls, TI rapidly achieved a position of dominant leadership in a market that became a source of large and rapidly growing profits.

Generally speaking, in order for learning to play an important role in an effective competitive strategy, a number of conditions must be satisfied. Learning must be significant, resulting in average cost savings of 20% to 30% as cumulative output doubles. If only modest effects of learning are present, relative product quality or customer service is likely to play a greater role in determining firm success than is a modest average cost advantage. Learning is also likely to be much more important in industries with an abundance of new products or new production techniques than in mature industries with stable and well-known production methods. Similarly, learning tends to be important in industries producing standardized products in which competition is based on price rather than product variety or service. It is important that the learning curve phenomenon must be managed. It is definitely not automatic. The beneficial effects of learning are realized only under management systems that tightly control costs and monitor potential sources of increased production efficiency. Continuous feedback of information between production and management personnel is essential. To ensure the flow of useful information and a cooperative attitude among all employees, incentive pay programs that reward increased productivity are often established. This allows employees and employers to jointly benefit through learning.

Economies of Scope

For many firms, cost analysis focuses not just on how much to produce but also on what combination of products to offer. By virtue of their efficiency in the production of a given product, firms often enjoy cost advantages in the production of related products. Identifying and taking advantage of such efficiencies is often crucial to long-run success.

THE ECONOMIES OF SCOPE CONCEPT

Economies of Scope
Cost reduction from producing complementary products.

Economies of scope exist for multiple outputs when the cost of joint production is less than the cost of producing each output separately. In other words, a firm will produce products that are complementary in the sense that producing them together costs less than producing them individually. Suppose that a regional airline offers regularly scheduled passenger service between midsize city pairs and that it expects some excess capacity. Also assume that there is a modest local demand for air parcel and small-package delivery service. Given current airplane sizes, configuration, and so on, it is often less costly for a single carrier to provide both passenger and cargo services in small regional markets than to specialize in one or the other. Thus, regional air carriers often provide both services. This can be seen as an example of economies of scope. Other examples of scope economies abound in the provision of both goods and services. In fact, the economies of scope concept seems to explain best why firms produce multiple rather than single products.

Studying economies of scope forces management to consider both the direct and indirect benefits associated with individual lines of business. For example, on a product line basis, some firms that offer financial services regard checking accounts and money market mutual funds as "loss leaders." When one considers just the revenues and costs associated with marketing and offering checking services or running a money market mutual fund, they may just break even or yield only a marginal profit. However, successful firms like Dreyfus, Fidelity, and Merrill Lynch correctly evaluate the profitability of their money market mutual funds within the context of overall operations. These funds are a valuable delivery vehicle for the vast array of financial products and services that they offer. By offering money market funds on an attractive basis, each of these financial services companies establishes a working relation with an ideal group of prospective customers for stocks, bonds, tax shelters, and so on. When viewed as a delivery vehicle or marketing device, money market mutual funds may be one of the industry's most profitable financial product lines.

EXPLOITING SCOPE ECONOMIES

Economies of scope are important because they permit a firm to translate superior skill or productive capability in a given product line into unique advantages in the production of complementary products. An effective competitive strategy emphasizes the development or extension of product lines related to a firm's current stars, or areas of recognized strength. For example, PepsiCo, Inc., has long been a leader in the soft drink market. Over time, the company has gradually broadened its product line to include various brands of regular and diet soft drinks, *Fritos* and *Doritos* corn chips, *Grandma's Cookies*, and other snack foods. PepsiCo can no longer be considered just a soft drink manufacturer. It is a widely diversified snack foods company for whom well over one-half of total current profits come from non-soft drink lines. PepsiCo's snack foods product line extension strategy was effective because it capitalized on the product development capabilities, distribution network, and marketing developed in the firm's soft drink business. In the case of PepsiCo, snack foods and soft drinks are a natural fit and a good example of how a firm has been able to take the skills gained in developing one star (soft drinks) and use them to develop a second (snack foods).

The economies of scope concept plays an important role in managerial decision making because it offers a useful means for evaluating the potential of current and prospective lines of business. It naturally leads to definition of those areas in which the firm has a comparative advantage and thus its greatest profit potential.

Cost-Volume-Profit Analysis

Cost-Volume-Profit Analysis
Analytical technique used to study relations among costs, revenues, and profits.

Cost-volume-profit analysis, sometimes called breakeven analysis, is an important analytical technique used to study relations among costs, revenues, and profits. Both graphic and algebraic methods are employed. The approach that should be used in any given situation depends on the complexity of the cost problem being analyzed. For simple problems, simple graphic methods work best. In more complex situations, analytic methods, possibly involving the use of *Lotus 1-2-3* or other spreadsheet software programs, are preferable.

COST-VOLUME-PROFIT CHARTS

The nature of cost-volume-profit analysis is depicted in Figure 8.12, a basic cost-volume-profit chart composed of a firm's total cost and total revenue curves. Volume of output is measured on the horizontal axis; revenue and cost are shown on the vertical axis. Since fixed costs are constant regardless of the output produced, they are indicated by a horizontal line. Variable costs at each output level are measured by the distance between the total cost curve and the constant fixed costs. The total revenue curve indicates the price/demand relation for the firm's product; profits or losses at each output are shown by the distance between total revenue and total cost curves.

In the example depicted in Figure 8.12, fixed costs of $60,000 are represented by a horizontal line. Variable costs are assumed to be $1.80 per unit, so total costs rise by that amount for each additional unit of output produced. The product is assumed to be sold for $3 per unit. Total revenue is a straight line through the origin. The slope of the total revenue line is steeper than that of the total cost line because the firm receives $3 per unit in revenue but spends only $1.80 on labor, materials, and other variable inputs.

Below the breakeven point, found at the intersection of the total revenue line and the total cost line, the firm suffers losses. Beyond that point, it begins to make profits. Figure 8.12 indicates a breakeven point at a sales and cost level of $150,000, which occurs at a production level of 50,000 units.

LINEAR COST-VOLUME-PROFIT CHART

Output levels below the breakeven point produce losses. As output grows beyond the breakeven point, increasingly higher profits result.

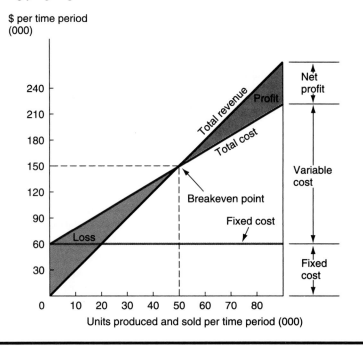

ALGEBRAIC COST-VOLUME-PROFIT ANALYSIS

Although cost-volume-profit charts are often used to portray profit/output relations, algebraic techniques are typically more efficient for analyzing decision problems. The algebra of cost-volume-profit analysis can be illustrated as follows. Let

$$P = \text{Price per unit sold;}$$

$$Q = \text{Quantity produced and sold;}$$

$$TFC = \text{Total fixed costs;}$$

$$AVC = \text{Average variable cost;}$$

$$\pi_C = \text{Profit contribution.}$$

As described previously, profit contribution, π_C, is the difference between revenues and variable cost. On a per unit basis, profit contribution equals price minus average variable cost ($\pi_C = P - AVC$). Profit contribution can be applied to cover fixed costs and then to provide profits. It is the foundation of cost-volume-profit analysis.

Breakeven Quantity
A zero profit activity level.

One useful application of cost-volume-profit analysis lies in the determination of breakeven activity levels for a product. A **breakeven quantity** is a zero profit activity level. At breakeven quantity levels, total revenue $(P \times Q)$ exactly equals total costs $(TFC + AVC \times Q)$:

$$Total\ Revenue = Total\ Cost$$

$$P \times Q = TFC + AVC \times Q$$

$$(P - AVC)Q = TFC.$$

It follows that breakeven quantity levels occur where:

$$Q_{BE} = \frac{TFC}{P - AVC}$$

$$= \frac{TFC}{\pi_C}.$$

(8.6)

Thus, breakeven quantity levels are found by dividing the per unit profit contribution into total fixed costs. In the example illustrated in Figure 8.12, $P = \$3$, $AVC = \$1.80$, and $TFC = \$60,000$. Profit contribution is $\$1.20 (= \$3.00 - \$1.80)$, and the breakeven quantity is

$$Q = \frac{\$60,000}{\$1.20}$$

$$= 50,000\ units.$$

TEXTBOOK PUBLISHING: A FURTHER COST-VOLUME-PROFIT EXAMPLE

A more extensive example of cost-volume-profit analysis is helpful in illustrating additional uses of the concept in managerial decision making. The textbook publishing business provides a good illustration of the effective use of cost-volume-profit analysis for new product decisions.

Consider the hypothetical cost-volume-profit analysis data shown in Table 8.2. Fixed costs can be estimated quite accurately. Variable costs are linear and set by contract. List prices are variable, but competition keeps prices within a sufficiently narrow range to make a linear total revenue curve reasonable. Variable costs for the proposed book are $52 a copy, and the price is $60. This means that each copy sold provides $8 in profit contribution. Applying the breakeven formula from Equation 8.6, the breakeven sales volume is 12,500 units, calculated as

$$Q = \frac{\$100,000}{\$8}$$

$$= 12,500\ units.$$

<table>
<tr><td>Table 8.2</td><td colspan="2">COST-VOLUME-PROFIT ANALYSIS FOR TEXTBOOK PUBLISHING</td></tr>
</table>

Cost Category	Dollar Amount
Fixed Costs	
Copy editing and other editorial costs	$ 15,750
Illustrations	32,750
Typesetting	51,500
Total fixed costs	$100,000
Variable Costs per Copy	
Printing, binding, and paper	$16.85
Bookstore discounts	12.50
Sales staff commissions	5.25
Author's royalties	4.80
General and administrative costs	12.60
Total variable costs per copy	$52.00
List price per copy	$60.00

Publishers can evaluate the size of the total market for a given book, competition, and other factors. With these data in mind, they estimate the probability that a given book will reach or exceed the breakeven point. If the publisher estimates that the book will neither meet nor exceed the breakeven point, it may consider cutting production costs by reducing the number of illustrations, doing only light copy editing, using a lower grade of paper, negotiating with the author to reduce the royalty rate, and so on.

Assume now that the publisher is interested in determining how many copies must sell to earn a $20,000 profit on the text. Because profit contribution is the amount available to cover fixed costs and provide profit, the answer is found by adding the profit requirement to the book's fixed costs and then dividing by the per unit profit contribution. The sales volume required in this case is 15,000 books, found as follows:

$$Q = \frac{Fixed\ Costs\ +\ Profit\ Requirement}{Profit\ Contribution}$$

$$= \frac{\$100,000\ +\ \$20,000}{\$8}$$

$$= 15,000\ units.$$

Consider yet another decision problem that might confront the publisher. Assume that a book club has indicated an interest in purchasing copies of the textbook for its members and has offered to buy 3,000 copies at a price of $45 per copy. Cost-volume-profit analysis can be used to determine the incremental effect of such a sale on the publisher's profits.

Since fixed costs do not vary with respect to changes in the number of textbooks sold, they should be ignored in the analysis. Variable costs per copy are $52, but note that $12.50 of this cost represents bookstore discounts. Since the 3,000 copies are being sold directly to the club, this cost will not be incurred and, hence, the relevant variable cost is $39.50. Profit contribution per book sold to the book club then is $5.50 (= $45 − $39.50), and $5.50 times the 3,000 copies sold indicates that the order will result in a total profit contribution of $16,500. Assuming that these 3,000 copies would not have been sold through normal sales channels, the $16,500 profit contribution indicates the increase in profits to the publisher from accepting this order.

THE DEGREE OF OPERATING LEVERAGE

Cost-volume-profit analysis is also a useful tool for analyzing the financial characteristics of alternative production systems. This analysis focuses on how total costs and profits vary with output as the firm operates in a more mechanized manner and substitutes fixed costs for variable costs. Operating leverage reflects the extent to which fixed production facilities, as opposed to variable production facilities, are used in the firm's operation.

The relation between operating leverage and profit variation is shown in Figure 8.13, which contrasts the experience of three firms, *A, B,* and *C,* with differing degrees of leverage. The fixed costs of Firm *B* are typical. Firm *A* uses relatively less capital equipment and has lower fixed costs, but it has a steeper rate of increase in variable costs. Firm *A* breaks even at a lower activity level than does Firm *B.* For example, at a production level of 40,000 units, *B* is losing $8,000, but *A* breaks even. Firm *C* is highly automated and has the highest fixed costs, but its variable costs rise slowly. Firm *C* has a higher breakeven point than either *A* or *B,* but once *C* passes the breakeven point, profits rise faster than those of the other two firms.

Degree of Operating Leverage
Percentage change in profit from a 1% change in output.

The **degree of operating leverage** is the percentage change in profit that results from a 1% change in units sold:

$$Degree\ of\ Operating\ Leverage = \frac{Percentage\ Change\ in\ Profit}{Percentage\ Change\ in\ Sales}$$

$$= \frac{\Delta\pi/\pi}{\Delta Q/Q} \qquad (8.7)$$

$$= \frac{\Delta\pi}{\Delta Q} \times \frac{Q}{\pi}.$$

The degree of operating leverage is an elasticity concept, and it can be understood as the elasticity of profits with respect to output. When based on linear cost and revenue curves, this elasticity varies depending on the point of the breakeven graph being considered. The degree of operating leverage is always greatest close to the breakeven point. There, a small change in volume produces a large percentage increase in profits, because base profits are near zero.

For firm B in Figure 8.13, the degree of operating leverage at 100,000 units of output is 2.0, calculated as follows:[4]

$$DOL_B = \frac{\Delta\pi/\pi}{\Delta Q/Q}$$

$$= \frac{(\$41,600 - \$40,000)/\$40,000}{(102,000 - 100,000)/100,000} = \frac{\$1,600/\$40,000}{2,000/100,000}$$

$$= \frac{4\%}{2\%} = 2.$$

Here, π is profit and Q is the quantity of output in units.

For linear revenue and cost relations, the degree of operating leverage can be calculated at any level of output. The change in output is ΔQ. Fixed costs are constant, so the change in profit is $\Delta Q(P - AVC)$, where P is price per unit and AVC is average variable cost.

Any initial profit level is $Q(P - AVC) - TFC$, so the percentage change in profit is:

$$\frac{\Delta\pi}{\pi} = \frac{\Delta Q(P - AVC)}{Q(P - AVC) - TFC}.$$

The percentage change in output is $\Delta Q/Q$, so the ratio of the percentage change in profits to the percentage change in output, or profit elasticity, is:

$$\frac{\Delta\pi/\pi}{\Delta Q/Q} = \frac{\Delta Q(P - AVC)/[Q(P - AVC) - TFC]}{\Delta Q/Q}$$

$$= \frac{\Delta Q(P - AVC)}{Q(P - AVC) - TFC} \times \frac{Q}{\Delta Q}.$$

After simplifying, the degree of operating leverage formula at any given level of output is:[5]

$$\textit{Degree of Operating Leverage at Point } Q = \frac{Q(P - AVC)}{Q(P - AVC) - TFC}. \qquad \textbf{(8.8)}$$

---

[4]This calculation arbitrarily assumes that $\Delta Q = 2,000$. If $\Delta Q = 1,000$ or $\Delta Q = 4,000$, the degree of operating leverage still equals 2, because these calculations are based on linear cost and revenue curves. However, if a base other than 100,000 units is chosen, the degree of operating leverage will vary.

[5]Since $TFC = Q(AFC)$ and $AC = AVC + AFC$, where AFC is average fixed cost, Equation 8.8 can be reduced further to a form that is useful in some situations:

$$DOL = \frac{Q(P - AVC)}{Q(P - AVC) - Q(AFC)}$$

$$= \frac{P - AVC}{P - AC}.$$

BREAKEVEN AND OPERATING LEVERAGE

The breakeven point for Firm C occurs at the highest output level. Once this level is reached, profits rise at a faster rate than for Firm A or B.

Firm A

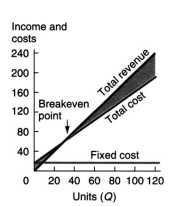

Selling price = $2.00
Fixed cost = $20,000
Variable cost = $1.50Q

Units sold (Q)	Sales	Cost	Profit
20,000	$ 40,000	$ 50,000	– $10,000
40,000	80,000	80,000	0
60,000	120,000	110,000	10,000
80,000	160,000	140,000	20,000
100,000	200,000	170,000	30,000
120,000	240,000	200,000	40,000

Firm B

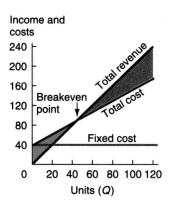

Selling price = $2.00
Fixed cost = $40,000
Variable cost = $1.20Q

Units sold (Q)	Sales	Cost	Profit
20,000	$ 40,000	$ 64,000	– $24,000
40,000	80,000	88,000	– 8,000
60,000	120,000	112,000	8,000
80,000	160,000	136,000	24,000
100,000	200,000	160,000	40,000
120,000	240,000	184,000	56,000

Firm C

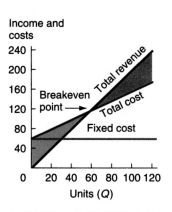

Selling price = $2.00
Fixed cost = $60,000
Variable cost = $1.00Q

Units sold (Q)	Sales	Cost	Profit
20,000	$ 40,000	$ 80,000	– $40,000
40,000	80,000	100,000	– 20,000
60,000	120,000	120,000	0
80,000	160,000	140,000	20,000
100,000	200,000	160,000	40,000
120,000	240,000	180,000	60,000

Using Equation 8.8, Firm *B*'s degree of operating leverage at 100,000 units of output is calculated as

$$DOL_B \text{ at } 100,000 \text{ units} = \frac{100,000\ (\$2.00 - \$1.20)}{100,000(\$2.00 - \$1.20) - \$40,000}$$

$$= \frac{\$80,000}{\$40,000} = 2.$$

Equation 8.8 can also be applied to Firms *A* and *C*. When this is done, Firm *A*'s degree of operating leverage at 100,000 units equals 1.67 and Firm *C's* equals 2.5. With a 2% increase in volume, Firm *C,* the firm with the most operating leverage, will experience a profit increase of 5%. For the same 2% gain in volume, the firm with the least leverage, Firm *A*, will have only a 3.3% profit gain. As seen in Figure 8.13, the profits of Firm *C* are most sensitive to changes in sales volume, whereas Firm *A*'s profits are relatively insensitive to volume changes. Firm *B*, with an intermediate degree of leverage, lies between these two extremes.

LIMITATIONS OF LINEAR COST-VOLUME-PROFIT ANALYSIS

Cost-volume-profit analysis helps explain relations among volume, prices, and costs. It is also useful for pricing, cost control, and other financial decisions. However, linear cost-volume-profit analysis has its limitations.

Linear cost-volume-profit analysis has a weakness in what it implies about sales possibilities for the firm. Linear cost-volume-profit charts are based on constant selling prices. To study profit possibilities with different prices, a whole series of charts is necessary, with one chart for each price. However, using sophisticated spreadsheet software such as *Lotus 1-2-3*, the creation of a wide variety of cost-volume-profit charts is relatively easy. Using such software, profit possibilities for different pricing strategies can be quickly determined. Alternatively, nonlinear cost-volume-profit analysis can be used to show the effects of changing prices.

Linear cost-volume-profit analysis is also somewhat limited by the underlying assumption of constant average costs. The linear cost relations assumed in cost-volume-profit charts cannot be expected to hold at all output levels. As unit sales increase, existing plant and equipment can be worked beyond capacity, thus reducing their efficiency. The need for additional workers, longer work periods, and, especially, overtime wages can also cause variable costs to rise sharply. If additional plant and equipment is required, fixed costs will also rise. Finally, over time the products sold by the firm change in quality and quantity. Such changes in product mix influence both the level and the slope of cost functions.

Although linear cost-volume-profit analysis has proved to be useful as a tool for managerial decision making, care must be taken to ensure that it is not applied in situations in which underlying assumptions are violated. Like any decision tool, cost-volume-profit analysis must be used with discretion.

Summary

Cost analysis plays a key role in most managerial decisions. This chapter introduces a number of cost concepts, shows the relation between cost functions and production functions, and examines several cost analysis issues.

- For tax purposes, actual **historical cost,** or historical cash outlay, is the relevant cost. This is also generally true for annual 10-K reports to the Securities and Exchange Commission and for reports to stockholders. **Current cost,** the amount that must be paid under prevailing market conditions, is typically much more relevant for decision-making purposes.

- Current costs are often determined by **replacement costs,** or the cost of duplicating productive capability using present technology. Another prime determinant of current cost is **opportunity cost,** or the foregone value associated with the current rather than the next-best use of a given asset. Both of these cost categories typically involve out-of-pocket costs, or **explicit costs,** and other noncash costs, called **implicit costs.**

- **Incremental cost** is the change in cost caused by a given managerial decision. Whereas marginal cost is the change in cost following a one-unit change in output, incremental costs often involve multiple units of output. Incremental costs are a prime determinant of the **profit contribution,** or profit before fixed charges, associated with a given managerial decision. Neither are affected by **sunk costs,** which do not vary across decision alternatives.

- Proper use of relevant cost concepts requires an understanding of the cost/output relation, or **cost function. Short-run cost functions** are used for day-to-day operating decisions; **long-run cost functions** are employed in the long-range planning process. The **short run** is the operating period during which the availability of at least one input is fixed. In the **long run,** the firm has complete flexibility with respect to input use. **Fixed costs** that do not vary with output are incurred only in the short run. **Variable costs** fluctuate with output in both the short and the long run.

- A **short-run cost curve** shows the minimum cost impact of output changes for a specific plant size and in a given operating environment. A **long-run cost curve** shows the minimum cost impact of output changes for the optimal plant size using current technology in the present operating environment.

- Increasing returns, or **economies of scale,** which originate from production and market-related sources, cause long-run average costs to decline. **Cost elasticity,** ϵ_C, measures the percentage change in total cost associated with a 1% change in output.

- **Capacity** refers to the output level at which short-run average costs are minimized. **Minimum efficient scale** (MES) is the output level at which long-run average costs are minimized.

- **Multiplant economies of scale** are cost advantages that arise from operating multiple facilities in the same line of business or industry. Conversely, **multiplant diseconomies of scale** are cost disadvantages that arise from managing multiple facilities in the same line of business or industry.

■ When knowledge gained from manufacturing experience is used to improve production methods so that output is produced with increasing efficiency, the resulting decline in average cost is said to reflect the effects of the firm's **learning curve.** **Economies of scope** exist for multiple outputs when the cost of joint production is less than the cost of producing each output separately.

■ **Cost-volume-profit analysis,** sometimes called breakeven analysis, is an important analytical technique used to study relations among costs, revenues, and profits. A **breakeven quantity** is a zero profit activity level. The **degree of operating leverage** is the percentage change in profit that results from a 1% change in units sold; it can be understood as the elasticity of profits with respect to output.

Cost analysis poses a continuing challenge to management in all types of organizations. Using the concepts and tools discussed in this chapter, successful managers are able to manage costs effectively.

QUESTIONS

Q8.1 The relevant cost for most managerial decisions is the current cost of an input. The relevant cost for computing income for taxes and stockholder reporting is the historical cost. What advantages or disadvantages do you see in using current costs for tax and stockholder reporting purposes?

Q8.2 What are the relations among historical costs, current costs, and opportunity costs?

Q8.3 What is the difference between marginal and incremental cost?

Q8.4 What is a sunk cost, and how is it related to a decision problem?

Q8.5 What is the relation between production functions and cost functions? Be sure to include in your discussion the effect of conditions in input factor markets.

Q8.6 Explain why $\epsilon_Q > 1$ and $\epsilon_C < 1$ both indicate increasing returns to scale. (See Chapter 7 for the definition of output elasticity.)

Q8.7 The president of a small firm has been complaining to his controller about rising labor and material costs. However, the controller notes that average costs have not increased during the past year. Is this possible?

Q8.8 Given the short-run total cost curve in Figure 8.1(b), explain why (a) Q_1 is the minimum of the *MC* curve, (b) Q_2 is the minimum of the *AVC* curve, (c) Q_3 is the minimum of the *ATC* curve, and (d) the *MC* curve cuts the *AVC* and *ATC* curves at their minimum points.

Q8.9 Will firms in industries in which high levels of output are necessary for minimum efficient scale tend to have substantial degrees of operating leverage?

Q8.10 Do operating strategies of average cost minimization and profit maximization always lead to identical levels of output?

SELF-TEST PROBLEMS AND SOLUTIONS

ST8.1 **Learning Curves.** Modern Merchandise, Inc., makes and markets do-it-yourself hardware, housewares, and industrial products. The company's new Aperture Miniblind is winning customers by virtue of its high quality and quick order turnaround time. The product also benefits because its price point bridges the gap between ready-made vinyl blinds and their high-priced custom counterpart. In addition, the company's expanding product line is sure to benefit from cross-selling across different lines. Given the success of the Aperture Miniblind product, Modern Merchandise plans to open a new production facility near Beaufort, South Carolina. Based on information provided by its chief financial officer, the company estimates fixed costs for this product of $50,000 per year and average variable costs of:

$$AVC = \$0.5 + \$0.0025Q,$$

where AVC is average variable cost (in dollars) and Q is output.

A.   Estimate total cost and average total cost for the projected first-year volume of 20,000 units.

B.   An increase in worker productivity because of greater experience or learning during the course of the year resulted in a substantial cost saving for the company. Estimate the effect of learning on average total cost if actual second-year total cost was $848,000 at an actual volume of 20,000 units.

ST8.1   **SOLUTION**

A.   The total variable cost function for the first year is:

$$TVC = AVC \times Q$$

$$= (\$0.5 + \$0.0025Q)Q$$

$$= \$0.5Q + \$0.0025Q^2$$

At a volume of 20,000 units, estimated total cost is:

$$TC = TFC + TVC$$

$$= \$50,000 + \$0.5Q + \$0.0025Q^2$$

$$= \$50,000 + \$0.5(20,000)$$
$$+ \$0.0025(20,000^2)$$

$$= \$1,060,000$$

Estimated average cost is:

$$AC = TC/Q$$

$$= \$1,060,000/20,000$$

$$= \$53 \text{ per case}$$

B.   If actual total costs were $848,000 at a volume of 20,000 units, actual average total costs were:

$$AC = TC/Q$$

$$= \$848,000/20,000$$

$$= \$42.40 \text{ per case}$$

Therefore, greater experience or learning has resulted in an average cost saving of $10.60 per case since:

$$\text{Learning effect} = \text{Actual } AC - \text{Estimated } AC$$

$$= \$42.40 - \$53$$

$$= -\$10.60 \text{ per case}$$

Alternatively,

$$\text{Learning rate} = \left(1 - \frac{AC_2}{AC_1}\right) \times 100$$

$$= \left(1 - \frac{\$42.40}{\$53}\right) \times 100$$

$$= 20\%$$

ST8.2   **Minimum Efficient Scale Estimation.** Kanata Corporation is a leading manufacturer of telecommunications equipment based in Ontario, Canada. Its main products are microprocessors controlled telephone switching equipment, called automatic private branch exchanges (PABXs), capable of handling 8 to 3,000 telephone extensions. Severe price cutting throughout the PABX industry continues to put pressure on sales and margins, even though the company eliminated over 500 jobs last year. To better compete against increasingly aggressive rivals, the company is contemplating the construction of a new production facility capable of producing 1.5 million units per year. Kanata's in-house engineering estimate of the total cost function for the new facility is:

$$TC = \$3,000 + \$1,000Q + \$0.003Q^2,$$

$$MC = \$1,000 + \$0.006Q$$

where TC = Total Costs in thousands of dollars, Q = Output in thousands of units, and MC = Marginal Costs in thousands of dollars.

A.   Estimate minimum efficient scale in this industry.

B.   In light of current PABX demand of 30 million units per year, how would you evaluate the future potential for competition in the industry?

ST8.2   **SOLUTION**

A.   Minimum efficient scale is reached when average costs are first minimized. This occurs at the point where $MC = AC$.

Average Costs $= AC = TC/Q$

$$= (\$3,000 + \$1,000Q + \$0.003Q^2)/Q$$

$$= \frac{\$3,000}{Q} + \$1,000 + \$0.003Q$$

Therefore,

$$MC = AC$$

$$\$1,000 + \$0.006Q = \frac{\$3,000}{Q} + \$1,000 + \$0.003Q$$

$$0.003Q = \frac{3,000}{Q}$$

$$\frac{3,000}{Q^2} = 0.003$$

$$Q^2 = 1,000,000$$

$$Q = 1,000(000)$$
or 1 million

[*Note:* AC is rising for $Q > 1,000(000)$].

Alternatively, MES can be calculated using the point cost elasticity formula, since MES is reached when $\epsilon_C = 1$.

$$\epsilon_C = \frac{\Delta TC}{\Delta Q} \times \frac{Q}{TC}$$

$$\frac{(\$1,000 + \$0.006Q)Q}{(\$3,000 + \$1,000Q + \$0.003Q^2)} = 1$$

$$1,000Q + 0.006Q^2 = 3,000 + 1,000Q + 0.003Q^2$$

$$0.003Q^2 = 3,000$$

$$Q^2 = 1,000,000$$

$$Q_{MES} = 1,000(000)$$
or 1 million

B. With a minimum efficient scale of 1 million units and total industry sales of 30 million units, up to 30 efficiently sized competitors are possible in Kanata's market.

$$\text{Potential Number of Efficient Competitors} = \frac{\text{Market Size}}{\text{MES Size}}$$

$$= \frac{30,000,000}{1,000,000}$$

$$= 30$$

Thus, it would appear that there is a real potential for $N = 30$ efficiently sized competitors and, therefore, vigorous competition in Kanata's industry.

PROBLEMS

P8.1 **Cost and Production Functions.** The total product curve shown on page 357 describes a production system in which X is the only variable input. Answer the following questions relating production to costs.

A. Over approximately what range of Input X will marginal costs be falling if P_X is not affected by the amount purchased?

B. At approximately what level of employment of Input X will average variable costs be minimized?

C. If $P_X = \$25$, what is the minimum average variable cost in this production system?

D. What is the marginal cost of production at 60 units of output?

E. If the price of output is $2 per unit, is employment of 3 units of X optimal for a profit-maximizing firm (assuming again that X costs $25 per unit)? Explain.

P8.2 **Cost Relations.** Determine whether each of the following is true or false. Explain why.

A. Average cost equals marginal cost at the minimum efficient scale of plant.

B. When total fixed cost and price are held constant, an increase in average variable cost will

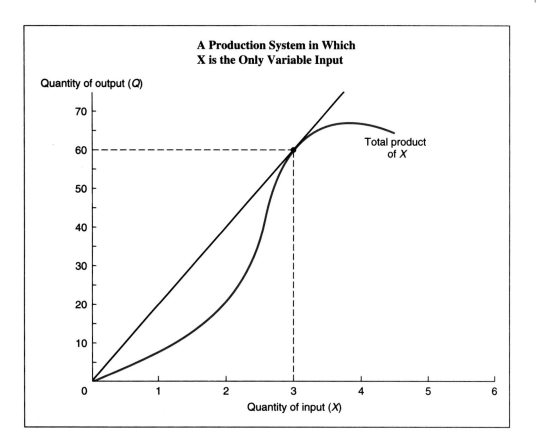

**A Production System in Which
X is the Only Variable Input**

Quantity of output (Q)

Total product of X

Quantity of input (X)

---

typically cause a reduction in the breakeven activity level.

C.   If $\epsilon_C > 1$, diminishing returns to scale and increasing average costs are indicated.

D.   When long-run average cost is decreasing, it can pay to operate larger plants with some excess capacity rather than smaller plants at their peak efficiency.

E.   An increase in average variable cost always increases the degree of operating leverage for firms making a positive net profit.

P8.3   **Cost Curves.** Indicate whether each of the following involves an upward or downward shift in the long-run average cost curve or, instead, involves a leftward or rightward movement along a given curve. Also indicate whether each will have an increasing, decreasing, or uncertain effect on the level of average cost.

A.   A rise in wage rates.

B.   A decline in output.

C.   An energy-saving technical change.

D.   A fall in interest rates.

E.   An increase in learning or experience.

P8.4   **Incremental Cost.** Paladin Instruments, Inc., produces precision measuring instruments that it sells to other manufacturers, who then customize and distribute the products to research laboratories. The yearly volume of output is 15,000 units. The selling price and costs per unit are as follows:

Selling Price		$250
Costs:		
Direct material	$40	
Direct labor	60	
Variable overhead	30	
Variable selling expenses	25	
Fixed selling expenses	20	−$175
Unit profit before tax		$ 75

Management is evaluating the alternative of performing the necessary customizing to allow Paladin to sell its output directly to laboratories for $300 per unit. Although no added investment is required in productive facilities, additional processing costs are estimated as follows:

Direct labor	$30 per unit
Variable overhead	$5 per unit
Variable selling expenses	$2 per unit
Fixed selling expenses	$20,000 per year

A. Calculate the incremental profit that Paladin would earn by customizing its instruments and marketing them directly to end users.

P8.5 **Accounting and Economic Costs.** Three graduate business students are considering operating a frozen yogurt stand in the Harbor Springs, Michigan, resort area during their summer break. This is an alternative to summer employment with a local firm, where they would each earn $6,000 over the three-month summer period. A fully equipped facility can be leased at a cost of $8,000 for the summer. Additional projected costs are $1,000 for insurance and 40 cents per unit for materials and supplies. Their frozen yogurt would be priced at $1 per unit.

A. What is the accounting cost function for this business?

B. What is the economic cost function for this business?

C. What is the economic breakeven number of units for this operation? (Assume a $1 price and ignore interest costs associated with the timing of the lease payments.)

P8.6 **Profit Contribution.** Diane Chambers is manager of a Quick Copy franchise in White Plains, New York. Chambers projects that by reducing copy charges from 5¢ to 4¢ each, Quick Copy's $600-per-week profit contribution will increase by one-third.

A. If average variable costs are 2¢ per copy, calculate Quick Copy's projected increase in volume.

B. What is Chambers's estimate of the arc price elasticity of demand for copies?

P8.7 **Cost Elasticity.** Power Brokers, Inc. (PBI), a discount brokerage firm, is contemplating opening a new regional office in Providence, Rhode Island. An accounting cost analysis of monthly operating costs at a dozen of its regional outlets reveals average fixed costs of $4,500 per month and average variable costs of

$$AVC = \$59 - \$0.006Q,$$

where AVC is average variable costs (in dollars) and Q is output measured by number of stock and bond trades.

A typical stock or bond trade results in $100 gross commission income, with PBI paying 35% of this amount to its sales representatives.

A. Estimate the trade volume necessary for PBI to reach a target return of $7,500 per month for a typical office.

B. Estimate and interpret the elasticity of cost with respect to output at the trade volume found in Part A.

P8.8 **Multiplant Operation.** Appalachia Beverage Company, Inc., a regional soft drink bottler operating in southeastern states, is considering two alternative proposals for expansion into the Midwest. *Alternative 1:* Construct a single plant in Indianapolis, Indiana, with a monthly production capacity of 300,000 cases, a monthly fixed cost of $262,500, and a variable cost of $3.25 per case. *Alternative 2:* Construct three plants, one each in Muncie, Indiana; Normal, Illinois; and Dayton, Ohio, with capacities of 120,000, 100,000, and 80,000, respectively, and monthly fixed costs of $120,000, $110,000, and $95,000 each. Variable costs would be only $3 per case because of lower distribution costs. To achieve these cost savings, sales from each smaller plant would be limited to demand within its home state. The total estimated monthly sales volume of 200,000 cases in these three midwestern states is distributed as follows: 80,000 cases in Indiana, 70,000 cases in Illinois, and 50,000 cases in Ohio.

A. Assuming a wholesale price of $5 per case, calculate the breakeven output quantities for each alternative.

B. At a wholesale price of $5 per case in all states, and assuming sales at the projected levels, which alternative expansion scheme provides Appalachia with the highest profit per month?

C. If sales increase to production capacities, which alternative would prove to be more profitable?

P8.9   **Learning Curves.** The St. Thomas Winery plans to open a new production facility in the Napa Valley of California. Based on information provided by the accounting department, the company estimates fixed costs of $250,000 per year and average variable costs of

$$AVC = \$10 + \$0.01Q,$$

where AVC is average variable cost (in dollars) and Q is output measured in cases of output per year.
A.   Estimate total cost and average total cost for the coming year at a projected volume of 4,000 cases.
B.   An increase in worker productivity because of greater experience or learning during the course of the year resulted in a substantial cost saving for the company. Estimate the effect of learning on average total cost if actual total cost was $522,500 at an actual volume of 5,000 cases.

P8.10   **Cost-Volume-Profit   Analysis.** Untouchable Package Service (UPS) offers overnight package delivery to Canadian business customers. UPS has recently decided to expand its facilities to better satisfy current and projected demand. Current volume totals two million packages per week at a price of $12 each, and average variable costs are constant at all output levels. Fixed costs are $3 million per week, and profit contribution averages one-third of revenues on each delivery. After completion of the expansion project, fixed costs will double, but variable costs will decline by 25%.
A.   Calculate the change in UPS's weekly breakeven output level that is due to expansion.
B.   Assuming that volume remains at two million packages per week, calculate the change in the degree of operating leverage that is due to expansion.
C.   Again assuming that volume remains at two million packages per week, what is the effect of expansion on monthly profit?

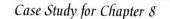

Case Study for Chapter 8

ESTIMATING THE COSTS OF NURSING CARE

Cost estimation and cost containment are an important concern for a wide range of for-profit and not-for-profit organizations offering health-care services. For such organizations, the accurate measurement of nursing costs per patient day (a measure of output) is necessary for effective management. Similarly, such cost estimates are of significant interest to public officials at the federal, state, and local government levels. For example, many state Medicaid reimbursement programs base their payment rates on historical accounting measures of average costs per unit of service. However, these historical average costs may or may not be relevant for hospital management decisions. During periods of substantial excess capacity, the overhead component of average costs may become irrelevant. When the facilities of providers are fully used and facility expansion becomes necessary to increase services, then all costs, including overhead, are relevant. As a result, historical average costs provide a useful basis for planning purposes only if appropriate assumptions can be made about the relative length of periods of peak versus off-peak facility usage. From a public-policy perspective, a further potential problem arises when hospital expense reimbursement programs are based on historical average costs per day, because the care needs and nursing costs of various patient groups can vary widely. For example, if the care received by the average publicly supported Medicaid patient actually costs more than that received by non-Medicaid patients, Medicaid reimbursement based on average costs for the entire facility would be inequitable to providers and could create access barriers for some Medicaid patients.

As an alternative to traditional cost estimation methods, one might consider using the engineering technique to estimate nursing costs. For example, the

Table 8.3

NURSING COSTS PER PATIENT DAY, NURSING SERVICES, AND PROFIT
STATUS FOR 40 HOSPITALS IN SOUTHEASTERN STATES

HOSPITAL	NURSING COSTS PER PATIENT DAY	SHOTS	IV THERAPY	PULSE TAKING	WOUND DRESSING	PROFIT STATUS (1 = FOR-PROFIT 0 = NOT-FOR-PROFIT)
1	125.00	1.50	0.75	2.25	0.75	0
2	125.00	1.50	0.75	2.25	0.75	0
3	115.00	1.50	0.50	2.00	0.50	1
4	125.00	2.00	0.75	2.25	0.75	0
5	122.50	1.50	0.50	2.25	0.75	0
6	120.00	1.50	0.75	2.25	0.75	1
7	125.00	1.75	0.75	2.00	0.50	0
8	130.00	1.75	0.75	2.25	0.75	0
9	117.50	1.50	0.50	2.25	0.50	0
10	130.00	1.75	0.75	3.25	0.75	0
11	125.00	1.50	0.75	3.00	0.50	0
12	127.50	1.50	0.75	2.50	0.75	0
13	125.00	1.75	0.75	2.50	0.50	0
14	125.00	1.50	0.50	2.50	0.75	0
15	120.00	1.50	0.75	2.25	0.50	0
16	125.00	1.50	0.50	2.25	0.75	0
17	130.00	1.75	0.75	2.50	0.75	0
18	120.00	1.50	0.50	2.25	0.50	0
19	125.00	1.50	0.75	2.25	0.75	0
20	122.50	1.50	0.50	2.50	0.75	0
21	117.50	1.75	0.50	2.00	0.50	1
22	120.00	1.50	0.50	2.50	0.50	0
23	122.50	1.50	0.75	2.50	0.75	1
24	117.50	1.50	0.50	2.50	0.50	0
25	132.50	1.75	0.75	2.50	0.75	0
26	120.00	1.75	0.50	2.25	0.50	1
27	122.50	1.75	0.50	2.50	0.50	0
28	125.00	1.50	0.75	2.50	0.75	0
29	125.00	1.50	0.50	2.00	0.75	0
30	130.00	1.75	0.75	2.25	0.75	0
31	115.00	1.50	0.50	2.00	0.50	0
32	115.00	1.50	0.50	2.25	0.50	0
33	130.00	1.75	0.75	2.50	0.75	0
34	132.50	1.75	0.75	3.00	0.75	0
35	117.50	1.50	0.50	2.00	0.50	1
36	122.50	1.50	0.50	2.50	0.75	0
37	112.50	1.50	0.50	2.00	0.50	0
38	130.00	1.50	0.75	3.25	0.75	0
39	130.00	1.50	0.75	3.25	0.75	1
40	125.00	1.50	0.75	3.00	0.75	1

labor cost of each type of service could be estimated as the product of an estimate of the time required to perform each service times the estimated wage rate per unit of time. Multiplying this figure by an estimate of the frequency of service provides an estimate of the aggregate cost of the service. A possible limitation to the accuracy of this engineering cost-estimation method is that treatment of a variety of illnesses often requires a combination of nursing services. To the extent that multiple services can be provided simultaneously, the engineering technique will tend to overstate actual costs unless the effect on costs of service "packaging" is allowed for.

Nursing cost estimation is also possible by means of a carefully designed regression-based approach using variable cost and service data collected at the ward, unit, or facility level. Weekly labor costs for registered nurses (RNs), licensed practical nurses (LPNs), and nursing aides might be related to a variety of patient services performed during a given measurement period. With sufficient variability in cost and service levels over time, useful estimates of variable labor costs become possible for each type of service and for each patient category (Medicaid, non-Medicaid, etc.). An important advantage of a regression-based approach is that it explicitly allows for the effect of service packaging on variable costs. For example, if shots and wound-dressing services are typically provided together, this will be reflected in the regression-based estimates of variable costs per unit.

Long-run costs per nursing facility can be estimated using either cross-section or time-series methods. By relating total facility costs to the service levels provided by a number of hospitals, nursing homes, or out-patient care facilities during a specific period, useful cross-section estimates of total service costs are possible. If case mixes were to vary dramatically according to type of facility, then the type of facility would have to be explicitly accounted for in the regression model analyzed. Similarly, if patient mix or service-provider efficiency is expected to depend, at least in part, on the for-profit or not-for-profit organization status of the care facility, the regression model must also recognize this factor. These factors plus price-level adjustments for inflation would be accounted for in a time-series approach to nursing cost estimation.

To illustrate a regression-based approach to nursing cost estimation, consider the following cross-section analysis of variable nursing costs conducted by the Southeast Association of Hospital Administrators (SAHA). Using confidential data provided by 40 regional hospitals, SAHA studied the relation between nursing costs per patient day and four typical categories of nursing services. These annual data appear in Table 8.3 The four categories of nursing services studied include shots, intravenous (IV) therapy, pulse taking and monitoring, and wound dressing. Each service is measured in terms of frequency per patient day. An output of 1.50 in the shots service category means that, on average, patients received one and one-half

Table 8.4

NURSING COSTS PER PATIENT DAY: COST ESTIMATION RESULTS

VARIABLE NAME	COEFFICIENT (1)	STANDARD ERROR OF COEFFICIENT (2)	T-STATISTIC (1) + (2) = (3)
Intercept	76.182	5.086	14.98
Shots	11.418	2.851	4.00
IV	10.052	3.646	2.76
Pulse	4.532	1.153	3.93
Wound dressing	18.933	3.370	5.62
For-profit status	−2.015	0.883	−2.38

Coefficient of determination = R^2 = 84.1%

Standard error of estimate = S.E.E. = $2.21

shots per day. Similarly, an output of 0.75 in the IV service category means that IV services were provided daily to 75% of a given hospital's patients, and so on. In addition to four categories of nursing services, the not-for-profit or for-profit status of each hospital is also indicated. Using a "dummy" (or binary) variable approach, the profit status variable equals 1 for the 8 for-profit hospitals included in the study and zero for the remaining 32 not-for-profit hospitals.

Cost estimation results for nursing costs per patient day derived using a regression-based approach are shown in Table 8.4.

A. Interpret the coefficient of determination (R^2) estimated for the nursing cost function.

B. Describe the economic and statistical significance of each estimated coefficient in the nursing cost function.

C. Average nursing costs for the eight for-profit hospitals in the sample are only $120.94 per patient day, or $3.28 per patient day less than the $124.22 average cost experienced by the 32 not-for-profit hospitals. How can this fact be reconciled with the estimated coefficient of −2.105 for the for-profit status variable?

D. Would such an approach for nursing cost estimation have practical relevance for publicly funded nursing cost reimbursement systems?

Linear Programming

Linear Programming
A solution method for maximization or minimization decision problems subject to underlying constraints.

Optimal Solution
Best answer.

A computer spreadsheet consists of electronically stored data in the form of an accounting income statement or balance sheet. Using sophisticated but easy-to-learn spreadsheet software such as Lotus 1-2-3 and powerful desktop computers, managers in both small and large organizations are able to use a proven optimization tool called **linear programming** *(LP) to isolate the best solution, or* **optimal solution,** *to decision problems. Linear programming is designed to solve problems that involve an objective function to be maximized or minimized, where the relevant objective function is subject to a variety of underlying constraints. Linear programming is a popular method because production decisions are often constrained by the availability of essential raw materials, equipment, or personnel. Plant location and delivery routing decisions must be made in light of production schedules, customer service requirements, and delivery costs. Inventory and cash management in accounting, capital budget decisions in finance, work scheduling and organization design in management, and media choice decisions in marketing all involve constraints on the allocation of scarce resources to achieve specific managerial goals. All are typical of the types of decision problems addressed using linear programming methods.*

Real-world constrained optimization problems seldom have a simple rule-of-thumb solution. Finding the optimal solution is complicated because careful analysis of all decision alternatives is required. Relations between the objective function and the constraint conditions can also be complex, as are relations among the constraint conditions themselves. This chapter illustrates how linear programming can be used to quickly and easily solve such real-world decision problems.[1]

Basic Assumptions

Many production or resource constraints faced by managers are inequalities. Constraints often limit resource use by specifying that the quantity employed must be less than or equal to ($\leq$) some fixed amount available. In other instances, constraints specify that the quantity or quality of output must be greater than or equal to ($\geq$) some minimum requirement. Linear programming handles constraint inequalities easily, making it a useful technique with several applications in managerial economics.

A typical linear programming problem might be to maximize output subject to the constraint that no more than 40 hours of skilled labor time per week be used. This labor

---

[1]See John W. Verity, "Coaxing Meaning Out of Raw Data," *Business Week,* February 3, 1997, 134-138.

constraint is expressed as an inequality where skilled labor $\leq$ 40 hours per week. Such an operating constraint means that although no more than 40 hours of skilled labor can be used, some excess capacity is permissible, at least in the short run. If 36 hours of skilled labor were fruitfully employed during a given week, the four hours per week of unused labor is called excess capacity. This is the type of production constraint that the linear programming approach is designed for.

As its name implies, linear programming can be applied only in situations in which the relevant objective function and constraint conditions are linear. Typical managerial decision problems that can be solved using the linear programming method involve revenue and cost functions and their composite, the profit function. Each of these must be linear; as output increases, revenues, costs, and profits must increase in a linear fashion. For revenues to be a linear function of output, product prices must be constant. For costs to be a linear function of output, both returns to scale and input prices must be constant. Constant input prices, when combined with constant returns to scale, result in a linear total cost function. If both output prices and unit costs are constant, then profit contribution and profits also rise in a linear fashion with output.

Product and input prices are relatively constant when a typical firm can buy unlimited quantities of input and sell unlimited amounts of output without changing prices. This occurs under conditions of pure competition. Therefore, linear programming methods are clearly applicable for firms in purely competitive industries in which constant returns to scale are operative. However, the linear programming method is also applicable in many instances when these conditions are not met over extensive ranges of output. Because linear programming is used for marginal analysis, it focuses on the effects of fairly modest output, price, and input changes. For moderate changes in current operating conditions, a constant-returns-to-scale assumption is often valid. Similarly, input and output prices are typically unaffected by modest changes from current levels. As a result, sales revenue, cost, and profit functions are often linear when only moderate changes in operations are contemplated, and the use of linear programming methods is entirely valid.

To illustrate, suppose that an oil company must choose the optimal output mix for a refinery with a capacity of 150,000 barrels of oil per day. The oil company may be perfectly valid in basing its analysis on the $20 per barrel prevailing market price for crude oil, regardless of how much is purchased or sold. This assumption might not be valid if the company were to quickly expand refinery output by a factor of 10, but within the 150,000 barrels per day range of feasible output, prices will be approximately constant. Up to capacity limits, it is also reasonable to expect that a doubling of crude oil input would lead to a doubling of refined output, and, therefore, returns to scale are constant. These same conditions hold for most services, as well as for both producer products and consumer goods.

In many instances, the underlying assumption of linearity is entirely valid, and the linear programming technique can be used to solve a wide variety of managerial decision problems. In other instances in which the objective function and constraint conditions can be usefully approximated by linear relations, the linear programming technique can also be fruitfully applied. Only when objective functions and constraint conditions are inherently nonlinear must more complicated *mathematical programming* techniques be applied. In most managerial applications, even when the assumption of linearity does not hold precisely, linear approximations seldom distort the analysis.

Production Planning for a Single Product

Although linear programming has been widely applied in managerial decision making, it has been developed most fully and used most frequently in production decisions. Often the decision problem is to determine the least-cost combination of inputs needed to produce a particular product. In other cases, the problem may be to obtain the maximum possible output from a fixed quantity of resources. Both problems can be readily solved using linear programming techniques. To illustrate the method, a simple two-input/one-output problem is examined. Later sections consider more realistic and complex problems.

PRODUCTION PROCESSES

Assume that a firm produces a single product, Q, using two inputs, L and K, which might represent labor and capital. Instead of assuming continuous substitution between L and K, as in Chapter 7, assume that Q can be produced using only four input combinations. In other words, four different production processes are available for making Q, each of which uses a different fixed combination of inputs L and K. In most industries, this is an entirely reasonable assumption, much more reasonable than the possibility of continuous input substitution. The production processes might represent four different plants, each with its own fixed asset configuration and labor requirements. Alternatively, they could be four different assembly stations or assembly lines, each using a different combination of capital equipment and labor.

The four production processes are illustrated as rays in Figure 9.1. Process A requires the combination of 15 units of L and 1 unit of K for each unit of Q produced. Process B uses 10 units of L and 2 units of K for each unit of output. Processes C and D use 7.5 units of L and 3 units of K, and 5 units of L with 5 units of K, respectively, for each unit of Q produced. Each point along the production ray for Process A combines L and K in the ratio 15 to 1; Process rays B, C, and D are developed in the same way. Each point along a single production ray combines the two inputs in a fixed ratio, with the ratios differing from one production process to another. If L and K represent labor and capital inputs, the four production processes might be different plants employing different production techniques. Process A is very labor intensive in comparison with the other production systems, whereas B, C, and D are based on increasingly capital-intensive technologies.

Point A_1 indicates the combination of L and K required to produce one unit of output using the A process. Doubling both L and K doubles the quantity of Q produced; this is indicated by the distance moved along ray A from A_1 to A_2. Line segment $0A_2$ is exactly twice the length of line segment $0A_1$ and thus represents twice as much output. Along production process ray A, the distance $0A_1 = A_1A_2 = A_2A_3 = A_3A_4 = A_4A_5$. Each

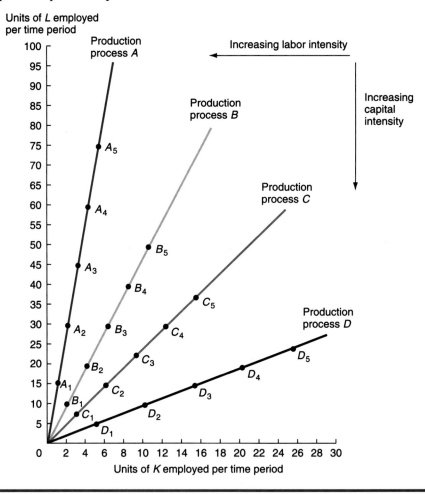

Figure 9.1

PRODUCTION PROCESS RAYS IN LINEAR PROGRAMMING

Points along each process ray represent combinations of inputs L and K required for that production process to produce output.

Units of L employed per time period

of these line segments indicates the addition of one unit of output using increased quantities of L and K in the fixed ratio of 15 to 1.

Output along the ray increases proportionately with increases in the input factors. If each input is doubled, output is doubled; if inputs increase by a factor of 10%, output increases by 10%. This follows from the linearity assumption noted previously: Each production process must exhibit constant returns to scale.

Output is measured in the same way along the three other production process rays in Figure 9.1. Point C_1 indicates the combination of L and K required to produce one unit of Q using Process C. The production of two units of Q using that process requires the combination of L and K indicated at point C_2; the same is true for points C_3, C_4, and C_5. Although production of additional units using Process C is indicated by line segments of equal length, just as for Process A, these line segments are of different lengths between the various production systems. Whereas each production process exhibits constant returns to scale, equal distances along *different* process rays do not ordinarily indicate equal output quantities.

PRODUCTION ISOQUANTS

Joining points of equal output on the four production process rays creates a set of isoquant curves. Figure 9.2 illustrates isoquants for $Q = 1, 2, 3, 4,$ and 5. These isoquants have the same interpretation as those developed in Chapter 8. Each isoquant represents combinations of input factors L and K that can be used to produce a given quantity of output. Production isoquants in linear programming are composed of linear segments connecting the various production process rays. Each of these isoquant segments is parallel to one another. For example, line segment A_1B_1 is parallel to segment A_2B_2; isoquant segment B_3C_3 is parallel to B_2C_2.

Points along each segment of an isoquant between two process rays represent a combination of output from each of the two adjoining production processes. Consider Point X in Figure 9.2, which represents production of 4 units of Q using 25 units of L and 16 units of K. None of the available production processes can manufacture Q using L and K in the ratio of 25 to 16, but that combination is possible by producing part of the output with Process C and part with Process D. In this case, 2 units of Q can be produced using Process C and 2 units using Process D. Production of 2 units of Q with Process C uses 15 units of L and 6 units of K. For the production of 2 units of Q with Process D, 10 units each of L and K are necessary. Although no single production system is available that can produce 4 units of Q using 25 units of L and 16 units of K, Processes C and D together can produce that combination.

All points lying along production isoquant segments can be interpreted in a similar manner. Each point represents a linear combination of output using the production process systems that bound the particular segment. Point Y in Figure 9.2 provides another illustration. At Y, 3 units of Q are produced, using a total of 38.5 units of L and 4.3 units of K.[2] This input-output combination is possible through a combination of Processes A and B. This can be analyzed algebraically. To produce 1 unit of Q by Process A requires 15 units of L and 1 unit of K. Therefore, to produce 1.7 units of Q requires 25.5 (1.7×15) units of L and 1.7 (1.7×1) units of K. To produce a single unit

---

[2] Another assumption of linear programming is that fractional variables are permissible. In many applications, this assumption is not important. For example, in the present illustration, we might be talking about labor hours and machine hours for the inputs. The solution value calling for $L = 38.5$ merely means that 38.5 hours of labor are required.

In some cases, however, inputs are large (whole plants, for example), and the fact that linear programming assumes divisible variables is important. In such cases, linear programming as described here may be inappropriate, and a more complex technique, integer programming, may be required.

PRODUCTION ISOQUANTS IN LINEAR PROGRAMMING

Each point along an isoquant represents the output level resulting from a given combination of inputs. For example, Point X depicts the production of 4 units of Q using 25 units of L and 16 units of K.

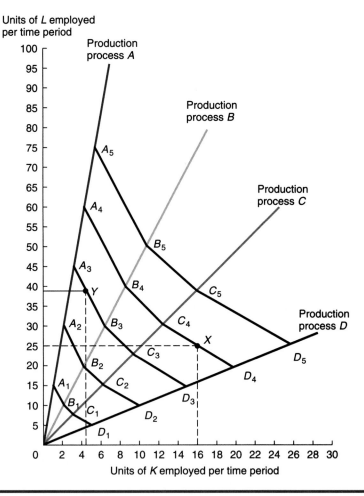

Units of L employed per time period

Units of K employed per time period

of Q by Process B requires 10 units of L and 2 units of K, so 1.3 units of Q requires 13 (10×1.3) units of L and 2.6 (2×1.3) units of K. Thus, Point Y calls for the production of 3 units of Q in total, 1.7 units by Process A and 1.3 units by Process B, using a total of 38.5 units of L and 4.3 units of K.

Relative Distance Method
Graphic technique used to solve linear programming problems.

One method of determining the quantity to be produced by each production process at varying points along the isoquant is called the relative distance method. The **relative distance method** is based on the fact that the location of a point along an isoquant determines the relative shares of production for the adjacent processes. If Point X in

Figure 9.2 were on process ray *C,* all output would be produced using Process *C.* Similarly, if *X* were on process ray *D,* all output would be produced using Process *D.* Since Point *X* lies between process rays *C* and *D,* both Processes *C* and *D* will be used to produce this output. Process *C* will be used relatively more than Process *D* if *X* is closer to process ray *C* than to process ray *D.* Similarly, Process *D* will be used relatively more than Process *C* if *X* is closer to process ray *D* than to process ray *C.* Because Point *X* in Figure 9.2 lies at the midpoint of the $Q = 4$ isoquant segment between C_4 and D_4, it implies production using Processes *C* and *D* in equal proportions. Thus, at Point *X,* $Q = 4$, $Q_C = 2$, and $Q_D = 2$.

The relative proportions of Process *A* and Process *B* used to produce $Q = 3$ at Point *Y* can be determined in a similar manner. Because *Y* lies closer to process ray *A* than to process ray *B,* Point *Y* entails relatively more output from Process *A* than from Process *B.* The share of total output produced using Process *A* is calculated by considering the distance B_3Y relative to B_3A_3. The share of total output produced using Process *B* is calculated by considering the distance A_3Y relative to A_3B_3. Starting from Point B_3, the segment B_3Y covers 56.6% of the total distance B_3A_3. This means that at Point *Y,* about 56.6% of total output is produced using Process *A* ($Q_A = 0.566 \times 3 = 1.7$) and 43.4% ($= 1.0 - 0.566$) using Process *B* ($Q_B = 0.434 \times 3 = 1.3$). Alternatively, starting from Point A_3, note that the segment A_3Y covers 43.4% of the total distance A_3B_3. At Point *Y,* 43.4% of total output is produced using Process *B* and 56.6% using Process *A.* Extreme accuracy would require painstaking graphic detail, but in many instances the relative distance method can adequately approximate production intensities along isoquants.

LEAST-COST INPUT COMBINATIONS

Adding isocost curves to a set of isoquants permits one to determine least-cost input combinations for the production of Product *Q.* This is shown in Figure 9.3 under the assumption that each unit of *L* costs $3 and each unit of *K* costs $10. The isocost curve illustrated indicates a total expenditure of $150.

The tangency between the isocost curve and the isoquant curve for $Q = 3$ at Point B_3 indicates that Process *B,* which combines Inputs *L* and *K* in the ratio 5 to 1, is the least-cost method of producing *Q.* For any expenditure level, production is maximized by using Process *B.* Alternatively, Process *B* is the least-cost method for producing any quantity of *Q,* given the assumed prices for *L* and *K.*

OPTIMAL INPUT COMBINATIONS WITH LIMITED RESOURCES

Frequently, firms faced with limited inputs during a production period find it optimal to use inputs in proportions other than the least-cost combination. To illustrate, consider the effect of limits on the quantities of *L* and *K* available in our example. Assume that only 20 units of *L* and 11 units of *K* are available during the current production period and that the firm seeks to maximize output of *Q.* These constraints are shown in Figure 9.4. The horizontal line drawn at $L = 20$ indicates the upper limit on the quantity of *L* that can be employed during the production period; the vertical line at $K = 11$ indicates a similar limit on the quantity of *K.*

DETERMINATION OF THE LEAST-COST PRODUCTION PROCESS

Figure 9.3

The tangency between the isoquant and isocost lines at Point B_3 reveals the least-cost combination of inputs.

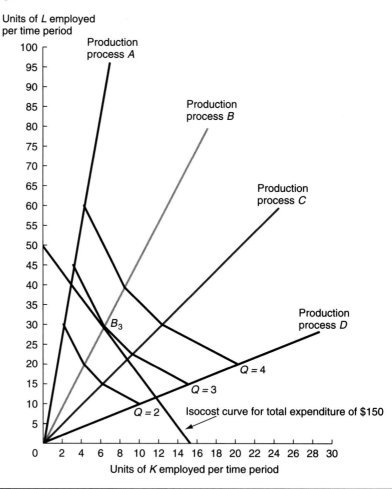

Units of L employed per time period

Production process A

Production process B

Production process C

Production process D

B_3

$Q = 4$

$Q = 3$

$Q = 2$

Isocost curve for total expenditure of $150

Units of K employed per time period

Feasible Space
Graphical region that is both technically and economically feasible and includes the optimal solution.

Production possibilities for this problem are determined by noting that, in addition to limitations on Inputs L and K, the firm must operate within the area bounded by production process rays A and D. Combining production possibilities with input constraints restricts the firm to operation within the shaded area on $0PRS$ in Figure 9.4. This area is known as the **feasible space** in the programming problem. Any point within this space combines L and K in a technically feasible ratio without exceeding availability limits on L and K. Because the firm is trying to maximize production of Q subject to constraints on the use of L and K, it should operate at the feasible space point that touches the highest possible isoquant. This is Point R in Figure 9.4, where $Q = 3$.

OPTIMAL INPUT COMBINATION WITH LIMITED RESOURCES

Figure 9.4

Given limited resources, output is maximized at Point R because this point lies on the highest iso-quant that intersects the feasible space.

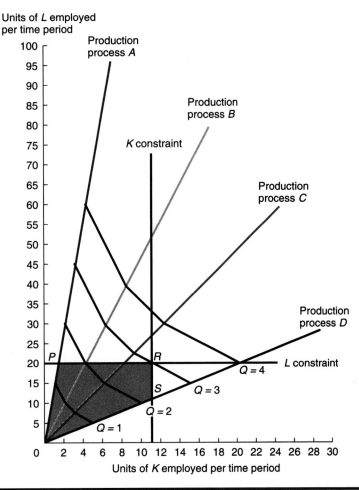

Although it is possible to solve problems like the foregoing example by using carefully drawn graphs, it is typically more useful to combine graphic analysis with analytical techniques to obtain accurate solutions efficiently. For example, consider Figure 9.4 again. Even if the isoquant for $Q = 3$ were not drawn, it would be apparent from the slopes of the isoquants for 2 or 4 units of output that the optimal solution to the problem must be at Point R. It is obvious from the graph that maximum production is obtained by operating at the point where both inputs are fully employed. Because R lies between production Processes C and D, the output-maximizing input combination uses only those two production processes. All 20 units of L and 11 units of

K will be employed, since Point R lies at the intersection of these two input constraints.

Using this information from the graph, it is possible to quickly and easily solve for the optimal quantities to be produced using Processes C and D. Recall that each unit of output produced using Process C requires 7.5 units of L. Thus, the total L required in Process C equals $7.5 \times Q_C$. Similarly, each unit produced using Process D requires 5 units of L, so the total L used in Process D equals $5 \times Q_D$. At Point R, 20 units of L are being used in Processes C and D together, and the following must hold:

$$7.5Q_C + 5Q_D = 20. \qquad (9.1)$$

A similar relation can be developed for the use of K. Each unit of output produced from Process C requires 3 units of K, whereas Process D uses 5 units of K to produce each unit of output. The total use of K in Processes C and D equals 11 units at Point R, so

$$3Q_C + 5Q_D = 11. \qquad (9.2)$$

Equations 9.1 and 9.2 both must hold at Point R. Output quantities from Processes C and D at that location are determined by solving these equations simultaneously. Subtracting Equation 9.2 from Equation 9.1 to eliminate the variable Q_D isolates the solution for Q_C:

$$7.5Q_C + 5Q_D = 20$$
$$\text{minus } \underline{3.0Q_C + 5Q_D = 11}$$
$$4.5Q_C = 9$$
$$Q_C = 2.$$

Substituting 2 for Q_C in Equation 9.2 determines output from Process D:

$$3(2) + 5Q_D = 11,$$
$$5Q_D = 5,$$
$$Q_D = 1.$$

Total output at Point R is 3 units, composed of 2 units from Process C and 1 unit from Process D.

The combination of graphic and analytic techniques allows one to obtain precise linear programming solutions with relative ease.

Production Planning for Multiple Products

Many production decisions are more complex than the preceding example. Consider the problem of finding the optimal output mix for a multiproduct firm facing restrictions on productive facilities and other inputs. This problem, which is faced by a host of companies producing consumer and producer goods alike, is readily solved with linear programming techniques.

Visualizing Higher Profits

Linear programming is often portrayed as a visual means of characterizing financial, management, marketing, and production problems. It is—at least when only a limited number of products or product dimensions are being analyzed. When the optimal level of production for two products is sought, for example, a simple graph of the appropriate linear programming problem offers managers a useful intuitive basis for considering the best means of meeting a variety of production constraints or criteria. However, when a multitude of products is offered, or when a large number of production characteristics must be considered, the typical linear programming problem becomes too complex to be visualized graphically. In such instances, computer-based solutions using spreadsheets offer a tractable alternative for analyzing and solving linear programming problems.

The intuitive appeal of graphic approaches to solving linear programming problems has encouraged companies to seek visual means for characterizing daunting problems. One of the newest such approaches is called Geographic Information Systems, or GIS, a computer-based display that makes it possible to view and analyze data on digitized maps. The GIS concept isn't new, but its widespread application is. Utilities, oil companies, and governments have long used such systems to plot transmission routes, manage natural resources, and track pollution. The GIS technology already accounts for more than $2 billion a year in hardware, software, and consulting sales. But the cost of GIS has fallen so dramatically it is now becoming one of the most useful business information tools. Diverse companies have adopted GIS mapping as an instinctive means for deciphering data that were previously analyzed only in the form of complex printouts, spreadsheets, and charts. Maps and graphs are intuitive ways to organize things, and people remember things about space that they don't remember about other ways of organizing information.

A GIS typically consists of a demographic database, digitized maps, a desktop computer, and software that enables the user to add customized corporate data. The annual cost of bringing together these elements has dropped sharply, from $125,000 per user in 1985 to just a few thousand dollars today. That's largely because desktop computers are now powerful enough to manage and analyze the masses of data that mapping involves. A host of startup companies have also emerged to offer low-cost business mapping data and software. For example, only a few years ago a complete set of U.S. street maps and census information was over $50,000; today, such maps can be downloaded at little or no cost from a number of sites on the worldwide web. A plethora of niche software manufacturers also use the internet to distribute specialized GIS software programs that can be extremely cost effective to adapt to meet firm-specific needs.

One of the most compelling uses of GIS is to wring value out of already developed customer databases. For example, computer mapping is one of the best ways to take advantage of marketing databases loaded with geographic information, such as customer addresses, and demographic information that reveals customer buying habits. With customized GIS software manufacturers can more effectively solicit distributors and better support their sales staffs. To persuade a retail outlet to allocate more shelf space to its products, for example, a sales rep might present retailers a demographic map of the store's clientele, along with information about their buying habits.

Business programs are now the most rapidly growing segment of the GIS software market. Businesses increasingly turn to GIS software programs to help with site selection, target marketing, sales support, disaster and fleet management, and regulatory compliance. In an interesting application, textile manufacturers can now use LP methods to help solve stock cutting problems, when pieces have irregular shapes and can be rotated. Research has shown that this problem becomes a parametric linear program with a nonlinear parameter corresponding to the orientation of the moving figure.

In sum, more and more companies are coming to learn that business graphics and LP methods are a useful means of visualizing higher profits.

See: Myron Orfield, "A Map is Worth a Thousand Words," *Brookings Review,* 15 (Winter 1997), 9.

OBJECTIVE FUNCTION SPECIFICATION

Consider a firm that produces Products X and Y and uses Inputs A, B, and C. To maximize total profit, the firm must determine optimal quantities of each product subject to constraints imposed on input availability. It is often useful to structure such a linear programming problem in terms of the maximization of profit contribution, or total revenue minus variable costs, rather than to explicitly maximize profits. Of course, fixed costs must be subtracted from profit contribution to determine net profits. However, because fixed costs are constant, maximizing profit contribution is tantamount to maximizing profit. The output mix that maximizes profit contribution also maximizes net profit.

An equation that expresses the goal of a linear programming problem is called the **objective function.** In the present example, assume that the firm wishes to maximize total profits from the two products, X and Y, during each period. If per-unit profit contribution (the excess of price over average variable costs) is \$12 for Product X and \$9 for Product Y, the objective function is

Objective Function
Equation that expresses the goal of a linear programming problem.

$$\text{Maximize } \pi = \$12Q_X + \$9Q_Y. \tag{9.3}$$

Q_X and Q_Y represent the quantities of each product produced. The total profit contribution, π, earned by the firm equals the per-unit profit contribution of X times the units of X produced and sold, plus the profit contribution of Y times Q_Y.

CONSTRAINT EQUATION SPECIFICATION

Table 9.1 specifies the available quantities of each input and their usage in the production of X and Y. This information is all that is needed to form the constraint equations.

The table shows that 32 units of Input A are available in each period. Four units of A are required to produce each unit of X, whereas 2 units of A are necessary to produce 1 unit of Y. Since 4 units of A are required to produce a single unit of X, the total amount of A used to manufacture X can be written as $4Q_X$. Similarly, 2 units of A are required to produce each unit of Y, so $2Q_Y$ represents the total quantity of A used to produce Product Y. Summing the quantities of A used to produce X and Y provides an expression for

Table 9.1

INPUTS AVAILABLE FOR PRODUCTION OF X AND Y

INPUT	QUANTITY AVAILABLE PER TIME PERIOD	QUANTITY REQUIRED PER UNIT OF OUTPUT	
		X	Y
A	32	4	2
B	10	1	1
C	21	0	3

the total usage of A. Because this total cannot exceed the 32 units available, the constraint condition for Input A is

$$4Q_X + 2Q_Y \leq 32. \qquad \qquad \textbf{(9.4)}$$

The constraint for Input B is determined in a similar manner. One unit of Input B is necessary to produce each unit of either X or Y, so the total amount of B employed is $1Q_X + 1Q_Y$. The maximum quantity of B available in each period is 10 units; thus, the constraint requirement associated with Input B is

$$1Q_X + 1Q_Y \leq 10. \qquad \qquad \textbf{(9.5)}$$

Finally, the constraint relation for Input C affects only the production of Y. Each unit of Y requires an input of 3 units of C, and 21 units of Input C are available. Usage of C is given by the expression $3Q_Y$, and the relevant constraint equation is

$$3Q_Y \leq 21. \qquad \qquad \textbf{(9.6)}$$

Constraint equations play a major role in solving linear programming problems. One further concept must be introduced, however, before the linear programming problem is completely specified and ready for solution.

NONNEGATIVITY REQUIREMENT

Because linear programming is merely a mathematical tool for solving constrained optimization problems, nothing in the technique itself ensures that an answer makes economic sense. In a production problem for a relatively unprofitable product, the mathematically optimal output level might be a *negative* quantity, clearly an impossible solution. In a distribution problem, an optimal solution might indicate negative shipments from one point to another, which again is impossible.

To prevent economically meaningless results, a nonnegativity requirement must be introduced. This is merely a statement that all variables in the problem must be equal to or greater than zero. For the present production problem, the following expressions must be added:

$$Q_X \geq 0,$$

and

$$Q_Y \geq 0.$$

Graphic Specification and Solution

Having specified all the component parts of the firm's linear programming problem, the problem can now be illustrated graphically and analyzed algebraically.

ANALYTIC EXPRESSION

The decision problem is to maximize total profit contribution, π, subject to resource constraints. This is expressed as

$$\text{Maximize} \qquad\qquad \pi = \$12Q_X + \$9Q_Y \qquad\qquad\qquad (9.3)$$

subject to the following constraints:

Input A:	$4Q_X + 2Q_Y \leq 32,$	**(9.4)**
Input B:	$1Q_X + 1Q_Y \leq 10,$	**(9.5)**
Input C:	$3Q_Y \leq 21,$	**(9.6)**

where

$$Q_X \geq 0 \text{ and } Q_Y \geq 0.$$

Each variable and coefficient is exactly as specified previously.

GRAPHING THE FEASIBLE SPACE

In Figure 9.5, the graph of the constraint equation for Input A, $4Q_X + 2Q_Y = 32$ indicates the maximum quantities of X and Y that can be produced given the limitation on the availability of Input A. A maximum of 16 units of Y can be produced if no X is manufactured; 8 units of X can be produced if the output of Y is zero. Any point along the line connecting these two outputs represents the maximum combination of X and Y that can be produced with no more than 32 units of A.

This constraint equation divides the XY plane into two half spaces. Every point lying on the line or to the left of the line satisfies the constraint expressed by the equation $4Q_X + 2Q_Y \leq 32$; every point to the right of the line violates that expression. Only points on the constraint line or to the left of it are in the feasible space. The shaded area of Figure 9.5 represents the feasible area limited by the constraint on Input A.

In Figure 9.6 the feasible space is limited further by adding constraints for Inputs B and C. The constraint on Input B is expressed as $Q_X + Q_Y = 10$. If no Y is produced, a maximum of 10 units of X can be produced; if output of X is zero, 10 units of Y can be manufactured. All combinations of X and Y lying on or to the left of the line connecting these two points are feasible with respect to utilization of Input B.

The horizontal line at $Q_Y = 7$ in Figure 9.6 represents the constraint imposed by Input C. Since C is used only in the production of Y, it does not constrain the production of X. Seven units are the maximum quantity of Y that can be produced with 21 units of C available.

These three input constraints, together with the nonnegativity requirement, completely define the feasible space shown as the shaded area of Figure 9.6. Only points within this area meet all constraints.

CONSTRAINT IMPOSED BY LIMITATIONS ON INPUT A.

The constraint equation for Input A represents the maximum combination of X and Y that can be produced with 32 units of A.

Figure 9.5

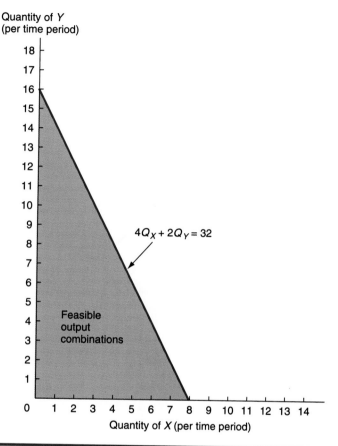

Quantity of Y
(per time period)

$4Q_X + 2Q_Y = 32$

Feasible output combinations

Quantity of X (per time period)

GRAPHING THE OBJECTIVE FUNCTION

The objective function, $\pi = \$12Q_X + \$9Q_Y$, can be graphed in $Q_X Q_Y$ space as a series of isoprofit curves. This is illustrated in Figure 9.7, where isoprofit curves for \$36, \$72, \$108, and \$144 are shown. Each isoprofit curve illustrates all possible combinations of X and Y that result in a constant total profit contribution. For example, the isoprofit curve labeled $\pi = \$36$ identifies each combination of X and Y that results in a total profit contribution of \$36; all output combinations along the $\pi = \$72$ curve provide a total profit contribution of \$72; and so on. It is clear from Figure 9.7 that isoprofit curves are a series of parallel lines that take on higher values as one moves upward and to the right.

Figure 9.6

FEASIBLE SPACE

The feasible space is reduced further by the addition of constraints on Inputs B and C. Only points within the shaded region meet all constraints.

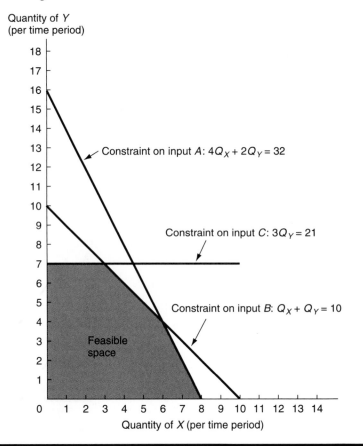

The general formula for isoprofit curves can be developed by considering the profit function $\pi = aQ_X + bQ_Y$, where a and b are the profit contributions of Products X and Y, respectively. Solving the isoprofit function for Q_Y creates an equation of the following form:

$$Q_Y = \frac{\pi}{b} - \frac{a}{b} Q_X.$$

Given the individual profit contributions, a and b, the Q_Y intercept equals the profit level of the isoprofit curve divided by the profit per unit earned on Q_Y, π/b. Slope of the objective function is given by the relative profitability of the two products, $-a/b$. Because the relative profitability of the products is not affected by the output level, the isoprofit

GRAPHIC SOLUTION OF THE LINEAR PROGRAMMING PROBLEM

Figure 9.7

Points along the isoprofit line represent all possible combinations of X and Y that result in the same profit level. Point M is on the highest isoprofit curve that intersects the feasible space. Thus, it represents the output combination that will maximize total profit given input constraints.

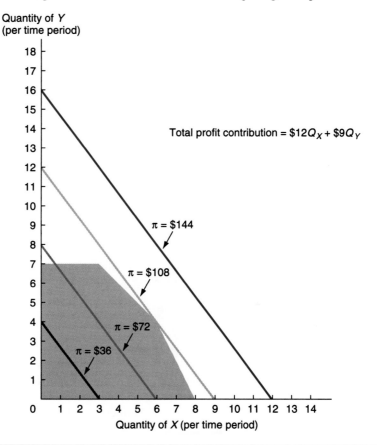

curves consist of a series of parallel lines. In this example, all isoprofit curves have a slope of $-12/9$, or -1.33.

GRAPHIC SOLUTION

Because the firm's objective is to maximize total profit, it should operate on the highest isoprofit curve obtainable. To see this point graphically, Figure 9.7 combines the feasible space limitations shown in Figure 9.6 with the family of isoprofit curves discussed above. Using this approach, point M in the figure is indicated as the optimal solution. At point M, the firm produces 6 units of X and 4 units of Y, and the total profit is $108 [=($12 × 6) + ($9 × 4)], which is the maximum available under the conditions stated in the problem. No other point within the feasible spaces touches so high an isoprofit curve.

Using the combined graphic and analytical method introduced in the preceding section, M can be identified as the point where $Q_X = 6$ and $Q_Y = 4$. At M, constraints on Inputs A and B are binding. At M, 32 units of Input A and 10 units of Input B are being completely used to produce X and Y. Thus, Equations 9.4 and 9.5 can be written as equalities and solved simultaneously for Q_X and Q_Y. Subtracting two times Equation 9.5 from Equation 9.4 gives

$$4Q_X + 2Q_Y = 32$$

$$\text{minus } 2Q_X + 2Q_Y = 20$$

$$2Q_X = 12$$

$$Q_X = 6.$$

Substituting 6 for Q_X in Equation 9.5 results in

$$6 + Q_Y = 10,$$

$$Q_Y = 4.$$

Corner Point
Spot in the feasible space where the X-axis, Y-axis, or constraint conditions intersect.

Notice that the optimal solution to the linear programming problem occurs at a **corner point** of the feasible space. A corner point is a spot in the feasible space where the X-axis, Y-axis, or constraint conditions intersect. When the objective function and all constraints are specified in linear form, as is always true in linear programming problems, the firm will always optimize at a point of capacity limitation on the feasible space boundary.

A final step is necessary to show that the optimal solution to any linear programming problem always lies at a corner of the feasible space. Because all of the relations in a linear programming problem must be linear by definition, every boundary of the feasible space is linear. Furthermore, the objective function is linear. Thus, the constrained optimization of the objective function takes place either at a corner of the feasible space or at one boundary face, as is illustrated by Figure 9.8.

In Figure 9.8 the linear programming example has been modified by assuming that each unit of either X or Y yields a profit of $5. In this case, the optimal solution to the problem includes any of the combinations of X and Y found along Line LM. All of these combinations are feasible and result in a total profit of $50. If all points along Line LM provide optimal combinations of output, the combinations found at Corners L and M are also optimal. Since the firm is indifferent about producing at Point L or at Point M, or at any point in between, any such location provides an optimal solution to the production problem. It is possible to achieve an optimal solution at a corner of the feasible space even when the highest obtainable isoprofit curve lies along a boundary of the feasible space.

As a result, the search for an optimal solution can be limited to just the corners of each linear programming problem's feasible space. In other words, the infinite number of points lying within the feasible space can be ignored and efforts can be concentrated solely on corner solutions. This greatly reduces the number of necessary computations.

Figure 9.8	GRAPHIC SOLUTION OF A LINEAR PROGRAMMING PROBLEM WHEN THE OBJECTIVE FUNCTION COINCIDES WITH A BOUNDARY OF THE FEASIBLE SPACE

When the objective function coincides with the boundary of the feasible space, several different output combinations will produce maximum profits.

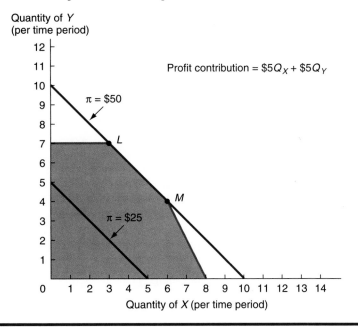

Algebraic Specification and Solution

The graphic technique just described illustrates the nature of linear programming, but it can be applied only in the two-output case. Because most linear programming problems contain far too many variables and constraints to allow solution by graphic analysis, algebraic methods must be employed. Algebraic techniques are of great practical relevance because they can be used to solve complex linear programming problems using modern computer software.

SLACK VARIABLES

Slack Variables
Factors that indicate the amount by which constraint conditions are exceeded.

The concept of **slack variables** must be introduced to solve linear programming problems algebraically. In the case of less-than-or-equal-to constraints, slack variables are used to *increase* the left side to equal the right side limits of the constraint conditions. In the illustrative problem, one slack variable is added to each constraint to account for excess capacity. The firm is faced with capacity constraints on Input Factors A, B, and C, so the algebraic specification of the problem contains three slack variables: S_A, indicating the units of A that are not used in any given solution; S_B, representing unused units of B; and S_C, which measures the unused units of C.

With slack variables, each constraint equation becomes an equality rather than an inequality. After adding the relevant slack variable, the constraint on Input A, $4Q_X + 2Q_Y \leq 32$, is

$$4Q_X + 2Q_Y + S_A = 32. \tag{9.7}$$

$S_A = 32 - 4Q_X - 2Q_Y$ is the amount of Input A not used to produce X or Y. Similar equality constraints can be specified for Inputs B and C. The equality form of the constraint on Input B is

$$1Q_X + 1Q_Y + S_B = 10. \tag{9.8}$$

The constraint equation for Input C is

$$3Q_Y + S_C = 21. \tag{9.9}$$

The introduction of slack variables not only simplifies algebraic analysis, but slack variables' solution values also provide useful information. In a production problem, for example, slack variables with *zero* values at the optimal solution indicate inputs that are limiting factors and cause bottlenecks. Slack variables with *positive* values at the optimal solution indicate excess capacity in the related input factor. Slack variables cannot take on negative values, since this would imply that the amount of resource use exceeds available supply. The information provided by slack variable solution values is important in long-range planning and is a key benefit derived from algebraic solution methods.

ALGEBRAIC SOLUTION

The complete specification of the illustrative programming problem is as follows:

$$\text{Maximize } \pi = \$12Q_X + \$9Q_Y, \tag{9.3}$$

subject to these constraints:

$$4Q_X + 2Q_Y + S_A = 32, \tag{9.7}$$

$$1Q_X + 1Q_Y + S_B = 10, \tag{9.8}$$

$$3Q_Y + S_C = 21, \tag{9.9}$$

where

$$Q_X \geq 0, \ Q_Y \geq 0, \ S_A \geq 0, \ S_B \geq 0, \ S_C \geq 0.$$

The problem is to find the set of values for Variables Q_X, Q_Y, S_A, S_B, and S_C that maximizes Equation 9.3 and at the same time satisfies the constraints imposed by Equations 9.7, 9.8, and 9.9.

As shown previously, a single exact solution to a system of three constraint equations with five unknown variables cannot be determined without further information. A simultaneous solution to the constraint equations must be found, but there are more unknowns (five) than constraint equations (three). In such circumstances, a unique solution does not exist; multiple solutions are possible. However, because the solution to any linear programming problem occurs at a corner of the feasible space, values can be determined for some of the unknown variables in Equations 9.7, 9.8, and 9.9. At each corner of the feasible space, the number of nonzero variables exactly equals the number of constraint equations. At each corner point, the number of known constraint conditions is exactly equal to the number of unknown variables. In such circumstances, a single unique solution can be found for each variable at each corner point of the feasible space. The optimal solution is that corner point solution with the most desirable value for the objective function.[3]

Consider Figure 9.9, in which the feasible space for the illustrative problem has been graphed once again. At the origin, where neither X nor Y is produced, Q_X and Q_Y both equal zero. Slack exists in all inputs, however, so S_A, S_B, and S_C are all greater than zero. Now move up the vertical axis to Point K. Here Q_X and S_C both equal zero, because no X is being produced and Input C is being used to the fullest extent possible. However, Q_Y, S_A, and S_B all exceed zero. At Point L, Q_X, Q_Y, and S_A are all positive, but S_B and S_C equal zero. The remaining corners, M and N, can be examined similarly, and at each of them the number of nonzero-valued variables exactly equals the number of constraints. At each corner point, the constraints can be expressed as a system with three equations and three unknowns that can be solved algebraically.

Solving the constraint equations at each corner point provides values for Q_X and Q_Y, as well as for S_A, S_B, and S_C. The total profit contribution at each corner is likewise determined by inserting relevant values for Q_X and Q_Y into the objective function (Equation 9.3). The corner solution that produces the maximum profit is the optimal solution to the linear programming problem.

Simplex Solution Method
Iterative technique used to provide algebraic solutions for linear programming problems.

This iterative process is followed in what is called the **simplex solution method.** Computer programs find solution values for all variables at each corner point, then isolate that corner point with the optimal solution to the objective function. Highly complex linear programming problems can be solved in only a few seconds when using the simplex method and high-speed desktop computers, whereas they are long and tedious when done by hand. While it is perhaps not worth delving into the simplex procedure in great detail, the method can be illustrated for the present example.

Although a unique solution for this problem is obtained when any two variables are set equal to zero, it is convenient to begin by setting Q_X and Q_Y equal to zero and examining the origin solution. Substituting zero values for Q_X and Q_Y into the constraint Equations 9.7, 9.8, and 9.9 results in a value for each slack variable that equals the total units available: $S_A = 32$, $S_B = 10$, and $S_C = 21$. At the origin, neither X nor Y is produced and no input is used in production. Total profit contribution at the origin corner of the feasible space is zero.

---

[3]In almost all linear programming problems, the number of nonzero-valued variables in all corner solutions exactly equals the number of constraints in the problem. Only under a particular condition known as *degeneracy,* when more than two constraints coincide at a single corner of the feasible space, are there fewer nonzero-valued variables. This condition does not hinder the technique of solution considered in this chapter.

Figure 9.9

DETERMINATION OF ZERO-VALUED VARIABLES AT
CORNERS OF THE FEASIBLE SPACE

At all corner points of the feasible space, the number of nonzero-valued variables equals the number of constraint equations.

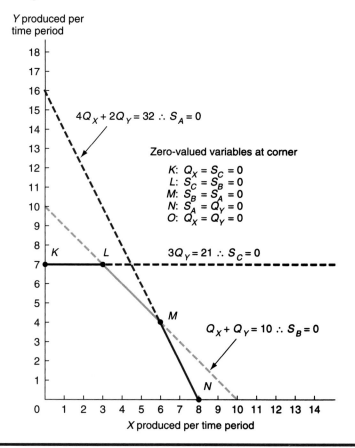

Similarly, it is possible to examine the solution at a second corner point, N in Figure 9.10, where Q_Y and S_A equal zero. After making the appropriate substitution into constraint Equation 9.7, the value for Q_X is

$$4Q_X + 2Q_Y + S_A = 32,$$

$$(4 \times Q_X) + (2 \times 0) + 0 = 32,$$

$$4Q_X = 32,$$

$$Q_X = 8.$$

(9.7)

With the value of Q_X determined, it is possible to substitute into Equations 9.8 and 9.9 and determine values for S_B and S_C:

$$Q_X + Q_Y + S_B = 10,$$
$$8 + 0 + S_B = 10, \tag{9.8}$$
$$S_B = 2,$$

and

$$3Q_Y + S_C = 21,$$
$$(3 \times 0) + S_C = 21, \tag{9.9}$$
$$S_C = 21.$$

Total profit contribution at this point is

$$\pi = \$12Q_X + \$9Q_Y$$
$$= (\$12 \times 8) + (\$9 \times 0) \tag{9.3}$$
$$= \$96.$$

Next, assign zero values to S_B and S_A to reach solution values for Point M. Substituting zero values for S_A and S_B in Equations 9.7 and 9.8 results in two equations with two unknowns:

$$4Q_X + 2Q_Y + 0 = 32. \tag{9.7}$$
$$Q_X + Q_Y + 0 = 10. \tag{9.8}$$

Multiplying Equation 9.8 by two and subtracting this result from Equation 9.7 provides the solution value for Q_X:

$$4Q_X + 2Q_Y = 32$$
$$\text{minus } \underline{2Q_X + 2Q_Y = 20}$$
$$2Q_X = 12 \tag{9.7}$$
$$Q_X = 6$$

Then, substituting 6 for Q_X in Equation 9.8 finds $Q_Y = 4$. Total profit contribution in this case is $108 [= (\$12 \times 6) + (\$9 \times 4)]$.

Similar algebraic analysis provides the solution for each remaining corner of the feasible space. However, rather than work through those corner solutions, the results are shown in Table 9.2. It is apparent, just as illustrated in the earlier graphic analysis, that the optimal solution occurs at Point M, where 6 units of X and 4 units of Y are produced. Total profit is $108, which exceeds the profit at any other corner of the feasible space.

Table 9.2

ALGEBRAIC SOLUTION TO A LINEAR PROGRAMMING PROBLEM

SOLUTION AT CORNER	VALUE OF VARIABLE					TOTAL PROFIT CONTRIBUTION
	Q_Y	Q_Y	S_A	S_B	S_C	
0	0	0	32	10	21	$ 0
N	8	0	0	2	21	96
M	6	4	0	0	9	108
L	3	7	6	0	0	99
K	0	7	18	3	0	63

SLACK VARIABLES AT THE SOLUTION POINT

At each corner point solution, values for each slack variable are also determined. For example, at the optimal solution (Corner M) reached in the preceding section, S_A and S_B both equal zero, meaning that Inputs A and B are used to the fullest extent possible. S_C is not equal to zero and must be solved for. To find the solution for S_C, $Q_Y = 4$ is substituted into Constraint Equation 9.9:

$$3 \times Q_Y + S_C = 21,$$
$$3 \times 4 + S_C = 21, \tag{9.9}$$
$$S_C = 9.$$

The optimal combination of X and Y completely exhausts available quantities of Inputs A and B, but 9 units of Input C remain unused. Because Inputs A and B impose effective constraints on the firm's profits, more of each must be acquired to expand output. Input C is in excess supply, so the firm would certainly not want more capacity of C; it might even attempt to reduce its purchases of C during future periods. If C is a fixed facility, such as a machine tool, the firm might offer some of that excess capacity to other companies.

COMPUTER-BASED SOLUTION METHODS

The linear programming problem illustrated thus far is simple by design. It can be solved graphically and algebraically to illustrate the linear programming technique using both methods. However, linear programming problems encountered in the real world are often quite complex and frequently involve a large number of constraints and output variables. Such problems are too complicated to solve graphically. The geometry is messy for three outputs and impossible for four or more. In real-world applications, computer software programs use algebraic techniques to handle large numbers of variables and constraints.

Karmarkar's LP Breakthrough

On a typical day, thousands of U.S. Air Force planes ferry cargo and military passengers around the globe. To keep those jets flying, the Military Airlift Command (MAC) must juggle schedules for pilots and other flight personnel. In addition, the MAC has to make literally millions of calculations to determine the most efficient flight route, cargo weight, fuel loading, and so on. After all of these details have been carefully accounted for, unexpected bad weather or emergency changes in priorities can force a complete recalculation of the entire flight plan.

Getting all of the pieces to fit together has been a classic linear programming (LP) dilemma. On the one hand, if an LP computer program could help increase fuel efficiency by just 2%, it would be worth millions of dollars per year. On the other hand, the underlying complexity of the Air Force's transportation problem is so great that, until recently, it defied the capabilities of even the most sophisticated supercomputers.

In 1984, Narendra K. Karmarkar, a young scientist for AT&T Bell Laboratories, discovered an algorithm, or mathematical formula, that greatly speeds the process of solving even the most complex LP problems. In the traditional approach to solving LP problems, one corner of the feasible solution space is solved and compared to the solutions for adjacent points. If a better solution is found, the computer is instructed to move off in that direction. This iterative process continues until the program finds itself boxed in by inferior solutions. Karmarkar's algorithm employs a radically different geometric approach that finds an optimal solution more efficiently. Working from within the interior of the feasible space, the Karmarkar method avoids the tedious surface route and uses projective geometry to reconfigure the solution structure. By studying this structure, the program determines the direction in which the optimal solution is likely to lie. Then the problem structure is allowed to return to its original shape, and the program moves toward the solution, pausing at intervals to repeat the process until it finds the optimal solution.

Despite early skepticism, there is a great deal of excitement today in both the scientific and business communities concerning the potential of Karmarkar's method for solving complex LP problems. For example, AT&T is using Karmarkar's formula to forecast the most cost-effective method for meeting future demands on the telephone network linking countries with shores on the Pacific Ocean. AT&T must estimate current and future telephone demand between every pair of switching points within the network. With a ten-year horizon, the AT&T planning model includes over 42,000 variables. Considering that many variables, using the traditional LP solution method requires four to seven hours of mainframe computer time to answer each what-if question. Karmarkar's method finds answers in just a few minutes.

The cost savings possible using the Karmarkar method make the LP approach practical in a host of new applications. For example, AT&T assesses its long-distance telephone network in an LP problem involving 800,000 variables. A multiprocessor supercomputer and a software version of Karmarkar's algorithm have been optimized for high-speed parallel processing and installed at St. Louis's Scott Air Force Base to help solve MAC logistics problems.

So fast have been recent developments in the area that many new and unanticipated applications are sure to emerge as new generations of software for the Karmarkar algorithm become available. The possibilities include a broad range of applications, from assessing risk factors in stock and bond portfolios to setting up production schedules in industrial factories. The accuracy of economic forecasting may also increase if Karmarkar's method allows economists to study the effects of economic factors on highly detailed input/output tables that include both firm-specific and economy-wide influences. When combined with the capabilities of amazingly powerful supercomputers, the Karmakar breakthrough promises to rapidly extend the application of LP techniques.

See: William G. Wild and Otis Port, "The Startling Discovery Bell Labs Kept in the Shadows," *Business Week,* September 21, 1987, 69-76; and G. Mosheiov and A. Reveh, "On Trend Estimation of Time Series: A Simple Linear Programming Approach," *Journal of the Operational Research Society,* 48 (January 1997), 90-96.

The Dual in Linear Programming

Primal
Original problem statement (symmetrical to dual).

Dual
Secondary problem statement (symmetrical to primal).

For every maximization problem in linear programming, there exists a symmetrical minimization problem; for every minimization problem, there exists a symmetrical maximization problem. These pairs of related maximization and minimization problems are known as the **primal** and **dual** linear programming problems. The symmetry or duality between constrained maximization and constrained minimization problems is a key concept in managerial economics.

THE DUALITY CONCEPT

The concept of duality demonstrates the symmetry between the value of a firm's products and the value of resources used in production. With the duality concept, it is possible to show that value maximization can be attained by focusing on either resource requirements and the revenue-generating capability of a firm's products or on the cost of resources and their productivity.

In addition to providing valuable insight into the economics of optimal resource employment, duality provides the key to solving difficult constrained optimization problems. Because of the symmetry between primal and dual problem specifications, either one can be constructed from the other and the solution to either problem can be used to solve both. This is helpful because it is sometimes easier to obtain the solution to the dual problem than to the original or primal problem.

Finally, the duality concept also allows one to evaluate the solution to a constrained decision problem in terms of the activity required for optimization and in terms of the economic impact of constraint conditions. Analysis of the constraint conditions and slack variable solutions frequently provides important information for long-range planning. In fact, the **primal solution** is often described as a tool for short-run operating decisions, whereas the **dual solution** is often seen as a tool for long-range planning. The duality concept demonstrates the need to recognize that operating decisions and long-range planning are related.

Primal Solution
Input for short-run operating decisions.

Dual Solution
Input for long-range planning.

SHADOW PRICES

Shadow Prices
Implicit values associated with linear-programming-problem decision variables.

To examine the duality concept, the idea of implicit values or **shadow prices** must be introduced. In the primal linear programming problem discussed previously, the values Q_X and Q_Y maximize the firm's profit subject to constraints imposed by limitations of Input Factors A, B, and C. Duality theory indicates that an identical operating decision would result if one had instead chosen to minimize the costs of resources employed in producing Q_X and Q_Y, subject to an output constraint.

The key to this duality is that relevant costs are not the acquisition costs of inputs but, rather, the economic costs of using them. For a resource that is available in a fixed amount, this cost is not acquisition cost but opportunity cost. Consider, for example, a skilled labor force employed by a firm. If workers are fully utilized producing valuable products, a reduction in skilled labor will reduce valuable output, and an increase in skilled labor will increase the production of valuable output. If some labor is shifted from the production of one product to another, the cost of using skilled labor in this new activity is the value of the original product that can no longer be produced. The marginal cost of a constrained resource that is fully utilized is its opportunity cost as measured by the value of foregone production. If a limited resource such as skilled labor is not fully utilized, then at least the last unit of that resource is not productive and its marginal value is zero. Acquiring additional excess resources does not increase valuable output. The firm would incur a zero opportunity cost if it applied currently unused resources in some different activity.

The economic value, or opportunity cost, of a constrained resource depends on the extent to which it is utilized. When a limited resource is fully utilized, its marginal value in use is positive. When a constrained resource is not fully utilized, its marginal value in use is zero. Minimizing the value of limited resources used to produce valuable output is nothing more than minimizing the opportunity cost of employing those resources. Minimization of opportunity costs is equivalent to maximizing the value of output produced with those resources.

Since the economic value of constrained resources is determined by their value in use rather than by historical acquisition costs, such amounts are called implicit values or shadow prices. The term *shadow price* is used because it represents the price that a manager would be willing to pay for additional units of a constrained resource. Comparing the shadow price of a resource with its acquisition price indicates whether the firm has an incentive to increase or decrease the amount acquired during future production periods. If shadow prices exceed acquisition prices, the resource's marginal value exceeds marginal cost and the firm has an incentive to expand employment. If acquisition cost exceeds the shadow price, there is an incentive to reduce employment. These relations and the importance of duality can be clarified by relating the dual to the linear programming problem discussed previously.

THE DUAL OBJECTIVE FUNCTION[4]

In the original or primal problem statement, the goal is to maximize profits, and the (primal) objective function is

$$\text{Maximize } \pi = \$12Q_X + \$9Q_Y. \tag{9.3}$$

The dual problem goal is to minimize implicit values or shadow prices for the firm's resources. Defining V_A, V_B, and V_C as the shadow prices for Inputs A, B, and C, respectively, and π^* as the total implicit value of the firm's fixed resources, the dual objective function (the dual) is

$$\text{Minimize } \pi^* = 32V_A + 10V_B + 21V_C. \tag{9.10}$$

---

[4]Rules for constructing the dual linear programming problem from its related primal are provided in Appendix 9A, at the end of this chapter.

Since the firm has 32 units of A, the total implicit value of Input A is 32 times A's shadow price, or $32V_A$. If V_A, or Input A's shadow price is found to be \$1.50 when the dual equations are solved, the implicit value of A is \$48 ($= 32 \times \$1.50$). Inputs B and C are handled in the same way.

THE DUAL CONSTRAINTS

In the primal problem, the constraints stated that the total units of each input used to produce X and Y must be equal to or less than the available quantity of input. In the dual, the constraints state that the total value of inputs used to produce one unit of X or one unit of Y must not be less than the profit contribution provided by a unit of these products. In other words, the shadow prices of A, B, and C times the amount of each of the inputs needed to produce a unit of X or Y must be equal to or greater than the unit profit contribution of X or of Y. Because resources have value only when used to produce output, they can never have an implicit value, or opportunity cost, that is less than the value of output.

In the example, unit profit is defined as the excess of price over variable cost, price and variable cost are both constant, and profit per unit for X is \$12 and for Y is \$9. As shown in Table 9.1, each unit of X requires 4 units of A, 1 unit of B, and 0 units of C. The total implicit value of resources used to produce X is $4V_A + 1V_B$. The constraint requiring that the implicit cost of producing X be equal to or greater than the profit contribution of X is

$$4V_A + 1V_B \geq 12. \tag{9.11}$$

Because 2 units of A, 1 unit of B, and 3 units of C are required to produce each unit of Y, the second dual constraint is

$$2V_A + 1V_B + 3V_C \geq 9. \tag{9.12}$$

Since the firm produces only two products, the dual problem has only two constraint equations.

DUAL SLACK VARIABLES

Dual slack variables can be incorporated into the problem, thus allowing the constraint conditions to be expressed as equalities. Letting L_X and L_Y represent the two slack variables, constraint Equations 9.11 and 9.12 become

$$4V_A + 1V_B - L_X = 12, \tag{9.13}$$

and

$$2V_A + 1V_B + 3V_C - L_Y = 9. \tag{9.14}$$

These slack variables are *subtracted* from the constraint equations, since greater-than-or-equal-to inequalities are involved. Using slack variables, the left-hand sides of the constraint conditions are thus *decreased* to equal the right-hand sides' profit contributions.

Dual slack variables measure the *excess* of input value over output value for each product. Alternatively, dual slack variables measure the opportunity cost associated with producing X and Y. This can be seen by examining the two constraint equations. Solving constraint Equation 9.13 for L_X, for example, provides

$$L_X = 4V_A + 1V_B - 12.$$

This expression states that L_X is equal to the implicit cost of producing 1 unit of X minus the profit contribution provided by that product. The dual slack variable L_X is a measure of the opportunity cost of producing Product X. It compares the profit contribution of Product X, $12, with the value to the firm of the resources necessary to produce it.

A zero value for L_X indicates that the marginal value of resources required to produce one unit of X is exactly equal to the profit contribution received. This is similar to marginal cost being equal to marginal revenue at the profit-maximizing output level. A positive value for L_X indicates that the resources used to produce X are more valuable, in terms of the profit contribution they can generate, when used to produce the other product Y. A positive value for L_X measures the firm's opportunity cost (profit loss) associated with production of Product X. The slack variable L_Y is the opportunity cost of producing Product Y. It will have a value of zero if the implicit value of resources used to produce 1 unit of Y exactly equals the $9 profit contribution provided by that product. A positive value for L_Y measures the opportunity loss in terms of the foregone profit contribution associated with product Y.

A firm would not choose to produce if the value of resources required were greater than the value of resulting output. It follows that a product with a positive slack variable (opportunity cost) is not included in the optimal production combination.

SOLVING THE DUAL PROBLEM

The dual programming problem can be solved with the same algebraic technique that was employed to obtain the primal solution. In this case, the dual problem is

Minimize $$\pi^* = 34V_A + 10V_B + 21V_C, \tag{9.10}$$

subject to

$$4V_A + 1V_B - L_X = 12, \tag{9.13}$$

and

$$2V_A + 1V_B + 3V_C - L_Y = 9, \tag{9.14}$$

where

$$V_A, \ V_B, \ V_C, \ L_X, \ \text{and} \ L_Y \ \text{all} \geq 0.$$

Because there are only two constraints in this programming problem, the maximum number of nonzero-valued variables at any corner solution is two. One can proceed with the solution by setting three of the variables equal to zero and solving the constraint equations for the values of the remaining two. By comparing the value of the objective function at each feasible solution, the point at which the function is minimized can be determined. This is the dual solution.

To illustrate the process, first set $V_A = V_B = V_C = 0$, and solve for L_X and L_Y:

$$(4 \times 0) + (1 \times 0) - L_X = 12, \tag{9.13}$$

$$L_X = -12.$$

$$(2 \times 0) + (1 \times 0) + 0 + (3 \times 0) - L_Y = 9, \tag{9.14}$$

$$L_Y = -9.$$

Since L_X and L_Y cannot be negative, this solution is outside the feasible set.

The values just obtained are inserted into Table 9.3 as Solution 1. All other solution values can be calculated in a similar manner and used to complete Table 9.3. It is apparent from the table that not all solutions lie within the feasible space. Only Solutions 5, 7, 9, and 10 meet the nonnegativity requirement while also providing a number of nonzero-valued variables that are exactly equal to the number of constraints. These four solutions coincide with the corners of the dual problem's feasible space.

At Solution 10, the total implicit value of Inputs A, B, and C is minimized. Solution 10 is the optimum solution, where the total implicit value of employed resources exactly equals the $108 maximum profit primal solution. Thus, optimal solutions to primal and dual objective functions are identical.

At the optimal solution, the shadow price for Input C is zero, $V_C = 0$. Because shadow price measures the marginal value of an input, a zero shadow price implies that the resource in question has a zero marginal value to the firm. Adding another unit of

Table 9.3

SOLUTIONS FOR THE DUAL PROGRAMMING PROBLEM

VALUE OF THE VARIABLE

SOLUTION NUMBER	V_A	V_B	V_C	L_X	L_Y	TOTAL VALUE IMPUTED TO THE FIRM'S Resources
1	0	0	0	−12	−9	a
2	0	0	3	−12	0	a
3	0	0	b	0	b	a
4	0	9	0	−3	0	a
5	0	12	0	0	3	$120
6	0	12	−1	0	0	a
7	4.5	0	0	6	0	$144
8	3	0	0	0	−3	a
9	3	0	1	0	0	$117
10	1.5	6	0	0	0	$108

[a]Outside the feasible space.

[b]No solution.

this input adds nothing to the firm's maximum obtainable profit. A zero shadow price for Input C is consistent with the primal solution that Input C is not a binding constraint. Excess capacity exists in C, so additional units of C would not increase production of either X or Y. The shadow price for Input A of $1.50 implies that this fixed resource imposes a binding constraint. If an additional unit of A is added, the firm can increase total profit by $1.50. It would increase profits to buy additional units of Input A at any price less than $1.50 per unit, at least up until the point at which A is no longer a binding constraint. This assumes that the cost of Input A is currently fixed. If those costs are variable, the firm would be willing to pay $1.50 *above* the current price of Input A to eliminate this constraint. Since availability of B also imposes an effective constraint, the firm can also afford to pay up to $6 for a marginal unit of B.

Finally, both dual slack variables equal zero at the optimal solution. This means that the implicit value of resources required to produce a single unit of X or Y is exactly equal to the profit contribution provided. The opportunity cost of producing X and Y is zero, meaning that the resources required for their production are not more valuable in some alternative use. This is consistent with the primal solution, since both X and Y are produced at the optimal solution. Any product with a positive opportunity cost is suboptimal and would not be produced.

USING THE DUAL SOLUTION TO SOLVE THE PRIMAL

The dual solution does not indicate optimal amounts of X and Y. It does, however, provide all the information necessary to determine the optimum output mix. The dual solution shows that Input C does not impose a binding constraint on output of X and Y. Further, it demonstrates that $\pi = \pi^* = \$108$ at the optimum output of X and Y. The dual solution also offers evidence on the value of primal constraint slack variables. To see this, recall the three constraints in the primal problem:

$$\text{Constraint on } A: \quad 4Q_X + 2Q_Y + S_A = 32,$$

$$\text{Constraint on } B: \quad 1Q_X + 1Q_Y + S_B = 10,$$

$$\text{Constraint on } C: \quad 3Q_Y + S_C = 21.$$

The dual solution indicates that the constraints on A and B are binding, because both inputs have positive shadow prices, and only resources that are fully utilized have a nonzero marginal value. Accordingly, the slack variables S_A and S_B equal zero, and the binding primal constraints can be rewritten as

$$4Q_X + 2Q_Y = 32,$$

and

$$1Q_X + 1Q_Y = 10.$$

With two equations and only two unknowns, this system can be solved for Q_X and Q_Y. Multiplying the second constraint by two and subtracting from the first provides

$\mathcal{LP}$ on the $\mathcal{PC}$!

Until recently, the complexity of real-world decision problems often made it impractical for the nonspecialist to use linear programming (LP) methods. As a result, the application of LP techniques had been largely restricted to managers of the relatively few firms that employ computer programmers and have expensive mainframe computers. Instead of using more appropriate LP methods, managers of many small to medium-sized companies still plug hypothetical financial and operating data into spreadsheet software programs, and then recalculate profit figures to see how various changes might affect the bottom line. A major problem with this popular "What if?" approach to decision analysis is the haphazard way in which various alternatives are considered. Dozens of time-consuming recalculations are often necessary before suggestions emerge that lead to a considerable improvement in operating efficiency. Even then, managers have no assurance that superior decision alternatives are not available.

The frustrations and limitations of the "What if?" approach to decision analysis are sure to become a thing of the past with the increasing popularity of new *Solver* LP programs, used in conjunction with popular spreadsheet software like *Lotus 1-2-3* and *Microsoft Excel*. Designed for use with *Lotus 1-2-3*, for example, *What-if Solver* constitutes a powerful user-friendly LP software program for the personal computer (PC) environment. *What-if Solver* is a powerful, yet easy to use, LP program that enables users to solve a wide range of optimization problems without leaving the spreadsheet environment. It uses the Simplex method for linear constrained optimization and the Generalized Reduced Gradient Method for nonlinear constrained optimization. A student edition of *What-if Solver* is also available at very modest cost that will solve most of the optimization problems that are typically encountered in business and government, including LP problems that involve up to 120 variables and 120 constraints. The student edition of *What-if Solver* provides a complete sensitivity analysis for LP problems that will indicate, for example, objective function coefficient ranges, the potential for cost reduction, shadow prices, and so on. More powerful professional versions of *What-if Solver*

LP programs, and others like the award-winning *What's Best* LP software, are available to easily solve highly complex business and government problems at a cost of only a few hundred dollars.

For users of the *Microsoft Windows* operating environment, LP software programs are often included as a basic feature of spreadsheet software. *Lotus 1-2-3 for Windows,* for example, incorporates a *Solver* LP tool that is capable of solving all but the toughest LP problems. *Solver* is extremely user-friendly for those with little LP training, and like most *Windows* programs, it requires little computer experience.

Of course, the practical value of any tool for managerial decision making is measured in terms of how well it actually works. Easy to follow linear programming applications in the student edition of *What-if Solver* illustrate how LP techniques are actually used to solve problems in transportation routing, staff scheduling, and financial planning. Whenever a company needs to move a quantity of goods from and to multiple locations, such as plants, regional warehouses, or retail stores, it faces a practical LP problem. By minimizing route mileage, operating costs can also be minimized and outlays for capital investment can often be avoided. Many companies routinely save thousands of dollars per year on shipping costs by solving linear programming problems of this type. Similarly, many types of businesses and government agencies use LP methods to solve the problem of scheduling employees' working hours to meet customer service demands, which might vary by the hour or the day, in light of employee availability and preferences. Other examples of practical applications include the use of LP techniques to help banks decide on the best use of loanable funds, and models to help investors decide on the optimal allocation of a stock and bond portfolio.

As new generations of user-friendly LP software emerge, appreciation of the value of the LP technique as a practical tool for decision analysis is bound to flourish.

See: Stephen H. Wildstrom, "Suites That Just Got Sweeter," *Business Week,* January 27, 1997, 16.

$$4Q_X + 2Q_Y = 32,$$

$$\text{minus } \underline{2Q_X + 2Q_Y = 20,}$$

$$2Q_X = 12,$$

$$Q_X = 6,$$

and

$$6 + Q_Y = 10,$$

$$Q_Y = 4.$$

These values of Q_X and Q_Y, found after learning from the dual which constraints were binding, are identical to the values found by solving the primal problem directly. Having obtained the value for Q_Y, it is possible to substitute Constraint C and solve for the amount of slack in that resource:

$$3Q_Y + S_C = 21,$$

$$S_C = 21 - 3 \times 4 = 9.$$

These relations, which allow one to solve either the primal or the dual specification of a linear programming problem and then quickly obtain the solution to the other, can be generalized by the two following expressions:

$$\text{Primal Objective Variable}_i \times \text{Dual Slack Variable}_i \equiv 0 \qquad \textbf{(9.15)}$$

$$\text{Primal Slack Variable}_j \times \text{Dual Objective Variable}_j \equiv 0 \qquad \textbf{(9.16)}$$

Equation 9.15 states that if an ordinary variable in the primal problem takes on a nonzero value in the optimal solution to that problem, its related dual slack variable must be zero. Only if a particular Q_i is zero valued in the solution to the primal can its related dual slack variable, L_i, take on a nonzero value. A similar relation exists between the slack variables in the primal problem and their related ordinary variables in the dual, as indicated by Equation 9.16. If the primal slack variable is nonzero valued, then the related dual variable will be zero valued, and vice versa.

Constrained Cost Minimization: Another Linear Programming Example

Constrained cost-minimization problems are frequently encountered in managerial decision making. One such example is the problem of minimizing advertising expenditures subject to certain audience exposure requirements. For example, consider a firm that is planning an advertising campaign for a new product. Goals set for the campaign include exposure to at least 100,000 individuals, no fewer than 80,000 of whom have an annual income of at least $50,000 and no fewer than 40,000 of whom are single. For simplicity, assume that the firm has only radio and television media available for this campaign. One television advertisement costs $10,000 and is expected to reach an average audience of 20,000 persons. Ten thousand of these individuals will have an income of $50,000 or more, and 4,000 will be single. A radio advertisement costs $6,000 and reaches a total audience of 10,000, all of whom have at least $50,000 in income. Eight thousand of those exposed to a radio advertisement are single. Table 9.4 summarizes these data.

THE PRIMAL PROBLEM

The objective is to minimize the cost of the advertising campaign. Since total cost is merely the sum of the amounts spent on radio and television advertisements, the objective function is

Minimize   Cost = $6,000R + $10,000TV,

where R and TV represent the number of radio and television ads, respectively, that are employed in the advertising campaign.

   This linear programming problem has three constraint equations, including the minimum audience exposure requirement, the audience income requirement, and the marital status requirement. The minimum audience exposure requirement states that the number of persons exposed to radio ads plus the number exposed to television ads must be equal to or greater than 100,000 persons. Algebraically, 10,000 times the number of radio ads plus 20,000 times the number of television advertisements must be equal to or greater than 100,000:

$$10,000R + 20,000TV \geq 100,000.$$

The two remaining constraints can be constructed in a similar fashion from the data in Table 9.4. The audience income constraint is written:

$$10,000R + 10,000TV \geq 80,000,$$

and the marital status constraint is given by

$$8,000R + 4,000TV \geq 40,000.$$

Combining the cost-minimization objective function with these three constraint conditions written in equality form using slack variables gives the complete linear programming problem:

Minimize   Cost = $6,000R + $10,000TV,

Table 9.4

ADVERTISING MEDIA RELATIONS

	RADIO	TELEVISION
Cost per ad	$ 6,000	$10,000
Total audience per ad	10,000	20,000
Audience per ad with income ≥$50,000	10,000	10,000
Unmarried audience per ad	8,000	4,000

subject to

$$10,000R + 20,000TV - S_A = 100,000,$$

$$10,000R + 10,000TV - S_I = 80,000,$$

$$8,000R + 4,000TV - S_S = 40,000,$$

and

$$R,\ TV,\ S_A,\ S_I,\ and\ S_S \geq 0.$$

S_A, S_I, and S_S are slack variables indicating the extent to which minimums on total audience exposure, exposure to individuals with incomes of at least $50,000, and exposure to single individuals, respectively, have been exceeded. Note that each slack variable is *subtracted* from the relevant constraint equation because greater-than-or-equal-to inequalities are involved. Excess capacity or nonzero slack variables for any of the constraints mean that audience exposure minimums have been exceeded.

The solution to this linear programming problem is easily obtained using a combination of graphic and analytical methods. Figure 9.10 illustrates this solution. The feasible space problem is bordered by the three constraint equations and the nonnegativity requirements. An isocost curve shows that costs are minimized at Point M, where the total audience exposure and income constraints are binding. With these constraints binding, slack variables $S_A = S_I = 0$. Thus,

$$10,000R + 20,000TV = 100,000,$$

$$minus\ \underline{10,000R + 10,000TV = 80,000,}$$

$$10,000TV = 20,000,$$

$$TV = 2,$$

and

$$10,000R + 20,000(2) = 100,000,$$

$$10,000\ R = 60,000,$$

$$R = 6.$$

The firm should employ 6 radio advertisements and 2 television advertisements to minimize costs while still meeting audience exposure requirements. Total cost for such a campaign is $56,000.

THE DUAL PROBLEM

The dual to the advertising-mix linear programming problem offers interesting and valuable information to management. The dual is a constrained-maximization problem, since the primal problem is a minimization problem. The objective function of the dual is expressed in terms of shadow prices or implicit values for the primal problem con-

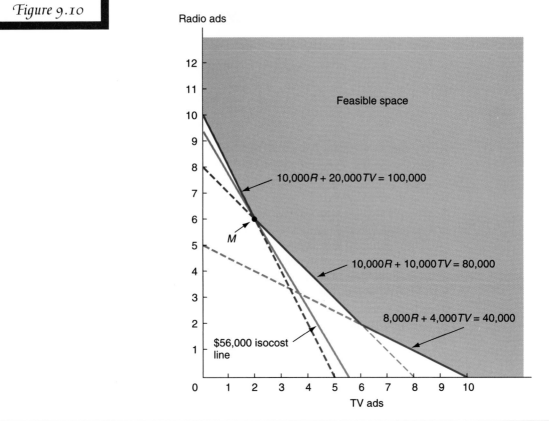

Figure 9.10

ADVERTISING COST-MINIMIZATION LINEAR PROGRAMMING PROBLEM

straint conditions. Thus, the dual objective function includes an implicit value, or shadow price, for the minimum audience exposure requirement, the audience income requirement, and the marital status requirement. Since constraint limits in the primal problem become the dual objective function coefficients, the dual objective function is

$$\text{Maximize } C^* = 100,000V_A + 80,000V_I + 40,000V_S,$$

where V_A, V_I, and V_S are shadow prices for the minimum audience exposure, audience income, and marital status requirements.

Dual constraints are based on the two variables from the primal objective function. Thus, there are two constraint conditions in the dual, the first associated with radio advertisements and the second with television advertisements. Both constraints are of the less-than-or-equal-to type, since primal constraints are of the greater-than-or-equal-to type.

The radio advertising constraint limit is the $6,000 radio advertisements coefficient from the primal objective function. Coefficients for each shadow price in this constraint equation are given by the advertising effectiveness measures for a single radio advertisement. The coefficient for the audience exposure shadow price, V_A, is 10,000, the number of individuals reached by a single radio advertisement. Similarly, the coefficient for V_I is 10,000 and that for V_S is 8,000. Thus, the dual radio advertisements constraint is

$$10,000V_A + 10,000V_I + 8,000V_S \leq \$6,000.$$

The dual television advertising constraint is developed in the same fashion. Since each TV advertisement reaches a total audience of 20,000, this is the coefficient for the V_A variable in the second dual constraint equation. Coefficients for V_I and V_S are 10,000 and 4,000, respectively, because these are the numbers of high-income and single persons reached by one TV advertisement. The $10,000 cost of a television advertisement is the limit to the second dual constraint, which can be written:

$$20,000V_A + 10,000V_I + 4,000V_S \leq \$10,000.$$

Following the introduction of constraint slack variables, the dual programming problem is

Maximize $\qquad C^* = 100,000V_A + 80,000V_I + 40,000V_S,$

subject to

$$10,000V_A + 10,000V_I + 8,000V_S + L_R = \$6,000$$

$$20,000V_A + 10,000V_I + 4,000V_S + L_{TV} = \$10,000$$

and

$$V_A, \ V_I, \ V_S, \ L_R, \ and \ L_{TV} \geq 0.$$

SOLVING THE DUAL

It is possible but difficult to solve this dual problem using a three-dimensional graph or the simplex method. However, because the primal problem has been solved already, information from this solution can be used to easily solve the dual. Remember that the solutions to the primal and dual of a single linear programming problem are complementary, and the following must hold:

Primal Objective Variable$_i$ × Dual Slack Variable$_i$ = 0.

Primal Slack Variable$_j$ × Dual Objective Variable$_j$ = 0.

In this linear programming problem,

$$R \times L_R = 0 \ and \ TV \times L_{TV} = 0,$$

and

$$S_A \times V_A = 0, \ S_I \times V_I = 0, \text{ and } S_S \times V_S = 0.$$

Because both R and TV have nonzero solutions in the primal, the dual slack variables L_R and L_{TV} must equal zero at the optimal solution. Furthermore, since there is excess audience exposure to the single marital status category in the primal solution, $S_S \neq 0$, the related dual shadow price variable V_S must also equal zero in the optimal solution. This leaves only V_A and V_I as two unknowns in the two-equation system of dual constraints:

$$10,000V_A + 10,000V_I = \$6,000,$$

$$20,000V_A + 10,000V_I = \$10,000.$$

Subtracting the second constraint equation from the first gives

$$-10,000V_A = -\$4,000,$$

$$V_A = \$0.40.$$

Substituting the value $0.40 for V_A in either constraint equation produces a value of $0.20 for V_I. Finally, substituting the appropriate values for V_A, V_I, and V_S into the dual objective function gives a value of $C^* = \$56,000 \ [= (\$0.40 \times 100,000) + (\$0.20 \times 80,000) + (\$0 \times 40,000)]$. This is the same figure as the $56,000 minimum cost solution to the primal.

INTERPRETING THE DUAL SOLUTION

The primal solution tells management the minimum-cost advertising mix. The dual problem results are equally valuable. Each dual shadow price indicates the change in cost that would accompany a one-unit change in the various audience exposure requirements. These prices show the marginal costs of increasing each audience exposure requirement by one unit. For example, V_A is the marginal cost of reaching the last individual in the overall audience. If there were a one-person reduction in the total audience exposure requirement, a cost saving of $V_A = \$0.40$ would be realized. The marginal cost of increasing total audience exposure from 100,000 to 100,001 individuals would also be 40¢.

Shadow prices for the remaining constraint conditions are interpreted in a similar manner. The shadow price for reaching individuals with incomes of at least $50,000 is $V_I = \$0.20$, or 20¢. It would cost an extra 20¢ per person to reach more high-income individuals. A zero value for V_S, the marital status shadow price, means that the proposed advertising campaign already reaches more than the 40,000 minimum required number of single persons. Thus, a small change in the marital status constraint has no effect on total costs.

By comparing these marginal costs with the benefits derived from additional exposure, management is able to judge the effectiveness of its media advertising campaign. If the expected profit per exposure exceeds 40¢, it would prove profitable to design an advertising campaign for a larger audience. Likewise, if the expected return per exposure to high-income individuals is greater than 20¢, promotion to this category of potential customers should be increased. Conversely, if marginal profitability is less than marginal cost, audience size and/or income requirements should be reduced.

Dual slack variables also have an interesting interpretation. They represent opportunity costs of using each advertising medium. L_R measures the excess of cost over benefit associated with using radio, whereas L_{TV} indicates the excess of cost over benefit for television. Since $L_R = L_{TV} = 0$, the marginal benefit derived just equals the marginal cost incurred for both media. Both radio and TV are included in the optimal media mix, as was indicated in the primal solution.

This example again demonstrates the symmetry of the primal and dual specifications of linear programming problems. Either specification can be used to describe and solve the same basic problem. Both primal and dual problem statements and solutions offer valuable insight for decision making.

Summary

Linear programming is a valuable technique for solving maximization or minimization problems in which inequality constraints are imposed on the decision maker. This chapter introduces graphic and analytic approaches for setting up, solving, and interpreting the solutions to such problems.

- **Linear programming** is a proven optimization tool used to isolate the best solution, or **optimal solution,** to decision problems. The technique is ideally suited to solving decision problems that involve an objective function to be maximized or minimized, where the relevant objective function is subject to underlying constraints.

- Simple linear programming problems can be solved graphically using the **relative distance method.** The **feasible space** is the graphical region showing the linear programming problem solution space that is both technically and economically feasible.

- An equation that expresses the goal of a linear programming problem is called the **objective function.**

- The optimal solution to a linear programming problem occurs at the intersection of the objective function and a **corner point** of the feasible space. A corner point is a spot in the feasible space where the X-axis, Y-axis, or constraint conditions intersect.

- **Slack variables** indicate the amount by which constraint conditions are exceeded. In the case of less-than-or-equal-to constraints, slack variables are used to *increase* the left side to equal the right side limits of the constraint conditions. In the case of greater-than-or-equal-to constraints, slack variables are used to *decrease* the left side to equal the right side limits of the constraint conditions.

- The **simplex solution method** is an iterative method used to solve linear programming problems. In this procedure, computer programs find solution values for all variables at each corner point, then isolate that corner point with the optimal solution to the objective function.

- For every maximization problem in linear programming, there exists a symmetrical minimization problem; for every minimization problem, there exists a symmetrical maximization problem. These pairs of related maximization and minimization problems are known as the **primal** and **dual** linear programming problems.
- The **primal solution** is often described as a tool for short-run operating decisions, whereas the **dual solution** is often seen as a tool for long-range planning. Both provide management with valuable insight for the decision-making process.
- **Shadow prices** are implicit values or opportunity costs associated with linear programming problem decision variables. In the case of output, shadow prices indicate the marginal cost of a one-unit increase in output. In the case of the constraints, shadow prices indicate the marginal cost of a one-unit relaxation in the constraint condition.

  During recent years, rapid advances in user-friendly computer software have allowed the widespread application of linear programming techniques to a broad range of complex managerial decision problems. With the background provided in this chapter, it is possible to apply this powerful technique to a wide array of problems in business, government, and the not-for-profit sector.

QUESTIONS

Q9.1 Give some illustrations of managerial decision situations in which you think the linear programming technique would be useful.

Q9.2 Why can't linear programming be used in each of the following circumstances?
A. Strong economies of scale exist.
B. As the firm expands output, the prices of variable factors of production increase.
C. As output increases, product prices decline.

Q9.3 Do equal distances along a given production process ray in a linear programming problem always represent an identical level of output?

Q9.4 Assume that output can be produced only using Processes A and B. Process A requires Inputs L and K to be combined in the fixed ratio $2L:4K$, and Process B requires $4L:2K$. Is it possible to produce output efficiently using $3L$ and $3K$? Why or why not?

Q9.5 Describe the relative distance method used in graphic linear programming analysis.

Q9.6 Is the number of isocost, isorevenue, or isoprofit lines in a typical two-input bounded feasible space limited?

Q9.7 In linear programming, why is it so critical that the number of nonzero-valued variables exactly equals the number of constraints at corners of the feasible space?

Q9.8 Will maximizing a profit contribution objective function always result in also maximizing total net profits?

Q9.9 The primal problem calls for determining the set of outputs that will maximize profit, subject to input constraints.
A. What is the dual objective function?
B. What interpretation can be given to the dual variables called the shadow prices or implicit values?
C. What does it mean if a dual variable or shadow price equals zero?

Q9.10 How are the solution values for primal and dual linear programming problems actually employed in practice?

SELF-TEST PROBLEMS AND SOLUTIONS

ST9.1 **Cost Minimization.** Idaho Natural Resources (INR) has two mines with different production capabilities for producing the same type of ore. After mining and crushing, the ore is graded into three classes: high, medium, and low. The company has contracted to provide local smelters with 24 tons of high-grade ore, 16 tons of medium-grade ore, and 48 tons of low-grade ore each week. It costs INR $10,000 per day to operate Mine A and $5,000 per day to run Mine B. In a day's time, Mine A produces 6 tons of high-grade ore, 2 tons of medium-grade ore, and 4 tons of low-grade ore. Mine B produces 2, 2, and 12 tons per day of each grade, respectively. Management's short-run problem is to determine how many days per week to operate each mine under current conditions. In the long run, management wishes to know how sensitive these decisions will be to changing economic conditions.

A report prepared for the company by an independent management consultant addressed the company's short-run operating concerns. The consultant claimed that the operating problem could be solved using linear programming techniques by which the firm would seek to minimize the total cost of meeting contractual requirements. Specifically, the consultant recommended that INR do the following:

Minimize Total Cost $= \$10,000A + \$5,000B$,

subject to

$6A + 2B \geq 24$ (high-grade ore constraint),

$2A + 2B \geq 16$ (medium-grade ore constraint),

$4A + 12B \geq 48$ (low-grade ore constraint),

$\quad A \leq 7$ (Mine A operating days in a week constraint),

$\quad B \leq 7$ (Mine B operating days in a week constraint),

or, in their equality form:

$$6A + 2B - S_H = 24,$$

$$2A + 2B - S_M = 16,$$

$$4A + 12B - S_L = 48,$$

$$A + S_A = 7,$$

$$B + S_B = 7,$$

where

$$A, B, S_H, S_M, S_L, S_A, \text{ and } S_B \geq 0.$$

Here, A and B represent the days of operation per week for each mine; S_H, S_M, and S_L represent excess production of high-, medium-, and low-grade ore, respectively; and S_A and S_B are days per week that each mine is not operated.

A graphic representation of the linear programming problem was also provided. The graph suggests an optimal solution at Point X, where Constraints 1 and 2 are binding. Thus, $S_H = S_M = 0$ and

$$6A + 2B - 0 = 24,$$

$$\text{minus } \underline{2A + 2B - 0 = 16,}$$

$$4A = 8,$$

$$A = 2 \text{ days per week.}$$

Substitute $A = 2$ into the high-grade ore constraint:

$$6(2) + 2B = 24,$$

$$12 + 2B = 24,$$

$$2B = 12,$$

$$B = 6 \text{ days per week.}$$

A minimum total operating cost per week of $50,000 is suggested, since

$$\text{Total Cost} = \$10,000A + \$5,000B$$

$$= \$10,000(2) + \$5,000(6)$$

$$= \$50,000.$$

The consultant's report did not discuss a variety of important long-run planning issues. Specifically, INR wishes to know the following, holding all else equal:

A. How much, if any, excess production would result if the consultant's operating recommendation were followed?

B. What would be the cost effect of increasing low-grade ore sales by 50%?

C. What is INR's minimum acceptable price per ton if it is to renew a current contract to provide one of its customers with six tons of high-grade ore per week?

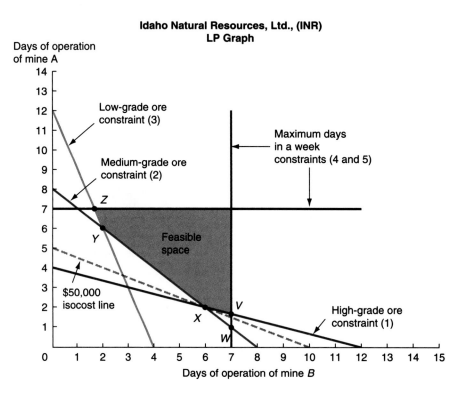

Idaho Natural Resources, Ltd., (INR)
LP Graph

D. With current output requirements, how much would the cost of operating Mine *A* have to rise before INR would change its operating decision?
E. What increase in the cost of operating Mine *B* would cause INR to change its current operating decision?

ST9.1 **SOLUTION**

A. If the consultant's operating recommendation of $A = 2$ and $B = 6$ were followed, 32 tons of excess low-grade ore production would result. No excess production of high- or medium-grade ore would occur. This can be shown by solving for S_H, S_M and S_L at the recommended activity level.

From the constraint equations, we find the following:

$$(1) \qquad 6(2) + 2(6) - S_H = 24,$$

$$S_H = 0.$$

$$(2) \qquad 2(2) + 2(6) - S_M = 16,$$

$$S_M = 0.$$

$$(3) \qquad 4(2) + 12(6) - S_L = 48,$$

$$S_L = 32.$$

B. There would be a *zero cost impact* of an increase in low-grade ore sales from 48 to 72 tons (= 1.5×48). With $A = 2$ and $B = 6$, 80 tons of low-grade ore are produced. A 50% increase in low-grade ore sales would simply reduce excess production from $S_L = 32$ to $S_L = 8$, since

$$(3') \qquad 4(2) + 12(6) - S_L = 72,$$

$$S_L = 8.$$

Graphically, the effect of a 50% increase in low-grade ore sales would be to cause a rightward shift in the low-grade ore constraint to a new constraint line with endpoints ($0B$, $18A$) and ($6B$, $0A$). While such a shift would reduce the feasible space, it would not affect the optimal operating decision of $A = 1$ and $B = 6$ (at Point X).

C. If INR didn't renew a contract to provide one of its current customers with 6 tons of high-grade ore per week, the high-grade ore constraint would fall from 24 to 18 tons per week. The new high-grade ore constraint, reflecting a parallel leftward shift, is written

$$(1') \quad 6A + 2B - S_H = 18$$

and has endpoints $(0B, 3A)$ and $(9B, 0A)$. With such a reduction in required high-grade ore sales, the high-grade ore constraint would no longer be binding and the optimal production point would shift to Point W, and $A = 1$ and $B = 7$ (since $S_M = S_B = 0$). At this point, high-grade ore production would equal 20 tons, or 2 tons more than the new high-grade ore requirement:

$$6(1) + 2(7) - S_H = 18,$$

$$S_H = 2,$$

with operating costs of

$$\text{Total Cost} = \$10,000A + \$5,000B$$
$$= \$10,000(1) + \$5,000(7)$$
$$= \$45,000.$$

Therefore, renewing a contract to provide one of its current customers with 6 tons of high-grade ore per week would result in our earlier operating decision of $A = 2$ and $B = 6$ and total costs of $50,000, rather than the $A = 1$ and $B = 7$ and total costs of $45,000 that would otherwise be possible. The marginal cost of renewing the 6-ton contract is $5,000, or $833 per ton.

$$\text{Marginal Cost} = \frac{\text{Change in Operating Costs}}{\text{Number of Tons}}$$
$$= \frac{\$50,000 - \$45,000}{6}$$
$$= \$833 \text{ per ton.}$$

D. In general, the isocost relation for this problem is

$$C_0 = C_A A + C_B B,$$

where C_0 is any weekly cost level, and C_A and C_B are the daily operating costs for Mines A and B,

respectively. In terms of the graph, A is on the vertical axis and B is on the horizontal axis. From the isocost formula, we find the following:

$$A = C_0/C_A - (C_B/C_A)B,$$

with an intercept of C_0/C_A and a slope equal to $-(C_B/C_A)$. The isocost line will become steeper as C_B increases relative to C_A. The isocost line will become flatter (slope will approach zero) as C_B falls relative to C_A.

If C_A increases to slightly more than $15,000, the optimal feasible point will shift from Point X $(6B, 2A)$ to Point V $(7B, 1.67A)$, since the isocost line slope will then be less than $-1/3$, the slope of the high-grade ore constraint $[A = 4 - (1/3)B]$. Thus, an increase in C_A from $10,000 to at least $15,000, or an increase of *at least $5,000*, is necessary before the optimal operating decision will change.

E. An increase in C_B of *at least $5,000* to slightly more than $10,000 will shift the optimal point from Point X to Point Y $(2B, 6A)$, since the isocost line slope will then be steeper than -1, the slope of the medium-grade ore constraint $(A = 8 - B)$.

An increase in C_B to slightly more than $30,000 will be necessary before Point Z $(1.67B, 7A)$ becomes optimal. With $C_B \geq \$30,000$ and $C_A = \$10,000$, the isocost line slope will be steeper than -3, the slope of the low-grade ore constraint, $A = 12 - 3B$.

As seems reasonable, the greater C_B is relative to C_A, the more Mine A will tend to be employed. The greater C_A is relative to C_B, the more Mine B will tend to be employed.

ST9.2 **Profit Maximization.** Interstate Bakeries, Inc., is an Atlanta-based manufacturer and distributor of branded bread products. Two leading products, Low Calorie, Q_A, and High Fiber, Q_B, bread, are produced using the same baking facility and staff. Low Calorie bread requires 0.3 hours of worker time per case, whereas High Fiber bread requires 0.4 hours of worker time per case. During any given week, a maximum of 15,000 worker hours are available for these two products. To meet grocery retailer demands for a full product line of branded bread products, Interstate must produce a minimum of 25,000 cases of Low Calorie bread and 7,500 cases of High Fiber bread per week. Given the popularity of low-calorie products in general, Interstate must also ensure that weekly production of Low Calorie bread is at least twice that of High Fiber bread.

Low Calorie bread is sold to groceries at a price of $42 per case; the price of High Fiber bread is $40 per case. Despite its lower price, the markup on High Fiber bread substantially exceeds that on Low Calorie bread. Variable costs are $30.50 per case for Low Calorie bread, but only $17 per case for High Fiber bread.

A. Set up the linear programming problem that the firm would use to determine the profit-maximizing output levels for Low Calorie and High Fiber bread. Show both the inequality and equality forms of the constraint conditions.

B. Completely solve the linear programming problem.

C. Interpret the solution values for the linear programming problem.

D. Holding all else equal, how much would variable costs per unit on High Fiber bread have to fall before the production level indicated in Part B would change?

ST9.2 **SOLUTION**

A. First, the profit contribution for Low Calorie bread, Q_A, and High Fiber bread, Q_B, must be calculated.

$$\text{Profit contribution per unit}$$
$$= \text{Price} - \text{Variable costs per unit}$$

Thus,

$$\pi_A = \$42 - \$30.50 = \$11.50 \text{ per case of } Q_A,$$

$$\pi_B = \$40 - \$17 = \$23 \text{ per case of } Q_B.$$

This problem requires maximization of profits, subject to limitations on the amount of each product produced, the acceptable ratio of production, and available worker hours. The linear programming problem is:

Maximize $\pi = \$11.50Q_A + \$23Q_B$

subject to

$$Q_A \geq 25,000$$

$$Q_B \geq 7,500$$

$$Q_A - 2Q_B \geq 0$$

$$0.3Q_A + 0.4Q_B \leq 15,000$$

In equality form, the constraint conditions are:

(1) $\qquad Q_A - S_A = 25,000$
(Low Calorie constraint)

(2) $\qquad Q_B - S_B = 7,500$
(High Fiber constraint)

(3) $\qquad Q_A - 2Q_B - S_R = 0$
(Acceptable ratio constraint)

(4) $\qquad 0.3Q_A + 0.4Q_B + S_W = 15,000$
(Worker hours constraint)

$$Q_A, Q_B, S_A, S_B, S_R, S_W \geq 0$$

Here, Q_A and Q_B are cases of Low Calorie and High Fiber bread, respectively. S_A, S_B, are variables representing excess production of Low Calorie and High Fiber bread, respectively. S_R is the amount by which the production of Low Calorie bread exceeds the minimally acceptable amount, given High Fiber production. S_W is excess worker capacity.

B. By graphing the constraints and the highest possible isoprofit line, the optimal Point X occurs where $S_R = S_W = 0$. Thus,

(1) $\qquad Q_A - S_A = 25,000$
(2) $\qquad Q_B - S_B = 0$
(3) $\qquad Q_A - 2Q_B - 0 = 0$
(4) $\qquad 0.3Q_A + 0.4Q_B + 0 = 15,000$

From (3), $Q_A = 2Q_B$. Substituting this value into (4) yields:

$$0.3(2Q_B) + 0.4Q_B = 15,000$$

$$Q_B = 15,000$$

From (3),

$$Q_A - 2(15,000) = 0$$

$$Q_A = 30,000$$

From (1),

$$30,000 - S_A = 25,000$$

$$S_A = 5,000$$

From (2),

$$15,000 - S_B = 7,500$$

$$S_B = 7,500$$

And the total profit contribution per week is:

$$\pi = \$11.50(30,000) + \$23(15,000)$$

$$= \$690,000$$

C.   Solution values can be interpreted as follows:

$Q_A = 30,000$	Optimal production of Low Calorie bread is 30,000 cases per week.
$Q_B = 15,000$	Optimal production of High Fiber bread is 15,000 cases per week.
$S_A = 5,000$	The production of Low Calorie bread exceeds the 25,000 case minimum by 5,000 units.
$S_B = 7,500$	The production of High Fiber bread exceeds the 7,500 case minimum by 7,500 units.
$S_R = 0$	The minimally acceptable 2:1 ratio of Low Calorie:High Fiber bread is produced.
$S_W = 0$	All worker hours are utilized; no excess worker capacity exists.
$\pi = \$690,000$	Maximum weekly profit contribution given constraints.

D. $7.67 per case. In the initial problem, there are two feasible solutions that are at the corners of the feasible space that is furthest away from the origin. The optimal solution Point X entails production of $Q_A = 30,000$, $Q_B = 15,000$, and $\pi = \$690,000$. An inferior cornerpoint solution is at Point Y where $Q_A = 40,000$, $Q_B = 7,500$, and $\pi = \$632,500$.

Analytically, Point X is preferred to Point Y because it emphasizes production of the higher-margin High Fiber bread. Graphically, Point X is preferred to Point Y because the slope of the iso-profit line (equal to -2) is "steeper" than the slope of the worker hours constraint (4) (equal to -1.33). If the slope of the isoprofit line became slightly less negative than the worker hours constraint, then the optimal production level would shift from Point X to Point Y.

In general, the isoprofit line formula is:

$$\pi = \pi_A Q_A + \pi_B Q_B,$$

or

$$Q_A = (\pi/\pi_A) - (\pi_B/\pi_A)Q_B.$$

In this specific case, the isoprofit line is:

$$Q_A = (\pi/\$11.50) - (\$23/\$11.50)Q_B.$$

To intersect the feasible space at Point Y rather than Point X, the slope of this line would have to become slightly less negative than -1.33. To solve for the required level for π_B, note that if:

$$\frac{\pi_B}{\$11.50} < 1.33$$

then

$$\pi_B < \$15.33$$

Given a price of High Fiber bread of $40 per unit, a profit contribution of $15.33 implies variable costs per unit of $24.67 because:

$$\pi_B = \text{Price} - \text{Variable Costs per Unit}$$

$$= \$40 - \$24.67$$

$$= \$15.33$$

Therefore, to change the optimal production point from Point X to Point Y, variable costs per unit on High Fiber bread would have to rise by *at least* $7.67 per unit:

Change in Variable Costs
$$= \textit{New Level} - \textit{Initial Level}$$

$$= \$24.67 - \$17$$

$$= \$7.67$$

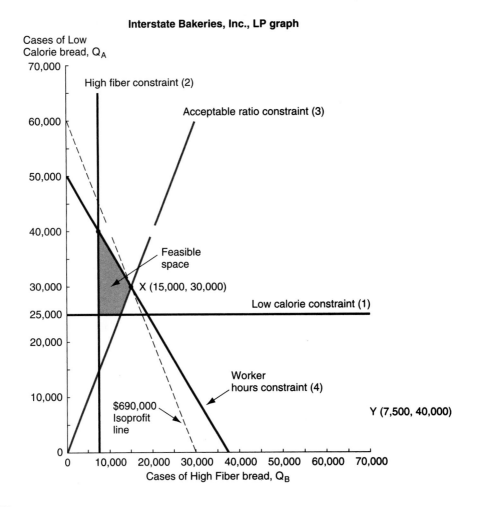

Interstate Bakeries, Inc., LP graph

PROBLEMS

P9.1 **LP Basics**. Indicate whether each of the following statements is true or false and explain why.

A. Constant returns to scale and constant input prices are the only requirements for a total cost function to be linear.

B. Changing input prices will always alter the slope of a given isocost line.

C. In profit-maximization linear programming problems, negative values for slack variables imply that the amount of an input resource employed exceeds the amount available.

D. Equal distances along a given process ray indicate equal output quantities.

E. Nonbinding constraints are constraints that intersect at the optimum solution.

P9.2 **Fixed Input Combinations**. Cherry Devices, Inc., assembles connectors and terminals for electronic products at a plant in New Haven, Connecticut. The plant uses labor (L) and capital (K) in an assembly line process to produce output (Q), where

$$Q = 0.025L^{0.5}K^{0.5}.$$

A. Calculate how many units of output can be produced with 4 units of labor and 400 units of capital and with 16 units of labor and 1,600 units of capital. Are returns to scale increasing, constant, or diminishing?

B.   Calculate the change in the marginal product of labor as labor grows from 4 to 16 units, holding capital constant at 400 units. Similarly, calculate the change in the marginal product of capital as capital grows from 400 to 1,600 units, holding labor constant at 4 units. Are returns to each factor increasing, constant, or diminishing?

C.   Assume now and throughout the remainder of the problem that labor and capital must be combined in the ratio $4L:400K$. How much output could be produced if Cherry has a constraint of $L = 4,000$ and $K = 480,000$ during the coming production period?

D.   What are the marginal products of each factor under the conditions described in Part C?

P9.3   **LP Setup and Interpretation**. The Syflansyd Nut Company has enjoyed booming sales following the success of its "Sometimes You Feel Like a Nut, Sometimes You Don't" advertising campaign. Syflansyd packages and sells four types of nuts in four different types of mixed-nut packages. These products include bulk (B), economy (E), fancy (F), and regular (R) mixed-nut packages. Each of these packages contains a different mixture of almonds (A), cashews (C), filberts (F), and peanuts (P). Based on its contracts with current suppliers, the company has the following daily inventory of each of the following nuts: almonds, 8,000 ounces; cashews, 7,000 ounces; filberts, 7,500 ounces; and peanuts, 10,000 ounces.

Given available inventory, it is management's goal to maximize profits by offering the optimum mix of the four package types. Profit earned per package type is as follows:

Bulk	$0.50
Economy	$0.25
Fancy	$1.25
Regular	$0.75

The composition of each of the four package types can be summarized as follows:

	OUNCES PER PACKAGE			
	BULK	ECONOMY	FANCY	REGULAR
Almonds	35	2	3	2
Cashews	35	1	4	2
Filberts	35	1	3	2
Peanuts	35	8	2	6
Total	140	12	12	12

Solution values for the optimal number of packages to produce (decision variables) and excess capacity (slack variables) are the following:

$$B = 0$$
$$E = 0$$
$$F = 1,100$$
$$R = 1,300$$
$$S_A = 2,100$$
$$S_C = 0$$
$$S_F = 1,600$$
$$S_P = 0$$

A.   Identify and interpret the appropriate Syflansyd objective function.

B.   Using both inequality and equality forms, set up and interpret the resource constraints facing the Syflansyd Company.

C.   Calculate optimal daily profit, and provide a complete interpretation of the full solution to this linear programming problem.

P9.4   **Cost Minimization**. Delmar Custom Homes (DCH) uses two different types of crews on home construction projects. Type A crews consist of master carpenters and skilled carpenters, whereas B crews include skilled carpenters and unskilled labor. Each home involves framing (F), roofing (R), and finish carpentry (FC). During recent months, A crews have demonstrated a capability of framing one home, roofing two, and doing finish carpentry for no more than four homes per month. Capabilities for B crews are framing three homes, roofing two, and completing finish carpentry for one during a month. DCH has agreed to build ten homes during the month of July but has subcontracted 10% of framing and 20% of finish carpentry requirements. Labor costs are $60,000 per month for A crews and $45,000 per month for B crews.

A.   Formulate the linear programming problem that DCH would use to minimize its total labor costs per month, showing both the inequality and equality forms of the constraint conditions.

B.   Solve the linear programming problem and interpret your solution values.

C.   Assuming that DCH can both buy and sell subcontracting services at prevailing prices of $8,000 per unit for framing and $14,000 per unit for finish carpentry, would you recommend that the company alter its subcontracting policy? If so, how much could the company save through such a change?

D.   Calculate the minimum increase in A-crew costs necessary to cause DCH to change its optimal employment combination for July.

P9.5   Optimal Credit Policy. Shirley Feeney is a senior loan officer with Citybank in Milwaukee, Wisconsin. Feeney has both corporate and personal lending customers. On average, the profit contribution margin or interest rate spread is 1.5% on corporate loans and 2% on personal loans. This return difference reflects the fact that personal loans tend to be riskier than corporate loans. Feeney seeks to maximize the total dollar profit contribution earned, subject to a variety of restrictions on her lending practices. To limit default risk, Feeney must restrict personal loans to no more than 50% of the total loans outstanding. Similarly, to ensure adequate diversification against business-cycle risk, corporate lending cannot exceed 75% of loaned funds. To maintain good customer relations by serving the basic needs of the local business community, Feeney has decided to extend at least 25% of her total credit authorization to corporate customers on an ongoing basis. Finally, Feeney cannot exceed her current total credit authorization of $100 million.

A.   Using the inequality form of the constraint conditions, set up and interpret the linear programming problem that Feeney would use to determine the optimal dollar amount of credit to extend to corporate (C) and personal (P) lending customers. Also formulate the LP problem using the equality form of the constraint conditions.

B.   Use a graph to determine the optimal solution, and check your solution algebraically. Fully interpret solution values.

P9.6   Optimal Portfolio Decisions. The James Bond Fund is a mutual fund (open-end investment company) with an objective of maximizing income from a widely diversified corporate bond portfolio. The fund has a policy of remaining invested largely in a diversified portfolio of investment-grade bonds. Investment-grade bonds have high investment quality and receive a rating of Baa or better by Moody's, a bond rating service. The fund's investment policy states that investment-grade bonds are to be emphasized, representing at least three times the amount of junk bond holdings. Junk bonds pay high nominal returns but have low investment quality, and they receive a rating of less than Baa from Moody's. To maintain the potential for high investor income, at least 20% of the fund's total portfolio must be invested in junk bonds. Like many funds, the James Bond Fund cannot use leverage (or borrowing) to enhance investor returns. As a result, total bond investments cannot total more than 100% of the portfolio. Finally, the current expected return for investment-grade (I) bonds is 9%, and it is 12% for junk (J) bonds.

A.   Using the inequality form of the constraint conditions, set up and interpret the linear programming problem that the James Bond Fund would use to determine the optimal portfolio percentage holdings of investment-grade (I) and junk (J) bonds. Also formulate the problem using the equality form of the constraint conditions. (Assume that the fund managers have decided to remain fully invested and therefore hold no cash at this time.)

B.   Use a graph to determine the optimal solution, and check your solution algebraically. Fully interpret solution values.

C.   Holding all else equal, how much would the expected return on junk bonds have to fall to alter the optimal investment policy determined in Part B? Alternatively, how much would the return on investment-grade bonds have to rise before a change in investment policy would be warranted?

D.   In anticipation of a rapid increase in interest rates and a subsequent economic downturn, the investment committee has decided to minimize the fund's exposure to bond price fluctuations. In adopting a defensive position, what is the maximum share of the portfolio that can be held in cash given the investment policies stated in the problem?

P9.7 **Cost Minimization**. Carolina Power and Light (CP&L) is a small electric utility located in the Southeast. CP&L currently uses coal-fired capacity to satisfy its base load electricity demand, which is the minimum level of electricity demanded 24 hours per day, 365 days per year.

CP&L currently burns both high-sulfur eastern coal and low-sulfur western coal. Each type of coal has its advantages. Eastern coal is more expensive ($50 per ton) but has higher heat-generating capabilities. Although western coal doesn't generate as much heat as eastern coal, western coal is less expensive ($25 per ton) and doesn't cause as much sulfur dioxide pollution. CP&L's base load requirements are such that at least 2,400 million BTUs must be generated per hour. Each ton of eastern coal burned generates 40 million BTUs, and each ton of western coal burned generates 30 million BTUs. To limit sulfur dioxide emissions, the state's Environmental Protection Agency (EPA) requires CP&L to limit its total burning of sulfur to no more than 1.5 tons per hour. This affects CP&L's coal usage, because eastern coal contains 2.5% sulfur and western coal contains 1.5% sulfur. The EPA also limits CP&L particulate emissions to no more than 900 pounds per hour. CP&L emits 10 pounds of particulates per ton of eastern coal burned and 15 pounds of particulates per ton of western coal burned.

A. Set up and interpret the linear program that CP&L would use to minimize hourly coal usage costs in light of its constraints.

B. Calculate and interpret all relevant solution values.

C. Holding all else equal, how much would the price of western coal have to rise before only eastern coal would be used? Explain.

P9.8 **Profit Maximization**. Creative Accountants, Ltd., is a small San Francisco-based accounting partnership specializing in the preparation of individual (*I*) and corporate (*C*) income tax returns. Prevailing prices in the local market are $125 for individual tax return preparation and $250 for corporate tax return preparation.

Five accountants run the firm and are assisted by four bookkeepers and four secretaries, all of whom work a typical 40-hour workweek. The firm must decide how to target its promotional efforts to best use its resources during the coming tax preparation season. Based on previous experience, the firm expects that an average of one hour of accountant time will be required for each individual return prepared. Corporate return preparation will require an average of two accountant hours and two bookkeeper hours. One hour of secretarial time will also be required for typing each individual or corporate return. In addition, variable computer and other processing costs are expected to average $25 per individual return and $100 per corporate return.

A. Set up the linear programming problem that the firm would use to determine the profit-maximizing output levels for preparing individual and corporate returns. Show both the inequality and equality forms of the constraint conditions.

B. Completely solve and interpret the solution values for the linear programming problem.

C. Calculate maximum possible net profits per week for the firm, assuming that the accountants earn $1,500 per week, bookkeepers earn $500 per week, secretaries earn $10 per hour, and fixed overhead (including promotion and other expenses) averages $5,000 per week.

D. After considering the preceding data, one senior accountant recommended letting two bookkeepers go while retaining the rest of the current staff. Another accountant suggested that if any bookkeepers were let go, an increase in secretarial staff would be warranted. Which is the more profitable suggestion? Why?

E. Using the equality form of the constraint conditions, set up, solve, and interpret solution values for the dual linear programming problem.

F. Does the dual solution provide information useful for planning purposes? Explain.

P9.9 **Revenue Maximization**. Architect Nick Yemana is managing partner of Designed for Sales (DFS), Inc., an Evanston, Illinois-based designer of single-family and multifamily housing units for real estate developers, building contractors, and so on. Yemana's challenge is to determine an optimal mix of output during the current planning period. DFS offers custom designs for single-family units,

Q_1, for \$3,000 and custom designs for multifamily units (duplexes, fourplexes, etc.), Q_2, for \$2,000 each. Both types of output make use of scarce drafting, artwork, and architectural resources. Each custom design for single-family units requires 12 hours of drafting, 2 hours of artwork, and 6 hours of architectural input. Each custom design for multifamily units requires 4 hours of drafting, 5 hours of artwork, and 6 hours of architectural input. Currently, DFS has 72 hours of drafting, 30 hours of artwork, and 48 hours of architectural services available on a weekly basis.

A.   Using the equality form of the constraint conditions, set up the primal linear program that Yemana would use to determine the sales revenue-maximizing product mix. Also set up the dual.

B.   Solve for and interpret all solution values.

C.   Would DFS's optimal product mix be different with a profit-maximization goal rather than a sales revenue-maximization goal? Why or why not?

P9.10   **Optimal Output**. Omaha Meat Products (OMP) produces and markets Cornhusker Plumpers, an extra-large frankfurter product being introduced on a test market basis into the St. Louis, Missouri, area. This product is similar to several others

offered by OMP, and it can be produced with currently available equipment and personnel using any of three alternative production methods. Method A requires 1 hour of labor and 4 processing-facility hours to produce 100 packages of plumpers, one unit of Q_A. Method B requires 2 labor hours and 2 processing-facility hours for each unit of Q_B, and Method C requires 5 labor hours and 1 processing-facility hour for each unit of Q_C. Because of slack demand for other products, OMP currently has 14 labor hours and 6 processing-facility hours available per week for producing Cornhusker Plumpers. Cornhusker Plumpers are currently being marketed to grocery retailers at a wholesale price of \$1.50 per package, and demand exceeds current supply.

A.   Using the equality form of the constraint conditions, set up the primal and dual linear programs that OMP would use to maximize production of Cornhusker Plumpers given currently available resources.

B.   Calculate and interpret all solution values.

C.   Should OMP expand its processing-facility capacity if it can do so at a cost of \$40 per hour?

D.   Discuss the implications of a new union scale calling for a wage rate of \$20 per hour.

Case Study for Chapter 9

AN LP PENSION FUNDING MODEL

Several companies have learned that a well-funded and comprehensive employee benefits package constitutes an important part of the compensation plan needed to attract and retain key personnel. An employee stock ownership plan, profit-sharing arrangements, and deferred compensation to fund employee retirement are all used to allow productive employees to share in the firm's growth and development. Among the fringe benefits offered under the cafeteria-style benefits plans are comprehensive medical and dental care furnished through local health maintenance organizations, on-site daycare centers for employee children, and "eldercare"

support for the aging parents and other dependents of workers.

Many companies also provide their employees with so-called "defined benefit" pension plans. Under defined benefit plans, employers usually offer workers a fixed percentage of their final salary as a retirement annuity. In a typical arrangement, a company might offer employees a retirement annuity of 1.5% of their final salary for each year employed. A 10-year veteran would earn a retirement annuity of 15% of final salary, a 20-year veteran would earn a retirement annuity of 30% of final salary, and so on. Since each employee's retirement benefits are defined by the company, the company itself is obligated to pay for promised benefits.

Over time, numerous firms have found it increasingly difficult to forecast the future rate of return on invested assets, the future rate of inflation, and the morbidity (death rate) of young, healthy, active retirees. As a result, several organizations have discontinued traditional defined benefit pension plans and instead have begun to offer new "defined contribution" plans. A defined contribution plan features a matching of company plus employee retirement contributions, with no prescribed set of retirement income benefits defined beforehand. Each employee is typically eligible to contribute up to 10% of their pre-tax income into the plan, with the company matching the first 5% or so of such contributions. Both company and employee contributions compound on a tax-deferred basis until the point of retirement. At that time, employees can use their pension funds to purchase an annuity, or draw a pension income from earned interest, plus dividends and capital gains.

Defined contribution plans have some obvious advantages over traditional defined benefit pension plans. From the company's perspective, defined benefit pension plans became much less attractive when accounting rule changes during the late 1980s required them to record as a liability any earned but not funded pension obligations. Unfunded pension liabilities caused gigantic one-time charges against operating income during the early 1990s for AT&T, General Motors, IBM, and a host of other large corporations. Faced with enormous one-time charges during an initial catch-up phase, plus the prospect of massive and rapidly growing retirement expenses over time, many large and small firms have simply elected to discontinue their defined contribution plan altogether. From the employee's perspective, defined contribution plans are attractive because they are portable from one employer to another. Rather than face the prospect of losing pension benefits after changing from one employer to another, employees appreciate the advantage of being able to take their pension plans with them as they switch jobs. Defined contribution plans are also attractive because they allow employees to tailor retirement funding contributions to fit individual needs. Younger employees faced with the necessity of buying a home or paying for children's educational expenses can limit pension contributions to minimal levels; older workers with greater discretionary income and a more imminent retirement can provide the maximum pension contribution allowed by law. An added benefit of defined contribution compensation plans is that individual workers can allocate pension investments according to individual risk preferences. Older workers who are extremely risk averse can focus their investments on short-term government securities; younger and more venturesome employees can devote a larger share of their retirement investment portfolio to common stocks.

Workers appreciate companies that offer flexible defined contribution pension plans and closely related profit-sharing and deferred compensation arrangements. To maximize plan benefits, firms must make modest efforts to educate and inform employees about retirement income needs and objectives. Until recently, compensation consultants suggested that employees could retire comfortably on a retirement income that totaled 80% of their final salary. However, concerns about the underfunding of federal Social Security and Medicaid programs and apprehension about the rapid escalation of medical care costs make retirement with sufficient assets to fund a pension income equal to 100% of final salary a worthy goal. To fund such a nest egg requires substantial regular savings and an impressive rate of return on pension plan assets. Workers who save 10% of income for an extended period, say, 30 years, have historically been able to fund a retirement income equal to 100% of final salary. This assumes, of course, that the pension plan portfolio is able to earn significant returns over time. Investing in a broadly diversified portfolio of common stocks has historically provided the best returns. Since 1926, the real (after-inflation) rate of return on NYSE stocks is 6.4% per year; the real return on bonds is only 0.5% per year. Indeed, over every 30-year investment horizon during that time interval, stocks have beat short-term bonds (money market instruments) and long-term bonds. The added return from common stocks is the predictable reward for assuming the greater risks of stock-market investing. However, to be sure of earning the market risk premium on stocks, one must invest in several different companies (at least 30) for several years (at least 30). For most pension plans, investments in no-load low-expense common stock index funds work best in the long run. However, bond market funds have a place in some pension portfolios, especially for those at or near the retirement age.

To illustrate the type of retirement income funding model that a company might make available to employees, consider the following scenario. Suppose that an individual employee has accumulated a pension portfolio worth $250,000 and hopes to receive initial post-retirement income of $500 per month, or $6,000 per year. To provide a total return from current income (yield) plus growth (capital gains) of at least 7%, a minimum of 25% of the portfolio should be invested in common stocks. To limit risk, stocks should total no more than 50% of the overall portfolio, and a minimum of 5% should be invested in long-term taxable bonds, 5% in medium-term tax-exempt bonds, and 5% in a short-term money-market mutual fund. Moreover, not more than 75% of the overall portfolio should be invested in stocks plus long-term taxable bonds, and at least $30,000 should be available in money markets plus medium-term tax-exempt bonds to provide sufficient liquidity to fund emergencies. Assume that common stocks have a before-tax dividend yield of 3.5%, with expected growth from capital appreciation of 6.5% per year. Similar figures for long-term taxable bonds are 6% plus 1.5%, 4% plus 1% for medium-term tax-exempt bonds, and 4.5% plus 0% for money market instruments. Also assume that the effective marginal tax rate is 30%.

A.   Set up the linear programming problem that a benefits officer might use to determine the total-return maximizing allocation of the employee's pension portfolio. Use the inequality forms of the constraint conditions.

B.   Solve this linear programming problem and interpret all solution values. Also determine the employee's expected before-tax and after-tax income levels.

C.   Calculate the amount of unrealized capital gain earned per year on this investment portfolio.

D.   What is the total return opportunity cost of the $6,000 after-tax income constraint?

Given the importance of duality, a list of simple rules that can be used to form the dual program to any given primal program would be useful. Four such rules exist. They are as follows:

1. Change a maximize objective to minimize, and vice versa.

2. Reverse primal constraint inequality signs in dual constraints (i.e., change $\geq$ to $\leq$, and $\leq$ to $\geq$).

3. Transpose primal constraint coefficients to get dual constraint coefficients.

4. Transpose objective function coefficients to get limits in dual constraints, and vice versa.
(The word *transpose* is a matrix algebra term that simply means that each row of coefficients is rearranged into columns so that Row 1 becomes Column 1, Row 2 becomes Column 2, and so on.)

To illustrate the rules for transformation from primal and dual, consider the following simple example.

PRIMAL PROBLEM

Maximize
$$\pi = \pi_1 Q_1 + \pi_2 Q_2,$$

subject to

$$a_{11}Q_1 + a_{12}Q_2 \leq r_1,$$
$$a_{21}Q_1 + a_{22}Q_2 \leq r_2,$$
$$Q_1, Q_2 \geq 0,$$

where π is profits and Q is output. Thus, π_1 and π_2 are unit profits for Q_1 and Q_2, respectively. The resource constraints are given by r_1 and r_2. The constants in the primal constraints reflect the input requirements for each type of output. For example, a_{11} is the amount of resource r_1 in one unit of output Q_1. Similarly, a_{12} is the amount of resource r_1 in one unit of output Q_2. Thus, $a_{11}Q_1 + a_{12}Q_2$ is the total amount of resource r_1 used in production. The remaining input requirements, a_{21} and a_{22}, have a similar interpretation. For convenience, this primal problem statement can be rewritten in matrix notation as follows:

PRIMAL PROBLEM

Maximize
$$\pi = \pi_1 Q_1 + \pi_2 Q_2,$$

subject to

$$\begin{bmatrix} a_{11} & a_{21} \\ a_{12} & a_{22} \end{bmatrix} \times \begin{bmatrix} Q_1 \\ Q_2 \end{bmatrix} \leq \begin{bmatrix} r_1 \\ r_2 \end{bmatrix}$$
$$Q, Q_2 \geq 0.$$

Matrix notation is just a convenient means for writing large systems of equations. In going from matrix form back to equation form, one just multiplies each row element by each column element. Thus, the left side of the first constraint equation is $a_{11} \times Q_1$ plus $a_{12} \times Q_2$, or $a_{11}Q_1 + a_{12}Q_2$, and this sum must be less than or equal to r_1.

Given the expression of the primal program in matrix notation, the four rules for transformation given previously can be used to convert from the primal to the dual. Following these rules, the dual is written as follows:

DUAL PROBLEM

Minimize
$$\pi^* = r_1 V_1 + r_2 V_2,$$

subject to

$$\begin{bmatrix} a_{11} & a_{12} \\ a_{21} & a_{22} \end{bmatrix} \times \begin{bmatrix} V_1 \\ V_2 \end{bmatrix} \geq \begin{bmatrix} \pi_1 \\ \pi_2 \end{bmatrix}$$

$$V_1, V_2 \geq 0.$$

Then, converting from matrix back to equation form gives the following:

DUAL PROBLEM

Minimize
$$\pi^* = r_1 V_1 + r_2 V_2,$$

subject to

$$a_{11} V_1 + a_{21} V_2 \geq \pi_1,$$

$$a_{12} V_1 + a_{22} V_2 \geq \pi_2,$$

$$V_1, V_2 \geq 0.$$

Here, V_1 and V_2 are the shadow prices for resources r_1 and r_2, respectively. Since r_1 and r_2 represent the quantities of the two resources available, the objective function measures the total implicit value of the resources available. Recalling the interpretation of a_{11} and a_{21} from the primal, it is obvious that $a_{11} V_1 + a_{21} V_2$ is the total value of inputs used to produce one unit of output Q_1. Similarly, $a_{12} V_1 + a_{22} V_2$ is the total value of inputs used in production of a unit of output Q_2.

Finally, the primal and dual linear programming problems can be fully specified through the introduction of slack variables. Remember that with less-than-or-equal-to constraints, the left side of the constraint equation must be brought up to equal the right side. Thus, slack variables must be added to the left side of such constraint equations. With greater-than-or-equal-to constraints, the left side of the constraint equation must be brought down to equal the right side. Thus, slack variables must be *subtracted from* the left side of such constraint equations. With this, the full specification of the preceding primal and dual linear programs can be written as follows:

PRIMAL PROBLEM	DUAL PROBLEM
Maximize $\pi = \pi_1 Q_1 + \pi_2 Q_2$, subject to $a_{11} Q_1 + a_{12} Q_2 + S_1 = r_1$, $a_{21} Q_1 + a_{22} Q_2 + S_2 = r_2$, $\qquad Q_1, Q_2, S_1, S_2 \geq 0$,	Minimize $\pi^* = r_1 V_1 + r_2 V_2$, subject to $a_{11} V_1 + a_{21} V_2 - L_1 = \pi_1$, $a_{12} V_1 + a_{22} V_2 - L_2 = \pi_2$, $\qquad V_1, V_2, L_1, L_2 \geq 0$,

where S_1 and S_2 are slack variables representing excess capacity of resources r_1 and r_2, respectively. L_1 and L_2 are also slack variables; they represent the amount by which the value of resources used in the production of Q_1 and Q_2 exceeds the value of output as measured by π_1 and π_2, respectively. Thus, L_1 and L_2 measure the opportunity cost, or foregone profit, as a result of producing the last unit of Q_1 and Q_2.

Understanding these basic rules simplifies construction of the dual, given a primal program, and facilitates understanding and interpretation of the constraints and coefficients found in both primal and dual linear programming problems.

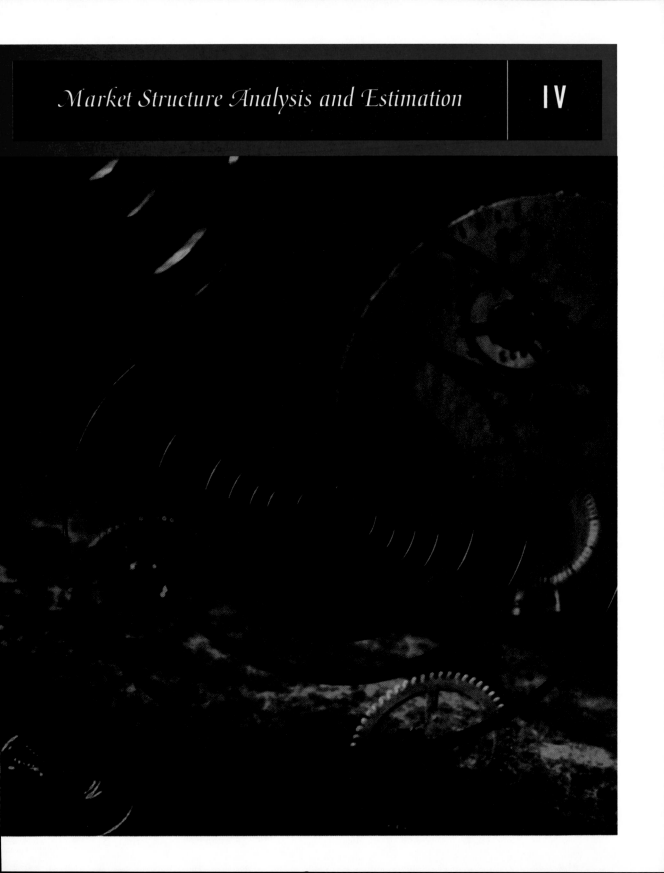

Market Structure Analysis and Estimation

IV

Firms operating in perfectly competitive industries find it very difficult to sustain attractive rates of return on investment. Take newsprint production, for example. When the economy is booming, newspapers are able to attract new advertisers for branded products, general merchandise, and want ads; and the demand for newsprint soars. During recessions, advertising falls as does the demand for newsprint. As the demand for newsprint rises and falls with trends in the overall economy, newsprint prices oscillate wildly. Because newsprint is a commodity-like product, newsprint manufacturers struggle to earn nominal rates of return of 8% to 10% on stockholders' equity. On the other hand, newspapers, the customers of newsprint manufacturers, often do much better. Local newspapers in one-newspaper towns have a limited monopoly on the provision of want ad advertising, regional news, and sports reporting. Local monopoly, or specialized monopoly power, permits distinctive newspapers to consistently earn above-normal profits of 15% to 20% and more on stockholders' equity. The simple lesson is that producers of commodity-like products earn only meager rates of return, while monopoly producers of distinctive goods and services have the potential for significant above-normal profits.[1]

This chapter considers the nature of rivalry in markets that might be described as perfectly competitive, and the behavior of firms in markets where little or no competition is present, or monopoly markets. Taken together, these market structures can be viewed as the endpoints along a continuum of decreasing competition, moving from perfect competition to monopolistic competition to oligopoly to monopoly. Monopolistic competition and oligopoly are the subjects of Chapter 11.

The Contrast Between Perfect Competition and Monopoly

Glaring differences between the perfect competition and monopoly models of buyer and seller behavior are evident along every important dimension of market structure. These differences are characterized briefly in this section and then developed more fully in the rest of the chapter.

---

[1] See Robert J. Sherwood, "The *Forbes* Profits 500," *Forbes,* April 21, 1997, 188-201.

WHAT IS MARKET STRUCTURE?

Market Structure
The competitive environment.

Market structure is the complete array of industry characteristics that directly affect the price/output decisions made by firms. One of the most important elements of market structure is the number and size distribution of sellers and buyers. Generally speaking, the greater the number of market participants, the more vigorous the price and product quality competition. Similarly, the more even the balance of power between sellers and buyers, the more likely it is that the competitive process will yield maximum benefits. However, a link between the numbers of market participants and the vigor of competition does not always hold true. For example, there are literally thousands of producers active in most major milk markets. Despite this large number of competitors, price competition is nonexistent given an industry cartel that is sustained by a federal program of milk price supports. In contrast, real-world experience shows that competition can be spirited in newspaper, cable television, long-distance telephone service, and other markets with as few as two competitors. This is particularly true in instances in which the actions of market participants are constrained by the viable threat of potential entrants. The mere threat of entry by potential entrants is sometimes enough to keep industry prices and profits in check and to maintain a high level of productive efficiency.

Market
Firms and individuals willing and able to buy or sell a given product.

Market structure describes the competitive environment in the market for any good or service. A **market** consists of all firms and individuals willing and able to buy or sell a particular product. This includes firms and individuals currently engaged in buying and selling a particular product, as well as potential entrants. Market structure is typically characterized on the basis of four important industry characteristics: the number and size distribution of active buyers and sellers and potential entrants, the degree of product differentiation, the amount and cost of information about product price and quality, and conditions of entry and exit. The effects of market structure are measured in terms of the prices paid by consumers, availability and quality of output, employment and career advancement opportunities, and the pace of product innovation, among other factors.

Potential Entrants
Firms and individuals with the economic resources to enter a particular market, given sufficient economic incentives.

A **potential entrant** is an individual or firm posing a sufficiently credible threat of market entry to affect the price/output decisions of incumbent firms. Potential entrants play extremely important roles in many industries. Some industries with only a few active participants might at first appear to hold the potential for substantial economic profits. However, a number of potential entrants can have a substantial effect on the price/output decisions of incumbent firms. For example, Compaq, Dell, Gateway, IBM, and other leading computer manufacturers are viable potential entrants into the computer component manufacturing industry. These companies use their threat of potential entry to obtain favorable prices from suppliers of microprocessors, video display terminals, and peripheral equipment. Despite having only a relative handful of active foreign and domestic participants, computer components manufacturing is both highly innovative and vigorously price competitive. When characterizing market structure, it is important to consider the effects of both current rivals and potential entrants.

PERFECT COMPETITION

Perfect Competition
A market structure characterized by a large number of buyers and sellers of an identical product.

Perfect competition is a market structure characterized by a large number of buyers and sellers of essentially the same product, where each market participant's transactions

Price Takers
Buyers and sellers whose
individual transactions are
so small that they do not
affect market prices.

are so small that they have no influence on the market price of the product. Individual buyers and sellers are **price takers.** This means that firms take market prices as given and devise their production strategies accordingly. Free and complete demand and supply information is available in a perfectly competitive market, and there are no meaningful barriers to entry and exit. As a result, vigorous price competition prevails, and only a normal rate of return on investment is possible in the long run. Economic profits are possible only during periods of short-run disequilibrium before rivals mount an effective competitive response.

MONOPOLY

Monopoly
A market structure
characterized by a single
seller of a highly
differentiated product.

Price Makers
Buyers and sellers whose
large transactions affect
market prices.

Monopoly is a market structure characterized by a single seller of a highly differentiated product. Because a monopolist is the sole provider of a desired commodity, the monopolist *is* the industry. Producers must compete for a share of the consumer's overall market basket of goods, but monopolists face no effective competition for specific product sales from either established or potential rivals. As such, monopolists are **price makers** that exercise significant control over market prices. This allows the monopolist to simultaneously determine price and output for the firm (and the industry). Substantial barriers to entry or exit often deter potential entrants and offer both efficient and inefficient monopolists the opportunity for economic profits, even in the long run.

Factors That Determine the Level of Competition

Two key conditions determine the level of competition in a given market: the number and relative size of buyers and sellers in the market and the extent to which the product is standardized. These factors, in turn, are influenced by the nature of the product and production systems, the scope of potential entry, and buyer characteristics.

EFFECT OF PRODUCT CHARACTERISTICS ON MARKET STRUCTURE

Good substitutes for a product increase the degree of competition in the market for that product. To illustrate, rail freight and passenger service between two points is typically supplied by only one railroad. Transportation service is available from several sources, however, and railroads compete with bus lines, truck companies, barges, airlines, and private autos. The substitutability of these other modes of transportation for rail service increases the degree of competition in the transportation service market.

It is important to realize that market structures are not static. In the 1800s and early 1900s—before the introduction of trucks, buses, automobiles, and airplanes—railroads faced very little competition. Railroads could charge excessive prices and earn monopoly profits. Because of this exploitation, laws were passed giving public authorities permission to regulate railroad prices. Over the years, such regulation became superfluous given intermodal competition. Other firms were enticed by railroad profits to develop competing transportation service systems, which ultimately led to a much more competitive market structure. Today, few would argue that railroads retain significant monopoly power, and public regulation of the railroads has been greatly reduced in recognition of this fact.

Physical characteristics of a product can also influence the competitive structure of its market. A low ratio of distribution cost to total cost, for example, tends to increase competition by widening the geographic area over which any particular producer can compete. Rapid perishability of a product produces the opposite effect. In considering the level of competition for a product, the national, regional, or local nature of the market must be considered.

EFFECT OF PRODUCTION CHARACTERISTICS ON COMPETITION

When minimum efficient scale is large in relation to overall industry output, only a few firms are able to attain the output size necessary for productive efficiency. In such instances, competitive pressures allow only a few firms to survive in an industry. On the other hand, when minimum efficient scale is small in relation to overall industry output, many firms are able to attain the size necessary for efficient operation. Holding all else equal, competition tends to be most vigorous when many efficient competitors are present in the market. This is especially true when firms of smaller-than-minimum-efficient scale face considerably higher production costs, as well as when the construction of minimum-efficient-scale plants involves the commitment of substantial capital, skilled labor, and material resources. When construction of minimum-efficient-scale plants requires the commitment of only modest resources or when smaller firms face no important production cost disadvantages, economies of scale have little or no effect on the competitive potential of new or entrant firms.

EFFECT OF ENTRY AND EXIT CONDITIONS ON COMPETITION

Barrier to Entry
Any advantage for industry incumbents over new arrivals.

Barrier to Mobility
Any advantage for large leading firms over small nonleading rivals.

Maintaining the above-normal profits or productive inefficiency of a monopolist over the long run requires substantial barriers to entry, mobility, or exit. A **barrier to entry** is any factor or industry characteristic that creates an advantage for incumbents over new arrivals. Legal rights such as patents and local, state, or federal licenses can present formidable barriers to new entry in pharmaceuticals, cable television, television and radio broadcasting, and other industries. A **barrier to mobility** is any factor or industry characteristic that creates an advantage for large leading firms over smaller nonleading rivals. Factors that sometimes create barriers to entry and/or mobility include substantial economies of scale, scope economies, large capital or skilled-labor requirements, and ties of customer loyalty created through advertising and other means.

Barriers to entry and mobility can sometimes result in compensating advantages for consumers. Even though patents can lead to monopoly profits for inventing firms, they also spur valuable new product and process development. Although extremely efficient or innovative leading firms make new entry and nonleading firm growth difficult, they can have the favorable effect of lowering industry prices and increasing product quality. Therefore, a complete evaluation of the economic effects of entry barriers involves a consideration of both costs and benefits realized by suppliers and customers.

Barrier to Exit
Any limit on asset redeployment from one line of business or industry to another.

Whereas barriers to entry have the potential to impede competition by making entry or nonleading firm growth difficult, competitive forces can also be diminished through barriers to exit. A **barrier to exit** is any restriction on the ability of incumbents to redeploy assets from one industry or line of business to another. During the late 1980s, for example, several state governments initiated legal proceedings to impede plant closures by large employers in the steel, glass, automobile, and other industries. By imposing large fines or severance taxes or requiring substantial expenditures for worker retraining, they created significant barriers to exit.

By impeding the asset redeployment that is typical of any vigorous competitive environment, barriers to exit can dramatically increase both the costs and risks of doing business. Even though one can certainly sympathize with the difficult adjustments faced by both individuals and firms affected by plant closures, government actions that create barriers to exit can have the unintended effect of impeding industrial development and market competition.

EFFECT OF BUYERS ON COMPETITION

Monopsony
A market with one buyer.

The degree of market competition is affected by buyers as well as sellers. Generally speaking, if there are only a few buyers in a given market, there will be less competition than if there are many buyers. **Monopsony** exists when a single firm is the sole buyer of a desired product or input. Monopsony characterizes local labor markets with a single major employer, as well as many local agricultural markets with a single feed mill or livestock buyer. Similarly, the federal government is a monopsony buyer of military weapons and equipment. Major retailers such as Wal-Mart, Kmart, and Sears all enjoy monopsony power in the purchase of apparel, appliances, auto parts, and other consumer products. Such buyer power is especially strong in the purchase of "house brand" goods, where suppliers might sell much if not all of their production to a single retailer.

Monopsony is perhaps more common in factor input markets than in markets for final demand. In terms of economic efficiency, monopsony is least harmful, and can sometimes even be beneficial, in those markets in which a monopsony buyer faces a monopoly or just a few sellers. For example, consider the case of the town in which one mill is the sole employer of unskilled labor. The mill is a monopsony since it is a single buyer of labor, and it may be able to use its power to reduce wage rates below competitive levels. If workers organize a union to bargain collectively with their employer, a single monopoly seller of labor is created that could offset the employer's monopsony power and increase wages toward competitive market norms. Not only is monopsony accepted in such situations, but it is sometimes encouraged by public policy.

EFFECT OF PRODUCT DIFFERENTIATION ON COMPETITION

In addition to the number and size distribution of actual and potential competitors, market structure is also described by the degree of product differentiation. Product differentiation includes any real or perceived differences in the quality of goods and services offered to consumers. Sources of product differentiation include all of the various forms of advertising promotion, plus new product and process developments made possible

Is the Stock Market Perfectly Competitive?

The New York Stock Exchange is the largest organized U.S. securities market. Established in 1817, the NYSE is the primary marketplace for investors in the common and preferred stocks of roughly 3,400 large and medium-size companies. Listed companies include AT&T Corp., General Electric Co., General Motors Corp., International Business Machines, and virtually every other major company with products that touch our lives on a daily basis. The NYSE enjoys near-monopoly status by virtue of the fact that NYSE trading accounts for roughly 80% of the composite volume in listed company shares. The remainder is off-the-floor electronic trading by pension funds and other institutions, and trading on eight smaller regional exchanges.

The National Association of Securities Dealers Automated Quotations service, or NASDAQ for short, is a stock trading system that involves a huge electronic trading system for thousands of over-the-counter stocks. OTC stocks are unlisted companies whose shares are traded on a negotiated basis among hundreds of brokers and other dealers. NASDAQ's National Market System is comprised of the common stocks of roughly 6,000 generally small companies; NASDAQ Small Cap Issues include another 3,000 smaller companies with at least two market makers. More than 10,000 inactively traded OTC stocks are listed in the "pink sheets." Interestingly, several large firms like Apple Computer, Cisco Systems Intel, Microsoft Corp., and cable TV giant Tele-Communications, Inc., choose to have their shares traded on NASDAQ rather than the NYSE. Their reasoning is that when even a handful of dealers make a market in any given stock, price competition among these dealers has the potential to force down the cost of trading for investors.

In any market, the *bid* price is the amount buyers are willing to pay, and the *ask* price is the price at which sellers are willing to sell. If a given dealer is willing to pay 100 for Microsoft, and willing to sell Microsoft for 100 1/4, the bid-ask spread of 25 cents represents the dealer markup and profit margin on its inventory of Microsoft stock. At least in theory, competition among even a handful of dealers using the NASDAQ system should produce lower bid-ask spreads than would be observed on the Big Board, given the NYSE's near-monopoly status in the trading of listed stocks.

Much to the chagrin of NASDAQ, in 1995 the Securities and Exchange Commission began looking into allegations that NASDAQ market-makers violate the "90-second rule," which requires them to report stock trades within 90 seconds. Any such violations would limit the amount of data available to investors, and possibly keep them from getting the details necessary to make informed buy or sell decisions. At the same time, the Justice Department investigated charges that NASDAQ dealers had colluded by refusing to honor quoted prices, or by refusing to "bust the spread" by failing to submit bids of 65 1/8 when a given stock is reported to have a bid-ask spread of 65 to 65 1/4. Starting in 1997, the SEC required that dealers display the highest bid and the lowest ask price offered by customers for NASDAQ stocks to minimize the possibility of dealer collusion. As a result, artificially wide bid-ask spreads on 100 of NASDAQ's most actively traded stocks narrowed dramatically.

While the NYSE was initially smug on learning of price-fixing charges against its prime competitor, it too has come under fire for the high cost of transacting. In a perfectly competitive market, upticks and downticks should occur only when the "information set" available to investors changes. Prices should be typically stable, especially when trades occur on almost a continuous basis. Looking at the market impact of trading, some market analysts have found that too many Big Board prices zigzag from second-to-second in increments of 1/8 to 1/4.

Thus, investigations of pricing practices on NASDAQ and the NYSE make clear that even in markets widely recognized as *near* perfectly competitive, elements of monopoly pricing are sometimes present. *Caveat emptor!*

See: Deborah Lohse, "Traders Fear SEC Rules' Expansion, *"The Wall Street Journal,* April, 21 1997, C1, C16.

by effective programs of research and development. The availability and cost of information about prices and output quality is a similarly important determinant of market structure. Competition is always most vigorous when buyers and sellers have ready access to detailed price/performance information. Finally, market structure is broadly determined by entry and exit conditions. Low regulatory barriers, modest capital requirements, and nominal standards for skilled labor and other inputs all increase the likelihood that competition will be vigorous. Because all of these elements of market structure have important consequences for the price/output decisions made by firms, the study of market structure is an important ingredient of managerial economics.

Perfect Competition

Market characteristics described in the preceding section determine the level of competition in the market for any good or service. This section focuses on the special features of perfectly competitive markets and illustrates why perfect competition is desirable from a social perspective. Monopoly is discussed in the subsequent section and is shown to be much less attractive than the perfectly competitive ideal.

CHARACTERISTICS OF PERFECTLY COMPETITIVE MARKETS

Perfect competition exists when the individual producers have no influence on market prices; they are price takers as opposed to price makers. This lack of influence on price typically requires that each of the following conditions be met.

- *Large numbers of buyers and sellers.* Each firm in the industry produces a small portion of industry output, and each customer buys only a small part of the total.
- *Product homogeneity.* The output of each firm is perceived by customers to be essentially the same as the output of any other firm in the industry.
- *Free entry and exit.* Firms are not restricted from entering or leaving the industry.
- *Perfect dissemination of information.* Cost, price, and product quality information is known by all buyers and all sellers in the market.

These basic conditions are too restrictive for perfect competition to be commonplace in actual markets. Although the stock market and commodity exchanges approach the perfectly competitive ideal, imperfections occur even there. For example, the acquisition or sale of large blocks of securities by institutional investors clearly affects stock market prices, at least in the short run. Nevertheless, because up to 1,000 shares of any stock listed on the New York Stock Exchange or American Stock Exchange can be bought or sold at the current market price, the stock market approaches the ideal of a perfectly competitive market. Similarly, many firms must make output decisions without any control over price, and examination of a perfectly competitive market structure provides insights into these operating decisions. A clear understanding of perfect competition also provides a reference point from which to analyze the more typically encountered market structures of monopolistic competition and oligopoly described in Chapter 11.

MARKET PRICE DETERMINATION

Market price in a competitive industry is determined by aggregate supply and demand; individual firms have no control over price. The total industry demand curve for a product reflects an aggregation of the quantities that individual purchasers will buy at each price. An industry supply curve reflects a summation of the quantities that individual firms are willing to supply at different prices. The intersection of industry demand and supply curves determines market price.

Data in Table 10.1 illustrate the process by which an industry supply curve is constructed. First, suppose that each of five firms in an industry is willing to supply varying quantities of the product at different prices. Summing the individual supply quantities of these five firms at each price determines their combined supply schedule, shown in the Partial Market Supply column. For example, at a price of $2, the output quantities supplied by the five firms are 15, 0, 5, 25, and 45 units, respectively, resulting in a combined supply of 90 units at that price. With a product price of $8, the supply quantities become 45, 115, 40, 55, and 75, for a total supply by the five firms of 330 units.

Now assume that the five firms, although representative of firms in the industry, account for only a small portion of the industry's total output. Assume that there are actually 5,000 firms in the industry, each with an individual supply schedule identical to one of the five firms illustrated in the table. There are 1,000 firms just like each one illustrated in Table 10.1; the total quantity supplied at each price is 1,000 times that shown under the Partial Market Supply schedule. This supply schedule is illustrated in Figure 10.1. Adding the market demand curve to the industry supply curve, as in Figure 10.2, allows one to determine the equilibrium market price.

Market price is found by equating market supply and market demand to find the equilibrium output level and then using either the demand or supply curve to find

Table 10.1

MARKET SUPPLY SCHEDULE DETERMINATION

QUANTITY SUPPLIED BY FIRM

PRICE ($)	1	+	2	+	3	+	4	+	5	=	PARTIAL MARKET SUPPLY	×	1,000	=	TOTAL MARKET SUPPLY
1	5		0		5		10		30		50				50,000
2	15		0		5		25		45		90				90,000
3	20		20		10		30		50		130				130,000
4	25		35		20		35		55		170				170,000
5	30		55		25		40		60		210				210,000
6	35		75		30		45		65		250				250,000
7	40		95		35		50		70		290				290,000
8	45		115		40		55		75		330				330,000
9	50		130		45		65		80		370				370,000
10	55		145		50		75		85		410				410,000

Figure 10.1

HYPOTHETICAL INDUSTRY SUPPLY CURVE

Industry supply is the sum of the quantities that individual firms supply at each price.

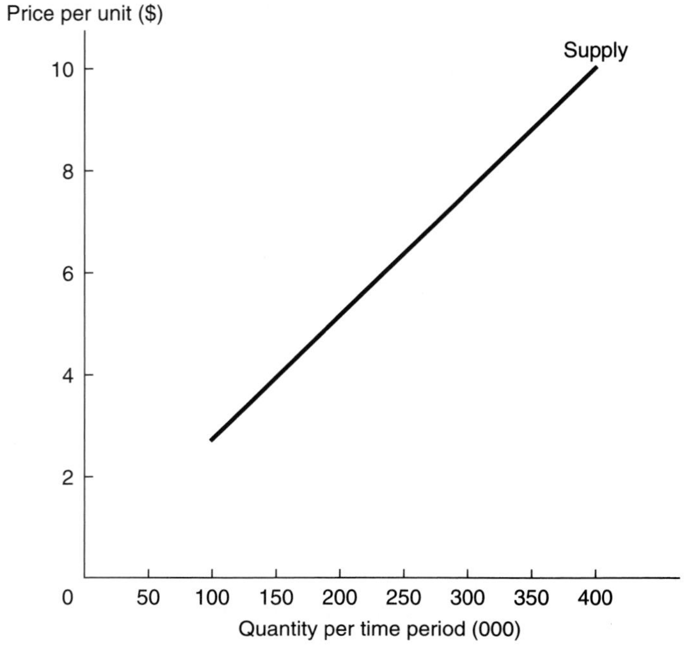

Price per unit ($)

the market clearing price at that activity level. From the curves in Figure 10.2 we have the following:

$$\text{Demand} = \text{Supply}$$

$$\$40 - \$0.0001Q = -\$0.254 + \$0.000025Q$$

$$\$0.000125Q = \$40.254$$

$$Q = 322{,}032$$

$$P = \$40 - \$0.0001(322{,}032)$$

$$= \$40 - \$32.20$$

$$= \$7.80.$$

Although it is apparent from Figure 10.2 that both the quantity demanded and supplied depend on price, a simple example demonstrates the inability of an individual firm to affect price. The total demand function in Figure 10.2, which represents the summation at each price of the quantities demanded by individual purchasers, is described by the equation

Figure 10.2

MARKET PRICE DETERMINATION IN PERFECT COMPETITION

The perfectly competitive market-equilibrium price/output combination can be determined by
equating the market demand and supply curves.

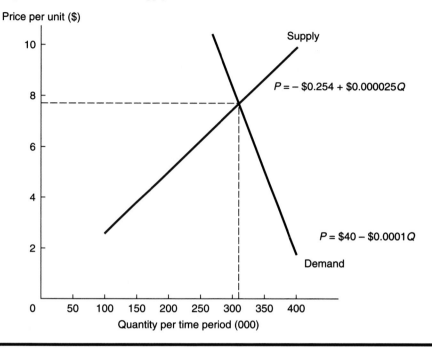

According to Equation 10.1a, a 100-unit change in output would cause only a $0.01
change in price. A $0.0001 price increase would lead to a one-unit decrease in total mar-
ket demand; a $0.0001 price reduction would lead to a one-unit increase in total market
demand.

The demand curve shown in Figure 10.2 is redrawn for an individual firm in Figure
10.3. The slope of the curve is -0.0001, the same as in Figure 10.2, only the scales have
been changed. The intercept $7.80 is the going market price as determined by the inter-
section of the market supply and demand curves in Figure 10.2.

At the scale shown in Figure 10.3, the firm's demand curve is seen to be, for all
practical purposes, a horizontal line. An output change of even 100 units by the individual firm results in only a $0.01 change in market price, and the data in Table 10.1

$$\text{Quantity Demanded} = Q = 400{,}000 - 10{,}000P, \qquad \textbf{(10.1)}$$

or, solving for price,

$$\$10{,}000P = \$400{,}000 - Q,$$

$$P = \$40 - \$0.0001Q. \qquad \textbf{(10.1a)}$$

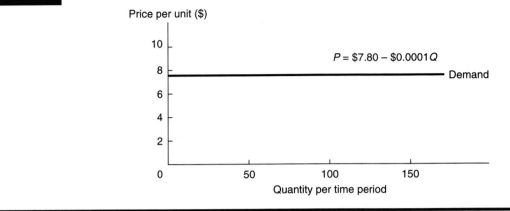

Figure 10.3

DEMAND CURVE FOR A SINGLE FIRM IN PERFECT COMPETITION

Firms face horizontal demand curves in perfectly competitive markets.

Note: With price constant at, say, P^*, $TR = P^* \times Q$, $AR = (P^* \times Q)/Q = P^*$, and $MR = dTR/dQ = P^*$.

indicate that the typical firm would not vary output by this amount unless the market price changed by more than $10 a unit. Thus, it is clear that under perfect competition, the individual firm's output decisions do not affect price in any meaningful way, and for pricing decisions, the demand curve is taken to be perfectly horizontal. Price is assumed to be constant irrespective of the output level at which the firm chooses to operate.

THE FIRM'S PRICE/OUTPUT DECISION

Figure 10.4 illustrates the firm's price/output decision in a competitive market. Assume for simplicity that the curves graphed are those of a representative firm. Thus, the cost curves in Figure 10.4 represent an average firm in a perfectly competitive industry.

Profit maximization requires that a firm operate at the output level at which marginal revenue and marginal cost are equal. With price constant, average revenue (or price) and marginal revenue must always be equal. To maximize profits, market price must equal marginal cost for a firm operating in a perfectly competitive industry. In the example shown in Figure 10.4, the firm chooses to operate at output level Q^*, where price (and hence marginal revenue) equals marginal cost, and profits are maximized.

This illustration shows that above-normal or economic profits can exist in the short run even under conditions of perfect competition. A normal profit, defined as the rate of return just sufficient to attract the capital investment necessary to operate and develop a firm (see Chapter 1) is included as a part of economic costs. Therefore, any profit shown in a graph such as Figure 10.4 is defined as economic profit and represents an above-normal rate of return. The firm incurs economic losses whenever it fails to earn a normal profit. A firm might show a small accounting profit but be suffering economic losses because these profits are insufficient to provide an adequate return to the firm's stockholders. In such instances, firms are unable to replace plant and equipment and will exit the industry in the long run.

COMPETITIVE FIRM'S OPTIONAL PRICE/OUTPUT COMBINATION

Figure 10.4

Given a horizontal demand curve, $P = MR$. Thus, short-run equilibrium occurs when $P = MR = MC$.

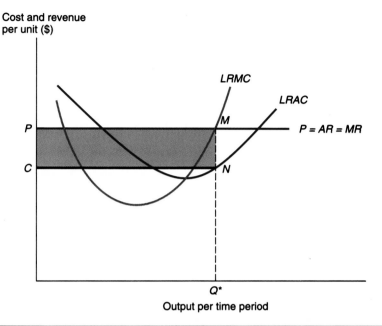

In Figure 10.4 the firm produces and sells Q^* units of output at an average cost of C dollars; with a market price P, the firm earns economic profits of $P - C$ dollars per unit. Total economic profit, $(P - C)Q^*$, is shown by the shaded rectangle *PMNC*.

Over the long run, positive economic profits attract additional firms into the industry, lead to increased output by existing firms, or both. Expanding industry supply puts downward pressure on market prices for the industry as a whole, since industry output can expand only by offering the product at a lower price. Expanded supply simultaneously pushes cost upward because of increased demand for factors of production. Long-run equilibrium is reached when all economic profits and losses have been eliminated and each firm in the industry is operating at an output that minimizes long-run average cost (*LRAC*). The long-run equilibrium for a firm under perfect competition is graphed in Figure 10.5. At the profit-maximizing output, price (or average revenue) equals average cost, so the firm neither earns economic profits nor incurs economic losses. When this condition exists for all firms in the industry, new firms are not encouraged to enter the industry nor are existing ones pressured into leaving it. Prices are stable, and each firm is operating at the minimum point on its short-run average cost curve. All firms must also be operating at the minimum cost point on the long-run average cost curve; otherwise, they will make production changes, decrease costs, and affect industry

Figure 10.5	**LONG-RUN EQUILIBRIUM IN A COMPETITIVE MARKET** Long-run equilibrium is reached when Q^* units of output are produced at minimum *LRAC*. Thus, $P = MR = MC = AC$, and economic (excess) profits equal zero.

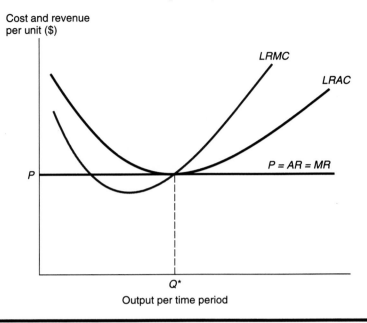

output and prices. Accordingly, a stable equilibrium requires that firms operate with op-
timally sized plants.

The optimal price/output level for a firm in a perfectly competitive market can
be further illustrated using a more detailed example. Assume that you are interested
in determining the profit-maximizing activity level for the Hair Stylist, Ltd., a
hairstyling salon in College Park, Maryland. Given the large number of competitors, the fact that stylists routinely tailor services to meet customer needs, and the
lack of entry barriers, it is reasonable to assume that the market is perfectly competitive and that the average $20 price equals marginal revenue, $P = MR = \$20$.
Furthermore, assume that the firm's operating expenses are typical of the 100 firms
in the local market and can be expressed by the following total and marginal cost
functions:

$$TC = \$5,625 + \$5Q + \$0.01Q^2,$$

$$MC = \$5 + \$0.02Q$$

where TC is total cost per month including capital costs and Q is the number of hairstylings provided.

The optimal price/output combination can be determined by setting marginal revenue equal to marginal cost and solving for Q:

$$MR = MC$$

$$\$20 = \$5 + \$0.02Q$$

$$\$0.02Q = \$15$$

$$Q = 750 \text{ hairstylings per month.}$$

At this output level, maximum economic profits are

$$\pi = TR - TC$$

$$= \$20Q - \$5,625 - \$5Q - \$0.01Q^2$$

$$= \$20(750) - \$5,625 - \$5(750) - \$0.01(750^2)$$

$$= \$0.$$

The $Q = 750$ activity level results in zero economic profits. This means that the Hair Stylist is just able to obtain a normal or risk-adjusted rate of return on investment since capital costs are already included in the cost function. The $Q = 750$ output level is also the point of minimum average production costs ($AC = MC = \$20$). Finally, with 100 identical firms in the industry, industry output totals 75,000 hairstylings per month.

THE FIRM SUPPLY CURVE

Market supply curves are the summation of supply quantities for individual firms at various prices. The perfectly competitive firm's short-run supply curve corresponds to that portion of the marginal cost curve that lies above the average variable cost curve. Since $P = MR$ under perfect competition, the quantity supplied by the perfectly competitive firm is found at the point where $P = MC$, as long as price exceeds average variable cost.

To clarify this point, consider the options available to the firm. Profit maximization under perfect competition requires that the firm operate at the output level at which marginal revenue equals marginal cost, if it produces any output at all. That is, the firm will either produce nothing and incur a loss equal to its fixed costs, or it will produce an output determined by the intersection of the horizontal demand curve and the marginal cost curve. It will choose the alternative that maximizes profits or minimizes losses, if losses must be incurred. If price is less than average variable costs, the firm should produce nothing and incur a loss equal to total fixed cost. Losses will increase if any output at all is produced and sold when $P < AVC$. If price exceeds average variable cost, then each unit of output provides at least some profit contribution to help cover fixed costs and provide profit. The firm should produce and sell its product under such conditions, because such production reduces losses or leads to profits. The minimum point on the firm's average variable cost curve determines the lower limit, or cutoff point, of its supply schedule.

This is illustrated in Figure 10.6. At a very low price such as $1, $MR = MC$ at 100 units of output. The firm has a total cost per unit of $2 and a price of only $1, so it is incurring a loss of $1 per unit. Since the difference between the *ATC* and the *AVC* curves represents the fixed cost per unit of output, the total loss consists of a fixed cost component ($2.00 − $1.40 = $0.60) and a variable cost component ($1.40 − $1.00 = $0.40). Thus, the total loss is

$$\text{Total Loss} = (100 \text{ Units}) \times (\$0.60 \text{ Fixed Cost Loss} + \$0.40 \text{ Variable Cost Loss})$$

$$= \$100.$$

If the firm simply shut down and terminated production, it would cease to incur variable costs, and its loss would be reduced to the level of fixed costs, or 100($0.60) = $60.

Variable cost losses occur at any price less than $1.25, the minimum point on the *AVC* curve, so this is the lowest price at which the firm will operate. Above $1.25, price more than covers variable costs. Even though total costs are not covered at prices less than $2, it is preferable to operate when $1.25 < P < $2 and earn at least some profit contribution to cover a portion of total fixed costs rather than to shut down and incur losses equal to total fixed costs.

To summarize, the perfectly competitive firm short-run supply curve is that portion of the marginal cost curve lying above the *AVC* curve. When marginal cost is below average cost but above average variable cost, losses can be reduced if the firm expands

Figure 10.6

PRICE, COST, AND OPTIMAL SUPPLY DECISIONS FOR A FIRM UNDER PURE COMPETITION

The minimum point of $1.25 on the *AVC* curve is the lowest price level at which the firm will supply output.

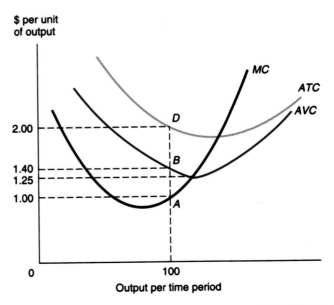

production. Despite losses, firms continue to produce when price exceeds average variable cost. Positive economic profits occur over that part of the supply function for which price (and marginal cost) exceeds average total cost. The firm's long-run supply function is similarly determined. Since all costs vary in the long run, firms shut down unless total costs are completely covered. The portion of the firm's long-run marginal cost curve that lies above its long-run average cost curve represents its long-run supply schedule.

Monopoly

Perfect monopoly lies at the opposite extreme from perfect competition on the market structure continuum. Monopoly exists when a single firm is the sole producer of a good that has no close substitutes; in other words, there is a single firm in the industry. Perfect monopoly, like perfect competition, is seldom observed.

CHARACTERISTICS OF MONOPOLY MARKETS

Monopoly exists when an individual producer has the ability to substantially dictate market price. Monopoly firms are price makers as opposed to price takers. Their control over price typically requires that each of the following conditions be met.

- *A single seller.* A single firm produces all industry output. The monopoly is the industry.
- *Unique product.* Monopoly output is perceived by customers to be distinctive and preferable to its imperfect substitutes.
- *Blockaded entry and exit.* Firms are heavily restricted from entering or leaving the industry.
- *Imperfect dissemination of information.* Cost, price, and product quality information is withheld from uninformed buyers.

As in the case of perfect competition, these basic conditions are too restrictive for monopoly to be commonplace in actual markets. Few goods are produced by single producers, and fewer still are free from competition of close substitutes. Even public utilities are imperfect monopolies in most of their markets. Electric companies, for example, typically approach a perfect monopoly in their residential lighting market, but they face strong competition from gas and oil suppliers in the heating market. In all industrial and commercial power markets, electric utilities face competition from gas- and oil-powered private generators. Even though perfect monopoly rarely exists, it is still worthy of careful examination. Many of the economic relations found under monopoly can be used to estimate optimal firm behavior in the less precise, but more prevalent, partly competitive and partly monopolistic market structures that dominate the real world. An understanding of monopoly also provides the background necessary to examine the economics of regulation, covered in Chapter 13, a topic of prime importance to business managers.

Is Ticketmaster a Monopoly?

In a breath-taking innovation, closely-held Ticketmaster Corp. has joined with Viacom, Inc., owner of MTV, to offer concert tickets and fan merchandise directly to MTV viewers. In April 1995, for example, the immense potential of their joint marketing agreement was aptly demonstrated when a phenomenal 4 *million* VH-1 viewers called in to spend $35 to $45 per ticket, or $1.8 million in total, for a Melissa Etheridge concert tour. Another $200,000 was spent on T-shirts, hats and other Melissa Etheridge paraphernalia. In January 1995, an estimated 500,000 calls were received during the first 15 minutes of a show devoted to selling 20,000 tickets to an upcoming Tom Petty and the Heartbreakers concert. Even after discounting caller numbers for repeat phone calls, Ticketmaster and MTV have clearly found a way to quickly and efficiently address an important audience for tickets to popular concerts. In the future, MTV and Ticketmaster may offer a series of special programs to promote concert tickets and related merchandise, or Ticketmaster may offer a TV channel exclusively devoted to concert ticket and merchandise promotions. In the present, the awesome marketing might displayed by Ticketmaster raises some fears that this ticket-selling goliath may come to further dominate the ticket selling industry.

In only few short years, Ticketmaster has converted computerized ticketing services from a minor $1 million per year business for sports and entertainment ticketing into a huge and profitable industry that generates billions of dollars per year in fees. As it has transformed this business, Ticketmaster has come to dominate the computerized ticket-buying industry. In the 1980s, Ticketmaster recognized that customers would pay much more for ticket-buying services than the typical service charge of $1 per ticket. Today, Ticketmaster charges typically run from $1.50 to $6.50 per ticket, depending upon location and event, and telephone handling fees run an additional $1.30-$2.05 per order. At a 1997 showing of Walt Disney's *Pocahontas on Ice* in Kansas City, for example, a $25 ticket carried an outlet service charge of $1.75 per ticket, or a $2 service charge when ordered by phone plus a $1.00 per order telephone handling fee (see table).

In defense of such high fees, Ticketmaster argues that the convenience to ticket buyers and facility operator services offered by the company don't come cheap. Continuously staffing toll-free telephone lines with informed ticket agents is expensive, and beyond the capability of any single concert hall or sports facility. In acting as the sole ticket vendor for such facilities, Ticketmaster can also assure facility operators that tickets to on-site events will be priced properly in light of booking alternatives. No single concert hall or sports facility has anywhere near the same data base concerning the ticket buying habits of the general public as does Ticketmaster. Ticketmaster uses this information in its own behalf, and on behalf of the on-site facilities that it represents. It is Ticketmaster's marketing savvy and choke-hold on information concerning the ticket-buying habits of the general public that has some trustbusters worried that the company has created significant monopoly power in the computerized ticketing services industry.

Arenas used to pay Ticketron, an early Ticketmaster competitor, for its ticket-selling services. As an innovative competitive strategy, Ticketmaster paid arenas millions of dollars for the right to sell their tickets and helped develop effective marketing tactics. With Ticketmaster's help, selling tickets went from being a costly headache to a care-free and a revenue-maximizing endeavor for on-site facilities. As its part of the bargain, Ticketmaster

PRICE/OUTPUT DECISION UNDER MONOPOLY

Under monopoly, the industry demand curve is identical to the firm demand curve. Because industry demand curves slope downward, monopolists also face a downward-sloping demand curve. In Figure 10.7, for example, 100 units can be sold at a price of $10 a unit. At an $8 price, quantity demanded rises to 150 units. If the firm decides to

Managerial Application 10.2 (continued)

THE COST OF BEING A FAN: SELECTED PRICES FOR TICKETS SOLD THROUGH TICKETMASTER

EVENT	TICKET PRICE	SERVICE CHARGE		TELEPHONE HANDLING FEE[3]
		OUTLET[1]	TELEPHONE[2]	
Alabama Concert	$25.50	$4.00	$5.00	$1.80
Andrew Lloyd Webber Musical (Terrace seating)	31.00	5.50	6.50	2.05
Blues & Jazz Festival in Penn Valley Park (Kansas City)	10.00	2.25	3.00	1.75
Boston Concert	25.00	4.00	5.00	1.80
Chicago Cubs Baseball (Club seats)	19.00	2.00	2.50	1.30
L.A. Dodgers Baseball (Middle-level loge)	11.00	1.75	2.00	1.55
L.A. Lakers Basketball Playoffs (Loge seats)	50.50	2.75	4.25	2.05
Milwaukee Summerfest	6.00	1.50	2.00	1.55
Minnesota Timberwolves Basketball (Upper level)	29.50	1.75	2.00	1.60
Walt Disney's Pocohantas On Ice	25.00	1.75	2.00	1.00
Ted Nugent & Bad Company Concert	20.00	4.00	5.00	1.80

[1]Per ticket; Ticketmaster outlets require cash.

[2]Per ticket; Ticketmaster phone service requires a credit card.

[3]Per order, regardless of number of tickets ordered, if tickets are mailed.

SOURCE: Phone survey, February 1997; see http://www.ticketmaster.com.

gained exclusive marketing rights for the initial hours of ticket sales for major concerts and other special events. Because on-site box offices open later, and only when tickets are left over, Ticketmaster often accounts for 85% to 90% of sales for hundreds on-site facilities.

All of this raises an important question: At what point does it become reasonable for society to limit the success of innovative companies like Ticketmaster that come to dominate their industry? Are such limits *ever* reasonable?

See: "Marketing & Media: Ticketmaster Goes On-line, Sells Tickets to Broadway on Web," *The Wall Street Journal*, October 29, 1996, B8.

sell 100 units, it will receive $10 a unit; if it wishes to sell 150 units, it must accept an $8 price. The monopolist can set either price or quantity, but not both. Given one, the value of the other is determined by the demand curve.

A monopoly uses the same profit-maximization rule as does any other firm: it operates at the output level at which marginal revenue equals marginal cost. The monopoly

FIRM'S DEMAND CURVE UNDER MONOPOLY

Figure 10.7

The demand curve for a monopolist is the industry demand curve.

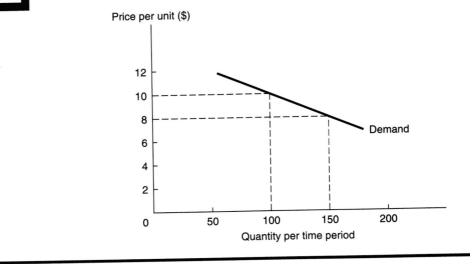

demand curve is not horizontal, however, so marginal revenue does not coincide with price at any but the first unit of output. Marginal revenue is always less than price for output quantities greater than one because of the negatively sloped demand curve. Since the demand (average revenue) curve is negatively sloped and hence declining, the marginal revenue curve must lie below it.

When a monopoly equates marginal revenue and marginal cost, it simultaneously determines the output level and the market price for its product. This decision is illustrated in Figure 10.8. The firm produces Q units of output at a cost of C per unit and sells this output at price P. Profits, which equal $(P - C)$ times Q, are represented by the area $PP'C'C$ and are at a maximum. Q is optimal short-run output only if average revenue, or price, is greater than average variable cost, as shown in Figure 10.8. If price is below average variable cost, losses are minimized by shutting down.

To further illustrate price/output decisions under monopoly, the previous Hair Stylist, Ltd., example can be modified to reflect an assumption that the firm has a monopoly in the College Park market, perhaps because of restrictive licensing requirements. In the earlier example, each of 100 perfectly competitive firms had a profit-maximizing activity level of 750 hairstylings per month, for a total industry output of 75,000 hairstylings per month.

As a monopoly, the Hair Stylist provides all industry output. For simplicity, assume that the Hair Stylist operates a chain of salons and that the cost function for each shop is the same as in the previous example. By operating each shop at its average cost-minimizing activity level of 750 hairstylings per month, the Hair Stylist can operate with Marginal Cost = Average Cost = $20.

PRICE/OUTPUT DECISION UNDER MONOPOLY

Figure 10.8

Monopoly equilibrium occurs where $MR = MC$. However, $P > ATC$, and the firm earns economic (excess) profits.

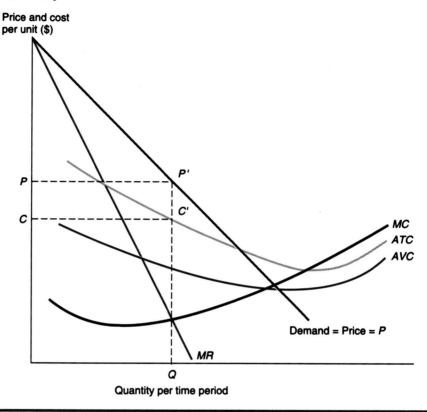

Assume that industry demand and marginal revenue curves for hair stylings in the College Park market are

$$P = \$80 - \$0.0008Q,$$

$$MR = \$80 - \$0.0016Q.$$

The monopoly profit-maximizing activity level is obtained by setting marginal revenue equal to marginal cost, or marginal profit equal to zero ($M\pi = 0$), and solving for Q:

$$MR = MC$$

$$\$80 - \$0.0016Q = \$20$$

$$\$0.0016Q = \$60$$

$$Q = 37,500 \text{ hairstylings per month.}$$

The optimal market price is

$$P = \$80 - \$0.0008(37,500)$$

$$= \$50.$$

At the $Q = 37,500$ activity level, the Hair Stylist will operate a chain of 50 salons ($= 37,500/750$). Although each outlet produces $Q = 750$ hairstylings per month, a point of optimum efficiency, the benefits of this efficiency accrue to the company in the form of economic profits rather than to consumers in the form of lower prices. Economic profits from each shop are

$$\pi = TR - TC$$

$$= P \times Q - AC \times Q$$

$$= \$50(750) - \$20(750)$$

$$= \$22,500 \text{ per month.}$$

With 50 shops, the Hair Stylist earns total economic profits of $1,125,000 per month. As a monopoly, the industry provides only 37,500 units of output, down from the 75,000 units provided in the case of a perfectly competitive industry. The new price of $50 per hairstyling is up substantially from the perfectly competitive price of $20. The effects of monopoly power are reflected in terms of higher consumer prices, reduced levels of output, and substantial economic profits for the Hair Stylist, Inc.

In general, any industry characterized by monopoly *sells less* output at *higher prices* than would the same industry if it were perfectly competitive. From the perspective of the firm and its stockholders, the benefits of monopoly are measured in terms of the economic profits that are possible when competition is reduced or eliminated. From a broader social perspective, however, these private benefits must be weighed against the costs borne by consumers in the forms of higher prices and reduced availability of desired products. Employees and suppliers also suffer from the reduced employment opportunities associated with the lower production of monopoly market structures.

Nevertheless, it is important to recognize that monopoly is not always as socially harmful as indicated in the previous example. In the case of Microsoft Corp., for example, the genius of Bill Gates and a multitude of research associates has created a dynamic computer software juggernaut. The tremendous stockholder value created through their efforts, including billions of dollars in personal wealth for Gates and his associates, can be viewed only as a partial index of their contribution to society in general. Other similar examples include the DeKalb Corporation (hybrid seeds), Kellogg Company (ready-to-eat cereal), Lotus Corporation (spreadsheet software), and the Reserve Fund (money market mutual funds), among others. In instances such as these, monopoly profits are the just rewards flowing from truly important contributions of unique firms and individuals.

It is also important to recognize that monopoly profits are often fleeting. Early profits earned by each of the firms mentioned previously attracted a host of competitors. For example, note the tremendous growth in the money market mutual fund business since the November 1971 birth of the Reserve Fund. Today the Reserve Fund is only one of roughly 500 money market mutual funds available, and it accounts for only a small fraction of the roughly $1 trillion in industry assets. The tremendous social value of invention and innovation often remains long after early monopoly profits have dissipated.

LONG-RUN EQUILIBRIUM UNDER MONOPOLY

In the long run, a monopoly continues to operate only if price at least equals long-run average cost. Because all costs are variable in the long run, the firm will not operate unless all costs are covered. No monopoly or perfectly competitive firm will operate in the long run if it suffers continual losses.

As shown earlier, in equilibrium, perfectly competitive firms must operate at the minimum point on the *LRAC* curve. This requirement does not hold under monopoly. For example, again consider Figure 10.8 and assume that the *ATC* curve represents the long-run average cost curve for the firm. The firm will produce *Q* units of output at an average cost of *C* per unit, somewhat above the minimum point on the *ATC* curve. Such a firm is a **natural monopoly,** since the market-clearing price, where $P = MC$, occurs at a point at which *long-run* average costs are still declining. In other words, market demand is insufficient to justify full utilization of even one minimum-efficient-scale plant. A single firm can produce the total market supply at a lower total cost than could any number of smaller firms, and competition naturally reduces the number of competitors until only a single supplier remains. Electric and local telephone utilities are classic examples of natural monopoly, since any duplication in production and distribution facilities would increase consumer costs.

Natural Monopoly
An industry in which the market-clearing price occurs at a point at which the monopolist's long-run average costs are still declining.

MONOPOLY REGULATION

Natural monopoly presents something of a dilemma. On the one hand, economic efficiency could be enhanced by restricting the number of producers to a single firm. On the other hand, monopolies have an incentive to underproduce and can earn economic profits. **Underproduction** results when a monopoly curtails output to a level at which the value of resources employed, as measured by the marginal cost of production, is less than the social benefit derived, where social benefit is measured by the price that customers are willing to pay for additional output. Under monopoly, marginal cost is less than price at the profit-maximizing output level. Although resulting economic profits serve the useful functions of providing incentives and helping allocate resources, it is difficult to justify above-normal profits that result from market power rather than from exceptional performance.

Underproduction
A situation that occurs when a monopolist curtails production to a level at which marginal cost is less than price.

How is it possible to escape the dilemma that monopoly can be efficient but can also lead to economic profits and underproduction? The answer sometimes lies in permitting monopolies to exist but regulating their prices and output quantity. The important topic of public regulation of natural monopolies is discussed in detail in Chapter 13. In other instances, market forces often emerge that effectively limit the profit potential of monopoly.

Countervailing Power: The Monopoly/Monopsony Confrontation

Unregulated monopoly sellers facing perfectly competitive market demand will typically limit production and offer their products to consumers at high prices. The private and social costs of this behavior are often measured by above-normal profits, inefficient production methods, and lagging rates of innovation. How is this inefficiency reduced, if not eliminated, in unregulated markets? Sometimes the answer lies in the development of countervailing forces within markets.

Countervailing Power
Buyer market power that offsets seller market power, and vice versa.

SELLER VERSUS BUYER POWER

Countervailing power is an economic influence that creates a closer balance between previously unequal sellers and buyers. The classic example is a single employer in a

Figure 10.9

MONOPOLY UNION AND MONOPSONY EMPLOYER CONFRONTATION IN THE LABOR MARKET

In a perfectly competitive labor market, the equilibrium wage is at W_C. A monopoly union facing competitive labor demand will seek a higher wage of W_U. A monopsony employer facing a competitive labor supply will offer a lower wage of W_M.

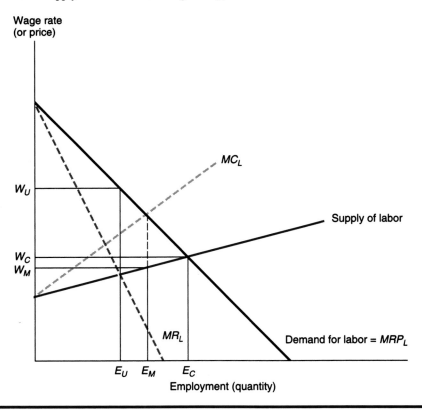

small town who might take advantage of the local labor force by offering less-than-competitive wages. As the single employer, the company has a monopsony in the local labor market. Workers might decide to band together and form a union, a monopoly seller in the local labor market, to offset the monopsony power of the employer.

To illustrate this classic confrontation, consider Figure 10.9, which shows demand and supply relations in a local labor market. The downward-sloping demand for labor is simply the marginal revenue product of labor curve as discussed in Chapter 7. The marginal revenue product of labor (MRP_L) is simply the amount of net revenue generated through employment of an additional unit of labor ($\Delta TR/\Delta L$). It is the product of the marginal product of labor (MP_L) and the marginal revenue of output (MR_Q). Thus, $MRP_L = \Delta TR/\Delta L = MP_L \times MR_Q$. MRP_L tends to fall as employment expands because of the labor factor's diminishing returns. An upward-sloping supply curve reflects that higher wages are typically necessary to expand the amount of labor offered. Perfectly competitive demand and supply conditions create an exact balance between demand and supply, and the competitive equilibrium wage, W_C, and employment level, E_C, are observed.

A monopsony employer facing a perfectly competitive supply of labor sets its marginal cost of labor, MC_L, equal to the marginal benefit derived from employment. Because the employer's marginal benefit is measured in terms of the marginal revenue product of labor, an unchecked monopsonist sets $MC_L = MRP_L$. Notice that the MC_L curve exceeds the labor supply curve at each point, based on the assumption that wages must be increased for all workers in order to hire additional employees. This is analogous to cutting prices for all customers in order to expand sales, causing the MR curve to lie below the demand curve. Since workers need to be paid only the wage rate indicated along the labor supply curve for a given level of employment, the monopsonist employer offers employees a wage of W_M and a less than competitive level of employment opportunities, E_M.

An unchecked union, or monopoly seller of labor, could command a wage of W_U if demand for labor were competitive. This solution is found by setting the marginal revenue of labor (MR_L) equal to the labor supply curve, which represents the marginal cost of labor to the union. Like any monopoly seller, the union can obtain higher wages (prices) only by restricting employment opportunities (output) for union members. A union is able to offer its members only the less than competitive employment opportunities, E_U, if it attempts to maximize labor income.

THE COMPROMISE SOLUTION

What is likely to occur in the case of the monopoly union/monopsony employer confrontation? Typically, wage/employment bargaining produces a compromise wage/employment outcome. Compromise achieved through countervailing power has the beneficial effect of moving the labor market away from the inefficient unchecked monopoly or monopsony solutions toward a more efficient labor market equilibrium. However, only in the unlikely event of perfectly matched monopoly/monopsony protagonists will the perfectly competitive outcome occur. Depending on the relative power of the union and the employer, either an above-market or a below-market wage outcome typically results, and employment opportunities are often somewhat below those under competitive conditions. Nevertheless, the countervailing power of monopoly/monopsony confrontation can have the beneficial effect of improving economic efficiency from that experienced under unchecked monopoly or monopsony.

The Measurement of Business Profit Rates

In long-run equilibrium, economic theory states that profit rates in perfectly competitive industries are just sufficient to provide investors with a normal risk-adjusted rate of return. In monopoly markets, barriers to entry or exit are thought sufficient to allow monopolists to earn above-normal profits, even over the long run. Nevertheless, high profit rates are sometimes observed in vigorously competitive markets over extended periods. At the same time, other firms that seem to enjoy many of the attributes of monopoly stumble from one year to the next without realizing superior rates of return. To appreciate the sources of observed differences in realized rates of return, it is necessary to understand conventional means for measuring business profits.

THE RATE OF RETURN ON STOCKHOLDERS' EQUITY

Return on Stockholders' Equity
Business profits expressed as a percentage of owner-supplied capital.

Business profit rates are best measured by the accounting rate of **return on stockholders' equity** measure. Simply referred to as ROE, the return on stockholders' equity measure is defined as net income divided by the book value of stockholders' equity, where stockholders' equity is the book value of total assets minus total liabilities. As seen in Table 10.2, ROE can also be described as the simple product of three common accounting ratios. ROE equals the firm's profit margin multiplied by the total asset turnover ratio, all times the firm's leverage ratio:

$$\text{ROE} = \frac{\text{Net Income}}{\text{Equity}}$$

$$= \frac{\text{Net Income}}{\text{Sales}} \times \frac{\text{Sales}}{\text{Total Assets}} \times \frac{\text{Total Assets}}{\text{Equity}} \qquad (10.2)$$

$$= \text{Profit Margin} \times \frac{\text{Total Asset}}{\text{Turnover}} \times \text{Leverage}.$$

Profit Margin
Net income expressed as a percentage of sales revenue.

Profit margin is defined as accounting net income expressed as a percentage of sales revenue and shows the amount of profit earned per dollar of sales. When profit margins are high, robust demand or stringent cost controls, or both, allow the firm to earn a significant profit contribution. Holding capital requirements constant, profit margin is a useful indicator of managerial efficiency in responding to rapidly growing demand and/or effective measures of cost containment. The outstanding profit margins reported by Cedar Fair, Great Northern Iron, Hong Kong Telecom, and others reported in Table 10.2 are an interesting case in point. However, rich profit margins do not necessarily guarantee a high rate of return on stockholders' equity. Despite high profit margins, firms in mining, construction, heavy equipment manufacturing, cable TV, and motion

| Table 10.2 | RETURN ON STOCKHOLDERS' EQUITY, PROFIT MARGIN, TOTAL ASSET TURNOVER, AND LEVERAGE FOR A SAMPLE OF TOP PERFORMING LARGE COMPANIES |

COMPANY NAME	INDUSTRY NAME	RETURN ON STOCK-HOLDERS' EQUITY (ROE)	PROFIT MARGIN	TOTAL ASSET TURNOVER RATIO	LEVER-AGE RATIO
Abbott Labs	Medical Supplies	38.4%	16.9%	1.06	2.14
Alliance Capital	Financial Services	38.2%	24.3%	1.11	1.41
Ametek Industries	Diversified Co	50.3%	5.2%	1.59	6.05
Billing Info.	Telecom Services	61.8%	16.2%	0.76	5.04
Bristol-Myers Squibb	Drug	58.2%	24.6%	0.99	2.39
Callaway Golf	Recreation	43.4%	17.7%	1.91	1.29
Cedar Fair, LP	Recreation	43.6%	30.3%	0.79	1.81
Ceridian Corp.	Computer Software & Services	89.4%	10.1%	1.18	7.51
Coca-Cola	Soft Drinks	55.4%	16.6%	1.20	2.79
Computer Associates	Computer Software & Services	50.7%	21.4%	0.70	3.39
Du Pont (E.I.)	Chemical: Basic	40.4%	8.1%	1.13	4.42
Dun & Bradstreet	Publishing	54.5%	11.9%	0.98	4.66
Eastmen Chemical	Chemical: Diversified	37.1%	11.3%	1.04	3.18
EQUIFAX, Inc.	Industrial Services	41.8%	9.1%	1.54	2.98
Freeport McMorman	Chemical: Diversified	44.3%	18.0%	0.81	3.04
Great Northern Iron	Steel: General	57.9%	83.5%	0.60	1.16
GTE Corp.	Telecom Services	36.8%	12.7%	0.54	5.39
Hong Kong Telecom	Foreign Telecom	43.0%	32.4%	0.80	1.65
ICN Pharmaceuticals	Drug	36.1%	11.5%	0.98	3.20
JLG Industries	Machinery: Construction & Mining	37.2%	10.2%	2.26	1.61
Jostens, Inc.	Publishing	42.4%	7.4%	1.81	3.15
Kellogg	Food Processing	47.9%	10.9%	1.59	2.77
Lamson & Sessions	Electrical Equipment	39.2%	4.0%	2.21	4.39
Luxottica Group	Retail: Specialty	37.6%	8.7%	0.62	6.96
McAfee Associates	Computer Software & Services	36.5%	25.7%	0.87	1.64
Medusa Corp.	Cement & Aggregates	45.2%	14.7%	1.34	2.30
Micron Technology	Semiconductor	44.5%	28.6%	1.06	1.46
Millipore Corp.	Chemical: Diversified	37.7%	14.4%	1.12	2.34
Northwest Airlines	Air Transport	52.6%	4.3%	1.08	11.29
Pacific Telesis	Telecom Services	47.9%	11.6%	0.57	7.23
Philip Morris	Tobacco	39.2%	8.3%	1.23	3.85
Plum Creek Timber	Paper & Forest Products	47.3%	18.9%	0.71	3.53
Quality Food Centers	Grocery	44.5%	2.8%	2.58	6.23
Ralston Purina	Household Products	47.5%	4.6%	1.58	6.61
Safeway Inc.	Grocery	41.0%	2.0%	3.16	6.53
Schering-Plough	Drug	64.9%	20.6%	1.09	2.87
Sealed Air	Packaging & Containers	49.6%	7.3%	1.63	4.17
Southern New England Telephone	Telecom Services	47.8%	9.2%	0.67	7.72
Stone Container	Paper & Forest Products	44.2%	6.0%	1.15	6.37
Tambrands, Inc.	Toiletries & Cosmetics	91.5%	13.8%	1.62	4.10

				TOTAL	
		RETURN ON		ASSET	LEVER-
		STOCK-			
		HOLDERS'	PROFIT	TURNOVER	AGE
COMPANY NAME	INDUSTRY NAME	EQUITY (ROE)	MARGIN	RATIO	RATIO
Triad Systems	Computer & Peripherals	59.2%	4.8%	1.32	9.35
Union Carbide	Chemical: Basic	42.2%	14.7%	0.94	3.06
WD-40 Co.	Chemical: Specialty	45.1%	16.3%	2.12	1.31
Zeigler Coal	Coal & Alternate Energy	49.9%	54.4%	0.73	12.70
Averages		47.8%	14.9%	1.24	4.25

Table 10.2

(continued)

Data Source: Value Line/Value Screen II Data Base, January 1, 1997.

picture production often earn only modest rates of return because significant capital expenditures are required before meaningful sales revenues can be generated. Thus, it is vitally important to consider the magnitude of capital requirements when interpreting the size of profit margins for a firm or an industry.

Total Asset Turnover
Sales revenue divided by the book value of total assets.

Total asset turnover is sales revenue divided by the book value of total assets. When total asset turnover is high, the firm is thought to display a wise use of assets because it is able to make its investments work hard in the sense of generating a large amount of sales volume. Many segments of the retailing industry, especially grocery and apparel retailing, are good examples of industries where high rates of total asset turnover, sometimes as high as 2.5 to 3 times per year, can allow efficient firms to earn an attractive rate of return on stockholders' equity despite modest profit margins. For example, consider grocery retailer Safeway, Inc. Despite below-average profit margins and a fairly conservative financial structure, Safeway reports a sterling ROE of 41% per year by virtue of the fact that it reports a total asset turnover rate of 3.16 times per year. Like other successful retailers, Safeway has learned that the wise use of assets is a key ingredient of success in the often cutthroat business of grocery retailing.

Leverage
The ratio of the book value of assets divided by stockholders' equity.

Leverage is often defined as the ratio of the book value of total assets divided by stockholders' equity. It reflects the extent to which debt and preferred stock is used in addition to common stock financing. Leverage is used to amplify firm profit rates over the business cycle. During economic booms, leverage can dramatically increase the firm's profit rate; during recessions and other economic contractions, leverage can just as dramatically decrease realized rates of return, if not lead to losses. Despite ordinary profit margins and modest rates of total asset turnover, ROE in the automobile and telecommunications industries can sometimes benefit through use of a risky financial strategy that employs significant leverage. However, it is worth remembering that a risky financial structure can lead to awe-inspiring profit rates during economic expansions, such as that experienced during the mid-1990s, but it can also lead to huge losses during economic contractions or recessions, such as that experienced during 1991.

TYPICAL BUSINESS PROFIT RATES

For both large and small firms in the United States and Canada, ROE ranges between 9% and 10% during a typical year. This average ROE is comprised of a typical profit margin on sales revenue of roughly 3.5%, a standard total asset turnover ratio of 0.8 times, and a common leverage ratio of roughly 3.5:1:

$$\text{Typical ROE} = \text{Profit Margin} \times \text{Total Asset Turnover} \times \text{Leverage}$$

$$= 3.5\% \times 0.8 \times 3.5 \qquad\qquad \textbf{(10.2a)}$$

$$= 9\% \text{ to } 10\%.$$

ROE is an attractive measure of firm performance because it shows the rate of profit earned on funds committed to the enterprise by its owners, the stockholders. When ROE is at or above 10% per year, the rate of profit is generally sufficient to compensate investors for the risk involved with a typical business enterprise. When ROE consistently falls far below 10% per year, profit rates are generally insufficient to compensate investors for the risks undertaken. Of course, when business risk is substantially higher than average, a commensurately higher rate of return is required. When business risk is somewhat lower than average, a somewhat lower than average profit rate is adequate.

This naturally suggests an important question: How is it possible to know if business profit rates in any given circumstance are sufficient to compensate investors for the risks undertaken? The answer to this difficult question turns out to be rather simple: just ask current and potential shareholders and bondholders. While it is difficult to accurately assess business risk, and the problem of accurately measuring profit rates is always vexing, shareholders and bondholders implicitly inform management of their risk/return assessment of the firm's performance on a daily basis. If firm performance is above the minimum required, the firm's bond and stock prices will rise; if firm performance is below the minimum required, bond and stock prices will fall. For privately held companies, the market's risk/return assessment comes at less frequent intervals, such as when new bank financing is required. If firm performance is above the minimum required, bank financing will be easy to obtain; if firm performance is below the minimum required, bank financing will be difficult or impossible to procure. Therefore, as a practical matter, firms must consistently earn a business profit rate or ROE of at least 10% per year in order to grow and prosper. If ROE consistently falls below this level, sources of financing tend to dry up and the firm withers and dies. If ROE consistently exceeds this level, new debt and equity financing is easy to obtain, and growth by new and established competitors is rapid.

Finally, while ROE is perhaps the most useful available indicator of business profits, other accounting measures can also be used to compare profit rates across different lines of business and/or lines of business. For example, the accounting **return on assets,** defined as net income divided by the book value of total assets, is another useful indicator of the business profit rate. Like ROE, ROA captures the effects of managerial operating decisions; unlike ROE, ROA is unaffected by the amount of leverage. Therefore, while ROA is a useful alternative indicator of the basic profitability of a business,

Return on Assets
Net income divided by the book value of total assets.

This Is Why They Call It "Hardball"?

The only employer of major-league baseball players in the U.S. and Canada is Major League Baseball. This association of 30 major league franchises and their owners operates in much the same way as does a large corporation with 30 different regional offices. Even though individual clubs compete with one another on the playing field, their financial competition is much different than that between true competitors. In a competitive market, the gain of one competitor comes at the expense of others. In baseball, the success of one franchise brings increased prosperity for all. Through revenue sharing, all clubs prospered when Hank Aaron chased and broke Babe Ruth's lifetime home-run mark, as well as when Pete Rose chased and broke Ty Cobb's lifetime record for hits. Conversely, ineptitude and poor gate sales at one franchise weaken the profit picture for everyone. Tight pennant races make for prosperity; blowouts result in lost profits.

Baseball players are covered by a single basic labor contract negotiated through collective bargaining between the Major League Players Association (the sole union representative of the baseball players) and the owners. The players' association is a monopoly seller of baseball player talent, and the owners are a monopsony employer. During recent years, economic power in this labor market has clearly shifted from the owners toward the players. A key element of this shift has been the advent of free agency. Any baseball player with six years of major league service is eligible to become a free agent and sign with any team, with only modest compensation in the form of draft choices due to the player's former club. While not eligible for free agency, any player with three to six years' service is eligible for impartial salary arbitration. Since free agency was developed, baseball players' salaries have exploded.

In the early 1980s, baseball teams' front offices were often outwitted by sharp player agents. Occasional efforts to turn back player salaries fizzled since most owners still cared more about winning pennants than losing money. During Peter Ueberroth's reign as baseball commissioner, the owners began to strike back. The commissioner urged teams not to offer contracts longer than three years for regulars, two years for pitchers, and none longer than one year for marginal players. As a result, most early free agents returned to their old teams after not having received competing offers. During this period, overall player salaries stagnated despite a jump in industry revenues, and owner profits skyrocketed from breakeven levels.

The owners' display of monopsony power proved that they were capable of limiting player salaries and enhancing employer profits in the short run. However, in the long run, the owners' use of monopsony power stiffened the resolve of union adversaries and led to charges of collusion. Suspecting that collusion among owners had violated their collective bargaining agreement, the players' union filed a grievance against the owners in 1986 and won millions of dollars in damages. In 1990, the owners were found guilty of collusion that ultimately cost more than $10 million per team to fund payments to free-agent players who were harmed by salary collusion. Without such collusion, player salaries jumped and widespread operating losses among small-city clubs were reported.

During 1994, in a poisoned collective bargaining atmosphere, the players' union scoffed at the notion of financial trouble among the owners, and flatly rejected the owners' salary cap and revenue-sharing proposals. With equally powerful and determined antagonists, a standoff ensued that resulted in a cancellation of one-third of the 1994 season, the playoffs, the World Series, and even resulted in postponement of the 1995 season. Both the owners and players have already lost hundreds of millions of dollars in revenue, and stand to lose more until labor peace is restored.

The labor-market standoff in major league baseball is a classic labor-market confrontation between a powerful monopsony employer (the owners) and an equally powerful monopoly employee group (the players' association). With such a standoff, there clearly is "no joy in Mudville," at least in terms of labor relations.

See: Stefan Fatsis, "Baseball Pact is Ratified by Owners," *The Wall Street Journal,* November 27, 1996, A3.

it fails to account for the effects of financial leverage decisions on firm performance. As such, ROE has some advantages over ROA as a fundamental measure of business profits. Irrespective of whether ROE, ROA, or some other measure of business profits is employed, consistency requires that comparisons be made using a common basis.

The Link Between Market Structure and Business Profit Rates

Generally speaking, high business profit rates are derived from some combination of high profit margins, quick total asset turnover, and a high rate of total assets to stockholders' equity. As a result, it is generally argued that high business profits as reflected by ROE indicate modest competition, a wise use of assets, and/or a risky financial structure. However, there is some dispute concerning this interpretation. It is generally agreed that a high rate of total asset turnover reflects wise conservation of corporate wealth. Similarly, a widespread consensus accepts the view of debt financing as risky. It is the argument that high profit margins reflect modest competition that is controversial.

BUSINESS PROFIT RATES BY INDUSTRY GROUP

In a perfectly competitive market, profit margins are low. This stems from the fact that in a perfectly competitive market, theory suggests that $P = MC$ and $MC = AC$. As a result, when average cost includes a risk-adjusted normal rate of return on investment, $P = AC$. This means that when profit margin is measured as $(P - AC)/P$, profit margins will tend to be low and reflect only a normal rate of return in perfectly competitive markets. On the other hand, theory asserts that $P > MC$ in monopoly markets. When profit margin is measured as $(P - AC)/P$, profit margins will tend to be high and reflect above-normal rates of return in monopoly markets. However, there is a real problem encountered when profit margins earned in the business world are used as indicators of the level of competition in the marketplace. Without detailed firm-specific data, how is it possible to know if higher profit margins are due to higher prices, and perhaps monopoly power, or instead due to lower marginal and average costs, and, therefore, superior efficiency?

The short answer is simple. It is impossible to know the source of above-normal profit margins without direct access to detailed firm-level price and cost data. That such data are not easy to come by is hardly surprising. For example, while McDonald's must disclose company-wide profit rates to conform with Securities and Exchange Commission reporting requirements, it jealously guards secret information for individual restaurants. McDonald's would never voluntarily disclose profit rates by location or per menu item for fear that such disclosures would attract or intensify unwanted competition. By simply making its location decisions and building new restaurants, McDonald's already sends out a signal that acts as a beacon to Pizza Hut, Hardee's, Burger King, and a host of other competitors. Why make the job easier for such competitors by telling them exactly where the gold is buried?

Table 10.3 shows business profit rates by industry group for a sample of large firms obtained from *Forbes* magazine. While such industry groups correspond only loosely

Table 10.3

PROFITABILITY AND GROWTH FOR 20 INDUSTRY GROUPS COVERED IN *FORBES* ANNUAL REPORT ON AMERICAN INDUSTRY

		RETURN ON CAPITAL			SALES GROWTH	
			5-YR LATEST			5-YR LATEST
		AVG.	12 MO.		AVG.	12 MO.
INDUSTRY	RANK	%	%	RANK	%	%
Health	1	14.1	9.7	1	15.3	12.8
Chemicals	2	12.3	14.2	16	5.5	2.7
Financial services	3	12.2	10.8	13	6.2	12.8
Consumer nondurables	4	12.2	9.8	6	8.6	3.0
Insurance	5	12.1	11.3	12	6.3	8.5
Capital goods	6	11.8	14.4	10	7.3	7.9
Computers & communications	7	11.7	12.4	1	18.5	12.4
Aerospace & defense	8	11.0	14.7	20	1.1	6.1
Business services & supplies	9	10.7	10.4	4	9.4	13.0
Consumer durables	10	10.5	10.7	7	8.4	4.8
Entertainment & information	11	10.1	8.0	9	7.6	10.9
Food, drink & tobacco	12	10.1	9.6	15	5.7	6.6
Food distribution	13	9.8	8.6	17	4.9	4.8
Retailing	14	9.2	7.9	3	10.6	8.4
Metals	15	8.5	9.7	14	5.8	3.7
Construction	16	8.0	11.2	5	8.7	12.7
Forrest products & packaging	17	7.7	7.8	11	6.8	−4.2
Energy	18	7.1	8.4	19	3.3	15.6
Travel & transport	19	7.0	8.7	8	7.7	8.8
Electric utilities	20	6.5	6.2	18	4.2	4.9
All-industry averages		9.8	9.6		7.2	8.1

Data Source: Robert J. Sherwood, "Who's Where in the Industry Groups," *Forbes,* January 13, 1997, 257-258.

with individual economic markets, these profit rate data do offer useful perspective on the variability of profits across a variety of important lines of business. In actual practice, reported profit rates vary widely among industries. As shown in Table 10.3, historical profit rates range from very low in the electric utility, travel and transport, and energy sectors to very high in health, chemicals, financial services and consumer nondurables (personal products, photography, toys). An interesting feature of Table 10.3 and Figure 10.10 is that they illustrate a phenomenon known as the **regression to the mean.**

Regression to the Mean
Over time, the tendency for business profit rates to revert toward a risk-adjusted normal rate of return.

Over time, entry into highly profitable industries and nonleading firm growth causes above-normal profits to regress toward the mean. Conversely, bankruptcy and exit allow the below-normal profits of depressed industries to rise toward the mean. For example, drugs, health-care services, and medical supplies were among our most profitable industries during the late-1980s as an aging population and government-sponsored health programs have caused the demand for health care to skyrocket. In the

Figure 10.10

PROFIT RATES DISPLAY A REGRESSION TO THE MEAN OVER TIME

Entry into high profit industries drives down both prices and profits. Over time, entry causes above-normal profits to regress toward normal profit-rate average, while exit allows the below-normal profits of depressed industries to rise toward the mean.

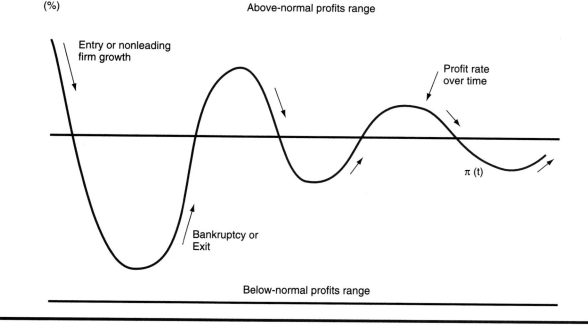

mid-1990s, however, a proliferation of new drug therapies, cost containment measures, and government regulations have conspired to limit profit-making opportunities in health care. As a result, profits and sales growth in the industry have turned downward during recent years. By the turn of the century, it is highly unlikely that health-care industry profits will dramatically exceed all-industry averages; they will have regressed towards the mean profit level. At the same time, major air carriers such as United, American, and Delta typically earn meager profits, at best, because they operate in an industry with a homogenous product (safe air travel) and huge fixed costs. As a result, price competition is vicious. Still, profit rates for the airlines and other travel industries were bound to rise during the mid-1990s because the industry cannot continue to sustain the enormous losses incurred during the early-1990s. Bankruptcy and exit will allow prices and profits to rise toward a risk-adjusted normal rate of return for survivors.

On an overall basis, the degree of competition in the market environment is an important contributor to the level of profitability that can be achieved by efficient firms. The level of profitability actually achieved is a function of both market structure and firm performance. To see the role played by firm-specific factors, it is informative to examine profit rates for top performers.

BUSINESS PROFIT RATES FOR TOP PERFORMING LARGE FIRMS

ROE is high to the extent that the firm enjoys a high profit margin on sales, a high rate of total asset turnover, or benefits from financial leverage. To see the relative importance of firm-specific factors as contributors to high rates of business profits, it is interesting to analyze the components of ROE for a sample of top performing large firms. Table 10.2 shows ROE data for a $n = 44$ sample of top performing firms taken from the *Value Line* database of roughly 1,600 large foreign and domestic firms. This sample is comprised of all *Value Line* firms able to earn ROE $> 35\%$ per year for the 1994 period. As a result, these data describe a sample of firms that are, at a minimum, roughly three times as profitable as the average company in the United States and Canada.

On average, the sample of top performing large firms displayed in Table 10.2 earns an ROE of 47.8% per year based on a 14.9% profit margin, 1.24 times per year total asset turnover ratio, and a leverage ratio of 4.25 times. Drug companies such as Abbott Labs, Bristol-Myers Squibb, ICN Pharmaceuticals, and Schering-Plough display the lofty profit margins associated with the marketing of innovative patent-protected pharmaceutical therapies. Other firms with special characteristics are also found among high profit margin firms. For example, Coca-Cola has a dominant market position in the soft drink industry; Great Northern Iron is a trust that pays high but diminishing royalties on shipments from iron ore mines in northern Minnesota; and Hong Kong Telephone enjoys a government-granted monopoly. When profit margins are substantial, high total asset turnover and leverage can amplify realized returns. As shown in Table 10.2, the boost to ROE can be substantial when total asset turnover and leverage exceed 2.0.

What is intriguing about the list of firms displayed in Table 10.2 is that they exemplify wide variety in terms of industry and in terms of the relative importance of profit margins, total asset turnover, and leverage as contributors to ROE. This diversity suggests that firm-specific factors, such as superior efficiency, and industry-related factors, such as market power, both contribute to the realization of above-normal rates of return.

Competitive Strategy in Perfectly Competitive and Monopoly Markets

Competitive Strategy
The search for a favorable competitive position in an industry or line of business.

The level of competition in the marketplace, and the firm's response to that competition, is at the core of business success or failure. The nature of competition determines both the appropriateness of managerial decisions and the speed with which they must be made. Survival of the fittest translates into success for the most able businesses, and extinction for the least capable. **Competitive strategy** is the search for a favorable competitive position in an industry or line of business. In perfectly competitive markets, the ready imitation of rivals makes ongoing success a constant struggle. In monopoly markets, entry and growth by nonleading firms often eat away at proprietary advantages. In both instances, development of an effective competitive strategy requires a careful response to market structure considerations.

COMPETITIVE STRATEGY IN PERFECTLY COMPETITIVE MARKETS

Economic Luck
Temporary good fortune due to unexpected changes in industry demand or cost conditions.

In perfectly competitive industries, above-normal returns sometimes reflect **economic luck,** or temporary good fortune due to unexpected changes in industry demand or cost conditions. For example, during the 1970s and 1980s, many small- to mid-size oil refineries and gasoline retailers benefited greatly when oil prices unexpectedly shot up following oil embargoes by the Oil and Petroleum Exporting Countries (OPEC) cartel. At the same time, many other firms experienced economic losses following the unanticipated rise in energy costs. Both sets of companies experienced a reversal of fortune when energy prices plummeted during the mid-1990s. Similarly, grain farmers benefited mightily during the 1970s and 1980s when export demand for agricultural products skyrocketed, and suffered during the 1990s when export demand withered.

Economic Rents
Profits due to uniquely productive inputs.

In other instances, above-normal returns in perfectly competitive industries reflect what is known as **economic rents,** or profits due to uniquely productive inputs. An exceptionally well-trained workforce, talented management, or superior land and raw materials can all lead to above-normal profits. For example, in parts of the country with school systems that provide outstanding primary and secondary education, firms are able to hire a basic workforce with a high rate of literacy and strong basic skills. Businesses that are able to employ such workers at a typical wage are able to earn superior profits when compared with the average rate of return for all competitors in the U.S. and Canada. Local tax subsidies designed to attract investment and job opportunities can also lower the cost of capital and create economic rents for affected firms. In many parts of the country, government initiatives often lead to economic rents for affected firms. On the other hand, if local taxes or government regulations prove to be especially onerous, economic losses can result for affected companies.

Disequilibrium Profits
Above-normal returns that can be earned in the time interval between when a favorable influence on industry demand or cost conditions first transpires and the time when competitor entry or growth finally develops.

Another important source of above-normal profits in perfectly competitive industries is **disequilibrium profits.** Disequilibrium profits are above-normal returns that can be earned in the time interval that often exists between when a favorable influence on industry demand or cost conditions first transpires and the time when competitor entry or growth finally develops.

Disequilibrium Losses
Below-normal returns that can be suffered in the time interval that often exists between when an unfavorable influence on industry demand or cost conditions first transpires and the time when exit or downsizing finally occurs.

Disequilibrium losses are below-normal returns that can be suffered in the time interval that often exists between when an unfavorable influence on industry demand or cost conditions first transpires, and the time when exit or downsizing finally occurs. When barriers to entry and exit are minimal, competitor reactions tend to be quick and disequilibrium profits are fleeting. When barriers to entry and exit are significant, competitor reactions tend to be slow and disequilibrium profits can persist for extended periods. In the quintessential perfectly competitive industry, disequilibrium profits are quickly dissipated. In real-world markets, disequilibrium profits can persist over an entire business cycle even in the most competitive industries. In retailing, for example, labor and inventory costs have been cut dramatically following the introduction of computerized price scanners. Despite the vigorously price-competitive nature of the retailing business, early innovators who first adopted the bar code technology have been able to earn above-normal profits for a number of years. Innovative grocery retailers have enjoyed dramatically lower costs and profit margins on sales of 2% to 3.5%, versus a more typical 1%, over a decade and more.

In equilibrium, perfectly competitive markets only offer the potential for a normal rate of return on investment. If many equally capable competitors offer identical products, vigorous price competition tends to eliminate disequilibrium profits. The only exception to this rule is that superior efficiency can sometimes lead to superior profits, even in perfectly competitive markets. Above-normal profits in perfectly competitive industries are transitory and reflect the influences of economic rents, luck, or disequilibrium conditions. If above-normal returns persist for extended periods in a given industry or line of business, then elements of uniqueness are probably at work.

COMPETITIVE STRATEGY IN MONOPOLY MARKETS

Above-normal returns tend to be fleeting in perfectly competitive industries, but can be durable for efficient firms that benefit from meaningful monopoly advantages. As in any perfectly competitive industry, above-normal profit rates can be observed if monopoly firms temporarily benefit from some unanticipated increase in demand or decrease in costs. Similarly, monopolists can benefit from temporary affluence due to unexpected changes in industry demand or cost conditions or uniquely productive inputs. What is unique about monopoly is the potential for durable long-term above-normal rates of return.

To be sure, in this age of instant global communication and rapid technical advance, no monopoly is permanently secure from the threat of current or potential competitors. Product characteristics, the local or regional limits of the market, the time necessary for reactions by established or new competitors, the pace of innovation, unanticipated changes in government regulation and tax policy, and a host of additional considerations all play an important role in defining the scope and durability of monopoly power. Therefore, when attempting to describe monopoly advantages, it is always helpful to consider the number and size of potential competitors, degree of product differentiation, level of information available in the marketplace, and conditions of entry.

Table 10.4 summarizes major characteristics typical of perfectly competitive and monopolistic markets. To develop an effective competitive strategy, it is necessary to assess the degree to which the characteristics of an individual market more or less embody elements of each. While the probability of successful entry is greater in perfectly competitive markets, monopoly markets lure new and established competitors with the promise of long-lasting, above-normal returns. Because the decision to enter any new market or line of business requires a careful balancing of expected costs and expected benefits, the advantages of monopoly can act as a powerful inducement to competitors. It follows that the protection of current monopoly advantages is only likely to succeed when firms can maintain the distinctive and valuable characteristics required by customers. Similarly, the search for above-normal profits is only likely to be successful when firms can offer customers products that are faster, cheaper, or better than those offered by rivals.

WHY MARKET NICHES ARE ATTRACTIVE

Entry into a perfectly competitive industry is not apt to result in above-normal rates of return under the best of circumstances. For example, a grain producer located along a

Table 10.4	SUMMARY OF PERFECT COMPETITION AND MONOPOLY (MONOPSONY) MARKET-STRUCTURE CHARACTERISTICS	
	PERFECT COMPETITION	MONOPOLY (MONOPSONY)
Number of actual or potential competitors	Many small buyers and sellers.	A single seller (buyer) of a valued product.
Product differentiation	None—each buyer and seller deals in an identical product.	Very high—no close substitutes available.
Information	Complete and free information on price and product quality.	Highly restricted access to price and product-quality information.
Conditions of entry and exit	Complete freedom of entry and exit.	Very high barriers caused by economies of scale (natural monopoly), patents, copyrights, government franchises, or other factors.
Profit potential	Normal profit in long run; economic profits (losses) in short run only.	Potential for economic profits in both short and long run.
Examples	Some agricultural markets (grain); commodity, stock, and bond markets; some nonspecialized input markets (unskilled labor).	Monopoly (sellers): Local telephone service (basic hook-up); municipal bus companies; gas, water, and electric utilities. Monopsony (buyers): state and local governments (roads); U.S. government (defense electronics).

river or on exceptionally fertile soil would enjoy lower-than-average irrigation costs and fertilizer expenses, and higher profits could result. However, potential buyers would have to pay a price premium for such productive land, and subsequent investors would earn only a normal rate of return on their investment. No landowner is going to sell highly productive or well-situated land at a bargain-basement price. Similarly, purchase of a business that enjoys recognized monopoly power is unlikely to lead to economic profits because anticipated abnormal returns on plant and equipment will be reflected in the purchase price. Much like fertile land brings a premium price in the real estate market, monopoly franchises bring a premium purchase price in the stock market. As a result, the purchase of a recognized monopoly leads to only a risk-adjusted normal rate of return for subsequent investors. Monopolists make money; investors in fully appreciated monopoly properties do not.

Market Niche
A segment of a market that can be successfully exploited through the special capabilities of a given firm or individual.

Only new and unique products or services have the potential to create monopoly profits. Imitation of such products may be protected by patents, copyrights, or other means. In many instances, these above-normal profits reflect the successful exploitation of a market niche. A **market niche** is a segment of a market that can be successfully exploited through the special capabilities of a given firm or individual. To be durable, the above-normal profits derived from a niche in the market for goods and services must not be vulnerable to imitation by competitors.

For example, Avon Products, Inc., is rightly famous for its veritable army of door-to-door sales representatives. "Avon Calling!" is a greeting that has long generated huge cash returns for the company in the United States and abroad. In Japan, for example, Avon's profit rate and popularity appears to exceed even that enjoyed in the U.S. market. Avon has succeeded where others have failed because it has developed and nurtured the market for in-home cosmetic sales. Better than anyone else, Avon knows the cosmetics, toiletries, costume jewelry, and other products that many women want and knows how much they are willing to pay for them. Avon keeps on growing despite numerous assaults from would-be competitors and regular predictions that its primary market is a sure-fire casualty of dual-income households. Indeed, its domestic and foreign business is so profitable that Avon has been the subject of repeated takeover speculation. To thwart such advances, the company has initiated a dramatic program to streamline operations in an effort to enhance already high profits. In the meantime, Avon keeps on dominating its market niche.

Another interesting example of a firm that successfully exploits a profitable market niche is the Templeton Group of mutual funds. Templeton has a dominant and extraordinarily profitable market niche in the worldwide mutual fund business. Founder John Templeton is a pioneer of the global diversification concept for mutual fund investors. Not only has the idea proved popular to U.S. investors, but Japanese and European investors have jumped on the Templeton bandwagon as well. As a result, Templeton, now a subsidiary of mutual fund giant Franklin Resources, Inc., enjoys double-digit growth, profit margins that average in excess of 35% of sales, and a rate of return on assets of over 50% per year.

Avon Products and the Templeton Group are only two examples of the many firms that enjoy tremendous success through market niche dominance. To attain similar success, a firm must first recognize the attractiveness of the market niche and then successfully apply the concept to its own business. Few firms achieve any great measure of success in trying to be all things to all customers. Lasting success requires exploitation of those segments of the market that can be best served using the special capabilities of a given firm or individual.

INFORMATION BARRIERS TO COMPETITIVE STRATEGY

Any use of market structure information as a guide to competitive strategy must address the challenge posed by measurement problems encountered in defining the magnitude and root cause of above-normal rates of return. To be sure, accounting profit data derived from a historical perspective give much useful information for operating decisions and tax purposes. However, these data sometimes measure economic profits only imperfectly. For example, advertising and research and development (R&D) expenditures are expensed for both reporting and tax purposes, even though each can give rise to long-term economic benefits. An expense as incurred treatment of advertising and R&D expenditures can lead to errors in profit measurement. While current net income is depressed when advertising and R&D and are written off before the end of their useful lives, intangible assets can be understated when they fail to reflect the value of brand names and other innovative products. Depending on the true rate of economic amortization for advertising and R&D and the rate of growth in expenditures for each, business profit rates can be either understated or overstated. In either event, reported business profit rates, such as ROE, can substantially misstate economic profits. At the same time, other imperfections in accrual accounting methods lead to imperfectly matched revenues and costs and, therefore, to some misstatement of economic profits over time.

Beyond these and other obvious limitations of accounting data, business practices are often expressly intended to limit the loss of valuable trade secret information. Why would anyone give competitors any more than the bare minimum of information? It is well known, for example, that firms patent only what they cannot otherwise keep secret. Combined with the limitations of publicly available data on profitability, business practices create an information barrier that hides the true details about economic profit rates. At the same time, such obfuscation makes defining the scope of monopoly power difficult, as it hides the costs and benefits of entry into monopoly markets from both private and public decision makers.

Summary

Market structure analysis begins with the study of perfect competition and monopoly. Competition is said to be perfect when producers offer what buyers want at prices just sufficient to cover the marginal cost of output. No profits above the minimum required to maintain investment are possible. Monopoly is socially less desirable given its tendency for underproduction, high prices, and excess profits.

- **Market structure** describes the competitive environment in the market for any good or service. A **market** consists of all firms and individuals willing and able to buy or sell a particular product. This includes firms and individuals currently engaged in buying and selling a particular product, as well as potential entrants. A **potential entrant** is an individual or firm posing a sufficiently credible threat of market entry to affect the price/output decisions of incumbent firms.

- **Perfect competition** is a market structure characterized by a large number of buyers and sellers of essentially the same product, where each market participant's transactions are so small that they have no influence on the market price of the product. Individual buyers and sellers are **price takers.** Such firms take market prices as given and devise their production strategies accordingly.

- **Monopoly** is a market structure characterized by a single seller of a highly differentiated product. Monopoly firms are **price makers** that exercise significant control over market prices.

- A **barrier to entry** is any factor or industry characteristic that creates an advantage for incumbents over new arrivals. A **barrier to mobility** is any factor or industry characteristic that creates an advantage for large leading firms over smaller nonleading rivals. A **barrier to exit** is any restriction on the ability of incumbents to redeploy assets from one industry or line of business to another.

- **Monopsony** exists when a single firm is the sole buyer of a desired product or input.

- A **natural monopoly** occurs when the market-clearing price, where $P = MC$, occurs at a point at which *long-run* average costs are still declining.

- **Underproduction** results when a monopoly curtails output to a level at which the value of resources employed, as measured by the marginal cost of production, is less than the social benefit derived, where social benefit is measured by the price customers are willing to pay for additional output.

- **Countervailing power** is an economic influence that creates a closer balance between previously unequal sellers and buyers.

- Business profit rates are best measured by the accounting rate of **return on stockholders' equity** measure. ROE is defined as net income divided by the book value of stockholders' equity, where stockholders' equity is the book value of total assets minus total liabilities. High ROE is derived from some combination of high **profit margins,** quick **total asset turnover,** and high **leverage** or a high rate of total assets to stockholders' equity. Business profits are also sometimes measured by the **return on assets,** defined as net income divided by the book value of total assets. While ROA is a useful alternative indicator of the basic profitability of a business, it fails to account for the effects of financial leverage decisions on firm performance.

- Business profit rates often display a phenomenon known as the **regression to the mean.** Over time, entry into highly profitable industries tends to cause above-normal profits to regress toward the mean, just as bankruptcy and exit allow the below-normal profits of depressed industries to rise toward the mean.

- The nature of competition determines the suitability of managerial decisions and the speed with which they must be made. Survival of the fittest translates into success for the most able and extinction of the least capable. **Competitive strategy** is the search for a favorable competitive position in an industry or line of business.

- In perfectly competitive industries, above-normal returns sometimes reflect **economic luck,** or temporary good fortune due to unexpected changes in industry demand or cost conditions. In other instances, above-normal returns in perfectly competitive industries reflect **economic rents,** or profits due to uniquely productive inputs. Another important source of above-normal profits in perfectly competitive industries is **disequilibrium profits.** Disequilibrium profits are above-normal returns that can be earned in the time interval between when a favorable influence on industry demand or cost conditions first transpires and the time when competitor reactions finally develop. **Disequilibrium losses** are below-normal returns that can be suffered in the time interval that often exists between when an unfavorable influence on industry demand or cost conditions first transpires and the time when exit or downsizing finally occurs.

- Only new and unique products or services have the potential to create monopoly profits. In many instances, these above-normal profits reflect the successful exploitation of a market niche. A **market niche** is a segment of a market that can be successfully exploited through the special capabilities of a given firm or individual.

Although the requirements for perfect competition and monopoly are quite restrictive and are seldom met exactly, these market structure concepts provide a crucial basis for understanding competition in all markets. Moreover, many real-world markets do in fact closely approximate the perfectly competitive ideal, but elements of monopoly are often encountered. As a result, these market structure concepts often provide a valuable guide to managerial decision making.

QUESTIONS

Q10.1   What are the primary elements of market structure?

Q10.2   Describe the perfectly competitive market structure and provide some examples.

Q10.3   Describe the monopoly market structure and provide some examples.

Q10.4   How are barriers to entry and exit similar? How are they different?

Q10.5   Why is the firm demand curve horizontal in perfectly competitive markets? Does this mean that the perfectly competitive industry demand curve is also horizontal?

Q10.6   Why are the perfectly competitive firm and the perfectly competitive industry supply curves upward sloping?

Q10.7   From a social standpoint, what is the problem with monopoly?

Q10.8   Why are both industry and firm demand curves downward sloping in monopoly market structure?

Q10.9   Give an example of monopoly in the labor market. Discuss such a monopoly's effect on wage rates and on inflation.

Q10.10   Describe the economic effects of countervailing power, and cite examples of markets in which countervailing power is observed.

SELF-TEST PROBLEMS AND SOLUTIONS

ST10.1   **Market Value and Profitability.** The Paper and Forest Products Industry, Standard Industrial Classification Code 2600, is dominated by large integrated manufacturers. According to data from the Census of Manufacturers, roughly 50% of industry output comes from giant plants with more than 500 employees. This is despite the fact that specialized minimills with as few as 20 to 49 employees have recently emerged in the industry to take advantage of market niches. On an overall basis, this major industry group is one of the largest and most important in our economy in terms of sales, profits, and employment. Low prices combined with innovative new products, such as recycled newspaper products, have swept the industry and given innovative competitors the means to earn above-average rates of return. In this highly competitive environment, the way to survive and prosper is to reduce operating expenses, increase product quality, and improve customer service. As much as any other single industry, paper and forest products companies have taken advantage of advances in computer-based methods of data collection and analysis to improve their relation with suppliers, keep inventories lean, and boost sales by better serving customer demands.

To learn how investors assess the investment potential of these companies, the table on page 460 shows the market value of common equity, the accounting book value of total assets, accounting net income, the five-year rate of growth in earnings per share, and total liabilities for an $n = 20$ sample of paper and forest product companies. The market value effects of accounting book values indicate how investors capitalize the current value of assets in place; valuation effects of net profits and earnings growth reflect investor views

Company Name	Market Value	Total Assets	Net Profit	5-Yr EPS Growth (%)	Total Debt
Chesapeake Corp.	$781.4	$919.3	$10.4	−16.0	$432.2
Consolidated Papers	2,052.2	1,467.1	67.8	−9.0	266.7
Federal Paperboard	1,217.0	2,570.3	20.8	−7.0	1,251.4
Gladfelter	692.8	842.1	32.2	0.0	231.5
International Paper	9,245.1	16,631.0	314.0	−5.0	7,610.0
Longview Fibre	829.3	1,022.1	33.4	−13.0	505.8
Louisiana-Pacific	3,016.2	2,466.3	258.8	9.5	605.8
Mead Corp.	2,944.5	4,164.5	131.7	−8.5	2,080.3
Mosinee Paper	178.7	252.1	6.6	−17.5	132.7
Pentair, Inc.	757.1	958.8	46.6	7.5	457.4
Potlatch Corp.	1,102.3	2,066.8	35.6	−10.5	886.2
Republic Gypsum	104.1	53.0	7.7	8.5	7.2
Scott Paper	5,108.1	6,625.1	116.5	−11.0	4,136.0
St. Joe Paper	1,658.4	1,491.3	12.1	−25.5	132.4
Temple-Inland	2,552.1	3,403.8	67.4	−2.5	1,380.4
Union Camp	3,369.4	4,685.0	68.8	−15.0	2,154.3
Wausau Paper	664.7	361.4	42.1	19.5	76.4
Westvaco Corp.	2,661.5	3,983.0	103.6	−10.0	1,595.9
Weyerhaeuser	7,793.4	9,589.0	462.7	−4.0	4,074.1
Willamette Industries	2,552.8	2,804.6	116.5	−8.5	1,317.3
Averages	$2,464.1	$3,317.8	$97.8	−5.9	$1,466.7

Data Source: Value Line/Value Screen II Database, January 1, 1995.

of the firms' longer-term growth potential (all dollar values are in millions).

A.   A multiple regression model with each paper and forest products company's market value of common stock (MV) as the dependent Y-variable, and total assets (A), net profit (NP), the five-year rate of growth in earnings per share (GR), and total debt (D) gives the following results (t-statistics in parentheses):

$$MV = \$262.986 + \$0.206A + \$8.245NP$$
$$(1.23) \qquad (5.57)$$

$$- \$16.964GR + \$0.416D,$$
$$(-1.78) \qquad (1.33)$$

$$R^2 = 97.8\%, \text{S.E.E.} = \$408.438$$

How would you interpret these findings?

B.   What suggestions might you make for a more detailed study of the determinants of the market value of common stock for paper and forest products companies versus other types of companies?

ST10.1   **SOLUTION**

A.   As is typically the case, the constant in such a regression has no economic meaning. Clearly, the intercept should not be used to suggest the market value of common stock for a paper and forest products company that has zero values for total assets, net profits, earnings growth, and total debt. Zero values for all of these variables are not observed for any of these paper and forest products companies, and extrapolation beyond the range of actual observations is always dangerous.

The coefficient estimate of 0.206 for total assets implies that a $1 rise in total assets leads to an average $0.206 increase in the market value of the firm. However, the total assets coefficient is *not* statistically significant at the $\alpha = 0.10$ level with a calculated t-statistic value of 1.23, meaning that it is *not* possible to be 90% confident that the current value of total assets affects the market value of common stock. Typically, investors regard the accounting book value of assets in place as a favorable indication of the firm's ability to earn attractive rates of return in the future. In this case, the downturn in industry profitability in the mid-1990s led to especially severe profit problems for industry leaders. Controversies tied to environmental concerns, like the spotted owl crisis, made matters even worse. Apparently, investors at the beginning of 1995 saw such problems as continuing and thereby accorded a less than typically strong link between accounting asset values and future profit potential.

The coefficient estimate of 8.245 for net profit implies that a $1 rise in net profit leads to an average $8.245 increase in the market value of the firm. The net profit coefficient is statistically significant at the $\alpha = 0.01$ level with a calculated t-statistic value of 5.57, meaning that it is possible to be more than 99% confident that current net profits affect the market value of common stock. This suggests that investors regard the current level of net profits as a favorable indication of the firm's ability to earn attractive rates of return in the future. The probability of observing such a large t-statistic when there is in fact no relation between total assets and the market value of common stock is less than 1%.

The coefficient estimate of -16.964 for EPS growth implies that a 1% rise in earnings growth leads to an average $16.964 *decrease* in the market value of the firm. Apparently, investors believed at the start of 1995 that good times were in store for large companies that had been poor recent performers (i.e., negative earnings growth). The coefficient estimate of 0.416 for total debt implies that a $1 rise in total debt leads to an average $0.416 increase in the market value of the firm. Again, this suggests that investors were counting on a turnaround in the fortunes of highly leveraged companies in the industry. However, neither of these two coefficient estimates are statistically significant at the $\alpha = 0.10$ level, meaning that it is not possible to be 90% confident that the current market value of the firm is simply and directly related to these two factors, after allowing for the market-value effects of total assets and net profits.

The $R^2 = 97.8\%$ indicates the share of market value variation that can be explained by the model as a whole. While this is a relatively high level of explained variation, it must be interpreted

in light of the very small sample size involved. The standard error of the Y-estimate of S.E.E. = $408.438 is the average amount of error encountered in estimating the market value of the firm using this multiple regression model (all figures in millions). If the u_i error terms are normally distributed about the regression equation, as would be true when large samples of more than 30 or so observations are analyzed, there is a 95% probability that observations of the dependent variable will lie within the range $\hat{Y}_i \pm (1.96 \times$ S.E.E.), or within roughly *two* standard errors of the estimate. The probability is 99% that any given $\hat{Y}_i$ will lie within the range $\hat{Y}_i \pm (2.576 \times$ S.E.E.), or within roughly *three* standard errors of its predicted value. When very small samples of data are analyzed, as is the case here, "critical" t-values slightly larger than two or three are multiplied by the S.E.E. to obtain the 95% and 99% confidence intervals.

Precise critical t-values obtained from a t-table, such as that found in Appendix C, are $t^*_{15,\alpha=0.05} = 2.131$ (at the 95% confidence level) and $t^*_{15,\alpha=0.01} = 2.947$ (at the 99% confidence level) for $df = 20 - 5 = 15$. This means that actual sales revenue Y_i can be expected to fall in the range $\hat{Y}_i \pm (2.131 \times \$408.433)$, or $\hat{Y}_i \pm \$870.370$, with 95% confidence; and within the range $\hat{Y}_i \pm (2.947 \times \$408.433)$, or $\hat{Y}_i \pm \$1,203.625$, with 99% confidence.

B.   Collection of a broader and more descriptive sample of data is a necessary first step in a more detailed study of the determinants of the market value of common stock for paper and forest products companies. With only 20 observations of annual data, the regression technique is clearly handicapped in this application. Perhaps a pooled cross-section sample of annual data over the past five years, or $n = 100 \, (= 20 \times 5)$ observations, would provide a sufficiently broad sample of data to offer a meaningful perspective on the determinants of the market value of common for retail firms. In addition, a larger sample of data would make it possible to investigate the potential role of additional independent variables, such as the level of advertising spending, the rate of growth in total assets, the role of regional economic growth, and so on.

ST10.2   **Perfect Competition and Monopoly.** The City of Columbus, Ohio, is considering two proposals to privatize municipal garbage collection. First, a leading waste disposal firm has offered to purchase the city's plant and equipment at an attractive price in return for an exclusive franchise on residential service. A second proposal would allow several individual workers and small companies to enter the business without any exclusive franchise agreement or competitive restrictions. Under this plan, individual companies would bid for the right to provide service in a given residential area. The city would then allocate business to the lowest bidder.

The city has conducted a survey of Columbus residents to estimate the amount that they would be willing to pay for various frequencies of service. The city has also estimated the total cost of service per resident. Service costs are expected to be the same whether or not an exclusive franchise is granted.

A. Complete the following table.

TRASH PICKUPS PER MONTH	PRICE PER PICKUP	TOTAL REVENUE	MARGINAL REVENUE	TOTAL COST	MARGINAL COST
0	$5.00			$0.00	
1	4.80			3.75	
2	4.60			7.45	
3	4.40			11.10	
4	4.20			14.70	
5	4.00			18.00	
6	3.80			20.90	
7	3.60			23.80	
8	3.40			27.20	
9	3.20			30.70	
10	3.00			35.00	

B. Determine price and the level of service if competitive bidding results in a perfectly competitive price/output combination.

C. Determine price and the level of service if the city grants a monopoly franchise.

ST10.2 **SOLUTION**

A.

TRASH PICKUPS PER MONTH	PRICE PER PICKUP	TOTAL REVENUE	MARGINAL REVENUE	TOTAL COST	MARGINAL COST
0	$5.00	$0.00	—	$0.00	—
1	4.80	4.80	$4.80	3.75	$3.75
2	4.60	9.20	4.40	7.45	3.70
3	4.40	13.20	4.00	11.10	3.65
4	4.20	16.80	3.60	14.70	3.60
5	4.00	20.00	3.20	18.00	3.30
6	3.80	22.80	2.80	20.90	2.90
7	3.60	25.20	2.40	23.80	2.90
8	3.40	27.20	2.00	27.20	3.40
9	3.20	28.80	1.60	30.70	3.50
10	3.00	30.00	1.20	35.00	4.40

B. In a perfectly competitive industry, $P = MR$, so the optimal activity level occurs where $P = MC$. Here, $P = MC = \$3.40$ at $Q = 8$ pickups per month.

C. A monopoly maximizes profits by setting $MR = MC$. Here, $MR = MC = \$3.60$ at $Q = 4$ pickups per month and $P = \$4.20$ per pickup.

PROBLEMS

P10.1 **Market Structure Concepts.** Indicate whether each of the following statements is true or false, and explain why.

A. In long-run equilibrium, every firm in a perfectly competitive industry earns zero profit. Thus, if price falls, none of these firms will be able to survive.

B. Perfect competition exists in a market when all firms are price takers as opposed to price makers.

C. A natural monopoly results when the profit-maximizing output level occurs at a point where long-run average costs are declining.

D. Downward-sloping industry demand curves characterize both perfectly competitive and monopoly markets.

E. A decrease in the price elasticity of demand would follow an increase in monopoly power.

P10.2 **Perfectly Competitive Firm Supply.** Mankato Paper, Inc., produces uncoated paper used in a wide variety of industrial applications. Newsprint, a major product, is sold in a perfectly competitive market. The following relation exists between the firm's newsprint output and total production costs:

TOTAL OUTPUT (TONS)	TOTAL COST (PER TON)
0	$25
1	75
2	135
3	205
4	285
5	375
6	475
7	600

A.   Construct a table showing Mankato's marginal cost of newsprint production.
B.   What is the minimum price necessary for Mankato to supply one ton of newsprint?
C.   How much newsprint would Mankato supply at industry prices of $75 and $100 per ton?

P10.3   **Perfectly Competitive Equilibrium.** Demand and supply conditions in the perfectly competitive market for unskilled labor are as follows:

$$Q_D = 120 - 20P \quad \text{(Demand)},$$

$$Q_S = 10P \quad \text{(Supply)},$$

where Q is millions of hours of unskilled labor and P is the wage rate per hour.
A.   Graph the industry demand and supply curves.
B.   Determine the industry equilibrium price/output combination both graphically and algebraically.
C.   Calculate the level of excess supply (unemployment) if the minimum wage is set at $5 per hour.

P10.4   **Perfectly Competitive Industry Supply.** Farm Fresh, Inc., supplies sweet peas to canners located throughout the Mississippi River Valley. Like some grain and commodity markets, the market for sweet peas is perfectly competitive. The company's total and marginal costs per ton are given by the following relations:

$$TC = \$250,000 + \$200Q + \$0.02Q^2,$$

$$MC = \$200 + \$0.04Q.$$

A.   Calculate the industry price necessary for the firm to supply 5,000, 10,000, and 15,000 tons of sweet peas.
B.   Calculate the quantity supplied by Farm Fresh at industry prices of $200, $500, and $1,000 per ton.

P10.5   **Perfectly Competitive Firm and Industry Supply.** New England Textiles, Inc., is a medium-sized manufacturer of blue denim that sells in a market for which it is perfectly competitive. The total cost function for this product is described by the following relation:

$$TC = \$25,000 + \$1Q + \$0.000008Q^2,$$

$$MC = \$1 + \$0.000016Q,$$

where Q is square yards of blue denim produced per month.
A.   Derive the firm's supply curve, expressing quantity as a function of price.
B.   Derive the industry's supply curve if New England Textiles is one of 500 competitors.
C.   Calculate industry supply per month at a market price of $2 per square yard.

P10.6   **Perfectly Competitive Equilibrium.** Yakuza, Ltd., supplies standard 16MB-RAM chips to the U.S. computer and electronics industry. Like the output of its competitors, Yakuza's chips must meet strict size, shape, and speed specifications. As a result, the chip-supply industry can be regarded as perfectly competitive. The total cost and marginal cost functions for Yakuza are

$$TC = \$1,000,000 + \$20 + \$0.0001Q^2,$$

$$MC = \$20 + \$0.0002Q,$$

where Q is the number of chips produced.
A.   Calculate Yakuza's optimal output and profits if chip prices are stable at $60 each.
B.   Calculate Yakuza's optimal output and profits if chip prices fall to $30 each.
C.   If Yakuza is typical of firms in the industry, calculate the firm's equilibrium output, price, and profit levels.

P10.7   **Monopoly Equilibrium.** Fluid Controls, Inc., is a major supplier of reverse osmosis and ultrafiltration equipment, which helps industrial and commercial customers achieve improved production processes and a cleaner work environment. The company has recently introduced a new line of ceramic filters that enjoy patent protection. Relevant cost and revenue relations for this product are as follows:

$$TR = \$300Q - \$0.001Q^2,$$

$$MR = \$300 - \$0.002Q,$$

$$TC = \$9,000,000 + \$20Q + \$0.0004Q^2,$$

$$MC = \$20 + \$0.0008Q,$$

where TR is total revenue, Q is output, MR is marginal revenue, TC is total cost, including a risk-adjusted normal rate of return on investment, and MC is marginal cost.

A. As a monopoly, calculate Fluid Controls' optimal price/output combination.

B. Calculate monopoly profits and the optimal profit margin at this profit-maximizing activity level.

P10.8 Monopoly versus Perfectly Competitive Equilibrium. Big Apple Music, Inc., enjoys an exclusive copyright on music written and produced by the Fab Four, a legendary British rock group. Total and marginal revenues for the group's records are given by the following relations:

$$TR = \$15Q - \$0.000005Q^2,$$

$$MR = \$15 - \$0.00001Q.$$

Marginal costs for production and distribution are stable at $5 per unit. All other costs have been fully amortized.

A. Calculate Big Apple's output, price, and profits at the profit-maximizing activity level.

B. What record price and profit levels would prevail following expiration of copyright protection based on the assumption that perfectly competitive pricing would result?

P10.9 Monopoly versus Perfectly Competitive Equilibrium. During recent years, the Big Blue Computer Company has enjoyed substantial economic profits derived from patents covering a wide range of inventions and innovations in the personal computer field. A recent introduction, the SP/2, has proved to be especially profitable. Market demand and marginal revenue relations for the SP/2 are as follows:

$$P = \$5,500 - \$0.005Q,$$

$$MR = \$5,500 - \$0.01Q.$$

Fixed costs are nil because research and development expenses have been fully amortized during previous periods. Average variable costs are constant at $4,500 per unit.

A. Calculate the profit-maximizing price/output combination and economic profits if Big Blue enjoys an effective monopoly on the SP/2 because of its patent protection.

B. Calculate the price/output combination and total economic profits that would result if competitors offer clones that make the SP/2 market perfectly competitive.

P10.10 Monopoly/Monopsony Confrontation. Safeguard Corporation offers a unique service. The company notifies credit card issuers after being informed that a subscriber's credit card has been lost or stolen. The Safeguard service is sold to card issuers on a one-year subscription basis. Relevant revenue and cost relations for the service are as follows:

$$TR = \$5Q - \$0.00001Q^2,$$

$$MR = \$5 - \$0.00002Q,$$

$$TC = \$50,000 + \$0.5Q + \$0.000005Q^2,$$

$$MC = \$0.5 + \$0.00001Q,$$

where TR is total revenue, Q is output measured in terms of the number of subscriptions in force, MR is marginal revenue, TC is total cost, including a risk-adjusted normal rate of return on investment, and MC is marginal cost.

A. If Safeguard has a monopoly in this market, calculate the profit-maximizing price/output combination and optimal total profit.

B. Calculate Safeguard's optimal price, output, and profits if credit card issuers effectively exert monopsony power and force a perfectly competitive equilibrium in this market.

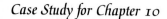

Case Study for Chapter 10

THE PROFITABILITY EFFECTS OF LARGE FIRM SIZE

Does large firm size, pure and simple, give rise to monopoly profits? This question has been a source of great interest in both business and government, as well as the basis for lively debate over the years. Monopoly theory states that large relative firm size within a given economic market gives rise to the potential for above-normal profits. Monopoly theory makes no prediction at all about a link between large absolute firm size and the potential for above-normal profits. By itself, it is not clear what economic advantages are gained from large firm size. Pecuniary or money-related economies of large size in the purchase of labor, raw materials, or other inputs are sometimes suggested. For example, some argue that large firms enjoy a comparative advantage in the acquisition of investment funds given their ready access to organized capital markets. Others contend that capital markets are themselves very efficient in the allocation of scarce capital resources and that all firms, both large and small, must offer investors a competitive rate of return.

Still, without a doubt, firm size is a matter of significant business and public interest. Membership in the *Fortune 500* roster of the largest industrial corporations in the United States is a matter of significant corporate pride for included companies and their top executives. Sales and profit levels achieved by such firms are widely reported and commented on in the business and popular press. At times, congressional leaders have called for legislation that would bar mergers among *Fortune 500* companies on the premise that such combinations create monolithic giants that impair competitive forces. Movements up and down the *Fortune 500* list are similarly chronicled, studied, and commented on. It is perhaps a little known fact that, given the dynamic nature of change in the overall economy, few companies are able to maintain, let alone enhance, their position in the *Fortune 500* over a 5- to 10-year period. As many as 30 to 50 companies are displaced from the *Fortune 500* in a typical year. With an annual attrition rate of 6% to 10%, it indeed appears to be "slippery" at the top.

To evaluate the link, if any, between profitability and firm size, it is interesting to consider the data contained in Table 10.5. These data on $n = 37$ of the largest companies in the world that have publicly traded common stock in the United States are taken from the *Value Line/Value Screen II* Database. Both industrial and nonindustrial companies are included, thus giving broad perspective on any possible link between firm size and profitability. The *Value Line* sample included all such companies that reported at least $25 billion in sales for the fiscal year ending prior to January 1, 1997.

Table 10.5 shows profitability as measured by net income, and three standard measures of firm size. Net worth, or stockholders' equity, is defined in accounting terms as total assets minus total liabilities. It is a useful measure of the total funds committed to the enterprise by stockholders through paid in capital plus retained earnings. Total assets is perhaps the most common accounting measure of firm size and indicates the book value of all tangible plant and equipment, plus the recognized intangible value of acquired assets with customer goodwill due to brand names, patents, and so on. Sales revenue is a third common measure of firm size. From an econometric perspective, sales is an attractive measure of firm size because it is not susceptible to accounting manipulation or bias, nor is it influenced by the relative capital or labor intensity of the enterprise. When size is measured by sales revenue, measurement problems tied to inflation, replacement cost errors, and so on are minimized.

The simplest means for studying the link between profitability and firm size is to regress profits on firm size, when size is measured along the different dimensions of stockholders' equity, total assets, and sales. *Fortune* magazine and many public sector analysts use sales as a preferred index of size, so the relation between profits and sales is of obvious interest. Nonlinearities can be investigated through the use of second-order (quadratic or squared) and third-order (cubic) terms for the size variable. For example, a positive and statistically significant coefficient

Table 10.5

NET PROFIT, NET WORTH, TOTAL ASSETS, AND SALES REVENUE FOR A SAMPLE OF LARGE COMPANIES WITH SALES REVENUE IN EXCESS OF $25 BILLION

COMPANY NAME	INDUSTRY NAME	NET PROFIT	NET WORTH	TOTAL ASSETS	SALES
Alcatel Alsthom	Foreign Telecom	−$2,457.4	$10,108.1	$52,183.3	$32,763.2
AMOCO Corp.	Integrated Petroleum	1,862.0	14,848.0	29,845.0	27,066.0
AT&T Corp.	Telecom Services	1,866.5	17,274.0	88,884.0	79,609.0
B.A.T. Industries	Tobacco	2,281.6	8,571.5	70,095.7	36,232.8
British Petroleum	Integrated Petroleum	2,070.0	16,899.0	51,601.0	57,047.0
Chevron Corp.	Integrated Petroleum	1,962.0	14,355.0	34,330.0	31,322.0
Chrysler Corp.	Auto & Truck	2,121.0	10,959.0	53,756.0	53,195.0
Daimler-Benz	Auto & Truck	−1,179.2	15,875.0	69,831.9	71,909.0
Du Pont	Basic Chemical	3,407.0	8,436.0	37,312.0	42,163.0
Elf Aquitaine	Integrated Petroleum	1,086.8	16,057.0	49,432.8	42,512.0
Exxon Corp.	Integrated Petroleum	6,380.0	40,436.0	91,296.0	107,893.0
Ford Motor	Auto & Truck	4,139.0	24,547.0	243,283.0	137,137.0
General Electric	Electrical Equipment	6,573.0	29,609.0	55,716.0	43,013.0
General Motors	Auto & Truck	6,932.5	23,345.5	217,123.4	168,828.6
Hewlett-Packard	Computer & Peripherals	2,433.0	11,839.0	24,427.0	31,519.0
Hitachi Ltd.	Electronics & Entertainment	1,345.3	29,907.2	91,620.9	75,923.5
Honda Motor	Auto & Truck	661.7	10,696.6	32,860.9	39,740.7
IBM	Computer & Peripherals	6,334.0	22,423.0	80,292.0	71,940.0
Kmart Corp.	Retail Store	−490.0	5,280.0	15,397.0	34,389.0
Matsushita Electronics	Electronics & Entertainment	1,003.1	31,753.2	74,876.9	63,503.3
Mobil Corp.	Integrated Petroleum	2,376.0	17,951.0	42,138.0	64,767.0
Motorola, Inc.	Semiconductor	1,781.0	11,048.0	22,801.0	27,037.0
NEC Corp.	Electronics & Entertainment	721.2	8,213.6	43,767.5	41,100.0
Nissan Motor	Auto & Truck	−826.3	12,679.2	66,276.6	56,440.3
Pepsico, Inc.	Soft Drinks	1,990.0	7,313.0	25,432.0	30,421.0
Philip Morris	Tobacco	5,478.0	13,985.0	53,811.0	66,071.0
Philips Electronics	Electronics & Entertainment	1,558.4	8,729.8	32,448.5	40,038.5
Procter & Gamble	Household Products	3,046.0	11,722.0	27,730.0	35,284.0
Royal Dutch Petroleum	Integrated Petroleum	7,492.0	58,781.0	117,602.0	109,872.0
Sears	Retail Store	1,025.0	4,385.0	33,130.0	34,925.0
Shell Transport	Integrated Petroleum	7,492.0	58,781.0	117,602.0	109,872.0
Sony Corp.	Electronics & Entertainment	507.0	10,926.9	47,156.3	40,555.2
Texaco, Inc.	Integrated Petroleum	1,152.0	9,519.0	24,937.0	35,551.0
Toyota	Auto & Truck	2,401.7	49,691.6	106,004.2	100,175.1
Uniliver	Food Processing	2,327.0	17,020.0	42,903.0	49,505.0
Volvo	Auto & Truck	1,684.3	10,292.8	23,371.9	25,636.9
Wal-Mart Stores	Retail Store	2,740.0	14,756.0	37,541.0	93,627.0
Averages		**$2,467.0**	**$18,622.0**	**$62,941.0**	**$59,691.5**

Data Source: *Value Line/Value Screen II* Data Base, January 1, 1997.

Table 10.6	ESTIMATION RESULTS FOR THE PROFITABILITY EFFECTS OF FIRM SIZE FOR SELECTED LARGE COMPANIES (t-STATISTICS IN PARENTHESES)					
			INDEPENDENT VARIABLES			
DEPENDENT VARIABLE (SIZE MEASURE)	CONSTANT	SIZE	SIZE^2	SIZE^3	R^2	S.E.E.
Profits (Net Worth)	−1,549.1	0.391 (1.41)	−1.0e-05 (−0.95)	1.0e-10 (0.89)	41.3%	1,935.4
Profits (Assets)	3,165.5	−0.094 (−1.24)	1.54e-06 (1.85)	−4.6e-12 (−2.00)	34.4%	2,046.1
Profit (Sales)	3,233.4	−0.105 (−0.74)	1.8e-06 (1.04)	−6.3e-12 (−1.02)	37.2%	2,001.9
ROE (Net Worth)	0.112	4.5e-06 (0.23)	−1.8e-10 (−0.24)	1.7e-15 (0.21)	0.6%	0.134
ROA (Assets)	0.087	−1.5e-06 (−1.06)	1.4e-11 (0.91)	−3.8e-17 (−0.87)	6.1%	0.039
Margin (Sales)	0.102	−2.6e-06 (−0.91)	3.0e-11 (0.86)	−1.0e-16 (−0.81)	2.6%	0.040

for the sales squared variable indicates that profit margins increase at a pace faster than the rate of change in sales. A positive and statistically significant coefficient for the sales cubed variable indicates a growing rate of increase in profit margins, and so on. Using this approach, estimation results for the data reported in Table 10.5 are shown in Table 10.6.

When firm size is measured using stockholders' equity, or the difference between total assets and total liabilities, it is worthwhile to consider the effect of stockholders' equity on relative profits measured by the return on stockholders' equity (ROE). Similarly, when firm size is measured using the book value of total assets, it is interesting to see if the return on assets (ROA) is affected by size (asset level). A significant link between profitability and firm size is suggested to the extent that profit margins, ROE, and/or ROA tend to be higher among larger companies, and highest among the very largest companies.

A. Use the data reported in Table 10.5 to compute the return on equity (ROE), return on assets (ROA), and return on sales, or profit margin (MGN), for each company. Discuss any differences among these alternative profit rate measures.

B. Use an ordinary least squares approach to replicate the nonlinearities in the firm size-profit relation reported in Table 10.6 using first-order, second-order (quadratic or squared) and third-order (cubic) terms for the size variable. In other words, regress profits on size, size^2, and size^3, where size is measured in three separate regression equations by stockholders' equity, total assets, and sales. Discuss your findings.

C. Use an ordinary least squares approach to replicate the nonlinearities in the firm size-profit rate relation reported in Table 10.6 using first-order, second-order (quadratic or squared), and third-order (cubic) terms for the size variable. That is, regress profit rates on size, size^2, and size^3, where size is measured in three separate regression equations by stockholders' equity, total assets, and sales. Discuss your findings.

D. Does the fact that German auto giant Daimler-Benz reported a net loss during 1997 make it more or less difficult to find a positive link between profitability and firm size for the entire sample during this period? Should this observation be dropped from the analysis? What other important determinants of profitability might be included in a more detailed study of the profitability/firm size relation?

Monopolistic Competition and Oligopoly

11

Anyone who believes that bigger is always better should consider the dreadful operating experience of four industrial and service giants from the U.S.: AT&T, Citicorp, General Motors, and IBM. Despite massive resources and compelling brand names, each of these behemoths has stumbled badly during recent years, wounding customers, employees, and stockholders in the process. After a decade of deregulation, massive writeoffs, layoffs, and reorganizations, AT&T is finally set to reap the benefits. It now hopes to generate $50 billion per year in revenues from new businesses, like the internet, by the year 2005. Citicorp, after stumbling badly on real estate lending during the 1980s, is now set to focus on its core consumer lending franchise built around its Visa card. GM, after shedding Electronic Data Systems, is placing renewed emphasis on its core car assembly operations and Direct TV, the consumer services arm of its Hughes Electronics. And Big Blue, after a near-death experience with the onslaught of PC competition, is rejuvenated with the resurgence of customer demand for internet and network computing products. As these and other industrial and service giants struggle to keep from becoming obsolete dinosaurs, they are finding that their large size is a disadvantage and that to survive they must become dramatically smaller—leaner and meaner organizations.[1]

Like Chapter 10, this chapter offers perspective on how the nature of competition is affected by the number and size distribution of buyers and sellers; it examines competition in the partly competitive, partly monopolistic world of monopolistic competition and oligopoly.

The Contrast Between Monopolistic Competition and Oligopoly

Monopolistic competition and oligopoly provide differing perspectives on the nature of competition in imperfectly competitive markets. Each entails important unique characteristics. Major attributes of the monopolistic competition and oligopoly market models are outlined in this section and then elaborated on in the rest of the chapter.

MONOPOLISTIC COMPETITION

The economic environment faced by a majority of firms in the economy cannot be described as perfectly competitive. Likewise, few firms have a clear monopoly in terms of

---

[1]See Melanie Warner, "Size Matters," *Fortune*, April 28, 1997, 200–201.

the goods and services they provide. Market structures encountered in the real world commonly embody elements of both perfect competition and monopoly. Firms often introduce valuable new products or process innovations that give rise to substantial economic profits or above-normal rates of return in the short run. In the long run, however, entry and imitation by new rivals erode the dominant market share enjoyed by early innovators, and profits eventually return to normal. Still, in sharp contrast to perfectly competitive markets, the unique product characteristics of individual firms often remain valued by consumers. Consumers often continue to prefer *Campbell's Soup, Dockers, Oil of Olay, Rubbermaid, Tide,* and other favorite brands long after comparable products have been introduced by rivals. The partly competitive, partly monopoly market structure encountered by firms in the apparel, food, hotel, retailing, and consumer products industries is called monopolistic competition. Given the lack of perfect substitutes, monopolistically competitive firms exercise some discretion in setting prices—they are not price takers. However, given vigorous competition from imitators offering close but not identical substitutes, such firms enjoy only a normal risk-adjusted rate of return on investment in long-run equilibrium.

Monopolistic Competition
A market structure characterized by a large number of sellers of differentiated products.

    Monopolistic competition is similar to perfect competition and entails vigorous price competition among a large number of firms and individuals. The major difference between these two market structure models is that consumers perceive important differences among the products offered by monopolistically competitive firms, whereas the output of perfectly competitive firms is homogeneous. This gives monopolistically competitive firms at least some discretion in setting prices. However, the presence of many close substitutes limits this price-setting ability and drives profits down to a normal risk-adjusted rate of return in the long run. As in the case of perfect competition, above-normal profits are possible only in the short run, before the monopolistically competitive firm's rivals can take effective countermeasures.

OLIGOPOLY

Other imperfectly competitive markets are characterized by rivalry among few rather than many competitors, as is true of perfectly competitive and monopolistically competitive markets. Oligopoly is the market structure model that describes competition among a handful of competitors sheltered by significant barriers to entry. Oligopolists might produce a homogeneous product, such as aluminum, steel, or semiconductors; or differentiated products such as *Cheerios, Coca-Cola, Marlboro, MTV,* and *Nintendo.* Firms in the ready-to-eat cereal, beverage, cigarette, and computer games software industries, among others, have the potential for economic profits even in the long run. With few competitors, economic incentives also exist for such firms to devise illegal agreements to limit competition, fix prices, or otherwise divide markets. The history of antitrust enforcement in the United States provides numerous examples of "competitors" who illegally entered into such agreements. Yet there are also examples of markets in which vigorous competition among a small number of firms generates obvious long-term benefits for consumers. It is therefore erroneous to draw a simple link between the number of competitors and the vigor of competition.

Oligopoly
A market structure characterized by few sellers and interdependent price/output decisions.

In an industry characterized by **oligopoly,** only a few large rivals are responsible for the bulk of industry output. As in the case of monopoly, high to very high barriers to entry are typical. Under oligopoly, the price/output decisions of firms are interrelated in the sense that direct reactions among rivals can be expected. As a result, decisions of individual firms are based in part on the likely responses of competitors. This competition among the few involves a wide variety of price and nonprice methods of rivalry, as determined by the institutional characteristics of each particular market. Even though limited numbers of competitors give rise to a potential for economic profits, above-normal rates of return are far from guaranteed. Competition among the few is sometimes vigorous.

THE DYNAMIC NATURE OF COMPETITION

In characterizing the descriptive relevance of the monopolistic competition and oligopoly models of seller behavior, it is important to recognize the dynamic nature of real-world markets. For example, as late as the mid-1980s it seemed quite appropriate to regard the automobile and personal computer manufacturing markets as oligopolistic in nature. Today, it seems fairer to regard each industry as monopolistically competitive. In the automobile industry, GM, Ford, and Chrysler have found Toyota, Honda, Nissan, Mazda, and a host of specialized competitors to be formidable foes. So-called clones of IBM and Apple computers have also dramatically reduced the relative attractiveness of *PS/2* and *Macintosh* computers. Compaq, Dell, Gateway, and a plethora of smaller computer manufacturers have dramatically cut prices and margins for desktop personal computers, while increasing both information processing capacity and reliability at the same time.

In many formerly oligopolistic markets, the market discipline provided by a competitive fringe of smaller domestic and foreign rivals has also become sufficient to limit the potential abuse of a few large competitors. In the long-distance telephone service market, for example, AT&T, MCI, and Sprint continue to dominate the industry. However, a host of specialized providers of long-distance phone service cause price and service quality competition to be spirited. Similarly, the competitive fringe in cellular communications and cable TV promise to force dramatic change during the years ahead. It is unfortunate, but public perceptions and government regulatory policy sometimes lag behind economic reality. It is essential that timely and accurate market structure information be available to form the basis for managerial investment decisions that relate to entry or exit from specific lines of business. Similarly, enlightened public policy requires timely information.

Monopolistic Competition

Perfect competition and monopoly rarely exist in actual markets. Most firms are subject to rivalry, though perhaps not as vigorous as would exist under perfect competition. Even though most firms compete with a large number of other firms producing highly substitutable products, many still have some control over the price of their product. They cannot sell all that they want at a fixed price, nor would they lose all their sales if they raised prices slightly. In other words, most firms face downward-sloping demand curves, signifying less-than-perfect competition.

CHARACTERISTICS OF MONOPOLISTICALLY COMPETITIVE MARKETS

Monopolistic competition exists in a market when individual producers have moderate influence over product prices, where each such product enjoys a degree of uniqueness in the perception of customers. This market structure has some important similarities and dissimilarities with perfectly competitive markets. Monopolistic competition is characterized by the following:

- *Large numbers of buyers and sellers.* Each firm in the industry produces a small portion of industry output, and each customer buys only a small part of the total.
- *Product heterogeneity.* The output of each firm is perceived by customers to be essentially different from, though comparable with, the output of other firms in the industry.
- *Free entry and exit.* Firms are not restricted from entering or leaving the industry.
- *Perfect dissemination of information.* Cost, price, and product quality information is known by all buyers and all sellers in the market.

These basic conditions are not as restrictive as those for perfect competition and are fairly commonplace in actual markets. Vigorous monopolistic competition is evident in the banking, container and packaging, discount and fashion retail, electronics, food manufacturing, office equipment, paper and forest products, and most personal and professional service industries. Although individual firms are able to maintain some control over pricing policy, their pricing discretion is severely limited by competition from firms offering close but not identical substitutes.

Monopolistic competition is a realistic description of the competition encountered by firms in a wide variety of industries. As in perfectly competitive markets, a large number of competitors make independent decisions in monopolistically competitive markets. A price change by any one firm does not cause other firms to change prices. If price reactions did occur, then an oligopoly market structure would be present. The most distinctive characteristic of monopolistic competition is that each competitor offers a unique product that is only an imperfect substitute for those offered by competitors. Each firm is able to differentiate its product, at least to some degree, from those of rival firms. Nevertheless, each firm's demand function is significantly affected by the presence of numerous competitors producing goods that consumers view as reasonably close substitutes. Exogenous changes in demand and cost conditions also tend to have a similar effect on all firms and frequently lead to comparable pricing influences.

Product differentiation takes many forms. Quality differentials, packaging, credit terms, or superior maintenance service can all differentiate products, as can advertising that leads to brand-name identification. Not only is a tube of *Crest* toothpaste different from *Colgate* toothpaste, a tube of *Crest* at a nearby convenience store is different from an identical tube available at a distant discount retailer. Since consumers evaluate products on the basis of their ability to satisfy specific wants, as well as when and where they have them, products involve not only quantity, quality, and price characteristics but time and place attributes as well. The important factor in all of these forms of product differentiation is that some consumers prefer the product of one seller to those of others.

The effect of product differentiation is to create downward sloping firm demand curves in monopolistically competitive markets. Unlike a price taker facing a perfectly horizontal demand curve, the firm is able to independently determine an optimal price/output combination. The degree of price flexibility enjoyed depends on the strength of product differentiation. The more differentiated a firm's product, the lower the substitutability of other products for it. Strong differentiation results in greater consumer loyalty and greater control over price. This is illustrated in Figure 11.1, which shows the demand curves of Firms *A* and *B*. Consumers view Firm *A*'s product as being only slightly differentiated from the bulk of industry output. Because many other firms offer acceptable substitutes, Firm *A* is close to being a price taker. Conversely, Firm *B* has successfully differentiated its product, and consumers are therefore less willing to accept substitutes for *B*'s output. Firm *B*'s demand is relatively less sensitive to price changes.

Figure 11.1

RELATION BETWEEN PRODUCT DIFFERENTIATION AND ELASTICITY OF DEMAND

Firm *B*'s steeper demand curve relative to Firm *A*'s reflects stronger product differentiation and hence less sensitivity to price changes.

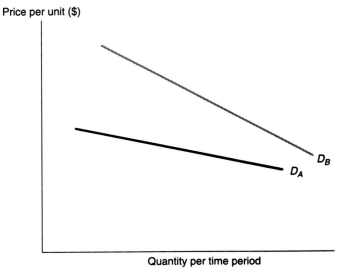

Intel: Running Fast to Stay in Place

Intel is the dominant and most profitable maker of integrated circuits, the microscopic pieces of silicon chips used to power electronic computers, calculators, video games, and a burgeoning array of other products. *intel inside*™ is a valued trademark that identifies products produced by a company whose microprocessors are the brains of more than 100 million IBM-compatible personal computers, more than five times that of its nearest rival. So complete has been Intel's grip on the PC market that its sales surged from $1.3 billion in 1986 to more than $20.8 billion in 1996, while profits exploded from a *deficit* of $183.3 million in 1986 to roughly $5.2 billion in 1996. Meanwhile, Intel's stock price skyrocketed from a split-adjusted 3 1/2 to more than 160 by early 1997.

Despite this enviable record of success, and despite obvious strengths, Intel's core business is facing its biggest challenge in a decade. Led by Advanced Micro Devices, Inc., Cyrix, Inc., International Business Machines, Inc., Texas Instruments, Inc., and a handful of foreign firms, competitors are rushing to produce competitors of Intel chips. High-quality clones can quickly erode the profits of early innovators like Intel, a company that has come to count on giant-sized profit margins of 60%. During recent years, investors and market analysts have both posed an important question: Is Intel's dominance of the integrated circuits market coming to an end?

Not without a fight, it won't. Intel is led by visionary CEO Andy Grove, author of the 1997 best-seller *Only the Paranoid Survive*. Driven by paranoia, Intel is striking back at competitors on multiple fronts, dragging competitors into court for patent infringement, slashing prices, and advertising its products on national television. Intel's strategic vision has also been revamped to focus on computer microprocessor products, the core of its business. The company is establishing a close working relationship with manufacturers of end-user products, like personal computers, to ensure compatibility and maximize the benefits of new microprocessor innovations. Perhaps most important, Intel has launched a campaign to speed product development and to thereby expand the potential market for Intel products.

Gordon Moore founded Intel with Robert Noyce, the co-inventor of the integrated circuit. Moore is credited with a prescient prediction in 1975, now referred to as

"Moore's Law," that the power of state-of-the-art computer chips would double every *18 months*. If anything, the pace of that advance is quickening. Intel is no longer satisfied to introduce one or two new-generations of chips annually and new microprocessor families every three or four years. In 1992, for example, it marketed roughly 30 variants of its cutting-edge 486 chip. By the summer of 1992, several months ahead of schedule, it unveiled its next-generation product, the Pentium microprocessor, a veritable one-chip mainframe that is roughly 30% faster than an i486 chip. In 1997, Grove confidently predicted that by the year 2011 Intel chips will contain *one billion* transistors (up from today's 5.5 million), and feature a clock speed of ten gigahertz (or 10,000 megahertz, up from today's 200 megahertz). This blistering tempo is one that Intel hopes will keep competitors in a perpetual catch-up mode.

Intel's speedup of microprocessor technology will affect everyone who uses computers and other electronic products. The ever-increasing power of microprocessors has already catapulted the spread of office automation, computer networks, and "user friendly" software that makes high-power computing available to even the novice. In the banking, retailing, and fast food industries, nearly every competitor already relies on microprocessors in cash registers or personal computers to track revenues, measure product demand, and control costs. Each new generation of technology has produced new products, services, and productivity in these and many sectors. It is therefore reasonable to expect that any speedup in microprocessor technology will produce widespread benefits as worldwide competition grows more feverish and intense in a wide variety of industries.

In the 21st century, Intel hopes to become a force in supercomputers, interactive digital video, and flash memory, a semiconductor alternative to storing data on magnetic disks. But none of these new products will have the support needed to bring them to market unless Intel can protect its main turf from increasingly aggressive rivals.

See: David Kirkpatrick, "Intel's Amazing Profit Machine," *Fortune*, February 17, 1997, 60-72.

PRICE/OUTPUT DECISIONS UNDER MONOPOLISTIC COMPETITION

As its name suggests, monopolistic competition embodies elements of both monopoly and perfect competition. The monopoly aspect of monopolistic competition is most forcefully observed in the short run. For example, consider Figure 11.2. With the demand curve, D_1, and its related marginal revenue curve, MR_1, the optimum output, Q_1, is found at the point where $MR_1 = MC$. Short-run monopoly profits equal to the area P_1LMATC_1 are earned. Such profits can be derived from new product introductions, product and process improvements, creative packaging and marketing, or other factors such as an unexpected rise in demand.

Over time, short-run monopoly profits attract competition, and other firms enter the industry. This competitive aspect of monopolistic competition is seen most forcefully in the long run. As competitors emerge to offer close but imperfect substitutes, the market share and profits of the initial innovating firm diminish. Firm demand and marginal revenue curves shift to the left, as for example, from D_1 to D_2 and from MR_1 to MR_2 in Figure 11.2. Optimal long-run output occurs at Q_2, the point where $MR_2 = MC$. Since the

Figure 11.2

PRICE/OUTPUT COMBINATIONS UNDER MONOPOLISTIC COMPETITION

Long-run equilibrium under monopolistic competition occurs when $MR = MC$ and $P = AC$. This typically occurs between (P_2, Q_2) (the high-price/low-output equilibrium) and (P_3, Q_3) (the low-price/high-output equilibrium).

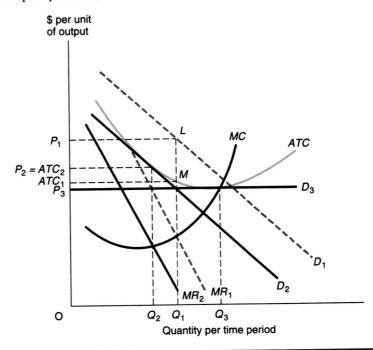

optimal price P_2 equals ATC_2, where cost includes a normal profit just sufficient to maintain capital investment, economic profits are zero.

The price/output combination (P_2Q_2) describes a monopolistically competitive market equilibrium characterized by a high degree of product differentiation. If new entrants offered perfect rather than close substitutes, each firm's long-run demand curve would become more nearly horizontal, and the perfectly competitive equilibrium, D_3 with P_3 and Q_3, would be approached. Like the (P_2Q_2) high-differentiation equilibrium, the (P_3Q_3) no-differentiation equilibrium is something of an extreme case. In most instances, competitor entry reduces but does not eliminate product differentiation. An intermediate price/output solution, one between (P_2Q_2) and (P_3Q_3), is often achieved in long-run equilibrium. Indeed, it is the retention of at least some degree of product differentiation that distinguishes the monopolistically competitive equilibrium from that achieved in perfectly competitive markets.

A firm will never operate at the minimum point on its average cost curve in monopolistically competitive equilibrium. Each firm's demand curve is downward sloping, so it is tangent to the ATC curve at some point above the minimum of the ATC curve. However, this does not mean that a monopolistically competitive industry is inefficient, except in a superficial sense. The very existence of a downward-sloping demand curve implies that consumers value an individual firm's products more highly than they do products of other producers. If the number of producers were somehow reduced so that all the remaining firms could operate at their minimum cost point, some consumers would clearly suffer a loss in welfare, *because the product variety they desire would no longer be available.* The higher prices and costs of monopolistically competitive industries, as opposed to perfectly competitive industries, reflect the economic cost of product variety. If consumers are willing to bear such costs, and often they are, then these costs must not be excessive. The success of many branded products in the face of generic competition is powerful testimony in support of this presumption.

Although the perfectly competitive and monopoly settings are comparatively rare in real-world markets, monopolistic competition is frequently observed. It often develops from the competitive forces that continually shape markets. For example, in 1960 a small ($37 million in sales) office-machine company, Haloid Xerox, Inc., revolutionized the copy industry with the introduction of the Xerox 914 copier. Xerography was a tremendous improvement over electrofax and other coated-paper copiers. It permitted the use of untreated paper, which produced not only a more desirable copy but one that was less expensive on a cost-per-copy basis as well. Invention of the dry copier established what is now Xerox Corporation at the forefront of a rapidly growing office-copier industry and propelled the firm to a position of virtual monopoly by 1970. Between 1970 and 1980, the industry's market structure changed dramatically because of an influx of both domestic and foreign competition as many of Xerox's original patents expired. IBM entered the copier market in April 1970 with its Copier I model and expanded its participation in November 1972 with Copier II. Eastman Kodak made its entry into the market in 1975 with its Ektaprint model. Of course, Minnesota Mining and Manufacturing (3M) has long been a factor in the electrofax copier segment of the market. A more complete list of Xerox's recent domestic and international competitors would include at least 30 firms. The effect of this entry on Xerox's market share and profitability was dramatic. Between 1970 and 1978, for example, Xerox's share of the domestic copier market fell from 98% to 56%, and its return on stockholders' equity fell from 23.6% to 18.2%.

The monopolistic dry-copier market of 1970 has evolved into a much more competitive industry in the 1990s. Because *Canon, Kodak, 3M, Panasonic,* and *Sharp* copiers are only close rather than perfect substitutes for Xerox machines, each company retains some price discretion, and today the industry can be described as monopolistically competitive.

The process of price/output adjustment and the concept of equilibrium in monopolistically competitive markets can be further illustrated by the following example. Assume that the Skyhawk Trailer Company, located in Toronto, Ontario, owns patents covering important design features of its Tomahawk II, an ultralight camping trailer that can safely be towed by high-mileage subcompact cars. Skyhawk's patent protection has made it very difficult for competitors to offer similar ultralight trailers. The Tomahawk II is a highly successful product, and a veritable flood of similar products can be expected within five years as Skyhawk's patent protection expires.

Skyhawk has asked its financial planning committee to identify both short- and long-run pricing and production strategies for the Tomahawk II. To facilitate the decision-making process, the committee has received the following revenue and cost data from Skyhawk's marketing and production departments:

$$TR = \$20,000Q - \$15.6Q^2,$$

$$MR = \Delta TR/\Delta Q = \$20,000 - \$31.2Q,$$

$$TC = \$400,000 + \$4,640Q + \$10Q^2,$$

$$MC = \Delta TC/\Delta Q = \$4,640 + \$20Q,$$

where *TR* is revenue (in dollars), *Q* is quantity (in units), *MR* is marginal revenue (in dollars), *TC* is total cost, including a risk-adjusted normal rate of return on investment (in dollars), and *MC* is marginal cost (in dollars).

As a first step in the analysis, one might determine the optimal price/output combination if the committee were to decide that Skyhawk should take full advantage of its current monopoly position and maximize short-run profits. To find the short-run profit-maximizing price/output combination, set Skyhawk's marginal revenue equal to marginal cost and solve for *Q*:

$$MR = MC,$$

$$\$20,000 - \$31.2Q = \$4,640 + \$20Q,$$

$$\$51.2Q = \$15,360,$$

$$Q = 300 \text{ units},$$

and

$$P = \$20,000 - \$15.6(300)$$

$$= \$15,320.$$

$$\pi = TR - TC$$
$$= -\$25.6(300^2) + \$15,360(300) - \$400,000$$
$$= \$1,904,000.$$

Therefore, the financial planning committee should recommend a \$15,320 price and 300-unit output level to Skyhawk management if the firm's objective is to maximize short-run profit. Such a planning decision results in roughly \$1.9 million in profit during those years when Skyhawk's patent protection effectively deters competitors.

Now assume that Skyhawk can maintain a high level of brand loyalty and product differentiation in the long run, despite competitor offerings of similar trailers but that such competition eliminates any potential for economic profits. This is consistent with a market in monopolistically competitive equilibrium, where $P = AC$ at a point above minimum long-run average costs. Skyhawk's declining market share is reflected by a leftward shift in its demand curve to a point of tangency with its average cost curve. Although precise identification of the long-run price/output combination is very difficult, the planning committee can identify the bounds within which this price/output combination can be expected to occur.

The high-price/low-output combination is identified by the point of tangency between the firm's average cost curve and a new demand curve reflecting a *parallel leftward* shift in demand (D_2 in Figure 11.2). This parallel leftward shift assumes that the firm can maintain a high degree of product differentiation in the long run. The low-price/high-output equilibrium combination assumes no residual product differentiation in the long run, and it is identified by the point of tangency between the average cost curve and a new horizontal firm demand curve (D_3 in Figure 11.2). This is, of course, also the perfectly competitive equilibrium price/output combination.

The equilibrium high-price/low-output combination that follows a parallel leftward shift in Skyhawk's demand curve can be determined by equating the slopes of the firm's original demand curve and its long-run average cost curve. Since a parallel leftward shift in firm demand results in a new demand curve with an identical slope, equating the slopes of the firm's initial demand and average cost curves identifies the monopolistically competitive high-price/low-output equilibrium.

For simplicity, assume that the previous total cost curve for Skyhawk also holds in the long run. To determine the slope of this average cost curve, one must find out how average costs vary with respect to output.

$$AC = TC/Q = (\$400,000 + \$4,640Q + \$10Q^2)/Q$$
$$= \frac{\$400,000}{Q} + \$4,640 + \$10Q$$
$$= \$400,000Q^{-1} + \$4,640 + \$10Q.$$

The slope of this average cost curve is given by the expression

$$\Delta AC/\Delta Q = -400,000Q^{-2} + 10.$$

The slope of the new demand curve is given by

$$\Delta P/\Delta Q = -15.6 \text{ (same as the original demand curve)}.$$

In equilibrium,

$$\text{Slope of } AC \text{ Curve} = \text{Slope of Demand Curve},$$

$$-400,000Q^{-2} + 10 = -15.6,$$

$$Q^{-2} = 25.6/400,000,$$

$$Q^2 = 400,000/25.6,$$

$$Q = 125 \text{ Units},$$

$$P = AC$$

$$= \frac{\$400,000}{125} + \$4,640 + \$10(125)$$

$$= \$9,090,$$

and

$$\pi = P \times Q - TC$$

$$= \$9,090(125) - \$400,000 - \$4,640(125) - \$10(125^2)$$

$$= \$0.$$

This high-price/low-output monopolistically competitive equilibrium results in a decrease in price from $15,320 to $9,090 and a fall in output from 300 to 125 units per year. Only a risk-adjusted normal rate of return will be earned, eliminating Skyhawk's economic profits. This long-run equilibrium assumes that Skyhawk would enjoy the same low price elasticity of demand that it experienced as a monopolist. This assumption may or may not be appropriate. New entrants often have the effect of both cutting a monopolist's market share and increasing the price elasticity of demand. It is often reasonable to expect entry to cause both a leftward shift of and some flattening in Skyhawk's demand curve. To see the extreme limit of the demand-curve flattening process, the case of a perfectly horizontal demand curve can be considered.

The low-price/high-output (perfectly competitive) equilibrium combination occurs at the point where $P = MR = MC = AC$. This reflects that the firm's demand curve is perfectly horizontal, and average costs are minimized. To find the output level of minimum average costs, set $MC = AC$ and solve for Q:

$$\$4,640 + \$20Q = \$400,000Q^{-1} + \$4,640 + \$10Q,$$

$$\$10Q = \$400,000Q^{-1},$$

$$Q^2 = 40,000,$$

$$Q = \sqrt{40,000}$$

$$= 200 \text{ units.}$$

$$P = AC$$

$$= \frac{\$400,000}{200} + \$4,640 + \$10(200)$$

$$= \$8,640,$$

and

$$\pi = P \times Q - TC$$

$$= \$8,640(200) - \$400,000 - \$4,640(200) - \$10(200^2)$$

$$= \$0.$$

Under this low-price equilibrium scenario, Skyhawk's monopoly price falls in the long run from an original $15,320 to $8,640, and output falls from the monopoly level of 300 units to the competitive equilibrium level of 200 units per year. The company would earn only a risk-adjusted normal rate of return, and economic profits would equal zero.

Following expiration of its patent protection, management can expect that competitor entry will reduce Skyhawk's volume from 300 units per year to a level between $Q = 125$ and $Q = 200$ units per year. The short-run profit-maximizing price of $15,320 will fall to a monopolistically competitive equilibrium price between $P = \$9,090$, the high-price/low-output equilibrium, and $P = \$8,640$, the low-price/high-output equilibrium. In deciding on an optimal short-run price/output strategy, Skyhawk must weigh the benefits of high near-term profitability against the long-run cost of lost market share resulting from competitor entry. Such a decision involves consideration of current interest rates, the speed of competitor imitation, and the future pace of innovation in the industry, among other factors.

Oligopoly

The theory of monopolistic competition recognizes that firms often have some control over price but that their price flexibility is limited by a large number of close substitutes for their products. The theory assumes, however, that in making decisions, firms do not consider competitor reactions. Such a behavioral assumption is appropriate for some industries but inappropriate for others. When individual firm actions cause competitors to react, oligopoly exists.

CHARACTERISTICS OF OLIGOPOLY MARKETS

Oligopoly exists when a handful of competitors dominate the market for a good or service and each firm makes pricing and marketing decisions in light of the expected response by rivals. Individual firms have the ability to set pricing and production strategy, and they enjoy the potential for economic profits in both the short run and the long run. Oligopoly describes markets that can be characterized as follows:

- *Few sellers.* A handful of firms produces the bulk of industry output.
- *Homogeneous or unique product.* Oligopoly output can be perceived as homogeneous (e.g., aluminum) or distinctive (e.g., ready-to-eat cereal).
- *Blockaded entry and exit.* Firms are heavily restricted from entering or leaving the industry.
- *Imperfect dissemination of information.* Cost, price, and product quality information is withheld from uninformed buyers.

In the United States, aluminum, cigarettes, electrical equipment, filmed entertainment production and distribution, glass, long-distance telecommunications, and ready-to-eat cereals are all produced and sold under conditions of oligopoly. In each of these industries, a small number of firms produces a dominant percentage of all industry output. In the ready-to-eat breakfast cereal industry, for example, Kellogg, General Mills, General Foods (Phillip Morris), RJR Nabisco, Quaker Oats, and Ralston Purina are responsible for almost all domestic production in the United States. Durable customer loyalty gives rise to fat profit margins and rates of return on assets that are two to three times food industry norms. *Corn Flakes, Sugar Frosted Flakes, Cheerios, Raisin Bran, Wheaties,* and a handful of other brands continue to dominate the industry year after year and make successful entry extremely difficult. Even multinational food giant Nestlé sought and obtained a joint venture agreement with General Mills rather than enter the potentially lucrative European breakfast cereal market by itself. Long-distance telephone service is also highly concentrated, with AT&T, MCI, and Sprint providing almost all domestic service to residential customers.

Oligopoly also is present in a number of local markets. In many retail markets for gasoline and food, for example, only a few service stations and grocery stores compete within a small geographic area. Drycleaning services are also sometimes provided by a relative handful of firms in small to medium-size cities and towns.

A limited number of sellers creates price/output decision interdependence under oligopoly. Consider the case of *duopoly,* a special form of oligopoly, under which only two firms provide a particular product. For simplicity, assume that a homogeneous product is offered and that customers choose between the firms solely on the basis of price. Assume also that both firms charge the same price and that each has an equal share of the market. Now suppose that Firm *A* attempts to increase its sales by lowering its price. All buyers will attempt to switch to Firm *A,* and Firm *B* will lose a substantial share of its market. To retain customers, *B* will react by lowering its price. Neither firm is free to act independently; actions taken by one lead to reactions by the other.

PRICE/OUTPUT DECISIONS UNDER OLIGOPOLY

Demand curves relate quantity demanded to price, *holding constant the effect of all other variables.* One variable that is typically assumed to remain fixed is the price charged by competing firms. In an oligopolistic market structure, however, if one firm changes its price, other firms react by changing their prices. The demand curve for the initial firm shifts position so that instead of moving along a single demand curve as it changes price, the firm moves to an entirely new demand curve.

The phenomenon of shifting demand curves is illustrated in Figure 11.3(a). Firm A is initially producing Q_1 units of output and selling them at a price of P_1. Demand curve D_1 applies here, assuming that prices charged by other firms remain fixed. Under this assumption, a price cut from P_1 to P_2 would increase demand to Q_2. Assume, however, that only a few firms operate in the market and that each has a fairly large share of total sales. If one firm cuts its price and obtains a substantial increase in volume, other firms lose a large part of their business. Furthermore, they know exactly why their sales have fallen and react by cutting their own prices. This action shifts Firm A down to the second demand curve, D_2, reducing its demand at P_2 from Q_2 to Q_3 units. The new curve is just as unstable as the old one, so knowledge of its shape is useless to Firm A; if it tries to move along D_2, competitors will react, forcing the company to yet another demand curve.

Shifting demand curves present no real difficulty in making price/output decisions *if each firm knows how rivals will react to price changes*. The reactions would just be built into the price/demand relation, and a new demand curve could be constructed to include interactions among firms. Curve D_3 in Figure 11.3(b) represents such a reaction-based demand curve; it shows how price reductions affect quantity demanded after competitive reactions have been taken into account. The problem with this approach is that different interfirm behavior leads to different pricing decision rules.

CARTEL ARRANGEMENTS

All firms in an oligopoly market benefit if they get together and set prices to maximize industry profits. In so doing, the firms set a monopoly price and extract the maximum amount of profit from consumers. A group of competitors operating under such a formal overt agreement is called a **cartel.** If an informal covert agreement is reached, the firms are said to be operating in **collusion.** Both practices are generally illegal in the United States. However, cartels are legal in many parts of the world, and multinational corporations often become involved with them in foreign markets. Several important domestic markets are also dominated by producer associations that operate like cartels and appear to flourish without interference from the government. Agricultural commodities such as milk are prime examples of products marketed under cartel-like arrangements.

Cartel
Firms operating with a formal agreement to fix prices and output.

Collusion
A covert, informal agreement among firms in an industry to fix prices and output levels.

A cartel that has absolute control over all firms in an industry can operate as a monopoly. To illustrate, consider the situation shown in Figure 11.4. The marginal cost curves of each firm are summed horizontally to arrive at an industry marginal cost curve. Equating the cartel's total marginal cost with the industry marginal revenue curve determines the profit-maximizing output and, simultaneously, the price, P^*, to be charged. Once this profit-maximizing price/output level has been determined, each individual firm finds its optimal output by equating its own marginal cost curve to the previously determined profit-maximizing marginal cost level for the industry.

Profits are often divided among firms on the basis of their individual level of production, but other allocation techniques can be employed. Market share, production capacity, and a bargained solution based on economic power have all been used in the

Figure 11.3

SHIFTING DEMAND UNDER OLIGOPOLY

(a) A price reduction to P_2 by Firm A temporarily increases output to Q_2. As other firms reduce prices, demand shifts back from D_1 to D_2 and Firm A's output drops to Q_3. (b) In contrast to D_1 and D_2, the demand curve D_3 reflects Firm A's projections of the price reactions of competitors.

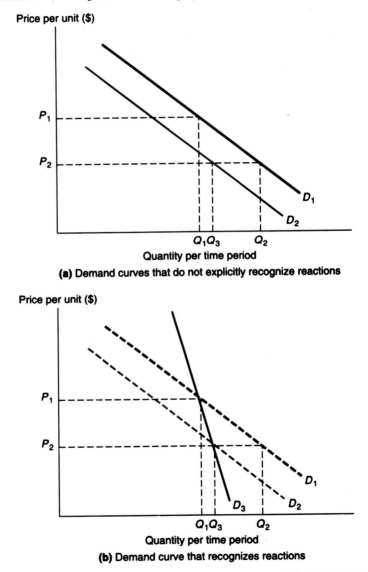

Price per unit ($)

P_1

P_2

D_1

D_2

Q_1Q_3 Q_2

Quantity per time period

(a) Demand curves that do not explicitly recognize reactions

Price per unit ($)

P_1

P_2

D_1

D_3 D_2

Q_1Q_3 Q_2

Quantity per time period

(b) Demand curve that recognizes reactions

PRICE/OUTPUT DETERMINATION FOR A CARTEL

| Figure 11.4

Horizontal summation of the *MC* curves for each firm gives the cartel's *MC* curve. Output for each firm is found by equating its own *MC* to the industry profit-maximizing *MC* level.

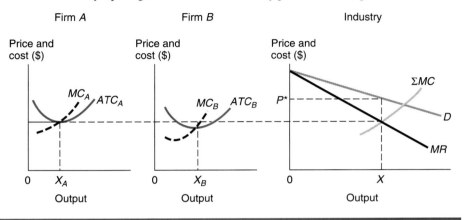

past. For a number of reasons, cartels are typically rather short-lived. In addition to the long-run problems of changing products and of entry into the market by new producers, cartels are subject to disagreements among members. Although firms usually agree that maximizing joint profits is mutually beneficial, they seldom agree on the equity of various profit-allocation schemes. This problem can lead to attempts to subvert the cartel agreement.

Cartel subversion can be extremely profitable to individual firms. With an industry operating at the monopoly price/output level, undetected secret price cutting can lead to a dramatic increase in profits for individual cartel members. The costs and benefits of such subversion are directly related to the number of firms included in the cartel. Consider a two-firm cartel in which each member serves 50% of the market. Cheating by either firm is very difficult, because any loss in market share is readily detected. The offending party can easily be identified and punished. Moreover, the potential profit and market share gain to successful cheating is exactly balanced by the potential profit and market share cost of detection and retribution. Conversely, a 20-member cartel promises substantial profits and market share gains to successful cheaters. At the same time, detecting the source of secret price concessions can be extremely difficult. History shows that cartels including more than a very few members have difficulty policing and maintaining member compliance. With respect to cartels, there appears to be little honor among thieves.

The OPEC cartel's loss of oil market control in the late 1980s is a classic example of a cartel that failed primarily because members could not agree on a profit- and market-sharing scheme. Unwieldy large size and pressure from new entrants attracted by relatively high oil prices added to the cartel's problems and caused it to become ineffective.

PRICE LEADERSHIP

Price Leadership
A situation in which one
firm establishes itself as the
industry leader and all other
firms in the industry accept
its pricing policy.

A less formal but still effective means of reducing oligopolistic uncertainty is through
price leadership. Price leadership results when one firm establishes itself as the industry leader and all other firms accept its pricing policy. This leadership may result from
the size and strength of the leading firm, from cost efficiency, or as a result of the recognized ability of the leader to forecast market conditions accurately and to establish
prices that produce satisfactory profits for all firms in the industry.

A typical case is price leadership by a dominant firm, usually the largest firm in the
industry. The leader faces a price/output problem similar to monopoly, while other firms
are price takers and face a competitive price/output problem. This is illustrated in Figure 11.5, where the total market demand curve is D_T, the marginal cost curve of the
leader is MC_L, and the horizontal summation of the marginal cost curves for all of the
price followers is labeled MC_f. Because price followers take prices as given, they
choose to operate at the output level at which their individual marginal costs equal
price, just as they would in a perfectly competitive market. Accordingly, the MC_f curve
represents the supply curve for following firms. At price P_3, followers would supply the
entire market, leaving nothing for the dominant firm. At all prices below P_3, the horizontal distance between the summed MC_f curve and the market demand curve represents the price leader's demand. At a price of P_1, for example, price followers provide
Q_2 units of output, leaving demand of $Q_5 - Q_2$ for the price leader. Plotting all of the

OLIGOPOLY PRICING WITH DOMINANT-FIRM PRICE LEADERSHIP

When the price leader has set an industry price of P_2, the price leader will maximize profits at Q_1
units of output. Price followers will supply a combined output of $Q_4 - Q_1$.

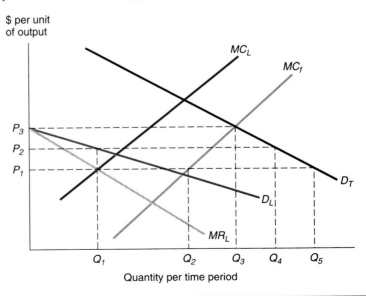

residual demand quantities for prices below P_3 produces the demand curve for the price leader, D_L, in Figure 11.5, and the related marginal revenue curve, MR_L.

More generally, the leader faces a demand curve of the following form:

$$D_L = D_T - S_f, \qquad \qquad (11.1)$$

where D_L is the leader's demand, D_T is total demand, and S_f is the followers' supply curve found by setting price $= MC_f$ and solving for Q_f, the quantity that will be supplied by the price followers. Since D_T and S_f are both functions of price, D_L is likewise determined by price.

Because the price leader faces the demand curve D_L as a monopolist, it maximizes profit by operating at the point where marginal revenue equals marginal cost, $MR_L = MC_L$. At this optimal output level for the leader, Q_1, market price is established at P_2. Price followers supply a combined output of $Q_4 - Q_1$ units. A stable short-run equilibrium is reached if no one challenges the price leader.

Barometric Price Leadership
A situation in which one firm in an industry announces a price change in response to what it perceives as a change in industry supply and demand conditions and other firms respond by following the price change.

A second type of price leadership is **barometric price leadership.** In this case, one firm announces a price change in response to what it perceives as a change in industry supply and demand conditions. This change could stem from cost increases that result from a new industry labor agreement, higher energy or material prices, higher taxes, or a substantial shift in industry demand. With barometric price leadership, the price leader is not necessarily the largest or the dominant firm in the industry. The price-leader role might even pass from one firm to another over time. To be effective, the price leader must only be accurate in reading the prevailing industry view of the need for price adjustment. If the price leader makes a mistake, other firms may not follow its price move, and the price leader may have to rescind or modify the announced price change to retain its leadership position.

KINKED DEMAND CURVE

An often-noted characteristic of oligopoly markets is "sticky" prices. Once a general price level has been established, whether through cartel agreement or some less formal arrangement, it tends to remain fixed for an extended period. Such rigid prices are often explained by what is referred to as the **kinked demand curve** theory of oligopoly prices. A kinked demand curve is a firm demand curve that has different slopes for price increases as compared with price decreases. The kinked demand curve describes a behavior pattern in which rival firms follow any decrease in price to maintain their respective market shares but refrain from following price increases, allowing their market shares to grow at the expense of the competitor increasing its price. The demand curve facing individual firms is kinked at the current price/output combination, as illustrated in Figure 11.6. The firm is producing Q units of output and selling them at a price of P per unit. If the firm lowers its price, competitors retaliate by lowering their prices. The result of a price cut is a relatively small increase in sales. Price increases, on the other hand, result in significant reductions in the quantity demanded and in total revenue, because customers shift to competing firms that do not follow the price increase.

Kinked Demand Curve
A theory assuming that rival firms follow any decrease in price in order to maintain their respective market shares but refrain from following increases, allowing their market share to increase at the expense of the firm making the initial price increase.

Associated with the kink in the demand curve is a point of discontinuity in the marginal revenue curve. As a result, the firm's marginal revenue curve has a gap at the

Government-Guaranteed Oligopoly

The Federal National Mortgage Association and the Federal Home Loan Mortgage Corp., or Fannie Mae and Freddie Mac, enjoy immense benefits from being government-sponsored entities that are also for-profit, publicly traded stockholder-owned corporations. Both are huge and highly profitable, despite the fact that they operate in a relatively simple and low-risk business. Fannie and Freddie purchase roughly $350 billion in home mortgages from thrifts and other financial institutions every year. Most of these loans are packaged and resold to investors as mortgage-backed securities, thus enabling home buyers to tap pension funds and other institutional money. Provided they can qualify, U.S. home buyers can get all the financing they need in the most liquid and efficient home-finance market in the world.

Fannie and Freddie are potent competitors for banks, savings and loans, and other lenders. Both are considering expansion into such markets as home equity lending and housing for the elderly, and Fannie has test-marketed construction lending programs for home builders. Fannie has also lent millions of dollars in home equity conversion loans, or "reverse mortgages," to people over 62 who have paid off most of their original mortgages. Fannie has also begun financing developers in the construction of single family and multifamily homes. It is no surprise that competing financial institutions are unhappy about continued Fannie and Freddie expansion. They claim that the firms compete unfairly because they get a subsidy from the U.S. government.

Fannie and Freddie, as government-sponsored enterprises, get noncash subsidies worth *billions* of dollars per year. Both have implied U.S. government guarantees on all of their liabilities. This earns them the highest possible credit ratings on their debt securities and allows them to attract institutional investors at the lowest possible interest rate. While the U.S. government charges nothing for its implied credit guarantee, Fannie and Freddie together reap more than $2.5 billion dollars per year in profits. In no small part, the amazingly good profit performance of Fannie and Freddie comes from the fact that they enjoy much lower interest costs on borrowed funds than the amount paid by their purely private-sector competitors.

Both Fannie and Freddie make a profit by selling packages of home loans to investors at an interest rate that is roughly 1% per year lower than that on the underlying pool of mortgages. In so doing, they earn an annual rate of return on stockholders' equity of roughly 20% per year, or nearly double the profit rate earned by financial institutions in general. These extraordinary profit rates have also remained remarkably stable as the scale of Fannie's and Freddie's operations has grown rapidly. During the past decade, earnings per share also grew by more than 15% per year for both; during coming decade, continued profit growth of 15-18% per year is anticipated. Stock-price performance has been sensational. Long-term investors saw their initial investments in Fannie and Freddie multiply more than ten-fold over the past decade, and look forward to continued gains of 12-15% per year over the coming ten-year period.

By congressional charter, Fannie and Freddie are supposed to provide liquidity to the mortgage market and help low-income and moderate-income families purchase adequate housing. Indeed, Fannie Mae has committed to guarantee loans to low-income renters with excellent credit. At the same time, to ensure a rapidly growing market for their services, Congress has allowed Fannie and Freddie to underwrite single-family home mortgages in excess of $200,000 each. This angers private-sector competitors because, in effect, taxpayers are subsidizing households that make more than $100,000 a year and can afford $250,000 homes. The fact that Fannie's and Freddie's implicit federal subsidies are "off the books" also concerns budget watchers concerned with the federal deficit.

In light of such criticism, Congress is pushing stronger capital requirements for Fannie and Freddie, and asking them to earmark more loans for low-income and moderate-income families. Despite such limits, Fannie and Freddie are likely to continue to prosper. There clearly are tangible rewards to government-guaranteed oligopoly!

See: I. Jeanne Dugan, "The Best Performers," *Business Week,* March 24, 1997, 80-90.

KINKED DEMAND CURVE

Figure 11.6

When price cuts are followed but price increases are not, a kink develops in the firm's demand curve. At the kink, the optimal price remains stable despite moderate changes in marginal costs.

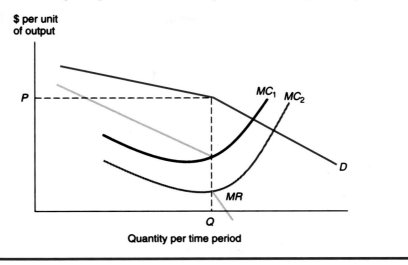

current price/output level, which results in price rigidity. To see why, recall that profit-maximizing firms always choose to operate at the point where marginal cost equals marginal revenue. Typically, any change in marginal cost leads to a new point of equality between marginal costs and marginal revenues and to a new optimal price. However, with a gap in the marginal revenue curve, the price/output combination at the kink can remain optimal despite fluctuations in marginal costs. As illustrated in Figure 11.6, the firm's marginal cost curve can vacillate between MC_1 and MC_2 without causing any change in the profit-maximizing price/output combination. Small changes in marginal costs have no effect; only large changes in marginal cost lead to price changes. In perfectly competitive grain markets, prices change every day. In the oligopolistic ready-to-eat cereals market, prices change only infrequently.

Nonprice Competition

New entrants to a market that hope to establish a position by merely cutting prices are often frustrated. Nonleading firms that hope to grow market share through price concessions alone are frequently thwarted. The problem in both instances is that price cuts are obvious and easily detected by competitors. "Meet it or beat it" is a pricing challenge that often results in quick competitor price reductions, and price wars favor the deep pockets of established incumbents. As a result, many successful firms find non-price methods of competition an effective means for growing market share and profitability in the face of entrenched rivals.

ADVANTAGES OF NONPRICE COMPETITION

Because rival firms are likely to retaliate against price cuts, oligopolists often emphasize nonprice competition to boost demand. To illustrate, assume that a firm demand function is given by Equation 11.2:

$$Q_A = f(P_A, P_X, Ad_A, Ad_X, SQ_A, SQ_X, I, Pop, \ldots)$$

$$= a - bP_A + cP_X + dAd_A - eAd_X + fSQA \tag{11.2}$$

$$- gSQ_X + hI + iPop + \ldots,$$

where Q_A is the quantity of output demanded from Firm A, P_A is A's price, P_X is the average price charged by other firms in the industry, Ad is advertising expenditures, SQ denotes an index of styling and quality, I represents income, and Pop is population. The firm can control three variables in Equation 11.2: P_A, Ad_A, and SQ_A. If it reduces P_A in an effort to stimulate demand, it will probably cause a reduction in P_X, offsetting the hoped-for effects of the initial price cut. Rather than boosting sales, Firm A may have simply started a price war.

Now consider the effects of changing Ad_A and SQ_A. Effective advertising shifts the firm's demand curve to the right, thus enabling the firm to increase sales at a given price or to sell the same quantity at a higher price. Any improvement in styling or quality would have a comparable effect, as would easier credit terms, better service, and more convenient retail locations. While competitors react to nonprice competition, their reaction is often slower and less direct than that for price changes. Nonprice changes are generally less obvious to rivals, and the design of an effective response is often time-consuming and difficult. Advertising campaigns have to be designed; media time and space must be purchased. Styling and quality changes frequently require long lead times, as do fundamental improvements in customer service. Furthermore, nonprice competition can alter customer buying habits, and regaining lost customers can prove to be difficult. Although it may take longer to establish a reputation through nonprice competition, its advantageous effects are likely to be more persistent than the fleeting benefits of a price cut.

The optimal level of nonprice competition is defined by resulting marginal benefits and marginal costs. Any form of nonprice competition should be pursued as long as marginal benefits exceed marginal costs. For example, suppose that a product has a market price of $10 per unit and a variable cost per unit of $8. If sales can be increased at an additional cost of less than $2 per unit, these additional expenditures will increase profits and should be made.

THE OPTIMAL LEVEL OF ADVERTISING

Advertising is but one of the many different methods of nonprice competition employed in imperfectly competitive markets. However, promotional and selling expenses constitute a considerable share of costs in many industries and therefore merit special consideration. In addition to helping determine an appropriate level of promotional and selling expenses, the method for determining an optimal level of advertising illustrates the technique for determining profit-maximizing levels of expenditures for other forms of nonprice competition, such as improvements in product quality, expansions in customer service, research and development expenditures, and so on.

The rule that must be followed to determine a profit-maximizing level of expenditures for nonprice methods of competition is to set the marginal cost of the activity involved just equal to the marginal revenue or marginal benefit derived from it. This follows because if the marginal cost of any activity equals the marginal revenue derived, the total net profit generated will be maximized. The optimal level of advertising occurs at that point where the additional marginal revenues derived from advertising just offset the marginal cost of advertising expenditures.

The marginal revenues per unit of output derived from advertising are measured by the marginal profit contribution generated. This is the difference between marginal revenues, MR, and the marginal costs of production and distribution, MC_Q, *before* advertising costs:

$$\frac{Marginal\ Revenue\ Derived}{from\ Advertising} = \frac{Marginal}{Revenue} - \frac{Marginal\ Cost}{of\ Output} \quad \textbf{(11.3)}$$

$$MR_A = MR - MC_Q.$$

The marginal cost of advertising, again expressed in terms of the marginal cost of selling one additional unit of output, can be written:

$$Marginal\ Cost\ of\ Advertising = \frac{Change\ in\ Advertising\ Expenditures}{One\ Unit\ Change\ in\ Demand},$$

$$MC_A = \frac{\Delta Advertising\ Expenditures}{\Delta Demand} = \frac{\Delta Ad}{\Delta Q}. \quad \textbf{(11.4)}$$

The optimal level of advertising is found where:

$$\frac{Marginal\ Revenue\ Derived}{from\ Advertising} = \frac{Marginal\ Cost}{of\ Advertising},$$

$$MR - MC_Q = \frac{\Delta Advertising\ Expenditures}{\Delta Demand},$$

$$MR_A = MC_A.$$

To illustrate, suppose that output in an individual line of business provides a profit contribution before advertising expenses of \$2,500 per unit. The net marginal revenue derived from advertising that expands demand by one unit is \$2,500. Marginal advertising and promotional expenditures up to this \$2,500 level could then be justified. If one more unit of demand could be generated with an additional \$1,000 in advertising expenditures, this additional advertising would be warranted because it generates an additional profit contribution of \$1,500. In contrast, if an additional advertising expenditure of \$3,000 were necessary to expand demand by one unit, the additional advertising expenditure would reduce firm profits and would not be justified.

In general, it will pay to expand advertising expenditures so long as $MR_A > MC_A$. Since the marginal profit derived from advertising is:

$$M\pi_A = MR_A - MC_A, \tag{11.5}$$

the optimal level of advertising occurs at the point where

$$M\pi_A = 0.$$

This relation is illustrated in Figure 11.7. As long as $MR_A > MC_A$, $M\pi_A > 0$, and it will pay to expand the level of advertising. Conversely, if $MR_A < MC_A$, then $M\pi_A < 0$, and it will pay to reduce the level of advertising expenditures. The optimal level of advertising is achieved when $MR_A = MC_A$, and $M\pi_A = 0$.

AN EXAMPLE OF OPTIMAL ADVERTISING

The effect of advertising on the optimal price/output combination can be further illustrated with a more detailed example. Suppose that Consumer Products, Inc., has a new prescription ointment called *Regain* that can be used to restore hair loss due to male pattern baldness in some patients. Currently, *Regain* is marketed through doctors without any consumer advertising. Given the newness of the product, demand for *Regain* is expected to increase rapidly following the initiation of consumer advertising. Samantha

---

Figure 11.7

OPTIMAL LEVEL OF ADVERTISING

A firm will expand the level of advertising up to the point where the net marginal revenue generated just equals the marginal cost of advertising.

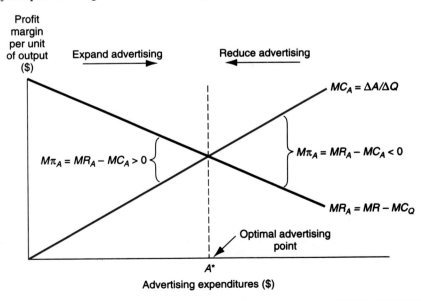

Stevens, an ad executive with the McMann & Tate Advertising Agency, projects that demand would double following the start of a $500,000 per month media advertising campaign developed by the agency. To illustrate the profit impact of the proposed television advertising campaign, it is necessary to identify the projected effect on demand and revenue relations.

Current monthly demand for the product is described by the following expressions:

$$Q = 25,000 - 100P,$$

or

$$P = \$250 - \$0.01Q.$$

This market demand implies total and marginal revenue functions of:

$$TR = P \times Q = \$250Q - \$0.01Q^2,$$

$$MR = \Delta TR/\Delta Q = \$250 - \$0.02Q.$$

Assume total and marginal costs are given by the expressions

$$TC = \$250,000 + \$50Q,$$

$$MC = \Delta TC/\Delta Q = \$50.$$

The optimal price/output combination is found by setting $MR = MC$ and solving for Q. Since marginal costs are constant at $50 per unit, the pre-advertising optimal activity level for *Regain* is

$$MR = MC$$

$$\$250 - \$0.02Q = \$50,$$

$$0.02Q = 200,$$

$$Q = 10,000,$$

and,

$$P = \$250 - \$0.01Q$$
$$= \$250 - \$0.01(10,000)$$
$$= \$150.$$

$$\pi = TR - TC$$
$$= \$250(10,000) - \$0.01(10,000^2) - \$250,000 - \$50(10,000)$$
$$= \$750,000 \text{ per month.}$$

Following a 100% advertising-inspired increase in demand, the new monthly demand relations for *Regain* are

$$Q = 2(25,000 - 100P)$$
$$= 50,000 - 200P,$$

or

$$P = \$250 - \$0.005Q.$$

This new advertising-induced market demand implies new total and marginal revenue functions of

$$TR = \$250Q - \$0.005Q^2,$$

$$MR = \$250 - \$0.01Q.$$

The new optimal price/output combination is found by setting the new $MR = MC$ and solving for Q. Since marginal costs remain constant at \$50 per unit, the new optimal activity level for *Regain* is

$$MR = MC$$

$$\$250 - \$0.01Q = \$50,$$

$$0.01Q = 200,$$

$$Q = 20{,}000,$$

and,

$$P = \$250 - \$0.005Q,$$

$$= \$250 - \$0.005(20{,}000),$$

$$= \$150.$$

$$\pi = TR - TC,$$

$$= \$250(20{,}000) - \$0.005(20{,}000^2) - \$250{,}000$$
$$- \$50(20{,}000) - \$500{,}000,$$

$$= \$1{,}250{,}000 \text{ per month.}$$

Notice that sales have doubled from 10,000 to 20,000 at the \$150 price. The effect on profits is dramatic, rising from \$750,000 to \$1.25 million, even after accounting for the additional \$500,000 in media expenditures. Therefore, the new advertising campaign appears fully warranted. In fact, given the \$1 million in profits that are generated by a doubling in unit sales at a price of \$150, Consumer Products would be willing to pay up to that full amount to double sales. From this perspective, the \$500,000 price charge for the advertising campaign represents a relative bargain. The profit implications of other forms of advertising, or other types of nonprice competition, can be measured in a similar fashion.

Market Structure Measurement

To formulate an effective competitive strategy, managers must accurately assess the current competitive environment for actual and potential products. Data gathered by the federal government, private market research firms, and trade associations are often useful for this purpose. This section shows the types of market structure data available from public sources and explains why they are important for decision-making purposes.

HOW ARE ECONOMIC MARKETS MEASURED?

An economic market consists of all individuals and firms willing and able to buy or sell competing products during a given period. The key criterion in identifying competing products is similarity in use. Precise determination of whether a specific good is a distinct economic product involves an evaluation of cross-price elasticities for broad classes of goods. When cross-price elasticities are large and positive, goods are substitutes for each other and can be thought of as competing products in a single market. Conversely, large negative cross-price elasticities indicate complementary products. Complementary products produced by a single firm must be evaluated as a single product line serving the same market. If complementary products are produced by other companies, evaluating the potential of a given product line involves incorporating exogenous influences beyond the firm's control. When cross-price elasticities are near zero, goods are in separate economic markets and can be separately analyzed as serving distinct consumer needs. Therefore, using cross-price elasticity criteria to desegregate the firm's overall product line into its distinct economic markets is an important task confronting managers.

To identify relevant economic markets and define their characteristics, firms in the United States make extensive use of economic data collected by the Bureau of the Census of the U.S. Department of Commerce. Because these data provide valuable information on economic activity across the broad spectrum of U.S. industry, it is worthwhile to briefly consider the method and scope of the economic censuses.

THE ECONOMIC CENSUSES

Economic Censuses
Data collected by the U.S. Department of Commerce that provide a comprehensive statistical profile of large segments of the U.S. economy.

Economic censuses provide a comprehensive statistical profile of large segments of the national economy. They are taken at five-year intervals during years ending with the digits 2 and 7—for example, 1987, 1992, 1997, 2002, and so on. Included are censuses of manufacturing, retail and wholesale trade, services, minerals, and construction. In 1987, for example, sectors covered by the economic censuses accounted for roughly 70% of total economic activity originating in the private sector. Principal industry groups not covered are finance, insurance, real estate, agriculture, forestry, communications, public utilities, and transportation. However, limited transportation-related information is collected, including the distance that commodities are shipped and the type of transport employed.

Economic censuses are the primary source of data concerning changes in the number and size distribution of competitors, output, and employment in the economy. They are used extensively by the government in compiling national income accounts and as a basis for current surveys of industrial production, productivity, and prices. Census data are also used extensively by government agencies in setting public policy and monitoring economic programs. Manufacturers and distributors rely on census data to analyze current and potential markets. The censuses provide data for demand and cost forecasting; market penetration analysis; layout of sales territories; allocation of advertising budgets; and locations of plants, warehouses, and retail outlets. Trade and professional associations rely on census information to learn about changes in the number, size, and geographic dispersion of firms in their industry. State and local governments and chambers of commerce use census data to assess the business climate, as well as to gauge the success of programs designed to increase business investment and employment opportunities in local areas.

A further important characteristic of the economic censuses is their coverage of geographic trends. Recent *Census of Manufacturers* surveys measure industrial activity for legally constituted geographic units such as states, counties, and cities. Manufacturing activity levels are also provided on hundreds of Standard Metropolitan Statistical Areas (SMSAs). SMSAs are integrated economic and social units with a large volume of daily travel and communication between the central city (having 50,000 or more population) and outlying areas. Each SMSA consists of one whole county or more and may include both industrialized counties and adjoining counties that are largely residential in character. Detail for various industries is shown at the SMSA level if data for individual companies would not be disclosed and if the industry has at least 250 employees.

In addition to being a comprehensive source of information on economic activity, census data have the compelling virtues of easy access and widespread availability. Census reports can be purchased directly from the Government Printing Office at modest cost or can be consulted free of charge at most major public and college libraries. In addition, census data and reports are often republished and distributed by trade associations, business magazines, and newspapers.

THE CENSUS CLASSIFICATION SYSTEM

Census data are collected at the establishment level—that is, at a single physical location engaged in a specific line of business. The establishment level is best suited for obtaining direct measures of output and inputs such as labor, materials, capital, and so on. It is also a useful level of aggregation for providing detailed industry and geographic tabulations. In contrast, statistics measuring overall income and balance sheet data are best collected at the company or enterprise level. Enterprise statistics on income and balance sheet data are made available to the public by the Internal Revenue Service in its *Statistics of Income* and by the Federal Trade Commission in its *Quarterly Financial Report for Manufacturing, Mining and Trade.*

The census classification of individual establishments by sector, industry group, industry, and products is called the Standard Industrial Classification (SIC) system. Table 11.1 shows the first step in this process and illustrates how the entire scope of economic activity is subdivided into sectors described by two-digit classifications. Below the two-digit major group or sector level, the SIC system proceeds to desegregated levels of increasingly narrowly defined activity. Currently, the SIC system proceeds from very general two-digit industry groups to very specific seven-digit product classifications. To illustrate, Table 11.2 shows the breakdown that occurs as one moves from the two-digit "food and kindred products" major group to the seven-digit "canned evaporated milk"

Table 11.1	**STANDARD INDUSTRIAL CLASSIFICATION OF ECONOMIC ACTIVITY**	

SECTOR	TWO-DIGIT SIC CODES
Agriculture, Forestry, and Fisheries	01–09
Mining	10–14
Contract Construction	15–17
Manufacturing	20–39
Transportation; Communication; Electric, Gas, and Sanitary Services	40–49
Wholesale and Retail Trade	50–59
Finance, Insurance, and Real Estate	60–67
Services	70–89
Public Administration	91–97
Nonclassifiable Establishments	99

product category. Economists generally agree that four-digit-level classifications correspond quite closely with the economic definition of a market. Establishments grouped at the four-digit level produce products that are ready substitutes for one another and thus function as competitors. Managers who analyze census data to learn about the number and size distribution of actual and potential competitors focus their attention primarily on data provided at the four-digit level. For this reason, attention is focused on four-digit-level concentration data in discussions of market structure.

Census Measures of Market Concentration

Market structure falls along the continuum from perfect competition to monopoly. Where an industry falls along this continuum is important for firms currently in the industry and for those contemplating entry. Price/output strategies vary markedly depending on the market structure encountered. Profit rates are also affected by the level of competitive pressures. Among the attributes describing market structure, perhaps the

Table 11.2	**CENSUS CLASSIFICATION EXAMPLE**	

DIGIT LEVEL	NUMBER OF CLASSIFICATIONS	EXAMPLE SIC CODE	DESCRIPTION
Two	20	20	Food and Kindred Products
Three	144	202	Dairy Products
Four	452	2023	Condensed and Evaporated Milk Industry
Five	1,500	20232	Canned Milk
Six			(Not currently utilized)
Seven	13,000	2023212	Canned Evaporated Milk

number and size distribution of competitors are most important. These data must be carefully considered in managerial decision making.

CONCENTRATION RATIOS

In addition to those directly engaged in business, both government and the public share an interest in the size distribution of firms. A small number of competitors can sometimes have direct implications for regulation and antitrust policy. Thus, considerable public resources are devoted to monitoring both the size distribution and economic performance of firms in several important sectors of the economy. Data that describe these characteristics of the U.S. economy are regularly compiled and circulated in economic census reports published by the Department of Commerce. Among those sectors covered by the economic censuses, manufacturing is clearly the largest, accounting for approximately 20% of aggregate economic activity in the United States. Firm sizes in manufacturing are also much larger than in other major sectors such as retail and wholesale trade, construction, legal and medical services, and so on. Among the more than 16 million business enterprises in the United States, manufacturing is the domain of the large corporation. Thus, the manufacturing sector provides an interesting basis for considering data that are available on the size distribution of firms.

> **Concentration Ratios**
> Data in the Census of Manufacturers that show the percentage market share held by an industry's leading firms.

Table 11.3 shows numbers of competitors, industry sales, and leading-firm market share data for a small sample of four-digit industries taken from a recent *Census of Manufacturers*. As is generally the case, leading-firm market shares are calculated from sales data for the top four or eight firms in an industry. These market share data are called **concentration ratios** because they measure the percentage market share held by (concentrated in) an industry's top four (CR_4) or eight (CR_8) firms. When concentration ratios are low, industries tend to be made up of many firms and competition tends to be vigorous. Industries in which the four leading firms are responsible for less than 20% of total industry sales (i.e., $CR_4 < 20$) are highly competitive and approximate the perfect competition model. On the other hand, when concentration ratios are high, leading firms dominate following firms in terms of size, and leading firms may have more potential for pricing flexibility and economic profits. Industries in which the four leading firms control more than 80% of total industry sales (i.e., $CR_4 > 80$) are highly concentrated, and market structure can tend toward monopoly. However, industries with a $CR_4 < 20$ or $CR_4 > 80$ are quite rare. Three-quarters of all manufacturing activity takes place in industries with concentration ratios falling in the range $20 \leq CR_4 \leq 80$. In terms of relative importance, market structures that can be described as monopolistically competitive are much more common than perfect competition or monopoly.

LIMITATIONS OF CENSUS CONCENTRATION RATIOS

Despite the obvious attraction of census concentration ratio data as a useful source of information on the number and size distribution of current competitors, it is prudent to remain cautious in their use and interpretation. Various limitations of concentration ratio data are important in terms of both business and public policy considerations. By not

Table 11.3

A REPRESENTATIVE SAMPLE OF FOUR-DIGIT CENSUS INDUSTRIES

STANDARD INDUSTRIAL CLASSIFICATION (SIC) CODE	DESCRIPTION	NUMBER OF FIRMS	INDUSTRY SALES (MILLIONS OF DOLLARS)	MARKET SHARES (%)	
				TOP FOUR FIRMS (CR_4)	TOP EIGHT FIRMS (CR_8)
2011	Meat Packing Plants	1,328	$5,266.9	32	50
2043	Cereal Breakfast Foods	33	6,565.7	87	99
2047	Dog, Cat, and Other Pet Food	130	5,069.3	61	78
2067	Chewing Gum	8	1,090.3	96	100
2095	Roasted Coffee	110	6,400.6	66	78
2371	Fur Goods	380	422.6	16	24
2387	Apparel Belts	263	627.8	21	31
2621	Paper Mills	122	28,918.0	33	50
2711	Newspapers	7,473	31,850.1	25	39
3425	Handsaws and Saw Blades	128	674.9	45	61
3711	Motor Vehicles and Car Bodies	352	$133,345.6	90	95
3721	Aircraft	137	39,092.7	72	92
3732	Boat Building and Repairing	2,108	5,352.5	33	41
3995	Burial Caskets	213	839.0	59	66

Data Source: U.S. Department of Commerce, Bureau of the Census, 1987 *Census of Manufactures: Concentration Ratios in Manufacturing* (Washington, D.C.: U.S. Government Printing Office, 1988).

recognizing these limitations, one might make incorrect judgments concerning market structure when relying on concentration ratio information.

A major drawback of concentration ratio data relates to the timing of their availability. It typically takes more than *five years* for detailed concentration ratio data to become widely available. Data for 1992 were not available until mid-1997; data for 1997 will not become available until mid-2002. In many fast-moving markets, these data are simply obsolete before they are published. Even in less dynamic markets, they provide only an imperfect guide to managerial decision making. As a result, most managers supplement census information with more current data available from market research firms.

A further important weakness of census concentration ratio data pertains to their coverage. Concentration data ignore domestic sales by foreign competitors (imports) as well as exports by domestic firms. Only data on domestic sales from *domestic production,* not total domestic sales, are reported. This means, for example, that if foreign imports have a market share of 25%, the four leading domestic automobile manufacturers account for 67.5% (= 90% of 75%) of total U.S. foreign plus domestic car sales, rather than the 90%, as Table 11.3 suggests. For industries in which import competition is important, concentration ratios significantly overstate the relative importance of leading domestic firms. Concentration ratios also overstate market power for several industries in which increasing foreign competition has been responsible for the liquidation or merger of many smaller domestic firms with older, less efficient production facilities. Despite reduced numbers of domestic firms and the consequent rise in concentration, an increase in foreign competition often makes affected industries more efficient and more competitive rather than less so. The impact of foreign competition is important in many industries, but it is particularly so in manufacturing industries such as apparel, steel, automobiles, cameras, copiers, motorcycles, and television sets.

Another limitation of concentration ratio data is that they are *national totals,* whereas a relevant economic market may be national, regional, or local in scope. If high transportation costs or other product characteristics keep markets regional or local rather than national in scope, concentration ratios can significantly understate the relative importance of leading firms. For example, the leading firm in many metropolitan newspaper markets often accounts for 90% or more of total market advertising and subscription revenues. Thus, a national CR_4 level for newspapers of 25% in 1987 significantly understates local market power in that industry. Whereas national concentration ratios in the 25% range usually suggest a highly competitive market structure, the local or regional character of some markets can make national concentration figures meaningless. Other examples of products with local or regional rather than national markets include milk, bread and bakery products, commercial printing, and ready-mix concrete.

Additional problems occur because concentration ratios provide an imperfect view of market structure by including only firms that are *currently active* in a particular industry. Recall that an economic market includes all firms willing and able to sell an identifiable product. Besides firms currently active in an industry, this includes those that can be regarded as likely potential entrants. Often the mere presence of one or more potential entrants constitutes a sufficient threat to force competitive market behavior in industries with only a handful of established competitors. Major retailers such as Wal-Mart, Kmart, and Sears, for example, use their positions as potential entrants into manufacturing to obtain attractive prices on a wide range of private-label merchandise such as clothing, lawn mowers, washing machines, and so on.

Finally, considering concentration ratio data in isolation can lead to deceptive conclusions regarding the vigor of competition in an industry because the degree of competitiveness appears in more than one dimension. Concentration ratios measure only one element of market structure; other elements include the market shares of individual firms, barriers to entry or exit, vertical integration, and so on. Under certain circumstances, even a very few large competitors can compete vigorously. Although concentration ratios are helpful indicators of the relative importance of leading firms and perhaps the potential for market power, it must be remembered that a high level of concentration does not necessarily imply a lack of competition. In some instances, *competition among the few can be vigorous.* In addition to considering the number and size distribution of competitors as measured by concentration, firms must judge the competitive environment in light of foreign competition, transportation costs, regional product differences, likely potential entrants, advertising, customer loyalty, research and development, demand growth, and economies of scale in production, among other factors, to

| *Corporate Dinosaurs or Go-Go Goliaths?* | MANAGERIAL APPLICATION 11.3 |

In 1963, a prestigious series of lectures was held at Columbia University's business school, and the speaker was arguably America's most renowned chief executive. The speaker talked about the difficulty successful corporations face in maintaining their success. Of the 25 largest U.S. industrial corporations in 1900, only two remained in that select company some 60 years later. One was General Electric Co. and the other a predecessor of U.S. Steel (now USX). Fully 23 out of 25 corporate giants had failed, been merged out of existence, or simply shrunk in size. "Figures like these," said the executive, "help to remind us that corporations are expendable and that success—at best—is an impermanent achievement which can always slip out of hand." The speaker? Thomas J. Watson Jr., chairman of IBM.

In 1963, IBM ruled the emerging computer business and was about to launch its renowned 360 family of computers. Watson could not have dreamed he was foreseeing his own company's demise. Neither could he have imagined the fading of two other corporate giants, General Motors and Sears Roebuck. GM was then suspected of trying to hold its market share *down,* so as not to invite antitrust scrutiny. Sears completely dominated retailing, selling more merchandise than its next four rivals combined. Had professional investors ranked the 1960s companies most likely to succeed, these three might well have headed the list. Yet in the early 1990s, each of them recorded billions of dollars in operating losses. As a result, each underwent a comprehensive management shakeup that led to replacement of its chairman and chief executive officer, and undertook massive corporate restructuring. In the world of big business, these companies are sometimes referred to as dinosaurs. While not yet extinct, IBM, GM, and Sears are, to varying degrees, onetime dominant creatures in the midst of a precipitous long-term decline. Incredibly, they all went lame in a remarkably similar way: through arrogance and bureaucracy each lost touch with the customer.

At the same time, some market leaders have found a simple formula to continued success:

- Use customers' input to help design better products.
- Make your own products obsolete before your competitors do.

- Decentralize authority to make quick decisions.
- Improve employee skills through training.
- Cut costs.

None of these strategies is new or surprising, but the mantra of staying close to the customer is a skill too soon forgotten in many organizations. In fact, the histories of IBM, GM, Sears, and other corporate dinosaurs lead one to ask if enormous success inevitably breeds failure.

Everyone is plainly aware of the advantages of large firm size, including purchasing muscle, easy access to financing, and deep managerial talent. Less commonly perceived are the ruinous problems of complacency and bureaucracy that slow reaction time. While adroit management ought to be able to cope with success, evidence often suggests otherwise. IBM sought to protect its mainframe turf by ignoring customer demands for powerful desktop computing. GM failed to answer customer calls for high mileage cars that are fun to drive, and Sears ignored customer demands for everyday low prices. By opening the door to competitors, each of them invited a loss in market share from which they can never fully recover. IBM has lost forever its claim to number one in the computing and software industries. Cisco, Compaq, Dell, Gateway, Microsoft, and a host of others are here to stay. GM faces reinvigorated challengers in Ford, Chrysler, and the imports. Sears has been outstripped by Wal-Mart, Kmart, and a legion of strong regional retailers.

Based upon profitability, the 5 largest companies in the U.S. today are the ever present GE, Exxon Corp., Philip Morris Co. Inc., GM, and IBM. Looking at market values and *future* profits, the 5 largest companies are GE, Coca-Cola Co., Exxon Corp., Intel Corp., and Microsoft. Thus, investors are betting that giants like GE and Exxon will grow and prosper, while goliaths like Philip Morris, GM and IBM may not. The next time someone suggests that large size is all you need for success in business, remind them about corporate dinosaurs.

See: Carol J. Loomis, "Dinosaurs?," *Fortune,* May 3, 1993, 36; and David Whitford, "Sale of the Century," *Fortune,* February 17, 1997, 92-100.

make accurate pricing and output decisions. All of these features of markets constitute important elements of market structure.

Competitive Strategy in Monopolistic Competition and Oligopoly Markets

Few real-world markets exactly fit the perfectly competitive model from economic theory, nor do many enjoy the full profit potential of unchecked monopoly. Most industries and lines of business offer some blend of competition and monopoly; they represent business opportunities in imperfectly competitive markets. Developing and implementing an effective competitive strategy in imperfectly competitive markets involves a never-ending search for uniquely attractive products. Not all industries offer the same potential for sustained profitability; not all firms are equally capable of exploiting the profit potential that is available.

COMPETITIVE STRATEGY IN IMPERFECTLY COMPETITIVE MARKETS

It is always helpful to consider the number and size distribution of competitors, degree of product differentiation, level of information available in the marketplace, and conditions of entry when attempting to define market structure. Unfortunately, these and other readily obtained data are seldom definitive. Conditions of entry and exit are subtle and dynamic, as is the role of unseen potential entrants. All of this contributes to the difficulty of correctly assessing the profit potential of current products or prospective lines of business.

Rather than consider simply what is, effective managers must contemplate what might be. This is especially true when seeking to develop an effective competitive strategy. An effective competitive strategy in imperfectly competitive markets must be founded on the firm's **competitive advantage.** A competitive advantage is a unique or rare ability to create, distribute, or service products valued by customers. It is the business-world analog to what economists call **comparative advantage,** or when one nation or region of the country is better suited to the production of one product than to the production of some other product. For example, when compared with the United States and Canada, Mexico enjoys a relative abundance of raw materials and cheap labor. As such, Mexico is in a relatively good position to export agricultural products, oil, and finished goods that require unskilled labor to the U.S. and Canadian market. At the same time, United States and Canada enjoy a relative abundance of highly educated people, capital goods, and investment resources. Therefore, the United States and Canada are in a relatively good position to export machine tools, computer equipment, education, and professional services to Mexico.

An effective competitive strategy in imperfectly competitive markets grows out of a sophisticated understanding of the rules of competition in a given line of business or industry. The ultimate aim of this strategy is to cope with or, better still, change those

Competitive Advantage
A unique or rare ability to create, distribute, or service products valued by customers.

Comparative Advantage
When one nation or region of the country is better suited to the production of one product than to the production of some other product.

rules in the company's favor. To do so, managers must understand and contend with the rivalry among existing competitors, entry of new rivals, threat of substitutes, bargaining power of suppliers, and the bargaining power of buyers. Just as all industries are not alike in terms of their inherent profit potential, all firms are not alike in terms of their capacity to exploit available opportunities. In the business world, long-lasting above-normal rates of return require a sustainable competitive advantage that, by definition, cannot be easily duplicated.

Nike's use of basketball superstar Michael Jordan as the focal point of an extensive media advertising and product development campaign during the early 1990s is an interesting case. Like other highly successful and innovative advertising campaigns, the Nike promotion captured the imagination of consumers and put competitors Reebok, L.A. Gear, and others at a distinct disadvantage. After all, there is only one Michael Jordan. Nike sales surged as consumers got caught up in the enthusiasm of Jordan's amazing basketball prowess, and the excitement generated as the Jordan-led Chicago Bulls marched to three straight NBA championships. However, this success proved to be rather short-lived, as Jordan's popularity and Nike sales plummeted following Jordan's surprise retirement from basketball during the summer of 1993. A subsequent promotion by Reebok, the second largest basketball shoe manufacturer in America, caught consumers' interest with the "Shaq Attack," an extensive media promotion and product development strategy built around NBA star Shaquille O'Neal. The risks of star-based advertising as an effective form of nonprice competition in the nondurable consumer products industries became even more readily apparent following the well documented failure of *Pepsi's* sponsorship of musical legend Michael Jackson during the mid-1990s. *Pepsi* not only lost the millions of dollars it spent on an obviously ineffective Michael Jackson-based advertising campaign, but it also lost valuable market share to rival *Coca-Cola.* Only time will tell if *Pepsi's* aging, but still popular, "Get Stuf" advertising campaign proves successful in displacing *Coca-Cola* as the most popular soft drink of the 1990s.

This is not to suggest that advertising and other nonprice methods of competition have not been used to great advantage by many successful firms in imperfectly competitive markets. In fact, these techniques are often a primary force in developing a strong basis for product differentiation. Table 11.4 summarizes major characteristics typical of the monopolistic competition and oligopoly market structures. To develop an effective competitive strategy, it is necessary to assess the degree to which an individual industry or line of business embodies elements of each of these market structures. Although the probability of successful entry is higher in monopolistically competitive markets, only difficult-to-enter oligopoly markets hold the potential for long-lasting above-normal returns.

In sum, firms in imperfectly competitive markets have the potential to earn economic profits in the long run only to the extent that they impart a valuable degree of uniqueness to the goods or services provided. Success, measured in terms of above-normal rates of return, requires a comparative advantage in production, distribution, or marketing that cannot easily be copied. That such success is difficult to achieve and is often rather fleeting is obvious when one considers the most profitable companies in America.

Table 11.4

SUMMARY OF MONOPOLISTIC COMPETITION AND OLIGOPOLY (OLIGOPSONY) MARKET-STRUCTURE CHARACTERISTICS

	MONOPOLISTIC COMPETITION	OLIGOPOLY
Number of actual or potential competitors	Many sellers	Few sellers whose decisions are directly related to those of competitors.
Product differentiation	Consumers perceive differences among the products of various competitors.	High or low, depending on entry and exit conditions.
Information	Low-cost information on price and product quality.	Restricted access to price and product-quality information; cost and other data are often proprietary.
Conditions of entry and exit	Easy entry and exit	High entry or exit barriers because of economies of scale, capital requirements, advertising, research and development costs, or other factors.
Profit potential	Economic (above-normal) profits in short run only; normal profit in long run.	Potential for economic (above-normal) profits in both short and long run.
Examples	Clothing, consumer financial services, professional services, restaurants.	Automobiles, bottled and canned soft drinks, investment banking, long-distance telephone service, pharmaceuticals.

THE MOST PROFITABLE COMPANIES IN AMERICA

Table 11.5 shows the profitability of *Forbes'* most profitable firms in American industry. Like Table 11.5, which shows business profit rates for a sample of top-performing large firms, these data demonstrate that market leaders earn truly extraordinary profits. In industries that produce distinctive goods and services, and in others that offer fairly mundane products, the most profitable firms in America earn an average rate of return on assets that is a whopping 252.3% of all-industry norms. This means that the most profitable firm in a typical industry earns roughly 24.7% on assets, or 2.52 times the five-year median ROA of 9.8% per year for *Forbes'* sample of 1,340 large and highly successful U.S. companies. Notice that this five-year median profit rate, which minimizes the effects of significant losses due to corporate restructuring, is very close to the long-term average return on equity (ROE) of 9% to 10% for all companies.

Using the ROA measure of business profits, it is obvious that the most profitable companies in America are able to outpace industry norms by a significant margin. Some of this variation in business profits represents the influence of risk premiums necessary to compensate investors if one business is inherently riskier than another. In the prescription pharmaceuticals industry, for example, hoped-for discoveries of effective therapies for important diseases are often a long-shot at best. However, apart from such risks, the observed intraindustry variation in profitability makes it clear that many firms earn significant economic profits or experience meaningful economic losses at any given point in time. As in perfectly competitive industries, some above-normal returns in monopolistically competitive and oligopoly markets also reflect temporary good fortune due to unexpected changes in industry demand or cost conditions, and/or profits

Table 11.5	THE RELATIVE PROFITABILITY OF TOP-PERFORMING COMPANIES ACROSS AMERICA			
INDUSTRY	TOP-PERFORMING COMPANIES	RETURN ON ASSETS (ROA) 5-YEAR AVG.	INDUSTRY ROA 5-YEAR MEDIAN	RELATIVE PROFITABILITY
Advertising	Omnicom	19.4%	12.3%	157.7%
Aerospace & Defense	General Dynamics	38.3%	11.0%	348.2%
Air Freight	Air Express International	20.4%	8.6%	237.2%
Airlines	Southwest Airlines	9.6%	3.7%	259.5%
Apparel	Gap	28.3%	11.8%	239.8%
Apparel & Shoes	Jones Apparel Group	34.1%	10.8%	315.7%
Appliances	Sunbeam	12.9%	7.5%	172.0%
Automobiles & Trucks	Chrysler	16.1%	6.4%	251.6%
Automotive Parts	Bandag	22.8%	12.1%	188.4%
Beverages	Coca-Cola	42.0%	10.7%	392.5%
Broadcasting & Cable	King World Productions	25.7%	4.7%	546.8%
Brokerage & Commodity	Charles Schwab	27.7%	12.6%	219.8%
Business Services	Ceridian	26.3%	11.1%	236.9%
Business Supplies	Viking Office Prods.	27.0%	12.5%	216.0%
Cement & Gypsum	Vulcan Materials	13.5%	6.4%	210.9%
Chemicals-Diversified	FMC	18.8%	12.3%	152.8%
Chemicals-Specialized	Cytec Industries	47.1%	12.8%	368.0%
Commercial Builders	Fluor	16.8%	8.1%	207.4%
Computer Peripherals & Equipment	Cisco Systems	61.7%	17.9%	344.7%
Computer Software	Oracle	42.1%	19.8%	212.6%
Computer Systems	Gateway 2000	50.6%	7.4%	683.8%
Consumer Electronics	Circuit City Stores	20.1%	9.5%	211.6%
Department Stores	Kohl's	19.0%	9.4%	202.1%
Drug & Discount	Dollar General	25.4%	9.1%	279.1%
Drugs	Schering-Plough	41.8%	14.3%	292.3%
Electric Utilities: North Central	DPL	8.3%	6.5%	127.7%
Electric Utilities: Northeast	Consolidated Edison	8.0%	6.4%	125.0%
Electric Utilities: South Central	Houston Industries	8.3%	6.9%	120.3%
Electric Utilities: Southeast	TECO Energy	7.9%	6.6%	119.7%
Electric Utilities: Western	Enova	7.7%	6.3%	122.2%
Electrical Equipment	Andrew	19.7%	11.4%	172.8%
Environmental & Waste	Thermo Electron	9.4%	8.1%	116.0%
Food Processors	Quaker Oats	34.5%	9.8%	352.0%
Food Wholesalers	Richfood Holding	14.1%	7.9%	178.5%
Gas Distributors	MCN	8.9%	7.6%	117.1%
Gas Products & Pipelines	Williams Cos.	19.8%	7.5%	264.0%
Health Care Services	Mid Atlantic Medical	51.9%	10.9%	476.1%
Heavy Equipment	AGCO	21.9%	12.0%	182.5%
Home Furnishings	Newell Co.	17.2%	9.6%	179.2%
Home Improvement	Home Depot	16.9%	10.1%	167.3%
Home Shopping	CUC International	23.9%	11.3%	211.5%
Hotels & Gaming	Carnival	15.0%	8.7%	172.4%

continued

continued

INDUSTRY	TOP-PERFORMING COMPANIES	RETURN ON ASSETS (ROA) 5-YEAR AVG.	INDUSTRY ROA 5-YEAR MEDIAN	RELATIVE PROFITABILITY
Industrial Services	Cintas	15.8%	9.1%	173.6%
Insurance Services	Marsh & McLennan	23.1%	16.2%	142.6%
Insurance: Diversified	Horace Mann	15.2%	12.9%	117.8%
Insurance: Life & Health	UICI	26.4%	12.9%	204.7%
Insurance: Property & Casualty	Commerce Group, Inc.	31.7%	11.3%	280.5%
Integrated Gas	Questar	8.8%	5.4%	163.0%
International Oils	Exxon	10.3%	8.6%	119.8%
Medical Supplies	Medtronic	27.3%	13.9%	196.4%
Movies	Walt Disney	14.5%	7.4%	195.9%
Multinational Banks	JP Morgan & Co.	11.3%	9.4%	120.2%
Mutual Fund Management	Franklin Resources	23.7%	8.7%	272.4%
Nonferrous Metals	Phelps Dodge	15.3%	8.5%	180.0%
Oilfield Services	Smith International	15.8%	7.5%	210.7%
Other Construction Materials	Owens Corning	82.9%	8.7%	952.9%
Other Energy	Holly Corp	16.0%	5.4%	296.3%
Other Industrial Equipment	Nordson	21.8%	11.3%	192.9%
Packaging	Sealed Air	28.1%	8.3%	338.6%
Paper & Lumber	Wilamette Industries	12.3%	7.2%	170.8%
Personal Products	Avon Products	51.5%	13.0%	396.2%
Photography & Toys	Mattel	23.0%	12.6%	182.5%
Publishing	Valassis	43.2%	11.0%	392.7%
Railroads	Illinois Central	13.8%	7.4%	186.5%
Recreation Equipment	Harley-Davidson	21.7%	10.1%	214.9%
Regional Banks	First Tennessee National	18.4%	12.7%	144.9%
Residential Builders	Clayton Homes	16.1%	8.5%	189.4%
Restaurant Chains	Shoney's	29.6%	12.5%	236.8%
Specialty Retailers	CellStar	41.8%	8.4%	497.6%
Steel	Rouge Steel	54.3%	8.4%	646.4%
Supermarkets & Convenience	Kroger	24.5%	9.5%	257.9%
Telecommunications	DSC Communications	17.9%	9.5%	188.4%
Textiles	Unifi	13.0%	6.1%	213.1%
Thrift Institutions	Washington Mutual	15.1%	6.4%	235.9%
Tobacco	UST Inc.	73.9%	11.6%	637.1%
Trucking & Shipping	Landstar System	20.5%	6.8%	301.5%
All Industries		24.7%	9.8%	252.3%

Data Source: "Annual Report on American Industry," *Forbes,* January 13, 1997, 109–183.

due to uniquely productive inputs. Be sure to note that the data shown in Table 11.5 are *five-year averages* that cannot be dismissed as aberrant returns due to occasional good luck. These superior performers clearly are doing something faster, better, or cheaper than the competition.

All of this leads to a fundamentally important question: What are the basic characteristics of a wonderful business? Since it is impossible to plan on being lucky, and it is improbable to expect that uniquely productive inputs will be routinely underpriced, how do managers go about discovering business opportunities with the real potential for above-normal returns?

THE CHARACTERISTICS OF WONDERFUL BUSINESSES

Since 1900, the rate of return on common stocks has averaged roughly 10% per year. Through depressions and economic booms, world wars and periods of peaceful prosperity, and following countless federal, state, and local elections, common stocks have allowed patient investors to double their money every seven years, on average. After accounting for average inflation of roughly 4% per year, common stocks have returned investors roughly 6% per year in inflation-adjusted, or "real," dollars. In real terms, common stocks have allowed patient investors to double their money every 12 years. These 10% nominal and 6% real rates of return reflect the yield that can be expected on the broad cross section of common stock investments. Of course, the challenge to stock-market investors is to identify and invest in superior stocks with the potential to earn in excess of 10% per year. Given the ferocious nature of stock-market competition, it is extraordinarily difficult for investors to consistently earn in excess of market norms. Steady returns of 12% to 15% per year are rare; consistent returns of 15% to 20% are almost unheard of over extended periods, say 15 to 20 years.

As discussed in Chapter 10, 10% per year is also the approximate average business profit rate, when business profits are measured using the ROE or ROA measures. A correspondence between the average ROE and average investor returns is to be expected: firms must generate a 10% profit rate if investors are to earn a 10% rate of return. The challenge to business managers is to identify and invest in lines of business or business opportunities with the potential to earn a minimum 10% rate of return per year, if not more. In the short run, trading skill or luck can increase investor returns just as the use of leverage can unexpectedly increase business profits. In the long run, superior investor and business returns are only possible given superior economic characteristics of invested assets.

An interesting perspective on the characteristics of "wonderful businesses" is given by legendary Wall Street investors T. Rowe Price and Warren E. Buffett. The late T. Rowe Price was founder of Baltimore-based T. Rowe Price and Associates, Inc., one of the largest no-load mutual fund organizations in the United States, and the father of the "growth stock" theory of investing. According to Price, attractive growth stocks have low labor costs, superior research to develop products and new markets, a high rate of return on stockholders' equity (ROE), elevated profit margins, rapid earnings per share (EPS) growth, lack cutthroat competition, and are comparatively immune from regulation. Omaha's Warren E. Buffett, the billionaire head of Berkshire Hathaway, Inc., also looks for companies that have strong franchises and enjoy pricing flexibility, high ROE, high cash flow, owner-oriented management, and predictable earnings that are not natural targets of regulation. Like Price, Buffett has profited enormously through his investments. Buffett's holdings in Berkshire alone were worth in excess of $16 billion in mid-1997.

Table 11.6 offers insight on the basic characteristics of wonderful businesses by showing major common stock holdings of Warren Buffett's Berkshire Hathaway as of mid-1997. For each of Berkshire's major holdings, a variety of financial and operating statistics are reported. With average total assets of $67 billion, these are large capital-intensive companies. More importantly, they display a wise use of assets by virtue of the fact that they report an average ROE of 30.9%, a level of profitability that is well above typical norms. Enhancing the attractiveness of these companies is the fact that they display an average 17.7% annual rate of growth in stockholders' equity. Thus, they can all be described as beneficiaries of high-margin growth. As is often the case, these attractive financial and operating statistics reflect essentially attractive economic characteristics of each company.

Berkshire holds a large stake in The American Express Company, a premier travel and financial services firm that is strategically positioned to benefit from aging baby boomers. The Coca-Cola Company, one of Berkshire's biggest and most successful holdings, typifies the concept of a wonderful business. Coca-Cola enjoys perhaps the world's strongest franchise, owner-oriented management, and a predictable and growing return of more than 55.4% on ROE; also, the company is not subject to price or profit regulation. From the standpoint of being a wonderful business, Coca-Cola is clearly the "real thing." Newspapers, banks, and cable TV companies, such as Gannett, The Washington Post Company, Wells Fargo & Company, and the Walt Disney Company, which translate immense economies of scale in production into dominating competitive advantages, also fit Buffett's criteria for wonderful businesses. In the case of the Federal Home Loan Mortgage Corporation, commonly referred to as Freddie Mac, a government charter that confers gigantic advantages is a dependable source of above-normal returns. In the cases of Gillette and Salomon, above-normal returns stem from unique products that are designed and executed by extraordinarily capable management.

To apply Price's and Buffett's investment criteria successfully, business managers and investors must be sensitive to the fundamental economic and demographic trends of the 1990s. Perhaps the most obvious of these is the aging of the population. Health-care demands will continue to soar. In recognition of the fact, investors have bid up the shares of companies offering prescription drugs, health care, and health-care cost containment (e.g., home health agencies). Perhaps less obvious is that an aging and increasingly wealthy population will save growing amounts for their children's education and retirement. This bodes well for mutual fund operators, insurance companies, and other firms that offer financial services.

As the overall population continues to enjoy growing income, spending on leisure activities is apt to grow; companies that offer distinctive goods and services in this area will do well. Helping well-heeled customers have fun has always been a good business. Productivity enhancement to combat economic stagnation is also likely to be a major thrust of the 1990s. In this area, it is perhaps easier to pick likely beneficiaries of emerging technologies than it is to chart the future course of technical advance. For example, catalog retailers, long-distance and cellular phone companies, and credit card providers are all major beneficiaries of the rapid pace of advance in computer and information technology. Similarly, major broadcasters, cable TV companies, movie makers, and

Table 11.6

FINANCIAL AND OPERATING STATISTICS FOR WARREN BUFFETT'S SAMPLE OF WONDERFUL COMPANIES

Company Name	Industry Name	Net Profit	Net Worth	Sales	Total Assets	Return on Equity (ROE)	Return on Sales (Profit Margin)	Return on Assets (ROA)	Expected Growth in Net Worth
American Express	Financial Services	$1,564.0	$8,220.0	$15,841.0	$107,405.0	19.0%	9.9%	1.5%	6.0%
Coca-Cola	Soft Drinks	2,986.0	5,392.0	18,018.0	15,041.0	55.4%	16.6%	19.9%	8.5%
Disney (Walt)	Entertainment	1,343.6	6,650.8	12,112.0	14,605.8	20.2%	11.1%	9.2%	
Federal Home Loan Mortgage	Thrift	1091.0	5,863.0	NA	137,181.0	18.6%	NA	0.8%	74.5%
Federal National Mortgage	Thrift	2,144.0	10,959.0	NA	316,550.0	19.6%	NA	0.7%	
Gannett	Newspaper	477.3	2,145.6	4,006.7	6,503.8	22.2%	11.9%	7.3%	3.0%
General Dynamics	Aerospace & Defense	247.0	1,567.0	3,067.0	3,164.0	15.8%	8.1%	7.8%	5.0%
Gillette	Toiletries & Cosmetics	823.5	2,513.3	6,794.7	6,340.3	32.8%	12.1%	13.0%	33.0%
McDonald's Corp.	Restaurant	1,427.3	7,861.3	9,794.5	15,414.6	18.2%	14.6%	9.3%	
PNC Bank Corp.	Bank	788.3	5,768.0	NA	73,404.0	13.7%	NA	1.1%	
Salomon, Inc.	Securities Brokerage	457.0	4,703.0	8,933.0	188,428.0	9.7%	5.1%	0.2%	8.5%
UST, Inc.	Tobacco	429.8	293.6	1,325.4	784.8	146.4%	32.4%	54.8%	
Washington Post	Newspaper	190.1	1,184.2	1,719.4	1,732.9	16.1%	11.1%	11.0%	11.5%
Wells Fargo	Bank	1,032.0	4,055.0	NA	50,316.0	25.5%	NA	2.1%	9.5%
Averages		$1,071.5	$4,798.3	$5,829.4	$66,919.4	30.9%	9.5%	9.9%	17.7%

Note: NA means not applicable.

Data Source: Value Line/Value Screen Data Base, January 1, 1997.

software providers are all prone to benefit from increasingly user-friendly technology for leisure-time activities.

To be sure, above-normal returns from investing in wonderful businesses are only possible to the extent that such advantages are not fully recognized by other investors. In the case of T. Rowe Price, early investments in Avon Products, Xerox, and IBM generated fantastic returns because Price saw their awesome potential far in advance of other investors. On the other hand, Buffett has profited by taking major positions in wonderful companies that suffer from some significant, but curable, malady. In 1991, for example, Buffett made a large investment in American Express when the company suffered unexpected credit card and real estate loan losses. When the company absorbed these losses without any lasting damage to its intrinsic profit-making ability, its stock price soared and Buffett cleaned up. Companies that are conservatively financed enjoy a similar ability to profit when an unexpected business downturn causes financially distressed rivals to sell valuable assets at bargain-basement prices.

WHEN LARGE SIZE IS A *DISADVANTAGE*

If economies of scale are substantial, larger firms are able to achieve lower costs of production or distribution than their smaller rivals. These cost advantages can translate into higher and more stable profits, and a permanent competitive advantage for larger firms in some industries. Diseconomies of large-scale organizations work in the opposite direction. When diseconomies of scale are operative, larger firms suffer a cost disadvantage when compared to smaller rivals. Smaller firms are then able to translate the benefits of small size into a distinct competitive advantage. Rather than losing profits and sales opportunities to larger rivals, smaller firms can enjoy higher profit rates and gain market share over time.

Industries dominated by large firms tend to be those in which there are significant economies of scale, important advantages to vertical integration, and a prevalence of mass marketing. As a result, large organizations with sprawling plants emphasize large quantities of output at low production costs. Use of national media, especially TV advertising, is common. Industries in which "small is beautiful" tend to be characterized by diseconomies of scale, "just in time" assembly and manufacturing, and niche marketing that emphasizes the use of highly skilled individuals adept at personal selling. Small factories with flexible production schedules are common. Rather than emphasize long production runs, many smaller companies focus on product quality. Instead of the sometimes slow-to-respond hierarchical organizations of large companies, smaller companies feature "flat" organizations with quick, decentralized decision making and authority.

The villain sometimes encountered by large-scale firms is not any diseconomy of scale in the production process itself, but rather the burden that size places on effective management. Big often means complex, and complexity results in inefficiencies and bureaucratic snarls that can strangle effective communication. In the former Soviet Union, a huge, highly centralized, run-from-the-top system came crashing down as a result of its own gigantic weight. Hoping to avoid a similar fate, many large organizations are now splitting assets into smaller independent operating units that can react quickly to customer needs without the typically long delays of large organizations. IBM, for example, has split into independent operating units that compete directly with each other to provide customers with the latest in computer equipment and software. GM, seeking to become more lean and agile like Japanese competitors, established Saturn as an independent operating unit. Exxon is selling domestic exploration and production operations to smaller independents that chop overhead and earn significant profits despite low volume and depressed oil prices. These examples suggest that the *Fortune 500* is going through a metamorphosis that will favor large organizations that are especially adept at reallocating capital among nimble, entrepreneurial operating units.

In the past, when foreign visitors wanted to experience firsthand the latest innovations in U.S. business and administrative practice, they found it mandatory to stop and visit major corporations in Chicago, Detroit, New York, and Pittsburgh. Today, it is more likely that they would make stops at Boston's Route 128, California's Silicon Valley, or North Carolina's Research Triangle. From electronics instrumentation to specialized steel, smaller companies have replaced larger companies in positions of industry leadership. The trend towards a higher level of efficiency for smaller companies has become so widespread that larger companies are now finding that meeting the needs of the customer sometimes requires a dramatic downsizing of the large-scale organization.

THE THREAT OF POTENTIAL COMPETITION

The potential for above-normal rates of return is a powerful inducement to the entry of new competitors and to the rapid growth of nonleading firms. Imitation may be the sincerest form of flattery, but it is also the most effective enemy of above-normal rates of return. Regression to the mean is the rule rather than the exception for above-normal corporate profit rates over time. During recent years, after-tax rates of return on stockholders' equity have usually been in the range of 9% to 10% per year. Just as in the stock market where investors rarely earn excess returns, individual companies rarely earn in excess of 15% to 20% for more than a decade. A consistent ROE $\geq$ 20% is simply unheard of for an entire industry with several competitors over a sustained period. Therefore, it seems reasonable to conclude that price and nonprice methods of competition are often vigorous, even in imperfectly competitive industries with few active or potential competitors.

Summary

This chapter extends the study of market structure to monopolistic competition and oligopoly. These models describe the behavior of competitors in imperfectly competitive markets across a broad spectrum of our economy in which both price competition and a wide variety of methods of nonprice competition are observed.

■ **Monopolistic competition** is similar to perfect competition in that it entails vigorous price competition among a large number of firms and individuals. The major difference is that consumers perceive important differences among the products offered by monopolistically competitive firms, whereas the output of perfectly competitive firms is homogeneous.

■ In an industry characterized by **oligopoly,** only a few large rivals are responsible for the bulk of industry output. High to very high barriers to entry are typical, and the price/output decisions of firms are interrelated in the sense that direct reactions from rivals can be expected. This "competition among the few" involves a wide variety of price and nonprice methods of rivalry.

■ A group of competitors operating under a formal overt agreement is called a **cartel.** If an informal covert agreement is reached, the firms are said to be operating in **collusion.** Both practices are generally illegal in the United States. However, cartels are legal in many parts of the world, and multinational corporations often become involved with them in foreign markets.

■ **Price leadership** results when one firm establishes itself as the industry leader and all other firms accept its pricing policy. This leadership may result from the size and strength of the leading firm, from cost efficiency, or as a result of the recognized ability of the leader to forecast market conditions accurately and to establish prices that produce satisfactory profits for all firms in the industry. Under a second type of price leadership, **barometric price leadership,** the price leader is not necessarily the largest or dominant firm in the industry. The price leader must only be accurate in reading the prevailing industry view of the need for price adjustment.

■ An often-noted characteristic of oligopoly markets is "sticky" prices. Once a general price level has been established, whether through cartel agreement or some less formal arrangement, it tends to remain fixed for an extended period. Such rigid prices are often explained by what is referred to as the **kinked demand curve** theory of oligopoly prices. A kinked demand curve is a firm demand curve that has different slopes for price increases versus price decreases.

■ **Economic censuses** provide a comprehensive statistical profile of large segments of the national economy. They are taken at five-year intervals during years ending with the digits 2 and 7—for example, 1987, 1992, 1997, 2002, and so on. Included are censuses of manufacturing, retail and wholesale trade, services, minerals, and construction.

■ **Concentration ratios** measure the percentage market share held by (concentrated in) an industry's top four (CR_4) or eight (CR_8) firms. When concentration ratios are low, industries tend to be made up of many firms, and competition tends to be vigorous. Industries in which the four leading firms are responsible for less than 20% of total industry sales (i.e., $CR_4 < 20$) are highly competitive and approximate the perfect competition model. On the other hand, when concentration ratios are high, leading firms dominate and sometimes have the potential for pricing flexibility and economic profits.

■ An effective competitive strategy in imperfectly competitive markets must be founded on the firm's **competitive advantage.** A competitive advantage is a unique or rare ability to create, distribute, or service products valued by customers. It is the business-world analog to what economists call **comparative advantage,** or when one nation or region of the country is better suited to the production of one product than to the production of some other product.

Public and private sources offer valuable service through their regular collection and publication of market structure data on the number and size distribution of competitors, market size, growth, capital intensity, investment, and so on. All of this information is useful to the process of managerial decision making and provides a useful starting point for the development of successful competitive strategy.

QUESTIONS

Q11.1 Describe the monopolistically competitive market structure and provide some examples.

Q11.2 Describe the oligopolistic market structure and provide some examples.

Q11.3 Explain the process by which economic profits are eliminated in a monopolistically competitive industry as compared to a perfectly competitive industry.

Q11.4 Would you expect the demand curve for a firm in a monopolistically competitive industry to be more or less elastic after economic profits have been eliminated?

Q11.5 "One might expect firms in a monopolistically competitive industry to experience greater swings in the price of their products over the business cycle than those in an oligopolistic industry. However, fluctuations in profits do not necessarily follow the same pattern." Discuss this statement.

Q11.6 Will revenue-maximizing firms have short-run profits as large as or larger than profit-maximizing firms? If so, when? If not, why not?

Q11.7 Is short-run revenue maximization necessarily inconsistent with the more traditional long-run profit-maximizing model of firm behavior? Why or why not?

Q11.8 Why is the four-firm concentration ratio only an imperfect measure of market power?

Q11.9 The statement "You get what you pay for" reflects the common perception that high prices indicate high product quality and low prices indicate low quality. Irrespective of market structure considerations, is this statement always correct?

Q11.10 "Economic profits result whenever only a few large competitors are active in a given market." Discuss this statement.

SELF-TEST PROBLEMS AND SOLUTIONS

ST11.1 Columbia Drug Stores, Inc., based in Seattle, Washington, operates a chain of 30 drug stores in the Pacific Northwest. During recent years, the company has become increasingly concerned with the long-run implications of competition from a new type of competitor, the so-called superstore.

Based on the French concept of the hypermarket, the superstore is a relatively new marketing concept in the United States. Often covering more than 125,000 square feet of display space, superstores allow shoppers to buy everything from groceries to prescription drugs to oil changes and haircuts. Relying on huge volume spurred by deeply discounted prices, superstores have proved to be very popular with cost-conscious consumers. Even if high levels of consumer acceptance prove to be relatively short-lived, a costly loss in walk-in traffic for area drug and grocery stores can occur. Because Columbia, like many regional drug chains, depends on such traffic for its highly profitable impulse-buying business, a serious decline in profitability can immediately follow the opening of a superstore. Moreover, once shoppers change their regular buying habits, drug stores need to run expensive advertising campaigns to reestablish lost customer loyalty.

Columbia is especially vulnerable to superstore competition since all of its stores are currently located in major metropolitan areas. In fact, the effects of superstore competition are already being felt in eight regional markets, where superstores have located within five miles of company outlets. Given the high level of success enjoyed by superstores in other parts of the country, Columbia believes that in only a short time it will face a direct challenge in many, if not all, of its current markets. To devise an effective competitive strategy, Columbia must first assess the profit implications of superstore competition and then consider whether a shift in marketing strategy seems in order. For example, Columbia might shift its mix of products away from those on which it has a distinct pricing disadvantage, or it might shift its plans for expansion to smaller markets, where the superstore concept is not feasible.

To measure the effects of superstore competition on current profitability, Columbia asked management consultant Mindy McConnell to conduct a statistical analysis of the company's profitability in its various markets. To net out size-related influences, profitability was measured by Columbia's gross profit margin, or earnings before interest and taxes divided by sales. Columbia provided proprietary company profit, advertising, and sales data covering the last year for all 30 outlets, along with public trade association and Census Bureau data concerning the number and relative size distribution of competitors in each market, among other market characteristics.

As a first step in the study, McConnell decided to conduct a regression-based analysis of the various factors thought to affect Columbia's profitability. The first is the relative size of leading competitors in the relevant market, measured at the Standard Metropolitan Statistical Area

(SMSA) level. Columbia's market share, MS, in each market area is expected to have a positive effect on profitability given the pricing, marketing, and average-cost advantages that accompany large relative size. The market concentration ratio, CR, measured as the combined market share of the four largest competitors in any given market, is expected to have a negative effect on Columbia's profitability given the stiff competition from large, well-financed rivals. Of course, the expected negative effect of high concentration on Columbia profitability contrasts with the positive influence of high concentration on industry profits that is sometimes observed.

Both capital intensity, K/S, measured by the ratio of the book value of assets to sales, and advertising intensity, A/S, measured by the advertising-to-sales ratio, are expected to exert positive influences on profitability. Given that profitability is measured by Columbia's gross profit margin, the coefficient on capital intensity measured Columbia's return on tangible investment. Similarly, the coefficient on the advertising variable measures the profit effects of advertising. Growth, GR, measured by the geometric mean rate of change in total disposable income in each market, is expected to have a positive influence on Columbia's profitability, since some disequilibrium in industry demand and supply conditions is often observed in rapidly growing areas.

PROFIT-MARGIN AND MARKET-STRUCTURE DATA FOR COLUMBIA DRUG STORES, INC.

STORE NO.	PROFIT MARGIN	MARKET SHARE	CONCEN-TRATION	CAPITAL INTENSITY	ADVER-TISING INTENSITY	GROWTH	SUPERSTORE ($S = 1$ IF SUPER-STORE PRESENT)
1	15.0	25.0	75.0	10.0	10.0	7.5	0
2	10.0	20.0	60.0	7.5	10.0	2.5	1
3	15.0	40.0	70.0	7.5	10.0	5.0	0
4	15.0	30.0	75.0	15.0	12.5	5.0	0
5	15.0	50.0	75.0	10.0	12.5	0.0	0
6	20.0	50.0	70.0	10.0	12.5	7.5	1
7	15.0	50.0	70.0	7.5	10.0	0.0	1
8	25.0	40.0	60.0	12.5	15.0	5.0	0
9	20.0	10.0	40.0	10.0	12.5	5.0	0
10	10.0	30.0	60.0	10.0	12.5	0.0	0
11	15.0	20.0	60.0	12.5	12.5	7.5	1
12	10.0	30.0	75.0	12.5	10.0	2.5	0
13	15.0	50.0	75.0	7.5	10.0	5.0	0

Store No.	Profit Margin	Market Share	Concen- tration	Capital Intensity	Adver- tising Intensity	Growth	Superstore (S = 1 if Super- store Present)
14	10.0	20.0	75.0	7.5	12.5	2.5	0
15	10.0	10.0	50.0	7.5	10.0	2.5	0
16	20.0	30.0	60.0	15.0	12.5	2.5	0
17	15.0	30.0	50.0	7.5	12.5	5.0	1
18	20.0	40.0	70.0	7.5	12.5	5.0	0
19	10.0	10.0	60.0	12.5	10.0	2.5	0
20	15.0	20.0	70.0	5.0	12.5	7.5	0
21	20.0	20.0	40.0	7.5	10.0	7.5	0
22	15.0	10.0	50.0	15.0	10.0	5.0	1
23	15.0	40.0	40.0	7.5	12.5	5.0	1
24	10.0	30.0	50.0	5.0	7.5	0.0	0
25	20.0	40.0	70.0	15.0	12.5	5.0	0
26	15.0	40.0	70.0	12.5	10.0	5.0	1
27	10.0	20.0	75.0	7.5	10.5	2.5	0
28	15.0	10.0	60.0	12.5	12.5	5.0	0
29	10.0	30.0	75.0	5.0	7.5	2.5	0
30	10.0	20.0	75.0	12.5	12.5	0.0	0

Finally, to gauge the profit implications of superstore competition, McConnell used a "dummy" (or binary) variable where $S = 1$ in each market in which Columbia faced superstore competition and $S = 0$ otherwise. The coefficient on this variable measures the average profit rate effect of superstore competition. Given the vigorous nature of superstore price competition, Mc-Connell expects the superstore coefficient to be both negative and statistically significant, indicating a profit-limiting influence. The Columbia profit-margin data and related information used in McConnell's statistical analysis are given in the preceding table. Regression model estimates for the determinants of Columbia's profitability are as follows:

DETERMINANTS OF PROFITABILITY FOR COLUMBIA DRUG STORES, INC.

Variable Name	Coefficient (1)	Standard Error of Coefficient (2)	t-Statistic (3) = (1) ÷ (1)
Intercept	7.846	3.154	2.49
Market share	0.214	0.033	6.50
Concentration	−0.203	0.038	−5.30
Capital intensity	0.289	0.123	2.35
Advertising intensity	0.722	0.233	3.09
Growth	0.842	0.152	5.56
Superstore	−2.102	0.828	−2.54

Coefficient of determination = R^2 = 84%
Standard error of the estimate = S.E.E. = 1.872%

A. Describe the overall explanatory power of this regression model, as well as the relative importance of each continuous variable.
B. Based on the importance of the binary or dummy variable that indicates superstore competition, do superstores pose a serious threat to Columbia's profitability?
C. What factors might Columbia consider in developing an effective competitive strategy to combat the superstore influence?

ST11.1 **SOLUTION**

A. The coefficient of determination $R^2 = 84\%$ means that 84% of the total variation in Columbia's profit-rate variability is explained by the regression model. This is a relatively high level of explanation for a cross section study such as this, suggesting that the model provides useful insight concerning the determinants of profitability. The intercept coefficient of 7.846 has no economic meaning since it lies far outside the relevant range of observed data. The 0.214 coefficient for the market-share variable means that, on average, a 1% (unit) rise in Columbia's market share leads to a 0.214% (unit) rise in Columbia's profit margin. Similarly, as expected, Columbia's profit margin is positively related to capital intensity, advertising intensity, and the rate of growth in the market area. Conversely, high concentration has the expected limiting influence. Because of the effects of leading-firm rivalry, a 1% rise in industry concentration will lead to a 0.203% decrease in Columbia's profit margin. This means that relatively large firms compete effectively with Columbia.

B. Yes, the regression model indicates that superstore competition in one of Columbia's market areas reduces Columbia's profit margin on average by 2.102%. Given that Columbia's rate of return on sales routinely falls in the 10% to 15% range, the profit-limiting effect of superstore competition is substantial. Looking more closely at the data, it appears that Columbia faces superstore competition in only one of the seven lucrative markets in which the company earns a 20 to 25% rate of return on sales. Both observations suggest that current and potential superstore competition constitutes a considerable threat to the company and one that must be addressed in an effective competitive strategy.

C. Development of an effective competitive strategy to combat the influence of superstores involves the careful consideration of a wide range of factors related to Columbia's business. It might prove fruitful to begin this analysis by more carefully considering market characteristics for Store No. 6, the one Columbia outlet able to earn a substantial 20% profit margin despite superstore competition. For example, this analysis might suggest that Columbia, like Store No. 6, should specialize in service (e.g., prescription drug delivery) or in a slightly different mix of merchandise. On the other hand, perhaps Columbia should follow the example set by Wal-Mart in its early development and focus its plans for expansion on small to medium-size markets. In the meantime, Columbia's still-profitable stores in major metropolitan areas could help fund future growth.

Although obviously only a first step, a regression-based study of market structure such as that described here can provide a very useful beginning to the development of an effective competitive strategy.

ST11.2 **Price Leadership.** The La Jolla Company is the world's leading manufacturer of commercial jet aircraft. La Jolla is the dominant, price-leading firm in the market for mid-range aircraft suitable for commercial service in the continental United States. Recently, La Jolla has faced competitive inroads from Minnesota Minuteman Manufacturing, Inc., (3M) and Nippon Aircraft, Ltd. Both of these new competitors offer aircraft that airline customers find comparable to La Jolla's Model 797. Total and marginal cost functions for 3M (M) and Nippon (N) aircraft are as follows:

$$TC_M = \$10,000,000 + \$35,000,000Q_M + \$250,000\,Q_M^2,$$

$$MC_M = \$35,000,000 + \$500,000Q_M,$$

$$TC_N = \$200,000,000 + \$20,000,000Q_N + \$500,000Q_N^2,$$

$$MC_N = \$20,000,000 + \$1,000,000Q_N.$$

La Jolla's total and marginal cost relations are as follows:

$$TC_L = \$4,000,000,000 + \$5,000,000Q_L + \$62,500Q_L^2$$

$$MC_L = \$5,000,000 + \$125,000Q_L$$

The industry demand curve for this type of jet aircraft is:

$$Q = 910 - 0.000017P.$$

Assume throughout this problem that the 3M and Nippon aircraft are perfect substitutes for La Jolla's Model 797, and that each total cost function includes a risk-adjusted normal rate of return on investment.

A. Determine the supply curves for the 3M and Nippon aircraft, assuming that the firms operate as price takers.

B. What is the demand curve faced by La Jolla?

C. Calculate La Jolla's profit-maximizing price and output levels. (Hint: La Jolla's total and marginal revenue relations are $TR_L = \$50,000,000Q_L - \$50,000Q_L^2$, and $MR_L = \$50,000,000 - \$100,000Q_L$.)

D. Calculate profit-maximizing output levels for 3M and Nippon.

E. Is the market for aircraft from these three firms in short-run equilibrium? Is this market also in long-run equilibrium? Why or why not?

ST11.2 **SOLUTION**

A. Because price followers take prices as given, they operate where individual marginal cost equals price. Therefore, the supply curves for 3M and Nippon aircraft are:

3M

$$P_M = MC_M = \$35,000,000 + \$500,000Q_M$$

$$500,000Q_M = -35,000,000 + P_M$$

$$Q_M = -70 + 0.000002P_M$$

Nippon

$$P_N = MC_N = \$20,000,000 + \$1,000,000Q_N$$

$$1,000,000Q_N = -20,000,000 + P_N$$

$$Q_N = -20 + 0.000001P_N$$

B. As the industry price leader, La Jolla's demand equals industry demand minus following firm supply. Remember that $P = P_L = P_M = P_N$ since La Jolla is a price leader for the industry:

$$Q_L = Q - Q_M - Q_N$$

$$= 910 - 0.000017P + 70 - \$0.000002P + 20 - \$0.000001P$$

$$= 1{,}000 - \$0.00002P_L$$

$$P_L = \$50{,}000{,}000 - \$50{,}000Q_L$$

C. To find La Jolla's profit-maximizing price and output levels, set $MR_L = MC_L$ and solve for Q:

$$MR_L = MC_L$$

$$\$50{,}000{,}000 - \$100{,}000Q_L = \$5{,}000{,}000 + \$125{,}000Q_L$$

$$45{,}000{,}000 = 225{,}000Q_L$$

$$Q_L = 200 \text{ units}$$

$$P_L = \$50{,}000{,}000 - \$50{,}000(200)$$

$$= \$40{,}000{,}000$$

D. Since La Jolla is a price leader for the industry,

$$P = P_L = P_M = P_N = \$40{,}000{,}000$$

Optimal supply for 3M and Nippon aircraft are:

$$Q_M = -70 + 0.000002P_M$$

$$= -70 + 0.000002(40{,}000{,}000)$$

$$= 10$$

$$Q_N = -20 + 0.000001P_N$$

$$= -20 + 0.000001(40{,}000{,}000)$$

$$= 20$$

E. Yes. The industry is in short-run equilibrium if the total quantity demanded is equal to total supply. The total industry demand at a price of $40 million is:

$$Q_D = 910 - 0.000017P$$

$$= 910 - 0.000017(\$40{,}000{,}000)$$

$$= 230 \text{ units}$$

The total industry supply is:

$$Q_S = Q_L + Q_M + Q_N$$

$$= 200 + 10 + 20$$

$$= 230 \text{ units}$$

Provided that each manufacturer is making at least a risk-adjusted normal rate of return on investment, the industry is also in long-run equilibrium. To check profit levels for each manufacturer, note that:

$$\pi_M = TR_M - TC_M$$

$$= \$40,000,000(10) - \$10,000,000$$
$$- \$35,000,000(10) - \$250,000(10^2)$$

$$= \$15,000,000$$

$$\pi_N = TR_N - TC_N$$

$$= \$40,000,000(20) - \$200,000,000$$
$$- \$20,000,000(20) - \$500,000(20^2)$$

$$= \$0$$

$$\pi_L = TR_L - TC_L$$

$$= -\$4,000,000,000 + 45,000,000(200)$$
$$- \$12,500(200^2)$$

$$= \$500,000,000$$

Since each firm is at least earning normal profits, and the marginal entrant (Nippon) is earning only normal profits, the industry is also in long-run equilibrium.

PROBLEMS

P11.1   **Market Structure Concepts.** Indicate whether each of the following statements is true or false and explain why.

A. Equilibrium in monopolistically competitive markets requires that firms be operating at the minimum point on the long-run average cost curve.

B. A high ratio of distribution cost to total cost tends to increase competition by widening the geographic area over which any individual producer can compete.

C. The price elasticity of demand tends to fall as new competitors introduce substitute products.

D. An efficiently functioning cartel achieves a monopoly price/output combination.

E. An increase in product differentiation tends to increase the slope of firm demand curves.

P11.2   **Monopolistically Competitive Demand.** Would the following factors increase or decrease the ability of domestic auto manufacturers to raise prices and profit margins? Why?

A. Decreased import quotas

B. Elimination of uniform emission standards

C. Increased automobile price advertising

D. Increased import tariffs (taxes)

E. A rising value of the dollar, which has the effect of lowering import car prices

P11.3   **Monopolistically Competitive Equilibrium.** Soft Lens, Inc., has enjoyed rapid growth in sales and high operating profits on its innovative extended-wear soft contact lenses. However, the company faces potentially fierce competition from a host of new competitors as some important basic patents expire during the coming year. Unless the company is able to thwart such competition, severe downward pressure on prices and profit margins is anticipated.

A. Use Soft Lens's current price, output, and total cost data to complete the table on page 517.
(Note: Total costs include a risk-adjusted normal rate of return.)

B. If cost conditions remain constant, what is the monopolistically competitive high-price/low-output long-run equilibrium in this industry? What are industry profits?

C. Under these same cost conditions, what is the monopolistically competitive low-price/high-output equilibrium in this industry? What are industry profits?

D. Now assume that Soft Lens is able to enter into restrictive licensing agreements with potential competitors and create an effective cartel in the industry. If demand and cost conditions remain constant, what is the cartel price/output and profit equilibrium?

P11.4   **Competitive Strategy.** Gray Computer, Inc., located in Colorado Springs, Colorado, is a privately held producer of high-speed electronic computers with immense storage capacity and

Price ($)	Monthly Output ($Million)	Total Revenue ($Million)	Marginal Revenue ($Million)	Total Cost ($Million)	Marginal Cost ($Million)	Average Cost ($Million)	Total Profit ($Million)
$20	0			$0			
19	1			12			
18	2			27			
17	3			42			
16	4			58			
15	5			75			
14	6			84			
13	7			92			
12	8			96			
11	9			99			
10	10			105			

computing capability. Although Gray's market is restricted to industrial users and a few large government agencies (e.g., Department of Health, NASA, National Weather Service, etc.), the company has profitably exploited its market niche.

Glen Gray, founder and research director, has recently announced his retirement, the timing of which will unfortunately coincide with the expiration of several patents covering key aspects of the Gray computer. Your company, a potential entrant into the market for supercomputers, has asked you to evaluate the short- and long-run potential of this market. Based on data gathered from your company's engineering department, user surveys, trade associations, and other sources, the following market demand and cost information has been developed:

$$P = \$54 - \$1.5Q,$$

$$MR = \$54 - \$3Q,$$

$$TC = \$200 + \$6Q + \$0.5Q^2,$$

$$MC = \$6 + \$1Q,$$

where P is price, Q is units measured by the number of supercomputers, MR is marginal revenue, TC is total costs including a normal rate of return, MC is marginal cost, and all figures are in millions of dollars.

A. Assume that these demand and cost data are descriptive of Gray's historical experience. Calculate output, price, and economic profits earned by the Gray Company as a monopolist. What is the

point price elasticity of demand at this output level?

B. Calculate the range within which a long-run equilibrium price/output combination would be found for individual firms if entry eliminated Gray's economic profits. (Note: Assume that the cost function is unchanged and that the high-price/low-output solution results from a parallel shift in the demand curve while the low-price/high-output solution results from a competitive equilibrium.)

C. Assume that the point price elasticity of demand calculated in Part A is a good estimate of the relevant arc price elasticity. What is the potential overall market size for supercomputers?

D. If no other near-term entrants are anticipated, should your company enter the market for supercomputers? Why or why not?

P11.5 **Cartel Behavior.** An oil cartel has been formed by the three leading oil producers. Total production costs at various levels of oil production per day are as follows:

	Total Cost ($ millions)		
Barrels per Day (millions)	Arabco (A)	Britannia (B)	Cinco (C)
0	$35	$50	$5
1	40	75	25
2	50	105	40
3	65	140	65
4	90	180	95
5	125	225	130

A. Construct a table showing the marginal cost of production per firm.

B. From the data in Part A, determine an optimal allocation of output and maximum profits if the cartel sets $Q = 8$ and $P = \$35$.

C. Is there an incentive for individual members to cheat by expanding output when the cartel sets $Q = 8$ and $P = \$35$?

P11.6 **Cartel Equilibrium.** The Hand Tool Manufacturing Industry Trade Association recently published the following estimates of demand and supply relations for hammers:

$$Q_D = 60,000 - 10,000P \quad \text{(Demand)},$$

$$Q_S = 20,000P \quad \text{(Supply)}.$$

A. Calculate the perfectly competitive industry equilibrium price/output combination.

B. Now assume that the industry output is organized into a cartel. Calculate the industry price/output combination that will maximize profits for cartel members. (Hint: As a cartel, industry $MR = \$6 - \$0.0002Q$.)

C. Compare your answers to Parts A and B. Calculate the price/output effects of the cartel.

P11.7 **Kinked Demand Curves.** Safety Service Products (SSP) faces the following segmented demand and marginal revenue curves for its new infant safety seat:

1. Over the range from 0 to 10,000 units of output,

$$P_1 = \$60 - Q,$$

$$MR_1 = \$60 - \$2Q.$$

2. When output exceeds 10,000 units,

$$P_2 = \$80 - \$3Q,$$

$$MR_2 = \$80 - \$6Q.$$

The company's total and marginal cost functions are as follows:

$$TC = \$100 + \$20Q + \$0.5Q^2,$$

$$MC = \$20 + \$1Q,$$

where P is price (in dollars); Q is output (in thousands); MR is marginal revenue; TC is total cost; and MC is marginal cost, all in thousands of dollars.

A. Graph the demand, marginal revenue, and marginal cost curves.

B. How would you describe the market structure of the industry in which SSP operates? Explain why the demand curve takes the shape indicated previously.

C. Calculate price, output, and profits at the profit-maximizing activity level.

D. How much could marginal costs rise before the optimal price would increase? How much could they fall before the optimal price would decrease?

P11.8 **Supply Reactions.** Anaheim Industries, Inc., and Binghampton Electronics, Ltd., are the only suppliers to the U.S. Weather Service of an important electronic instrument. The Weather Service has established a fixed-price procurement policy, however, so $P = MR$ in this market. Total and marginal cost relations for each firm are as follows:

$$TC_A = \$7,000 + \$250Q_A + \$0.5Q_A^2, \quad \text{(Anaheim)}$$

$$MC_A = \frac{\Delta TC_A}{\Delta Q_A} = \$250 + \$1Q_A,$$

$$TC_B = \$8,000 + \$200Q_B + \$1Q_B^2, \quad \text{(Binghampton)}$$

$$MC_B = \frac{\Delta TC_B}{\Delta Q_B} = \$200 + \$2Q_B,$$

where Q is output in units, and $MC > AVC$ for each firm.

A. What is the minimum price necessary for each firm to supply output?

B. Determine the supply curve for each firm.

C. Based on the assumption that $P = P_A = P_B$, determine industry supply curves when $P < \$200$, $\$200 < P < \$250$, and $P > \$250$.

P11.9 **Nonprice Competition.** General Cereals, Inc. (GCI), produces and markets *Sweeties!*, a popular ready-to-eat breakfast cereal. In an effort to expand sales in the Secaucus, New Jersey, market, the company is considering a one-month promotion whereby GCI would distribute a coupon for a free daily pass to a local amusement park in exchange for three box tops, as sent in by retail customers. A 25% boost in demand is anticipated, even though only 15% of all eligible customers are expected to redeem their coupons. Each redeemed coupon costs GCI $6, so the expected cost of this promotion is 30¢ (= 0.15 × $6 ÷ 3) per unit sold. Other marginal costs for cereal production and distribution are constant at $1 per unit.

Current demand and marginal revenue relations for *Sweeties!* are

$$Q = 16,000 - 2,000P,$$

$$MR = \$8 - \$0.001Q.$$

Demand and marginal revenue relations that reflect the expected 25% boost in demand for *Sweeties!* are the following:

$$Q = 20,000 - 2,500P,$$

$$MR = \$8 - \$0.0008Q.$$

A. Calculate the profit-maximizing price/output and profit levels for *Sweeties!* prior to the coupon promotion.
B. Calculate these same values subsequent to the *Sweeties!* coupon promotion and following the expected 25% boost in demand.

P11.10 **Price Leadership.** Louisville Communications, Inc., offers 24-hour telephone answering service for individuals and small businesses in southeastern states. Louisville is a dominant, price-leading firm in many of its markets. Recently, Memphis Answering Service, Inc., and Nashville Recording, Ltd., have begun to offer services with the same essential characteristics as Louisville's service. Total and marginal cost functions for Memphis (*M*) and Nashville (*N*) services are:

$$TC_M = \$75,000 - \$7Q_M + \$0.0025Q_M^2,$$

$$MC_M = -\$7 + \$0.005Q_M,$$

$$TC_N = \$50,000 + \$3Q_N + \$0.0025Q_N^2,$$

$$MC_N = \$3 + \$0.005Q_N.$$

Louisville's total and marginal cost relations are as follows:

$$TC_L = \$300,000 + \$5Q_L + \$0.0002Q_L^2,$$

$$MC_L = \$5 + \$0.0004Q_L.$$

The industry demand curve for telephone answering service is

$$Q = 500,800 - 19,600P.$$

Assume throughout this problem that the Memphis and Nashville services are perfect substitutes for Louisville's service.
A. Determine the supply curves for the Memphis and Nashville services, assuming that the firms operate as price takers.
B. What is the demand curve faced by Louisville?
C. Calculate Louisville's profit-maximizing price and output levels. (Hint: Louisville's total and marginal revenue relations are $TR_L = \$25Q_L - \$0.00005Q_L^2$, and $MR_L = \$25 - \$0.0001Q_L$.)
D. Calculate profit-maximizing output levels for the Memphis and Nashville services.
E. Is the market for service from these three firms in short-run equilibrium?

Case Study for Chapter 11

THE PROFITABILITY OF MULTINATIONAL OPERATIONS

Like market power in domestic markets, market power in foreign markets will have positive effects on the market value of the firm to the extent that such power is an important determinant of future above-normal returns. In fact, greater valuation effects may be associated with market power in foreign as opposed to domestic operations. It is important to remember that the U.S. market is the largest free trade area in the world. While substantial numbers of efficiently sized competitors are available in an overwhelming share of U.S. markets, generally smaller foreign markets tend to be dominated by few large competitors. Entry barriers due to economies of scale tend to be more onerous, and the advantages to established leading firms are greater in foreign as opposed to U.S. markets. Antitrust and other policies limiting monopoly power also tend to be more vigorously pursued in the United States than in many foreign countries. In fact, some foreign governments encourage monopoly to gain a comparative advantages in foreign trade. Such public advantages are often viewed as a substantial offset to the monopoly power and monopoly profits that make them possible. Thus, the valuation effects of market power in foreign operations can be interesting in isolation, as well as in contrast with perhaps smaller effects due to market power in domestic operations.

While the effects of market power are often indirectly measured using concentration ratios in studies conducted at the industry level of aggregation, studies using firm level data often consider profit rate data directly. Generally speaking, concentration ratios for a firm's primary product industry are only a poor measure of market power when widely diversified firms are considered. Even weighted average concentration ratios reflecting firm involvement in a number of industries can fail to capture market power influences since the possibility of a critical concentration ratio is neglected. Either or both reasons help explain why concentration ratios seldom have any discernible influence on the market value of the firm.

Of course, high profit rates can show the influences of relatively higher prices, lower costs, or both. By themselves, it is impossible to determine if high profit rates reflect the presence of market power or superior efficiency. As such, profit rate data are an imperfect proxy for market power. They remain, however, a useful index of the relative attractiveness of one line of business or industry. If profit rates for foreign operations consistently exceed profit rates for U.S. operations, one might conclude that foreign markets are generally more attractive because they entail relatively less product market competition than U.S. markets. If profit rates for foreign operations have market value effects that invariably exceed the valuation effects of profit rates for U.S. operations, one might conclude that profit rates from foreign markets tend to be both higher and more long-lasting than profit rates earned in U.S. markets.

To estimate the effects of profit rates on the market value of the firm, it is necessary to build a simple economic model. To illustrate, consider the simple accounting identity that total assets equal the value of stockholders' equity plus total liabilities:

$$\text{Total Assets} = \text{Stockholders' Equity} + \text{Total Liabilities} \quad \textbf{(11.6)}$$

This means that the total assets of any corporation are financed either through the sale of common stock and retained earnings, or through debt financing. When the market value of common stock is used as an economic measure of the value of stockholder equity, then Equation 11.6 implies:

$$\frac{\text{Market Value of}}{\text{Common Stock}} = \frac{\text{Total}}{\text{Assets}} - \frac{\text{Total}}{\text{Liabilities}} + \epsilon \quad \textbf{(11.7)}$$

The error term ϵ (epsilon) allows for the fact that the market value of common stock seldom equals the difference between assets and liabilities, which is defined as the book value of stockholders' equity. As such, ϵ reflects the combined influence of accounting errors and bias. For example, since the accounting profession does not typically assign a superior value to assets or operations able to generate above-normal returns, the market price of common stock is often 1.5 to 2 times greater than the accountant's book value of stockholders' equity. So-called price/book ratios in the 1.5:1 to 2:1 range clearly imply that valuable economic assets go unmeasured in current accounting practice. When the price/book ratio is 1.5, for example, fully one-third of the market value of the firm relates to factors that are either unmeasured or improperly measured according to current accounting practice.

The effects of profit rates on the market value of the firm can be estimated by expanding the number of independent X-variables in Equation 11.7 to include profit rates on domestic and foreign operations. If current profit rates are a useful indicator of the multinational firm's future profit-making potential, an impact on the current market value of the firm can be anticipated. If profit rates on foreign operations are higher and/or more stable than profit rates on domestic operations, a somewhat greater influence of foreign profit rates on the market value of the firm can also be contemplated.

Table 11.7   MARKET VALUE EFFECTS OF FOREIGN OPERATIONS FOR 25 TOP U.S. MULTINATIONALS

RANK	COMPANY	MARKET VALUE/ASSETS RATIO	1/ASSETS RATIO	DEBT/ASSETS RATIO	ROA	FOREIGN ROA	DOMESTIC ROA	GROWTH	FOREIGN/DOMESTIC ASSETS
1	Exxon	89.28%	0.0012%	60.28%	6.35%	8.73%	3.24%	100.30%	130.90%
2	General Motors	11.94%	0.0005%	96.39%	0.00%	4.91%	-1.49%	106.97%	30.37%
3	IBM	33.20%	0.0012%	68.14%	0.00%	-3.10%	3.60%	99.58%	116.18%
4	Mobil	62.07%	0.0025%	59.22%	4.22%	6.56%	1.27%	101.49%	125.75%
5	Ford	11.62%	0.0006%	91.83%	0.00%	-2.06%	0.77%	113.42%	37.68%
6	Texaco	51.86%	0.0034%	53.73%	4.98%	6.38%	4.15%	98.77%	59.79%
7	Chevron	62.05%	0.0027%	55.57%	6.07%	7.08%	5.55%	102.75%	51.06%
8	Citicorp	3.61%	0.0004%	89.67%	0.32%	1.20%	-0.45%	100.34%	87.80%
9	du Pont (E.I.) de Nemours	81.84%	0.0026%	69.73%	2.51%	4.28%	1.27%	97.53%	70.04%
10	Procter & Gamble	129.97%	0.0042%	62.24%	7.79%	4.12%	10.59%	108.64%	76.19%
11	Philip Morris Cos	137.67%	0.0020%	74.88%	9.88%	8.55%	10.38%	104.23%	38.13%
12	General Electric	37.92%	0.0005%	87.84%	2.23%	1.84%	2.29%	94.77%	14.38%
13	Dow Chemical	61.54%	0.0039%	68.16%	2.32%	2.11%	2.48%	100.87%	74.28%
14	Xerox	21.59%	0.0029%	85.34%	0.00%	2.64%	-1.04%	101.76%	39.57%
15	Hewlett-Packard	104.13%	0.0073%	45.26%	6.43%	5.67%	7.01%	113.22%	75.53%
16	Eastman Kodak	57.05%	0.0043%	71.66%	4.30%	6.27%	3.47%	103.93%	42.16%
17	Digital Equipment	39.22%	0.0089%	56.30%	0.00%	-5.97%	9.94%	100.14%	166.51%
18	United Technologies	37.40%	0.0063%	77.89%	0.77%	7.35%	-1.86%	103.28%	40.09%
19	Coca-Cola	495.12%	0.0090%	64.82%	17.05%	25.99%	8.83%	112.98%	91.81%
20	American International Group	30.75%	0.0013%	83.99%	2.04%	2.37%	1.81%	109.99%	65.90%
21	Motorola	132.58%	0.0094%	51.60%	5.42%	13.82%	0.99%	117.30%	52.69%
22	Johnson & Johnson	278.50%	0.0084%	56.49%	13.67%	17.94%	10.35%	110.49%	77.96%
23	Minn Mining & Mfg	184.36%	0.0084%	44.80%	10.54%	7.04%	12.90%	104.07%	67.48%
24	ITT	14.59%	0.0017%	87.67%	0.00%	2.40%	-0.34%	106.02%	14.15%
25	Amoco	85.03%	0.0035%	54.45%	2.99%	2.56%	3.18%	99.82%	45.29%
Averages		90.20%	0.0039%	68.72%	4.39%	5.55%	3.96%	104.51%	67.67%

Data Source: "The 100 Largest U.S. Multinationals," *Forbes*, July 19, 1993, 182–186; Standard & Poor's Compustat Database, December 31, 1993.

To properly isolate the market value effects of profit rates in both foreign and domestic markets, it is important to control for the risk implications of multinational involvement. In many instances, multinational involvement not only allows firms to expand product markets, but also provides a "portfolio" of regulatory environments, economic conditions, and trade currencies. While exchange risk can be limited at minimal cost through participation in highly developed currency markets, limiting risks associated with political intervention (increased taxation, expropriation, etc.) and localized economic fluctuations can be costly. Thus, a firm's degree of "multinationalism" may have important implications for its overall risk level. To the extent that conventional measures fail to reflect the greater risks associated with multinational activity, the degree of multinational involvement can convey additional risk information. If multinationals face greater than typical levels of risk, or involve substantial hedging expenses, a firm's degree of multinational involvement can have important negative valuation effects. In addition, one might expect positive valuation effects to accompany high expected growth because a firm's options for future investment are largely determined by expected growth in demand.

Based on the previous considerations, a regression model that can be used to learn the relative market-value impacts of domestic versus foreign profit rates can be written:

$$\text{Market Value/Assets} = b_0 + b_1 \text{ 1/Assets} \\ + b_2 \text{ Debt/Assets} \\ + b_3 \text{ } ROA_i + b_4 \qquad \textbf{(11.8)} \\ \text{Growth} + b_5 \text{ Foreign/} \\ \text{Domestic} + u,$$

In this equation, notice that each size-related variable has been deflated, or normalized, by the book value of total assets. Without deflation of size-related variables, the link between market value and profits could be dominated by size effects: by definition, large firms have high market values and profits. The deflation of all size-related variables makes it possible to focus on the valuation effects of profit rate differences between foreign and domestic operations. In this model, the profit rate of interest is called the

---

Table 11.8

THE MARKET VALUE EFFECTS OF MULTINATIONAL OPERATIONS (t-STATISTICS IN PARENTHESES)

INDEPENDENT VARIABLES	THE DEPENDENT VARIABLE IS THE MULTINATIONAL FIRM'S PRICE/BOOK RATIO:	
	A.	**B.**
Constant	−1.068	−1.531
1/Assets	11,988.017	5,513.498
	(3.04)	(1.30)
Debt/Assets	2.021	1.663
	(2.71)	(2.01)
Return on Assets (ROA)	20.493	—
	(9.46)	
Foreign ROA	—	11.990
		(7.95)
Domestic ROA	—	9.813
		(4.08)
Growth	−0.750	−0.243
	(−0.47)	(−0.14)
Foreign/Domestic	—	0.410
		(0.25)
R^2	89.5%	89.9%

return on total assets, or ROA, and defined as net income (profits) divided by the book value of total assets. Like ROE, ROA is a basic measure of the firm's rate of return on investment; unlike ROE, the ROA measure does not directly reflect the firm's use of financial leverage.

For exploratory purposes, the simple economic model described in Equation 11.8 is estimated over a sample of the $n = 25$ largest U.S. multinationals taken from *Forbes*. In an annual survey, *Forbes* shows foreign sales, foreign profits, and foreign assets for top multinationals. To estimate Equation 11.8, it is necessary to supplement these *Forbes* data with market value, leverage, and growth information from the *Compustat* data base. Table 11.7 shows the actual data used in the regression analysis.

Table 11.8 shows the market value effects of multinational operations for 25 top U.S. multinationals. In Panel A, the simple positive effect of ROA on the market value of the firm is illustrated. Panel B depicts the differential positive effects of profit rates from foreign versus domestic operations.

A. Describe the overall explanatory power of both regression models, as well as the relative importance of each continuous variable.

B. Based on the importance of the ROA variable in Panel A, is it reasonable to conclude that stock-market investors believe that current rates of return will persist into future periods?

C. Based on the importance of the ROA variables for foreign versus domestic operations in Panel B, is it reasonable to suggest that foreign markets may be more competitive than the U.S. market?

Pricing Practices

The pricing practices of successful firms sometimes seem a bit peculiar. For example, when first-class hotel rooms in London, Tokyo, or Paris go for $300 to $500 per night, Holiday Inns offers summertime "Great Rates" from as low as $39 per room per night to families of weekend vacationers—more than 50% off regular prices. Not to be outdone, Howard Johnson's says vacations are more fun when "Kids Go HoJo" and offers summertime family rates as low as $29 per night. Meanwhile, Marriott offers low 21-day nonrefundable advance purchase summer rates for $79 per night in downtown Chicago or $114 at San Francisco's Fisherman's Wharf and $69 weekday, $39 weekend rates at the Raleigh Research Triangle Park. What is going on here?

Rather than a mad scramble to build market share at any cost, these hotel-chain rates represent a shrewd use of information technology. Any night that hotel rooms stand empty represents lost revenue, and since hotel costs are largely fixed, revenue losses translate directly into lost profits. A room rate of $39 per night doesn't begin to cover fixed construction, maintenance, and interest costs, but it makes a nice profit contribution when the alternative is weekend vacancy. By segmenting their markets, hotels are able to charge the maximum amount the market will bear on weekdays and on weekends.[1] Similarly, hotel marketing gets fierce for convention business, especially when conventions meet at traditionally slack periods. Is it any wonder why the American Economic Association holds its annual meeting around New Year's Day and typically in cold-weather cities?

This chapter examines common pricing practices and illustrates their value as a practical means for achieving profit-maximizing prices under a wide variety of demand and cost conditions.

Markup Pricing

Surveys indicate that markup pricing is the most commonly employed pricing method. Given the popularity of the technique, it behooves managers to fully understand markup pricing methods and their underlying rationale. When the underlying rationale of markup pricing methods is fully understood, they can be seen as the practical means for achieving optimal prices under a wide variety of demand and cost conditions.

---

[1]See Andrew J. Kessler, "Price Fix," *Forbes,* August 12, 1996, 141.

MARKUP PRICING TECHNOLOGY

The development of pricing practices to profitably segment markets has reached a fine art with the advent and use of high-speed computer technology. Why do *Business Week, Forbes, Fortune,* and *The Wall Street Journal* offer bargain rates to students but not to business executives? It is surely not because it costs less to deliver the *Journal* to students, and it's not out of benevolence; it's because students aren't willing or able to pay the standard rate. Even at 50% off regular prices, student bargain rates more than cover marginal costs and make a significant profit contribution. Similarly, senior citizens who eat at Holiday Inns enjoy a 10 to 15% discount and make a meaningful contribution to profits. Conversely, relatively high prices for popcorn at movie theaters, peanuts at the ball park, and clothing at the height of the season reflect the fact that customers can be insensitive to price changes at different places and at different times of the year. Regular prices, discounts, rebates, and coupon promotions all represent different pricing mechanisms used to discover the breadth and depth of customer demand and to maximize profitability.

Interestingly, effective pricing practices can be employed with little direct reference to marginal analysis. While profit maximization requires that prices be set so that marginal revenues equal marginal cost, it is not necessary to calculate both to set optimal prices. Just using information on marginal costs and the point price elasticity of demand, the calculation of profit-maximizing prices is quick and easy. Many firms derive an optimal pricing policy using a technique called **markup pricing,** whereby prices are set to cover all direct costs plus a percentage markup for profit contribution. Flexible markup pricing practices that reflect differences in marginal costs and demand elasticities constitute an efficient method for ensuring that $MR = MC$ for each line of products sold. Similarly, peak and off-peak pricing, price discrimination, and joint product pricing practices are efficient means for operating so that $MR = MC$ for each customer or customer group and product class.

Markup Pricing
Setting prices to cover direct costs plus a percentage profit contribution.

MARKUP ON COST

In a conventional approach, firms estimate the average variable costs of producing and marketing a given product, add a charge for variable overhead, and then add a percentage markup, or profit margin. The charge for variable overhead costs is usually determined by allocating these expenses among all products on the basis of their average variable costs. For example, if total variable overhead costs are projected at $1.3 million per year and variable costs for planned production total $1 million, then variable overhead is allocated to individual products at the rate of 130% of variable cost. If the average variable cost of a product is estimated to be $1, the firm adds a charge of 130% of variable costs, or $1.30, for variable overhead, obtaining a fully allocated cost of $2.30. To this figure the firm might add a 30% markup for profits, or 69¢, to obtain a price of $2.99 per unit.

Markup on cost is the profit margin for an individual product or product line expressed as a percentage of unit cost. The markup-on-cost, or *cost-plus,* formula is given by the expression:

Markup on Cost
The difference between price and cost, measured relative to cost, expressed as a percentage.

$$Markup\ on\ Cost = \frac{Price\ -\ Cost}{Cost}. \tag{12.1}$$

The numerator of this expression, called the **profit margin,** is measured by the difference between price and cost. In the example cited previously, the 30% markup on cost is calculated as:

$$Markup \; on \; Cost = \frac{Price - Cost}{Cost}$$

$$= \frac{\$2.99 - \$2.30}{\$2.30}$$

$$= 0.30, \; or \; 30\%.$$

Solving Equation 12.1 for price provides the expression that determines price in a cost-plus pricing system:

$$Price = Cost \; (1 + Markup \; on \; Cost). \qquad \textbf{(12.2)}$$

Continuing with the previous example, the product selling price is found as:

$$Price = Cost \; (1 + Markup \; on \; Cost)$$

$$= \$2.30(1.30)$$

$$= \$2.99.$$

MARKUP ON PRICE

Profit margins, or markups, are sometimes calculated as a percentage of price instead of cost. **Markup on price** is the profit margin for an individual product or product line expressed as a percentage of price, rather than unit cost as in the markup-on-cost formula. This alternative means of expressing profit margins can be illustrated by the markup-on-price formula:

$$Markup \; on \; Price = \frac{Price - Cost}{Price}. \qquad \textbf{(12.3)}$$

Profit margin is the numerator of the markup-on-price formula, as in the markup-on-cost formula. However, unit cost has been replaced by price in the denominator.

The markup-on-cost and markup-on-price formulas are simply alternative means for expressing the relative size of profit margins. To convert from one markup formula to the other, just use the following expressions:

$$Markup \; on \; Cost = \frac{Markup \; on \; Price}{1 - Markup \; on \; Price}. \qquad \textbf{(12.4)}$$

$$Markup \; on \; Price = \frac{Markup \; on \; Cost}{1 + Markup \; on \; Cost}. \qquad \textbf{(12.5)}$$

Therefore, the 30% markup on cost described in the previous example is equivalent to a 23% markup on price:

$$Markup\ on\ Price = \frac{0.3}{1 + 0.3} = 0.23\ or\ 23\%.$$

An item with a cost of $2.30, a 69¢ markup, and a price of $2.99 has a 30% markup on cost and a 23% markup on price. This illustrates the importance of being consistent in the choice of a cost or price basis when comparing markups among products or sellers.

Markup pricing is sometimes criticized as a naive pricing method based solely on cost considerations—and the wrong costs at that. Some who employ the technique may ignore demand conditions, emphasize fully allocated accounting costs rather than marginal costs, and arrive at suboptimal price decisions. However, a categorical rejection of such a popular and successful pricing practice is clearly wrong. Although inappropriate use of markup pricing formulas will lead to suboptimal managerial decisions, successful firms typically employ the method in a way that is consistent with profit maximization. In fact, markup pricing can be viewed as an efficient rule-of-thumb approach to setting optimal prices.

THE ROLE OF COST IN MARKUP PRICING

Although a variety of cost concepts are employed in markup pricing, most firms use a standard, or fully allocated, cost concept. Fully allocated costs are determined by first estimating direct costs per unit, then allocating the firm's expected indirect expenses, or overhead, assuming a standard or normal output level. Price is then based on standard costs per unit, irrespective of short-term variations in actual unit costs.

Unfortunately, use of the standard cost concept can create several problems. Sometimes, firms fail to adjust historical costs to reflect recent or expected price changes for key inputs. Unadjusted historical accounting costs have little relevance for current pricing decisions. Also, accounting costs may not reflect true economic costs. The concept of opportunity cost must be employed for optimal decision making. For example, fully allocated costs can be appropriate when a firm is operating at full capacity. During **peak** periods, when facilities are fully utilized, expansion is required to increase production. Under such conditions, an increase in production requires an increase in all plant, equipment, labor, materials, and other expenditures. However, if a firm has excess capacity, as during **off-peak** periods, only those costs that actually rise with production—the incremental costs per unit—should form a basis for setting prices. Successful firms that employ markup pricing base prices on fully allocated costs under normal conditions but offer price discounts or accept lower margins during off-peak periods when excess capacity is available. In this way, prices accurately reflect the effects of capacity utilization.

In some instances, output produced during off-peak periods is much cheaper than output produced during peak periods. When fixed costs represent a substantial share of total production costs, discounts of 30% to 50% for output produced during off-peak periods can often be justified on the basis of lower costs.

"Early Bird" or afternoon matinee discounts at movie theaters provide an interesting example. Except for cleaning expenses, which vary according to the number of customers, most movie theater expenses are fixed. As a result, the revenue generated by

Peak
Period of full capacity usage.

Off-Peak
Period of excess capacity.

adding customers during off-peak periods can significantly increase the theater's profit contribution. When off-peak customers buy regularly priced candy, popcorn, and soda, even lower afternoon ticket prices can be justified. Conversely, on Friday and Saturday nights when movie theaters operate at peak capacity, a small increase in the number of customers would require a costly expansion of facilities. Ticket prices during these peak periods reflect fully allocated costs. Similarly, McDonald's, Burger King, Hardee's, and many other fast-food outlets have increased their profitability substantially by introducing breakfast menus. If fixed restaurant expenses are covered by lunch and dinner business, even promotionally priced breakfast items can make a notable contribution to profits.

THE ROLE OF DEMAND IN MARKUP PRICING

Successful companies are willing to adjust prices or profit margins on specific products as market conditions vary. Efficient firms differentiate the markup charged on different products or product lines on the basis of competitive pressure as reflected in varying demand elasticities. Foreign and domestic automobile companies regularly offer rebates or special equipment packages for slow-selling models. Similarly, airlines promote different pricing schedules for business and vacation travelers. The airline and automobile industries are only two examples of sectors in which vigorous competition requires a careful reflection of demand and supply factors in pricing practice. Efforts to assess cost and revenue relations among products are by no means limited to these industries. In the production and distribution of many goods and services, successful firms demonstrate the ability to quickly adjust prices to different market conditions.

Examining the margins set by a successful regional grocery store chain provides interesting evidence that demand conditions play an important role in cost-plus pricing. Table 12.1 shows the firm's typical markup on cost and markup on price for a variety of products sold in its stores. A field manager with over 20 years' experience in the grocery business provided the authors with useful insight into the firm's pricing practices. He stated that the "price sensitivity" of an item is the primary consideration in setting margins. Staple products like bread, coffee, ground beef, milk, and soup are highly price sensitive and carry relatively low margins. Products with high margins tend to be those for which demand is less price sensitive.

Note the wide range of margins applied to different items. The 0% to 10% markup on cost for ground beef, for example, is substantially lower than the 15% to 35% margin on steak. Hamburger is a relatively low-priced meat with wide appeal to families, college students, and low-income groups whose price sensitivity is high. In contrast, relatively expensive sirloin, T-bone, and porterhouse steaks appeal to higher-income groups with lower price sensitivity.

It is also interesting to see how seasonal factors affect the demand for grocery items like fruits and vegetables. When a fruit or vegetable is in season, spoilage and transportation costs are at their lowest levels, and high product quality translates into enthusiastic consumer demand, which leads to high margins. Consumer demand tends to shift away from high-cost/low-quality fresh fruits and vegetables when they are out of season, thereby reducing margins on these items.

	MARKUPS CHARGED ON A VARIETY OF GROCERY ITEMS		
Table 12.1	ITEM	MARKUP ON COST (%)	MARKUP ON PRICE (%)
	Bread—private label	0–5	0–5
	Bread—brand name	30–40	23–29
	Breakfast cereals (dry)	5–15	5–13
	Cake mixes	15–20	13–17
	Coffee	0–10	0–9
	Cold cuts (processed meats)	20–45	17–31
	Cookies	20–30	17–23
	Delicatessen items	35–45	26–31
	Fresh fruit—in season	40–50	29–33
	Fresh fruit—out of season	15–20	13–17
	Fresh vegetables—in season	40–50	29–33
	Fresh vegetables—out of season	15–20	13–17
	Ground beef	0–10	0–9
	Ice cream	15–20	13–17
	Laundry detergent	5–10	5–9
	Milk	0–5	0–5
	Nonprescription drugs	33–55	26–35
	Pastries (cakes, pies, etc.)	20–30	17–23
	Pet foods	15–20	13–17
	Snack foods	20–25	17–20
	Soft drinks	0–10	0–9
	Spices	30–60	23–38
	Soup	0–15	0–13
	Steak	15–35	13–26
	Toilet tissue	10–15	9–13
	Toothpaste	15–20	13–17

In addition to seasonal factors that affect margins over the course of a year, some market forces affect margins within a given product class. In breakfast cereals, for example, the markup on cost for highly popular corn flakes averages only 5% to 6%, with brands offered by Post (General Foods Corporation) and Kellogg's competing with a variety of local store brands. *Cheerios* and *Wheaties,* both offered only by General Mills, Inc., enjoy a markup on cost of 15% to 20%. Thus, availability of substitutes directly affects the markups on various cereals. Finally, it is interesting to note that among the wide variety of items sold in a typical grocery store, the product class with the highest margin is spices. Apparently, consumer demand for nutmeg, cloves, thyme, bay leaves, and other spices is quite insensitive to price. The manager interviewed said that in more than 20 years in the grocery business, he could not recall a single store coupon or special offered on spices.

This retail grocery store pricing example provides valuable insight into how markup pricing rules can be used in setting an efficient pricing policy. Although the words "price elasticity" were never used in the discussion, it is clear that this concept

Market-Based Pricing Practices for Pharmaceutical Drugs

Pharmaceutical companies have long had one of the best deals in business, a foolproof formula for success. Ever since the advent of Medicare in the mid-1960s, the industry has been able to follow its own set of rules and raise prices virtually at will. With Medicare, Medicaid, and a plethora of state-run health-care cost reimbursement schemes, U.S. buyers have federal and state dollars to help share the burden of exploding health care costs. What is not generally understood is that these very same government-sponsored programs contribute to the explosion of health care prices.

If the market for prescription drugs were a typical free market, demand would be limited by the extent to which consumers were willing to pay for innovative therapies. When government enters the picture, the link between the consumer and the industry is weakened. If each dollar of consumer demand is matched by federal and state funds, the demand for health care skyrockets. For example, suppose a given prescription costs $15, but that 80% of this cost is borne by the government or other third-party payers. Most consumers focus on the $3 cost that they themselves must pay, rather than the overall cost of $15. As government health-care benefits rise, it is the matching share paid by consumers that constrains demand in the industry. Rather than cut the cost to consumers of high-priced drugs, government matching schemes allow drug companies and other health care providers to raise prices at will. The 1980s explosion in prescription drug prices and other health care costs coincides exactly with the explosion of government-sponsored cost sharing in the health care industry.

In the late-1990s, a revolution is turning the sheltered world of pills and prescriptions into a rough and turbulent business. No matter what happens in Washington, market forces are already bringing the lower drug prices that consumers seek. Two factors have converged to change the prognosis for the industry: the onset of managed care has altered demand, and a profusion of low-cost alternatives to high-priced drugs has increased supply. Managed care encourages the formation of large buying groups among hospitals, health maintenance organizations (HMO), and mail-order drug houses to drive down the cost of pharmaceuticals. HMOs are under intense pressure to control drug costs for their corporate clients. To help corporations restrain drug costs, HMOs and other large buyers are shifting market share from one product to another in exchange for deep discounts. They can do this because shelves now teem with generic low-priced, exact copies of brand-name drugs. Why should an HMO allow its doctors to prescribe branded prescription drugs which cost perhaps hundreds of dollars per month, when generic equivalents are available for just pennies on the dollar? Competition for pioneering patented products also comes from so-called therapeutic equivalents. These drugs are chemically different from patented versions, but treat the same ailment effectively and less expensively.

In the 1980s, drug producers had three ways to boost earnings: introduce innovative therapies, launch me-too products, or raise prices on all drugs. In the 1990s, consolidation is the clear choice of industry leaders facing an aging product line, patent expirations, and powerful managed care providers with the clout to trim prices. An extremely cost-conscious environment demands that drug company management eliminate overhead, cut marketing expenses, consolidate production facilities, and close obsolete plants. Clearly, the economics of pricing practices in the drug industry have changed radically. Burgeoning demand spurred by government and other third-party co-payment plans led to rapid price increases and high profit margins during the 1980s. During the late-1990s, heightened competitive pressures, including new-found buyer power, and ongoing consolidation will dramatically cut profit margins and trim the overall rate of price increases.

What remains to be seen is the impact, if any, on the amazing pace of new and improved drug therapies, and on the rate of growth in health care quality.

See: Ron Winslow, "Health-Care Costs May Be Heading Up Again," *The Wall Street Journal,* January 21, 1997, B1, B6.

plays a key role in the firm's markup pricing decisions. To examine those decisions further, it is necessary to develop a method for determining optimal markups in practical pricing policy.

Markup Pricing and Profit Maximization

Demand analysis plays an important role in the markup pricing practices of successful firms. In fact, there is a simple inverse relation between the optimal markup and the price sensitivity of demand. The optimal markup is large when the underlying price elasticity of demand is low; the optimal markup is small when the underlying price elasticity of demand is high. To identify the precise relation between the price elasticity of demand and the optimal markups on cost and price, two relations developed previously must be reconsidered.

THE OPTIMAL MARKUP ON COST

Recall from Chapter 5 that there is a direct relation among marginal revenue, price elasticity of demand, and the profit-maximizing price for a product. This relation was expressed as

$$MR = P\left(1 + \frac{1}{\epsilon_P}\right). \tag{12.6}$$

To maximize profit, a firm must operate at the activity level at which marginal revenue equals marginal cost. Since marginal revenue always equals the right side of Equation 12.6, at the profit-maximizing output level, it follows that

$$P\left(1 + \frac{1}{\epsilon_P}\right) = MC, \tag{12.7}$$

or

$$P = MC\left(\frac{1}{1 + \frac{1}{\epsilon_P}}\right). \tag{12.8}$$

Equation 12.8 provides a formula for the profit-maximizing price for any product in terms of its price elasticity of demand. The equation states that the profit-maximizing price is found by multiplying marginal cost by the term

$$\left(\frac{1}{1 + \frac{1}{\epsilon_P}}\right).$$

To derive the optimal markup-on-cost formula, recall from Equation 12.2 that the price established by a cost-plus method equals cost multiplied by the expression

(1 + Markup on Cost). Equation 12.7 implies that marginal cost is the appropriate cost basis for cost-plus pricing and that

$$MC(1 + \textit{Markup on Cost}) = MC\left(\frac{1}{1 + \frac{1}{\epsilon_P}}\right).$$

By dividing each side of this expression by MC and subtracting 1 yields the expression

$$\textit{Markup on Cost} = \left(\frac{1}{1 + \frac{1}{\epsilon_P}}\right) - 1.$$

Optimal Markup on Cost
The profit-maximizing cost markup, equal to minus one divided by the quantity one plus the price elasticity of demand.

After simplifying, the **optimal markup on cost,** or profit-maximizing markup on cost, formula can be written

$$\textit{Optimal Markup on Cost} = OMC^* = \frac{-1}{\epsilon_P + 1}. \qquad (12.9)$$

The optimal markup on cost formula can be illustrated through use of a simple example. Consider the case of a leading catalog retailer of casual clothing and sporting equipment that wishes to offer a basic two strap design of *Birkenstock* leather sandals for easy on and off casual wear. Assume the catalog retailer pays a wholesale price of $25 per pair for *Birkenstock* sandals and markets them at a regular catalog price of $75 per pair. This typical $50 profit margin implies a standard markup on cost of 200% since:

$$\textit{Markup on Cost} = \frac{Price - Cost}{Cost}$$

$$= \frac{\$75 - \$25}{\$25}$$

$$= 2, \text{ or } 200\%.$$

In a preseason sale, the catalog retailer offered a discounted "early bird" price of $70 on *Birkenstock* sandals and noted a moderate increase in weekly sales from 275 to 305 pairs per week. This $5 discount from the regular price of $75 represents a modest 6.7% markdown. Using the arc price elasticity formula, the implied arc price elasticity of demand on *Birkenstock* sandals is:

$$E_P = \frac{Q_2 - Q_1}{P_2 - P_1} \times \frac{P_2 + P_1}{Q_2 + Q_1}$$

$$= \frac{305 - 275}{\$70 - \$75} \times \frac{\$70 + \$75}{305 + 275}$$

$$= -1.5.$$

In the absence of direct evidence on the point price elasticity of demand, it can be assumed that this arc price elasticity of demand $E_P = -1.5$ is the best available estimate of the current point price elasticity of demand. Using Equation 12.9, the $75 regular catalog price reflects an optimal markup on cost of 200% since:

$$\textit{Optimal Markup on Cost} = \frac{-1}{\epsilon_P + 1}$$

$$= -\frac{-1}{-1.5 + 1}$$

$$= 2.0 \text{ or } 200\%.$$

THE OPTIMAL MARKUP ON PRICE

Optimal Markup on Price
The profit-maximizing price markup, equal to minus one times the inverse of the price elasticity of demand.

Just as there is a simple inverse relation between a product's price sensitivity and the optimal markup on cost, so too is there a simple inverse relation between price sensitivity and the **optimal markup on price.** The profit-maximizing markup on price is easily determined using relations derived previously. Dividing each side of Equation 12.7 by P yields the expression

$$\frac{MC}{P} = 1 + \frac{1}{\epsilon_P}.$$

Subtracting 1 from each side of this equation and simplifying gives

$$\frac{MC - P}{P} = \frac{1}{\epsilon_P}.$$

Then, multiplying each side of this expression by -1 yields

$$\frac{P - MC}{P} = \frac{-1}{\epsilon_P}. \qquad \textbf{(12.10)}$$

Notice that the left side of Equation 12.10 is an expression for markup on price. Thus, the optimal markup-on-price formula is

$$\textit{Optimal Markup on Price} = OMP^* = \frac{-1}{\epsilon_P}. \qquad \textbf{(12.11)}$$

The optimal markup on price formula can be illustrated by continuing with the previous example of a catalog retailer and its optimal pricing policy for *Birkenstock* leather sandals. As you may recall from that example, the catalog retailer pays a wholesale price of $25 per pair for *Birkenstock* sandals, markets them at a regular catalog price of $75 per pair, and the arc price elasticity of demand $E_P = -1.5$ is the best available estimate of the current point price elasticity of demand. This typical $50 profit margin implies a standard markup on price of 66.7% since:

$$Markup\ on\ Price = \frac{Price - Cost}{Price}$$

$$= \frac{\$75 - \$25}{\$75}$$

$$= 0.667,\ or\ 66.7\%.$$

If it can again be assumed that the arc price elasticity of demand $E_P = -1.5$ is the best available estimate of the current point price elasticity of demand, the $75 regular catalog price reflects an optimal markup on price since:

$$Optimal\ Markup\ on\ Price = \frac{-1}{\epsilon_P}$$

$$= \frac{-1}{-1.5}$$

$$= 0.667\ or\ 66.7\%.$$

Table 12.2 shows the optimal markup on marginal cost and on price for products with varying price elasticities of demand. As the table indicates, the more elastic the demand for a product, the more price sensitive it is and the smaller the optimal margin. Products with relatively less elastic demand have higher optimal markups. In the retail grocery example, a very low markup is consistent with a high price elasticity of demand for milk. Demand for fruits and vegetables during their peak seasons is considerably less price sensitive, and correspondingly higher markups reflect this lower price elasticity of demand.

Far from being a naive rule of thumb, markup pricing practices allow firms to arrive at optimal prices in an efficient manner. Markup pricing seems to be one of the best

Table 12.2

OPTIMAL MARKUP ON MARGINAL COST AND PRICE AT VARIOUS PRICE ELASTICITY LEVELS

PRICE ELASTICITY OF DEMAND ϵ_P	OPTIMAL MARKUP ON MARGINAL COST (%), $\dfrac{-1}{\epsilon_P + 1}$	OPTIMAL MARKUP ON PRICE (%), $\dfrac{-1}{\epsilon_P}$
−1.5	200.0	66.7
−2.0	100.0	50.0
−2.5	66.7	40.0
−5.0	25.0	20.0
−10.0	11.1	10.0
−25.0	4.2	4.0

methods available for implementing marginal analysis in pricing practice, especially when one considers the high cost of market demand information for many individual products. The process of generating marginal revenue and marginal cost information will itself increase costs. The marginal concept requires that firms weigh any added expense against the added gain and act accordingly. In its pricing policy, the firm must determine whether the added expense associated with obtaining more complete estimates of marginal relations is more than offset by the expected gain in revenues from increased pricing precision. In many instances, markup pricing practices represent an efficient method for setting optimal prices over broad categories of products when one considers the expense involved with obtaining detailed marginal revenue and marginal cost information.

A FURTHER OPTIMAL MARKUP EXAMPLE

The use of the optimal markup formulas can be further illustrated by considering the case of Betty's Boutique, a small specialty retailer located in a suburban shopping mall. In setting its initial $36 price for a new spring line of blouses, Betty's added a 50% markup on cost. Costs were estimated at $24 each: the $12 purchase price of each blouse, plus $6 in allocated variable overhead costs, plus an allocated *fixed* overhead charge of $6. Customer response was so strong that when Betty's raised prices from $36 to $39 per blouse, sales only fell from 54 to 46 blouses per week. Was Betty's initial $36 price optimal? Is the new $39 price suboptimal? If so, what is the optimal price?

At first blush, Betty's pricing policy seems clearly inappropriate. It is always improper to consider allocated fixed costs in setting prices for any good or service; only marginal or incremental costs should be included. However, by adjusting the amount of markup on cost or markup on price employed, Betty's can implicitly compensate for the inappropriate use of fully allocated costs. Thus, it is necessary to carefully analyze both the cost categories included and the markup percentages chosen before judging a given pricing practice.

To determine Betty's optimal markup for blouses, it is necessary to calculate an estimate of the point price elasticity of demand and relevant marginal cost, and then apply the optimal markup formula. Betty's standard cost per blouse includes the $12 purchase cost, plus $6 allocated variable costs, plus $6 fixed overhead charges. However, for pricing purposes, only the $12 purchase cost plus the allocated variable overhead charge of $6 are relevant. Thus, the relevant marginal cost for pricing purposes is $18 per blouse. The allocated fixed overhead charge of $6 is irrelevant for pricing purposes since fixed overhead costs are unaffected by blouse sales.

The $3 price increase to $39 represents a moderate 7.7% escalation in price. Using the arc price elasticity formula, the implied arc price elasticity of demand for Betty's blouses is:

$$E_P = \frac{Q_2 - Q_1}{P_2 - P_1} \times \frac{P_2 + P_1}{Q_2 + Q_1}$$

$$= \frac{46 - 54}{\$39 - \$36} \times \frac{\$39 + \$36}{46 + 54}$$

$$= -2.$$

If it can be assumed that this arc price elasticity of demand $E_P = -2$ is the best available estimate of the current point price elasticity of demand, the $36 price reflects an optimal markup of 100% on relevant marginal costs of $18 since:

$$Optimal\ Markup\ on\ Cost = \frac{-1}{\epsilon_P + 1}$$

$$= \frac{-1}{-2 + 1}$$

$$= 1\ or\ 100\%.$$

Similarly, the $36 price reflects an optimal markup on price since

$$Optimal\ Markup\ on\ Price = \frac{-1}{\epsilon_P}$$

$$= \frac{-1}{-2}$$

$$= 0.5\ or\ 50\%.$$

Betty's actual markup on relevant marginal costs per blouse is an optimal 100%, because

$$Markup\ on\ Cost = \frac{\$36 - \$18}{\$18}$$

$$= 1\ (or\ 100\%).$$

Similarly, Betty's markup on price is an optimal 50%, since

$$Markup\ on\ Price = \frac{\$36 - \$18}{\$36}$$

$$= 0.5\ (or\ 50\%).$$

Therefore, Betty's initial $36 price on blouses is optimal, and the subsequent $3 price increase should be rescinded.

This simple example teaches an important lesson. Despite the improper consideration of fixed overhead costs and a markup that might at first appear unsuitable, Betty's pricing policy is entirely consistent with profit-maximizing behavior because the end result is an efficient pricing policy. Given the prevalence of markup pricing in everyday business practice, it is important that these pricing practices be carefully analyzed before they are judged suboptimal. The widespread use of markup pricing methods among highly successful firms suggests that the method is employed in ways that are consistent with profit maximization.

Price Discrimination

Pricing decisions are more complex when the firm sells products in a variety of markets. With multiple markets or customer groups, the potential exists to enhance profits by charging different prices and markups to each relevant market segment. Market segmentation is an important fact of life for firms in the airline, entertainment, hotel, medical, legal, and consulting services industries. Firms that offer goods also often segment their market between wholesale and retail buyers and between business, educational, not-for-profit, and government customers.

REQUIREMENTS FOR PROFITABLE PRICE DISCRIMINATION

Price Discrimination
A pricing practice that sets prices in different markets that are not related to differences in costs.

Price discrimination occurs whenever different classes of customers are charged different markups for the same product. Price discrimination is evident whenever identical customers are charged different prices or when price differences are not proportional to cost differences. Thus, price discrimination can occur when different customers are charged the same price despite underlying cost differences or when price differentials fail to reflect cost discrepancies.

For price discrimination to be profitable, different price elasticities of demand must exist in the various submarkets. Unless price elasticities differ among submarkets, there is no point in segmenting the market. With identical price elasticities and identical marginal costs, profit-maximizing pricing policy calls for the same price and markup to be charged in all market segments. A **market segment**

Market Segment
A division or fragment of the overall market with essentially unique characteristics.

is a division or fragment of the overall market with unique demand or cost characteristics. For example, wholesale customers tend to buy in large quantities, are highly familiar with product costs and characteristics, and are well informed about available alternatives. Wholesale buyers are highly price sensitive. Conversely, retail customers tend to buy in small quantities, are sometimes poorly informed about product costs and characteristics, and are often ignorant about available alternatives. As a group, retail customers are often less price sensitive than wholesale buyers. Markups charged to retail customers usually exceed those charged to wholesale buyers.

For price discrimination to be profitable, the firm must also be able to efficiently identify relevant submarkets and prevent transfers among affected customers. Detailed information must be obtained and monitored concerning customer buying habits, product preferences, and price sensitivity. Just as important, the price-discriminating firm must be able to monitor customer buying patterns to prevent reselling among customer subgroups. A highly profitable market segmentation between wholesale and retail customers can be effectively undermined if retail buyers are able to obtain discounts through willing wholesalers. Similarly, price discrimination among buyers in different parts of the country can be undermined if customers are able to resell in high-margin territories those products obtained in bargain locales.

THE ROLE PLAYED BY CONSUMERS' SURPLUS

The underlying motive for price discrimination can be better understood by introducing the concept of **consumers' surplus.** Consumers' surplus (or customers' surplus) is the value of purchased goods and services above and beyond the amount paid to sellers. To illustrate, consider Figure 12.1, in which a market equilibrium price/output combination of P^* and Q^* is shown. The total value of output to customers is given by the area under the demand curve, or area $0ABQ^*$. Since the total revenue paid to producers is price times quantity, equal to area $0P^*BQ^*$, the area P^*AB represents the value of output above the amount paid to producers—that is, the consumers' surplus. For example, if a given customer is willing to pay $200 for a certain overcoat but is able to obtain a bargain price of $150, the buyer enjoys $50 worth of consumers' surplus. If another customer places a value of only $150 on the overcoat, he or she would enjoy no consumers' surplus following a purchase for $150.

Consumers' surplus arises because individual consumers place different values on goods and services. Customers who place a relatively high value on a product will pay high prices; customers who place a relatively low value on a product are only willing to pay low prices. As one proceeds from Point A downward along the market marginal curve in Figure 12.1, customers who place a progressively lower marginal value (utility) on the product enter the market. At low prices, both high-value and low-value customers are buyers; at high prices, only customers that place a relatively high value on a given product are buyers.

When product value differs greatly among various groups of customers, a motive for price discrimination is created. By charging higher prices to customers with a high marginal value of consumption, revenues will increase without affecting costs. Sellers

AN ILLUSTRATION OF CONSUMERS' SURPLUS

Consumers' surplus is shown by the area P^*AB and represents the value of output to consumers above and beyond the amount they pay to producers.

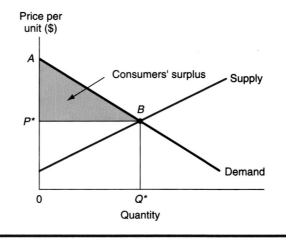

with the ability to vary prices according to the value placed on their products by buyers are able to capture at least some of the value represented by consumers' surplus. Such price discrimination will always increase profits because it allows the firm to increase total revenue without affecting costs. A firm that is precise in its price discrimination practices always charges the maximum each market segment is willing to pay. Price discrimination is charging what the market will bear.

Finally, it is important to recognize that price discrimination does not carry any evil connotation in a moral sense. It is merely a pricing practice that must be judged good or bad on the merits of each specific situation. In some circumstances, price discrimination leads to lower prices for some customer groups and to a wider availability of goods and services. For example, a municipal bus company might charge lower prices for easily identifiable consumer groups, such as the elderly and the handicapped. In such circumstances, the bus company is price discriminating in favor of elderly and handicapped riders and against other customers. This type of price discrimination provides elderly and handicapped customers a greater opportunity to ride the bus. Because of incremental revenues provided by elderly and handicapped riders, the bus company may also be able to offer routes that could not be supported by revenues from full-fare customers alone, or it may be able to operate with a lower subsidy from taxpayers.

DEGREES OF PRICE DISCRIMINATION

First-Degree Price Discrimination
Charging different prices to each customer.

The extent to which a firm can engage in price discrimination is classified into three major categories. Under **first-degree price discrimination,** the firm extracts the maximum amount each customer is willing to pay for its products. Each unit is priced separately at the price indicated along each product demand curve. Such pricing precision is rare because it requires that sellers know the maximum price each buyer is willing to pay for each unit of output. Purchase decisions must also be monitored closely to prevent reselling among customers. Although first-degree price discrimination is uncommon, it has the potential to emerge in any market where discounts from posted prices are standard and effective prices are individually negotiated between buyers and sellers. When sellers possess a significant amount of market power, consumer purchases of big-ticket items such as appliances, automobiles, homes, and both personal and professional services all have the potential to involve first-degree price discrimination.

Second-Degree Price Discrimination
Charging different prices based on use rates of quantities purchased.

Second-degree price discrimination, a more frequently employed type of price discrimination, involves setting prices on the basis of the quantity purchased. Bulk rates are typically set with high prices and markups charged for the first unit or block of units purchased, but progressively greater discounts are offered for greater quantities. Quantity discounts that lead to lower markups for large versus small customers are a common means of discriminating in price between retail and wholesale customers. Book publishers often charge full price for small purchases but offer 40 to 50% off list price when 20 or more units are purchased. Public utilities, such as electric companies, gas companies, and water companies, also frequently charge block rates that are discriminatory. Consumers pay a relatively high markup for residential service, whereas commercial and industrial customers pay relatively low markups. Office equipment such as copy machines and mainframe computers (or "servers") are other examples of products for

Do Colleges Price Discriminate?

A number of economists have become vocal critics charging that the financial aid policies of major colleges and universities have changed the whole character of tuition pricing practices. Most of the students attending elite colleges receive so-called financial aid. At many Ivy League colleges, for example, the average financial aid recipient comes from a family with an annual income of roughly $50,000—and dozens came from families with incomes exceeding $100,000. They are not unique in this respect. Similar patterns can be found at other private colleges across the country. As a result, some economists charge that college financial aid is not about "needy students" but is instead a means of price discrimination designed to extract all that the traffic will bear, both from students, their families, and from the government.

As with some commercial sellers of products and services, economists argue that colleges levy a list price (tuition), set far above what most people can or will pay, and then offer varying discounts (financial aid), so that each customer is charged what the traffic will bear. That is why financial aid recipients enjoy incomes far above what most Americans consider "needy," and often fall into a range that many might regard as wealthy. Unlike ordinary businesses that risk prosecution under the Robinson-Patman Act for price discrimination practices, academic institutions appear to engage in price discrimination as an accepted norm. Moreover, while a commercial enterprise may be able to separate its customers into only a few categories, to be charged different prices, Ivy League schools have been investigated by the Justice Department for colluding to charge every single student a different price. Although there were thousands of students who applied to more than one college, any given student would be charged the same net price (tuition minus financial aid). Classmates might be charged different net prices, but each price would be the same from any college in the group. Some students even found that individual schools would only consider altering the financial aid package offered after consulting with other schools the student was considering. Economists say that such practices amount to carrying collusion and price discrimination right down to the individual customer level.

In addition to the kind of financial aid that is simply a paper discount, some financial aid involves money actually changing hands. Much of the latter is provided in the form of federal government grants and student loans. Unfortunately, the system virtually guarantees that tuition will rise to unaffordable levels. At the heart of government aid formulas is an "expected family contribution" based on family income, assets, the number of children, and so on. Government aid is available when the cost of college exceeds this "expected family contribution." Even a small college could lose millions of dollars annually in federal aid if it kept tuition affordable. According to critics, federal subsidies and virtual exemption from antitrust laws have produced skyrocketing tuition, collusion, and price discrimination. Economist Milton Friedman estimates that colleges could operate at a profit by charging half what the Ivy League schools charge. But why should they, as long as parents and taxpayers are willing to pay more?

In defense of current financial aid practices, school administrators point out that many would be unable to afford college without some cross-subsidization among students. Private schools use endowment income to supplement student tuition and fees whereas public colleges and universities enjoy substantial tax-revenue income. Even the premiums paid by out-of-state students at leading state universities fail to cover fully allocated costs per student. However, average costs may not be relevant for pricing purposes. The marginal cost per student is often nearly zero, and even very low net tuition-plus-fee income can often make a significant contribution to overhead. From an economic perspective, the pricing practices of colleges and universities may in fact be consistent with the theory of price discrimination.

See: Lynn Asinoff, "In Paying College Costs, Parents Discover They Can Negotiate About Financial Aid," *The Wall Street Journal*, April 16, 1997, C1.

which second-degree price discrimination is practiced, especially when time sharing among customers is involved.

Third-Degree Price Discrimination
Charging different prices to each customer class.

The most commonly observed form of price discrimination, **third-degree price discrimination,** results when a firm separates its customers into several classes and sets a different price for each customer class. Customer classifications can be based on for-profit or not-for-profit status, regional location, or customer age, for example. IBM, Apple, Compaq, and other major computer manufacturers routinely offer educational discounts that can be in excess of 30 to 40% off list prices. These manufacturers are eager to penetrate the classroom on the assumption that student users will become loyal future customers. Auto companies, magazine and newspaper publishers, and others also prominently feature educational discounts as part of their marketing strategy. Many hospitals also offer price discounts to various patient groups. If unemployed and uninsured patients are routinely charged only what they can easily afford to pay for medical service, whereas employed and insured medical patients are charged maximum allowable rates, the hospital is price discriminating in favor of the unemployed and against the employed. Widespread price discounts for senior citizens represent a form of price discrimination in favor of older customers but against younger customers.

A Price Discrimination Example

Price discrimination is profitable because it allows the firm to enhance revenues without increasing costs. It is an effective means for increasing profits because it allows the firm to more closely match marginal revenues and marginal costs. A firm that can segment its market maximizes profits by operating at the point where marginal revenue equals marginal cost in each market segment. A detailed example is a helpful means for illustrating this process.

PRICE/OUTPUT DETERMINATION

Suppose that Midwest State University (MSU) wants to reduce the athletic department's operating deficit and increase student attendance at home football games. To achieve these objectives, a new two-tier pricing structure for season football tickets is being considered.

A market survey conducted by the school suggests the following market demand and marginal revenue relations:

Public Demand

$$P_P = \$225 - \$0.005Q_P$$

$$MR_P = \Delta TR_P/\Delta Q_P = \$225 - \$0.01Q_P.$$

Student Demand

$$P_S = \$125 - \$0.00125Q_S$$

$$MR_S = \Delta TR_S/\Delta Q_S = \$125 - \$0.0025Q_S.$$

From these market demand and marginal revenue curves, it is obvious that the general public is willing to pay higher prices than are students. The general public is willing to purchase tickets up to a market price of $225, above which point market demand equals zero. Students are willing to enter the market only at ticket prices below $125.

During recent years, the football program has run on an operating budget of $1.5 million per year. This budget covers fixed salary, recruiting, insurance, and facility-maintenance expenses. In addition to these fixed expenses, the university incurs variable ticket-handling, facility-cleaning, insurance, and security costs of $25 per season ticketholder. The resulting total cost and marginal cost functions are

$$TC = \$1,500,000 + \$25Q,$$

$$MC = \Delta TC/\Delta Q = \$25.$$

What are the optimal football ticket prices and quantities for each market, assuming that MSU adopts a new season ticket pricing policy featuring student discounts? To answer this question, one must realize that since $MC = \$25$, the athletic department's operating deficit is minimized by setting $MR = MC = \$25$ in each market segment and solving for Q. This is also the profit-maximizing strategy for the football program. Therefore

Public Demand

$$MR_P = MC$$

$$\$225 - \$0.01Q_P = \$25$$

$$\$0.01Q_P = \$200$$

$$Q_P = 20,000,$$

and

$$P_P = \$225 - \$0.005(20,000)$$

$$= \$125.$$

Student Demand

$$MR_S = MC$$

$$\$125 - \$0.0025Q_S = \$25$$

$$\$0.0025Q_S = \$100$$

$$Q_S = 40,000,$$

and,

$$P_S = \$125 - \$0.00125(40,000)$$

$$= \$75.$$

The football program's resulting total operating surplus (profit) is

Operating Surplus (Profit) $= TR_P + TR_S - TC$

$$= \$125(20{,}000) + \$75(40{,}000)$$
$$-\$1{,}500{,}000 - \$25(60{,}000)$$

$$= \$2.5 \text{ million.}$$

To summarize, the optimal price/output combination with price discrimination is 20,000 in unit sales to the general public at a price of \$125 and 40,000 in unit sales to students at a price of \$75. This two-tier pricing practice results in an optimal operating surplus (profit) of \$2.5 million.

COMPARISON WITH THE ONE-PRICE ALTERNATIVE

To gauge the implications of this new two-tier ticket pricing practice, it is interesting to contrast the resulting price/output and surplus levels with those that would result if MSU maintained its current one-price ticket policy.

If tickets are offered to students and the general public at the same price, the total amount of ticket demand equals the sum of student plus general public demand. The student and general public market demand curves are

$$Q_P = 45{,}000 - 200P_P \text{ and } Q_S = 100{,}000 - 800P_S.$$

Under the assumption $P_P = P_S$, total demand (Q_T) equals

$$Q_T = Q_P + Q_S$$
$$= 145{,}000 - 1{,}000P,$$

and

$$P = \$145 - \$0.001Q,$$

which implies that

$$MR = \$145 - \$0.002Q.$$

These aggregate student-plus-general-public market demand and marginal revenue curves hold only for prices below \$125, a level at which both the general public and students purchase tickets. For prices above \$125, only nonstudent purchasers buy tickets, and the public demand curve $P_P = \$225 - \$0.005Q_P$ represents total market demand as well. This causes the actual total demand curve to be kinked at a price of \$125, as shown in Figure 12.2.

The uniform season ticket price that maximizes operating surplus (or profits) is found by setting $MR = MC$ for the total market and solving for Q:

$$MR = MC$$

$$\$145 - \$0.002Q = \$25$$

$$\$0.002Q = \$120$$

$$Q = 60,000,$$

$$P = \$145 - \$0.001(60,000)$$

$$= \$85,$$

and

$$Q_P = 45,000 - 200(\$85) \qquad Q_S = 100,000 - 800(\$85)$$

$$= 28,000 \qquad\qquad\qquad = 32,000$$

$$\text{Operating surplus (profit)} = TR - TC$$

$$= \$85(60,000) - \$1,500,000$$
$$-\$25(60,000)$$

$$= \$2.1 \text{ million.}$$

Observe that the total number of tickets sold equals 60,000 under both the two-tier and the single-price policies. This results because the marginal cost of a ticket is the same under each scenario. Ticket-pricing policies featuring student discounts increase student attendance from 32,000 to 40,000 and maximize the football program's operating surplus at $2.5 million (rather than $2.1 million). It is the preferred pricing policy when viewed from MSU's perspective. However, such price discrimination creates both "winners" and "losers." Winners following adoption of student discounts include students and MSU. Losers include members of the general public, who pay higher football ticket prices or find themselves priced out of the market.

GRAPHIC ILLUSTRATION

The MSU pricing problem and the concept of price discrimination can be illustrated graphically. Figure 12.2 shows demand curves for the general public in part (a) and for students in part (b). The aggregate demand curve in part (c) represents the horizontal sum of the quantities demanded at each price in the public and student markets. The associated marginal revenue curve, MR_{P+S}, has a similar interpretation. For example, marginal revenue equals $25 at an attendance level of 20,000 in the public market and $25 at an attendance level of 40,000 in the student market. Accordingly, one point on the total marginal revenue curve represents output of 60,000 units and marginal revenue of $25. From a cost standpoint, it does not matter whether tickets are sold to the public or to students. The single marginal cost curve $MC = \$25$ applies to each market.

**PRICE DISCRIMINATION FOR AN IDENTICAL PRODUCT
SOLD IN TWO MARKETS**

Figure 12.2

Price discrimination results in higher prices for market segments with low price elasticity (public)
and lower prices for market segments with high price elasticity (students).

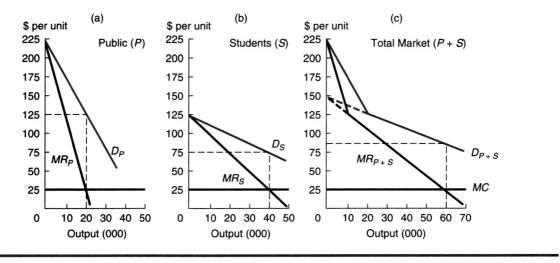

Graphically solving this pricing problem is a two-part process. The profit-maximizing total output level must first be determined, and then this output must be allocated between submarkets. Profit maximization occurs at the aggregate output level at which marginal revenue and marginal cost are equal. Figure 12.2(c) shows a profit-maximizing output of 60,000 tickets, where marginal cost and marginal revenue both equal $25. Proper allocation of total output between the two submarkets is determined graphically by drawing a horizontal line to indicate that $25 is the marginal cost in each market at the indicated aggregate output level. The intersection of this horizontal line with the marginal revenue curve in each submarket indicates the optimal distribution of sales and pricing structure. In this example, profits are maximized at an attendance (output) level of 60,000, selling 20,000 tickets to the public at a price of $125 and 40,000 tickets to students at a price of $75.

PRICE DISCRIMINATION EXAMPLE SUMMARY

The price charged in the less elastic public market is two-thirds higher than the price charged to students, whose demand is relatively elastic. This price differential adds substantially to MSU's profits. In the case of a uniform pricing policy, the school acts as though it faced only the single total market demand curve shown in Figure 12.2(c). Profit maximization requires operation at the output level where $MR = MC$—that is, at 60,000 tickets. The single price that would prevail is $85, the price determined by the intersection of a vertical line at 60,000 tickets with the total market demand curve, D_{P+S}.

Pricing Practices in the Airline Industry

The airline industry is often criticized for pricing practices that vacation travelers and business customers regard as confusing at best, and sometimes as downright unfair. High on the customer list of concerns is the typical airline pricing practice of charging different customers widely differing fares depending upon the time lag between the point of ticket purchase and the scheduled time of departure. At United Airlines, for example, during early-1997 the cheapest 21-day advance "excursion" fare between Chicago, Illinois and Los Angeles, California was $318, or 83% below the normal unrestricted round trip coach fare of $1,902. Somewhat more modest pricing differentials are common on shorter routes with heavy traffic. For example, early in 1997 Southwest Airlines charged $91 one way, $182 round trip, for urestricted flights between Kansas City and Chicago (Midway), and only $88 round trip for seven-day advance purchase fares.

Because complicated pricing practices have a tendency to alienate leisure and business travelers, individual carriers periodically attempt to simplify the industry's complicated domestic fare structure. Such plans are often described as good for consumers because they typically cut unrestricted fares dramatically. They are often better for the airlines, because average fares typically rise under simplified pricing plans when steep discounts for vacation travelers are eliminated. Unfortunately for the industry, various simplified but higher air fares routinely fail to generate the hoped-for additional business. Airlines have lured travelers with special discounts and other promotions for years, and they balk when the industry attempts to eliminate them. Travelers are used to taking advantage of brutal price wars by airlines teetering on the brink of bankruptcy under mountains of financial leverage. "One time" fare promotions such as free companion tickets for any adult traveling on a full-fare ticket, or 50% off the lowest fare price, are now industry staples during low traffic periods. Discounting has been especially prevalent among carriers operating under bankruptcy court protection, thereby sheltered from creditors.

Why do the airlines rush to sell discounted tickets? The answer to this question lies in the basic economics of

the airline industry. Air travel is a capital-intensive business where cash flow is king. Given Federal Aviation Administration regulation of airline safety, customers are apt to travel on whichever carrier offers the lowest price and most convenient departure schedule. With uniformly high safety standards, airline passenger service becomes an essentially commodity-like business. To attract passengers and build market share with "hub and spoke" travel networks, carriers must order and pay for millions of dollars in new planes and other equipment, sometimes years in advance. This gives rise to huge fixed costs that must be met regardless of passenger traffic. *Any* revenue growth has the potential to make an important contribution toward covering fixed expenses and making a profit contribution. This makes the airlines fight like mad for revenue.

As long as excess capacity and at least a few competitors exist in important markets, recurrent fare wars and dismal operating profits are probable. Taking the industry's gigantic losses during the early-1990s into account, the airlines have actually *lost* money in accounting terms since the time of Kitty Hawk, when the industry began. This is an amazing record when one considers that passenger miles, a measure of industry output, and revenue grow consistently. Stockholders typically reap only meager dividends, if any, and little in the way of capital gains. While bondholders of nonbankrupt carriers receive timely bond interest and principal payments, total indebtedness in the industry continues to grow. In real terms, the return to investors in the airline industry has been bleak.

Prices will continue to fall as the airlines are forced to eliminate services that have a low priority with consumers. Years ago, the airlines used to offer security check-in services for passenger luggage. Today, luggage loss and theft is up at airports as passengers handle their own bags. In the future, it will be interesting to see if continuing cost pressures bring the airlines to completely eliminate meals, beverages, and other low-value services.

See: Scott McCartney, "Strike Threat at American Gives Travelers Jitters," *The Wall Street Journal,* January 31, 1997, B1, B6.

Optimal price discrimination requires that marginal revenue equal marginal cost in each market. When an identical product is sold in two markets, as in this example, marginal revenue in each market is also equal, $MR_P = MR_S = MC$. This results because the products sold are indistinguishable from a production standpoint. If marginal costs of production and distribution are different in each market, profit maximization requires equating marginal revenues to marginal costs in each separate market.

Multiple-Product Pricing

It is difficult to think of even a single firm that does not produce a variety of products. Almost all companies produce multiple models, styles, or sizes of output, and each of these variations can represent a separate product for pricing purposes. Although multiple-product pricing requires the same basic analysis as for a single product, the analysis is complicated by demand and production interrelations.

DEMAND INTERRELATIONS

Demand interrelations arise because of competition or complementarity among various products or product lines. If products are interrelated, either as substitutes or complements, a change in the price of one affects demand for the other. Multiple-product pricing decisions must reflect such influences. In the case of a two-product firm, the marginal revenue functions for each product can be written as:

$$MR_A = \frac{\Delta TR}{\Delta Q_A} = \frac{\Delta TR_A}{\Delta Q_A} + \frac{\Delta TR_B}{\Delta Q_A}, \tag{12.12}$$

$$MR_B = \frac{\Delta TR}{\Delta Q_B} = \frac{\Delta TR_B}{\Delta Q_B} + \frac{\Delta TR_A}{\Delta Q_B}. \tag{12.13}$$

Equations 12.12 and 12.13 are general statements describing the marginal revenue/output relations for the two products. The first term on the right side of each equation represents the marginal revenue directly associated with each product. The second term depicts the indirect marginal revenue associated with each product and indicates the change in revenues due to a change in sales of the alternative product. For example, $\Delta TR_B/\Delta Q_A$ in Equation 12.12 shows the effect on Product B revenues of an additional unit sold of Product A. Likewise, $\Delta TR_A/\Delta Q_B$ in Equation 12.13 represents the change in revenues received from Product A when an additional unit of Product B is sold.

Cross-marginal revenue terms that reflect demand interrelations can be positive or negative. For complementary products, the net effect is positive in that increased sales of one product lead to increased revenues from another. For substitute products, increased sales of one product reduce demand for another, and the cross-marginal revenue term is negative. Accurate price determination in the case of multiple products requires a complete analysis of pricing decision effects. This often means that optimal pricing requires an application of incremental analysis to ensure that the total implications of pricing decisions are reflected.

PRODUCTION INTERRELATIONS

By-Product
Output that is customarily produced as a direct result of an increase in the production of some other output.

Whereas many products are related to one another through demand relationships, others are related in terms of the production process. A **by-product** is any output that is customarily produced as a direct result of an increase in the production of some other output. While it is common to think of by-products as resulting only from physical production processes, they are also generated in the process of providing services. One of the primary reasons why top accounting firms have become such a leading force in the management information systems (MIS) consulting business is that information generated in the auditing process has natural MIS implications, and *vice versa*. In this way, auditing and consulting services are joint products produced in variable proportions. The cost of providing each service depends greatly on the extent to which the other is also provided. Given the efficiencies of joint production, it is common for an accounting firm's auditing clients to also become MIS consulting clients.

Multiple products are produced in variable proportions for a wide range of goods and services. In the refining process for crude oil, gasoline, diesel fuel, heating oil, and other products are produced in variable proportions. The cost and availability of any single by-product depends on the demand for others. By-products are also sometimes the unintended or unavoidable consequence of producing certain goods. Whenever lumber is produced, scrap bark and sawdust are also created and used in gardening and paper production. Whenever paper is produced, residual chemicals and polluted water are created that must be treated and recycled. Indeed, pollution can be thought of as the necessary by-product of many production processes. Since pollution is, by definition, a "bad" with harmful social consequences rather than a "good" with socially redeeming value, production processes must often be altered to minimize this type of negative joint product.

Production interrelations are sometimes so strong that the degree of jointness in production is relatively constant and unchanging. For example, many agricultural products are jointly produced in a fixed ratio. Wheat and straw, beef and hides, milk and butter are all produced in relatively fixed proportions. In mining, gold and copper, silver and lead, and other precious metals and minerals are often produced jointly in fixed proportions. Appropriate pricing and production decisions are possible only when such interrelations are accurately reflected.

JOINT PRODUCTS PRODUCED IN VARIABLE PROPORTIONS

Firms can often vary the proportions in which joint products are created. Even the classic example of fixed proportions in the joint production of beef and hides holds only over short periods: leaner or heavier cattle can be bred to provide differing proportions of these two products. When the proportions of joint output can be varied, it is possible to construct separate marginal cost relations for each product. This is illustrated in Table 12.3, a schedule of cost/output relations for two joint products, A and B. Since the marginal cost of either product is defined as the increase in total costs associated with a unit increase in that product, *holding constant the quantity of the other product produced,* the marginal costs of producing *A* can be determined by examining the data in each row of the table, and the marginal costs of *B* are obtained from each column. For example, the marginal cost of the fourth unit of *A*, holding the production of *B* at 2 units, is \$5 (= \$23 − \$18); the marginal cost of the fifth unit of *B* when output of *A* is 3 units is \$25 (= \$78 − \$53).

Optimal price/output determination for joint products in this case requires a simultaneous solution of cost and revenue relations. This process can be illustrated graphically through the construction of isorevenue and isocost curves, as in Figure 12.3. The isocost curves map out the locus of all production combinations that can be produced for a given total cost. The isorevenue curves indicate all combinations of the products that, when sold, result in a given revenue. The isorevenue relations in Figure 12.3 have been drawn as straight lines for simplicity. This reflects an underlying assumption that each product is sold in a competitive market. Only with a horizontal demand curve do prices not vary with respect to changing output. If pure competition does not exist and prices vary as output changes, isorevenue lines will be curved rather than straight, but the optimal output combination is still indicated by tangencies between isocost and isorevenue curves.

At points of tangency between isocost and isorevenue curves, the marginal costs of producing each product are proportionate to marginal revenues. Therefore, these tangencies indicate optimal proportions in which to produce the products. Because profit equals revenue minus cost, the firm maximizes profit by operating at the tangency between the isorevenue and isocost curves whose positive difference is greatest. At that tangency, the marginal cost of producing each product just equals the marginal revenue it generates. Point Q^* in Figure 12.3 indicates the profit-maximizing combination of Products *A* and *B* in the illustrated example. Production and sale of A^* units of *A* and B^* units of *B* result in a profit of 12, the maximum possible under the conditions shown.

While the preceding discussion demonstrates the possibility of determining the separate marginal costs of goods produced in variable proportions, it is impossible to determine their individual average costs. This is because **common costs** or expenses are necessary for manufacture of a joint product. Common costs of production—raw material and equipment costs, management expenses, and other overhead—cannot be

Common Costs
Expenses that are necessary for manufacture of a joint product.

Table 12.3

COST/OUTPUT SCHEDULE FOR TWO JOINT PRODUCTS

OUTPUT OF B	OUTPUT OF A				
	1	2	3	4	5
1	\$ 5	\$ 7	\$10	\$15	\$22
2	10	13	18	23	31
3	20	25	33	40	50
4	35	43	53	63	75
5	55	67	78	90	105

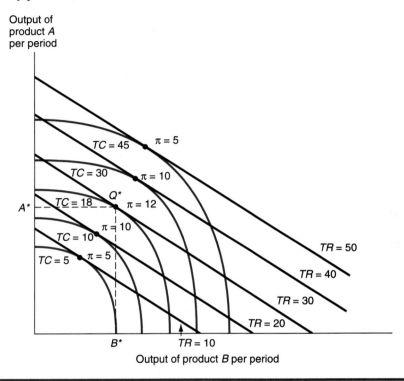

Figure 12.3

OPTIMAL PRICE/OUTPUT COMBINATIONS FOR JOINT PRODUCTS PRODUCED IN VARIABLE PROPORTIONS

If joint products can be produced in variable proportions, profits are maximized where $MR = MC$ for each by-product. (All values are in dollars.)

allocated to each individual by-product on any economically sound basis. Only costs that can be separately identified with a specific by-product can be allocated. For example, tanning costs for hides and refrigeration costs for beef are separate identifiable costs of each by-product. Feed costs are common and cannot be allocated between hide and beef production. Any allocation of common costs is wrong and arbitrary.

JOINT PRODUCTS PRODUCED IN FIXED PROPORTIONS

An interesting case of joint production is that of by-products produced in fixed proportions. In this situation, it makes no sense to attempt to separate the products from a production or cost standpoint. Products that must be produced in fixed proportions should be considered as a package or bundle of output. This is because it is impossible to determine the costs of each individual by-product. When by-products are jointly produced in fixed proportions, all costs are common, and there is no economically sound method of allocation. Optimal price/output determination for output produced in fixed proportions requires analysis of the relation between marginal revenue and marginal cost for the combined output package. As long as the sum of marginal revenues obtained from each by-product is greater than the marginal cost of production, the firm gains by expanding output.

Figure 12.4 illustrates the pricing problem for two products produced in fixed proportions. Demand and marginal revenue curves for each by-product and the single marginal cost curve for production of the combined output package are shown. *Vertical* summation of the two marginal revenue curves indicates the total marginal revenue generated by both by-products. Marginal revenue curves are summed vertically because each unit of output provides revenues from the sale of both by-products. The intersection of the total marginal revenue curve MR_T with the marginal cost curve identifies the profit-maximizing output level.

The optimal price for each by-product is determined by the intersection of a vertical line at the profit-maximizing output level with each by-product's demand curve. Q_1

OPTIMAL PRICING FOR JOINT PRODUCTS PRODUCED IN FIXED PROPORTIONS

Figure 12.4

For joint products produced in fixed proportions, the optimal activity level occurs at the point where the marginal revenues derived from both products (MR_T) equal the marginal cost of production.

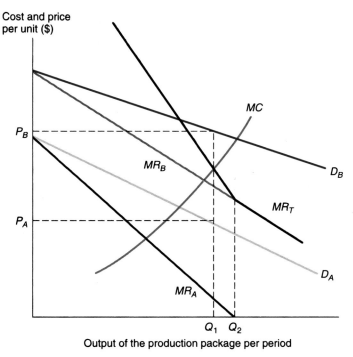

Output of the production package per period

represents the optimal quantity of the output package to be produced, and P_A and P_B are the prices to be charged for each by-product. If this graph dealt with cattle, the joint package would consist of one hide and two sides of beef. Q_1 for the firm in question might be 3,000 steers, resulting in 6,000 sides of beef sold at a price of P_A and 3,000 hides sold at P_B per unit.

Notice that the MR_T curve in Figure 12.4 coincides with the marginal revenue curve for Product B at all output quantities greater than Q_2. This is because M_A becomes negative at that point, and the firm would not sell more than the quantity of Product A represented by Output Package Q_2. The total revenue generated by Product A is maximized at output Q_2; sales of any larger quantity of Product A would reduce revenues and profits.

If the marginal cost curve for the output package intersects the total marginal revenue curve to the right of Q_2, profit maximization requires that the firm raise output up to this point of intersection. At that point, Product B must be priced as indicated by its demand and marginal revenue curves. Since Product B sales offer the sole motivation for production beyond the Q_2 level, the marginal revenue generated from Product B sales must be sufficient to cover the marginal costs of producing the entire output package. In this instance, profit maximization requires that $MR_B = MC$. Beyond the Q_2 level, the marginal cost of Product A is zero; Product A is the unavoidable by-product of Product B production. Beyond the Q_2 level, the price of Product A is set in order to maximize profits in that $MR_A = MC_A = 0$. This pricing situation is illustrated in Figure 12.5, which shows the same demand and marginal revenue curves presented in Figure 12.4, along with a new marginal cost curve. The optimal output quantity is Q_3, determined by the intersection of the marginal cost curve and the total marginal revenue curve. Product B is sold in the amount indicated by Output Package Q_3 and is priced at P_B. The sales quantity of Product A is limited to the amount in output Q_2 and is priced at P_A. The excess quantity of Product A produced, shown as $Q_3 - Q_2$, must be destroyed or otherwise kept out of the market so that its price and total revenue is not lowered below that indicated at Q_2.

An example of joint output that is sometimes destroyed or otherwise held off the market is provided by sliced pineapple and pineapple juice; juice is produced as a by-product as pineapples are peeled and sliced. Some years ago, an excessive amount of pineapple juice was produced, and rather than put it on the market and depress prices, the excess was destroyed. Seeing a profit-making opportunity, Dole, Del Monte, and other producers advertised heavily to shift the demand curve for juice outward. New products were also created, such as pineapple-grapefruit juice, to spur demand for the waste by-product. Canning machinery was also improved to reduce the amount of juice. Today, little if any pineapple excess juice by-product is produced. Similarly, firms in many other industries have discovered new and valuable uses for previously discarded by-products.

An Example of Joint Product Pricing

A graphic approach offers a useful introduction to the solution of joint product pricing problems, but many real-world problems require a more detailed analytic treatment. An

Figure 12.5

OPTIMAL PRICING FOR JOINT PRODUCTS PRODUCED IN FIXED PROPORTIONS WITH EXCESS PRODUCTION OF ONE PRODUCT

When all of by-product A cannot be sold at a price that generates positive marginal revenue, its sales will be limited to the point where $MR_A = 0$. Excess production, shown as $Q_3 - Q_2$, will be destroyed or otherwise held off the market.

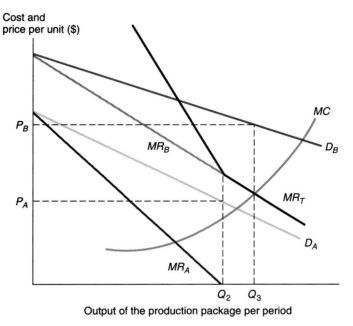

Output of the production package per period

example of a price/output decision for two products produced in fixed proportions will help clarify the technique.

JOINT PRODUCTS WITHOUT EXCESS BY-PRODUCT

The Vancouver Paper Company, located in Vancouver, B.C., produces newsprint and packaging materials in a fixed 1:1 ratio, or one ton of packaging materials per one ton of newsprint. These two products, A (newsprint) and B (packaging materials), are produced in equal quantities because newsprint production leaves scrap by-product that is useful only in the production of lower-grade packaging materials. The total and marginal cost functions for Vancouver can be written

$$TC = \$2,000,000 + \$50Q + \$0.01Q^2,$$

$$MC = \Delta TC/\Delta Q = \$50 + \$0.02Q,$$

where Q is a composite package or bundle of output consisting of one ton of Product A and one ton of Product B. Given current market conditions, demand and marginal revenue curves for each product are as follows:

Newsprint   *Packaging Materials*

$$P_A = \$400 - \$0.01Q_A \qquad\qquad P_B = \$350 - \$0.015Q_B$$

$$MR_A = \Delta TR_A/\Delta Q_A = \$400 - \$0.02Q_A \quad MR_B = \Delta TR_B/\Delta Q_B = \$350 - \$0.03Q_B$$

For each unit of Q produced, the firm obtains one unit of Product A and one unit of Product B for sale to customers. The revenue derived from the production and sale of one unit of Q is composed of revenues from the sales of one unit of Product A plus one unit of Product B. Therefore, the total revenue function is merely a sum of the revenue functions for Products A and B:

$$TR = TR_A + TR_B$$
$$= P_AQ_A + P_BQ_B.$$

Substituting for P_A and P_B results in the total revenue function:

$$TR = (\$400 - \$0.01Q_A)Q_A + (\$350 - \$0.015Q_B)Q_B$$
$$= \$400Q_A - \$0.01Q_A^2 + \$350Q_B - \$0.015Q_B^2.$$

Because one unit of Product A and one unit of Product B are contained in each unit of Q, $Q_A = Q_B = Q$. This allows substitution of Q for Q_A and Q_B to develop a total revenue function in terms of Q, the unit of production:

$$TR = \$400Q - \$0.01Q^2 + \$350Q - \$0.015Q^2$$
$$= \$750Q - \$0.025Q^2.$$

This total revenue function assumes that all quantities of Product A and B produced are also sold. It assumes no dumping or withholding from the market for either product. It is the appropriate total revenue function if, as in Figure 12.4, the marginal revenues of both products are positive at the profit-maximizing output level. When this occurs, revenues from each product contribute toward covering marginal costs.

The profit-maximizing output level is found by setting $MR = MC$ and solving for Q:

$$MR = MC$$
$$\$750 - \$0.05Q = \$50 + \$0.02Q$$
$$0.07Q = 700$$
$$Q = 10,000 \text{ units.}$$

At the activity level $Q = 10,000$ units, marginal revenues for each product are positive:

$$MR_A = \$400 - \$0.02Q_A \qquad\qquad MR_B = \$350 - \$0.03Q_B$$
$$= \$400 - \$0.02(10,000) \qquad\qquad = \$350 - \$0.03(10,000)$$
$$= \$200 \text{ (at 10,000 Units)}. \qquad = \$50 \text{ (at 10,000 Units)}.$$

Each product makes a positive contribution toward covering the marginal cost of production, where:

$$MC = \$50 + \$0.02Q$$
$$= \$50 + \$0.02(10,000)$$
$$= \$250.$$

There is no reason to expand or reduce production because $MR = MR_A + MR_B = MC = \$250$, and each product generates positive marginal revenues.

Prices for each product and total profits for Vancouver can be calculated from the demand and total profit functions:

$$P_A = \$400 - \$0.01Q_A \qquad\qquad P_B = \$350 - \$0.015Q_B$$
$$= \$400 - \$0.01(10,000) \qquad\qquad = \$350 - \$0.015(10,000)$$
$$= \$300, \qquad\qquad = \$200,$$

and

$$\pi = P_AQ_A + P_BQ_B - TC$$
$$= \$300(10,000) + \$200(10,000) - \$2,000,000$$
$$-\$50(10,000) - \$0.01(10,000^2)$$
$$= \$1,500,000.$$

Vancouver should produce 10,000 units of output and sell the resulting 10,000 units of Product A at a price of $300 per ton and 10,000 units of Product B at a price of $200 per ton. An optimum total profit of $1.5 million is earned at this activity level.

JOINT PRODUCTION WITH EXCESS BY-PRODUCT (DUMPING)

The determination of a profit-maximizing activity level is only slightly more complex if a downturn in demand for either Product A or B causes marginal revenue for one product to be negative when all output produced is sold to the marketplace.

Suppose that an economic recession causes the demand for Product B (packaging materials) to fall dramatically, while the demand for Product A (newsprint) and marginal cost conditions hold steady. Assume new demand and marginal revenue relations for Product B of

$$P_B' = \$290 - \$0.02Q_B,$$
$$MR_B' = \$290 - \$0.04Q_B.$$

A dramatically lower price of $90 per ton [= $290 − $0.02(10,000)] is now required to sell 10,000 units of Product B. However, this price and activity level is suboptimal.

To see why, the profit-maximizing activity level must again be calculated, assuming that all output is sold. The new marginal revenue curve for Q is

$$MR = MR_A + MR'_B$$
$$= \$400 - \$0.02Q_A + \$290 - \$0.04Q_B$$
$$= \$690 - \$0.06Q.$$

If all production is sold, the profit-maximizing level for output is found by setting $MR = MC$ and solving for Q:

$$MR = MC$$
$$\$690 - \$0.06Q = \$50 + \$0.02Q$$
$$0.08Q = 640$$
$$Q = 8,000.$$

At $Q = 8,000$, the sum of marginal revenues derived from both by-products and the marginal cost of producing the combined output package each equal $210, since

$$MR = \$690 - \$0.06Q \qquad\qquad MC = \$50 + \$0.02Q$$
$$= \$690 - \$0.06(8,000) \qquad\qquad = \$50 + \$0.02(8,000)$$
$$= \$210. \qquad\qquad\qquad\qquad = \$210.$$

However, the marginal revenue of Product B is no longer positive:

$$MR_A = \$400 - \$0.02Q_A \qquad\qquad MR'_B = \$290 - \$0.04Q_B$$
$$= \$400 - \$0.02(8,000) \qquad\qquad = \$290 - \$0.04(8,000)$$
$$= \$240. \qquad\qquad\qquad\qquad = -\$30.$$

Even though $MR = MC = \$210$, the marginal revenue of Product B is negative at the $Q = 8,000$ activity level. This means that the price reduction necessary to sell the last unit of Product B causes Vancouver's total revenue to decline by $30. Rather than sell Product B at such unfavorable terms, Vancouver would prefer to withhold some from the marketplace. In contrast, Vancouver would like to produce and sell more than 8,000 units of Product A since $MR_A > MC$ at the 8,000 unit activity level. It would be profitable for the company to expand production of Q just to increase sales of Product A, even if it had to destroy or otherwise withhold from the market the unavoidable added production of Product B.

Under these circumstances, set the marginal revenue of Product A, the only product sold at the margin, equal to the marginal cost of production to find the profit-maximizing activity level:

$$MR_A = MC$$

$$\$400 - \$0.02Q = \$50 + \$0.02Q$$

$$\$0.04Q = \$350$$

$$Q = 8{,}750 \text{ units.}$$

Under these circumstances, Vancouver should produce 8,750 units of $Q = Q_A = Q_B$. Since this activity level is based on the assumption that only Product A is sold at the margin and that the marginal revenue of Product A covers all marginal production costs, *the effective marginal cost of Product B is zero.* As long as production is sufficient to provide 8,750 units of Product A, 8,750 units of Product B are also produced without any additional cost.

With an effective marginal cost of zero for Product B, its contribution to firm profits is maximized by setting the marginal revenue of Product B equal to zero (its effective marginal cost):

$$MR_B' = MC_B$$

$$\$290 - \$0.04Q_B = \$0$$

$$\$0.04Q_B = \$290$$

$$Q_B = 7{,}250.$$

Whereas a total of 8,750 units of Q should be produced, only 7,250 units of Product B will be sold. The remaining 1,500 units of Q_B must be destroyed or otherwise withheld from the market.

Optimal prices and the maximum total profit for Vancouver are as follows:

$$
\begin{aligned}
P_A &= \$400 - \$0.01Q_A & P_B' &= \$290 - \$0.02Q_B \\
&= \$400 - \$0.01(8{,}750) & &= \$290 - \$0.02(7{,}250) \\
&= \$312.50, & &= \$145,
\end{aligned}
$$

$$
\begin{aligned}
\pi &= P_A Q_A + P_B' Q_B - TC \\
&= \$312.50(8{,}750) + \$145(7{,}250) - \$2{,}000{,}000 \\
&\quad - \$50(8{,}750) - \$0.01(8{,}750^2) \\
&= \$582{,}500.
\end{aligned}
$$

No other price/output combination has the potential to generate as large a profit for Vancouver.

Transfer Pricing

Expanding markets brought about by improvements in communication and transportation, as well as falling trade barriers, have led to the development of large, multidivision firms that cut across national boundaries. The advantages of large-scale enterprises are often obvious; common problems are sometimes less apparent. A vexing difficulty encountered is the challenge to set an appropriate price for the transfer of goods and services among divisions.

THE TRANSFER PRICING PROBLEM

Vertical Relation
Where the output of one division or company is the input to another.

Vertical Integration
When a single company controls various links in the production chain from basic inputs to final output.

The transfer pricing problem results from the difficulty of establishing profitable relationships among divisions of a single company when each separate business unit stands in **vertical relation** to the other. A vertical relation is one where the output of one division or company is the input to another. **Vertical integration** occurs when a single company controls various links in the production chain from basic inputs to final output. A cable TV company like Telecommunications, Inc. (TCI) is vertically integrated because it owns a number of cable TV systems plus a number of programming properties. Thus, vertically integrated companies in this field own and operate the distribution channel and the software that is sold over the distribution channel.

Transfer Pricing
The pricing of products transferred among divisions of a firm.

To combat the problems of coordinating large-scale enterprises that are vertically integrated, separate profit centers are typically established for each important product or product line. Despite obvious advantages, this decentralization has the potential to create problems. The most critical of these is the problem of **transfer pricing,** or the pricing of intermediate products transferred among divisions. To maximize profits for the vertically integrated firm, it is essential that a profit margin or markup only be charged at the final stage of production. All intermediate products transferred internally must be transferred at marginal cost.

TRANSFER PRICING FOR PRODUCTS WITHOUT EXTERNAL MARKETS

Think of the divisionalized firm as a type of internal market. Like external markets, the internal markets of divisionalized firms act according to the laws of supply and demand. Supply is offered by various downstream suppliers to meet the demand of upstream users. Goods and services must be transferred and priced each step along the way from basic raw materials to finished products.

For simplicity, consider the problem faced by a vertically integrated firm that has different divisions at distinct points along the various steps of the production process, and assume for the moment that no external market exists for transferred inputs. If each separate division is established as a profit center to provide employees with an efficiency incentive, a transfer pricing problem can occur. Suppose each selling division adds a markup over its marginal cost for inputs sold to other divisions. Each buying division would then set its marginal revenue from output equal to the division's marginal cost of input. This process would culminate in a marginal cost to the ultimate upstream user that is in excess of the sum total of marginal costs for each transferring division. All of the markups charged by each transferring division drive a wedge between the firm's true marginal cost of production and the marginal cost to the last or ultimate upstream user. As a result, the ultimate upstream user buys less than the optimal amount of input and produces less than the profit-maximizing level of output.

For example, it would be inefficient if TCI, a major cable TV distributor, paid more than the marginal cost of programming produced by its own subsidiaries. If each subsidiary added a markup to the marginal cost of programming sold to the parent company, TCI would buy less than a profit-maximizing amount of its own programming. In fact, TCI would have an incentive to seek programming from other purveyors so long as the external market price was less than the internal transfer price. Such an incentive could create extreme inefficiencies, especially when the external market price is less than the transfer price, but greater than the marginal cost of programming produced by TCI's own subsidiaries.

An effective transfer pricing system leads to activity levels in each division that are consistent with profit maximization for the overall enterprise. This observation leads to the first and most basic rule for optimal transfer pricing: *when transferred products cannot be sold in external markets, the marginal cost of the transferring division is the optimal transfer price.* One practical means for ensuring that an optimal amount of input is transferred at an optimal transfer price is to inform buying divisions that the marginal cost curve of supplying divisions is to be treated like a supply schedule. Alternatively, supplying divisions could be informed about the buying division's marginal revenue or demand curve and told to use this information in determining the quantity supplied. In either case, each division would voluntarily choose to transfer an optimal amount of input at the optimal transfer price.

TRANSFER PRICING WITH PERFECTLY COMPETITIVE EXTERNAL MARKETS

The transfer pricing problem is only sightly more complicated when transferred inputs can be sold in external markets. When transferred inputs can be sold in a perfectly competitive external market, the external market price represents the firm's opportunity cost of employing such inputs internally. As such, it would never pay to use inputs internally unless their value to the firm is at least as great as their value to others in the external market. This observation leads to a second key rule for optimal transfer pricing: *when transferred products can be sold in perfectly competitive external markets, the external market price is the optimal transfer price.* If downstream suppliers wish to supply more than upstream users desire to employ at a perfectly competitive price, excess input can be sold in the external market. If upstream users wish to employ more than downstream suppliers seek to furnish at a perfectly competitive price, excess input demand can be met through purchases in the external market. In either event, an optimal amount of input is transferred internally.

Of course, it is hard to imagine why a firm would be vertically integrated in the first place if all inputs could be purchased in perfectly competitive markets. Neither Kellogg's nor McDonald's, for example, have extensive agricultural operations to ensure a steady supply of foodstuffs. Grains for cereal and beef for hamburgers can both be purchased at prices that closely approximate marginal cost in perfectly competitive input markets. On the other hand, if an input market is typically competitive but punctuated by periods of scarcity and shortage, it can pay to maintain some input producing capability. For example, Exxon has considerable production facilities that supply its extensive distribution network with gasoline, oil, and petroleum products. These production facilities offer Exxon some protection against the threat of supply stoppages. Similarly, Coca-Cola has long-term supply contracts with orange growers to ensure a steady supply of product for its *Minute Maid* juice operation. Both Exxon and Coca-Cola offer examples of vertically integrated firms with inputs offered in markets that are usually, but not always, perfectly competitive.

TRANSFER PRICING WITH IMPERFECTLY COMPETITIVE EXTERNAL MARKETS

The typical case of vertical integration involves firms with inputs that can be transferred internally or sold in external markets that are not perfectly competitive. Again, it never pays to use inputs internally unless their value to the firm is at least as great as their value to others in the external market. This observation leads to a third and final fundamental rule for optimal transfer pricing: *when transferred products can be sold in imperfectly competitive external markets, the optimal transfer price equates the marginal cost of the transferring division to the marginal revenue derived from the combined internal and external markets.* In other words, when inputs can be sold in imperfectly competitive external markets, internal input demand must reflect the opportunity to supply input to the external market at a price in excess of marginal cost. If downstream suppliers wish to offer more input than upstream users desire to employ when input $MC = MR$ from the combined market, excess supply can be sold in the external market. If upstream users want to employ more than downstream suppliers seek to furnish when $MC = MR$, excess internal demand can be met through added purchases in the external market. In both cases, an optimal amount of input is transferred internally.

A Global Transfer Pricing Example

Transfer pricing is an important responsibility of management. This is particularly true in the case of vertically integrated firms that have dispersed global operations. While the transfer pricing concept can be introduced conceptually through the use of graphic analysis, most real-world applications are complex and must be solved algebraically. For this reason, examination of a detailed numerical example can be fruitful.

PROFIT MAXIMIZATION FOR AN INTEGRATED FIRM

Hope Steadman & Sons, Inc., is a small integrated domestic manufacturer of material handling equipment. Demand and marginal revenue curves for the firm are

$$P = \$100 - \$0.001Q,$$

$$MR = \$100 - \$0.002Q.$$

Relevant total cost, marginal cost, and profit functions are

$$TC = \$312,500 + \$25Q + \$0.0015Q^2,$$
$$MC = \$25 + \$0.003Q.$$
$$\pi = TR - TC$$
$$= \$100Q - \$0.001Q^2 - \$312,500 - \$25Q - \$0.0015Q^2$$
$$= -\$0.0025Q^2 + \$75Q - \$312,500.$$

Profit maximization occurs at the point where $MR = MC$, so the optimal output level is

$$MR = MC,$$
$$\$100 - \$0.002Q = \$25 + \$0.003Q,$$
$$75 = 0.005Q,$$
$$Q = 15,000.$$

This implies that

$$P = \$100 - \$0.001(15,000)$$
$$= \$85.$$
$$\pi = TR - TC$$
$$= -\$0.0025(15,000^2) + \$75(15,000) - \$312,500$$
$$= \$250,000.$$

Therefore, the optimal price/output combination is $85 and 15,000 units for this integrated firm, and profits total $250,000. To be optimal, transfer prices must ensure operation at these same levels.

TRANSFER PRICING WITH NO EXTERNAL MARKET

Consider how the situation changes if the firm is reorganized into separate manufacturing and distribution division profit centers, and no external market exists for the transferred product. The demand curve facing the distribution division is precisely the same as the firm's output demand curve. While the total cost function of the firm is unchanged, it can be broken down into the costs of manufacturing and distribution.
    Assume that such a breakdown results in the following divisional cost functions:

$$TC_{Mfg} = \$250,000 + \$20Q + \$0.001Q^2,$$
$$MC_{Mfg} = \$20 + \$0.002Q,$$

and

$$TC_{Distr} = \$62,500 + \$5Q + \$0.0005Q^2,$$
$$MC_{Distr} = \$5 + \$0.001Q.$$

With divisional operation, the total and marginal cost functions for the firm are

$$TC = TC_{Mfg} + TC_{Distr},$$
$$MC = MC_{Mfg} + MC_{Distr},$$

and precisely the same as before. No substantive change has occurred.

To demonstrate the derivation of an appropriate activity level, the net marginal revenue for the distribution division is set equal to the marginal cost of the manufacturing division:

$$MR - MC_{Distr} = MC_{Mfg},$$
$$\$100 - \$0.002Q - \$5 - \$0.001Q = \$20 + \$0.002Q,$$
$$75 = 0.005Q,$$
$$Q = 15,000.$$

The 15,000-unit output level remains optimal for profit maximization. If the distribution division determines the quantity it will purchase by movement along its marginal revenue curve, and the manufacturing division supplies output along its marginal cost curve, then the market-clearing transfer price is the price that results when $MR - MC_{Distr} = MC_{Mfg}$. At 15,000 units of output, the optimal transfer price is

$$P_T = MC_{Mfg}$$
$$= \$20 + \$0.002(15,000)$$
$$= \$50.$$

At a transfer price of $P_T = \$50$, the quantity supplied by the manufacturing division equals 15,000. This is the same quantity demanded by the distribution division at a $P_T = \$50$, since

$$MR - MC_{Distr} = P_T,$$
$$\$100 - \$0.002Q - \$5 - \$0.001Q = \$50,$$
$$45 = 0.003Q,$$
$$Q = 15,000.$$

At a transfer price of $P_T > \$50$, the distribution division will accept fewer units of output than the manufacturing division wants to supply. If $P_T < \$50$, the distribution division will seek to purchase more units than the manufacturing division desires to produce. Only at a $50 transfer price are supply and demand in balance in the firm's internal market.

A COMPETITIVE EXTERNAL MARKET
WITH EXCESS INTERNAL DEMAND

To consider the effects of an external market for the transferred product, assume that the company is able to *buy* an unlimited quantity of a comparable product from a foreign supplier at a price of $35. The product supplied by the foreign manufacturer meets the exact same specifications as that produced by Hope Steadman & Sons. Since an unlimited quantity can be purchased for $35, a perfectly competitive external market exists for the transferred product, and the optimal transfer price equals the external market price. For $P_T = \$35$, the quantity demanded by the distribution division is

$$MR - MC_{Distr} = P_T,$$

$$\$100 - \$0.002Q - \$5 - \$0.001Q = \$35,$$

$$60 = 0.003Q,$$

$$Q = 20,000,$$

whereas the quantity supplied by the manufacturing division is

$$P_T = MC_{Mfg},$$

$$\$35 = \$20 + \$0.002Q,$$

$$15 = 0.002Q,$$

$$Q = 7,500.$$

In this case of excess internal demand, the distribution division will purchase all 7,500 units produced internally plus an additional 12,500 units from the foreign supplier. The price impact for customers and the profit impact for Hope Steadman & Sons are dramatic. Domestic customer prices and total profits are now calculated as

$$P = \$100 - \$0.001(20,000)$$

$$= \$80,$$

and

$$\pi = TR - TC_{Mfg} - TC_{For.} - TC_{Distr}$$

$$= \$100(20,000) - \$0.001(20,000^2) - \$250,000 - \$20(7,500)$$
$$-\$0.001(7,500^2) - \$35(12,500) - \$62,500 - \$5(20,000)$$
$$-\$0.0005(20,000^2)$$

$$= \$343,750.$$

Hope Steadman & Sons' domestic customers benefit from the increased availability of goods, 20,000 versus 15,000 units, and lower prices, $80 versus $85 per unit. The opportunity to purchase goods at a price of $35 from a foreign supplier benefits the company since profits grow from $250,000 to $343,750. The firm now manufactures only 7,500 of the units sold to customers and has become much more of a distributor than an integrated manufacturer and distributor. Hope Steadman & Sons has been able to make its business and profits grow by focusing efforts on distribution, where it enjoys a comparative advantage.

A COMPETITIVE EXTERNAL MARKET WITH EXCESS INTERNAL SUPPLY

It is interesting to contrast these results with those achieved under somewhat different circumstances. For example, assume that Hope Steadman & Sons is able to *sell* an unlimited quantity of its goods to a foreign distributor at a price of $80. For simplicity, also assume that sales to this new market have no impact on the firm's ability to sell to current domestic customers and that this market can be supplied under the same cost conditions as previously. If $P_T = \$80$, the quantity demanded by the distribution division is

$$MR - MC_{Dist.} = P_T,$$

$$\$100 - \$0.002Q - \$5 - \$0.001Q = \$80,$$

$$15 = 0.003Q,$$

$$Q = 5,000,$$

whereas the quantity supplied by the manufacturing division is

$$P_T = MC_{Mfg},$$

$$\$80 = \$20 + \$0.002Q,$$

$$60 = 0.002Q,$$

$$Q = 30,000.$$

In this instance of excess internal supply, the distribution division will purchase all 5,000 units desired internally, while the manufacturing division will offer an additional 25,000 units to the new foreign distributor. Again, the price impact for customers and the profit impact for Hope Steadman & Sons are dramatic. Domestic customer prices and total profits are now as follows:

$$P = \$100 - \$0.001(5,000)$$

$$= \$95,$$

and

$$\pi = TR_{Dom} + TR_{For} - TC_{Mfg} - TC_{Distr}$$

$$= \$100(5,000) - \$0.001(5,000^2) + \$80(25,000) - \$250,000$$
$$-\$20(30,000) - \$0.001(30,000^2) - \$62,500 - \$5(5,000)$$
$$-\$0.0005(5,000^2)$$

$$= \$625,000.$$

Under this scenario, Hope Steadman & Sons' domestic market shrinks from an initial 15,000 to 5,000 units, and prices rise somewhat from $85 to $95 per unit. At the same time, foreign customers benefit from the increased availability of goods, 25,000 versus none previously, and the attractive purchase price of $80 per unit. The opportunity to sell at a price of $80 to a foreign distributor has also benefited the company, since profits grew from $250,000 to $625,000. The company now distributes only 5,000 of 30,000 units sold to customers and has become much more of a manufacturer than a distributor. By emphasizing manufacturing, Hope Steadman & Sons makes its business and profits grow by focusing efforts on what it does best.

Summary

This chapter examines a number of popular pricing practices. It becomes apparent that, when studied in detail, the methods commonly employed by successful firms reflect a careful appreciation of the use of marginal analysis to derive profit-maximizing prices.

- Many firms derive an optimal pricing policy using a technique called **markup pricing,** whereby prices are set to cover all direct costs plus a percentage markup for profit contribution. Flexible markup pricing practices that reflect differences in marginal costs and demand elasticities constitute an efficient method for ensuring that $MR = MC$ for each line of products sold.

- **Markup on cost** is the profit margin for an individual product or product line expressed as a percentage of unit cost. The numerator of this expression, called the **profit margin**, is the difference between price and cost. **Markup on price** is the profit margin for an individual product or product line expressed as a percentage of price, rather than unit cost.

- During **peak** periods, facilities are fully utilized. A firm has excess capacity during **off-peak** periods. Successful firms that employ markup pricing typically base prices on fully allocated costs under normal conditions but offer price discounts or accept lower margins during off-peak periods when substantial excess capacity is available.

- The **optimal markup on cost** formula is $OMC^* = -1/(\epsilon_P + 1)$. The **optimal markup-on-price** formula is $OMP^* = -1/\epsilon_P$. Either formula can be used to derive profit-maximizing prices solely on the basis of marginal cost and price elasticity of demand information.

- **Price discrimination** occurs whenever different market segments are charged different price markups for the same product. A **market segment** is a division or fragment of the overall market with essentially different or unique demand or cost characteristics. Price discrimination is evident whenever identical customers are charged different prices, or when price differences are not proportional to cost differences. Through price discrimination, sellers are able to increase profits by appropriating the **consumers' surplus.** Consumers' surplus (or customers' surplus) is the value of purchased goods and services above and beyond the amount paid to sellers.

- The extent to which a firm can engage in price discrimination is classified into three major categories. Under **first-degree price discrimination,** the firm extracts the maximum amount each customer is willing to pay for its products. Each unit is priced separately at the price indicated along each product demand curve. **Second-degree price discrimination** involves setting prices on the basis of the quantity purchased. Quantity discounts that lead to lower markups for large versus small customers are a common means for second-degree price discrimination. The most commonly observed form of price discrimination, **third-degree price discrimination,** results when a firm separates its customers into several classes and sets a different price for each customer class.

- A **by-product** is any output that is customarily produced as a direct result of an increase in the production of some other output. Profit maximization requires that marginal revenue be set equal to marginal cost for each by-product. While the marginal costs of by-products produced in variable proportions can be determined, it is impossible to do so for by-products produced in fixed proportions. **Common costs,** or expenses that are necessary for manufacture of a joint product, cannot be allocated on any economically sound basis.

- A **vertical relation** is one where the output of one division or company is the input to another. **Vertical integration** occurs when a single company controls various links in the production chain from basic inputs to final output. **Transfer pricing** deals with the problem of pricing intermediate products transferred among divisions of vertically integrated firms. When transferred products cannot be sold in competitive external markets, the marginal cost of the transferring division is the optimal transfer price. When transferred products can be sold in perfectly competitive external markets, the external market price is the optimal transfer price. When transferred products can be sold in imperfectly competitive external markets, the optimal transfer price equates the marginal cost of the transferring division to the marginal revenue derived from the combined internal and external markets.

Throughout the chapter, it has been shown that efficient pricing practices require a careful analysis of marginal revenues and marginal costs for each relevant product or product line. Among the most relevant marginal costs that must be considered are those costs involved with generating useful information on product demand and cost conditions. Rule-of-thumb pricing practices employed by successful firms can be reconciled with profit-maximizing behavior when the costs and benefits of pricing information are properly understood. These practices add tremendous value to the managerial decision-making process.

QUESTIONS

Q12.1 What is markup pricing?

Q12.2 Develop and explain the relation between the markup-on-cost and the markup-on-price formulas.

Q12.3 Identify and interpret the relation between the optimal markup on cost and the point price elasticity of demand.

Q12.4 Illustrate the relation between the optimal markup on price and the point price elasticity of demand.

Q12.5   "One of the least practical suggestions that economists have offered to managers is that they set marginal revenues equal to marginal costs." Discuss this statement.

Q12.6   "Marginal cost pricing, as well as the use of incremental analysis, is looked upon with favor by economists, especially those on the staffs of regulatory agencies. With this encouragement, regulated industries do indeed employ these rational techniques quite frequently. Unregulated firms, on the other hand, use marginal or incremental cost pricing much less frequently, sticking to cost-plus, or full-cost, pricing except under unusual circumstances.

In my opinion, this goes a long way toward explaining the problems of the regulated firms vis-à-vis unregulated industry." Discuss this statement.

Q12.7   What is price discrimination?

Q12.8   What conditions are necessary before price discrimination is both possible and profitable? Why does price discrimination result in higher profits?

Q12.9   Discuss the role of common costs in pricing practice.

Q12.10   Why is it possible to determine the marginal costs of joint products produced in variable proportions but not those of joint products produced in fixed proportions?

SELF-TEST PROBLEMS AND SOLUTIONS

ST12.1   Cliff Claven is a project coordinator at Norm Peterson & Associates, Ltd., a large Boston-based painting contractor. Claven has asked you to complete an analysis of profit margins earned on a number of recent projects. Unfortunately, your predecessor on this project was abruptly transferred, leaving you with only sketchy information on the firm's pricing practices.

A.   Use the available data to complete the following table:

PRICE	MARGINAL COST	MARKUP ON COST (%)	MARKUP ON PRICE (%)
$100	$25	300.0	75.0
240	72		
680	272	150.0	60.0
750		100.0	
2,800			40.0
	2,700	33.3	
	3,360		20.0
5,800			10.0
6,250		5.3	
	10,000		0.0

B.   Calculate the missing data for each of the following proposed projects, based on the available estimates of the point price elasticity of demand, optimal markup on cost, and optimal markup on price:

PROJECT	PRICE ELASTICITY	OPTIMAL MARKUP ON COST (%)	OPTIMAL MARKUP ON PRICE (%)
1	−1.5	200.0	66.7
2	−2.0		
3		66.7	
4			25.0
5	−5.0	25.0	
6		11.1	10.0
7	−15.0		
8	−20.0		5.0
9			4.0
10	−50.0	2.0	

ST12.1   **SOLUTION**

A.

PRICE	MARGINAL COST	MARKUP ON COST (%)	MARKUP ON PRICE (%)
$100	$25	300.0	75.0
240	72	233.3	70.0
680	272	150.0	60.0
750	375	100.0	50.0
2,800	1,680	66.7	40.0
3,600	2,700	33.3	25.0
4,200	3,360	25.0	20.0
5,800	5,220	11.1	10.0
6,250	5,938	5.3	5.0
10,000	10,000	0.0	0.0

B.

PROJECT	PRICE ELASTICITY	OPTIMAL MARKUP ON COST (%)	OPTIMAL MARKUP ON PRICE (%)
1	−1.5	200.0	66.7
2	−2.0	100.0	50.0
3	−2.5	66.7	40.0
4	−4.0	33.3	25.0
5	−5.0	25.0	20.0
6	−10.0	11.1	10.0
7	−15.0	7.1	6.7
8	−20.0	5.3	5.0
9	−25.0	4.2	4.0
10	−50.0	2.0	2.0

ST12.2 **Optimal Markup on Price.** TLC Lawncare, Inc., provides fertilizer and weed control lawn services to residential customers. Its seasonal service package, regularly priced at $250, includes several chemical spray treatments. As part of an effort to expand its customer base, TLC offered $50 off its regular price to customers in the Dallas area. Response was enthusiastic, with sales rising to 5,750 units (packages) from the 3,250 units sold in the same period last year.
A.   Calculate the arc price elasticity of demand for TLC service.
B.   Assume that the arc price elasticity (from Part A) is the best available estimate of the point price elasticity of demand. If marginal cost is $135 per unit for labor and materials, calculate

TLC's optimal markup on price and its optimal price.

ST12.2 **SOLUTION**

A. $E_P = \dfrac{\Delta Q}{\Delta P} \times \dfrac{P_2 + P_1}{Q_2 + Q_1}$

$= \dfrac{5,750 - 3,250}{\$200 - \$250} \times \dfrac{\$200 + \$250}{5,750 + 3,250}$

$= -2.5$

B.   Given $\epsilon_P = E_P = -2.5$, the optimal TLC markup on price is:

$$Optimal\ Markup\ on\ Price = \dfrac{-1}{\epsilon_P}$$

$$= \dfrac{-1}{-2.5}$$

$$= 0.4\ or\ 40\%$$

Given $MC = \$135$, the optimal price is:

$$Optimal\ Markup\ on\ Price = \dfrac{P - MC}{P}$$

$$0.4 = \dfrac{P - \$135}{P}$$

$$0.4P = P - \$135$$

$$0.6P = \$135$$

$$P = \$225$$

PROBLEMS

P12.1   **Markup Calculation.** Controller Bailey Porter has asked you to review the pricing practices of Cincinnati Novelty Products, Inc., an importer and regional distributor of low-priced trinkets and curios. Use the following data to calculate the relevant markup on cost and markup on price for the following five items in the next column.

PRODUCT	PRICE	MARGINAL COST	MARKUP ON COST (%)	MARKUP ON PRICE (%)
A	10¢	1¢		
B	29	6		
C	59	18		
D	89	31		
E	99	40		

P12.2 **Optimal Markup.** Management consultant David Addison has been retained to assess the pricing practices of Maddie Hayes' Moonlight Cafe. As Addison's assistant, use the following demand elasticity estimates to calculate the profit-maximizing markup on cost and markup on price for a variety of luncheon and dinner entrées.

ENTRÉ	PRICE ELASTICITY	OPTIMAL MARKUP ON COST	OPTIMAL MARKUP ON PRICE
A.	−1		
B.	−2		
C.	−3		
D.	−4		
E.	−5		

P12.3 **Optimal Price.** Payless Shoe Stores, Inc., cut prices on women's dress shoes by 2% during the first quarter and enjoyed a 4% increase in unit sales over the period compared with a year earlier.
A.   Calculate the point price elasticity of demand for Payless shoes.
B.   Calculate the company's optimal shoe price if marginal cost is $10 per unit.

P12.4 **Markup on Cost.** Brake-Checkup, Inc., offers automobile brake analysis and repair at a number of outlets in the Philadelphia area. The company recently initiated a policy of matching the lowest advertised competitor price. As a result, Brake-Checkup has been forced to reduce the average price for brake jobs by 3%, but it has enjoyed a 15% increase in customers. Marginal costs have held steady at $120 per brake job.
A.   Calculate the point price elasticity of demand for brake jobs.
B.   Calculate Brake-Checkup's optimal price and markup on cost.

P12.5 **Optimal Markup on Cost.** The Bristol, Inc. is an elegant dining establishment that features French cuisine at dinner six nights per week, and brunch on weekends. To boost traffic from shoppers during the Christmas season, the Bristol offered Saturday customers $2 off its $8 regular price for brunch. The promotion proved successful, with brunch sales rising from 250 to 750 units per day.

A.   Calculate the arc price elasticity of demand for brunch at the Bristol.
B.   Assume that the arc price elasticity (from Part A) is the best available estimate of the point price elasticity of demand. If marginal cost is $4.28 per unit for labor and materials, calculate the Bristol's optimal markup on cost and its optimal price.

P12.6 **Peak/Off-Peak Pricing.** Simon & Simon Construction Company is a building contractor serving the Gulf Coast region. The company recently bid on a new office building construction project in Mobile, Alabama. Simon & Simon has incurred bid development and job cost-out expenses of $25,000 prior to submission of the bid. The bid was based on the following projected costs:

COST CATEGORY	AMOUNT
Bid development and job cost-out expenses	$25,000
Materials	881,000
Labor (50,000 hours @ $26)	1,300,000
Variable overhead (40% of direct labor)	520,000
Allocated fixed overhead (6% of total costs)	174,000
Total costs	$2,900,000

A.   What is Simon & Simon's minimum acceptable (breakeven) contract price, assuming that the company is operating at peak capacity?
B.   What is the Simon & Simon's minimum acceptable contract price if an economic downturn has left the company with substantial excess capacity?

P12.7 **Incremental Pricing Analysis.** The General Eclectic Company manufactures an electric toaster. Sales of the toaster have increased steadily during the previous five years, and, because of a recently completed expansion program, annual capacity is now 500,000 units. Production and sales during the upcoming year are forecast to be 400,000 units, and standard production costs are estimated as follows:

Materials	$6.00
Direct labor	4.00
Variable indirect labor	2.00
Fixed overhead	3.00
Allocated cost per unit	$15.00

In addition to production costs, General incurs fixed selling expenses of $1.50 per unit and variable warranty repair expenses of $1.20 per unit. General currently receives $20 per unit from its customers (primarily retail department stores), and it expects this price to hold during the coming year.

After making the preceding projections, General received an inquiry about the purchase of a large number of toasters by a discount department store. The inquiry contained two purchase offers:

- Offer 1: The department store would purchase 80,000 units at $14.60 per unit. These units would bear the General label and be covered by the General warranty.
- Offer 2: The department store would purchase 120,000 units at $14.00 per unit. These units would be sold under the buyer's private label, and General would not provide warranty service.

A. Evaluate the incremental net income potential of each offer.

B. What other factors should General consider when deciding which offer to accept?

C. Which offer (if either) should General accept? Why?

P12.8 **Price Discrimination.** Coach Industries, Inc., is a leading manufacturer of recreational vehicle products. Its products include travel trailers, fifth-wheel trailers (towed behind pick-up trucks), and van campers, as well as parts and accessories. Coach offers its fifth-wheel trailers to both dealers (wholesale) and retail customers. Ernie Pantusso, Coach's controller, estimates that each fifth-wheel trailer costs the company $10,000 in variable labor and material expenses. Demand and marginal revenue relations for fifth-wheel trailers are

Wholesale
$$P_W = \$15,000 - \$5Q_W$$
$$MR_W = \Delta TR_W/\Delta Q_W = \$15,000 - \$10Q_W.$$

Retail
$$P_R = \$50,000 - \$20Q_R$$
$$MR_R = \Delta TR_R/\Delta Q_R = \$50,000 - \$40Q_R.$$

A. Assuming that the company can price discriminate between its two types of customers, calculate the profit-maximizing price, output, and profit contribution levels.

B. Calculate point price elasticities for each customer type at the activity levels identified in Part A. Are the differences in these elasticities consistent with your recommended price differences in Part A? Why or why not?

P12.9 **Joint Product Pricing.** Each ton of ore mined from the Baby Doe Mine in Leadville, Colorado, produces one ounce of silver and one pound of lead in a fixed 1:1 ratio. Marginal costs are $10 per ton of ore mined.

The demand and marginal revenue curves for silver are

$$P_S = \$11 - \$0.00003Q_S,$$
$$MR_S = \Delta TR_S/\Delta Q_S = \$11 - \$0.00006Q_S,$$

and the demand and marginal revenue curve for lead are

$$P_L = \$0.4 - \$0.000005Q_L,$$
$$MR_L = \Delta TR_L/\Delta Q_L = \$0.4 - \$0.00001Q_L,$$

where Q_S is ounces of silver and Q_L is pounds of lead.

A. Calculate profit-maximizing sales quantities and prices for silver and lead.

B. Now assume that wild speculation in the silver market has created a fivefold (or 500%) increase in silver demand. Calculate optimal sales quantities and prices for both silver and lead under these conditions.

P12.10 **Transfer Pricing.** Simpson Flanders, Inc., is a Motor City-based manufacturer and distributor of valves used in nuclear power plants. Currently, all output is sold to North American customers. Demand and marginal revenue curves for the firm are as follows:

$$P = \$1,000 - \$0.015Q,$$
$$MR = \Delta TR/\Delta Q = \$1,000 - \$0.03Q.$$

Relevant total cost, marginal cost, and profit functions are

$$TC = \$1,500,000 + \$600Q$$
$$+ \$0.005Q^2,$$

$$MC = \Delta TC/\Delta Q = \$600 + \$0.01Q,$$

$$\pi = TR - TC$$

$$= -\$0.02Q^2 + \$400Q$$
$$- \$1,500,000.$$

A. Calculate the profit-maximizing activity level for Simpson Flanders when the firm is operated as an integrated unit.

B. Assume that the company is reorganized into two independent profit centers with the following cost conditions:

$$TC_{Mfg} = \$1,250,000 + \$500Q + \$0.005Q^2,$$

$$MC_{Mfg} = \$500 + \$0.01Q,$$

and,

$$TC_{Distr} = \$250,000 + \$100Q,$$

$$MC_{Distr} = \$100.$$

Calculate the transfer price that ensures a profit-maximizing level of profit for the firm, with divisional operation based on the assumption that all output produced is to be transferred internally.

C. Now assume that a major distributor in the European market offers to buy as many valves as Simpson Flanders wishes to offer at a price of $645. No impact on demand from the company's North American customers is expected, and current facilities can be used to supply both markets. Calculate the company's optimal price(s), output(s), and profits in this situation.

Case Study for Chapter 12

PRICING PRACTICES IN THE MADISON, WISCONSIN, AND DENVER, COLORADO, LOCAL NEWSPAPER MARKETS

Why do you read the newspaper? Studies show that significant numbers of newspaper purchases from vending machines are motivated by the headline appearing on the front page. During the recent presidential election, for example, newspaper sales grew rapidly as readers sought the information on their favorite candidate. Others read the paper to get the latest sports information, business news, or weather report. Perhaps *The Wall Street Journal* is best known for providing timely and comprehensive business news, whereas *USA Today* is known for providing broad coverage of general news, sports, and entertainment. Both compete against the *New York Times,* the *Washington Post,* and other leading newspapers, as well as against *Business Week, Forbes, Fortune, Newsweek, Time,* and a host of specialized magazines. It is quite surprising that national newspapers compete to a much lesser degree with local newspapers. Local newspapers have a formidable niche in the provision of local news. If you want to read up on

the latest Wall Street rumor, you can read the *Journal.* If you want to read up on the latest high school basketball scores, you must read the local newspaper. Similarly, the local newspaper is the only place to go for local classified ads.

An interesting illustration of price discrimination can be found in the classified-ad pricing policies of local newspapers. The value of classified-ad advertising varies according to the value of the item advertised. Real estate advertising has a much greater value to customers than advertising of lower-priced household items, boats, pets, and so on. Given these differences, customers are willing to pay much more to advertise a personal residence, for example, than to seek new homes for Spotty and her kittens. Local newspapers satisfy the requirements necessary for profitable price discrimination, since they can easily identify the value of the item advertised and often enjoy a monopoly position in the sale of local advertising. Indeed, it is rare to find more than one newspaper company serving a local market, given the significant economies of scale in the industry.

Table 12.4 shows pricing practices at the start of 1997 for local newspapers in the Madison, Wisconsin, and Denver, Colorado, markets. This comparison yields insight because of the difference in market structure. The Madison market is typical of local newspaper markets in the United States in that it is served by a single newspaper company, Madison Newspapers, Inc., with the *Wisconsin State Journal* (morning and Sunday) and the *Capital Times* (evening) editions. The Denver market, however, is served by two independent newspaper companies, the *Denver Post* and the *Rocky Mountain News.*

It is interesting that the monopoly position of Madison Newspapers is reflected in higher single-copy and subscription prices than either the *Denver Post* or *Rocky Mountain News.* The 15¢ (42.9%) price premium on daily single-copy sales and the $1.25 (250%) price premium on Sunday single-copy sales

in the Madison market is dramatic, as is the corresponding premium on daily plus Sunday subscription sales. These price differentials suggest that, by virtue of its monopoly position, Madison Newspapers enjoys a substantial pricing advantage in its market when compared with the pricing discretion of either the *Post* or *News* in the Denver market.

The advantages of Madison Newspapers' monopoly position are even more apparent when classified-ad pricing practices are considered. Madison Newspapers' real estate classified-ad prices consistently exceed those charged by the *Post* and *News,* despite having an overall market size is only 30% to 40% as large. This means that on a cost-per-exposure basis, Madison Newspapers' real estate classified-ad prices are roughly two and one-half to three times higher than those charged by the *Post* and *News.* Although all three papers engage in price discrimination for classified ads, Madison Newspapers' non–real estate merchandise (automobiles, etc.) classified-ad pricing

---

Table 12.4   PRICING PRACTICES AND MARKET SHARES IN THE MADISON, WISCONSIN, AND DENVER, COLORADO, LOCAL NEWSPAPERS MARKETS

	MADISON NEWSPAPERS	DENVER POST	ROCKY MOUNTAIN NEWS
Newspaper Prices			
Single copy—Daily	50¢	25¢	35¢
Single copy—Sunday	$1.75	50¢	50¢
Subscription—Daily	$9.14 (mo.)	$6.80 (mo.)	$10.28 (mo.)
Subscription—Daily + Sunday	$15.94 (mo.)	$6.80 (mo.)	$11.45 (mo.)
Want-Ad Prices (3-line ad)			
Real estate	$36.90 (3 days)	$23.99 (3 days)	$21.24 (3 days)
	$59.85 (7 days)	$60.00 (10 days)	$70.80 (10 days)
	$109.20 (14 days)	$120.00 (20 days)	$141.60 (20 days)
	$234.00 (30 days)	$180.00 (30 days)	$212.40 (30 days)
Merchandise	$21.00 (10 days, ≤ $2,000 value)	$20.00 (10 days)	$28.95 (21 days)
	$29.00 (10 days, $2,000 < value ≤ $20,000)		
Circulation			
Daily (market share)	107,815 (100%)	334,436 (51.3%)	316,919 (48.7%)
Sunday (market share)	162,607 (100%)	461,837 (53.2%)	406,473 (46.8%)

Source: Phone survey by the authors, December 23, 1996.

structure is much more closely tied to the value of the item advertised than in the case of either the *Post* or *News*.

A.   What is the motivation for local newspaper price discrimination in classified-ad advertising?

B.   Widely differing fares for business and vacation travelers on the same flight have led some to accuse the airlines of price discrimination. Do airline fare differences or local newspaper classified-ad rate differences provide stronger evidence of price discrimination?

C.   Is price discrimination by local newspapers as likely in the case of locally placed national ads for *Nike* shoes as it is in the case of local classified-ad advertising?

Long-Term Investment Decisions

V

Government Regulation of the Market Economy

The collapse of communism in Eastern Europe and the former Soviet Union has led to a rebirth of capitalism and to renewed faith in free-market solutions to economic problems. This global revolution has not gone unnoticed in Washington, D.C., Ottawa, Ontario, and in national capitals throughout the world. After decades of exponential growth, the U.S. Congress and Canadian Parliament are both moving to dramatically reduce government spending and budget deficits by downsizing the role of government.

In the U.S., welfare benefits are apt to be cut as states are asked to assume a greater responsibility for designing and paying for "safety net" entitlement programs. Housing subsidies and job training programs are liable to shrink as federal efforts are trimmed to save costs. Politically motivated agricultural subsidy payments are being cut for certain grains and commodities, while critics question the fairness of continuing to subsidize other farmers, like milk producers. Other federal programs, such as the air traffic control system, may be privatized to shift costs from taxpayers to those who directly benefit from such services, like air travelers. And finally, a comprehensive review of federal, state, and local regulation has been set in motion to ensure regulatory effectiveness.[1]

This chapter considers the economic and social rationale for regulation. Because public policy trades off efficiency and equity considerations, both the process and results of regulation are controversial. This makes historical methods of regulation, regulatory reform, and the deregulation movement among the most fascinating and important subject areas in the study of managerial economics.

Competition and the Role of Government

When considering the role of government in the market economy, it has been traditional to focus on how government influences economic activity through tax policies, law enforcement, and infrastructure investments in highways, water treatment facilities, and the like. More recently, interest has shifted to how and why the government regulates private market activity. Government regulation of the market economy consists of rules that constrain the way private companies operate and the types of products that they produce. The subject is interesting because tax policies, rules, and regulations fundamentally shape the competitive environment.

---

[1]See Howard Banks, "Global Deregulation," *Forbes*, May 5, 1997, 130-133.

HOW GOVERNMENT INFLUENCES BUSINESS

Government affects what and how firms produce, influences conditions of entry and exit, dictates marketing practices, prescribes hiring and personnel policies, and imposes a host of other requirements on private enterprise. Government regulation of the market economy is a controversial topic because the power to tax or compel has direct economic consequences.

For example, local telephone service monopolies are protected by a web of local and federal regulation that gives rise to above-normal rates of return while providing access to below-market financing. Franchises that confer the right to offer cellular telephone service in a major metropolitan area are literally worth millions of dollars and can be awarded in the United States only by the Federal Communications Commission (FCC). The federal government also spends hundreds of millions of dollars per year to maintain artificially high price supports for selected agricultural products such as milk and grain, but not chicken and pork. At the same time, natural gas prices in the United States are held far below market prices. Careful study of the motivation and methods of such regulation is essential to the study of managerial economics because of regulation's key role in shaping the managerial decision-making process.

The pervasive and expanding influence of government in the market economy can be illustrated by considering the growing role played by the FCC, a once obscure agency known only for regulation of the broadcast industry and AT&T. The FCC currently holds the keys to success for a number of emerging communications technologies. In the immediate future, the FCC will determine the fate of digital audio broadcasting, which does away with static on car radio channels; personal communication networks that make users reachable anywhere with a pocket phone; and interactive television, which lets customers order goods and communicate with others through a television set. Rapid advances in communications technology will be obvious if you soon find yourself talking to your TV, if your car stereo sounds like a CD player, and if you can phone home from the top of Glacier National Park. If not, the FCC and overly restrictive regulation of the airwaves will be to blame.

Although all sectors of the U.S. economy are regulated to some degree, the method and scope of regulation vary widely. Most companies escape price and profit restraint, except during periods of general wage-price control, but they are subject to operating regulations governing pollution emissions, product packaging and labeling, worker safety and health, and so on. Other firms, particularly in the financial and the public utility sectors, must comply with financial regulation in addition to such operating controls. Banks and savings and loan institutions, for example, are subject to state and federal regulation of interest rates, fees, lending policies, and capital requirements. Unlike firms in the electric power and telecommunications industries, banks and savings and loans face no explicit limit on profitability. For this reason, regulation of depository institutions, insurance companies, and the securities business encompasses more than regulation in the nonfinancial sector but is less comprehensive than the regulation of public utilities.

Both economic and social considerations enter into decisions of what and how to regulate. Economic considerations relate to the cost and efficiency implications of

Efficiency
Production of what consumers demand in a least-cost fashion.

Regulation
Government control of the market economy.

Equity
Concern for a just distribution of wealth.

regulatory methods. From an economic **efficiency** standpoint, a given mode of **regulation** or government control is desirable to the extent that benefits exceed costs. In terms of efficiency, the question is whether market competition by itself is sufficient, or if it needs to be supplemented with government regulation. **Equity,** or fairness, criteria must also be carefully weighed when social considerations bear on the regulatory decision-making process. Therefore, the incidence, or placement, of costs and benefits of regulatory decisions is important. If a given change in regulatory policy provides significant benefits to the poor, society may willingly bear substantial costs in terms of lost efficiency.

ECONOMIC CONSIDERATIONS

Competitive markets have several compelling advantages. Perhaps most important, the discipline of competition encourages economic efficiency. In the short run, efficient firms gain market share from higher-cost competitors and earn above-normal profits. Ultimately, competition forces inefficient firms from the marketplace. Competition also ensures that the types of products preferred by customers are offered. In competitive markets, firms must react to customer preferences rather than dictate the quantity and quality of goods and services provided. A further advantage of competition is that profits and wage rates reflect the productive capability of firms and workers. Companies that earn higher profits tend to be those that best serve customer needs; high-wage workers tend to be those who are most productive. As a result, competition is desirable from both efficiency and equity perspectives.

Economic regulation began and continues in part because of the public's perception of market imperfections. It is sometimes believed that unregulated market activity can lead to inefficiency and waste or to market failure. **Market failure** is the inability of a system of market institutions to sustain socially desirable activities or to eliminate undesirable ones.

Market Failure
The inability of market institutions to sustain desirable activity or eliminate undesirable activity.

Failure by Market Structure
Insufficient market participants for active competition.

A first cause of market failure is **failure by market structure.** For a market to realize the beneficial effects of competition, it must have many producers (sellers) and consumers (buyers), or at least the ready potential for many to enter. Some markets do not meet this condition. Consider, for example, water, power, and some telecommunications markets. If customer service in a given market area can be most efficiently provided by a single firm (a natural monopoly situation), such providers would enjoy market power and could earn economic profits by limiting output and charging high prices. As a result, utility prices and profits were placed under regulatory control, which has continued with the goal of preserving the efficiency of large-scale production while preventing the higher prices and economic profits of monopoly. When the efficiency advantages of large size are not thought to be compelling, antitrust policy limits the market power of large firms.

Failure by Incentive
Breakdown of the pricing mechanism as a reflection of all costs and benefits of production and consumption.

Externalities
Differences between private and social costs or benefits.

A second kind of market failure is **failure by incentive.** In the production and consumption of goods and services, social values and costs often differ from the private costs and values of producers and consumers. Differences between private and social costs or benefits are called **externalities.** A negative externality is a cost of producing, marketing, or consuming a product that is not borne by the product's producers or consumers. A positive externality is a benefit of production, marketing, or consumption that is not reflected in the product pricing structure and, hence, does not accrue to the product's producers or consumers.

Environmental pollution is one well-known negative externality. Negative externalities also arise when employees are exposed to hazardous working conditions for which they are not fully compensated. Similarly, a firm that dams a river or builds a solar collector to produce energy and thereby limits the access of others to hydropower or solar power creates a negative externality. Positive externalities can result if an increase in a firm's activity reduces costs for its suppliers, who pass these cost savings on to their other customers. The rapid growth of the computer industry has, for example, reduced input costs for both the computer and electronics industries. Economies of scale in semiconductor production made possible by increased computer demand lowered input costs for all users of semiconductors. As a result, prices have fallen for computers as well as a wide variety of "intelligent" electronic appliances, calculators, toys, and so on. Positive externalities in production can result when a firm trains employees who later apply their knowledge in work for other firms. Positive externalities also arise when an improvement in production methods is transferred from one firm to another without compensation. The dam cited previously for its potential negative externalities might also provide positive externalities by offering flood control or recreational benefits.

In short, externalities lead to a difference between the private and social costs and benefits of a given product or activity. These differences often have a notable effect on the economy. Firms that provide substantial positive externalities without compensation are unlikely to produce at the socially optimal level. Similarly, consumption activities that confer positive externalities may not reach the socially optimal level. In contrast, negative externalities can channel too many resources to a particular activity. Producers or consumers that generate negative externalities do not pay the full costs of production or consumption and tend to overutilize social resources. Instances in which market prices do not fully reflect costs or benefits provide an impetus for government intervention.

SOCIAL CONSIDERATIONS

Consumer Sovereignty
Buyer supremacy in the marketplace.

Competition promotes efficiency by giving firms incentives to produce the types and quantities of products that consumers want. Competitive pressures force each firm to use resources wisely to earn at least a normal profit. The market-based resource allocation system is efficient when it responds quickly and accurately to consumer preferences. Not only are these features of competitive markets attractive on an economic basis, but they are also consistent with basic democratic principles. Preservation of consumer choice or **consumer sovereignty** is an important feature of competitive markets. By encouraging and rewarding individual initiative, competition greatly enhances personal freedom. For this reason, less vigorous competitive pressure indicates diminishing buyer supremacy in the marketplace. Firms with market power can limit output and raise prices to earn economic profits, whereas firms in competitive markets refer to market prices to determine optimal output quantities. Regulatory policy can be a valuable tool with which to control monopolies, restoring control over price and quantity decisions to the public.

Is Civil Litigation Too Expensive?

One of the most important hidden charges of doing business in the U.S. and Canada is the mushrooming expense of civil litigation. When employees, companies, and their customers face the constant threat of frivolous litigation, the cost of doing business can skyrocket. For example, doctors who fear being sued for overlooking some rare or unanticipated malady often order unnecessary tests and otherwise practice what is known as "defensive medicine." Stanford economists Daniel Kessler and Mark McClellan recently reported that this expensive practice is most common for patients in states that place no limits on the right to sue. Critics argue that because Congress has generally left medical practice reform to the states, federal taxpayers in Montana pay for unnecessarily high Medicare and Medicaid expenditures in Mississippi. Recent estimates suggest that if tort reform passed in various states were to become common across the country, medical cost savings could total as much as *$50 billion* per year. By themselves, such savings would place the Medicare and Medicaid systems on firm financial footing for years to come.

Of course, problems posed by frivolous litigation expenses extend far beyond the health care sector. Rather than face the unknown probability of being sued by dissatisfied customers, many companies restrict their hours of operation or otherwise limit the types of products and services provided. Because the popular reliance on lawyers and the legal system differs from one locale to another, the costs to business from civil litigation can and does vary widely according to local laws and customs. Regrettably, companies seeking to gain information about the relative cost of doing business in various regions face a significant roadblock. There is no central data base that details the cost of civil litigation for business by region or locale.

In quantifying the amount of civil litigation in each of the fifty states, one might consider the percentage of automobile accidents where lawyers get involved, the average annual cost of malpractice insurance, the number of trial lawyers per 100,000 population, judicial election campaign contributions, the amount of civil damage awards, and other such factors. In some states and in some

industries, it is clear that unnecessary costs of civil litigation have grown burdensome. For example, few single-engine and twin-engine planes are manufactured today because of potential liability to the manufacturer. Older and more dangerous aircraft stay in use longer than they otherwise would because manufacturers cannot bear the burden of projected legal expenses under the current system. Many public swimming pools have removed diving boards, snow skiers often face gentler slopes, and many kids don't have the opportunity to play football and other contact sports—all because of the fear of legal liability.

How much of the roughly $150 billion spent every year on tort liability in the U.S. is unnecessary? How much of the billions more spent to avoid getting sued is a waste? No one knows for sure. Paul H. Rubin, an economics professor at Emory University, suggests that looking at the amount spent on the tort system in other countries can give an interesting perspective. Suppose that European and other developed countries spend roughly the right amount on insurance and deterrence through the tort system; then the difference between U.S. tort costs and this average would be an indicator of waste in the U.S. system. From this perspective the amount of waste is a staggering 1.5% of GDP, or roughly $1,000 per household in the U.S.

To help reform the system and curb abuse, frivolous lawsuits, arbitrary punitive damages, and "junk science" in the courtroom have all been targeted. Among the proposals being seriously considered are a ban on contingency fees for expert witnesses, limits on punitive damages, and a requirement that losers pay the winners' court costs (as is the case in England). Fairness considerations demand for everyone the right to have a "day in court" when significant injury is encountered. At the same time, efficiency considerations require that the legal process reflect a careful balancing of system-wide costs and benefits. Both are important.

See: Brigid McMenamin, "Un-Natural Justice," *Forbes*, May 5, 1997, 122-128.

Limit Concentration
A social goal of regulation is to restrict undue influence.

A second social purpose of regulatory intervention is to **limit concentration** of economic and political power. It has long been recognized that economic and social relations become intertwined and that concentrated economic power is generally inconsistent with the democratic process. The laws of incorporation, first passed during the 1850s, play an important role in the U.S. economic system. These laws have allowed owners of capital (stockholders) to pool economic resources without also pooling political resources, thereby allowing big business and democracy to coexist. Of course, the large scale of modern corporations has sometimes diminished the controlling influence of individual stockholders. In these instances, regulatory and antitrust policy have limited the growth of large firms to avoid undue concentration of political power.

Important social considerations often constitute compelling justification for government intervention in the marketplace. Deciding whether a particular regulatory reform is warranted is complicated because social considerations can run counter to efficiency considerations. This is not to say that policies should never be pursued when the expected benefits are exceeded by expected costs. Costs in the form of lost efficiency may sometimes be borne to achieve more equitable economic solutions.

Regulatory Response to Incentive Failures

One of the roles of government is to help preserve the competitive environment. To reach this objective, government regulation responds to problems created by both positive and negative externalities in production, marketing, and consumption. In the effort to limit the frequency of market failure that is due to incentive problems, government frequently grants property rights and employs a variety of tax policies. In granting patents and operating subsidies, government provides compensation to reward activity that provides positive externalities. Local, state, and federal governments levy taxes (a form of negative subsidy) and set operating requirements or controls to limit the creation of negative externalities. Property rights, grants, taxes, and operating control policies are common responses by government to incentive failures and provide a good introduction to this area of government/business interaction.

PROPERTY RIGHTS REGULATION

Property Rights
The license to limit use by others.

Property rights give the prerogative to limit use by others of specific land, plant and equipment, and other assets. The deed to a piece of land, for example, explicitly defines a property right and gives the owner access to the courts if someone tries to use the property without the owner's permission. The establishment and maintenance of private property rights is essential to the workings of a competitive market. Property rights are so fundamental to the free market economy and democratic form of government that they are protected in the United States by the Fifth Amendment to the Constitution. While local zoning laws limit property rights by restricting the types of buildings allowed in a particular neighborhood, these laws cannot be so burdensome as to deprive owners from the rightful use of their property. Although the public interest might be served by regulations designed to preserve wetlands or endangered species, owners are entitled to compensation for any loss they might suffer as a result.

Regulation of property rights is a common, though seldom discussed, method of giving firms an incentive to promote service in the public interest. Common examples are FCC control of local television and radio broadcasting rights; federal and state regulatory bodies that govern national or state chartering of banks and savings and loan institutions; and insurance commissions that oversee insurance company licensing at the state level. In each of these instances, firms must be able to demonstrate fiscal responsibility and to provide evidence that they are meeting the needs of their service areas. Should firms fail to meet established criteria, public franchises in the form of broadcasting rights, charters, or licenses can be withdrawn, or new franchises can be offered to potential competitors. While such drastic action is rare, the mere threat of these sanctions is often sufficient to compel compliance.

Although control of property rights can be an effective form of regulation, it often falls short of its full potential because of imprecise operating criteria. For example, is a television station that broadcasts poorly rated local programming 20 hours per week responding better to the needs of its service area than a station that airs highly popular reruns of hit shows? How progressive an attitude should a local bank take toward electronic funds transfer services? Without clear, consistent, and workable standards of performance, operating grant regulation is hampered by inefficiency and waste. The cost of this inefficiency is measured by the low quality and limited quantity of desired goods and services and by the excessive profits and/or high costs of firms sheltered from competition by regulatory policies.

PATENTS AND THE TORT SYSTEM

Patents
Exclusive property rights to produce, use, or sell an invention or innovation for a limited period.

With **patents,** the government grants an exclusive property right to produce, use, or sell an invention or innovation for a limited period of time (17 years in the United States). These valuable grants of legal monopoly power are intended to stimulate research and development. Without patents, competitors could quickly exploit and develop close, if not identical, substitutes for new products or processes, and inventing firms would fail to reap the full benefit of their technological breakthroughs. Patent policy is a regulatory attempt to achieve the benefits of both monopoly and competition in the field of research and development. In granting the patent, the public confers a limited opportunity for monopoly profits to stimulate research activity and the economic growth that it creates. By limiting the patent monopoly, competition is encouraged to extend and develop the common body of knowledge.

The patent monopoly is subject to other restrictions besides the time limit. Firms cannot use patents to unfairly monopolize or otherwise limit competition. For example, in 1973 the Federal Trade Commission (FTC) charged Xerox with dominating the office-copier industry through unfair marketing and patent practices. In its complaint, the FTC alleged that Xerox, in association with Battelle Memorial Institute, a private research corporation, had created an artificial "patent barrier to competition." A final consent order in 1975 resolved the FTC's monopolization suit against Xerox. The consent order required Xerox to license competitors to use its more than 1,700 copier patents with little or no royalty payments and restricted Xerox's freedom to acquire such rights from competitors. Partially because of this action, entry into the copier industry grew rapidly during the late 1970s.

The rules of contract law provide for the enforcement of patents and other legal agreements among firms. Because it is impossible to specify all possible outcomes in writing a legal contract, the court system provides an open forum for dispute resolution. Even if all possible outcomes could be specified beforehand, legal enforcement would still be necessary to ensure that all parties honor their agreements. If a manufacturer fails to deliver goods to a wholesaler as promised, the wholesaler can go to the courts to enforce its agreement with the manufacturer. Without such enforcement, firms would have no recourse but to depend exclusively on the goodwill of others. The legal system also includes a body of law designed to provide a mechanism for victims of accidents and injury to receive just compensation for their loss. Called the **tort system,** these laws create an incentive for firms and other parties to act responsibly in commerce. Because of the threat of being sued for their transgressions, firms are encouraged to prevent accidents and resulting economic damages.

Tort System
A body of law that provides a means for victims of accidents and injury to receive just compensation for their loss.

Like patents that are difficult and costly to enforce in the courts, the tort system can itself result in significant costs. For example, both sides to a legal dispute have almost unlimited ability to take sworn depositions from witnesses and seek documents in the pretrial "discovery" process. Since discovery must be provided without payment from the requesting party, there is no incentive to limit the size of any request. Requesting parties can and have used the discovery process to impose significant litigation costs on the other side, even in lawsuits that later prove frivolous. As a result, proposals have been made to place limits on the amount of free discovery that can be requested, set caps on the amount of punitive damages, foster proper use of expert testimony, and encourage other means of dispute resolution.

SUBSIDY POLICY

Subsidy Policy
Government grants that benefit firms and individuals.

Government also responds to positive externalities by providing subsidies to private business firms. **Subsidy policy** can be indirect, like government construction and highway maintenance grants that benefit the trucking industry. They can also take the form of direct payments, such as agricultural payment-in-kind (PIK) programs, special tax treatments, and government-provided low-cost financing.

Tax credits on business investment and depletion allowances on natural resource development are examples of tax subsidies that government sometimes gives in recognition of social benefits such as job creation and energy independence. Positive externalities associated with industrial parks induce government to provide local tax incremental or industrial revenue bond financing for such facilities. This low-cost financing is thought to provide some compensation for the external benefits of economic development.

Pollution Emission Allowances
A controversial form of government subsidy that gives firms the property right to pollute and then sell that right to others.

Pollution emission allowances are a new and controversial form of government subsidy because they are pollution licenses granted by the government to firms and other individuals. When firms and consumers pollute the environment, some of the costs of production or consumption are shifted onto third parties. Rather than spend millions of dollars on new equipment, raw materials, or production methods to meet pollution abatement regulations, firms sometimes purchase emission allowances from other companies. Therefore, pollution emission allowances are a valuable commodity that can be worth millions of dollars. Opponents of the pollution emission allowance system argue that they infringe on the public's right to a clean and safe environment. Proponents contend that the costs of pollution abatement become prohibitive as emissions are reduced toward zero, thus making some trade-offs inevitable. Moreover, they argue that an allowance trading system does not confer new licenses to pollute; it merely transfers licenses from one polluter to another. Nevertheless, by awarding pollution emission allowances worth millions of dollars to the worst offenders of a clean environment, environmentally sensitive firms and consumers have been hurt, at least on a relative basis.

TAX POLICY

Tax Policy
Fines and penalties that limit undesirable performance.

Whereas subsidy policy gives firms positive incentives for desirable performance, **tax policy** contains penalties, or negative subsidies, designed to limit undesirable performance. Tax policy includes both regular tax payments and fines or penalties that may be assessed intermittently.

Local, state, or federal fines for exceeding specified weight limits on trucks, pollution taxes, and effluent charges are common examples of tax policies intended to limit negative externalities by shifting external costs of production back to firms and their customers. The appropriate tax level is extremely difficult to determine because of problems associated with estimating the magnitude of negative externalities. For example, calculating some of the social costs of air pollution, such as more frequent house painting, is relatively straightforward. Calculating the costs of increased discomfort—even death—for, say, emphysema patients is more difficult. Nevertheless, regulators must consider the full range of consequences of negative externalities to create appropriate and effective incentives for pollution control.

Although tax policy may appear simply to mirror subsidy and property rights grant policies, an important distinction should not be overlooked. If society wants to limit the harmful consequences of air pollution, either subsidies for pollution reduction or taxes on pollution can provide effective incentives. Implied property rights are, however, considerably different under the two approaches. The subsidy mechanism implies a firm's right to pollute, because society pays to reduce pollution. In contrast, a system of pollution tax penalties asserts society's right to a clean environment. Firms must reimburse society for the damage caused by their pollution. The difference is a distinction about who owns the environment. Many prefer tax policy as a method for pollution reduction on the grounds that it explicitly recognizes the public's right to a clean and safe environment.

OPERATING CONTROLS

Operating Controls
Regulation by government directive.

Operating control regulation, or control by government directive, is an important and growing form of regulation. **Operating controls** are standards that limit undesirable

Is Microsoft Too Big?

The history of computer software maker Microsoft Corporation and Chairman Bill Gates is the stuff of economic legends. During the late 1980s and early 1990s, this software upstart dethroned IBM as the king of operating and applications software to become an industry titan. Microsoft first went public in 1986, when it generated $197.5 million in revenues and $39.3 million in net income. Microsoft exploded to more than $10 billion in revenues and $2.5 billion in profits by the end of 1997. Its +40% rate of growth in annual revenues and sky-high profit margins of 25% on sales have made Microsoft the darling of Wall Street. During the 1990s, after Microsoft had emerged as a power to contend with, investors saw the value of their stock multiply. Early investors saw a more than 150:1 return on their initial investment as Microsoft rose from a split-adjusted 60 cents in 1986 to over $100 per share by 1997. To top things off, Bill Gates emerged in 1997 as the richest man in America with a net worth approaching *$30 billion.*

Microsoft's amazing success stems from its ability to efficiently capitalize on the obvious consumer appeal of the graphical-user interface (GUI). The GUI is an object-oriented rather than command-driven approach to computer programming. Rather than memorize a series of arcane computer commands, users of Microsoft object-oriented software use a "mouse" pointing device to point and click (turn) on desired computer functions. Click a garbage can icon to delete text, click a chart icon to draw a graph, and so on. So compelling are the advantages of the GUI approach, rival command-drive computer software is rapidly becoming obsolete. Meanwhile, Microsoft continues to introduce innovative and popular database management systems, word processing, spreadsheets, and graphics software applications. Increasingly important are internet programs that facilitate the development and transfer of such business documents across the worldwide web.

More often than not, Microsoft's new product introductions are facilitated through a two-pronged strategy. First and foremost, Microsoft deploys a huge research and development effort funded by more than $1.6 billion per year, or roughly 16.5% of sales. During recent years, nobody has outspent Microsoft on software R&D, and nobody has gotten more out of its R&D spending. In addition to the efforts of Microsoft's mammoth research and development operation, Microsoft has deployed an aggressive campaign to invest in or acquire start-up software companies with innovative software or capabilities.

Some of Microsoft's competitors contend that they are at a disadvantage in the production of highly profitable applications software because Microsoft controls the underlying operating software used on most personal computers. Operating software is the basic set of instructions used to tell the computer how to operate and how to interface with user applications software. By controlling the pace of new operating software introductions, and proprietary information regarding key features, competitors have charged that Microsoft unfairly monopolizes the operating software and applications software markets. Among the accusations levelled against Microsoft is the charge that the company engages in "vaporware," or the preliminary announcement of new and innovative software that is not yet available in an attempt to preempt rivals, and coerce users to delay their adoption of innovative products offered by rivals. Others retort that Microsoft's competitors are trying to achieve in court what they cannot achieve in the marketplace, namely: to hamstring this software juggernaut.

The ultimate result of the ongoing Microsoft-antitrust battle may be years away from resolution. Whatever the final result, it raises fundamental questions about the ability of regulatory agencies and the courts to regulate a rapidly changing economic environment. For example, with the convergence of computers, copy equipment, fax machines, home appliances, televisions, and telephones, how big is the market for applications and operating-systems software? With the advent of the worldwide web, how does Microsoft's dominance of PC operating software limit the competitive capability of application software providers? Does Microsoft dominate this exploding business? Is Microsoft even a big player in such a gigantic market?

See: Kathy Rebello, "Bill's Quiet Shopping Spree," *Business Week,* January 13, 1997, 34-35; Holman W. Jenkins, Jr., "What's a Little Antitrust Between Friends?," *The Wall Street Journal,* January 28, 1997, A17.

behavior by prohibiting certain actions while compelling others. Operating control regulation that achieves 100% compliance creates a situation similar to that reached under a prohibitive tax policy. In each instance, the undesirable activity in question is completely eliminated, and no tax revenues are collected. When operating controls result in less than full compliance, operating control regulation becomes much like tax policy because fines and levies increase the costs to violators.

What kinds of operating controls are imposed on business firms? Controls over environmental pollution immediately come to mind, but businesses are also subject to many other kinds of constraints. Federal legislation limits automobile emissions and sets fuel efficiency and safety standards; firms handling foods, drugs, and other controlled substances are constrained under the Pure Food and Drug Act. Working conditions are governed under labor laws and health regulations, including provisions related to noise levels, noxious gases and chemicals, and safety standards. Antidiscrimination laws designed to protect minority groups and women can cause firms to modify their hiring and promotion policies. Wage and price controls, imposed during times of rapid inflation, restrict pricing practices and production decisions.

Like property rights regulation, the effectiveness of operating control regulations is often limited by vague or imprecise statutory specifications. If sanctions against violators are poorly defined or overly lenient, incentives for compliance can be weak. Beyond the difficulties created by poorly defined regulations and sanctions, problems can also result if conflicting operating controls are imposed. For example, mandatory safety standards and pollution controls have increased passenger car costs by several hundred dollars per unit. These expenses are an obvious direct cost of meeting auto safety and pollution regulations, but other less obvious indirect costs are also incurred. Auto safety and pollution standards have the effect of reducing fuel efficiency and thus make more serious the U.S. dependence on imported oil.

Perhaps the clearest difference between operating control regulation and regulation via tax or subsidy policies is the reliance on nonmonetary incentives for compliance. There are no easy alternatives to operating control regulation in instances in which social costs are prohibitively great (e.g., nuclear disaster, ground water contamination, and so on) or difficult, if not impossible, to measure (e.g., public health, worker death, or serious injury). In some instances, however, operating control regulations can cause firms to direct their efforts toward being exempted from regulation rather than toward reducing the negative externalities of concern to society. It is not clear if operating controls are more or less effective than tax and subsidy policies in ensuring that the results of regulatory efforts are both effective and equitable. Each approach has its place.

Who Pays the Costs of Regulation?

Among its many benefits, the legal system provides a mechanism for resolving disputes and establishes the ground rules for market transactions. This process is not without its expense, however. The regulatory system can retard economic growth if dispute resolution is slow, costs of litigation are high, and the outcomes of legal proceedings are risky. Socially beneficial regulatory reform, and reform of the legal system in particular, involves creating a set of rules that provides the basis for a fair and efficient settlement of disputes.

DEMAND AND SUPPLY EFFECTS

Tax Incidence
Point of tax collection.

Tax Burden
Economic cost of tax.

The question of who pays the costs of regulation designed to mitigate incentive failures is an important one. Although the point of tax collection, or the **tax incidence,** of pollution charges may be a heavily polluting foundry, the economic cost of pollution taxes, or the **tax burden,** may be passed on to customers or suppliers. The question of who pays for specific regulations can seldom be determined merely by identifying the fined, taxed, or otherwise regulated party.

In general, who pays for operating control regulation depends on the elasticity of demand for the final products of affected firms. Figure 13.1 illustrates this issue by considering the theoretically polar extremes of perfectly elastic demand for final products, [Fig. 13.1(a)], and perfectly inelastic demand for final products, [Fig. 13.1(b)]. Identically upward-sloping *MC* curves are assumed in each instance. Here, as is often the case, regulation is assumed to increase marginal costs by a fixed amount per unit. This amount, t, can reflect pollution taxes per unit of output or regulation-induced cost increases.

Figure 13.1(a) shows that good substitutes for a firm's product and highly elastic demand prevent producers from passing taxes or regulation-induced cost increases on to customers. As a result, producers (including investors, employees, and suppliers) are forced to bear the burden of regulatory costs, at least in the short run. In these instances, falling industry rates of return on invested capital and high rates of industry unemployment are symptomatic of regulatory influences.

Figure 13.1(b) shows the effect of regulation-induced cost or tax increases in the case of perfectly inelastic final-product demand. Without effective substitute products, producers can pass the burden of regulation on to customers. In contrast to the case of perfectly elastic demand, producers may encounter relatively few disadvantages because of regulation-induced cost increases.

Although the preceding analysis is greatly simplified, it points out that taxes or regulation-induced cost increases have widely differing effects on industries if demand relationships vary. Similarly, the effect of regulation on industries with similar product-demand elasticities varies to the extent that supply characteristics differ. For example, in industries in which marginal costs per unit are constant, per-unit taxes will increase output prices by an amount greater than in the case of rising marginal costs but by less than in the instance of falling marginal costs.

A REGULATION COST SHARING EXAMPLE

To illustrate the effects of regulation-induced cost or tax increases, consider the possible effects on consumers and producers of a new regulation prohibiting herbicide usage in corn production, perhaps because of fears about groundwater contamination. Assume that the industry is perfectly competitive, so the market price of $3 represents both

Figure 13.1

REGULATORY BURDEN ALLOCATION UNDER ELASTIC
AND INELASTIC DEMAND

(a) Highly elastic product demand places the burden of regulation-induced cost increases on producers, who must cut production from Q_1 to Q_2. (b) Low elasticity of product demand allows producers to raise prices from P_1 to P_2, and consumers bear the burden of regulation-induced cost increases.

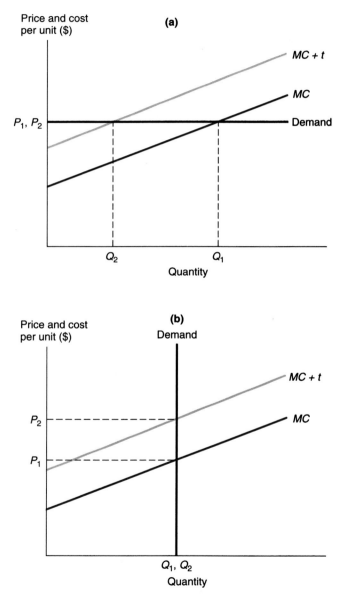

average and marginal revenue per bushel ($P = MR = \$3$). The marginal cost relation for each farmer, before any new regulations are imposed, is

$$MC = \Delta TC/\Delta Q = \$0.6 + \$0.04Q,$$

where Q is bushels of corn (in thousands). The optimal level of corn production per farm is calculated by setting $MR = MC$ and solving for Q:

$$MR = MC$$
$$\$3 = \$0.6 + \$0.04Q$$
$$\$0.04Q = \$2.4$$
$$Q = 60(000) \text{ or } 60,000 \text{ bushels.}$$

Given a perfectly competitive market, the supply curve for each producer is given by the marginal cost curve. From the marginal cost relation, the quantity of corn supplied by each farmer is

$$Supply\ Price = Marginal\ Cost$$
$$P = \$0.6 + \$0.04Q,$$

or

$$Q = -15 + 25P.$$

If the corn industry consists of 200,000 farmers with farms of equal size, total industry supply is

$$Q_S = 200,000(-15 + 25P)$$
$$= -3,000,000 + 5,000,000P. \qquad \text{(Supply)}$$

To complete the industry profile prior to the new regulation on herbicides, assume that industry demand is given by the relation

$$Q_D = 15,000,000 - 1,000,000P. \qquad \text{(Demand)}$$

In equilibrium,

$$Q_S = Q_D$$
$$-3,000,000 + 5,000,000P = 15,000,000 - 1,000,000P$$
$$6,000,000P = 18,000,000$$
$$P = \$3 \text{ per bushel,}$$

and

$$Q_S = -3,000,000 + 5,000,000(3)$$
$$= 12,000,000(000), \text{ or } 12 \text{ billion bushels,}$$
$$Q_D = 15,000,000 - 1,000,000(3)$$
$$= 12,000,000(000), \text{ or } 12 \text{ billion bushels.}$$

Now assume that reducing herbicide usage increases the amount of tillage needed to keep weed growth controlled and causes the yield per acre to drop, resulting in a 25% increase in the marginal costs of corn production. For individual farmers, the effect on marginal costs is reflected as

$$MC' = 1.25(\$0.6 + \$0.04Q)$$
$$= \$0.75 + \$0.05Q.$$

If only a few farmers in a narrow region of the country are subject to the new regulation, as would be true in the case of state or local pollution regulations, then market prices would remain stable at $3, and affected farmers would curtail production dramatically to 45,000 bushels each, because

$$MR = MC'$$
$$\$3 = \$0.75 + \$0.05Q$$
$$\$0.05Q = \$2.25$$
$$Q = 45(000), \text{ or } 45,000 \text{ bushels.}$$

Given a perfectly competitive industry and, therefore, a perfectly elastic demand for corn, local pollution regulations will force producers to bear the entire burden of regulation-induced cost increases.

A different situation arises when all producers are subject to the new herbicide regulation. In this instance, the revised individual-firm supply curve is

$$Supply\ Price = Marginal\ Cost$$
$$P = \$0.75 + \$0.05Q,$$

or

$$Q = -15 + 20P.$$

Total industry supply, assuming that all 200,000 farmers remain in business (something that may not happen if the resulting changes in profit levels are substantial), equals

$$Q'_S = 200,000(-15 + 20P)$$
$$= -3,000,000 + 4,000,000P. \quad \text{(New Supply)}$$

The equilibrium industry price/output combination is found where

$$Q_S' = Q_D$$

$$-3{,}000{,}000 + 4{,}000{,}000P = 15{,}000{,}000 - 1{,}000{,}000P$$

$$5{,}000{,}000P = 18{,}000{,}000$$

$$P = \$3.60 \text{ per bushel,}$$

and

$$Q_S' = -3{,}000{,}000 + 4{,}000{,}000(3.60)$$

$$= 11{,}400{,}000(000), \text{ or } 11.4 \text{ billion bushels,}$$

$$Q_D = 15{,}000{,}000 - 1{,}000{,}000(3.60)$$

$$= 11{,}400{,}000(000), \text{ or } 11.4 \text{ billion bushels.}$$

At the new market price, each individual farm produces 57,000 bushels of corn:

$$Q = -15 + 20(3.60)$$

$$= 57(000), \text{ or } 57{,}000 \text{ bushels.}$$

Thus, industry-wide regulation of herbicides has a relatively smaller impact on producers because the effects of regulation are partially borne by consumers through the price increase from \$3 to \$3.60 per bushel. This example illustrates why state and local authorities find it difficult to regulate firms, such as farms, that operate in highly competitive national or worldwide markets. Such regulations usually are initiated at the national level.

EFFICIENT REGULATION

Regulations that affect the marginal costs of production typically have some combination of adverse price and output effects for producers and consumers. Realizing this, some policy makers have promoted taxes or regulations with fixed or "lump sum" charges for producers. Any tax that increases fixed costs affects neither price nor output levels for profit-maximizing firms in the short run. The idea is to promote a form of taxation that cannot be shifted forward onto consumers or backward onto employees or suppliers. Even this approach to regulation is far from painless, however, since heavily regulated producers may be compelled to leave the industry in the long run, should profitability be forced below the cost of capital.

As a result, both per unit and lump sum taxes used to pay the costs of economic regulation tend to have important economic consequences. This is not to suggest that even costly regulation cannot sometimes be justified. It simply means that all forms of regulation have costs that must be paid. To be efficient, these costs must be weighed carefully and justified by the benefits of regulation.

Efficient regulation of the market economy depends on a balancing of all regulatory costs with the resulting benefits to society in general. While the intentions of many regulations are admirable, they can have unintended adverse impacts on firms and the general public. Obvious administrative costs plus hidden costs to consumers and industry must both be justified by the benefits provided. Deregulation is appropriate in markets that can be vigorously competitive; regulatory changes are fitting when they allow markets to function more efficiently and better serve consumers. From an efficiency perspective, regulation is only desirable when there can be a strong presumption that the net benefits to society are positive.

Regulatory Response to Structural Failures

Chapters 10 and 11 illustrate that monopoly or oligopoly in an industry can result in too little output and in economic profits. Regulation intended to reduce or eliminate the socially harmful consequences of such structural failures can seek to control preexisting monopoly power or to prevent its emergence. Public utility regulation, which controls the prices and profits of established monopolies, is an important example of the effort to enjoy the benefits of low-cost production by large firms while avoiding the social costs of unregulated monopoly. Tax and antitrust policies also address the problem of structural failures by limiting not only the abuse of monopoly but also its growth.

THE DILEMMA OF NATURAL MONOPOLY

In some industries, the average costs of production continue to decline as output expands. A single large firm can produce total industry output more efficiently than any group of smaller producers. Demand equals supply at a point where the long-run average cost curve for a single firm is still declining. The term *natural monopoly* describes this situation, because monopoly naturally results from the superior efficiency of a single large producer.

For example, consider Figure 13.2. Here the firm will produce Q units of output at an average cost of C per unit. Note that this cost level is above the minimum point on the long-run average cost curve, and average costs are still declining. As a monopolist, the firm can earn an economic profit equal to the rectangle $PP'C'C$, or $Q(P - C)$. Local electric, gas, and water companies are classic examples of natural monopolies, since the duplication of production and distribution facilities would greatly increase costs if more than one firm served a given area.

This situation presents something of a dilemma. Economic efficiency could be enhanced by restricting the number of producers to a single firm. However, this entails certain risks, since monopolists tend to earn economic profits or incur unnecessary costs and also tend to underproduce. Recall that economic profits are profits so large that the firm earns an above-normal risk-adjusted rate of return on invested capital. Such profits are useful both for allocating resources and as an incentive for efficiency, but it is difficult to justify above-normal profits derived from market power rather than from exceptional performance.

Underproduction occurs when the firm curtails production to a level at which the marginal value of resources needed to produce an additional unit of output (marginal

PRICE/OUTPUT DECISION UNDER MONOPOLY

Figure 13.2

Without regulation, monopolies would charge too much and produce too little output.

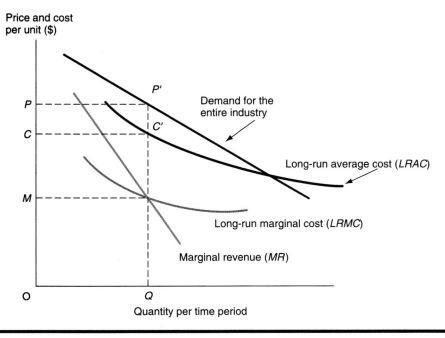

cost) is less than the benefit derived from the additional unit, as measured by the price that consumers are willing to pay for it. In other words, at output levels just greater than Q in Figure 13.2, consumers are willing to pay approximately P dollars per unit, so the value of additional units is P. However, the marginal cost of producing an additional unit is slightly less than M dollars and well below P, so cost does not equal value. Accordingly, society finds an expansion of output desirable.

Besides earning economic profits and withholding production, an unregulated natural monopolist could be susceptible to operating inefficiency. In competitive markets, firms must operate efficiently to remain in business. A natural monopoly feels no pressure for cost efficiency from established competitors. This means that the market power of the natural monopolist permits some inefficiency and waste. Even though excessive amounts of operating inefficiency attract new competitors, substantial losses in economic efficiency can persist for extended periods in the case of natural monopoly.

A real dilemma is posed because monopoly has the potential for greatest efficiency but unregulated monopoly can lead to economic profits, underproduction, and resource waste. One possible solution is to allow natural monopoly to persist but to impose price and profit regulations.

UTILITY PRICE AND PROFIT REGULATIONS

The most common method of monopoly regulation is price and profit control. Such regulations typically result in larger output quantities than would be the case with unrestricted monopoly, reduced dollar profit, and a lower rate of return on investment. This situation is illustrated in Figure 13.3. A monopolist operating without regulation would produce Q_1 units of output and charge a price of P_1. If regulators set a ceiling on prices at P_2, the firm's effective demand curve becomes the kinked curve P_2AD. Since price is a constant from 0 to Q_2 units of output, marginal revenue equals price in this range; that is, P_2A is the marginal revenue curve over the output range $0Q_2$. For output beyond Q_2, marginal revenue is given by the original marginal revenue function. The marginal revenue curve is now discontinuous at Output Q_2, with a gap between Points A and L. This

Figure 13.3

MONOPOLY PRICE REGULATION: OPTIMAL PRICE/OUTPUT DECISION MAKING

Monopoly regulation imposes a price ceiling at P_2 just sufficient to provide a fair return (area P_2AEC on investment. Under regulation, price falls from P_1 to P_2 and output expands from Q_1 to Q_2.

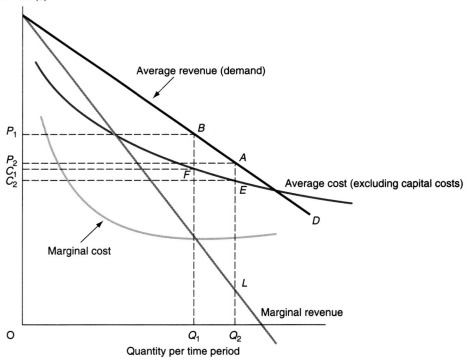

regulated firm maximizes profits by operating at Output Q_2 and charging the ceiling price, P_2. Marginal revenue is greater than marginal cost up to that output but is less than marginal cost beyond it.

Profits are also reduced by this regulatory action. Without price regulation, price P_1 is charged, a cost of C_1 per unit is incurred, and Output Q_1 is produced. Profit is $(P_1 - C_1) \times (Q_1)$, which equals the area P_1BFC_1. With price regulation, the price is P_2, the cost is C_2, Q_2 units are sold, and profits are represented by the smaller area P_2AEC_2.

To determine a fair price, the regulatory commission must estimate a fair or normal rate of return, given the risk inherent in the enterprise. The commission then approves prices that produce the target rate of return on the required level of investment. In the case illustrated by Figure 13.3, if the profit at Price P_2, when divided by the investment required to produce Q_2, were to produce more than the target rate of return, price would be reduced until actual and target rates of return became equal. This assumes, of course, that cost curves in Figure 13.3 do not include equity capital costs. The profit that the regulator allows is business profit, not economic profit.

A UTILITY PRICE AND PROFIT REGULATION EXAMPLE

To further illustrate the concept of public utility regulation, consider the case of the Malibu Beach Telephone Company, a small telephone utility serving urban customers in southern California. At issue is the monthly rate for local telephone service, or basic hookup. The monthly demand for service is given by the relation

$$P = \$22.50 - \$0.00004Q,$$

where P is service price in dollars and Q is the number of customers served. Annual total cost and marginal cost curves, excluding a normal rate of return, are given by the following expressions:

$$TC = \$3,750,000 + \$70Q + 0.00002Q^2,$$

$$MC = \Delta TC/\Delta Q = \$70 + \$0.00004Q,$$

where cost is expressed in dollars.

To find the profit-maximizing level of output, demand and marginal revenue curves for annual service must be derived. This will give all revenue and cost relations a common annual basis. The demand curve for annual service is 12 times monthly demand:

$$P = 12(\$22.5 - \$0.00004Q)$$

$$= \$270 - \$0.00048Q.$$

Total and marginal revenue curves for this annual demand curve are

$$TR = \$270Q - \$0.00048Q^2,$$

$$MR = \Delta TR/\Delta Q = \$270 - \$0.00096Q.$$

The profit-maximizing level of output is found by setting $MC = MR$ (where $M\pi = 0$) and solving for Q:

$$MC = MR,$$

$$\$70 + \$0.00004Q = \$270 - \$0.00096Q,$$

$$\$0.001Q = \$200,$$

$$Q = 200,000.$$

The monthly service price is

$$P = \$22.50 - \$0.00004(200,000)$$

$$= \$14.50 \text{ per month (or } \$174 \text{ per year).}$$

This price/output combination generates annual total profits of

$$\pi = \$270Q - \$0.00048Q^2 - \$3,750,000 - \$70Q - \$0.00002Q^2$$

$$= -\$0.0005Q^2 + \$200Q - \$3,750,000$$

$$= -\$0.0005(200,000^2) + \$200(200,000) - \$3,750,000$$

$$= \$16,250,000.$$

If the company has $125 million invested in plant and equipment, the annual rate of return on investment is

$$Return\ on\ Investment = \frac{\$16,250,000}{\$125,000,000} = 0.13,\ or\ 13\%.$$

Now assume that the State Public Utility Commission decides that a 12% return is fair given the level of risk taken and conditions in the financial markets. With a 12% return on total assets, Malibu Beach would earn business profits of

$$\pi = Allowed\ Return \times Total\ Assets$$

$$= 0.12 \times \$125,000,000$$

$$= \$15,000,000.$$

To determine the level of output that would generate this level of total profits, total profit must be set equal to $15 million:

$$\pi = TR - TC$$

$$\$15,000,000 = -\$0.0005Q^2 + \$200Q - \$3,750,000.$$

This implies that

$$-\$0.0005Q^2 + \$200Q - \$18,750,000 = 0,$$

which is a function of the form $aQ^2 + bQ - c = 0$. Solving for the roots of this equation provides the target output level. We use the quadratic equation as follows:

$$Q = \frac{-b \pm \sqrt{b^2 - 4ac}}{2a}$$

$$= \frac{-200 \pm \sqrt{200^2 - 4(-0.0005)(18,750,000)}}{2(-0.0005)}$$

$$= \frac{-200 \pm \sqrt{2,500}}{-0.001}$$

$$= 150,000 \text{ or } 250,000.$$

Because public utility commissions generally want utilities to provide service to the greatest possible number of customers at the lowest possible price, the upper figure $Q = 250,000$ is the appropriate output level. To induce Malibu Beach Telephone to operate at this output level, regulatory authorities would determine the maximum allowable price for monthly service as

$$P = \$22.50 - \$0.00004(250,000)$$

$$= \$12.50.$$

This $12.50-per-month price provides service to the broadest customer base possible, given the need to provide Malibu Beach with the opportunity to earn a 12% return on investment.

PROBLEMS WITH UTILITY PRICE AND PROFIT REGULATION

Although the concept of utility price and profit regulation is simple, several practical problems arise in public utility regulation. In practice it is impossible to exactly determine cost and demand schedules, or the minimum investment required to support a given level of output. Moreover, since utilities serve several classes of customers, many different rate schedules could produce the desired profit level. If profits for the local electric power company are too low, should rates be raised for summer (peak) or for winter (off-peak) users? Should industrial, commercial, or residential customers bear the burden of higher rates? These questions have no easy answers.

Further problems with utility regulation are involved because regulators make mistakes with regard to the optimal level and growth of service. For example, if a local telephone utility is permitted to charge excessive rates, system expansion will grow at a faster-than-optimal rate. Similarly, when the allowed rate of return exceeds the cost of capital, electric, gas, and water utilities have an incentive to overexpand fixed assets and shift to overly capital intensive methods of production. In contrast, if prices allowed to natural gas producers are too low, consumers will be encouraged to deplete scarce gas supplies, producers will limit exploration and development, and gas shortages can occur. If gas prices are too low and offer only a below-market rate of return on capital, necessary expansion will be thwarted.

Regulatory Lag
The delay between when a change in regulation is appropriate and the date it becomes effective.

A related problem is that of **regulatory lag,** or the delay between when a change in regulation is appropriate and the date it becomes effective. During the 1970s and 1980s, inflation exerted constant upward pressure on costs. At the same time, consumers and voters were able to reduce, delay, or even deny reasonable rate increases. This caused severe financial hardship for a number of utilities and their stockholders.

Traditional forms of regulation can also lead to inefficiency. If a utility is guaranteed a minimum return on investment, operating inefficiencies can be offset by higher prices. Consider the situation portrayed in Figure 13.4. A regulated utility faces the demand curve AR and the marginal revenue curve MR. If the utility operates at peak efficiency, the average cost curve AC_1 applies. At a regulated price, P_1, the quantity demanded is Q_1, cost per unit is C_1, and profits equal the rectangle $P_1P_1'C_1'C_1$. Assume that these profits are just sufficient to provide a reasonable return on invested capital.

Now suppose that another utility with less capable managers is operating under similar conditions. Because management is less efficient, the firm's cost curve is represented by AC_2. If price is set at P_1, the firm will still sell Q_1 units, but average cost equals C_2; profits equal only $P_1P_1'C_2'C_2$; and the company earns less than the required rate of return. Under regulation, the inefficient utility can request—and probably will receive—a rate increase to P_2. Here it can sell Q_2 units of output, incur an average cost of C_3 per unit, and earn profits of $P_2P_2'C_3'C_3$, resulting in a rate of return on investment approximately equal to that of the efficient company. Utility regulation sometimes has the unfortunate effect of reducing the free market profit incentive for efficiency.

Figure 13.4

EFFICIENT AND INEFFICIENT UTILITY COMPANIES

Inefficient utilities harm consumers through higher prices, P_2 versus P_1, and lower output, Q_2 versus Q_1. (Here, AC_1 and AC_2 do not include equity capital costs.)

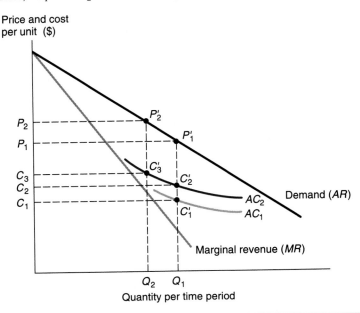

Finally, the process of utility regulation itself is costly. Detailed demand and cost analyses are necessary to provide a reasonable basis for rate decisions. It is expensive to pay regulatory officials, full-time utility commission staffs, record-keeping costs, and the expense of processing rate cases. All of these expenses are ultimately borne by consumers. Although many economists can see no reasonable alternative to utility regulation for electric, gas, local telephone, and private water companies, the costs and inefficiency of such regulation is troubling to all.

NONUTILITY PRICE CONTROLS AND WINDFALL PROFITS TAXES

Price Controls
Short-term limits on prices charged by nonutilities.

Windfall Profits
Economic profits due to unwarranted good fortune.

Another method of monopoly regulation is through the use of short-term **price controls** and **windfall profits** taxes on nonutilities to limit perceived abuses of monopoly power. Windfall profits are above-normal returns that result from unexpected and unwarranted good fortune, as opposed to economic profits that result from superior operating efficiency, innovation, economies of scale, and so on. Windfall profit taxes have frequently been imposed during wartime to eliminate the excess profits earned by providers of critical goods and services. More recently, the federal government imposed price controls and windfall profits taxes on U.S. oil companies.

The intent of oil price controls and windfall profits taxes on the oil companies was to reduce the harm to consumers from the rapid increase in crude oil prices that took place during the 1970s. Unfortunately, oil price controls, begun in 1971 and abandoned during 1981, had the unintended effect of aggravating the effects of the two oil crises experienced during the 1970s. Spot shortages of gasoline erupted and long gasoline lines resulted. In contrast, during the 1990–91 Persian Gulf crisis, a short-term spike in oil prices reflected the potential scarcity of oil created by Iraq's invasion of Kuwait. Higher prices encouraged consumers to conserve, thus avoiding the need for government allocation. Once the crisis passed, it became apparent that future supply disruptions were unlikely, and prices receded.

The most serious challenge to a successful windfall profits tax policy is the problem of correctly determining the magnitude of unwarranted profits. Prices, operating expenses, and investment policies of affected firms must be carefully scrutinized. Industry expertise is necessary to avoid potential abuses of a windfall profits tax policy. If firms perceive that a windfall profits tax is only temporary, they may incur unnecessary operating expenses or undertake unwarranted investments in anticipation of future benefits. For example, the railroad industry substantially rebuilt or replaced its right-of-way (track and related) investments during World War II. Although some reinvestment in plant and equipment was necessary to meet wartime demands for freight and passenger service, one can only speculate about how much investment was undertaken simply to avoid wartime windfall profits taxes.

Beyond the obvious problem of defining the magnitude of windfall profits to be taxed, windfall profits taxes can increase the level of risk or uncertainty in doing business. If oil company executives perceive that profits from successful exploration activities will be taxed severely, the risk of obtaining a satisfactory return from the firm's entire drilling program would rise. Higher required profits and industry prices would naturally result. Following the collapse of worldwide oil prices in the late 1980s, it was ironic that many domestic oil companies, especially smaller operators, reported large after-tax losses, or even filed bankruptcy, while paying substantial windfall profits taxes.

SMALL COMPANY TAX PREFERENCES

During recent years, the U.S. corporate income tax system has become relatively more favorable to small business. The stated rationale is quite broad. Growth in small business is consistent with democratic principles of self-determination and individual decision making. Small firms also form an important competitive fringe in many industries, exerting downward pressure on the prices and profits of leading firms. In addition, small firms are an important source of invention and innovation. To some extent, progressive taxes partially offset the relatively high costs that regulation and government reporting requirements impose on small businesses.

Whatever the rationale, it is clear that small business plays an important role in the U.S. economy. The extent to which tax and other regulatory preferences enhance the competitive positions of small firms is not fully known, but use of these preferences to ensure continued success of small business seems likely.

NEW FORMS OF INCENTIVE-BASED REGULATION

Incentive-Based Regulation
Rules that benefit firms and customers through enhanced efficiency.

State and federal regulators have begun to address the problems of price and profit regulations through new methods of **incentive-based regulation.** For example, a particular commission might believe that 12% is a reasonable rate of return on stockholders' equity, but it might allow efficient companies to earn up to 12.5% and penalize inefficient companies by holding them to returns of less than 12%. The problem with this approach is that each utility operates in a unique setting, so it is extremely difficult to make valid comparisons. One electric company might have a cost of 2¢ per kilowatt hour, and another in the same state might have a cost of 2.5¢. It is difficult to determine if the first company is more efficient than the second or if it merely benefits from cost advantages that result from differences in fuel type, plant size, labor costs, customer mix, and so on. Until recently, such difficulties have limited the explicit use of efficiency differentials in setting profit rates for local electric utilities.

However, federal regulators have already begun incentive-based regulation for long-distance telephone service. Since January 1991, the FCC has adopted a "price cap" for the seven regional Baby Bells and other local telephone companies. By limiting prices rather than the rate of return that monopoly local phone companies can earn on long-distance calls, the FCC hopes to accelerate the Bell companies' efforts to reduce their work forces and streamline operations. Such price caps have worked well in the case of regulating industry-leader AT&T. Since 1990, long-distance price increases for AT&T have been regulated to the general rate of inflation as measured by the gross domestic product price index *minus* 3% per year. That adjustment represents an expected 2.5% annual productivity gain based on AT&T's past experience, plus a 0.5% "consumer dividend."

American, Canadian, European, and Japanese multinational giants are learning how to juggle multiple identities and myriad loyalties. Pressed by the emergence of regional trading blocs in North America, Europe, and East Asia, these global corporations are developing chameleon-like abilities to resemble insiders no matter where they operate. At the same time, global manufacturers move factories and labs around the world without particular reference to national boundaries.

The global focus of modern corporations represents a striking evolution from the U.S. multinationals alternately feared and courted by developing countries around the globe since the 1960s. These giants treated foreign operations as subsidiaries for producing products designed and engineered back home. The chain of command and nationality of the company were clear. This is obviously not the case today. With the U.S. no longer dominating the world economy or holding a monopoly on innovation, new technologies, capital, and talents flow in multiple directions. In the 1990s, the most sophisticated manufacturing companies often make breakthroughs in foreign labs, place shares with foreign investors, and put foreigners on the fast track to the top. The late 1980s wave of mergers, acquisitions, and strategic alliances has further clouded traditional corporate/national relations. International competitors seeking cost efficiencies and product-quality improvements now often find themselves working together to efficiently penetrate new and emerging markets. At the same time, the pro-capitalism revolution of the late 1980s and 1990s has resulted in market-driven policies that make social, political, and cultural differences among companies less significant.

Many in both the private and public sectors believe the current trend toward globalization is bound to accelerate in the next millennium. Major advantages to global operations are obvious, including an ability to:

- *Optimize location of manufacturing and distribution facilities.* Global operations allow companies to minimize costs and improve product quality.
- *Achieve labor gains.* Workers must be responsive when companies can take advantage of low-cost employment opportunities elsewhere.
- *Sidestep legal and regulatory entanglement.* Regulators tend to be sensible when firms can relocate to avoid burdensome regulation.
- *Take advantage of global research capabilities.*

Despite obvious benefits to globalization, nagging questions remain concerning corporate/national relations in the new global environment. Now that the era of East-West military and ideological conflict is fading, does corporate nationality matter? Does it make any difference what a company's nationality is so long as it provides jobs? What nation controls the technology developed by global companies? What obligation do global corporations have to follow rules imposed by Washington, Ottawa, Paris, or Tokyo on their foreign operations? If a U.S. company makes copiers in Japan and exports them to the U.S., should they be counted in the trade deficit the same way as Toyotas from Japan, or are international accounting rules outmoded?

Washington, Ottawa, and other capitals around the globe are only beginning to come to terms with these issues. If all the industrialized nations submerge parochial interests in pursuit of a global economy where everyone benefits, then giving foreign corporations the same treatment as their domestic counterparts makes sense. But if U.S. and Canadian companies are headed into tougher competition with Japan, for example, giving Japanese companies preferential tax benefits for research and development is economic foolishness. Similarly, providing low-cost government financing for new Japanese-owned auto factories in southeastern states can harm domestic companies that must finance their own facilities in the Midwest.

Global companies obviously raise important questions for governments seeking to shape their nations' economic identity. Sorting out national economic interests is harder than ever before given lightening-quick financial markets that punish neighbor currencies, like the U.S. and Canadian dollar, when major trading partners, like Mexico, run into trouble. Washington and Ottawa can barely monitor the international trade and investment activities of U.S. and Canadian businesses, and are nearly impotent when it comes to determining the domestic implications of foreign operations. Local, state, and national governments are clearly struggling to come to grips with companies that know no national boundaries.

Source: David P. Goldman, "A Report Card on Asia," *Forbes,* February 24, 1997, 122-127.

The Bush Administration was clearly committed to the incentive regulation concept and the movement to deregulate or reduce regulation in markets that had the potential for workable competition. In a broad regulatory reform initiative issued during 1992, the Bush Administration asked federal agencies to rely as much as possible on market incentives to achieve regulatory goals. Following the precedent set by incentive-based telecommunications regulation, the Bush Administration proposed allowing natural gas pipelines to set transmission prices equal to the average cost of other similar pipelines. Under this scheme, all pipelines would want to lower average costs to achieve greater profits. Similarly, the Department of Transportation is considering guidelines for local airport authorities to permit use of "peak/off-peak" takeoff and landing fees as a means for reducing airport congestion. In a demonstration of how broadly the incentive-based regulation concept can be applied, the Environmental Protection Agency (EPA) "cash for clunkers" program was begun to remove older cars from the highway. By offering cash to owners of pre-1980 automobiles, the EPA targeted removal of the 29% of all vehicles that cause 53% of hydrocarbon and 61% of carbon monoxide emissions.[2] This program has the potential to dramatically reduce harmful pollution by directly targeting the source of harmful emissions.

At this point the future for incentive-based regulation is uncertain in the United States. Whereas the Bush Administration was solidly behind the incentive regulation concept, the Clinton Administration is less clearly committed to regulatory reform. Nevertheless, the future for incentive-based regulation would appear bright since such methods have become increasingly popular. This is an exciting innovation in regulation and holds great promise for both consumers and the stockholders of regulated companies.

Antitrust Policy

In the late nineteenth century, industrial growth was rapid and oligopoly emerged in several important industries. In some instances, pricing decisions were made by industry leaders who formed voting trusts to achieve monopoly profits. The oil and tobacco trusts of the 1880s are well-known examples. Although profitable, the trusts were socially unacceptable. Public indignation resulted in the 1890 passage of the Sherman Act, the first important U.S. antitrust statute. Other notable antitrust legislation includes the Clayton Act (1914), the Federal Trade Commission Act (1914), the Robinson-Patman Act (1936), and the Celler-Kefauver Act (1950). Each of these acts is designed to prevent anticompetitive behavior.

OVERVIEW OF ANTITRUST LAW

Antitrust Laws
Laws that promote competition and prevent monopoly.

Antitrust laws are designed to promote competition and prevent unwarranted monopoly. These laws seek to improve economic efficiency by enhancing consumer

---

[2]*Economic Report of the President,* United States Government Printing Office, 1993, 174.

sovereignty and the impartiality of resource allocation while limiting concentrations in economic and political power.

There is no single antitrust statute in the United States. Federal antitrust law is based on two important statutes—the Sherman Act and the Clayton Act—and their amendments. An important characteristic of these laws is that they broadly ban, but never define, "restraints of trade," "monopolization," "unfair competition," and so on. By never precisely defining such key terms, the statutes left the courts to decide the specific legality or illegality of various business practices. Because of this, many principles in antitrust law rest on judicial interpretation. Individual court decisions, called case law, and statutory standards, called statutory law, must be consulted to assess the legality of business behavior.

SHERMAN ACT

The Sherman Act of 1890 was the first federal antitrust legislation. It is brief and to the point. Section 1 forbade contracts, combinations, or conspiracies in restraint of trade, which were then offenses under common law. Section 2 forbade monopolies. Both sections could be enforced through civil court actions or by criminal proceedings, with the guilty liable to pay fines or serve jail sentences. In 1974, an amendment to the Sherman Act made violations felonies rather than misdemeanors. The Act now provides for up to $1 million fines against corporations and up to $100,000 in fines and three years' imprisonment for individuals. Firms and individuals violating the Sherman Act also face the possibility of paying triple damages to injured parties who bring civil suits.

The Sherman Act is often characterized as being too vague. Even with landmark decisions against the tobacco, powder, and oil trusts, enforcement has been sporadic. On the one hand, business people claim not to know what is legal; on the other, the Justice Department is sometimes criticized as being ignorant of monopoly-creating practices and failing to act in a timely fashion.

Despite its shortcomings, the Sherman Act remains one of the government's main weapons against anticompetitive behavior. In 1978 a federal judge imposed some of the stiffest penalties in U.S. antitrust history on eight firms and eleven of their officers when they were convicted of violating the Sherman Act. These convictions for price fixing in the electrical wiring devices industry resulted in fines totaling nearly $900,000 and jail terms for nine of the eleven officers charged.

CLAYTON ACT

Congress passed two measures in 1914 to overcome weaknesses in the Sherman Act. The more important of these, the Clayton Act, addressed problems of mergers, interlocking directorates, price discrimination, and tying contracts. The Federal Trade Commission (FTC) Act outlawed unfair methods of competition in commerce and established the FTC, an agency intended to enforce the Clayton Act.

Section 2 of the Clayton Act prohibited sellers from discriminating in price among business customers, unless cost differentials or competitive pressure justified the price differentials. As a primary goal, the act sought to prevent a strong regional or national firm from employing selective price cuts to drive weak local firms out of business. It was thought that once competitors in one market were eliminated, national firms could then charge monopoly prices and use resulting excess profits to subsidize cutthroat competition in other areas. The Robinson-Patman Act, passed in 1936, amended the section of the Clayton Act dealing with price discrimination. It declared specific forms of price discrimination illegal, especially those related to chain-store purchasing practices.

Section 3 of the Clayton Act forbade tying contracts that reduce competition. A firm, particularly one with a patent on a vital process or a monopoly on a natural resource, could use licensing or other arrangements to restrict competition. One such method was the tying contract, whereby a firm tied the acquisition of one item to the purchase of another. For example, IBM once refused to sell its business machines. It only rented machines to customers and then required them to buy IBM punch cards, materials, and maintenance service. This had the effect of reducing competition in these related industries. The IBM lease agreement was declared illegal under the Clayton Act, and the company was forced to offer machines for sale and to separate leasing arrangements from agreements to purchase other IBM products.

Finally, although the Sherman Act prohibited voting trusts that lessened competition, interpretation of the act did not always prevent one corporation from acquiring the stock of competing firms and then merging these firms into itself. Section 7 of the Clayton Act prohibited stock mergers that were found to reduce competition. Either the antitrust division of the Justice Department or the FTC can bring suit under Section 7 to prevent mergers. If mergers have been consummated prior to the suit, divestiture can be ordered. The Clayton Act also prevents individuals from serving on the boards of directors of two competing companies. So-called competitors having common directors would obviously not compete very hard. Although the Clayton Act made it illegal for firms to merge through stock transactions when the effect is to lessen competition, the law left a loophole. A firm could purchase the assets of a competing firm, integrate the operations into its own, and thus reduce competition. The Celler-Kefauver Act closed this loophole, making asset acquisitions illegal when the effect of such purchases is to reduce competition. By a slight change in wording, it made clear Congress's intent to attack all mergers that threatened competition, whether vertical mergers between buyers and sellers, horizontal and market extension mergers between actual or potential competitors, or purely conglomerate mergers between unrelated firms.

ANTITRUST ENFORCEMENT

Public enforcement of the antitrust laws is the dual responsibility of the antitrust division of the Department of Justice and the FTC. Generally speaking, the Justice Department concerns itself with significant or flagrant offenses under the Sherman Act, as well as with mergers for monopoly covered by Section 7 of the Clayton Act. In most instances, the Justice Department brings charges under the Clayton Act only when broader Sherman Act violations are also involved. In addition to policing law violations, the Sherman Act assigns the Justice Department the duty of restraining possible future violations. Firms found to be in violation of the law often receive detailed federal court injunctions that regulate future business activity. Injunctive relief in the form of dissolution or divestiture decrees is a much more typical outcome of Justice Department suits than are criminal penalties.

Although the Justice Department can institute civil proceedings in addition to the criminal proceedings discussed previously, civil proceedings are typically the responsibility of the FTC. The FTC is an administrative agency of the executive branch that has quasi-judicial powers with which it enforces compliance with the Clayton Act. Because the substantive provisions of the Clayton Act do not create criminal offenses, the FTC has no criminal jurisdiction. The FTC holds hearings about suspected violations of the law and issues cease and desist orders if violations are found. Cease and desist orders under the Clayton Act are subject to review by appellate courts.

ECONOMIC ANALYSIS IN ANTITRUST ACTIONS

Antitrust policy is applied if a specific business practice is thought to substantially lessen competition. Mergers are not illegal if they do not affect the vigor of competition. However, it is very difficult to accurately predict the competitive implications of a given merger. If two firms, each with 1% of a market served by 100 competitors, merge, few would argue that the merger reduces competition. After the merger, 99 firms remain, and the 1% market share advantage of the merged firm is not likely to be significant. However, merger of two firms that each had a substantial share of the market, leaving only a few firms after the merger, might affect competition. The problem lies in defining a "substantial" share of the market and quantifying a "few" remaining firms. Where should these lines be drawn? Furthermore, if a particular merger would not itself reduce competition but a series of similar mergers would do so, should the original merger be permitted? Assume that 20 firms, each with a 5% share of the market, are in competition. Suppose that two of these firms merge, and a judgment is made that competition suffers no harm. The approval of the merger might induce other firms to seek to merge, with the ultimate result being reduced competition. At what point should the trend toward concentration be stopped?

Market concentration is a key element in making judgments about the effect of a merger on competition, but drawing industry boundaries is often difficult. Suppose that two banks in lower Manhattan seek to merge. More than 10,000 banks operate in the United States, and the national banking concentration ratio is low. However, the entire United States is not a relevant market for most banking services; a local area is the relevant market. But what local area? Should metropolitan New York be deemed the market? The City of New York? The Borough of Manhattan? Lower Manhattan only? For certain classes of services, especially loans to major national corporations, the nation as a whole constitutes the appropriate market. For personal checking account and loan services, the local market area is much more relevant.

The problem is even more complex when competing products or industries are considered. A particular bank might, for example, be the only one serving a given neighborhood, but the bank might still face intense competition from savings and loan associations, credit unions, and money market mutual funds that offer service by mail and toll-free telephone numbers. Similar problems are found in other aspects of antitrust policy. Given the difficulties in estimating costs for multiproduct firms, determining the presence and magnitude of price discrimination becomes difficult.

As these examples illustrate, antitrust policy is complex, and generalizations are difficult. Nevertheless, because antitrust policy constitutes a serious constraint to many business decisions, antitrust considerations are an important, if nebulous, aspect of managerial economics.

Problems with Regulation

For effective decision making, managers must be aware of the causes and effects of regulatory processes. The need for regulation stems from economic and social factors that stimulate market failures due to incentive or structural problems. However, despite obvious benefits, there are costs to various regulatory methods. It is therefore useful to look closely at both the problems and the unfilled promise of economic regulation.

COSTS OF REGULATION

Every government program and policy has economic costs. Economic costs of regulatory policies are measured in terms of administrative burdens for regulatory agencies, deviations from optimal methods of production, and the misallocation of economic resources. An obvious cost of regulation is the cost to local, state, and federal governments for supervisory agencies. Federal government estimates for administrative expenditures on business regulation have grown from roughly $3.5 billion per year in 1970 to roughly $10 billion per year in the mid-1990s (see Figure 13.5). Billions more are spent annually by local and state agencies. It is interesting that the largest regulatory budgets at the federal level are not those of traditional regulatory agencies, such as the Securities and Exchange Commission (SEC) or Interstate Commerce Commission (ICC), but are those devoted to the broader regulatory activities of the Department of Labor for employment and job safety standards and the Department of Agriculture for food inspection.

Although the direct costs of regulation are substantial, they may be far less than hidden or indirect costs borne by the private sector. For example, the extensive reporting requirements of the Occupational Safety and Health Administration (OSHA) drive up administrative costs and product prices. Consumers also bear the cost of auto emission standards mandated by the Environmental Protection Agency (EPA). In the case of auto emissions, the National Academy of Sciences and the National Academy of Engineering estimate the annual benefits of the catalytic converter at only one-half the billions of dollars in annual costs. One might ask if the noneconomic, social advantages of this method of pollution control are sufficient to offset what appear to be significant economic disadvantages. Similarly, the economic and noneconomic benefits of regulation must be sufficient to offset considerable private costs for pollution control, OSHA-mandated noise reductions, health and safety equipment, FTC-mandated business reports, and so on.

Figure 13.5

ADMINISTRATIVE COSTS OF FEDERAL REGULATION

The administrative costs of federal regulation have increased greatly since 1970.

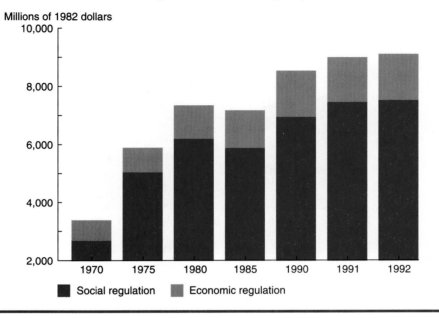

Millions of 1982 dollars

Social regulation   Economic regulation

Neither business nor the public can regard the economic costs of regulation as insignificant. In a recent study, Thomas D. Hopkins, professor of economics at the Rochester Institute of Technology, argues that laws already on the books guarantee that federal regulations will cost at least $662 billion (in 1991 dollars) by the year 2000 (see Figure 13.6).[3] Costs of environmental regulation, such as clean air and water controls, could easily top $122 billion and rachet upwards after 2000 when the full effects of the 1990 clean air amendments are felt. Indirect regulation, which transfers costs from producers to consumers, is another big regulatory cost item. "Voluntary" controls over imports of autos, textiles, and agricultural products such as sugar cost billions, while entrenched pressure groups make them hard to eliminate. A third major source of regulatory costs is paperwork, now estimated to require up to 6 billion worker hours per year. Other social programs cost billions for health and safety and affirmative action regulation.

With roughly 250 million Americans and $662 billion in direct and indirect expenses tied to regulation, the current cost of federal regulations is roughly $2,650 per year for every man, woman, and child in the United States. Local and state regulations already cost consumers billions of additional dollars; new federal regulations on health

---

[3]See Howard Banks, "What's Ahead for Business?" *Forbes,* February 15, 1993, 39.

Figure 13.6

TOTAL DIRECT AND INDIRECT COSTS OF FEDERAL
GOVERNMENT REGULATION

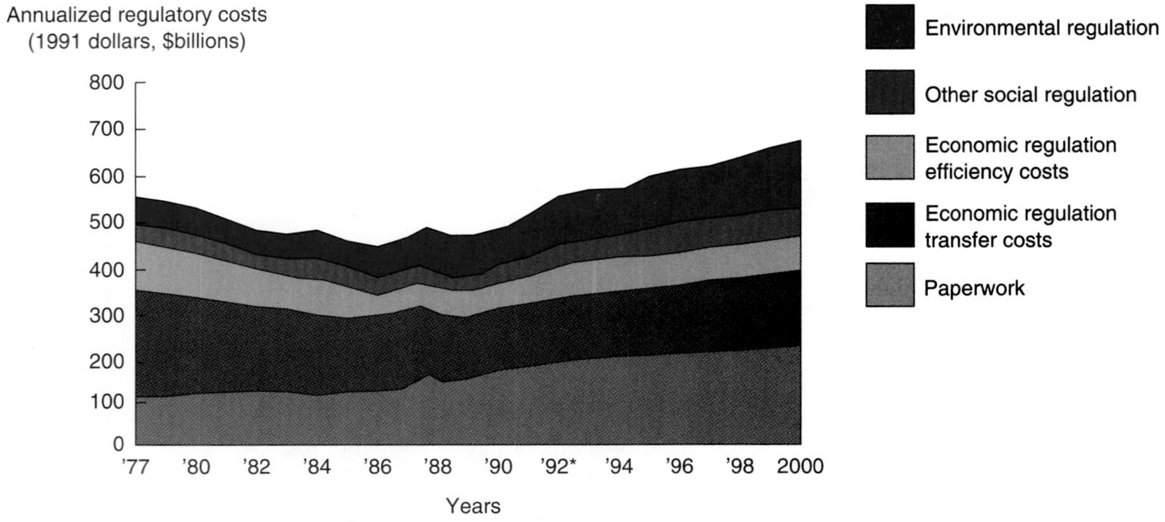

Annualized regulatory costs
(1991 dollars, $billions)

Legend:
- Environmental regulation
- Other social regulation
- Economic regulation efficiency costs
- Economic regulation transfer costs
- Paperwork

(Chart: Years from '77 to 2000 on x-axis; values 0 to 800 on y-axis)

Years

Note: Data after 1992 are estimates; all costs are in billions of 1991 dollars.

Source: Howard Banks, "What's Ahead for Business?" *Forbes*, February 15, 1993, 39.

care, worker safety, and the environment will add billions more. **Given this magnitude, consideration of the total costs of regulation must play a prominent role in decisions about what and how to regulate.**

THE SIZE-EFFICIENCY PROBLEM

Natural monopoly creates a dilemma because a single seller can achieve superior cost efficiency but may also restrict output, raise prices, and earn economic profits. This conflict between the superior efficiency of large firms and the harmful consequences of limited numbers of competitors is one of the oldest controversies in antitrust and regulation. Federal legislation proposed during recent years would limit mergers between firms of a certain size, say $100 million or more in annual sales. These proposals reflect the belief that such mergers increase monopoly power and have no offsetting advantages in terms of economic efficiency. However, research on the economic causes and consequences of mergers indicates that unfriendly takeovers are especially unfriendly to inefficient management, which is subsequently replaced. Perhaps one of the greatest dangers to a blanket prohibition of all large mergers is that it could protect inefficient management.

Antitrust policy concerning the breakup of long-established firms is especially complex, as illustrated by the classic Justice Department case against IBM. Although it did not invent the electronic computer, IBM was one of the first companies to realize the enormous opportunities the computer offered. IBM's involvement with the computer transformed the company into the dominant firm in a rapidly expanding industry. During the 1950s and 1960s, IBM became the leader in the mainframe equipment sector of the industry while playing a lesser role in peripherals and terminal equipment, software services, and other areas. Concerned with the potentially anti-competitive effects of IBM's market position, the antitrust division of the Justice Department filed suit in 1969 to break up the firm. The case foundered. No one could doubt that IBM was a large and highly profitable company, but the sources of its success were a matter of dispute. Was IBM highly profitable merely because of its leadership position (monopoly power), or was IBM a highly profitable industry leader by virtue of its ability to offer innovative products at attractive prices (efficiency)? In the first case, breaking up IBM could lead to lower prices, eliminate monopoly profits, and increase consumer welfare. In the second case, breaking up IBM would penalize the type of efficiency that competitive markets are meant to encourage. Determining the source of IBM's success and the costs and benefits from a possible breakup became a problem with no obvious answer. In 1982, after more than a decade of litigation costing both sides tens of millions of dollars, the Justice Department dismissed its suit. Free from antitrust concerns, IBM clearly became more aggressive in terms of pricing and new-product development during the 1980s.

A second interesting example is the 1974 Justice Department suit to break up AT&T. The Department argued that breaking up AT&T would stimulate competition in the telephone equipment and long-distance sectors of the industry and provide consumers with improved goods and services at lower prices. To avoid the expense and uncertainty of a prolonged antitrust case, AT&T agreed to divest itself of its local phone companies. On January 1, 1984, a "new" AT&T was created, consisting largely of AT&T communications (long-distance phone service), AT&T information systems (computer systems), AT&T international (foreign operations), Bell Labs (research and development), and Western Electric (telephone equipment). The seven local companies created were Ameritech, Bell Atlantic, Bell South, Nynex, Pacific Telesis, Southwestern Bell, and U S West.

An early indication of increasing competition in the telecommunications industry was provided by the slump in AT&T's sales of telephone exchange equipment for use within businesses, as its market share plummeted from 80% in 1970 to 28% in 1980. Since the 1984 breakup, AT&T's share of the long-distance telephone service market has fallen from in excess of 85%, to roughly 60% in 1992 (see Figure 13.7). As a direct benefit to consumers, long distance prices *declined* 9.8% per year over the 1983 to 1989 period due to increased competition and technological improvements.[4] Today, there are almost 500 firms that provide long-distance telephone services to consumers and specialized business customers. While near-term results are promising, the ultimate implications of this reorganization of the telecommunications industry remains to be seen. In the meantime, the enormous costs and risks involved make it clear why such antiturest "experiments" are rare.

---

[4]*Economic Report of the President,* United States Government Printing Office, 1993, 1182–1183.

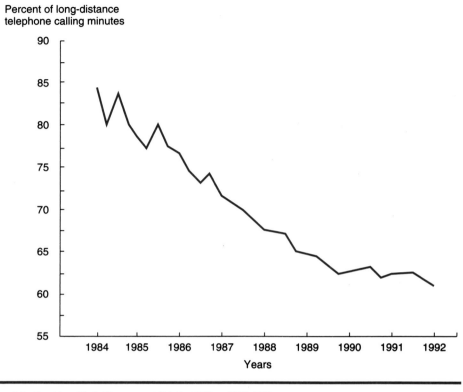

**AT&T'S SHARE OF THE LONG-DISTANCE TELEPHONE
SERVICE MARKET, 1984–1992**

AT&T's market share has declined significantly since the 1984 breakup of the Bell system.

Data Source: *Economic Report of the President*, U. S. Government Printing Office, 1993, 189.

THE "CAPTURE" PROBLEM

It is a widely held belief that regulation is in the public interest and influences firm behavior toward socially desirable ends. However, in the early 1970s, Nobel laureate George Stigler introduced an alternative **capture theory** of economic regulation. According to Stigler, the machinery and power of the state are a potential resource to every industry. With its power to prohibit or compel, to take or give money, the state can and does selectively help or hurt a vast number of industries. Because of this, regulation may be actively sought by industry. Stigler contended that regulation is typically *acquired* by industry and is designed and operated primarily for industry's benefit.

Stigler asserted that the types of state favors commonly sought by regulated industries include direct money subsidies, control over entry by new rivals, control over of substitutes and complements, and price fixing. Domestic "air mail" subsidies, Federal Deposit Insurance Corporation (FDIC) regulation that reduces the rate of entry into commercial banking, suppression of margarine sales by butter producers, price fixing in

Capture Theory
Economic hypothesis suggesting that regulation is sometimes sought to limit competition and obtain government subsidies.

motor carrier (trucking) regulation, and American Medical Association control of medical training and licensing can be interpreted as historical examples of control by regulated industries.

In summarizing his views on regulation, Stigler suggested that local, state, and federal regulators should be criticized for pro-industry policies no more than the Great Atlantic and Pacific Tea Company (A&P) should be criticized for selling groceries or politicians for seeking popular support. Current methods of enacting and carrying out regulations only make the pro-industry stance of regulatory bodies more likely. Stigler contended that the only way to get different results from regulation is to change the political process of regulator selection and to provide economic rewards to regulators who serve the public interest effectively.

Public Interest Theory
A view of regulation as a government-imposed means of private-market control.

Capture theory is in stark contrast to more traditional **public interest theory,** which sees regulation as a government-imposed means of private-market control. Rather than viewing regulation a "good" to be obtained, controlled, and manipulated, public interest theory views regulation as a method for improving economic performance by limiting the harmful effects of market failure. Public interest theory is silent on the need to provide regulators with economic incentives to improve regulatory performance. Unlike capture theory, a traditional view has been that the public can trust regulators to make a good-faith effort to establish regulatory policy in the public interest.

To be sure, suggestions of a capture problem are debatable. The need to provide regulators with positive economic incentives to ensure regulation in the public interest is also highly controversial. Nevertheless, growing dissatisfaction with traditional approaches to government regulation has led to a deregulation movement that continues in the 1990s.

The Deregulation Movement

Deregulation
The reduction of government control of the free market.

Growing concern with the costs and problems of government regulation gave birth in the early 1970s to a **deregulation** movement that has grown to impressive dimensions. Although it is difficult to pinpoint a single catalyst for the movement, it is hard to overlook the role played by Stigler and other economists (notably, Alfred E. Kahn) who illustrated that the regulatory process can sometimes harm consumer interests.

MAJOR STEPS TOWARD DEREGULATION

Table 13.1 highlights some of the major steps taken toward deregulation since 1970. Although many industries have felt the effects of changing state and local regulation, changing federal regulation has been most pronounced in the financial, telecommunications, and transportation sectors. Since 1975, for example, it has been illegal for securities dealers to fix commission rates. This broke a 182-year tradition under which the New York Stock Exchange (NYSE) set minimum rates for each 100-share ("round lot") purchase. Until 1975, everyone charged the minimum rate approved by the NYSE. Purchase of 1,000 shares cost a commission of ten times the minimum, even though

Table 13.1		
	RECENT MAJOR STEPS TOWARD DEREGULATION	
	1970	Federal Reserve Board frees interest rates on large bank deposits with short maturities ($100,000 or more for six months or less).
	1971	Federal Communications Commission (FCC) allows companies to set up long-distance telephone networks and compete with AT&T by offering private-line services.
	1975	Securities and Exchange Commission prohibits fixed commissions on stock and bond sales.
	1978	Congress deregulates prices for airline passenger service.
	1979	FCC allows AT&T to sell a limited range of unregulated services (e.g., data processing).
	1980	Congress allows banks to pay interest on checking, increases competition for commercial loans. Interstate Commerce Commission begins to dismantle trucking and railroad regulation.
	1981	FCC allots airwave space for two cellular phone franchises in every city—one for the local telephone company and one for a competing provider.
	1982	Congress allows savings and loans to make commercial loans and related investments.
	1982	Department of Justice and Federal Trade Commission relax merger guidelines.
	1984	Department of Justice order splitting off AT&T's seven operating subsidiaries becomes effective. Judge Harold Greene retains indefinite control of the "Baby Bells."
	1986	Congress deregulates interest rates for passbook and statement savings accounts.
	1989	FCC caps AT&T's long-distance rates and institutes limited profit-rate deregulation.
	1991	FCC caps long-distance rates and institutes limited profit-rate deregulation for the interstate services of local telephone companies; eliminates price caps for AT&T's large business customers.
	1992	FCC eases caps on radio and TV station ownership. Sets in motion the process to allow networks full access to syndication revenues from reruns of hit shows in U.S. and abroad.
	1995	Congress votes to require all regulations that cost the economy in excess of $25 million to be subject to cost-benefit analysis.
	1997	Clinton Administration and Congress put in motion plans to eliminate Glass-Steagall Act limits on competition among banks, insurance, and financial service companies; Congress cuts telecommunications regulations dramatically.

the overhead and work involved are roughly the same for small and large stock transactions. Following deregulation, commission rates tumbled, and, predictably, some of the least efficient brokerage firms merged or otherwise went out of business. Today, more than a decade later, commission rates (prices) have fallen by 50% or more, and the industry is noteworthy for its increasing productivity and variety of new product introductions. It is also worth mentioning that during the 1975 to 1982 period, the number of sales offices in the industry increased by 80%, total employment rose by two-thirds, and profits increased to $1.5 billion per year, more than ten times the 1974 level. All of this may lead many observers to conclude that deregulation can benefit consumers without causing any lasting damage to industry. In fact, a leaner, more efficient industry may be one of the greatest benefits of deregulation.

THE REGULATION VERSUS DEREGULATION CONTROVERSY

In evaluating the effects of deregulation, and in gauging the competitive implications of market exit by previously viable firms, it is important to remember that protecting competition is definitely not the same thing as protecting competitors. Without regulation, it is inevitable that some competitors will fall by the wayside and that concentration will rise in some markets. Although such trends must be watched closely for anticompetitive effects, they are sometimes characteristics of a vigorously competitive environment. Although some think that there is simply a question of regulation versus deregulation, this is seldom the case. On grounds of economic and political feasibility, it is often most fruitful to consider approaches to improving existing methods of regulation.

An important problem with regulation is that regulators seldom have the information or expertise to specify, for example, the correct level of utility investment, the minimum transportation costs, or the optimum method of pollution control. Because technology changes rapidly in most regulated industries, only industry personnel working at the frontier of current technology have such specialized knowledge. One method for dealing with this technical expertise problem is to have regulators focus on the preferred outcomes of regulatory processes, rather than on the technical means that industry adopts to achieve those ends. The FCC's decision to adopt downward-adjusting price caps for long-distance rates is an example of this developing trend. If providers of long-distance telephone service are able to reduce costs faster than the FCC-mandated decline in prices, they will enjoy an increase in profitability. By setting price caps that fall over time, the FCC ensures that consumers share in expected cost savings while companies enjoy a positive incentive to innovate. This approach to regulation focuses on the objectives of regulation while allowing industry to meet those goals in new and unique ways. Tying regulator rewards and regulated industry profits to objective, output-oriented performance criteria has the potential to create a desirable win/win situation for regulators, utilities, and the general public. For example, the public has a real interest in safe, reliable, and low-cost electric power. State and federal regulators who oversee the operations of utilities could develop objective standards for measuring utility safety, reliability, and cost efficiency. Tying firm profit rates to such performance-oriented criteria could stimulate real improvements in utility and regulator performance.

Regulatory Reform for the 1990s

Competitive forces provide a persistent and socially desirable constraining influence on firm behavior. When vigorous competition is absent, government regulation can be justified through both efficiency and equity criteria. When regulation is warranted, business, government, and the public must work together to ensure that regulatory processes represent the public interest. The unnecessary costs of antiquated regulations dictate

Regulatory Reform
Improvement in government control to enhance efficiency and fairness.

that **regulatory reform** is likely to remain a significant social concern throughout the 1990s.

PROMOTING COMPETITION IN ELECTRIC POWER GENERATION

The electric power industry comprises three different components: the generation of electric power, the transmission of electric power from generators to local utilities, and the distribution of electricity by local utilities to commercial and residential customers. All three segments of the industry are currently subject to some state and federal regulation. Competition has generally been regarded as unlikely in the transmission and local distribution of electricity given their natural monopoly characteristics. However, competition has emerged in the wholesale generation of electric power, and regulators now face the question of how to foster and encourage such competition.

The ability to buy and sell electric power permits utilities to efficiently employ existing capacity. By buying power from unregulated sources, utilities can meet peak-load demands on hot days or during winter storms and avoid the need to invest in additional production facilities. When utilities purchase power from others, the Federal Power Act of 1935 requires the Federal Energy Regulatory Commission (FERC) to ensure that prices charged on interstate sales are "just and reasonable" in light of necessary costs. With the emergence of competition in the electric power generation market, however, the need for FERC regulation of all interstate sales on a cost-of-service basis has diminished.

When purchasers of electric power have a number of alternative sources, a competitive market can develop and market prices can take the place of prices based on cost-of-service regulation. Indeed, by the early 1990s, the availability of alternative power sources had encouraged more than a dozen states to use competitive procurement policies for intrastate acquisition of electric power, rather than cost-of-service regulation. Competition in the electric power generation industry can be promoted by allowing local utilities access to transmission facilities that link them with alternative energy sources, provided that the owners of transmission facilities are compensated for their use. In addition, federal legislation may be required to repeal sections of the Public Utility Holding Company Act of 1935 that create barriers to entry and obstacles to the development of new wholesale power sources.

FOSTERING COMPETITION IN THE CABLE TELEVISION INDUSTRY

Cable television is available to more than 90% of U.S. households, and more than 60% of all such households subscribe to cable service. Services historically provided include improved reception for television programs broadcast over the air on advertiser-supported networks such as CBS, NBC, ABC, and the FOX network, and specialized programming from cable networks such as CNN, MTV, and the Disney Channel. In the 1990s, much of the growth in cable TV revenues will come from the provision of new shopping and data communication services. The problem is that consumers in most communities receive these services from a single monopoly provider. Regulators must decide how to encourage continued innovation in programming and in the development of new cable services, while at the same time restraining industry prices.

One possible competitor for existing cable companies is the local telephone company, although they might have to install new fiberoptic cable to provide competitive services. Standing in the way, however, are regulations that prohibit competition from telephone companies. Rules that would allow telephone companies to carry television programming and other video services would clearly enhance competition in the industry. Similarly, requiring local cable companies to transmit programming provided by others would free up access to local markets. Rules would have to be put in place to guarantee open access to local cable markets and reasonable fees to the local cable companies for program transmission.

Another potential competitor for existing cable companies is provided by "sky cable" and new emerging technologies for over-the-air transmission of specialized programming and data. Such technologies are an effective competitor for local cable companies, especially in large cities and residential areas with dense population. If such forms of competition are allowed to meet their potential, the local cable monopoly problem may become moot before the turn of the century.

IMPROVING REGULATION OF HEALTH AND SAFETY

Decisions to smoke cigarettes, go scuba diving in Baja, California, or ride a roller coaster at an amusement park involve risk. Similarly, decisions to take a job as a management consultant, as an ironworker in the construction trades, or as a commodities broker involve a trade-off between the risks and perceived benefits of employment. In the United States, government seeks to control these risks by offering consumers and employees redress for wrongful injury through the tort system and by an extensive and growing policy of health and safety regulation.

Proponents of expanded government health and safety regulation assert that consumers and employees either do not have sufficient information or are incapable of making appropriate decisions in these areas. If certain risks are extremely high or prohibitively expensive, society sometimes assumes the burden of paying for them out of equity considerations. Public concern over risk has also given rise to legislation that requires risk to be eliminated. For example, the Delaney Clause of the Food, Drug, and Cosmetics Act prohibits the use in food of substances shown to cause *any* cancer in animals or humans.

However, just as firms and individuals must balance risk and benefits when making decisions, so too must regulators. While regulators often target catastrophic risks that have a small probability of occurring, they can overlook modest risks that occur frequently. It may be good politics to target products with a very small chance of leading to cancer, but it may be more economic to focus on methods for increasing consumer awareness on the dangers of obesity. In regulating health and safety, government must focus on regulations with benefits that outweigh unavoidable costs.

REFORMING ENVIRONMENTAL REGULATION

Environmental regulation expanded greatly during the 1970s and 1980s. By requiring firms and consumers to account for pollution costs, the Clean Air Act, the Clean Water

Act, and the Resource Conservation and Recovery Act have all limited environmental waste. At the same time, each of these environmental regulations imposes significant costs on the private economy. While the U.S. already spends more on pollution abatement than any industrialized nation, this total is sure to rise sharply in the years ahead. For example, economists estimate that the Clean Air Amendments of 1990 will cost between $25 billion and $30 billion per year when fully implemented in 2005.

Still, significant uncertainties surround environmental issues, and the costs and benefits of various means of environmental regulation. For example, in the case of acid rain, studies show that simple mitigation strategies can be much more cost effective than the types of regulatory controls favored by Congress. Similarly, there may exist more efficient alternatives for correcting externalities associated with gasoline consumption. A rise in gasoline consumption increases the nation's vulnerability to oil price shocks and pollution. The most direct way of dealing with such problems would be to impose a user fee per gallon on gasoline consumption that is commensurate with resulting externalities.

The scope and importance of environmental concerns will become clearer as better information becomes available and more effective methods of regulation begin to yield results. At this point, it seems clear that economic incentives decrease compliance costs by allowing firms the flexibility to meet environmental regulations in the most efficient manner possible. With economic incentives tied to environmental objectives, rather than to the means used to achieve them, firms and society in general benefit through a practical approach to protecting the environment.

Summary

Government rules, regulations, and tax policy play a key role in shaping competitive forces. By understanding the rationale for government involvement in the market economy, a better appreciation of the part played by business is gained. For this reason, study of the role of government in the market economy is an important component of managerial economics.

- From an economic **efficiency** standpoint, a given mode of **regulation** or government control is desirable to the extent that benefits exceed costs. In terms of efficiency, the question is whether market competition by itself is adequate or if government regulation is desirable. **Equity,** or fairness, criteria must also be carefully weighed when social considerations bear on the regulatory decision-making process.
- **Market failure** is the failure of market institutions to sustain socially desirable activities or to eliminate undesirable ones. **Failure by market structure** occurs in markets with too few buyers and sellers for effective competition. **Failure by incentive** occurs when some important benefits or costs of production and consumption are not reflected in industry prices. Differences between private and social costs or benefits are called **externalities.** For example, air pollution is a type of negative externality.

- Competitive markets are also attractive because they are consistent with basic democratic principles. Preservation of consumer choice or **consumer sovereignty** is an important feature of competitive markets. A second social purpose of regulatory intervention is to **limit concentration** of economic and political power.

- **Property rights** give firms the prerogative to limit use by others of specific land, plant and equipment, and other assets. The establishment and maintenance of private property rights is essential to the workings of a competitive market. With **patents,** government grants an exclusive property right to produce, use, or sell an invention or innovation for a limited period (17 years in the United States). These valuable grants of legal monopoly power are intended to stimulate research and development. The **tort system** includes a body of law designed to provide a mechanism for victims of accidents and injury to receive just compensation for their loss. These laws create an incentive for firms and other parties to act responsibly in commerce.

- Government also responds to positive externalities by providing subsidies to private business firms. **Subsidy policy** can be direct or indirect, like government construction and highway maintenance grants that benefit the trucking industry. **Pollution emission allowances** are a new and controversial form of government subsidy that give firms the property right to pollute and to sell that right to others if they wish. Whereas subsidy policy gives firms positive incentives for desirable performance, **tax policy** contains penalties, or negative subsidies, designed to limit undesirable performance. Tax policy includes both regular tax payments and fines or penalties that may be assessed intermittently.

- **Operating controls** are regulations or standards that limit undesirable behavior by compelling certain actions while prohibiting others. The question of who pays for such regulation is seldom answered by simply referring to the point of tax collection, or point of **tax incidence.** The economic cost of regulation, or the **tax burden,** is often passed on to customers or suppliers.

- The process of regulation is expensive in terms of administrative costs, lost operating efficiency, and the misallocation of scarce resources. Contributing to these costs is the problem of **regulatory lag,** or delay between the time a change in regulation is appropriate and the date it becomes effective. Another method of monopoly regulation is through the use of short-term **price controls** and **windfall profits** taxes on nonutilities to limit perceived abuses of monopoly power. Like other forms of regulation, such rules are often imposed or maintained long after they are economically appropriate.

- State and federal regulators have begun to address the high cost and other problems of utility price regulation through new methods of **incentive-based regulation,** whereby both utilities and their customers benefit through enhanced efficiency.

- **Antitrust laws** are designed to promote competition and prevent unwarranted monopoly. These laws seek to improve economic efficiency by enhancing consumer sovereignty and the impartiality of resource allocation while limiting concentrations in both economic and political power.

- The **capture theory** of economic regulation says that the power of the state to prohibit or compel and to take or give money is often manipulated to selectively help or hurt a vast number of industries. Because of this, regulation may be actively *sought* by an industry. Capture theory contrasts sharply with the more traditional **public interest theory** view of regulation as a government-imposed means of private-market control.

■ In recognition that the regulatory process can sometimes harm rather than help consumer interests, a **deregulation** movement has sprung up and has grown to impressive dimensions. Similarly, the unnecessary costs of other forms of regulation dictate that **regulatory reform** is likely to remain a significant social concern throughout the 1990s.

Government regulation of the market economy is a natural by-product of public concern that unrestricted market competition has the potential to harm economic performance. As the benefits and costs of government/business interaction become better understood, the potential grows for a more constructive approach to government regulation.

QUESTIONS

Q13.1 Define the term *market failure* and cite some causes. Also, cite some examples of market failure.

Q13.2 What role does the price elasticity of demand play in determining the short-run effects of regulations that increase fixed costs? What if they lead to increased variable costs?

Q13.3 Given the difficulties encountered with utility regulation, it has been suggested that nationalization might lead to a more socially optimal allocation of resources. Do you agree? Why or why not?

Q13.4 Antitrust statutes in the United States have been used to attack monopolization by big business. Does labor monopolization by giant unions have the same potential for the misallocation of economic resources?

Q13.5 When will an increase in the minimum wage increase employment income for unskilled laborers?

When will it cause this income to fall? Based on your experience, which is more likely?

Q13.6 Explain why state tax rates on personal income vary more on a state-by-state basis than do corresponding tax rates on corporate income.

Q13.7 Do the U.S. antitrust statutes protect competition or competitors? What is the distinction between the two?

Q13.8 Define price discrimination. When is it legal? When is it illegal? Cite some common examples of price discrimination.

Q13.9 Is the deregulation movement of the 1970s and 1980s consistent or inconsistent with the capture theory of economic regulation?

Q13.10 "Regulation is often proposed on the basis of equity considerations and opposed on the basis of efficiency considerations. As a result, the regulation versus deregulation controversy is not easily resolved." Discuss this statement.

SELF-TEST PROBLEMS AND SOLUTIONS

ST13.1 During each 24-hour period, coal-fired electricity-generating plants emit substantial amounts of sulfur dioxide and particulate pollution into the atmosphere. Concerned citizens are appalled at the aesthetic and environmental implications of such

pollution, as well as the potential health hazard to the local population.

In analyzing remedies to the current situation, three general methods used to control pollution are generally considered:

- Regulations—licenses, permits, compulsory standards, and so on.
- Payments—various types of government aid to help companies install pollution-control equipment. Aid can take the form of forgiven local property taxes, income tax credits, special accelerated depreciation allowances for pollution-control equipment, low-cost government loans, and so on.
- Charges—excise taxes on polluting fuels (e.g., coal, oil, and so forth), pollution discharge taxes, and other taxes.

Answer the following questions in light of these alternative methods of pollution control.

A.   Pollution is a negative production externality and an example of market failure. Why do markets fail?

B.   What is the incentive provided to polluters under each method of pollution control?

C.   Who pays for a clean environment under each form of control?

D.   On the basis of both efficiency and equity considerations, which form of pollution control is most attractive?

ST13.1   SOLUTION

A.   Market failure sometimes occurs because the number of buyers and sellers is too small to ensure vigorous competition. Small numbers of sellers are sometimes caused by economies of scale in production, distribution, or marketing; barriers to entry caused by high capital, skilled labor, or other input requirement; or government-imposed barriers due to franchise grants, rules, or regulations.

Market failure can also occur if some of the costs or benefits of production or consumption are not reflected in market prices. Air, water, and noise pollution that emits from an industrial facility represent a cost of production that is imposed on society in general. Without appropriate charges for such pollution, producers, suppliers, and customers receive an implicit subsidy from the public at large. By failing to pay such environmental costs, they avoid paying the full cost of production

and consumption. In general, if some product benefit (cost) is not reflected in firm revenues (costs), then suboptimal production quantities and output prices will result and provide both firms and their customers improper economic incentives.

B.   Each alternative method of pollution control provides producers with a different set of incentives. With rules and regulations, producers often have an incentive to litigate or otherwise petition to be made a "special case" and thereby avoid regulatory costs. Rules and regulations are also sometimes difficult to monitor and enforce given the problems of determining legislative intent and regulated firm compliance. With a scheme of payments to reduce the flow of pollution, polluters have positive incentives to reduce emissions and improve economic performance. A benefit of this approach is that firms often respond better to the "carrot" of promised rewards than to the "stick" of threatened penalties. Under a pollution control method of fines or dollar penalties for noncompliance, firms have an economic incentive to reduce pollution in order to avoid charges. However, this method of forcing compliance is sometimes regarded as coercive and met with resistance.

C.   When polluters are forced to respond to rules and regulations, the company, customers, employees, and stockholders are all faced with the prospect of paying the costs of pollution reduction. The incidence of pollution cleanup costs depends on the elasticity of demand for the firm's products and on the elasticity of supply. When product demand is highly inelastic, customers have no good substitutes for the products of the polluting firm and therefore must ultimately pay the costs of cleanup. When product demand is highly elastic, customers are able to avoid the costs of pollution reduction by transferring their business to other providers who needn't charge for such expenses. In such circumstances, the firm, suppliers, employees, and stockholders bear the costs of pollution reduction. This situation is very similar to that faced by firms subject to pollution charges. In both instances, society's right to a clean environment is implied.

A system of payments to encourage pollution reduction contrasts in fundamental ways with rules and regulations and pollution charges and taxes. This method of pollution reduction is obviously attractive to polluters in that it is free and voluntary, rather than compulsory. It even provides a profit-making opportunity in pollution reduction that increases according to the scope of pollution. Moreover, when society pays a firm to reduce the level of its own pollution, the company's right to pollute is implicitly recognized.

D. Efficiency considerations typically favor payments and charges over rules and regulations as the more efficient methods of pollution control. From an efficiency standpoint, pollution charges are especially attractive in that they recognize pollution as a sometimes necessary cost of doing business, and they force cleanup costs to be borne by those who benefit most directly.

However, equity considerations make the choice among pollution control methods less certain. The regulatory process is attractive from an equity standpoint in that it ensures due process (a day in court) for the polluter. All parties are also treated equitably in the sense that all polluters are equal before the law. Payments for pollution reduction are sometimes favored on an equity basis in that it avoids penalizing polluters with "sunk" investment costs, and employees who work in older production facilities that face new domestic and foreign competitors. Pollution charges are often favored on an equity basis in that they force a close link between prices and full economic costs. Pollution charges, like payments for pollution reduction, are sometimes criticized as favoring large companies versus their smaller competitors.

Therefore, there is no single "best" method of pollution regulation. All are employed because each has the ability to meet efficiency and equity criteria in specific circumstances.

ST13.2 **Pollution Control Costs.** Fred Ziffel, Inc., processes hogs at a large facility in Hooterville, Iowa. Each hog processed yields both pork and a render by-product in a fixed 1:1 ratio. Although the by-product is unfit for human consumption, some can be sold to a local pet food company for further processing. Relevant annual demand and cost relations are as follows:

$$P_P = \$110 - \$0.00005Q_P,$$
(Demand for pork)

$$MR_P = \$110 - \$0.0001Q_P,$$
(Marginal revenue from pork)

$$P_B = \$10 - \$0.0001Q_B,$$
(Demand for render by-product)

$$MR_B = \$10 - \$0.0002Q_B,$$
(Marginal revenue from render by-product)

$$TC = \$10,000,000 + \$60Q,$$
(Total cost)

$$MC = \$60.$$
(Marginal cost)

Here, P is price in dollars, Q is the number of hogs processed (with an average weight of 100 pounds), and Q_P and Q_B are pork and render by-product per hog, respectively; both total and marginal costs are in dollars. Total costs include a risk-adjusted normal return of 15% on a $50 million investment in plant and equipment.

Currently, the city allows the company to dump excess by-product into its sewage treatment facility at no charge, viewing the service as an attractive means of keeping a valued employer in the area. However, the sewage treatment facility is quickly approaching peak capacity and must be expanded at an expected operating cost of $3 million per year. This is an impossible burden on an already strained city budget.

A. Calculate the profit-maximizing price/output combination and optimal total profit level for Fred Ziffel.

B. How much by-product will the company dump into the Hooterville sewage treatment facility at the profit-maximizing activity level?

C. Calculate output and total profits if the city imposes a $35 per unit charge on the amount of by-product Fred Ziffel dumps.

D. Calculate output and total profits if the city imposes a fixed $3-million-per-year tax on Fred Ziffel to pay for the sewage treatment facility expansion.

E. Will either tax alternative permit Fred Ziffel to survive in the long run? In your opinion, what should the city of Des Moines do about its sewage treatment problem?

ST13.2 **SOLUTION**

A. Solution to this problem requires that one look at several production and sales options available to the firm. One option is to produce and sell equal quantities of pork (P) and by-product (B). In this case, the firm sets relevant $MC = MR$.

$$MC = MR_P + MR_B = MR$$

$$\$60 = \$110 - \$0.0001Q + \$10 - \$0.0002Q$$

$$0.0003Q = 60$$

$$Q = 200,000 \text{ hogs}$$

Thus, the profit-maximizing output level for production and sale of equal quantities of P and B would be 200,000 hogs. However, the marginal revenues of both products must be positive at this sales level for this to be an optimal activity level. Evaluated at 200,000 hogs:

$$MR_P = \$110 - \$0.0001(200,000)$$

$$= \$90$$

$$MR_B = \$10 - \$0.0002(200,000)$$

$$= -\$30$$

Since the marginal revenue for B is negative, and Fred Ziffel can costlessly dump excess production, the sale of 200,000 units of B is suboptimal. This invalidates the entire solution developed above since output of P is being held down by the negative marginal revenue associated with B. The problem must be set up to recognize that Fred Ziffel will stop selling B at the point where its marginal revenue becomes zero since, given production for P, the marginal cost of B is zero.
Set:

$$MR_B = MC_B$$

$$\$10 - \$0.0002Q_B = \$0$$

$$0.0002Q_B = 10$$

$$Q_B = 50,000 \text{ units}$$

Thus, 50,000 units of B are the maximum that would be sold. Any excess units will be dumped into the city's sewage treatment facility. The price for B at 50,000 units is:

$$P_B = \$10 - \$0.0001Q_B$$

$$= 10 - 0.0001(50,000)$$

$$= \$5$$

To determine the optimal production of P (pork), set the marginal revenue of P equal to the marginal cost of hog processing and since pork production is the only motive for processing more than 50,000 units:

$$MR_P = MC_P = MC_Q$$

$$\$110 - \$0.0001Q_P = \$60$$

$$0.0001Q_P = 50$$

$$Q_P = 500,000 \text{ units}$$

$$(\text{Remember } (Q_P = Q)$$

and

$$P_P = \$110 - \$0.00005Q_P$$

$$= 110 - 0.00005(500,000)$$

$$= \$85$$

Excess profits at the optimal activity level for Fred Ziffel are:

$$\text{Excess profits} = \pi = TR_P + TR_B - TC$$

$$= P_P \times Q_P + P_B \times Q_B - TC_Q$$

$$= \$85(500,000) + \$5(50,000) - \$10,000,000 - \$60(500,000)$$

$$= \$2,750,000$$

Since total costs include a normal return of 15% on \$50 million in investment,

$$Total\ profits = Required\ return + Excess\ profits$$

$$= 0.15(\$50,000,000) + \$2,750,000$$

$$= \$10,250,000$$

B.   With 500,000 hogs being processed, but only 50,000 units of B sold, dumping of B is:

Units B dumped = Units produced − Units sold

$$= 500,000 - 50,000$$

$$= 450,000 \text{ units}$$

C.   In Part A, it is shown that if all P and B produced is sold, an activity level of $Q = 200,000$ results in $MR_B = -\$30$. A dumping charge of $35 per unit of B will cause Fred Ziffel to prefer to sell the last unit of B produced (and lose $30) rather than pay a $35 fine. Therefore, this fine, as does any fine greater than $30, will eliminate dumping and cause Fred Ziffel to reduce processing to 200,000 hogs per year. This fine structure would undoubtedly reduce or eliminate the need for a new sewage treatment facility.

While eliminating dumping is obviously attractive in the sense of reducing sewage treatment costs, the $35 fine has the unfortunate consequence of cutting output substantially. Pork prices rise to $P_P = \$110 - \$0.00005(200,000) = \$100$, and by-product prices fall to $P_B = \$10 - \$0.0001(200,000) = -\$10$. This means Fred Ziffel will pay the pet food company $10 per unit to accept all of its by-product sludge. Employment will undoubtedly fall as well. In addition to these obvious short-run effects, long-run implications may be especially serious. At $Q = 200,000$, Fred Ziffel's excess profits are:

Excess profits $= TR_P + TR_B - TC$

$$= \$110Q - \$0.00005Q^2$$
$$+ \$10Q - \$0.0001Q^2$$
$$- \$10,000,000 - \$60Q$$

$$= \$110(200,000)$$
$$- \$0.00005(200,000^2)$$
$$+ \$10(200,000)$$
$$- \$0.0001(200,000^2)$$
$$- \$10,000,000$$
$$- \$60(200,000)$$

$$= -\$4,000,000 \text{ (a loss)}$$

This means that total profits are:

Total profits = Required return + Excess profits

$$= 0.15(\$50,000,000)$$
$$+ (-\$4,000,000)$$

$$= \$3,500,000$$

This level of profit is insufficient to maintain investment. While a $35 dumping charge will eliminate dumping, it is likely to cause the firm to close down or move to some other location. The effect on employment in Hooterville could be disastrous.

D.   In the short run, a $3 million tax on Fred Ziffel has no effect on dumping, output, or employment. At the $Q = 500,000$ activity level, a $3 million tax would reduce Fred Ziffel's total profits to $7,250,000, or $250,000 below the required return on investment. However, following imposition of a $3 million tax, the firm's survival and total employment would be imperiled in the long run.

E.   No. Fred Ziffel is not able to bear the burden of either tax alternative. Obviously, there is no single best alternative here. The highest fixed tax the company can bear in the long run is $2.75 million, the full amount of excess profits. If the city places an extremely high priority on maintaining employment, perhaps a $2.75 million tax on Fred Ziffel plus $250,000 in general city tax revenues could be used to pay for the new sewage system treatment facility.

PROBLEMS

P13.1   **Costs of Regulation.** People of many different age groups and circumstances take advantage of part-time employment opportunities provided by the fast-food industry. Given the wide variety of different fast-food vendors, the industry is fiercely competitive, as is the so-called unskilled labor market. In each of the following circumstances, indicate whether the proposed changes in government policy are likely to have an increasing, a decreasing, or an uncertain effect on employment opportunities in this industry.

A.   Elimination of minimum wage law coverage

for those working less than 20 hours per week.

B.   An increase in spending for education that raises basic worker skills.

C.   An increase in the employer portion of federally mandated FICA insurance costs.

D.   A requirement that employers install expensive new worker-safety equipment.

E.   A state requirement that employers pay 8% of wages to fund a new national health-care program.

P13.2 Advertising Regulation. The Tobacco Products Control Act bans all print and broadcast advertising of tobacco products in Canada. The Act also orders the phase-out of all existing billboard and in-store tobacco advertising and requires stronger health warnings on tobacco packaging. Explain why this legislation is likely to increase, decrease, or have no effect on the following:

A.   Consumption of tobacco products

B.   Industry advertising costs

C.   Short-run industry profits

D.   Nonadvertising methods of competition

E.   Barriers to entry.

P13.3 Price Fixing. The Ivy League, comprised of Brown, Columbia, Cornell, Harvard, Princeton, and Yale universities, Dartmouth College, and the University of Pennsylvania, is one of the most distinguished academic associations in the U.S. and the world. Long noted for celebrated academic programs at both the undergraduate and graduate levels, each of these schools can rightfully boast about its superb faculty and extremely talented students.

Over the years, Ivy League members have come to regard one another as colleagues with a common goal of providing the highest quality education possible. However, in an economic sense, members of the Ivy League might be regarded as competitors rather than collaborators. Members compete among themselves to attract and retain talented faculty members and capable students. The academic job market is often highly competitive, and bidding for coveted faculty members can be spirited. Higher salaries, reduced teaching loads, research assistants, and sophisticated laboratory equipment are often used to attract the best young talent, or to entice senior faculty to move from one institution to another. Similarly, scholarships, student loans, and work-study arrangements are often provided as a means for encouraging

National Merit Scholars and other gifted students to enroll in one institution versus another.

Against this backdrop, it is interesting to consider a May 8, 1992, article in *The Wall Street Journal* (p. A1) titled "Ivy League Discussions on Finances Extended to Tuition and Salaries." The article described a May 1991 consent decree between the Justice Department and Ivy League members who admitted no wrongdoing in the settlement but agreed not to collude on tuition, salaries, or financial aid in the future.

According to Justice Department reports, Ivy League presidents gathered at the Harvard Club in New York on Dec. 3, 1986, to discuss their "common concerns." Ostensibly competitors, the eight private schools openly examined each other's plans for increasing tuition and faculty salaries during the coming year. In other words, they openly discussed plans for raising prices (tuition) and limiting costs (faculty salaries) in an effort to control competition among themselves for prized students and faculty. Except for Dartmouth, each school was planning tuition increases in a tight range between 5.8% and 7.5%, and salary increases of 5% to 6.5%. When Dartmouth told of plans for tuition and salary increases of 8% to 8.5%, an audible gasp escaped from the crowd. Quickly, Dartmouth brought its tuition and salary increases into line with the others. The net result was that final 1987–1988 charges, including room, board, and fees, were bunched closely between $16,841 and $17,100 at seven of the eight schools, leaving students and their families no financial reason to shop around. Cornell, an exception at $16,320, receives subsidies from New York state.

A.   How would you determine whether the outcome of the presidents' meeting is an example of price fixing?

B.   If price fixing did indeed occur at these meetings, which laws in particular might be violated?

P13.4 Price Discrimination. During recent years, U.S. car manufacturers have charged lower car prices in western states in an effort to head off competition by popular Japanese imports. Subcompacts produced by GM, Ford, and others have cost consumers $100 to $150 less in western states than in other parts of the country. This two-tier pricing scheme has raised the ire of eastern dealers, who view it as discriminatory and a violation of antitrust laws.

A. Is this pricing scheme discriminatory in the economic sense? What conditions would be necessary for it to be profitable to the automakers?

B. Carefully describe how price discrimination could violate U.S. antitrust laws, and be sure to mention which laws in particular might be violated.

P13.5 **Benefits of Regulation.** Three leading concrete suppliers have entered into a secret cartel to fix prices and allocate repair business for the Garden State Parkway. The marginal costs per unit for supplying concrete are as follows:

CUBIC YARDS OF CONCRETE (THOUSANDS)	ATLANTIC CITY SUPPLY, INC. (A)	BRUNSWICK CONTRACTORS, LTD. (B)	CAMDEN CONSTRUCTION, INC. (C)
1	$10	$20	$20
2	15	20	15
3	20	30	10
4	25	40	25
5	30	50	35

A. Determine the cartel's optimal allocation of output and maximum profits if it sets $Q = 8$ and $P = \$25$.

B. Calculate the perfectly competitive industry price for $Q = 8$.

C. How much output would a perfectly competitive industry supply at $P = \$25$?

D. Describe the value to society of breaking up the cartel.

P13.6 **Costs of Regulation.** Kildare Gillespie Instruments, Inc., manufactures an innovative piece of diagnostic equipment used in medical laboratories and hospitals. OSHA has determined that additional safety precautions are necessary to bring radioactive leakage occurring during use of this equipment down to acceptable levels. Total and marginal production costs, including a normal rate of return on investment but before additional safeguards are installed, are as follows:

$$TC = \$5,000,000 + \$5,000Q,$$

$$MC = \Delta TC/\Delta Q = \$5,000.$$

Market demand and marginal revenue relations are the following:

Medical Laboratory Demand
$$P_L = \$15,000 - \$12.5Q_L,$$

$$MR_L = \Delta TR/\Delta Q_L = \$15,000 - \$25Q_L.$$

Hospital Demand
$$P_H = \$10,000 - \$1Q_H,$$

$$MR_H = \Delta TR/\Delta Q_H = \$10,000 - \$2Q_H.$$

A. Assuming that the company faces two distinct markets, calculate the profit-maximizing price/output combination in each market and Kildare Gillespie's level of economic profits.

B. Describe the short- and long-run implications of meeting OSHA standards if doing so raises Kildare Gillespie's marginal cost by $1,000 per machine.

C. Calculate the point price elasticity at the initial (Part A) profit-maximizing activity level in each market. Are the differential effects on sales in each market that were seen in Part B typical or atypical?

P13.7 **Incidence of Regulation Costs.** The Smokey Mountain Coal Company sells coal to electric utilities in the southeast. Unfortunately, Smokey's coal has a high particulate content, and, therefore, the company is adversely affected by state and local regulations governing smoke and dust emissions at its customer's electricity-generating plants. Smokey's total and marginal cost relations are

$$TC = \$1,000,000 + \$5Q + \$0.0001Q^2,$$

$$MC = \$5 + \$0.0002Q,$$

where Q is tons of coal produced per month and TC includes a risk-adjusted normal rate of return on investment.

A. Calculate Smokey's profit at the profit-maximizing activity level if prices in the industry are stable at $25 per ton and therefore $P = MR = \$25$.

B. Calculate Smokey's optimal price, output, and profit levels if a new state regulation results in a $5-per-ton cost increase that can be fully passed on to customers.

C. Determine the effect on output and profit if

Smokey must fully absorb the $5-per-ton cost increase.

P13.8 **Cost of Import Tariffs.** Topo Gigo Imports, Ltd., located in San Francisco, California, is an importer and distributor of a leading Japanese-made desktop dry copier. The U.S. Commerce Department recently informed the company that it will be subject to a new 5.75% tariff on the import cost of copiers. Topo Gigo is concerned that the tariff will slow its sales, given the highly competitive nature of the copier market. Relevant market demand and marginal revenue relations are as follows:

$$P = \$13,800 - \$0.23Q,$$

$$MR = \$13,800 - \$0.46Q.$$

Topo Gigo's marginal cost per copier equals the import cost of $8,000 per unit, plus 15% to cover transportation, insurance, and related selling expenses. In addition to these costs, Topo Gigo's fixed costs, including a normal rate of return, come to $15 million per year.

A. Calculate Topo Gigo's optimal price/output combination and economic profits before imposition of the tariff.

B. Calculate Topo Gigo's optimal price/output combination and economic profits after imposition of the tariff.

C. Compare your answers to Parts A and B. Who pays the economic burden of the import tariff?

P13.9 **Utility Regulation.** The Woebegone Water Company, a small water utility serving rural customers in Minnesota, is currently engaged in a rate case with the regulatory commission under whose jurisdiction it operates. At issue is the monthly rate that the company will charge for unmetered sewer and water service. The demand curve for monthly service is $P = \$40 - \$0.01Q$. This implies annual demand and marginal revenue curves of

$$P = \$480 - \$0.12Q,$$

$$MR = \$480 - \$0.24Q,$$

where P is service price in dollars and Q is the number of customers served. Total and marginal costs per year (before investment return) are described by the following function:

$$TC = \$70,000 + \$80Q + \$0.005Q^2,$$

$$MC = \$80 + \$0.01Q.$$

The company has assets of $2 million and the utility commission has authorized an 11.5% return on investment.

A. Calculate Woebegone's profit-maximizing price (monthly and annually), output, and rate-of-return levels.

B. Woebegone has requested a monthly price of $22. Calculate Woebegone's output and total return on investment if the request were to be granted. Why are these values different from those calculated in Part A?

C. What monthly price should the commission grant to limit Woebegone to an 11.5% rate of return?

P13.10 **Costs of Regulation.** The Klamath Paper Company produces corrugated boxes for industrial packaging at a plant located in Klamath Falls, Oregon. For each ton of packaging materials produced, 100 gallons of waste water pollutant is dumped into the Klamath River. Klamath's revenue and manufacturing cost relations for corrugated boxes are:

$$TR = \$6,000Q - \$0.15Q^2,$$

$$MR = \$6,000 - \$0.3Q,$$

$$TC = \$18,000,000 + \$2,000Q + \$0.05Q^2,$$

$$MC = \$2,000 + \$0.1Q.$$

Both price and total manufacturing cost (which includes capital costs) are in dollars, and Q is in tons of output. The Oregon Department of Natural Resources (DNR) is considering various pollution tax schemes designed to provide funding for clean-up operations as well as reduce Klamath's waste water pollution. The DNR has determined that discharges into the river must be cut to meet new federal water-quality guidelines. Alternatively, the Klamath Water District water-treatment facility could be expanded to deal with water-treatment needs at a public cost of $2.5 million per year—costs that must be met through pollution charges, other taxes, or both.

A. Calculate Klamath's optimal output, price, discharge, and profit levels based on the assumption of no pollution taxes nor disposal costs.

B.   Calculate these same levels if a $2 per gallon waste water disposal charge is imposed on the company.

C.   If Klamath is required to recycle all waste water, Klamath calculates total recycling costs (in dollars) as:

$$TC_R = \$2W + \$0.000005W^2,$$

$$= \$2(100Q) - \$0.000005(100Q)^2,$$

$$= \$200Q + \$0.05Q^2$$

where W is gallons of recycled waste water. This implies a marginal recycling cost per ton of production of :

$$MC_R = \$200 + \$0.1Q.$$

Calculate optimal output, price, discharge, and profit levels in this situation.

D.   Describe the advantages and disadvantages of the disposal charge and recycling alternatives.

Case Study for Chapter 13

THE NETWORK TELEVISION REGULATION VERSUS DEREGULATION CONTROVERSY

When viewers think of FCC regulation of network television, they might think of censorship or of the FCC controlling the renewal of local broadcast licenses. While TV censors are the butt of frequent jokes by David Letterman on CBS's "Late Show" and Jay Leno on NBC's "The Tonight Show," TV censorship in the United States is very mild when compared with that in many foreign countries, and it has little economic or political impact. Although more important, FCC control over the renewal of local broadcast licenses also has little direct effect on the network broadcasting business. To be sure, local affiliates must be careful to merit license renewal by serving the special community interests of local viewing areas.

It might come as a big surprise to many viewers that network television has been subject to heavy economic regulation in terms of what are referred to as financial interest and network syndication rules. These so-called fin/syn rules were adopted in the early 1970s to prevent ABC, CBS, and NBC from collectively dominating the broadcast industry. The financial interest rule long prohibited networks from having an ownership interest in shows produced for them by others. The network syndication rule prohib-

ited networks from selling internally produced programs into the domestic syndication or rerun market. Limits on network access to the rerun market were an important disincentive to network production of new television shows. A single half-hour episode of prime-time programming can sometimes cost up to $1 million. Given these tremendous costs, few television programs, even popular hit shows like "Seinfeld," "Roseanne," and "The Simpsons," make money on their initial runs. The big profits come from subsequent syndication sales of reruns to network affiliates or independent stations in the late afternoon or early evening hours.

Fin/syn rules effectively brought about a separation between the production of television entertainment programming and broadcasting. This was especially true following a 1980 consent decree that limited the amount of prime-time programming that the networks could produce internally. With the exception of prime-time sports and news coverage, which they can offer without restriction, the networks serve as distributors of entertainment programs produced by independent Hollywood producers and others. The networks paid fees for the rights to distribute specific shows and they hope to make enough money from selling advertising time on their initial run to more than offset fees and earn a profit.

Back in the 1970s and early 1980s, this method of regulation made much more sense than it does in the 1990s. Without it, Hollywood producers would have been at a big disadvantage in negotiating terms with the networks, since there were only three major networks that could buy their shows. Today, things are much different. Not only has the number of independent stations proliferated, but cable TV has become a major power. CNN offers stiff competition for network news programming, while ESPN gives the networks a run for their money in sports programming. Of most direct relevance to fin/syn regulation is the proliferation of entertainment programming outlets such as A&E, the Disney Channel, Lifetime, Nickelodeon, TNT, and the USA network, among others.

Consistent with the Bush Administration's push for deregulation, then FCC chairman Alfred C. Sikes argued in early 1991 that the fin/syn rules were antiquated and should be repealed. However, in a startling rebuke of the chairman, the FCC voted 3-2 in April 1991 to retain the fin/syn rules with only modest changes. Effective June 15, 1991, the networks gained the opportunity to acquire foreign-syndication rights for network programs, but only after giving independent producers the opportunity to make other distribution deals. The networks were also allowed into the domestic-syndication market for entertainment programming, but only for programs produced in-house and for no more than 40% of the networks' prime-time schedule. By failing to abolish fin/syn rules, the FCC ruling represented a major victory for Jack Valenti, head of the Motion Picture Association of America, and a stunning defeat for the networks. Like a real-life soap opera, the fin/syn regulatory drama seems to never end. In November 1993, fin/syn rules were further loosened to allow the networks to own and produce as much of their prime-time schedules as they want, own stakes in shows produced by outsiders, and syndicate reruns of their shows abroad. As of November 1995, the networks have been freed to enter the U.S. syndication market as well and will no longer be barred from merging with Hollywood studios that have extensive syndication operations.

Meanwhile, the networks' cable rivals have suffered some recent setbacks at the hands of the regulators. In the past, only CNN, ESPN, MTV, and other exclusively cable stations have received compensation from the cable operators to help cover programming expenses. Until recently, regulators had required the networks to allow cable to carry network shows without compensation. This changed with the Cable Act of 1992, when cable systems were ordered to compensate broadcast stations for the right to retransmit their broadcast signals. In the short run, this rule change has had little practical effect since cable operators that dominate local markets have largely refused to pay the broadcasters. In light of the cable operator's threat to drop network stations from cable packages, the broadcasters caved in, and most continue to allow cable operators to carry their stations for free, at least for the time being.

Briefly explain the following:

A. The causes and consequences of regulation according to the public interest theory of regulation;

B. The causes and consequences of regulation according to the capture theory of regulation; and

C. How the network television regulation versus deregulation controversy supports or contradicts each theory.

Risk Analysis

Effective managerial decision making in the late 1990s requires that managers make correct choices in the midst of a risky economic environment. To succeed in an environment where moves and counter moves by local and global competitors must be correctly anticipated, managers must employ dynamic new decision methods. One of the most useful of these tools is game theory, a technique originally devised to help World War II military leaders deal with wartime uncertainty. Fortune 500 firms, like Bell Atlantic, have found that game theory concepts give managers a way of analyzing and responding to the impact of sometimes contradictory market forces. Because managers cannot control the economic environment as shaped by competitor pricing and output decisions, it is essential that the managerial decision-making process allow for the effects of competitor counter measures. Game theory concepts give managers the tools necessary to identify decision alternatives that eliminate the possibility of catastrophic outcomes and to isolate other choices that minimize the chance of foregoing dynamic new economic opportunities. Managers at Bell Atlantic and other firms argue that the greatest benefit earned through application of game theory techniques is that it forces managers to see opportunities through the eyes of actual and potential competitors.[1]

This chapter introduces techniques helpful for measuring the risk or uncertainty associated with a given managerial decision. Then, certainty equivalent and risk-adjusted discount rate approaches are shown as practical ways for adapting the basic valuation model to account for uncertainty. Finally, decision trees, simulation, and game theory techniques are discussed as further aids to decision making under conditions of risk and uncertainty.

The Concepts of Risk and Uncertainty

Let's face it, risk is a four-letter word. When it comes to investing, managers and other investors often prefer not to hear much about the chance of loss. That's why billions of dollars sit in low-yielding certificates of deposit or Treasury securities "backed by the full faith and credit of the U.S. government." However, while the local bank can guarantee savers that their funds will be returned intact, it does nothing to protect them from the risk that inflation will reduce the real value of their assets. To make effective investment decisions, managers must understand the many faces of risk.

---

[1]See Raymond W. Smith, "Business as War Game: A Report from the Battlefront," *Fortune,* September 30, 1996, 190–193.

ECONOMIC RISK AND UNCERTAINTY

Managers sometimes know with certainty the outcomes that each possible course of action will produce. A firm with $100,000 in cash that can be invested in a 30-day Treasury bill yielding 6% ($493 interest for 30 days) or used to prepay a 10% bank loan ($822 interest for 30 days) can determine with certainty that prepayment of the bank loan provides a $329 higher one-month return. A retailer can just as easily predict the cost savings earned by placing a given order directly with the manufacturer versus through an independent wholesaler; manufacturers can often forecast the precise cost effect of meeting a rush order when overtime wages rather than standard labor rates are required. Order backlogs give a wide variety of consumer and producer goods manufacturers a clear indication of product demand conditions. Similarly, book, magazine, and trade journal publishers accurately judge product demand conditions on the basis of subscription revenues. Resort hotels can often foretell with a high degree of accuracy the amount of food, beverages, and linen service required to meet the daily needs of a 1,500-person convention, especially when such conventions are booked on a regular basis. Even when events cannot be predicted exactly, only a modest level of decision uncertainty is present in such situations.

Economic Risk
The chance of loss due to the fact that all possible outcomes and their probability of occurrence are unknown.

Uncertainty
When the outcomes of managerial decisions cannot be predicted with absolute accuracy but all possibilities and their associated probabilities of occurrence are known.

Many other important managerial decisions are made under conditions of risk or uncertainty. **Economic risk** is the chance of loss because all possible outcomes and their probability of happening are unknown. Actions taken in such a decision environment are purely speculative, such as the buy and sell decisions made by traders and other speculators in commodity, futures, and options markets. All decision makers are equally likely to profit as well as to lose; luck is the sole determinant of success or failure. **Uncertainty** exists when the outcomes of managerial decisions cannot be predicted with absolute accuracy but all possibilities and their associated probabilities are known. Under conditions of uncertainty, informed managerial decisions are possible. Experience, insight, and prudence allow managers to devise strategies for minimizing the chance of failing to meet business objectives. While luck still plays a role in determining ultimate success, managers can deal effectively with an uncertain decision environment by limiting the scope of individual projects and developing contingency plans for dealing with failure.

To assume that all future possibilities and their associated probabilities are known with certainty involves an obvious abstraction from reality. Decision makers are seldom, if ever, able to precisely gauge future prospects and the chance that various end results will occur. However, practical experience is a powerful aid to decision making under uncertainty, and the range of probable outcomes can often be estimated with a high degree of reliability. Successful companies incorporate risk analysis into their everyday decision making. When the level of risk and the attitudes toward risk taking are known, the effects of uncertainty can be directly reflected in the basic valuation model of the firm. The certainty equivalent method converts expected risky profit streams to their certain sum equivalents to eliminate value differences that result from different risk levels. For risk-averse decision makers, the value of a risky stream of payments is less than the value of a certain stream, and the application of certainty equivalent adjustment factors results in a downward adjustment in the value of expected returns. For risk-seeking decision makers, the value of a risky stream of payments is greater than that of a certain stream, and application of certainty equivalent adjustment factors results in an upward adjustment in the value of expected returns. In both cases, risky dollars are converted into certain-sum equivalents. Another method used to reflect uncertainty in the basic valuation model is the risk-adjusted discount rate approach. In this technique, the interest rate used in the denominator of the basic valuation model depends on the level of risk. For highly risk-averse decision makers, higher discount rates are implemented; for less risk-averse decision makers, lower discount rates are employed. Using this technique, discounted expected profit streams reflect risk differences and become directly comparable.

GENERAL RISK CATEGORIES

Business risk is the chance of loss associated with a given managerial decision. Such losses are a normal by-product of the unpredictable variation in product demand and cost conditions. Business risk must be dealt with effectively; it seldom can be eliminated.

In a globally competitive environment with instant communication, managers face a wide variety of risks. For managers, a main worry is something called **market risk,** or the chance that a portfolio of investments can lose money because of overall swings in the financial markets. Managers must be concerned about market risk because it influences the cost and timing of selling new debt and equity securities to investors. When a bear market ensues, investors are not the only ones to lose. Companies unable to raise funds for new plant and equipment must forego profitable investment opportunities when the cost of financing escalates. **Inflation risk** is the danger that a general increase in the price level will undermine the real economic value of corporate agreements that involve a fixed promise to pay a specified amount over an extended period. Leases, rental agreements, and corporate bonds are all examples of business contracts that can be susceptible to inflation risk. **Interest-rate risk** is another type of market risk that can severely affect the value of corporate investments and obligations. This stems from the fact that a fall in interest rates will increase the value of any contract that involves a fixed promise to pay over an extended time frame. Conversely, a rise in interest rates will decrease the value of any agreement that involves fixed interest and principal payments.

Credit risk is the chance that another party will fail to abide by its contractual obligations. A number of companies have lost substantial sums because other parties were either unable or unwilling to provide raw commodities, rental space, or financing at agreed upon prices. Like other investors, corporations must also consider the problem of **liquidity risk,** or the difficulty of selling corporate assets or investments that are not easily transferable at favorable prices under typical market conditions. Another type of risk is related to the rapidly expanding financial derivatives market. A financial derivative is a security that derives value from price movements in some other security. **Derivative risk** is the chance that volatile financial derivatives such as commodities futures and index options could create losses in underlying investments by increasing price volatility.

Business Risk
The chance of loss associated with a given managerial decision.

Market Risk
The chance that a portfolio of investments can lose money because of swings in the financial markets as a whole.

Inflation Risk
The danger that a general increase in the price level will undermine real economic value.

Interest-Rate Risk
Market risk that stems from the fact that changing interest rates affect the value of any agreement that involves a fixed promise to pay over a specified period.

Credit Risk
The chance that another party will fail to abide by contractual obligations.

Liquidity Risk
The difficulty of selling corporate assets or investments that have only a few willing buyers or are otherwise not easily transferable at favorable prices under typical market conditions.

Derivative Risk
The chance that volatile financial derivatives such as commodities futures and index options could create losses in underlying investments by increasing price volatility.

SPECIAL RISKS OF GLOBAL OPERATIONS

Cultural Risk
The chance of loss because of product market differences due to distinctive social customs.

Cultural risk is borne by companies that pursue a global investment strategy. Product market differences due to distinctive social customs make it difficult to predict which products might do well in foreign markets. For example, breakfast cereal is extremely popular and one of the most profitable industries in the United States, Canada, and the United Kingdom. However, in France, Germany, Italy, and many other foreign countries, breakfast cereal is much less popular and less profitable. In business terms, breakfast cereal doesn't "travel" as well as U.S.-made entertainment like movies, videos, and television programming.

Currency Risk
Loss due to changes in the domestic-currency value of foreign profits.

Currency risk is another important danger facing global businesses since most companies wish to eventually repatriate foreign earnings back to the domestic parent. When the U.S. dollar rises in value against foreign currencies such as the Canadian dollar, foreign profits translate into fewer U.S. dollars. Conversely, when the U.S. dollar falls in value against the Canadian dollar, profits earned in Canada translate into more U.S. dollars. Because price swings in the relative value of currencies are unpredictable and can be significant, many multinational firms hedge against currency price swings using financial derivatives in the foreign currency market. This hedging is not only expensive but can be risky during volatile markets.

Government Policy Risk
The chance of loss because foreign government grants of monopoly franchises, tax abatements, and favored trade status can be tenuous.

Global investors also experience **government policy risk** because foreign government grants of monopoly franchises, tax abatements, and favored trade status can be tenuous. In the "global friendly" 1990s, many corporate investors seem to have forgotten the widespread confiscations of private property owned by U.S. corporations in Mexico, Cuba, Libya, the former Soviet Union, and in a host of other countries. **Expropriation risk,** or the risk that business property located abroad might be seized by host governments, is a risk that global investors must not forget. During every decade of the twentieth century, U.S. and other multinational corporations have suffered from expropriation, and probably will in the years ahead.

Expropriation Risk
The danger that business property located abroad might be seized by host governments.

Probability Concepts

A clear understanding of probability concepts provides a background for discussing various methods of effective risk analysis. Marketing directors cannot accurately assess the potential of new products or pricing strategies without data. Managers cannot make insightful investment decisions without reliable information about risk.

THE PROBABILITY DISTRIBUTION

Probability
The chance of occurrence.

Probability Distribution
A list of possible events and probabilities.

The **probability** of an event is the chance, or odds, that the incident will occur. If all possible events or outcomes are listed, and if a probability is assigned to each event, the listing is called a **probability distribution.** For example, suppose a sales manager observes that there is a 70% chance that a given customer will place a specific order, versus a 30% chance that the customer will not. This situation is described by the probability distribution shown in Table 14.1.

Table 14.1

A SIMPLE PROBABILITY DISTRIBUTION

EVENT (1)	PROBABILITY OF OCCURRENCE (2)
Receive order	0.7 = 70%
Do not receive order	0.3 = 30%
Total	1.0 = 100%

Table 14.2

PAYOFF MATRIX FOR PROJECTS A AND B

	PROFITS	
STATE OF THE ECONOMY	PROJECT A	Project B
Recession	$4,000	$ 0
Normal	5,000	5,000
Boom	6,000	12,000

Both possible outcomes are listed in Column 1, and the probabilities of each outcome, expressed as decimals and percentages, appear in Column 2. Notice that the probabilities sum to 1.0, or 100%, as they must if the probability distribution is complete. In this simple example, risk can be read from the probability distribution as the 30% chance of the firm not receiving the order. For most managerial decisions the relative desirability of alternative events or outcomes is not absolute. A more general measure of the relation between risk and the probability distribution is typically required to adequately incorporate risk considerations into the decision-making process.

Suppose a firm is able to choose only one of two investment projects, each calling for an outlay of $10,000. Assume also that profits earned from the two projects are related to the general level of economic activity during the coming year, as shown in Table 14.2. This table is known as a **payoff matrix** since it illustrates the dollar outcome associated with each possible state of nature. Both projects provide a $5,000 profit in a normal economy, higher profits in an economic boom, and lower profits if a recession occurs. However, Project B profits vary far more according to the state of the economy than do profits from Project A. In a normal economy, both projects return $5,000 in profit. Should the economy be in a recession next year, Project B will produce nothing, whereas Project A will still provide a $4,000 profit. If the economy is booming next year, Project B's profit will increase to $12,000, but profit for Project A will increase only moderately, to $6,000.

Project A is clearly more desirable if the economy is in recession, whereas Project B is superior in a boom. In a normal economy the projects offer the same profit potential, and both are equally desirable. To choose the best project, one needs to know the

Payoff Matrix
A table that shows outcomes associated with each possible state of nature.

likelihood of a boom, a recession, or normal economic conditions. If such probabilities can be estimated, the expected profits and variability of profits for each project can be determined. These measures make it possible to evaluate each project in terms of expected return and risk, where risk is measured by the deviation of profits from expected values.

EXPECTED VALUE

Expected Value
Anticipated realization.

The **expected value** is the anticipated realization from a given payoff matrix and probability distribution. It is the *weighted-average* payoff, where the weights are defined by the probability distribution.

To continue with the previous example, assume that forecasts based on the current trend in economic indicators suggest a two in ten chance of recession, a six in ten chance of a normal economy, and a two in ten chance of a boom. As probabilities, the probability of recession is 0.2, or 20%; the probability of normal economic activity is 0.6, or 60%; and the probability of a boom is 0.2, or 20%. These probabilities add up to 1.0 (0.2 + 0.6 + 0.2 = 1.0), or 100%, and thereby form a complete probability distribution, as shown in Table 14.3.

If each possible outcome is multiplied by its probability and then summed, the weighted average outcomes are determined. In this calculation, the weights are the probabilities of occurrence, and the weighted average is called the expected outcome. Column 4 of Table 14.3 illustrates the calculation of expected profits for Projects A and B. Each possible profit level in Column 3 is multiplied by its probability of occurrence from Column 2 to obtain weighted values of the possible profits. Summing Column 4 of the table for each project gives a weighted average of profits under various states of the economy. This weighted average is the expected profit from the project.

Table 14.3

CALCULATION OF EXPECTED VALUES

	STATE OF THE ECONOMY (1)	PROBABILITY OF THIS STATE OCCURRING (2)	PROFIT OUTCOME IF THIS STATE OCCURS (3)	EXPECTED PROFIT OUTCOME (4) = (2) × (3)
Project A	Recesson	0.2	$4,000	$ 800
	Normal	0.6	5,000	3,000
	Boom	0.2	6,000	1,200
		1.0	Expected Profit A =	$5,000
Project B	Recession	0.2	$ 0	$ 0
	Normal	0.6	5,000	3,000
	Boom	0.2	12,000	2,400
		1.0	Expected Profit B =	$5,400

The expected-profit calculation is expressed by the equation

$$Expected\ Profit = E(\pi) = \sum_{i=1}^{N} \pi_i \times p_i. \qquad (14.1)$$

Here, π is the profit level associated with the ith outcome, p_i is the probability that outcome i will occur, and N is the number of possible outcomes or states of nature. Thus, $E(\pi)$ is a weighted average of possible outcomes (the π_i values), with each outcome's weight equal to its probability of occurrence.

The expected profit for Project A is obtained as follows:

$$E(\pi_A) = \sum_{i=1}^{3} \pi_i \times p_i$$
$$= \pi_1 \times p_1 \times \pi_2 \times p_2 \times \pi_3 \times p_3$$
$$= \$4,000(.2) + \$5,000(0.6) + \$6,000(0.2)$$
$$= \$5,000.$$

The results in Table 14.3 are shown as a bar chart in Figure 14.1. The height of each bar signifies the probability that a given outcome will occur. The probable outcomes for Project A range from $4,000 to $6,000, with an average, or expected, value of $5,000. For Project B, the expected value is $5,400 and the range of possible outcomes is from $0 to $12,000.

For simplicity, this example assumes that only three states of nature can exist in the economy: recession, normal, and boom. Actual states of the economy range from deep depression, as in the early 1930s, to tremendous booms, such as in the mid- to late 1980s, with an unlimited number of possibilities in between. Suppose sufficient information exists to assign a probability to each possible state of the economy and a monetary outcome in each circumstance for every project. A table similar to Table 14.3 could then be compiled that would include many more entries for Columns 1, 2, and 3. This table could be used to calculate expected values as shown, and the probabilities and outcomes could be approximated by the continuous curves in Figure 14.2.

Figure 14.2 is a graph of the probability distribution of returns for Projects A and B. In general, the tighter the probability distribution, the more likely it is that actual outcomes will be close to expected values. The more loose the probability distribution, the less likely it is that actual outcomes will be close to expected values. Because Project A has a relatively tight probability distribution, its actual profit is more likely to be close to its expected value than is that of Project B.

ABSOLUTE RISK MEASUREMENT

Risk is a complex concept, and some controversy surrounds attempts to define and measure it. Common risk measures that are satisfactory for most purposes are based on the observation that tight probability distributions imply low risk because of the correspondingly small chance that actual outcomes will differ greatly from expected values.

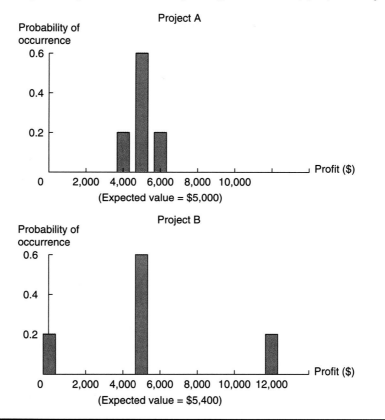

RELATION BETWEEN STATE OF THE ECONOMY AND PROJECT RETURNS

Figure 14.1

Project *B* has a greater expected return and a higher dispersion in returns (risk) than Project *A*.

From this perspective, Project *A* is less risky than Project *B*.

Standard deviation, shown as σ (sigma), is a popular and useful measure of ab-

Absolute Risk
Overall dispersion of
possible payoffs.

solute risk. **Absolute risk** is the overall dispersion of possible payoffs. The smaller the standard deviation, the tighter the probability distribution and the lower the risk in absolute terms. To calculate standard deviation using probability information, the expected value or mean of the return distribution must first be calculated as

$$Expected\ Value\ =\ E(\pi)\ =\ \sum_{i=1}^{N}\ (\pi_i p_i).\tag{14.2}$$

In this calculation, π_i is the profit or return associated with the ith outcome; p_i is the probability that the ith outcome will occur; and $E(\pi)$, the expected value, is a weighted average of the various possible outcomes, each weighted by the probability of its occurrence.

Figure 14.2

PROBABILITY DISTRIBUTIONS SHOWING RELATION BETWEEN STATE
OF THE ECONOMY AND PROJECT RETURNS

The actual return form Project *A* is likely to be close to the expected value. It is less likely that the
actual return from Project *B* will be close to the expected value.

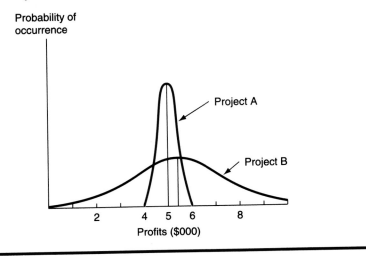

The deviation of possible outcomes from the expected value must then be derived:

$$Deviation_i = \pi_i - E(\pi).$$

The squared value of each deviation is then multiplied by the relevant probability and
summed. This arithmetic mean of the squared deviations is the variance of the probability distribution:

$$Variance = \sigma^2 = \sum_{i=1}^{N} [\pi_i - E(\pi)]^2 p_i. \qquad (14.3)$$

The standard deviation is found by obtaining the square root of the variance:

$$Standard\ Deviation = \sigma = \sqrt{\sum_{i=1}^{N} [\pi_i - E(\pi)]^2 p_i.} \qquad (14.4)$$

The standard deviation of profit for Project *A* can be calculated to illustrate this procedure:

DEVIATION $[\pi_i - E(\pi)]$	DEVIATION^2 $[\pi_i - E(\pi)]^2$	DEVIATION^2 × PROBABILITY $[\pi_i - E(\pi)]^2 \times p_i$
$4,000 − $5,000 = −$1,000	$1,000,000	$1,000,000(0.2) = $200,000
$5,000 − $5,000 = 0	0	$0(0.6) = $0
$6,000 − $5,000 = $1,000	$1,000,000	$1,000,000(0.2) = $200,000
		Variance = σ^2 = $400,000

$$\textit{Standard deviation} = \sigma = \sqrt{\sigma^2} = \sqrt{\$400,000} = \$632.46$$

Using the same procedure, the standard deviation of Project *B*'s profit is \$3,826.23. Since Project *B* has a larger standard deviation of profit, it is the riskier project.

RELATIVE RISK MEASUREMENT

Problems sometimes arise when standard deviation is used to measure risk. If an investment project is relatively expensive and has large expected cash flows, it will have a large standard deviation of returns without being truly riskier than a smaller project. Suppose a project has an expected return of \$1 million and a standard deviation of only \$1,000. Some might reasonably argue that it is less risky than an alternative investment project with expected returns of \$1,000 and a standard deviation of \$900. The *absolute* risk of the first project is greater; the risk of the second project is much larger relative to the expected payoff. **Relative risk** is the variation in possible returns compared with the expected payoff amount.

Relative Risk
The variation in possible returns compared with the expected payoff amount.

A popular method for determining relative risk is to calculate the coefficient of variation. Using probability concepts, the coefficient of variation is

$$\textit{Coefficient of Variation} = v = \frac{\sigma}{E(\pi)}. \qquad \textbf{(14.5)}$$

In general, when comparing decision alternatives with costs and benefits that are not of approximately equal size, the coefficient of variation measures relative risk better than does the standard deviation.

OTHER RISK MEASURES

The standard deviation and coefficient of variation risk measures are based on the *total* variability of returns. In some situations, however, a project's total variability overstates its risk. This is because projects with returns that are less than perfectly correlated can be combined, and the variability of the resulting portfolio of investment projects is less than the sum of individual project risks. Much recent work in finance is based on the idea that project risk should be measured in terms of its contribution to total return variability for the firm's asset portfolio. The contribution of a single investment project to the overall variation of the firm's asset portfolio is measured by a concept known as *beta*. **Beta** is a measure of the systematic variability or covariance of one asset's returns with returns on other assets.

Beta
A measure of the systematic variability of one asset's returns with returns on other assets.

The concept of beta should be employed when the returns from potential investment projects are likely to greatly affect or be greatly affected by current projects. However, in most circumstances the standard deviation and coefficient of variation measures provide adequate assessments of risk.

The Standard Normal Concept

Managers often estimate the scope of investment project payoff possibilities to construct a range of optimistic to pessimistic scenarios. Once this has been done, the risk of a given course of action can be characterized in terms of the distribution of possible outcome values. The standard normal concept is an intuitive and practical means for assessing the dispersion of possible outcomes in terms of expected value and standard deviation measures.

THE NORMAL DISTRIBUTION

Normal Distribution

A symmetrical distribution about the mean or expected value.

The relation among risk, standard deviation, and the coefficient of variation can be clarified by examining the characteristics of a normal distribution, as shown in Figure 14.3. A **normal distribution** has a symmetrical distribution about the mean or expected value. If a probability distribution is normal, the actual outcome will lie within ± 1 standard deviation of the mean roughly 68% of the time; the probability that the actual outcome will be within ± 2 standard deviations of the expected outcome is approximately 95%; and there is a greater than 99% probability that the actual outcome will occur within ± 3 standard deviations of the mean. The smaller the standard deviation, the tighter the distribution about the expected value and the smaller the probability of an outcome that is very different from the expected value.

Probability distributions can be viewed as a series of *discrete values* represented by a bar chart, such as in Figure 14.1, or as a *continuous function* represented by a smooth curve, such as that in Figure 14.2. Probabilities associated with the outcomes in Figure

Figure 14.3

PROBABILITY RANGES FOR A NORMAL DISTRIBUTION

When returns display a normal distribution, actual outcomes will lie within ± 1 standard deviation of the mean 68.26 percent of the time, within ± 2 standard deviations 95.46 percent of the time, and within ± 3 standard deviations 99.74 percent of the time.

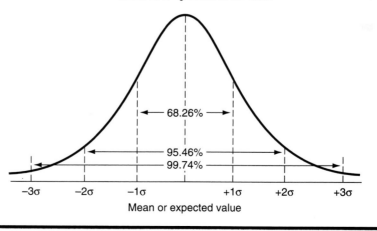

14.1 are given by the *heights* of the bars, whereas in Figure 14.2, the probabilities must be found by calculating the area under the curve between points of interest. Consider, for example, the continuous probability distribution shown in Figure 14.4. This is a normal curve with a mean of 20 and a standard deviation of 5; x could be dollars of sales, profits, or costs; units of output; percentage rates of return; or any other units. To learn the probability that an outcome will fall between 15 and 30, one must calculate the area beneath the curve between these points, the shaded area in the diagram.

The area under the curve between 15 and 30 can be determined by painstaking graphic analysis or, since the distribution is normal, by reference to tables of the area under the normal curve, such as Table 14.4 or Appendix B of this book. To use these tables, it is necessary to know only the mean and standard deviation of the distribution.

STANDARDIZED VARIABLES

Standardized Variable
A variable with a mean of 0 and a standard deviation equal to 1.

Any distribution of costs or revenues to be investigated must first be transformed or standardized. A **standardized variable** has a mean of 0 and a standard deviation equal to 1. Any distribution of revenue, cost, or profit data can be standardized with the following formula:

$$z = \frac{x - \mu}{\sigma}, \tag{14.6}$$

where z is the standardized variable, x is the outcome of interest, and μ and σ are the mean and standard deviation of the distribution, respectively. If the point of interest is 1σ away from the mean, then $x - \mu = \sigma$, so $z = \sigma/\sigma = 1.0$. When $z = 1.0$, the point of interest is 1σ away from the mean; when $z = 2$, the value is 2σ away from the mean; and so on.

Figure 14.4

CONTINUOUS PROBABILITY DISTRIBUTION

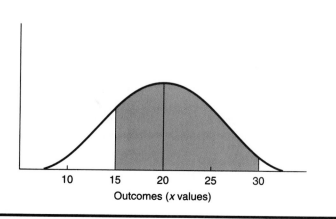

Outcomes (x values)

Table 14.4

AREA UNDER THE NORMAL CURVE

z	AREA FROM THE MEAN TO THE POINT OF INTEREST	ORDINATE
0.0	0.0000	0.3989
0.5	0.1915	0.3521
1.0	0.3413	0.2420
1.5	0.4332	0.1295
2.0	0.4773	0.0540
2.5	0.4938	0.0175
3.0	0.4987	0.0044

In the present example, the probability that an outcome will fall between 15 and 30 can be easily calculated. Using Equation 14.6, these points of interest are normalized as follows:

$$z_1 = \frac{15 - 20}{5} = -1, \qquad z_2 = \frac{30 - 20}{5} = 2.$$

The negative sign on z_1 is ignored, since the normal curve is symmetrical around the mean; the minus sign merely indicates that the point of interest lies to the left of the mean. A plus sign (or no sign) indicates that a point of interest lies to the right of the mean. The areas under the normal curve associated with these z values are found in Table 14.4 to be 0.3413 and 0.4773. This means that the probability is 0.3413, or 34.13%, that the actual outcome will fall between 15 and 20, and 0.4773, or 47.73%, that it will fall between 20 and 30. Summing these probabilities shows that the probability of an outcome falling between 15 and 30 is 0.8186, or 81.86%.

Suppose that one is interested in determining the probability that an actual outcome would be greater than 15. Note that the probability is 0.3413, or 34.13%, that an outcome will be between 15 and 20. Then observe that the probability is 0.5000, or 50%, of an outcome greater than the mean, 20. The probability is 0.3413 + 0.5000 = 0.8413, or 84.13%, that a given outcome will exceed 15.

Some interesting properties of normal probability distributions can be seen by examining Table 14.4 and Figure 14.3, which is a graph of the normal curve. For any normal distribution, the probability of an outcome falling within ±1 standard deviation from the mean is 0.6826, or 68.26% (= 0.3413 × 2.0); the probability of an outcome falling within 2 standards of the mean is 95.46%; and 99.74% of all outcomes will fall within 3 standard deviations of the mean. Although the standard normal distribution theoretically runs from minus infinity to plus infinity, the probability of occurrences beyond 3 standard deviations is very near zero.

USE OF THE STANDARD NORMAL CONCEPT: AN EXAMPLE

An example illustrates use of the standard normal concept in managerial decision making. Suppose that the Harry Morton Realty is considering a boost in advertising to reduce a large inventory of unsold homes. The firm's management plans to make its media decision using the data shown in Table 14.5 on the expected success of television versus newspaper promotions. For simplicity, assume that the returns from each promotion are normally distributed. If the television promotion costs $4,000 and the newspaper promotion costs $3,000, what is the probability that each will generate a profit?

To calculate the probability that each promotion will generate a profit, it is necessary to calculate the portion of the total area under the normal curve that is to the right of (greater than) each breakeven point. Using methods described earlier, relevant expected values and standard deviations are $E(R_{TV}) = \$6,000$, $\sigma_{TV} = \$2,828.43$, $E(R_N) = \$6,000$, and $\sigma_N = \$1,414.21$. For the television promotion, the breakeven revenue level of $4,000 is 0.707 standard deviations to the left of the expected revenue level of $6,000 because

$$z = \frac{x_{TV} - E(R_{TV})}{\sigma_{TV}}$$

$$= \frac{\$4,000 - \$6,000}{\$2,828.43}$$

$$= -0.707.$$

The standard normal distribution function value for $z = -0.707$ is between that for $z = -0.70$ and $z = -0.71$:

z	Pr
-0.70	0.2580
-0.707	$0.2580 + a$
-0.71	0.2611

To find the precise probability value for $z = -0.707$, it is necessary to interpolate, where

$$\frac{a}{(0.2611 - 0.2580)} = \frac{(-0.707 + 0.70)}{(-0.71 + 0.70)}$$

$$\frac{a}{0.0031} = \frac{0.007}{0.01}$$

$$a = 0.0022,$$

and the probability value for $z = -0.707$ is $0.2580 + 0.0022 = 0.2602$. This means that 0.2602, or 26.02%, of the total area under the normal curve lies between x_{TV} and $E(R_{TV})$, and implies a profit probability for the television promotion of $0.2602 + 0.5 = 0.7602$, or 76.02%.

Table 14.5	RETURN DISTRIBUTIONS FOR TELEVISION AND NEWSPAPER PROMOTIONS		
	MARKET RESPONSE	PROBABILITY OF OCCURRING (P_i)	RETURN (R_i) (COMMISSION REVENUES)
Television	Poor	0.25	$ 2,000
	Good	0.50	6,000
	Very Good	0.25	10,000
Newspaper	Poor	0.25	4,000
	Good	0.50	6,000
	Very Good	0.25	8,000

In calculating the newspaper promotion profit probability, z is calculated as

$$z = \frac{x_N - E(R_N)}{\sigma_N}$$

$$= \frac{\$3,000 - \$6,000}{\$1,414.21}$$

$$= -2.121,$$

and the probability value for $z = -2.121$ is 0.4830. This means that 0.483, or 48.3%, of the total area under the normal curve lies between x_N and $E(R_N)$, and it implies a profit probability for the newspaper promotion of $0.483 + 0.5 = 0.983$, or 98.3%. In terms of profit probability, the newspaper advertisement is obviously the less risky alternative.

Utility Theory and Risk Analysis

The assumption of risk aversion is basic to many decision models in managerial economics. Because this assumption is so crucial, it is appropriate to examine attitudes toward risk and discuss why risk aversion holds in general.

POSSIBLE RISK ATTITUDES

Risk Aversion
A desire to avoid or minimize uncertainty.

Risk Neutrality
A focus on expected values, not return dispersion.

Risk Seeking
A preference for speculation.

In theory, three possible attitudes toward risk are present: aversion to risk, indifference to risk, and preference for risk. **Risk aversion** characterizes individuals who seek to avoid or minimize risk. **Risk neutrality** characterizes decision makers who focus on expected returns and disregard the dispersion of returns (risk). **Risk seeking** characterizes decision makers who prefer risk. Given a choice between more risky and less risky investments with identical expected monetary returns, a risk averter selects the less risky investment and a risk seeker selects the riskier investment. Faced with the same choice, the risk-neutral investor is indifferent between the two investment projects. Some individuals prefer high-risk projects and the corresponding potential for substantial returns, especially when relatively small sums of money are involved.

Risk Seekers Get Gambling Fever

The success of state-run lotteries is convincing evidence that many people display risk-seeking behavior, especially when small sums of money are involved. The profitability of state-run lotteries stems from the fact that ticket buyers are willing to pay $1 for a bet that has an expected return of less than $1. When only 50% of lottery-ticket revenues are paid out in the form of prizes, for example, each $1 ticket has an expected return of only 50 cents. In such circumstances, the "price" of $1 in expected return is $2 in certain dollars. The willingness to pay such a premium for the unlikely chance at a lottery payoff that might reach into the millions of dollars stems from the fact that such opportunities are rare and lottery-ticket buyers value them highly. Many have no opportunity for hitting the jackpot in their careers. The lottery is their only chance, however remote, at a substantial sum of money. The success of state-run lottery promotions is noteworthy because it is fairly unusual. Typically, consumers and investors display risk-averse behavior, especially when substantial sums of money are involved.

Gambling is one of America's great growth industries. Over the past decade, the gambling industry has enjoyed average yearly growth in per-capita spending and gross revenues of roughly 10% per year. With such impressive results, it's little wonder that several Midwestern and Southern states have licensed gambling on river boats, many of them anchored in some of the nation's poorest towns along the Mississippi Delta. Roughly 100 river boats and dockside casinos are afloat as more than a dozen states from Texas to Rhode Island search for more jobs and revenue. Some 20 states now have Indian gambling, ranging from bingo parlors to casinos as big and glamorous as those in Nevada. Interestingly, gambling fever has spread to states with long traditions of fiscal conservatism. For example, the state of Minnesota, with its Native American gambling halls, has more casinos than Atlantic City.

If legislative agendas are any indication, Americans can expect to see even more river boat gambling, card clubs, off-track betting parlors, and casinos in their own backyards. Indian-run casinos are also becoming increasingly popular. Americans are so eager to gamble that they are shifting long-established leisure-time expenditures. Today, U.S. consumers spend more on legal games of chance than on movie theaters, books, amusement attractions, and recorded music combined! According to some Wall Street and industry forecasts, spending on gambling will double by the year 2000.

Some of the recent surge in gambling's popularity can be traced to demographics and broader spending trends. The population is aging, and an older population tends to favor participant amusements that aren't strenuous. Pouring quarters into a slot machine is easy, and apparently quite appealing to a growing number of Americans. The growth in gambling has also coincided with a glacial shift in social attitudes. Within a generation, gambling has gone from being a moral vice to mass-market entertainment. Analysts contend that it was church and charity "Las Vegas Nights" and "Bingo Nights" that laid the legal groundwork for Indian tribes to broaden their gambling operations.

Critics regard all of this as unfortunate. They contend that in the pell-mell rush to scoop up gambling revenues, the seeds of potential problems are being planted. Compulsive and underage gambling are mostly ignored. In Minnesota, for example, obsessive gambling among the poor has become a major problem with some calling for a tax on gambling casino profits to pay for treatment centers. The problem that gambling can attract crime and corruption also tends to be overlooked. Any high turnover all-cash business invites problems, and casino gambling is no exception. At least for the time being, no one even seems worried by the potential for over building in the industry. However, when one considers the likelihood of future shakeouts, it's easy to see that investors and government sponsors—not just the players—stand to lose.

See: Ronald Grover, "Hilton Could Hit the Jackpot," *Business Week*, February 10, 1997, 40-41.

Entrepreneurs, innovators, inventors, speculators, and lottery ticket buyers are all examples of individuals who sometimes display risk-seeking behavior. Risk-neutral behavior is exhibited in some business decision making. However, both logic and observation suggest that business managers and investors are predominantly risk averters, especially when substantial dollar amounts are involved.

RELATION BETWEEN MONEY AND ITS UTILITY

Diminishing Marginal Utility
When additional increments of money bring ever smaller increments of added benefit.

At the heart of risk aversion is the notion of **diminishing marginal utility** for money. If someone with no money receives $5,000, it can satisfy his or her most immediate needs. If such a person then receives a second $5,000, it will obviously be useful, but the second $5,000 is not quite so necessary as the first $5,000. Thus, the value, or *utility,* of the second, or *marginal,* $5,000 is less than the utility of the first $5,000, and so on. Diminishing marginal utility of money implies that the marginal utility of money diminishes for additional increments of money. Figure 14.5 graphs the relation between money and its utility, or value. In the figure, utility is measured in units of value or satisfaction, an index that is unique to each individual.

For risk averters, money has diminishing marginal utility. If such an individual's wealth were to double suddenly, he or she would experience an increase in happiness or satisfaction, but the new level of well-being would not be twice the previous level. In cases of diminishing marginal utility, a less than proportional relation holds between total utility and money. Accordingly, the utility of a doubled quantity of money is less than twice the utility of the original level. In contrast, those who are indifferent to risk perceive a strictly proportional relationship between total utility and money. Such a

AN EXAMPLE OF A MONEY/UTILITY RELATION

Figure 14.5

A risk seeker's marginal utility of money increases. A risk-indifferent individual has a constant marginal utility of money. A risk averter displays a diminishing marginal utility of money.

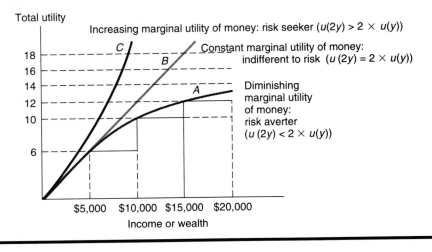

relation implies a constant marginal utility of money, and the utility of a doubled quantity of money is exactly twice the utility of the original level. Risk seekers perceive a more than proportional relation between total utility and money. In this case, the marginal utility of money increases. With increasing marginal utility of money, the utility of doubled wealth is more than twice the utility of the original amount. These relations are illustrated in Figure 14.5.

Even though total utility increases with increased money for risk averters, risk seekers, and those who are indifferent to risk, the relation between total utility and money is quite different for each group. These differences lead to dissimilar risk attitudes. Because individuals with a diminishing marginal utility for money suffer more pain from a dollar lost than the pleasure derived from a dollar gained, they seek to avoid risk. Risk averters require a very high return on any investment that is subject to much risk. In Figure 14.5, for example, a gain of $5,000 from a base of $10,000 brings 2 units of additional satisfaction, but a $5,000 loss causes a 4-unit loss in satisfaction. A person with this utility function and $10,000 would be unwilling to make an investment with a 50/50 chance of winning or losing $5,000. The 9-unit expected utility of such a gamble [$E(u)$ = 0.5 times the utility of $5,000 + 0.5 times the utility of $15,000 = $0.5 \times 6 +$ $0.5 \times 12 = 9$] is less than the 10 units of utility obtained by forgoing the gamble and keeping $10,000 in certain wealth.

Since an individual with a constant marginal utility for money values a dollar gained just as highly as a dollar lost, the expected utility from a fair gamble always exactly equals the utility of the expected outcome. An individual indifferent to risk makes decisions on the basis of expected monetary outcomes and is not concerned with possible variation in the distribution of outcomes.

AN EXAMPLE OF RISK AVERSION

A second and more detailed example should clarify the relation between utility and risk aversion. Assume that government bonds are riskless securities that currently offer a 9% rate of return. If an individual buys a $10,000 U.S. Treasury bond and holds it for one year, he or she will end up with $10,900, a gain of $900.

Suppose that in an alternative investment opportunity, the $10,000 would back a wildcat oil-drilling venture. If the drilling venture is successful, the investment will be worth $20,000 at the end of the year. If it is unsuccessful, investors can liquidate their holdings and recover $5,000. There is a 60% chance that oil will be discovered and a 40% chance of a dry hole. Should an investor with only $10,000 to invest choose the riskless government bond or the risky drilling operation?

To analyze this question, the expected monetary values of the two investments must be calculated, as in Table 14.6. The calculation in the table is not really necessary for the government bond; a $10,900 outcome occurs regardless of what happens in the oil field. The oil venture calculation shows that the $14,000 expected value of this venture is higher than that of the bond. However, this does not necessarily mean that the investor should invest in the wildcat well. That depends on the investor's utility function. If an investor's marginal utility for money diminishes sharply, thus indicating strong risk aversion, then the utility from a producing well might not compensate for the

Table 14.6

EXPECTED RETURNS FROM TWO PROJECTS

		DRILLING OPERATION			GOVERNMENT BOND	
STATE OF NATURE	PROBABILITY (1)	OUTCOME (2)	(3) = (1) × (2)	PROBABILITY (1)	OUTCOME (2)	(3) = (1) × (2)
Oil	0.6	$20,000	$12,000	0.6	$10,900	$ 6,540
No Oil	0.4	5,000	2,000	0.4	10,900	4,360
		Expected value	$14,000		Expected value	$10,900

Table 14.7

EXPECTED UTILITY OF THE OIL-DRILLING PROJECT

STATE OF NATURE	PROBABILITY (1)	MONETARY OUTCOME (2)	ASSOCIATED UTILITY (3)	WEIGHTED UTILITY (4) = (1) × (3)
Oil	0.6	$20,000	13.0	7.8
No Oil	0.4	5,000	6.0	2.4
			Expected utility	10.2

potential loss of utility from a dry hole. This is precisely the case if the risk averter's utility function shown in Figure 14.5 applies. Four units of utility will be lost if no oil is found, and only three will be gained if the well produces.

The expected monetary value calculation can be modified to reflect utility considerations. Reading from Figure 14.5, this particular risk-averse investor will enjoy 13 units of utility if he or she invests in the wildcat venture and oil is found, but only 6 units of utility will be experienced if no oil is found. This information is used in Table 14.7 to calculate the expected utility for the oil investment. No calculation is needed for the government bond; its utility is 10.7 units regardless of the outcome of the oil venture. The investor will have 10.7 units of utility with certainty by choosing the government bond.

Because the expected utility from the wildcat venture is only 10.2 units, versus 10.7 from the government bond, the government bond is the preferred investment. Even though the expected monetary value for the oil venture is higher, expected utility is greater for the bond investment. Risk considerations dictate that the investor should buy the government bond.

Adjusting the Valuation Model for Risk

Diminishing marginal utility leads directly to risk aversion, and risk aversion is reflected in the basic valuation model used to determine the worth of a firm. If a managerial decision affects the firm's risk level, the value of the firm is impacted. Two primary methods are used to adjust the basic valuation model to account for decision making under conditions of uncertainty.

THE BASIC VALUATION MODEL

The basic valuation model developed in Chapter 1 is

$$V = \sum_{t=1}^{N} \frac{\pi_t}{(1 + i)^t} \qquad (14.7)$$

This model states that the value of the firm is equal to the discounted present worth of future profits. Under conditions of certainty, the numerator is profit, and the denominator is a time-value adjustment using the risk-free rate of return i. After time-value adjustment, the profits to be earned from various projects are strictly and completely comparable.

Under conditions of uncertainty, the profits shown in the numerator of the valuation model as π equal the expected value of profits during each future period. This expected value is the best available estimate of the amount to be earned during any given period. However, since profits cannot be predicted with absolute precision, some variability is to be anticipated. If the firm must choose between two alternative methods of operation, one with high expected profits and high risk and another with smaller expected profits and lower risks, some technique must be available for making the alternative investments comparable. An appropriate ranking and selection of projects is possible only if each respective investment project can be adjusted for considerations of both time value of money and risk. At least two popular methods are employed to make such adjustments. In the first, expected profits are adjusted to account for risk. In the second, the interest rate used in the denominator of the valuation model is increased to reflect risk considerations. Either method can be used to ensure that value-maximizing decisions are made.

CERTAINTY EQUIVALENT ADJUSTMENTS

Certainty Equivalent
The assured sum that equals an expected risky amount in utility terms.

The **certainty equivalent** method is an adjustment to the numerator of the basic valuation model to account for risk. Under the certainty equivalent approach, decision makers specify the certain sum that they regard comparable to the expected value of a risky investment alternative. The certainty equivalent of an expected risk amount typically differs in dollar terms but not in terms of the amount of utility provided. To illustrate, suppose that you face the following choices:

- Invest $100,000. From a successful project, you receive $1,000,000; if it fails, you receive nothing. If the probability of success is 0.5, or 50%, the investment's expected payoff is $500,000 (= 0.5 × $1,000,000 + 0.5 × $0).
- You do not make the investment; you keep the $100,000.

If you find yourself indifferent between the two alternatives, $100,000 is your certainty equivalent for the risky expected return of $500,000. In other words, a certain or riskless amount of $100,000 provides exactly the same utility as the 50/50 chance to earn $1,000,000 or $0. You are indifferent between these two alternatives.

In this example, any certainty equivalent of less than $500,000 indicates risk aversion. If the maximum amount that you are willing to invest in the project is less than $500,000, you are exhibiting very risk-averse behavior. Each certain dollar is "worth" five times as much as each risky dollar of expected return. Alternatively, each risky dollar of expected return is worth only 20¢ in terms of certain dollars. In general, any risky investment with a certainty equivalent less than the expected dollar value indicates risk aversion. A certainty equivalent greater than the expected value of a risky investment indicates risk preference.

Any expected risky amount can be converted to an equivalent certain sum using the **certainty equivalent adjustment factor, α**, calculated as the ratio of a certain sum divided by an expected risky amount, where both dollar values provide the same level of utility:

Certainty Equivalent Adjustment Factor, α
The ratio of a certain sum divided by an expected risky amount, where both dollar values provide the same level of utility.

$$Certainty\ Equivalent\ Adjustment\ Factor = \alpha = \frac{Equivalent\ Certain\ Sum}{Expected\ Risky\ Sum}. \quad \textbf{(14.8)}$$

The certain sum numerator and expected return denominator may vary in dollar terms, but they provide the exact same reward in terms of utility. In the previous investment problem, in which a certain sum of $100,000 provides the same utility as an expected risky return of $500,000, the certainty equivalent adjustment factor $\alpha = 0.2 = $100,000/$500,000. This means that the "price" of one dollar in risky expected return is 20¢ in certain dollar terms.

The following general relations enable managers to use the certainty equivalent adjustment factor to analyze risk attitudes:

IF	THEN	IMPLIES
Equivalent certain sum < Expected risky sum	$\alpha < 1$	Risk aversion
Equivalent certain sum = Expected risky sum	$\alpha = 1$	Risk indifference
Equivalent certain sum > Expected risky sum	$\alpha > 1$	Risk preference

The appropriate α value for a given managerial decision varies according to the level of risk and degree of the decision maker's risk aversion. Figure 14.6 shows a series of risk-return combinations among which the decision maker is indifferent. For example, Point A represents an investment with a perceived degree of risk v_A and expected dollar return of $3,000. The risk-return tradeoff function, or indifference curve, shows a person who is indifferent to a certain $1,000, an expected $2,000 with risk v_B, and an expected $3,000 with risk v_A.

The indifference curve shown in Figure 14.6 can be used to construct a risk-aversion function such as the one illustrated in Figure 14.7. This conversion is obtained

CERTAINTY EQUIVALENT RETURNS

Figure 14.6

An indifference curve shows risk-return trade-offs that provide the same utility to a given individual.

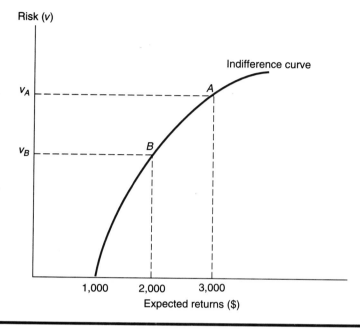

by dividing each risky return into its certainty equivalent amount to obtain a certainty equivalent adjustment factor, α, for each level of risk, v. For example, the certainty equivalent adjustment factor for risk level v_A is

$$\alpha_A = \frac{\$1,000}{\$3,000} = 0.33.$$

For risk level v_B, the relevant calculation is

$$\alpha_B = \frac{\$1,000}{\$2,000} = 0.5.$$

Conceptually, α values could be developed for all possible levels of v (risk). Assuming risk aversion, the range for α is from $\alpha = 1$ for $v = 0$, to $\alpha \approx 0$ for extremely large values of v.

Given complete information from an appropriate risk-aversion function and evidence on the degree of risk inherent in a given risky return, the certainty equivalent of the expected return is calculated as

Certainty Equivalent of $E(\pi_t) = \alpha E(\pi_t)$,

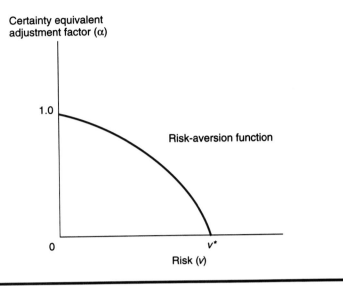

HYPOTHETICAL RISK-AVERSION FUNCTION

For a risk-averse individual, the acceptable certainty equivalent adjustment factor will decline as risk increases.

Risk-Adjusted Valuation Model
A valuation model that reflects time-value and risk considerations.

The basic valuation model (Equation 14.7) can then be converted into a **risk-adjusted valuation model,** one that explicitly accounts for risk:

$$V = \sum_{t=1}^{N} \frac{\alpha E(\pi_t)}{(1 + i)^t}. \tag{14.9}$$

In this risk-adjusted valuation model, expected future profits, $E(\pi_t)$, are converted to their certainty equivalents, $\alpha E(\pi_t)$, and are discounted at a risk-free rate, i, to obtain the risk-adjusted present value of a firm or project. With the valuation model in this form, one can appraise the effects of different courses of action with different risks and expected returns.

To use Equation 14.9 for real-world decision making, managers must estimate appropriate αs for various investment opportunities. Deriving such estimates can prove difficult, since α varies according to the size and riskiness of investment projects as well as according to the risk attitudes of managers and investors. In many instances, however, the record of past investment decisions offers a guide that can be used to determine appropriate certainty equivalent adjustment factors. The following example illustrates how managers use certainty equivalent adjustment factors in practical decision making.

A CERTAINTY EQUIVALENT ADJUSTMENT EXAMPLE

Assume that operations at Burns & Allen Industries have been seriously disrupted by problems with a faulty boiler at its main fabrication facility. In fact, state fire marshals shut the facility down for an extended period recently following repeated overheating and minor explosions. The boiler problem was solved when it was discovered that a design flaw had made the pilot light safety switch inoperable.

Burns & Allen retained the Denver law firm of Dewey, Cheetum & Howe to recover economic damages from the boiler manufacturer. The company has filed suit in state court for $250,000 in damages. Prior to filing suit, the attorney estimated legal, expert witness, and other litigation costs to be $10,000 for a fully litigated case, for which Burns & Allen had a 10% chance of receiving a favorable judgment. For simplicity, assume that a favorable judgment will award Burns & Allen 100% of the damages sought, whereas an unfavorable judgment will result in the firm receiving zero damages. Also assume that $10,000 is the most Burns & Allen would be willing to pay to sue the boiler manufacturer.

In filing suit against the boiler manufacturer, Burns & Allen has made a risky investment decision. By its willingness to bear litigation costs of $10,000, the company has implicitly stated that it regards these out-of-pocket costs to be *at least* equivalent to the value of the risky expectation of receiving a favorable judgment against the boiler manufacturer. In other words, Burns & Allen is willing to exchange $10,000 in certain litigation costs for the possibility of receiving a $250,000 judgment against the boiler manufacturer.

Burns & Allen's investment decision can be characterized using the certainty equivalent adjustment method. To do this, it is important to realize that the $10,000 in litigation costs is incurred irrespective of the outcome of a fully litigated case. This $10,000 represents a certain sum that the company must value as highly as the expected risky outcome to be willing to file suit. The expected risky outcome, or expected return from filing suit, is

$$\text{Expected Return} = \text{Favorable Judgment Payoff} \times \text{Probability}$$
$$+ \text{Unfavorable Judgment Payoff} \times \text{Probability}$$

$$= \$250,000(0.1) + \$0(0.9)$$

$$= \$25,000.$$

To justify filing suit, Burns & Allen's certainty equivalent adjustment factor for investment projects of this risk class must be

$$\alpha = \frac{\text{Certain Sum}}{\text{Expected Risky Sum}}$$

$$= \frac{\text{Litigation Costs}}{\text{Expected Return}}$$

$$= \frac{\$10,000}{\$25,000}$$

$$= 0.4.$$

Therefore, each risky dollar of expected return from the litigation effort is worth, in terms of utility, *at least* 40¢ in certain dollars. Alternatively, $10,000 is the certain sum equivalent of the risky expected return of $25,000.

Now assume that after Burns & Allen goes to court, incurring $5,000 in litigation costs, especially damaging testimony by an expert witness dramatically changes the outlook of the case in Burns & Allen's favor. In response, the boiler manufacturer's attorney offers an out-of-court settlement in the amount of $30,000. However, Burns & Allen's attorney recommends that the company reject this offer, estimating that it now has a 50/50 chance of obtaining a favorable judgment in the case. Should Burns & Allen follow the attorney's advice and reject the settlement offer?

In answering this question, one must keep in mind that having already spent ("sunk") $5,000 in litigation costs, Burns & Allen must consider as relevant litigation costs only the additional $5,000 necessary to complete litigation. These $5,000 litigation costs, plus the $30,000 out-of-court settlement offer, represent the relevant certain sum, since proceeding with the suit will require an "investment" of these additional litigation plus opportunity costs. Given the revised outlook for a favorable judgment, the expected return to full litigation is

$$\text{Expected Return} = (\$250,000)(0.5) + (\$0)(0.5)$$

$$= \$125,000.$$

In light of Burns & Allen's earlier decision to file suit on the basis that each dollar of expected risky return was "worth" 40¢ in certain dollars, this expected return would have a $50,000 certainty equivalent value ($125,000 × 0.4). Since this amount exceeds the settlement offer plus remaining litigation costs, the settlement offer seems deficient and should be rejected. On the basis of Burns & Allen's revealed risk attitude, an out-of-court settlement offer has to be at least $45,000 to receive favorable consideration. At that point the settlement plus saved litigation costs of $5,000 would equal the certainty equivalent value of the expected return from continuing litigation.

This simple example illustrates that historical investment decisions offer a useful guide to current risky investment decisions. If a potential project's required investment and risk levels are known, the α implied by a decision to accept the investment project can be calculated. This project-specific α can then be compared with αs for prior projects with similar risks. Risk-averse individuals should invest in projects if calculated αs are *less* than or equal to those for accepted historical projects in the same risk class. Furthermore, given an estimate of expected return and risk, the maximum amount that the firm should be willing to invest in a given project can also be determined from the certainty equivalent adjustment factor. Risk-averse management will accept new projects if the level of required investment per dollar of expected return is less than or equal to that for historical projects of similar risk.

RISK-ADJUSTED DISCOUNT RATES

Another way to incorporate risk in managerial decision making is to adjust the discount rate or denominator of the basic valuation model (Equation 14.7). Like certainty

Risk-Adjusted Discount Rate

The risk-free rate of return plus the required risk premium.

equivalent factors, **risk-adjusted discount rates** are based on the trade-off between risk and return for individual investors. Suppose risk-averse investors are willing to trade between risk and return, as shown in Figure 14.8. This curve is called a market indifference curve or a risk-return tradeoff function. The average investor is indifferent to a riskless asset with a sure 5% rate of return, a moderately risky asset with a 10% expected return, and a very risky asset with a 15% expected return. As risk increases, higher expected returns on investment are required to compensate investors for the additional risk.

Risk Premium

The added expected return for a risky asset over that of a riskless asset.

The difference between the expected rate of return on a risky asset and the rate of return on a riskless asset is the **risk premium** on the risky asset. In the example shown in Figure 14.8, the riskless rate is assumed to be 5%. A 2% risk premium is required to compensate for the level of risk indicated by $\sigma = 0.5$; a 10% risk premium is required for an investment with a risk of $\sigma = 1.5$. Observe that the required risk premium is directly related to the level of risk associated with a particular investment.

The basic valuation model shown in Equation 14.7 can be adapted to account for risk through adjustment of the discount rate, i, where

$$V = \sum_{t=1}^{N} \frac{E(\pi_t)}{(1 + k)^{t}}.$$

(**14.10**)

Figure 14.8

RELATION BETWEEN RISK AND RATE OF RETURN

As risk rises, investors typically demand higher expected returns to compensate for the increased risk.

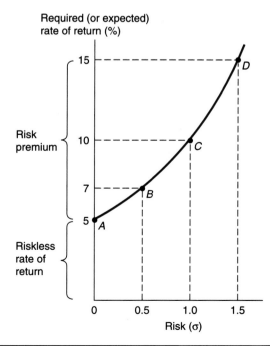

The risk-adjusted discount rate k is the sum of the risk-free rate of return, R_F, plus the required risk premium, R_p:

$$k = R_F + R_p.$$

In Equation 14.10, value is measured by the present worth of expected future income or profits, $E(\pi_t)$, discounted at a risk-adjusted rate. If the risk-return trade-off illustrated in Figure 14.8 is appropriate, returns for a project with risk level $\sigma = 0.5$ should be adjusted using a 7% discount rate, comprised of the 5% risk-free rate plus a 2% risk premium. A riskier project with $\sigma = 1.5$ requires a risk premium of 10% and should be evaluated using a 15% discount rate or the 5% risk-free rate plus a 10% risk premium.

A RISK-ADJUSTED DISCOUNT RATE EXAMPLE

The following example further illustrates the use of risk-adjusted discount rates in managerial decision making. Suppose the Property & Casualty Insurance Company is contemplating purchase of one of the two data base and file management computer software programs offered by Rockford Files, Inc. System A is specifically designed for P&C's current computer software system and cannot be used with those of other providers; System B is compatible with a broad variety of computer software systems, including P&C's and those of other software providers. The expected investment outlay is $600,000 for each alternative. Expected annual cost savings (cash inflows) over five years are $220,000 per year for System A and $260,000 per year for System B. The standard deviation of expected annual returns from System A is $10,000, whereas that of System B is $15,000. In view of this risk differential, P&C management has decided to evaluate System A with a *before-tax* 20% cost of capital and System B with a 30% cost of capital.

The risk-adjusted value for each system is as follows:[2]

$$Value_A = \sum_{t=1}^{5} \frac{\$220,000}{(1.20)^t} - \$600,000$$

$$= \$220,000 \times \left(\sum_{t=1}^{5} \frac{1}{(1.20)^t} \right) - \$600,000$$

---

[2] The terms

$$\sum_{t=1}^{5} \frac{1}{(1.20)^t} = 2.991$$

and

$$\sum_{t=1}^{5} \frac{1}{(1.30)^t} = 2.436$$

are present-value-of-an-annuity interest factors. Tables of interest factors for various interest rates and years (t values) appear in Appendix A. And finally, if state-plus-federal corporate income tax rates average roughly 40%, a *before-tax* cost of capital in the 20% to 30% range implies an *after-tax* required rate of return of 12% to 18%.

$$= \$220,000 \times 2.991 - \$600,000$$

$$= \$58,020.$$

$$Value\ _B = \sum_{t=1}^{5} \frac{\$260,000}{(1.30)^t} - \$600,000$$

$$= \$260,000 \times \left(\sum_{t=1}^{5} \frac{1}{(1.30)^t} \right) - \$600,000$$

$$= \$260,000 \times 2.436 - \$600,000$$

$$= \$33,360.$$

Because the risk-adjusted value of System A is larger than that for System B, P&C should choose System A. This choice maximizes the value of the firm.

Decision Trees and Computer Simulation

A variety of additional techniques for decision making under uncertainty supplement the use of probability concepts, certainty equivalents, and risk-adjusted discount rate methods. Decision trees that follow the sequential nature of the decision-making process provide a logical framework for decision analysis under conditions of uncertainty. When a high degree of uncertainty exists and data are not readily available, computer simulation often provides the basis for reasonable conjecture. Application of these methods was once arduous and time-consuming. Today, new computer software fully automates the process of decision tree analysis and computer simulation. More than ever before, these techniques constitute useful and practical means for risk assessment and effective managerial decision making.

DECISION TREES

Decision Tree
A map of a sequential decision-making process.

A **decision tree** is a sequential decision-making process. Decision trees are designed for analyzing decision problems that involve a series of choice alternatives that are constrained by previous decisions. They illustrate the complete range of future possibilities and their associated probabilities in terms of a logical progression from an initial decision point, through each subsequent constrained decision alternative, to an ultimate outcome.

Decision trees are widely employed because many important decisions are made in stages. For example, a pharmaceutical company considering expansion into the generic prescription drug market might take the following steps:

- Spend $100,000 to survey supply and demand conditions in the generic drug industry.
- If survey results are favorable, spend $2 million on a pilot plant to investigate production methods.
- Depending on cost estimates and potential demand, either abandon the project, build a large plant, or build a small one.

Fast Company

Forbes's annual list of 200 hot growth stocks, dubbed "The Best Small Companies in America," is compiled from a universe of roughly 3,000 publicly traded U.S. corporations with sales of at least $5 million but no more than $350 million per year. Companies in all industries are considered, except for banks and savings and loans where high leverage makes predictions of future earnings growth tenuous, at best. *Forbes* ranks its top 200 small companies based on their five-year average rate of return on stockholders' equity. A minimum of 15% per year ROE is typically required to make the *Forbes* list, in addition to five-year average growth in sales and earnings per share of 10% to 15% per year. During a typical year, the median *Forbes* 200 company boasts five-year annualized earnings growth of 40%, and a five-year average ROE of more than 20%. In short, these rapid growers earn sky-high profit rates by outperforming rivals by a significant margin.

To appreciate the significance of such torrid rates of growth one need only recall what financial analysts refer to as the "Rule of 72." Just take any growth rate and divide that amount into 72 to determine the number of years required to double in size. For example, a firm that grows by 7.2% per year will double in roughly 10 years; a firm that grows by 14.4% per year will double in roughly 5 years, and so on. This means that any firm growing at say 35% to 40% per year will double in size in roughly two years. Stated differently, approximately one-half of the people that will be working for such a firm in just two years have not been hired yet! Any company that is able to maintain such scorching rates of growth is running an educational institution as much as it is a typical business. The rookie sales trainee hired today will be a member of the company's veteran sales staff within a year, and a marketing director before too long after that. The potential for employee growth and development is enormous in rapidly growing companies; so too is the potential for hiring mistakes and minor snafus that snowball into major disasters. The corporate landscape is littered with examples of once rapid growers that were highly profitable un-

til they seemingly spun out of control, crashed, and burned.

Forbes annual survey reflects a number of hot companies that are prone to suffer flameouts. Rapid high-margin growth attracts competitors that can make life difficult for smaller companies with limited financial resources. Medical software company Cerner Corp., for example, was a regular fixture on the *Forbes* list during the mid-1990s. Cerner stumbled in 1997, however, as its sophisticated software system used to link hospitals, doctor's offices, and clinics attracted competition from well-financed larger rivals like HBO & Co. Declining market share led to dwindling stock prices for cosmetics and fragrance maker Jean Philippe Fragrances, Norstan telecommunications systems, and computer hardware and software maker Digi International. Others, like First Team Sports, a major producer of in-line roller skates, ride a fad until it crashes. By their nature, *Forbes* hot growth companies can be an ephemeral lot. Of the 200 small companies that appear on *Forbes* list in any given year, only about one-third to one-half return for an encore the following year. A few companies, usually 5 or 10, outgrow the list as company sales rise to exceed the $350 million threshold. A handful of others, sometimes as many as a dozen, are gobbled up by large companies. The rest just don't make the grade. When a company is growing at a rate that will double its size in less than 3 years, as is common among the *Forbes* 200, it's easy to stumble.

Before investors put any hard-earned money in a rapidly growing small company, it's prudent to ask a simple question: Does the company enjoy a significant advantage over actual and potential rivals that is prone to be sustainable? If not, it's probably riding a wave of popularity that is apt to be temporary. Even among highly successful risk takers, only the strongest survive.

See: Steve Kitchen and Michelle Conlin, "Fast Company," *Forbes*, November 4, 1996, 222-223.

These decisions are made in stages; subsequent determinations depend on prior judgments. The sequence of events can be mapped out to visually resemble the branches of a tree—hence the term *decision tree.*

Figure 14.9 illustrates the decision-tree method for the pharmaceutical company decision problem. Assume that the company has completed its industry supply and demand analysis and determined that it should develop a full-scale production facility. Either a large plant or a small plant can be built. The probability is 50% for high demand, 30% for medium demand, and 20% for low demand. Depending on actual demand, the present value of net cash flows, defined as sales revenue minus operating costs, ranges from $8.8 million to $1.4 million for a large plant and from $2.6 million to $1.4 million for a small plant.

Because demand probabilities are known, the expected value of cash flow can be determined, as in Column 5 of Figure 14.9. Investment outlays are deducted from expected net cash flow to obtain the expected net present value for each decision. The expected net present value is $730,000 for the large plant and $300,000 for the small one. Notice the wide range of possible outcomes for the large plant. Actual net present values for the large plant investment equal the present value of cash flows (Column 4) minus the large plant investment cost of $5 million. These values vary from $3.8 million to −$3.6 million. Actual net present values for the small plant investment range only

ILLUSTRATIVE DECISION TREE

Figure 14.9

The expected net present value of each investment alternative (Column 5) is determined by linking possible outcomes (Column 2), probabilities (Column 3), and monetary values (Column 4).

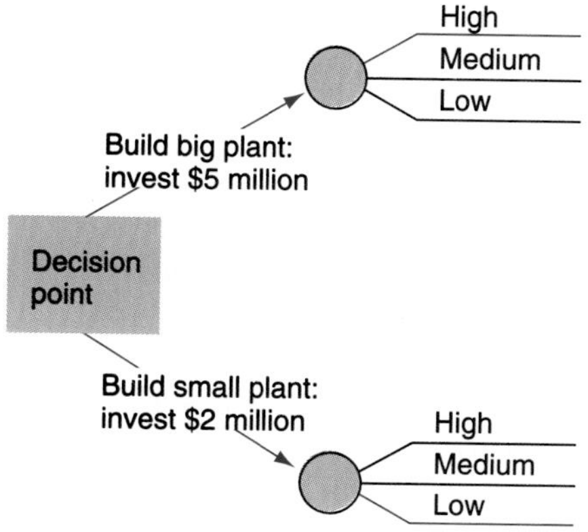

Action (1)	Demand conditions (2)	Probability (3)	Present value of cash flows[a] (4)	(5) = (3) × (4)
	High	0.5	$8,800,000	$4,400,000
	Medium	0.3	$3,500,000	1,050,000
	Low	0.2	$1,400,000	280,000
Build big plant: invest $5 million			Expected value of cash flows	$5,730,000
			Cost	5,000,000
Decision point			Expected net present value	$ 730,000
Build small plant: invest $2 million	High	0.5	$2,600,000	$1,300,000
	Medium	0.3	$2,400,000	720,000
	Low	0.2	$1,400,000	280,000
			Expected value of cash flows	$2,300,000
			Cost	2,000,000
			Expected net present value	$ 300,000

from $600,000 to −$600,000. Clearly, the smaller plant appears less risky based on the width of the range of possible net present value outcomes. Because the investment requirement differs for each plant, the coefficient of variation for each plant's net present value can be examined to provide an alternate measure of relative risk. The coefficient of variation for the large plant's present value is 4.3, whereas that for the small plant is only 1.5.[3] Again, risk appears greater for the large plant alternative.

These risk and expected return differentials can be incorporated into the decision-making process in a variety of ways. Assigning utility values to the cash flows given in Column 4 of Figure 14.9 would state Column 5 in terms of expected utility. The company could then choose the plant size that provided the greatest expected utility. Alternatively, present values given in Column 4 could be adjusted using the certainty equivalent or risk-adjusted discount rate method. The plant that offers the largest risk-adjusted net present value is the optimal choice.

A MORE COMPLEX DECISION TREE EXAMPLE

The decision tree illustrated in Figure 14.9 is quite simple; actual decision trees are frequently complex and involve several sequential decision points. An example of a more complex tree is illustrated in Figure 14.10. Numbered boxes represent **decision points,** or instances where management must select among several choice alternatives. The circles represent **chance events,** or possible outcomes following each decision point. At Decision Point 1, the firm has three choices: invest $3 million in a large plant, invest $1.3 million in a small plant, or spend $100,000 on market research. If the large plant is built, the firm follows the upper branch, and its position is fixed; it can only hope that demand will be high. If it builds the small plant, it follows the lower branch. If demand is low, no further action is required. If demand is high, Decision Point 2 is reached, and the firm can either do nothing or expand the plant at a cost of an additional $2.2 million. Notice that if the company obtains a large plant through expansion, the cost is $500,000 greater than if it had built a large plant in the first place.

If the decision at Point 1 is to pay $100,000 for more information, the firm moves to the center branch. This research modifies the firm's information about potential demand. Initially, the probabilities were 70% for high demand and 30% for low demand. The research survey will show either favorable or unfavorable demand prospects. If they are favorable, the probability for high final demand is 87% and for low demand is 13%. If demand prospects are unfavorable, the odds on high final demand are only 35% and on low demand are 65%.

If the firm builds a large plant and demand is high, sales and profits will be substantial. If it builds a large plant and demand is low, sales will be depressed and it will incur losses. If the company builds a small plant and demand is high, sales and profits will be lower than they could have been had a large plant been built, yet the chance of

Decision Points
Instances when management must select among choice alternatives.

Chance Events
Possible outcomes following each decision point.

---

[3]Using Equation 14.4 and data on possible returns in Figure 14.9, the standard deviation for the big plant is $3.155 million and for the small plant it is $458,260. Dividing these standard deviations by the appropriate expected return for each respective plant size, as in Equation 14.5, gives the coefficient of variation.

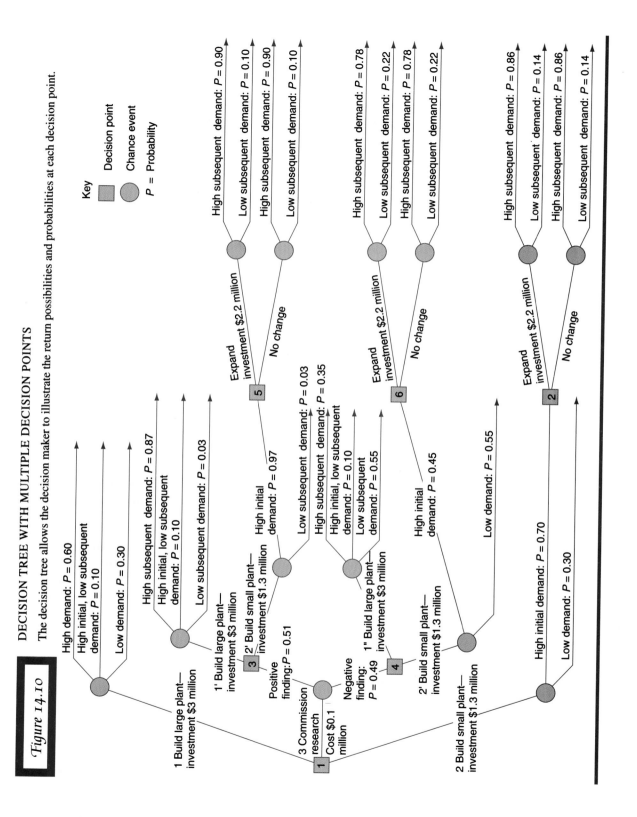

Figure 14.10

DECISION TREE WITH MULTIPLE DECISION POINTS

The decision tree allows the decision maker to illustrate the return possibilities and probabilities at each decision point.

Key

■ Decision point

● Chance event

P = Probability

High demand: P = 0.60
High initial, low subsequent demand: P = 0.10
Low demand: P = 0.30

High subsequent demand: P = 0.87
High initial, low subsequent demand: P = 0.10
Low subsequent demand: P = 0.03

1' Build large plant—investment $3 million

3 2' Build small plant—investment $1.3 million

High initial demand: P = 0.97

Low subsequent demand: P = 0.03
High subsequent demand: P = 0.35
High initial, low subsequent demand: P = 0.10
Low subsequent demand: P = 0.55

Positive finding: P = 0.51

3 Commission research Cost $0.1 million

Negative finding: P = 0.49

1" Build large plant—investment $3 million

4 2' Build small plant—investment $1.3 million

High initial demand: P = 0.45

High initial demand: P = 0.55
Low demand: P = 0.55

1 Build large plant—investment $3 million

2 Build small plant—investment $1.3 million

High initial demand: P = 0.70
Low demand: P = 0.30

5 Expand investment $2.2 million
No change

High subsequent demand: P = 0.90
Low subsequent demand: P = 0.10
High subsequent demand: P = 0.90
Low subsequent demand: P = 0.10

6 Expand investment $2.2 million
No change

High subsequent demand: P = 0.78
Low subsequent demand: P = 0.22
High subsequent demand: P = 0.78
Low subsequent demand: P = 0.22

2 Expand investment $2.2 million
No change

High subsequent demand: P = 0.86
Low subsequent demand: P = 0.14
High subsequent demand: P = 0.86
Low subsequent demand: P = 0.14

loss in the event of low demand can be eliminated. Building the large plant is obviously riskier than building the small plant. The cost of market research is, in effect, an expenditure serving to reduce the degree of uncertainty.

The decision tree in Figure 14.10 is incomplete because no dollar outcomes (or utility values) are assigned to each point on the decision tree. If dollars are assigned, similar to the way values are shown in the last two columns of Figure 14.9, the expected value and risk of each decision alternative could be calculated to help arrive at an appropriate managerial decision.

COMPUTER SIMULATION

Computer Simulation
The use of computer software and workstations or sophisticated desktop computers to create outcome scenarios.

Another technique designed to assist managers in making decisions under uncertainty is **computer simulation.** Computer simulation involves the use of computer software and sophisticated desktop computers to create a wide variety of decision outcome scenarios. These simulations illustrate a broad range of possible outcomes to help managers assess the possible and probable consequences of decision alternatives. Using the computer simulation technique, a variety of hypothetical "What if?" questions can be asked and answered on the basis of measurable differences in underlying assumptions. More than just informed conjecture, computer simulation allows managers to make precise judgments concerning the desirability of various choices on the basis of highly detailed probability information.

Computer simulations require probability distribution estimates for a number of variables, such as investment outlays, unit sales, product prices, input prices, and asset lives. In some instances, full-scale simulations are expensive and time consuming and therefore restricted to projects such as major plant expansions or new-product decisions. When a firm is deciding whether to accept a major undertaking involving an outlay of millions of dollars, full-scale computer simulations provide valuable insights that are well worth their cost. Somewhat less expensive, limited-scale simulations are used to project outcomes for projects or strategies. Instead of using complete probability distributions for each variable included in the problem, results are simulated based on best-guess estimates for each variable. Changes in the values of each variable are then considered to see the effects of such changes on project returns. Typically, returns are highly sensitive to some variables, less so to others. Attention is then focused on the variables to which profitability is most sensitive. This technique, known as **sensitivity analysis,** is less expensive and less time consuming than full-scale computer simulation, but it still provides valuable insight for decision-making purposes.

Sensitivity Analysis
A limited form of computer simulation that focuses on important decision variables.

A COMPUTER SIMULATION EXAMPLE

To illustrate the computer simulation technique, consider the evaluation of a new mini-mill investment project by Remington Steel, Inc. The exact cost of the plant is not known, but it is expected to be about $150 million. If no difficulties arise in construction, this cost can be as low as $125 million. An unfortunate series of events such as strikes, greater than projected increases in material costs, and/or technical problems could drive the required investment outlay as high as $225 million. Revenues from the new facility depend on the growth of regional income and construction, competition, developments in the field of metallurgy, steel import quotas and tariffs, and so on. Operating costs depend on production efficiency, the cost of raw materials, and the trend in wage rates. Because sales revenues and operating costs are uncertain, annual profits are unpredictable.

Assuming that probability distributions can be developed for each major cost and revenue category, a computer program can be constructed to simulate the pattern of future events. Computer simulation randomly selects revenue and cost levels from each relevant distribution and uses this information to estimate future profits, net present values, or the rate of return on investment. This process is repeated a large number of times to identify the central tendency of projected returns and their expected values. When the computer simulation is completed, the frequency pattern and range of future returns can be plotted and analyzed. While the expected value of future profits is of obvious interest, the range of possible outcomes is similarly important as a useful indicator of risk.

The computer simulation technique is illustrated in Figures 14.11 and 14.12. Figure 14.11 is a flow chart that shows the information flow pattern for the simulation procedure just described. Figure 14.12 illustrates the frequency distribution of rates of return generated by such a simulation for two alternative projects, X and Y, each with an expected cost of \$20 million. The expected rate of return on Investment X is 15%, and 20% on Investment Y. However, these are only average rates of return derived by the computer simulation. The range of simulated returns is from -10% to 45% for Investment Y, and from 5% to 25% for Investment X. The standard deviation for X is only 4%; that for Y is 12%. Based on this information, the coefficient of variation is 0.267 for Project X and 0.60 for Project Y. Investment Y is clearly riskier than Investment X. A decision about which alternative to choose can be made on the basis of expected utility, or on the basis of a present value determination that incorporates either certainty equivalents or risk-adjusted discount rates.

Game Theory

Game Theory
A decision framework for making choices in hostile environments and under extreme uncertainty.

In an uncertain economic environment, value maximization is achieved using the risk-adjusted valuation models described in this chapter. Under certain circumstances, especially when the decision environment is hostile rather than neutral and when extreme uncertainty exists, other **game theory** decision criteria may be appropriate.

GAME THEORY AND AUCTION STRATEGY

Game theory dates from the 1940s, when mathematician John von Neuman and economist Oskar Morgenstern decided to turn their card playing ability into a more general theory of decision making under uncertainty. They discovered that deciding when to bluff, fold, stand pat, or raise is not only relevant when playing cards, but also when opposed by aggressive competitors in the market place. Rules they developed are increasingly regarded as relevant for analyzing competitive behavior in a wide variety of settings. One of the most interesting uses of game theory in the 1990s is to analyze bidder strategy in auctions.

Figure 14.11

SIMULATION FOR INVESTMENT PLANNING

Computer simulation allows detailed analysis of managerial problems involving complex cost and revenue relations.

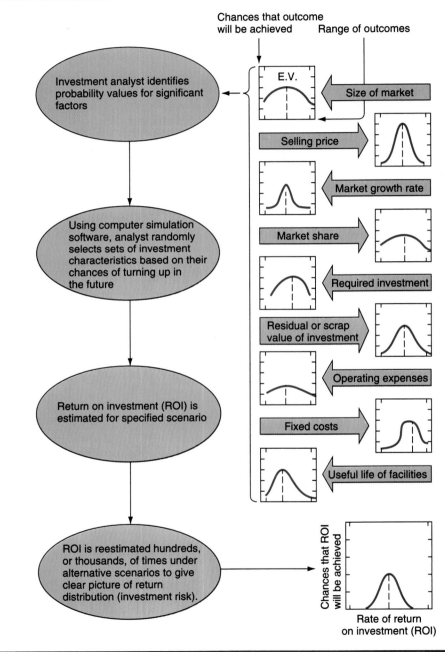

EXPECTED RATES OF RETURN ON INVESTMENTS X AND Y

Figure 14.12

Investments X and Y both have continuous distributions of returns around their expected values.

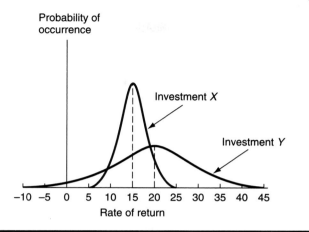

The most familiar type of auction is an **English auction,** where an auctioneer keeps raising the price until a single highest bidder remains. The advantage of an English auction is that it is widely regarded as a fair and open process. It is an effective approach for obtaining high winning bid prices. Because participants can see and hear what rivals are doing, bidders often act aggressively. In fact, winners sometimes overpay for their winning bids. The so-called **winner's curse** results when overly aggressive bidders pay more than the economic value of auctioned off items. During the 1970s and 1980s, for example, participants in the bidding process for off-shore oil properties in the Gulf of Mexico routinely seemed to overestimate the amount of oil to be found.

English Auction
The most familiar type of auction where an auctioneer keeps raising the price until a single highest bidder remains.

Winner's Curse
Where overly aggressive bidders pay more than the economic value of auctioned off items.

Another commonly employed auction method is a **sealed-bid auction,** where all bids are secret, and the highest bid wins. Local and state governments, for example, employ the sealed-bid approach to build roads, buy fuel for schools and government offices, and to procure equipment and general supplies. A compelling advantage of the sealed-bid approach is that it is relatively free from the threat of collusion since, at least ostensibly, no one knows what anyone else is doing. The downside to the approach is that it could yield less to the government when airwave space is auctioned off since the approach often encourages bidders to act cautiously.

Sealed-Bid Auction
An auction where all bids are secret, and the highest bid wins.

A relatively rare sealed-bid auction method is a **Vickrey auction,** where the highest sealed bid wins, but the winner pays the price of the second-highest bid. The reason for this design is that the technique tends to produce high bids since participants know beforehand that they will not be forced to pay the full amount of their winning bid. A disadvantage of the technique is that it creates the perception that the buyer is taking advantage of the seller by paying only the second highest price.

Vickrey Auction
Where the highest sealed bid wins, but the winner pays the price of the second-highest bid.

Another uncommon auctioning method is the so-called reverse or **Dutch auction.** In a Dutch auction, the auctioneer keeps lowering a very high price until a winning bidder emerges. The winning bidder is the first participant willing to pay the auctioneer's

Dutch Auction
In a Dutch auction, the winning bidder is the first participant willing to pay the auctioneer's price.

Game Theory Helps Public Policy

Australian bureaucrats thought they had struck it rich when Ucom Proprietary Ltd. submitted a blockbuster sealed bid of $152 million for the right to use the airwaves for a satellite-TV service. Trouble is, Ucom had no intention of paying that much, defaulted on its bid, and forced the government to proceed to the next lower amount. The company proceeded to default on one bid after another before settling on $84 million, a number just higher than its closest rival. The resulting uproar almost cost Australia's communications minister his job.

The U.S. Federal Communications Commission was determined to avoid such mistakes when it began to auction off licenses for new wireless phone systems known as Personal Communications Services (PCS). To encourage PCS competition, the FCC decided to auction PCS spectrum to three "A-block," "B-block," and "C-block" competitors in each market, all of which would provide competition for cellular telephone service providers. FCC Chairman Reed Hundt was behind the decision to restrict the C-block auction process to smaller companies in the interest of promoting diversity. To help with financing costs, C-block bidders were given exceedingly generous financing terms: only 5% of the bid was due at the close of the auction, 5% was due at the time the PCS license was granted, and the remainder was financed at low interest rates tied to the federal government's 30-year bond rate.

In designing the auction process, the FCC relied heavily on advice from top game theorists at Stanford, Yale, and other leading universities. The agency adopted a standard English auction in which the winner pays what it bids, and everyone can see all bids as they are made. Game theory research shows that such open auctions tend to stimulate bidding, whereas sealed auctions foster restraint for fear of needlessly paying too much. While the FCC initially favored auctioning off all airwave licenses at once to make it easier for bidders to assemble efficient blocs of adjoining areas, this approach entails a nightmare of complexity. Complicating the problem is the fact that bidders must be allowed some flexibility to withdraw bids when adjoining areas are sold to others. If all offers could

be withdrawn easily, however, the integrity of the process suffers, as illustrated in the Australian case. A sequential auction, where areas are put up for bid one at a time, also involves problems because it denies participants the opportunity to bid more for economically efficient blocks of service areas. Once the New York City service area franchise has been sold, the value of the adjoining New Jersey market will fall for everyone except the winning bidder for the New York City service area. For the winner of the New York City franchise, the value of the New Jersey market grows, and so on. Thus, winning bidders in a sequential auction have the potential for a snowballing effect where one success leads to another, and another, and another.

After considering a wide variety of options, the FCC adopted a modified sequential bidding approach. The 1995 auction of A-block and B-block PCS spectrum was a smash hit, bringing taxpayers a windfall of $7 billion. The C-block spectrum auction in 1996 brought even more. A stunning $10.2 billion was bid for C-block spectrum, despite the fact that each C-block PCS provider must compete against two well-capitalized and already entrenched PCS companies plus two cellular phone service providers. Apparently, exceedingly generous financing terms led many bidders to overpay for C-block spectrum. By early 1997, the FCC began to face the knotty problem of having to renegotiate C-block spectrum prices to help over enthusiastic buyers from defaulting on their bids.

The PCS auction process taught the FCC two important lessons. First, game theory has clearly arrived as a practical tool for analysis of decisions involving risk and uncertainty. And second, funds for winning bids must come from bidders, not the government. When it comes to risk and uncertainty, the "other people's money" problem still exists.

See: Mark Lewyn, "What Price Air?," *Business Week*, March 14, 1994, 48-50; and Peter Spiegel, "Hollow Victory," *Forbes*, January 27, 1997, 50-52.

price. A disadvantage of this approach is that bidders tend to act cautiously out of fear of overpaying for auctioned items. In terms of the FCC's sale of airwave space, a Dutch auction might yield less to the government than an English auction. Offsetting this disadvantage is the fact that winning bidders would then be left with greater resources to quickly build a viable service network.

In planning auctions of airwave space for new communications services, the FCC uses a number of auction strategies to achieve a variety of sometimes conflicting goals. To raise the most money while creating efficient service areas and encouraging competitive bidding, the FCC uses all four basic auction strategies. To better understand the motives behind these auction strategies, it is necessary to examine game theory rules for decision making under uncertainty.

MAXIMUM DECISION RULE

Maximin Criterion
Decision choice method that provides the best of the worst possible outcomes.

One decision standard that is sometimes applicable for decision making under uncertainty is the **maximin criterion.** This criterion states that the decision maker should select the alternative that provides the best of the worst possible outcomes. This is done by finding the worst possible (minimum) outcome for each decision alternative and then choosing the option whose worst outcome provides the highest (maximum) payoff. This criterion instructs one to maximize the minimum possible outcome.

To illustrate, consider Table 14.8, which shows the weekly profit contribution payoffs from alternative gasoline pricing strategies by the self-service U-Pump gas station in Jackson, Wyoming. Assume that U-Pump has just been notified of a 3¢ reduction in the wholesale price of gas. If U-Pump reduces its current self-service price by 3¢ per gallon, its weekly profit contribution will depend on the reaction, if any, of its nearest competitor. If U-Pump's competitor matches the price reduction, a $2,500 profit contribution will result. Without any competitor reaction, U-Pump would earn $3,000. If U-Pump and its competitor both maintain current prices, U-Pump will earn $5,000, whereas if U-Pump did not match the competitor's price cut, U-Pump would earn only $1,000. The worst possible outcome following a price reduction by U-Pump is $2,500, but a $1,000 outcome is possible if U-Pump maintains its current price. The maximin criterion requires U-Pump to reduce its price, since the minimum possible outcome from this decision is greater than the minimum $1,000 payoff possible by maintaining the current price.

Although the maximin criterion suffers from the obvious shortcoming of focusing on the most pessimistic outcome for each decision alternative, it should not be dismissed as naive and unsophisticated. The maximin criterion implicitly assumes a very strong aversion to risk and is appropriate for decisions involving the possibility of catastrophic outcomes. When decision alternatives involve outcomes that endanger worker lives or the survival of the organization, for example, the maximin criterion can be an appropriate technique. Similarly, if the state of nature that prevails depends on the course of action taken by the decision maker, the maximin criterion might be appropriate. In the preceding example, one might expect that a decision by U-Pump to reduce prices would cause the competitor to follow suit, resulting in the worst possible outcome for that decision alternative.

Table 14.8

U-PUMP'S WEEKLY PROFIT CONTRIBUTION PAYOFF MATRIX

	STATES OF NATURE	
DECISION ALTERNATIVES	COMPETITOR REDUCES PRICES	COMPETITOR MAINTAINS CURRENT PRICE
Reduce price	$2,500	$3,000
Maintain current price	$1,000	$5,000

U-PUMP'S WEEKLY PROFIT CONTRIBUTION OPPORTUNITY LOSS OR REGRET MATRIX

	STATES OF NATURE	
DECISION ALTERNATIVES	COMPETITOR REDUCES PRICES	COMPETITOR MAINTAINS CURRENT PRICE
Reduce price	$0 (= $2,500 − $2,500)	$2,000 (= $5,000 − $3,000)
Maintain current price	$1,500 (= $2,500 − $1,000)	$0 (= $5,000 − $5,000)

MINIMAX REGRET DECISION RULE

Minimax Regret Criterion
Decision choice method that minimizes the maximum possible regret (opportunity loss) associated with a wrong decision *after the fact.*

Opportunity Loss
The difference between a given payoff and the highest possible payoff for the resulting state of nature.

A second useful decision criterion focuses on the opportunity loss associated with a decision rather than on its worst possible outcome. This decision rule, known as the **minimax regret criterion,** states that the decision maker should minimize the maximum possible regret (opportunity loss) associated with a wrong decision *after the fact.* This criterion instructs one to minimize the difference between possible outcomes and the best outcome for each state of nature.

To illustrate this decision technique, the concept of opportunity loss, or regret, must be examined in greater detail. In game theory, **opportunity loss** is defined as the difference between a given payoff and the highest possible payoff for the resulting state of nature. Opportunity losses result because returns actually received under conditions of uncertainty are frequently lower than the maximum return that would have been possible had perfect knowledge been available beforehand.

Table 14.8 shows the opportunity loss or regret matrix associated with U-Pump's gasoline pricing problem. It was constructed by finding the maximum payoff for a given state of nature and then subtracting from this amount the payoffs that would result from various decision alternatives. Opportunity loss is always a positive figure or zero, since each alternative payoff is subtracted from the largest payoff possible in a given state of nature. For example, if U-Pump's competitor reduced its price, the best possible decision for that state of nature would be for U-Pump to have also reduced prices. After the fact, U-Pump would have no regrets had it done so. Should

U-Pump maintain its current price, the firm would experience a $1,500 opportunity loss, or regret. To calculate this amount, subtract the $1,000 payoff associated with U-Pump's maintaining its current price despite a competitor price reduction from the $2,500 payoff that it would have received from matching the competitor's price reduction. Similarly, if U-Pump would reduce its price while its competitor maintains the current price, U-Pump would experience a $2,000 opportunity loss or regret after the fact.

The minimax regret criterion would cause U-Pump to maintain the current retail price of gasoline because this decision alternative minimizes the maximum regret, or opportunity loss. The maximum regret in this case is limited to the $1,500 loss that would result if the competitor reduced its current price. If U-Pump were to reduce its price while the competitor maintained its current price, U-Pump's opportunity loss would be $2,000 per week, $500 more than the maximum regret from U-Pump maintaining its current price.

THE COST OF UNCERTAINTY

An unavoidable opportunity loss is the cost associated with uncertainty. Therefore, the expected opportunity loss associated with a decision provides a measure of the expected monetary gain from the removal of all uncertainty about future events. From the opportunity loss or regret matrix, the **cost of uncertainty** is measured by the minimum expected opportunity loss. From the payoff matrix, the cost of uncertainty is measured by the difference between the expected payoff associated with choosing the correct alternative under each state of nature (which will be known only after the fact) and the highest expected payoff available from among the decision alternatives. The cost of uncertainty is the unavoidable economic loss that is due to chance. Using this concept, it becomes possible to judge the value of gaining additional information before choosing among decision alternatives.

Cost of Uncertainty
The minimum expected opportunity loss.

The previous gasoline pricing problem can illustrate this use of opportunity loss. On the basis of the data in Table 14.8, the expected opportunity loss of each decision alternative can be calculated as shown in Table 14.9. Here it is assumed that U-Pump projects a 50/50, or 50%, chance of a competitor price reduction. The minimum expected opportunity cost in this case is $750 and represents U-Pump's loss from not knowing its competitor's pricing reaction with certainty. This cost of uncertainty represents the $750 value to U-Pump of resolving doubt about its competitor's pricing policy. U-Pump would be better off if it could eliminate this uncertainty by making an expenditure of less than $750 on information gathering.

Firms often engage in activities aimed at reducing the uncertainty of various alternatives before making an irrevocable decision. For example, a food-manufacturing company will employ extensive marketing tests in selected areas to gain better estimates of sales potential before going ahead with large-scale introduction of a new product. Manufacturers of consumer goods frequently install new equipment in a limited number of models to judge reliability and customer reaction before including the equipment in all models. Similarly, competitors often announce price changes well in advance of their effective date to elicit the reaction of rivals.

Table 14.9

U-PUMP'S CALCULATION OF EXPECTED OPPORTUNITY LOSS
FROM THE LOSS MATRIX

	REDUCE PRICE			MAINTAIN CURRENT PRICE		
STATE OF NATURE	PROBABILITY OF THIS STATE OF NATURE (1)	OPPORTUNITY LOSS OF THIS OUTCOME (2)	EXPECTED OPPORTUNITY LOSS (3) = (1) × (2)	PROBABILITY OF THIS STATE OF NATURE (1)	OPPORTUNITY LOSS OF THIS OUTCOME (2)	EXPECTED OPPORTUNITY LOSS (3) = (1) × (2)
Competitor reduces price	0.5	$ 0	$ 0	0.5	$1,500	$750
Competitor maintains current price	0.5	$2,000	$1,000	0.5	$ 0	$ 0
			$1,000			$750

Cost of uncertainty = Minimum expected opportunity loss = $750.

FROM THE PAYOFF MATRIX

	REDUCE PRICE			MAINTAIN CURRENT PRICE		
STATE OF NATURE	PROBABILITY (1)	OUTCOME (2)	(3) = (1) × (2)	PROBABILITY (1)	OUTCOME (2)	(3) = (1) × (2)
Competitor reduces price	0.5	$2,500	$1,250	0.5	$1,000	$ 500
Competitor maintains current price	0.5	$3,000	$1,500	0.5	$5,000	$2,500
			$2,750			$3,000

Expected value of a correct decision after the fact = $2,500(0.5) + $5,000(0.5) = $3,750.
Cost of uncertainty = Expected value of a correct decision − Expected value of best alternative
= $3,750 − $3,000 = $750.

Summary

Risk analysis plays an integral role in the decision process for most business problems. This chapter defines the concept of economic risk and illustrates how the concept can be dealt with in the managerial decision making process.

- **Economic risk** is the chance of loss due to the fact that all possible outcomes and their probability of occurrence are unknown. **Uncertainty** exists when the outcomes of managerial decisions cannot be predicted with absolute accuracy but all possibilities and their associated probabilities of occurrence are known.
- **Business risk** is the chance of loss associated with a given managerial decision. Many different types of business risk are apparent in the globally competitive 1990s. **Market risk** is the chance that a portfolio of investments can lose money because of swings in the stock market as a whole. **Inflation risk** is the danger that a general increase in the price level will undermine real economic values. **Interest-rate risk** stems from the fact that a fall in interest rates will increase the value of

any agreement that involves a fixed promise to pay interest and principal over a specified period. **Credit risk** is the chance that another party will fail to abide by its contractual obligations. Corporations must also consider the problem of **liquidity risk,** or the difficulty of selling corporate assets or investments that have only a few willing buyers or that are otherwise not easily transferable at favorable prices under typical market conditions. **Derivative risk** is the chance that volatile financial derivatives could create losses in underlying investments by increasing rather than decreasing price volatility.

■ **Cultural risk** is borne by companies that pursue a global rather than solely a domestic investment strategy. Product market differences due to distinctive social customs make it difficult to predict which products might do well in foreign markets. **Currency risk** is another important danger facing global businesses since most companies wish to eventually repatriate foreign earnings back to the domestic parent. And finally, global investors also experience **government policy risk** because foreign government grants of monopoly franchises, tax abatements, and favored trade status can be tenuous. **Expropriation risk,** or the risk that business property located abroad might be seized by host governments, is another type of risk that global investors must not forget.

■ The **probability** of an event is the chance, or odds, that the incident will occur. If all possible events or outcomes are listed, and if a probability of occurrence is assigned to each event, the listing is called a **probability distribution. A payoff matrix** illustrates the outcome associated with each possible state of nature. The **expected value** is the anticipated realization from a given payoff matrix.

■ **Absolute risk** is the overall dispersion of possible payoffs. The smaller the standard deviation, the tighter the probability distribution and the lower the risk in absolute terms. **Relative risk** is the variation in possible returns compared with the expected payoff amount. **Beta** is a measure of the systematic variability or covariance of one asset's returns with returns on other assets.

■ A **normal distribution** has a symmetrical distribution about the mean or expected value. If a probability distribution is normal, the actual outcome will lie within ± 1 standard deviation of the mean roughly 68% of the time. The probability that the actual outcome will be within ± 2 standard deviations of the expected outcome is approximately 95%; and there is a greater than 99% probability that the actual outcome will occur within ± 3 standard deviations of the mean. A **standardized variable** has a mean of 0 and a standard deviation equal to 1.

■ **Risk aversion** characterizes individuals who seek to avoid or minimize risk. **Risk neutrality** characterizes decision makers who focus on expected returns and disregard the dispersion of returns (risk). **Risk seeking** characterizes decision makers who prefer risk. At the heart of risk aversion is the notion of **diminishing marginal utility,** where additional increments of money bring ever smaller increments of marginal utility.

■ Under the **certainty equivalent** approach, decision makers specify the certain sum that they regard comparable to the expected value of a risky investment alternative. Any expected risky amount can be converted to an equivalent certain sum using the **certainty equivalent adjustment factor,** α, calculated as the ratio of a certain sum divided by an expected risky amount, where both dollar values provide the same level of utility. The **risk-adjusted valuation model** reflects both time value and risk considerations.

■ The difference between the expected rate of return on a risky asset and the rate of return on a riskless asset is the **risk premium** on the risky asset. The **risk-adjusted discount rate** k is the sum of the risk-free rate of return, R_F, plus the required risk premium, R_p.

■ A **decision tree** is a map of a sequential decision-making process. Decision trees are designed for analyzing decision problems that involve a series of choice alternatives that are constrained by previous decisions. **Decision points** represent instances when management must select among several choice alternatives. **Chance events** are possible outcomes following each decision point.

■ **Computer simulation** involves the use of computer software and workstations or sophisticated desktop computers to create a wide variety of decision outcome scenarios. **Sensitivity analysis** focuses on those variables that most directly affect decision outcomes, and it is less expensive and less time consuming than full-scale computer simulation.

■ **Game theory** is a useful decision framework employed to make choices in hostile environments and under extreme uncertainty. A variety of auction strategies are based on game theory principles.

■ The most familiar type of auction is an **English auction,** where an auctioneer keeps raising the price until a single highest bidder remains. A **winner's curse** results when overly aggressive bidders pay more than the economic value of auctioned items. In a **sealed-bid** auction, all bids are secret and the highest bid wins. A relatively rare sealed-bid auction method is a **Vickrey auction,** where the highest sealed bid wins, but the winner pays the price of the second-highest bid. Another auctioning method is the so-called reverse or **Dutch auction.** In a Dutch auction, the auctioneer keeps lowering a very high price until a winning bidder emerges. The winning bidder is the first participant willing to pay the auctioneer's price.

■ A game-theory decision standard that is sometimes applicable for decision making under uncertainty is the **maximin criterion,** which states that the decision maker should select the alternative that provides the best of the worst possible outcomes. The **minimax regret criterion** states that the decision maker should minimize the maximum possible regret (opportunity loss) associated with a wrong decision *after the fact.* In game theory, **opportunity loss** is defined as the difference between a given payoff and the highest possible payoff for the resulting state of nature. From the opportunity loss or regret matrix, the **cost of uncertainty** is measured by the minimum expected opportunity loss.

Decision making under conditions of uncertainty is greatly facilitated by use of the tools and techniques discussed in this chapter. While uncertainty can never be eliminated, it can be assessed and dealt with to minimize its harmful consequences.

QUESTIONS

Q14.1 Define the following terms:
A. Probability distribution
B. Expected value
C. Standard deviation
D. Coefficient of variation
E. Risk
F. Diminishing marginal utility of money
G. Certainty equivalent
H. Risk-adjusted discount rate
I. Decision tree
J. Simulation

Q14.2 What is the main difficulty associated with making decisions solely on the basis of comparisons of expected returns?

Q14.3 The standard deviation measure of risk implicitly gives equal weight to variations on both sides of the expected value. Can you see any potential limitations of this treatment?

Q14.4 "Utility is a theoretical concept that cannot be observed or measured in the real world. Hence, it has no practical value in decision analysis." Discuss this statement.

Q14.5 Graph the relation between money and its utility for an individual who buys both household fire insurance and state lottery tickets.

Q14.6 When the basic valuation model is adjusted using the risk-free rate, i, what economic factor is being explicitly accounted for?

Q14.7 If the expected net present value of returns from an investment project is $50,000, what is the maximum price that a risk-neutral investor would pay for it? Explain.

Q14.8 "Market estimates of investors' reactions to risk cannot be measured precisely, so it is impossible to set risk-adjusted discount rates for various classes of investment with a high degree of precision." Discuss this statement.

Q14.9 What is the value of decision trees in managerial decision making?

Q14.10 When is it most useful to use game theory in decision analysis?

SELF-TEST PROBLEMS AND SOLUTIONS

ST14.1 Certainty Equivalent Method. Federal-Magnate, Inc., is a Texas-based manufacturer and distributor of components and replacement parts for the auto, machinery, farm, and construction equipment industries. The company is presently funding a program of capital investment that is necessary to reduce production costs and thereby meet an onslaught of competition from low-cost suppliers located in Mexico and throughout Latin America. Federal-Magnate has a limited amount of capital available and must carefully weigh both the risks and potential rewards associated with alternative investments. In particular, the company seeks to weigh the advantages and disadvantages of a new investment project, Project X, in light of two other recently adopted investment projects, Project Y and Project Z:

A. Using a 5% risk-free rate, calculate the present value of expected cash flows after tax (CFAT) for the ten-year life of Project X.

	EXPECTED CASH FLOWS AFTER TAX (CFAT) PER YEAR		
YEAR	PROJECT X	Project Y	Project Z
1999	$10,000	$20,000	$0
2000	10,000	18,000	2,500
2001	10,000	16,000	5,000
2002	10,000	14,000	7,500
2003	10,000	12,000	10,000
2004	10,000	10,000	12,500
2005	10,000	8,000	15,000
2006	10,000	6,000	17,500
2007	10,000	4,000	20,000
2008	10,000	2,000	22,500
PV of Cash Flow @5%		$91,131	$79,130
Investment Outlay in 1997:	$60,000	$60,000	$50,000

B. Calculate the minimum certainty equivalent adjustment factor for each project's CFAT that would justify investment in each project.

C. Assume that the management of Federal-Magnate is risk averse and uses the certainty equivalent method in decision making. Is Project X as attractive or more attractive than Projects Y and Z?

D. If the company would not have been willing to invest more than $60,000 in Project Y nor more than $50,000 in Project Z, should Project X be undertaken?

ST14.1 **SOLUTION**

A. Using a 5% risk-free rate, the present value of expected cash flows after tax (CFAT) for the ten-year life of Project X is $77,217, calculated as follows:

EXPECTED CASH FLOWS AFTER TAX (CFAT) PER YEAR

YEAR	PROJECT X	PV OF $1 AT 5%	PV OF CFAT AT 5%
1999	$10,000	0.9524	$9,524
2000	10,000	0.9070	9,070
2001	10,000	0.8638	8,638
2002	10,000	0.8227	8,227
2003	10,000	0.7835	7,835
2004	10,000	0.7462	7,462
2005	10,000	0.7107	7,107
2006	10,000	0.6768	6,768
2007	10,000	0.6446	6,446
2008	10,000	0.6139	6,139
PV of Cash Flow @ 5%			$77,217

B. To justify each investment alternative, the company must have a certainty equivalent adjustment factor of at least $\alpha_X = 0.777$ for Project X, $\alpha_Y = 0.658$ for Project Y, and $\alpha_Z = 0.632$ for Project Z, since:

$$\alpha = \frac{Certain\ Sum}{Expected\ Risky\ Sum}$$

$$= \frac{Investment\ Outlay\ (Opportunity\ Cost)}{Present\ Value\ CFAT}$$

Project X

$$\alpha_X = \frac{\$60,000}{\$77,217} = 0.777$$

Project Y

$$\alpha_Y = \frac{\$60,000}{\$91,131} = 0.658$$

Project Z

$$\alpha_Z = \frac{\$50,000}{\$79,130} = 0.632$$

In other words, each risky dollar of expected profit contribution from Project X must be "worth" at least (valued as highly as) 77.7¢ in certain dollars to justify investment. For Project Y, each risky dollar must be worth at least 65.8¢ in certain dollars; each risky dollar must be worth at least 63.2¢ to justify investment in Project Z.

C. Given managerial risk aversion, Project X is the least attractive investment since it has the highest "price" on each risky dollar of expected CFAT. In adopting Projects Y and Z, Federal-Magnate implicitly asserted that it is willing to pay between 63.2¢ (Project Z) and 65.8¢ (Project Y) per each expected dollar of CFAT.

D. No. If the prices described previously represent the maximum price the company is willing to pay for such risky returns, then Project X should not be undertaken.

ST14.2 **Project Valuation.** Quality Foods, Inc., is a leading grocery retailer in the greater Washington, D.C., metropolitan area. The company is currently engaged in an aggressive store refurbishing program and is contemplating expansion of its in-store delicatessen department. A number of investment alternatives are being considered, including the construction of facilities for a new restaurant-quality carryout service for Chinese food. This investment project is to be evaluated using the certainty equivalent adjustment factor method and the risk-adjusted discount rate method. If the project has a positive value when both methods are employed, the project will be undertaken. The project will not be undertaken if either evaluation method suggests that the investment will fail to increase the value of the firm. Expected cash flow after tax (CFAT) values over the five-year life of the investment project and relevant certainty equivalent adjustment factor information are as follows:

HOT FOOD CARRYOUT COUNTER
INVESTMENT PROJECT

TIME PERIOD (YEARS)	ALPHA	PROJECT E(CFAT)
0	1.00	($75,000)
1	0.95	22,500
2	0.90	25,000
3	0.85	27,500
4	0.75	30,000
5	0.70	32,500
Total		$62,500

At the present time, an 8% annual rate of return can be obtained on short-term U.S. government securities; the company uses this rate as an estimate of the risk-free rate of return.

A.   Use the 8% risk-free rate to calculate the present value of the investment project.

B.   Using this present value as a basis, utilize the certainty equivalent adjustment factor information given previously to determine the risk-adjusted present value of the project.

C.   Use an alternative risk-adjusted discount rate method of project valuation on the assumption that a 15% rate of return is appropriate in light of the level of risk undertaken.

D.   Compare and contrast your answers to Parts B and C. Should the investment be made?

ST14.2   SOLUTION

A.   The present value of this investment project can be calculated easily using a hand-held calculator with typical financial function capabilities or by using the tables found in Appendix A. Using the appropriate discount factors corresponding to an 8% risk-free rate, the present value of the investment project is calculated as follows:

HOT FOOD CARRYOUT COUNTER INVESTMENT PROJECT

TIME PERIOD (YEARS)	PRESENT VALUE OF $1 AT 8%	PROJECT E (CFAT)	PRESENT VALUE OF E (CFAT) AT 8%
0	1.0000	($75,000)	($75,000)
1	0.9259	22,500	20,833
2	0.8573	25,000	21,433
3	0.7938	27,500	21,830
4	0.7350	30,000	22,050
5	0.6806	32,500	22,120
Total		$62,500	$33,266

B.   Using the present value given in Part A as a basis, the certainty equivalent adjustment factor information given previously can be employed to determine the risk-adjusted present value of the project. See table at the bottom of this page.

C.   An alternative risk-adjusted discount rate method of project valuation based on a 15% rate of return gives the project valuation on page 674.

D.   The answers to Parts B and C are fully compatible; both suggest a positive risk-adjusted present value for the project. In Part B, the certainty equivalent adjustment factor method reduces the

HOT FOOD CARRYOUT COUNTER INVESTMENT PROJECT

TIME PERIOD (YEARS)	PRESENT VALUE OF $1 AT 8%	PROJECT E(CFAT)	PRESENT VALUE OF E(CFAT) AT 8%	ALPHA	RISK-ADJUSTED VALUE
0	1.0000	($75,000)	($75,000)	1.00	($75,000)
1	0.9259	22,500	20,833	0.95	19,791
2	0.8573	25,000	21,433	0.90	19,290
3	0.7938	27,500	21,830	0.85	18,556
4	0.7350	30,000	22,050	0.75	16,538
5	0.6806	32,500	22,120	0.70	15,484
Total		$62,500	$33,266		$14,659

HOT FOOD CARRYOUT COUNTER INVESTMENT PROJECT

TIME PERIOD (YEARS)	PRESENT VALUE OF $1 AT 15%	PROJECT E(CFAT)	PRESENT VALUE OF E(CFAT) AT 15%
0	1.0000	($75,000)	($75,000)
1	0.8696	22,500	19,566
2	0.7561	25,000	18,903
3	0.6575	27,500	18,081
4	0.5718	30,000	17,154
5	0.4972	32,500	16,159
Total		$62,500	$14,863

present value of future receipts to account for risk differences. As is typical, the example assumes that money to be received in the more distant future has a greater risk, and hence, a lesser certainty equivalent value. In the risk-adjusted discount rate approach of Part C, the discount rate of 15% entails a time-factor adjustment of 8% plus a risk adjustment of 7%. Like the certainty equivalent adjustment factor approach, the risk-adjusted discount rate method gives a risk-adjusted present value for the project. Since the risk-adjusted present value of the project is positive under either approach, the investment should be made.

PROBLEMS

P14.1 **Risk Preferences.** Identify each of the following as being consistent with risk-averse, risk-neutral, or risk-seeking behavior in investment project selection. Explain your answers.
A. Larger risk premiums for riskier projects
B. Preference for smaller, as opposed to larger, coefficients of variation
C. Valuing certain sums and expected risky sums of equal dollar amounts equally
D. Having an increasing marginal utility of money
E. Ignoring the risk levels of investment alternatives

P14.2 **Certainty Equivalents.** The certainty equivalent concept can be widely employed in the analysis of personal and business decision making. Indicate whether each of the following statements is true or false and explain why:
A. The appropriate certainty equivalent adjustment factor, α, indicates the minimum price in certain dollars that an individual should be willing to pay per risky dollar of expected return.
B. An $\alpha \neq 1$ implies that a certain sum and a risky expected return of different dollar amounts provide equivalent utility to a given decision maker.
C. If previously accepted projects with similar risk have αs in a range from $\alpha = 0.4$ to $\alpha = 0.5$, an investment with an expected return of $150,000 is acceptable at a cost of $50,000.

D. A project for which NPV > 0 using an appropriate risk-adjusted discount rate has an implied α factor that is too large to allow project acceptance.
E. State lotteries that pay out 50% of the revenues that they generate require players who place at least a certain $2 value on each $1 of expected risky return.

P14.3 **Expected Value.** Duddy Kravitz, a broker with Caveat Emptor, Ltd., offers free investment seminars to local PTA groups. On average, Kravitz expects 1% of seminar participants to purchase $25,000 in tax-sheltered investments and 5% to purchase $5,000 in stocks and bonds. Kravitz earns a 4% net commission on tax shelters and a 1% commission on stocks and bonds. Calculate Kravitz's expected net commissions per seminar if attendance averages ten persons.

P14.4 **Probability Concepts.** Aquarius Products, Inc., has just completed development of a new line of skin-care products. Preliminary market research indicates two feasible marketing strategies: (1) creating general consumer acceptance through media advertising or (2) creating distributor acceptance through intensive personal selling by company representatives. The marketing manager has developed the following estimates for sales under each alternative at the top of page 675.
A. Assume that the company has a 50% profit margin on sales (that is, profits equal one-half of sales revenue). Calculate expected profits for each plan.

MEDIA ADVERTISING STRATEGY		PERSONAL SELLING STRATEGY	
PROBABILITY	SALES	PROBABILITY	SALES
0.1	$ 500,000	0.3	$1,000,0000
0.4	1,500,000	0.4	1,500,000
0.4	2,500,000	0.3	2,000,000
0.1	3,500,000		

B. Construct a simple bar graph of the possible profit outcomes for each plan. Which plan appears to be riskier?

C. Assume that management's utility function resembles the one illustrated in the figure at the bottom of this page. Which strategy should the marketing manager recommend?

P14.5 **Probability Concepts.** Sam Malone, marketing director for Narcissism Records, Inc., has just completed an agreement to rerelease a recording of "The Boss's Greatest Hits." (The Boss had a number of hits on the rock and roll charts during the early 1980s.) Preliminary market research indicates two feasible marketing strategies: (1) concentration on developing general consumer acceptance by advertising on late-night television or (2) concentration on developing distributor acceptance through intensive sales calls by company representatives. Malone developed estimates for sales under each alternative plan and has constructed payoff matrices according to his assessment of the likelihood of product acceptance under each plan. These data are at the top of page 676.

A. Assuming that the company has a 50% profit margin on sales, calculate the expected profits for each plan.

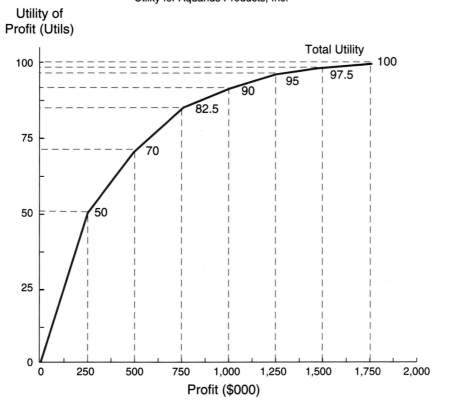

The Relation Between Total Profit and Utility for Aquarius Products, Inc.

STRATEGY 1 CONSUMER TELEVISION PROMOTION		STRATEGY 2 DISTRIBUTOR ORIENTED PROMOTION	
PROBABILITY	OUTCOME (SALES)	PROBABILITY	OUTCOME (SALES)
0.32	$ 250,000	0.125	$ 250,000
0.36	1,000,000	0.750	750,000
0.32	1,750,000	0.125	1,250,000

B. Construct a simple bar graph of the possible profit outcomes for each plan. Which plan appears to be riskier?

C. Calculate the standard deviation of the profit distribution associated with each plan.

D. Assume that the management of Narcissism has a utility function like the one illustrated in the following figure. Which marketing strategy should Malone recommend?

P14.6 **Risk-Adjusted Discount Rates.** One-Hour Dryclean, Inc., is contemplating replacing an obsolete dry cleaning machine with one of two innovative pieces of equipment. Alternative 1 requires a current investment outlay of $25,373, whereas Alternative 2 requires an outlay of $24,199. The following cash flows (cost savings) will be generated each year over the new machines' four-year lives:

	PROBABILITY	CASH FLOW
Alternative 1	0.18	$5,000
	0.64	10,000
	0.18	15,000
Alternative 2	0.125	$8,000
	0.75	10,000
	0.125	12,000

A. Calculate the expected cash flow for each investment alternative.

The Relation Between Total Utility and Profit for Narcissism Records, Inc.

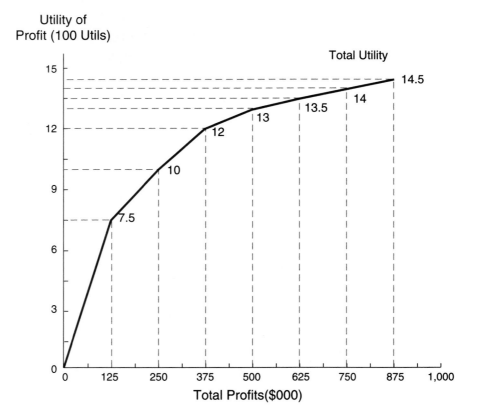

B. Calculate the standard deviation of cash flows (risk) for each investment alternative.

C. The firm will use a discount rate of 12% for the cash flows with a higher degree of dispersion and a 10% rate for the less risky cash flows. Calculate the expected net present value for each investment. Which alternative should be chosen?

P14.7 **Certainty Equivalent Method.** Tex-Mex, Inc., is a rapidly growing chain of Mexican food restaurants. The company has a limited amount of capital for expansion and must carefully weigh available alternatives. Currently, the company is considering opening restaurants in Santa Fe or Albuquerque, New Mexico. Projections for the two potential outlets are as follows:

CITY	OUTCOME	ANNUAL PROFIT CONTRIBUTION	PROBABILITY
Albuquerque	Failure	$100,000	0.5
	Success	200,000	0.5
Santa Fe	Failure	$60,000	0.5
	Success	340,000	0.5

Each restaurant would require a capital expenditure of $700,000, plus land acquisition costs of $500,000 for Albuquerque and $1 million for Santa Fe. The company uses the 10% yield on riskless U.S. Treasury bills to calculate the risk-free annual opportunity cost of investment capital.

A. Calculate the expected value, standard deviation, and coefficient of variation for each outlet's profit contribution.

B. Calculate the minimum certainty equivalent adjustment factor for each restaurant's cash flows that would justify investment in each outlet.

C. Assuming that the management of Tex-Mex is risk averse and uses the certainty equivalent method in decision making, which is the more attractive outlet? Why?

P14.8 **Decision Trees.** Keystone Manufacturing, Inc., is analyzing a new bid to supply the company with electronic control systems. Alpha Corporation has been supplying the systems and Keystone is satisfied with its performance. However, a bid has just been received from Beta Controls, Ltd., a firm that is aggressively marketing its products. Beta has offered to supply systems for a price of $120,000. The price for the Alpha system is

$160,000. In addition to an attractive price, Beta offers a money-back guarantee. That is, if Beta's systems do not match Alpha's quality, Keystone can reject and return them for a full refund. However, if it must reject the machines and return them to Beta, Keystone will suffer a delay costing the firm $60,000.

A. Construct a decision tree for this problem and determine the maximum probability that Keystone could assign to rejection of the Beta system before it would reject that firm's offer, assuming that it decides on the basis of minimizing expected costs.

B. Assume that Keystone assigns a 50% probability of rejection to the Beta Controls. Would Keystone be willing to pay $15,000 for an assurance bond that would pay $60,000 in the event that the Beta Controls fail the quality check? (Use the same objective as in Part A.) Explain.

P14.9 **Standard Normal Concept.** Speedy Business Cards, Inc., supplies customized business cards to commercial and individual customers. The company is preparing a bid to supply cards to the Nationwide Realty Company, a large association of independent real estate agents. Since paper, ink, and other costs cannot be determined precisely, Speedy anticipates that costs will be normally distributed around a mean of $20 per unit (each 500-card order) with a standard deviation of $2 per unit.

A. What is the probability that Speedy will make a profit at a price of $20 per unit?

B. Calculate the unit price necessary to give Speedy a 95% chance of making a profit on the order.

C. If Speedy submits a successful bid of $23 per unit, what is the probability that it will make a profit?

P14.10 **Game Theory.** Sierra Mountain Bike, Inc., is a producer and wholesaler of rugged bicycles designed for mountain touring. The company is considering an upgrade to its current line by making high-grade chrome alloy frames standard. Of course, the market response to this upgrade in product quality depends on the competitor's reaction, if any. The company's comptroller projects the following annual profits (payoffs) following resolution of the upgrade decision on page 678.

A. Which decision alternative would Sierra choose given a maximin criterion? Explain.

SIERRA'S DECISION ALTERNATIVES	STATES OF NATURE	
	COMPETITOR UPGRADE	NO COMPETITOR UPGRADE
Upgrade	$1,000,000	$1,500,000
Do not upgrade	800,000	2,000,000

B. Calculate the opportunity loss or regret matrix.

C. Which decision alternative would Sierra choose given a minimax regret criterion? Explain.

Case Study for Chapter 14

TIME WARNER IS PLAYING GAMES WITH STOCKHOLDERS

Time Warner, Inc., the world's largest media and entertainment company, was created through the July 1989 merger of Time, Inc. and Warner Communications, Inc. The company is best known as the publisher of magazines such as *Fortune, Time, Life, People,* and *Sports Illustrated* as well as owner of the highly profitable Book-of-the-Month Club. Perhaps less well known is the fact that Time Warner also owns leading pay TV networks such as *Home Box Office* and *Cinemax,* and it controls one of the nation's largest cable TV systems through its American Television and Communications subsidiary. The company also has a leading position in the recorded music business and enjoys major interests in both movie making and TV entertainment program production. Time Warner has the potential to profit whether people go to theaters, buy or rent videocassettes, watch cable or broadcast TV, or listen to records.

Just as impressive as Time Warner's commanding presence in the entertainment field is its potential for better capitalizing on its recognized strengths during coming years. Time Warner is a leader in terms of embracing new entertainment-field technology, as typified by its installation of the world's first fiber-optic 150-channel two-way cable TV system in Queens, New York. This revolutionary cable system allows subscribers to rent movies, purchase a wide array of goods and services, and participate in game shows and consumer surveys—all within the privacy of their own homes. Wide channel flexibility also gives the company the opportunity to expand pay-per-view TV offerings to meet demand from specialized market niches. In areas where cable systems have sufficient capacity, HBO subscribers are now offered a choice of programming on different channels. Time Warner also set up a TVKO network to offer boxing events on a regular pay-per-view basis following its success with the Holeyfield-Foreman fight during the spring of 1991. More examples of specialized programming are sure to follow during the late-1990s.

Time Warner is an interesting case study in decision making under uncertainty given the company's controversial plan during 1991 to raise new equity capital through use of a complex "contingent" rights offering. After months of assuring Wall Street that it was close to raising new equity from other firms through strategic alliances, Time Warner instead asked its shareholders to ante up more cash. Under the plan, the company granted holders of its 57.8 million shares of common stock the rights to 34.5 million shares of new common, or 0.6 rights per share. Each right enabled a shareholder to pay Time Warner $105 for an unspecified number of new common shares. Since the number of new shares that might be purchased for $105 was unspecified, so too was the price per share. In an unusual twist, Time Warner's Wall Street advisers structured the offer so that the new stock would be offered at cheaper prices if fewer shareholders chose to exercise their rights.

In an unusual arrangement, the rights from all participating shareholders were to be placed in a pool to determine their pro rata share of the 34.45 million shares to be distributed. If 100% of Time Warner shareholders chose to exercise their rights, the price per share would be $105, the number of shares owned by each shareholder would increase by 60%, and each shareholder would retain his or her same proportionate ownership in the company. In the event that less than 100% of the shareholders chose to participate, participating shareholders would receive a discount price and increase their proportionate interest in the company. If only 80% of Time Warner shareholders chose to exercise their rights, the price per share would be $84; if 60% chose to exercise their rights, the price per share would be $63. These lower prices reflect the fact that if only 80% of Time Warner shareholders chose to exercise their rights, each $105 right would purchase 1.25 shares; if 60% chose to exercise their rights, each $105 right would purchase roughly 1.667 shares. Finally, to avoid the possibility of issuing equity at fire-sale prices, Time Warner reserved the privilege to cancel the equity offering entirely if fewer than 60% of holders chose to exercise their rights.

The terms of the offer were designed to make Time Warner shareholders feel compelled to exercise their rights in hopes of getting cheap stock and avoiding seeing their holdings diluted. Although such contingent rights offerings are a common capital-raising technique in Britain, prior to the Time Warner offering they had never been proposed on such a large scale in the United States. Wall Street traders and investment bankers lauded the Time Warner offer as a brilliant coercive device—a view that might have been colored by the huge fees they stood to make on the offering. Advisory fees for Merrill Lynch and Time Warner's seven other key advisers were projected at $41.5 million to $145 million, depending on the number of participating shareholders. An additional $20.7 million to $34.5 million was set aside to pay other investment bankers for soliciting shareholders to exercise their rights. Time Warner's advisers argued that their huge fees totaling 5.22% of the proceeds to the company were justified because the offering entered uncharted ground in terms of Wall Street experience. Disgruntled shareholders noted that a similar contingent rights offering by Bass PLC of Britain involved a fee of only 2.125% of the proceeds to the company, despite the fact that the lead underwriter Schroders PLC agreed to buy and resell any new stock that wasn't claimed by rights holders. This led to charges that Time Warner's advisers were

charging underwriters' fees without risking any of their own capital.

Proceeds from the offering were earmarked to help pay down the $11.3 billion debt Time Inc. took on to buy Warner Communications Inc. two years previously when Time Warner was formed. Time Warner maintained that it was in intensive talks with potential strategic partners and that the rights offering would strengthen its hand in those negotiations by improving the company's balance sheet. Time Warner said that the rights offering would enhance its ability to enter into strategic alliances or joint ventures with partners overseas. Such alliances would help the company penetrate markets in Japan, Europe, and elsewhere. Critics of the plan argued that the benefits from strategic alliances come in small increments and that Time Warner had failed to strike any such deals previously because it wants both management control and a premium price from potential partners. These critics also maintained that meaningful revenue from any such projects is probably years away.

Stockholder reaction to the Time Warner offering was immediate and overwhelmingly negative. On the day the offering was announced, Time Warner shares closed at $99.50, down $11.25, in New York Stock Exchange composite trading. This is in addition to a decline of $6 suffered the previous day on the basis of a report in *The Wall Street Journal* that some form of equity offering was being considered. After trading above $120 per share in the days prior to the first reports of a pending offer, Time Warner shares plummeted by more than 25% to $88 per share within a matter of days. This is yet one more disappointment for the company's long-suffering common stockholders. During the summer of 1989, Time cited a wide range of synergistic benefits to be gained from a merger with Warner Communications and spurned a $200 per share buyout offer from Paramount Communications, Inc. This is despite the fact that the Paramount offer represented a fat 60% premium to the then prevailing market price of $125 for Time stock. During the succeeding two-year period, Time Warner stock failed to rise above this $125 level and traded as low as $66 per share during the fall of 1990. Meanwhile, the hoped-for Time Warner synergy has yet to emerge.

A. Was Paramount's above-market offer for Time, Inc. consistent with the notion that the prevailing market price for common stock is an accurate reflection of the discounted net present value of future cash flows? Was management's rejection of Paramount's above-market offer for Time, Inc. consistent with the value-maximization concept?

B. Assume that a Time Warner shareholder could buy additional shares at a market price of $90 or participate in the company's rights offering. Construct the payoff and regret matrices per share that correspond to a $90 per share purchase decision versus a decision to partic-

ipate in the rights offering with subsequent 100%, 80%, and 60% participation by all Time Warner shareholders.

C. Describe the relevant maximin and minimax shareholder strategies.

D. Explain why the price of Time Warner common stock fell following the announcement of the company's controversial rights offering. Is such an offering in the best interests of current shareholders?

Capital Budgeting

Who are the real wealth creators among the industrial giants? If Coca-Cola, General Electric, Merck, Philip Morris, or Microsoft come to mind, you're on the right track. These companies are standout performers when financial results are measured according to the amount of wealth created for shareholders.

For example, General Electric Chairman Jack Welch is widely regarded as among the most astute financial managers. By redeploying assets from lower- to higher-valued uses within the GE empire, Welch has been able to maintain high rates of growth and an enviable rate of return on invested capital. At the cornerstone of Welch's capital budgeting process is a concept known as "economic value added." EVA measures the wealth managers have created, or lost, for GE shareholders in running their businesses. To determine EVA, GE deducts the explicit or implicit cost of capital employed in the business from the after-tax profit earned on operations. What's left over is the dollar amount of "value added" for shareholders. Like any basic measure of economic profitability, EVA measures returns from a marginal project-by-project perspective. Its usefulness stems from the fact that it focuses managers' attention on the incremental value created through the capital budgeting process.[1]

This chapter describes the mechanics of capital budgeting as an application of marginal analysis. In capital budgeting, marginal revenue is measured in terms of the incremental cash flows generated by investment projects; marginal cost is measured by the marginal cost of new investment capital.

The Capital Budgeting Process

Management invests hundreds of billions of dollars per year in fixed assets. By their very nature, these investment decisions have the potential to affect a firm's fortunes over several years. A good decision can boost earnings sharply and dramatically increase the value of the firm. A bad decision can lead to bankruptcy. Effective planning and control is essential if the health and long-run viability of the firm is to be assured.

WHAT IS CAPITAL BUDGETING?

The term *capital* refers to the funds employed to finance fixed assets used in production, while a budget is a detailed plan of projected inflows and outflows over future periods.

---

[1] See Ronald B. Lieber, "Who Are the Real Wealth Creators?" *Fortune,* December 9, 1996, 107–116.

Capital Budgeting
Long-term investment planning process.

Capital budgeting is the process of planning expenditures that generate cash flows expected to extend beyond one year. The choice of one year is arbitrary, of course, but it is a convenient cutoff for distinguishing between classes of expenditures. Examples of capital outlays are expenditures for land, buildings and equipment, and for additions to working capital (e.g., inventories and receivables) made necessary by expansion. New advertising campaigns or research and development programs are also likely to have impacts beyond one year and come within the classification of capital budgeting expenditures.

Capital budgeting integrates the various elements of the firm. Although the financial manager generally has administrative control of the capital budgeting process, the effectiveness of a firm's capital investments depends on input from all major departments. The marketing department makes a key contribution by providing sales forecasts. Because operating costs must be estimated, the accounting, production, engineering, and purchasing departments are also involved. The initial outlay, or investment cost, must be estimated; again engineering and purchasing typically provide input. Obtaining funds and estimating their cost are major tasks of the financial manager. Finally, these various estimates must be drawn together in the form of a project evaluation. Although the finance department generally writes up the evaluation report, top management ultimately sets standards of acceptability.

THE PROJECT SELECTION PROCESS

A firm's growth and development, even its ability to remain competitive and to survive, depend on a constant flow of ideas for new products and ways to make existing products better and at a lower cost. A well-managed firm goes to great lengths to develop good capital budgeting proposals. For example, a sales representative may report that customers are asking for a particular product that the company does not now produce. The sales manager then will discuss the idea with the marketing research group to determine the size of the market for the proposed product. If it appears likely that a substantial market does exist, cost accountants and engineers will be asked to estimate production costs. If it appears that the product can be produced and sold to yield a sufficient profit, the project will be undertaken.

If a firm has capable and imaginative managers and other employees, and if its incentive system is working properly, several ideas for capital investment will be advanced. Some ideas will be both practical and profitable, whereas others will not. As a result, procedures must be established for screening project alternatives.

PROJECT CLASSIFICATION TYPES

Analyzing capital expenditure proposals is not a costless operation; benefits can be gained from careful analysis, but such investigations are costly. For certain types of projects, a relatively detailed analysis may be warranted; for others, cost/benefit studies suggest that simpler procedures should be used. Firms generally classify projects into a number of categories and analyze those projects in each category somewhat differently.

Replacement Projects
Maintenance of business investments.

Replacement projects, or maintenance of business projects, consist of expenditures necessary to replace worn-out or damaged equipment used to produce profitable products. These projects are necessary if the firm is to continue in its current businesses. The relevant issues are (a) Should the company continue to offer current products and services? and (b) Should existing plant and equipment be employed for this purpose? Usually, the answers to both questions are yes, so maintenance decisions are typically routine and made without going through an elaborate decision process.

Cost Reduction Projects
Expenditures to replace obsolete plant and equipment.

Cost reduction projects include expenditures to replace serviceable but obsolete plant and equipment. The purpose of these investment projects is to lower production costs by lowering expenses for labor, raw materials, heat, or electricity. These decisions are often discretionary, so a more detailed analysis is generally required to support the expenditure. Decision-making authority usually rests at the manager or higher level in the organization.

Safety and Environmental Projects
Mandatory nonrevenue-producing investments.

Capital expenditures made necessary by government regulation, collective bargaining agreements, or insurance policy requirements fall into a further **safety and environmental projects** category. Such capital expenditures are sometimes called "mandatory" investments because they often are nonrevenue-producing in nature. How they are handled depends on their size and complexity; most often they are quite routine and their treatment is similar to replacement and cost reduction projects.

Expansion Projects
Expenditures to increase availability of existing products.

Expansion projects involve expenditures to increase the availability of existing products and services. For example, investment projects to expand the number of service outlets or distribution facilities are included in this category. These investment decisions are relatively complex because they require an explicit forecast of the firm's future supply and demand conditions. Mistakes are quite possible, so detailed analysis is required and the final decision is made at a high level within the firm, perhaps at the level of the controller or chief financial officer.

Expansion into new products or markets requires expenditures necessary to produce new products and services or to expand into new geographic areas. Strategic decisions that could change the fundamental nature of the firm's business are involved. Expenditures of large sums over extended investment horizons are often necessary. Detailed analysis is invariably required, and final decisions are often made by the chief executive officer or board of directors.

To summarize, relatively simple calculations and only a few supporting documents are required for replacement decisions, especially maintenance-type investments in profitable plants. More complete analysis is required for cost reduction projects, for expansion of existing product lines, and especially for investments in new product lines or geographic areas. Within each capital investment project category, projects are treated differently, depending on the level of expenditure required. The larger the required investment, the more detailed the analysis and the higher the level of decision-making authority required. A plant manager may be authorized to approve maintenance expenditures costing less than $10,000 to $25,000 on the basis of a relatively cursory analysis. At the other extreme, the entire board of directors may review decisions that involve more than $1 million or that entail a major strategic shift in the firm's focus. Highly detailed and thorough analysis is typically required in such instances.

Steps in Capital Budgeting

If an individual investor identifies and invests in a stock or bond whose expected return is greater than the cost of funds, the investor's portfolio will increase in value. Similarly, if a firm identifies or creates an investment opportunity with a present value greater than its cost, the value of the firm will increase. This increase in the firm's value as a result of successful capital budgeting will be reflected in the firm's future growth. The more effective the firm's capital budgeting process, the higher its growth rate and the greater its future value. In theory, the capital budgeting process involves six logical steps.

THE SEQUENCE OF PROJECT VALUATION

First, the cost of the project must be determined. This is similar to finding the price that must be paid for a stock or bond. Next, management must estimate the expected cash flows from the project, including the value of the asset at a specified terminal date. This is similar to estimating the future dividend or interest payment stream on a stock or bond. Third, the riskiness of projected cash flows must be estimated. To do this, management needs information about the probability distributions of future cash flows. Fourth, given the riskiness of projected cash flows and the cost of funds under prevailing economic conditions as reflected by the riskless rate, R_F, the firm must determine the appropriate discount rate, or cost of capital, at which the project's cash flows are to be discounted. This is equivalent to finding the required rate of return on a stock or bond investment. Fifth, expected cash flows are converted to a present value to obtain a clear estimate of the investment project's value to the firm. This is equivalent to finding the present value of expected future dividends or interest plus principal payments. Finally, the present value of expected cash inflows is compared with the required outlay, or cost, of the project. If the present value of cash flows derived from a project exceeds the cost of the investment, the project should be accepted. Otherwise, the project should be rejected.

CASH FLOW ESTIMATION

The most important and difficult step in the analysis of a capital budgeting project is estimating its cash flows—the investment outlays and the annual net cash inflows after the project goes into operation. Many variables are involved in cash flow forecasting, and several individuals and departments participate in the process. For example, forecasts of unit sales and sales prices are normally made by the marketing department, based on its knowledge of price elasticity, advertising effects, the state of the economy, competitors' reactions, and trends in consumers' tastes. The size of necessary capital outlays associated with a new product are generally obtained from the engineering and product development staffs, while operating costs are estimated by cost accountants, production experts, personnel specialists, purchasing agents, and so forth.

It is difficult to make accurate forecasts of the costs and revenues associated with a large, complex project, so forecast errors can be large. For example, when several major oil companies decided to build the Alaska pipeline, the original cost forecasts were in the neighborhood of $700 million, but the final cost was closer to $7 billion. Similar, and sometimes even worse, miscalculations are common in forecasts of product design costs, such as the costs to develop a new personal computer. As difficult as plant and equipment costs are to estimate, sales revenues and operating costs over the life of the project are generally even more uncertain. For example, when AT&T originally developed the *Videophone,* it envisaged large sales in both the residential and business markets. As of the mid-1990s, such sales have yet to materialize. Because of its financial strength, AT&T has been able to absorb losses on the project, but the *Videophone* venture would have forced a weaker firm into bankruptcy.

The financial staff's role in the forecasting process involves coordinating the efforts of the other departments, such as engineering and marketing, ensuring that everyone involved with the forecast uses a consistent set of economic assumptions, and making sure that no biases are inherent in the forecasts. This last point is extremely important, because division managers often become emotionally involved with pet projects or develop empire-building complexes, leading to cash flow forecasting biases that make bad projects look good—on paper. The AT&T *Videophone* project is an example of this problem. For the capital budgeting process to be successful, the pattern of expected cash inflows and outflows must be established within a consistent and unbiased framework.

INCREMENTAL CASH FLOW EVALUATION

Accounting income statements reflect a mix of cash and noncash expenses and revenues. Accountants deduct labor costs, which are cash outflows, from revenues, which may or may not be entirely in cash because sales are often made on credit. At the same time, accountants do not deduct capital outlays, which are cash outflows, but they do deduct depreciation expenses, which are not cash outflows. In capital budgeting, it is critical that decisions are based strictly on cash flows, the actual dollars that flow into and out of the company during each time period.

Incremental Cash Flows

Change in net cash flows due to an investment project.

The relevant cash flows for capital budgeting purposes are the incremental cash flows attributable to a project. **Incremental cash flows** are the period-by-period changes in net cash flows that are due to an investment project:

$$Project\ CF_t = \frac{CF_t\ for\ Corporation}{with\ Project} - \frac{CF_t\ for\ Corporation}{without\ Project} \qquad \textbf{(15.1)}$$

It is possible to construct a firm's pro forma cash flow statements with and without a project for each year of the project's life and then measure annual project cash flows as the differences in cash flows between the two sets of statements. In practice, a number of problems must be addressed successfully if the incremental cash flows from a given investment project are to be estimated successfully.

As described in Chapter 9, a sunk cost is any expenditure outlay that has already occurred or has been agreed to on a contractual basis. Sunk costs are not incremental costs, they are not relevant to subsequent investment decisions, and they should not be included in the analysis of such decisions. Suppose, for example, that Gourmet Foods, Ltd., is evaluating the possibility of opening a retail store in a newly developed section of Albuquerque. A year ago, Gourmet Foods hired a consulting firm to perform an on-site analysis at a cost of $100,000, and this $100,000 has already been paid and expensed for tax purposes. Is this expenditure a relevant cost with respect to Gourmet's still-pending capital budgeting decision? The answer is no. The $100,000 represents a sunk cost. Gourmet Foods cannot recover this amount regardless of whether the new facility is opened. This money is gone. Whether the pending investment project should be accepted or rejected depends on the incremental costs and revenues associated with the project from this point *forward*. Whether the earlier commitment of $100,000 looks good or bad in hindsight is irrelevant. It is essential that irrelevant sunk costs not confound investment decisions. It sometimes turns out that a project looks unprofitable when all costs, including sunk costs, are considered. On an incremental basis, however, many of these same projects have the potential to generate a significant profit contribution when only incremental cash flows are included. An investment project should be undertaken only when incremental cash flows exceed the cost of investment on a present-value basis. It is essential that irrelevant sunk costs be deleted from the analysis so that correct forward-looking investment decisions can be made.

A second potential problem relates to the improper treatment of opportunity costs. All relevant opportunity costs must be included in the capital budgeting process. For example, suppose Gourmet Foods already owns a piece of land that is suitable for the new store. When evaluating the new retail facility, should the cost of the land be disregarded because no additional cash outlay would be required? Certainly not, because there is an opportunity cost inherent in the use of the property. Suppose that the land could be sold to net $150,000 after commissions and taxes. Use of the site for the new store would require foregoing this inflow, so the $150,000 must be charged as an opportunity cost against the project. The proper land cost is the $150,000 market-determined value, irrespective of historical acquisition costs.

A further potential problem involves the effects of the project on other parts of the firm. For example, suppose that some of the new outlet's customers are already customers at Gourmet Foods' downtown store. Revenues and profits generated by these customers would not be new to the firm but would represent transfers from one outlet to another. Cash flows produced by such customers should not be treated as incremental in the capital budgeting analysis. On the other hand, having a new suburban store might actually increase customer awareness in the local market and thereby attract additional customers to the downtown outlet. In this case, additional revenues projected to flow to the downtown store should be attributed to the new suburban facility. Although they are often difficult to identify and quantify, externalities such as these are important and must be considered.

A fourth problem relates to the timing of cash flows. Year-end accounting income statements seldom reflect exactly when revenues or expenses occur. Because of the time value of money, capital budgeting cash flows should be analyzed according to when they occur. A time line of daily cash flows would in theory be most accurate but it is sometimes costly to construct and unwieldy to use. In the case of Gourmet Foods, it may be appropriate to measure incremental cash flows on a quarterly or monthly basis

Market-Based Capital Budgeting

The real key to creating corporate wealth is to apply a market-based approach to capital budgeting. A common technique is to build the capital budgeting process around a concept called market-based capital budgeting. Its greatest virtue lies in the fact that focusing on the market value implications of the capital budgeting process forces management to act like shareholders. For managers who wish to boost profits while cutting capital investment, market-based capital budgeting has become an indispensable tool. The power of the market-based capital budgeting concept stems from the fact that managers can't know if an operation is really creating value for the corporation until they calculate and apply the true cost of capital to all assets employed. To grow the company in a value-maximizing manner, the firm must weigh the answers to two important questions.

Question No. 1: What is the true cost of capital employed in a business? The cost of borrowed capital is typically easy to estimate. It is the interest paid, adjusted to reflect the tax deductibility of interest payments. The cost of equity capital is more difficult to estimate, but companies must ask: What is the cost of money provided by shareholders? The true cost of equity capital is the return shareholders could be getting in price appreciation and dividends if they invested instead in a portfolio of companies about as risky as the company itself. From this perspective, the relevant cost of equity is its opportunity cost.

Some managers resist this notion and seem to argue: How can the cost of equity be real if managers don't have to write a check to shareholders on a regular basis? Think of the cost of equity from the point of view of the shareholder who has committed funds to your company instead of to Coca-Cola. If you're not employing shareholder money as successfully as they are—and not showing any promise of doing so—shareholders will take their money back by selling your stock, sending its price down. Other investors will be similarly less inclined to supply any capital. So as long as any company fails to at least match investor opportunity costs, it is on the road to oblivion.

So what is the cost of equity capital today? Over the past 60 years, ever since reliable data have been available, shareholders have received an average rate of return that is 6% higher on stocks than on risk-free government bonds. With short-term Treasury Bill rates around 6% in mid-1997, the current average cost of equity is roughly 12% per year, though it goes much higher for especially volatile companies and slightly lower for those with more stable prospects. If a firm uses debt as well as equity financing, the cost of capital is simply the weighted average of the two.

Question No. 2: How much capital is tied up in the operation? Capital traditionally consists of the current value of real estate, machines, vehicles, and the like, plus working capital. Proponents of market-based capital budgeting say there's more. What about the money spent on R&D and on employee training? Those are investments meant to pay off for years, but accounting rules say you can't treat them that way. Many companies say forget the accounting rules. For internal purposes the return on these investments must also be calculated over a reasonable life, say three to five years.

When both questions are answered, one simply multiplies the amount of capital from *Question No. 2* by the rate of return from *Question No. 1* to get the dollar cost of capital. The market value added by the capital budgeting process is then calculated as operating earnings minus taxes minus capital costs. If the amount of market value added is positive, the operation is creating wealth. If market value added is negative, the operation is destroying capital.

Don't assume that because capital costs a lot, it's a bad thing. The cost of equity capital at Coca-Cola exceeds 20% per year. What's important is not the cost or amount of capital employed—it's how capital is managed that counts.

See: Roger Lowenstein, "Testing the Latest Economic Elixer," *The Wall Street Journal,* February 13, 1997, C1.

using an electronic spreadsheet such as *Lotus 1-2-3* or *Microsoft Excel.* In other cases, it may be appropriate simply to assume that all cash flows occur at the end or midpoint of every year.

Finally, tax considerations are often important because they can have a major impact on cash flows. In some cases, tax effects can make or break a project. It is critical that taxes be dealt with correctly in capital budgeting decisions. This is difficult because the tax laws are extremely complex and are subject to interpretation and change. For example, salvage value has no effect on the depreciable basis and hence on the annual depreciation expense that can be taken. Still, when performing a cash flow analysis, the market value of an asset at the end of the project represents a relevant expected cash inflow. Any difference between salvage value and depreciated book value at the end of a project is currently treated as ordinary income and is taxed at the firm's marginal tax rate. The staff in charge of evaluating capital investment projects must rely heavily on the firm's accountants and tax lawyers and also must develop a working knowledge of current tax law.

Accounting income statements provide a crucial basis for estimating the relevant cash flows from investment projects. This information must be adjusted, however, to carefully reflect the economic pattern of inflows and outflows so that value-maximizing investment decisions can be made. Though a formidable task, firms can and do overcome problems posed by sunk costs, opportunity costs, spillovers, and tax considerations. To illustrate, the following section offers a simplified example of cash flow estimation.

A Cash Flow Estimation Example

To illustrate several important aspects of cash flow analysis and see how they relate to one another, consider a capital budgeting decision that faces Silicon Valley Controls Corp. (SVCC), a California-based high-tech firm. SVCC's research and development department has been applying its expertise in microprocessor technology to develop a small computer specifically designed to control home appliances. Once programmed, the computer system automatically controls the heating and air-conditioning systems, security system, hot water heater, and even small appliances such as a coffee maker. By increasing the energy efficiency of a home, the appliance control computer can save on energy costs and hence pay for itself. The project evaluation effort has reached the stage at which a decision about whether to go forward with production must be made.

SVCC's marketing department plans to target sales of the appliance control computer to the owners of larger homes; the computer is cost-effective only for homes with 2,000 or more square feet of heated and air-conditioned space. The marketing vice-president believes that annual sales would be 25,000 units if the appliance control computers were priced at $2,200 each. The engineering department has estimated that the firm would need a new manufacturing facility. Such a plant could be built and made ready for production in two years, once the "go ahead" decision is made. The plant would require a 25-acre site, and SVCC currently has an option to purchase a suitable tract of land for $1.2 million. If the decision is made to go ahead with the project, building construction could begin immediately and would continue for two years. Since the project has an estimated economic life of six years, the overall planning period is eight years: two years for plant construction (Years 1 and 2) plus six years for operation (Years 3 through 8). The building would cost $8 million and have a 31.5-year life for tax purposes. A $4 million payment would be due the building contractor at the end of each year of construction. Manufacturing equipment, with a cost of $10 million and a seven-year life for tax purposes, is to be installed and paid for at the end of the second year of construction, just prior to the beginning of operations.

The project also requires a working capital investment equal to 12% of estimated sales during the coming year. The initial working capital investment is to be made at the end of Year 2 and is increased at the end of each subsequent period by 12% of the expected increase in the following year's sales. After completion of the project's six-year operating period, the land is expected to have a market value of $1.7 million; the building, a value of $1 million; and the equipment, a value of $2 million. The production department has estimated that variable manufacturing costs would total 65% of dollar sales and that fixed overhead costs, excluding depreciation, would be $8 million for the first year of operations. Sales prices and fixed overhead costs, other than depreciation, are projected to increase with inflation, which is expected to average 6% per year over the six-year production period.

SVCC's marginal federal-plus-state tax rate is 40%, and its weighted average cost of capital is 15%. For capital budgeting purposes, the company's policy is to assume that cash flows occur at the end of each year. Since the plant would begin operations at the start of Year 3, the first operating cash flows would be realized at the end of Year 3. As one of the company's financial analysts, you have been assigned the task of supervising the capital budgeting analysis. For now, you may assume that the project has the same risk as the firm's current average project, and hence you may use the 15% corporate cost of capital for this project.

The first step in the analysis is to summarize the investment outlays required for the project; this is done in Table 15.1. Note that the land cannot be depreciated, and hence its depreciable basis is $0. Because the project will require an increase in net working capital during Year 2, this is shown as an investment outlay for that year.

	Table 15.1	INVESTMENT OUTLAY ANALYSIS FOR NEW PLANT INVESTMENT PROJECT				
		YEAR				
FIXED ASSETS	0	1	2	TOTAL COSTS	DEPRECIABLE BASIS	
Land	$1,200,000	$ 0	$ 0	$ 1,200,000	$ 0	
Building	0	4,000,000	4,000,000	8,000,000	8,000,000	
Equipment	0	0	10,000,000	10,000,000	10,000,000	
Total fixed assets	$1,200,000	$4,000,000	$14,000,000	$19,200,000		
Net working capital[a]	0	0	6,600,00	6,600,000		
Total investment	$1,200,000	$4,000,000	$20,600,000	$25,800,000		

[a]Twelve percent of first year's sales, or 0.12 ($55,000,000) = $6,600,000.

Table 15.2

NET CASH FLOWS FROM OPERATIONS FOR NEW PLANT INVESTMENT PROJECT

	YEAR					
	3	4	5	6	7	8
Unit sales	25,000	25,000	25,000	25,000	25,000	25,000
Sale price[a]	$ 2,200	$ 2,332	$ 2,472	$ 2,620	$ 2,777	$ 2,944
Net sales[a]	$55,000,000	$58,300,000	$61,800,000	$65,500,000	$69,425,000	$73,600,000
Variable costs[b]	35,750,000	37,895,000	40,170,000	42,575,000	45,126,250	47,840,000
Fixed costs (overhead)[a]	8,000,000	8,480,000	8,988,800	9,528,128	10,099,816	10,705,805
Depreciation (building)[c]	120,000	240,000	240,000	240,000	240,000	240,000
Depreciation (equipment)[c]	2,000,000	3,200,000	1,900,000	1,200,000	1,100,000	600,000
Earnings before taxes	$ 9,130,000	$ 8,485,000	$10,501,200	$11,956,872	$12,858,934	$14,214,195
Taxes (40%)	3,652,000	3,394,000	4,200,480	4,782,749	5,143,574	5,685,678
Projected net operating income	$ 5,478,000	$ 5,091,000	$ 6,300,720	$ 7,174,123	$ 7,715,360	$ 8,528,517
Add back noncash expenses[d]	2,120,000	3,440,000	2,140,000	1,440,000	1,340,000	840,000
Cash flow from operations[e]	$ 7,598,000	$ 8,531,000	$ 8,440,720	$ 8,614,123	$ 9,055,360	$ 9,368,517
Investment in net working capital (NWC)[f]	(396,000)	(420,000)	(444,000)	(471,000)	(501,000)	8,832,000
New salvage value[g]						5,972,000
Total projected cash flows	$ 7,202,000	$ 8,111,000	$ 7,996,720	$ 8,143,123	$ 8,554,360	$24,172,517

[a]Year 3 estimate increased by the assumed 6 percent inflation rate.

[b]Sixty-five percent of net sales.

[c]ACRS depreciation rates were estimated as follows:

	YEAR					
	3	4	5	6	7	8
Building	1.5%	3%	3%	3%	3%	3%
Equipment	20	32	19	12	11	6

These percentages are multiplied by the depreciable basis to get the depreciation expense for each year. Note that the allowances have been rounded for ease of computation.

[d]In this case, depreciation on building and equipment.

[e]Net operating income plus noncash expenses.

[f]Twelve percent of next year's increase in sales. For example, Year 4 sales are $3.3 million over Year 3 sales, so the addition to NWC in Year 3 required to support Year 4 sales is (0.12)($3,300,000) = $396,000. The cumulative working capital investment is recovered when the project ends.

[g]See Table 15.3 for the net salvage value calculation.

Once capital requirements have been identified, operating cash flows that will occur once production begins must be estimated; these are set forth in Table 15.2. The operating cash flow estimates are based on information provided by SVCC's various departments. Note that the sales price and fixed costs are projected to increase each year by the 6% inflation rate, and since variable costs are 65% of sales, they too will rise by 6% each year. The changes in net working capital (NWC) represent the additional investments required to support sales increases (12% of the next year's sales increase, which in this case results only from inflation) during Years 3 through 7, as well as the recovery of the cumulative net working capital investment in Year 8. Amounts for depreciation were obtained by multiplying the depreciable basis by the Accelerated Cost Recovery System (ACRS) depreciation allowance rates set forth in footnote c to Table 15.2.

The analysis also requires an estimation of the cash flows generated by salvage values. Table 15.3 summarizes this analysis. First is a comparison between projected market and book values for salvageable assets. Land cannot be depreciated and has an estimated salvage value greater than the initial purchase price. Thus, SVCC would have to pay taxes on the profit. The building has an estimated salvage value less than the book value; it will be sold at a loss for tax purposes. This loss will reduce taxable income and thus will generate a tax savings; in effect, the company has been depreciating the building too slowly, so it will write off the loss against ordinary income. Equipment,

| Table 15.3 | NET SALVAGE VALUE CALCULATION FOR NEW PLANT INVESTMENT PROJECT |

	LAND	BUILDING	EQUIPMENT
Salvage (ending market) value	$1,700,000	$1,000,000	$ 2,000,000
Initial cost	1,200,000	8,000,000	10,000,000
Depreciable basis (Year 2)	0	8,000,000	10,000,000
Book value (Year 8)[a]	1,200,000	6,680,000	0
Capital gains income	$ 500,000	$ 0	$ 0
Ordinary income (loss)[b]	0	(5,680,000)	2,000,000
Taxes[c]	$ 200,000	($2,272,000)	$ 800,000
Net salvage value (Salvage Value − Taxes)	$1,500,000	$3,272,000	$ 1,200,000

Total Cash Flow from Salvage Value = $1,500,000 + $3,272,000 + $1,200,000 = $5,972,000.

[a]Book value for the building in Year 8 equals depreciable basis minus accumulated ACRS depreciation of $1,320,000. The accumulated depreciation on the equipment is $10,000,000. See Table 16.2.

[b]Building: $1,000,000 market value − $6,680,000 book value = $5,680,000 depreciation shortfall, which is treated as an operating expense in Year 8.

Equipment: $2,000,000 market value − $0 book value = $2,000,000 depreciation recapture, which is treated as ordinary income in Year 8.

[c]Since capital gains are now taxed at the ordinary income rate, all taxes are based on SVCC's 40 percent marginal federal-plus-state rate. The table is set up to differentiate ordinary income from capital gains because Congress may reinstate different tax rates on those two income sources.

however, will be sold for more than book value, so the company will have to pay ordinary taxes on the $2 million profit. In all cases, the book value is the depreciable basis minus accumulated depreciation, and the total cash flow from salvage is merely the sum of the land, building, and equipment components.

As illustrated by this SVCC example, cash flow estimation involves a detailed analysis of demand, cost, and tax considerations. Even for fairly simple projects, such as that described here, the analysis can become complicated. Innovative, powerful spreadsheet software such as *Lotus 1-2-3* and *Microsoft Excel* make possible the accurate estimation of cash flows under a variety of operating assumptions, for even the most complex projects. More than just allowing managers to enter and manipulate data in several useful ways, these spreadsheet programs also incorporate various effective techniques for project evaluation. Among these techniques are a number of valuable capital budgeting decision rules.

Capital Budgeting Decision Rules

An economically sound capital budgeting decision rule must consistently lead to the acceptance of projects that will increase the value of the firm. When the discounted present value of expected future cash flows exceeds the cost of investment, a project represents a worthy use of scarce resources and should be accepted for investment. When the discounted present value of expected future cash flows is less than the cost of investment, a project represents an inappropriate use of scarce resources and should be rejected. An effective capital budgeting decision rule must also lead to a consistent ranking of projects from most to least desirable and should be easy to apply.

NET PRESENT VALUE ANALYSIS

Net Present Value (*NPV*)
Current-dollar difference between marginal revenues and marginal costs.

Perhaps the most commonly employed method for long-term investment project evaluation is called **net present value** (*NPV*) analysis. *NPV* analysis is the difference between the marginal revenues and marginal costs for individual investment projects, when both revenues and costs are expressed in present value terms. *NPV* analysis meets all of the criteria for an effective capital budgeting decision rule cited previously. As a result, it is the most routinely applied capital budgeting decision rule. However, the *NPV* method is only one of four capital budgeting decision rules that might be encountered in practice. Other techniques that are sometimes used to rank capital investment projects include the profitability index or benefit/cost ratio method, the internal rate of return approach, and the payback period. Each of these alternative capital budgeting decision rules, with the possible exception of the payback period, incorporates the essential features of *NPV* analysis and can be used to provide useful information on the desirability of individual projects. A comparison across methods is useful.

NPV analysis is based on the timing and magnitude of cash inflows and outflows, since traditional accounting data can obscure differences between cash and noncash expenses and revenues, tax considerations, and so on. *NPV* analysis is commonly used by managers to correctly employ marginal analysis in the capital budgeting process. To see

NPV analysis as a reflection of marginal analysis and the value-maximization theory of the firm, recall from Chapter 2 the basic valuation model:

$$
\begin{aligned}
Value &= \sum_{t=1}^{N} \frac{\pi_t}{(1 + k)^t} \\
&= \sum_{t=1}^{N} \frac{Total\ Revenue_t - Total\ Cost_t}{(1 + k)^t} \\
&= \sum_{t=1}^{N} \frac{Net\ Cash\ Flow_t}{(1 + k)^t}.
\end{aligned}
\qquad \textbf{(15.2)}
$$

In this equation, *Net Cash Flow_t* represents the firm's total after-tax profit plus noncash expenses such as depreciation; k, which is based on an appraisal of the firm's overall riskiness, represents the average cost of capital to the firm. The value of the firm is simply the discounted present value of the difference between total cash inflows and total cash outflows. Any investment project is desirable if it increases the firm's net present value, and it is undesirable if accepting it causes the firm's net present value to decrease.

  The use of net present value analysis in capital budgeting involves the application of the present value model described in Equation 15.2 to individual projects rather than to the firm as a whole. The procedure starts with an estimation of the expected net cash flows. Depending on the nature of the project, these estimates will have a greater or lesser degree of risk. For example, the benefits from replacing a piece of equipment used to produce a stable, established product can be estimated more accurately than those from an investment in equipment to produce a new and untried product. Next, the expected cost or investment outlay of the project must be estimated. This cost estimate will be quite accurate for purchased equipment, since cost equals the invoice price plus delivery and installation charges. Cost estimates for other kinds of projects may be highly uncertain or speculative. The next step involves the determination of an appropriate discount rate, or **cost of capital,** for the project. A high discount rate is used for high-risk projects, and a low discount rate is used for low-risk projects. The cost of capital is considered in detail later in this chapter, but for now it may be thought of as being determined by the riskiness of the project—that is, by the uncertainty of the expected cash flows and the investment outlay. Finally, the present value of expected cash outflows must be subtracted from the present value of expected cash inflows to determine the net present value of the project. If *NPV* > 0, the project should be accepted. If *NPV* < 0, the project should be rejected. In equation form, the net present value of an individual project can be written as follows:

Cost of Capital
Discount rate.

$$
NPV_t = \sum_{t=1}^{N} \frac{E(CF_{it})}{(1 + k_i)^t} - \sum_{t=1}^{N} \frac{C_{it}}{(1 + k_i)^t},
\qquad \textbf{(15.3)}
$$

where NPV_i is the *NPV* of the ith project, $E(CF_{it})$ represents the expected cash inflows of the ith project in the tth year, k_i is the risk-adjusted discount rate applicable to the ith project, and C_i is the project's investment cost or cash outflow.

Table 15.4			CONSOLIDATED END-OF-YEAR NET CASH FLOW ANALYSIS FOR NEW PLANT INVESTMENT PROJECT EXAMPLE		
YEAR (1)	NET NOMINAL CASH FLOWS (2)	CUMULATIVE NET NOMINAL CASH FLOWS (3)	PRESENT-VALUE INTEREST FACTOR (*PVIF*) AT 15% (4)	NET DISCOUNTED CASH FLOWS (5) = (2) × (4)	CUMULATIVE NET DISCOUNTED CASH FLOWS (6)
0	($1,200,000)	($1,200,000)	1.0000	($1,200,000)	($1,200,000)
1	(4,000,000)	(5,200,000)	0.8696	(3,478,261)	(4,678,261)
2	(20,600,000)	(25,800,000)	0.7561	(15,576,560)	(20,254,820)
3	7,202,000	(18,598,000)	0.6575	4,735,432	(15,519,389)
4	8,111,000	(10,487,000)	0.5718	4,637,491	(10,881,898)
5	7,996,720	(2,490,280)	0.4972	3,975,783	(6,906,115)
6	8,143,123	5,652,843	0.4323	3,520,497	(3,385,618)
7	8,554,360	14,207,203	0.3759	3,215,901	(169,717)
8	24,172,517	38,379,720	0.3269	7,902,039	7,732,321
Sum	$38,379,720			$7,732,321	

Note: Negative net cash flows represent net cash outlays and are shown within parentheses.

To illustrate the *NPV* method, consider the SVCC capital investment project discussed earlier. Table 15.4 shows net cash flows per year over the entire eight-year planning period in nominal dollars, as well as in dollars discounted using the firm's 15% cost of capital. Overall, the net cash flow earned on the project expressed in nominal dollars is $38,379,720. This amount is the sum of Column 2 and is equal to the last entry in Column 3, which shows the culmination of net cash flows over the life of the project. Net nominal cash flow is a misleading measure of the attractiveness of the project, however, since cash outlays necessary to fund the project must be made substantially before cash inflows are realized. A much more relevant measure of the attractiveness of this project is net cash flow expressed in present-value terms, where each dollar of cash outflow and inflow is converted on a common current-dollar basis. In Column 5, net nominal cash flows from Column 2 are multiplied by present-value interest factors from Column 4 that reflect a 15% cost of capital assumption. These present value interest factors are used to convert the nominal dollar outlays and returns from various periods on a common present-value basis.

The *NPV* for this investment project is given by the cumulative net discounted cash flow of $7,732,321 earned over the entire life of the project. This amount is given at the base of Column 5 and is the sum of net discounted cash flows over the life of the project. Note also that this amount is given as the last entry in Column 6, because it reflects the cumulative net discounted cash flow earned by the end of the project, Year 8. Alternatively, *NPV* is simply the difference between the $27,987,141 present value of cash inflows from Column 5, Year 3 through Year 8, minus the $20,254,820 present value of cash outflows from Column 5, Year 0 through 2. In equation form, the *NPV* for this project is calculated as follows:

$$NPV = PV \text{ of Cash Inflows} - PV \text{ of Cash Outflows}$$

$$= \$27,987,141 - \$20,254,820 \qquad \textbf{(15.4)}$$

$$= \$7,732,321.$$

Because dollar inflows received in the future are worth less than necessary dollar outlays at the beginning of the project, the *NPV* for the project is much less than the $38,379,720 received in net nominal cash flows (see Columns 2 and 3). This divergence between nominal and discounted cash flow figures reflects the time value of money. In present-value terms, the difference between the incremental costs and incremental revenues derived from this project is $7,732,321. This is a desirable project that if undertaken would increase the value of the firm by this amount.

Firms typically make investments in projects showing positive net present values, reject those with negative net present values, and choose between mutually exclusive investments on the basis of higher net present values. For many capital budgeting problems, the use of the *NPV* method is far more complex than the preceding description suggests. The capital budgeting problem may require analysis of mutually exclusive projects with different expected lives or with substantially different initial costs. A complication also arises when the size of the firm's capital budget is limited. Under these conditions, a variant of the simple *NPV* is used to select projects that maximize the value of the firm.

PROFITABILITY INDEX OR BENEFIT/COST RATIO ANALYSIS

Although individual projects might promise relatively attractive yields, combining them can create unforeseen difficulties. Undertaking a large number of projects simultaneously can require a very fast rate of expansion. Additional personnel requirements and organizational problems can arise that diminish overall rates of return. At some point in the capital budgeting process, management must decide what total volume of favorable projects the firm can successfully undertake without significantly reducing projected returns. Another reason for limiting the capital budget at some firms is the reluctance or inability to obtain external financing by issuing debt or selling stock. For example, considering the plight of firms with substantial amounts of debt during economic recession, management may simply refuse to use high levels of debt financing. Such capital rationing complicates the capital budgeting process and requires more complex tools of analysis.

A variant of *NPV* analysis that is often used in complex capital budgeting situations is called the **profitability index** (*PI*), or the benefit/cost ratio method. The profitability index is calculated as follows:

Profitability Index (*PI*)
Benefit/cost ratio.

$$PI = \frac{PV \text{ of Cash Inflows}}{PV \text{ of Cash Outflows}} = \frac{\sum_{t=1}^{N} [E(CF_{it})/(1 + k_i)^t]}{\sum_{t=1}^{N} [C_{it}/(1 + k_i)^t]} \qquad \textbf{(15.5)}$$

The *PI* shows the *relative* profitability of any project, or the present value of benefits per dollar of cost.

In the SVCC example described in Table 15.4, *NPV* > 0 implies a desirable investment project and *PI* > 1. To see that this is indeed the case, we can use the profitability index formula, given in Equation 15.5, and the present value of cash inflows and outflows from the project, given in Equation 15.4. The profitability index for the SVCC project is

$$PI = \frac{PV \ of \ Cash \ Inflows}{PV \ of \ Outflows}$$

$$= \frac{\$27,987,141}{\$20,254,820}$$

$$= 1.38.$$

This means that the SVCC capital investment project returns $1.38 in cash inflows for each dollar of cash outflow, when both figures are expressed in present-value terms.

In *PI* analysis, a project with *PI* > 1 should be accepted and a project with *PI* < 1 should be rejected. Projects will be accepted provided that they return more than a dollar of discounted benefits for each dollar of cost. Thus, the *PI* and *NPV* methods always indicate the same accept/reject decisions for independent projects, since *PI* > 1 implies *NPV* > 0 and *PI* < 1 implies *NPV* < 0. However, for alternative projects of unequal size, *PI* and *NPV* criteria can give different project rankings. This can sometimes cause problems when mutually exclusive projects are being evaluated. Before investigating the source of such conflicts, however, it is worthwhile to introduce two additional capital budgeting decision rules.

INTERNAL RATE OF RETURN ANALYSIS

Internal Rate of Return (IRR)
Discount rate that equates present value of cash inflows and outflows.

The **internal rate of return** (*IRR*) is the interest or discount rate that equates the present value of the future receipts of a project to the initial cost or outlay. The equation for calculating the internal rate of return is simply the *NPV* formula set equal to zero:

$$NPV_i = 0 = \sum_{t=1}^{N} \frac{E(CF_{it})}{(1 + k_i^*)^t} - \sum_{t=1}^{N} \frac{C_{it}}{(1 + k_i^*)^t}. \qquad (15.6)$$

Here the equation is solved for the discount rate, k^*_i, that produces a zero net present value or causes the sum of the discounted future receipts to equal the initial cost. That discount rate is the internal rate of return earned by the project.

Because the net present value equation is complex, it is difficult to solve for the actual internal rate of return on an investment without a computer or sophisticated calculator. For this reason, trial and error is sometimes employed. One begins by arbitrarily selecting a discount rate. If it yields a positive *NPV*, the internal rate of return must be greater than the interest or discount rate used, and another higher rate is tried. If the chosen rate yields a negative *NPV*, the internal rate of return on the project is lower than the discount rate, and the *NPV* calculation must be repeated using a lower discount rate.

This process of changing the discount rate and recalculating the net present value continues until the discounted present value of the future cash flows equals the initial cost. The interest rate that brings about this equality is the yield, or internal rate of return on the project.

Using trial and error, an electronic financial calculator, or a spreadsheet software program such as *Lotus 1-2-3* or *Microsoft Excel,* the internal rate of return for the SVCC investment project is *IRR* = 25.1%. Since this *IRR* exceeds the 15% cost of capital, the project is attractive and should be undertaken. In general, internal rate of return analysis suggests that projects should be accepted when the *IRR* > k and rejected when the *IRR* < k. When the *IRR* > k, the marginal rate of return earned on the project exceeds the marginal cost of capital. As in the case of projects with an *NPV* > 0 and *PI* > 1, the acceptance of all investment projects with *IRR* > k will lead management to maximize the value of the firm. In instances in which capital is scarce and only a limited number of desirable projects can be undertaken at one point in time, the *IRR* can be used to derive a rank ordering of projects from most desirable to least desirable. Like a rank ordering of all *NPV* > 0 projects from highest to lowest *PI*s, a rank ordering of potential investment projects from highest to lowest *IRR*s allows managers to effectively employ scarce funds.

PAYBACK PERIOD ANALYSIS

Payback Period
Number of years required to recover initial investment.

The **payback period** is the expected number of years of operation required to recover an initial investment. When project cash flows are discounted using an appropriate cost of capital, the discounted payback period is the expected number of years required to recover the initial investment from discounted net cash flows. Payback period calculation is quick and easy using actual or discounted net cash flows. In equation form, the payback period is

$$Payback\ Period = Number\ of\ Years\ to\ Recover\ Investment. \qquad (15.7)$$

The payback period can be thought of as a breakeven time period. The shorter the payback period, the more desirable the investment project. The longer the payback period, the less desirable the investment project.

To illustrate, consider the SVCC capital investment project discussed earlier. Table 15.4 shows net cash flows per year over the entire eight-year planning period in nominal dollars, as well as in dollars discounted using the firm's 15% cost of capital. In nominal dollars, the total amount of investment is $25.8 million, which is the sum of the dollar outlays given in the first three rows of Column 2. As shown in the third row of Column 3, a negative $25.8 million is also the cumulative value of the nominal net cash flow as of the end of Year 2, just prior to the beginning of plant operations. When the nominal cash outlay of $25.8 million is discounted using the firm's 15% cost of capital, the present value of the investment cash outlay is $20,254,820, the sum of discounted cash outlays given in the first three rows of Column 5. As shown in the third row of Column 6, a negative $20,254,820 is also the cumulative value of net discounted cash flow as of the end of Year 2, just prior to the beginning of plant operations.

Based on nominal dollar cash outflows and inflows, the payback period is completed between the end of Year 5, when the cumulative net nominal cash flow is a

Is the Sun Setting on Japan's Vaunted MOF?

MANAGERIAL APPLICATION
15.2

More and more these days, Japan's Ministry of Finance (MOF) is castigated by Japanese politicians, bankers, and foreign governments. Long the power center of Japanese government, the MOF finds itself under attack for manipulating the Japanese economy, stock market, real estate values, and surpluses with trade partners. At risk is not only its bureaucratic authority over policymaking, but the whole concept of the managed Japanese economy. MOF officials argue that relinquishing control over the economy would imperil full employment and perhaps cause another stock market crash in Japan. However, continued trade surpluses with Canada, the U.S., and other trade partners will clearly push up the Japanese currency, spur ongoing trade friction, and stifle worldwide economic growth.

The aura of infallibility that the MOF cultivated during Japan's postwar "economic miracle" has all but disappeared in the gloom of Japan's deepening recession of the late-1990s. No longer can supporters point to a continuing series of economic triumphs as justification for the MOF's ongoing existence. Instead, the ministry has made a number of highly visible and foolish public errors by failing to deal effectively with stock manipulation scandals, and by botching privatization plans for highly visible government monopolies. It also alienated Japan's biggest banks and brokerages throughout a series of embarrassing scandals. Politicians whom the MOF used to dominate now openly challenge the ministry's role in Japanese government. Their goal is to make economic policy themselves, a radical concept in Japan. If they succeed, consequences for the MOF, Japan, and Japan's trading partners will be momentous. The new antibureaucracy campaign in Japan seeks to end the practice of having economic policy decisions percolate up through bureaucratic consensus with no one taking responsibility. In a global era of expanding democracy and free-market reforms, Japanese critics of the MOF argue that bureaucrats should no longer be able to feel they can do things on their own without the oversight of elected representatives.

While the MOF remains powerful, winds of change are blowing strongly. The entire bureaucratic community in Japan has been outraged by recent proposals that cut to the heart of the MOF's power. Elected party leaders in Japan have suggested that politically appointed deputy and vice ministers take charge of the ministries, and recommended barring bureaucrats from answering questions in the Diet, Japan's parliament. Many people, including charismatic Japanese politician Ryutaro Hashimoto, think that the new beat-the-bureaucrats crusade will make deep inroads by the end of the decade. Change is inevitable if the Japanese government is to better respond to growing popular dissatisfaction with high consumer prices and depressed employment opportunities. Invigorated trade partners are also apt to seek continuing change in terms of greater access to Japanese markets. The breakup of so-called collusion among politicians, bureaucrats, and industrialists may be an inevitable byproduct of growing free-market reforms on a worldwide basis.

Clearly the process of economic change in Japan is just in the beginning; it may be years before fundamental reforms take hold. It is also important for foreigners to realize that none of the current upheaval means that Japan is suddenly going to become integrated with the rest of the world. Many Japanese politicians and business leaders remain fervent nationalists who believe that Japan continues to work superbly as a society simply because it is Japanese. It is a common view that the extent to which the country becomes less Japanese, or more integrated globally, it can no longer be Japan. In a real sense, the MOF sees itself as guardian of Japan's conservative heritage. Thus, while there is a clear move under way in Japan to make the MOF more accountable, any severe undermining of its authority seems years away, at best. While Japanese bureaucracy, elected officials, and industry are strongly motivated to change, they remain even more tightly bound to Japanese tradition and culture.

See: David P. Hamilton and Norihiko Shirouzu, "A Conservative Pushes For Vast Changes in Japanese Economy, *The Wall Street Journal,* January 29, 1997, A1, A6.

negative $2,490,280, and the end of Year 6, when the cumulative net nominal cash flow is a positive $5,652,843. Using nominal dollars, the payback period of years is calculated as

$$Nominal\ Payback\ Period = 5.00 + \$2,490,280/\$8,143,123$$

$$= 5.30\ years.$$

Based on cash outflows and inflows discounted using the firm's 15% cost of capital, the payback period is completed between the end of Year 7, when the cumulative net discounted cash flow is a negative $169,717, and the end of Year 8, when the cumulative net discounted cash flow is a positive $7,732,321. Using discounted net cash flows, the payback period of years is calculated as

$$Discounted\ Payback\ Period = 7.00 + \$169,717/\$7,902,039$$

$$= 7.02\ years.$$

Of course, these payback period calculations are based on the typical assumption that cash inflows are received continuously throughout the operating period. If cash inflows are received only at the end of the operating period, then the nominal payback period in this example would be six years and the discounted payback period would be eight years. The exact length of the payback period depends on underlying assumptions concerning the pattern of cash inflows.

Note that the payback period is a breakeven calculation in that if cash flows come in at the expected rate until the payback year, the project will break even in an accounting sense. However, the nominal payback period does not take into account the cost of capital; the cost of the debt and equity used to undertake the project is not reflected in the cash flow calculation. The discounted payback period does take account of capital costs—it shows the breakeven year after covering debt and equity costs. Both payback methods have the serious deficiency of not taking into account any cash flows beyond the payback year. Other capital budgeting decision rules are more likely to lead to better project rankings and selections. The discounted payback period, however, does provide useful information about how long funds will be tied up in a project. The shorter the discounted payback period, the greater the project's liquidity. Also, cash flows expected in the distant future are generally regarded as riskier than near-term cash flows. Therefore, the discounted payback period is a useful but rough measure of liquidity and project risk.

Choosing Among Alternative Projects

The preceding section shows how application of the net present value method in the capital budgeting process permits a rank ordering of investment projects from most attractive to least attractive. An investment project is attractive and should be pursued as long as the discounted net present value of cash inflows is greater than the discounted net present value of the investment requirement, or net cash outlay. Because the attractiveness of individual projects increases with the magnitude of this difference, high *NPV* projects are inherently more appealing and are preferred to low *NPV* projects. Any investment project that is incapable of generating sufficient cash inflows to cover necessary cash outlays, when both are expressed on a present-value basis, should not be undertaken. In the case of a project with *NPV* = 0, project acceptance would neither increase nor decrease the value of the firm. Management would be indifferent to pursuing such a project. *NPV* analysis represents a practical application of the marginal concept, in which the marginal revenues and marginal costs of investment projects are considered on a present-value basis. Use of the *NPV* technique in the evaluation of alternative investment projects allows managers to apply the principles of marginal analysis in a simple and clear manner. The widespread practical use of the *NPV* technique also lends support to the view of value maximization as the prime objective pursued by managers in the capital budgeting process.

THE DECISION RULE CONFLICT PROBLEM

Just as acceptance of *NPV* > 0 projects will enhance the value of the firm, so too will acceptance of projects for which the *PI* > 1 and the *IRR* > k. Acceptance of projects for which *NPV* < 0, *PI* < 1, or *IRR* < k would be unwise and would reduce the value of the firm. Because each of these project evaluation techniques shares a common focus on the present value of net cash inflows and outflows, these techniques display a high degree of consistency in terms of the project accept/reject decision. This high degree of consistency might even lead one to question the usefulness of having these alternative ways of project evaluation when only one, the *NPV* method, seems sufficient for decision-making purposes. However, even though these alternative capital budgeting decision rules will consistently lead to the same project accept/reject decision, they involve important differences in terms of project ranking. Projects ranked most favorably using the *NPV* method may appear less so when analyzed using the *PI* or *IRR* methods. Projects ranked most favorably using the *PI* or *IRR* methods may appear less so when analyzed using the *NPV* technique. The purpose of this section is to identify the reasons for these differences in project rankings and to illustrate how such differences can be dealt with.

If the application of a capital budgeting decision rule is to consistently lead to correct investment decisions, it must consider the time value of money in the evaluation of all cash flows and must rank projects according to their ultimate impact on the value of the firm. *NPV*, *PI*, and *IRR* methods satisfy both criteria, and each can be used to value and rank capital budgeting projects. The payback method does not meet both of the preceding criteria and should be used only as a complement to the other techniques. However, each of the *NPV*, *PI*, and *IRR* methods incorporate certain assumptions that can and do affect project rankings. Understanding the sources of these differences and learning how to deal with them is an important part of knowing how to correctly evaluate alternative investment projects.

REASONS FOR DECISION RULE CONFLICT

As discussed earlier, *NPV* is the difference between the marginal revenues and marginal costs of an individual investment project, when both revenues and costs are expressed in present-value terms. *NPV* measures the relative attractiveness of alternative investment projects by the discounted dollar difference between revenues and costs. *NPV* is an *absolute* measure of the attractiveness of a given investment project. Conversely, the *PI* reflects the difference between the marginal revenues and marginal costs of an individual project in ratio form. The *PI* is the ratio of the discounted present value of cash inflows divided by the discounted present value of cash outflows. *PI* is a *relative* measure of project attractiveness. It follows that application of the *NPV* method leads to the highest ranking for large profitable projects. Use of the *PI* method leads to the highest ranking for projects that return the greatest amount of cash inflow per dollar of outflow, regardless of project size. At times, application of the *NPV* method can create a bias for larger as opposed to smaller projects—a problem when all favorable *NPV* > 0 projects cannot be pursued. When capital is scarce, application of the *PI* method has the potential to create a better project mix for the firm's overall investment portfolio.

Both *NPV* and *PI* methods differ from the *IRR* technique in terms of their underlying assumptions regarding the reinvestment of cash flows during the life of the project. In the *NPV* and *PI* methods, excess cash flows generated over the life of the project are "reinvested" at the firm's cost of capital. In the *IRR* method, excess cash flows are reinvested at the *IRR*. For especially attractive investment projects that generate an exceptionally high rate of return, the *IRR* can actually overstate project attractiveness because reinvestment of excess cash flows at a similarly high *IRR* is not possible. When reinvestment at the project-specific *IRR* is not possible, the *IRR* method must be adapted to take into account the lower rate of return that can actually be earned on excess cash flows generated over the life of individual projects. Otherwise, use of the *NPV* or *PI* methods is preferable.

THE RANKING REVERSAL PROBLEM

A further and more serious conflict can arise between *NPV* and *IRR* methods when projects differ significantly in terms of the magnitude and timing of cash flows. When the size or pattern of alternative project cash flows differs greatly, each project's *NPV* can react quite differently to changes in the discount rate. As a result, changes in the appropriate discount rate can sometimes lead to reversals in project rankings.

To illustrate the potential for conflict between *NPV* and *IRR* rankings and the possibility of ranking reversals, Table 15.5 shows a further development of the SVCC plant investment project example. Assume that the company is considering the original new plant investment project in light of an alternative proposal to buy and remodel an existing plant. Old plant and equipment can be purchased for an initial cash outlay of $11.5 million and can be remodeled at a cost of $2 million per year over the next two years. As before, a net working capital investment of $6.6 million will be required just prior to opening the remodeled production facility. For simplicity, assume that after Year 2, all cash inflows and outflows are the same for the remodeled and new plant facilities.

Note that the new plant proposal involves an initial nominal cash outlay of $25.8 million, whereas the remodeled plant alternative involves a nominal cash outlay of $22.1 million. In addition to this difference in project size, the two investment alternatives differ in terms of the timing of cash flows. The new plant alternative involves a larger but later commitment of funds. To see the implications of these differences,

Table 15.5	A COMPARISON OF THE "BUILD NEW PLANT" VERSUS "REMODEL OLD PLANT" INVESTMENT PROJECT EXAMPLE USING ALTERNATIVE CAPITAL BUDGETING DECISION RULES

A. INVESTMENT PROJECT CASH FLOW PROJECTIONS

YEAR	BUILD NEW PLANT PROJECT NEW NOMINAL CASH FLOWS	REMODEL OLD PLANT PROJECT NET NOMINAL CASH FLOWS
0	($1,200,000)	($11,500,000)
1	(4,000,000)	(2,000,000)
2	(20,600,000)	(8,600,000)
3	7,202,000	7,202,000
4	8,111,000	8,111,000
5	7,996,720	7,996,720
6	8,143,123	8,143,123
7	8,554,360	8,554,360
8	24,172,517	24,172,517
Sum	($38,379,720)	$42,079,720
IRR	25.06%	23.57%

Note: Negative net cash flows represent net cash outlays and are shown within parentheses.

B. EVALUATION USING ALTERNATIVE CAPITAL BUDGETING DECISION RULES

	BUILD NEW	REMODEL OLD
0% Discount Rate:		
PV of cash inflows	$64,179,720	$64,179,720
PV of cash outflows	($25,800,000)	($22,100,000)
NPV	$38,379,720	$42,079,720
PI	2.49	2.90
Discounted payback period	5.30	4.85
15% Discount Rate:		
PV of cash inflows	$27,987,142	$27,987,142
PV of cash outflows	($20,254,820)	($19,741,966)
NPV	$7,732,321	$8,245,176
PI	1.38	1.42
Discounted payback period	7.02	6.89
25% Discount Rate:		
PV of cash inflows	$17,614,180	$17,614,180
PV of cash outflows	($17,584,000)	($18,604,000)
NPV	$30.180	($989,820)
PI	1.00	0.95
Discounted payback period	7.99	—

Net Present Value Profile
Graph relating *NPV* to the discount rate.

notice how the "remodel old plant" alternative is preferred at and below the firm's 15% cost of capital using *NPV* and *PI* methods, even though the *IRR* of 25.06% for the new plant project exceeds the *IRR* of 23.57% for the "remodel old plant" alternative. Also troubling is the fact that the relative ranking of these projects according to *NPV* and *PI* methods is reversed at higher discount rates. Notice how the "build new plant" alternative is preferred using *NPV* and *PI* techniques when a 25% discount rate is employed.

Figure 15.1 displays the potential conflict between *NPV, PI,* and *IRR* project rankings at various interest rates by showing the effect of discount rate changes on the *NPV* of each alternative investment project. This **net present value profile** relates the *NPV* for each project to the discount rate used in the *NPV* calculation. Using a $k = 0\%$ discount rate, the *NPV* for the "build new plant" investment project is $38.4 million, and it is $42.1 million for the "remodel old plant" alternative. These *NPV* values correspond to the difference between nominal dollar cash inflows and outflows for each project and also coincide with *NPV* line *Y*-axis intercepts of $38.4 million for the "build new plant" project and $42.1 million for the "remodel old plant" alternative. The *X*-axis intercept for each curve occurs at the discount rate where $NPV = 0$ for each project. Since $NPV = 0$ when the discount rate is set equal to the *IRR*, or when $IRR = k$, the *X*-axis

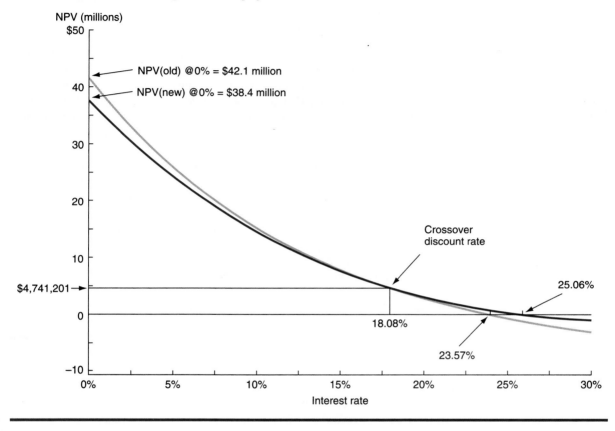

Figure 15.1

NPV PROFILES FOR THE "BUILD NEW PLANT" VERSUS "REMODEL OLD PLANT" INVESTMENT PROJECT ALTERNATIVES

Each profile relates project *NPV* to the discount rate used in the *NPV* calculation.

NPV (millions)

NPV(old) @0% = $42.1 million

NPV(new) @0% = $38.4 million

Crossover discount rate

$4,741,201

25.06%

18.08%

23.57%

Interest rate

intercept for the "build new plant" alternative is at the *IRR* = 25.06% level, and it is at the *IRR* = 23.57% level for the "remodel old plant" alternative.

Figure 15.1 illustrates how ranking reversals can occur at various *NPV* discount rates. Given higher nominal dollar returns and, therefore, a higher *Y*-axis intercept, the "remodel old plant" alternative is preferred when very low discount rates are used in the *NPV* calculation. Given a higher *IRR* and, therefore, a higher *X*-axis intercept, the "build new plant" alternative is preferred when very high discount rates are used in the calculation of *NPV*. Between very high and low discount rates is an interest rate where *NPV* is the same for both projects. A reversal of project rankings occurs at the **crossover discount rate,** where *NPV* is equal for two or more investment alternatives. In this example, the "remodel old plant" alternative is preferred when using the *NPV* criterion and a discount rate k that is less than the crossover discount rate. The "build new plant" alternative is preferred when using the *NPV* criterion and a discount rate k that is

Crossover Discount Rate
Interest factor that equates *NPV* for two or more investments.

greater than the crossover discount rate. This ranking reversal problem is typical of situations in which investment projects differ greatly in terms of their underlying *NPV* profiles. Hence, a potentially troubling conflict exists between *NPV*, *PI*, and *IRR* methods.

MAKING THE CORRECT INVESTMENT DECISION

The ranking reversal problem and suggested conflict between *NPV*, *PI*, and *IRR* methods are actually much less serious than one might imagine. Many comparisons between alternative investment projects involve neither crossing *NPV* profiles nor crossover discount rates as shown in Figure 15.1. Some other project comparisons involve crossover discount rates that are either too low or too high to affect project rankings at the current cost of capital. As a result, there is often no meaningful conflict between *NPV* and *IRR* project rankings.

When crossover discount rates are relevant, they can be easily calculated as the *IRR* of the cash-flow *difference* between two investment alternatives. To see that this is indeed the case, consider how cash flows differ between each of the two plant investment alternatives considered previously. The "build new plant" alternative involves a smaller initial cash outflow of $1.2 million versus $11.5 million, a $10.3 million saving, but it requires additional outlays of $2 million at the end of Year 1 plus an additional $12 million at the end of Year 2. Except for these differences, the timing and magnitude of cash inflows and outflows from the two projects are identical. The *IRR* for the cash flow difference between two investment alternatives exactly balances the present-value cost of higher cash outflows with the present-value benefit of higher cash inflows. At this *IRR*, the cash flow difference between the two investment alternatives has an *NPV* equal to zero. When k is less than this crossover *IRR*, the investment project with the greater nominal dollar return will have a larger *NPV* and will tend to be favored. In the present example, this is the "remodel old plant" alternative. When k is greater than the crossover *IRR*, the project with an earlier cash flow pattern will have the larger *NPV* and be favored. In the current example, this is the "build new plant" alternative. When k equals the crossover *IRR*, the cash flow difference between projects has an $NPV = 0$, and each project has exactly the same *NPV*.

Once an economically relevant crossover discount rate has been determined, management must decide whether to rely on *NPV* or *IRR* decision rules in the resolution of the ranking reversal problem. Logic suggests that the *NPV* ranking should dominate because that method will result in a value-maximizing selection of projects. In most situations, it is also more realistic to assume reinvestment of excess cash flows during the life of a project at the current cost of capital k. This again favors *NPV* over *IRR* rankings. As a result, conflicts between *NPV* and *IRR* project rankings are usually resolved in favor of the *NPV* rank order.

Finally, given the size-based conflict between the *NPV* and *PI* methods, which one should be relied on in the ranking of potential investment projects? Alternatively stated: Is it better to use the net present value approach on an absolute basis (*NPV*) or on a relative basis (*PI*)? For a firm with substantial investment resources and a goal of maximizing shareholder wealth, the *NPV* method is better. For a firm with limited resources, the *PI* approach allocates scarce resources to the projects with the greatest relative effect on value. Using the *PI* method, projects are evaluated on the basis of their *NPV* per dollar of investment, avoiding a possible bias toward larger projects. In some cases, this leads to a better combination of investment projects and higher firm value. The *PI*, or benefit/cost ratio, approach has also proved to be a useful tool in public-sector decision making, where allocating scarce public resources among competing projects is a typical problem.

As seen in the evaluation of alternative capital budgeting decision rules, the attractiveness of investment projects varies significantly depending on the interest rate used to discount future cash flows. Determination of the correct discount rate is a vitally important aspect of the capital budgeting process. This important issue is the subject of the next section.

The Cost of Capital

If firms typically considered projects one by one and raised investment funds for each project separately, calculation of a suitable discount rate would be easy. The correct discount rate to employ for each investment project would simply be the marginal cost of capital for that project. However, determination of the correct discount rate for individual projects is seldom that straightforward. Firms rarely consider individual projects in isolation but instead tend to evaluate *portfolios* of potential investment projects to be funded from an ongoing stream of new capital funds generated by retained earnings and new capital-raising efforts. New projects are funded by a mix of debt and equity financing, and each debt and equity component of new capital can be expected to have different costs. Calculation of the correct discount rate for any given potential investment project typically involves weighing the relative importance of each component cost of new financing.

THE COMPONENT COST OF DEBT FINANCING

Component Cost of Debt
Interest rate investors require on debt, adjusted for taxes.

The **component cost of debt** is the interest rate that investors require on debt, adjusted for taxes. If a firm borrows $100,000 for one year at 10% interest, the before-tax cost is $10,000 and the before-tax interest rate is 10%. However, interest payments on debt are deductible for income tax purposes. It is necessary to account for this tax deductibility by adjusting the cost of debt to an after-tax basis. The deductibility of interest payments means, in effect, that the government pays part of a firm's interest charges. This reduces the firm's cost of debt financing. The after-tax component cost of debt is given by the following expression:

$$k_d = (Interest\ Rate) \times (1.0 - Tax\ Rate). \qquad \textbf{(15.8)}$$

Assuming that the firm's marginal federal-plus-state tax rate is 40%, the after-tax cost of debt will be 60% (= 1.0 − 0.4) of the nominal interest rate.

The relevant component cost of debt applies only to *new* debt, not to the interest on old or previously outstanding debt. In other words, the cost of new debt financing is what is relevant in terms of the *marginal cost of debt.* It is irrelevant that the firm borrowed at higher or lower rates in the past.

THE COMPONENT COST OF EQUITY FINANCING

Component Cost of Equity
Rate of return stockholders require on common stock.

Risk-Free Rate of Return (R_F)
Investor reward for postponing consumption.

Risk Premium (R_P)
Investor reward for risk taking.

The **component cost of equity** is the rate of return stockholders require on common stock. This return includes a compensation to investors for postponing their consumption, plus a return to compensate for risk taking. Therefore, the component cost of equity consists of a **risk-free rate of return,** R_F, plus a **risk premium,** R_P:

$$k_e = R_F + R_P. \qquad (15.9)$$

The risk-free return is typically estimated by the interest rate on short-term U.S. government securities. On a daily basis, these rates of return can be obtained from *The Wall Street Journal* and other sources. Various methods can be used to estimate R_P for different securities. Because dividends paid to stockholders are not deductible for income tax purposes, dividend payments must be made with after-tax dollars. There is no tax adjustment for the component cost of equity capital.

A first method for estimating k_e and R_P is based on the capital asset pricing model, or CAPM. This method assumes that the risk of a stock depends on the sensitivity of its return to changes in the return on all securities. A stock that is twice as risky as the overall market would entail twice the market risk premium; a security that is one-half as risky as the overall market would earn one-half the market risk premium, and so on. In the CAPM approach, the riskiness of a given stock is measured in terms of the variability of its return relative to the variability of returns on all stocks, perhaps as represented by the volatility in the *Standard and Poor's 500 Index*. A firm's **beta coefficient,** β, is a measure of this variability. In a simple regression model, the beta coefficient for an individual firm, β_i, is estimated as

Beta Coefficient
A measure of relative stock-price variability.

$$R_i = \alpha_i + \beta_i R_M + e, \qquad (15.10)$$

where R_i is the weekly or monthly return on a given stock and R_M is a similar return on the market as a whole (e.g., the *Standard and Poor's 500 Index*). A stock with average risk has a beta of 1.0. Low-risk stocks have betas less than 1.0; high-risk stocks have betas greater than 1.0. Although beta estimation is a relatively simple task, managers seldom need to actually run such regressions. Analysts at Merrill Lynch and other leading brokerage houses, as well as investment advisory services such as *The Value Line Investment Survey*, provide beta estimates that can be used for equity capital cost estimation for individual companies and/or operating divisions.

In addition to data on the R_F rate and β_i for a given company, the CAPM approach requires an estimate of the expected rate of return on the market as a whole. This return, k_M, is a relative benchmark for measuring the risk premium on the market. With these three inputs, R_F, β_i, and k_M, the CAPM estimate of the required rate of return on any given stock is

$$k_e = R_F + \beta_i(k_M - R_F), \qquad (15.11)$$

where the value $(k_M - R_F)$ is the market risk premium, or risk premium on an average stock. Multiplying this market risk premium by the index of risk for a particular stock, or β_i, gives the risk premium for that stock.

To illustrate, assume that $R_F = 8\%$, $k_M = 14\%$, and $\beta_i = 0.5$ for a given stock. Remember, $\beta_i = 0.5$ means that a given stock is only one-half as risky as the overall market. Under such circumstances, the stock's required return is

$$k_e = 8 + 0.5(14 - 8) = 8 + 3 = 11\%.$$

If $\beta_i = 1.5$, indicating that a stock is 50% riskier than the average security, then k_e is

$$k_e = 8 + 1.5(14 - 8) = 8 + 9 = 17\%.$$

A second common technique adds a premium of 4% or 5% onto the risk premium paid on a firm's long-term bonds. Using this approach, the total risk premium on equity equals the difference between the yield on the firm's debt and that on risk-free government bonds, *plus* 4% to 5%. For example, if risk-free government bonds yield 8%, and a firm's bonds are priced to yield 10%, the cost of equity, k_e, is

$$k_e = Firm\ Bond\ Rate + 4\%\ to\ 5\%\ Risk\ Premium$$

$$= 10\% + (4\%\ to\ 5\%) = 14\%\ to\ 15\%.$$

Given an 8% return on risk-free government bonds, this implies a total risk premium for equity of 6% to 7%, since:

$$14\%\ to\ 15\% = 8\% + R_p$$

$$R_p = 6\%\ to\ 7\%.$$

Managers who rely on this method often cite historical studies suggesting that the long-term 1900 to 1997 annual risk premium on investments in common stocks is generally 6% to 7% over that earned on government bonds. The primary difficulty with estimating risk premiums from historical returns is that historical returns differ depending on the beginning and ending dates of the estimation period, and past differences in stock and bond returns may not precisely indicate future required risk premiums.

Yet another method for determining the cost of equity is to use a constant growth model. If earnings, dividends, and the stock price all grow at the same rate, then

$$\frac{Required\ Return}{on\ Equity} = Dividend\ Yield + Capital\ Gains$$

$$= \frac{Expected\ Dividend}{Current\ Stock\ Price} + \frac{Expected}{Growth\ Rate}$$

$$= \frac{Dividend}{Price} + \frac{Expected}{Growth\ Rate} \qquad \textbf{(15.12)}$$

$$k_e = \frac{D_1}{P_0} + g.$$

The rationale for this equation is that stockholder returns are derived from dividends and capital gains. If past growth rates in earnings and dividends have been relatively stable, and if investors expect a continuation of past trends, then g may be based on the firm's historic growth rate. However, if the company's growth has been abnormally high or low, either because of its own unique situation or because of general economic conditions, investors cannot project historical growth rate into the future. Security analyst estimates of g must then be relied on. These earnings forecasts are regularly published by *Business Week, Forbes, Value Line,* and other sources and offer a useful proxy for the growth expectations of investors in general. When security analyst growth projections are combined with the dividend yield expected during the coming period, k_e can be estimated as

$$k_e = \frac{D_1}{P_0} + \begin{array}{c} \textit{Growth Rate Projected} \\ \textit{by Security Analysts} \end{array}. \qquad \textbf{(15.13)}$$

In practice, it is often best to use all of these methods and try to arrive at a consensus estimate of the component cost of equity financing.

THE WEIGHTED AVERAGE COST OF CAPITAL

Suppose that the interest rate on new debt is 7.5% and the firm's marginal federal-plus-state income tax rate is 40%. This implies a 4.5% after-tax component cost of debt. Also assume that the firm has decided to finance next year's projects by selling debt. Does this mean that next year's investment projects have a 4.5% cost of capital? The answer is no, at least not usually. In financing a particular set of projects with debt, the firm typically uses up some of its potential for obtaining further low-cost debt financing. As expansion takes place, the firm typically finds it necessary to raise additional high-cost equity to avoid unacceptably high leverage. As a result, the current component cost of debt seldom measures the true long-term opportunity cost of debt financing. To illustrate, suppose that the firm has a current 4.5% cost of debt and a 10% cost of equity. In the first year it borrows heavily, using up its debt capacity in the process, to finance projects yielding 6%. In the second year it has projects available that yield 9%, or substantially above the return on first-year projects, but it cannot accept them because they would have to be financed with 10% equity. To avoid this problem, the firm should be viewed as an ongoing concern, and the cost of capital should be calculated as a weighted average of the various types of funds it uses.

Weighted Average Cost of Capital

The marginal cost of a composite dollar of debt and equity financing.

Optimal Capital Structure

Combination of debt and equity that minimizes the firm's weighted average cost of capital.

The **weighted average cost of capital** is the interest rate necessary to attract additional funds for new capital investment projects. It is the marginal cost of a composite dollar of debt and equity financing. The proper set of weights to employ in computing the weighted average cost of capital is determined by the firm's optimal capital structure. The **optimal capital structure** is the combination of debt and equity financing that minimizes the firm's overall weighted average cost of capital.

In general, the risk to investors is lower on debt and higher on common stock. Risk aversion among investors makes debt the lowest component-cost source of funds and equity the highest component-cost source. However, the firm's risk increases as debt financing grows, because the higher the debt level, the greater the probability that under adverse conditions the firm will not make interest and principal payments. Because interest rates on debt are lower than the expected rate of return (dividends plus capital gains) on common stock, this can cause the weighted average cost of capital to decline with modest amounts of debt financing. More debt means higher financial risk, which offsets this effect to some extent. As a result, the weighted average cost of capital first declines as a firm moves from zero debt to some positive amount of debt, hits a minimum (perhaps over a range rather than at some specific amount of debt), and then rises as an increasing level of debt drives the firm's risk position beyond acceptable levels. Thus, each firm has an optimal amount of debt that minimizes its cost of capital and maximizes its value.

Figure 15.2 shows how the cost of capital changes as the debt ratio increases for a hypothetical industry with about average risk. The average cost of capital figures in the graph are calculated in Table 15.6. In the figure, each dot represents one of the firms in the industry. For example, the dot labeled "one" represents Firm 1, a company with no debt. Because its projects are financed entirely with 10% equity money, Firm 1's average cost of capital is 10%. Firm 2 raises 10% of its capital as debt, and it has a 4.5% after-tax cost of debt and a 10% cost of equity. Firm 3 also has a 4.5% after-tax cost of debt and 10% cost of equity, even though it uses 20% debt. Firm 4 has an 11% cost of equity and a 4.8% after-tax cost of debt. Because it uses 30% debt, a before-tax debt risk premium of 0.5% and an equity risk premium of 1% have been added to account for the additional risk of financial leverage. Notice that the required return on both debt and

Figure 15.2	HYPOTHETICAL COST-OF-CAPITAL SCHEDULES FOR AN INDUSTRY

A U-shaped weighted average cost of capital curve reflects, first, lower capital costs because of the tax benefits of debt financing and, second, increasing capital costs as bankruptcy risk increases for highly leveraged firms.

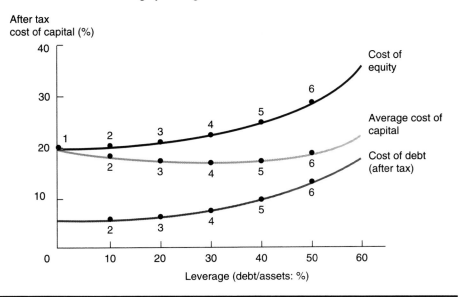

equity rises with increasing leverage for firms 5, 6, and 7. Providers of debt and equity capital typically believe that because of the added risk of financial leverage, they should obtain higher yields on the firm's securities. In this particular industry, the threshold debt ratio that begins to worry creditors is about 20%. Below the 20% debt level, creditors are unconcerned about any risk induced by debt; above 20%, they are aware of higher risks and require compensation in the form of higher expected rates of return.

In Table 15.6, the debt and equity costs of the various firms are averaged on the basis of their respective proportions of the firm's total capital. Firm 1 has a weighted average cost of capital equal to 10%, Firm 2 has a weighted average cost of 9.45%, Firm 3 has a weighted average cost of 8.9%, and Firm 4 has a weighted average cost of 9.14%. These weighted costs, together with those of the other firms in the industry, are plotted in Figure 15.2. Firms with approximately 20% debt in their capital structure have the lowest weighted-average after-tax cost of capital, equal to 8.9%. Accordingly, proper calculation of the cost of capital requires that the cost of equity for a firm in the industry be given a weight of 0.8 and the cost of debt be given a weight of 0.2—the firm's optimal capital structure.

Table 15.6

CALCULATION OF AVERAGE COST OF CAPITAL FOR HYPOTHETICAL FIRMS WITH DIFFERENT DEBT RATIOS

		PERCENTAGE OF TOTAL (1)	COMPONENT COST (2)		WEIGHTED COST $\frac{(1) \times (2)}{100}$ (3)
FIRM 1	DEBT	0	6.0		0.0
	EQUITY	100	20.0		20.00
		100%		AVERAGE COST	20.00%
FIRM 2	DEBT	10	6.0		0.60
	EQUITY	90	20.0		18.00
		100%		AVERAGE COST	18.60%
FIRM 3	DEBT	20	6.0		1.20
	EQUITY	80	20.0		16.00
		100%		AVERAGE COST	17.20%
FIRM 4	DEBT	30	7.0		2.10
	EQUITY	70	21.0		14.70
		100%		AVERAGE COST	16.80%
FIRM 5	DEBT	40	9.0		3.60
	EQUITY	60	22.5		13.50
		100%		AVERAGE COST	17.10%
FIRM 6	DEBT	50	12.0		6.00
	EQUITY	50	24.0		12.00
		100%		AVERAGE COST	18.00%
FIRM 7	DEBT	60	17.0		10.20
	EQUITY	40	27.5		11.00
		100%		AVERAGE COST	21.20%

| *Capital Allocation at Berkshire Hathaway, Inc.* | MANAGERIAL APPLICATION 15.3 |

Warren E. Buffett, then 34 years old, gained control of textile manufacturer Berkshire Hathaway in 1965. Buffett gradually built Berkshire into a conglomerate with a string of property casualty insurance companies, *See's Candies*, the *Buffalo News, World Book Encyclopedia,* and so on. During more than 25 years of Buffett's stewardship, Berkshire's net worth per share has compounded at 24% per year. In an era when median *Fortune 500* companies count themselves lucky to earn half that much, Buffett's accomplishment can only be viewed as amazing—especially for a debt-free company.

In addition to being uniquely capable as an investor and manager, Buffett has the uncommon ability to communicate his insights on management in a disarmingly modest and humorous fashion that is equally important for stock-market investors and experienced business managers. Among the most important do's and don'ts learned by Buffett are the following ten lessons.

- *It is far better to buy a wonderful company at a fair price than a fair company at a wonderful price.* In a difficult business, no sooner is one problem solved than another surfaces. "There is never just one cockroach in the kitchen."
- *When a management with a reputation for brilliance tackles a business with a reputation for bad economics, it is the reputation of the business that remains intact.* According to Buffett, attractive economics include a 20% plus rate of return on capital without leverage or accounting gimmicks, high margins, high cash flow, low capital investment requirements, a lack of government regulation, and strong prospects for continuing growth. "Good jockeys do well on good horses," Buffett says, "but not on broken down old nags."
- *Management does better by avoiding dragons, not slaying them.* Buffett attributes his success to avoiding, rather than solving, tough business problems. As Buffett says, "We have been successful because we concentrated on identifying one-foot hurdles that we could step over rather than because we acquired any ability to clear seven-footers."

- *As if governed by Newton's first law of motion, an institution will resist any change in its current direction.* Too often, the call for necessary change is blithely ignored.
- *Just as work expands to fill available time, corporate projects or acquisitions will materialize to soak up available funds.* Even when plainly called for, dividends or share buybacks are seldom seen as the best use of funds.
- *Any business craving of the leader, however foolish, will be quickly supported by detailed rate-of-return and strategic studies prepared by the troops.* Rationality frequently wilts when the institutional imperative comes into play.
- *The behavior of peer companies, whether they are expanding, acquiring, setting compensation, or whatever, will be mindlessly imitated.* Institutional dynamics often set management on a misguided course.
- *It is not a sin to miss a business opportunity outside one's area of expertise.* By inference, it is a sin to miss opportunities that you are fully capable of understanding.
- *If your actions are sensible, you are certain to get good results.* Leverage moves things along faster, but at the unavoidable risk of anguish or default.
- *Do not join with managers who lack admirable qualities, no matter how attractive the prospects of their business.* When searching for businesses to buy, Buffett looks for first-class businesses accompanied by first-class management.

How well do these capital allocation rules work in practice? Consider that when Buffett gained control of Berkshire Hathaway in 1965 the company had a stock price of $12 per share. By mid-1997, Berkshire's stock price had risen to roughly $37,500 per share, making Buffett's personal stake worth about *$16 billion.* All in all, not too shabby!

See: Warren E. Buffett, *Berkshire Hathaway Annual Report* (Omaha, NE: May, 1997).

The Optimal Capital Budget

A profit-maximizing firm operates at the point where marginal revenue equals marginal cost. In terms of the capital budgeting process, this implies that projects will be accepted as long as they return a cash inflow that is at least equal to the required cash outflow, when both are expressed in present value terms. At the margin, the present value of inflows is exactly equal to the present value of cash outflows. Alternatively, the marginal rate of return earned on the last acceptable investment project is just equal to the firm's relevant marginal cost of capital. The **optimal capital budget** is the funding level required to underwrite a value-maximizing level of new investment. In a complete analysis of the capital budgeting process, it is necessary to show how investment project returns and costs can be integrated to help define the optimal capital budget.

Optimal Capital Budget
Funding required to underwrite a value-maximizing level of new investment.

INVESTMENT OPPORTUNITY SCHEDULE

Investment Opportunity Schedule (*IOS*)
Pattern of returns for all potential investment projects.

The **investment opportunity schedule** (*IOS*) shows the pattern of returns for all of the firm's potential investment projects. Figure 15.3(a) shows an investment opportunity schedule for a hypothetical firm. The horizontal axis measures the dollar amount of investment commitments made during a given year. The vertical axis shows both the rate of return earned on each project and the percentage cost of capital. Each box denotes a given project. Project *A*, for example, calls for an outlay of $3 million and promises a 17% rate of return; Project *B* requires an outlay of $1 million and promises a 16% yield, and so on. The last investment, Project *E*, simply involves buying 9% government bonds. By displaying this stepwise pattern of potential returns on a single graph, the firm's *IOS* is depicted. Figure 15.3(b) generalizes the *IOS* concept to show a smooth pattern of potential returns. The curve labeled *IRR* shows the internal rate of return potential for each project in the portfolio of investment projects available to the firm. It is important to remember that these projects are arrayed from left to right in terms of declining attractiveness as measured by the *IRR* criterion. Therefore, Project *A* is more attractive than Project *E*, and the *IRR* schedule is downward sloping from left to right.

Although the *IOS* provides important input into the capital budget decision-making process, by itself it is insufficient for determining the optimal capital budget. Both the returns *and* costs of potential projects must be considered. To define the optimal capital budget, a means for evaluating the marginal cost of funds must be incorporated into the process.

MARGINAL COST OF CAPITAL

Marginal Cost of Capital
Financing cost of an additional investment project, expressed on a percentage basis.

The **marginal cost of capital** (*MCC*) is the extra financing cost necessary to fund an additional investment project, expressed on a percentage basis. When the firm is considering an entire portfolio of potential investment projects, the marginal cost of capital is the incremental financing cost of a relevant mix of debt and equity financing. Therefore, the *MCC* is typically given by the firm's weighted average cost of capital. As drawn in Figure 15.3(b), the marginal cost of capital is constant at 10% up until the point where the firm

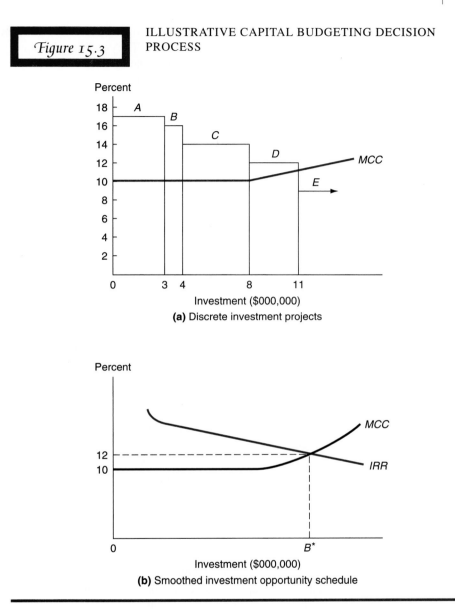

Figure 15.3

ILLUSTRATIVE CAPITAL BUDGETING DECISION
PROCESS

Percent

(a) Discrete investment projects

Percent

(b) Smoothed investment opportunity schedule

has raised an additional $8 million. After this point, capital costs begin to rise. Given these *IOS* and *MCC* schedules, the firm should accept Projects *A* through *D*, obtaining and investing $11 million. Project *E*, the government bond investment alternative, should be rejected. The smooth curves in Figure 15.3(b) indicate that the firm should invest *B** dollars, the optimal capital budget. At this investment level, the marginal cost of capital is 12%, exactly the same as the *IRR* on the marginal investment project.

Whenever the optimal capital budget B^* is determined, the *IRR* always equals the *MCC* for the last project undertaken. The condition that must be met for any budget to be optimal is that *IRR* = *MCC*. This means that the final project accepted for investment is a breakeven project, in that it provides an *IRR* that is just equal to the discount rate. For this project, *NPV* = 0, *PI* = 1, and *IRR* = *k*. By accepting all earlier and more attractive projects, value maximization is assured because the firm has accepted all projects where *NPV* > 0, *PI* > 1, and *IRR* > *k*. This means that the area above the *MCC* schedule but below the *IRR* (or *IOS* schedule) represents the net profit earned on the firm's new investment projects. The *IRR* = *MCC* optimal capital budget condition is completely analogous to the *MR* = *MC* requirement for profit maximization. When *MR* = *MC*, all profitable units have been produced and sold. When *IRR* = *MCC*, all profitable investment projects have likewise been accepted.

THE POSTAUDIT

Postaudit
Careful reconciliation of actual and predicted results.

To assure that an optimal capital budget has indeed been determined, the methods and data employed must often be carefully reexamined at the end of the capital budgeting process. The **postaudit** is a careful examination of actual and predicted results, coupled with a detailed reconciliation of any differences.

One of the most important advantages of the postaudit is that managerial forecasts of revenues and costs tend to improve when decision makers systematically compare projections to actual outcomes. Conscious or subconscious biases can be observed and eliminated, and new forecasting methods can be sought as their need becomes apparent. People simply tend to work better if they know that their actions are being monitored. It is important to remember that businesses are run by people, and people can perform at higher or lower levels of efficiency. When a divisional team has made a forecast in a capital budgeting proposal, it is putting its reputation on the line. Because of the postaudit, these managers have every incentive to make good on their projections. If costs rise above predicted levels or sales fall below expectations, managers in production, sales, and related areas have incentives to strive to bring results into line with earlier forecasts.

Of course, it must be recognized that each element of the cash flow forecast is subject to uncertainty, so a percentage of all projects undertaken by a reasonably aggressive firm will prove to be unsuccessful. This must be considered when appraising the performances of managers who submit capital expenditure requests. Projects also sometimes fail to meet expectations for reasons that no one could realistically have anticipated. For example, wild fluctuations in both oil prices and interest rates during recent years have made long-term forecasts of any sort very difficult. It is also sometimes hard to separate the operating results of one investment from those of contemporaneous projects. If the postaudit process is not used carefully, managers may be reluctant to suggest potentially profitable but risky projects. Because of these difficulties, some firms tend to play down the importance of the postaudit. However, the best-run and most successful organizations in business and government are those that put the greatest emphasis on postaudits. Accordingly, the postaudit process is one of the most important elements in an effective capital budgeting system.

Summary

Long-term investment decisions are among the most important and difficult of those faced by managers in all types of organizations. They are important because substantial amounts of funds are often committed for extended periods. They are difficult because they entail forecasts of uncertain future events that must be relied on heavily. To minimize obvious risks, the process of planning long-term investment decisions must itself become an important concern of management.

- **Capital budgeting** is the process of planning expenditures that generate cash flows expected to extend beyond one year. Several different types of investment projects may be involved, including **replacement projects,** or maintenance of business projects; **cost reduction projects** to replace obsolete plant and equipment; mandatory nonrevenue-producing **safety and environmental projects;** and **expansion projects** to increase the availability of existing products and services.
- In all cases, the focus is on **incremental cash flows,** or the period-by-period changes in net cash flows that are due to the investment project. The most common tool for project valuation is **net present value** (*NPV*) analysis, where *NPV* is the difference between project marginal revenues and marginal costs, when both are expressed in present-value terms. The conversion to present-value terms involves use of an appropriate discount rate, or **cost of capital.**
- Alternative decision rules include the **profitability index** (*PI*), or benefit/cost ratio; **internal rate of return** (*IRR*), or discount rate that equates the present value of receipts and outlays; and the **payback period,** or number of years required to recover the initial investment.
- Managers must be aware of the **net present value profile** for individual projects, a graph that relates the *NPV* for each project to the discount rate used in the *NPV* calculation. A reversal of project rankings occurs at the **crossover discount rate,** where *NPV* is equal for two or more investment alternatives.
- To properly value cash flows over the life of a project, the cost of capital funds must be determined. The **component cost of debt** is the interest rate that investors require on debt, adjusted for taxes. The **component cost of equity** is the rate of return stockholders require on common stock. This includes a **risk-free rate of return** to compensate investors for postponing their consumption, plus a **risk premium** to compensate them for risk taking. The riskiness of a given stock is measured in terms of the firm's **beta coefficient,** a measure of return variability.
- The **weighted average cost of capital** is the marginal cost of a composite dollar of debt and equity financing. The proper set of weights to employ in computing the weighted average cost of capital is determined by the firm's **optimal capital structure,** or combination of debt and equity financing that minimizes the firm's overall weighted average cost of capital.
- The **optimal capital budget** is the funding level required to underwrite a value-maximizing level of new investment. Graphically, the optimal capital budget is determined by the intersection of the **investment opportunity schedule** (*IOS*), or

pattern of returns for all of the firm's potential investment projects, and the **marginal cost of capital** (*MCC*), or *IRR* schedule.

■ The **postaudit** is the final step in the capital budgeting process and consists of a careful examination of actual and predicted results, coupled with a detailed reconciliation of any differences.

Taken as a whole, the capital budgeting process is one in which the principles of marginal analysis are applied in a systematic way to long-term investment decision making. As such, the process provides further evidence of managers actually going through the process of value maximization.

QUESTIONS

Q15.1 What is capital budgeting?

Q15.2 What major steps are involved in the capital budgeting process?

Q15.3 Why do accounting income statements provide only an imperfect basis for investment decisions, and what steps must be taken to adjust these data?

Q15.4 Explain the underlying rationale for using the NPV approach to investment project selection.

Q15.5 Why do the *NPV*, *PI*, and *IRR* capital budgeting decision rules sometimes provide conflicting rank orderings of investment project alternatives?

Q15.6 How is a crossover discount rate calculated, and how does it affect capital budgeting decisions?

Q15.7 In an earlier chapter, it was argued that factors should be used in such proportions that the marginal product/price ratios for all inputs are equal. In terms of capital budgeting, this implies that the marginal net cost of debt should equal the marginal net cost of equity in the optimal capital structure. Yet firms often issue debt at interest rates substantially below the yield that investors require on the firm's equity shares. Does this mean that such firms are not operating with optimal capital structures? Explain.

Q15.8 Explain why the intersection of the *IOS* and *MCC* curves defines an economically optimal capital budget.

Q15.9 Recent academic studies in financial economics conclude that stockholders of target firms in takeover bids "win" (earn abnormal returns) and that stockholders of successful bidders do not lose subsequent to takeovers, even though takeovers usually occur at substantial premiums over prebid market prices. Is this observation consistent with capital market efficiency?

Q15.10 What important purposes are served by the postaudit?

SELF-TEST PROBLEMS AND SOLUTIONS

ST15.1 *NPV and Payback Period Analysis.* Suppose that your college roommate has approached you with an opportunity to invest $25,000 in her fledgling home health-care business. The business, called Home Health Care, Inc., plans to offer home infusion therapy and monitored in-the-home health-care services to surgery patients in the Brainerd, Minnesota area. The funds would be used to lease a delivery vehicle, to purchase supplies, and for working capital. The terms of the proposal are that you would receive $5,000 at the end of each year in interest on a $25,000 loan to be repaid in full at the end of a ten-year period.

A. Assuming a 10% required rate of return, calculate the present value of cash flows and the net present value of the proposed investment.

B. Based on this same interest-rate assumption, calculate the cumulative cash flow of the proposed investment for each period in both nominal and present-value terms.

C. What is the payback period in both nominal and present-value terms?

D. What is the difference between the nominal and present-value payback period? Can the present-value payback period ever be shorter than the nominal payback period?

ST15.1 **SOLUTION**

A. The present value of cash flows and the net present value of the proposed investment can be calculated as follows:

YEAR	CASH FLOW	PRESENT VALUE INTEREST FACTOR	PRESENT VALUE CASH FLOW
0	($25,000)	1.0000	($25,000)
1	5,000	0.9091	4,545
2	5,000	0.8264	4,132
3	5,000	0.7513	3,757
4	5,000	0.6830	3,415
5	5,000	0.6209	3,105
6	5,000	0.5645	2,822
7	5,000	0.5132	2,566
8	5,000	0.4665	2,333
9	5,000	0.4241	2,120
10	5,000	0.3855	1,928

Cost of Capital	10.0%
Present Value of Benefits	$30,723
Present Value of Cost	$25,000
Net Present Value	$5,723

B. The cumulative cash flow of the proposed investment for each period in both nominal and present-value terms is:

C. Based on the information provided in Part B, it is clear that the cumulative cash flow in nominal dollars reached $0 at the end of Year 5. This means that the nominal payback period is 5 years. The cumulative cash flow in present-value dollars exceeds $0 when the Year 8 interest payment is received. This means that the present-value payback period is roughly 8 years. If cash flows were received on a continuous basis, the present-value payback period would be 8.28 years (= $658/$2,333).

D. Assuming a positive rate of interest, the present-value payback period is always longer than the nominal payback period. This stems from the fact that present-value dollars are always less than nominal dollars, and it therefore takes longer to receive a fixed dollar amount back in terms of present-value dollars rather than in nominal terms.

ST15.2 **Decision Rule Conflict.** Assume that you have been retained as a financial consultant by a small local retailer to analyze two proposed capital investments, Projects X and Y. Project X is a sophisticated working capital and inventory control system based upon a powerful personal computer, called a system server, and PC software specifically designed for inventory processing and control in the retailing business. Project Y is a similarly sophisticated working capital and inventory control system based upon a powerful personal computer, and general purpose PC software. Each project has a cost of $10,000, and the cost of

YEAR	CASH FLOW	PRESENT VALUE INTEREST FACTOR	PRESENT VALUE CASH FLOW	CUMULATIVE CASH FLOW	CUMULATIVE PV CASH FLOW
0	($25,000)	1.0000	($25,000)	($25,000)	($25,000)
1	5,000	0.9091	4,545	(20,000)	(20,455)
2	5,000	0.8264	4,132	(15,000)	(16,322)
3	5,000	0.7513	3,757	(10,000)	(12,566)
4	5,000	0.6830	3,415	(5,000)	(9,151)
5	5,000	0.6209	3,105	0	(6,046)
6	5,000	0.5645	2,822	5,000	(3,224)
7	5,000	0.5132	2,566	10,000	(658)
8	5,000	0.4665	2,333	15,000	1,675
9	5,000	0.4241	2,120	20,000	3,795
10	5,000	0.3855	1,928	25,000	5,723

Payback Period	5 years
Present Value Payback Period	8.28 years (= 8 + $658/$2,333).

capital for both projects is 12%. The projects' expected net cash flows are as follows:

EXPECTED NET CASH FLOW

YEAR	PROJECT X	PROJECT Y
0	($10,000)	($10,000)
1	6,500	3,500
2	3,000	3,500
3	3,000	3,500
4	1,000	3,500

A. Calculate each project's nominal payback period, net present value (NPV), internal rate of return (IRR), and profitability index (PI).
B. Should both projects be accepted if they are interdependent?
C. Which projects should be accepted if they are mutually exclusive?
D. How might a change in the cost of capital produce a conflict between the NPV and IRR rankings of these two projects? At what values of k would this conflict exist? (Hint: Plot the NPV profiles for each project to find the crossover discount rate k.)
E. Why does a conflict exist between NPV and IRR rankings?

ST15.2 **SOLUTION**
A. *Payback:*
To determine the nominal payback period, construct the cumulative cash flows for each project:

CUMULATIVE CASH FLOW

YEAR	PROJECT X	PROJECT Y
0	($10,000)	($10,000)
1	(3,500)	(6,500)
2	(500)	(3,000)
3	2,500	500
4	3,500	4,000

$$\text{Payback}_X = 2 + \frac{\$500}{\$3,000} = 2.17 \text{ years.}$$

$$\text{Payback}_Y = 2 + \frac{\$3,000}{\$3,500} = 2.86 \text{ years.}$$

Net Present Value (NPV):

$$NPV_X = -\$10,000 + \frac{\$6,500}{(1.12)^1} + \frac{\$3,000}{(1.12)^2}$$
$$+ \frac{\$3,000}{(1.12)^3} + \frac{\$1,000}{(1.12)^4}$$

$$= \$966.01.$$

$$NPV_Y = -\$10,000 + \frac{\$3,500}{(1.12)^1} + \frac{\$3,500}{(1.12)^2}$$
$$+ \frac{\$3,500}{(1.12)^3} + \frac{\$3,500}{(1.12)^4}$$

$$= \$630.72.$$

Internal Rate of Return (IRR):
To solve for each project's IRR, find the discount rates that set NPV to zero:

$$IRR_X = 18.0\%.$$

$$IRR_Y = 15.0\%.$$

Profitability Index (PI):

$$PI_X = \frac{PV \ Benefits}{PV \ Costs} = \frac{\$10,966.01}{\$10,000} = 1.10.$$

$$PI_Y = \frac{\$10,630.72}{\$10,000} = 1.06.$$

B. Using all methods, Project X is preferred over Project Y. Since both projects are acceptable under the NPV, IRR, and PI criteria, both projects should be accepted if they are interdependent.
C. Choose the project with the higher NPV at $k = 12\%$, or Project X.
D. To determine the effects of changing the cost of capital, plot the NPV profiles of each project. The crossover rate occurs at about 6 to 7%. To find this rate exactly, create a Project Δ, which is the difference in cash flows between Projects X and Y:

YEAR	PROJECT X − PROJECT Y = PROJECT Δ NET CASH FLOW
0	$0
1	3,000
2	(500)
3	(500)
4	(2,500)

Then find the *IRR* of Project Δ:

$$IRR_\Delta = Crossover\ Rate = 6.2\%.$$

Thus, if the firm's cost of capital is less than 6.2%, a conflict exists, since $NPV_Y > NPV_X$ but $IRR_X > IRR_Y$.

Graphically, the crossover discount rate is illustrated below.

E.   The basic cause of conflict is the differing reinvestment rate assumptions between *NPV* and *IRR*. The conflict occurs in this situation because the projects differ in their cash flow timing.

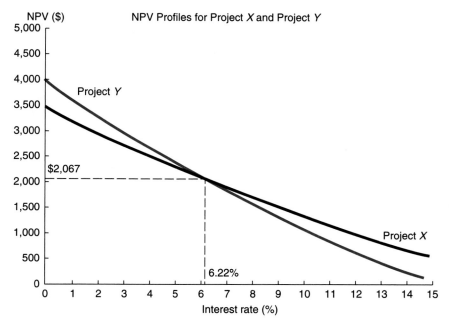

PROBLEMS

P15.1   Cost of Capital. Identify each of the following statements as true or false, and explain your answers.

A.   Information costs both increase the marginal cost of capital and reduce the internal rate of return on investment projects.

B.   Depreciation expenses involve no direct cash outlay and can be safely ignored in investment-project evaluation.

C.   The marginal cost of capital will be less elastic for larger firms than for smaller firms.

D.   In practice, the component costs of debt and equity are jointly rather than independently determined.

E.   Investments necessary to replace worn-out or damaged equipment tend to have low levels of risk.

P15.2   Decision Rule Criteria. The net present value (*NPV*), profitability index (*PI*), and internal rate of return (*IRR*) methods are often employed in project valuation. Identify each of the following statements as true or false, and explain your answers.

A.   The *IRR* method can tend to understate the relative attractiveness of superior investment projects when the opportunity cost of cash flows is below the *IRR*.

B.   A $PI = 1$ describes a project with an $NPV = 0$.

C.   Selection solely according to the *NPV* criterion will tend to favor larger rather than smaller investment projects.

D.   When $NPV = 0$, the *IRR* exceeds the cost of capital.

E.   Use of the *PI* criterion is especially

appropriate for larger firms with easy access to capital markets.

P15.3 **Cost of Capital.** Indicate whether each of the following would increase or decrease the cost of capital that should be used by the firm in investment project evaluation. Explain.

A. Interest rates rise because the Federal Reserve System tightens the money supply.

B. The stock market suffers a sharp decline, as does the company's stock price, without (in management's opinion) any decline in the company's earnings potential.

C. The company's home state eliminates the corporate income tax in an effort to keep or attract valued employers.

D. In an effort to reduce the federal deficit, Congress raises corporate income tax rates.

E. A merger with a leading competitor increases the company's stock price substantially.

P15.4 **Present Value.** New York City licenses taxicabs in two classes: (1) for operation by companies with fleets and (2) for operation by independent driver-owners having only one cab. The city also fixes the rates that taxis charge. For many years, no new licenses have been issued in either class. There is an unofficial market for licenses (medallions), the market value of which is currently more than $100,000.

A. Discuss the factors determining the value of a license. To make your answer concrete, estimate numerical values for the various components that together can be summarized in a price of $100,000.

B. What factors would determine whether a change in the fare fixed by the city would raise or lower the value of a license?

C. Cab drivers, whether hired by companies or as owners of their own cabs, seem unanimous in opposing any increase in the number of cabs licensed. They argue that an increase in the number of cabs would increase competition for customers and drive down what they regard as an already unduly low return to drivers. Is their economic analysis correct? Who would benefit and who would lose from an expansion in the number of licenses issued at a nominal fee?

P15.5 **NPV and PI.** The Pacific Princess luxury cruise line is contemplating leasing an additional cruise ship to expand service from the Hawaiian Islands to Long Beach or San Diego. A financial analysis by staff personnel resulted in the following projections for a five-year planning horizon:

	LONG BEACH	SAN DIEGO
Cost	$2,000,000	$3,000,00
PV of expected cash flow @ $k = 15\%$	2,500,000	3,600,000

A. Calculate the net present value for each service. Which is more desirable according to the *NPV* criterion?

B. Calculate the profitability index for each service. Which is more desirable according to the *PI* criterion?

C. Under what conditions would either or both of the services be undertaken?

P15.6 **NPV and PI.** Louisiana Drilling and Exploration, Inc. (LD&E), has the funds necessary to complete one of two risky oil and gas drilling projects. The first, Permian Basin 1, involves the recovery of a well that was plugged and abandoned five years ago but that may now be profitable, given improved recovery techniques. The second, Permian Basin 2, is a new onshore exploratory well that appears to be especially promising. Based on a detailed analysis by its technical staff, LD&E projects a ten-year life for each well with annual net cash flows as follows:

PROJECT	PROBABILITY	ANNUAL CASH FLOW
Permian Basin 1	0.08	$500,000
	0.84	1,000,000
	0.08	1,500,000
Permian Basin 2	0.18	300,000
	0.64	900,000
	0.18	1,500,000

In the recovery-project valuation, LD&E uses an 8% riskless rate and a standard 12% risk premium. For exploratory drilling projects, the company uses larger risk premiums proportionate to project risks as measured by the project coefficient of variation. For example, an exploratory project with a coefficient of variation one and one-half times that for recovery projects would require a risk premium of 18% (= 1.5 × 12%). Both projects involve land acquisition, as well as surface preparation and subsurface drilling costs of $3 million each.

A. Calculate the expected value, standard deviation, and coefficient of variation for annual net operating revenues from each well.

B. Calculate and evaluate the *NPV* for each project using the risk-adjusted discount rate method.

C. Calculate and evaluate the *PI* for each project.

P15.7 Investment Project Choice. The Green Acres Hotel is considering investment in two alternative capital budgeting projects. Project *A* is an investment of $75,000 to replace working but obsolete refrigeration equipment. Project *B* is an investment of $150,000 to expand dining room facilities. Relevant cash flow data for the two projects over their expected two-year lives are as follows:

PROJECT *A*

YEAR 1		YEAR 2	
PROBABILITY	CASH FLOW	PROBABILITY	CASH FLOW
0.18	$0	0.08	$0
0.64	50,000	0.84	50,000
0.18	100,000	0.08	100,000

PROJECT *B*

YEAR 1		YEAR 2	
PROBABILITY	CASH FLOW	PROBABILITY	CASH FLOW
0.50	$0	0.125	$0
0.50	200,000	0.75	100,000
		0.125	200,000

A. Calculate the expected value, standard deviation, and coefficient of variation of cash flows for each project.

B. Calculate the risk-adjusted *NPV* for each project using a 15% cost of capital for the riskier project and a 12% cost of capital for the less risky one. Which project is preferred using the *NPV* criterion?

C. Calculate the *PI* for each project, and rank the projects according to the *PI* criterion.

D. Calculate the *IRR* for each project, and rank the projects according to the *IRR* criterion.

E. Compare your answers to Parts B, C, and D, and discuss any differences.

P15.8 Cash Flow Estimation. Cunningham's Drug Store, a medium-size drug store located in Milwaukee, Wisconsin, is owned and operated by Richard Cunningham. Cunningham's sells pharmaceuticals, cosmetics, toiletries, magazines, and various novelties. Cunningham's most recent annual net income statement is as follows:

Sales revenue	$1,800,000
Total costs	
Cost of goods sold	$1,260,000
Wages and salaries	200,000
Rent	120,000
Depreciation	60,000
Utilities	40,000
Miscellaneous	30,000
Total	1,710,000
Net profit before tax	$90,000

Cunningham's sales and expenses have remained relatively constant over the past few years and are expected to continue unchanged in the near future. To increase sales, Cunningham is considering using some floor space for a small soda fountain. Cunningham would operate the soda fountain for an initial three-year period and then would reevaluate its profitability. The soda fountain would require an incremental investment of $20,000 to lease furniture, equipment, utensils, and so on. This is the only capital investment required during the three-year period. At the end of that time, additional capital would be required to continue operating the soda fountain, and no capital would be recovered if it were shut down. The soda fountain is expected to have annual sales of $100,000 and food and materials expenses of $20,000 per year. The soda fountain is also expected to increase wage and salary expenses by 8% and utility expenses by 5%. Because the soda fountain will reduce the floor space available for display of other merchandise, sales of non-soda fountain items are expected to decline by 10%.

A. Calculate net incremental cash flows for the soda fountain.

B. Assume that Cunningham has the capital necessary to install the soda fountain and that he places a 12% opportunity cost on those funds. Should the soda fountain be installed? Why or why not?

P15.9   **Cash Flow Analysis.** The Patriotic Press, Inc. (PPI), is analyzing the potential profitability of three printing jobs put up for bid by the State Department of Revenue:

	JOB A	JOB B	JOB C
Projected winning bid (per unit)	$5.00	$8.00	$7.50
Direct cost per unit	$2.00	$4.30	$3.00
Annual unit sales volume	800,000	650,000	450,000
Annual distribution costs	$90,000	$75,000	$55,000
Investment required to produce annual volume	$5,000,000	$5,200,000	$4,000,000

Assume that: (1) the company's marginal city-plus-state-plus-federal tax rate is 50%; (2) each job is expected to have a six-year life; (3) the firm uses straight-line depreciation; (4) the average cost of capital is 14%; (5) the jobs have the same risk as the firm's other business; and (6) the company has already spent $60,000 on developing the preceding data. This $60,000 has been capitalized and will be amortized over the life of the project.

A.   What is the expected net cash flow each year? (Hint: Cash flow equals net profit after taxes plus depreciation and amortization charges.)

B.   What is the net present value of each project? On which project, if any, should PPI bid?

C.   Suppose that PPI's primary business is quite cyclical, improving and declining with the economy, but that Job A is expected to be countercyclical. Might this have any bearing on your decision?

P15.10   **Cost of Capital.** Eureka Membership Warehouse, Inc., is a rapidly growing chain of retail outlets offering brand-name merchandise at discount prices. A security analyst's report issued by a national brokerage firm indicates that debt yielding 13% composes 25% of Eureka's overall capital structure. Furthermore, both earnings and dividends are expected to grow at a rate of 15% per year.

Currently, common stock in the company is priced at $30, and it should pay $1.50 per share in dividends during the coming year. This yield compares favorably with the 8% return currently available on risk-free securities and the 14% average for all common stocks, given the company's estimated beta of 2.

A.   Calculate Eureka's component cost of equity using both the capital asset pricing model and the dividend yield plus expected growth model.

B.   Assuming a 40% marginal federal-plus-state income tax rate, calculate Eureka's weighted average cost of capital.

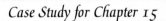

Case Study for Chapter 15

INVESTMENT PROJECT ANALYSIS AT FLIGHTSAFETY INTERNATIONAL, INC.

FlightSafety International, Inc., trains more than 30,000 corporate, commercial, and military pilots per year and has found its niche business to be enormously profitable. Net profit margins have averaged roughly 30% of sales during the 1980s and mid-1990s. It is the only company to have earned a spot on *Forbes'* annual list of the best Up & Comers in every year since the magazine started tracking such companies in 1979. Over this period, FlightSafety's profits rose more than fivefold, and the company racked up an average rate of return on common equity of 18% to 20% per year. Its stock was up from $7 a share (split-adjusted) in 1982 to more than $50 in 1996, at which point FlightSafety was purchased by Berkshire Hathaway, Inc. in a cash and stock transaction worth $1.5 billion. Among the 9,500 stockholders that benefited from the company's amazing success is company founder, chairman, and president Albert Ueltschi—Ueltschi and his family owned roughly one-third of FlightSafety common stock prior to the Berkshire buyout.

What separates FlightSafety from other small companies that look good for a couple of years and then crash and burn is the quality of top management. Ueltschi is widely regarded as dedicated, highly intelligent, and honest. He started FlightSafety in 1951, while working as a pilot for Pan American Airways. Since 1946 he had served as the personal pilot to Pan Am's colorful founder, Juan Trippe, flying Trippe around in a converted B-23 military transport. During the early years of this association, Ueltschi noticed that other corporate CEOs were buying surplus military planes and converting them into corporate aircraft. He also noticed that many of the former military pilots who were signing on as corporate pilots had little or no training on the specific planes they were being hired to fly. Ueltschi reasoned that corporations would pay to rectify this dangerous situation.

Ueltschi opened an office next to Pan Am's La-Guardia terminal and began hiring moonlighting pilots from Pan Am and United to train corporate pilots. Actual flight instruction was done in the clients' aircraft. Additional instrument training was done on instrument trainers, rented by the hour from United Airlines. Early clients included Kodak, Burlington Industries, and National Distillers. Ueltschi poured all the profits back into the business, a practice he still abides by. During the past decade, the company has spent ever-increasing amounts on new plant and equipment; current capital expenditures total roughly $100 million per year.

Today FlightSafety is the largest independent flight trainer in the United States. So complete is its grip on the market that 20 aircraft manufacturers, among them Gulfstream, Cessna, and Learjet, include its training with the price of a new plane. The com-

pany trains pilots on sophisticated flight simulators at training centers located adjacent to manufacturers' plants, military bases, and commercial airports. Flight simulators not only re-create the look, feel, and sound of flying specific planes but also simulate emergency flight conditions—such as wind shear or the loss of a hydraulic system—that one does not want to attempt with an actual plane. Training on a simulator is also significantly cheaper than training in an actual plane. FlightSafety's simulator time for a Boeing 737, for example, costs about $550 an hour. Operating costs for an actual 737 are about $3,000 an hour. The company, which now builds most of its own simulators at a cost of $8 million to $12 million each, is putting new ones into service at a rate of three per quarter.

To illustrate the company's capital budgeting process, assume that FlightSafety had built a given simulator for $8 million two years ago. The company uses straight-line depreciation over the simulator's projected 12-year life. Therefore, the used flight simulator has a present depreciated book value of $6.5 million; it has a current market value of $7.5 million (before taxes). If kept, the used simulator will last ten more years and produce an expected net cash flow before tax (CFBT) of $2.5 million per year. A new flight simulator costs $12 million to build but has greater capabilities and is expected to generate CFBT of $4 million per year over a useful life of 15 years. Assume that neither the new nor the used flight simulator has any salvage value at the end of its projected useful life, a marginal state-plus-federal tax rate of 40%, a current after-tax discount rate of 20%, and straight-line depreciation.

A. Calculate the expected *NPV* for retention of the used flight simulator equipment.

B. Calculate the expected *NPV* for construction of the new flight simulator equipment.

C. Based on the *NPV* criterion, should FlightSafety retain the used flight simulator equipment, build new equipment, or both? Why?

Public Management

The information age has revolutionized the competitive environment and led to gut-wrenching corporate change. Instant awareness and accountability now demand the same level of dramatic, structural change in government. Rising demands for a balanced federal budget mark a fundamental shift in taxpayer attitudes towards the public management of economic resources. No longer is government seen as the clear and easy solution to all economic and social problems. Instead, it is sometimes viewed as an unnecessary impediment to lower taxes, lower interest rates, and more growth in a freer and more vibrant economy.[1] Like corporate executives who must justify investment decisions to increasingly wary stockholders, public-sector managers often find themselves before restive taxpayers defending basic duties and responsibilities that had long been taken for granted.

This chapter focuses on how national, state, and local governments can pursue wise public policies that have the potential to improve economic performance. Such policies have the capacity to lay a better foundation for economic growth, a healthy environment, and the necessary balance between the private and public sectors. A balanced view is presented that recognizes limitations of public policy without precluding the possibility that well-articulated policy can be immensely helpful. From this perspective, the methodology of managerial economics provides a practical framework for effectively comparing the relative costs and benefits of social programs and public-sector investment decisions. As such, managerial economics can help improve both the efficiency and equity of the public-sector decision-making process.

The Rationale for Public Management

Managers in the public and not-for-profit sectors must optimize resource use under a variety of operating constraints. When issues of economic efficiency are encountered, the decision tools and criteria discussed throughout managerial economics can be applied across the entire spectrum of the economy. As issues of economic equity or fairness are addressed, economic theory and methodology can be used to understand and improve the public decision-making process.

---

[1]Micheal M. Phillips, "More States Reassess Business Incentives," *The Wall Street Journal,* March 20, 1997, A2, A4.

PUBLIC VERSUS PRIVATE GOODS

Government regulation and antitrust policy is often used to protect consumers, workers, and the environment; to discourage and regulate monopoly; and to overcome the problems posed by externalities such as pollution. Another important function of government is to provide goods and services that cannot be provided and allocated in optimal quantities by the private sector.

Public Good
Products or services where consumption by one individual does not reduce the amount available for others.

If the consumption of a product by one individual does not reduce the amount available for others, the product is a **public good.** Once public goods are provided for a single consumer, they become available to all consumers at no additional marginal cost. Classic examples of public goods include national defense and police and fire protection. Over-the-air radio and TV broadcasts are typical examples of public goods provided by the private sector in the U.S., even though radio and TV programming is provided by the public sector in many foreign countries. By way of contrast, a **private good** is one where consumption by one individual precludes or limits consumption by others. Food, clothing, and shelter are all private goods because the number of potential consumers of a fixed amount is strictly limited. The distinguishing characteristic of public goods is that they share the attribute of **nonrival consumption.** In the case of public goods, use by certain individuals does not reduce availability for others. For example, when an individual watches a network broadcast of a popular TV program such as *The Simpsons,* this does not interfere with the enjoyment of that same TV program by others. In contrast, if an individual consumes a 12-ounce can of *Diet Coke,* this same can of soda is not available for others to consume.

Private Good
Products or services where consumption by one individual precludes or limits consumption by others.

Nonrival Consumption
Where use by certain individuals does not reduce availability for others.

The concept of nonrival consumption must be distinguished from the **nonexclusion concept.** A good or service is characterized as nonexclusionary if it is impossible or prohibitively expensive to confine the benefits of consumption to paying customers. While nonrival consumption and nonexclusion often go hand-in-hand, theory defines public goods only in terms of the nonrival consumption concept. Since national defense and network TV broadcasts can be enjoyed equally by more than one consumer at the same point in time, they are both public goods. National defense also exhibits the characteristic of nonexclusion because when it is provided for by taxpayers, nontax-paying citizens cannot be excluded from also enjoying the benefits of a strong national defense. On the other hand, the enjoyment of TV broadcasts can be made exclusive by restricting viewership, as is true with cable TV customers. Public goods that are nonrival in consumption would not be provided in the optimal amount by the private sector.

Nonexclusion Concept
When it is impossible or prohibitively expensive to confine the benefits of consumption to paying customers.

Since public goods can be enjoyed by more than one consumer at the same point in time, the aggregate or total demand for a public good is determined through the vertical summation of the demand curves of all consuming individuals. As shown in Figure 16.1, D_A is the demand curve of consumer A, and D_B is the demand curve of consumer B for Public Good Y. If consumers A and B are the only two individuals in the market, the aggregate demand curve for Public Good Y, D_T is obtained by the vertical summation of D_A and D_B. This contrasts with the market demand curve for any private good, which is determined by the horizontal summation of individual demand curves. Given market supply curve S_Y for Public Good Y in Figure 16.1, the optimal amount of Y is Q_Y units per time period given by the intersection of D_T and S_Y at point T. At point T, the

Figure 16.1

THE OPTIMAL AMOUNT OF A PUBLIC GOOD

Aggregate demand curve D_T for public good Y is obtained by the *vertical* summation of individual demand curves D_A and D_B. The reason for this is that each unit of public good Y can be consumed by both individuals at the same time. Given market supply curve S_Y, the optimal amount of Y is Q_Y units per time period (indicated by the intersection of D_T and S_Y). At Q_Y, the sum of the individual's marginal benefits equals the marginal social costs (that is, $P_A + P_B = P_T = MSC_Y$).

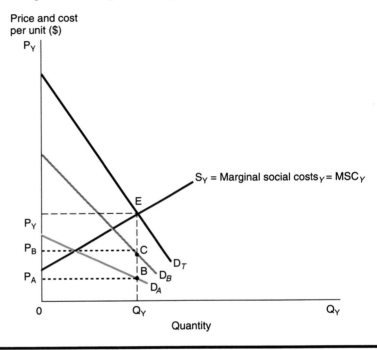

sum of marginal benefits enjoyed by both consumers equals the marginal social cost of producing Q_Y units of the public good. That is, $P_A + P_B = P_T = MC_Y$.

While the optimal quantity is Q_Y units in Figure 16.1, there are two related reasons why less than this amount is likely to be supplied by the private sector. First, because individuals not paying for Public Good Y cannot be excluded from consumption, there is a tendency for consumers to avoid payment responsibility. A **free-rider problem** emerges because each consumer believes that the public good will be provided irrespective of his or her contribution toward covering its costs. When several people share the cost of providing public goods, consumers often believe that their individual failure to provide financial support will have no effect on the provision of the good. When many individuals behave this way, however, less than the optimal amount of the public good will be provided. This problem is generally overcome when the government initiates a tax on the general public to pay for the provision of important public goods, like national defense. In the private sector, free-rider problems are sometimes resolved

Free-Rider Problem
The tendency of consumers to avoid making any contribution towards covering the costs of public goods.

through group consensus to support local zoning covenants, charitable associations, and so on.

Hidden Preferences Problem
The difficulty of determining true desires for public goods.

A **hidden preferences problem** also emerges in the provision of public goods because individuals have no economic incentive to accurately reveal their true demand. Consumers are reluctant to reveal high demand for public goods because they fear similarly high payment demands. With private goods, the price that consumers are willing to pay provides a credible signal to producers regarding the quantity and quality that should be produced. No such pricing signals are available in the case of public goods and services. As a result, it is difficult to determine the optimal amount that should be provided.

Of course, many goods and services do not fit neatly within the categories of pure private goods and pure public goods. Examples of goods and services with some but not all of the characteristics of public goods include: airports, basic research programs, day-care centers, highways, hospital facilities, immunization programs, the judicial system, parks, primary and secondary education, and trash collection. Given the many difficulties involved with accurately determining the demand for these and other quasi public goods, it is necessary to be cautious when using the power of government to tax or otherwise compel popular support. Public policy must focus narrowly on the source of any perceived private-market imperfections and address these impediments directly. For example, trash collection involves elements of a public good because the timely removal of trash and other debris limits the propagation of insects and rodents and, therefore, the spread of infectious diseases. Moreover, there are immense economies of density in trash collection. It is far more efficient for a monopoly trash hauler to service an entire neighborhood on a weekly basis than it is to have multiple competitors serve a single area. In recognition of the potential for problems with unregulated private-market trash collection, some local governments regulate private suppliers while others pay for this service out of general tax revenues. In theory, either approach has the potential to result in better trash collection services. In practice, regulation is seldom perfect, and local governments often find it difficult to maintain a high level of efficiency in the public provision of trash collection services.

And finally, it must be recognized that some goods and services provided by the public and not-for-profit sectors are designed to meet social goals of equity or fairness, rather than efficiency-oriented objectives. These purposes include redistributing income by giving assistance to the poor, sick, and uneducated; stabilizing economic growth, and providing for the national defense. However, efficiency considerations remain important even when these alternative objectives are important concerns of a government-sponsored or regulated program. Government has an obligation to use public funds wisely.

Public Choice Theory
The philosophy of how government decisions are made and implemented.

Government Failure
Circumstances where public policies reflect narrow private interests, rather than the general public interest.

PUBLIC CHOICE THEORY

Public choice theory is a philosophy of how government decisions are made and implemented. Public choice theory considers how government and the political process actually work, rather than how they should work. It explicitly recognizes the possibility of **government failure,** or circumstances where public policies reflect narrow private interests, rather than the public interest. Just because unregulated market activity does not always work perfectly does not mean that government policies will improve the situation. It is possible that government intervention will make a bad situation worse. Similarly, the fact that government policies are inefficient does not necessarily mean that private markets can do better. For example, substantial waste in government defense expenditures does not necessarily mean that the provision of national defense should be left to private interests.

The theory of public choice is based on the premise that individuals attempt to further personal interests in the political arena just as they seek to further private economic interests in the marketplace. Economists have long recognized that when an individual pursues private economic interests in the marketplace, that person is moved by an "invisible hand" to also promote the welfare of society as a whole. The study of public choice theory seeks to learn whether such an invisible hand mechanism is also at work in the political system. In other words, when individuals attempt to further personal interests through political activity, is the welfare of society also promoted?

Public choice theory examines how government decisions are made and implemented by analyzing the behavior of four broad groups of participants in the political system. **Voters** in the political process are the counterpart of consumers in the marketplace. Instead of purchasing goods and services in the marketplace, voters elect government representatives who make and enforce government policies. Other things being equal, voters support candidates who favor policies that further their personal economic interests. According to public choice theory, however, voters are less informed about political decisions than about market decisions due to their **rational ignorance.** Because elected officials act for the community as a whole, there is less of a need for individual voters to be fully informed about public choices. It is also generally more expensive for individuals to gather information about public choices than about market choices. Moreover, as a voter, each individual has relatively little ability to directly influence public choices. For all of these reasons, voters find it sensible to remain relatively uninformed about public policy decisions.

Politicians are the political-system counterpart of entrepreneurs and managers in the private market system. While the entrepreneur or manager of a private firm seeks to maximize the value of the firm, politicians seek to maximize chances for reelection. In doing so, politicians must respond to the desires of well-organized, well-informed, and well-funded special-interest groups. Examples of such interest groups in the U.S. include associations of primary and secondary school teachers, farmers, medical doctors, and many others. Faced with the rational ignorance of the majority of voters, politicians often support policies that greatly benefit special-interest groups who contribute heavily to reelection campaigns at the expense of the mostly silent and uninformed majority.

Perhaps the most maligned and misunderstood groups participating in the political process are **special-interest groups.** Organized lobbyists actively support the passage of laws and regulations that further narrow economic interests. For example, the National Education Association has successfully blocked the advance of innovative voucher systems of public school financing, and maintained a public school monopoly on public financing of primary and secondary education. The American Medical

Voters
Persons who elect public officials.

Rational Ignorance
The tendency to remain relatively uninformed about public policy decisions.

Politicians
Elected representatives or leaders.

Special-Interest Groups
Organized lobbyists who actively support the passage of laws and regulations that further their own narrow economic interests.

Association has succeeded in limiting admissions to medical schools, thereby reducing the supply of medical doctors and increasing doctors' incomes. Grain and dairy farmers have successfully lobbied the government to provide billions of dollars in subsidies each year, while poultry and pork producers fail to share in such benefits. Restrictions on auto and truck imports from Japan and other countries benefit General Motors, Ford, and Chrysler, while consumers pay higher than necessary prices. The success of special-interest groups is explained by the fact that such bodies provide millions of dollars in financial support to politicians who advocate their cause. While special-interest groups play a valuable role in the democratic process, problems are often obvious. Unfortunately, when large economic benefits for special interests are weighed against individually small but collectively huge social costs, it is the economic interest of special-interest groups that often prevails.

Bureaucrats
Appointed government employees and civil servants.

Bureaus are government agencies that carry out policies enacted by Congress and other legislative bodies. According to public choice theory, public employees, or **bureaucrats,** are not passive executors of adopted policies; they actively seek to influence policies to further personal interests. They do so by seeking to increase the magnitude and scope of bureau activity and funding. This stems from the fact that the income, power, and prestige of top bureaucrats are directly related to the employment size and growth of the bureau. Bureaucrats can become a separate special-interest group within government.

POLICY IMPLICATIONS OF PUBLIC CHOICE THEORY

The characterization of the political process by public choice theorists is sometimes viewed as cynical. Many voters are well informed and unselfish in their political beliefs. Politicians also sometimes refuse to compromise basic principles simply to maximize chances for reelection. Collectively important public interests prevail more often than one might expect; powerful special-interest groups are sometimes defeated. Government bureaucracies are often staffed by well-intentioned and committed public servants. For example, a majority of high-income voters consistently support social welfare programs that involve a redistribution of income to poor people. During the 1990s, large cuts in defense spending occurred despite the best efforts of the military-industrial complex; the tobacco lobby has suffered one defeat after another. The American Medical Association is no longer able to restrict admissions to medical schools; milk and grain price supports are under attack. Even the Civil Aeronautics Board, a large and influential agency of the federal government, proposed its own elimination following airline deregulation and, as such, no longer exists.

Nevertheless, these contradictions do not invalidate the theory of public choice. While public policy can improve the economic system in the presence of market failures, the public policy process itself is subject to systematic influences that can lead to government failure. The theory of public choice can be used to suggest institutional changes that can lead to improvements in public sector performance.

One method that public choice theory suggests for improving public sector performance is to subject government bureaus and agencies to private-market competition

Does the U.S. Need an Industrial Policy?

Should the U.S. have an industrial policy? Yes, contend prominent members of the Clinton Administration. Advocates argue that the federal government can help industry become a key player in the "knowledge economy." They advocate a boost in government research spending across a wide range of technologies and in financial support to the next generation of scientists and engineers. Supporters also assert that the U.S. needs tax laws that make it cheaper for the private sector to invest in research and development (R&D) and new plant and equipment. They encourage giving smaller companies technical assistance to learn the latest manufacturing techniques. Government spending to enhance productivity by building up the infrastructure, especially by encouraging the development of high-speed communications networks, is also proposed. A new trade policy that focuses on opening up foreign markets while resisting protectionism at home is also favored.

Interest in an industrial policy for the U.S. has surged given the anemic rates of economic growth experienced during much of the last part of the 20th century. When matched against the historical record, the U.S.

economy has turned in dismal productivity performance over the past decade. Based on data in the *Economic Report of the President*, "real," or inflation-adjusted, Gross Domestic Product is projected to grow at an annual rate of less than 2.2% during the 1990s, down sharply from the 3.1% rate of growth over the 1960–90 period. While the difference between 2.2% and 3.1% rates of growth may seem minor, it can lead to significant differences in GDP and family incomes over time. Starting from a base median family income of $32,142 in 1990 (in 1992 dollars), a 3.1% rate of growth would lead to a median family income of $43,617 by the year 2000. A 2.2% rate of growth leads to a year 2000 median family income of $39,956. To make matters worse, while economic growth is stagnant in the U.S., other industrial nations are enjoying rapidly improving living standards. These countries, especially China and Pacific Basin competitors, have been planning for even better economic performance by boosting productivity growth.

Advocates of a government-based industrial policy for the U.S. recommend that the federal government do the following:

whenever possible. For example, families could be provided with vouchers to finance primary and secondary education at public or private institutions. This would stimulate competition among private and public schools, just like student-specific federal support for higher education stimulates competition among private and public colleges and universities. Still another means for increasing government efficiency is to encourage interagency competition. While streamlining government eliminates some duplication and waste, it also eliminates competition and incentives for efficient operation. For example, the cost effectiveness of the Department of Defense might actually have declined following the consolidation of the three branches of the armed forces to a single department.

Public choice theory also proposes at least two ways for reducing the leverage of special-interest groups. One is to rely more on referenda to decide important political issues. When important decisions are subject to popular referendum, special-interest groups must focus their energy on influencing the general public rather than curry favor with important politicians. Another method for reducing the influence of special-interest groups is to specify the total amount of public funds budgeted for the year and

Managerial Application 16–1 continued

- *Boost industrial R&D support.* Increase federal spending on civilian R&D; cut defense R&D. Support a wide range of projects, from basic research to new manufacturing technologies.
- *Provide technical assistance to industry.* Increase funding for programs to help smaller manufacturers adopt up-to-date technologies and production methods. Provide training grants and low-cost equipment loans.
- *Improve data collection.* Spread information on the successful R&D and manufacturing practices of foreign competitors. Identify emerging technologies that merit support.
- *Rebuild infrastructure.* Rebuild roads and bridges, and increase funding for high-speed data networks, to encourage new high-tech industries.
- *Expand exports.* Make export financing easier to obtain for creditworthy small and midsize exporters. Boost export promotion for nonagricultural products.
- *Fund education.* Raise funding for all levels of science, mathematics, and engineering education.
- *Cut taxes.* Institute permanent R&D and investment tax credits, so companies can do long-range planning.

Advocates of an alternative market-based approach to economic development reject the notion of government-inspired industrial policy. Free-market advocates have little confidence in government policy that reallocates resources from one sector to another. Despite some successes, problems are evident with past attempts at industrial policy in the U.S. In the case of nineteenth century land grants to help build the railroads, public policy created wasteful excess capacity plus an immense and inefficient regulatory bureaucracy. While farm policy helps U.S. farmers develop and promote agriculture, many lavish government programs become entrenched and live for decades beyond the point where they can be justified.

A market-based growth policy doesn't call on government to pick winning and losing industries. It asks government to provide an appropriate legal and tax environment and asks the private sector to risk its own money to develop commercially viable ideas. In an enlightened industrial policy, it's the market, not government, that picks the winners and losers.

See: Howard Gleckman and Mike McNamee, "Life Under a Balanced Budget," *Business Week,* February 10, 1997, 32–38.

encourage different groups to compete for government funding and support. When the total amount of public expenditures is fixed, one group can gain only at the expense of others. Each group is then likely to present its best case for funding while exposing the weakness in competitor funding requests.

Benefit-Cost Analysis

As the trustees of valuable public resources, public-sector managers must administer economic resources in a responsible manner. This task is made difficult by problems involved with assessing the true level of public demand for government-provided or government-administered goods and services. As a result, a variety of nonmarket-based mechanisms have evolved that can be used to effectively administer government programs and investment expenditures. The most prevalent of these methods compares relative costs and benefits.

BENEFIT-COST ANALYSIS THEORY

Pareto Satisfactory
If investment in a public project makes at least one individual better off and no one worse off.

Pareto Optimal
When all Pareto satisfactory programs and investment projects have been undertaken.

Potential Pareto Improvement
When an anticipated program or project involves positive *net* benefits.

Many public programs are promoted on the premise that all citizens will benefit. If investment in a public project makes at least one individual better off and no one worse off, then the project is described as **Pareto satisfactory,** after the noted Italian economist Vilfredo Pareto. When all such projects have been undertaken, the situation is deemed **Pareto optimal.** In practice, most public expenditures increase the welfare of some individuals while reducing the welfare of others. As a result, it is often regarded as too stringent to require that all public works fit the Pareto satisfactory criterion. Instead, it is often required that they meet the criteria of a **potential Pareto improvement,** where there are positive *net* benefits. In other words, a government program or project is deemed attractive under the potential Pareto improvement criterion when beneficiaries could fully compensate losers and still receive positive net benefit.

The potential Pareto improvement criterion provides the rationale for benefit-cost analysis: Public programs and projects are desirable from a social standpoint so long as benefits exceed costs. Whether or not beneficiaries actually compensate losers is immaterial. The allocation of benefits and costs among various individuals is a separate equity issue. Much like the distribution of tax burdens, the allocation of costs and benefits from public programs and projects is thought to depend upon popular notions of fairness, rather than upon efficiency considerations.

In theory, any public good or service should be supplied up to the amount that equates marginal social costs and marginal social benefits. This principle is similar to the profit-maximizing standard that output should increase to the point where marginal revenue equals marginal cost. For purposes of public-sector analysis, social benefits play the role of revenue and social costs play the role of production expenditures. As in the process of profit maximization, benefit-cost analysis presumes that all relevant pluses and minuses associated with public programs and projects can be measured in present-day dollar terms.

Marginal Social Costs
Added private and public expenses.

Marginal External Costs
Expenses that are not directly borne by producers or their customers.

Marginal Private Costs
Production expenses borne by producers and their customers.

Marginal Social Benefits
Added private and public advantages.

Marginal Private Benefits
Value enjoyed by those who directly pay for any good or service.

Marginal External Benefits
Value enjoyed by nonpurchasers and not reflected in market prices.

The **marginal social costs** of any good or service equal the marginal cost of production plus any **marginal external costs,** such as pollution, that are not directly borne by producers or their customers. Production costs borne by producers and their customers represent private economic costs; external costs include the value of foregone alternative goods and services. In the absence of marginal external costs, **marginal private costs** and marginal social costs are equal at all levels of output. **Marginal social benefits** are the sum of **marginal private benefits** plus **marginal external benefits.** Marginal private benefits are enjoyed by those who directly pay for any good or service; marginal external benefits are enjoyed by purchasers and non-purchasers alike and are not reflected in market prices. When no externalities are present, marginal social benefits equal marginal private benefits.

The optimal allocation of social resources is shown in Figure 16.2 where the marginal social cost curve intersects the marginal social benefit curve at Q^*. Marginal social cost and marginal social benefit curves show that for all levels of output greater than Q^*, additional social costs exceed additional social benefits. For output levels less than Q^*, the marginal *net* benefit to society is positive. For output levels greater than Q^*, the marginal *net* benefit to society is negative.

The optimal production of public-sector goods and services follows the same rules as optimal private-sector production. For example, consider the simplified case of two

	MAXIMIZATION OF SOCIAL BENEFITS FROM GOVERNMENT PROGRAMS
Figure 16.2	AND PUBLIC-SECTOR INVESTMENTS

Social benefits are maximized from government programs and public-sector investments when the marginal social cost equals marginal social benefits. Output level Q^* maximizes society's net benefits.

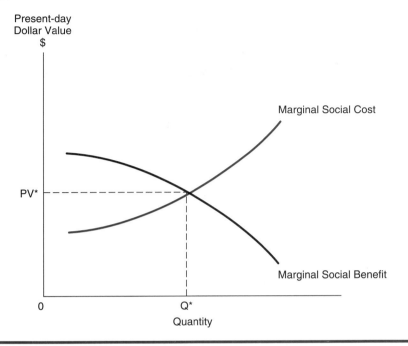

government programs or public-sector investment projects, Project X and Project Y. Optimal relative amounts of X and Y are made available to consumers so long as the ratio of marginal social benefits equals the ratio of marginal social costs for both projects:

$$\frac{Marginal\ Social\ Benefit_X}{Marginal\ Social\ Benefit_Y} = \frac{Marginal\ Social\ Cost_X}{Marginal\ Social\ Cost_Y}. \qquad (16.1)$$

When the ratio of marginal social benefits is equal to the ratio of marginal social costs across all government programs and public-sector investment projects, each respective program and/or project represents an equally effective use of taxpayer funds in that it results in an identical payoff per dollar of marginal social cost.

Alternatively, optimal relative amounts of X and Y are made available to consumers so long as the marginal social benefit to marginal social cost ratio is equal for each respective program or public-sector investment project:

$$\frac{Marginal\ Social\ Benefit_X}{Marginal\ Social\ Cost_X} = \frac{Marginal\ Social\ Benefit_Y}{Marginal\ Social\ Cost_Y}. \qquad (16.2)$$

Notice that each side of Equation 16.2 shows the dollar amount of marginal social benefit relative to the dollar amount of marginal social cost for each project. When the MSB/MSC ratio is equal across all government programs and public-sector investment projects, each respective program and/or project represents an equally effective use of taxpayer funds and results in an identical payoff per dollar of marginal social cost. When the ratio $MSB/MSC > 1$, the value of marginal social benefits exceeds the value of marginal social costs. When the ratio $MSB/MSC < 1$, then the value of marginal social benefits is less than the value of marginal social costs. If the ratio $MSB/MSC = 1$, the value of marginal social benefits exactly equals the value of marginal social costs.

When $MSB/MSC = 1$, a dollar's worth of social benefit is received for each additional dollar spent on government programs and public-investment projects. This relationship implies an important decision rule, assuming that marginal social benefits fall and marginal social costs rise with an increase in the number of government programs and public-sector investment projects. If resources are fully employed throughout the economy, society's net benefit will be maximized when $MSB/MSC = 1$ for the last or *marginal* government program or public-sector investment project. Further net marginal benefits to society are possible through an expansion in the public sector when $MSB/MSC > 1$ for the marginal public-sector project; resources are being squandered in the public sector when $MSB/MSC < 1$ for the marginal public-sector project. Only when $MSB/MSC = 1$ for the marginal public-sector project and private-sector project are resources effectively allocated between the public and private sectors.

BENEFIT-COST ANALYSIS METHODOLOGY

Benefit-cost analysis is often used when the economic consequences of a project or a policy change are apt to extend beyond one year. When compared to the capital budgeting process employed by a private firm, benefit-cost analysis is more complex because it seeks to measure both direct and indirect effects of government programs and public-sector investment projects. While the activities of both private firms and public agencies produce externalities, private firms do not typically consider external effects because they are not able to charge for them. Since public agencies seek to maximize social benefits, they must measure both direct and indirect benefits and costs.

The guiding principle of benefit-cost analysis is economic efficiency in a global sense. Resources are allocated efficiently when they lead to the maximization of total social benefits. The purpose of benefit-cost analysis is to determine if a given public expenditure would produce greater benefits than if such funds were invested in an alternative public program, or if they were instead left in the private sector. The method has been used to determine whether a public-sector program should be undertaken or expanded, and the funding level at which such programs should be supported. While benefit-cost analysis was first applied in France in the 1840s, it was not until the early part of the 20th century that it was used extensively in the U.S. to evaluate river and harbor projects. It has also been applied to projects involving defense, hydroelectric power, water supply availability, recreational facilities, transportation systems, urban renewal projects, educational systems, health, and job creation programs. All benefit-cost analyses consist of five major elements: (1) statement of objectives, (2) discussion of alternatives, (3) quantification of related costs and benefits, (4) selection of a criterion for acceptable project determination and, (5) specification of an appropriate social discount rate.

And finally, benefit-cost analysis objectives must be stated clearly. Objectives should specify a target group, problem, or condition and the nature of the change expected as a result of implementing the program. For example, reducing the nighttime crime rate is not a clear enough objective for effective police department management. A clear objective would be to reduce burglaries by 20% and car thefts by 10%, following an increase in nighttime patrol hours by 50%. The discussion of project alternatives may consist of a choice between one project and no project, or among several public projects differing in purpose, scope, location, and size. If no public project is chosen, the implicit decision is to leave resources in the private sector. A common criticism of benefit-cost analysis is that sophisticated models are applied to poorly chosen alternatives. Since the goal of benefit-cost analysis is the efficient use of social resources, it is necessary to include all realistic alternatives.

THE SOCIAL RATE OF DISCOUNT

Social Rate of Discount
The interest-rate cost of public funds.

Since the benefits and costs of most government programs and public-sector investment projects extend beyond one year, it is necessary to convert these benefits and costs into present-day dollars to accurately compare decision alternatives. Determining the appropriate **social rate of discount,** or interest-rate cost of public funds, is critical to the selection of appropriate alternatives. A low rate favors long-term investments with substantial future benefits; a higher rate favors short-term projects with benefits that accrue soon after the initial investment.

A common approach is to discount the benefits and costs associated with public projects based on the government's cost of borrowed funds. Because government loans are considered risk-free, the government's cost of borrowing is much lower than the private cost of borrowing. An important disadvantage of these low public-sector rates is that they fail to recognize the opportunity cost of funds transferred from the private sector to the public sector. Competition between public-sector and private-sector projects for resources is essential to the efficient allocation of investment capital. Most economists argue that because private-sector resources are used to fund public-sector projects, the marginal private-sector opportunity cost of funds of roughly 10% is the appropriate social rate of discount. The opportunity cost of funds transferred from private investment to the public sector is computed from the average pretax rate of return on private corporate investments. This rate includes a risk premium for the uncertainty about the returns accruing as a result of allocating funds for a given venture. The pretax rate of return for private investments must be used because returns from public-sector projects are not taxed.

The average pretax rate of return on government securities is a very conservative estimate of the opportunity cost of private-sector consumption that is diverted to public use. This is a conservative basis because the interest rate on government securities does not embody any default risk premium, as would be true of long-term corporate bonds. The average pretax rate of return on private-sector investment is a similarly useful estimate of the opportunity cost of funds diverted from private investment. In both cases, the pretax rate of return is used because personal and corporate income taxes simply represent a redistribution of income from the private to the public sector. Since funds for public investments are likely to come from both private consumption and private investments, the weighted average of the opportunity cost of funds coming from these two components of the private sector should be used to compute the social rate of discount.

During the 1990s, a typical pretax rate of return on long-term government bonds is 7.5%, a standard after-tax return on investment in the private sector is 10%, the marginal corporate and individual tax rate is roughly 40%, and consumption averages 94% of total income. Using the assumptions provided, an appropriate average social rate of discount of 8.0% is calculated as follows:

$$
\begin{aligned}
\text{Social rate} \atop \text{of discount} &= \left(\begin{array}{c} \textit{Percentage of funds} \\ \textit{diverted from private-sector} \\ \textit{consumption} \end{array} \right) \times \left(\begin{array}{c} \textit{Before-tax opportunity} \\ \textit{cost of private-sector} \\ \textit{consumption} \\ \textit{(Govt. bond rate)} \end{array} \right) \\
&+ \left(\begin{array}{c} \textit{Pecentage of funds} \\ \textit{diverted from private-sector} \\ \textit{investment} \end{array} \right) \times \left(\begin{array}{c} \textit{After-tax opportunity} \\ \textit{cost of private-sector} \\ \textit{investment} \\ \hline (1 - \textit{Tax rate}) \end{array} \right) \quad \textbf{(16.3)} \\
&= (94\%) \times (7.5\%) + (6\%) \times \left(\frac{10\%}{(1 - 40\%)} \right) \\
&= 8\%.
\end{aligned}
$$

SOCIAL NET PRESENT VALUE ANALYSIS

If adequate public funds are available for all decision alternatives, the appropriate decision criterion must rank-order decision alternatives so that net social benefits are maximized. If public funds are inadequate to fund all desirable decision alternatives, the appropriate decision criterion must rank-order decision alternatives so that marginal social benefits are maximized per dollar of marginal social cost.

Social Net Present Value
The present-value difference between marginal social benefits and marginal social costs.

Under the **social net present value** (*SNPV*) criterion, marginal social benefits and marginal social costs are discounted back to the present using an appropriate social discount rate. Individual government programs and public-sector investment projects are acceptable if the present value of marginal social benefits is greater than or equal to the present value of marginal social costs. In other words, public-sector projects are desirable when the *difference* between the present value of direct and indirect benefits and the present value of direct and indirect costs is greater than or equal to zero. Like net present value analysis in private-sector project evaluation, the social net present value criterion establishes a rank-order of acceptable projects according to the magnitude of the net present value of resulting benefits. Whereas all projects with *SNPV* > 0 represent a productive use of public sector resources, the highest-value projects are those with the highest *SNPV*.

In equation form, the social net present value of an individual government program or public-sector investment project can be written as

$$SNPV_i = \sum_{t=1}^{N} \frac{Marginal\ Social\ Benefits_{it}}{(1 + k_i)^t} - \sum_{t=1}^{N} \frac{Marginal\ Social\ Costs_{it}}{(1 + k_i)^t}, \quad \textbf{(16.4)}$$

where $SNPV_i$ is the $SNPV$ of the ith project, *Marginal Social Benefits*$_{it}$ represent the expected direct and indirect social benefits of the ith project in the tth year, k_i is the appropriate risk-adjusted social discount rate applicable to the ith public-sector project, and *Marginal Social Cost*$_i$ is the government program's or public-sector investment project's cost or initial cash outflow.

As with the profitability index method described in Chapter 15, the social net present value criterion employs an appropriate interest-rate discount factor. In the social net present value approach, the appropriate interest-rate discount factor is the social rate of discount. This rate is comprised of a risk-free component to compensate taxpayers for the economic cost of waiting, plus a risk premium that reflects the level of uncertainty surrounding the realization of program benefits. In equation form, the social rate of discount factor is

$$Social\ Rate\ of\ Discount\ (k_i) = \frac{Risk\text{-}free\ Rate}{of\ Return\ (R_F)} + \frac{Risk\ Premium}{(R_p)}. \quad \textbf{(16.5)}$$

To illustrate the $SNPV$ method, consider the data contained in Table 16.1 for three hypothetical 20-year government programs. Dollar values of marginal social benefits are shown for each year over the projected 20-year life of each program. For simplicity, assume that these values are net of all ongoing costs for program administration; they can be thought of as net marginal social benefits per year. The present values of marginal social costs for each program are comprised of the initial cash outlay required. Notice that Program *A* and Program *C* have an identical investment requirement of $5 million, whereas Program *B* has a somewhat smaller initial outlay of $3 million. Marginal social benefits in nominal terms, or before discounting, total $8.65 million for Program *A*, $10 million for Program *B*, and $24 million for Program *C*. Marginal social benefits before discounting are a misleading measure of the attractiveness of each project because they do not reflect differences in the time frame over which program benefits and costs are generated.

A relevant measure of the attractiveness of each respective program is the social net present value of each program, where each dollar of marginal social benefits and marginal social costs is converted into a common current-dollar basis. The social rate of discount used to convert nominal dollar values into present-value terms is 8% for Program *A*, 10% for Program *B*, and 12% for Program *C*. Each respective social discount rate plays the role of a present-value interest factor that can be used to convert nominal dollar costs and benefits to a common present-value basis. If a 5% yield to maturity on short-term Treasury Bills is taken as a proxy for the risk-free rate, Program *A* involves a 3% risk premium, Program *B* entails a 5% risk premium, and Program *C* employs a 7% risk premium.

| Table 16.1 | HYPOTHETICAL BENEFIT-COST RATIO ANALYSIS FOR THREE GOVERNMENT PROGRAMS |

ANNUAL DOLLAR VALUE OF MARGINAL SOCIAL BENEFIT
ARISING FROM THREE GOVERNMENT PROGRAMS

YEARS	A	B	C
	−$5,000,000	−$3,000,000	−$5,000,000
1	$575,000	$500,000	$250,000
2	560,000	500,000	350,000
3	545,000	500,000	450,000
4	530,000	500,000	550,000
5	515,000	500,000	650,000
6	500,000	500,000	750,000
7	485,000	500,000	850,000
8	470,000	500,000	950,000
9	455,000	500,000	1,050,000
10	440,000	500,000	1,150,000
11	425,000	500,000	1,250,000
12	410,000	500,000	1,350,000
13	395,000	500,000	1,450,000
14	380,000	500,000	1,550,000
15	365,000	500,000	1,650,000
16	350,000	500,000	1,750,000
17	335,000	500,000	1,850,000
18	320,000	500,000	1,950,000
19	305,000	500,000	2,050,000
20	290,000	500,000	2,150,000
Marginal social benefits (in nominal terms)	$8,650,000	$10,000,000	$24,000,000
Present value of marginal social cost (PV of MSC)	$5,000,000	$3,000,000	$5,000,000
Social rate of discount (interest rate)	8%	10%	12%
Present value of marginal social benefits (PV of MSB)	$4,609,087.90	$4,256,781.86	$6,364,117.84
Social net present value (= PV of MSB − PV of MSC)	−$390,912.10	$1,256,781.86	$1,364,117.84
Benefit-cost ratio [= (PV of MSB)/(PV of MSC)]	0.92	1.42	1.27

Because social benefits received in the future are worth less than social costs incurred at the beginning of the program, the *SNPV* for any public program tends to be much less than the nominal dollar amount of social benefits. Using a program-specific social rate of discount, the present value of marginal social benefits is $4,609,087.90 for Program *A*, $4,256,781.86 for Program *B*, and $6,364,117.84 for Program *C*. After considering the present value of marginal social cost for each program, the *SNPV* for Program *A* is $SNPV_A = -\$390,912.10$, calculated as follows:

$$SNPV_A = PV \; of \; MSB - PV \; of \; MSC$$

$$= \$4,609,087.90 - \$5,000,000 \qquad \textbf{(16.6)}$$

$$= -\$390,912.10.$$

The $SNPV_A = -\$390,912.10$ means that the present value of marginal social costs for this program exceeds the present value of marginal social benefits. Funding Program A would represent an unwise use of public resources. Whenever $SNPV < 0$, program funding is unwise on an economic basis. A judicious use of social resources requires that $SNPV > 0$ for every public program or public investment project.

Again using an appropriate program-specific social rate of discount, the present value of marginal social benefits is $4,256,781.86 for Program B and $6,364,117.84 for Program C. After considering the present value of marginal social cost for each program, the $SNPV$ for Program B is $1,256,781.86 and for Program C is $1,364,117.84. Both Programs B and C represent a wise use of public resources since $SNPV_B > 0$ and $SNPV_C > 0$. If public funding is sufficient to fund both projects at the same time, both should be underwritten. If public funding is scarce and both programs cannot be funded, Program C is preferred to Program B since $SNPV_C > SNPV_B$.

As discussed in Chapter 15, large projects tend to be favored through the use of net present value criterion since large net present values usually require the commitment of significant capital resources. In a similar fashion, the $SNPV$ can result in a bias toward larger projects since a large social net present value typically requires the commitment of significant marginal social costs. This has the potential to result in a bias toward larger as opposed to smaller social programs and public-sector investment projects when the $SNPV$ criterion is employed. To avoid such a bias, it becomes necessary to introduce two additional public-sector capital budgeting decision rules.

BENEFIT-COST RATIO ANALYSIS

Benefit-Cost Ratio Analysis
The present value of marginal social benefits per dollar of marginal social cost.

A variant of $SNPV$ analysis that is often used in complex capital budgeting situations is called **benefit-cost (B/C) ratio analysis.** The benefit-cost ratio is calculated as follows:

$$B/C \ ratio_i = \frac{PV \ of \ MSB_i}{PV \ of \ MSC_i} = \frac{\sum\limits_{t=1}^{N} [MSB_{it}/(1 + k_i)^t]}{\sum\limits_{t=1}^{N} [MSC_{it}/(1 + k_i)^t]}. \tag{16.7}$$

The *B/C ratio* shows the *relative* attractiveness of any social program or public-sector investment project, or the present value of marginal social benefits per dollar of marginal social cost.

In Table 16.1, $SNPV > 0$ implies a desirable investment program and *B/C ratio* > 1. For example, the benefit-cost ratio for Program B is:

$$B/C \ ratio = \frac{PV \ of \ MSB}{PV \ of \ MSC}$$

$$= \frac{\$4,256,781.86}{\$3,000,000}$$

$$= 1.42$$

This means that Program *B* returns $1.42 in marginal social benefits for each dollar of marginal social costs, when both figures are expressed in present-value terms. On the other hand, Program *A* returns only 92¢ in marginal social benefits for each dollar of marginal social costs, whereas Program *C* returns $1.27 in marginal social benefits for each dollar of marginal social cost.

In *B/C ratio* analysis, any social program with *B/C ratio* > 1 should be accepted; any program with *B/C ratio* < 1 should be rejected. Programs will be accepted provided that they return more than a dollar of discounted benefits for each dollar of cost. The *B/C ratio* and *SNPV* methods always indicate the same accept/reject decisions for independent programs, since *B/C ratio* > 1 implies *SNPV* > 0 and *B/C ratio* < 1 implies *SNPV* < 0. However, for alternative programs of unequal size, *B/C ratio* and *SNPV* criteria can give different program rankings.

INTERNAL RATE OF RETURN ANALYSIS

Social Internal Rate of Return
The interest or discount rate that equates the present value of the future benefits to the initial cost or outlay.

The **social internal rate of return** (*SIRR*) is the interest or discount rate that equates the present value of the future receipts to the initial cost or outlay. The equation for calculating the social internal rate of return is simply the *SNPV* formula set equal to zero:

$$SNPV_i = 0 = \sum_{t=1}^{N} \frac{MSB_{it}}{(1 + k_i^*)^t} - \sum_{t=1}^{N} \frac{MSC_{it}}{(1 + k_i^*)^t}. \tag{16.8}$$

This equation is solved for the discount rate, k_i^*, that produces a zero net present value by setting discounted future marginal social benefits equal to marginal social costs. That discount rate is the social internal rate of return earned by the program, that is, $SIRR_i = k_i^*$.

Because the social net present value equation is complex, it is difficult to solve for the actual social internal rate of return on an investment without a computer spreadsheet. For this reason, trial and error is sometimes employed. One begins by arbitrarily selecting a social discount rate, such as 10%. If it yields a positive *SNPV*, the social internal rate of return must be greater than the interest or discount rate used, and another higher rate is tried. If the chosen rate yields a negative *SNPV*, the internal rate of return on the program is lower than the social discount rate, and the *SNPV* calculation must be repeated using a lower social discount rate. This process of changing the social discount rate and recalculating the net present value continues until the discounted present value of future marginal social benefits equals the present value of marginal social costs. The interest rate that brings about this equality is the yield, or social internal rate of return on the program.

Using trial and error, an electronic financial calculator, or a spreadsheet software program such as *Lotus 1-2-3* or *Microsoft Excel,* the internal rate of return for Program *A* is $SIRR_A$ = 6.79%. Similarly, $SIRR_B$ = 15.78% and $SIRR_C$ = 14.81%. Since $SIRR_B$ and $SIRR_C$ exceed the cost of capital, Program *B* and Program *C* are attractive and should be undertaken. Since $SIRR_A$ is less than the cost of capital, Program *A* is unattractive and should *not* be undertaken. In general, social internal rate of return analysis suggests that programs should be accepted when the *SIRR* > *k* and rejected when the

The NAFTA Debate

In the early 1990s, backers of the North American Free Trade Agreement (NAFTA) argued that free trade would further open Mexico's economy, causing a surge in exports from the United States and Canada. It was also argued that NAFTA would reduce illegal immigration by raising the standard of living for Mexican workers. The case against NAFTA was most forcefully carried by former head of Electronic Data Systems, ex-presidential candidate Ross Perot. In Perot's view, NAFTA will cost high-wage U.S. jobs by accelerating the migration of "greedy" U.S. corporations to Mexico. Talk-show host and former presidential candidate Pat Buchanan spearheaded conservative opposition by arguing that NAFTA "surrenders" U.S. sovereignty. Veteran consumer activist Ralph Nader portrayed the pact as a prop for a "corrupt" Mexican oligarchy; Democratic Party leader Jesse Jackson argued that low-wage workers would lose jobs because of Mexican imports. Lane Kirkland, president of the AFL-CIO, North America's largest trade union, opposed NAFTA because of fears it would hasten the decline in union membership. More than anything, it was Ross Perot's suggestion of "a giant sucking sound" that fueled the debate. That's the sound one would supposedly hear as, in one great whoosh, the U.S. lost millions of jobs to low-wage Mexicans. Happily, the economic facts are much less scary than the political rhetoric.

When NAFTA went into effect on January 1, 1994, the U.S. and Canada already had a free trade agreement. NAFTA merely extended that agreement to include Mexico and permit duty-free and quota-free movement of goods across all of North America. Perhaps the most glaring irony of the NAFTA debate is that much of the job opportunity transfer feared by Ross Perot and other critics had already occurred prior to NAFTA ratification. In the 1960s, the Johnson Administration reached an agreement with Mexico to allow U.S. companies to locate *maquiladoras,* Spanish for manufacturing plants, in Mexico. These plants imported parts from the U.S. on a duty-free basis, and then exported finished products back to the U.S. for a negligible duty. By 1994, more than 2,000 maquiladoras employed more than a half-million Mexican workers. Why only a half-million Mexican workers in the *maquiladoras* rather than the millions projected by Ross Perot? The answer is productivity. The gap between the productivity of U.S. versus Mexican workers is approximately 8:1, an amount that equals the 8:1 gap in salaries between U.S. and Mexican workers.

When productivity differences are considered, Mexican labor is no cheaper than higher-priced but more efficient labor from the U.S. and Canada. Free trade is enormously beneficial to all Americans, whether they be from Canada, Mexico, or the U.S. Before NAFTA, the tariff imposed by the U.S. on Mexican goods averaged about 4%, while the tariff imposed by Mexico on U.S. goods averaged about 11%. With NAFTA, Mexican, U.S., and Canadian export industries and their workers benefit enormously from the increased access across national boundaries that follows from the abolition of all such tariffs. To extend the many benefits of free and open trade, Congress is now considering bills that would extend NAFTA privileges to Caribbean nations. Such a pact would make way for broad trade agreements that might encompass the southern hemisphere, and eventually our European and Asian trade partners as well.

It is now abundantly clear that free trade agreements like NAFTA do not retard new investment; they spur economic growth. Scare stories about NAFTA and the perils of free trade ignore the experience of other countries with low wages and duty free access to the U.S. market, like Puerto Rico. If low wages were all that mattered, then why haven't all U.S. factories moved to Puerto Rico? Better yet, why isn't *everything* marked "Made in Bangladesh" or "Made in Haiti"? The answer is obvious. With free trade, economic activity flows to where business is most efficient in producing the high-quality goods and services that customers demand. Talented and well-educated U.S. workers compete effectively with low-wage competitors.

See: Christopher Palmeri and Jose Aguayo, "Good Bye Guangdong, Hello Jalisco," *Forbes,* February 10, 1997, 76-77.

$SIRR < k$. When the $SIRR > k$, the marginal rate of return exceeds the marginal cost of capital. As in the case of programs with an $SNPV > 0$ and $B/C\ ratio > 1$, the acceptance of all investment programs with $SIRR > k$ will lead public-sector managers to maximize net social benefits. In instances in which capital is scarce and only a limited number of desirable programs can be undertaken at one point in time, the $SIRR$ can be used to derive a rank ordering of programs from most desirable to least desirable. Like a rank ordering of all $SNPV > 0$ programs from highest to lowest B/C ratios, a rank ordering of potential investment programs from highest to lowest $SIRR$s allows public-sector managers to effectively employ scarce public funds.

LIMITATIONS OF BENEFIT-COST ANALYSIS

Although the benefit-cost analysis is conceptually appealing, it has several limitations that must be considered. Primary among these is the fact that existing measurement techniques are sometimes inadequate for comparing diverse public programs. Without competitive markets for public goods and services, it is difficult to ascertain the social value placed on public programs. How much is it worth to society to provide food stamps and other financial support to poor parents and their children? Is this value reduced when the poor refuse minimum-wage employment opportunities, or when government funds are used for unintended purposes (e.g., to buy alcohol, cigarettes, or illegal drugs)? How do you measure the social value of sophisticated new defense weapons, and how do you compare this value to the value of social programs? What is the social value of the agricultural milk-price support program?

Benefit-cost analysis requires public-sector managers to quantify all relevant factors in dollar terms. Where dollar-value estimation is not possible, qualitative factors must still be considered to prevent the omission of important indirect and intangible impacts. However, the inclusion of qualitative factors makes benefit-cost analysis more complex and its conclusions more ambiguous. At times, analytical results cannot be summarized in a single comparable ratio. Evaluation problems also occur when a non-efficiency objective, such as reducing the level of highway noise pollution around a school yard, must be considered alongside an efficiency objective, such as increasing business activity along a new highway corridor.

Despite these and other obvious problems, benefit-cost analysis enjoys well-documented success as a vital tool for public-sector decision making. At a minimum, benefit-cost analysis forces the itemization and computation of costs and benefits in a manner that is far more precise and useful than many other methods of public-sector decision making. As a result, benefit-cost analysis allows for a more thorough analysis of public policy alternatives than other more limited techniques.

Additional Methods for Improving Public Management

Whereas benefit-cost studies attempt to measure all relevant factors in dollar terms, measurement problems sometimes preclude this possibility. In such situations, alternative means for assessing the effectiveness of decision alternatives must be explored.

The most popular of such methods allow public-sector managers to focus attention on narrowly monitoring the results of existing programs.

COST-EFFECTIVENESS ANALYSIS

Cost-Effectiveness Analysis
A method used to determine how to best employ resources in a given social program or public-sector investment project.

Another technique commonly used to improve public-sector performance is **cost-effectiveness analysis.** The purpose of cost-effectiveness analysis is to determine how to best employ resources in a given social program or public-sector investment project. One common approach is to hold output or service levels constant and then evaluate cost differences resulting from alternative program strategies. For example, a local school board might be interested in evaluating alternative special education programs and their respective costs. The cost-effectiveness analysis approach might compare mainstreaming, separate classrooms, or itinerant teaching in terms of their effectiveness in meeting important special education goals. The most cost-effective method is the decision alternative that meets specific educational goals at minimum cost.

Cost-effectiveness analysis is useful for evaluating the effectiveness of social programs and public-sector investment projects where output can be identified and measured in qualitative terms, but it is difficult to express in monetary terms. For example, cost-effectiveness analysis can be used to evaluate the success of alternative transportation programs such as taxis or social service vehicles for the handicapped, but cannot be used to determine if providing transportation for the handicapped is worthwhile from a resource allocation standpoint. Cost-effectiveness studies are also useful in situations where significant externalities or other intangibles exist that cannot be easily measured in dollar terms. In such cases, negative impacts of social programs can be dealt with by excluding from consideration all decision alternatives that generate negative impacts beyond a certain level. The selection of a preferred alternative is made on the basis of differences in tangible performance measures.

PRIVATIZATION

Privatization
The transfer of public-sector resources to the private sector.

During the 1980s, a **privatization** movement began and accelerated in Europe, the former Soviet Union, and former Eastern Bloc countries. With privatization, public-sector resources are transferred to the private sector in the hope that the profit motive might spur higher product quality, better customer service, and lower costs. The privatization movement has gained momentum during the 1990s in response to growing dissatisfaction with the low quality of many government services and increasing dissatisfaction with cost overruns at the federal, state, and local levels of government.

In the U.S., the privatization movement has thus far failed to generate the type of enthusiasm seen in many foreign countries. Nevertheless, local municipalities across the U.S. are increasing the amount of private-sector contracting for snow removal, garbage collection, and transit services. Since the late-1980s, a majority of state and local governments have greatly increased the amount of public goods and services contracted out to private providers. At the federal level, the U.S. Postal Service, now a quasi-private monopoly, has long used private carriers for rural deliveries. Similarly, the Department of Health and Human Services uses private contractors to process Medicare claims. The privatization movement has clearly made dramatic inroads in countries throughout Europe and Latin America, where government control over the economy has traditionally been comprehensive. During the early-1990s, European and Latin American governments greatly increased the pace at which previously nationalized companies have been returned to the private sector. Prominent examples include electrical utilities, railroads, telecommunications businesses, and steel companies.

The economic justification for privatization is that cheaper and better goods and services result as the profit motive entices firms to improve quality and cut costs. Public agencies and government employees that face competition from the private sector also display an encouraging tendency to improve performance and operating efficiency. In Chicago, for example, competitive bidding between private contractors and city clean-up and repair crews creates incentives for public employees and public managers to become more effective. In a similar situation, the City of Phoenix Public Works department won back a number of garbage collection districts previously lost to private bidders after instituting innovations that lowered operating costs below that of private competitors. Several city and county administrators have reported similar cost savings as a result of privatizing public services. In Milwaukee, school vouchers are given to low-income children to select the private school of their choice. While parental satisfaction with Milwaukee's school voucher program is high, it is too early to tell whether or not educational quality has risen for both private-school and public-school children.

Opponents of privatization argue that the transfer of government programs to the private sector does not necessarily lead to smaller government and fewer budget deficits. Profit-seeking firms who become dependent on public financing lobby for an expansion of public-sector spending with as much vigor as public-sector employees. Evaluating the success of private firms in providing public goods is also made difficult by inadequate performance measures and lax performance monitoring. For example, after the federal government relinquished direct control for job training, under the Job Training Partnership Act, measures used to evaluate program quality appeared to show the program was a success. Fully two-thirds of adult trainees found jobs. These performance measures were biased, however, because training contractors boosted their measured performance by only selecting the most promising job applicants. Similarly, in 1963, the federal government gave millions of dollars to private firms to build and staff mental health centers without developing a process to track results. By the 1980s, many of these centers were converted to for-profit status and served only those able to pay, leaving the poor and indigent without adequate mental health care.

A final argument against privatization is that the goal of public services is not just to achieve a high level of efficiency, but to provide benefits that private markets cannot or do not provide. A private firm may, for example, find it unprofitable to educate unruly children from single-parent homes with little commitment to education. For-profit hospitals may find it prohibitively expensive to offer emergency room care to violent teens from inner-city neighborhoods. As a result, questions of what and how much to privatize must focus on those instances where privatization can work best. Successful privatization also requires specific goals and measurement criteria that clearly define the public interest. And finally, successful privatization efforts depend upon a direct link between the achievement of recognized goals and the compensation of public-sector *and* private-sector managers.

Macroeconomic Growth and Stabilization Policy

Macroeconomic policies shape the environment within which households and businesses make decisions. These policies are also important tools used to pursue the goals of economic growth, full employment, and stable purchasing power for the national currency. Economic growth increases social welfare because it leads to improved living standards for rich and poor alike. An economic environment that includes fee markets, well-designed and efficient regulation where necessary, and legal protection of property rights fosters such progress.

BUSINESS CYCLES AND LONG-TERM ECONOMIC PERFORMANCE

Business Cycle
Fluctuations of output around a long-term trend, or recessions followed by recoveries and expansions.

Stabilization Policy
Strategy designed to offset temporary economic disruptions.

The **business cycle** refers to fluctuations of output around a long-term trend, or recessions followed by recoveries and expansions. However, there is nothing regular about the timing and magnitude of these fluctuations. The relative economic stability of the post-World War II era may reflect fewer or less severe economic disturbances. It also may be due to the development of **stabilization policy** designed to offset temporary economic disruptions. These policies are particularly important in light of the fact that the costs of recessions are not shared evenly across the population. For most families, incomes remain roughly the same or continue to grow during a recession; the economic and social costs of recessions fall disproportionately on those who experience unemployment. While carefully chosen stabilization policies cannot eliminate recessions, they have the potential to reduce the frequency and severity of economic downturns.

To understand the limitations of policy, factors that contribute to recessions must be taken into account. A sharp reduction in national defense expenditures, for example, gives rise to structural adjustments in production and employment. Such reductions followed World War II, the Korean, and Vietnam wars and are now taking place in response to the end of the Cold War. While society as a whole is obviously better off when conflict ends and the resources devoted to national defense can be put to better use, large decreases in military spending disrupt employment as production patterns adjust to meet changing demands. External shocks in the form of large and sudden oil price increases have also been an important factor in several recent recessions. The partial embargo on oil exports by the Organization of Petroleum Exporting Countries in 1973 tripled world oil prices. Since oil is an important input in production, oil price shocks forced many industries to change production methods. Moreover, since the U.S. is a net oil importer, oil price shocks transfer income and wealth to oil exporting countries and thereby reduce the overall demand for domestic output. It is important to recognize that even if no policy mistakes are made, structural adjustments and external shocks may cause occasional periods of declining output. It is unrealistic to expect that well-chosen public policies can compensate completely for all types of economic disturbances.

MONETARY POLICY

Monetary Policy
Actions taken by the Federal Reserve (the Fed) that influence bank reserves, the money stock, and interest rates.

Monetary policy refers to actions taken by the Federal Reserve (the Fed) that influence bank reserves, the money stock, and interest rates. An expansionary monetary policy lowers short-term interest rates by increasing the availability of money and credit. Lower interest rates encourage spending, particularly on investment projects. If the economy is operating well below capacity, increased spending is likely to lead to increased output. Once the economy is at or near capacity, however, rapid monetary expansion leads to inflation (a sustained increase in prices) rather than output growth. Conversely, tight monetary policy reduces the growth rate of the money stock, increases short-term interest rates, and eventually lowers inflation. In the short run, the Fed can use monetary policy to increase the availability of credit and to lower interest rates. In the long run, an excessively expansionary monetary policy leads to inflation and higher nominal interest rates. While interest rates, monetary aggregates, and other indicators help the Fed assess the effects of its actions, no set of indicators provides a reliable forecast of the future consequences of current monetary policy choices.

The goal of using monetary policy to increase output without increasing inflation is inherently difficult to achieve. When the Fed increases or decreases bank reserves, the path from reserve changes to interest rates to output and prices is often unpredictable. In recent years, a number of factors have further complicated the task of setting monetary policy. The weakening in the relation among the money supply, interest rates, and nominal GDP has decreased the reliability of monetary aggregates as indicators of policy. Transitory problems in financial markets and structural changes in the global economy have also altered the response of the U.S. economy to Fed policy. As such, the use of monetary policy to fine tune the U.S. economy has become increasingly problematic.

FISCAL POLICY

Fiscal Policy
Spending and taxing policies of the government.

Fiscal policy refers to the spending and taxing policies of the federal government. Fiscal policy can influence total demand in the economy by changing taxes and government spending. Expansionary fiscal policy, for example, implements tax cuts, increases government spending, or both, to increase economic activity during business downturns. Fiscal policy can also affect incentives to work, save, invest, and innovate. Changes in taxes on capital, for example, affect the after-tax return on investment in physical assets and thus the incentive for capital accumulation.

Automatic Stabilizers
Buffers designed to smooth the pace of economic activity.

Automatic stabilizers act as buffers when the economy weakens by automatically reducing taxes and increasing government spending. Mandatory spending for programs such as unemployment insurance, food stamps, welfare programs, and medicaid increases when the economy slows down since benefit criteria depend upon income or employment status. These transfer payments help consumers maintain spending. The tax system as a whole also acts as an automatic stabilizer. In an economic slump, personal income and corporate profits are lower, so tax payments fall, thus helping to reduce the decline in after-tax incomes that might otherwise occur. Government revenues from excise and other sales-based taxes also fall when purchases decline. In fact, taxes typically change by a larger proportion than GDP, primarily because average income tax rates fall with income levels. This feature of the tax system makes after-tax income more stable than pretax income, which helps insulate consumption spending from changes in income.

Discretionary Policy
Unrestricted changes in spending and taxes.

Discretionary policy refers to new changes in spending and taxes. Classic examples of discretionary fiscal policy include the 1964 tax cut intended to stimulate spending and economic expansion, and the income tax surcharge of 1968 designed to curb rising inflation. Since the change in total expenditures determines whether policy has been expansionary or contractionary, it is difficult to attribute expansionary fiscal policy to specific acts of spending. For example, increased highway spending is expansionary only if it is not offset by a decline in some other appropriation. Nevertheless, changes in discretionary spending by federal, state, and local governments can have significant effects on the overall economy.

THE LIMITS OF MONETARY AND FISCAL POLICY

Support for activist economic policy was weakened considerably by the historical experience of the 1960s and 1970s. Output grew rapidly in the 1960s, but inflation, as measured by the rate of change in the consumer price index, rose from 0.7% during 1961 to 6.20% during 1969. In the 1970s, the economy experienced simultaneous increases in inflation and unemployment. This contradicted the idea of a stable trade-off between inflation and unemployment and led to a rethinking of the efficacy of fine-tuning. Given recent failures in fine-tuning the U.S. economy, some have taken the position that there is no predictable benefit to countercyclical policies. This argument is based on the belief that policy changes increase costly uncertainty among private-sector decision makers.

Economic Expectations
Anticipated financial considerations.

To be sure, changes in **economic expectations** place severe limits on the effectiveness of fiscal and monetary stabilization policy. People's actions depend not only on their current situation but also on their expectations for the future. For example, when the government introduces a temporary investment tax credit, businesses have an incentive to shift investment expenditures to the period in which the credit applies. However, if they merely shift capital spending from one period to another rather than increase the overall amount of investment, the positive effect on economic growth will be limited.

Crowding Out
The reduction in private investment associated with an increase in government spending.

Changes in government purchases may also have limited effects on total spending. For example, if an appropriation for the construction of a new highway system is not accompanied by a corresponding increase in tax revenues, the budget deficit and government borrowing will increase. Such an increase in government borrowing may put upward pressure on interest rates and discourage investment spending, thus offsetting at least part of the increase in total demand resulting from the construction project. The reduction in private investment associated with an increase in government spending is known as the **crowding out** phenomenon. Given the enormous budget deficits of the 1990s, further increases in government spending might create expectations of higher future deficits and tighter conditions in credit markets and exacerbate the crowding out problem.

A Canadian-style plan for health care reform in the U.S. is gaining some acceptance among policy makers and others. The single-payer, or Canadian-style, solution to health-care reform has long been dismissed by those who cringe at the idea of turning over one-seventh of the U.S. economy to the federal government. However, given the flaws of President Clinton's health care reform plan, some are taking another look (north) at the single-payer system.

A single-payer system would decimate the U.S. health-insurance industry in one swift stroke. Moreover, the Congressional Budget Office estimates that such a method for providing U.S. health-care services would cost a breathtaking $556 billion in federal spending by 1998. With roughly 265 million Americans, this amounts to more than $2,000 for each man, woman, and child in the U.S. On the positive side, such a plan would preserve the freedom to choose your own doctor and the freedom of physicians to order care as they see fit. Both these principles are seriously compromised by managed-care plans that would force most Americans to choose among narrow treatment options. Under the leading single-payer proposal, sponsored by Representative Jim McDermott (D-Wash.), the federal government would become responsible for virtually all medical bills, including prescription drugs, mental-health treatment, and long-term nursing-home care. So-called frills, like private hospital rooms, would not be covered. As in Canada, taxpayers would pick up the entire tab for covered procedures.

McDermott would finance a U.S. single-payer system with stiff federal tax increases, which might be at least partially offset by a decline in insurance premiums. Businesses with more than 75 workers and wages averaging more than $24,000 per employee would face an 8.4% payroll tax. Smaller businesses would pay 4%, while individuals would pay 2.1% directly. In addition, McDermott would increase the federal cigarette tax to $2 a pack from 24¢ and impose a new 50% excise tax on handguns and ammunition. With projected cost savings, McDermott estimates that 75% of Americans would pay less than they do presently for health-care coverage.

Critics challenge McDermott's underlying assumption that the government is capable of eliminating much of the bureaucracy of American medicine. Due to the paperwork and complexity of private insurance, some 24% of U.S. health-care spending now goes to administration, compared with only 11% in Canada. In fact, the Congressional Budget Office (CBO) estimates that a single-payer system would trim U.S. medical overhead by up to $100 billion a year, an amount large enough to provide coverage for 40 million uninsured Americans. Still others fear that a single-payer system would lead to runaway demand for services and then rationing. It would also give the government exclusive power to make life-and-death decisions. To control spending, a U.S. single-payer system would establish a national health budget indexed to economic growth. While Canada and other nations have proven that such budgets can work, the CBO predicts that a single-payer system in the U.S. would cause demand to surge for physician services by 30%, home health care by 50%, and triple demand for drug-abuse treatment. The legitimate fear is that the states would then have to ration care by imposing waiting lines and spending limits on new technology.

All in all, the pros of a single-payer U.S. system can be summarized as:

- *Potential administrative and paperwork cost savings.*
- *Universal coverage.*
- *Preservation of some consumer choice.*
- *Maintenance of some physician autonomy.*

The cons of such a system for U.S. health care are:

- *The projected $500 billion explosion in federal spending and taxes.*
- *Rationing and waiting lines for some treatments, as has happened in Canada.*
- *Quality deterioration as spending caps squeeze R&D and the adoption of new innovations.*
- *Political upheaval as health-care insurers and some providers are forced out of business.*

As the health-care debate unfolds, it will be interesting to see if the U.S. adopts a Canadian solution!

See: William C. Symonds, "Whither a Health Care Solution? Oh, Canada," *Business Week,* March 21, 1994, 82-85; and Ron Winslow, "Health-Care Costs May Be Heading Up Again," *The Wall Street Journal,* January 21, 1997, B1, B6.

Economic Growth Policy

Americans enjoy a remarkably high average standard of living. Retirees today enjoy roughly three times the level of real personal consumption expenditures typical when they were born. At this same rate of growth, our current standard of living will rise by 50% in less than 25 years and double in roughly 40 years. Such is the power of economic growth.

PUBLIC AND PRIVATE BENEFITS OF GROWTH

Productive investments in institutions, technology, education, and physical capital all contribute to growth. Resources for investment are obtained when people save and invest. Growth can be accomplished by encouraging current generations to sacrifice so that future generations may be better off. Conversely, growth can be reduced when the capital stock is run down or when governments borrow from future generations to increase consumption today.

Some argue that because future generations are not represented in the political process, government actions that reduce their well-being are inherently unfair. The national debt, a liability passed on to the future, is sometimes cited as indicative of a government financial policy that is unjust in this sense. Future generations, however, inherit stocks of private and public capital, technology, knowledge, and institutions. Government-sponsored public schools and financial aid to college and university students represent transfers from older to younger generations. Government-sponsored scientific research also provides benefits to both current and future generations. With a constantly growing stock of productive assets, consumers on average are likely to be better off in the future than they are today. Some argue that given rising income, it is proper for the government to redistribute income from future generations to the current generation, much like any income redistribution from the rich to the poor. Others seek to increase the ability of future generations to raise living standards, as have past generations.

Few people, however, would argue that ever-higher economic growth rates are worthwhile regardless of cost. Even if such increases were desirable, current sacrifice alone does not ensure rapid growth. For example, the former Soviet Union directed massive amounts of resources away from consumption and into investment, but such investments were so poorly managed that this sacrifice went largely unrewarded. The collapse of communism in Eastern Europe and the former Soviet Union is in large part the result of the failure of that economic system to raise living standards.

ECONOMIC GROWTH AND THE ENVIRONMENT

Properly understood, economic growth means not just "more" but "better." Living standards rise not just because people consume more goods and services, but because the quality of those goods and services improves. This includes the services of a sound environment. As the U.S. has grown economically, it has also devoted an increasing share of national income to environmental protection.

To ensure economic progress consistent with environmental concerns, some have advocated the concept of "sustainable development." To some, sustainable development means that each generation should pass on to future generations an undiminished stock of natural resources. However, such a definition fails to take into account the fact that a reduction in the stock of one resource can be worthwhile for present and future generations if it generates more valuable increases in another resource. For example, future generations could benefit if part of a forest is harvested to build a school, yet they might be harmed if the school were built with the last remaining ancient forest. A better definition of sustainable development is growth in which every generation passes on a stock of "net resources" no lower in per capita value than the stock it received. Net resources include natural and environmental resources as well as knowledge, technology, and physical capital.

LIMITS TO GROWTH?

Some believe that economic growth is severely constrained by finite natural resources. This view traces its roots at least as far back as Thomas Malthus, who wrote in the 18th century that the population has a natural tendency to grow faster than food production, and hence is constrained by starvation, pestilence, and war. The "limits-to-growth" view, however, neglects the fact that competitive markets adjust to scarcity. When goods, services, or raw materials become scarce, prices rise and both consumers and producers are motivated to find more efficient ways of obtaining and using them. Rising energy prices encourage conservation; rising land prices encourage improvements in agricultural techniques that increase food output. Contrary to the Malthusian view, world cereal production has actually grown faster than the global population for nearly 200 years.

Nevertheless, when markets do not operate well, valuable resources can be consumed too rapidly or be exhausted. Inadequate property rights in water or forest resources, for example, can result in their future value being neglected. In such cases, establishing reliable property rights or, where markets are seriously deficient, establishing appropriate fees or regulations constitute the economically sensible approach.

Public policies designed to enhance the skills and productivity of the labor force are critical to ensuring that the rising living standards made possible by economic growth are spread throughout the economy. Increased funding for Head Start, a program aimed at developing learning skills at an early age; promoting school choice for elementary and secondary education; better access to higher education; and improved job training all have the potential to spur economic growth. Sound policies to protect the environment and manage natural resources can also strengthen the framework for growth. The current income tax system can also be reformed to eliminate aspects that inhibit growth. Among these modifications are cutting the tax rate on savings and entrepreneurship, depreciation reform, and eliminating the double taxation of corporate dividends.

Trade Policy

International trade, or the voluntary exchange of goods and services across national boundaries, increases the well-being of all participants by promoting economic efficiency in a variety of ways. International trade allows each country to concentrate on its most productive activities. Trade also gives firms access to the large international market, allowing them to increase output and lower average costs by taking advantage of scale economies. Access to world markets for raw materials, capital goods, and technology also improves productivity. Foreign competition forces domestic monopolies or oligopolies to lower prices, and imported goods provide consumers with greater choice. Finally, a liberal trade environment can provide a better climate for investment and innovation, thus raising the rate of economic growth.

PUBLIC BENEFITS OF FREE TRADE

International trade has grown much faster than world production during recent years. The rapid recent increase in world trade is, in part, the result of the General Agreement on Tariffs and Trade (GATT), which was created after World War II to reduce tariffs and remove other nontariff barriers to international trade. Expanding opportunities for international trade have effects similar to those of technological improvements: For the same amount of input more output will be produced. Open trade is especially beneficial to developing economies that have less competitive markets and need modern capital goods. By creating new competition, providing domestic producers with access to large international markets, and improving the environment for investment, international trade can make a vital contribution to economic development.

An important counterpart to an integrated global trade system is a well-functioning international financial system. The international financial system serves several important functions. It provides traders with access to foreign exchange and credit, thereby expanding the scope for commercial transactions. It also allows nations to finance trade imbalances through private capital flows, government borrowing and lending, or changes in reserves. The international financial system also encourages capital to move to countries where it is more productive. Capital inflows can finance domestic investment and thereby enable a country to invest more than it saves. Finally, international finance allows investors to diversify investment portfolios and reduce the risk of loss due to poor economic performance or political upheaval in any single country.

The growth in international finance is the result not only of the increase in international trade but also of improvements in technology, financial innovations, and changes in regulation. As an important example, the removal of external capital restrictions in Europe contributed to the creation in the 1950s and 1960s of **Eurodollar markets,** in which banks outside the U.S. accept deposits and make loans denominated in dollars. More recently, Eurodollar markets have developed into **Eurocurrency markets** with transactions in a variety of currencies in addition to dollars and have expanded throughout much of the globe. Both markets play an important role in taking deposits from countries running trade surpluses and lending those funds to nations needing funds to pay for trade deficits.

THE NORTH AMERICAN FREE TRADE AGREEMENT (NAFTA)

In 1992, the U.S., Canada, and Mexico reached an agreement to create a free-trade area with more than 360 million consumers and over $6 trillion in annual output. The so-called NAFTA accord will stimulate growth, promote investment in North America, enhance the ability of North American producers to compete, and raise the standard of living of all three countries. NAFTA will also speed technological progress and provide innovating companies with a larger market. Many economic studies show that NAFTA will lead to higher wages, lower prices, and higher economic growth.

NAFTA is an important recent example of the worldwide move to open trade among countries. NAFTA eliminates most barriers to trade among Canada, Mexico, and the U.S.; opens markets in banking, insurance, and telecommunications; ensures nondiscriminatory treatment for global investors; protects intellectual property rights; and provides dispute settlement mechanisms. Like any free-trade agreement, NAFTA reinforces the market-based economic reforms under way in Mexico. As the Mexican economy grows, it will provide the U.S. with a valuable and growing market for exports. Benefits derived from NAFTA, and lessons learned in its negotiation, will help in the 21st century as the global community struggles to define the relationship between trade and competition policy, a code of conduct for government support of high-technology industries, and the clarification of trade and environmental issues.

Public Management of Health Care

Americans are living longer, healthier lives than ever before. Since 1960, average life expectancy has increased by more than five years. American physicians have access to the best technology in the world, and more than one-half of the world's medical research is funded by private and public sources in the U.S. At the same time, the share of national income devoted to health care has been growing rapidly. Concern about rising expenditures and reduced access to insurance has led to the development of a variety of proposals for health-care reform, from market-based managed care to calls for a government-run national health insurance program. Economic analysis is very helpful in understanding the potential of these alternative approaches.

THE ECONOMICS OF HEALTH CARE

Two features of health-care services have significant economic implications. First, it is difficult for consumers to independently evaluate the quality of health-care services. Consumers typically rely on the advice of service providers in deciding what to buy. While the lack of independent information is not unique to the health-care market (car owners often rely on mechanics), it can lead to the purchase of poor quality, unnecessary, or high-cost services. Second, to protect consumers from unscrupulous or incompetent providers, licensing boards in every state regulate those who work in the health-care field. Such licensing procedures can increase the cost of health-care services by limiting price and product quality competition.

Physicians have much more information about treating particular illnesses than do patients. Patients often find it difficult to evaluate the efficacy of their treatment. Even if they get better, they may not be able to tell whether they have enjoyed a natural recovery or have benefited from especially effective treatment. Lack of service quality information also makes it difficult for people to make rational decisions about purchasing health-care services. Without an accurate way to measure quality, health care plans, hospitals, and providers have a difficult time competing on the basis of the price of services they offer. To address this problem, insurers and employers have recently been working together to develop systems for measuring the quality of health care provided.

In some instances, health-care costs have risen because of restrictive government regulations. Industry costs typically rise when skilled personnel and materials are in short supply. In most cases, short-term shortages cause wages to rise, attracting new supplies of skilled workers. As a result, extreme personnel shortages and the high wages that they produce are not likely to persist. Historically, high physician incomes didn't lead to an increased supply of doctors because the medical profession limited the number of new physicians receiving licenses. For many years, professional associations also controlled advertising and the types of fee arrangements that doctors could accept. These problems are less serious today. With new and more enlightened government regulation, the number of practicing doctors and price competition has increased greatly.

A further problem stems from the fact that all medical insurance, whether privately or publicly provided, affects the incentives of the insured. Because they are protected against the full cost of a serious illness or injury, insureds have less incentive to take steps to limit the losses associated with such events. The change in incentives that results from the purchase of insurance is known as the **moral hazard problem,** or the difficulty encountered when the full costs of economic activity are not directly borne by the consumer. This term carries no connotation of dishonesty; it simply refers to the typical reduction in the economic incentive to avoid undesirable events. For example, people insured against car theft may leave their doors unlocked, increasing the chance that their cars may be stolen. While people with health insurance may be careful about avoiding health risks, they are prone to go to the doctor often and choose complex medical procedures. Among health economists, the term *moral hazard* has come to explain why insurance provides incentives for the overconsumption of health-care services.

Moral Hazard Problem
Change in incentives that results from the purchase of insurance.

MARKET-BASED HEALTH-CARE REFORM

Uncontrollable increases in health-care expenditures and the growing number of uninsured have led to a proliferation of proposals for U.S. health-care reform. While most of these plans seek to alleviate the symptoms of trouble in the health-care market, relatively few address underlying causes of health-care cost increases and gaps in insurance coverage. Because the health-care sector is flexible and responsive, health reforms that address underlying economic problems and provide sound incentives can be effective.

Reforms that ignore the economics of health care are likely to lead to unexpected and undesirable results. Table 16.2 summarizes general features of four leading proposals for health-care reform.

Among the most promising health-care reform proposals is a market-based reform plan designed to expand access to health insurance and to improve the private markets for health-care services. The market-based plan would provide low-income Americans with a transferable tax credit for purchasing health insurance. Those who do not file tax returns would receive the credit in the form of a transferable health insurance certificate. Because low-income Americans would be able to purchase basic health insurance using tax credits, they would no longer have to rely on the public hospital safety net. At the same time, the fixed-dollar nature of the credit or deduction would discourage overconsumption of health insurance. The market-based plan would expand health insurance coverage by promoting the use of health insurance networks to act as group purchasing

SIDE-BY-SIDE COMPARISON OF HEALTH-CARE REFORM PROPOSALS

Table 16.2 ISSUE	MARKET-BASED PROPOSAL	MANAGED COMPETITION PROPOSAL	PAY-OR-PLAY	NATIONAL HEALTH INSURANCE
MORAL HAZARD	Encourages managed care for public programs.	Promotes use of basic benefit package.	—	—
COST CONTAINMENT	Increases competition in small group market and public programs. Improves availability of health-care quality information. Simplifies recordkeeping and billing. Reduces malpractice litigation costs.	Increases competition in small group market.	Provider and hospital fee schedule.	Global budgets. Physician and hospital fee schedule.
ACCESS TO POOR	Provides low and middle income people with insurance certificate/deduction.	Mandates coverage through employers. Provides subsidies to low income people who are not employed and to part-time workers.	Requires employers to offer insurance or pay into public plan.	Universal coverage.
ACCESS FOR THOSE IN ILL HEALTH	Implements health risk adjusters for high-risk people in individual and small group health insurance markets.	Provides age-adjusted community-rated coverage in individual and small group health insurance markets.	Covers employed persons in ill health.	Universal coverage.

Source: "The Economics of Health Care," *Economic Report of the President* (Washington, D.C.: Government Printing Office, 1993), 155.

agents for smaller employers, thus obtaining more favorable premiums and reducing administrative costs. The plan would incorporate health risk pools that spread the cost of serious health problems among all those purchasing health insurance. Low- and middle-income people with chronic health problems would have greatly improved access to health-care through this combination of tax credits and health risk pools. Under the market-based plan, everyone would not be required to purchase health insurance. Those eligible for only a partial credit or deduction could decide not to purchase health insurance, and continue to pay their own expenses or rely on the existing health-care safety net.

PUBLIC MANAGEMENT OF HEALTH-CARE REFORM

In an evolving plan for comprehensive health-care reform, the Clinton Administration proposed an alternative "managed competition" approach. Although managed competition has some market-oriented features, it would greatly increase the role of government in the health-care system and limit the range of health insurance options available. The concept of managed competition is built around the "accountable health partnership," an organization similar to a health maintenance organization (HMO) that would provide both health benefits and consumer information. Each accountable health partnership would be registered with a national health board that would define "uniform effective health benefits" that each partnership would be required to provide. All insurers, both private and public, would be required to offer the same basic benefit plan.

The mechanism for cost containment under this plan is competition among accountable health partnerships over the price of a minimum benefit package. Although taxpayers could choose any minimum benefits insurance package offered by any participating accountable health partnership, they would not be able to deduct from taxable income more than the cost of the minimum benefit package offered by the cheapest accountable health partnership. Theoretically, this tax subsidy limit would encourage taxpayers to choose less comprehensive health insurance and efficiently run insurance plans. With managed competition the government would take an active role in selecting the basic benefit package and in defining the type of insurance that most people would be able to purchase.

THE OUTLOOK FOR HEALTH-CARE REFORM

It is speculative to project that the U.S. health-care system will evolve along the lines of market-based proposals, managed competition plans, or by more traditional "play-or-pay" or national health insurance proposals. Pay-or-play plans require firms to provide basic health insurance to employees and their dependents ("play") or pay a payroll tax to cover enrollment in a public health-care plan ("pay"). Proposals for national health insurance envision replacing the private health insurance market with a single national health insurer. National health insurance would be funded through taxes and care would be free (as in Canada) or provided at a low cost-sharing level.

Clearly, no plan for health-care reform is without its pluses and minuses, costs and benefits. While managed competition would encourage rivalry among health insurers providing a basic benefit package, the government would become responsible for defining the benefits that most Americans would receive. On the other hand, play-or-pay proposals would improve access to insurance by mandating employer coverage, but they do not address the problem of rising medical costs and may cause firms to lay off low-wage workers. National health insurance proposals would provide insurance for all Americans, but could lead to a cost explosion. Reforms that give consumers, insurers, and providers appropriate incentives are likely to be most effective in controlling costs, improving access, and giving consumers the quality of health care that they want.

Summary

Public and not-for-profit organizations face many of the same problems that challenge companies in the for-profit sector. Competing demands on public funds and not-for-profit organization budgets force responsible managers to consider the marginal social benefits and marginal social costs of each alternative program and investment project. Like managers of companies in the for-profit sector, government officials and managers of not-for-profit organizations must optimize resource use under a variety of operating constraints.

- A traditional rationale for public management of economic resources is the perception of private market failures to efficiently provide and equitably allocate economic goods and services. If the consumption of a product by one individual does not reduce the amount available for others, the product is referred to as a **public good.** A **private good** is one where consumption by one individual precludes or limits consumption by others. The distinguishing characteristic of public goods is the concept of **nonrival consumption.** In the case of public goods, use by certain individuals does not reduce availability for others. A good or service is characterized by the **nonexclusion concept** if it is impossible or prohibitively expensive to confine the benefits of consumption to paying customers.

- A **free-rider problem** often materializes in the case of public goods because each consumer believes that the public good will be provided irrespective of his or her contribution towards covering its costs. A **hidden preferences problem** also emerges in the provision of public goods because individuals have no economic incentive to accurately reveal their true demand for public goods.

- **Public choice theory** is the philosophy of how government decisions are made and implemented. The study of public choice theory considers how government and the political process actually work, rather than how they should work. It explicitly recognizes the possibility of **government failure,** or circumstances where public policies reflect narrow private interests, rather than the general public interest.

- **Voters** in the political process are the counterpart of consumers in the marketplace. According to public choice theory, voters are less informed about political decisions than about market decisions due to their **rational ignorance.** Because elected officials act for the community as a whole, high information costs and each individual's low ability to directly influence public choices, voters often find it sensible to remain relatively uninformed about public policy decisions. **Politicians** are the political-system counterpart of entrepreneurs and managers in the private market system. **Special-interest groups** are organized lobbyists that actively support the passage of laws and regulations that further their own narrow economic interests. According to public choice theory, public employees, or **bureaucrats,** are not passive executors of adopted policies; they actively seek to influence these policies to further personal interests.

■ If investment in a public project makes at least one individual better off and no one worse off, then the project is described as **Pareto satisfactory.** When all such government programs and investment projects have been undertaken, the situation is deemed to be **Pareto optimal.** In practice, it is often deemed adequate when public programs and projects meet the criteria of a **potential Pareto improvement,** where there are positive *net* benefits.

■ The **marginal social costs** of any good or service equal the marginal cost of production plus any **marginal external costs** that are not directly borne by producers or their customers. Production costs that are borne by producers and their customers represent private economic costs; external costs include the value of foregone alternative goods and services. In the absence of marginal external costs, **marginal private costs** and marginal social costs are equal at all levels of output. **Marginal social benefits** are the sum of **marginal private benefits** plus **marginal external benefits.** Marginal private benefits are enjoyed by those who directly pay for any good or service; marginal external benefits are enjoyed by purchasers and non-purchasers alike and are not reflected in market prices. When no externalities are present, marginal social benefits equal marginal private benefits.

■ The **social rate of discount** is the interest-rate cost of public funds. According to the **social net present value** (*SNPV*) criterion, social programs and public-sector investment projects are acceptable if the present value of marginal social benefits is greater than or equal to the present value of marginal social costs. **Benefit-cost ratio analysis** shows the *relative* attractiveness of any social program or public-sector investment project, or the present value of marginal social benefits per dollar of marginal social cost. The **social internal rate of return** (*SIRR*) is the interest or discount rate that equates the present value of the future receipts of a program to the initial cost or outlay.

■ Once the resource allocation decision has been made, the purpose of **cost-effectiveness analysis** is to determine how to best employ resources in a given social program or public-sector investment project. With **privatization,** public-sector resources are sold or otherwise transferred to the private sector in the hope that the profit motive might spur higher product quality, better customer service, and lower costs for production and distribution.

■ **Monetary policy** refers to actions taken by the Federal Reserve (the Fed) that influence bank reserves, the money stock, and interest rates. **Fiscal policy** refers to the spending and taxing policies of the federal government. The **business cycle** refers to fluctuations of output around a long-term trend, or recessions followed by recoveries and expansions. Recent reductions in the volatility of economic activity may be due to the development of **stabilization policy** designed to offset temporary economic disruptions. **Automatic stabilizers** act as buffers when the economy weakens by automatically reducing taxes and increasing government spending. **Discretionary policy** refers to new changes in spending and taxes.

■ **International trade,** or the voluntary exchange of goods and services across national boundaries, increases the well-being of all participants by promoting economic efficiency in a variety of ways. The **Eurodollar market** is a market in which banks outside the U.S. accept deposits and make loans denominated in dollars. Eurodollar markets have developed into **Eurocurrency markets** with transactions in a variety of currencies in addition to dollars.

■ While sometimes effective, changes in **economic expectations** and certain indirect effects of government actions place severe limits on the effectiveness of fiscal and monetary stabilization policy. The reduction in private investment associated with an increase in government spending is known as the **crowding out** phenomenon. Change in incentives that results from the purchase of insurance is known as the **moral hazard problem,** or the difficulty encountered when the full costs of economic activity are not directly borne by the consumer.

During the 1990s, microeconomic and macroeconomic policies are employed by all levels of government as a means for improving upon private-sector price and output decisions. At the same time, government agencies and not-for-profit organizations find themselves besieged by competing demands for scarce goods and services. This chapter illustrates how the tools and techniques of managerial economics can be employed to improve decision making in the not-for-profit sector and refine the management of scarce public resources.

QUESTIONS

Q16.1 Describe the traditional rationale for public management of economic resources. Is this rationale viable during the 1990s in light of massive government deficits?

Q16.2 Describe the essential difference between public and private goods. Give some examples of each and some examples of goods and services that involve elements of both.

Q16.3 Does the fact that public decisions are sometimes made by self-interested politicians and bureaucrats undermine the basic premise of public choice theory?

Q16.4 Describe some of potential causes of the Great Depression and the range of factors that influence the timing and magnitude of economic fluctuations in general.

Q16.5 One of the most vexing issues to complicate the health-care debate is the problem that there is no simple link between general health and well-being and the amount spent on health care. Briefly describe why the connection between health care and health is not a simple one. Does the weakness of the link between health and health care have any implications for mandatory universal coverage proposals?

Q16.6 What features of the health-care services market can lead to the purchase of poor quality, unnecessary, or high-cost services?

Q16.7 Among health economists, the term *moral hazard* has come to explain why insurance provides incentives for the overconsumption of health-care services. Describe this idea and its economic implications.

Q16.8 Describe why government policy that increases the well-being of one generation at the expense of another may or may not be just in the ethical sense.

Q16.9 "Economic growth is ultimately constrained by finite natural resources. In a capitalist system, the population has a natural tendency to grow faster than food production and hence is only constrained by starvation, pestilence, and war. It is the proper role of government to own and manage natural re-

sources so that the limits-to-growth are managed in a humane manner." Discuss this statement.

Q16.10 Describe some of the social benefits of international trade.

SELF-TEST PROBLEMS AND SOLUTIONS

ST16.1 **Benefit-Cost Analysis Methodology.** The benefit-cost approach is not new: the concept first surfaced in France in 1844. In this century, benefit-cost analysis has been widely used in the evaluation of river and harbor projects since as early as 1902. In the U.S., the 1936 Flood Control Act authorized federal assistance in developing flood-control programs "if the benefits to whomsoever they may accrue are in excess of the estimated costs." By 1950, federal agency practice required the consideration of both direct and indirect benefits and costs and that unmeasured intangible influences be listed. Despite this long history of widespread use, it has only been since 1970 that public-sector managers have sought to broadly apply the principles of benefit-cost analysis to the evaluation of agricultural programs, rapid transit projects, highway construction, urban renewal projects, recreation facility construction, job training programs, health-care reform, education, research and development projects, and defense policies.

A. Briefly describe major similarities and differences between public-sector benefit-cost analysis and the private-sector capital budgeting process.

B. What major questions must be answered before meaningful benefit-cost analysis is possible?

C. While the maximization of society's wealth is the primary objective of benefit-cost analysis, it is important to recognize that constraints often limit government's ability to achieve certain objectives. Enumerate some of the common economic, political, and social constraints faced in public-sector benefit-cost analysis.

D. In light of these constraints, discuss some of the pluses and minuses associated with the use of benefit-cost analysis as the foundation for a general approach to the allocation of government-entrusted resources.

ST16.1 **SOLUTION**

A. Benefit-cost analysis is a method for assessing the desirability of social programs and public-

sector investment projects when it is necessary to take a long view of the public and private repercussions of such expenditures. As in the case of private-sector capital budgeting, benefit-cost analysis is frequently used in cases where the economic consequences of a program or project are likely to extend beyond one year in time. Unlike capital budgeting, however, benefit-cost analysis seeks to measure both direct private effects and indirect social implications of public-sector investment decisions and policy changes.

B. *Before* meaningful benefit-cost analysis is possible, a number of important policy questions must be answered. Among these policy questions are:

- What is the social objective function that is to be maximized?
- What constraints are placed on the decision-making process?
- What marginal social benefits and marginal social costs are to be included, and how are they to be measured?
- What social investment criterion should be used?
- What is the appropriate social rate of discount?

C. A number of constraints impinge upon society's ability to maximize the social benefits derived from public expenditures. Among these constraints are:

- *Physical constraints.* Program alternatives are limited by the available state of technology and by current production possibilities. For example, it is not yet possible to cure AIDS. Therefore, major emphasis for public policy in this area must be directed toward prevention, early detection and treatment, and research.

■ *Legal constraints.* Domestic laws and international agreements place limits on property rights, the right of eminent domain, due process, constitutional limits on a particular agency's activities, and so on. These legal constraints often play an important role in shaping the realm of public policy.

■ *Administrative constraints.* Effective programs require competent management and execution. Qualified individuals must be available to carry out social objectives. Even the best-conceived program is doomed to failure unless managers and workers with the proper mix of technical and administrative skill are available.

■ *Distributional constraints.* Social programs and public-sector investment projects affect different groups in different ways. The "gainers" are seldom the same as "losers." When distributional impacts of public policy are of paramount concern, the objective of benefit-cost analysis might maximize subject to the constraint that equity considerations be met.

■ *Political constraints.* That which is optimal may not be feasible because of slowness and inefficiency in the political process. Often what is *best* is tempered by what is *possible,* given the existence of strong competing special-interest groups.

■ *Budget constraints.* Public agencies often work within the bounds of a predetermined budget. As a result, virtually all social programs and public-sector investment projects have some absolute financial ceiling above which the program cannot be expanded, irrespective of social benefits.

■ *Social or religious constraints.* Social or religious constraints may limit the range of feasible program alternatives. It is futile to attempt to combat teen pregnancy with public support for family planning if religious constraints prohibit the use of modern birth control methods.

D. An important potential use of benefit-cost analysis is as the structure for a general philosophy of government resource allocation. As such, the results of benefit-cost studies have the potential to serve as a guide for resource-allocation de-

cisions within and among government programs and investment projects in agriculture, defense, education, health care, welfare, and other areas. The objective of such a comprehensive benefit-cost approach to government would be to maximize the net present value of the difference between the marginal social benefits and the marginal social costs derived from *all* social programs and public-sector investment projects.

Although a benefit-cost approach to evaluating all levels and forms of government is conceptually appealing on an efficiency basis, it suffers from a number of serious practical limitations. Perhaps most importantly, the measurement of marginal social benefits and marginal social costs for goods and services that are not or cannot be provided by the private sector is often primitive, at best. Measurement systems have not been sufficiently refined or standardized to permit meaningful comparisons among the social net present value of "Star Wars" defense systems, the guaranteed student loan program for college students, funding for AIDS research, Medicare, and Medicaid. A further problem arises because benefit-cost analysis is largely restricted to a consideration of the efficiency objective; equity-related considerations are seldom accorded full treatment in benefit-cost analysis. In addition, as discussed previously, a number of important economic, political, and social constraints limit the effectiveness of benefit-cost analysis. As a result, significant problems arise when a given social program or public-sector investment project is designed to meet efficiency and equity-related objectives.

For these reasons, benefit-cost analysis is traditionally viewed within the narrow context of a decision technique that is helpful in focusing interest on the economic consequences of proposed social programs and public-sector investment projects. Its greatest use is in comparing programs and projects that are designed to achieve the same or similar objectives, and as a tool for focusing resources on the best use of resources intended to meet a given social objective.

ST16.2 **Trade Policy.** In 1992, the U.S., Canada, and Mexico reached an agreement to create a free-trade area with more than 360 million consumers and over $6 trillion in annual output. This so-called North American Free Trade (NAFTA) accord links the U.S. with its first- and third-largest trading partners.

A. Summarize the main economic features of the NAFTA Agreement.

B. In the years prior to the NAFTA Agreement, Mexico had opened its markets and implemented sweeping economic reforms. Briefly describe some of the economic and political benefits derived from these reforms.

C. In light of this experience, what economic and political benefits do you project as a result of the NAFTA Agreement?

ST16.2 **SOLUTION**

A. According to the NAFTA Agreement, existing duties on most goods and services will be either eliminated or phased out. NAFTA will also eliminate quotas along with import licenses unless they are essential for such purposes as protecting human health. In addition to dismantling trade barriers in industrial goods, NAFTA includes agreements in services, investment, intellectual property rights, agriculture, and the strengthening of trade rules. There are also side agreements on labor provisions and protection of the environment.

Under NAFTA, the three countries extend most-favored-nation treatment in services to each other. Each NAFTA country must treat service providers from other NAFTA countries no less favorably than it treats its own service providers and no less favorably than it treats service providers from non-NAFTA countries. In addition, a NAFTA country may not require that a service provider of another NAFTA country establish or maintain a residence as a condition for providing the service.

B. In recent years, Mexico has opened its markets and implemented sweeping economic reforms. In 1986, Mexico joined the General Agreement on Tariffs and Trade (GATT) and began to unilaterally lower its tariffs and other trade barriers. Mexico's reforms have raised its economic growth rate and helped make it an important export market for the U.S. As an added economic benefit, as economic opportunities in Mexico improve, Mexican workers will have fewer incentives to migrate to the U.S. Thus, a stable and prosperous Mexico is important from both an economic and a political standpoint.

C. NAFTA will stimulate growth, promote investment in North America, enhance the ability of North American producers to compete, and raise the standard of living of all three countries. NAFTA will also speed up technological progress and provide innovating companies with a larger market. Many economic studies show that NAFTA will lead to higher wages, lower prices, and higher economic growth rates. NAFTA will also reinforce market reforms already under way in Mexico.

Perhaps most importantly, passage of the NAFTA Agreement strengthens peaceful ties among the U.S., Canada, and Mexico. As important partners in mutually beneficial trade, these three countries have a common interest in maintaining a strong peaceful coexistence.

PROBLEMS

P16.1 **Public versus Private Goods.** Publicly funded lighthouses provide a valuable service along coastal waterways and in the Great Lakes Region. Through visual light beam signals, lighthouses mark the route of safe passage for cargo ships and pleasure craft 24 hours per day, 365 days per year. The service provided by such lighthouses is an often-cited classic example of a public good. Once a lighthouse is built, it can send signals to additional cargo ships and pleasure craft at practically zero marginal cost. Thus, lighthouse signals are said to be an excellent example of a government-provided service that is nonrival in consumption.

As such, proponents of government funding for lighthouses argue that such services would not be provided by the private sector.

A. Briefly describe and contrast the nonrival consumption and nonexclusion concepts.

B. Do lighthouse services display both nonrival consumption and nonexclusion characteristics?

C. Explain how private-sector providers of public goods can operate profitably when such goods and services do not embody the nonexclusion concept.

P16.2 **Goal Setting in Public Management.** The objectives of social programs are set by the public through their support for various political representatives. In the election process, policy alternatives are enumerated, explored, and revised in light of popular preferences and operative constraints. These alternatives are then evaluated by comparing the present-value size of marginal social benefits and marginal social costs. According to the social net present value criterion, any social program or public-sector investment project is desirable so long as the present-value of marginal social benefits exceeds the present-value of marginal social costs.

A. Explain how the social net present value criterion is related to the Pareto satisfactory concept.

B. Do you see any problems with the adoption of the Pareto satisfactory criterion?

C. Is there any straightforward method for overcoming the limitations of the Pareto satisfactory criterion?

P16.3 **The Social Rate of Discount.** Because resources for social programs and public-sector investment projects come from private-sector consumption and/or investment, economists typically advocate the use of a social rate of discount that reflects this private-sector opportunity cost. A good estimate of the opportunity cost of funds diverted from private consumption is the rate of return on government securities that is available to individual investors. Similarly, the average rate of return on private investments can be taken as the opportunity cost of private-sector investment funds.

A. Should pretax or after-tax rates of return be used to estimate the opportunity cost of resources diverted from the private sector to fund social programs or public-sector investment projects? Why?

B. Assume that the rate of return on long-term government bonds is 8%, a typical after-tax return on investment in the private sector is 10%, the marginal corporate and individual tax rate is 30%, and consumption averages 95% of total income. Based on the information provided, calculate an economically appropriate social rate of discount.

P16.4 **Equity and Efficiency in Benefit-Cost Analysis.** In benefit-cost analysis, public-sector managers seek to learn if society as a whole will be better off by the adoption of a specific social program or public-sector investment project. Rather than seeking to maximize profits or the value of the firm, public-sector managers use benefit-cost analysis to maximize, or at least move toward a maximization of, the excess of marginal social benefits over marginal social costs. With this goal in mind, from an efficiency perspective, the distribution of any social net present value is of no importance. For example, when the city of Denver sponsors a new Denver International Airport at an initial cost of $3.5 billion dollars, it makes no difference whether the city pays the entire cost or whether the city, the state of Colorado, and the federal government split these costs. Similarly, if the city of Denver is motivated by the desire to lure business and tourist traffic from Chicago or Los Angeles, the benefits of increased economic activity in Denver that has merely shifted from other transportation centers should not be counted. In both instances, the proper concern is the increase in aggregate social wealth, not aggregate local wealth.

A. Assume that the city of Denver and local airline customers must pay only 10% of the costs of Denver International Airport, with the federal government picking up the other 90% of the tab. Describe how a local benefit-cost analysis of the airport project might be distorted by this cost-sharing arrangement.

B. Under the federal revenue sharing program, the federal government collects tax revenues that are then returned to states and other local units of government to support a wide variety of social programs. Can you see any problems for an efficient allocation of public expenditures when the spending and taxing authority of government is divided in this manner?

C. As a practical matter, can the equity and efficiency implications of social programs and public-sector investment projects be completely separated?

P16.5 **Benefit-Cost Analysis.** A February 1994 study published in *The Journal of the American Medical Association* reported on the economic consequences of a chicken pox vaccination program. The study considered an assortment of costs arising from the disease, including the costs of medication, hospitalizations, emergency-room visits, and physician visits. Those costs were then compared with the cost of a vaccination program, estimated at $88 million annually (or $35 a dose).

The vaccination program would prevent 3.7 million chicken pox cases, 9,300 hospitalizations, and 52 deaths annually, the researchers predicted. However, the study reported that the chicken pox vaccination program would cost $8 million per year more than it would save in direct medical costs.

A. From an economic standpoint, can you explain how public-sector managers might place a dollar value on the lives saved through chicken pox vaccination?

B. What other indirect personal and social benefits might be associated with such a chicken pox vaccination program?

P16.6   **Privatization.** In Massachusetts, a state education law authorized the establishment of up to 25 so-called charter schools. Charter schools are public schools that receive state funding as well as some measure of autonomy from local school boards and the rules that govern conventional schools. As a result students and educators in Boston face the ready prospect of classrooms with politicians as lecturers, academic instruction aided by yoga, school doors open from dawn to dusk, and public schools run on a for-profit basis.

Charter schools already are operating in Minnesota and California, and five other states promise to join the trend with recently enacted charter-school legislation. Advocates of such schools argue that they provide badly needed competition for existing public schools. Under the charter-school concept, anyone with a good education idea gets access to government funding, so long as they can attract and effectively train students.

A. Explain how breaking the public-school monopoly on access to public funding could help improve the quality of public- and private-school primary education.

B. Explain why primary-school privatization might not create such benefits.

P16.7   **Growth Implications of the Federal Deficit.** The amount of federal debt held by the public is the sum total of all previous deficits minus any surpluses. Federal debt held by the public equals the value of outstanding Treasury Bills, notes, and bonds, U.S. savings bonds, and other financial obligations of the federal government that the Treasury sells to the public. Debt held by the pub-

lic does not include debt held in government trust funds. This debt is owed by the government to itself, so economists generally use the debt held by the public as the economically meaningful measure of the national debt. At the beginning of 1998, government debt held by the public was roughly $4 trillion, or roughly $15,000 for every man, woman, and child in the U.S.

Of the many government activities that may affect future living standards, considerable attention has focused on the federal debt and the large and persistent federal budget deficits.

A. Explain how government debt and deficits can affect intergenerational equity and, under certain conditions, adversely affect the economy's productive capacity.

B. Explain why government debt and deficits may not affect intergenerational equity and adversely affect the economy's productive capacity.

C. Illustrate how balancing the budget might actually harm the economy, and why zero deficits are not a prerequisite to reducing the debt-to-GDP ratio.

P16.8   **Trade Policy.** The past half century has been marked by a number of experiments with different international exchange-rate arrangements. Under the Bretton Woods system, designed at the end of World War II, currencies of participating nations were pegged to the dollar and only occasionally adjusted. Since that system was abandoned in the early 1970s, exchange rates of major industrialized countries have generally "floated" against each other in response to market forces. However, a number of European countries revived the pegged exchange-rate system when they created the European Monetary System (EMS) in 1979.

In the Maastricht Treaty of 1991, members of the European Community agreed to replace their national currencies with a single currency by the year 2000, thereby superseding the present system of pegged exchange rates under the EMS and permanently ruling out exchange-rate changes. Ironically, events in 1992, including the temporary withdrawal of a number of countries from the EMS exchange rate mechanism, underscored the shortcomings of a pegged exchange-rate system in the face of economic disturbances.

A. Explain why progress toward a single European currency might be viewed as complementary to the increasing integration of the European market for goods and services.

B.   Contrast the economic benefits of a single European currency with the economic benefits of an elimination of European trade barriers. Is a single European currency necessary for a complete integration of the European market?

P16.9   **The Economics of Health Care.** Since 1960, U.S. health-care financing has undergone a major change. In 1960, most medical care was paid for directly by consumers, but by 1990 only 23% of health-care expenses were paid for directly by consumers. Thirty-two percent were covered by private health insurers and 41% by the government. This change can be traced to the expansion of employer-provided benefits, development of Medicare (a government program that finances care for the elderly and disabled), and the initiation of Medicaid, a program that extended and formalized existing programs to finance health care for the poor. Americans no longer bear most of the financial responsibility for their own health care decisions; most have relatively little direct exposure to the health-care costs.

Still, in many other developed countries, the government plays a larger part in financing and, in many cases, delivering health care than in the U.S. Germany, the United Kingdom, Canada, and many other industrialized countries experienced large increases in health-care spending between 1960 and 1990. Spending in Germany increased rapidly between 1960 and 1980, but slowed dramatically during the 1980s. In Canada, the United Kingdom, and the U.S., expenditures increased rapidly in all three decades. Although outlays for health care have increased substantially in all four countries, per capita health-care spending in the U.S. has been considerably higher than in the other three countries. Consumers in the U.S. currently spend about 1.5 times as much on per capita health care as do Canadians, about 1.7 times as much as Germans, and about 2.6 times as much as people in the United Kingdom.

A.   Why is health-care demand different from the demand for many other services?

B.   Consumers buy health care to improve their health and well-being, but research suggests that the connection between health-care and health is not a simple one. Explain why there is no direct link between health care expenditures and health.

C.   Rapid growth in health care spending in the U.S., Canada, Germany, and the United Kingdom is somewhat surprising in light of the fact that these countries have very different systems for financing and furnishing health-care services. Why do you believe health-care spending has risen so rapidly worldwide?

P16.10   **Health-Care Reform.** As a key part of its managed competition approach to health-care reform, the Clinton Administration proposed the creation of a national pricing board to oversee the pricing of pharmaceuticals. A motivating concern was the Administration's perception that high pharmaceutical prices lead to an overinvestment in cures for certain rare diseases.

As the Clinton Administration seeks a plan to provide Americans with universal health care, its strategy appears to stress cutting costs more than reducing human afflictions. The Administration's plan embraces the concept that Americans cannot afford all the recent investment in new drugs, nor can government afford to pay for all these products.

A.   Explain how price controls might affect the availability of pharmaceuticals as well as new and innovative drug therapies.

B.   Many health economists argue that advances in pharmaceutical technology are not an obstacle to cost control; they are essential to the process. Explain how market forces limit the ability of advances in medical technology to increase health-care costs.

```
╔══════════════════════════════╗
║   Case Study for Chapter 16   ║
╚══════════════════════════════╝
```

OH, LORD, WON'T YOU BUY ME A MERCEDES-BENZ (FACTORY)?[2]

On October 1, 1993, Alabama emerged victorious as the site of Mercedes-Benz AG's first U.S. car plant. States like Alabama are vying more desperately than ever to lure new industrial jobs and hold on to those they have. To start with, they give away millions of dollars in free land. After that come fat checks for site clearance, training, even employee salaries. Both foreign and domestic companies are finding ingenious ways to cash in.

Mercedes initially had so little interest in Alabama that Andreas Renschler, who headed Mercedes's site-selection team and is expected to run the new factory, says he didn't even plan to visit. Of more than 20 states that Mercedes looked at seriously, it initially leaned toward North Carolina, where Mercedes's parent, Daimler-Benz AG, already builds Freightliner trucks. And North Carolina officials say Governor Jim Hunt pursued Mercedes harder than he ever had pursued a potential investor. Mercedes officials were reportedly surprised at the various states' ardor, but they quickly cashed in on it. Mercedes would get offers for certain things from certain states, put it on their ideal contract proposal, and then come back to the other states and ask if they would be willing to do the same. For example, Mercedes persuaded all the main competitors to offer $5 million for a welcome center next to the factory, where customers could pick up cars, have them serviced, and visit an auto museum. It got commitments for free 18-month employee-training programs. It also got state governments and utilities to promise to buy large quantities of the four-wheel-drive recreational vehicles that the new factory will produce. Perhaps the biggest bombshell, Mercedes officials even asked the states to pick up the salaries of its 1,500 workers for their first year

or so on the job, at a cost of $45 million. The workers would be in a training program and wouldn't be producing anything, Mercedes explained. While North Carolina and other state officials said no, Alabama said yes, even to the salary request. "The Mercedes project simply was worth more to us than it was to any other state," says Billy Joe Camp, Alabama's economic-development director.

When Mercedes found North Carolina proposing to build a $35 million training center at the company's plant, the German automaker enticed Alabama to more than match the North Carolina offer. To outbid the competition, the Alabama governor hurriedly won legislative approval for special, lavish tax concessions—dubbed Alabama's Mercedes Law—and offered to spend tens of millions of dollars buying more than 2,500 Mercedes vehicles for state use. In the bargain, Mercedes says it agreed to limit itself to using just $42.6 million per year in income and payroll tax credits; Alabama officials say that was all Mercedes expected to be able to use, based on profit projections. It also will be allowed, however, to escape more than $9 million a year in property taxes and other fees, as permitted under existing law. While South Carolina offered $80 million in tax credits over a period of 20 years, Alabama granted Mercedes a more attractive tax credit, available in advance in the form of an interest-free loan. Mercedes officials also say Alabama's promised education spending was double any other state's promise. Alabama officials even agreed to place Mercedes's distinctive emblem atop a local scoreboard in time for the big, televised Alabama-Tennessee football game. The price? Why, free, of course.

In all, Alabama wound up promising Mercedes over $300 million in incentives, which economic-development experts call a record package for a foreign company. Given the ardor with which states are pursuing foreign and domestic investment, it is a record that may not stand very long. In the 1980s, after Japanese automakers pulled in then-record subsidies in exchange for new plants in Ohio, Tennessee, and Kentucky, state and local politicians vowed to

---

[2]See: E.S. Browning and Helene Cooper, "Ante Up: States' Bidding War Over Mercedes Plant Made for Costly Chase; Alabama Won the Business, But Some Wonder if it Also Gave Away the Farm, Will Image Now Improve?" *The Wall Street Journal,* November 24, 1993, A1; and Bill Vlasic, "In Alabama, The Soul of a New Mercedes," *Business Week,* March 31, 1997, 70-71.

bring the bidding wars to an end. If anything, they have escalated instead. In 1992, South Carolina offered Bayerische Motoren Werke (BMW) AG at least $130 million in incentives to build a BMW automotive factory there. The state even paid to move 100 families from their homes so BMW could have the exact site it wanted, and then agreed to lease BMW the land for a dollar a year. More recently, Northwest Airlines won $270 million in loans from Minnesota to prop up the airline's shaky finances. At the same time, Walt Disney Co. threatened to cancel a planned Disneyland expansion in Southern California unless it got $800 million in city, state, and federal infrastructure spending. New York City also awarded tax cuts worth $30 million each to securities firms Morgan Stanley Group and the Kidder, Peabody Group, Inc., which threatened to move to the New Jersey and Connecticut suburbs. In what New York officials view as fitting retribution, Connecticut's suburban towns now are having to offer tax cuts to their own major employers to keep them from migrating to the Sun Belt.

Government officials worry that such handouts can have the effect of eroding the tax base at the state and local level. Money that perhaps could have gone to repair crumbling highways or help underpaid teachers is targeted instead for industrial development. The state of Alabama, for example, was under court order in 1993 to spend more than $500 million a year upgrading its schools. If Mercedes would have located in Alabama without such generous aid, the company's corporate income taxes could have been used to help pay those bills. As it is, Mercedes will be exempt from state and local taxes for years.

In August 1993, the National Governors' Association adopted voluntary guidelines intended to de-escalate bidding wars that have penalized existing businesses and squandered precious state resources. In fact, Alabama passed its tax-incentive law almost exactly at the moment the Governors' Association was condemning the idea. Governor Folsom says that with neighboring states competing all-out, Alabama would have been naive to do otherwise. He also says the investment was worth every penny. "Because of our image problems, we were continually being written off when people were looking for factory sites," he explains. "Mercedes's decision to come to Alabama is worth billions of dollars in public relations to us. Now I think we'll be looked at in a different light." As the Mercedes case illustrates, little de-escalation is evident in the bidding war among the states. Indiana

Governor Evan Bayh, for example, won election in 1988 after accusing predecessors of over-paying to attract a Japanese auto plant. By 1991, Governor Bayh himself was being attacked by neighboring governors for offering United Airlines $291 million in incentives to build a new maintenance facility in Indianapolis. In 1993, Indiana began work on an aggressive new tax-credit law to help it compete with similar laws in Kentucky and Ohio. "We view this as a necessary evil," says a Bayh spokesman.

Meanwhile the modest size of economic benefits attached to the Mercedes plant construction project is somewhat sobering. For its part, Mercedes plans to hire just 1,500 workers. Alabama economists say they expect ripple effects to create a total of 10,000 new jobs in just five years. A study by economists at Alabama's Troy State University says Mercedes will pull in autoparts and service companies, beefing up local salaries, the local tax base, and even local retail sales in an area that badly needs new investment. Mercedes says it expects ultimately to invest a total of $1 billion in Alabama, far more than the original $300 million it will cost to put up its initial plant.

A. With $300 million in state aid to attract 1,500 new jobs, the marginal social cost to Alabama taxpayers of attracting the Mercedes plant is $200,000 per job. Estimate the minimum marginal social benefit required to make this a reasonable expenditure from the perspective of Alabama taxpayers. Do the facts of this case lead you to believe that it is more likely that Alabama underbid or overbid for this project? Explain.

B. Does the fact that the bidding process for the Mercedes plant took place at the state and local level of government have any implications for the amount of inducements offered? Would these numbers change dramatically if only the federal government could offer tax breaks for industrial development? Explain.

C. In 1993, Ypsilanti, Michigan, lost a court battle to reverse General Motors Corp.'s 1991 decision to close a plant. Local authorities had just given it a $13 million tax credit in a vain attempt to keep the plant open. In its ruling, the Michigan Court of Appeals said, "It has never been held that . . . an abatement carries a promise of continued employment." Explain how such risks could be accounted for in a benefit-cost analysis of the Alabama-Mercedes project.

D. Explain how a benefit-cost analysis of the Alabama-Mercedes project could account for any potential erosion of the local tax base at the state and local level.

Appendix A / Compounding and the Time Value of Money

The concepts of compound growth and the time value of money are widely used in all aspects of business and economics. Compounding is the principle that underlies growth, whether it is growth in value, growth in sales, or growth in assets. The time value of money—the fact that a dollar received in the future is worth less than a dollar in hand today—also plays an important role in managerial economics. Cash flows occurring in different periods must be adjusted to their value at a common point in time to be analyzed and compared. Because of the importance of these concepts in economic analysis, thorough understanding of the material on future (compound) and present values in the appendix is important for the study of managerial economics.

Future Value (or Compound Value)

Suppose that you deposit $100 in a bank savings account that pays 5% interest compounded annually. How much will you have at the end of one year? Let us define terms as follows:

PV = Present value of your account, or the beginning amount, $100;

i = Interest rate the bank pays you = 5% per year, or, expressed in decimal terms, 0.05;

I = Dollars of interest earned during the year;

FV_N = Future value, or ending amount, of your account at the end of N years. Whereas PV is the value now, at the present time, FV_N is the value N years into the future, after compound interest has been earned. Note also that FV_0 is the future value zero years into the future, which is the present, so $FV_0 = PV$.

In our example, $N = 1$, so $FV_N = FV_1$, and it is calculated as follows:

$$
\begin{aligned}
FV_1 &= PV + I \\
&= PV + PV \times i \qquad\qquad \textbf{(A.1)} \\
&= PV(1 + i).
\end{aligned}
$$

We can now use Equation A.1 to find how much the account is worth at the end of one year:

$$FV_1 = \$100(1 + 0.05) = \$100(1.05) = \$105.$$

Your account earned $5 of interest ($I = \$5$), so you have $105 at the end of the year.

767

COMPOUND INTEREST CALCULATIONS

Table A.1

YEAR	BEGINNING AMOUNT, PV	$\times (1 + i) =$	ENDING Amount, FV_N
1	$100.00	1.05	$105.00
2	105.00	1.05	110.25
3	110.25	1.05	115.76
4	115.76	1.05	121.55
5	121.55	1.05	127.63

Now suppose that you leave your funds on deposit for five years; how much will you have at the end of the fifth year? The answer is $127.63; this value is worked out in Table A.1.

Notice that the Table A.1 value for FV_2, the value of the account at the end of Year 2, is equal to

$$FV_2 = FV_1(1 + i) = PV(1 + i)(1 + i) = PV(1 + i)^2.$$

FV_3, the balance after three years, is

$$FV_3 = FV_2(1 + i) = PV(1 + i)^3.$$

In general, FV_N, the future value at the end of N years, is found as:

$$FV_N = PV(1 + i)^N. \tag{A.2}$$

Applying Equation A.2 in the case of a five-year account that earns 5% per year gives

$$PV_5 = \$100(1.05)^5$$
$$= \$100(1.2763)$$
$$= \$127.63$$

which is the same as the value in Table A.1.

If an electronic calculator is handy, it is easy enough to calculate $(1 + i)^N$ directly.[1] However, tables have been constructed for values of $(1 + i)^N$ for wide ranges of i and N, as Table A.2 illustrates. Table B.1 in Appendix B contains a more complete set of compound value interest factors. Interest compounding can occur over periods of time different from one year. Thus, although compounding is often on an annual basis, it can be quarterly, semiannually, monthly, or for any other period.

The term *future value interest factor* ($FVIF_{i,N}$) equals $(1 + i)^N$. Therefore, Equation A.2 may be written as $FV_N = PV(FVIF_{i,N})$. One need only to go to an appropriate interest table to find the proper interest factor. For example, the correct interest factor for our five-year, 5% illustration can be found in Table A.2. Simply look down the Period

---

[1]For example, to calculate $(1 + i)^N$ for $i = 5\% = 0.05$ and $N = 5$ years, simply multiply $(1 + i) = (1.05)$ times (1.05); multiply this product by (1.05); and so on: $(1 + i)^N = (1.05)(1.05)(1.05)(1.05)(1.05) = (1.05)^5 = 1.2763$.

Table A.2	**FUTURE VALUE OF $1 AT THE END OF N PERIODS: $FVIF_{i,N} = (1 + i)^N$**									
PERIOD (N)	1%	2%	3%	4%	5%	6%	7%	8%	9%	10%
0	1.0000	1.0000	1.0000	1.0000	1.0000	1.0000	1.0000	1.0000	1.0000	1.0000
1	1.0100	1.0200	1.0300	1.0400	1.0500	1.0600	1.0700	1.0800	1.0900	1.1000
2	1.0201	1.0404	1.0609	1.0816	1.1025	1.1236	1.1449	1.1664	1.1881	1.2100
3	1.0303	1.0612	1.0927	1.1249	1.1576	1.1910	1.2250	1.2597	1.2950	1.3310
4	1.0406	1.0824	1.1255	1.1699	1.2155	1.2625	1.3108	1.3605	1.4116	1.4641
5	1.0510	1.1041	1.1593	1.2167	1.2763	1.3382	1.4026	1.4693	1.5386	1.6105
6	1.0615	1.1262	1.1941	1.2653	1.3401	1.4185	1.5007	1.5869	1.6771	1.7716
7	1.0721	1.1487	1.2299	1.3159	1.4071	1.5036	1.6058	1.7138	1.8280	1.9487
8	1.0829	1.1717	1.2668	1.3686	1.4775	1.5938	1.7182	1.8509	1.9926	2.1436
9	1.0937	1.1951	1.3048	1.4233	1.5513	1.6895	1.8385	1.9990	2.1719	2.3579
10	1.1046	1.2190	1.3439	1.4802	1.6289	1.7908	1.9672	2.1589	2.3674	2.5937
11	1.1157	1.2434	1.3842	1.5395	1.7103	1.8983	2.1049	2.3316	2.5804	2.8531
12	1.1268	1.2682	1.4258	1.6010	1.7959	2.0122	2.2522	2.5182	2.8127	3.1384
13	1.1381	1.2936	1.4685	1.6651	1.8856	2.1329	2.4098	2.7196	3.0658	3.4523
14	1.1495	1.3195	1.5126	1.7317	1.9799	2.2609	2.5785	2.9372	3.3417	3.7975
15	1.1610	1.3459	1.5580	1.8009	2.0789	2.3966	2.7590	3.1722	3.6425	4.1772

column to 5, then across this row to the 5% column to find the interest factor, 1.2763. Then, using this interest factor, we find the value of $100 after five years as $FV_N = PV(FVIF_{i,N}) = \$100(1.2763) = \$127.63$, which is identical to the value obtained by the long method in Table A.1.

GRAPHIC VIEW OF THE COMPOUNDING PROCESS: GROWTH

Figure A.1 shows how $1 (or any other initial quantity) grows over time at various rates of interest. The higher the rate of interest, the faster the rate of growth. The interest rate is, in fact, the growth rate: If a sum is deposited and earns 5%, then the funds on deposit grow at the rate of 5% per period. Similarly, the sales of a firm or the Gross Domestic Product (GDP) of a country might be expected to grow at a constant rate. Projections of future sales or GDP could be obtained using the compound value method.

Future value curves could be drawn for any interest rate, including fractional rates. In Figure A.1, we have plotted curves for 0%, 5%, and 10%, using the data from Table A.2.

Present Value

Suppose that you are offered the alternative of receiving either $127.63 at the end of five years or X dollars today. There is no question that the $127.63 will be paid in full

RELATIONS AMONG FUTURE VALUE INTEREST FACTORS,
INTEREST RATES, AND TIME

The future value interest factor rises with increases in the interest rate and in the number of periods for interest compounding.

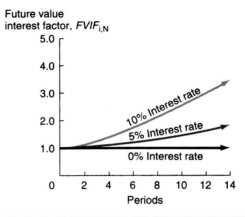

(perhaps the payer is the U.S. government). Having no current need for the money, you would deposit it in a bank account that pays 5% interest. (Five percent is your *opportunity cost,* or the rate of interest you could earn on alternative investments of equal risk.) What value of X will make you indifferent between X dollars today or the promise of $127.63 five years hence?

Table A.1 shows that the initial amount of $100 growing at 5% a year yields $127.63 at the end of five years. Thus, you should be indifferent in your choice between $100 today and $127.63 at the end of five years. The $100 is the present value, or *PV,* of $127.63 due in five years when the applicable interest rate is 5%. Therefore, if X is anything less than $100, you would prefer the promise of $127.63 in five years to X dollars today.

In general, the present value of a sum due N years in the future is the amount that, if it were invested today, would grow to equal the future sum over a period of N years. Since $100 would grow to $127.63 in five years at a 5% interest rate, $100 is the present value of $127.63 due five years in the future when the appropriate interest rate is 5%.

Finding present values (or *discounting,* as it is commonly called) is simply the reverse of compounding, and Equation A.2 can readily be transformed into a present value formula:

$$FV_N = PV(1 + i)^N,$$

which, when solved for PV, gives

$$PV = \frac{FV_N}{(1 + i)^N} = FV_N \left[\frac{1}{(1 + i)^N} \right]. \qquad \textbf{(A.3)}$$

Tables have been constructed for the term in brackets for various values of i and N; Table A.3 is an example. For a more complete table, see Table B.2 in Appendix B. For

Table A.3

PRESENT VALUES OF $1 DUE AT THE END OF N PERIODS

$$PVIF_{i,N} = \frac{1}{(1 + i)^N} = \left[\frac{1}{(1 + i)}\right]^N$$

PERIOD (N)	1%	2%	3%	4%	5%	6%	7%	8%	9%	10%	12%	14%	15%
1	.9901	.9804	.9709	.9615	.9524	.9434	.9346	.9259	.9174	.9091	.8929	.8772	.8696
2	.9803	.9612	.9426	.9246	.9070	.8900	.8734	.8573	.8417	.8264	.7972	.7695	.7561
3	.9706	.9423	.9151	.8890	.8638	.8396	.8163	.7938	.7722	.7513	.7118	.6750	.6575
4	.9610	.9238	.8885	.8548	.8227	.7921	.7629	.7350	.7084	.6830	.6355	.5921	.5718
5	.9515	.9057	.8626	.8219	.7835	.7473	.7130	.6806	.6499	.6209	.5674	.5194	.4972
6	.9420	.8880	.8375	.7903	.7462	.7050	.6663	.6302	.5963	.5645	.5066	.4556	.4323
7	.9327	.8706	.8131	.7599	.7107	.6651	.6227	.5835	.5470	.5132	.4523	.3996	.3759
8	.9235	.8535	.7894	.7307	.6768	.6274	.5820	.5403	.5019	.4665	.4039	.3506	.3269
9	.9143	.8368	.7664	.7026	.6446	.5919	.5439	.5002	.4604	.4241	.3606	.3075	.2843
10	.9053	.8203	.7441	.6756	.6139	.5584	.5083	.4632	.4224	.3855	.3220	.2697	.2472

the case being considered, look down the 5% column in Table A.3 to the fifth row. The figure shown there, 0.7835, is the *present value interest factor (PVIF$_{i,N}$)* used to determine the present value of $127.63 payable in five years, discounted at 5%:

$$PV = FV_5(PVIF_{i,N})$$

$$= \$127.63(0.7835)$$

$$= \$100.$$

GRAPHIC VIEW OF THE DISCOUNTING PROCESS

Figure A.2 shows how the interest factors for discounting decrease as the discounting period increases. The curves in the figure were plotted with data taken from Table A.3; they show that the present value of a sum to be received at some future date decreases (1) as the payment date is extended further into the future and (2) as the discount rate increases. If relatively high discount rates apply, funds due in the future are worth very little today. Even at relatively low discount rates, the present values of funds due in the distant future are quite small. For example, $1 due in ten years is worth about 61¢ today if the discount rate is 5%. It is worth only 25¢ today at a 15% discount rate. Similarly, $1 due in five years at 10% is worth 62¢ today, but at the same discount rate, $1 due in ten years is worth only 39¢ today.

Future Value Versus Present Value

Notice that Equation A.2, the basic equation for compounding, was developed from the logical sequence set forth in Table A.1; the equation merely presents in mathematical

Figure A.2

RELATIONS AMONG PRESENT VALUE INTEREST FACTORS, INTEREST RATES, AND TIME

The present value interest factor falls with increases in the interest rate and in the number of periods prior to payment.

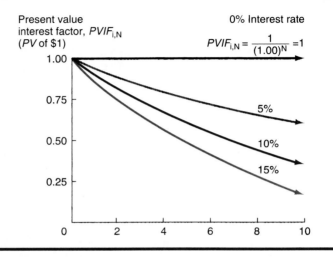

form the steps outlined in the table. The present value interest factor ($PVIF_{i,N}$) in Equation A.3, the basic equation for discounting or finding present values, was found as the *reciprocal* of the future value interest factor ($FVIF_{i,N}$) for the same i, N combination:

$$PVIF_{i,N} = \frac{1}{FVIF_{i,N}}.$$

For example, the *future value interest factor* for 5% over five years is seen in Table A.2 to be 1.2763. The *present value interest factor* for 5% over five years must be the reciprocal of 1.2763:

$$PVIF_{5\%, \ 5 \ years} = \frac{1}{1.2763} = 0.7835.$$

The $PVIF_{i,N}$ found in this manner does, of course, correspond with the $PVIF_{i,N}$ shown in Table A.3.

The reciprocal relation between present value and future value permits us to find present values in two ways—by multiplying or by dividing. Thus, the present value of $1,000 due in five years and discounted at 5% may be found as

$$PV = FV_N \left[\frac{1}{1 + i} \right]^N = FV_N(PVIF_{i,N}) = \$1,000(0.7835) = \$783.50,$$

Figure A.3	**TIME LINE FOR AN ANNUITY: FUTURE VALUE ($i = 4\%$)**

When the interest rate is 4%, the future value of $1,000 annuity to be paid over 3 years is $3,121.60.

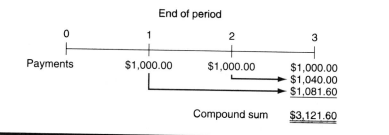

or as

$$PV = \frac{FV_N}{(1 + i)^N} = \frac{FV_N}{FVIF_{i,N}} = \frac{\$1,000}{1.2763} = \$783.50.$$

To conclude this comparison of present and future values, compare Figures A.1 and A.2.[2]

Future Value of an Annuity

An annuity is defined as a series of payments of a fixed amount for a specified number of periods. Each payment occurs at the end of the period.[3] For example, a promise to pay $1,000 a year for three years is a three-year annuity. If you were to receive such an annuity and were to deposit each annual payment in a savings account paying 4% interest, how much would you have at the end of three years? The answer is shown graphically as a *time line* in Figure A.3. The first payment is made at the end of Year 1, the second at the end of Year 2, and the third at the end of Year 3. The last payment is not compounded at all, the second payment is compounded for one year, and the first is compounded for two years. When the future values of each of the payments are added, their total is the sum of the annuity. In the example, this total is $3,121.60.

---

[2]Notice that Figure A.2 is not a mirror image of Figure A.1. The curves in Figure A.1 approach ∞ as *n* increases; in Figure A.2 the curves approach zero, not −∞.

[3]Had the payment been made at the beginning of the period, each receipt would simply have been shifted back one year. The annuity would have been called an *annuity due;* the one in the present discussion, with payments made at the end of each period, is called a *regular annuity* or, sometimes, a *deferred annuity.*

FUTURE VALUE OF AN ANNUITY OF $1 PER PERIOD FOR N PERIODS

Table A.4

$$FVIFA_{i,N} = \sum_{t=1}^{N} (1+i)^{t-1}$$

$$= \frac{(1+i)^N - 1}{i}$$

NUMBER OF PERIODS	1%	2%	3%	4%	5%	6%	7%	8%
1	1.0000	1.0000	1.0000	1.0000	1.0000	1.0000	1.0000	1.0000
2	2.0100	2.0200	2.0300	2.0400	2.0500	2.0600	2.0700	2.0800
3	3.0301	3.0604	3.0909	3.1216	3.1525	3.1836	3.2149	3.2464
4	4.0604	4.1216	4.1836	4.2465	4.3101	4.3746	4.4399	4.5061
5	5.1010	5.2040	5.3091	5.4163	5.5256	5.6371	5.7507	5.8666
6	6.1520	6.3081	6.4684	6.6330	6.8019	6.9753	7.1533	7.3359
7	7.2135	7.4343	7.6625	7.8983	8.1420	8.3938	8.6540	8.9228
8	8.2857	8.5830	8.8923	9.2142	9.5491	9.8975	10.2598	10.6366
9	9.3685	9.7546	10.1591	10.5828	11.0266	11.4913	11.9780	12.4876
10	10.4622	10.9497	11.4639	12.0061	12.5779	13.1808	13.8164	14.4866

Expressed algebraically, with S_N defined as the future value, R as the periodic receipt, N as the length of the annuity, and $FVIFA_{i,N}$ as the future value interest factor for an annuity, the formula for S_N is:

$$S_N = R(1+i)^{N-1} + R(1+i)^{N-2} + \ldots + R(1+i)^1 + R(1+i)^0$$

$$= R[(1+i)^{N-1} + (1+i)^{N-2} + \ldots + (1+i)^1 + (1+i)^0]$$

$$= R\sum_{t=1}^{N} (1+i)^{N-t} \text{ or } = R\sum_{t=1}^{N} (1+i)^{t-1} \tag{A.4}$$

$$= R(FVIFA_{i,N}).$$

The expression in parentheses, $FVIFA_{i,N}$, has been calculated for various combinations of i and N.[4] An illustrative set of these annuity interest factors is given in Table A.4.[5] To

---

[4]The third equation is simply a shorthand expression in which sigma (Σ) signifies *sum up* or add the values of N factors. The symbol $\sum_{t=1}^{N}$ simply says, "Go through the following process: Let $t = 1$ and find the first factor. Then let $t = 2$ and find the second factor. Continue until each individual factor has been found, and then add these individual factors to find the value of the annuity."

[5]The equation given in Table A.4 recognizes that the *FVIFA* factor is the sum of a geometric progression. The proof of this equation is given in most algebra texts. Notice that it is easy to use the equation to develop annuity factors. This is especially useful if you need the *FVIFA* for some interest rate not given in the tables (for example, 6.5%).

TIME LINE FOR AN ANNUITY: PRESENT VALUE ($i = 4\%$)

When the interest rate is 4%, the present value of a $1,000 annuity to be paid over 3 years is $2,775.10.

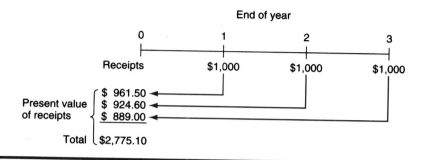

find the answer to the three-year, $1,000 annuity problem, simply refer to Table A.4, look down the 4% column to the row of the third period, and multiply the factor 3.1216 by $1,000. The answer is the same as the one derived by the long method illustrated in Figure A.3:

$$S_N = R(FVIFA_{i,N}),$$

$$S_3 = \$1,000(3.1216) = \$3,121.60$$

Notice that for all positive interest rates, the $FVIFA_{i,N}$ for the sum of an annuity is always equal to or greater than the number of periods the annuity runs.[6]

Present Value of an Annuity

Suppose that you were offered the following alternatives: a three-year annuity of $1,000 per year or a lump-sum payment today. You have no need for the money during the next three years, so if you accept the annuity, you would simply deposit the receipts in a savings account paying 4% interest. How large must the lump-sum payment be to make it equivalent to the annuity? The time line shown in Figure A.4 will help explain the problem.

---

[6]It is worth noting that the entry for each period t in Table A.4 equals the sum of the entries in Table A.2 up to the period $N - 1$. For example, the entry for Period 3 under the 4% column in Table A.4 is equal to 1.000 + 1.0400 + 1.0816 = 3.1216.

Also, had the annuity been an *annuity due*, with payments received at the beginning rather than at the end of each period, the three payments would have occurred at $t = 0$, $t = 1$, and $t = 2$. To find the future value of an annuity due, look up the $FVIFA_{i,N}$ for $N + 1$ years, then subtract 1.0 from the amount to get the $FVIFA_{i,N}$ for the annuity due. In the example, the annuity due $FVIFA_{i,N}$ is 4.2465 − 1.0 = 3.2465, versus 3.1216 for a regular annuity. Because payments on an annuity due come earlier, it is a little more valuable than a regular annuity.

The present value of the first receipt is $R[1/(1 + i)]$, the second is $R[1/(1 + i)]^2$, and so on. Designating the present value of an annuity of N years as A_N and the present value interest factor for an annuity as $PVIFA_{i,N}$, we may write the following equation:

$$A_N = R\left(\frac{1}{1 + i}\right)^1 + R\left(\frac{1}{1 + i}\right)^2 + \ldots + R\left(\frac{1}{1 + i}\right)^N$$

$$= R\left(\frac{1}{(1 + i)^1} + \frac{1}{(1 + i)^2} + \ldots + \frac{1}{(1 + i)^N}\right) \qquad \text{(A.5)}$$

$$= R\sum_{t=1}^{N} \frac{1}{(1 + i)^t}$$

$$= R(PVIFA_{i,N}).$$

Again, tables have been worked out for $PVIFA_{i,N}$, the term in parentheses in Equation A.5, as Table A.5 illustrates; a more complete listing is found in Table B.4 in Appendix B. From Table A.5, the $PVIFA_{i,N}$ for a three-year, 4% annuity is found to be 2.7751. Multiplying this factor by the $1,000 annual receipt gives $2,775.10, the present value of the annuity. This figure is identical to the long-method answer shown in Figure A.4:

$$A_N = R(PVIFA_{i,N}),$$

$$A_3 = \$1,000(2.7751)$$

$$= \$2,775.10$$

Table A.5

PRESENT VALUE OF AN ANNUITY OF $1 PER PERIOD FOR N PERIODS

$$PVIFA_{i,N} = \sum_{t=1}^{N} \frac{1}{(1 + i)^t} = \frac{1 - \dfrac{1}{(1 + i)^N}}{i}$$

PERIOD	1%	2%	3%	4%	5%	6%	7%	8%	9%	10%
1	0.9901	0.9804	0.9709	0.9615	0.9524	0.9434	0.9346	0.9259	0.9174	0.9091
2	1.9704	1.9416	1.9135	1.8861	1.8594	1.8334	1.8080	1.7833	1.7591	1.7355
3	2.9410	2.8839	2.8286	2.7751	2.7232	2.6730	2.6243	2.5771	2.5313	2.4869
4	3.9020	3.8077	3.7171	3.6299	3.5460	3.4651	3.3872	3.3121	3.2397	3.1699
5	4.8534	4.7135	4.5797	4.4518	4.3295	4.2124	4.1002	3.9927	3.8897	3.7908
6	5.7955	5.6014	5.4172	5.2421	5.0757	4.9173	4.7665	4.6229	4.4859	4.3553
7	6.7282	6.4720	6.2303	6.0021	5.7864	5.5824	5.3893	5.2064	5.0330	4.8684
8	7.6517	7.3255	7.0197	6.7327	6.4632	6.2098	5.9713	5.7466	5.5348	5.3349
9	8.5660	8.1622	7.7861	7.4353	7.1078	6.8017	6.5152	6.2469	5.9952	5.7590
10	9.4713	8.9826	8.5302	8.1109	7.7217	7.3601	7.0236	6.7101	6.4177	6.1446

Table A.6			

PRESENT VALUE OF AN UNEVEN STREAM OF RECEIPTS ($i = 6\%$)

YEAR	STREAM OF RECEIPTS	$\times\ PVIF_{i,N} =$	PV OF INDIVIDUAL RECEIPTS
1	$ 100	0.9434	$ 94.34
2	200	0.8900	178.00
3	200	0.8396	167.92
4	200	0.7921	158.42
5	200	0.7473	149.46
6	0	0.7050	0
7	1,000	0.6651	665.10
		$PV = $ Sum $=$	$1,413.24

Notice that the entry for each period N in Table A.5 is equal to the sum of the entries in Table A.3 up to and including period N. For example, the $PVIFA$ for 4%, three periods as shown in Table A.5, could have been calculated by summing values from Table A.3:

$$0.9615 + 0.9246 + 0.8890 = 2.7751.$$

Notice also that for all positive interest rates, $PVIFA_{i,N}$ for the *present value* of an annuity is always less than the number of periods.[7]

Present Value of an Uneven Series of Receipts

The definition of an annuity includes the words *fixed amount*—in other words, annuities involve situations in which cash flows are *identical* in every period. Although many managerial decisions involve constant cash flows, some important decisions are concerned with uneven cash flows. Consequently, it is necessary to deal with varying payment streams.

The PV of an uneven stream of future income is found as the sum of the PVs of the individual components of the stream. For example, suppose that we are trying to find the PV of the stream of receipts shown in Table A.6, discounted at 6%. As shown in the table, we multiply each receipt by the appropriate $PVIF_{i,N}$, then sum these products to obtain the PV of the stream, $1,413.24. Figure A.5 gives a graphic view of the cash-flow stream.

The PV of the receipts shown in Table A.6 and Figure A.5 can also be found by using the annuity equation; the steps in this alternative solution process are as follows:

■ *Step 1:* Find PV of $100 due in one year:

$$\$100(0.9434) = \$94.34.$$

---

[7]To find the $PVIFA_{i,N}$ for an *annuity due,* look up the $PVIFA_{i,N}$ for $n - 1$ periods; then add 1.0 to this amount to obtain the $PVIFA_{i,N}$ for the annuity due. In the example, the $PVIFA_{i,N}$ for a 4%, three-year annuity due is $1.8861 + 1.0 = 2.8861$.

Figure A.5

TIME LINE FOR AN UNEVEN CASH FLOW STREAM (i = 6%)

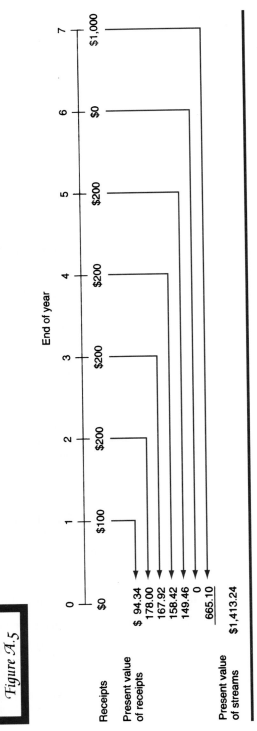

End of year	0	1	2	3	4	5	6	7
Receipts	$0	$100	$200	$200	$200	$200	$0	$1,000

Present value of receipts	
	$ 94.34
	178.00
	167.92
	158.42
	149.46
	0
	665.10

Present value of streams $1,413.24

- *Step 2:* Recognize that a $200 annuity will be received during Years 2 through 5. Thus, we can determine the value of a five-year annuity, subtract from it the value of a one-year annuity, and have remaining the value of a four-year annuity whose first payment is due in two years. This result is achieved by subtracting the *PVIFA* for a one-year, 6% annuity from the *PVIFA* for a five-year annuity and then multiplying the difference by $200:

$$PV \text{ of the Annuity} = (PVIFA_{6\%, \ 5yrs.} - PVIFA_{6\%, \ 1yr.})(\$200)$$

$$= (4.2124 - 0.9434)(\$200)$$

$$= \$653.80.$$

Thus, the present value of the annuity component of the uneven stream is $653.80.

- *Step 3:* Find the *PV* of the $1,000 due in Year 7:

$$\$1,000(0.6651) = \$665.10.$$

- *Step 4:* Sum the components:

$$\$94.34 + \$653.80 + \$665.10 = \$1,413.24.$$

Either of the two methods can be used to solve problems of this type. However, the alternative (annuity) solution is easier if the annuity component runs for many years. For example, the alternative solution would be clearly superior for finding the *PV* of a stream consisting of $100 in Year 1, $200 in Years 2 through 29, and $1,000 in Year 30.

Annual Payments for Accumulation of a Future Sum

Suppose that you want to know the amount of money that must be deposited at 5% for each of the next five years in order to have $10,000 available to pay off a debt at the end of the fifth year. Dividing both sides of Equation A.4 by *FVIFA* obtains:

$$R = \frac{S_N}{FVIFA_{i,N}} \tag{A.6}$$

Looking up the future value of an annuity interest factor for five years at 5% in Table A.4 and dividing this figure into $10,000 gives:

$$R = \frac{\$10,000}{5.5256} = \$1,810.$$

Thus, if $1,810 is deposited each year in an account paying 5% interest, at the end of five years the account will have accumulated to $10,000.

Annual Receipts from an Annuity

Suppose that on September 1, 1998, you received an inheritance of $7,500. The money is to be used for your education and is to be spent during the academic years beginning September 1999, 2000, and 2001. If you place the money in a bank account paying 6% annual interest and make three equal withdrawals at each of the specified dates, how large can each withdrawal be so as to leave you with exactly a zero balance after the last one has been made?

The solution requires application of the present value of an annuity formula, Equation A.5. Here, however, we know that the present value of the annuity is $7,500, and the problem is to find the three equal annual payments when the interest rate is 6%. This calls for dividing both sides of Equation A.5 by $PVIFA_{i,N}$ to derive Equation A.7:

$$R = \frac{A_N}{PVIFA_{i,N}}. \tag{A.7}$$

The interest factor is found in Table A.5 to be 2.6730, and substituting this value into Equation A.7, the three annual withdrawals are calculated to be $2,806:

$$R = \frac{\$7,500}{2.6730} = \$2,806.$$

This particular calculation is used frequently to set up insurance and pension-plan benefit schedules and to find the periodic payments necessary to retire a loan within a specified period. For example, if you want to retire in three equal annual payments a $7,500 bank loan accruing interest at 6% on the unpaid balance, each payment would be $2,806. In this case, the bank is acquiring an annuity with a present value of $7,500.

Determining Interest Rates

We can use the basic equations developed earlier to determine the interest rates implicit in financial contracts.

Example 1. A bank offers to lend you $1,000 if you sign a note to repay $1,610.50 at the end of five years. What rate of interest are you paying? To solve the problem, recognize that $1,000 is the PV of $1,610.50 due in five years, and solve Equation A.3 for the present value interest factor ($PVIF_{i,N}$).

$$PV = FV_N\left[\frac{1}{(1 + i)^N}\right] = FV_N(PVIF_{i,N})$$

$$\$1,000 = \$1,610.50(PVIF_{i,N} \text{ for 5 years}) \tag{A.3}$$

$$\$1,000/\$1,610.50 = 0.6209 = PVIF_{i,5 \ years}.$$

Now, go to Table A.3 and look across the row for Year 5 until you find 0.6209. It is in the 10% column, so you would be paying a 10% rate of interest.

Example 2. A bank offers to lend you $100,000 to buy a house. You must sign a mortgage calling for payments of $8,882.73 at the end of each of the next 30 years, equivalent to roughly $740.23 per month. What interest rate is the bank charging you?

1. Recognize that $100,000 is the PV of a 30-year, $8,882.73 annuity:

$$\$100,000 = PV = \sum_{t=1}^{30} \$8,882.73\left[\frac{1}{(1+i)^t}\right] = \$8,882.73(PVIFA_{i,30\ yrs}).$$

2. Solve for $PVIFA_{i,30\ yrs}$:

$$PVIFA_{i,30\ yrs} = \$100,000/\$8,882.73 = 11.2578.$$

3. Turn to Table B.4 in Appendix B, since Table A.5 does not cover a 30-year period. Looking across the row for 30 periods, find 11.2578 under the column for 8%. Therefore, the rate of interest on this mortgage is 8%.

Semiannual and Other Compounding Periods

All of the examples thus far have assumed that returns were received once a year, or annually. Suppose, however, that you put your $1,000 in a bank that offers to pay 6% interest compounded *semiannually*. How much will you have at the end of one year? Semiannual compounding means that interest is actually paid every six months, a fact taken into account in the tabular calculations in Table A.7. Here the annual interest rate is divided by two, but twice as many compounding periods are used because interest is paid twice a year. Comparing the amount on hand at the end of the second six-month period, $1,060.90, with what would have been on hand under annual compounding, $1,060, shows that semiannual compounding is better from the standpoint of the saver. This result occurs because you earn interest on interest more frequently.

Throughout the economy, different types of investments use different compounding periods. For example, bank and savings and loan accounts generally pay interest quarterly, some bonds pay interest semiannually, and other bonds pay interest annually. Thus, if we are to compare securities with different compounding periods, we need to put them on a common basis. This need has led to the development of the terms *nominal,* or *stated, interest rate* and *effective annual,* or *annual percentage rate (APR).* The stated, or nominal, rate is the quoted rate; thus, in our example the nominal rate is 6%. The annual percentage rate is the rate that would have produced the final compound

Table A.7

COMPOUND INTEREST CALCULATIONS WITH
SEMIANNUAL COMPOUNDING

	BEGINNING AMOUNT (PV)	$\times (1 + i/2) =$	ENDING AMOUNT, FV_N
Period 1	$1,000.00	(1.03)	$1,030.00
Period 2	1,030.00	(1.03)	1,060.90

value, $1,060.90, under annual rather than semiannual compounding. In this case, the effective annual rate is 6.09%:

$$\$1,000(1 + i) = \$1,060.90,$$

$$i = \frac{\$1,060.90}{\$1,000} - 1 = 0.0609 = 6.09\%$$

Thus, if one bank offered 6% with semiannual compounding, whereas another offered 6.09% with annual compounding, they would both be paying the same effective rate of interest. In general, we can determine the effective annual rate of interest, given the nominal rate, as follows:

- *Step 1:* Find the *FV* of $1 at the end of one year, using the equation

$$FV = 1\left(1 + \frac{i_n}{M}\right)^M.$$

Here i_n is the nominal rate, and M is the number of compounding periods per year.

- *Step 2:* Subtract 1.0 from the result in Step 1; then multiply by 100. The final result is the effective annual rate.

Example. Find the effective annual rate if the nominal rate is 6%, compounded semiannually:

$$Effective\ Annual\ Rate = \left(1 + \frac{0.06}{2}\right)^2 - 1.0$$
$$= (1.03)^2 - 1.0$$
$$= 1.0609 - 1.0$$
$$= 0.0609$$
$$= 6.09\%$$

The points made about semiannual compounding can be generalized as follows. When compounding periods are more frequent than once a year, use a modified version of Equation A.2:

$$FV_N = PV(1 + i)^N, \tag{A.2}$$

$$FV_N = PV\left(1 + \frac{i}{M}\right)^{MN}. \tag{A.2a}$$

Here M is the number of times per year compounding occurs. When banks compute daily interest, the value of M is set at 365, and Equation A.2a is applied.

The interest tables can be used when compounding occurs more than once a year. Simply divide the nominal, or stated, interest rate by the number of times compounding occurs, and multiply the years by the number of compounding periods per year. For example, to find the amount to which $1,000 will grow after six years with semiannual compounding and a stated 8% interest rate, divide 8% by 2 and multiply the six years by 2. Then look in Table A.2 under the 4% column and in the row for Period 12. You will find an interest factor of 1.6010. Multiplying this by the initial $1,000 gives a value of $1,601, the amount to which $1,000 will grow in six years at 8% compounded semiannually. This compares with $1,586.90 for annual compounding.

The same procedure applies in all of the cases covered—compounding, discounting, single payments, and annuities. To illustrate semiannual discounting in finding the present value of an annuity, consider the case described in the section "Present Value of an Annuity"—$1,000 a year for three years, discounted at 4%. With annual discounting, the interest factor is 2.7751, and the present value of the annuity is $2,775.10. For semiannual discounting, look under the 2% column and in the Period 6 row of Table A.5 to find an interest factor of 5.6014. This is now multiplied by half of $1,000, or the $500 received each six months, to get the present value of the annuity, $2,800.70. The payments come a little more rapidly—the first $500 is paid after only six months (similarly with other payments)—so the annuity is a little more valuable if payments are received semiannually rather than annually.

Summary

Managerial decisions often require determining the present value of a stream of future cash flows. Also, we often need to know the amount to which an initial quantity will grow during a specified time period, and at other times we must calculate the interest rate built into a financial contract. The basic concepts involved in these processes are called compounding and the time value of money.

The key procedures covered in this appendix are summarized below:

- *Future Value:* $FV_N = PV(1 + i)^N$, where FV_N is the future value of an initial amount, PV, compounded at the rate of i percent for N periods. The term $(1 + i)^N$ is the future value interest factor, $FVIF_{i,N}$. Values for $FVIF$ are contained in tables.

- *Present Value:* $PV = FV_N[1/(1 + i)]^N$. This equation is simply a transformation of the future value equation. The term $[1/(1 + i)]^N$ is the present value interest factor, $PVIF_{i,N}$.

- *Future Value of an Annuity:* An annuity is defined as a series of constant or equal payments of R dollars per period. The sum, or future value of an annuity, is given the symbol S_N, and it is found as follows:

$$S_N = R\left[\sum_{t=1}^{N} (1 + i)^{t-1}\right].$$

The term $\left[\sum_{t=1}^{N}(1 + i)^{t-1}\right]$ is the future value interest factor for an annuity, $FVIFA_{i,N}$.

■ *Present Value of an Annuity:* The present value of an annuity is identified by the symbol A_N, and it is found as follows:

$$A_N = R\left[\sum_{t=1}^{N}(1/1 + i)^t\right].$$

The term $\left[\sum_{t=1}^{N}(1/1 + i)^t\right] = PVIFA_{i,N}$ is the present value interest factor for an annuity.

Table B.1

Future Value of $1: $FVIF_{i,N} = (1 + i)^N$

PERIOD	1%	2%	3%	4%	5%	6%	7%	8%	9%	10%
1	1.0100	1.0200	1.0300	1.0400	1.0500	1.0600	1.0700	1.0800	1.0900	1.1000
2	1.0201	1.0404	1.0609	1.0816	1.1025	1.1236	1.1449	1.1664	1.1881	1.2100
3	1.0303	1.0612	1.0927	1.1249	1.1576	1.1910	1.2250	1.2597	1.2950	1.3310
4	1.0406	1.0824	1.1255	1.1699	1.2155	1.2625	1.3108	1.3605	1.4116	1.4641
5	1.0510	1.1041	1.1593	1.2167	1.2763	1.3382	1.4026	1.4693	1.5386	1.6105
6	1.0615	1.1262	1.1941	1.2653	1.3401	1.4185	1.5007	1.5869	1.6771	1.7716
7	1.0721	1.1487	1.2299	1.3159	1.4071	1.5036	1.6058	1.7138	1.8280	1.9487
8	1.0829	1.1717	1.2668	1.3686	1.4775	1.5938	1.7182	1.8509	1.9926	2.1436
9	1.0937	1.1951	1.3048	1.4233	1.5513	1.6895	1.8385	1.9990	2.1719	2.3579
10	1.1046	1.2190	1.3439	1.4802	1.6289	1.7908	1.9672	2.1589	2.3674	2.5937
11	1.1157	1.2434	1.3842	1.5395	1.7103	1.8983	2.1049	2.3316	2.5804	2.8531
12	1.1268	1.2682	1.4258	1.6010	1.7959	2.1022	2.2522	2.5182	2.8127	3.1384
13	1.1381	1.2936	1.4685	1.6651	1.8856	2.1329	2.4098	2.7196	3.0658	3.4523
14	1.1495	1.3195	1.5126	1.7317	1.9799	2.2609	2.5785	2.9372	3.3417	3.7975
15	1.1610	1.3459	1.5580	1.8009	2.0789	2.3966	2.7590	3.1722	3.6425	4.1772
16	1.1726	1.3728	1.6047	1.8730	2.1829	2.5404	2.9522	3.4259	3.9703	4.5950
17	1.1843	1.4002	1.6528	1.9479	2.2920	2.6928	3.1588	3.7000	4.3276	5.0545
18	1.1961	1.4282	1.7024	2.0258	2.4066	2.8543	3.3799	3.9960	4.7171	5.5599
19	1.2081	1.4568	1.7535	2.1068	2.5270	3.0256	3.6165	4.3157	5.1417	6.1159
20	1.2202	1.4859	1.8061	2.1911	2.6533	3.2071	3.8697	4.6610	5.6044	6.7275
21	1.2324	1.5157	1.8603	2.2788	2.7860	3.3996	4.1406	5.0338	6.1088	7.4002
22	1.2447	1.5460	1.9161	2.3699	2.9253	3.6035	4.4304	5.4365	6.6586	8.1403
23	1,2572	1.5769	1.9736	2.4647	3.0715	3.8197	4.7405	5.8715	7.2579	8.9543
24	1.2697	1.6084	2.0328	2.5633	3.2251	4.0489	5.0724	6.3412	7.9111	9.8497
25	1.2824	1.6406	2.0938	2.6658	3.3864	4.2919	5.4274	6.8485	8.6231	10.834
26	1.2953	1.6734	2.1566	2.7725	3.5557	4.5494	5.8074	7.3964	9.3992	11.918
27	1.3082	1.7069	2.2213	2.8834	3.7335	4.8223	6.2139	7.9881	10.245	13.110
28	1.3213	1.7410	2.2879	2.9987	3.9201	5.1117	6.6488	8.6271	11.167	14.421
29	1.3345	1.7758	2.3566	3.1187	4.1161	5.4184	7.1143	9.3173	12.172	15.863
30	1.3478	1.8114	2.4273	3.2434	4.3219	5.7435	7.6123	10.062	13.267	17.449
40	1.4889	2.2080	3.2620	4.8010	7.0400	10.285	14.974	21.724	31.409	45.259
50	1.6446	2.6916	4.3839	7.1067	11.467	18.420	29.457	46.901	74.357	117.39
60	1.8167	3.2810	5.8916	10.519	18.679	32.987	57.946	101.25	176.03	304.48

continued

Table B.1

continued

PERIOD	12%	14%	15%	16%	18%	20%	24%	28%	32%	36%
1	1.1200	1.1400	1.1500	1.1600	1.1800	1.2000	1.2400	1.2800	1.3200	1.3600
2	1.2544	1.2996	1.3225	1.3456	1.3924	1.4400	1.5376	1.6384	1.7424	1.8496
3	1.4049	1.4815	1.5209	1.5609	1.6430	1.7280	1.9066	2.0972	2.3000	2.5155
4	1.5735	1.6890	1.7490	1.8106	1.9388	2.0736	2.3642	2.6844	3.0360	3.4210
5	1.7623	1.9254	2.0114	2.1003	2.2878	2.4883	2.9316	3.4360	4.0075	4.6526
6	1.9738	2.1950	2.3131	2.4364	2.6996	2.9860	3.6352	4.3980	5.2899	6.3275
7	2.2107	2.5023	2.6600	2.8262	3.1855	3.5832	4.5077	5.6295	6.9826	8.6054
8	2.4760	2.8526	3.0590	3.2784	3.7589	4.2998	5.5895	7.2058	9.2170	11.703
9	2.7731	3.2519	3.5179	3.8030	4.4355	5.1598	6.9310	9.2234	12.166	15.916
10	3.1058	3.7072	4.0456	4.4114	5.2338	6.1917	8.5944	11.805	16.059	21.646
11	3.4785	4.2262	4.6524	5.1173	6.1759	7.4301	10.657	15.111	21.198	29.439
12	3.8960	4.8179	5.3502	5.9360	7.2876	8.9161	13.214	19.342	27.982	40.037
13	4.3635	5.4924	6.1528	6.8858	8.5994	10.699	16.386	24.758	36.937	54.451
14	4.8871	6.2613	7.0757	7.9875	10.147	12.839	20.319	31.691	48.756	74.053
15	5.4736	7.1379	8.1371	9.2655	11.973	15.407	25.195	40.564	64.358	100.71
16	6.1304	8.1372	9.3576	10.748	14.129	18.488	31.242	51.923	84.953	136.96
17	6.8660	9.2765	10.761	12.467	16.672	22.186	38.740	66.461	112.13	186.27
18	7.6900	10.575	12.375	14.462	19.673	26.623	48.038	85.070	148.02	253.33
19	8.6128	12.055	14.231	16.776	23.214	31.948	59.567	108.89	195.39	344.53
20	9.6463	13.743	16.366	19.460	27.393	38.337	73.864	139.37	257.91	468.57
21	10.803	15.667	18.821	22.574	32.323	46.005	91.591	178.40	340.44	637.26
22	12.100	17.861	21.644	26.186	38.142	55.206	113.57	228.35	449.39	866.67
23	13.552	20.361	24.891	30.376	45.007	66.247	140.83	292.30	593.19	1178.6
24	15.178	23.212	28.625	35.236	53.108	79.496	174.63	374.14	783.02	1602.9
25	17.000	26.461	32.918	40.874	62.668	95.396	216.54	478.90	1033.5	2180.0
26	19.040	30.166	37.856	47.414	73.948	114.47	268.51	612.99	1364.3	2964.9
27	21.324	34.389	43.535	55.000	87.259	137.37	332.95	784.63	1800.9	4032.2
28	23.883	39.204	50.065	63.800	102.96	164.84	412.86	1004.3	2377.2	5483.8
29	26.749	44.693	57.575	74.008	121.50	197.81	511.95	1285.5	3137.9	7458.0
30	29.959	50.950	66.211	85.849	143.37	237.37	634.81	1645.5	4142.0	10143.
40	93.050	188.88	267.86	378.72	750.37	1469.7	5455.9	19426.	66520.	*
50	289.00	700.23	1083.6	1670.7	3927.3	9100.4	46890.	*	*	*
60	897.59	2595.9	4383.9	7370.1	20555.	56347.	*	*	*	*

*FVIF > 99,999.

Table B.2

PRESENT VALUE OF \$1: $PVIF_{i,N} = 1/(1 + i)^N = 1/FVIF_{i,N}$

PERIOD	1%	2%	3%	4%	5%	6%	7%	8%	9%	10%
1	.9901	.9804	.9709	.9615	.9524	.9434	.9346	.9259	.9174	.9091
2	.9803	.9612	.9426	.9246	.9070	.8900	.8734	.8573	.8417	.8264
3	.9706	.9423	.9151	.8890	.8638	.8396	.8163	.7938	.7722	.7513
4	.9610	.9238	.8885	.8548	.8227	.7921	.7629	.7350	.7084	.6830
5	.9515	.9057	.8626	.8219	.7835	.7473	.7130	.6806	.6499	.6209
6	.9420	.8880	.8375	.7903	.7462	.7050	.6663	.6302	.5963	.5645
7	.9327	.8706	.8131	.7599	.7107	.6651	.6227	.5835	.5470	.5132
8	.9235	.8535	.7894	.7307	.6768	.6274	.5820	.5403	.5019	.4665
9	.9143	.8368	.7664	.7026	.6446	.5919	.5439	.5002	.4604	.4241
10	.9053	.8203	.7441	.6756	.6139	.5584	.5083	.4632	.4224	.3855
11	.8963	.8043	.7224	.6496	.5847	.5268	.4751	.4289	.3875	.3505
12	.8874	.7885	.7014	.6246	.5568	.4970	.4440	.3971	.3555	.3186
13	.8787	.7730	.6810	.6006	.5303	.4688	.4150	.3677	.3262	.2897
14	.8700	.7579	.6611	.5775	.5051	.4423	.3878	.3405	.2992	.2633
15	.8613	.7430	.6419	.5553	.4810	.4173	.3624	.3152	.2745	.2394
16	.8528	.7284	.6232	.5339	.4581	.3936	.3387	.2919	.2519	.2176
17	.8444	.7142	.6050	.5134	.4363	.3714	.3166	.2703	.2311	.1978
18	.8360	.7002	.5874	.4936	.4155	.3503	.2959	.2502	.2120	.1799
19	.8277	.6854	.5703	.4746	.3957	.3305	.2765	.2317	.1945	.1635
20	.8195	.6730	.5537	.4564	.3769	.3118	.2584	.2145	.1784	.1486
21	.8114	.6598	.5375	.4388	.3589	.2942	.2415	.1987	.1637	.1351
22	.8034	.6468	.5219	.4220	.3418	.2775	.2257	.1839	.1502	.1228
23	.7954	.6342	.5067	.4057	.3256	.2618	.2109	.1703	.1378	.1117
24	.7876	.6217	.4919	.3901	.3101	.2470	.1971	.1577	.1264	.1015
25	.7798	.6095	.4776	.3751	.2953	.2330	.1842	.1460	.1160	.0923
26	.7720	.5976	.4637	.3607	.2812	.2198	.1722	.1352	.1064	.0839
27	.7644	.5859	.4502	.3468	.2678	.2074	.1609	.1252	.0976	.0763
28	.7568	.5744	.4371	.3335	.2551	.1956	.1504	.1159	.0895	.0693
29	.7493	.5631	.4243	.3207	.2429	.1846	.1406	.1073	.0822	.0630
30	.7419	.5521	.4120	.3083	.2314	.1741	.1314	.0994	.0754	.0573
35	.7059	.5000	.3554	.2534	.1813	.1301	.0937	.0676	.0490	.0356
40	.6717	.4529	.3066	.2083	.1420	.0972	.0668	.0460	.0318	.0221
45	.6391	.4102	.2644	.1712	.1113	.0727	.0476	.0313	.0207	.0137
50	.6080	.3715	.2281	.1407	.0872	.0543	.0339	.0213	.0134	.0085
55	.5785	.3365	.1968	.1157	.0683	.0406	.0242	.0145	.0087	.0053

continued

Table B.2

continued

PERIOD	12%	14%	15%	16%	18%	20%	24%	28%	32%	36%
1	.8929	.8772	.8696	.8621	.8475	.8333	.8065	.7813	.7576	.7353
2	.7972	.7695	.7561	.7432	.7182	.6944	.6504	.6104	.5739	.5407
3	.7118	.6750	.6575	.6407	.6086	.5787	.5245	.4768	.4348	.3975
4	.6355	.5921	.5718	.5523	.5158	.4823	.4230	.3725	.3294	.2923
5	.5674	.5194	.4972	.4761	.4371	.4019	.3411	.2910	.2495	.2149
6	.5066	.4556	.4323	.4104	.3704	.3349	.2751	.2274	.1890	.1580
7	.4523	.3996	.3759	.3538	.3139	.2791	.2218	.1776	.1432	.1162
8	.4039	.3506	.3269	.3050	.2660	.2326	.1789	.1388	.1085	.0854
9	.3606	.3075	.2843	.2630	.2255	.1938	.1443	.1084	.0822	.0628
10	.3220	.2697	.2472	.2267	.1911	.1615	.1164	.0847	.0623	.0462
11	.2875	.2366	.2149	.1954	.1619	.1346	.0938	.0662	.0472	.0340
12	.2567	.2076	.1869	.1685	.1372	.1122	.0757	.0517	.0357	.0250
13	.2292	.1821	.1625	.1452	.1163	.0935	.0610	.0404	.0271	.0184
14	.2046	.1597	.1413	.1252	.0985	.0779	.0492	.0316	.0205	.0135
15	.1827	.1401	.1229	.1079	.0835	.0649	.0397	.0247	.0155	.0099
16	.1631	.1229	.1069	.0930	.0708	.0541	.0320	.0193	.0118	.0073
17	.1456	.1078	.0929	.0802	.0600	.0451	.0258	.0150	.0089	.0054
18	.1300	.0946	.0808	.0691	.0508	.0376	.0208	.0118	.0068	.0039
19	.1161	.0829	.0703	.0596	.0431	.0313	.0168	.0092	.0051	.0029
20	.1037	.0728	.0611	.0514	.0365	.0261	.0135	.0072	.0039	.0021
21	.0926	.0638	.0531	.0443	.0309	.0217	.0109	.0056	.0029	.0016
22	.0826	.0560	.0462	.0382	.0262	.0181	.0088	.0044	.0022	.0012
23	.0738	.0491	.0402	.0329	.0222	.0151	.0071	.0034	.0017	.0008
24	.0659	.0431	.0349	.0284	.0188	.0126	.0057	.0027	.0013	.0006
25	.0588	.0378	.0304	.0245	.0160	.0105	.0046	.0021	.0010	.0005
26	.0525	.0331	.0264	.0211	.0135	.0087	.0037	.0016	.0007	.0003
27	.0469	.0291	.0230	.0182	.0115	.0073	.0030	.0013	.0006	.0002
28	.0419	.0255	.0200	.0157	.0097	.0061	.0024	.0010	.0004	.0002
29	.0374	.0224	.0174	.0135	.0082	.0051	.0020	.0008	.0003	.0001
30	.0334	.0196	.0151	.0116	.0070	.0042	.0016	.0006	.0002	.0001
35	.0189	.0102	.0075	.0055	.0030	.0017	.0005	.0002	.0001	*
40	.0107	.0053	.0037	.0026	.0013	.0007	.0002	.0001	*	*
45	.0061	.0027	.0019	.0013	.0006	.0003	.0001	*	*	*
50	.0035	.0014	.0009	.0006	.0003	.0001	*	*	*	*
55	.0020	.0007	.0005	.0003	.0001	*	*	*	*	*

*The factor is zero to four decimal places.

Table B.3

FUTURE VALUE OF AN ANNUITY OF $1 FOR N PERIODS

$$FVIFA_{i,N} = \sum_{t=1}^{N} (1 + i)^{t-1}$$

$$= \frac{(1 + i)^N - 1}{i}$$

NUMBER OF PERIODS	1%	2%	3%	4%	5%	6%	7%	8%	9%	10%
1	1.0000	1.0000	1.0000	1.0000	1.0000	1.0000	1.0000	1.0000	1.0000	1.0000
2	2.0100	2.0200	2.0300	2.0400	2.0500	2.0600	2.0700	2.0800	2.0900	2.1000
3	3.0301	3.0604	3.0909	3.1216	3.1525	3.1836	3.2149	3.2464	3.2781	3.3100
4	4.0604	4.1216	4.1836	4.2465	4.3101	4.3746	4.4399	4.5061	4.5731	4.6410
5	5.1010	5.2040	5.3091	5.4163	5.5256	5.6371	5.7507	5.8666	5.9847	6.1051
6	6.1520	6.3081	6.4684	6.6330	6.8019	6.9753	7.1533	7.3359	7.5233	7.7156
7	7.2135	7.4343	7.6625	7.8983	8.1420	8.3938	8.6540	8.9228	9.2004	9.4872
8	8.2857	8.5830	8.8923	9.2142	9.5491	9.8975	10.259	10.636	11.028	11.435
9	9.3685	9.7546	10.159	10.582	11.026	11.491	11.978	12.487	13.021	13.579
10	10.462	10.949	11.463	12.006	12.577	13.180	13.816	14.486	15.192	15.937
11	11.566	12.168	12.807	13.486	14.206	14.971	15.783	16.645	17.560	18.531
12	12.682	13.412	14.192	15.025	15.917	16.869	17.888	18.977	20.140	21.384
13	13.809	14.680	15.617	16.626	17.713	18.882	20.140	21.495	22.953	24.522
14	14.947	15.973	17.086	18.291	19.598	21.015	22.550	24.214	26.019	27.975
15	16.096	17.293	18.598	20.023	21.578	23.276	25.129	27.152	29.360	31.772
16	17.257	18.639	20.156	21.824	23.657	25.672	27.888	30.324	33.003	35.949
17	18.430	20.012	21.761	23.697	25.840	28.212	30.840	33.750	36.973	40.544
18	19.614	21.412	23.414	25.645	28.132	30.905	33.999	37.450	41.301	45.599
19	20.810	22.840	25.116	27.671	30.539	33.760	37.379	41.446	46.018	51.159
20	22.019	24.297	26.870	29.778	33.066	36.785	40.995	45.762	51.160	57.275
21	23.239	25.783	28.676	31.969	35.719	39.992	44.865	50.422	56.764	64.002
22	24.471	27.299	30.536	34.248	38.505	43.392	49.005	55.456	62.873	71.402
23	25.716	28.845	32.452	36.617	41.430	46.995	53.436	60.893	69.531	79.543
24	26.973	30.421	34.426	39.082	44.502	50.815	58.176	66.764	76.789	88.497
25	28.243	32.030	36.459	41.645	47.727	54.864	63.249	73.105	84.700	98.347
26	29.525	33.670	38.553	44.311	51.113	59.156	68.676	79.954	93.323	109.18
27	30.820	35.344	40.709	47.084	54.669	63.705	74.483	87.350	102.72	121.09
28	32.129	37.051	42.930	49.967	58.402	68.528	80.697	95.338	112.96	134.20
29	33.450	38.792	45.218	52.966	62.322	73.639	87.346	103.96	124.13	148.63
30	34.784	40.568	47.575	56.084	66.438	79.058	94.460	113.28	136.30	164.49
40	48.886	60.402	75.401	95.025	120.79	154.76	199.63	259.05	337.88	442.59
50	64.463	84.579	112.79	152.66	209.34	290.33	406.52	573.76	815.08	1163.9
60	81.669	114.05	163.05	237.99	353.58	533.12	813.52	1253.2	1944.7	3034.8

continued

Table B.3   *continued*

NUMBER OF PERIODS	12%	14%	15%	16%	18%	20%	24%	28%	32%	36%
1	1.0000	1.0000	1.0000	1.0000	1.0000	1.0000	1.0000	1.0000	1.0000	1.0000
2	2.1200	2.1400	2.1500	2.1600	2.1800	2.2000	2.2400	2.2800	2.3200	2.3600
3	3.3744	3.4396	3.4725	3.5056	3.5724	3.6400	3.7776	3.9184	4.0624	4.2096
4	4.7793	4.9211	4.9934	5.0665	5.2154	5.3680	5.6842	6.0156	6.3624	6.7251
5	6.3528	6.6101	6.7424	6.8771	7.1542	7.4416	8.0484	8.6999	9.3983	10.146
6	8.1152	8.5355	8.7537	8.9775	9.4420	9.9299	10.980	12.135	13.405	14.798
7	10.089	10.730	11.066	11.413	12.141	12.915	14.615	16.533	18.695	21.126
8	12.299	13.232	13.726	14.240	15.327	16.499	19.122	22.163	25.678	29.731
9	14.775	16.085	16.785	17.518	19.085	20.798	24.712	29.369	34.895	41.435
10	17.548	19.337	20.303	21.321	23.521	25.958	31.643	38.592	47.061	57.351
11	20.654	23.044	24.349	25.732	28.755	32.150	40.237	50.398	63.121	78.998
12	24.133	27.270	29.001	30.850	34.931	39.580	50.894	65.510	84.320	108.43
13	28.029	32.088	34.351	36.786	42.218	48.496	64.109	84.852	112.30	148.47
14	32.392	37.581	40.504	43.672	50.818	59.195	80.496	109.61	149.23	202.92
15	37.279	43.842	47.580	51.659	60.965	72.035	100.81	141.30	197.99	276.97
16	42.753	50.980	55.717	60.925	72.939	87.442	126.01	181.86	262.35	377.69
17	48.883	59.117	65.075	71.673	87.068	105.93	157.25	233.79	347.30	514.66
18	55.749	68.394	75.836	84.140	103.74	128.11	195.99	300.25	459.44	700.93
19	63.439	78.969	88.211	98.603	123.41	154.74	244.03	385.32	607.47	954.27
20	72.052	91.024	102.44	115.37	146.62	186.68	303.60	494.21	802.86	1298.8
21	81.698	104.76	118.81	134.84	174.02	225.02	377.46	633.59	1060.7	1767.3
22	92.502	120.43	137.63	157.41	206.34	271.03	469.05	811.99	1401.2	2404.6
23	104.60	138.29	159.27	183.60	244.48	326.23	582.62	1040.3	1850.6	3271.3
24	118.15	158.65	184.16	213.97	289.49	392.48	723.46	1332.6	2443.8	4449.9
25	133.33	181.87	212.79	249.21	342.60	471.98	898.09	1706.8	3226.8	6052.9
26	150.33	208.33	245.71	290.08	405.27	567.37	1114.6	2185.7	4260.4	8233.0
27	169.37	238.49	283.56	337.50	479.22	681.85	1383.1	2798.7	5624.7	11197.9
28	190.69	272.88	327.10	392.50	566.48	819.22	1716.0	3583.3	7425.6	15230.2
29	214.58	312.09	377.16	456.30	669.44	984.06	2128.9	4587.6	9802.9	20714.1
30	241.33	356.78	434.74	530.31	790.94	1181.8	2640.9	5873.2	12940.	28172.2
40	767.09	1342.0	1779.0	2360.7	4163.2	7343.8	22728.	69377.	*	*
50	2400.0	4994.5	7217.7	10435.	21813.	45497.	*	*	*	*
60	7471.6	18535.	29219.	46057.	*	*	*	*	*	*

*FVIFA > 99,999.

Table B.4

PRESENT VALUE OF AN ANNUITY OF $1 FOR N PERIODS

$$PVIFA_{i,N} = \sum_{t=1}^{N} \frac{1}{(1 + i)^t} = \frac{1 - \dfrac{1}{(1 + i)^N}}{i}$$

NUMBER OF PAY- MENTS	1%	2%	3%	4%	5%	6%	7%	8%	9%
1	0.9901	0.9804	0.9709	0.9615	0.9524	0.9434	0.9346	0.9259	0.9174
2	1.9704	1.9416	1.9135	1.8861	1.8594	1.8334	1.8080	1.7833	1.7591
3	2.9410	2.8839	2.8286	2.7751	2.7232	2.6730	2.6243	2.5771	2.5313
4	3.9020	3.8077	3.7171	3.6299	3.5460	3.4651	3.3872	3.3121	3.2397
5	4.8534	4.7135	4.5797	4.4518	4.3295	4.2124	4.1002	3.9927	3.8897
6	5.7955	5.6014	5.4172	5.2421	5.0757	4.9173	4.7665	4.6229	4.4859
7	6.7282	6.4720	6.2303	6.0021	5.7864	5.5824	5.3893	5.2064	5.0330
8	7.6517	7.3255	7.0197	6.7327	6.4632	6.2098	5.9713	5.7466	5.5348
9	8.5660	8.1622	7.7861	7.4353	7.1078	6.8017	6.5152	6.2469	5.9952
10	9.4713	8.9826	8.5302	8.1109	7.7217	7.3601	7.0236	6.7101	6.4177
11	10.3676	9.7868	9.2526	8.7605	8.3064	7.8869	7.4987	7.1390	6.8052
12	11.2551	10.5753	9.9540	9.3851	8.8633	8.3838	7.9427	7.5361	7.1607
13	12.1337	11.3484	10.6350	9.9856	9.3936	8.8527	8.3577	7.9038	7.4869
14	13.0037	12.1062	11.2961	10.5631	9.8986	9.2950	8.7455	8.2442	7.7862
15	13.8651	12.8493	11.9379	11.1184	10.3797	9.7122	9.1079	8.5595	8.0607
16	14.7179	13.5777	12.5611	11.6523	10.8378	10.1059	9.4466	8.8514	8.3126
17	15.5623	14.2919	13.1661	12.1657	11.2741	10.4773	9.7632	9.1216	8.5436
18	16.3983	14.9920	13.7535	12.6593	11.6896	10.8276	10.0591	9.3719	8.7556
19	17.2260	15.6785	14.3238	13.1339	12.0853	11.1581	10.3356	9.6036	8.9501
20	18.0456	16.3514	14.8775	13.5903	12.4622	11.4699	10.5940	9.8181	9.1285
21	18.8570	17.0112	15.4150	14.0292	12.8212	11.7641	10.8355	10.0168	9.2922
22	19.6604	17.6580	15.9369	14.4511	13.1630	12.0416	11.0612	10.2007	9.4424
23	20.4558	18.2922	16.4436	14.8568	13.4886	12.3034	11.2722	10.3711	9.5802
24	21.2434	18.9139	16.9355	15.2470	13.7986	12.5504	11.4693	10.5288	9.7066
25	22.0232	19.5235	17.4131	15.6221	14.0939	12.7834	11.6536	10.6748	9.8226
26	22.7952	20.1210	17.8768	15.9828	14.3752	13.0032	11.8258	10.8100	9.9290
27	23.5596	20.7069	18.3270	16.3296	14.6430	13.2105	11.9867	10.9352	10.0266
28	24.3164	21.2813	18.7641	16.6631	14.8981	13.4062	12.1371	11.0511	10.1161
29	25.0658	21.8444	19.1885	16.9837	15.1411	13.5907	12.2777	11.1584	10.1983
30	25.8077	22.3965	19.6004	17.2920	15.3725	13.7648	12.4090	11.2578	10.2737
35	29.4086	24.9986	21.4872	18.6646	16.3742	14.4982	12.9477	11.6546	10.5668
40	32.8347	27.3555	23.1148	19.7928	17.1591	15.0463	13.3317	11.9246	10.7574
45	36.0945	29.4902	24.5187	20.7200	17.7741	15.4558	13.6055	12.1084	10.8812
50	39.1961	31.4236	25.7298	21.4822	18.2559	15.7619	13.8007	12.2335	10.9617
55	42.1472	33.1748	26.7744	22.1086	18.6335	15.9905	13.9399	12.3186	11.0140

continued

Table B.4

continued

NUMBER OF PAY- MENTS	10%	12%	14%	15%	16%	18%	20%	24%	28%	32%
1	0.9091	0.8929	0.8772	0.8696	0.8621	0.8475	0.8333	0.8065	0.7813	0.7576
2	1.7355	1.6901	1.6467	1.6257	1.6052	1.5656	1.5278	1.4568	1.3916	1.3315
3	2.4869	2.4018	2.3216	2.2832	2.2459	2.1743	2.1065	1.9813	1.8684	1.7663
4	3.1699	3.0373	2.9137	2.8550	2.7982	2.6901	2.5887	2.4043	2.2410	2.0957
5	3.7908	3.6048	3.4331	3.3522	3.2743	3.1272	2.9906	2.7454	2.5320	2.3452
6	4.3553	4.1114	3.8887	3.7845	3.6847	3.4976	3.3255	3.0205	2.7594	2.5342
7	4.8684	4.5638	4.2883	4.1604	4.0386	3.8115	3.6046	3.2423	2.9370	2.6775
8	5.3349	4.9676	4.6389	4.4873	4.3436	4.0776	3.8372	3.4212	3.0758	2.7860
9	5.7590	5.3282	4.9464	4.7716	4.6065	4.3030	4.0310	3.5655	3.1842	2.8681
10	6.1446	5.6502	5.2161	5.0188	4.8332	4.4941	4.1925	3.6819	3.2689	2.9304
11	6.4951	5.9377	5.4527	5.2337	5.0286	4.6560	4.3271	3.7757	3.3351	2.9776
12	6.8137	6.1944	5.6603	5.4206	5.1971	4.7932	4.4392	3.8514	3.3868	3.0133
13	7.1034	6.4235	5.8424	5.5831	5.3423	4.9095	4.5327	3.9124	3.4272	3.0404
14	7.3667	6.6282	6.0021	5.7245	5.4675	5.0081	4.6106	3.9616	3.4587	3.0609
15	7.6061	6.8109	6.1422	5.8474	5.5755	5.0916	4.6755	4.0013	3.4834	3.0764
16	7.8237	6.9740	6.2651	5.9542	5.6685	5.1624	4.7296	4.0333	3.5026	3.0882
17	8.0216	7.1196	6.3729	6.0472	5.7487	5.2223	4.7746	4.0591	3.5177	3.0971
18	8.2014	7.2497	6.4674	6.1280	5.8178	5.2732	4.8122	4.0799	3.5294	3.1039
19	8.3649	7.3658	6.5504	6.1982	5.8775	5.3162	4.8435	4.0967	3.5386	3.1090
20	8.5136	7.4694	6.6231	6.2593	5.9288	5.3527	4.8696	4.1103	3.5458	3.1129
21	8.6487	7.5620	6.6870	6.3125	5.9731	5.3837	4.8913	4.1212	3.5514	3.1158
22	8.7715	7.6446	6.7429	6.3587	6.0113	5.4099	4.9094	4.1300	3.5558	3.1180
23	8.8832	7.7184	6.7921	6.3988	6.0442	5.4321	4.9245	4.1371	3.5592	3.1197
24	8.9847	7.7843	6.8351	6.4338	6.0726	5.4510	4.9371	4.1428	3.5619	3.1210
25	9.0770	7.8431	6.8729	6.4642	6.0971	5.4669	4.9476	4.1474	3.5640	3.1220
26	9.1609	7.8957	6.9061	6.4906	6.1182	5.4804	4.9563	4.1511	3.5656	3.1227
27	9.2372	7.9426	6.9352	6.5135	6.1364	5.4919	4.9636	4.1542	3.5669	3.1233
28	9.3066	7.9844	6.9607	6.5335	6.1520	6.5016	4.9697	4.1566	3.5679	3.1237
29	9.3696	8.0218	6.9830	6.5509	6.1656	5.5098	4.9747	4.1585	3.5687	3.1240
30	9.4269	8.0552	7.0027	6.5660	6.1772	5.5168	4.9789	4.1601	3.5693	3.1242
35	9.6442	8.1755	7.0700	6.6166	6.2153	5.5386	4.9915	4.1644	3.5708	3.1248
40	9.7791	8.2438	7.1050	6.6418	6.2335	5.5482	4.9966	4.1659	3.5712	3.1250
45	9.8628	8.2825	7.1232	6.6543	6.2421	5.5523	4.9986	4.1664	3.5714	3.1250
50	9.9148	8.3045	7.1327	6.6605	6.2463	5.5541	4.9995	4.1666	3.5714	3.1250
55	9.9471	8.3170	7.1376	6.6636	6.2482	5.5549	4.9998	4.1666	3.5714	3.1250

THE DISTRIBUTION OF A VARIABLE z (PERCENT OF TOTAL AREA UNDER THE
NORMAL CURVE BETWEEN x AND μ)

Table C.1

z^1	0.00	0.01	0.02	0.03	0.04	0.05	0.06	0.07	0.08	0.09
0.0	.0000	.0040	.0080	.0120	.0160	.0199	.0239	.0279	.0319	.0359
0.1	.0398	.0438	.0478	.0517	.0557	.0596	.0636	.0675	.0714	.0753
0.2	.0793	.0832	.0871	.0910	.0948	.0987	.1026	.1064	.1103	.1141
0.3	.1179	.1217	.1255	.1293	.1331	.1368	.1406	.1443	.1480	.1517
0.4	.1554	.1591	.1628	.1664	.1700	.1736	.1772	.1808	.1844	.1879
0.5	.1915	.1950	.1985	.2019	.2054	.2088	.2123	.2157	.2190	.2224
0.6	.2257	.2291	.2324	.2357	.2389	.2422	.2454	.2486	.2517	.2549
0.7	.2580	.2611	.2642	.2673	.2704	.2734	.2764	.2794	.2823	.2852
0.8	.2881	.2910	.2939	.2967	.2995	.3023	.3051	.3078	.3106	.3133
0.9	.3159	.3186	.3212	.3238	.3264	.3289	.3315	.3340	.3365	.3389
1.0	.3413	.3438	.3461	.3485	.3508	.3531	.3554	.3577	.3599	.3621
1.1	.3643	.3665	.3686	.3708	.3729	.3749	.3770	.3790	.3810	.3830
1.2	.3849	.3869	.3888	.3907	.3925	.3944	.3962	.3980	.3997	.4015
1.3	.4032	.4049	.4066	.4082	.4099	.4115	.4131	.4147	.4162	.4177
1.4	.4192	.4207	.4222	.4236	.4251	.4265	.4279	.4292	.4306	.4319
1.5	.4332	.4345	.4357	.4370	.4382	.4394	.4406	.4418	.4429	.4441
1.6	.4452	.4463	.4474	.4484	.4495	.4505	.4515	.4525	.4535	.4545
1.7	.4554	.4564	.4573	.4582	.4591	.4599	.4608	.4616	.4625	.4633
1.8	.4641	.4649	.4656	.4664	.4671	.4678	.4686	.4693	.4699	.4706
1.9	.4713	.4719	.4726	.4732	.4738	.4744	.4750	.4756	.4761	.4767
2.0	.4773	.4778	.4783	.4788	.4793	.4798	.4803	.4808	.4812	.4817
2.1	.4821	.4826	.4830	.4834	.4838	.4842	.4846	.4850	.4854	.4857
2.2	.4861	.4864	.4868	.4871	.4875	.4878	.4881	.4884	.4887	.4890
2.3	.4893	.4896	.4898	.4901	.4904	.4906	.4909	.4911	.4913	.4916
2.4	.4918	.4920	.4922	.4925	.4927	.4929	.4931	.4932	.4934	.4936
2.5	.4938	.4940	.4941	.4943	.4945	.4946	.4948	.4949	.4951	.4952
2.6	.4953	.4955	.4956	.4957	.4959	.4960	.4961	.4962	.4963	.4964
2.7	.4965	.4966	.4967	.4968	.4969	.4970	.4971	.4972	.4973	.4974
2.8	.4974	.4975	.4976	.4977	.4977	.4978	.4979	.4979	.4980	.4981
2.9	.4981	.4982	.4982	.4982	.4984	.4984	.4985	.4985	.4986	.4986
3.0	.4987	.4987	.4987	.4988	.4988	.4989	.4989	.4989	.4990	.4990

[1]z is the standardized variable, where $z = x - \mu/\sigma$ and x is the point of interest, μ is the mean, and σ is the standard deviation of a distribution. Thus, z measures the number of standard deviations between a point of interest x and the mean of a given distribution. In the table above, we indicate the percentage of the total area under the normal curve between x and μ. Thus, .3413 or 34.13% of the area under the normal curve lies between a point of interest and the mean when $z = 1.0$.

Table C.2

CRITICAL F VALUES AT THE 90 PERCENT CONFIDENCE LEVEL (α = .10)[1]

DEGREES OF FREEDOM IN THE NUMERATOR ($d.f. = k - 1$)

$d.f. = N - k$	1	2	3	4	5	6	7	8	9	10	12	15	20	24	30	40	60	120	∞
1	39.86	49.50	53.59	55.83	57.24	58.20	58.91	59.44	59.86	60.19	60.71	61.22	61.74	62.00	62.26	62.53	62.79	63.06	63.33
2	8.53	9.00	9.16	9.24	9.29	9.33	9.35	9.37	9.38	9.39	9.41	9.42	9.44	9.45	9.46	9.47	9.47	9.48	9.49
3	8.54	5.46	5.39	5.34	5.31	5.28	5.27	5.25	5.24	5.23	5.22	5.20	5.18	5.18	5.17	5.16	5.15	5.14	5.13
4	4.54	4.32	4.19	4.11	4.05	4.01	3.98	3.95	3.94	3.92	3.90	3.87	3.84	3.83	3.82	3.80	3.79	3.78	3.76
5	4.06	3.78	3.62	3.52	3.45	3.40	3.37	3.34	3.32	3.30	3.27	3.24	3.21	3.19	3.17	3.16	3.14	3.12	3.10
6	3.78	3.46	3.29	3.18	3.11	3.05	3.01	2.98	2.96	2.94	2.90	2.87	2.84	2.82	2.80	2.78	2.76	2.74	2.72
7	3.59	3.26	3.07	2.96	2.88	2.83	2.78	2.75	2.72	2.70	2.67	2.63	2.59	2.58	2.56	2.54	2.51	2.49	2.47
8	3.46	3.11	2.92	2.81	2.73	2.67	2.62	2.59	2.56	2.54	2.50	2.46	2.42	2.40	2.38	2.36	2.34	2.32	2.29
9	3.36	3.01	2.81	2.69	2.61	2.55	2.51	2.47	2.44	2.42	2.38	2.34	2.30	2.28	2.25	2.23	2.21	2.18	2.16
10	3.29	2.92	2.73	2.61	2.52	2.46	2.41	2.38	2.35	2.32	2.28	2.24	2.20	2.18	2.16	2.13	2.11	2.08	2.06
11	3.23	2.86	2.66	2.54	2.45	2.39	2.34	2.30	2.27	2.25	2.21	2.17	2.12	2.10	2.08	2.05	2.03	2.00	1.97
12	3.18	2.81	2.61	2.48	2.39	2.33	2.28	2.24	2.21	2.19	2.15	2.10	2.06	2.04	2.01	1.99	1.96	1.93	1.90
13	3.14	2.76	2.56	2.43	2.35	2.28	2.23	2.20	2.16	2.14	2.10	2.05	2.01	1.98	1.96	1.93	1.90	1.88	1.85
14	3.10	2.73	2.52	2.39	2.31	2.24	2.19	2.15	2.12	2.10	2.05	2.01	1.96	1.94	1.91	1.89	1.86	1.83	1.80
15	3.07	2.70	2.49	2.36	2.27	2.21	2.16	2.12	2.09	2.06	2.02	1.97	1.92	1.90	1.87	1.85	1.82	1.79	1.76
16	3.05	2.67	2.46	2.33	2.24	2.18	2.13	2.09	2.06	2.03	1.99	1.94	1.89	1.87	1.84	1.81	1.78	1.75	1.72
17	3.03	2.64	2.44	2.31	2.22	2.15	2.10	2.06	2.03	2.00	1.96	1.91	1.86	1.84	1.81	1.78	1.75	1.72	1.69
18	3.01	2.62	2.42	2.29	2.20	2.13	2.08	2.04	2.00	1.98	1.93	1.89	1.84	1.81	1.78	1.75	1.72	1.69	1.66
19	2.99	2.61	2.40	2.27	2.18	2.11	2.06	2.02	1.98	1.96	1.91	1.86	1.81	1.79	1.76	1.73	1.70	1.67	1.63
20	2.97	2.59	2.38	2.25	2.16	2.09	2.04	2.00	1.96	1.94	1.89	1.84	1.79	1.77	1.74	1.71	1.68	1.64	1.61
21	2.96	2.57	2.36	2.23	2.14	2.08	2.02	1.98	1.95	1.92	1.87	1.83	1.78	1.75	1.72	1.69	1.66	1.62	1.59
22	2.95	2.56	2.35	2.22	2.13	2.06	2.01	1.97	1.93	1.90	1.86	1.81	1.76	1.73	1.70	1.67	1.64	1.60	1.57
23	2.94	2.55	2.34	2.21	2.11	2.05	1.99	1.95	1.92	1.89	1.84	1.80	1.74	1.72	1.69	1.66	1.62	1.59	1.55
24	2.93	2.54	2.33	2.19	2.10	2.04	1.98	1.94	1.91	1.88	1.83	1.78	1.73	1.70	1.67	1.64	1.61	1.57	1.53
25	2.92	2.53	2.32	2.18	2.09	2.02	1.97	1.93	1.89	1.87	1.82	1.77	1.72	1.69	1.66	1.63	1.59	1.56	1.52
26	2.91	2.52	2.31	2.17	2.08	2.01	1.96	1.92	1.88	1.86	1.81	1.76	1.71	1.68	1.65	1.61	1.58	1.54	1.50
27	2.90	2.51	2.30	2.17	2.07	2.00	1.95	1.91	1.87	1.85	1.80	1.75	1.70	1.67	1.64	1.60	1.57	1.53	1.49
28	2.89	2.50	2.29	2.16	2.06	2.00	1.94	1.90	1.87	1.84	1.79	1.74	1.69	1.66	1.63	1.59	1.56	1.52	1.48
29	2.89	2.50	2.28	2.15	2.06	1.99	1.93	1.89	1.86	1.83	1.78	1.73	1.68	1.65	1.62	1.58	1.55	1.51	1.47
30	2.88	2.49	2.28	2.14	2.05	1.98	1.93	1.88	1.85	1.82	1.77	1.72	1.67	1.64	1.61	1.57	1.54	1.50	1.46
40	2.84	2.44	2.23	2.09	2.00	1.93	1.87	1.83	1.79	1.76	1.71	1.66	1.61	1.57	1.54	1.51	1.47	1.42	1.38
60	2.79	2.39	2.18	2.04	1.95	1.87	1.82	1.77	1.74	1.71	1.66	1.60	1.54	1.51	1.48	1.44	1.40	1.35	1.29
120	2.75	2.35	2.13	1.99	1.90	1.82	1.77	1.72	1.68	1.65	1.60	1.55	1.48	1.45	1.41	1.37	1.32	1.26	1.19
∞	2.71	2.30	2.08	1.94	1.85	1.77	1.72	1.67	1.63	1.60	1.55	1.49	1.42	1.38	1.34	1.30	1.24	1.17	1.00

DEGREES OF FREEDOM IN THE DENOMINATOR ($d.f. = N - k$)

Continued

[1]The F statistic provides evidence on whether or not a statistically significant proportion of the total variation in the dependent variable Y has been explained. The F statistic can be calculated in terms of the coefficient of determination as: $F_{k-1, n-k} = R^2/(k-1) \div (1 - R^2)/n - k$, where R^2 is the coefficient of determination, k is the number of estimated coefficients in the regression model (including the intercept), and n is the number of data observations. When the critical F value is exceeded, we can conclude with a given level of confidence (e.g., α = 0.01 or 90 percent confidence) that the regression equation, taken as a whole, significantly explains the variation in Y.

Table C.2

DEGREES OF FREEDOM IN THE NUMERATOR ($d.f. = k - 1$)

$d.f. = N - k$	1	2	3	4	5	6	7	8	9	10	12	15	20	24	30	40	60	120	∞
1	161.4	199.5	215.7	224.6	230.2	234.0	236.8	238.9	240.5	241.9	243.9	245.9	248.0	249.1	250.1	251.1	252.2	253.3	254.3
2	18.51	19.00	19.16	19.25	19.30	19.33	19.35	19.37	19.38	19.40	19.41	19.43	19.45	19.45	19.46	19.47	19.48	19.49	19.50
3	10.13	9.55	9.28	9.12	9.01	8.94	8.89	8.85	8.81	8.79	8.74	8.70	8.66	8.64	8.62	8.59	8.57	8.55	8.53
4	7.71	6.94	6.59	6.39	6.26	6.16	6.09	6.04	6.00	5.96	5.91	5.86	5.80	5.77	5.75	5.72	5.69	5.66	5.63
5	6.61	5.79	5.41	5.19	5.05	4.95	4.88	4.82	4.77	4.74	4.68	4.62	4.56	4.53	4.50	4.46	4.43	4.40	4.36
6	5.99	5.14	4.76	4.53	4.39	4.28	4.21	4.15	4.10	4.06	4.00	3.94	3.87	3.84	3.81	3.77	3.74	3.70	3.67
7	5.59	4.74	4.35	4.12	3.97	3.87	3.79	3.73	3.68	3.64	3.57	3.51	3.44	3.41	3.38	3.34	3.30	3.27	3.23
8	5.32	4.46	4.07	3.84	3.69	3.58	3.50	3.44	3.39	3.35	3.28	3.22	3.15	3.12	3.08	3.04	3.01	2.97	2.93
9	5.12	4.26	3.86	3.63	3.48	3.37	3.29	3.23	3.18	3.14	3.07	3.01	2.94	2.90	2.86	2.83	2.79	2.75	2.71
10	4.96	4.10	3.71	3.48	3.33	3.22	3.14	3.07	3.02	2.98	2.91	2.85	2.77	2.74	2.70	2.66	2.62	2.58	2.54
11	4.84	3.98	3.59	3.36	3.20	3.09	3.01	2.95	2.90	2.85	2.79	2.72	2.65	2.61	2.57	2.53	2.49	2.45	2.40
12	4.75	3.89	3.49	3.26	3.11	3.00	2.91	2.85	2.80	2.75	2.69	2.62	2.54	2.51	2.47	2.43	2.38	2.34	2.30
13	4.67	3.81	3.41	3.18	3.03	2.92	2.83	2.77	2.71	2.67	2.60	2.53	2.46	2.42	2.38	2.34	2.30	2.25	2.21
14	4.60	3.74	3.34	3.11	2.96	2.85	2.76	2.70	2.65	2.60	2.53	2.46	2.39	2.35	2.31	2.27	2.22	2.18	2.13
15	4.54	3.68	3.29	3.06	2.90	2.79	2.71	2.64	2.59	2.54	2.48	2.40	2.33	2.29	2.25	2.20	2.16	2.11	2.07
16	4.49	3.63	3.24	3.01	2.85	2.74	2.66	2.59	2.54	2.49	2.42	2.35	2.28	2.24	2.19	2.15	2.11	2.06	2.01
17	4.45	3.59	3.20	2.96	2.81	2.70	2.61	2.55	2.49	2.45	2.38	2.31	2.23	2.19	2.15	2.10	2.06	2.01	1.96
18	4.41	3.55	3.16	2.93	2.77	2.66	2.58	2.51	2.46	2.41	2.34	2.27	2.19	2.15	2.11	2.06	2.02	1.97	1.92
19	4.38	3.52	3.13	2.90	2.74	2.63	2.54	2.48	2.42	2.38	2.31	2.23	2.16	2.11	2.07	2.03	1.98	1.93	1.88
20	4.35	3.49	3.10	2.87	2.71	2.60	2.51	2.45	2.39	2.35	2.28	2.20	2.12	2.08	2.04	1.99	1.95	1.90	1.84
21	4.32	3.47	3.07	2.84	2.68	2.57	2.49	2.42	2.37	2.32	2.25	2.18	2.10	2.05	2.01	1.96	1.92	1.87	1.81
22	4.30	3.44	3.05	2.82	2.66	2.55	2.46	2.40	2.34	2.30	2.23	2.15	2.07	2.03	1.98	1.94	1.89	1.84	1.78
23	4.28	3.42	3.03	2.80	2.64	2.53	2.44	2.37	2.32	2.27	2.20	2.13	2.05	2.01	1.96	1.91	1.86	1.81	1.76
24	4.26	3.40	3.01	2.78	2.62	2.51	2.42	2.36	2.30	2.25	2.18	2.11	2.03	1.98	1.94	1.89	1.84	1.79	1.73
25	4.24	3.39	2.99	2.76	2.60	2.49	2.40	2.34	2.28	2.24	2.16	2.09	2.01	1.96	1.92	1.87	1.82	1.77	1.71
26	4.23	3.37	2.98	2.74	2.59	2.47	2.39	2.32	2.27	2.22	2.15	2.07	1.99	1.95	1.90	1.85	1.80	1.75	1.69
27	4.21	3.35	2.96	2.73	2.57	2.46	2.37	2.31	2.25	2.20	2.13	2.06	1.97	1.93	1.88	1.84	1.79	1.73	1.67
28	4.20	3.34	2.95	2.71	2.56	2.45	2.36	2.29	2.24	2.19	2.12	2.04	1.96	1.91	1.87	1.82	1.77	1.71	1.65
29	4.18	3.33	2.93	2.70	2.55	2.43	2.35	2.28	2.22	2.18	2.10	2.03	1.94	1.90	1.85	1.81	1.75	1.70	1.64
30	4.17	3.32	2.92	2.69	2.53	2.42	2.33	2.27	2.21	2.16	2.09	2.01	1.93	1.89	1.84	1.79	1.74	1.68	1.62
40	4.08	3.23	2.84	2.61	2.45	2.34	2.25	2.18	2.12	2.08	2.00	1.92	1.84	1.79	1.74	1.69	1.64	1.58	1.51
60	4.00	3.15	2.76	2.53	2.37	2.25	2.17	2.10	2.04	1.99	1.92	1.84	1.75	1.70	1.65	1.59	1.53	1.47	1.39
120	3.92	3.07	2.68	2.45	2.29	2.17	2.09	2.02	1.96	1.91	1.83	1.75	1.66	1.61	1.55	1.50	1.43	1.35	1.25
∞	3.84	3.00	2.60	2.37	2.21	2.10	2.01	1.94	1.88	1.83	1.75	1.67	1.57	1.52	1.46	1.39	1.32	1.22	1.00

DEGREES OF FREEDOM IN THE DENOMINATOR ($d.f. = N - k$)

Table C.2

CRITICAL F VALUES AT THE 99 PERCENT CONFIDENCE LEVEL (α = .01)

DEGREES OF FREEDOM IN THE NUMERATOR (d.f. = k − 1)

	1	2	3	4	5	6	7	8	9	10	12	15	20	24	30	40	60	120	∞
1	4052	4999.5	5403	5625	5764	5859	5928	5982	6022	6056	6106	6157	6209	6235	6261	6287	6313	6339	6366
2	98.50	99.00	99.17	99.25	99.30	99.33	99.36	99.37	99.39	99.40	99.42	99.43	99.45	99.46	99.47	99.47	99.48	99.49	99.50
3	34.12	30.82	29.46	28.71	28.24	27.91	27.67	27.49	27.35	27.23	27.05	26.87	26.69	26.60	26.50	26.41	26.32	26.22	26.13
4	21.20	18.00	16.69	15.98	15.52	15.21	14.98	14.80	14.66	14.55	14.37	14.20	14.02	13.93	13.84	13.75	13.65	13.56	13.46
5	16.26	13.27	12.06	11.39	10.97	10.67	10.46	10.29	10.16	10.05	9.89	9.72	9.55	9.47	9.38	9.29	9.20	9.11	9.02
6	13.75	10.92	9.78	9.15	8.75	8.47	8.26	8.10	7.98	7.87	7.72	7.56	7.40	7.31	7.23	7.14	7.06	6.97	6.88
7	12.25	9.55	8.45	7.85	7.46	7.19	6.99	6.84	6.72	6.62	6.47	6.31	6.16	6.07	5.99	5.91	5.82	5.74	5.65
8	11.26	8.65	7.59	7.01	6.63	6.37	6.18	6.03	5.91	5.81	5.67	5.52	5.36	5.28	5.20	5.12	5.03	4.95	4.86
9	10.56	8.02	6.99	6.42	6.06	5.80	5.61	5.47	5.35	5.26	5.11	4.96	4.81	4.73	4.65	4.57	4.48	4.40	4.31
10	10.04	7.56	6.55	5.99	5.64	5.39	5.20	5.06	4.94	4.85	4.71	4.56	4.41	4.33	4.25	4.17	4.08	4.00	3.91
11	9.65	7.21	6.22	5.67	5.32	5.07	4.89	4.74	4.63	4.54	4.40	4.25	4.10	4.02	3.94	3.86	3.78	3.69	3.60
12	9.33	6.93	5.95	5.41	5.06	4.82	4.64	4.50	4.39	4.30	4.16	4.01	3.86	3.78	3.70	3.62	3.54	3.45	3.36
13	9.07	6.70	5.74	5.21	4.86	4.62	4.44	4.30	4.19	4.10	3.96	3.82	3.66	3.59	3.51	3.43	3.34	3.25	3.17
14	8.86	6.51	5.56	5.04	4.69	4.46	4.28	4.14	4.03	3.94	3.80	3.66	3.51	3.43	3.35	3.27	3.18	3.09	3.00
15	8.68	6.36	5.42	4.89	4.56	4.32	4.14	4.00	3.89	3.80	3.67	3.52	3.37	3.29	3.21	3.13	3.05	2.96	2.87
16	8.53	6.23	5.29	4.77	4.44	4.20	4.03	3.89	3.78	3.69	3.55	3.41	3.26	3.18	3.10	3.02	2.93	2.84	2.75
17	8.40	6.11	5.18	4.67	4.34	4.10	3.93	3.79	3.68	3.59	3.46	3.31	3.16	3.08	3.00	2.92	2.83	2.75	2.65
18	8.29	6.01	5.09	4.58	4.25	4.01	3.84	3.71	3.60	3.51	3.37	3.23	3.08	3.00	2.92	2.84	2.75	2.66	2.57
19	8.18	5.93	5.01	4.50	4.17	3.94	3.77	3.63	3.52	3.43	3.30	3.15	3.00	2.92	2.84	2.76	2.67	2.58	2.49
20	8.10	5.85	4.94	4.43	4.10	3.87	3.70	3.56	3.46	3.37	3.23	3.09	2.94	2.86	2.78	2.69	2.61	2.52	2.42
21	8.02	5.78	4.87	4.37	4.04	3.81	3.64	3.51	3.40	3.31	3.17	3.03	2.88	2.80	2.72	2.64	2.55	2.46	2.36
22	7.95	5.72	4.82	4.31	3.99	3.76	3.59	3.45	3.35	3.26	3.12	2.98	2.83	2.75	2.67	2.58	2.50	2.40	2.31
23	7.88	5.66	4.76	4.26	3.94	3.71	3.54	3.41	3.30	3.21	3.07	2.93	2.78	2.70	2.62	2.54	2.45	2.35	2.26
24	7.82	5.61	4.72	4.22	3.90	3.67	3.50	3.36	3.26	3.17	3.03	2.89	2.74	2.66	2.58	2.49	2.40	2.31	2.21
25	7.77	5.57	4.68	4.18	3.85	3.63	3.46	3.32	3.22	3.13	2.99	2.85	2.70	2.62	2.54	2.45	2.36	2.27	2.17
26	7.72	5.53	4.64	4.14	3.82	3.59	3.42	3.29	3.18	3.09	2.96	2.81	2.66	2.58	2.50	2.42	2.33	2.23	2.13
27	7.68	5.49	4.60	4.11	3.78	3.56	3.39	3.26	3.15	3.06	2.93	2.78	2.63	2.55	2.47	2.38	2.29	2.20	2.10
28	7.64	5.45	4.57	4.07	3.75	3.53	3.36	3.23	3.12	3.03	2.90	2.75	2.60	2.52	2.44	2.35	2.26	2.17	2.06
29	7.60	5.42	4.54	4.04	3.73	3.50	3.33	3.20	3.09	3.00	2.87	2.73	2.57	2.49	2.41	2.33	2.23	2.14	2.03
30	7.56	5.39	4.51	4.02	3.70	3.47	3.30	3.17	3.07	2.98	2.84	2.70	2.55	2.47	2.39	2.30	2.21	2.11	2.01
40	7.31	5.18	4.31	3.83	3.51	3.29	3.12	2.99	2.89	2.80	2.66	2.52	2.37	2.29	2.20	2.11	2.02	1.92	1.80
60	7.08	4.98	4.13	3.65	3.34	3.12	2.95	2.82	2.72	2.63	2.50	2.35	2.20	2.12	2.03	1.94	1.84	1.73	1.60
120	6.85	4.79	3.95	3.48	3.17	2.96	2.79	2.66	2.56	2.47	2.34	2.19	2.03	1.95	1.86	1.76	1.66	1.53	1.38
∞	6.63	4.61	3.78	3.32	3.02	2.80	2.64	2.51	2.41	2.32	2.18	2.04	1.88	1.79	1.70	1.59	1.47	1.32	1.00

DEGREES OF FREEDOM IN THE DENOMINATOR (d.f. = N − k)

Table C.3

STUDENTS' T DISTRIBUTION[1]

DEGREES OF FREEDOM	AREA IN THE REJECTION REGION (TWO-TAIL TEST)												
	0.9	0.8	0.7	0.6	0.5	0.4	0.3	0.2	0.1	0.05	0.02	0.01	0.001
1	0.158	0.325	0.510	0.727	1.000	1.376	1.963	3.078	**6.314**	**12.706**	31.821	**63.657**	636.619
2	0.142	0.289	0.445	0.617	0.816	1.061	1.386	1.886	**2.920**	**4.303**	6.965	**9.925**	31.598
3	0.137	0.277	0.424	0.584	0.765	0.978	1.250	1.638	**2.353**	**3.182**	4.541	**5.841**	12.924
4	0.134	0.271	0.414	0.569	0.741	0.941	1.190	1.533	**2.132**	**2.776**	3.747	**4.604**	8.610
5	0.132	0.267	0.408	0.559	0.727	0.920	1.156	1.476	**2.015**	**2.571**	3.365	**4.032**	6.869
6	0.131	0.265	0.404	0.553	0.718	0.906	1.134	1.440	**1.943**	**2.447**	3.143	**3.707**	5.959
7	0.130	0.263	0.402	0.549	0.711	0.896	1.119	1.415	**1.895**	**2.365**	2.998	**3.499**	5.408
8	0.130	0.262	0.399	0.546	0.706	0.889	1.108	1.397	**1.860**	**2.306**	2.896	**3.355**	5.041
9	0.129	0.261	0.398	0.543	0.703	0.883	1.100	1.383	**1.833**	**2.262**	2.821	**3.250**	4.781
10	0.129	0.260	0.397	0.542	0.700	0.879	1.093	1.372	**1.812**	**2.228**	2.764	**3.169**	4.587
11	0.129	0.260	0.396	0.540	0.697	0.876	1.088	1.363	**1.796**	**2.201**	2.718	**3.106**	4.437
12	0.128	0.259	0.395	0.539	0.695	0.873	1.083	1.356	**1.782**	**2.179**	2.681	**3.055**	4.318
13	0.128	0.259	0.394	0.538	0.694	0.870	1.079	1.350	**1.771**	**2.160**	2.650	**3.012**	4.221
14	0.128	0.258	0.393	0.537	0.692	0.868	1.076	1.345	**1.761**	**2.145**	2.624	**2.977**	4.140
15	0.128	0.258	0.393	0.536	0.691	0.866	1.074	1.341	**1.753**	**2.131**	2.602	**2.947**	4.073
16	0.128	0.258	0.392	0.535	0.690	0.865	1.071	1.337	**1.746**	**2.120**	2.583	**2.921**	4.015
17	0.128	0.257	0.392	0.534	0.689	0.863	1.069	1.333	**1.740**	**2.110**	2.567	**2.898**	3.965
18	0.127	0.257	0.392	0.534	0.688	0.862	1.067	1.330	**1.734**	**2.101**	2.552	**2.878**	3.922
19	0.127	0.257	0.391	0.533	0.688	0.861	1.066	1.328	**1.729**	**2.093**	2.539	**2.861**	3.883
20	0.127	0.257	0.391	0.533	0.687	0.860	1.064	1.325	**1.725**	**2.086**	2.528	**2.845**	3.850
21	0.127	0.257	0.391	0.532	0.686	0.859	1.063	1.323	**1.721**	**2.080**	2.518	**2.831**	3.819
22	0.127	0.256	0.390	0.532	0.686	0.858	1.061	1.321	**1.717**	**2.074**	2.508	**2.819**	3.792
23	0.127	0.256	0.390	0.532	0.685	0.858	1.060	1.319	**1.714**	**2.069**	2.500	**2.807**	3.767
24	0.127	0.256	0.390	0.531	0.685	0.857	1.059	1.318	**1.711**	**2.064**	2.492	**2.797**	3.745
25	0.127	0.256	0.390	0.531	0.684	0.856	1.058	1.316	**1.708**	**2.060**	2.485	**2.787**	3.725
26	0.127	0.256	0.390	0.531	0.684	0.856	1.058	1.315	**1.706**	**2.056**	2.479	**2.779**	3.707
27	0.127	0.256	0.389	0.531	0.684	0.855	1.057	1.314	**1.703**	**2.052**	2.473	**2.771**	3.690
28	0.127	0.256	0.389	0.530	0.683	0.855	1.056	1.313	**1.701**	**2.048**	2.467	**2.763**	3.674
29	0.127	0.256	0.389	0.530	0.683	0.854	1.055	1.311	**1.699**	**2.045**	2.462	**2.756**	3.659
30	0.127	0.256	0.389	0.530	0.683	0.854	1.055	1.310	**1.697**	**2.042**	2.457	**2.750**	3.646
40	0.126	0.255	0.388	0.529	0.681	0.851	1.050	1.303	**1.684**	**2.021**	2.423	**2.704**	3.551
60	0.126	0.254	0.387	0.527	0.679	0.848	1.046	1.296	**1.671**	**2.000**	2.390	**2.660**	3.460
120	0.126	0.254	0.386	0.526	0.677	0.845	1.041	1.289	**1.658**	**1.980**	2.358	**2.617**	3.373
∞	0.126	0.253	0.385	0.524	0.674	0.842	1.036	1.282	**1.645**	**1.960**	2.326	**2.576**	3.291

[1]Columns in bold-face type indicate critical t-values for popular levels of significance for two-tail hypothesis testing. Thus, critical t-values for $\alpha = 0.1$ (90 percent confidence), $\alpha = 0.05$ (95 percent confidence), and $\alpha = 0.01$ (99 percent confidence) are highlighted. When the calculated t-statistic $= b/\sigma_b$ exceeds the relevant critical t-value, we can reject the hypothesis that there is no relationship between the dependent variable Y and a given independent variable X. For simple t-tests, the relevant number of degrees of freedom (column row) is found as follows: $d.f. = N - k$, where N is the number of data observations and k is the number of estimated coefficients (including the intercept).

Source: Ya-lun Chou. *Probability and Statistics for Decision Making* (New York: Holt, Rinehart and Winston, 1972), p. 612.

2.1
B. Q = 5.

2.2
B. Q = 5.
C. Q = 8.

2.4
B. ME = 5, NH = 3, VT = 2.
C. Commission Income = $3,000.

2.5
B. I = 3.
C. I = 4.

2.6
A. Q = 8,000.
B. π = $50,000.

2.7
A. Q = 25,000.
B. π = $625,000, MGN = 3.3%.

2.8
A. Q = 4,000, Surplus = $500,000.
B. Q = 3,800, Surplus = $110,000.
C. Q = 4,000, Surplus = $100,000.

2.9
A. Q = 500, P = $500, π = $150,000.
B. Q = 450, P = $550, π = $152,500.

2.10
A. Q = 6,000, MC = $3,000, AC = $3,000,
P = $3,600, π = $3,600,000.
B. Q = 5,000, MC = $2,600, AC = $3,040,
P = $3,850, π = $4,050,000.

3.1
A. $\overline{X}$ = 5, Median = Mode = 3.
B. Range = 2 to 23, σ^2 = 40.45, σ = 6.36.

3.2
A. $\overline{X}$ = 3.9, Median = 4, Mode = 3.

B. Range = 3 to 5, σ^2 = 0.767,
σ = 0.876, 95% CI = 3.273 to 4.527.

3.3
A. 99% CI = 5.17 to 5.23.
B. 99% CI = 4.97 to 5.03.

3.4
A. 95% CI = A: 5.108 to 6.892;
95% CI = B: 5.663 to 6.337.

3.5
A. 95% CI = Last year: 4.394 to 5.606;
95% CI = This year: 7.394 to 8.606.

3.8
A. Output: $\overline{X}$ = 975, Median = 1,100,
σ = 643, Range = 0 to 1,900;
Cost 1: $\overline{X}$ = 12,833, Median = 14,000,
σ = 4,648, Range = 6,000 to 20,000;
Cost 2: $\overline{X}$ = 15,667, Median = 15,500,
σ = 5,483, Range = 7,000 to 25,000;
Cost 3: $\overline{X}$ = 11,750, Median = 12,000,
σ = 8,226, Range = 0 to 24,000.

4.2
A. P = $10.
B. P = $1.
C. P = $4, Q = 300,000.

4.5
A. Q = 15,000.
B. Q = 22,500.

4.6
B. Q = 20,000, TR = $2,000,000.

4.7
B. P = $50, Q = 0;
P = $60, Q = 5,000,000;
P = $70, Q = 10,000,000.

C. $Q = 4,000,000$, $P = \$58$;
  $Q = 6,000,000$, $P = \$62$;
  $Q = 8,000,000$, $P = \$66$.

4.8
B. $P = \$325$, $Q_O = 0$, $Q_P = 875,000$;
  $P = \$350$, $Q_O = 0$, $Q_P = 1,000,000$;
  $P = \$375$, $Q_O = 500,000$, $Q_P = 1,125,000$.

4.9
B. $P = \$8$, $Q_C = 0$, $Q_P = 0$;
  $P = \$10$, $Q_C = 0$, $Q_P = 250$;
  $P = \$12$, $Q_C = 500$, $Q_P = 500$.

4.10
B. $P = \$1.50$, Shortage $= 50,000,000$;
  $P = \$2$, Surplus $=$ Shortage $= 0$;
  $P = \$2.50$, Surplus $= 50,000,000$.
C. $P = \$2$, $Q = 50,000,000$.

5.5
A. $Q = 600$.
B. $P = \$3$.
C. $P = \$7.50$.
D. $Q = 1,500$.
E. $\epsilon_P = -2$.

5.6
A. $\epsilon_P = -4$.
B. $P = \$14,500$.

5.7
A. $E_P = -2$.
B. $E_{PX} = -2.67$.

5.8
A. $E_I = 6$.
B. $E_P = -8$.

5.9
A. $E_{PX} = 1.5$.
B. $E_P = -3$.
C. $\Delta P = -\$20$.

5.10
A. $E_P = -2$.
B. $\Delta P = -\$2$.
C. $E_A = 1$.

6.1
A. $g = 32\%$.
B. $g = 28\%$.

6.2
B. $g = 0\%$.
C. $g = 11\%$.

6.3
A. $g = 10\%$.
B. $S_5 = \$104,715,000 + u$, $S_{10} = \$168,610,000 + u$.

6.4
A. $g = 7.4\%$.
B. $t = 2 + u$ years.

6.5
B. $A_t = 80 + u$.

6.6
B. $S_{t+1} = \$295,000 + u$.

6.7
B. $D_{t+1} = 375 + u$.

6.8
B. $S_{t+1} = 12,500 + u$.

6.9
B. Regular price: TR $= \$3,875 + u$,
  Special price: TR $= \$7,125 + u$.
C. Regular price: $\pi = \$1,450 + u$,
  Special price: $\pi = \$3,225 + u$.

6.10
  $I = \$1,000 + u$ billion.
  GDP $= \$7,000 + u$ billion.
  $C = \$4,500 + u$ billion.
  $T = \$1,400 + u$ billion.
  $Y = \$5,600 + u$ billion.

7.1
C. $Y = 3$.

7.5
A. Bates $= 3.75\%$, Belker $= 4.5\%$, Coffey $= 4\%$,
  Esterhaus $= 3.33\%$.
B. Bates $= \$8,000$, Belker $= \$5,000$,
  Coffey $= \$4,500$, Esterhaus $= \$3,750$.

7.6
B. Inquiries $= 4,000$.

7.7
B. Attendants $= 4$.
C. Wage $= \$80$.

7.8
C. Advertising = 50.

7.9
A. MRP_P = $62,500, MRP_A = $35,000.

7.10
A. $\Delta Q/Q$ = −1.12%.
B. $\Delta Q/Q$ = −2.88%.

8.1
A. X = 0 to X = 2.
B. X = 3.
C. Minimum AC = $1.25.
D. MC = $1.25.

8.4
A. π = $175,000.

8.5
C. Q_{BE} = 45,000.

8.6
A. ΔQ = 20,000.
B. E_P = −3.

8.7
A. Q_{BE} = 1,000.
B. σ_C = 0.82.

8.8
A. Q_M = 60,000;
$\quad Q_N$ = 55,000;
$\quad Q_D$ = 47,500.

8.9
A. TC = $450,000, AC = $112.50.
B. Learning = −$5,50, or 5%.

8.10
A. ΔQ_{BE} = 250,000.
B. ΔDOL = 0.4.
C. $\Delta\pi$ = $1,000,000.

9.2
A. L = 4, K = 400, Q = 1;
$\quad$ L = 16, K = 1,600, Q = 4.
B. ΔMP_L = −0.0625, ΔMP_K = −0.000625.
C. Q = 1,000.
D. MP_L = 0.25, MP_K = 0.

9.3
C. π = $2,350.

9.4
B. A = 1, B = 4, L_F = 4, L_R = 0, L_{FC} = 0,
$\quad$ C = $240,000.
C. ΔTC = −$32,000.
D. ΔC_A > $120,000.

9.5
B. C = $50,000,000, P = $50,000,000, S_D = $0,
$\quad S_B$ = $100,000,000, S_C = $25,000,000,
$\quad S_A$ = $0, π = $1,750,000.

9.6
B. I = 0.75, J = 0.25, L_I = 0, L_J = 0.05, L_L = 0,
$\quad$ i = 0.0975.
C. ΔR_J > −3%.
D. Maximum cash = 20%.

9.7
B. E = 30, W = 40, S_H = 0, S_S = 0.15, S_P = 0,
$\quad$ C = $2,500.
C. ΔP_W = $12.50.

9.8
B. I = 120, C = 40, S_A = 0, S_B = 80, S_S = 0,
$\quad \pi$ = $18,000.
C. π = $1,900.
D. π = $5,500.
E. L_I = L_C = 0, V_A = $50, V_B = $0, V_S = $50,
$\quad \pi^*$ = $18,000.

9.9
B. Q_1 = 5, Q_2 = 3, S_D = 0, S_A = 5, S_{AR} = 0,
$\quad$ R = $21,000;
$\quad L_1$ = L_2 = 0, V_D = $125, V_A = $0,
$\quad V_{AR}$ = $250, R^* = $21,000.

9.10
B. Q_A = 0, Q_B = 2, Q_C = 2, S_L = S_P = 0, Q = 4;
$\quad L_A$ = 0.625, L_B = L_C = 0, V_L = 0.125,
$\quad V_P$ = 0.375, Q^* = 4.

10.2
B. P = MC = $50.
C. P = $75, Q = 3;
$\quad$ P = $100, Q = 6.

10.3
B. P = $4, Q = 40.
C. Excess supply = 30.

10.4

A. $Q = 5,000, P = \$400$;
   $Q = 10,000, P = \$600$;
   $Q = 15,000, P = \$800$.
B. $P = \$200, Q = 0$;
   $P = \$500, Q = 7,500$;
   $P = \$1,000, Q = 20,000$.

10.5

C. $Q_S = 31,250,000$.

10.6

A. $Q = 50,000, \pi = -\$75,000$.
B. $Q = 200,000, \pi = \$300,000$.
C. $Q = 100,000, P = \$4, \pi = \$0$.

10.7

A. $P = \$200, Q = 100,000$.
B. $\pi = \$5,000,000, MGN = 25\%$.

10.8

A. $Q = 1,000,000, P = \$10, \pi = \$5,000,000$.
B. $P = MC = \$5, \pi = 0$.

10.9

A. $Q = 100,000, P = \$5,000, \pi = \$50,000,000$.
B. $Q = 200,000, P = \$4,500, \pi = \$0$.

10.10

A. $Q = 150,000, P = \$3.50, \pi = \$287,500$.
B. $Q = 100,000, P = \$1.50, \pi = \$0$.

11.3

B. $Q = 6,000,000, P = \$14, \pi = \$0$.
C. $Q = 9,000,000, P = \$11, \pi = \$0$.
D. $Q = 3,000,000, P = \$17, \pi = \$9,000,000$.

11.4

A. $Q = 12, P = \$36$ million, $\pi = \$88$ million,
   $\epsilon_P = -2$.
B. High-price/low-output:
   $Q = 10, P = \$31$ million, $\pi = \$0$;
   Low-price/high-output:
   $Q = 20, P = \$26$ million, $\pi = 0$.
C. $Q_2 = 16.2$, high-price/low-output;
   $Q_2 = 23.4$, low-price/high-output.

11.5

B. $A = 4, B = 1, C = 3, \pi = \$50$ million.

11.6

A. $P = \$2, Q = 40,000$.
B. $P = \$3.60, Q = 24,000$.

11.7

C. $P = \$50, Q = 10(000), \pi = \$150(000)$.

11.8

A. $P_A > \$250, P_B > \$200$.

11.9

A. $P = \$4.50, Q = 7,000$.
B. $P = \$4.65, Q = 8,375$.

11.10

C. $Q_L = 40,000, P_L = \$23$.
D. $P = \$23, Q_M = 6,000, Q_N = 4,000$.

12.3

A. $\epsilon_P = -2$.
B. $P = \$20$.

12.4

A. $\epsilon_P = -5$.
B. Optimal Markup on Cost $= 25\%, P = \$150$.

12.5

A. $E_P = -3.5$.
B. Optimal Markup on Price $= 40\%, P = \$5.99$.

12.6

A. $P = \$2,875,000 + \epsilon$.
B. $P = \$2,701,000 + \epsilon$.

12.7

A. $\pi_1 = \$112,000, \pi_2 = \$104,000$.

12.8

A. $Q_W = 500, P_W = \$12,500, Q_R = 1,000, P_R = \$30,000, \pi = \$21,250,000$.
B. $\epsilon_{PW} = -5, \epsilon_{PR} = -1.5$.

12.9

A. $Q_S = Q_L = 20,000, P_S = \$10.40, P_L = \$0.30$.
B. $Q_S = 150,000, P_S = \$32.50, Q_L = 40,000,$
   $P_L = 20¢$.

12.10

A. $Q = 10,000, P = \$850, \pi = \$500,000$.
B. $P_T = \$600$.
C. $Q_{NA} = 8,500, P_{NA} = \$872.50, Q_E = 6,000,$
   $P_E = \$645, \pi = \$635,000$.

13.5

A. $A = 3, B = 2, C = 3, \pi = \$80$.
B. $P = \$20$.

C. $Q = 10$.
D. $40 or $50.

13.6
A. $Q_L = 400$, $P_L = \$10,000$, $Q_H = 2,500$, $P_H = \$7,500$, $\pi = \$3,250,000$.
B. $Q_L = 360$, $P_L = \$10,500$, $Q_H = 2,000$, $P_H = \$8,000$, $\pi = \$620,000$.
C. $\epsilon_{PL} = -2$, $\epsilon_{PH} = -3$.

13.7
A. $Q = 100,000$, $\pi = \$0$.
B. $Q = 100,000$, $\pi = \$0$.
C. $Q = 75,000$, $\pi = -\$437,500$ (a loss).

13.8
A. $Q = 10,000$, $P = \$11,500$, $\pi = \$8,000,000$.
B. $Q = 9,000$, $P = \$11,730$, $\pi = \$3,630,000$.

13.9
A. $Q = 1,600$, $P_M = \$24$, $P_A = \$288$, $i = 12.5\%$.
B. $Q = 1,800$, $i = 12.25\%$.
C. $Q = 2,000$, $P_M = \$20$.

13.10
A. $Q = 10,000$, $P = \$4,500$, $D = 1,000,000$, $\pi = \$2,000,000$.
B. $Q = 9,500$, $P = \$4,575$, $D = 950,000$, $\pi = \$50,000$.
C. $Q = 7,600$, $P = \$4,860$, $D = 0$, $\pi = -\$3,560,000$ (a loss).

14.3
A. $E(NC) = \$125$.

14.4
A. $E(\pi_{MA}) = \$1,000,000$, $E(\pi_{PS}) = \$750,000$.

14.5
A. $E(\pi_1) = \$500,000$, $E(\pi_2) = \$375,000$.
C. $\sigma_1 = \$300,000$, $\sigma_2 = \$125,000$.
D. $E(u_1) = 1,172$, $E(u_2) = 1,162.50$.

14.6
A. $E(CF_1) = \$10,000$, $E(CF_2) = \$10,000$.
B. $\sigma_1 = \$3,000$, $\sigma_2 = \$1,000$.
C. $NPV_1 = \$5,000$, $NPV_2 = \$7,500$.

14.7
A. $E(\pi_A) = \$150,000$, $\sigma_A = \$50,000$, $V_A = 0.33$, $E(\pi_{SF}) = \$200,000$, $\sigma_{SF} = \$140,000$, $V_{SF} = 0.7$.
B. $\alpha_A = 0.8$, $\alpha_{SF} = 0.85$.

14.8
A. $Pr = 40\%$.

14.9
A. $Pr = 50\%$.
B. $P = \$23.29$.
C. $Pr = 93.32\%$.

15.5
A. $NPV_{LB} = \$500,000$, $NPV_{SD} = \$600,000$.
B. $PI_{LB} = 1.25$, $PI_{SD} = 1.2$.

15.6
A. $E(CF_1) = \$1,000,000$, $\sigma_1 = \$200,000$, $V_1 = 0.2$; $E(CF_2) = \$900,000$, $\sigma_2 = \$360,000$, $V_2 = 0.4$.
B. $NPV_1 = \$1,192,500$, $NPV_2 = -\$362,640$ (a loss).
C. $PI_1 = 1.40$, $PI_2 = 0.88$.

15.7
A. $E(CF_{A1}) = \$50,000$, $\sigma_{A1} = \$30,000$, $V_{A1} = 0.6$; $E(CFA_2) = \$50,000$, $\sigma_{A2} = \$20,000$, $V_{A2} = 0.4$; $E(CF_{B1}) = \$100,000$, $\sigma_{B1} = \$100,000$, $V_{B1} = 1$; $E(CF_{B2}) = \$100,000$, $\sigma_{B2} = \$50,000$, $V_{B2} = 0.5$.
B. $NPV_A = \$9,505$, $NPV_B = \$12,570$.
C. $PI_A = 1.13$, $PI_B = 1.08$.
D. $IRR_A = IRR_B = 21.6\%$.

15.8
A. $CF = \$8,000$.

15.9
A. Net Cash inflow: $A = \$1,576,667$, $B = \$1,603,333$, $C = \$1,323,333$.
B. $NPV_A = \$1,131,132$, $NPV_B = \$1,034,830$, $NPV_C = \$1,146,003$.

15.10
A. $k_e = 20\%$.
B. $k = 16.95\%$.

16.7
B. Social rate of discount $= 8.3\%$.

Selected References

CHAPTER 1

Alexander, Cindy R., and Cohen, Mark A. "New Evidence on the Origins of Corporate Crime." *Managerial & Decision Economics* 17 (July/August 1996): 421-435.

Andrews, Katherine Zoe. "Executive Bonuses: Two Kinds of Performance Measures." *Harvard Business Review* 74 (January/February 1996): 8-9.

Andrews, Katherine Zoe. "The Stock Market Does Not Always Approve." *Harvard Business Review* 74 (May/June 1996): 12.

Bhide, Amar. "The Questions Every Entrepreneur Must Answer." *Harvard Business Review* 74 (November-December 1996): 120-130.

Chen, Ming-Jer. "Competitor Analysis and Interfirm Rivalry: Toward a Theoretical Integration." *Academy of Management Review* 21 (Jan 1996): 100-134.

Drumwright, Minette E. "Company Advertising with a Social Dimension: The Role of Noneconomic Criteria." *Journal of Marketing* 60 (October 1996): 71-87.

Firth, Michael, Lohne, Johan Chr., Ropstad, Ruth, and Sjo, Jarle. "The Remuneration of CEOs and Corporate Financial Performance in Norway." *Managerial & Decision Economics* 17 (May/June 1996): 291-301.

Fraser, Niall M. "Lessons From the Marketplace." *Interfaces* 24 (November-December 1994): 100-106.

Gates, Bill. "What I Learned from Warren Buffett." *Harvard Business Review* 74 (January/February 1996): 148-152.

Goering, Gregory E. "Managerial Style and the Strategic Choice of Executive Incentives." *Managerial & Decision Economics* 17 (January/February 1996): 71-82.

Harrington, L. Katharine. "Ethics and Public Policy Analysis: Stakeholders' Interests and Regulatory Policy." *Journal of Business Ethics* 15 (April 1996): 373-382.

Hotchkiss, Edity Shwalb. "Postbankruptcy Performance and Management Turnover." *Journal of Finance* 50 (March 1995): 3-22.

Kampmeier, Curt. "Managerial Excellence: McKinsey Award Winners from the Harvard Business Review, 1980-1994." *Journal of Management Consulting* 9 (November 1996): 69.

Kole, Stacey R. "The Complexity of Compensation Contracts." *Journal of Financial Economics* 43 (January 1997): 79-104.

Miller, Kent D., and Leiblein, Michael J. "Corporate Risk-return Relations: Returns Variability versus Downside Risk." *Academy of Management Journal* 39 (February 1996): 91-122.

Rangan, V. Kasturi; Karim, Sohel; and Sandberg, Sheryl K. "Do Better at Doing Good." *Harvard Business Review* 74 (May/June 1996): 42-54.

Romer, Paul M. "Why, Indeed, in America? Theory, History, and the Origins of Modern Economic Growth." *American Economic Review* 86 (May 1996): 202-206.

Snidal, Duncan. "Political Economy and International Institutions." *International Review of Law & Economics* 16 (March 1996): 121-137.

Teal, Thomas. "The Human Side of Management." *Harvard Business Review* 74 (November-December 1996): 35-44.

Ulen, Thomas. "The Economics of Corporate Criminal Liability." *Managerial & Decision Economics* 17 (July/August 1996): 351-362.

CHAPTER 2

Bakshi, Gurdip S., and Chen, Zhiwu. "The Spirit of Capitalism and Stock-market Prices." *American Economic Review* 86 (March 1996): 133-157.

Becker, William E., and Watts, Michael. "Chalk and Talk: A National Survey on Teaching Undergraduate Economics." *American Economic Review* 86 (May 1996): 448-453.

Berk, Jonathan B.; Hughson, Eric; and Vandezande, Kirk. "The Price is Right, But Are the Bids? An Investigation of Rational Decision Theory." *American Economic Review* 86 (September 1996): 954-970.

Cornelli, Francesca. "Optimal Selling Procedures with Fixed Costs." *Journal of Economic Theory* 71 (October 1996): 1-30.

De Fraja, Gianni. "Entrepreneur or Manager: Who Runs the Firm?" *Journal of Industrial Economics* 44 (March 1996): 89-98.

Farzin, Y. H. "Optimal Pricing of Environmental and Natural Resource use with Stock Externalities." *Journal of Public Economics* 62 (October 1996): 31-57.

Heifetz, Ronald A., and Laurie, Donald L. "The Work of Leadership." *Harvard Business Review* 75 (January-February 1997): 124-134.

Jackwerth, Jens Carsten, and Rubinstein, Mark. "Recovering Probability Distributions from Option Prices." *Journal of Finance* 51 (December 1996): 1611-1631.

Leon, Linda; Przasnyski, Zbigniew; Seal, Kala Chand. "Spreadsheets and OR/MS Models: An End-user Perspective," *Interfaces,* 26 (March/April 1996): 92-104.

Levin, Dan, and Smith, James L. "Optimal Reservation Prices in Auctions." *Economic Journal: The Journal of the Royal Economic Society* 106 (September 1996): 1271-1283.

Lott, John R. Jr. "The Level of Optimal Fines to Prevent Fraud when Reputations Exist and Penalty Clauses are Unenforceable." *Managerial & Decision Economics* 17 (July/August 1996): 363-380.

Remus, William. "Will Behavioral Research on Managerial Decision Making Generalize to Managers?" *Managerial & Decision Economics* 17 (January/February 1996): 93-101.

Salemi, Michael K.; Saunders, Phillip; and Walstad, William B. "Teacher Training Programs in Economics: Past, Present, and Future." *American Economic Review* 86 (May 1996): 460-464.

Stinnett, Aaron A., and Paltiel, A. David. "Mathematical Programming for the Efficient Allocation of Health Care Resources." *Journal of Health Economics* 15 (October 1996): 641-653.

Stone, Nan. "The Value of Vision." *Harvard Business Review* 74 (September/October 1996): 14.

Szymanski, Stefan. "Making Hay While the Sun Shines." *Journal of Industrial Economics* 44 (March 1996): 1-16.

Tahvonen, Olli, and Withagen, Cees. "Optimality of Irreversible Pollution Accumulation." *Journal of Economic Dynamics & Control* 20 (September/October 1996): 1775-1795.

Tofallis, Chris. "Introduction to Global Optimization." *Journal of the Operational Research Society* 47 (October 1996): 1314-1315.

Walsh, Vivian. "Rationality as Self-interest versus Rationality as Present Aims." *American Economic Review* 84 (May 1994): 401-405.

Winston, Wayne L., "The Teachers' Forum: Management Science with Spreadsheets for MBAs at Indiana University." *Interfaces,* 26 (March/April 1996): 105-111.

CHAPTER 3

Bahmani-Oskooee, Mohsen. "The Black Market Exchange Rate and Demand for Money in Iran." *Journal of Macroeconomics* 18 (Winter 1996): 171-176.

Blanchard, Olivier, and Katz, Lawrence F. "What We Know and Do Not Know about the Natural Rate of Unemployment." *Journal of Economic Perspectives* 11 (Winter 1997): 51-72.

Crafts, Nicholas F. R. "The First Industrial Revolution: A Guided Tour for Growth Economists." *American Economic Review* 86 (May 1996): 197-201.

Docking, Diane; Hirschey, Mark; and Jones, Elaine. "Information and Contagion Effects of Loan-Loss Reserve Announcements." *Journal of Financial Economics* 43 (February 1997): 219-229.

Dutkowsky, Donald H. "Macroeconomic Price Stickiness: Evidence from the Postwar United States." *Journal of Economics & Business* 48 (December 1996): 427-442.

Foster, Andrew D., and Rosenzweig, Mark R. "Technical Change and Human-capital Returns and Investments: Evidence from the Green Revolution." *American Economic Review* 86 (September 1996): 931-953.

Frey, Bruno S., Oberholzer-Gee, Felix, and Eichenbach, Reiner. "The Old Lady Visits your Backyard: A Tale of Morals and Markets." *Journal of Political Economy* 104 (December 1996): 1297-1313.

Golan, Amos; Judge, George; and Perloff, Jeffrey M. "Estimating the Size Distribution of Firms Using Government Summary Statistics." *Journal of Industrial Economics* 44 (March 1996): 69-80.

Grosh, Margaret E., and Glewwe, Paul. "Household Survey Data from Developing Countries: Progress and Prospects." *American Economic Review* 86 (May 1996): 15-19.

Hoch, Stephen J. "How Should National Brands Think About Private Labels?" *Sloan Management Review* 37 (Winter 1996): 89-102.

Klepper, Steven. "Entry, Exit, Growth, and Innovation Over the Product Life Cycle." *American Economic Review* 86 (June 1996): 562-583.

Landers, Renee M.; Rebitzer, James B.; and Taylor, Lowell J. "Rat Race Redux: Adverse Selection in the Determination of Work Hours in Law Firms." *American Economic Review* 86 (June 1996): 329-348.

Light, David A. "Introducing New Products." *Harvard Business Review* 74 (November-December 1996): 8-9.

Loughran, Tim, and Ritter, Jay R. "Long-term Market Overreaction: The Effect of Low-priced Stocks." *Journal of Finance* 51 (December 1996): 1959-1970.

Majumdar, Sumit K., and Chang, Hsi-hui. "Scale Efficiencies in U.S. Telecommunications: An Empirical Investigation." *Managerial & Decision Economics* 17 (May/June 1996): 303-318.

McCloskey, Dierdre N., and Ziliak, Stephen T. "The Standard Error of Regressions." *Journal of Economic Literature* 34 (March 1996): 97-114.

Oulton, Nicholas. "Increasing Returns and Externalities in UK Manaufacturing: Myth or Reality?" *Journal of Industrial Economics* 44 (March 1996): 99-113.

Rao, Spuma M., and Hamilton, J. Brooke III. "The Effect of Published Reports of Unethical Conduct on Stock Prices." *Journal of Business Ethics* 15 (December 1996): 1321-1330.

Ross, Judith A. "Spreadsheet Risk." *Harvard Business Review* 74 (September/October 1996): 10-12.

Strauss, John, and Thomas, Duncan. "Measurement and Mismeasurement of Social Indicators." *American Economic Review* 86 (May 1996): 30-34.

CHAPTER 4

Barton, Stephen E. "Social Housing versus Housing Allowances." *Journal of the American Planning Association* 62 (Winter 1996): 108-119.

Bishop, John H. "Is the Market for College Graduates Headed for a Bust? Demand and Supply Responses to Rising College Wage Premiums." *New England Economic Review* (May/June 1996): 115-135.

Borjas, George J.; Freeman, Richard B.; and Katz, Lawrence F. "Searching for the Effect of Immigration on the Labor Market." *American Economic Reivew* 86 (May 1996): 246-251.

Bulinskaya, E. V. "Stability Problems in Inventory Management." *International Journal of Production Economics* 45 (August 1, 1996): 353-359.

Buongiorno, Joseph. "Forest Sector Modeling: A Synthesis of Econometrics, Mathematical Programming, and System Dynamics Methods." *International Journal of Forecasting* 12 (September 1996): 329-343.

Chambers, Marcus J., and Bailey, Roy E. "A Theory of Commodity Price Fluctuations." *Journal of Political Economy* 104 (October 1996): 924-957.

Chao, Chi-Chur, and Yu, Eden S. H. "Product Differentiation, Voluntary Export Restraints, and Profits." *Managerial & Decision Economics* 17 (January/February 1996): 103-110.

Coad, Leonard A., and van de Panne, Cornelis. "Computer Simulation for Supply-demand Interaction." *Canadian Journal of Economics* 29 (April 1996): S308-S312.

Davidson, Paul. "What Revolution? The Legacy of Keynes." *Journal of Post Keynesian Economics* 19 (Fall 1996): 47-60.

Deaton, Angus, and Laroque, Guy. "Competitive Storage and Commodity Price Dynamics." *Journal of Political Economy* 104 (October 1996): 896-923.

Dunn, L. F. "Loss Aversion and Adaptation in the Labor Market: Empirical Indifference Functions and Labor Supply." *Review of Economics & Statistics* 78 (August 1996): 441-450.

Fowler, Thomas B. "The International Narcotics Trade: Can it be Stopped by Interdiction?" *Journal of Policy Modeling* 18 (June 1996): 233-270.

Holmstrom, Bengt, and Tirole, Jean. "Modeling Aggregate Liquidity." *American Economic Review* 86 (May 1996): 187-191.

Ireland, Peter N. "The Role of Countercyclical Monetary Policy." *Journal of Political Economy* 104 (August 1996): 704-723.

Irwin, Douglas A. "The United States in a New Global Economy? A Century's Perspective." *American Economic Review* 86 (May 1996): 41-46.

Kranton, Rachel E. "Reciprocal Exchange: A Self-sustaining System." *American Economic Review* 86 (September 1996): 830-851.

Landry, John T. "Positioning the Product." *Harvard Business Review* 74 (November-December 1996): 13.

Nicol, Christopher J. "Some Model Specification Issues in Applied Demand Analysis." *Canadian Journal of Economics* 29 (April 1996): S592-S597.

Quelch, John A., and Harding, David. "Brands versus Private Labels: Fighting to Win." *Harvard Business Review* 74 (January/February 1996): 99-109.

Roach, Stephen S. "The Hollow Ring of the Productivity Revival." *Harvard Business Review* 74 (November-December 1996): 81-89.

CHAPTER 5

Arnott, Richard. "Time for Revisionism on Rent Control." *Journal of Economic Perspectives* 9 (Winter 1995): 99-120.

Avery, Rosemary J. and Haynes, George W. "Estimation of Consumer Savings from Coupon Redemption." *Journal of Managerial Issues* 8 (Winter 1996): 405-424.

Banks, James, Blundell, Richard, and Lewbel, Arthur. "Tax Reform and Welfare Measurement: Do We Need Demand System Estimation?" *Economic Journal: The Journal of the Royal Economic Society* 106 (September 1996): 1227-1241.

Bernard, Jean-Thomas; Bolduc, Denis; and Belanger, Donald. "Quebec Residential Electricity Demand: A Microeconometric Approach." *Canadian Journal of Economics* 29 (February 1996): 92-113.

Caminal, Ramon. "Price Advertising and Coupons in a Monopoly Model." *Journal of Industrial Economics* 44 (March 1996): 33-52.

Carone, Giuseppe. "Modeling the U.S. Demand for Imports through Cointegration and Error Correction." *Journal of Policy Modeling* 18 (February 1996): 1-48.

Dutkowsky, Donald H. "Macroeconomic Price Stickiness: Evidence from the Postwar United States." *Journal of Economics & Business* 48 (December 1996): 427-442.

Espey, Molly. "Explaining the Variation in Elasticity Estimates of Gasoline Demand in the United States: A Meta-analysis." *Energy Journal* 17 (1996): 49-60.

Haas-Wilson, Deborah. "The Impact of State Abortion Restrictions on Minors' Demand for Abortions." *Journal of Human Resources* 31 (Winter 1996): 140-158.

Hackl, Peter, and Westlund, Anders H. "Demand for International Telecommunication: Time-varying Price Elasticity." *Journal of Econometrics* 70 (January 1996): 243-260.

Hamermesh, Daniel S., and Pfann, Gerard A. "Adjustment Costs in Factor Demand." *Journal of Economic Literature* 34 (September 1996): 1264-1292.

Haug, Alfred A., and Lucas, Robert F. "Long-run Money Demand in Canada: In Search of Stability." *Review of Economics & Statistics* 78 (May 1996): 345-348.

Joachimsthaler, Erich, and Aaker, David A. "Building Brands Without Mass Media." *Harvard Business Review* 75 (January-February 1997): 39-50.

Koenig, Evan F. "Long-term Interest Rates and the Recent Weakness in M2." *Journal of Economics & Business* 48 (May 1996): 81-101.

Laird, Karylee, and Williams, Nicolas. "Employment Growth in the Temporary Help Supply Industry." *Journal of Labor Research* 17 (Fall 1996): 663-681.

Lewbel, Arthur. "Demand Estimation with Expenditure Measurement Errors on the Left and Right Hand Side." *Review of Economics & Statistics* 78 (November 1996): 718-725.

Ley, Eduardo, and Steel, Mark F. J. "On the Estimation of Demand Systems through Consumption Efficiency." *Review of Economics & Statistics* 78 (August 1996): 539-543.

Niklitschek, Mario, and Leon, Javier. "Combining Intended Demand and Yes/No Responses in the Estimation of Contingent Valuation Models." *Journal of Environmental Economics & Management* 31 (November 1996): 387-402.

Serageldin, Ismail. "Surviving Scarcity—Sustainable Management of Water Resources." *Harvard International Review* 18 (Summer 1996): 50-53.

Spencer, David E. "Interpreting the Cyclical Behavior of the Price Level in the U.S." *Southern Economic Journal* 63 (July 1996): 95-105.

CHAPTER 6

Andolfatto, David. "Business Cycles and Labor-market Research." *American Economic Review* 86 (March 1996): 112-132.

Baghestani, Hamid, and Nelson, David. "How Accurate are Professional Economic Forecasts?" *Journal of Applied Business Research* 10 (Winter 1994): 1-5

Chase, Charles W. Jr. "What you Need to Know When Building a Sales Forecasting System." *Journal of Business Forecasting Methods & Systems* 15 (Fall 1996): 2, 23.

Cho, Dong W. "Forecast Accuracy: Are Some Business Economists Consistently Better Than Others?" *Business Economics* 31 (October 1996): 45-49.

Fader, Peter S., and Hardie, Bruce G. S. "Modeling Consumer Choice Among SKUs." *Journal of Marketing Research* 33 (November 1996): 442-452.

Ferderer, J. Peter. "Oil Price Volatility and the Macroeconomy." *Journal of Macroeconomics* 18 (Winter 1996): 1-26.

Fortune, Peter. "Do Municipal Bond Yields Forecast Tax Policy?" *New England Economic Review* (September/October 1996): 29-48.

Geurts, Michael D., and Whitlark, David. "Improving Sales Forecasts by Improving the Input Data." *Journal of Business Forecasting Methods & Systems* 15 (Fall 1996): 15-18.

Goeldner, C. R. "The 1996 Travel Outlook." *Journal of Travel Research* 34 (Winter 1996): 102-106.

Guo, Dajiang. "The Predictive Power of Implied Stochastic Variance from Currency Options." *Journal of Futures Markets* 16 (December 1996): 915-942.

Hoffman, Dennis L., and Rasche, Robert H. "Assessing Forecast Performance in a Cointegrated System." *Journal of Applied Econometrics* 11 (September/October 1996): 495-517.

Ilmakunnas, Pekka. "Use of Macroeconomic Forecasts in Corporate Forecasting: A Note on Aggregation Problems." *International Journal of Forecasting* 12 (September 1996): 383-388.

Islam, Towhidul, and Meade, Nigel. "Forecasting the Development of the Market for Business Telephones in the UK." *Journal of the Operational Research Society* 47 (July 1996): 906-918.

Kim, Jeong-Bon; Lee, Jason; and Park, Tae H. "Transaction Responses to Analysts' Earnings Forecasts, News Type and Trader Type." *Journal of Business Finance & Accounting* 23 (September 1996): 1043-1058.

Kolb, R. A., and Stekler, H. O. "How Well Do Analysts Forecast Interest Rates?" *Journal of Forecasting* 15 (September 1996): 385-394.

McCullough, B. D. "Consistent Forecast Intervals When the Forecast-period Exogenous Variables are Stochastic." *Journal of Forecasting* 15 (July 1996): 293-304.

Phillips, Robert F. "Forecasting in the Presence of Large Shocks." *Journal of Economic Dynamics & Control* 20 (September/October 1996): 1581-1608.

Simos, Evangelos O., and Triantis, John E. "The World Economy in 2005." *Journal of Business Forecasting Methods & Systems* 15 (Fall 1996): 30-33.

Tayman, Jeff. "The Accuracy of Small-area Population Forecasts Based on a Spatial Interaction Land-use Modeling System." *Journal of the American Planning Association* 62 (Winter 1996): 85-98.

West, Carol Taylor. "System-based Weights versus Series-specific Weights in the Combination of Forecasts." *Journal of Forecasting* 15 (September 1996): 369-383.

CHAPTER 7

Adler, Paul S.; Mandelbaum, Avi; Nguyen, Vien; and Schwerer, Elizabeth. "Getting the Most Out of Your Product Development Process." *Harvard Business Review* 74 (March/April 1996): 134-152.

Audretsch, David B., and Feldman, Maryann P. "R&D Spillovers and the Geography of Innovation and Production." *American Economic Review* 86 (June 1996): 630-640.

Fahy, John, and Fuyuki Taguchi. "Reassessing the Japanese Distribution System." *Sloan Management Review* 36 (Winter 1995): 49-61.

Färe, Rolf; Grosskopf, Shawna; Norris, Mary; and Zhang, Zhongyang. "Productivity Growth, Technical Progress, and Efficiency Change in Industrialized Countries." *American Economic Review* 84 (March 1994): 66-83.

Gardner, Everett S., and Ivancevich, John M. "Productivity in the US and Japan." *Interfaces* 24 (November-December 1994): 66-78.

Gilmore, James H., and Pine, B. Joseph II. "The Four Faces of Mass Customization." *Harvard Business Review* 75 (January-February 1997): 91-101.

Henderson, David R. "Myth and Measurement: The New Economics of the Minimum Wage." *Managerial & Decision Economics* 17 (May/June 1996): 339-344.

Kalwani, Manohar, and Sari, Narake. "Long-Term Manufacturer-Supplier Relationships: Do They Pay Off for Supplier Firms?" *Journal of Marketing* 59 (January 1995): 1-16.

Majumdar, Sumit K., and Venkatram Ramaswamy. "Explaining Downstream Integration." *Managerial and Decision Economics* 15 (March-April 1994): 119-129.

Maruca, Regina Fazio. "How Do You Grow a Premium Brand?" *Harvard Business Review* 73 (March-April 1995): 22-43.

Metcalf, Gilbert E. "Value-Added Taxation: A Tax Whose Time Has Come?" *Economic Perspectives* 9 (Winter 1995): 121-140.

Ostrom, Amy, and Iacobucci, Dawn. "Consumer Trade-Offs and the Evaluation of Services." *Journal of Marketing* 59 (January 1995): 17-28.

Pine, B. Joseph II; Peppers, Don; and Rogers, Martha. "Do You Want to Keep Your Customers Forever?" *Harvard Business Review* 73 (March-April 1995): 120-133.

Pitelis, Christos. "Effective Demand, Outward Investment and the (Theory of the) Transnational Corporation: An Empirical Investigation." *Scottish Journal of Political Economy* 43 (May 1996): 192-206.

Richardson, James, and Roumasset, James. "Sole Sourcing, Competitive Sourcing, Parallel Sourcing: Mechanisms for Supplier Performance." *Managerial and Decision Economics* 16 (January 1995): 71-84.

Riley, Richard. "Educating the Workforce of the Future." *Harvard Business Review* 72 (March-April 1994): 39-51.

Ronnen, Uri. "The Effects of Mandated versus Voluntary Auditing Policy on the Quality of Auditing." *Journal of Accounting, Auditing & Finance* 11 (Summer 1996): 393-419.

Salafatinos, Chris. "Modeling Resource Supply and Demand: Expanding the Utility of ABC." *International Journal of Production Economics* 43 (May 1, 1996): 47-57.

Samaddar, Subhashish, "The Limits of Japanese Production Systems." *Interfaces,* 26 (July/August 1996): 66-68.

Van Ophem, Hans; Joop Hartog; and Vijverberg, Wim. "Job Complexity and Wages." *International Economic Review* 34 (November 1993): 853-872.

CHAPTER 8

Arthur, W. Brian. "Increasing Returns and the New World of Business." *Harvard Business Review* 74 (July/August 1996): 100-109.

Avery, Rosemary J., and Haynes, George W. "Estimation of Consumer Savings from Coupon Redemption." *Journal of Managerial Issues* 8 (Winter 1996): 405-424.

Bereskin, C. Gregory. "Econometric Estimation of the Effects of Deregulation on Railway Productivity Growth." *Transportation Journal* 35 (Summer 1996): 34-43.

Black, Sandra E., and Lynch, Lisa M. "Human-capital Investments and Productivity." *American Economic Review* 86 (May 1996): 263-267.

Bukh, Per Nikolaj D. "Activity Costing for Engineers." *Interfaces,* 26 (March/April 1996): 120-122.

Chou, Ray Y., and Cebula, Richard J. "Determinants of Geographic Differentials in the Savings and Loan Failure Rate: A Heteroskedastic TOBIT Estimation." *Journal of Financial Services Research* 10 (March 1996): 5-25.

Grant, James. "Too Big to Fail? Walter Wriston and Citibank." *Harvard Business Review* 74 (July/August 1996): 146-151.

Keeler, Theodore E., and Ying, John S. "Hospital Costs and Excess Bed Capacity: A Statistical Analysis." *Review of Economics & Statistics* 78 (August 1996): 470-481.

Lamm-Tennant, Joan; Starks, Laura; and Stokes, Lynne. "Considerations of Cost Trade-offs in Insurance Solvency Surveillance Policy." *Journal of Banking & Finance* 20 (June 1996): 835-852.

Levy, Frank, and Murnane, Richard J. "With What Skills are Computers a Complement?" *American Economic Review* 86 (May 1996): 258-262.

Liebeskind, Julia Porter; Opler, Tim C.; and Hatfield, Donald E. "Corporate Restructuring and the Consolidation of US Industry." *Journal of Industrial Economics* 44 (March 1996): 53-68.

Macarthur, John B. "From Activity-based Costing to Throughput Accounting," *Management Accounting,* 77 (April 1996): 30-38.

Nevis, Edwin C.; Di Bella, Anthony J.; and Gould, Janet M. "Understanding Organizations as Learning Systems." *Sloan Management Review* 36 (Winter 1995): 73-86.

Pope, Rulon D. and Just, Richard E. "Empirical Implementation of Ex Ante Cost Functions." *Journal of Econometrics* 72 (May/June 1996): 231-249.

Salafatinos, Chris, "Modeling Resource Supply and Demand: Expanding the Utility of ABC." *International Journal of Production Economics,* 43 (May 1, 1996): 47-57.

Sherman, H. David. "The Gaps in GAAP." *Harvard Business Review* 74 (March/April 1996): 103.

Simpson, Wayne K. "Activity-Based Models for Cost Management Systems." *Government Finance Review,* 12 (June 1996): 66-67.

Snow, Arthur, and Warren, Ronald S. Jr. "The Marginal Welfare Cost of Public Funds: Theory and Estimates." *Journal of Public Economics* 61 (August 1996): 289-305.

Udpa, Suneel, "Activity-Based Costing for Hospitals." *Health Care Management Review,* 21 (Summer 1996): 83-96.

Weiss, Andrew A. "Estimating Time Series Models Using the Relevant Cost Function." *Journal of Applied Econometrics* 11 (September/October 1996): 539-560.

CHAPTER 9

Atan, Tankut S.; Pandit, Ram, "Auxiliary Tool Allocation in Flexible Manufacturing Systems." *European Journal of Operational Research,* 89 (March 22, 1996): 642-659.

Bartmess, Andrew D. "The Plant Location Puzzle." *Harvard Business Review* 72 (March-April 1994): 20-22.

Billionnet, Alain; Calmels, Frederic, "Linear Programming for the 0-1 Quadratic Knapsack Problem." *European Journal of Operation Research,* 92 (July 19, 1996): 310-325.

Brown, Gerald G.; Dell, Robert F.; Farmer, Robert A., "Scheduling Coast Guard District Cutters," *Interfaces,* 26 (March/April 1996): 59-72.

Collaud, Gerald, and Pasquier-Boltuck, Jacques. "GLPS: A Graphical Tool for the Definition and Manipulation of Linear Problems." *European Journal of Operational Research* 72 (January 27, 1994): 277-286.

Greenberg, Harvey J. "How to Analyze the Results of Linear Programs—Part 1: Preliminaries." *Interfaces* 23 (July/August 1993): 56-67.

Greenberg, Harvey J. "How to Analyze the Results of Linear Programs—Part 2: Price Interpretation." *Interfaces* 23 (September/October 1993): 97-114.

Greenberg, Harvey J. "How to Analyze the Results of Linear Programs—Part 3: Infeasibility Diagnosis." *Interfaces* 23 (November/December 1993): 120-129.

Grinde, Roger B.; Cavalier, Tom M., "Containment of a Single Polygon Using Mathematical Programming." *European Journal of Operational Research,* 92 (July 19, 1996): 368-386.

Hemmer, Thomas. "Allocations of Sunk Capacity Costs and Joint Costs in a Linear Principal-agent Model." *Accounting Review* 71 (July 1996): 419-432.

Jacobs, Derya A.; Silan, Murat N.; Clemson, Barry A., "An Analysis of Alternative Locations and Service Areas of American Red Cross Blood Facilities." *Interfaces,* 26 (May/June 1996): 40-50.

Jones, Chris; Baker, Thomas E., "MIMI/G: A Graphical Environment for Mathematical Programming and Modeling." *Interfaces,* 26 (May/June 1996): 90-106.

Kouvelis, Panagiotis; Chiang, Wen-Chyuan, "Optimal and Heuristic Procedures for Row Layout Problems in Automated Manufacturing Systems." *Journal of the Operational Research Society,* 47 (June 1996): 803-816.

Martin, Warren S.; Stanford, Robert E.; Swan, John E.; Wren, Brent M.; et al. "Mail Surveys: A Linear Programming Solution." *Journal of Business Research* 29 (January 1994): 39-45.

Metters, Richard D., "Interdependent Transportation and Production Activity at the United States Postal Service." *Journal of the Operational Research Society,* 47 (January 1996): 27-37.

Mosheiov, Gur. "The Travelling Salesman Problem with Pick-Up and Delivery." *European Journal of Operational Research* 79 (December 8, 1994): 299-310.

Munson, Charles L., "Fine Tuning Regulated Telephone Prices." *Interfaces,* 26 (May/June 1996): 26-34.

Orden, Alex. "LP from the '40s to the '90s." *Interfaces* 23 (September/October 1993): 2-12.

Weintraub, Andres; Epstein, Rafael; Morales, Ramiro; Seron, Jorge; Traverso, Pier, "A Truck Scheduling System Improves Efficiency in the Forest Industries." *Interfaces,* 26 (July/August 1996): 1-12.

Zappe, Christopher, Webster, William; and Horowitz, Ira. "Using Linear Programming to Determine Post-Facto Consistency in Performance Evaluations of Major League Baseball Players." *Interfaces* 23 (November/December 1993): 107-113.

CHAPTER 10

Baland, Jean-Marie, and Francois, Patrick. "Innovation, Monopolies and the Poverty Trap." *Journal of Development Economics* 49 (April 1996): 151-178.

Beard, T. Randolph, and Thompson, Henry. "Efficient versus 'Popular' Tariffs for Regulated Monopolies." *Journal of Business* 69 (January 1996): 75-87.

Bensaid, Bernard, and Lesne, Jean-Philippe. "Dynamic Monopoly Pricing with Network Externalities." *International Journal of Industrial Organization* 14 (October 1996): 837-855.

Bughin, Jacques. "Trade Unions and Firms' Product Market Power." *Journal of Industrial Economics* 44 (September 1996): 289-307.

Caballero, Ricardo J. and Hammour, Mohamad L. "The 'Fundamental Transformation' in Macroeconomics." *American Economic Review* 86 (May 1996): 181-186.

Cameron, Duncan, and Glick, Mark. "Market Share and Market Power in Merger and Monopolization Cases." *Managerial & Decision Economics* 17 (March/April 1996): 193-201.

Chezum, Brian, and Garen, John. "A Model of Monopoly and 'Efficient' Unions with Endogenous Union Coverage: Positive and Normative Implications." *Journal of Labor Research* 17 (Summer 1996): 497-513.

Dudey, Marc. "Dynamic Monopoly with Nondurable Goods." *Journal of Econimic Theory* 70 (August 1996): 470-488.

Elbasha, Elamin H., and Roe, Terry L. "On Endogenous Growth: The Implications of Environmental Externalities." *Journal of Environmental Economics & Management* 31 (September 1996): 240-268.

Felder, Stefan. "Fire Insurance in Germany: A Comparison of Price-performance Between State Monopolies and Competitive Regions." *European Economic Review* 40 (April 1996): 1133-1141.

Hulett, Stanley W. "Universal Service: Theory or Reality?" *Public Utilities Fortnightly* 134 (October 15, 1996): 18-19.

Karp, Larry. "Monopoly Power can be Disadvantageous in the Extraction of a Durable Nonrenewable Resource." *International Economic Review* 37 (November 1996): 825-849.

Kehoe, Michael R. "Quality Uncertainty and Price in Monopoly Markets." *Journal of Industrial Economics* 44 (March 1996): 25-32.

Klein, Benjamin. "Market Power in Aftermarkets." *Managerial & Decision Economics* 17 (March/April 1996): 143-164.

Mantell, Edmund H. "The Social Costs of Monopoly and Regulation: Posner Reconsidered Again." *Quarterly Review of Economics & Finance* 36 (Summer 1996): 249-268.

Morrison, Clarence C. "Price Makers and Nonclearing Markets." *Atlantic Economic Journal* 24 (March 1996): 19-32.

Noronha, Gergory M.; Sarin, Atulya; and Saudagaran, Shahrokh M. "Testing for Micro-structure Effects of International Dual Listings using Intraday Data." *Journal of Banking & Finance* 20 (July 1996): 965-983.

Owen, Bruce M. "Telecommunication Policy for the Information Age: From Monopoly to Competition." *Journal of Economic Literature* 34 (June 1996): 797-798.

Sadanand, Asha B. "Bargaining and Waiting." *Canadian Journal of Economics* 29:Part 1 (April 1996): S281-S287.

CHAPTER 11

Arthur, W. Brian. "Increasing Returns and the New World of Business." *Harvard Business Review* 74 (July/August 1996): 100-109.

Beers, Michael C. "The Strategy that Wouldn't Travel." *Harvard Business Review* 74 (November-December 1996): 18-22.

D'Aspremont, Claude; Dos Santos Ferreira, Rodolphe; and Gerard-Varet, Louis-Andre. "On the Dixit-Stiglitz Model of Monopolistic Competition." *American Economic Review* 86 (June 1996): 623-629.

Degryse, Hans. "On the Interaction Between Vertical and Horizontal Product Differentiation: An Application to Banking." *Journal of Industrial Economics* 44 (June 1996): 169-186.

Devereux, Michael B.; Head, Allen C.; and Lapham, Beverly J. "Monopolistic Competition, Increasing Returns, and the Effects of Government Spending." *Journal of Money, Credit & Banking* 28 (May 1996): 233-254.

Dick, Andrew R. "Identifying Contracts, Combinations and Conspiracies in Restraint of Trade." *Managerial & Decision Economics* 17 (March/April 1996): 203-216.

Encaoua, David; Moreaux, Michel; and Perrot, Anne. "Compatibility and Competition in Airlines Demand Side Network Effects." *International Journal of Industrial Organization* 14 (October 1996): 701-726.

Felder, Stefan. "Fire Insurance in Germany: A Comparison of Price-performance Between State Monopolies and Competitive Regions." *European Economic Review* 40 (April 1996): 1133-1141.

Fethke, Gary, and Jagannathan, Raj. "Habit Persistence, Geterogeneous Tastes, and Imperfect Competition." *Journal of Economic Dynamics & Control* 20 (June/July 1996): 1193-1207.

Granitz, Elizabeth, and Klein, Benjamin. "Monopolization by 'Raising Rivals' Costs': The Standard Oil Case." *Journal of Law & Economics* 39 (April 1996): 1-47.

Green, Richard. "Increasing Competition in the British Electricity Spot Market." *Journal of Industrial Economics* 44 (June 1996): 205-216.

Hamel, Gary. "Strategy as Revolution." *Harvard Business Review* 74 (July/August 1996): 69-71.

Heijdra, Ben J. and van der Ploeg, Frederick. "Keynesian Multipliers and the Cost of Public Funds under Monopolistic Competition." *Economic Journal: The Journal of the Royal Economic Society* 106 (September 1996): 1284-1296.

Keuschnigg, Christian, and Kohler, Wilhelm. "Commercial Policy and Dynamic Adjustment Under Monopolistic Competition." *Journal of International Economics* 40 (May 1996): 373-409.

Nyahoho, Emmanuel. "Hayekian Approach to Competition in Monies and the New Dynamic of Financial Markets." *Canadian Journal of Economics* 29 (April 1996): S242-S248.

Philips, Louis. "On the Detection of Collusion and Predation." *European Economic Review* 4 (April 1996): 495-510.

Porter, Michael E. "What is Strategy?" *Harvard Business Review* 74 (November-December 1996): 61-78.

von Ungern-Sternberg, Thomas. "The Limits of Competition: Housing Insurance in Switzerland." *European Economic Review* 40 (April 1996): 1111-1121.

Wong, Herbert S. "Market Structure and the Role of Consumer Information in the Physician Services Industry: An Empirical Test." *Journal of Health Economics* 15 (April 1996): 139-160.

Yun, Tack. "Nominal Price Rigidity, Money Supply Endogeneity, and Business Cycles." *Journal of Monetary Economics* 37 (April 1996): 345-370.

CHAPTER 12

Andrews, Katherine Zoe. "Advertising Strategies." *Harvard Business Review* 74 (March/April 1996): 10-11.

Barros, Pedro P. "Competition Effects of Price Liberalization in Insurance." *Journal of Industrial Economics* 44 (September 1996): 267-287.

Bergman, Yaacov Z.; Grundy, Bruce D.; and Wiener, Zvi. "General Properties of Option Prices." *Journal of Finance* 51 (December 1996): 1573-1610.

Chevalier, Judith A., and Scharfstein, David S. "Capital-market Imperfections and Countercyclical Markups: Theory and Evidence." *American Economic Review* 86 (September 1996): 703-725.

Dopuch, Nicholas, and King, Ronald R. "The Effects of Lowballing on Audit Quality: An Experimental Markets Study." *Journal of Accounting, Auditing & Finance* 11 (Winter 1996): 45-68.

Engle, Howard S. "International Developments: Final Section 482 Cost-sharing Regulations." *Journal of Corporate Taxation* 23 (Winter 1997): 395-400.

Engle, Howard S. "International Developments: Final Section 6662 Transfer Pricing Penalty Rules." *Journal of Corporate Taxation* 23 (Winter 1997): 392-395.

Fama, Eugene F. "Discounting Under Uncertainty." *Journal of Business* 69 (October 1996): 415-428.

Fama, Eugene F., and French, Kenneth R. "The CAPM is Wanted, Dead or Alive." *Journal of Finance* 51 (December 1996): 1947-1958.

Han, Ki C., and Khaksari, Shahriar. "Dividends, Taxes, and Returns: Empirical Evidence." *Quarterly Journal of Business & Economics* 35 (Winter 1996): 3-15.

Horvitz, Paul M. "ATM Surcharges: Their Effect on Competition and Efficiency." *Journal of Retail Banking Services* 18 (Autumn 1996): 57-62.

Hurley, William J., and Johnson, Lewis D. "On the Pricing of Bond Default Risk." *Journal of Portfolio Management* 22 (Winter 1996): 66-70.

Huston, John, and Kamdar, Nipoli. "$9.99: Can 'Just-below' Pricing Be Reconciled with Rationality?" *Eastern Economic Journal* 22 (Spring 1996): 137-145.

Jacob, John. "Taxes and Transfer Pricing: Income Shifting and the Volume of Intrafirm Transfers." *Journal of Accounting Research* 34 (Autumn 1996): 301-312.

Kadiyali, Vrinda; Vilcassim, Naufel J.; and Chintagunta, Pradeep K. "Empirical Analysis of Competitive Product Line Pricing Decisions: Lead, Follow, or Move Together?" *Journal of Business* 69 (October 1996): 459-487.

Kehoe, Michael R. "Quality Uncertainty and Price in Monopoly Markets." *Journal of Industrial Economics* 44 (March 1996): 25-32.

Marvel, Howard P., and McCafferty, Stephen. "Comparing Vertical Restraints." *Journal of Economics & Business* 48 (December 1996): 473-486.

Rao, Akshay R., and Monroe, Kent B. "Causes and Consequences of Price Premiums." *Journal of Business* 69 (October 1996): 511-535.

Sethuraman, Raj. "A Model of How Discounting High-priced Brands Affects the Sales of Low-priced Brands." *Journal of Marketing Research* 33 (November 1996): 399-409.

Thompson, Sarahelen; Garcia, Philip; and Wildman, Lynne Dallafior. "The Demise of the High Fructose Corn Syrup Futures Contract: A Case Study." *Journal of Futures Markets* 16 (September 1996): 697-724.

CHAPTER 13

Bearne, Andrew. "Economic Analysis of Environmental Policy and Regulation." *Economic Journal: The Journal of the Royal Economic Society* 106 (July 1996): 1144.

Blair, Roger D., and Page, William H. "The Role of Economics in Defining Antitrust Injury and Standing." *Managerial & Decision Economics* 17 (March/April 1996): 127-142.

Crepas, Kenneth J. "The Regulation of Insurance." *Journal of Risk & Insurance* 63 (September 1996): 542-544.

Dick, Andrew R. "Identifying Contracts, Combinations and Conspiracies in Restraint of Trade." *Managerial & Decision Economics* 17 (March/April 1996): 203-216.

Haas-Wilson, Deborah. "The Impact of State Abortion Restrictions on Minors' Demand for Abortions." *Journal of Human Resources* 31 (Winter 1996): 140-158.

Henderson, J. Vernon. "Effects of Air Quality Regulation." *American Economic Review* 86 (September 1996): 789-813.

Hulett, Stanley W. "Universal Service: Theory or Reality?" *Public Utilities Fortnightly* 134 (October 15, 1996): 18-19.

Kabir, Rezaul, and Vermaelen, Theo. "Insider Trading Restrictions and the Stock Market: Evidence from the Amsterdam Stock Exchange." *European Economic Review* 40 (November 1996): 1591-1603.

Kaplan, David P. "The Nuts and Bolts of Antitrust Analysis: Some Thoughts on How to Develop the Facts." *Managerial & Decision Economics* 17 (March/April 1996): 179-192.

Keeler, Theodore E.; Hu, Teh-wei; Barnett, Paul G.; Manning, Willard G.; and Sung, Hai-Yen. "Do Cigarette Producers Price-discriminate by State? An Empirical Analysis of Local Cigarette Pricing and Taxation." *Journal of Health Economics* 15 (August 1996): 499-512.

Kuhn, Thomas R.; Mehra, Pradeep; Ball Robert L.; and Green, Richard C. Jr., et al. "Electric Utility Deregulation Sparks Controversy." *Harvard Business Review* 74 (May/June 1996): 150-162.

Lang, Neil S., and Gardner, Linda M. "The SEC's Attempt to Impose a Regulatory Regime on Municipal Securities Issuers." *Securities Regulation Law Journal* 24 (Fall 1996): 229-258.

Loudder, Martha L.; Khurana, Inder K.; and Boatsman, James R. "Market Valuation of Regulatory Assets in Public Utility Firms." *Accounting Review* 71 (July 1996): 357-373.

MacDonald, James M., and Cavalluzzo, Linda C. "Railroad Deregulation: Pricing Reforms, Shipper Responses, and the Effects on Labor." *Industrial & Labor Relations Review* 50 (October 1996): 80-91.

Marakovits, Donita M., and Considine, Timothy J. "An Empirical Analysis of Exposure-based Regulation to Abate Toxic Air Pollution." *Journal of Environmental Economics & Management* 31 (November 1996): 337-351.

Mitchell, Mark L., and Mulherin, J. Harold. "The Impact of Industry Shocks on Takeover and Restructuring Activity." *Journal of Financial Economics* 41 (June 1996): 193-229.

Navarro, Peter. "Electric Utilities: The Argument for Radical Deregulation." *Harvard Business Review* 74 (January/February 1996): 112-125.

Pargal, Sheoli, and Wheeler, David. "Informal Regulation of Industrial Pollution in Developing Countries: Evidence from Indonesia." *Journal of Political Economy* 104 (December 1996): 1314-1327.

Popper, Andrew F. "In Defense of Antitrust Immunity for Collective Ratemaking: Life after the ICC Termination Act of 1995." *Transportation Journal* 35 (Summer 1996): 26-33.

Posner, Eric A. "The Regulation of Groups: The Influence of Legal and Nonlegal Sanctions on Collective Action." *University of Chicago Law Review* 63 (Winter 1996): 133-197.

CHAPTER 14

Asness, Clifford S. "Why Not 100% Equities?" *Journal of Portfolio Management* 22 (Winter 1996): 29-34.

Blumenfeld, Stephen B. and Partridge, Mark D. "The Long-run and Short-run Impacts of Global Competition on U.S. Union Wages." *Journal of Labor Research* 17 (Winter 1996): 149-171.

Bulow, Jeremy, and Klemperer, Paul. "Auctions versus Negotiations." *American Economic Review* 86 (March 1996): 180-194.

Chang, Fwu-Ranq. "Uncertainty and Investment in Health." *Journal of Health Economics* 15 (June 1996): 369-376.

Dickie, Mark, and Gerking, Shelby. "Formation of Risk Beliefs, Joint Production and Willingness to Pay to Avoid Skin Cancer." *Review of Economics & Statistics* 78 (August 1996): 451-463.

Erb, Claude B.; Harvey, Campbell R.; and Viskanta, Tadas E. "The Influence of Political, Economic, and Financial Risk on Expected Fixed-income Returns." *Journal of Fixed Income* 6 (June 1996): 7-30.

Gangopadhyay, Partha, and Reinganum, Marc R. "Interpreting Mean Reversion in Stock Returns." *Quarterly Review of Economics & Finance* 36 (Fall 1996): 377-394.

Gibbons, Robert. "An Introduction to Applicable Game Theory." *Journal of Economic Perspectives* 11 (Winter 1997): 127-149.

Gollier, Christian. "Optimum Insurance of Approximate Losses." *Journal of Risk & Insurance* 63 (September 1996): 369-380.

Hutchison, David E., and Pennacchi, George G. "Measuring Rents and Interest Rate Risk in Imperfect Financial Markets: The Case of Retail Bank Deposits." *Journal of Financial & Quantitative Analysis* 31 (September 1996): 399-417.

Ilmanen, Antti. "When Do Bond Markets Reward Investors for Interest Rate Risk?" *Journal of Portfolio Management* 22 (Winter 1996): 52-64.

Laitner, John, and Juster, F. Thomas. "New Evidence on Altruism: A Study of TIAA-CREF Retirees." *American Economic Review* 86 (September 1996): 893-908.

Lee, Youngho; Elcan, Amie, "Simulation Modeling for Process Reengineering in the Telecommunications Industry," *Interfaces,* 26 (May/June 1996): 1-9.

Manning, Willard G., and Marquis, M. Susan. "Health Insurance: The Tradeoff Between Risk Pooling and Moral Hazard." *Journal of Health Economics* 15 (October 1996): 609-639.

Murphy, Frederic H., "The Occasional Observer: College Athletics, a Dollar Auction Game." *Interfaces,* 26 (May/June 1996): 22-25.

Perloff, Jeffrey M.; Rubinfeld, Daniel L.; and Ruud, Paul. "Antitrust Settlements and Trial Outcomes." *Review of Economics & Statistics* 78 (August 1996): 401-409.

Perroni, Carlo, and Whalley, John. "How Severe is Global Retaliation Risk Under Increasing Regionalism?" *American Economic Review* 86 (May 1996): 57-61.

Pratt, John W., and Zeckhauser, Richard J. "Willingness to Pay and the Distribution of Risk and Wealth." *Journal of Political Economy* 104 (August 1996): 747-763.

Swaney, James A. "Comparative Risk Analysis: Limitations and Opportunities." *Journal of Economic Issues* 30 (June 1996): 463-473.

Trippi, Robert R. "The AIM Game: Learning Investment Management Priciples Through Monte Carlo Simulation." *Interfaces,* 26 (May/June 1996): 66-76.

CHAPTER 15

Arya, Anil; Glover, Jonathan; and Young, Richard A. "Capital Budgeting in a Multidivisional Firm." *Journal of Accounting, Auditing & Finance* 11 (Fall 1996): 519-533.

Bar-Ilan, Avner, and Strange, William C. "Investment Lags." *American Economic Review* 86 (June 1996): 610-622.

Blose, Laurence E. "Gold Price Risk and the Returns on Gold Mutual Funds." *Journal of Economics & Business* 48 (December 1996): 499-513.

Buffett, Warren. "Acquiring the Warren Buffett Way." *Harvard Business Review* 74 (January/February 1996): 150.

Chan, Louis K.C.; Jegadeesh, Narasimhan; and Lakonishok, Josef. "Momentum Strategies." *Journal of Finance* 51 (December 1996): 1681-1713.

Deneffe, Daniel, and Wakker, Peter. "Mergers, Strategic Investments and Antitrust Policy." *Managerial & Decision Economics* 17 (May/June 1996): 231-240.

Elston, Julie Ann. "Dividend Policy and Investment: Theory and Evidence from US Panel Data. *Managerial & Decision Economics* 17 (May/June 1996): 267-275.

Fletcher, Donna J., and Taylor, Larry W. " 'Swap' Covered Interest Parity in Long-date Capital Markets." *Review of Economics & Statistics* 78 (August 1996): 530-538.

Hendel, Igal. "Competition Under Financial Distress." *Journal of Industrial Economics* 44 (September 1996): 309-324.

Ho, Thomas S. Y., and Pfeffer, David M. "Convertible Bonds: Model, Value Attribution, and Analytics." *Financial Analysts Journal* 52 (September/October 1996): 35-44.

Lee, Ahyee; Moy, Ronald L.; and Lee, Cheng F. "A Multivariate Test of the Covariance—Co-skewness Restriction for the Three Moment CAPM." *Journal of Economics & Business* 48 (December 1996): 515-523.

Lessard, Donald R., and Zaheer, Srilata. "Breaking the Silos: Distributed Knowledge and Strategic Responses to Volatile Exchange Rates." *Strategic Management Journal* 17 (July 1996): 513-533.

Maruca, Regina Fazio. "Successful Acquisitions." *Harvard Business Review* 74 (November-December 1996): 10-11.

Maruca, Regina Fazio. "The Cost of Capital." *Harvard Business Review* 74 (September/October 1996): 9-10.

Pike, Richard, "A Longitudinal Survey on Capital Budgeting Practices." *Journal of Business Finance & Accounting* 23 (January 1996): 79-92.

Sick, Gordon A. "Real Options." *Journal of Finance* 51 (December 1996): 1974-1977.

Slater, Stanley F., and Zwirlein, Thomas J. "The Structure of Financial Strategy: Patterns in Financial Decision Making." *Managerial & Decision Economics* 17 (May/June 1996): 253-266.

Stein, Jeremy C. "Rational Capital Budgeting in an Irrational World." *Journal of Business* 69 (October 1996): 429-455.

Stole, Lars A., and Zwiebel, Jeffrey. "Organizational Design and Technology Choice Under Intrafirm Bargaining." *American Economic Review* 86 (March 1996): 195-222.

White, John B. and Miles, Morgan P. "The Financial Implications of Advertising as an Investment." *Journal of Advertising Research* 36 (July/August 1996): 43-52.

CHAPTER 16

Andreasen, Alan R. "Profits for Nonprofits: Find a Corporate Partner." *Harvard Business Review* 74 (November-December 1996): 47-59.

Boyne, George A. "Scale, Performance and the New Public Management: An Empirical Analysis of Local Authority Services." *Journal of Management Studies* 33 (November 1996): 809-826.

Cohen, Mark A. "Theories of Punishment and Empirical Trends in Corporate Criminal Sanctions." *Managerial & Decision Economics* 17 (July/August 1996): 399-411.

Dougherty, Chrys, and Jorgenson, Dale W. "International Comparisons of the Sources of Economic Growth." *American Economic Review* 86 (May 1996): 25-29.

Feldstein, Martin. "The Missing Piece in Policy Analysis: Social Security Reform." *American Economic Review* 86 (May 1996): 1-14.

Findlay, Ronald. "Modeling Global Interdependence: Centers, Peripheries, and Frontiers." *American Economic Review* 86 (May 1996): 47-51.

Fuchs, Victor R. "Economics, Values, and Health Care Reform." *American Economic Review* 86 (March 1996): 1-24.

Galbraith, James K. "Time to Ditch the NAIRU." *Journal of Economic Perspectives* 11 (Winter 1997): 93-108.

Hart, Stuart L. "Beyond Greening: Strategies for a Sustainable World." *Harvard Business Review* 75 (January-February 1997): 66-76.

Koch, Rainer. "Public Management and Productivity Towards an Appraisal of the Productivity of Alternative Forms of Public Service Delivery." *International Journal of Public Administration* 19 (November/December 1996): 2035-2058.

Levitt, Steven D. "How do Senators Vote? Disentangling the Role of Voter Preferences, Party Affiliation, and Senator Ideology." *American Economic Review* 86 (June 1996): 425-441.

Lichtenberg, Frank R. "Do (More and Better) Drugs Keep People Out of Hospitals?" *American Economic Review* 86 (May 1996): 384-388.

Mintzberg, Henry. "Managing Government, Governing Management." *Harvard Business Review* 74 (May/June 1996): 75-83.

Newhouse, Joseph P. "Reimbursing Health Plans and Health Providers." *Journal of Economic Literature* 34 (September 1996): 1236-1263.

Rodriguez-Clare, Andres. "Multinationals, Linkages, and Economic Development." *American Economic Review* 86 (September 1996): 852-873.

Rogerson, Richard. "Theory Ahead of Language in the Economics of Unemployment." *Journal of Economic Perspectives* 11 (Winter 1997): 73-92.

Stephan, Paula. "The Economics of Science." *Journal of Economic Literature* 34 (September 1996): 1199-1235.

Stiglitz, Joseph. "Reflections on the Natural Rate Hypothesis." *Journal of Economic Perspectives* 11 (Winter 1997): 310.

Wonnacott, Ronald J. "Free-trade Agreements: For Better or Worse?" *American Economic Review* 86 (May 1996): 62-66.

Yanow, Dvora. "Engineering Public Management." *Public Administration Review* 56 (March/April 1996): 211-212.

Absolute risk
Overall dispersion of possible payoffs.

Antitrust laws
Laws that promote competition and prevent monopoly.

Arc elasticity
Average elasticity over a given range of a function.

Automatic stabilizers
Buffers designed to smooth the pace of economic activity.

Average cost minimization
Activity level that generates lowest average cost, $MC = AC$.

Average product
Total product divided by units of input employed.

Barometric forecasting
Predictive method based on the observed relation among economic time series.

Barometric price leadership
A situation in which one firm in an industry announces a price change in response to what it perceives as a change in industry supply and demand conditions and other firms respond by following the price change.

Barrier to entry
Any advantage for industry incumbents over new arrivals.

Barrier to exit
Any limit on asset redeployment from one line of business or industry to another.

Barrier to mobility
Any advantage for large leading firms over small nonleading rivals.

Behavioral equations
Economic relations that are hypothesized to be true.

Benefit-cost ratio analysis
The present value of marginal social benefits per dollar of marginal social cost.

Beta
A measure of the systematic variability of one asset's returns with returns on other assets.

Beta coefficient
A measure of relative stock-price variability.

Breakeven point
Output level where total profit is zero.

Breakeven quantity
A zero profit activity level.

Budget line
All combinations of products that can be purchased for a fixed dollar amount.

Bureaucrats
Appointed government employees and civil servants.

Business cycle
Fluctuations of output around a long-term trend, or recessions followed by recoveries and expansions.

Business cycle
Rhythmic pattern of contraction and expansion in the overall economy.

Business profit
Residual of sales revenue minus the explicit accounting costs of doing business.

Business risk
The chance of loss associated with a given managerial decision.

By-product
Output that is customarily produced as a direct result of an increase in the production of some other output.

Capacity
Output level at which short-run average costs are minimized.

Capital budgeting
Long-term investment planning process.

Capture theory
Economic hypothesis suggesting that regulation is sometimes sought to limit competition and obtain government subsidies.

Cartel
Firms operating with a formal agreement to fix prices and output.

Certainty equivalent
The assured sum that equals an expected risky amount in utility terms.

Certainty equivalent adjustment factor, α
The ratio of a certain sum divided by an expected risky amount, where both dollar values provide the same level of utility.

Chance events
Possible outcomes following each decision point.

Change in the quantity demanded
Movement along a given demand curve reflecting a change in price and quantity.

Change in the quantity supplied
Movement along a given supply curve reflecting a change in price and quantity.

Coefficient of determination
Goodness of fit measure for a multiple regression model.

Coefficient of variation
Standard deviation divided by the mean.

Collusion
A covert, informal agreement among firms in an industry to fix prices and output levels.

Common costs
Expenses that are necessary for manufacture of a joint product.

Comparative advantage
When one nation or region of the country is better suited to the production of one product than to the production of some other product.

Comparative statics analysis
The study of changing demand and supply conditions.

Compensatory profit theory
Above-normal rates of return that reward efficiency.

Competitive advantage
A unique or rare ability to create, distribute, or service products valued by customers.

Competitive strategy
The search for a favorable competitive position in an industry or line of business.

Complements
Related products for which a price increase for one leads to a reduction in demand for the other.

Component cost of debt
Interest rate investors require on debt, adjusted for taxes.

Component cost of equity
Rate of return stockholders require on common stock.

Composite index
A weighted average of leading, coincident, or lagging economic indicators.

Computer simulation
The use of computer software and workstations or sophisticated desktop computers to create outcome scenarios.

Concentration ratios
Data in the Census of Manufacturers that show the percentage market share held by an industry's leading firms.

Constant returns to scale
When a given percentage increase in all inputs leads to an identical percentage increase in output.

Consumer interview
Questioning customers or potential customers to estimate demand.

Consumer sovereignty
Buyer supremacy in the marketplace.

Consumers' surplus
The value to customers of goods and services above and beyond the amount they pay sellers.

Consumption path
Optimal combinations of products as consumption increases.

Continuous production function
A production function where inputs can be varied in a unbroken marginal fashion.

Corner point
Spot in the feasible space where the X-axis, Y-axis, or constraint conditions intersect.

Correlation coefficient
Goodness of fit measure for a simple regression model.

Cost elasticity
Percentage change in total cost associated with a 1% change in output.

Cost function
The cost-output relation.

Cost of capital
Discount rate.

Cost of uncertainty
The minimum expected opportunity loss.

Cost reduction projects
Expenditures to replace obsolete plant and equipment.

Cost-effectiveness analysis
A method used to determine how to best employ resources in a given social program or public-sector investment project.

Cost-volume-profit analysis
Analytical technique used to study relations among costs, revenues, and profits.

Countercyclical
Inferior goods whose demand falls with rising income, and rises with falling income.

Countervailing power
Buyer market power that offsets seller market power, and vice versa.

Credit risk
The chance that another party will fail to abide by its contractual obligations.

Cross-price elasticity
Responsiveness of demand for one product to changes in the price of another.

Cross-section
Data from a common point in time.

Crossover discount rate
Interest factor that equates NPV for two or more investments.

Crowding out
The reduction in private investment associated with an increase in government spending.

Cultural risk
The chance of loss because of product market differences due to distinctive social customs.

Currency risk
Loss due to changes in the domestic-currency value of foreign profits.

Current cost
Amount paid under prevailing market conditions.

Cyclical fluctuation
Rhythmic fluctuation in an economic series due to expansion or contraction in the overall economy.

Cyclical normal goods
Products for which demand is strongly affected by changing income.

Decision points
Instances when management must select among choice alternatives.

Decision tree
A map of a sequential decision-making process.

Decreasing returns to scale
When output increases at a rate less than the proportionate increase in inputs.

Degree of operating leverage
Percentage change in profit from a 1% change in output.

Degrees of freedom
Number of observations beyond the minimum required to calculate a statistic.

Delphi method
Method that uses forecasts derived from an independent analysis of expert opinion.

Demand
The total quantity customers are willing and able to purchase.

Demand curve
The relation between price and the quantity demanded, holding all else constant.

Demand function
The relation between demand and factors influencing its level.

Dependent variable
Y-variable determined by X values.

Deregulation
The reduction of government control of the free market.

Derivative risk
The chance that volatile financial derivatives such as commodities futures and index options could create losses in underlying investments by increasing rather than decreasing price volatility.

Derived demand
Demand for inputs used in production.

Deterministic relation
A relation known with certainty.

Diffusion index
Percentage of leading, coincident, or lagging indicators that are rising at any point in time.

Diminishing marginal utility
When additional increments of money bring ever smaller increments of added benefit.

Direct demand
Demand for consumption products.

Discrete production function
A production function with distinct input patterns.

Discretionary policy
Unrestricted changes in spending and taxes.

Disequilibrium losses
Below-normal returns that can be suffered in the time interval that often exists between when an unfavorable influence on industry demand or cost conditions first transpires, and the time when exit or downsizing finally occurs.

Disequilibrium profits
Above-normal returns that can be earned in the time interval between when a favorable influence on industry demand or cost conditions first transpires, and the time when competitor entry or growth finally develops.

Dual
Secondary problem statement (symmetrical to primal).

Dual solution
Input for long-range planning.

Durbin-Watson statistic
Measure that indicates significance of serial correlation.

Dutch auction
In a Dutch auction, the winning bidder is the first participant willing to pay the auctioneer's price.

Econometric methods
Use of economic theory and mathematical and statistical tools to forecast economic relations.

Economic censuses
Data collected by the U.S. Department of Commerce that provide a comprehensive statistical profile of large segments of the U.S. economy.

Economic efficiency
Achieved when all firms equate input marginal revenue product and marginal cost (maximize profits).

Economic expectations
Anticipated financial considerations.

Economic indicators
Data that describe projected, current, or past economic activity.

Economic luck
Temporary good fortune due to unexpected changes in industry demand or cost conditions.

Economic profit
Business profit minus the implicit costs of capital and any other owner-provided inputs.

Economic rents
Profits due to uniquely productive inputs.

Economic risk
The chance of loss due to the fact that all possible outcomes and their probability of occurrence are unknown.

Economies of scale
Decreasing long-run average costs.

Economies of scope
Cost reduction from producing complementary products.

Efficiency
Production of what consumers demand in a least-cost fashion.

Elastic demand
A situation in which a price change leads to a more than proportionate change in quantity demanded.

Elasticity
The percentage change in a dependent variable resulting from a 1% change in an independent variable.

Endogenous variables
Factors controlled by the firm.

English auction
The most familiar type of auction, where an auctioneer keeps raising the price until a single highest bidder remains.

Equation
Analytical expressions of functional relationships.

Equilibrium
Perfect balance in demand and supply.

Equity
Concern for a just distribution of wealth.

Eurocurrency markets
Markets in which bank transactions are denominated in a variety of currencies.

Eurodollar market
A market in which banks outside the U.S. accept deposits and make loans denominated in dollars.

Exogenous variables
Factors outside the control of the firm.

Expansion path
Optimal input combinations as the scale of production expands.

Expansion projects
Expenditures to increase availability of existing products.

Expected value
Anticipated realization.

Expected value maximization
Optimization of profits in light of uncertainty and the time value of money.

Explicit cost
Out-of-pocket expenditures.

Exponential smoothing
Averaging method for forecasting time series of data.

Expropriation risk
The danger that business property located abroad might be seized by host governments.

Externalities
Differences between private and social costs or benefits.

***F*-statistic**
Offers evidence if explained variation in Y is significant.

Failure by incentive
Breakdown of the pricing mechanism as a reflection of all costs and benefits of production and consumption.

Failure by market structure
Insufficient market participants for active competition.

Feasible space
Graphical region that is both technically and economically feasible and includes the optimal solution.

First-degree price discrimination
Charging different prices to each customer.

Fiscal policy
Spending and taxing policies of the government.

Fixed cost
Expense that does not vary with output.

Forecast group
Subsample of data used to test a forecast model.

Forecast reliability
Predictive consistency.

Free-rider problem
The tendency of consumers to avoid making any contribution toward covering the costs of public goods.

Frictional profit theory
Abnormal profits observed following unanticipated changes in demand or cost conditions.

Game theory
A decision framework for making choices in hostile environments and under extreme uncertainty.

Government failure
Circumstances where public policies reflect narrow private interests, rather than the general public interest.

Government policy risk
The chance of loss because foreign government grants of monopoly franchises, tax abatements, and favored trade status can be tenuous.

Graph
Visual representation of data.

Growth trend analysis
Assumes constant *percentage* change over time.

Heteroskedasticity
Nonconstant variance in the error term.

Hidden preferences problem
The difficulty of determining true demand for public goods.

Historical cost
Actual cash outlay.

Hypothesis test
Statistical experiment.

Identities
Economic relations that are true by definition.

Implicit cost
Noncash costs.

Incentive-based regulation
Rules that benefit firms and customers through enhanced efficiency.

Income effect
Shift to a new indifference curve following a change in aggregate consumption caused by a price change.

Income elasticity
Responsiveness of demand to changes in income, holding constant the effect of all other variables.

Increasing returns to scale
When the proportional increase in output is larger than an underlying proportional increase in input.

Incremental cash flows
Change in net cash flows due to an investment project.

Incremental change
Comprehensive impact resulting from a decision.

Incremental cost
Change in cost caused by a given managerial decision.

Incremental profit
Gain or loss associated with a given managerial decision.

Independent variable
X-variable determined separately from the Y-variable.

Indifference curve
A curve that identifies all combinations of goods and services that provide the same utility.

Inelastic demand
A situation in which a price change leads to a less than proportionate change in quantity demanded.

Inferior goods
Products for which consumer demand declines as income rises.

Inflation risk
The danger that a general increase in the price level will undermine the real economic value of any legal agreement that involves a fixed promise to pay over an extended period.

Inflection point
A point of maximum slope.

Innovation profit theory
Above-normal profits that follow successful invention or modernization.

Input substitution
The systematic replacement of productive factors.

Input-output analysis
Forecasting method that shows the interrelated nature of economic data.

Interest-rate risk
Market risk that stems from the fact that changing interest rates affect the value of any agreement that involves a fixed promise to pay over a specified period.

Internal rate of return (IRR)
Discount rate that equates present value of cash inflows and outflows.

International trade
The voluntary exchange of goods and services across national boundaries.

Investment opportunity schedule
Pattern of returns for all potential investment projects.

Irregular or random influences
Unpredictable shocks to the economic system.

Isocost curve
Line of constant costs.

Isoquant
Different input combinations used to efficiently produce a specified output.

Kinked demand curve
A theory assuming that rival firms follow any decrease in price in order to maintain their respective market shares but refrain from following increases, allowing their market share to increase at the expense of the firm making the initial price increase.

Law of diminishing marginal utility
As consumption of a given product increases, the added benefit derived diminishes.

Law of diminishing returns
As the quantity of a variable input increases, the resulting rate of output increase eventually diminishes.

Learning curve
Average cost reduction over time due to production experience.

Leverage
The ratio of the book value of assets divided by stockholders' equity.

Limit concentration
A social goal of regulation is to restrict undue influence.

Linear model
A straight-line relation.

Linear programming
A solution method for maximization or minimization decision problems subject to underlying constraints.

Linear trend analysis
Assumes constant *unit* change over time.

Liquidity risk
The difficulty of selling corporate assets or investments that have only a few willing buyers or are otherwise not easily transferable at favorable prices under typical market conditions.

Long run
Planning period with complete input flexibility.

Long-run cost curve
Cost-output relation for the optimal plant in the present operating environment.

Long-run cost functions
Basis for long-range planning.

Macroeconomic forecasting
Prediction of aggregate economic activity.

Managerial economics
Applies economic tools and techniques to business and administrative decision making.

Marginal
Change in the dependent variable caused by a one-unit change in an independent variable.

Marginal cost
Change in total cost following a one-unit change in output.

Marginal cost of capital
Financing cost of an additional investment project, expressed on a percentage basis.

Marginal external benefits
Value enjoyed by non-purchasers and not reflected in market prices.

Marginal external costs
Expenses that are not directly borne by producers or their customers.

Marginal private benefits
Value enjoyed by those who directly pay for any good or service.

Marginal private costs
Production expenses borne by producers and their customers.

Marginal product
Change in output associated with a one-unit change in a single input.

Marginal profit
Change in total profit due to a one-unit change in output.

Marginal rate of substitution
The amount of one product that must be substituted for another if utility is to remain unchanged.

Marginal rate of technical substitution (MRTS)
The amount of one input that must be substituted for another to maintain constant output.

Marginal revenue
Change in total revenue associated with a one-unit change in output.

Marginal revenue product
The amount of revenue generated by employing the last input unit.

Marginal social benefits
Added private and public advantages.

Marginal social costs
Added private and public expenses.

Marginal utility
The added utility derived from increasing consumption of a particular product by one unit.

Market
Firms and individuals willing and able to buy or sell a given product.

Market equilibrium price
Market clearing price.

Market experiments
Examining consumer behavior in actual or laboratory markets.

Market failure
The inability of market institutions to sustain desirable activity or eliminate undesirable activity.

Market niche
A segment of a market that can be successfully exploited through the special capabilities of a given firm or individual.

Market risk
The chance that a portfolio of investments can lose money because of swings in the financial markets as a whole.

Market segment
A division or fragment of the overall market with essentially unique characteristics.

Market structure
The competitive environment.

Markup on cost
The difference between price and cost, measured relative to cost, expressed as a percentage.

Markup on price
The difference between price and cost, measured relative to price, expressed as a percentage.

Markup pricing
Setting prices to cover direct costs plus a percentage profit contribution.

Maximum criterion
Decision choice method that provides the best of the worst possible outcomes.

Mean
Average.

Median
"Middle" observation.

Microeconomic forecasting
Prediction of partial economic data.

Minimax regret criterion
Decision choice method that minimizes the maximum possible regret (opportunity loss) associated with a wrong decision *after the fact.*

Minimum efficient scale
Output level at which long-run average costs are minimized.

Mode
Most common value.

Monetary policy
Actions taken by the Federal Reserve (the Fed) that influence bank reserves, the money stock, and interest rates.

Monopolistic competition
A market structure characterized by a large number of sellers of differentiated products.

Monopoly
A market structure characterized by a single seller of a highly differentiated product.

Monopoly profit theory
Above-normal profits caused by barriers to entry that limit competition.

Monopsony
A market with one buyer.

Moral hazard problem
Changes in incentives that result from the purchase of insurance.

Multicollinearity
High correlation among X-variables.

Multiplant diseconomies of scale
Cost disadvantages from managing multiple facilities in the same line of business or industry.

Multiplant economies of scale
Cost advantages from operating multiple facilities in the same line of business or industry.

Multiple regression model
A relation with one dependent Y-variable and more than one independent X-variable.

Multiplicative model
A log-linear relation.

Natural monopoly
An industry in which the market-clearing price occurs at a point at which the monopolist's long-run average costs are still declining.

Net marginal revenue
Marginal revenue after all variable costs.

Net present value *(NPV)*
Current-dollar difference between marginal revenues and marginal costs.

Net present value profile
Graph relating *NPV* to the discount rate.

Noncyclical normal goods
Products for which demand is relatively unaffected by changing income.

Nonexclusion concept
When it is impossible or prohibitively expensive to confine the benefits of consumption to paying customers.

Nonrival consumption
Where use by certain individuals does not reduce availability for others.

Normal distribution
A symmetrical distribution about the mean or expected value.

Normal or superior goods
Products for which demand is positively related to income.

Normal rate of return
Minimum profit necessary to attract and retain investment.

Objective function
Equation that expresses the goal of a linear programming problem.

Off-peak
Period of excess capacity.

Oligopoly
A market structure characterized by few sellers and interdependent price/output decisions.

One-parameter (simple) exponential smoothing
Method for forecasting slowly changing levels.

Operating controls
Regulation by government directive.

Opportunity cost
Foregone value associated with current rather than next-best use of an asset.

Opportunity loss
The difference between a given payoff and the highest possible payoff for the resulting state of nature.

Optimal capital budget
Funding required to underwrite a value-maximizing level of new investment.

Optimal capital structure
Combination of debt and equity that minimizes the firm's weighted average cost of capital.

Optimal decision
The choice alternative that produces a result most consistent with managerial objectives.

Optimal markup on cost
The profit-maximizing cost markup, equal to minus one divided by the quantity one plus the price elasticity of demand.

Optimal markup on price
The profit-maximizing price markup, equal to minus one times the inverse of the price elasticity of demand.

Optimal solution
Best answer.

Optimize
Seek the best solution.

Output elasticity
The percentage change in output associated with a 1% change in all inputs.

Panel consensus
Forecast method based on the informed opinion of several individuals.

Pareto optimal
When all pareto satisfactory programs and investment projects have been undertaken.

Pareto satisfactory
If investment in a public project makes at least one individual better off and no one worse off.

Patents
Exclusive property rights to produce, use, or sell an invention or innovation for a limited period.

Payback period
Number of years required to recover initial investment.

Payoff matrix
A table that shows outcomes associated with each possible state of nature.

Peak
Period of full capacity usage.

Perfect competition
A market structure characterized by a large number of buyers and sellers of an identical product.

Personal insight
Forecast method based on personal or organizational experience.

Point elasticity
Elasticity at a given point on a function.

Politicians
Elected representatives or leaders.

Pollution emission allowances
A controversial form of government subsidy that gives firms the property right to pollute and then sell that right to others.

Population parameters
Summary and descriptive measures for the population.

Population standard deviation
Square root of the population variance.

Population variance
Average squared deviation from the overall mean.

Postaudit
Careful reconciliation of actual and predicted results.

Potential Pareto improvement
When an anticipated program or project involves positive *net* benefits.

Potential entrants
Firms and individuals with the economic resources to enter a particular market, given sufficient economic incentives.

Power production function
A multiplicative relation between input and output.

Present value
Worth in current dollars.

Price controls
Short-term limits on prices charged by nonutilities.

Price discrimination
A pricing practice that sets prices in different markets that are not related to differences in costs.

Price elasticity of demand
Responsiveness of the quantity demanded to changes in the price of the product,

holding constant the values of all other variables in the demand function.

Price leadership
A situation in which one firm establishes itself as the industry leader and all other firms in the industry accept its pricing policy.

Price makers
Buyers and sellers whose large transactions affect market prices.

Price takers
Buyers and sellers whose individual transactions are so small that they do not affect market prices.

Primal
Original problem statement (symmetrical to dual).

Primal solution
Input for short-run operating decisions.

Private good
Products or services where consumption by one individual precludes or limits consumption by others.

Privatization
The transfer of public-sector resources to the private sector.

Probability
The chance of occurrence.

Probability distribution
A list of possible events and probabilities.

Production function
The maximum output that can be produced for a given amount of input.

Profit contribution
Profit before fixed charges.

Profit margin
Net income expressed as a percentage of sales revenue.

Profit margin
Net profit divided by sales.

Profit margin
The difference between the price and cost of a product.

Profit maximization
Activity level that generates highest profit, $MR = MC$ and $M\pi = 0$.

Profitability index *(PI)*
Benefit/cost ratio.

Property rights
The license to limit use by others.

Public choice theory
The philosophy of how government decisions are made and implemented.

Public good
Products or services where consumption by one individual does not reduce the amount available for others.

Public interest theory
A view of regulation as a government-imposed means of private-market control.

Qualitative analysis
An intuitive judgmental approach to forecasting based on opinion.

Range
Scope from largest to smallest observations.

Rational ignorance
The tendency to remain relatively uninformed about public policy decisions.

Regression analysis
Statistical method for describing *XY* relations.

Regression to the mean
Over time, the tendency for business profit rates to revert toward a risk-adjusted normal rate of return.

Regulation
Government control of the market economy.

Regulatory lag
The delay between when a change in regulation is appropriate and the date it becomes effective.

Regulatory reform
Improvement in government control to enhance efficiency and fairness.

Relative distance method
Graphic technique used to solve linear programming problems.

Relative risk
The variation in possible returns compared with the expected payoff amount.

Replacement cost
The cost of duplicating productive capability using current technology.

Replacement projects
Maintenance of business investments.

Residual
Error term.

Return on assets
Net income divided by the book value of total assets.

Return on stockholders' equity
Accounting net income divided by the book value of the firm.

Return on stockholders' equity
Business profits expressed as a percentage of owner-supplied capital.

Returns to a factor
The relation between output and variation in only one input.

Returns to scale
The output effect of a proportional increase in all inputs.

Revenue maximization
Activity level that generates highest revenue, $MR = 0$.

Ridge lines
Graphic bounds for positive marginal products.

Risk aversion
A desire to avoid or minimize uncertainty.

Risk neutrality
A focus on expected values, not return dispersion.

Risk premium
Investor reward for risk taking.

Risk premium *(R_P)*
The added expected return for a risky asset over that of a riskless asset.

Risk seeking
A preference for speculation.

Risk-adjusted discount rate
The risk-free rate of return plus the required risk premium.

Risk-adjusted valuation model
A valuation model that reflects time-value and risk considerations.

Risk-free rate of return *(R_F)*
Investor reward for postponing consumption.

Safety and environmental projects
Mandatory nonrevenue-producing investments.

Sample mean forecast error
Estimate of average forecast error.

Sample standard deviation
Square root of the population variance.

Sample statistics
Summary and descriptive measures for a sample.

Sample variance
Average squared deviation from the sample mean.

Satisfice
Seek satisfactory rather than optimal results.

Scatter diagram
A plot of *XY* data.

Sealed-bid auction
An auction where all bids are secret, and the highest bid wins.

Seasonality
Rhythmic annual patterns in sales or profits.

Second-degree price discrimination
Charging different prices based on use rates of quantities purchased.

Secular trend
Long-run pattern of increase or decrease.

Sensitivity analysis
A limited form of computer simulation that focuses on important decision variables.

Serial correlation
A time-series relation among error terms.

Shadow prices
Implicit values associated with linear-programming-problem decision variables.

Shift in demand
Switch from one demand curve to another following a change in a nonprice determinant of demand.

Shift in supply
Movement from one supply curve to another following a change in a nonprice determinant of supply.

Short run
Operating period during which at least one input is fixed.

Short-run cost curve
Cross-output relation for a specific plant and operating environment.

Short-run cost functions
Basis for day-to-day operating decisions.

Shortage
Excess demand.

Simple regression model
A relation with one dependent Y-variable and one independent X-variable.

Simplex solution method
Iterative technique used to provide algebraic solutions for linear programming problems.

Shewness
A lack of balance.

Slack variables
Factors that indicate the amount by which constraint conditions are exceeded.

Slope
A measure of steepness of a line.

Social internal rate of return
The interest or discount rate that equates the present value of the future benefits to the initial cost or outlay.

Social net present value
The present-value difference between marginal social benefits and marginal social costs.

Social rate of discount
The interest-rate cost of public funds.

Special-interest groups
Organized lobbyists that actively support the passage of laws and regulations that further their own narrow economic interests.

Spreadsheet
A table of electronically stored data.

Stabilization policy
Strategy designed to offset temporary economic disruptions.

Standard error of the estimate
Standard deviation of the dependent Y-variable after controlling for all X-variables.

Standardized variable
A variable with a mean of 0 and a standard deviation equal to 1.

Statistical relation
An inexact relation.

Subsidy policy
Government grants that benefit firms and individuals.

Substitutes
Related products for which a price increase for one leads to an increase in demand for the other.

Substitution effect
Movement along an indifference curve reflecting the substitution of cheaper products for more expensive ones.

Sunk cost
Cost that does not vary across decision alternatives.

Supply
The total quantity offered for sale.

Supply curve
The relation between price and the quantity supplied, holding all else constant.

Supply function
The relation between supply and all factors influencing its level.

Surplus
Excess supply.

Survey techniques
An interview or mailed questionnaire approach to forecasting.

Symmetrical
A balanced distribution.

***t*-statistic**
Approximately normal test statistic.

Tables
A list of economic data.

Tangent
A line that touches but does not intersect a given curve.

Tax burden
Economic cost of tax.

Tax incidence
Point of tax collection.

Tax policy
Fines and penalties that limit undesirable performance.

Technical efficiency
Least-cost production of a target level of output.

Test group
Subsample of data used to generate a forecast model.

Theory of the firm
The basic model of the business enterprise.

Third-degree price discrimination
Charging different prices to each customer class.

Three-parameter (Winters) exponential smoothing
Method for forecasting seasonally-adjusted growth.

Time series
A daily, weekly, monthly, or annual sequence of data.

Tort system
A body of law that provides a means for victims of accidents and injury to receive just compensation for their loss.

Total asset turnover
Sales revenue divided by the book value of total assets.

Total product
The whole output from a production system.

Transfer pricing
The pricing of products transferred among divisions of a firm.

Trend
Long-run pattern of increase or decrease.

Trend analysis
Forecasting the future path of economic variables based on historical patterns.

Two-parameter (Holt) exponential smoothing
Method for forecasting stable growth.

Type I error
Incorrect rejection of a true hypothesis.

Type II error
Failure to reject a false hypothesis.

Uncertainty
When the outcomes of managerial decisions cannot be predicted with absolute accuracy but all possibilities and their associated probabilities of occurrence are known.

Underproduction
A situation that occurs when a monopolist curtails production to a level at which marginal cost is less than price.

Unitary elasticity
A situation in which price and quantity changes exactly offset each other.

Utility
Value.

Utility function
A descriptive statement that relates satisfaction or well-being to the consumption of goods and services.

Value of the firm
The present value of the firm's expected future net cash flows.

Variable cost
Expense that fluctuates with output.

Vertical integration
When a single company controls various links in the production chain from basic inputs to final output.

Vertical relation
Where the output of one division or company is the input to another.

Vickrey auction
Where the highest sealed bid wins, but the winner pays the price of the second-highest bid.

Voters
Persons who elect public officials.

Weighted average cost of capital
The marginal cost of a composite dollar of debt and equity financing.

Windfall profits
Economic profits due to unwarranted good fortune.

Winner's curse
Where overly aggressive bidders pay more than the economic value of auctioned off items.

z-statistic
Normally distributed test statistic with zero mean and standard deviation of one.

Index